introduction to

PSYCHOLOGY

SIXTH EDITION

ERNEST R. HILGARD
Stanford University
RICHARD C. ATKINSON
Stanford University
RITA L. ATKINSON
Stanford University

introduction to PSYCHOLOGY

SIXTH EDITION

Oxford & IBH Publishing Co. Pvt. Ltd.
New Delhi

CBS

(A Unit of CBS Publishers & Distributors Pvt Ltd)

New Delhi • Bengaluru • Chennai • Kochi • Kolkata • Mumbai
Hyderabad • Jharkhand • Nagpur • Patna • Pune • Uttarakhand

Indian edition 1976 published pursuant to an agreement with the original American publisher, Harcourt Brace Jovanovich, Inc., New York, USA

CBS Publishers & Distributors Pvt Ltd
204 FIE, Patparganj Industrial Area, Delhi-110 092
E-mail: delhi@cbspd.com, cbspubs@airtelmail.in

24-Y17-11

Acknowledgments and Copyrights

Cover: A detail from Robert Delaunay, *Circular Forms—Sun and Moon* (1912–1913), Stedelijk Museum, Amsterdam

Tables

3-1 Sigel, I. E., The attainment of concepts. In M. L. Hoffman and L. W Hoffman (eds.), *Review of child development research,* Vol. 1. New York: Russell Sage Foundation, 1964. **3-2** Data in chart compiled from *Identity, youth and crisis* by Erik H. Erikson, p. 94. Copyright © 1968 by W. W. Norton & Company, Inc. And from *Childhood and society,* Second edition, Revised, by Erik H. Erikson, p. 274. Copyright © 1950, 1963 by W. W. Norton & Company, Inc. By permission of W. W. Norton & Company, Inc. New York, N.Y. The Hogarth Press; Faber & Faber, Ltd. **3-3** Kohlberg, L., The development of children's orientations toward a moral order: I. Sequence in the development of moral thought. *Vita humana, 6:* 11–33. By permission of S. Karger, Basel, Switzerland, 1963. **3-4** Hilgard, J. R., *Personality and hypnosis.* Chicago: The University of Chicago Press, 1970. Data from Table 33, p. 191 and Table 34, p. 192. Copyright © 1970 by The University of Chicago. All rights reserved. **3-5** Sorenson, Robert C., *Adolescent sexuality in contemporary America.* New York: World Publishing Co., 1973, p. 122. **3-6** Kandel, B., and Lesser, Gerald S., *Youth in two worlds.* San Francisco: Jossey-Bass Inc., 1972, p. 17. **3-7** Same as above (Table 3-6), p. 15.

4-1 Adapted from Table 1, p. 97, Some approximate detection threshold values, from "Contemporary psychophysics" by Eugene Galanter. In *New directions in psychology* by Roger Brown, Eugene Galanter, Eckhard H. Hess, and George Mandler. Copyright © 1962 by Holt, Rinehart and Winston, Inc. Reprinted by permission of Holt, Rinehart and Winston, Inc.

5-1 Soal, S. G., and Bateman, F., *Modern experiments in telepathy.* New Haven, Conn.: Yale University Press, 1954. Reprinted by permission of Yale University Press and Faber and Faber Ltd. (London) from *Modern experiments in telepathy.*

6-1 Weitzenhoffer, A. M., and Hilgard, E. R., *Stanford Hypnotic Susceptibility Scales,* Forms A and B. Stanford, Calif.: Stanford University Press, 1959. **6-3** Tart, C. T., *On being stoned: A psychological study of marijuana intoxication.* Palo Alto, Calif.: Science & Behavior Books, 1971.

10-2 Slobin, Dan I., Functions of two-word sentences in child speech, with examples from several languages. *Psycholinguistics.* Glenview, Ill.: Scott, Foresman and Co., 1971, pp. 44–45. **10-3** Modified from Limber, John, Representative examples of complex sentences taken from the records of one child between two and three years of age. In T. E. Moore (ed.), *Cognitive development and the acquisition of language.* New York: Academic Press, 1973, p. 181. **10-4** Gardner, B., and Gardner, R. A., Two-way communication with an infant chimpanzee. In A. Schrier and F. Stollnitz (eds.), *Behavior of nonhuman primates,* Vol. III. New York: Academic Press, 1969. Copyright © by Academic Press.

11-1 Hunt, Morton, "Sexual behavior in the 1970's," *Playboy,* November 1973, p. 74. Reproduced by special permission of *Playboy Magazine;* © 1973 by *Playboy.*

13-1 Norman, W. T., "Toward an adequate taxonomy of personality attributes: Replicated factor structure in peer nomination personality ratings." *Journal of Abnormal and Social Psychology, 66* (1963): 574–83.

14-4 Guilford, J. P., *The nature of intelligence.* New York: McGraw-Hill Book Company, 1967. **14-5** Thurstone, L. L., and Thurstone, T. G., *SRA primary abilities.* Chicago: Science Research Associates, 1963. **14-6** Flanagan, J. C., The definition and measurement of ingenuity. In C. W. Taylor and F. Barron (eds.), *Scientific creativity: its recognition and development.* New York: John Wiley and Sons, 1963. Guilford, J. P., A factor analytic study across the domains of reasoning, creativity, and evaluation I: Hypotheses and description of tests. *Reports from the Psychology Laboratory.* Los Angeles, Calif.: University of Southern California, 1954. Used by permission of the author. Getzels, J. W., and Jackson, P. W., *Creativity and intelligence: Explorations with gifted students.* New York: John Wiley and Sons, 1962. Torrance, E. Paul, *Torrance Tests of Creative Thinking,* Verbal Forms A and B. Princeton, N.J.: Personnel Press, Inc., 1966. Wallach, M. A., and Kogan, N., *Modes of thinking in young children: A study of the creativity-intelligence distinction.* Copyright © 1965 by Holt, Rinehart and Winston, Inc. Reprinted by permission of Holt, Rinehart and Winston, Inc. Mednick, S. A., The associative bases of creative process. *Psychology Review, 69:* 220–32. Copyright 1962 by the American Psychological Association and reproduced by permission. **14-7** Jensen, A. R., *Educability and group differences.* New York: Harper & Row, 1973.

continued on page 641

preface

In preparing the sixth edition of *Introduction to Psychology* we have relied on the experience of instructors who used earlier editions and who reported on the strengths and weaknesses of those editions. This record of experience was invaluable, but it did not solve one of the major problems encountered in writing a textbook representative of contemporary psychology. Psychology's dramatic growth in recent years has been accompanied by a staggering increase in research. With more than 12,000 research papers reported annually in *Psychological Abstracts,* the task of selection was formidable. The rapid expansion of the field and the importance of new findings are indicated by the fact that more than half the references in this edition appeared since the fifth edition went to press early in 1971.

To keep abreast of theory and research in psychology, as well as in related disciplines, we have relied more heavily on consultation with experts than we have in previous editions. Each chapter was reviewed thoroughly by specialists, all outstanding in their area. As many as five experts read the manuscript for a chapter at different stages of preparation. By such extensive reviewing we sought to ensure that the material presented in this book represents accurately the current state of knowledge in psychology.

Equally important was our concern for readability and student interest. Introductory psychology students have changed over the years in their interests, knowledge, and scientific sophistication. To make certain that our subject matter was readily comprehensible to students and relevant to the human issues with which they are concerned, we asked students to comment on each section of the text in terms of interest value, clarity, and level of difficulty. This is the first edition in which we sought detailed student feedback, and we found their responses enlightening and extremely helpful.

As a third source of information, several college instructors who specialize in teaching the introductory course read the manuscript as it evolved, commenting on its relevance to the problems they encountered in teaching beginning psychology students.

The feedback from these three sources—experts, students, and teachers—was invaluable in guiding our efforts.

Although this version is clearly the outgrowth of earlier editions, the entire book has been revised and many sections rewritten. Users of previous editions will recognize certain changes in the sequence of presentation, the consolidation of some topics, and the addition of a number of totally new topics. Developments and issues in psychology that have been newly introduced or given increased coverage include humanistic psychology, cognitive processes, obesity, changing sex roles and sexual behavior, child language learning, biofeedback, behavior modification, mnemonics, split-brain research, drug use, the IQ–race controversy, meditation and psychopathology. These are only a few of the topics that we hope will give the student some feeling for the scope and vitality of psychology and its relevance to the human condition.

In order to incorporate new material without lengthening the book some curtailing has been necessary. The two chapters on infancy, childhood, adolescence, and adulthood have been combined into a single chapter entitled "Developmental Psychology." As in previous editions, this material appears early in the text to give the student an overview of the kinds of problems with which psychology is concerned. The developmental aspects of specific functions (e.g., perception and language) are covered in more detail in later chapters.

Behavior genetics is no longer treated as a separate chapter. Because this rapidly growing area contributes to our understanding of many psychological phenomena (e.g., intelligence, personality, and mental illness), its findings are introduced appropriately throughout the text. The basic principles of behavior genetics are summarized in Chapter 2, "Biological Basis of Psychology."

The section on motivation and emotion has been entirely rewritten. Chapter 11 is concerned with physiological motives: it presents the latest research on mechanisms of hunger and thirst as well as interesting new material on sex and obesity. Chapter 12 now combines socially based motives with material on emotion; it devotes considerable space to aggression, considering aggressive behavior from several viewpoints and focusing on both innate and learned aspects.

Social psychology is another section that has been completely rewritten. Here we turned to Professor Daryl J. Bem of Stanford University, a leading social psychologist, and asked him to contribute two chapters. Chapter 18, "Social Psychology," and Chapter 19, "Psychology and Society," provide an engaging and thought-provoking finale to the book. Chapter 18 includes lively discussions of such topics as interpersonal attraction, bystander apathy, and attribution processes. Chapter 19 gives some intriguing examples of the way psychological facts and theories influence public policy; and, conversely, the way societal prejudices influence the objectivity of behavioral science.

We have tried to cover contemporary psychology in a textbook of reasonable length. But each instructor must design his or her course according to course objectives, type of students, and available time. Even if all chapters are not assigned, students will at least have them for reference. For a short course we believe that it is better to treat a reduced number of chapters fully than to attempt to cover the entire text. Two possible 14-chapter courses are proposed below, one for a course with an experimental-biological emphasis, the other for a course with a personal-social emphasis. These outlines only illustrate possible combinations.

EXPERIMENTAL-BIOLOGICAL EMPHASIS	PERSONAL-SOCIAL EMPHASIS
1. The nature of psychology (Chapter 1)	1. The nature of psychology (Chapter 1)
2. Biological basis of psychology (Chapter 2)	2. Developmental psychology (Chapter 3)

3. Developmental psychology (Chapter 3)
4. Sensory processes (Chapter 4)
5. Perception (Chapter 5)
6. States of consciousness (Chapter 6)
7. Conditioning and learning (Chapter 7)
8. Memory and forgetting (Chapter 8)
9. Language and thought (Chapter 10)
10. Physiological basis of motivation (Chapter 11)
11. Human motivation and emotion (Chapter 12)
12. Personality and its assessment (Chapter 13)
13. Ability testing and intelligence (Chapter 14)
14. Social psychology (Chapter 18)

3. States of consciousness (Chapter 6)
4. Conditioning and learning (Chapter 7)
5. Memory and forgetting (Chapter 8)
6. Language and thought (Chapter 10)
7. Human motivation and emotion (Chapter 12)
8. Personality and its assessment (Chapter 13)
9. Ability testing and intelligence (Chapter 14)
10. Conflict, anxiety, and defense (Chapter 15)
11. Psychopathology (Chapter 16)
12. Psychotherapy and other treatment methods (Chapter 17)
13. Social psychology (Chapter 18)
14. Psychology and society (Chapter 19)

The order of topics can be changed. For example, some instructors feel that student interest can be better aroused by beginning the course with material on social psychology, personality, and psychopathology, while leaving some of the more difficult subject matter (experimental methods, learning, physiological and sensory psychology) until later. The authors have experimented with such a scheme in their own teaching and have not found it entirely satisfactory. Beginning with the more personally relevant and intriguing topics may get the course off to a fast start, but it often gives the students a distorted idea of what psychology is all about. In addition, many students are ill prepared for, and disgruntled by, the more difficult material when it is sprung on them later in the course. Our preferred approach is to cover the chapter on developmental psychology early in the course, thereby exposing the student to a broad range of provocative topics in psychology. Then turn to some of the more technical areas like perception, learning, and motivation, and end the course with personality, psychopathology, and social psychology. But each instructor must choose the order of topics he or she finds most congenial; the book has been written so that a variety of chapter orders are possible.

The many decisions that must be made in teaching the introductory psychology course are skillfully discussed by Professor John C. Ruch of Mills College in the *Instructor's Handbook*. Instructors using the sixth edition are urged to obtain a copy of this handbook. It provides invaluable information for both the beginning and experienced instructor, as well as for teaching assistants. As further instructional aids, we have again provided a thoroughly revised *Study Guide with Programmed Units and Learning Objectives*—now including chapter-by-chapter learning objectives and key terms—and three series of *Test Item Files*.

A recurrent theme introduced throughout this edition is that psychological problems can be studied from different viewpoints. Chapter 1 introduces five approaches to the study of psychology—neurobiological, behavioristic, cognitive, psychoanalytic, and humanistic. These approaches are reintroduced in later chapters whenever a particular topic (e.g., personality, motivation, or perception) has been studied from several viewpoints. A consideration of alternative approaches provides a thread of cohesiveness and helps the student understand why theories about a given psychological topic often seem to be saying quite different things.

Our debt of gratitude to those who influenced earlier editions continues. Critical reviews of fifth edition chapters or drafts of revised chapters (or both) have been prepared by the following people.

Albert Bandura, Stanford University
Richard H. Blum, Stanford University
John D. Bonvillian, Vassar College
John B. Carroll, University of North Carolina, Chapel Hill
Isidor Chein, New York University
Joseph Church, Brooklyn College
Eve Clark, Stanford University
Herbert Clark, Stanford University
Ruth Cline, Los Angeles Valley College
David Elkind, University of Rochester
Shirley Feldman, Stanford University
John H. Flavell, University of Minnesota
Ronald H. Forgus, Lake Forest College
Leo Ganz, Stanford University
James Geiwitz, Santa Barbara, California
Norma Graham, Columbia University
J. P. Guilford, University of Southern California
Ralph N. Haber, University of Rochester
William S. Hall, The Rockefeller University
John P. Hill, Cornell University
Bartley G. Hoebel, Princeton University
Irving L. Janis, Yale University
Arthur R. Jensen, University of California, Berkeley
Harold H. Kelley, University of California, Los Angeles
Raymond Kesner, University of Utah
Frederick A. King, University of Florida
Walter Kintsch, University of Colorado
Benjamin Kleinmuntz, University of Illinois, Chicago Circle
John C. Loehlin, University of Texas
Arnold M. Ludwig, University of Kentucky Medical Center
Ruth Lyell, De Anza College
Brendan A. Maher, Harvard University
Edward J. Murray, University of Miami
Daniel Osherson, Stanford University
Ellis B. Page, University of Connecticut
Eugene Raxten, Los Angeles Valley College
Gary Robertson, Harcourt Brace Jovanovich, Inc.
Barbara Sakitt, Stanford University
Stanley Schachter, Columbia University
K. Warner Schaie, West Virginia University
Edward Smith, Stanford University
Charles T. Tart, University of California, Davis
Jared Tinklenberg, Stanford University
Wilse B. Webb, University of Florida
Burton White, Harvard University
Jeffrey Wine, Stanford University
Robert B. Zajonc, University of Michigan

Special thanks are due Professor Smith for his thoughtful review of the entire manuscript and Professor Cline, who reviewed both text material and the *Instructor's Handbook*.

We are gratefully indebted to Carolyn Young and Janine Ziemelis for secretarial assistance far beyond the call of duty, and to the patient and efficient staff of our publisher.

ERNEST R. HILGARD
RICHARD C. ATKINSON
RITA L. ATKINSON

contents

part three perception and awareness

part four learning and thinking

CONTENTS

part six personality and individuality

part seven conflict, adjustment, and mental health

part one

psychology as a scientific and humanistic endeavor

1

the nature of psychology

Psychology touches almost every facet of our lives. As society has become progressively more complex, psychology has assumed an increasingly important role in solving human problems. Psychologists are concerned with an astonishing variety of problems. Some are specific and practical. What is the best treatment for drug addiction or obesity? How should a survey be designed and administered to measure public opinion accurately? How can people be persuaded to give up smoking? What is the most effective method for teaching children to read? How should the dials on the instrument panel of a jet aircraft be arranged to minimize pilot error? Can a blind person be given artificial sight by electrical stimulation of small wires implanted in the brain?

Other problems are of broader concern. What child-rearing methods produce happy and effective adults? How can mental illness be prevented? What can be done to eliminate race prejudice? What family and social conditions contribute to alienation, aggression, and crime? Psychologists are working, along with other experts, on these and many more problems.

Psychology also affects our lives through its influence on laws and public policy. Laws concerning discrimination, capital punishment, pornography, sexual behavior, and the conditions under which a person may be held legally responsible for his actions are influenced by psychological theories of human nature. For example, laws pertaining to sexual deviancy have changed markedly in the past 20 years as research has shown that many sexual acts, previously classed as perversions, are quite "normal" in the sense that most people engage in them.

The effect of television violence on children is of concern to parents and psychologists. Only after studies provided evidence of the harmful effects of such programs has it been possible to modify television programming policies. More brutal TV fare is gradually being replaced by shows like *Sesame Street* and *The Electric Company,* which represent concerted efforts by psychologists and educators to make learning interesting, fun, and effective.

Because psychology affects so many aspects of our lives it is important, even for those who do not intend to specialize in the field, to know something about its basic facts and research methods. An introductory course in psychology should give you a better understanding of why people behave as they do and should provide insights into your own attitudes and reactions. It should also help you evaluate the many claims made in the name of psychology. Headlines like the following appear everyday in the newspapers.

Anxiety controlled by self-regulation of brain waves.
Psychclogist devises sure-fire method for curing impotency.
Violent crimes related to defective genes.
Proof of mental telepathy found.
Homosexuality linked to hormone levels.
Experiences in early infancy determine adult intelligence.
Emotional stability and family size closely related.

How can you judge the validity of such claims? In part, by knowing what psychological facts have been firmly established and by being familiar with the kind of evidence necessary to give credence to a new "discovery." This book reviews the current state of knowledge in psychology. It also examines the nature of research—how a psychologist formulates a hypothesis and designs a procedure to prove or disprove it.

Psychology is relatively young compared to other scientific disciplines, and recent years have seen a virtual explosion in psychological research. As a result, psychological theories and concepts have been continuously evolving and changing. For this reason, it is difficult to give a precise definition of psychology. Basically, psychologists are interested in finding out "why people act as they do." But there are different ways of explaining human actions. Before we provide a formal definition of psychology, it will be useful to consider alternative approaches to explaining psychological phenomena.

Psychological Conceptions of Man

Any action a person takes can be described or explained from several different points of view. Suppose, for example, you walk across the street. This act can be described in terms of the firing of the nerves that activate the muscles that move the legs that transport you across the street. It can also be described without reference to anything within the body; the green light is a stimulus to which you respond by crossing the street. Or your action might be explained in terms of its ultimate purpose or goal: you plan to visit a friend and crossing the street is one of many acts involved in carrying out the plan.

Just as there are different ways of describing such a simple act as crossing the street, there are also different approaches to the psychological study of man. The following discussion describes five approaches to psychology. Other schemes or categories are possible, but the ones presented here provide an insight into the major approaches of modern psychology. Because these diverse viewpoints will appear repeatedly throughout the book, we will provide only a brief description of some main points.

Fig. 1-1 Social behavior controlled by brain stimulation

Electrodes surgically implanted in the brain of these chimpanzees can be stimulated by remote radio control. Depending upon how the animals are stimulated, the experimenter can make one dominant and the other submissive in their social interactions.

Neurobiological Approach

The human brain with its twelve billion nerve cells and almost infinite number of interconnections and pathways may well be the most complex structure in the universe. In principle, all psychological events are represented in some manner by the activity of the brain and nervous system in conjunction with the other body systems. One approach to the study of man attempts to relate his actions to events taking place inside his body, particularly within the brain and nervous system. This approach tries to reduce observable (overt) behavior and mental events, such as thoughts and emotions, to neurobiological processes. For example, a psychologist studying learning from the biological approach is interested in the changes that take place in the nervous system as the result of learning how to perform a new task. Visual perception can be studied by recording the activity of nerve cells in the brain as the eye is exposed to simple patterns of lines.

Recent discoveries have made it dramatically clear that there is an intimate relationship between brain activity and behavior and experience. Emotional reactions, such as fear and rage, have been produced in animals and humans by mild electrical stimulation of specific areas deep in the brain (see Figure 1-1) Electrical stimulation of certain areas [illegible] the human brain will produce sensations of pleasure and pain, and even vivid memories of past events (see Figure 1-2).

Ultimately, it may be possible to specify the neurobiological mechanisms underlying even the most complex human actions. However, a comprehensive neurobiological theory of man is at present only a remote possibility.

Because of the complexity of the brain and the fact that live human brains are seldom available for study, tremendous gaps exist in our knowledge of neural functioning. A psychological conception of man based solely on neurobiology would be inadequate indeed. For this reason, other methods are used to investigate psychological phenomena. In many instances it is more practical to study antecedent conditions and their consequences without worrying about what goes on inside the organism.

John B. Watson

Behavioral Approach

A person eats breakfast, rides a bicycle, talks, blushes, laughs, and cries. All these are forms of *behavior,* those activities of an organism that can be observed. With the behavioral approach a psychologist studies an individual by looking at his *behavior* rather than his internal workings. The view that behavior should be the sole subject matter of psychology was first advanced by the American psychologist John B. Watson in the early 1900s. Before that, psychology had been defined as the study of mental experiences or activities, and its data were largely self-observations in the form of *introspection.* Introspection refers to a very careful observing and recording of one's own perceptions and feelings. The early psychologists trained themselves to analyze their own reactions in minute detail, hoping to unravel the mysteries of the mind. Watson felt that introspection was a futile approach. He argued that if psychology were to be a science, its data must be observable and measurable. Only you can observe your perceptions and feelings, but someone else can observe your actions. Watson maintained that only if you study what a person *does* can you have an objective science of psychology.

Behaviorism, as Watson's position came to be called, helped shape the course of psychology during the first half of this century and its outgrowth, stimulus-response psychology, is still strong in America, particularly through the work of Harvard psychologist B. F. Skinner. Stimulus-response psychology (or S-R psychology for short) studies the stimuli that elicit

Fig. 1-2 A brain wired for pleasure

Microelectrodes implanted in specific areas deep in the brain (left x-ray) of this young man produce a sensation of pleasure when stimulated by mild current. He had previously been driven to the brink of suicide by spells of deep depression. When the wired cap is attached to the microelectrodes (right photo), the man can produce pleasurable sensations by pressing a button on a control box. Brain stimulation studies with microelectrodes in animals are helping psychologists understand emotion-producing centers of the brain. Diagnostic procedures with humans, such as the one depicted here, are employed only when other methods fail to relieve serious suffering.

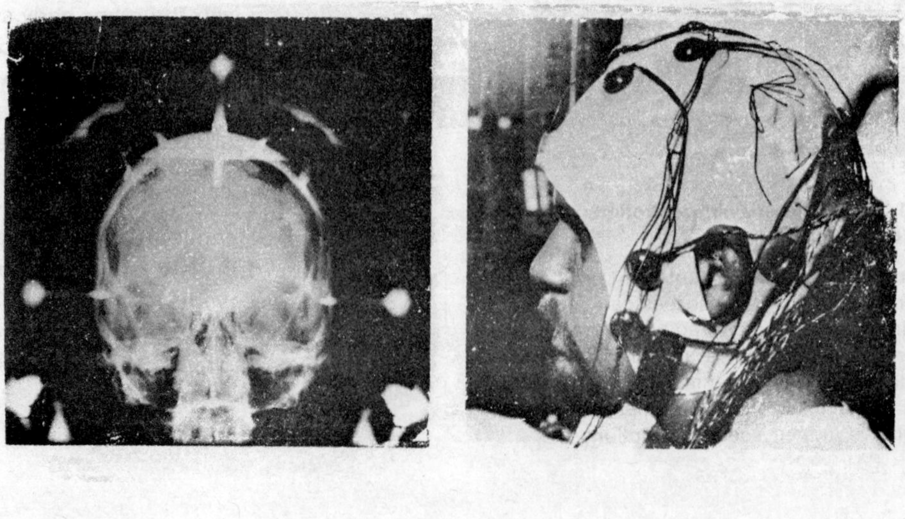

B. F. Skinner

behavioral responses, the rewards and punishments that maintain these responses, and the modifications in behavior obtained by changing the patterns of rewards and punishments. Stimulus-response psychology is *not* concerned with what goes on inside the organism; for this reason it has sometimes been called the "black box" approach. S-R psychologists maintain that although the brain and nervous system may carry on complex activities that the psychologist cannot see (inside the black box), a science of psychology can be based strictly on what goes into the box and what comes out, without worrying about what goes on inside. Thus, a theory of learning can be developed by observing how learned behavior varies with environmental conditions, for example, what stimulus conditions and patterns of reward and punishment lead to the fastest learning with the fewest errors. The theory need not specify the changes learning produces in the nervous system in order to be valuable.

A strict S-R approach does not consider the individual's *conscious experiences.* Conscious experiences are simply those events of which the experiencing person is fully aware. You may be aware of the various thoughts and hypotheses that go through your mind as you solve a difficult problem. You know what it feels like to be angry, or frightened, or excited. An observer may judge from your actions the kind of emotion you are experiencing, but the conscious process—the actual awareness of the emotion—is yours alone. A psychologist can record what a person *says* about his conscious experiences (his verbal report) and from this objective data can make *inferences* about the person's mental activity. But, by and large, S-R psychologists have not chosen to study the mental processes that intervene between the stimulus and the observable response.

Cognitive Approach

Cognitive psychologists argue that we are not merely passive receptors of stimuli; the mind actively processes the information it receives and transforms it into new forms and categories (see Figure 1-3). What you are looking at on this page is an arrangement of ink particles. At least, that is the physical stimulus. But the sensory input to the visual system is a pattern of light rays reflected from the page to the eye. The neural processes initiated are transmitted to the brain and eventually result in seeing, reading, and (perhaps) remembering. Numerous transformations occur between the stimulus and your experience of seeing and reading. These involve not only transformations of the light rays into some kind of visual image, but also processes that compare that image with others stored in memory. (What if you had never seen a book or the printed word before? Your response to the stimulus, which is the array of ink particles that forms the words on this page, would be quite different. What you perceive depends on past experience.)

Cognition refers to those mental processes that transform the sensory input in various ways, code it, store it in memory, and retrieve it for later use Perception, imagery, problem-solving, remembering, and thinking are all terms that describe hypothetical stages of cognition (Neisser, 1967).[1]

Fig. 1-3 Perception as an active process

We continually extract patterns from objects we see, trying to match them with something meaningful. Stare at the little bar in the center between the cubes to establish for yourself the fluctuating nature of perception. Your mind performs all sorts of transformations, seeking out the different patterns inherent in the cubes.

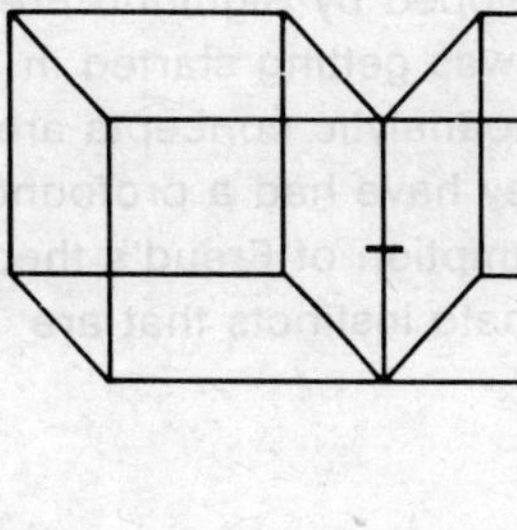

[1] Throughout this book, the reader will find references, cited by author and date, that document or expand the statements made here. Detailed publishing information on these studies appears in the bibliography at the end of the book. The bibliography also serves as an index to the pages on which the citations appear.

The cognitive approach to the study of man developed partly in reaction to the narrowness of the S-R view. To conceive of human actions solely in terms of stimulus input and response output may be adequate for the study of very simple forms of behavior, but this approach neglects too many interesting areas of human functioning. People can think, plan, make decisions on the basis of remembered information, and selectively choose among those environmental stimuli that require attention.

Behaviorism rejected the subjective study of "mental life" in order to make psychology a science. It provided a valuable service by making psychologists aware of the need for objectivity and measurement. Cognitive psychology attempts to investigate internal mental processes but, as later chapters will show, in an objective and scientific manner.

An analogy has sometimes been made between S-R psychology and a telephone switchboard; the stimulus goes in and, after a few cross connections and circuits through the brain, the response comes out. Cognitive psychology can be considered analogous to an electronic computer. Incoming information is processed in various ways—selected, compared and combined with other information already in memory, transformed and rearranged, and so on; the response output depends on the nature of these internal processes.

Psychoanalytic Approach

The psychoanalytic conception of man was developed by Sigmund Freud in Europe at about the same time that behaviorism was getting started in America. Unlike the ideas discussed thus far, psychoanalytic concepts are not based on experimental studies; nevertheless they have had a profound influence on psychological thinking. The basic assumption of Freud's theory is that much of man's behavior is determined by innate instincts that are

Drawing by Opie. © 1973 by The New Yorker Magazine, Inc.

Sigmund Freud

largely unconscious. By *unconscious processes* Freud meant thoughts, fears, and wishes of which the person is unaware but which influence his behavior. He believed that many forbidden or punished impulses of childhood are driven out of awareness into the unconscious where they still affect behavior. According to Freud, unconscious impulses find expression in dreams, slips of speech, mannerisms, and symptoms of neurotic illness, as well as through such socially approved behavior as artistic, literary, or scientific activity.

Most psychologists do not completely accept Freud's view of the unconscious. They would probably agree that the individual is not fully aware of some aspects of his personality. But they prefer to speak of degrees of awareness rather than assume that a sharp distinction exists between conscious and unconscious thoughts.

Freud's theories of personality and motivation and the psychoanalytic method for treating mental illness will be discussed in later chapters. At this point we will note only that Freud believed that all of man's actions have a cause, but the cause is often some unconscious motive rather than the rational reason the individual might give for his behavior. Freud's view of human nature was essentially negative. Man is driven by the same basic instincts as animals (primarily sex and aggression), and he is continually struggling against a society that stresses the control of these impulses. Because Freud believed that aggression was a basic instinct, he was pessimistic about the possibility of men ever living together peacefully.

Humanistic Approach

An individual is free to choose and to determine his actions. Consequently, each person is responsible for his actions and cannot blame the environment, his parents, or circumstances for what he does. This humanistic conception of man developed from the ideas of existential philosophers (Kierkegaard, Nietzsche, Sartre). It emphasizes those "human" qualities that distinguish man from the animals—primarily his *free will* and his drive toward *self-actualization.* The humanistic viewpoint rejects the concept of man as a mechanism controlled by external stimuli or by unconscious instincts. Rather than view man as being "acted on" by forces outside of his control, humanists prefer to see man as an "actor" capable of controlling his own destiny and changing the world around him.

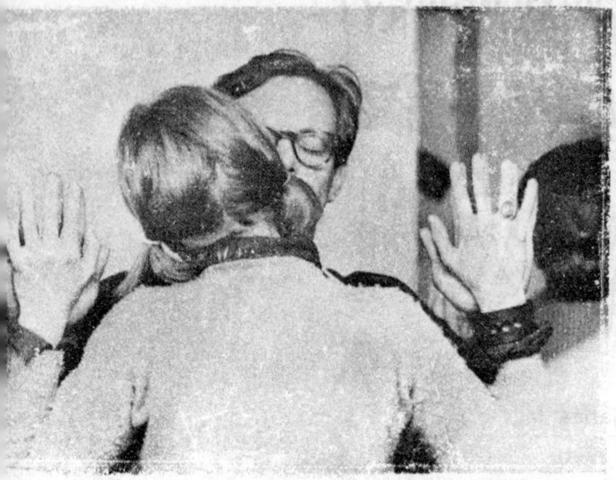

Sensory awareness in an encounter group

According to humanistic psychology an individual's main motivational force is a tendency toward growth and self-actualization. Every person has a basic need to develop his potential to the fullest, to progress beyond what he is now. He may not know which path leads to growth, and he may be blocked by all kinds of environmental and cultural obstacles, but his natural tendency is toward actualization of his potential.

Humanistic psychology evolved partly as a reaction against those aspects of a technological society that tend to dehumanize man. Emphasis on experiences that make life meaningful in the here and now—sensory awareness, interpersonal communication, and love—has led to an interest in encounter groups and various types of "consciousness-expanding" and mystical experiences.

The main concern of the humanistic psychologist is the individual's *subjective experience.* An individual's perceptions of himself and the world are considered a more important concern for study than his actions. Within his viewpoint, some humanists would even reject scientific psychology, claiming that its methods can contribute nothing worthwhile to an understanding of the nature of man.

As a warning that psychology needs to focus its attention on solving problems relevant to human welfare rather than studying isolated bits of behavior in the laboratory, the humanistic view makes a valuable point. But to assume that the difficult problems in today's highly complicated society can be solved by discarding all that we have learned about the scientific methods of investigation is fallacious indeed. To quote one psychologist concerned with this issue, "we can no more afford a psychology that is humanistic at the expense of being scientific than we can afford one that is 'scientific' at the expense of human relevance" (M. Brewster Smith, 1973).

Application of Different Conceptions

The details of each of these different psychological conceptions will become clearer as we encounter them in subsequent chapters. Any given area of study in psychology may be approached from several viewpoints. For example, in studying aggression the physiological psychologist would be interested in investigating the brain mechanisms responsible for such behavior. As we shall see in Chapter 12, aggressive behavior in animals has been provoked and controlled by electrical and chemical stimulation of specific areas deep in the brain. An S-R psychologist might be interested in determining the kinds of learning experiences that make one person more aggressive than another. Or he might study the specific stimuli that provoke hostile acts in a particular situation. A cognitive psychologist might focus on how individuals perceive certain events (in terms of their anger-arousing characteristics) and how these perceptions can be modified by providing the person with different types of information. A psychoanalyst might want to find out what childhood experiences foster the control of aggression or its channeling into socially acceptable forms. The humanistic psychologist might focus on those aspects of society that promote aggression by blocking the individual's progress toward self-actualization.

Each approach would attempt to modify behavior in a different way. For example, the neurobiologist would look for a drug or some other physical means, such as surgery, for controlling aggression. The behaviorist would try to modify the environmental conditions to provide new learning experiences that reward nonaggressive types of behavior. The cognitive psychologist would use an approach similar to that of the behaviorist, although he might focus more on the individual's thought processes and his reasoning when confronted with anger-arousing situations. The psychoanalyst might probe the individual's unconscious to discover why his hostility is directed toward certain people or situations and then try to redirect it into more acceptable channels. The humanistic psychologist would probably be concerned with changing society's priorities to place more emphasis on improving interpersonal relationships and providing conditions that promote the development of man's potential for constructive and cooperative actions.

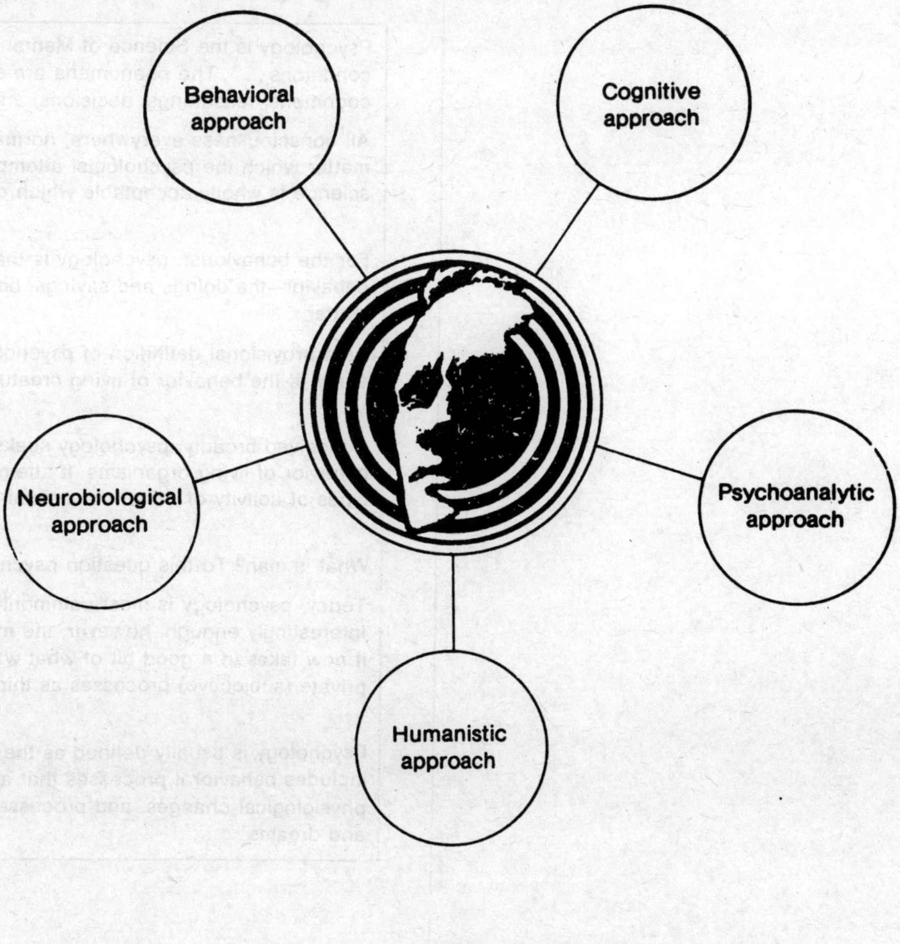

Fig. 1-4 Viewpoints in psychology

The analysis of psychological phenomena can be approached from several viewpoints. Each offers a somewhat different explanation of why a person acts as he does, and each makes a contribution to our conception of the total person.

The Broad Province of Contemporary Psychology

Throughout its brief history, psychology has been defined in many different ways (see Table 1-1). The early psychologists defined their field as "the study of mental activity." With the rise of behaviorism at the beginning of this century, and its concern for studying only those phenomena that could be objectively measured, psychology came to be defined as "the study of behavior." This definition usually included the investigation of animal as well as human behavior on the assumption that (1) information from experiments with subhuman species could be generalized to the human organism and (2) animal behavior was of interest in its own right. Most psychology textbooks of the 1930s through the 1960s used this definition. The cycle has come around again with the development of cognitive and humanistic psychology; most current definitions of psychology include references to both behavior and mental processes.

For our purposes, we will define psychology as *the science that studies behavior and mental processes.* But from a practical viewpoint, you can get a better idea of what psychology *is* from looking at what psychologists *do.*

About half the people who have advanced degrees in psychology work in colleges and universities; others work in the government and in private

TABLE 1-1
Changing definitions of psychology

Psychology is the Science of Mental Life, both of its phenomena and of their conditions. . . . The phenomena are such things as we call feelings, desires, cognitions, reasonings, decisions, and the like.	William James, 1890.
All consciousness everywhere, normal or abnormal, human or animal, is the subject matter which the psychologist attempts to describe or explain; and no definition of his science is wholly acceptable which designates more or less than just this.	James Angell, 1910.
For the behaviorist, psychology is that division of natural science which takes human behavior—the doings and sayings, both learned and unlearned—as its subject matter.	John B. Watson, 1919.
As a provisional definition of psychology, we may say that its problem is the scientific study of the behavior of living creatures in their contact with the outer world.	Kurt Koffka, 1925.
Conceived broadly, psychology seeks to discover the general laws which explain the behavior of living organisms. It attempts to identify, describe, and classify the several types of activity of which the animal, human or other, is capable.	Arthur Gates, 1931.
What is man? To this question psychology seeks an answer.	Edwin Boring, 1939.
Today, psychology is most commonly defined as "the science of behavior." Interestingly enough, however, the meaning of "behavior" has itself expanded so that it now takes in a good bit of what was formerly dealt with as experience . . . such private (subjective) processes as thinking are now dealt with as "internal behavior."	Norman Munn, 1951.
Psychology is usually defined as the scientific study of behavior. Its subject matter includes behavioral processes that are observable, such as gestures, speech, and physiological changes, and processes that can only be inferred such as thoughts and dreams.	Kenneth Clark and George Miller, 1970.

agencies—business, industry, clinics, and guidance centers. Those in private practice who offer their services to the public for a fee represent only a small minority. Psychologists do a variety of things, depending on their fields of specialization and their work locations.

One estimate of the proportion of psychologists who classify themselves in each of a number of specialties is found in Figure 1-5. The various fields of specialization are described below.

Experimental Psychologists

This term is really a misnomer because psychologists in many other areas of specialization carry out experiments too. But this category usually consists of those psychologists who use experimental methods to find out how people react to sensory stimuli, perceive the world around them, learn and remember, respond emotionally, and are motivated to action, whether by hunger or the desire to become president. Experimental psychologists also work with animals. Sometimes they attempt to relate animal and human behavior; sometimes they study animals in order to compare the behavior of different species (comparative psychology). Whatever their interest, experimental psychologists are concerned with developing precise methods of measurement and control.

Fig. 1-5 Fields of specialization within psychology (After Cates, 1970)

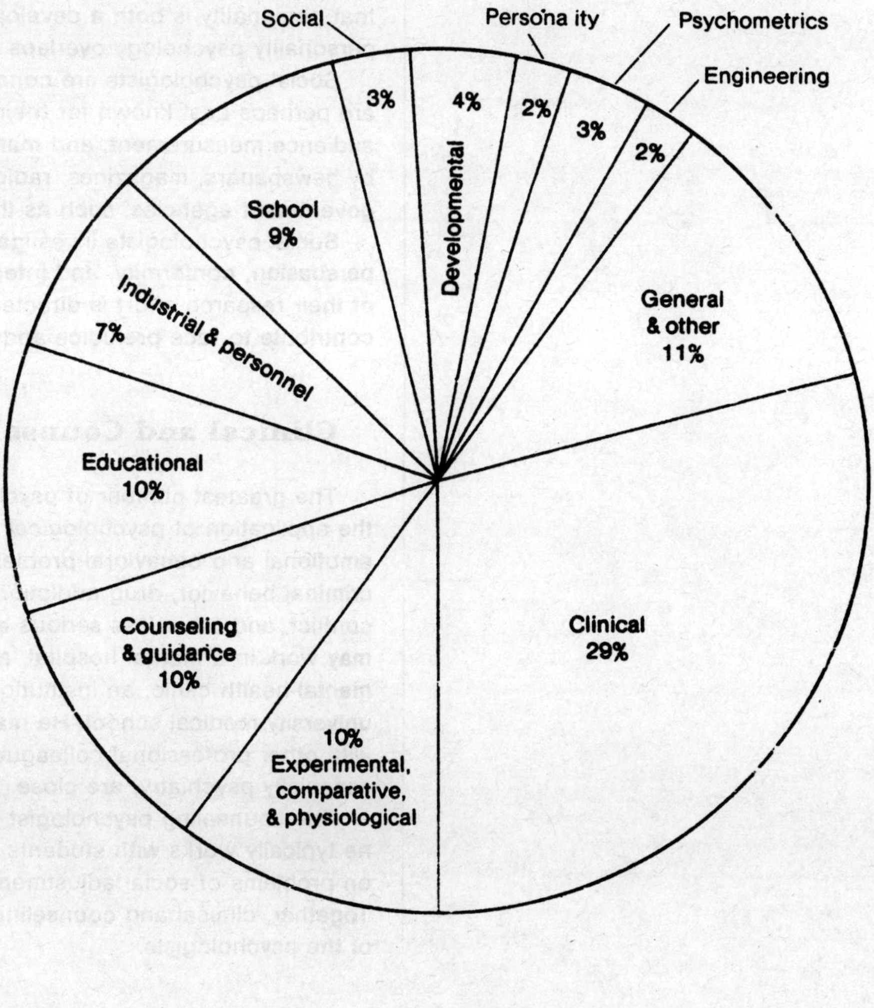

Physiological Psychologists

Closely related to experimental psychology is physiological psychology. The physiological psychologist wants to discover the relationship between bodily processes and behavior. How do sex hormones influence behavior? What area of the brain controls speech? How do drugs like marihuana and LSD affect coordination and memory? The physiological psychologist studies man from the neurobiological viewpoint.

Developmental, Personality, and Social Psychologists

The categories of developmental psychology, personality psychology, and social psychology overlap. A developmental psychologist is concerned with human growth and the factors that shape human behavior from birth to old age. He might study a specific ability such as how language develops and changes in the growing child, or a particular period of life, such as infancy, the preschool years, or adolescence.

Because human development takes place in the context of other persons—parents, siblings, playmates, and school companions—a large part of development is social. Social psychology is interested in the ways that interactions with other people influence attitudes and behavior. To the extent that personality is both a developmental and social product, the province of personality psychology overlaps both the other categories.

Social psychologists are concerned also with the behavior of groups. They are perhaps best known for their work in public opinion and attitude surveys, audience measurement, and market research. Surveys are now widely used by newspapers, magazines, radio and television networks, as well as by government agencies, such as the Bureau of the Census.

Social psychologists investigate such topics as propaganda and persuasion, conformity, and intergroup conflict. At present, a significant part of their research effort is directed toward identifying the factors that contribute to race prejudice and to aggression.

Clinical and Counseling Psychologists

The greatest number of psychologists are engaged in clinical psychology, the application of psychological principles to the diagnosis and treatment of emotional and behavioral problems—mental illness, juvenile delinquency, criminal behavior, drug addiction, mental retardation, marital and family conflict, and other less serious adjustment problems. A clinical psychologist may work in a mental hospital, a juvenile court or probation office, a mental-health clinic, an institution for the mentally retarded, a prison, or a university medical school. He may also practice privately, often in association with other professional colleagues. His affiliations with the medical profession, especially psychiatry, are close.

The counseling psychologist serves many of the same functions, although he typically works with students in high schools or universities giving advice on problems of social adjustment and vocational and educational goals. Together, clinical and counseling psychologists account for about 40 percent of the psychologists.

A school psychologist administering a test

School and Educational Psychologists

The public schools provide a wide range of opportunities for psychologists. Because the beginnings of serious emotional problems often appear in the early grades, many elementary schools employ psychologists whose training combines courses in child development, education, and clinical psychology. These school psychologists work with individual children to evaluate learning and emotional problems; administering and interpreting intelligence, achievement, and personality tests is part of their job. In consultation with parents and teachers, they plan ways of helping the child both in the classroom and at home. They also provide a valuable resource for teachers, offering suggestions for coping with classroom problems.

The educational psychologist is a specialist in learning and teaching. He may work in the school system, but more often he is employed by a university's school of education where he does research on teaching methods and helps train teachers and school psychologists.

Industrial and Engineering Psychologists

Industrial society makes available many goods that add to the comforts and satisfactions of living, but it also creates a number of problems. Modern technologies make warfare more destructive and more frightening; misuse of technology pollutes air and water, drains natural resources, and may drastically change the values by which people regulate their lives. Many of these problems are being brought to the attention of the public and are causing such strong reactions that some perceive this period as a evolutionary era—not necessarily a violent revolution in the political sense, but one that will force our institutions to adapt to the changes associated with a postindustrial society.

Industrial and engineering psychologists are deeply involved with these problems. At one level they serve the technological process—they are concerned with human factors in industry, such as personnel selection, employee morale, and the design of complex machines so that human errors are minimized. At another level, however, they are concerned with the larger problems of an industrial civilization. Here they join social psychologists and other scientists in planning for the future with shared concerr about our resources, environmental pollution, overcrowding, and other influences on the quality of life. A new term for this area of investigation is *environmental psychology.*

Methodologists

With the development of modern methods of experimentation and treatment of data—symbolized by the high-speed computer—problems of research design, statistics, and computation have become so complex that the methodologist has become a specialist. Whenever any large-scale research enterprise is undertaken, at least one statistical expert is needed, and often many more.

Statisticians in psychology formerly were associated chiefly with test construction and the interpretation of test results. As experts in sampling theory, they may now be called on to design a systematic procedure to locate people for questioning in a survey of public opinion or of voting behavior. As experts in experimental design, they may be asked to help research psychologists arrange procedures for gathering and analyzing data.

Methods of Psychology

Above all else, the aim of science is to provide new and useful information in the form of verifiable data: data obtained under conditions such that other qualified people can make similar observations and obtain the same results. This task calls for orderliness and precision in uncovering relationships and in communicating them to others. The scientific ideal is not always reached, but as a science becomes better established it rests on an increasing number of relationships that can be taken for granted because they have been validated so often.

Experimental Method

The experimental method can be used outside the laboratory as well as inside. Thus it is possible in an experiment in economics to investigate the effects of different taxation methods by trying these methods out on separate but similar communities. The experimental method is a matter of logic, not of location. Even so, most experimentation takes place in special laboratories, chiefly because the control of conditions commonly requires special equipment that is best housed and used in one place. The laboratory is generally located in a university or a research institute of some kind, where it is accessible to scientists who work on a variety of topics.

The distinguishing characteristic of a laboratory is that it is a place where the experimenter can carefully control conditions and take measurements in order to discover orderly *relationships among variables.* A *variable* is something that can occur with different values. For example, in an experiment seeking to discover the relationship between learning ability and age, both learning ability and age can have different values, learning being either slow or fast and the learner being either young or old. To the extent that learning ability changes systematically with increasing age, we can discover an orderly relationship between them.

The ability to exercise precise control over variables distinguishes the experimental method from other methods of observation. If the experimenter seeks to discover whether learning ability depends on the amount of sleep a person has had, he can control the amount of sleep by arranging to have several groups of subjects spend the night in the laboratory. One group might be allowed to go to sleep at 11:00 P.M., another at 1:00 A.M., and the third group might be kept awake until 4:00 A.M. By waking all the subjects at the same time and giving each the same learning task, the experimenter can determine whether the subjects with more sleep master the task more quickly than those with less sleep.

In this study, the different amounts of sleep are the antecedent conditions; the learning performances are the results of these conditions. We call the antecedent condition the *independent variable* because it is independent of what the subject does. The variabie affected by changes in the antecedent conditions is called the *dependent variable;* in psychological research the dependent variable is usually some measure of the subject's behavior. The phrase "*is a function of*" is used to express the dependency of one variable on another. Thus, for the experiment above, we could say the subject's ability to master a task is a function of the amount of sleep he has had.

A discussion of an experiment concerned with the effect of marihuana on memory may make the distinction between independent and dependent variables clearer (Darley and others, 1973). Male subjects were assigned to four groups comparable in age and educational level. When a subject arrived at the laboratory he was given an oral dose of marihuana in the form of a "brownie cookie." All subjects were given the same type of cookie and the same instructions. But the dosage level of the marihuana varied depending on the group: 5, 10, 15, or 20 milligrams of THC, the active ingredient in marihuana.

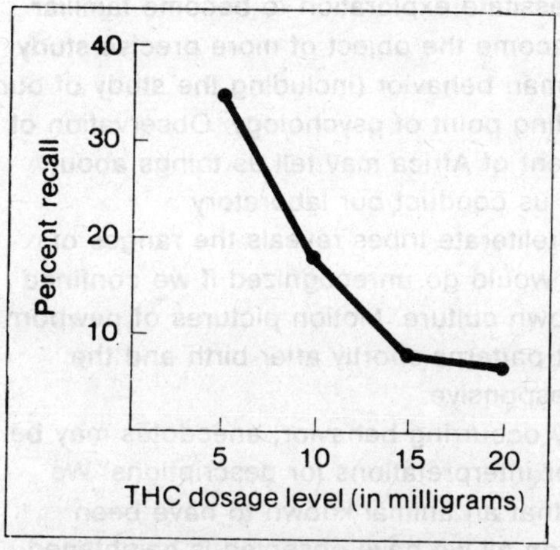

Fig. 1-6 Marihuana and memory

Word lists were memorized after varying dosages of THC (the active ingredient in marihuana) were taken; recall tests administered a week later measured how much of the memorized material was retained. The figure shows the relationship between dosage level (independent variable) and recall score (dependent variable). (After Darley and others, 1973)

After consuming the marihuana, the subject engaged in a series of tasks; the one of interest here was to memorize 10 lists of words. Each list contained 20 unrelated words, so the memorization task was quite difficult. The subject was allowed 30 minutes to memorize the word lists. One week later the subject was brought back to the laboratory and asked to recall as many words as possible from the lists. Figure 1-6 gives the percentage of words recalled for each of the four groups. Note that recall decreases as a function of the amount of marihuana taken at the time the subject studied the lists. (There was more to the experiment, but this description is sufficient for our purposes.)

The experimenters had worked out a careful *plan* before bringing the subjects to the laboratory. Except for the dosage of marihuana, they held all conditions constant: the general setting for the experiment, the instructions to the subjects, the material to be memorized, the time allowed for memorization, and the conditions under which recall was tested. The only factor permitted to vary across groups was the dosage of marihuana—the *independent variable.* The *dependent variable* was the amount of material recalled one week later. The marihuana dosage was measured in milligrams of THC; memory was measured in terms of percentage of words recalled a week later. The experimenters could plot the relationship between the independent and dependent variables as shown in Figure 1-6. Finally, the experimenters used enough subjects (20 per group) so that they could count on similar results if the experiment were repeated with a different sample of subjects.

The degree of control possible in the laboratory makes a laboratory experiment the preferred scientific method when it can be used appropriately. Precision instruments are usually necessary in order to control stimuli and to obtain exact data. The experimenter may need to produce colors of known wavelengths in vision studies, or sounds of known frequency in audition studies. It may be necessary to expose a pattern in an aperture of a viewing screen for a fraction of a second. With precision instruments, time can be measured in thousandths of a second, and physiological activity can be studied by means of very slight electrical currents amplified from the brain. Thus, the psychological laboratory has audiometers, photometers, oscilloscopes, electronic timers, electroencephalographs, and computers.

The value of an experiment is not determined, however, by the amount of apparatus used. If the logic of experimentation requires precision apparatus, then such apparatus should be used; if it does not, good experimentation can be carried out with pencil-and-paper procedures.

Moreover, for psychology to develop as a science it is not essential that all its problems be brought into the laboratory. Some sciences, such as geology and astronomy, are experimental only to a very limited extent. Now that we have recognized the value of the laboratory approach, without establishing its claims as exclusive, we turn to other methods used in psychological investigations.

Observational Method

Fig. 1-7 Chimpanzees observed in their natural habitat

Such naturalistic studies tell more about social behavior than strictly experimental studies can. For example, grooming behavior, as shown in the picture, is a common form of social contact among chimpanzees in the wild.

The early stages of a science necessitate exploration to become familiar with the relationships that later will become the object of more precise study. Careful observation of animal and human behavior (including the study of our own conscious processes) is the starting point of psychology. Observation of chimpanzees in their native environment of Africa may tell us things about their social organization that will help us conduct our laboratory investigations (Figure 1-7). Study of preliterate tribes reveals the ranges of variation in human institutions, which would go unrecognized if we confined our study to men and women of our own culture. Motion pictures of newborn babies reveal the details of movement patterns shortly after birth and the types of stimuli to which babies are responsive.

In making observations of naturally occurring behavior, anecdotes may be substituted for genuine observation, or interpretations for descriptions. We may be tempted, for example, to say that an animal known to have been without food is "looking for food" when all we have observed is heightened activity. Investigators must be trained to observe and record accurately in order to avoid projecting their own wishes or biases into what they report.

Observational methods have also been brought into the laboratory. In their extensive study of the physiological aspects of human sexuality, Masters and Johnson (1966) developed techniques that permitted direct observation of the sexual response in the laboratory. The intimate nature of the research required careful planning to devise procedures for making the subjects feel at ease in the laboratory, and to develop appropriate methods for observing and recording their responses. The data included (1) observations of behavior, (2) recordings of bodily changes, and (3) responses to questions asked about the subject's sensations before, during, and after sexual stimulation.

Masters and Johnson would be the first to agree that human sexuality has many dimensions in addition to the biological one. But, as they point out, we need to know the basic anatomical and physiological facts of sexual response before we can understand the psychological aspects. Their research has shown that some of the psychological hypotheses regarding sex (for example, the nature of the female orgasm and factors that contribute to sexual adequacy) are based on false biological assumptions. We will return to this topic in a later chapter.

Survey Method

Some problems that are difficult to study by direct observation may be studied through the use of questionnaires or interviews. For example, prior to the Masters and Johnson research on sexual response, most of the information on how people behaved sexually (as opposed to how laws,

church, or society said they should behave) came from extensive surveys conducted by the late Alfred Kinsey and his associates some 25 years ago. Information from thousands of individual interviews was analyzed to form the basis of *Sexual Behavior in the Human Male* (Kinsey et al., 1948) and *Sexual Behavior in the Human Female* (Kinsey et al., 1953).

Surveys have also been used to obtain information on political opinions, consumer preferences, health care needs, and many other topics. The Gallup poll and the U.S. Census are probably the most familiar surveys. An adequate survey requires a carefully pretested questionnaire, a group of interviewers trained in its use, a sample carefully selected to ensure that the respondents are representative of the population to be studied, and appropriate methods of data analysis and reporting so that the results are properly interpreted.

Test Method

The test is an important research instrument in contemporary psychology. It is used to measure all kinds of abilities, interests, attitudes, and accomplishments. Tests enable the psychologist to obtain large quantities of data from people with minimum disturbance of their living routines and without elaborate laboratory equipment. A test essentially presents a uniform situation to a group of people who vary in aspects relevant to the situation (such as intelligence, manual dexterity, anxiety, and perceptual skills). An analysis of the results then relates variations in test scores to variations among people.

Test construction and use are, however, no simple matters. They involve many steps in item preparation, scaling, and establishing norms. Later chapters will explore the problems of testing in some detail.

Case Histories

Scientific biographies, known as case histories, are important sources of data for psychologists studying individuals. There can, of course, be case histories of institutions or groups of people as well.

Most case histories are prepared by *reconstructing the biography* of a person according to remembered events and records. Reconstruction is necessary because the person's earlier history often does not become a matter of interest until he develops some sort of problem; at such time understanding of the past is thought to be important to comprehension of present behavior. The retrospective method may result in distortions of events or oversights, but it is often the only method available.

Case histories may also be based on a longitudinal study. This type of study follows an individual or group of individuals over an extended period of time, with measurements made at periodic intervals. Thus the case history is constructed from actual observations made by the investigator according to a plan. The advantage of a longitudinal study is that it does not depend on the memories of those interviewed at a later date. The disadvantage is that in most studies a large amount of data has to be collected from many individuals in the hope that some of the data will eventually show the characteristics of interest to the investigator—perhaps unusual creative abilities or some forms of mental disturbance.

"How would you like me to answer that question? As a member of my ethnic group, educational class, income group, or religious category?"

Measurement in Psychology

Whatever methods psychologists use, sooner or later they find it necessary to make statements about *amounts* or *quantities*. Variables have to be assessed in some clear manner, so that investigations can be repeated and confirmed by others. Occasionally variables can be grouped into *classes* or *categories*, as when separating boys and girls for the study of sex differences. Sometimes the variables are subject to ordinary *physical measurement:* for example, hours of sleep deprivation, dosage level of a drug, or time required to press a brake pedal when a light flashes. Sometimes variables have to be *scaled* in a manner that places them in some sort of order. For example, a psychotherapist in rating a patient's feelings of insecurity might use a five-point scale ranging from never to rarely, sometimes, often, and always. Usually, for purposes of precise communication, *numbers* are assigned to variables; in that case we are dealing with *quantitative variables*. The term *measurement* can be used whenever numerical values are assigned to independent and dependent variables, or indeed to any variable.[2]

Experimental Design

An investigator must plan his experiments. He must know how he will gather his data, how he will treat the data in order to discover the relationships involved, and the inferences he can reasonably make from what he finds. The expression *experimental design* is used to describe any of the more formal patterns according to which experiments are planned. The same design might be used for an experiment in vision, one in learning, and perhaps one in psychotherapy. The total plan includes more than the design, for it involves the substance of the particular experiment.

The simplest designs are those in which the investigator manipulates one variable (the independent variable) and studies its effects on another variable (the dependent variable). The ideal is to hold everything constant except the variable in question, in order to obtain an assertion of the form, "With everything else constant, when X increases, Y also increases." Or, in other cases, "When X increases, Y decreases." Note that almost any content can fit into this kind of statement—the subjective experience of loudness related to the physical energy of the sound source, the rate of learning related to the age of the learner, the fear of snakes related to prior experience with snakes.

The method of *graphical representation* is a convenient one, with the independent variable plotted on the horizontal axis (the abscissa) and the dependent variable plotted on the vertical axis (the ordinate) as shown in Figure 1-6. We shall see later that some psychological theories attempt to predict what form such a curve will take. The orderly relation between the variables can be stated more precisely by fitting a mathematical equation to the relationship. In other words, we are interested in more than the fact that when X increases, Y also increases; we want to know what the precise relationship is.

[2] The discussion of measurement and statistics here is designed to give the student a general introduction to the problems involved in order to facilitate understanding of the tables and charts in later chapters. A more thorough discussion of statistics is provided in the appendix.

Sometimes an experiment focuses only on the influence of a single condition, which can be either present or absent. (Such a condition is simply a variable with only two values, one representing its presence, the other its absence.) In this case, the experimental design commonly calls for an *experimental* group with the condition present and a *control* group with the condition absent. The results of such an experiment are presented in Figure 1-8. Inspecting the figure, we see that the experimental group, which received computer-assisted instruction, scored higher on reading achievement tests than the control group, which did not receive such instruction.

In some instances it is necessary to investigate the simultaneous effects of several variables. Suppose, for example, that you are studying the effects of moisture, temperature, and illumination on plant growth. You could hold two of these variables constant and study the effect of the third. A little reflection will show how limited this design would be. Unless *favorable* levels of the other variables were chosen, the plant would not live, and the experiment could not be performed at all; but *how* favorable the other variables must be cannot be determined in advance. A better procedure would be to vary moisture, temperature, and illumination in different combinations. Then the effect of one variable would be studied not against a *constant* value of other variables, but against an *array* of other values. Many behavioral science problems have this multivariable character. School performance, for example, is affected by the child's native ability, diet, family background, school facilities, teacher skill, and so on. The statistical problems of such a *multivariate design* are more complex than those of a design involving changes in only one independent variable at a time, but the yield in information is often greater for the same amount of experimental effort.

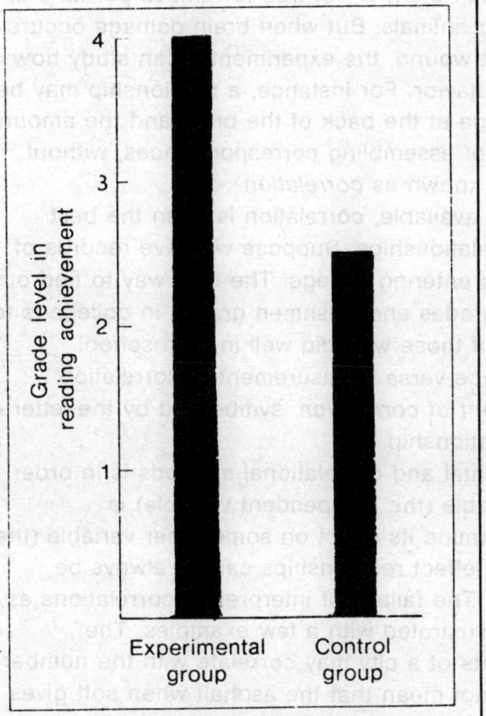

Fig. 1-8 Experimental and control groups

Each day grade-school children in the experimental group were given computer-assisted instruction (CAI) in reading. The computer presented the instructional materials to the children and then tested them on how much they had learned. CAI has the advantage of working with each student in a highly individualized way, concentrating on those areas where he is having the most difficulty. The control group had no supplementary CAI in reading. At the end of the third grade, all students in both groups were given a standardized reading test. As the figure indicates, students in the experimental group scored higher on the test than students in the control group, suggesting that CAI has been beneficial. In this experiment, the independent variable is the presence or absence of CAI, the dependent variable is the student's score on the reading test. (After Atkinson, 1974)

Interpreting Statistical Statements

Because descriptions of the results of psychological studies usually include statistical assertions, it is well to be familiar with the most common of these so that the reports will appear less baffling.

The most common statistic is the *mean,* or *arithmetic average,* which is the sum of the measures divided by the number of these measures. In experiments with a control group there are often two means to be compared: a mean for the sample of subjects run under the experimental condition and a mean for the sample of subjects run under the control condition. The difference between these two means is, of course, what interests us. If the difference is large, we may accept it at face value. But what if the difference is small? What if our measures are somewhat crude and subject to error? What if a few extreme cases are producing the difference? Statisticians solve these problems by producing tests of the *significance of a difference.* A psychologist who says that the difference between the experimental and the control group is "statistically significant" means that certain statistical tests have been applied to the data and that the observed difference is *trustworthy.* The psychologist is not commenting on the importance or practical significance of the results but is telling us that the statistical tests indicate that the difference observed is likely to occur again if the experiment is repeated. Many chance factors can influence the results of an experiment. By using statistical tests, psychologists can judge the likelihood that the observed difference is, in fact, due to the effect of the independent variable rather than an unhappy accident of chance factors.

Correlation as an Alternative to Experimentation

Sometimes strict experimental control is not possible. For example, the experimenter interested in the human brain is not free to remove portions at will, as he does with those of lower animals. But when brain damage occurs through disease, injury, or gunshot wound, the experimenter can study how parts of the brain are related to behavior. For instance, a relationship may be found between the extent of damage at the back of the brain and the amount of difficulty in vision. This method of assembling correspondences, without experimental control over them, is known as *correlation.*

When large masses of data are available, correlation is often the best available method for discovering relationships. Suppose we have records of the high-school grades of students entering college. The best way to find out the relation between high-school grades and freshmen grades in college is to *correlate* them, that is, to find out if those who did well in high school generally do well in college, and vice versa. Measurement in correlation studies is provided by the *coefficient of correlation,* symbolized by the letter *r*, which expresses the degree of relationship.

A distinction between experimental and correlational methods is in order. In an experimental study, one variable (the independent variable) is systematically manipulated to determine its effect on some other variable (the dependent variable). Similar cause-effect relationships cannot always be inferred from correlational studies. The fallacy of interpreting correlations as implying cause and effect is best illustrated with a few examples. The softness of the asphalt in the streets of a city may correlate with the number of sunstroke cases, but this does not mean that the asphalt when soft gives off some kind of poison that sends people to hospitals. We understand the cause in this example—a hot sun both softens the asphalt and produces sunstroke. Another common example is the high positive correlation obtained for the number of storks seen nesting in French villages and the number of child births recorded in the same communities. We shall leave it to the reader's ingenuity to figure out possible reasons for such a correlation, without postulating a cause-effect relation between babies and storks. These examples provide sufficient warning against giving a causal interpretation to a correlation. When two variables are correlated, variation in one may *possibly* be the cause of variation in the other, but in the absence of evidence no such conclusion is justified.

Interpreting a Coefficient of Correlation

The relationships expressed by a coefficient of correlation are made clearer by a diagram of actual test results (Figure 1-9). Forty-nine subjects were given a test of their susceptibility to hypnosis on two separate days.

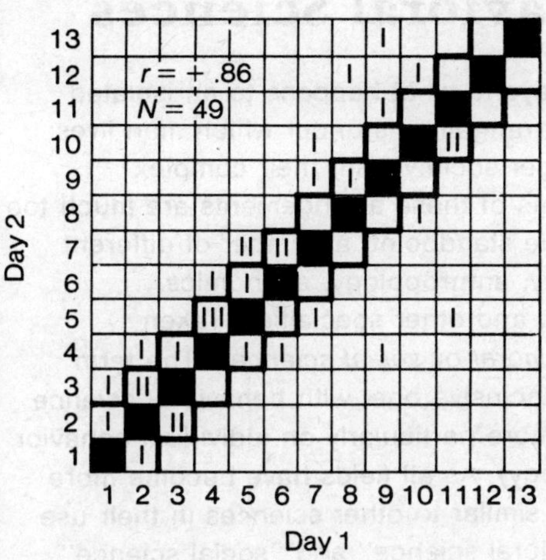

Fig. 1-9 A scatter diagram illustrating correlation

Each tally indicates the combined scores of one subject on two separate days of testing hypnotic susceptibility. Tallies in the shaded area indicate identical scores on both tests; those between the solid lines indicate a difference of no more than one point between the two scores. The correlation of $r = +.86$ means that the performances were fairly consistent on the two days. (After Hilgard, 1961)

Each tally in the diagram represents the *combined* score of one subject on the two tests. Thus two subjects made scores of 1 on both days, and two other subjects made scores of 13 on both days. But one subject (see the lower right-hand portion of the diagram) made a score of 11 on the first test but only 5 on the second one.

If all subjects had repeated their original scores on the second day, all the tallies would have fallen in the diagonal shaded squares, and the correlation would have been $r = +1.00$. Enough tallies fall to either side, however, so in this case the correlation drops to $r = +.86$. The interpretation of the coefficient of correlation requires a few words of explanation. Here are some rules of thumb:

1. A correlation of $r = +1.00$ means a perfect *positive* relationship between two variables. If weight corresponded exactly to height, so that you could precisely state a person's weight if you knew his height, then height and weight would be perfectly correlated. When the correlation is positive, the plus sign is often omitted.
2. A correlation of $r = -1.00$ means a perfect *negative* relationship. For example, if the price of a used car decreased as its age increased, so that one could precisely specify the price if the age were known, then the relation between the car's age and price would be expressed by a correlation of $r = -1.00$.
3. A correlation of $r = .00$ signifies no relation. Thus one would expect a zero correlation between the number of freckles on a person's face and his score on an intelligence test. Knowing the value of one variable in no way helps predict the value of the other variable.
4. A correlation between $r = .00$ and either $+1.00$ or -1.00 indicates an imperfect relationship. The *degree of relationship* is specified by the extent to which the value of the correlation approaches 1.00, plus or minus. Negative and positive correlations of the same size represent the same degree of relationship.
5. A correlation is *not* a percent, so a correlation of $r = .25$ cannot be interpreted as being half as great as one of $r = .50$. The relationship expressed by a correlation coefficient varies more nearly with its *square*. Thus a correlation of $r = .70$ (note that $.70^2 = .49$) expresses nearly double the relationship of $r = .50$ (note that $.50^2 = .25$). It helps to have some idea of the sizes of correlations commonly reported: (a) a correlation of $r = .50$ between the height of a parent and the adult height of a child of that parent; (b) correlations of about $r = .40$ between scholastic aptitude tests and freshman grades in college; (c) correlations of about $r = .75$ between grades in the first semester of the freshman year and those in the second semester.
6. Some supplementary information is needed to indicate whether or not a given correlation is *statistically significant.* This is the same problem met in determining whether a difference between two means is significant. For example, if too few cases have been studied, a few extreme cases might produce a high correlation, although none actually exists in the total population. Hence statisticians have developed formulas for stating the significance of a correlation; the most dependable correlations are based on a large number of cases.

The Family of Behavioral Sciences

A study of human activity should go beyond what happens to an isolated person and consider the institutional arrangements under which man lives: the family, the community, and the larger society, with their complex interrelationships. Because the problems of these arrangements are much too varied to be understood from any single standpoint, a number of different fields of inquiry have developed: history, anthropology, economics, geography, political science, sociology, and other specialties. Taken together, these are known as the *behavioral* or *social sciences.* The term "social science" used to be the more inclusive one, with behavioral science restricted to those fields that focused more particularly on individual behavior (anthropology, psychology, and sociology). As all fields have become more alike in their use of empirical data and similar to other sciences in their use of rigorous methods, the terms "behavioral science" and "social science" have come to be used interchangeably.

Just as there are divisions of labor among the specialties within psychology, so there are divisions of labor among and within the other behavioral sciences. As methods of study became more sophisticated and tools of inquiry were refined, it was inevitable that specialization should proceed in this manner, but there is a price to pay for such specialization. What is lost is a common attack on important human problems. This now has to come about from some new act of synthesis or integration that brings back together the results obtained from the divergent and specialized approaches.

Basic and Applied Aspects

All sciences have two foci of interest, basic research and applied research. *Basic research* is concerned with the quest for knowledge, regardless of whether it has immediate practical value. A psychologist studying learning in the laboratory may not be concerned primarily with improving methods of teaching, although his findings may eventually have applications to education. He wants to satisfy his curiosity about the laws that govern learning. His results may have practical consequences, but that is not his chief concern.

Applied research seeks to improve the human condition by discovering something that can be put to practical use. A psychologist trying out two different methods for teaching algebra in a school classroom is concerned with finding the most effective way of teaching mathematics. His results may have implications for a theory of learning, but his goal is the practical one of improving teaching methods. Of course, the methods that the psychologist wants to test in the classroom may be suggested by the theories and research of the laboratory scientist.

All sciences have their basic and applied aspects: botany and agriculture, physics and engineering, physiology and medicine, chemistry and pharmacology, to name a few. Although the applied-basic distinction is meaningful, it is somewhat artificial because research often serves both scientific curiosity and practical goals at the same time. A clinical psychologist may gather data in his treatment of patients that is pertinent to theories about the cause of mental disorders.

Psychology, along with the other behavioral sciences, seeks to develop facts and theories in an orderly way so as to provide a general understanding of man and his place in nature. It seeks also ways of designing human arrangements to alleviate suffering, increase general well-being, and improve the quality of life.

Organization of the Book

Psychologists today are in the process of investigating thousands of different problems ranging from microelectrode studies of how individual brain cells communicate to studies of the effects of population density and overcrowding on behavior. Deciding how to classify these problems into topics and how to present the topics in the most meaningful order is difficult. In sciences where facts and theories are fairly well established, such as physics and chemistry, most introductory textbooks arrange their topics in approximately the same order—starting with basic concepts and proceeding to the most complex. In a science as young as psychology, however, where theories are still very preliminary and so much remains unknown, the natural order of topics is not always clear. If you examine a number of introductory psychology texts you will find considerable variation in the grouping and ordering of topics. Should we know how people perceive the world around them in order to understand how they learn new things? Or does learning determine how we perceive our environment? Should we discuss what motivates a person to action so that we can understand his personality? Or can motivation be better understood if we look first at the way personality develops as a function of basic needs?

Despite such unresolved questions we have tried to arrange the topics in this book so that the understanding of the issues in each chapter will provide a background for the study of problems in the next.

Since we need to know something of a person's biological equipment—his brain, nervous system, endocrine glands—before we can understand how he interacts with his environment, these features will be discussed in the next chapter.

Part Two (Biological and Developmental Processes) will provide an overview of the individual's development from infancy through adolescence and adulthood. By noting how abilities, attitudes, and personality develop, and the problems that must be faced at different stages of life, we can appreciate more fully the kinds of questions to which psychology seeks answers.

We know the world around us through our senses. To understand how the individual reacts to his world we should know how the sense organs mediate the sensations of light, sound, touch, and taste; how the organism interprets and reacts to patterns of stimuli; and the characteristics of human consciousness under both normal and altered states of awareness. These topics are the substance of Part Three (Perception and Awareness).

Part Four (Learning and Thinking) is concerned with the processes by which we acquire skills and knowledge, remember them, and use them for purposes of communication, problem-solving, and thinking.

Part Five (Motivation and Emotion) deals with the forces that energize and direct behavior; these include biological needs as well as psychological motives and emotions.

The way in which individuals differ from one another, both in personal characteristics and abilities, is the substance of Part Six (Personality and Individuality). The development and treatment of abnormal behavior patterns provide the topics for Part Seven (Conflict, Adjustment, and Mental Health).

Part Eight (Social Behavior), is concerned with man in his social interactions—how he influences others and is influenced by them, and how he functions in groups.

Summary

1. The study of man can be approached from several viewpoints. The *neurobiological approach* attempts to relate human actions to events taking place inside the body, particularly in the brain and nervous system. The *behavioral approach* focuses on those external activities of the organism that can be observed and measured. *Cognitive psychology* is concerned with the way the brain actively processes incoming information by transforming it internally in various ways. The *psychoanalytic approach* emphasizes unconscious motives stemming from repressed sexual and aggressive impulses in childhood. *Humanistic psychology* focuses on the person's subjective experiences, freedom of choice, and motivation toward self-actualization. A particular area of psychological investigation can be approached from several of these viewpoints.
2. Psychology is defined as *the science that studies behavior and mental processes.* Its numerous areas of specialization include clinical and counseling psychology; experimental psychology; developmental, personality, and social psychology; industrial and engineering psychology; school and educational psychology. Some psychologists are chiefly methodologists whose expertise is primarily in mathematics, statistics, and computation.
3. When applicable, the *experimental method* is preferred for studying problems because it seeks to control all variables, except the one being studied, and provides for precise measurement of the *independent* and *dependent* variables. The independent variable is the one manipulated by the experimenter; the dependent variable, usually some measure of the subject's behavior, is affected by changes in the independent variable.
4. Other methods for investigating psychological problems include the observational method, the survey method, the test method, and case histories.
5. Measurement in psychology requires arranging observations so that numerical values can be assigned to the resulting data. One approach is through experimental design, in which experiments are so arranged that changes in the dependent variable can be studied in relation to changes in the independent variable (or to several variables at once). If the independent variable is something that is either present or absent, the control group method is appropriate; then the experimenter compares what happens in a given setting when the variable is present and when it is absent. Any differences in means can be tested for significance by appropriate statistical tests.
6. Another approach to research is by way of *correlation*. When the experimenter does not have control of the independent variable, he can make widely ranging observations and then study how one variable changes as another one changes. This method often is used with scores

from psychological tests. A correlation between *X* and *Y* tells how a change in *X* is related to a change in *Y*. If the relation is one-to-one, then the correlation is either $r = +1.00$ or $r = -1.00$; correlations between zero and ± 1.00 represent imperfect relationships.

Further Reading

The topical interests and theories of any contemporary science can often be understood best according to their history. Several useful books are Boring, *A history of experimental psychology* (2nd ed., 1950); Murphy and Kovach, *Historical introduction to modern psychology* (3rd ed., 1972); Herrnstein and Boring, *A sourcebook in the history of psychology* (1965); Wertheimer, *A brief history of psychology* (1970); and Watson, *The great psychologists: from Aristotle to Freud* (3rd ed., 1971).

A short paperback by Deese, *Psychology as science and art* (1972), discusses the problems involved in the search for psychological knowledge. The methods of psychological research are presented in Hyman, *The nature of psychological inquiry* (1964), and Myers and Grossen, *Behavioral research* (1974). More detailed accounts of research procedures in various areas of psychology may be found in Kling and Riggs, *Experimental psychology* (3rd ed., 1971).

The relation of psychology to the other behavioral or social sciences is considered in National Academy of Sciences/Social Science Research Council, *Behavioral and social sciences: outlook and needs* (1969), and in Clark and Miller (eds.), *Psychology: behavioral and social science survey* (1970).

To find out more about the specialty areas in psychology and the training required to become a psychologist, write to the American Psychological Association (1200 Seventeenth Street, N.W., Washington, D.C. 20036) for a copy of their booklet, *A career in psychology.*

part two

2. biological basis of psychology
3. developmental psychology

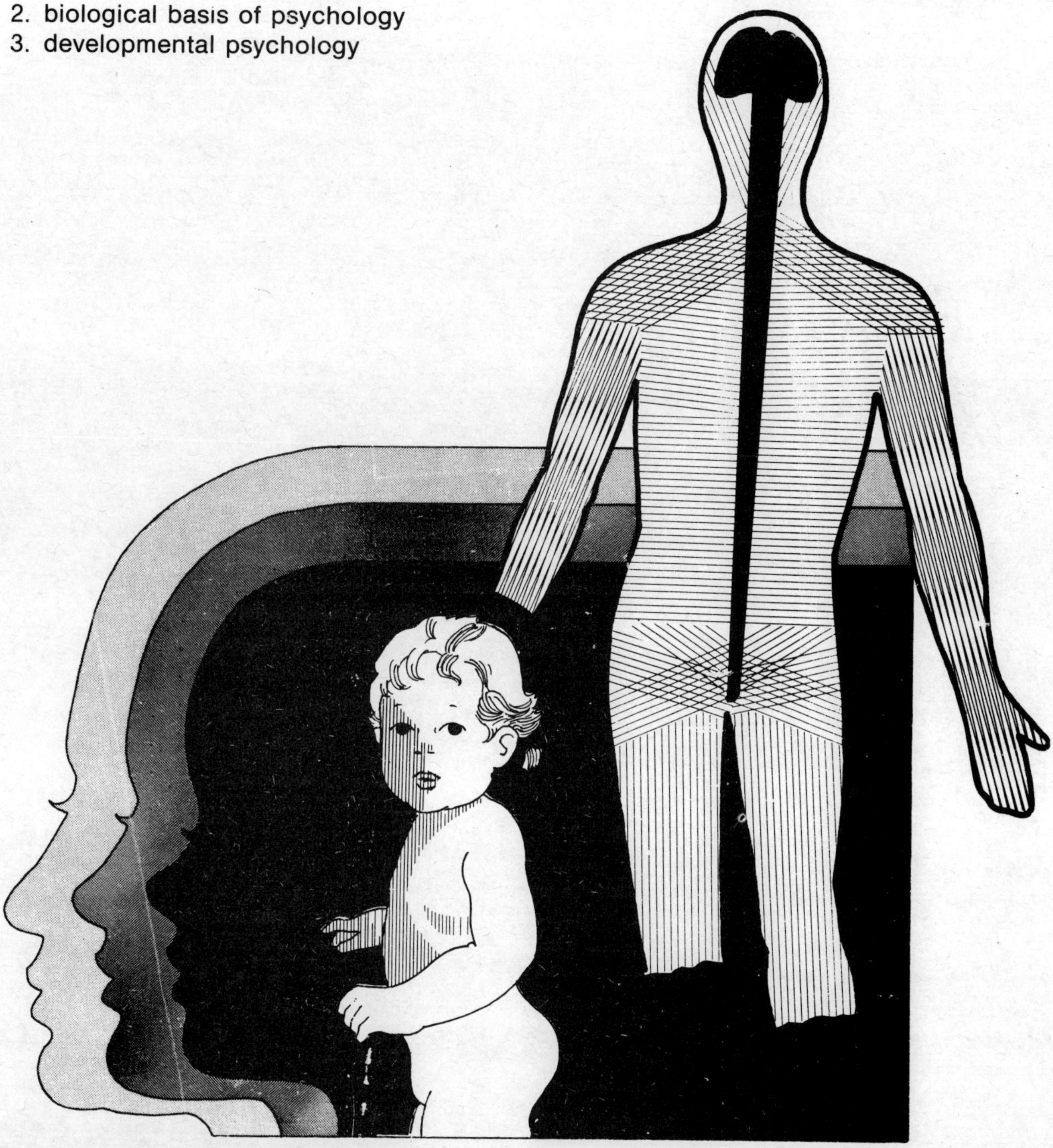

biological and developmental processes

biological basis of psychology

2

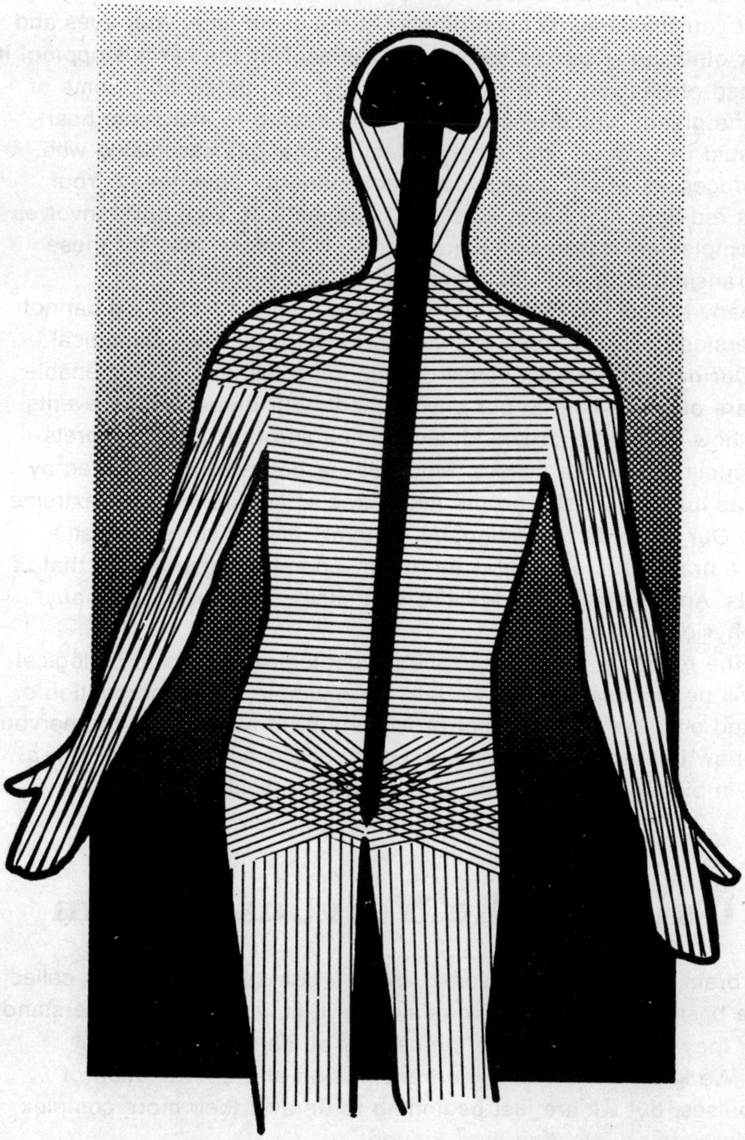

Behavior, from blinking an eyelid to driving a car or solving a mathematical equation, depends on the integration of numerous processes within the body. This integration is provided by the nervous system with the help of the endocrine glands.

Consider, for example, all the processes that must coordinate effectively for you to stop your car at a red light. First of all, you must *see* the light; this means that the light must attract the attention of one of your sense organs, your eye. Neural impulses from your eye are relayed to your brain where various features of the stimulus are analyzed and compared with information about past events stored in your memory. (You recognize that a red light in a certain context means "stop.") The process of pressing the brake pedal begins when the motor area of the brain signals the muscles of your leg and foot to respond. But you do not stop the car with one sudden movement of your leg. You receive continual *feedback* from muscles to a specialized part of your brain so that you are aware of how much pressure you are exerting and can alter your movements accordingly. At the same time, your eyes and some of your other body senses tell you how effectively the car is stopping. If the light turned red as you were speeding toward the intersection, some of your endocrine glands would also be activated, leading to increased heart rate, more rapid respiration, and other metabolic changes associated with fear; these processes would speed your reactions in an emergency. Your stopping at a red light may seem quick and automatic to you, but it involves numerous complex messages and adjustments. The information for these activities is transmitted by individual nerve cells, or *neurons.*

In fact, many aspects of human behavior and mental functioning cannot be fully understood without some knowledge of the underlying biological processes. Our nervous system, sense organs, muscles, and glands enable us to be aware of and adjust to our environment. Our perception of events depends on how our sense organs detect stimuli and our brain interprets information coming from the senses. Much of our behavior is motivated by such needs as hunger, thirst, and the avoidance of fatigue, pain, or extreme temperature. Our ability to use language, to think, and to solve problems depends on a brain structure that is incredibly complex compared to that of lower animals. And these unique abilities can easily be influenced by any number of physiological changes.

Some of the research relating specific psychological events to biological processes will be discussed when we talk, for example, about perception or motivation and emotion. This chapter provides a brief overview of the nervous system and how it integrates the various bodily processes. Students with a background in biology will find most of the material familiar.

Basic Units of the Nervous System

The human brain is composed of some 10–12 billion specialized cells called *neurons,* the basic units of the nervous system. It is important to understand neurons, for they undoubtedly hold the secrets of learning and mental functioning. We know their role in the transmission and coordination of nervous impulses, but we are just beginning to unravel their more complex functioning in learning, emotion, and thought.

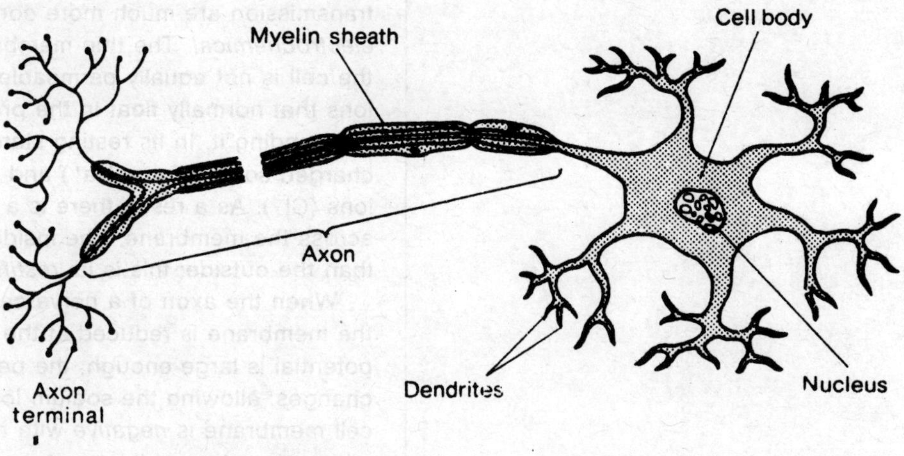

Fig. 2-1 A nerve cell

An idealized diagram of a neuron. Stimulation of the dendrites activates a neural impulse that travels through the cell body to the end of the axon. The myelin sheath covers the axons of some, but not all, neurons; it helps to increase the speed of nerve impulse conduction.

Nerves and Synapses

Each neuron is a living cell with a nucleus and other parts common to all cells. As a specialized structure the neuron consists of three main parts: the *cell body,* containing the nucleus; the *dendrites,* the many short fibers projecting from the cell body that receive activity from adjacent cells; and the *axon,* a single fiber extending away from one side of the cell body that transmits activity to other neurons or to muscles and glands (see Figure 2-1). Nerve impulses normally move in one direction—from the dendrites through the cell body and along the axon to the dendrites or cell body of the next neuron, or to a muscle or gland. All neurons have these general features, but they vary greatly in dimension and construction. A neuron in the spinal cord may have an axon 2–3 feet long running from the tip of the spine to the big toe; a neuron in the brain may cover only a few thousandths of an inch with all its parts. Closely interwoven among the neurons are a large number of cells, called *glia* cells. Until recently glia cells were thought to have only a nutritive and supportive function. New evidence suggests that they may be actively involved in the metabolic processes related to neural activity, but their exact role is as yet unknown.

A *nerve* is a bundle of elongated axons belonging to hundreds or thousands of neurons. The axons from a great many neurons (perhaps about 1,000) may connect with the dendrites and cell body of a single neuron (see Figure 2-2). A junction between neurons is a *synapse.* The synapse is not a direct connection; a slight physical separation exists across which the nervous impulse is transmitted by a chemical intermediary.

Fig. 2-2 Synapses at the cell body of a neuron

Many different axons, each of which branches repeatedly, synapse on the dendrites and cell body of a single neuron. Each branch of an axon terminates in a swelling called a synaptic knob. Inside each synaptic knob are numerous synaptic vesicles containing the chemical intermediary that transmits the nerve impulse across the synapse to the dendrite or cell body of the next cell.

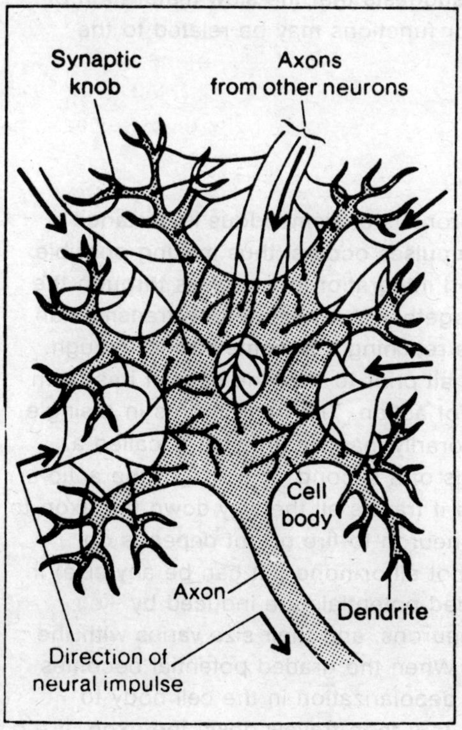

Transmission of Neural Impulses

The movement of a neural impulse along a nerve is quite different from the flow of electric current through a wire. Electricity travels at the speed of light (186,300 miles per second), whereas a nerve impulse in the human body may travel at anywhere from 2–200 miles per hour, depending on the diameter of the axon and other factors. The analogy of a fuse has sometimes been used; when a fuse is lighted, one part of the fuse lights the next part, the impulse being regenerated along the way. However, the details of neural transmission are much more complex than this. The process is *electrochemical.* The thin membrane that holds together the protoplasm of the cell is not equally permeable to the different types of electrically charged ions that normally float in the protoplasm of the cell and in the liquid surrounding it. In its resting state the cell membrane keeps out positively charged sodium ions (Na^+) and allows in potassium ions (K^+) and chloride ions (Cl^-). As a result there is a small electrical potential, or difference, across the membrane. The inside of a nerve cell is slightly more negative than the outside; this is its *resting potential.*

When the axon of a nerve cell is stimulated, the electric potential across the membrane is reduced at the point of stimulation. If the reduction in potential is large enough, the permeability of the cell membrane suddenly changes, allowing the sodium ions to enter the cell. Now the outside of the cell membrane is *negative* with respect to the inside. This change affects the adjacent portion of the axon, causing its membrane to permit the inflow of sodium ions. This process, repeating itself down the length of the axon, is the nerve impulse. The nerve impulse is also known as the *action potential,* in contrast to the *resting potential,* of the neuron. Because the nerve impulse is generated anew at each stage along the axon, it does not diminish in size during transmission.

Some nerve fibers have an insulating sheath called a *myelin sheath;* such fibers are known as *myelinated* fibers. The sheath is interrupted approximately every two millimeters by constrictions called *nodes,* where the myelin sheath is very thin or absent. Because conduction jumps along the fiber from node to node, it is much more rapid in myelinated fibers than in nonmyelinated fibers. The myelin sheath was a late development in evolution and is characteristic of the nervous systems of higher animals. The fact that the formation of the myelin sheath of many nerve fibers in the brain is not completed until some time after birth suggests that the slow maturation of some of the infant's sensory and motor functions may be related to the gradual process of myelination.

Photograph of nerve fibers and synaptic knobs.

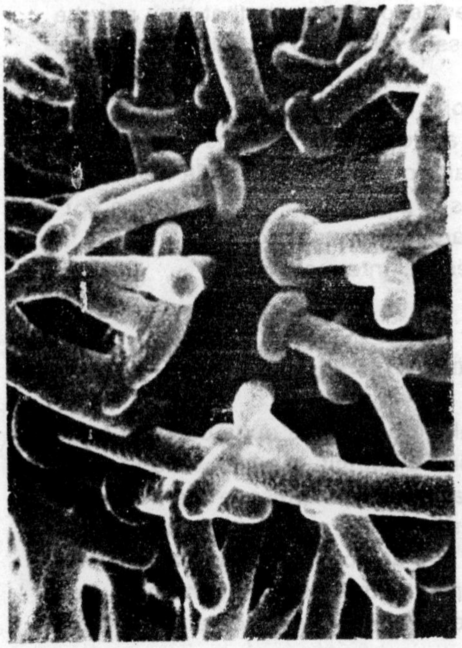

Synaptic Transmission

The synaptic junction between neurons is of tremendous importance because it is there that switching of impulses occurs, thus making possible facilitation, inhibition, coordination, and integration of impulses through the way in which groups of neurons act together. A single neuron transmits an impulse, or "fires," when the impulses reaching it become strong enough. Because its axon does not transmit at all prior to this, the neuron has been said to follow an *all-or-none* principle of action. The neuron fires in a single brief, transient burst and is then temporarily inactive (in what is called a *refractory phase*) for a few thousandths of a second. The size of the action potential is constant, and once started it travels all the way down the axon to the synapses. But the decision of the neuron to fire or not depends on *graded* potentials (potentials that are not all-or-none but can be any size) in the dendrites or cell body. These graded potentials are induced by stimulation at the synapses by other neurons, and their size varies with the amount and kind of incoming activity. When the graded potential becomes sufficiently large, it generates enough depolarization in the cell body to trigger the all-or-none action potential that then travels down the axon. If the graded potential does not reach the discharge threshold of the action potential, no activity occurs. Thompson (1967) has likened the occurrence of the graded potentials in the nerve cell to a decision-making process. The neuron considers all incoming activity and, depending on the amount and kind of this activity, decides to fire or not.

Since the size of the action potential is constant—that is, it does not vary with the strength of the stimulus—how is information concerning stimulus strength conveyed? The answer is that a strong stimulus will (1) cause the individual neuron to fire more frequently and (2) excite more neurons than a weaker stimulus.

An interesting new area of research studies the relationship between neuron activity and behavior. The electrical activity of a single neuron can be recorded by a microelectrode whose diameter at the tip is less than $\frac{1}{50,000}$ of an inch. Numerous microelectrodes implanted in different areas of an animal's brain make it possible to determine which nerve cells respond to a particular stimulus (such as touching a certain spot on the animal's body) or how the pattern of neuron firing changes as the animal becomes more proficient in learning to perform a new task. By examining nerve tissue with an electron microscope it is possible to count and measure synapses. Recent studies have shown that synapses change in both number and size as the result of an animal's early experience.

Although still in the pioneering stage, this research may provide the key to understanding the changes that occur in the brain as the result of learning. It may well be that anatomical changes in the number and structure of synapses account for our ability to remember things over long periods of time.

CHEMICAL TRANSMITTERS. As we have said, the nerve cells do not connect directly at the synapse; there is a slight gap across which the neural impulse must leap (see Figure 2-3). Although in a few areas of the nervous system the electrical activity in one neuron can stimulate another neuron directly, in most instances a chemical serves as the transmitter agent. The chemical is stored in tiny vesicles at the end of the axon until it is released into the synaptic gap when a neural impulse reaches it. The transmitter chemical combines with a receptor chemical in the receiving cell. This chemical reaction increases the membrane permeability and hence decreases the membrane potential. This *graded depolarization* may be strong enough to discharge the receiving neuron.

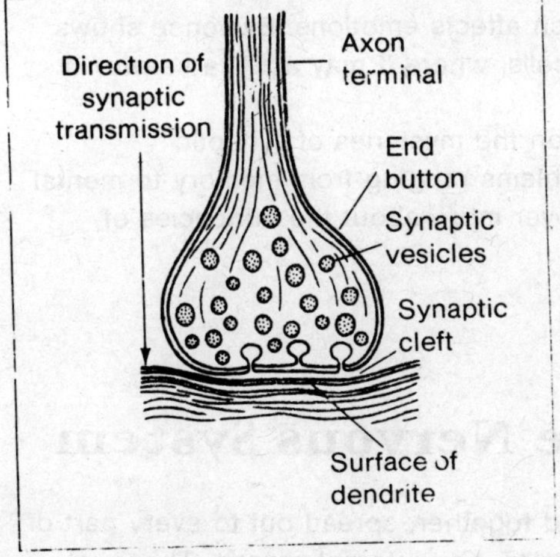

Fig. 2-3 Synaptic junction

When a neural impulse reaches the end of an axon it stimulates the synaptic vesicles to discharge their chemical contents into the synaptic cleft. This transmitter chemical combines with a receptor chemical in the receiving cell, setting up an electrical charge that may excite the receiving cell.

There appear to be two types of synapses: *excitatory* and *inhibitory*. Release of the chemical transmitter at an excitatory synapse produces a small graded shift in the cell membrane potential of the receiving neuron that is in the same direction as the action potential. When this depolarization is large enough, the cell fires an all-or-none action potential down its own axon to influence other cells.

The inhibitory synapse works in an analogous but opposite manner. Release of the chemical transmitter at an inhibitory synapse produces a small graded shift in the receiving neuron that is opposite in direction to the action potential. During this brief period, it is considerably more difficult for excitatory synapses to fire the neuron. Remember that any one neuron may connect with dendrites from many other neurons. Some of these synapses may be excitatory and some inhibitory. The constant interplay of excitation and inhibition determines the likelihood that a given neuron will fire an all-or-none action potential at any given moment.

If the brain were composed entirely of excitatory synapses, then any stimulus that excited a neuron would quickly build up excitation to the point where there would be massive discharges of brain neurons as in an epileptic seizure. For the brain to function properly, a balance must be maintained between excitatory and inhibitory processes. The complex organization of inhibitory and excitatory synapses may be the basis for the fine adjustments that occur in learning, memory, and thought.

The chemical changes take place on a minute scale. The energy involved in firing a neuron is something like a billionth of a watt; with 10 billion neurons in the human brain, and assuming every neuron is active simultaneously (which is hardly likely), the whole brain can operate on a power supply of about 10 watts. This is a remarkably low energy requirement for such a complex operating mechanism.

Several chemical transmitters have been identified, but others probably exist. Acetylcholine (ACh) is the chemical transmitter at every synapse where a nerve axon terminates at a skeletal muscle fiber and hence is responsible for muscle contraction. (It is also the transmitter at other synapses in the nervous system.) Certain drugs that block the release of ACh can cause fatal muscular paralysis. For example, *botulinus toxin,* which can form in improperly canned foods, can cause death when the muscles involved in breathing become paralyzed. *Curare,* a poison once used by South American Indians to tip their arrows, occupies the receptor site in the receiving cell, thus preventing ACh from acting, and resulting in paralysis. Some of the nerve gases developed for warfare cause paralysis by destroying the enzyme (acetylcholinesterase) that normally inactivates ACh once a nerve has fired. This produces a buildup of ACh to a point at which further synaptic transmission is impossible.

Some of the mood-altering drugs (such as tranquilizers and LSD) probably create their effects by changing the activity of the synapses. The tranquilizer chlopromazine blocks the release of the synaptic transmitter norepinephrine and thus allows fewer messages to get through. LSD is similar in composition to the neural transmitter serotonin, which affects emotions. Evidence shows that LSD accumulates in certain brain cells, where it may act like serotonin and overstimulate the cells.

Much research remains to be done on the mysteries of synaptic transmission. The answers to many problems ranging from memory to mental illness may become clearer as we discover more about the intricacies of neural communication.

Organization of the Nervous System

Nerves, groups of neuron fibers bundled together, spread out to every part of the body: to sense receptors, skin, muscles, and internal organs. Those nerves that carry sensory information from the periphery of the body and the internal organs to the spinal cord and brain are called *afferent* (sensory) nerves. Nerves transmitting impulses from the brain and spinal cord to the muscles and organs are called *efferent* (motor) nerves. The neuron cell bodies are not part of the long nerves but are grouped together into *nuclei* or *ganglia* which are found in or near the spinal cord, the brain, and some of the internal organs.

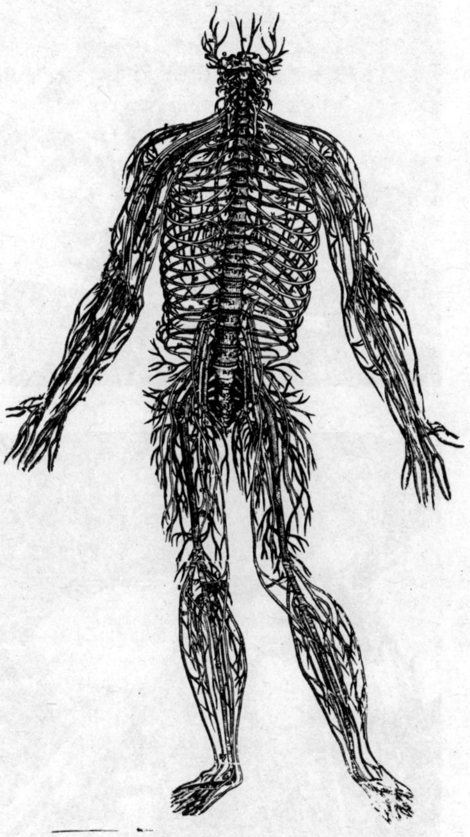

A woodcut showing the delineation of the spinal nerves done in 1543 by Andreas Vesalius.

Divisions of the Nervous System

All parts of the nervous system are interrelated. However, for purposes of anatomical discussion the nervous system can be separated into the following divisions and subdivisions:

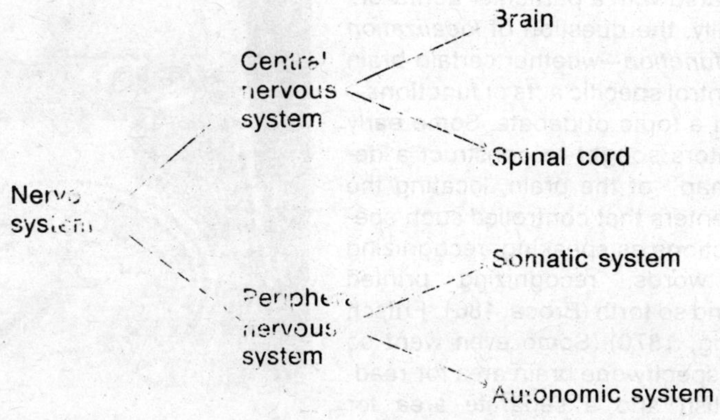

The *central nervous system* includes all the nerves in the brain and spinal cord, and contains the majority of the body's neurons. The *peripheral nervous system* consists of the nerves leading from the brain and spinal cord to the other parts of the body. The peripheral nervous system is further subdivided into the *somatic system,* whose nerves carry messages to and from the sense receptors, muscles, and body surface, and the *autonomic system,* whose nerves run to the internal organs regulating such body processes as respiration, heart rate, and digestion. The autonomic system, which plays a major role in emotion, will be discussed in a later section.

The nerves of the somatic system transmit information about external stimulation from the skin, muscles, and joints to the central nervous system; they make us aware of pain, pressure, and temperature variations. Nerves of the somatic system also carry impulses from the central nervous system back to the body parts where they initiate action. All the muscles we use in making voluntary movements, as well as involuntary adjustments in posture and balance, are controlled by these nerves. The axons of the motor neurons end, not on other neurons, but on certain especially sensitive regions in the muscles. The release of the neural transmitter ACh from the vesicles at the end of the axons stimulates the muscles to contract.

Spinal Cord

The nerve fibers running from various parts of the body to and from the brain are gathered together in the spinal cord, where they are protected by the bony spinal vertebrae. Some of the very simplest stimulus-response sequences are carried out within the spinal cord. One example is the knee jerk, the extension of the leg in response to a tap on the tendon that runs

CRITICAL DISCUSSION[1]

How the Brain Is Studied

The brain is a very complex structure, and great ingenuity is required to discover how it operates. How can we tell whether a particular part of the brain is associated with a particular behavior? Historically, the question of *localization of brain function*—whether certain brain areas control specific acts or functions—has been a topic of debate. Some early investigators sought to construct a detailed "map" of the brain, locating the neural centers that controlled such specific functions as speaking, recognizing spoken words, recognizing printed words, and so forth (Broca, 1861; Fritsch and Hitzig, 1870). Some even went so far as to specify one brain area for reading English and a separate area for reading French (Hinshelwood, 1900). Others took the view that the brain acts as a total mass with few localized functions—all areas were assumed to be "equipotential." They based their conclusions on experiments with monkeys and rats in which varying amounts and locations of brain tissue were destroyed surgically. The *amount* of tissue destruction appeared to be much more important to the animal's behavior than the specific area involved (Lashley, 1929).

Technological advances in recent years have made it possible to study the brain more precisely than ever before. It is now well established that some functions are localized in fairly circumscribed brain areas; speech, recognition of spoken words, and the production of motor responses are examples. All areas of the human brain are not equipotential. On the other hand, many different brain regions are involved in such higher mental processes as reasoning and problem solving. In addition, many functions are duplicated in more than one brain area. Thus, if one part of the brain is damaged by concussion or stroke, other areas can often take over its functions.

A

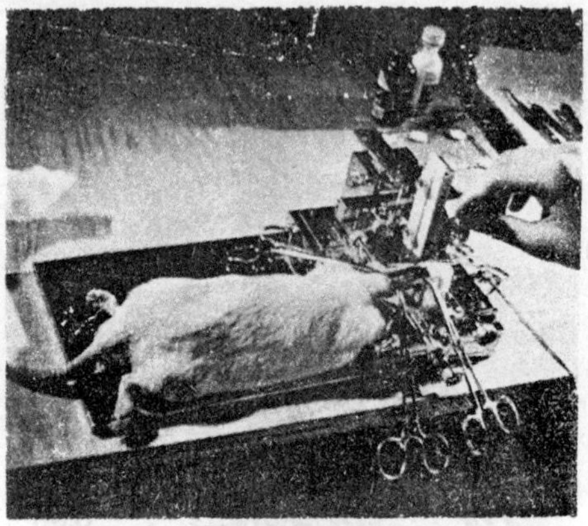

B

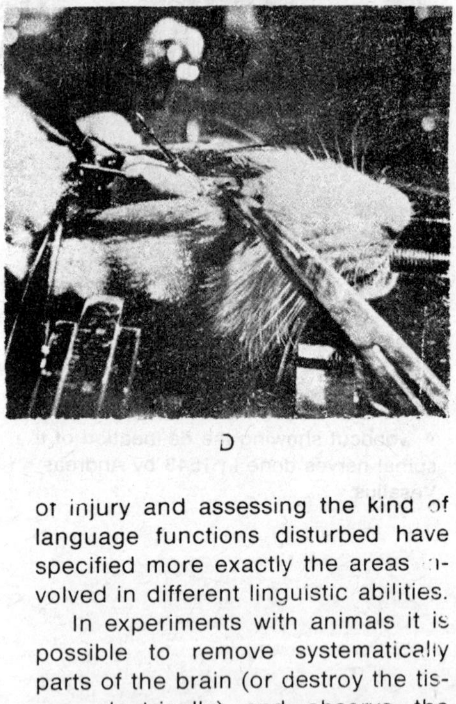

D

Fig. 2-4 Electrodes implanted in the brain

A. Rat being weighed before operation to determine the proper dose of anesthetic. **B.** Anesthetized rat under the stereotaxic instrument, which implants the electrodes through tiny holes in the skull. **C.** Insertion of screws that help to anchor dental cement to skull. **D.** Electrodes are cemented and connected to pins that project from the cement. **E.** Rat with electrodes implanted.

The following four methods are the ones used most often by physiological psychologists and neurophysiologists in studying the brain.

1. *Injury or surgical ablation.* Noting the kinds of symptoms produced when tumors or injuries damage certain parts of the brain may give clues about functions controlled by the area. Early observations that injury to the left side of the brain usually resulted in speech defects, whereas damage to the right side did not, led to localization of a speech center in the left cerebral hemisphere. Improved methods of locating the area of injury and assessing the kind of language functions disturbed have specified more exactly the areas involved in different linguistic abilities.

   In experiments with animals it is possible to remove systematically parts of the brain (or destroy the tissue electrically) and observe the kinds of defects that result. Sometimes ablation operations are performed on human patients when the removal of abnormal brain tissue is essential to their well-being (for example, to remove tumors or control epilepsy). Such patients are carefully studied to assess the effects of the operation on their abilities.

2. *Electrical or chemical stimulation.* Stimulating parts of the brain with

[1] Critical discussions are introduced from time to time to point up controversial issues or to treat a topic in more detail. They may be omitted at the discretion of the instructor.

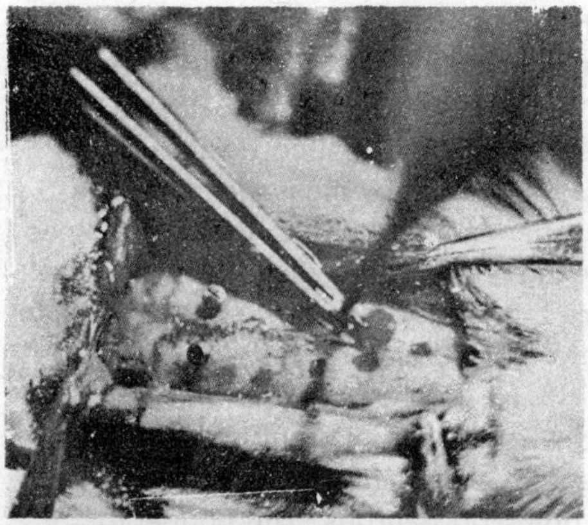

C

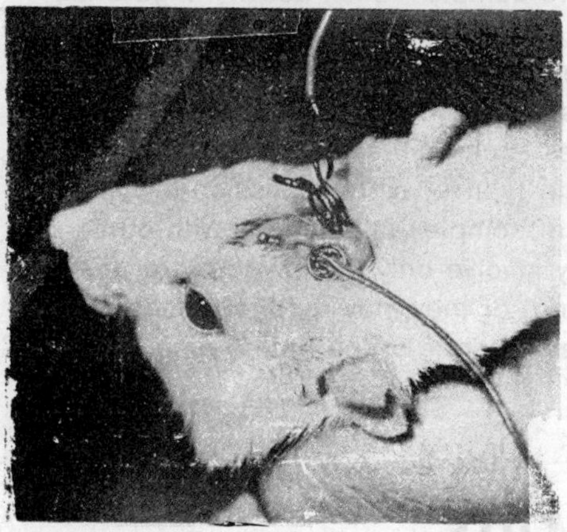

E

mild electrical currents produces effects on behavior. Brain surgery on human patients is often done under local anesthesia so the surgeon can tell (by the patient's responses when different points are stimulated electrically) which area to remove. From patient reports of sensations during stimulation fairly accurate maps of the cortex have been obtained.

Experimenters have used permanently implanted electrodes in animals to produce repeated stimulation of a local part of the brain (Figure 2-4). Studies with such electrodes help determine where sensory effects occur and where various types of muscular activity are controlled.

Chemical stimulation has also been used to affect behavior. A small tube is inserted into the animal's brain so that its end touches the area of interest. A minute amount of some chemical, often one that resembles a neural transmitter, is delivered through the tube and the behavioral effects are observed.

3. *Electrical effects of neural activity.* When neural action occurs, slight electrical currents are produced. By inserting at appropriate places electrodes connected to measuring devices, the experimenter can detect whether impulses starting at, say, the ear reach the part of the brain where the electrodes are inserted.

The brain as a whole also produces rhythmical electrical discharges. The record of these total brain discharges, known as an *electroencephalogram* (EEG), plays its part in the study of central nervous system activity. For example, if a particular kind of stimulation changes the rhythmic discharges picked up from one part of the brain and does not affect the discharges from another part, we can assume that the stimulation affected that particular region (see Figure 2-5).

4. *Single neuron activity.* The development of extremely refined microelectrodes (about one thousandth of a millimeter in size) has made it possible to record the nerve impulse from a single neuron. This technique which permits the investigator to study the activity of a single nerve cell while the organism is being exposed to different stimuli, yields information that cannot be obtained by recording massed electrical discharges.

These methods are merely noted here; later chapters will give examples of how results obtained by these methods further our psychological understanding.

Fig. 2-5 Electrical action of the brain

Through electrodes attached to the outside of the skull, the electroencephalograph measures the pattern of electrical activity within the brain. When the brain is at rest, the basic pattern is a large-amplitude "alpha" wave of about 10 cycles per second, as shown in the extreme left column of A and the first six columns of B and C. When the brain responds to sensory inputs, such as vision or touch, or when it is engaged by a mental problem, the alpha waves give way to irregular waves that are higher in frequency and lower in amplitude. (After Eccles, 1958)

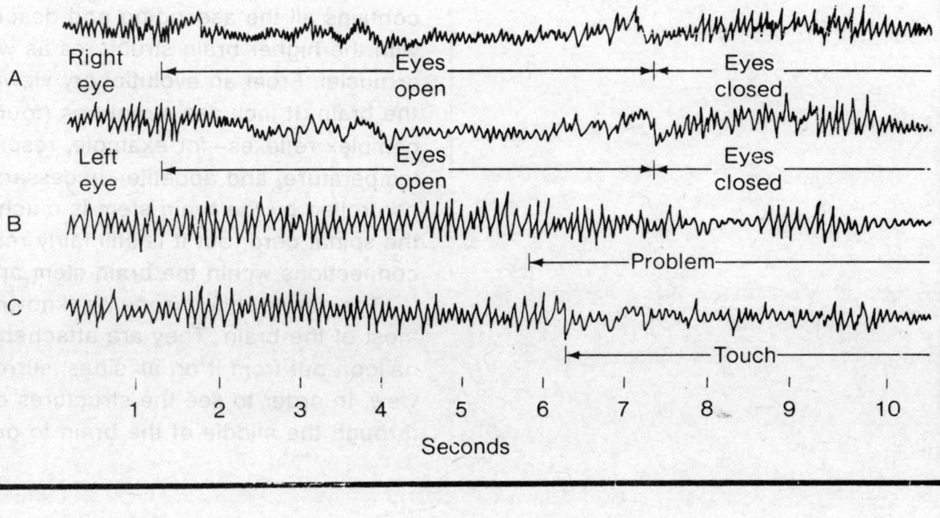

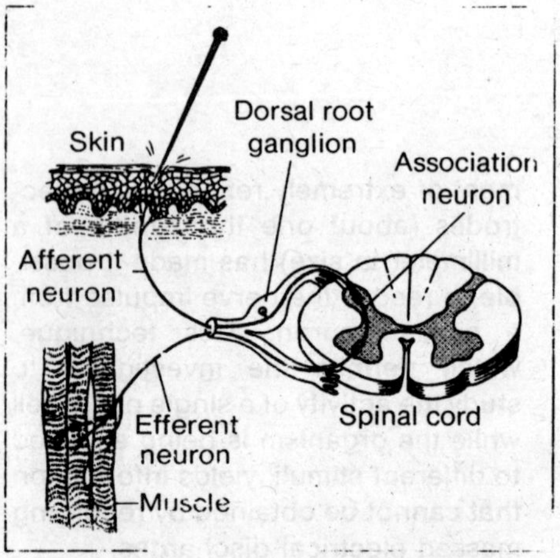

Fig. 2-6 Three-neuron reflex arc Diagram illustrates how nerve impulses from a sense organ in the skin reach a skeletal muscle by a three-neuron arc at the level of entrance to the spinal cord. Awareness of this automatic reflex occurs because impulses also reach the cerebral hemisphere by way of an ascending tract. The H-shaped portion is gray matter at the center of the spinal cord, consisting largely of cell bodies and their interconnections.

front of the knee cap. Frequently a doctor makes this test to determine the efficiency of the spinal reflexes. The natural function of this reflex is to insure that the leg will extend when the knee is bent by the force of gravity so that the organism remains standing. When the knee tendon is tapped, a message from sensory cells embedded in the attached muscle is transmitted through an afferent nerve to the spinal cord where it synapses directly with many motor neurons whose axons run in the efferent nerve back to the same muscle and cause it to extend.

Although this response *can* occur solely in the spinal cord without any assistance from the brain, it normally is modulated by messages from the higher nervous centers. If you grip your hands together just before the knee is tapped, the extension movement is exaggerated. And if you want to consciously inhibit the reflex just before the doctor taps the tendon, you can do so. The basic mechanism is built into the spinal cord, but it is under the control of the brain.

The simplest reflex may involve only afferent and efferent neurons, but most reflexes also involve one or more *connector neurons* in the spinal cord, which mediate between incoming and outgoing neurons. The connector neurons increase the possibility of more complex reflex activity. Figure 2-6 shows a basic three-neuron reflex arc.

Some reflexes are controlled at the level of the spinal cord by arcs of this type. For example, if the spinal cord is severed from the brain, as in the case of a paraplegic accident victim, reflexes such as the knee jerk and erection of the penis still function. But most activity involves transmission of nerve impulses to the brain, where all kinds of complex interactions with other neurons occur. These interactions may involve only the lower, more primitive sections of the brain stem (as in walking) or they may require numerous complicated circuits through the higher sections of the brain (as in thinking and problem solving).

Hierarchical Structure of the Brain

As the spinal cord enters the bony skull it enlarges into the *brain stem,* which contains all the ascending and descending nerve fibers that link the body with the higher brain structures as well as some important nerve cell centers or nuclei. From an evolutionary viewpoint, the brain stem is the oldest part of the brain. It includes structures (found in all vertebrates) that regulate the complex reflexes—for example, respiration, heart rate, balance of body fluids, temperature, and appetite—necessary for the maintenance of life. The activity controlled by the brain stem is much more complex than that controlled by the spinal cord, but it is still fairly reflexive in nature. That is, the neural connections within the brain stem are largely fixed and automatic.

The *cerebral hemispheres* (known collectively as the *cerebrum*) constitute most of the brain. They are attached to a small part of the brain stem and balloon out from it on all sides, surrounding and concealing most of it from view. In order to see the structures of the brain stem, it is necessary to slice through the middle of the brain to get the view shown in Figure 2-7. The

Fig. 2-7 The human brain

This schematic drawing shows the main subdivisions of man's central nervous system and their functions. (Only the upper portion of the spinal cord, which is also part of the central nervous system, is shown here.)

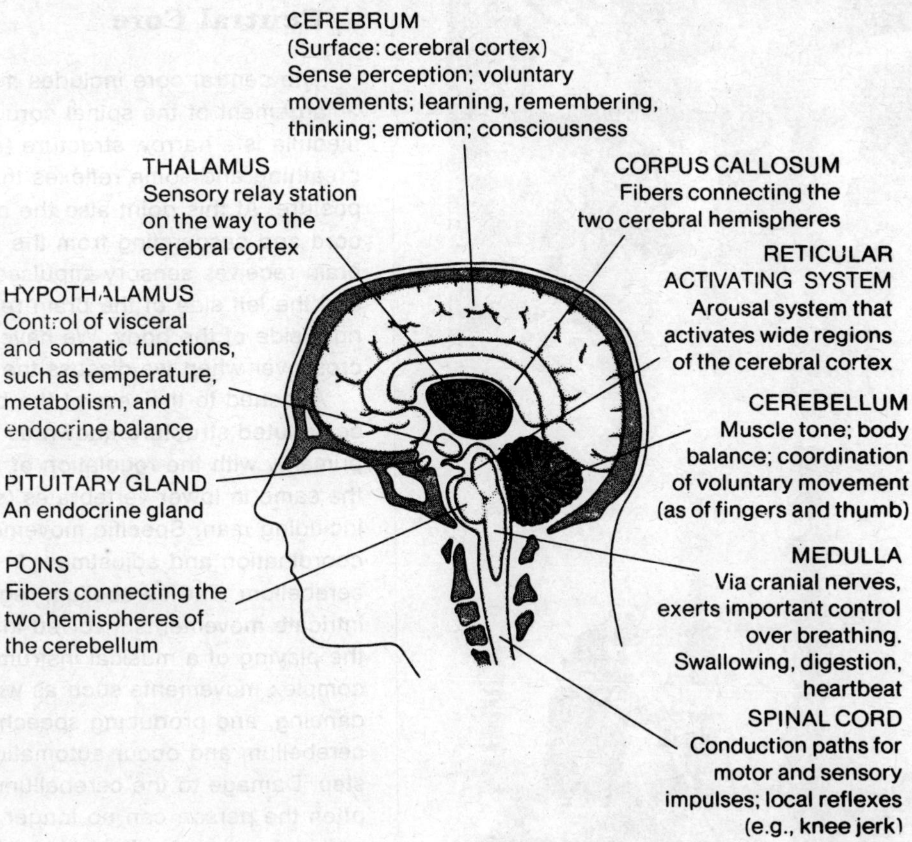

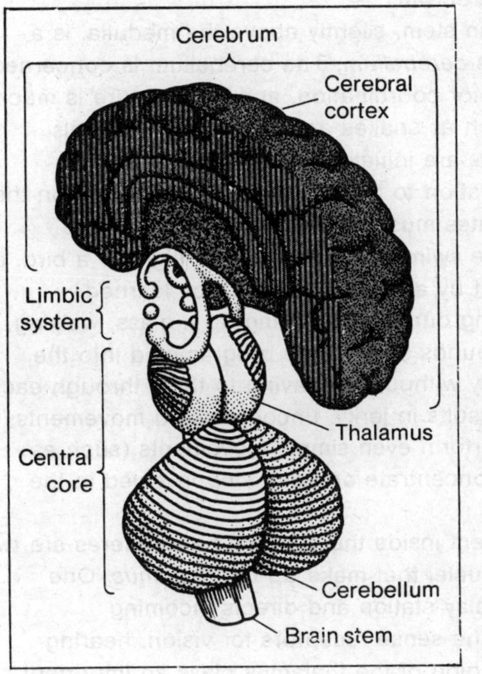

Fig. 2-8 The three concentric layers of the human brain

The primitive core and the limbic system are shown in their entirety, but the left cerebral hemisphere has been removed. The cerebellum of the primitive core controls balance and muscular coordination; the thalamus serves as a switchboard for messages coming from the sense organs; the hypothalamus (not shown but located in front of the thalamus) regulates endocrine activity and such life-maintaining processes as metabolism and temperature control. The limbic system is concerned with emotion and sequential activity. The cerebral cortex, an outer layer of cells covering the cerebrum, is the center of higher mental processes, where sensations are registered, voluntary actions initiated, decisions made, and memories stored.

cerebrum, which developed later than the brain stem in the evolutionary process, is the center for nonreflexive mental processes, which distinguish higher animals from lower ones.

The brain is incredibly complex in structure, and a hundred years from now researchers will probably still be trying to trace all its neural interconnections. We will present only the information needed to understand the psychological processes discussed in later chapters. (The student of neuroanatomy or neurophysiology may find the presentation oversimplified.)

Some brain structures are clearly demarcated; others gradually merge into each other and cause considerable debate about their exact boundaries and the neural functions they control. For our purposes it will be helpful to think of the human brain as composed of three concentric layers: (1) a primitive central core, (2) the limbic system that later evolved upon this core, and (3) the cerebrum that, as the latest evolutionary development, is the center for all higher mental processes—from perception of and response to changes in the environment to the most complex creative thinking. Figure 2-8 shows how these layers fit together and are closely interconnected. The three concentric layers may be compared with the more detailed cross section of the human brain in Figure 2-7.

Central Core

The central core includes most of the brain stem. The first slight enlargement of the spinal cord as it enters the skull is the *medulla.* The medulla is a narrow structure (about an inch and a half long) that controls breathing and some reflexes that help the organism maintain an upright posture. At this point also the major nerve tracts coming up from the spinal cord and descending from the brain cross over so that the right side of the brain receives sensory impulses from and controls the left side of the body, and the left side of the brain receives sensory impulses from and controls the right side of the body. We have more to say about the significance of this crossover when we discuss the cerebrum.

Attached to the rear of the brain stem, slightly above the medulla, is a convoluted structure known as the *cerebellum.* The cerebellum is concerned primarily with the regulation of motor coordination, and its structure is much the same in lower vertebrates (such as snakes and fish) as in mammals, including man. Specific movements are initiated in the cortex, but their coordination and adjustment in relation to the environment depend upon the cerebellum. The cerebellum regulates muscle tone and controls all the intricate movements involved in the swimming of a fish, the flight of a bird, or the playing of a musical instrument by a human being. Once learned, complex movements such as writing our name, picking up a glass, walking, dancing, and producing speech sounds seem to be programmed into the cerebellum and occur automatically without our having to think through each step. Damage to the cerebellum results in jerky, uncoordinated movements; often the person can no longer perform even simple movements (such as walking) automatically, but must concentrate on each step involved in the total action.

Located just above the brain stem inside the cerebral hemispheres are two egg-shaped groups of nerve cell nuclei that make up the *thalamus.* One region of the thalamus acts as a relay station and directs incoming information to the cerebrum from the sense receptors for vision, hearing, touch, taste, and smell. Another region of the thalamus plays an important role in the control of sleep and wakefulness and is considered part of the *limbic system.*

The *hypothalamus* is a much smaller structure just below the thalamus. Despite its size, the hypothalamus plays an extremely important role in many different kinds of motivation. Centers in the hypothalamus govern eating, drinking, sexual behavior, sleeping, and temperature control. The hypothalamus regulates endocrine activity and maintains *homeostasis.* Homeostasis refers to the general level of functioning characteristic of the healthy organism, such as normal body temperature, standard concentration of salt in the blood, and normal heart rate and blood pressure. Under stress the usual equilibrium is disturbed, and processes are set into motion to correct the disequilibrium and return the body to its normal level of functioning. For example, if we are too warm we perspire and if we are too cool we shiver. Both these processes tend to restore normal temperature and are controlled by the hypothalamus. The hypothalamus appears to contain control mechanisms that detect changes in body systems and correct the imbalance; these control mechanisms are just beginning to be understood.

The hypothalamus also plays an important role in emotion. We noted i.

Chapter 1 that mild electrical stimulation of certain areas in the hypothalamus produces feelings of pleasure, while stimulation in adjacent regions produces sensations that appear to be unpleasant or painful. By its influence on the pituitary gland which lies just below it (refer to Figure 2-7), the hypothalamus controls reactions to fear and stress.

One system of neural circuits that extends from the lower brain stem up to the cerebrum, traversing through some of the other central core structures, is the *reticular activating system* (RAS). Many incoming and outgoing nerves pass through the RAS either directly or by means of smaller branches off the main nerves. The RAS controls the state of arousal or awareness, as in changing from sleep to waking or from diffuse awareness to alert attention.

According to Woolridge (1968), the RAS acts as a "consciousness switch," turning consciousness on or off by sending suitable signals to those brain parts involved in conscious processes. When an electric current of a certain voltage is sent through electrodes implanted in the reticular formation of a cat or dog, sleep is produced; stimulation by a current with a more rapidly changing wave form always awakens the sleeping animal. Lesions in the RAS may produce permanent coma. The effects of general anesthesia result from the deactivation of the neurons of the RAS. A stimulus, such as a loud sound or a pin prick to the skin, will produce electrical activity in the appropriate regions of the brain as clearly when a person is anesthesized as when he is conscious and alert. But he is unaware of these actions because under the influence of the drug the RAS fails to send to the cortex the additional signals needed to turn on the state of consciousness.

The RAS also appears to play a role in attention. When several messages enter the nervous system simultaneously, the RAS apparently decides which is most urgent. Some messages may be toned down; others may never reach the higher centers at all. Thus, in a moment of intense concentration you may be unaware of the noises around you or the pain that was previously quite noticeable.

Both playing (upper photo) and fighting (lower photo) appear to be controlled by the limbic system.

Limbic System

Around the central core of the brain, lying along the innermost edge of the cerebral hemispheres, are a number of structures which grouped together are called the *limbic system.* From an evolutionary view, the limbic system is more recent than the central core; it is not found in organisms below mammals on the phylogenetic scale. This system is closely interconnected with the hypothalamus and seems to program the *sequential activities* necessary to satisfy some of the basic motivational and emotional needs regulated by the hypothalamus. The "instinctive" activities of lower animals, such as feeding, attacking, fleeing from danger, and mating, appear to be governed by the limbic system. Human patients with lesions in parts of the limbic system are unable to carry out an intended sequence of actions; a small distraction makes them forget what they have set out to do. The limbic system seems to build upon the homeostatic mechanisms of the hypothalamus, regulating the organisms' ability to engage in sequences of activities related to the basic adaptive functions.

The limbic system also is closely involved in emotional behavior. Monkeys with lesions in some regions of the limbic system show rage reactions at the slightest provocation. Monkeys with lesions in other areas lose aggressive behavior and show no hostility when attacked. They simply ignore the attacker and act as if nothing had happened.

Treating the brain as three concentric structures—a central core, the limbic system, and an outer core—must not lead us to think of these interrelated structures as independent. We might use the analogy of a bank of interrelated computers. Each has specialized functions, but they still work together to produce the most effective result. Similarly, the analysis of information coming from the senses requires one kind of computation and decision process (for which the cortex is well adapted) differing from that which controls a sequence of activities (limbic system). The finer adjustments of the muscles (as in writing or in playing a musical instrument) require another kind of control system, in this case mediated by the cerebellum. All these activities are ordered into complex subordinate and superordinate systems that maintain the integrity of the organism.

Cerebral Cortex

Structure of Cerebral Cortex

The two large cerebral hemispheres that envelop the brain stem are the most recent part of the nervous system to evolve, and they are more highly developed in man than in any other organism. The *cerebral cortex* is the thick layer of nerve cell bodies covering the cerebrum; in Latin the word cortex means "bark." If you look at a preserved brain, the cortical layer appears gray because it consists largely of nerve cell bodies and unmyelinated fibers; hence the term "gray matter." The inside of the cerebrum beneath the cortex is composed mostly of myelinated axons, and appears white. (A live brain appears slightly pinkish because of the blood supply.) It is in the cerebral cortex that all complex mental activity takes place.

The cerebral cortex of a primitive mammal such as the rat is small and relatively smooth. As we ascend the phylogenetic scale toward the higher mammals, the amount of cortex relative to the amount of total brain tissue increases accordingly, and the cortex becomes progressively more wrinkled and convoluted so that its actual surface is far greater than it would be if it were a smooth covering over the surface of the cerebrum. There is a general correlation between the cortical development of a species, its position on the phylogenetic scale, and the complexity of its behavior. Two-thirds of the cortex of the human brain is buried in the fissures. If the cortical tissue in the average human brain were spread flat, it would cover more than two square feet.

There are indications that the development of the cerebral cortex can be influenced by the organism's early experience. A rat raised in an "enriched" environment (in a large cage with playmates and all kinds of equipment to climb on and investigate) develops a heavier and thicker cerebral cortex than a rat raised alone in a bare cage; and such a rat will learn more readily (Rosenzweig and others, 1972).

Our clearest knowledge of the cortex has to do with those functions related to specific areas of the brain. Functions that can be mapped are *localized functions;* the places where they appear on a map of the cortex are called *projection areas.* Electrical stimulation of some areas of the cortex will produce specific kinds of *motor responses* (those involving motion or activity in parts of the body) or *sensory effects* (those involving sensation, feeling, awareness).

Tumors that exert pressure on these projection areas disturb the responses. When these areas are destroyed by disease or injury, the same functions are altered or obliterated. Yet we would be making an error in logic if we assumed that these functions are *controlled* by these areas alone. Even though an area is essential to a function, it may not be sufficient to control that function.

Before examining some illustrations of localization of function, we need a few landmarks by which to describe areas of the *cerebral hemispheres.* The two hemispheres are symmetrical, one on the right and one on the left, with a deep division between them, running from front to rear. So our first classification is the division into *right* and *left hemispheres.* For the most part, functions of the right side of the body are controlled by the left hemisphere and functions of the left side by the right hemisphere. Each hemisphere is divided into four *lobes:* the *frontal, parietal, occipital,* and *temporal.* The landmarks dividing these lobes are shown in Figure 2-9. The frontal lobe is separated from the parietal lobe by the *central fissure,* running down from the part of the cerebrum near the top of the head sideways toward the ears. The division between the parietal lobe and the occipital lobe is not as clear-cut; it suffices for our purpose to know that the parietal lobe is at the top of the brain, behind the central fissure, while the occipital lobe is at the rear of the brain. The temporal lobe is well set off by a deep fissure at the side of the brain, the *lateral fissure.*

Fig. 2-9 Localization of function in the human cortex

Left: the lobes of the cerebral hemispheres and the landmarks separating them. Right: the projection areas.

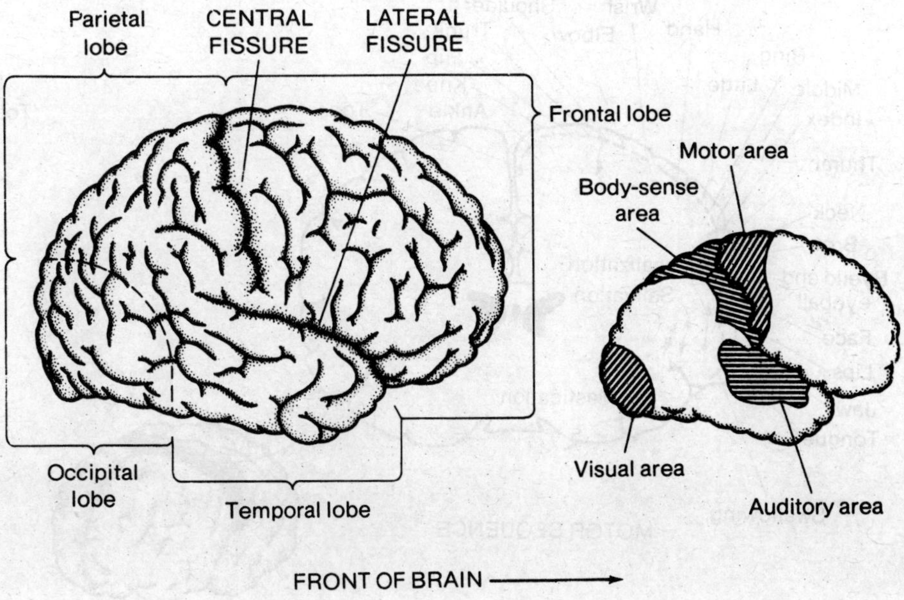

Cortical Areas and Their Functions

MOTOR AREA. The motor area, which controls all movements of the body, lies just in front of the central fissure, half of the body being represented by each side. When stimulated electrically, parts of the motor area cause movements in the extremities; when these parts are injured, the same extremities are paralyzed. The body is represented in approximately upside-down form, movement of the toes being mediated by the part near the top of the head, and tongue and mouth movements by the part near the bottom of the area toward the side of the brain (Figure 2-10). Movements on the right side of the body originate through stimulation of the motor area of the left hemisphere; movements on the left side through stimulation of the right hemisphere.

BODY-SENSE AREA. In the parietal lobe, separated from the motor area by the central fissure, lies an area that if stimulated electrically gives rise to sensory experiences, as though a part of the body were being touched or moved. Heat, cold, touch, pain, and the sense of body movement are all represented in this area. The lower extremities of the body are represented high on the area of the opposite hemisphere; the face, low.

It seems to be a general rule that the amount of cortex corresponding to a particular region of the body surface is directly related to the sensitivity and use of that region. We can see from Figure 2-10 that the area devoted to the hands and fingers, for example, is much larger than that devoted to the feet and toes. We may note that among four-footed mammals, the dog has only a small amount of cortical tissue representing the forepaws, whereas the raccoon, which makes extensive use of its forepaws in exploring and manipulating its environment, has a much larger representative cortical area, including regions for the separate fingers of the forepaw (Welker, Johnson, and Pubols, 1964).

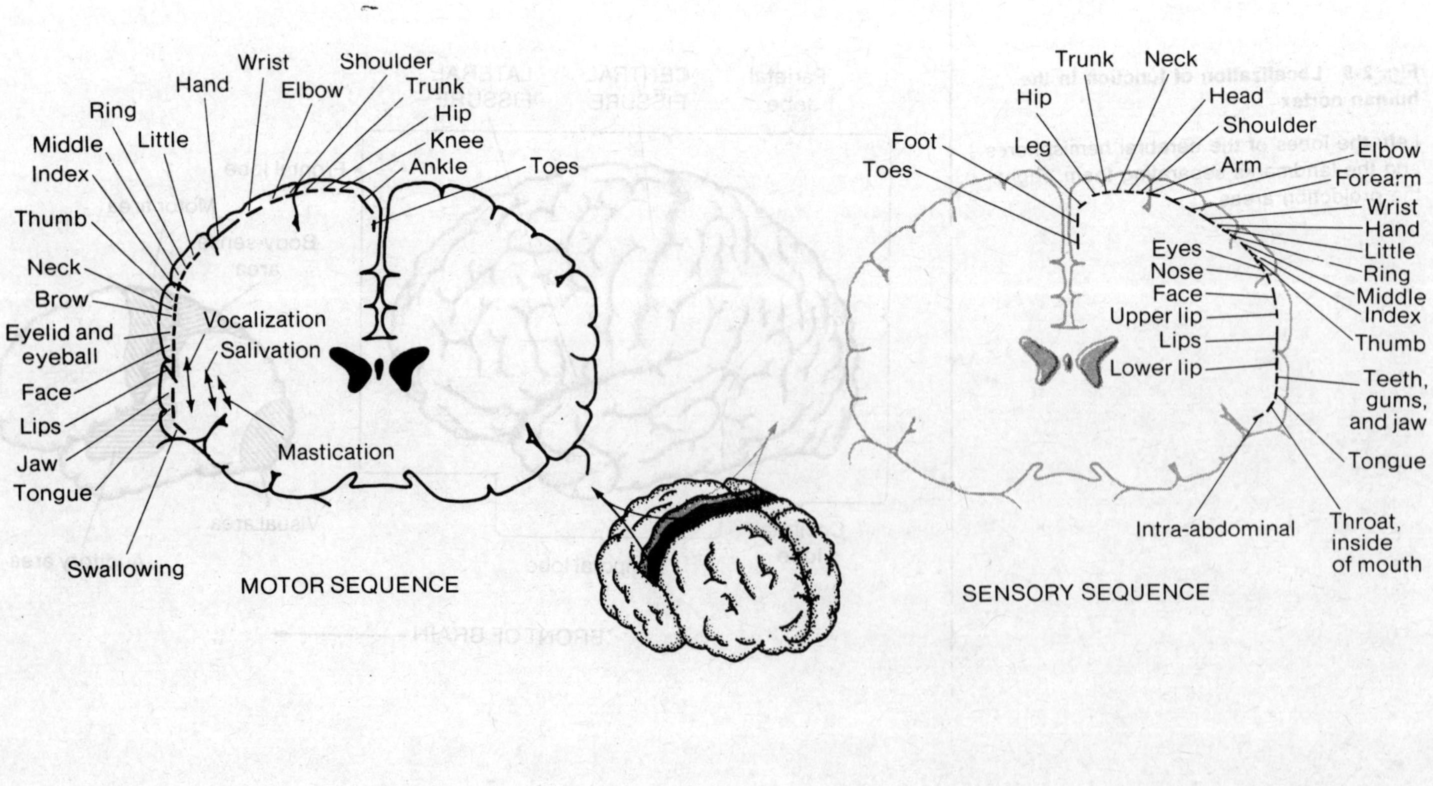

Fig. 2-10 Localization of function within the motor and body-sense areas

Two cross sections through the cerebrum are indicated: one for the motor cortex (in red) and the other for the body-sense cortex (in black). The various functions are represented in mirror image in both hemispheres, but in the figure only one side is labeled. (After Penfield and Rasmussen, 1950)

Fig. 2-11 Artificial vision

The figure on the left shows the experimental setup. A thin strip of Teflon with 64 electrode contacts is inserted against the visual cortex. Wires from each electrode connect to a computer. By stimulating pairs of electrodes at a time, it is possible to map on a television screen (with the aid of a computer) the relative position of each stimulated light spot, or phosphene, in the subject's visual cortex. Once the phosphene makeup of the subject's visual field is known, the experimenters stimulate the electrodes to present patterns and letters to the visual field. The subject draws what he "sees" on a pad. A potential artificial vision device is shown on the right.

Disease or injury in the body-sense area produces disturbances of sensory processes but seldom results in complete absence of sensation (*anesthesia*). The injured person may lose the ability to tell the positions of his arms or hands when his eyes are closed or to recognize objects by touch. Although he may still be able to detect extremes of temperature, he may be at a loss to judge finer gradations of warmth and coolness.

VISUAL AREA. At the very back of each cerebral hemisphere, in the part of the occipital lobe known as the *striate area,* lie centers important in vision. Knowledge of the functioning of the visual cortex has come through studies of the electrical responses of single cells in the cortex, chiefly in cats and monkeys, either unrestrained and mobile or lightly anesthetized (Hubel and Wiesel, 1965). When slits of light are presented in different positions in the animal's visual field, the response from cells within the visual cortex differs in orderly ways. For example, some cells will respond to a horizontal light slit but not to slits that differ from the horizontal by as much as 45°. Other cells will respond only to vertical slits of light. It appears that the sensory system is organized to perceive aspects of form and movement, and not simply points of light. We will have more to say about this intriguing area of research when perception is discussed in Chapter 5.

When the visual cortex is stimulated electrically during the course of brain surgery, the patient (who is under local anesthetic) reports seeing flashes or spots of light. This phenomenon forms the basis for research that may eventually provide "artificial vision" for blind people (Dobelle and others, 1974). An array of electrodes were implanted in the visual cortex of two blind subjects. When different groups of these electrodes were stimulated electrically, the blind subject experienced patterns of visual sensations. Although these sensations were a crude approximation of real sight, further research may provide a practical device that will enable blind persons to perceive objects and to read (see Figure 2-11).

AUDITORY AREA. The auditory area is found on the surface of the temporal lobe at the side of each hemisphere. There is some spatial distribution, one part being sensitive to high tones and a different part sensitive to low tones. Both ears are represented in the auditory areas on both sides, so that the loss of one temporal lobe has very little effect upon hearing.

The relation between the auditory projection area and behavior is illustrated by an experiment in which monkeys with electrodes implanted in their auditory cortex were trained to press a key in response to a tone. When the tone was turned on, the animal required approximately 200 milliseconds to respond. When, however, direct electrical stimulation of the auditory cortex was substituted for the tone, the response time was 185 milliseconds. The 15-millisecond difference between responses to acoustic and cortical stimulation presumably reflects the time required for the nerve impulse to reach the auditory cortex. The fact that recordings of action potentials in the auditory cortex also show a 15-millisecond delay following onset of the tone supports this assumption (Miller, Moody, and Stebbins, 1969).

LANGUAGE AREAS. Although most functions are localized equally in both cerebral hemispheres, speech, in most cases, is controlled by the left hemisphere. As early as 1861, the neurologist Paul Broca examined the brain of a patient with speech loss and found damage in an area of the left hemisphere just above the lateral fissure in the frontal lobe (see Figure 2-9). This region, known as Broca's area, is involved in the production of speech sounds—that is, in the control of the tongue and jaws in speaking. Destruction of the equivalent region in the right hemisphere usually does not result in speech impairment. A nearby region of the left hemisphere is concerned with understanding speech. Other areas, in the frontal lobes, are involved in the ability to write and to understand written words. Although the psychological functions involved in linguistic abilities are complicated and not precisely located, in most cases the brain regions concerned with spoken or written language are located in the left hemisphere. Thus, a person who suffers a stroke that damages the left hemisphere is more likely to show language impairment than one whose damage is confined to the right hemisphere. This is usually the case for right-handed individuals because their left hemisphere is almost always dominant. (Remember that the left hemisphere controls the motor functions of the right side of the body.) Some left-handed people have speech centers located in the right hemisphere or equally divided between the two; but most left-handed people apparently have "normal" left hemisphere speech centers.

ASSOCIATION AREAS. The many large areas of the cerebral cortex that are not directly concerned with sensorimotor processes have been called *association areas.* They are distinguished from the primary projection areas in that they integrate inputs from more than one sensory channel and also function in learning, memory, and thinking.

Although our knowledge about the association areas is still fragmentary, recent research makes it clear that they perform a number of different functions. The *frontal association areas* (those parts of the frontal lobes anterior to the motor area) appear to play an important role in the thought processes required for problem solving. In monkeys, for example, the ability to solve a delayed-response problem is destroyed by lesions in the frontal lobes. In this kind of problem, food is placed in one of two cups while the monkey watches, and the cups are covered with identical objects. An opaque screen is then placed between the monkey and the cups; after a specified time (from 5–60 seconds) the screen is removed and the monkey is allowed to choose one of the cups. Normal monkeys can "remember" the correct cup after delays of several minutes, but monkeys with frontal lobe lesions cannot solve the problem if the delay is more than a second or so (French and Harlow, 1962). This delayed-response deficit following brain lesions is unique to the frontal cortex; it does not occur if lesions are made in other cortical regions.

Human beings who have suffered damage to the frontal lobes can perform normally on many intellectual tasks, but they do show a deficit similar to that of the monkeys when delay is involved or when it is necessary to shift frequently from one method of working on a problem to another method (Milner, 1964).

The *posterior association areas* are located among the various primary sensory areas and appear to consist of subareas, each serving a particular sense. For example, the lower portion of the temporal lobe is related to visual perception. Lesions in this area produce deficits in the ability to recognize and discriminate different forms. The lesion does not cause loss of visual acuity as would be true of a lesion in the primary visual area of the occipital lobe; the individual "sees" the forms (and can trace the outline with his finger) but cannot identify the shape or distinguish it from a different form. Pribram (1969) has suggested that the function of this part of the temporal lobe is to organize the information coming in through the primary visual area.

Several areas, also in or near the temporal lobe, are concerned with language. Tissue damage in these areas does not interfere with the motor production of speech but results in certain types of language problems (called *aphasias*), in which the individual may have trouble recalling words or naming objects or have difficulty understanding what is said to him.

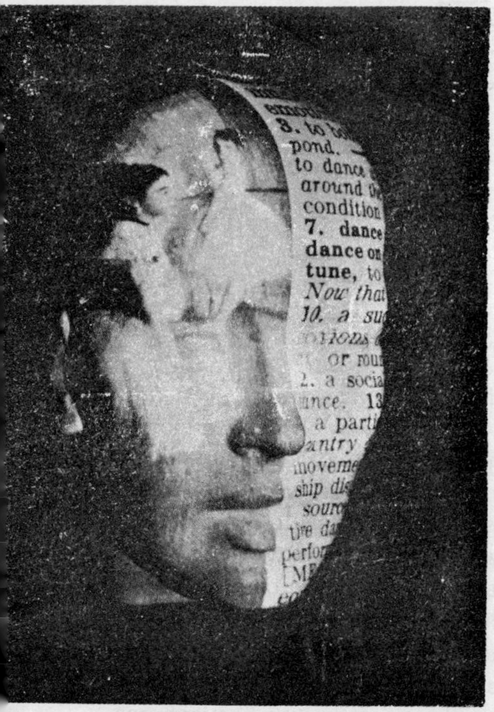

Very vivid memories can be elicited by electrical stimulation of some of the association areas in the temporal lobes. The experiences relived by the subject when the electrical stimulus is applied appear to be real events from the past, such as recollections of a childhood scene or of a tune once heard and only vaguely remembered. The tune can be "turned on" or "turned off" through electrical stimulation. These recalled events are always much more vivid than ordinary memories; it is as if the electrical current had started a filmstrip on which were registered the details of a past event long since forgotten by the subject (Penfield, 1969).

These results are intriguing, but their interpretation is baffling. Is the memory of this experience really localized in this small spot? When the spot is surgically removed it is no longer possible to secure the effect formerly produced by stimulating that spot. But the excision does not destroy the subject's ability to tell what the tune sounded like when the spot was earlier stimulated. Evidently other parts of the brain are involved in the total memory experience.

A Divided Brain

We have noted that the two cerebral hemispheres seem symmetrical in many respects; both have sensory, motor, visual, and auditory areas. Recent research indicates some dramatic differences between the psychological functions of the two cerebral hemispheres.

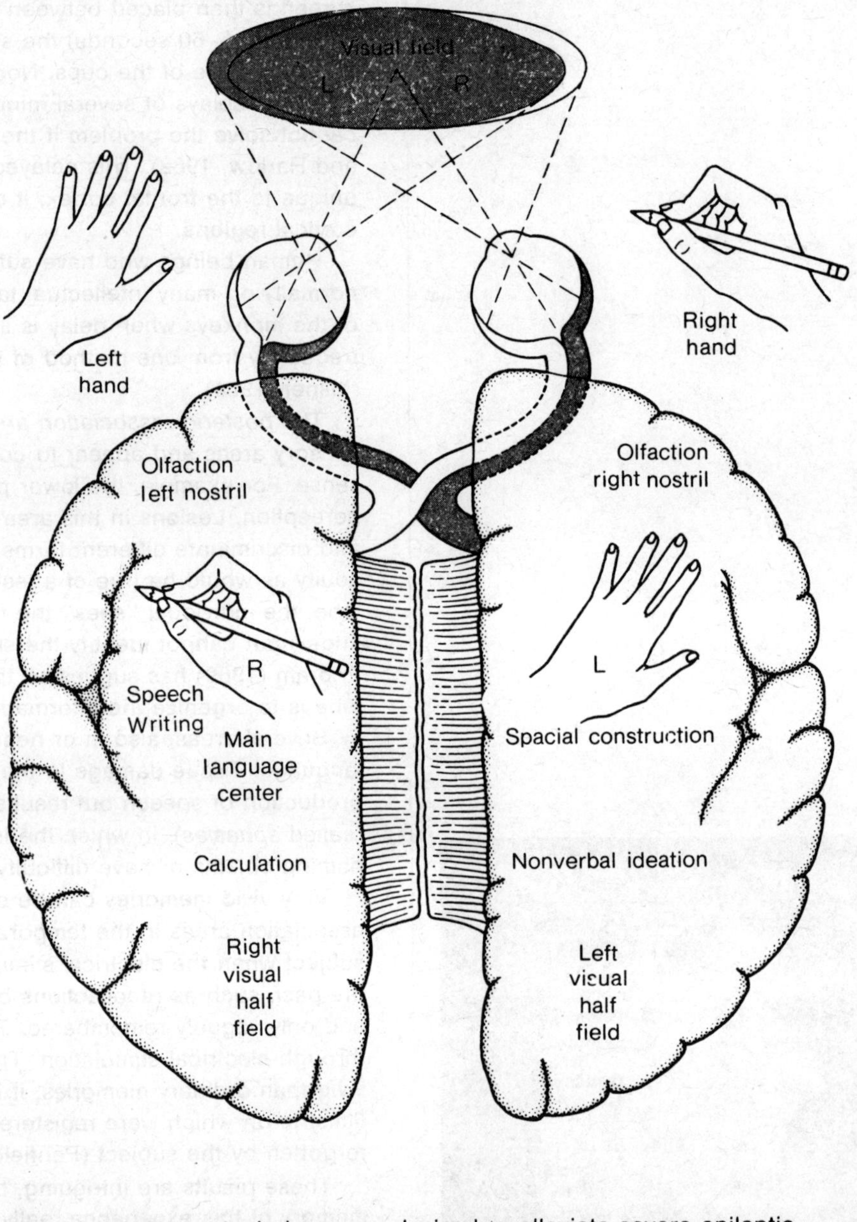

Fig. 2-12 Sensory inputs to the two hemispheres

With the eyes fixated straight ahead, stimuli to the left of the fixation point go to the right cerebral hemisphere and stimuli to the right go to the left hemisphere. The left hemisphere controls movements of the right hand, and the right hemisphere controls the left hand. Hearing is largely crossed in its input, but some sound representation goes to the same hemisphere as the ear. Olfaction is received on the same side as the nostril. The left hemisphere is dominant for most people; it controls written and spoken language and mathematical calculations. The minor, right hemisphere can understand only simple language. Its main ability seems to involve spatial construction and pattern sense. (After Sperry, 1970)

Some years ago a technique was devised to alleviate severe epileptic seizures in patients who did not respond to medication or other forms of treatment. It was hypothesized that cutting the *corpus callosum,* the broad band of fibers connecting the two cerebral hemispheres, would prevent a seizure starting in one hemisphere from spreading rapidly to the other and becoming generalized over the entire brain. The operation was quite successful. There was a significant decrease in seizures in both hemispheres, apparently because they reciprocally excite each other. There also appeared to be no undesirable aftereffects; the patients seemed able to function as well as individuals whose hemispheres were still connected. It took some very special tests to demonstrate the differences between the two hemispheres and the effect that separating them has on the individual's mental processes. A little more background information is needed to understand the experiments we are about to describe.

We have seen that the major motor nerves cross over as they leave the brain so that the left cerebral hemisphere controls the right side of the body and the right hemisphere controls the left. We noted also that the area for the production of speech (Broca's area) is located in the left hemisphere. Another fact to remember is that when the eyes are fixated directly ahead images to the left of the fixation point go through both eyes to the right side of the brain, and images to the right of the fixation point go to the left side of the brain (see Figure 2-12). In the normal brain, stimuli entering one hemisphere are rapidly communicated, by way of the corpus callosum, to the other so that our brain functions as a unit. We will see what happens when the corpus callosum is severed so that the two hemispheres cannot communicate.

Experiments with Split-Brain Subjects

In one test situation the subject with the "split brain" is seated in front of a screen that hides his hands from view (see Figure 2-13). His gaze is fixed at a spot on the center of the screen and the word "nut" is flashed very briefly (for one-tenth of a second) on the left side of the screen. Remember that this visual image goes to the right side of the brain which controls the left side of the body. With his left hand the subject can easily pick out the nut from a pile of objects hidden from view. But he cannot tell the experimenter what word flashed on the screen because language depends on the left hemisphere and the visual image "nut" was not transmitted to the left side. When questioned, the split-brain subject seems unaware of what his left hand is doing! Since the sensory input from the left hand goes to the right hemisphere, the left hemisphere receives no information about what the left hand is feeling or doing. All information is fed back to the right hemisphere which received the original visual input of the word "nut" (Sperry, 1970).

It is important that the word be flashed on the screen for no more than one-tenth of a second. If it remains longer the subject can move his eyes so that the word is also projected to the left hemisphere. If the split-brain subject can move his eyes freely, information goes to both cerebral hemispheres; this is one reason why the deficiencies caused by severing the corpus callosum are not readily apparent in a person's daily activities.

Further experiments support the idea that the split-brain subject is only aware of what is going on in his left hemisphere because it is that hemisphere alone that can communicate through language. Figure 2-13B shows another test situation. The word "hatband" is flashed on the screen so that "hat" goes to the right hemisphere and "band" to the left. When asked what word he saw the subject replies "band." When asked what kind of band he makes all sorts of guesses—"rubber band," "rock band," "band of robbers," etc., and only hits upon "hatband" by chance. Tests with other word combinations (such as keycase and suitcase), split so that half is projected to each hemisphere, show similar results. What is perceived by the right hemisphere does not transfer over to the left into the conscious awareness of the split-brain subject. With the corpus callosum severed, each hemisphere seems oblivious of the experiences of the other.

If a split-brain subject is blindfolded and a familiar object (such as a comb, toothbrush, or keycase) is placed in his left hand, he appears to know

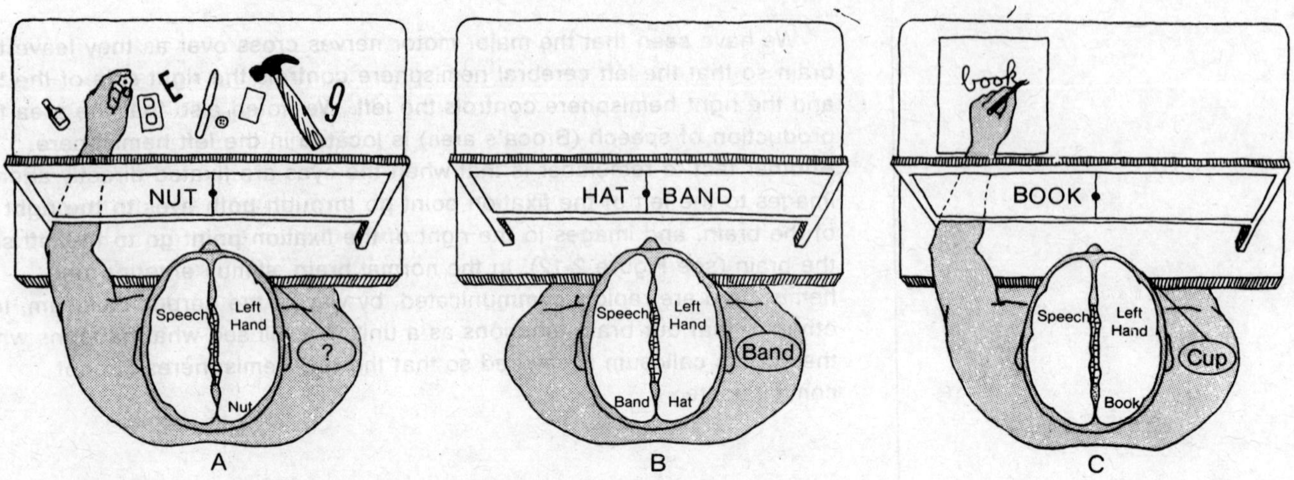

Fig. 2-13 Testing the abilities of the two hemispheres

A. The split-brain subject correctly retrieves an object by touch with the left hand when its name is flashed to the right hemisphere, but he cannot name the object or describe what he has done. **B.** The word "hatband" is flashed so that "hat" goes to the right cerebral hemisphere and "band" goes to the left hemisphere. The subject reports that he sees the word "band" but has no idea what kind of band. **C.** A list of common objects (including book and cup) is initially shown to both hemispheres. One word from the list (book) is then projected to the right hemisphere. When given the command to do so, the left hand begins writing the word "book," but when questioned the subject doesn't know what his left hand has written and guesses "cup." (After Sperry, 1970; and Nebes and Sperry, 1971)

what it is. For example, he can demonstrate its use by appropriate gestures; but he cannot express this knowledge in speech. If asked what is going on while he is manipulating the object, he has no idea. This is true as long as any sensory input from the object to the left (talking) hemisphere is blocked. But if the subject's right hand inadvertently touches the object, or if it makes a characteristic sound (like the jingling of a keycase), then the speaking hemisphere immediately gives the right answer.

Although the right hemisphere cannot speak, it does have some linguistic capabilities. It recognized the meaning of the word "nut," as we saw in our first example, and it can write a little. In the experiment illustrated in Figure 2-13C the subject is first shown a list of common objects such as a cup, knife, book, and glass. This list is not flashed on the screen but is displayed for a long enough time so the words can be projected to both hemispheres. Next, the list is removed and one of the words, for example, "book," is flashed briefly on the left side of the screen so that it goes to the right hemisphere. If asked to write what he sees, the left hand of the split-brain subject will begin writing the word "book." If asked what his left hand has written, he has no idea and will guess at any of the words on the original list. The subject knows he has written something, because he feels the writing movements through his body. But because there is no communication between the right hemisphere that saw and wrote the word and the left hemisphere that controls speech, the subject has no awareness of what he wrote (Nebes and Sperry, 1971).

Major and Minor Hemispheres

Such studies with split-brain subjects, supported by extensive research with split-brain animals, have made clear the striking differences between the functions of the two hemispheres and have raised some intriguing speculations about the nature of consciousness. The major, left hemisphere governs our ability to express ourselves in language. It can perform many complicated sequential and analytic activities and is skilled in mathematical computations. The minor, right hemisphere can comprehend very simple language. It can respond to simple nouns by selecting objects such as a nut or comb, and it can even respond to associations of these objects. For example, if the right hemisphere is asked to retrieve from a group of objects the one used "for lighting fire" it will instruct the left hand to select a match. But it cannot comprehend more abstract linguistic forms. If the right hemisphere is presented with such simple commands as wink, nod, shake head, or smile, it seldom responds. The right hemisphere can add simple two-digit numbers, but can do little beyond this in the way of calculation.

Although the right hemisphere may deserve the term "minor," it is not without special abilities of its own. The right hemisphere appears to have a highly developed spatial and pattern sense. It is superior to the left hemisphere in constructing geometric and perspective drawings (see Figure 2-14). It can assemble colored blocks to match a complex design much more effectively than the left hemisphere. When a split-brain subject is asked to use his right hand to assemble the blocks according to a picture design, he makes numerous mistakes. Sometimes he has trouble keeping his left hand from automatically correcting the mistakes being made by the right hand. There is some evidence too that the right hemisphere is the center for musical ability (Milner, 1962).

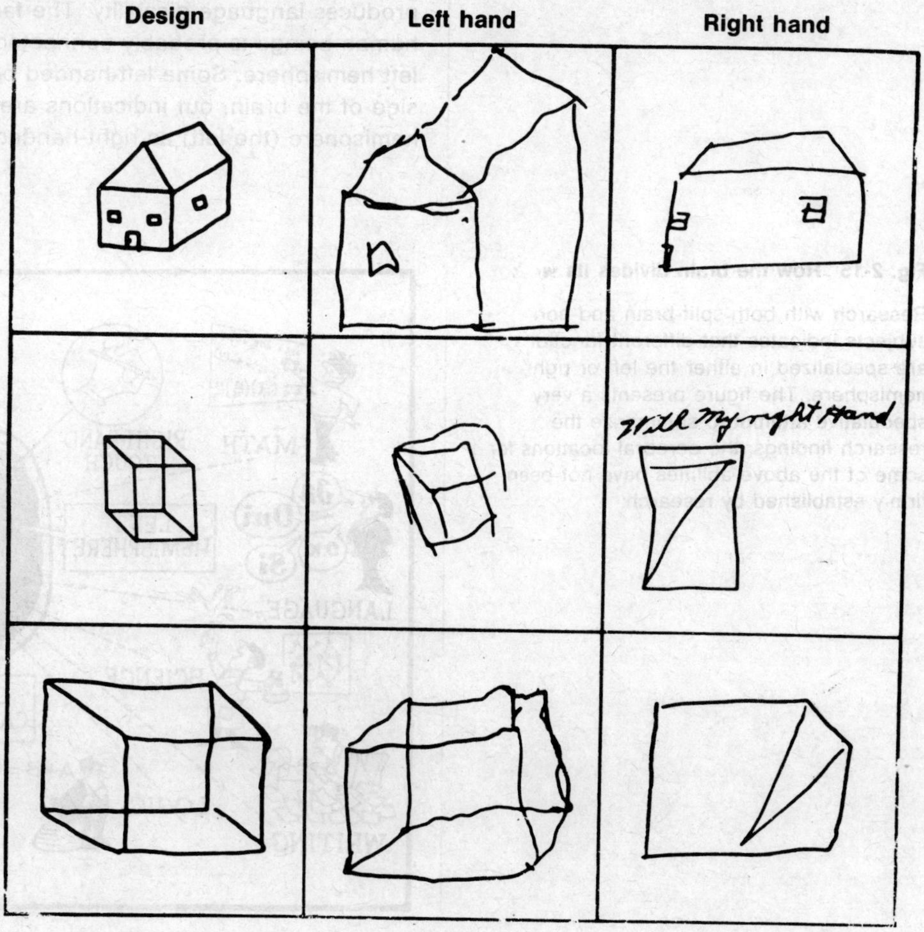

Fig. 2-14 Spatial drawing by split-brain subject

The left hand, guided by the right hemisphere, can copy three-dimensional designs (although somewhat crudely because the subject was right-handed). The right hand, guided by the dominant left hemisphere, is unable to reproduce the geometric designs (although it can write words with ease). (After Gazzaniga, 1970)

Studies with normal individuals tend to confirm the different specializations of the two hemispheres. For example, when information is flashed briefly to the right hemisphere and either a verbal or nonverbal response is required, the nonverbal response comes quicker than the verbal response. A verbal response apparently requires the information to be sent across the corpus callosum to the left hemisphere, which takes time (Gazzaniga, 1972). And studies of the electrical impulses given off by the brain (EEG) suggest that during a verbal task activity increases in the left hemisphere, whereas during a spatial task activity increases in the right (Ornstein, 1972). (See Figure 2-15.)

Split-brain research has led some psychologists to conclude that the conscious self, which is based on our linguistic memories of the past, resides in the left hemisphere. The right hemisphere itself is unconscious, but it normally achieves consciousness by communication with the left hemisphere across the corpus callosum. Experiences happening in the right hemisphere are quickly transmitted to the left hemisphere and become part of the conscious self. When the linkage between the two hemispheres is broken, the right hemisphere remains mute, and its experiences are not part of our conscious awareness (Eccles, 1973).

The specialization of the two hemispheres appears to develop along with language development. If the left hemisphere of a young child is damaged, the right one can take over the language functions without too much difficulty. Left hemisphere damage in an adult, however, almost invariably produces language disability. The fact that right-handedness is the norm for human beings is probably connected with the occurrence of speech in the left hemisphere. Some left-handed people have their speech areas in the right side of the brain, but indications are that most have the same dominant hemisphere (the left) as right-handed people.

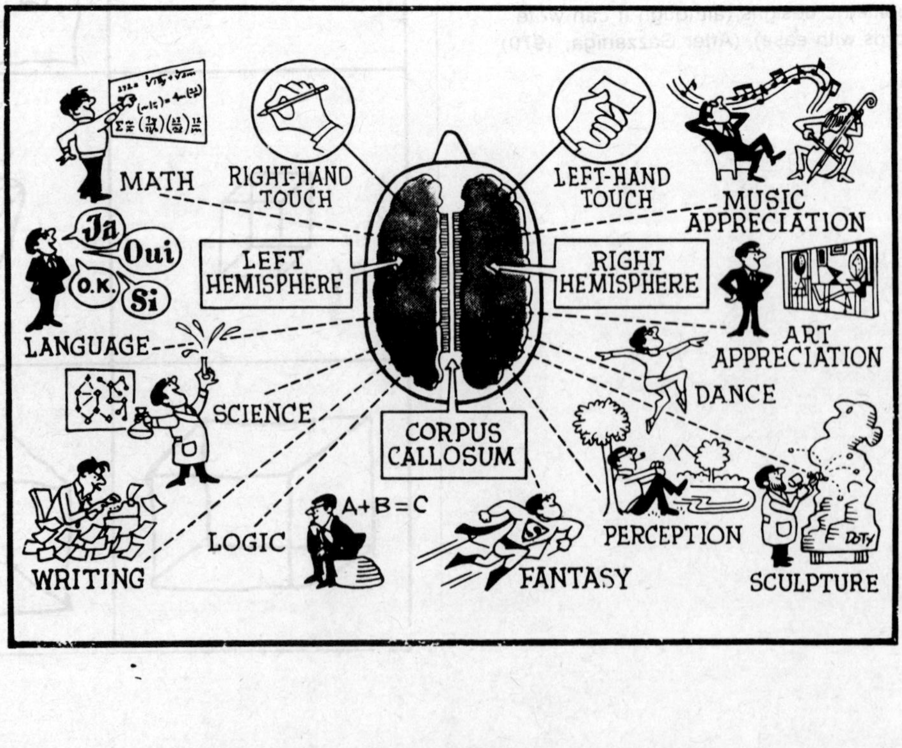

Fig. 2-15 How the brain divides its w k

Research with both split-brain and nor subjects indicates that different functio are specialized in either the left or righ hemisphere. The figure presents a very speculative attempt to summarize the research findings; the cerebral locations for some of the above abilities have not been firmly established by research.

Autonomic Nervous System

We noted earlier that the peripheral nervous system, which includes those nerves connecting the brain and spinal cord with the outlying regions of the body, consists of two divisions. The somatic system controls the skeletal muscles and receives sensory information from the skin, muscles, and various receptors. The autonomic system controls the glands and the smooth muscles that comprise the heart, blood vessels, and the lining of the stomach and intestines. These muscles are called smooth because microscopic examination shows that they lack the striated appearance characteristic of skeletal muscles. The somatic system then controls the striated muscles; the autonomic system controls the smooth muscles. The autonomic nervous system derives its name from the fact that many of the activities it controls are autonomous or self-regulating, such as digestion and circulation, which continue even when a person is asleep or unconscious.

The autonomic nervous system has two divisions—the *sympathetic* and the *parasympathetic*—which are often antagonistic in their action.

Sympathetic Division

On either side of the spinal column, closely connected with it through the spinal nerves, lie chains of nerve fibers and masses of cell bodies from which fibers extend to the various visceral organs. These chains are known as the *sympathetic chains.* The fibers coming from the spinal cord to the sympathetic chains originate in the thoracic and lumbar portions of the spine, between the cervical (neck) and the sacral (lower spine) regions. All the fibers and ganglia together constitute the sympathetic division of the autonomic system (Figure 2-16).

The sympathetic division tends to act as a unit. In emotional excitement it simultaneously speeds up the heart, dilates the arteries of the muscles and heart, and constricts the arteries of the skin and digestive organs; its action leads also to perspiration and to secretion of certain hormones that increase emotional arousal.

Parasympathetic Division

The parasympathetic division has two parts, some of its fibers originating in the cranial region (above those of the sympathetic system) and others originating in the sacral region (below those of the sympathetic system).

Unlike the sympathetic system, the parasympathetic system tends to act in a piecemeal fashion, affecting one organ at a time. If the sympathetic system is thought of as dominant in violent and excited activity, the parasympathetic system may be thought of as dominant in quiescence. It participates in digestion and, in general, maintains the functions that conserve and protect bodily resources.

Interaction between the Divisions

When both sympathetic and parasympathetic fibers are connected to the same muscle or gland, they usually act in opposite manners. Thus the

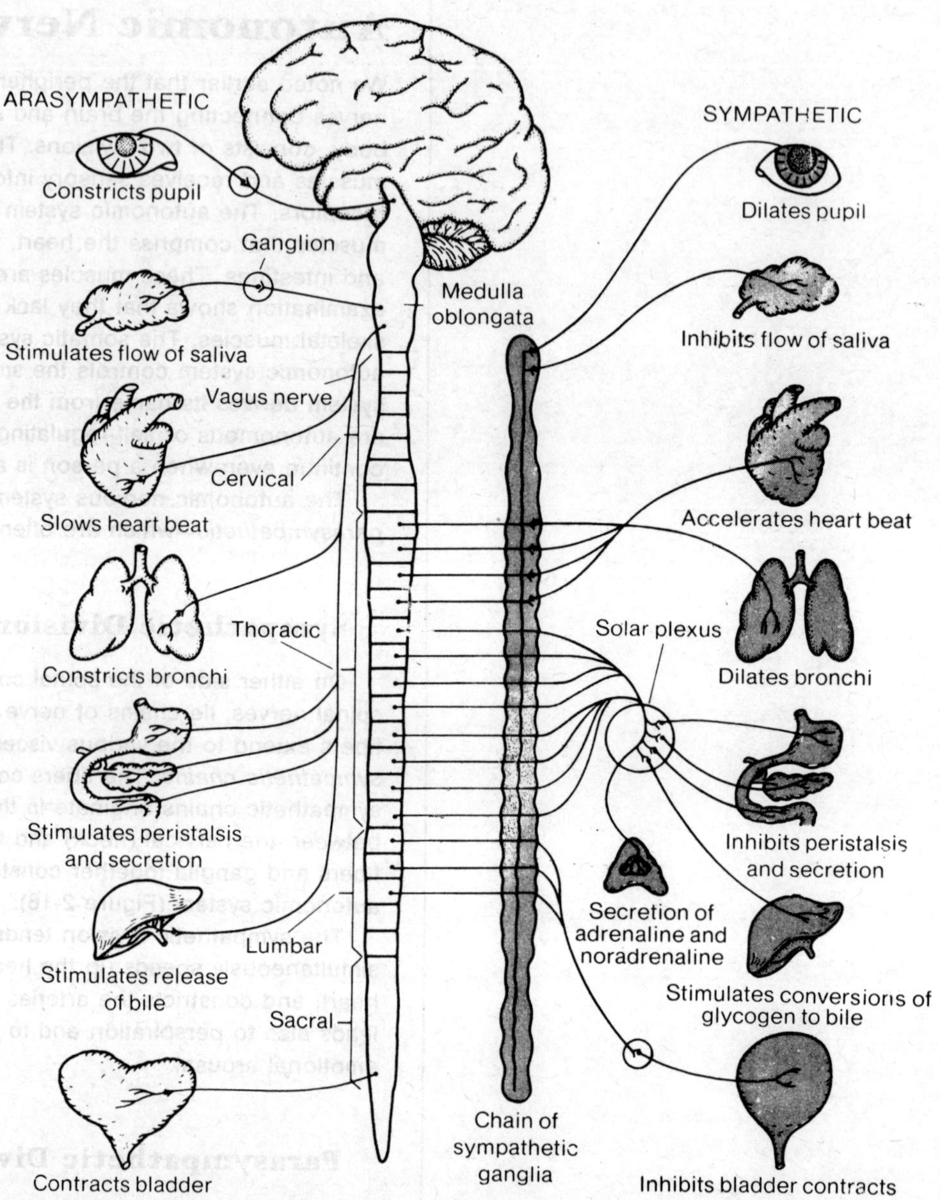

Fig. 2-16 The autonomic nervous system

Neurons of the sympathetic system originate in the thoracic and lumbar regions of the spinal cord; they form synaptic junctions with ganglia lying just outside the cord. Neurons of the parasympathetic system exit from the medulla region of the brain stem and from the lower (sacral) end of the spinal cord; they connect with ganglia near the organs stimulated, thus acting in a somewhat piecemeal fashion. Most, but not all, internal organs are innervated by both systems, which function in opposition to each other. The normal state of the body, somewhere between extreme excitement and vegetative placidity, results from the interplay of these two systems.

sympathetic system speeds the heart rate, the parasympathetic system slows it; the sympathetic system inhibits digestive processes, the parasympathetic system facilitates them; the sympathetic system dilates the pupil of the eye, the parasympathetic system constricts it.

There are some exceptions to the principle that the two systems are antagonistic. Both divisions may be active at once, and in some cases they act together in sequence. Although the sympathetic system is usually dominant in fear and excitement, a not uncommon parasympathetic symptom in extreme emotion is the involuntary discharge of the bladder or bowels. Another example is the complete sex act in the male, which requires erection (parasympathetic) followed by ejaculation (sympathetic). Thus, while the two divisions are often antagonistic, they interact in complex ways, and their interaction is not yet fully understood.

Endocrine System

Many of the bodily reactions that result from activity of the autonomic nervous system are produced by the action of that system on the endocrine glands. The endocrine glands secrete hormones, special chemical messengers, that are carried throughout the body by the blood stream.[2] These chemicals are as essential as the nervous system to the integration of the organism's activities and to the maintenance of homeostasis. Indeed, the functioning of the nervous system depends upon them. For example, some neurons use a hormone, norepinephrine, as their chemical transmitter. Other hormones serve to modify the excitability of neurons. The endocrine glands are responsible for growth, sexual and maternal behavior, the individual's characteristic level of energy and mood, and reaction to stress. Some endocrine glands are controlled by the nervous system, whereas others respond directly to the internal state of the body.

Pituitary Gland

One of the major endocrine glands, the pituitary, is partly an outgrowth of the brain and is joined to it just below the hypothalamus (refer back to Figure 2-7). The pituitary gland has been called the "master gland" because it produces the largest number of different hormones and controls the secretion of several other endocrine glands. The pituitary has two independently functioning parts.

The *posterior pituitary* is a direct extension of the nervous system. Two hormones produced in the hypothalamus are transported along nerve axons for release by the posterior pituitary. One hormone influences the contraction of the uterus during childbirth and the production of milk in the mammary glands; the other regulates the amount of water in the body cells and indirectly controls blood pressure.

The *anterior pituitary* is also controlled by the hypothalamus but in a different way. Certain hormones released by the hypothalamus are carried to the anterior pituitary by a system of tiny blood vessels. They stimulate the anterior pituitary to release its own hormones.

One of the anterior pituitary hormones has the crucial job of controlling the timing and amount of body growth. Too little of this hormone can create a dwarf, while oversecretion can produce a giant. A number of other hormones released by the anterior pituitary trigger the action of other endocrine glands—the thyroid, the sex glands or gonads, and one part of the adrenal glands. Courtship, mating, and reproductive behavior in many animals involve a complex interaction between the activity of the nervous system and the influence of the anterior pituitary on the sex glands.

Adrenal Glands

The adrenal glands located just above the kidneys are extremely important to neural functioning and to the ability of the body to cope with stress. Each

[2] Endocrine glands are distinguished from the other glands by the fact that they secrete directly into the blood stream. *Exocrine* glands, such as the salivary and tear glands, have ducts that enable them to secrete fluids directly onto the body surface or into body cavities; their influence is thus less widespread.

adrenal gland has two parts. The inner core, the medulla, secretes *epinephrine* (also known as adrenalin) and *norepinephrine* (noradrenalin). Epinephrine acts in a number of ways to prepare the organism for an emergency; it is closely involved with the action of the sympathetic division of the autonomic nervous system. Epinephrine, for example, acts on the smooth muscles and the sweat glands in a way similar to the sympathetic system. It causes nervous perspiration, constriction of the blood vessels in the stomach and intestines, and makes the heart beat faster (as anyone who has ever had a shot of adrenalin will know). It also acts on part of the reticular activating system, which excites the sympathetic system, which in turn stimulates the adrenals to secrete more epinephrine. Hence, a closed circuit maintaining emotional arousal is formed. Such a closed system is one reason why strong emotional excitement takes a while to subside even after the disturbing cause is removed. Some wild animals on being captured suffer such an intense stress reaction that their physiological system never returns to a state of homeostasis; they go into shock and die.

Norepinephrine also acts to prepare the organism for emergency action. As it reaches the pituitary in its travels through the blood stream, it stimulates the pituitary to release a hormone that acts on the outer part of the adrenal glands (the adrenal cortex), stimulating the release of *adrenocortical hormones.* These hormones, called *steroids,* promote the release of sugar stored in the liver so the body has energy for quick action. The steroids also help to maintain the normal metabolic processes of the body. One of the adrenal steroids is *cortisol;* a synthetic form of cortisol, cortisone, is used in the treatment of allergic reactions, arthritis, and shock. Patients treated with cortisone sometimes develop mental symptoms—for example, severe depression. Cortisol and some other steroids may play a role in the treatment of mental illness.

This description of the complex action of the pituitary and adrenal glands and their interaction with the nervous system indicates the endocrine systems's crucial role in the integration of bodily responses.

Genetic Influences on Behavior

To understand the biological foundations of behavior we need to know something about hereditary influences. The field of *behavior genetics* combines the methods of genetics and psychology to study the inheritance of behavioral characteristics. We know that many physical characteristics, such as height, bone structure, and hair and eye color, are inherited. Behavioral geneticists are interested in the degree to which psychological characteristics, such as ability, temperament, and emotional stability, are transmitted from parent to offspring.

All behavior depends upon the *interaction* between heredity and environment. The old heredity *versus* environment issue is no longer a meaningful question. Instead, researchers ask how heredity limits the individual's potential and to what degree favorable or unfavorable environmental conditions can change the inherited potential.

Chromosomes and Genes

The hereditary units we receive from our parents and transmit to our offspring are carried by microscopic particles, known as chromosomes, found in the nucleus of each cell in the body. Most body cells contain 46 chromosomes. At conception the human being receives 23 chromosomes from the father's sperm and 23 chromosomes from the mother's ovum. These 46 chromosomes form 23 pairs, which are duplicated in every cell of the body as the individual develops (Figure 2-17). Each chromosome is composed of many individual hereditary units called *genes,* which also occur in pairs—one gene of each pair comes from the sperm chromosomes and one gene from the ovum chromosomes.[3] We have no exact way of counting genes, for unlike the chromosomes they do not show up under the microscope as separate particles. The total number of genes in each human chromosome is on the order of 1000, perhaps higher. Because the number of genes is so high, it is extremely unlikely that two human beings would have the same heredity, even with the same parents. One exception is identical twins, who, having developed from the same ovum, have the same chromosomes and genes.

An important attribute of some genes is *dominance* or *recessiveness.* If both members of a gene pair are dominant, the individual will manifest the trait determined by the genes. If one is dominant and the other recessive, the individual will show the form of the trait expressive of the dominant gene, but will also carry the recessive gene, which may be expressed in a different way as a trait in offspring. A recessive form of the trait will be expressed only if both genes are recessive. The genes determining eye color, for example, act in a pattern of dominance and recessiveness. Blue eyes are recessive. Thus for a child to be blue-eyed both parents must be blue-eyed, or if one parent is brown-eyed, that parent must carry a recessive gene for blue eyes. Two brown-eyed parents can produce a blue-eyed child only if both carry a gene for blue eyes.

Some of the characteristics that are carried by recessive genes are baldness, albinism, hemophilia, and a susceptibility to poison ivy. Not all gene pairs follow the dominant-recessive pattern and, as we shall see later, most human characteristics are determined by many genes acting together rather than a single gene pair.

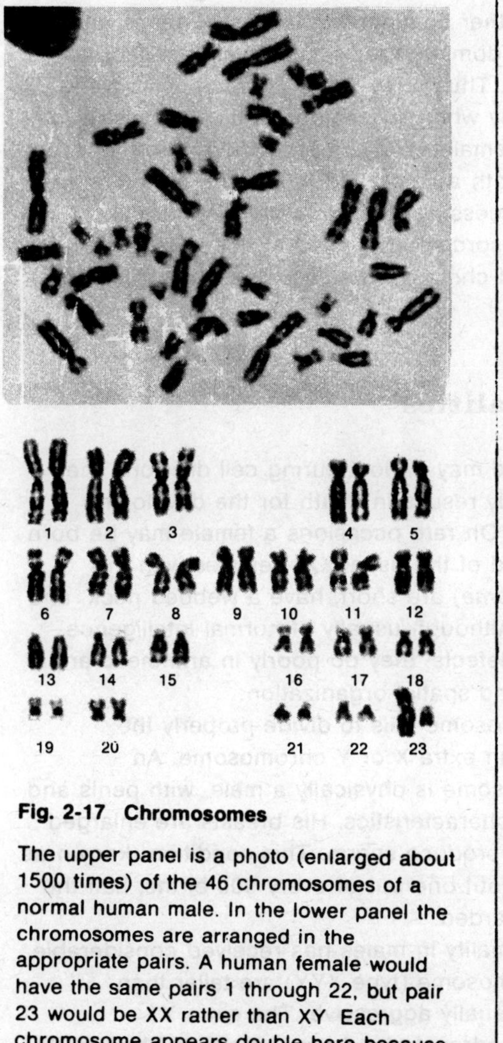

Fig. 2-17 Chromosomes

The upper panel is a photo (enlarged about 1500 times) of the 46 chromosomes of a normal human male. In the lower panel the chromosomes are arranged in the appropriate pairs. A human female would have the same pairs 1 through 22, but pair 23 would be XX rather than XY Each chromosome appears double here because the preparation was made at a stage during mitosis in which each chromosome has duplicated itself and is about to split apart.

SEX-LINKED GENES. Chromosome pair number 23 determines the sex of the individual and carries genes for certain traits that are called "sex-linked." A normal female has two similar appearing chromosomes in pair 23, called X chromosomes. A normal male has one X chromosome in pair 23 and one that looks slightly different, called a Y chromosome (see Figure 2-17). Thus the normal female chromosome pair 23 is represented by the symbol XX and the normal male pair by XY.

When most body cells reproduce (by a process called mitosis), the resulting cells have the same number of chromosomes (46) as the parent cell. However, when sperm and egg cells reproduce (by a process called meiosis) the chromosome pairs separate and half go to each "daughter" cell. Thus, egg and sperm cells have only 23 chromosomes and do not survive more than a few days unless they join to complete the 46 chromosomes necessary for proper cell functioning.

Each egg cell has an X chromosome and each sperm cell has either an X

[3]The actual carrier of hereditary information within the genes is a complex nucleic acid called DNA (deoxyribonucleic acid). The discovery in 1953 of the molecular structure of DNA and the method by which this molecule could duplicate itself during cell division and could transfer its genetic code from the ovum to direct the development of other body cells was a major break-through in understanding the genetic basis of plant and animal life.

or a Y chromosome. If an X-type sperm is the first to enter an egg cell the fertilized ovum will have an XX chromosome pair; the child will be a female. If a Y-type sperm fertilizes the egg, the 23rd chromosome will be of the XY type and the child will be a male. The adult male usually produces an equal number of X- and Y-type sperm, so that the chances of his producing male or female children are essentially equal. The female inherits one X-chromosome from the mother, one from the father; the male inherits his X-chromosome from his mother, his Y-chromosome from his father.

The X-chromosome may carry either dominant or recessive genes; the Y-chromosome carries a few genes dominant for sexual characteristics but is not known to carry recessive genes. Thus a recessive characteristic in the male like color blindness occurs only when the male inherits a recessive color-blind gene from his mother. Females are less often color-blind, because to be so they would have to have both a colorblind father and a mother who was either colorblind or carried a recessive gene for colorblindness. A number of genetically determined disorders are linked to abnormalities of, or recessive genes carried by, the 23rd chromosome pair. These disorders are called sex-linked.

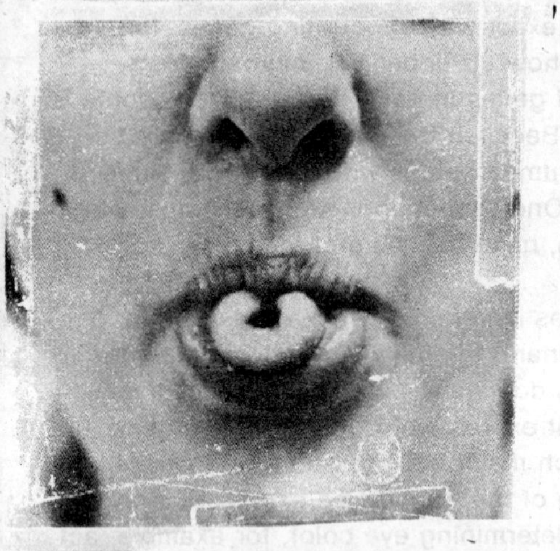

Seven out of ten people have the tongue-rolling ability transmitted by a dominant gene. You can perform a simple experiment in genetics by checking to see if the members of your family can do it.

Chromosomal Abnormalities

Sometimes part of a chromosome may be lost during cell division. The loss of an entire chromosome usually results in death for the developing organism, but there are exceptions. On rare occasions a female may be born with only one X chromosome instead of the usual XX. Females with this condition (known as *Turner's syndrome*) are short, have a webbed neck, and fail to develop sexually at puberty. Although usually of normal intelligence, they show some specific cognitive defects: they do poorly in arithmetic and on tests of visual form perception and spatial organization.

Sometimes when the 23rd chromosome fails to divide properly the developing organism ends up with an extra X or Y chromosome. An individual with an XXY 23rd chromosome is physically a male, with penis and testicles, but with marked feminine characteristics. His breasts are enlarged and his testes are small and do not produce sperm. This condition (known as *Klinefelter's syndrome*) occurs in about one out of every 900 births; half the persons so afflicted are mentally retarded.

Another sex chromosome abnormality in males has received considerable publicity. Men with an extra Y chromosome (type XYY) are taller than average and are reported to be unusually aggressive. The extra Y chromosome apparently causes the adrenal glands to secrete an abnormally large amount of the male hormone (testosterone) so that such individuals reach sexual maturity early and may have a higher than normal sex drive. In a sense they are "super male."

Early studies reported that the incidence of XYY males institutionalized because of violent crimes was much higher than in the population at large (Jacobs and others, 1965, 1968). On the basis of these studies several individuals with XYY abnormality were acquitted of criminal charges on the grounds of insanity. But more recent research questions the conclusion that XYY males are particularly aggressive (Kessler and Moos, 1970; Owen, 1972).

The incidence of XYY males in the general population has not been clearly determined to provide an accurate comparison with prison

"You can't talk to that crowd—they've all got extra Y chromosomes."

Source: Playboy, April, 1970. Reproduced by special permission of PLAYBOY Magazine; © 1970 by Playboy.

populations. Then too, greater-than-average height may alter the individual's psychological environment so as to predispose him to aggressive behavior. In other words, the cause of the aggression may be social rather than physiological. At present the association between aggressive behavior and the XYY chromosome type remains an unresolved issue. To understand how the XYY males differ from XY males requires careful studies in which XYY infants are identified at birth and their development over the years compared with a group of XY controls.

Deviations from the usual number of chromosomes in pairs other than the sex chromosomes have also been linked to specific disorders. For example, an extra chromosome on pair 21 results in a form of mental deficiency commonly called *mongolism.* The name derives from the characteristic upward slant of the eyelid and the small folds of skin over the inner corners of the eyes which makes these individuals look "oriental" or "mongoloid" to us. Mongolism, or Down's syndrome as it is now called, will be discussed in Chapter 14.

Genetic Studies of Behavior

A few disorders result from chromosomal abnormalities, and some traits are determined by single genes. But most human characteristics are determined by many sets of genes; they are *polygenic*. Traits such as intelligence, height, and emotionality do not fall into distinct categories but show continuous variation. People are not either dull or bright; intelligence is distributed over a broad range, with most individuals located near the middle. It is true that a single gene can, through its control of the production of certain enzymes, result in mental retardation (see Chapter 14). But in most instances a person's intellectual potential is determined by many genes that influence the factors underlying different abilities. And, of course, what happens to this genetic potential depends upon environmental conditions.

We do not as yet know the exact means of genetic transmission of many human characteristics even though research indicates the importance of heredity in their determination.

SELECTIVE BREEDING. One method of studying the heritability of traits in animals is by means of selective breeding. Animals that are high in a certain trait or low in a certain trait are mated with each other. For example, to study the inheritance of learning ability in rats the females that do poorly in learning to run a maze are mated with males that do poorly; the skilled maze-running females are mated with the skilled maze-running males. The offsprings of these matings are tested on the same maze. On the basis of performance the brightest are mated with the brightest and the dullest with the dullest. (To insure that environmental conditions are kept constant the offspring of "dull" mothers are sometimes given to "bright" mothers to raise so that genetic endowment rather than adequacy of maternal care is being tested.) After a few rodent generations a "bright" and a "dull" strain of rats can be produced (see Figure 2-18). When tested a year later the descendents of the maze-bright rats are still superior to the descendents of the maze-dull rats in learning several different types of mazes (Rosenzweig, 1969).

Selective breeding has been used to show the inheritance of a number of characteristics with many different animal species. Dogs have been bred to

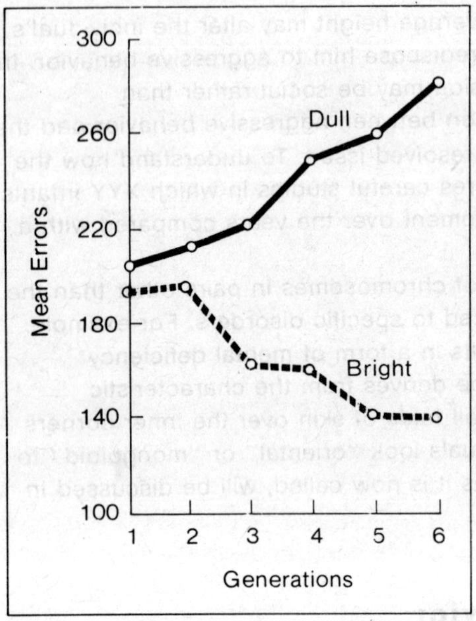

Fig. 2-18 Inheritance of maze learning in rats

Mean error scores of "bright" and "dull" rats selectively bred for maze-running ability. (After Thompson, 1954)

be excitable or lethargic, chickens to be aggressive and sexually active, and fruit flies to be more or less attracted to light (Scott and Fuller, 1965; McClearn and De Fries, 1973). It has even been possible to breed a strain of mice that prefer alcohol and a strain that does not; the preference may be based on genetic differences in the level of a liver enzyme that aids in the metabolic breakdown of alcohol (Eriksson, 1972).

If a trait is influenced by heredity, then it should be possible to change it by selective breeding. If selective breeding does not alter a trait, then we assume that trait is primarily dependent upon environmental factors and is not differentially influenced by the genes.

TWIN STUDIES. Since carefully controlled breeding experiments cannot be carried out with human beings, the behavior geneticist has had to look instead at similarities and differences in behavior among individuals who are related genetically. Family pedigrees often show that certain traits run in families. (See Figure 2-19.) The problem, however, is that families are not only linked genetically, but also share the same environment over a period of time. Thus, if musical talent runs in the family, is it because of genetic potential or the importance parents place on music and the training they provide? Do children of alcoholics become alcoholics because of genetic tendencies or environmental conditions? To alleviate this problem behavioral geneticists prefer to study genetic influences on behavior in twins.

Identical twins develop from a single fertilized egg and thus share the same heredity. (They are called *monozygotic* since they result from a single zygote or fertilized ovum.) Fraternal twins develop from different egg cells and are no more alike genetically than ordinary siblings. (They are called *dizygotic* or two-egged.) Studies comparing identical and fraternal twins help to partial out the influence of environment and heredity. Identical twins are found to be much more similar in intelligence than fraternal twins, even when they are separated at birth and reared in different homes (see Chapter 14). Identical twins are also more similar than fraternal twins in some personality characteristics and in susceptibility to the mental disorder of *schizophrenia* (see Chapter 16). Twin studies have proved one of the most useful methods of investigating genetic influences on human behavior, and we shall encounter them in later chapters.

Environmental Influences on Gene Action

The hereditary potential with which an individual enters the world is very much influenced by the environment that he encounters. This reciprocal interaction will be made clear in the following chapters. At this point two examples will suffice to illustrate the point. The tendency to develop *diabetes mellitus* is hereditary, although the exact method of transmission is unknown. Diabetes is manifested as an elevation of the blood sugar level. The assumption is that the genes determine the production of insulin which, in turn, affects the metabolism of carbohydrates, and hence the level of sugar in the blood. But people who carry the genetic potential for diabetes do not always develop the disease. One study of identical twins (one or the other of whom had diabetes) found that in 15 percent of the pairs only one twin developed the disease. The unafflicted twin clearly carried the genes for

Fig. 2-19 Is musical talent inherited?

The unusually high percentage of musicians in the Bach family seems to point to the inheritance of musical talent, although there was also environmental encouragement. All those listed in black type are known to have been competent musicians, and all but two of them gained their livelihood in music. (After Sandiford, 1938)

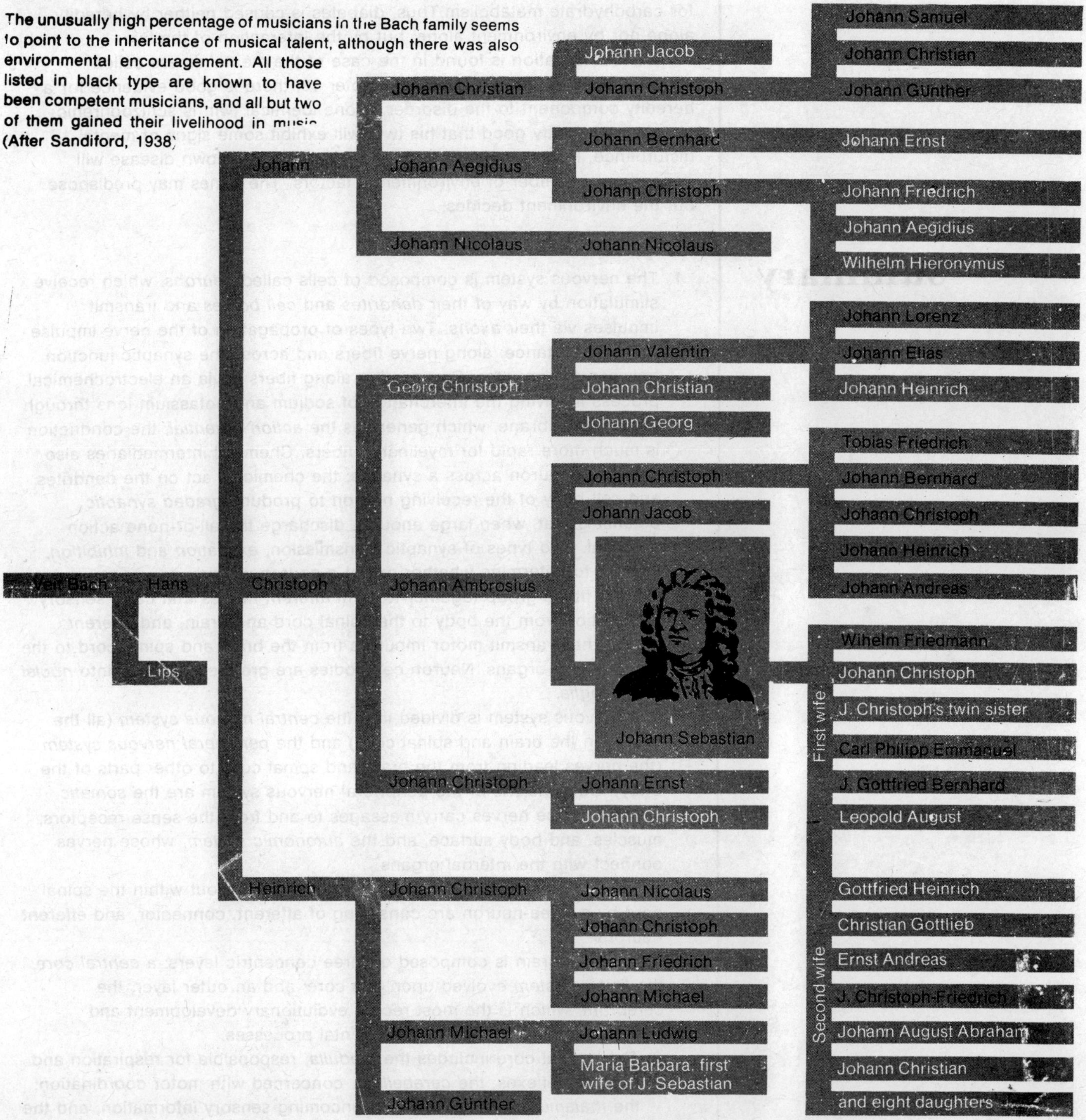

diabetes, but apparently was spared because his diet made fewer demands for carbohydrate metabolism. Thus, diabetes is caused neither by heredity alone nor by environment alone, but by the interaction of the two.

A similar situation is found in the case of the mental illness called *schizophrenia*. As we shall see in Chapter 16, there is good evidence for a heredity component to the disorder. If one identical twin is schizophrenic, chances are pretty good that his twin will exhibit some signs of mental disturbance. But whether or not he develops the full-blown disease will depend on a number of environmental factors. The genes may predispose but the environment decides.

Summary

1. The nervous system is composed of cells called *neurons*, which receive stimulation by way of their *dendrites* and *cell bodies* and transmit impulses via their *axons*. Two types of propagation of the nerve impulse are of importance: along nerve fibers and across the synaptic junction between the neurons. Propagation along fibers is via an electrochemical process involving the interchange of sodium and potassium ions through the cell membrane, which generates the *action potential;* the conduction is much more rapid for myelinated fibers. Chemical intermediaries also activate a neuron across a synapse; the chemicals act on the dendrites and cell body of the receiving neuron to produce *graded synaptic potentials* that, when large enough, discharge the all-or-none action potential. Two types of synaptic transmission, *excitation* and *inhibition*, interact to determine whether or not a neuron will fire.
2. Neuron fibers group together to form *afferent nerves* that carry sensory information from the body to the spinal cord and brain, and *efferent nerves* that transmit motor impulses from the brain and spinal cord to the muscles and organs. Neuron cell bodies are grouped together into *nuclei* and *ganglia*.
3. The nervous system is divided into the *central nervous system* (all the nerves in the brain and spinal cord) and the *peripheral nervous system* (the nerves leading from the brain and spinal cord to other parts of the body). Subdivisions of the peripheral nervous system are the *somatic system*, whose nerves carry messages to and from the sense receptors, muscles, and body surface, and the *autonomic system*, whose nerves connect with the internal organs.
4. Simple reflexes, such as the knee jerk, are carried out within the spinal cord by a three-neuron arc consisting of afferent, connector, and efferent neurons.
5. The human brain is composed of three concentric layers: a *central core;* the *limbic system* evolved upon this core; and an outer layer, the *cerebrum*, which is the most recent evolutionary development and constitutes the center for higher mental processes.
   a. The central core includes the *medulla*, responsible for respiration and postural reflexes; the *cerebellum*, concerned with motor coordination; the *thalamus*, a relay station for incoming sensory information; and the *hypothalamus*, important in emotion and in maintaining homeostasis. The *reticular activating system*, which crosses through several of the above structures, controls the organism's state of arousal.
   b. The *limbic system* controls sequential activities—feeding, attacking,

fleeing from danger, mating—necessary to satisfy the basic motivational and emotional needs regulated by the hypothalamus.

c. The *cerebrum* is divided into two *cerebral hemispheres.* The convoluted surface of these hemispheres, the *cerebral cortex,* controls discrimination, choice, learning, and thinking—the "higher mental processes" which are the most flexible and least stereotyped aspects of behavior. Certain areas of the cortex, called *projection areas,* represent centers for specific sensory inputs or for control of specific movements. The remainder of the cortex consists of *association areas.*

6. When the *corpus callosum* (the band of nerve fibers connecting the two cerebral hemispheres) is severed, significant differences in the functioning of the cerebral hemispheres can be observed. The major, left hemisphere is skilled in language and mathematical abilities. The minor, right hemisphere can understand some language but cannot communicate through speech; it has a highly developed spatial and pattern sense.
7. The *autonomic nervous system* is made up of two parts, a *sympathetic* and a *parasympathetic* division. Because its fibers mediate the action of the smooth muscles and of the glands, the autonomic system is particularly important in emotional reactions. The sympathetic division is usually involved in excited action and the parasympathetic in quiescent states. But the antagonism between the two divisions is not universal; they do cooperate in complex ways.
8. The *endocrine glands* secrete hormones into the blood stream which are important for emotional and motivational behavior and for some aspects of personality. They are an essential partner to the nervous system in integrating behavior, and their action is closely tied to the activity of the hypothalamus and the autonomic nervous system. The *pituitary* and the *adrenal glands* are two of the most important endocrine glands.
9. An individual's hereditary potential, carried by the *chromosome* and *genes,* will influence psychological as well as physical characteristics. Some genes are *dominant,* some *recessive,* and some *sex-linked.* Most human characteristics are *polygenic,* that is, determined by many sets of genes.
10. *Selective breeding,* mating animals that are high in a certain trait or low in a certain trait, is one method of studying the influence of heredity. Another method for partialing out the effects of environment and heredity is the *twin study* in which the characteristics of identical or *monozygotic* twins (who share the same heredity) are compared with those of fraternal or *dizygotic* twins (who are no more alike genetically than ordinary siblings).
11. All behavior depends upon the *interaction* between heredity and environment; the genes set the limits of the individual's potential but what happens to this potential depends upon the environment.

Further Readings

An overview of physiological psychology is given in a paperback by Teitelbaum, *Physiological psychology* (1967). More comprehensive treatments are Thompson, *Foundations of physiological psychology* (1967); Morgan, *Physiological psychology* (1965); Milner, *Physiological psychology* (1970); and Schwartz, *Physiological psychology* (1973).

Stevens, *Explorers of the brain* (1971), traces the history of attempts to understand brain functions from the 18th century to the present. Details of the split-brain research may be found in Gazzaniga, *The bisected brain* (1970). A comprehensive survey of genetic influences on behavior is provided by McClearn and DeFries, *Introduction to behavioral genetics* (1973).

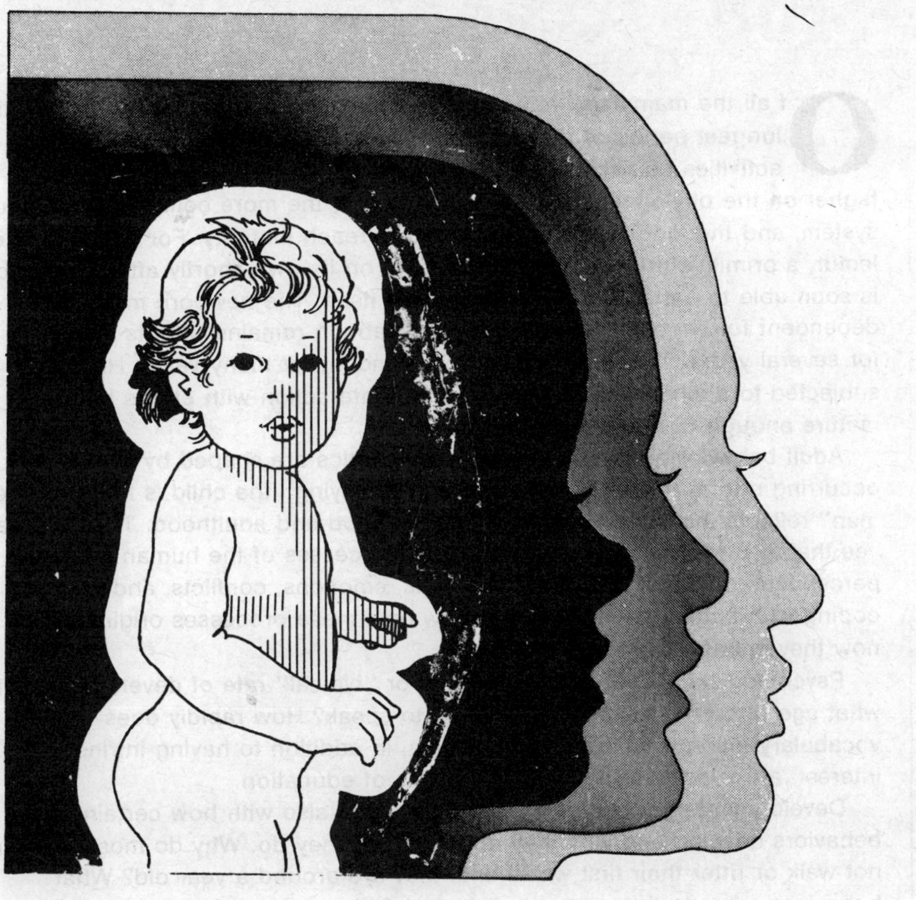

3

developmental psychology

Of all the mammals, man is the most immature at birth and requires the longest period of development before he is capable of all the activities and skills characteristic of his species. In general, the higher on the phylogenetic scale the organism, the more complex its nervous system, and the longer the time required to reach maturity. For example, the lemur, a primitive primate, can move about on its own shortly after birth and is soon able to eat adult food and fend for itself. The newborn monkey is dependent for several months; the infant baboon remains with its mother for several years. The human baby is dependent for many years. He is subjected to a long period of learning and interaction with others before he is mature enough to be fully "on his own."

Adult behavior and personality characteristics are shaped by events occurring during the early years of life. The saying "the child is father of the man" reflects this continuity between childhood and adulthood. Thus, we can see that to understand the psychological processes of the human adult—his perceptions, patterns of thinking, motives, emotions, conflicts, and ways of coping with conflicts—we need to know how these processes originate and how they change over time.

Psychologists may study the average or "typical" rate of development. At what age does the average child begin to speak? How rapidly does vocabulary increase with age? Such data, in addition to having intrinsic interest, are important in solving problems of education.

Developmental psychologists are concerned also with how certain behaviors develop and why they appear when they do. Why do most children not walk or utter their first world until they are around a year old? What behaviors precede these accomplishments? Can normal development be accelerated? What factors produce abnormal development, such as mental illness or retardation?

From a practical standpoint, knowing how early experiences mold an individual may make us wiser in the way we raise our children. Many problems confronting society—aggression, alienation, suicide, and mental illness—could perhaps be averted if we better understood how parental behavior and attitudes affect the child, how some of these problems originate, and how they might be dealt with at an early age.

In this chapter we will discuss several general principles of development as well as some behavior and attitude changes that occur as the individual matures from infancy to adulthood. Our purpose is to provide an overview of psychological development. The development of certain specific abilities, such as language and perception, will be covered later in the chapters devoted to these topics.

Factors Governing Development

One of the factors influencing development is *maturation,* an innately governed sequence of physical changes that does not depend on particular environmental events. Many behavioral changes that occur in the early months of life are clearly related to maturation of the nervous system, muscles, and glands. These changes represent a continuation of the growth processes that guided the development of the fetus within the uterus.

The environmental conditions to which the infant is exposed are, of

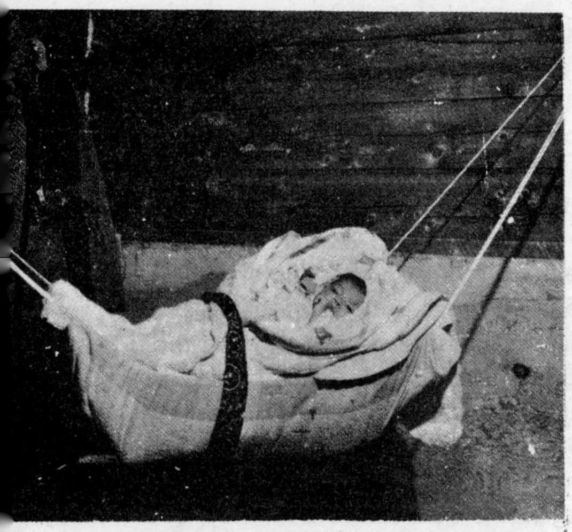

A typical baby hammock used by the Vanta Kuchin Indians of Canada.

course, another major influence on development. Each culture differs in its methods of child-rearing, and each family within a culture has its own schedules and ways of doing things. An infant is exposed to many different conditions—some are shared with other infants in his culture, some are common only to his family group, and some are uniquely his own.

To what extent does a certain skill (such as walking or speaking) develop through maturation and to what extent does its appearance depend on experience or environmental conditions? It is difficult to separate the effects of "nature" and "nurture." Maturation can be accelerated or impeded by the quality of the environment; and environmental conditions or special training can stimulate behavior only when the organism possesses the appropriate neural and muscular equipment.

Stages and Critical Periods in Development

Many skills follow a natural sequence of development. An infant is able to reach for an object before he can pick it up. We learn to walk before we run; we learn to speak words before sentences. Later skills build upon more basic ones in a fairly logical way.

The observation of such natural sequences of behavior has led some psychologists to suggest that development proceeds in orderly, definable *stages*. Certain behaviors, interests, and ways of thinking or coping with problems are characteristic of a certain stage of development, and these may change as the child progresses to the next stage. Failure to deal adequately with the developmental problems at a particular stage may interfere with development at the next stage. The various developmental stages proposed by several noted psychologists will be discussed in detail later.

Related to the notion of stages in development is the concept that there are *critical periods* during which both favorable and unfavorable circumstances have lasting and perhaps irreversible consequences. The concept of critical periods originated in the study of embryological development. As the embryo grows, the various organ systems develop in a fixed time sequence, and each system has a critical period during which it is maximally sensitive to growth stimulation and maximally vulnerable to disruptive factors. The organ system that does not develop normally during its critical period does not get a second chance, because the focus of growth shifts to other systems. Thus, if the mother contracts German measles during the first three months of pregnancy, the effect on the embryo depends on the exact time of infection. The infant may be born blind, deaf, or brain-damaged, depending on which organ system was in its critical phase of development at the time of the infection.

Critical periods have been identified in the postnatal emotional development of animals. There appears to be a critical period for taming dogs so that they will respond to human beings. Puppies were raised in a large field with tame mothers but without human contact. They were removed at various ages to spend 10 minutes a day with a handler who was passive and waited for them to approach him. If this experience was delayed as long as 14 weeks the puppies had become wild dogs, fearful of human beings. The best time for taming was between five to seven weeks of age. When tamed at these ages, the dogs remained tame, as was seen when they were tested again 14 weeks later.

It is possible, but much harder to demonstrate, that the psychological development of the child has critical periods. It has been suggested that a child must form a satisfactory emotional attachment to an adult during the first three years of life in order to be capable of normal affectional relationships in later life (Bowlby, 1969). If this hypothesis is true, then these years would constitute a critical period for the development of social relations.

A study of children born with sexual organs inappropriate to their true (genotypic) sex suggests that there is a critical period for sexual identification. These children (called *pseudohermaphrodites*) can often be helped by surgery. If the sex-change operation takes place before the child is two there appear to be no personality difficulties; that is, a boy who has been initially raised as a girl can assume the male sex role and vice versa. In a child older than two, however, switching identity to the opposite sex usually causes serious problems in adapting to the new sex role (Money, et al., 1957).

The notion of a critical period in development implies that at a certain time during a person's development he is optimally ready to acquire certain behavior. If the appropriate experiences do not occur during this period, then the behavior can be learned later only with great difficulty, if at all. As we examine different areas of development we will look for evidence of critical periods.

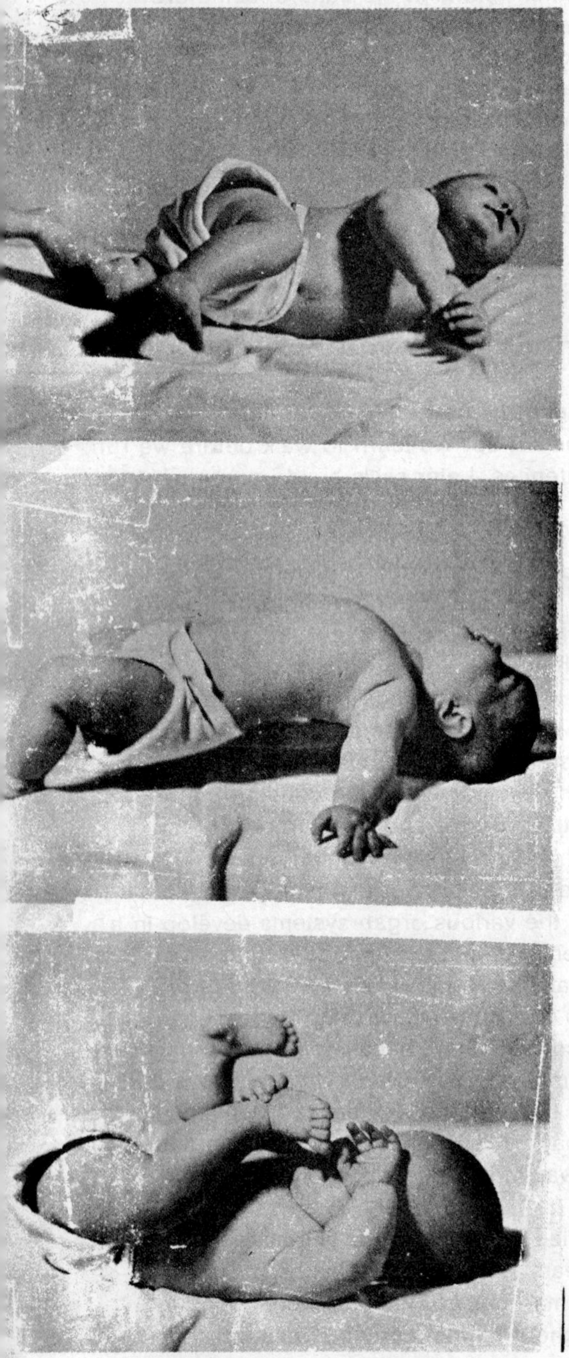

Fig. 3·1 Muscular activity of babies at the rolling stage

This six-month-old baby discovers movements that prepare him for further development and lead to his ability to walk later on.

Motor Development as an Example of Maturation

The human fetus develops within the mother's body according to a relatively fixed time schedule, and fetal behavior (such as turning and kicking) also follows an orderly sequence, depending on the stage of growth. Premature infants who are kept alive in an incubator develop at much the same rate as infants who remain in the uterus full term. The regularity of development before birth provides a clear picture of what is meant by maturation.

Motor development after birth—using the hands and fingers, standing, walking—also follows a regular sequence. For example, activities, such as rolling over, crawling, and pulling up to a standing position, that prepare the child for walking occur in the same order in most children. Unless we believe that all parents subject their offspring to the same training regime (an unlikely possibility), we must assume that growth processes determine the order of behavior. As you can see from Figure 3-2, not all children go through the sequence at the same rate; some infants are more than four or five months ahead of others in standing alone or walking. But the *order* in which they go from one stage to the next is generally the same from one infant to the next.

Effects of Early Experiences

Because the child's mastery of the movements necessary for sitting, standing, walking, and using hands and fingers follows such an orderly sequence, and because children in all cultures accomplish these skills at *roughly* the same age, motor development appears to be primarily a maturational process little influenced by the culture in which the child is reared. Although no special training is required for a child to walk at the appropriate time, a certain amount of environmental stimulation is necessary. Children raised in institutions who are handled infrequently and given little opportunity to move about will sit, stand, and walk much later than normal. One study of an orphanage in Iran found that only 42 percent of the children were able to sit alone at two years, and only 15 percent could walk alone at age four (Dennis, 1960). Contrast these percentages with the norms given for home-reared children in Figure 3-2.

A few of the orphaned children may have been mentally retarded, but most were not. A comparative study of three different foundling homes in Iran showed a direct relationship between the amount of stimulation and experience provided and the children's rate of motor development. Thus, although motor development is largely dependent upon maturation, experiences of moving about freely and being carried in different positions are also necessary.

Psychologists have done much research on the roles maturation and experience play in development. The most reasonable conclusion from the available data is that human development involves a continuous interaction between the organism and its environment. No behavior develops solely because of maturation or solely because of learning. Certain brain and body structures must mature before a particular behavior can occur, but experience is required to develop the brain's capacity to organize and process incoming information and to signal the appropriate response.

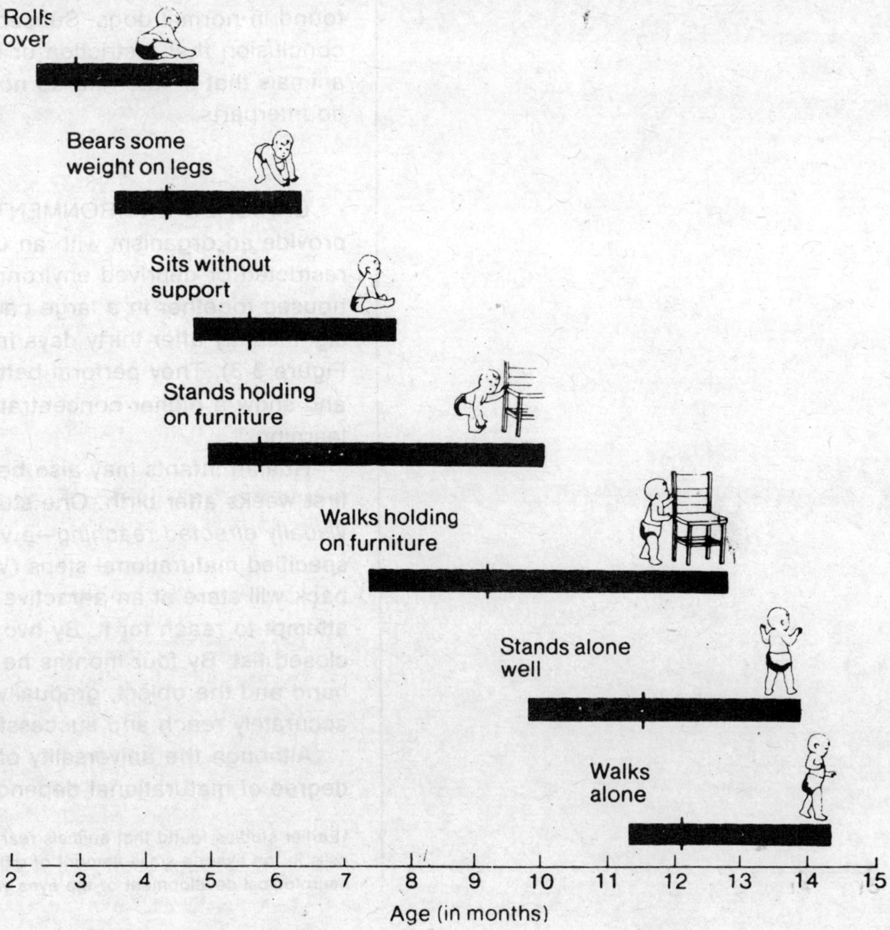

Fig. 3-2 Babies develop at different rates

Although development is orderly, some infants reach each stage ahead of others. The left end of the bar indicates the age by which 25 percent of infants have achieved the stated performance, whereas the right end gives the age by which 90 percent have accomplished the behavior. The vertical mark on each bar gives the age by which 50 percent have achieved it. (After Frankenburg and Dodds, 1967)

EARLY DEPRIVATION. Infant monkeys were reared in total darkness from birth to three months, except for a brief period each day when they were exposed to light while wearing special goggles that permitted only diffuse, unpatterned light to reach the eyes.[1] When the monkeys were first exposed to light without goggles, they showed serious deficiencies in visual-motor behavior. They could not track moving objects with their eyes, did not blink when threatened by a blow to the face, nor put out their arms when moved rapidly toward a wall. However, these skills improved with continued visual exposure, and by the end of several weeks the dark-reared monkeys were performing as well as normal monkeys. In most instances they acquired the responses in less time than had the normal monkeys at an earlier age. This study provides evidence for the importance of both maturation and experience. Fully adequate use of vision depends on neuromuscular growth continuing after birth as well as on practice in the use of vision. The dark-reared monkeys required experience in light before they could develop the proper response; but the fact that they required much less experience than newborn monkeys once the goggles were removed is evidence of the role of maturation (Riesen, 1965).

In another experiment, dogs reared in confined quarters were perfectly healthy but in some respects appeared "stupid" (Scott, 1968). For example, they seemed insensitive to pain. They did not respond to a pin prick or to having their tail stepped on. Time after time, they would investigate a lighted match by putting their nose into the flame. Whatever the felt experience may have been, certainly the pain stimulus did not evoke the avoidance responses found in normal dogs. Subsequent studies with other species have led to the conclusion that restriction or deprivation of stimulation generally produces animals that in later life do not learn new tasks as quickly as their normal counterparts.

ENRICHED ENVIRONMENTS. What will be the psychological effects if we provide an organism with an unusual amount of stimulation instead of a restricted or deprived environment? Young gerbils (small mouse-like rodents) housed together in a large cage equipped with various kinds of toys differ significantly after thirty days from gerbils kept singly in small, bare cages (see Figure 3-3). They perform better on learning tasks; their brains weigh more and show a higher concentration of some of the chemicals associated with learning.

Human infants may also benefit from an enriched environment, even in the first weeks after birth. One study showed the effect of early stimulation upon *visually directed reaching*—a visual-motor response that develops in clearly specified maturational steps (White, 1971). A month-old baby lying on his back will stare at an attractive object held above him but will make no attempt to reach for it. By two months he will swipe at it accurately but with a closed fist. By four months he will alternate glances between his raised open hand and the object, gradually narrowing the gap. By five months he will accurately reach and successfully grasp the object.

Although the universality of this response sequence indicates a large degree of maturational dependence, the rate of development can be

[1] Earlier studies found that animals reared in total darkness suffered some degeneration of nerve cells in the eyes; a small amount of diffuse light through plastic goggles is sufficient for normal neurological development of the eyes yet does not provide experience with visual patterns.

Fig. 3-3 An enriched environment
Animals raised together in this cage, which provides a complex and enriched environment, show better learning ability and have better developed brains than gerbils reared singly in bare cages. (Rosenzweig and Bennett, 1969)

accelerated. The environment of a group of month-old infants in a state hospital was enriched by

1. increasing the amount of handling,
2. placing the infants on their stomachs with the crib liners removed for several periods each day so they could observe the activities around them,
3. replacing white crib sheets and liners with patterned ones,
4. hanging an elaborate ornament over the cribs featuring contrasting colors and forms to look at and explore with the hands.

Infants receiving this kind of treatment succeeded in visually directed reaching at an average age of three and a half months as contrasted with five months for a control group reared in the relatively unstimulating conditions of normal hospital routine. Interestingly enough, the enriched-environment infants were delayed in one aspect of their development; they did not begin visually studying their hands until around two months, as contrasted with a month and a half for the control infants. With virtually nothing else to look at, the control group discovered their hands earlier than the experimental group.

Note, however, that increased stimulation will not result in accelerated development unless the infant is maturationally ready. In fact, too much stimulation too soon may be upsetting. During the first five weeks of the above experiment, infants in the enriched group spent less time looking at their surroundings (seeming to ignore the ornament and patterned bumpers) and engaged in much more crying than did the control infants. It may be that a month-old infant is actually distressed by being surrounded by more stimulation than he is able to respond to. A subsequent study found that providing infants with only a simple but colorful object mounted on the crib rails for the first two months of life and then introducing more complex ornaments during the third month seemed to produce optimal development. These infants showed no signs of unusual distress, were consistently attentive to their surroundings, and achieved visually directed reaching at *less* than three months. Thus we see the importance of providing stimulation appropriate to the level of maturation (White, 1971).

EARLY STIMULATION AND LATER DEVELOPMENT. Early experiences seem to be important in providing the background necessary to cope with the environment at a later age. The parents who are proud of the "good baby" lying quietly in the crib may not be giving that baby what is best for him. The importance of a stimulating environment in the early years can be further illustrated by a classic study by Skeels and Dye (1939).

A group of orphaned children (whose development at the age of nineteen months was so retarded that adoption was out of the question) was transferred to an institution for the mentally retarded. In this institution, in contrast to the overcrowded orphanage, each child was placed in the care of an older, mildly retarded girl who served as a surrogate mother, spending great amounts of time playing with the child, talking to him, and informally training him. In addition, the living quarters were spacious and well equipped with toys. As soon as the children could walk, they began to attend a nursery school where additional play materials and stimulation were provided. After a period of four years, this experimental group showed an average gain in intelligence of 32 I.Q. points; a control group that remained in the orphanage showed a loss of 21 points. A follow-up study over 20 years later found the experimental group to be still superior to the control group (Skeels, 1966). Most of the experimental group had completed high school (one-third had gone to college), were self-supporting, and had married and produced children of normal intelligence. Most of the control group, on the other hand, had not progressed beyond third grade and either remained institutionalized or did not earn enough to be self-supporting.

Although the number of subjects in this study was small and the possibility of some innate intellectual differences between the experimental and control groups cannot be completely ruled out, the results are sufficiently impressive to indicate the importance of a stimulating early environment for later intellectual development.

Stages in Development

As we already mentioned, some psychologists find it useful to conceive of development as proceeding in definite *stages* rather than as a continuous process. The stage concept implies that the course of development is divided into step-wise levels, with clear-cut changes in behavior from one stage to the next.

As a developmental concept, a stage usually defines a set of behaviors that occur together. As a group, they characterize a quality of behavior that differs appreciably from the quality of behavior in earlier and later stages. Stages follow each other in an orderly sequence, and the transition from one stage to the next usually involves a process of integration, whereby the behavior from the earlier stage is transformed into the next, along with some new elements. While environmental factors may speed up or slow down development, they do not change its sequence.

Stages in Cognitive Development

Swiss psychologist Jean Piaget has done the most to make the stage concept of development plausible. His interest for many years has focused on the cognitive or intellectual development of children. Piaget's main stages of intellectual development are presented in Table 3-1.

SENSORIMOTOR STAGE. Noting the close interplay between motor activity and perception in infants, Piaget designated the first two years as a *sensorimotor stage*. During this period the infant is busy discovering the relationships between sensations and motor behavior. He learns, for example, how far he has to reach to grasp an object, what happens when he pushes

TABLE 3-1
Piaget's stages of intellectual development

STAGE	APPROXIMATE AGES*	CHARACTERIZATION
1. Sensorimotor	Birth–2 years	Infant differentiates himself from objects; gradually becomes aware of the relationship between his actions and their effects on the environment so that he can act intentionally and make interesting events last longer (if he shakes a rattle it will make a noise); learns that objects continue to exist even though no longer visible (object permanence).
2. Preoperational	2–7	Uses language and can represent objects by images and words; is still *egocentric*, the world revolves around him and he has difficulty taking the viewpoint of others; classifies objects by single salient features: if A is like B in one respect, must be like B in other respects; toward the end of this stage begins to use numbers and develop conservation concepts.
3. Concrete operational	7–12	Becomes capable of logical thought; achieves conservation concepts in this order: number (age 6), mass (age 7), weight (age 9); can classify objects, order them in series along a dimension (such as size), and understand relational terms (A is longer than B).
4. Formal operational	12 and up	Can think in abstract terms, follow logical propositions, and reason by hypothesis; isolates the elements of a problem and systematically explores all possible solutions; becomes concerned with the hypothetical, the future, and ideological problems.

*The ages given are averages. They may vary considerably depending upon intelligence, cultural background, and socioeconomic factors, but the order of progression is the same for all children. Piaget has described more detailed phases within each stage; only a very general characterization of each stage is given here.

Jean Piaget

his food dish to the edge of the table, and that his hand is part of himself while the crib rail is not. Through countless "experiments" he begins to separate himself from external reality. An important discovery during this stage is the concept of *object permanence*—an awareness that an object continues to exist even when it is not present to the senses. If a cloth is placed over a toy for which an eight-month-old infant is reaching, he immediately stops his motion and appears to lose interest. He seems neither surprised nor upset, makes no attempt to search for the toy, and acts as if it ceased to exist (see Figure 3-4). In contrast, a ten-month-old infant will actively search for an object that has been hidden under a cloth or behind a screen. He seems to realize that the object exists even though he can no longer see it. He has attained the concept of object permanence. But even at this age his search is limited; if he has had repeated success in retrieving a toy hidden in one place, he will continue to look for it in that spot even though he has watched while it was being concealed in a new location. Not until about one year of age will he consistently look for an object where it was last seen to disappear regardless of what has happened on previous trials.

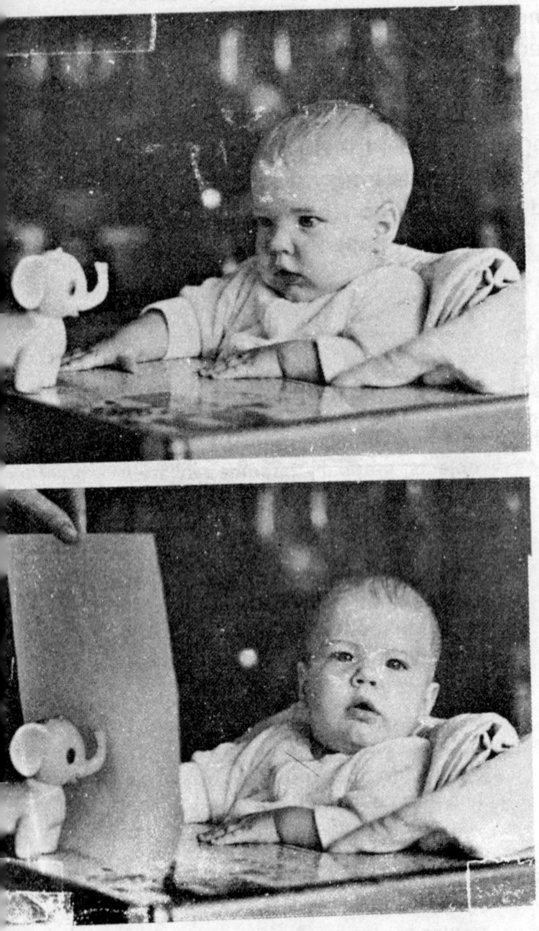

Fig. 3-4 Object permanence

When the toy is hidden by a screen, the infant acts as if it no longer exists. He does not yet have the concept of object permanence.

PREOPERATIONAL STAGE. The kinds of evidence that Piaget and his co-workers have used in studying children's cognitive processes in the *preoperational stage* can be illustrated by the development of what he calls *conservation.* As adults we take conservation principles for granted: the amount (mass) of a substance is not changed when its shape is changed or when it is divided into parts; the total weight of a set of objects will remain the same no matter how they are packaged together, and liquids do not change in amount when they are poured from a container of one shape to that of another. For children, however, attainment of these concepts is an aspect of intellectual growth requiring several years.

In a study of the conservation of mass, a child is given some clay to make into a ball equal to another ball of the same material; he declares them to be "the same." Now, leaving one for reference, the other is rolled out into a long sausage shape while the child watches. If the child is about four years old, he no longer considers the two objects to contain the same amount of clay: to him the longer one contains more (Figure 3-5). Not until the age of seven do the majority of children reach the stage where the clay in the longer object is perceived to be equal in amount to that in the reference ball.

The same kind of experiment can be used to study the conservation of weight. For example, the child who knows that equal things will balance on a scale (he can test this with the two balls to begin with) is then asked whether the sausage-shaped form will keep the scale arm balanced as did the original ball. Conservation of weight is a more difficult concept to conceive than conservation of mass, and it comes a year or so later in development.

A child younger than seven has difficulty with conservation concepts because his thinking is still dominated by visual impressions. A change in the perceptual quality of the clay mass means more to him than subtle qualities such as the volume the clay occupies regardless of its shape. The young child's reliance on visual impressions is made clear by a somewhat different conservation experiment. If a row of black checkers is matched one for one against an equal row of red checkers, the five or six year old will say there are the same number of each. If the black checkers are brought closer together to form a cluster, the five year old says there are now more red

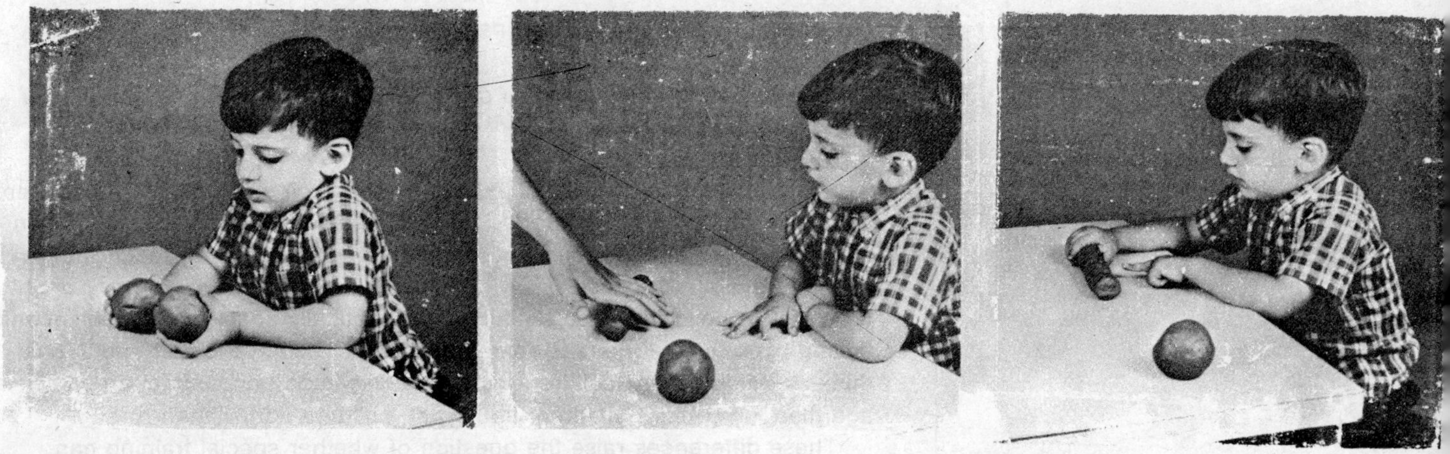

ones—even though no checkers have been removed (see Figure 3-6), impression of the length of the row of red checkers overrides the numerical equality that was obvious when the objects were matched. In contrast, a seven year old assumes that if the number of objects were equal before, they must remain equal. For him, numerical equality is more significant than visual impression.

Fig. 3-5 Concept of conservation

A four year old acknowledges that the two balls of clay are the same size. But when one ball is rolled into a long thin shape, he says that it has more clay. Not until he is several years older will he state that the two different shapes contain the same amount of clay.

OPERATIONAL STAGES. Between the ages of seven and twelve, the *concrete operational stage,* the child masters the various conservation concepts and begins to perform still other logical manipulations. For example, he can order objects on the basis of a dimension such as height or weight. He can also form a mental representation of a series of actions. A five year old can find his way to a friend's house, but he cannot direct you there nor can he trace the route with paper and pencil. He can find the way because he knows he has to turn at certain places, but he has no overall picture of the route. In contrast, an eight year old can readily draw a map of the route.

Piaget calls this period the *concrete operational stage* because, although the child is using abstract terms, he is doing so only in relation to concrete objects. Not until the final stage of cognitive development, the *formal operational stage,* which begins around 11 or 12, is the youngster able to reason in purely symbolic terms.

One test for formal operational thinking has the subject try to discover what determines the period of oscillation of a simple pendulum. The subject is presented with a length of string suspended from a hook and several weights that can be attached to the lower end. He can vary the length of the string, change the attached weight, and alter the height from which the bob is released.

A child still in the concrete operational stage will experiment changing some of the variables, but not in a systematic way. An adolescent of even average ability will set up a series of hypotheses and proceed to systematically test each one. He reasons that if a particular variable (weight) affects the period of oscillation, then the effect will appear only if he varies one variable and holds all others constant. If this variable seems to have no effect on the time of swing, he rules it out and tries another. Considering all the possibilities, working out the consequences for each hypothesis, and confirming or denying these consequences is the essence of what Piaget calls formal operational thought.

This ability to conceive of possibilities beyond what is present in reality—to think of alternatives to the way things are—permeates the adolescent's thinking and is tied in with his tendency to be concerned with metaphysical

Fig. 3-6 Conservation experiment

When the two rows of seven checkers are evenly spaced, most children report that they contain the same amount. When one row is then clustered into a smaller space children under six or seven will say the original row contains more.

and ideological problems and to question the way in which adults run the world.

EVALUATION OF PIAGET'S THEORY. Research with children of different ages and backgrounds supports Piaget's observations of the *sequences* in cognitive development. However, the *ages* at which children reach the different levels vary considerably depending on many factors. A very bright ten-year-old child might be skillful at systematically analyzing a problem and testing hypotheses, whereas some adults never achieve formal operational thinking. Middle-class children master conservation concepts at an earlier age than lower-class children; and urban children earlier than rural.

These differences raise the question of whether special training can accelerate progress through the cognitive stages. Different techniques have been used to try to speedup the transition from one stage to the next, with most of the studies focusing on conservation concepts. The usual procedure is to test a group of children on a conservation problem (for example, conservation of amount, using either water or clay), divide those who are nonconservers into an experimental and a control group, provide the experimental group with special training, and retest both groups to see whether the performance of children in the trained group differs from the performance of those who received no training. The training may involve direct teaching of conservation principles–for example, showing the child that different shapes of clay weigh the same on a scale. Or it may be indirectly related to conservation–for example, drawing attention to the fact that objects simultaneously possess a number of characteristics by having the child practice naming the characteristics of objects and noting the ways in which they are similar or different.

Studies on the training of conservation principles have had conflicting results. Some report no success; others claim that the concept can be taught. Probably the safest conclusion is that instruction can yield some acceleration in cognitive development; however, progress from one stage to the next depends upon maturational changes so that training is most effective if it occurs when the child is ready (Glaser and Resnick, 1972).

Psychosexual and Psychosocial Stages

A quite different theory of stages, proposed by Sigmund Freud, deals with the emotional and motivational (rather than the intellectual) aspects of personality. Like Piaget's, however, it assumes clearly definable stages.

Freud considered the childhood stages as having to do with deriving pleasure from different body zones at different ages, leading to the gratifications of adult sexuality. By using a very broad definition of sexuality, these stages became known as *psychosexual* stages. The chief ones are *oral* (gratification through stimulation of the lips and mouth region, as in nursing or thumbsucking), *anal* (gratification through withholding and expelling feces), *phallic* (gratification through fondling the sex organs), *latent* (in which sexual interests are no longer active, so that the child of elementary-school age turns his interests to the environment), and, finally, *genital* (at which point normal heterosexual interests arise). Each of the earlier stages is normally outgrown. In the event of arrested development (or *fixation*), some

Erik H. Erikson

problems associated with an earlier stage persist beyond their normal time; in this respect the theory is also a critical period theory. This classification of stages, while it has been influential, is not generally accepted by psychologists as a precise statement of development, whatever partial truths there may be within it.

Years later, the psychoanalyst Erikson (1963) felt that the social problems encountered in the course of development were more important than the biological ones. He described a progression of *psychosocial* stages in which the child faces a wider range of human relationships as he grows up and has specific problems to solve at each of these stages. Again, as with Freud's theory, how well the child solves his problems at any one stage may determine how adequate a person he will become later and how well he will cope with new problems.

Erikson's psychosocial stages of development are listed in Table 3-2. There is enough plausibility to the issues raised within Erikson's stages to make his scheme a useful one in calling attention to social development problems. The scheme lacks, however, the rigor of a strictly scientific delineation of stages, and its appeal must be thought of as speculative.

The concept of developmental stages has helped psychologists group problems to be studied into manageable segments. Evidence indicates, however, that (1) the overlapping of one stage with another is more common than a sharp transition, and (2) usually a deficiency from an earlier period can be corrected later. For example, although it is doubtless advantageous to learn to read early in life, people do learn to read as adults. The concept of developmental stages is interesting, however, and the issues involved are important enough to deserve investigation.

TABLE 3-2 Eight stages of psychosocial development

STAGES (AGES ARE APPROXIMATE)	PSYCHOSOCIAL CRISES	RADIUS OF SIGNIFICANT RELATIONS	PSYCHOSOCIAL MODALITIES	FAVORABLE OUTCOME
1. Birth–first year	Trust vs. mistrust	Mother or mother substitute	To get To give in return	Drive and hope
2. Second year	Autonomy vs. shame, doubt	Parents	To hold (on) To let (go)	Self-control and willpower
3. Third year–fifth year	Initiative vs. guilt	Basic family	To make (going after) To "make like" (playing)	Direction and purpose
4. Sixth year–onset of puberty	Industry vs. inferiority	Neighborhood; school	To make things (competing) To make things together	Method and competence
5. Adolescence	Identity and repudiation vs. identity diffusion	Peer groups and outgroups; models of leadership	To be oneself (or not to be) To share being oneself	Devotion and fidelity
6. Early adulthood	Intimacy and solidarity vs. isolation	Partners in friendship, sex, competition, cooperation	To lose and find oneself in another	Affiliation and love
7. Young and middle adulthood	Generativity vs. self-absorption	Divided labor and shared household	To make be To take care of	Production and care
8. Later adulthood	Integrity vs. despair	"Mankind" "My Kind"	To be, through having been To face not being	Renunciation and wisdom

Source: Erikson (1963); modified from original.

CRITICAL DISCUSSION

Are There Universal Stages in the Development

The possibility that children's views on moral issues change with age according to predictable stages has been the subject of extensive research by Lawrence Kohlberg at Harvard University. Using as a background Piaget's work on moral reasoning (Piaget, *The Moral Judgment of the Child,* 1932), Kohlberg sought to determine whether there are universal stages in the development of moral judgments. He presented stories such as the following to children and adults of various ages and cultural backgrounds.

> In Europe, a lady was dying because she was very sick. There was one drug that the doctors said might save her. This medicine was discovered by a man living in the same town. It cost him $200 to make it, but he charged $2,000 for just a little of it. The sick lady's husband, Heinz, tried to borrow enough money to buy the drug. He went to everyone he knew to borrow the money. But he could borrow only half of what he needed. He told the man who made the drug that his wife was dying, and asked him to sell the medicine cheaper or let him pay later. But the man said, "No, I made the drug and I'm going to make money from it." So Heinz broke into the store and stole the drug.

The subject is asked, "Should Heinz have done that? Was it actually wrong or right? Why?" By analyzing the answers to a series of stories of this type—each portraying a moral dilemma—Kohlberg arrived at six developmental stages of moral judgment grouped into three broad levels (see Table 3-3). The answers are stage-assigned, not on the basis of whether the action is judged right or wrong, but on the reasons given for the decision. For example, agreeing that Heinz should have stolen the drug because "If you let your wife die, you'll get in trouble" or condemning him for his actions because "If you steal the drug you'll be caught and sent to jail" are both scored at Stage 1. In both instances the man's actions are evaluated as right or wrong on the basis of anticipated punishment.

Kohlberg's studies indicate that the moral judgments of children who are seven and younger are predominantly at Level I—actions are evaluated in terms of whether they avoid punishment or lead to rewards. By age 13, a majority of the moral dilemmas are resolved at Level II—actions are evaluated in terms of maintaining a good image in the eyes of other people. This is the level of conventional morality. In the first stage at this level (Stage 3) one seeks approval by being "nice"; this orientation expands in the next stage (Stage 4) to include "doing one's duty," showing respect for authority, and conforming to the social order in which one is raised.

According to Kohlberg, many individuals never progress beyond Level II. He sees the stages of moral development as closely tied to Piaget's stages of cognitive development, and only if a person has achieved the later stages of formal operational thought is he capable of the kind of abstract thinking necessary for postconventional morality at Level III. The highest stage of moral development (Level III, Stage 6) requires formulating abstract ethical principles and conforming to them to avoid self-condemnation. Kohlberg reports that less than 10 percent of his subjects over age 16 show the kind of "clear-principled" Stage 6 thinking exemplified by the following response of a 16 year old to Heinz's dilemma: "By the law of society he was wrong but by the law of nature or of God the druggist was wrong and the husband was justified. Human life is above financial gain. Regardless of who was dying, if it was a total stranger, man has a duty to save him from dying" (Kohlberg, 1969, p. 244).

Kohlberg describes the child as a "moral philosopher" who develops moral standards of his own; these standards do not necessarily come from parents or peers but emerge from the cognitive interaction of the child with his social environment. Movement from one stage to the next involves an internal cognitive reorganization rather than a

TABLE 3-3
Stages in the development of moral values

LEVELS AND STAGES	ILLUSTRATIVE BEHAVIOR
Level I. Premoral	
1. Punishment and obedience orientation	Obeys rules in order to avoid punishment
2. Naive instrumental hedonism	Conforms to obtain rewards, to have favors returned
Level II. Morality of conventional role-conformity	
3. "Good-boy" morality of maintaining good relations, approval of others	Conforms to avoid disapproval, dislike by others
4. Authority maintaining morality	Conforms to avoid censure by legitimate authorities, with resultant guilt
Level III. Morality of self-accepted moral principles	
5. Morality of contract, of individual rights, and of democratically accepted law	Conforms to maintain the respect of the impartial spectator judging in terms of community welfare
6. Morality of individual principles of conscience	Conforms to avoid self-condemnation

Source: Kohlberg (1967).

of Moral Values?

simple acquisition of the moral concepts prevalent in his culture.

Other psychologists disagree, pointing out that the development of conscience is not simply a function of maturing cognitive abilities; a child's identification with his parents and the way in which he is rewarded or punished for behavior in specific situations will determine his moral views. Moreover, *moral reasoning*—as measured by verbal responses to moral dilemmas—may not correlate highly with *moral behavior.* Kohlberg claims that moral thought and moral action are closely related. For proof he cites a study in which college students were given an opportunity to cheat on a test. Only 11 percent of those who reached Level III on the moral dilemmas test cheated. In contrast, 42 percent of the students at the lower levels of moral judgment cheated (Schwartz and others, 1969). Other investigators, however, are not convinced that the correspondence between what people *say* and what they *do* is quite so close. And some believe that the specific situation is an important determiner of moral behavior; people cheat in some situations and not in others (Mischel and Mischel, 1974).

Kohlberg's studies, while controversial, raise interesting questions about the teaching of moral principles. If moral values are *relative* to the culture in which one is raised, as many people assume, then the task of the educator is to present the cultural values, point out their relativity, and tell each child that he must form his own values while bearing in mind the good of society. Within this view, it is not the educator's job to teach moral principles. Kohlberg, on the other hand, believes that moral values are universal and that each child should be helped to reach the highest stage possible. He suggests presenting moral dilemmas in the classroom and, through discussion, helping each child to understand the moral principles at the stage just above his own (Kohlberg, 1973).

Personality Development in Early Childhood

An infant's first social contacts are normally with his mother. The manner in which she responds to his needs—patiently with warmth and concern, or brusquely with little sensitivity to his discomfort—will greatly influence his attitudes toward other people.

Development of Social Attachments

By two months of age the average child will smile at the sight of his mother's face. Most mothers, delighted with this response, will go to great lengths to encourage its repetition. But she is not its only stimulus. At this age the infant will smile at the sight of any human face and at pictures of human faces. His behavior seems to indicate that he has acquired a mental image of the human face and can distinguish it from other objects. Smiling reaches a peak at about four months. If a strange infant bestows upon you a beauteous smile with little provocation on your part, you can estimate his age at between four and six months. At about eight months the appearance of a strange face will often fail to elicit a smile and may produce signs of wariness or distress. By this time the infant has begun to distinguish familiar faces from strange ones.

While there are individual differences, evidence indicates that specific attachments to the mother and other familiar persons has formed by about four months, and fear of strangers develops several months later. One theory proposes three stages in the development of attachments. In the first stage, the infant seeks stimulation of any kind from the environment. In the second stage, he begins to find people the most interesting and satisfying agents in his environment and seeks closeness to them, without expressing preferences among them. Finally, his interests narrow to selected persons; at this stage his reactions are truly social (Schaffer and Emerson, 1964).

It was formerly believed that the beginning of social attachment came about because the mother (as a source of food) met the infant's needs, reduced tensions, and hence was satisfying. However, it now appears that attachment may have relatively little to do with the mother as a source of food; attachments to the mother are commonly accompanied by attachments to others, usually, but not exclusively, the father. Observations of animals also confirm this interpretation. Some species of animals, such as young ducklings, feed themselves from birth, but still closely follow their mothers and spend a great deal of time in contact with them. The comfort the ducklings derive from the mother cannot come from her role in feeding.

More dramatic are some experiments with young monkeys reared in isolation from their true mothers but permitted to feed from and cling to artificial mothers (Harlow and Harlow, 1966; Harlow and Suomi, 1970). Two "laboratory mothers" were provided with devices permitting the young monkeys to obtain milk by sucking. Both "mothers" were immobile and, although they had torsos, heads, and faces, they did not resemble monkey mothers (see Figures 3-7). One of the laboratory mothers was constructed wire. The other, covered with soft terry cloth, was more "cuddly" than the wire model.

Fig. 3-7 A monkey's response to artificial mother

Although fed via the wire mother, the infant spends more time with the terry-cloth mother. The terry-cloth mother provides security and a safe base from which to explore strange objects.

The experiment sought to determine whether the "mother" that was always the source of food would be the one to which the young monkey would cling. The results were clear-cut: no matter which mother was the source of food, the infant monkey spent its time clinging to the terry-cloth, "cuddly" mother. This purely passive but soft-contact mother was a source of security. For example, the obvious fear of the infant monkey placed in a strange environment was allayed if the infant could make contact with the cloth mother. While holding on to the cloth mother with one hand or foot, the monkey was willing to explore objects that were otherwise too terrifying to approach. Similar responses can be observed in one- to two-year-old children who are willing to explore strange territory as long as mother is only a few feet away.

Although contact with an artificial mother provides an important aspect of "mothering," it is not sufficient to produce satisfactory development. Lack of contact with other monkeys during the first six months of life produces various types of bizarre behavior in adulthood. Monkeys raised in early isolation rarely engage in positive interactions with other monkeys later on and are very difficult to mate. When females deprived of early social contact are successfully mated (after considerable effort), they make poor mothers, tending to neglect or abuse their infants. The effects on adult social behavior of isolation during the first six months of life are so striking that these early months would seem to constitute a *critical period* for the development of social attachments in monkeys. Regardless of the amount of exposure to other monkeys that occurs during the intervening years, these early isolates never develop normal social behavior (Sackett, 1967).

Effects of Mother-Child Separation

Experimental data for human infants on the effect of early social attachments indicate that a close relationship with the mother serves the same important functions—it provides the security necessary for the child to explore his environment, and it forms the basis for interpersonal relationships in later years. Young children are much more willing to investigate strange surroundings when mother is nearby (Rheingold and Echerman, 1970). The failure to form an attachment to one or a few primary persons in the early years has been related to an inability to develop close personal relationships in adulthood (Bowlby, 1969).

In the normal course of events, attachment to the mother—as measured by seeking to remain near her and crying when separated—reaches a peak at about age two; from then on the child becomes progressively more willing to *detach* himself from the mother. By about age three, he is sufficiently secure in her absence to be able to play with peers or relate to other adults (see Figure 3-8).

A series of studies designed to investigate attachment in young children has revealed some interesting differences in the quality of the mother-child relationship. The laboratory setup, called the "strange situation," involves the following episodes

1. The mother brings the child into the experimental room, places him on a small chair surrounded by toys, and goes to sit at the opposite end of the room.

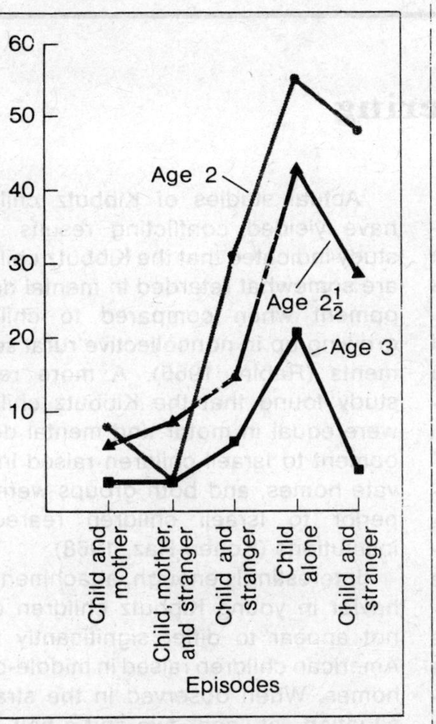

Fig. 3-8 Mother-attachment and age

The "strange situation" was used to study age changes in attachment behavior. The child was observed through a one-way mirror and the frequency of his crying recorded during the sequence of episodes noted along the baseline. The episodes are described more fully in the text; no data was reported for episodes 4 and 7. Note that crying in response to being left with a stranger or left alone decreases from ages 2–3, indicating that the child is more willing to be detached from the mother. (After Maccoby and Feldman, 1972)

2. After a few minutes a stranger enters the room, sits quietly for a while, and then attempts to engage the child in play with a toy.
3. The mother leaves the room.
4. Mother returns and engages the child in play while the stranger slips out.
5. Mother leaves and child is left alone for three minutes.
6. Stranger returns.
7. Mother returns.

The child is observed through a one-way mirror during the entire sequence, and any number of different measures can be recorded—child's activity level and play involvement, crying or other distress signs, proximity to and attempts to gain attention of mother, proximity to and willingness to interact with stranger, etc.

One study using the "strange situation" with one-year olds found that some of the most significant individual differences showed up in the baby's reaction to the mother when she returned. Almost all the babies were uneasy during the mother's absence, whether left with the stranger or completely alone; signs of distress ranged from fussing and visually searching for the mother to loud crying. On the mother's return more than half of the babies immediately sought close contact and interaction with her and continued to show a need for closeness for a while thereafter. But some babies conspicuously ignored the mother upon her return and avoided interaction with her; and some displayed seemingly ambivalent behavior—for example, they would cry to be picked up and then squirm angrily to get down.

Observation of the same babies in the home revealed that those babies who sought contact with the mother upon reunion were much more secure (cried less often, were more responsive to mother's verbal commands and less upset by mother's coming and going) than babies who were either avoidant or ambivalent upon reunion in the strange situation.

The investigator concluded, on the basis of these and other data, that all babies become attached to the mother by the time they are one year old, but the quality of the attachment differs depending upon the mother's responsiveness to the baby's needs. Most babies show *secure attachment,* but some show *anxious attachment.* The avoidant or ambivalent behavior shown by anxiously attached babies upon reunion with the mother is assumed to be a defense against the anxiety occasioned by a mother who cannot be depended upon. It is a mild form of the more extreme kind of detachment observed in young children who have had to endure long separations from the parents. Such children often appear indifferent to their parents when they are first reunited (Ainsworth, 1973).

Anxious attachment is associated with insensitive or unresponsive mothering during the first year. The mothers of babies who show anxious attachment tend to respond more on the basis of their own wishes or moods than to signals from the baby. For example, they will respond to the baby's cries for attention when they feel like cuddling him but will ignore such cries at other times. Such insensitivity produces feelings of insecurity in the infant (Stayton, 1973).

Anxious attachment also can be produced by repeated separations at an early age regardless of how responsive the mother may be. Two and three year olds attending a day-care center for eight or nine hours each week day were compared with home-reared children of the same ages in the strange

CRITICAL DISCUSSION

Intermittent Mothering

In some countries, such as Russia and Israel, mothers are encouraged to work while their children are cared for in state-run institutions. For example, on the collective farms, or *Kibbutzim,* of Israel, the children are cared for from earliest infancy by professional caretakers in houses separate from those of the parents. Practices differ somewhat from one Kibbutz to another, but the following arrangement is typical.

During the first year of life, the mother provides the major portion of the feeding and care of her infant, although the infant is still housed in the communal nursery. After the first year, the mother works full time and sees her child mainly during the evening and on Saturdays. This combination of institutional and maternal care, sometimes called *intermittent mothering,* has been closely studied to determine if these children differ from those raised in single-family homes. Because earlier studies had shown that children raised in orphanages were markedly retarded in social and intellectual development, those responsible for setting up communal child-care centers were especially concerned with providing a warm relationship with a mother-substitute as well as sufficient intellectual stimulation. They realized that adequate physical care was not enough to produce a healthy child. Consequently, the caretakers received special training in all areas of child development.

Reports from those who have observed life among Kibbutz children indicate that the approach to such situations as toilet training and self-care is warm and permissive, and independence is encouraged. The observers note that Kibbutz-raised children seem to develop early a feeling of group concern and identification, supporting their group against others and excluding others from play. The fact that discipline and training are handled primarily by the caretaker, so that the child's daily visits with his parents involve mostly pleasurable activities, is assumed to do much to reduce parent-child conflicts (Rabkin and Rabkin, 1969).

Actual studies of Kibbutz children have yielded conflicting results. One study indicated that the Kibbutz children are somewhat retarded in mental development when compared to children growing up in noncollective rural settlements (Rabin, 1965). A more recent study found that the Kibbutz children were equal in motor and mental development to Israeli children raised in private homes, and both groups were superior to Israeli children reared in institutions (Kohen-Raz, 1968).

Interestingly enough, attachment behavior in young Kibbutz children does not appear to differ significantly from American children raised in middle-class homes. When observed in the strange situation at age two-and-a-half, the Kibbutz youngsters were just as concerned over separation from the mother as their American counterparts. And despite their exposure to multiple caretakers, they were less willing to interact with strangers (Maccoby and Feldman, 1972). The latter findings may be due to the fact that Kibbutz-reared children live

situation. Although no differences were found between the two groups in the nature of the mother-child interaction at home, the day-care children showed significantly more signs of anxious attachment (as measured by ambivalent or avoidant responses on reunion) than the home-reared children (Blehar, 1973). The disruptive effects of frequent daily separations were more evident in those children who started day care at age two than those who started at age three. These findings must be viewed as tentative until further substantiated, but they suggest that starting day care either at birth or at age three may be preferable to separating the child from the mother at age two when attachment is strongest. Both insensitive mothering and repeated separations undermine the child's trust that his attachment figure will be accessible and responsive to him.

Child-rearing Practices and Later Behavior

Child-rearing methods vary tremendously from country to country, and from one social class to another. Even within middle-class homes in the United States attitudes have tended to fluctuate in cycles on such matters as

in a fairly closed community where they are familiar with most of the members; they seldom encounter total strangers as American children do when visiting supermarkets with their parents.

The majority of Kibbutz-raised 17 and 18 year olds questioned about their feelings concerning Kibbutz life expressed satisfaction with communal living. The girls, however, regretted the fact that they had not spent more time with their parents as children and expressed a desire to care for their own children more than their parents had cared for them (Rabin, 1968a).

One potential advantage of the Kibbutz is that by keeping records of the various training methods used, it is easier to determine which is most effective in the long run. To the extent that this can be accomplished, it should be possible to identify more accurately the important factors in an effective child-rearing program.

Mealtime at a Kibbutz

toilet training, feeding schedules, bottle versus breast feeding, and permissiveness versus firm control. At the turn of the century, the approach was permissive—the infant was fed when he was hungry and bowel and bladder control occurred naturally when the child was mature enough to control these functions and understand what was expected. In the 1920s under the influence of behaviorism, the trend swung toward systematic and strict training procedures. The goal was to build "good" habits and avoid teaching bad ones. The following quote from John B. Watson, the father of behaviorism, carries to a ridiculous extreme this notion of a controlled, objective, unemotional way of handling the child.

> There is a sensible way of treating children. Treat them as though they were young adults. Dress them, bathe them with care and circumspection. Let your behavior always be objective and kindly firm. Never hug and kiss them, never let them sit on your lap. If you must, kiss them once on the forehead when they say goodnight. Shake hands with them in the morning. Give them a pat on the head if they have made an extraordinarily good job of a difficult task. Try it out. In a week's time you will find how easy

it is to be perfectly objective with your child and at the same time kindly. You will be utterly ashamed of the mawkish, sentimental way you have been handling it (Watson, 1928).

Children under this regime were supposed to be fed on a rigid schedule (whether hungry or not), never picked up when they cried, and given a minimum of cuddling for fear they would become spoiled. It is doubtful whether many parents followed such a rigid program, but this was the advice of the "experts" at the time.

During the 1940s the trend shifted to more permissive and flexible child-care methods. Under the guidance of Dr. Spock, parents were advised to follow their own inclinations and adapt schedules to both the child's and their needs.

That children flourish under a wide variety of rearing methods is a tribute to the adaptability of the young organism, and probably an indication that specific methods are less important than the basic attitude of the parents. Nevertheless, psychologists are concerned with whether specific child-rearing methods have predictable effects on the development of the child.

Much research has been devoted to investigating the relationship between child-rearing methods and later personality characteristics. One approach is to obtain information from the parents about how they handle their children and then correlate that information with some measure of the child's behavior. For example, age of weaning (as reported by the mother) might be correlated with teacher's rating of "dependency" behavior in nursery school. Or the type of discipline the parents report using might be related to observations of the child's aggressiveness in school. Several large-scale studies have attempted to relate personality characteristics of the school-age child to child-rearing techniques as reported by the parents (e.g., Sears, Maccoby, and Levin, 1957). Unfortunately, the results are far from consistent, and the relationships found by one study are seldom supported by the next.

A number of reasons account for such inconsistent results. For one thing, parents' reports of how they handle their child may be quite inaccurate, particularly when memory for the child's early days is required. Parents tend to report what they *think they should do* in dealing with their offspring, rather than what they actually do. And, there are numerous ways of applying any specific child-rearing method. For example, two children may be toilet trained at the same early age; one mother is firm but patient, while the other is firm and impatient, making the child feel that he has failed to live up to her expectations when he does not perform at the proper time and place. Both mothers toilet train "early" but communicate quite different attitudes to the child.

In addition, evidence shows that children imitate or model much of their behavior after the important adults in their lives. A father who tells his four-year-old son it is bad to hit one's playmates and then proceeds to spank him for doing so provides a model of the very behavior he is criticizing. Will the boy learn from his father's words or from his actions?

Because of such complications it is difficult to predict what kind of child will be produced by a specific child-rearing method. Undoubtedly the attitudes and examples of the parents have a significant influence on the personality development of the child. But it is difficult to isolate the results of specific child-rearing methods from other dimensions of the parent-child relationship.

One thing seems clear—the most important factor in child rearing is an affectionate relationship with a parent (or parent substitute) in the early years. The absence of warmth and affection leads to many undesirable personality characteristics; neuroticism, aggressiveness, extreme submissiveness, and inability to control impulses have all been shown to be related to a lack of affection in the home. We cannot predict what kind of child rejecting parents will produce, but we can be fairly sure that the outcome will not be favorable.

In addition, studies concerned with moral behavior indicate the types of discipline that seem most conducive to self-control and the development of moral standards. Giving reasons why a child should change his behavior by explaining how it harms someone else, or appealing to the child's desire to be "grown up" and "competent," is generally better than using physical punishment, depriving him of privileges or material objects, or showing disapproval by love withdrawal (that is, isolating the child or refusing to speak to him). Using physical punishment or deprivation are power plays; they are apt to produce a child who is obedient in the presence of the parents but not elsewhere (Bandura and Walters, 1963). Love withdrawal is generally not as effective as reasoning, and is apt to produce a child who is overly dependent on adult approval (Hoffman, 1970).

The Process of Identification

As the child develops, he acquires many attitudes and behavior patterns that are similar to those of his parents. Sometimes the resemblance between a youngster and one of his parents in such characteristics as manner of walking, gestures, and voice inflection is striking. The child is said to *identify* with the parent (see Figure 3-9).

Fig. 3-9

A child identifies with the parent.

The concept of identification comes from psychoanalysis and played an important role in Freud's theorizing. In psychoanalytic theory identification refers to the unconscious process by which an individual takes on the characteristics (attitudes, patterns of behavior, emotions) of another person. The young child, by duplicating the attitudes and attributes of the parent, comes to feel that he has absorbed some of his parent's strength and adequacy. In the course of growing up, identification serves to relieve the anxiety produced by gradual separation from the parent since, in a sense, the child carries part of the parent with him.

Identification, according to the psychoanalytic view, involves more than simply imitating parental behavior; the child responds as if he *were* the parent. Thus, a young girl who identifies with her mother feels proud when her mother receives an award or honor—as if she, herself, had been the recipient. She feels sad when her mother suffers a disappointment. Through the process of identification the child acquires the diverse behaviors involved in developing self-control, a conscience, and the appropriate sex role. The child's conscience, for example, is formed by incorporating parental standards of conduct so that the child acts in accordance with these standards even when the parent is absent, and experiences guilt when he violates them.

Some psychologists question the psychoanalytic view of identification as an unconscious, unitary process. They point out that not all children identify with their parents in all respects. A girl, for example, may emulate her mother's social skills and sense of humor but not her moral values. They view identification as a form of learning; the child imitates certain parental behaviors because he is rewarded for doing so. Peers, teachers, and television heroes are other models who serve as sources of imitation or identification. According to this view, identification is a continuous process in which new responses are acquired as a function of both direct and vicarious experiences with parents and other models.

Most psychologists—regardless of how they define it—view identification as the basic process in the socialization of the child. By modeling behavior after the important people in his environment, the child acquires the attitudes and behaviors expected of an adult in his particular society. Parents, because they are the child's earliest and most frequent associates, serve as the primary source of identification. The parent of the opposite sex serves as the model for sex-typed behavior. Psychologists are interested in how the characteristics of the parents influence the child's tendency to identify.

Sex-Role Identification

Each culture sets certain approved ways in which men and women are expected to behave; these may be called the *sex-role standards* for that culture. The standards for masculine and feminine behavior vary from culture to culture and may change over time within a culture. Certainly our view of what is appropriate behavior today is radically different from what it was fifty years ago. Women are no longer expected to be dependent, submissive, and noncompetitive; men are not criticized for enjoying such domestic activities as cooking and sewing, or for expressing artistic and tender feelings. And standards of dress and appearances have certainly changed. But within each culture the roles of men and women still differ, and these roles are transmitted in large part by the parents. The man a boy knows best is his father and a girl's first exposure to the woman's role is through her mother. Parental attitudes toward themselves and one another are major influences on the child's view of masculine and feminine roles.

SEX-TYPING. Even before they are old enough to realize that there are two sexes, children are treated differently depending upon their sex. A female infant is often dressed in so-called feminine colors such as pink and is more frequently handled, touched, and talked to by her mother than is a boy. A male infant may be dressed in blue and allowed to express aggression more freely than a girl. Parents, without meaning to, tend to reinforce dependency in girls, and achievement and assertiveness in boys. By providing "sex-appropriate" toys and encouraging "sex-appropriate" play activities, parents instill sex-role stereotypes at an early age.

One method of measuring sex-typed behavior is to have the child choose between various toys and activities. Doll carriages and dishes are arbitrarily classified as feminine; dump trucks and tools as masculine. Examples of neutral toys (appropriate to either sex) are a wading pool and roller skates. Studies using this method indicate that boys as young as three prefer sex-appropriate toys. Many girls show an early preference for masculine toys and games; in kindergarten more girls show a preference for masculine toys than boys do for feminine toys. With increasing age, both girls and boys make increasingly more sex-appropriate choices, but boys consistently make more of them than do girls (see Figure 3-10).

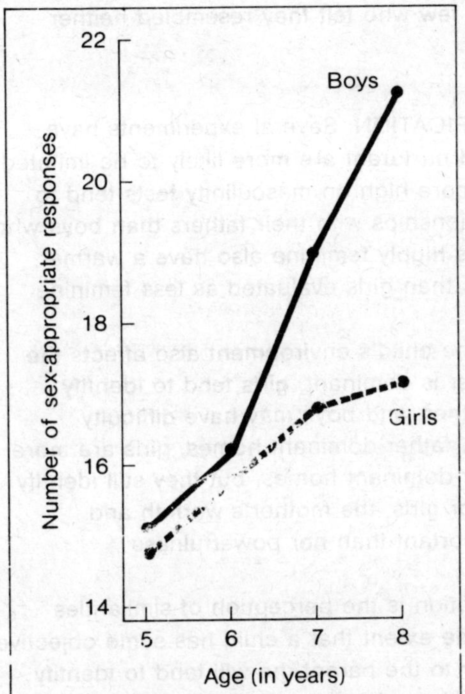

Fig. 3-10 Sex-typing in young children

When a choice is given between two toys (one masculine and the other feminine) the number of sex-appropriate responses increases with age for both boys and girls. Note that boys consistently make more of these responses than do girls, although the difference is very small at ages five and six (Data from DeLucia, 1963)

How do we account for these differences? For one thing, there is an unfortunate tendency for both sexes to view "masculine" activities as superior to "feminine" ones. And, in our culture the taboos against effeminate behavior for boys are stronger than those against masculine behavior for girls. Learning how to be masculine seems to be largely a matter of avoiding any behavior regarded as "sissyish." When kindergarten boys were individually permitted to play with a group of attractive feminine toys and unattractive neutral toys, most of them avoided the feminine toys, spending their time with the unattractive and dilapidated neutral toys. The presence of an adult increased avoidance of the feminine toys, whereas observation of another boy playing with the feminine toys reduced avoidance. Observing a girl play with the feminine toys brought no change in behavior (Kobasigawa, Arakaki, and Awiguni, 1966).

Current attempts to prevent sex-role stereotyping by encouraging children to engage in a wide range of activities, without implying that any activity is either masculine or feminine, may change the results in future studies of this kind. While there may be some innate sex differences in abilities and interests, sex-role standards are primarily culturally determined.

Personal (Non-Sex-Role) Identification

Many personal qualities are not strongly sex-typed (such as enthusiasm, sense of humor, personal warmth) and many moral qualities (such as integrity and considerateness) are shared by both men and women. The child may thus learn and imitate qualities of *either* parent in these areas without violating the cultural sex standards.

Personality, temperament, and attitudes toward work and play can come from either parent. A mother's standards of housekeeping may be reflected in the son's work, even though he models after his father and enters his profession; a daughter may imitate her mother's social graces but still tell a story in the hearty way her father does. Both parents are important in determining how a boy or girl will develop.

University students who were interviewed about their behavioral similarities to their parents in temperament and recreational interests often reported similarity to the parent of the opposite sex. A fourth or more of the boys thought that they resembled their mothers in these respects, and a similar proportion of the girls thought they resembled their fathers; many reported resemblances to both parents (Table 3-4). That identifications are probably

TABLE 3-4
Non-sex-role identifications of university students with their parents

University students give many indications of resemblance to the parent of the opposite sex in temperament and recreational interests, in which sex-typing is of little importance.

	MALE STUDENTS		FEMALE STUDENTS	
REPORTED SIMILARITY	TEMPERAMENT	RECREATIONAL INTERESTS	TEMPERAMENT	RECREATIONAL INTERESTS
To father only	47%	44%	29%	31%
To both parents	19	11	33	25
To mother only	30	25	35	33
To neither parent	3	18	3	10
Not ascertained	1	2	—	1
Total	100%	100%	100%	100%

Source: J. R. Hilgard (1970).

present is evident from the relatively few who felt they resembled neither parent (Hilgard, 1970).

FACTORS INFLUENCING IDENTIFICATION. Several experiments have shown that adults who are warm and nurturant are more likely to be imitated than those who are not. Boys who score high on masculinity tests tend to have warmer, more affectionate relationships with their fathers than boys who score low. And girls who are rated as highly feminine also have a warmer, closer relationship with their mothers than girls evaluated as less feminine (Mussen and Rutherford, 1963).

The adult's power in controlling the child's environment also affects the tendency to identify. When the mother is dominant, girls tend to identify much more with her than with the father, and boys may have difficulty developing the masculine sex-role. In father-dominant homes, girls are more similar to their fathers than in mother-dominant homes, but they still identify to a large degree with the mother. For girls, the mother's warmth and self-confidence seem to be more important than her powerfulness (Hetherington and Frankie, 1967).

A third factor influencing identification is the perception of similarities between oneself and the model. To the extent that a child has some objective basis for perceiving himself as similar to the parent, he will tend to identify with that parent. A girl who is tall and large-boned with facial features similar to those of her father may have more difficulty identifying with her petite mother than a younger sister who is similar to the mother in build.

To the extent that both parents are seen as nurturant, powerful, and competent the child will identify with both, although the stronger identification generally will be with the parent of the same sex.

IDENTIFICATION WITH SIBLINGS AND PEERS. Although parents are the primary identification figures, siblings play an important role too. The sex of the other siblings influences the child's interests and behavior; girls with older brothers are likely to be more masculine (tomboyish) and competitive than girls with older sisters. Similarly, boys with older sisters tend to be less aggressive than boys with older brothers.

Birth order also affects the child's relationships within the family. One study of large families identified three personality roles that were related to birth order: the responsible child (often the first born), the sociable, well-liked child (often the second), and the spoiled child (often the youngest) (Bossard and Ball, 1955).

First-born or only children occupy a unique position in the family for several reasons. Parents have more time and attention to devote to their first child and are apt to be more cautious, indulgent, and protective. The first born does not have to compete with older siblings; and for a while he has only adult models to copy and adult standards of conduct to emulate, while later-borns have siblings with whom to identify.

Research indicates that these factors do have an effect. First-born or only children are more likely to score at the upper extremes on intelligence tests, do well in college, and achieve eminence. Among finalists for the National Merit Scholarship from two-children families, there are twice as many first-born as second-born. Among finalists from three-child families there are

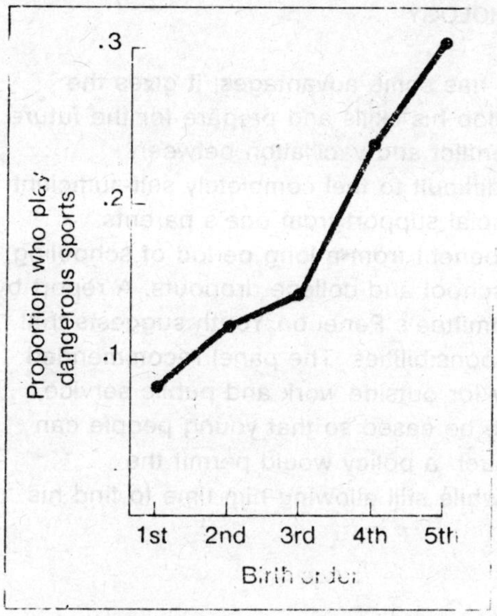

Fig. 3-11 Birth order and participation in dangerous sports

The graph shows the proportion of male undergraduates who play dangerous sports (football, rugby, soccer) in relation to their birth order. Note that the first-born is less likely to engage in a dangerous sport than later-borns. The study found no relationship between birth order and participation in nondangerous sports such as baseball or crew. (Data from Nisbett, 1968a).

Fig. 3-12 Age changes in conformity

Conformity to peer judgments reaches its highest level in the 11–13 year-old group and declines with increasing age. Girls show more conformity at all ages than boys. (After Costanzo and Shaw, 1966)

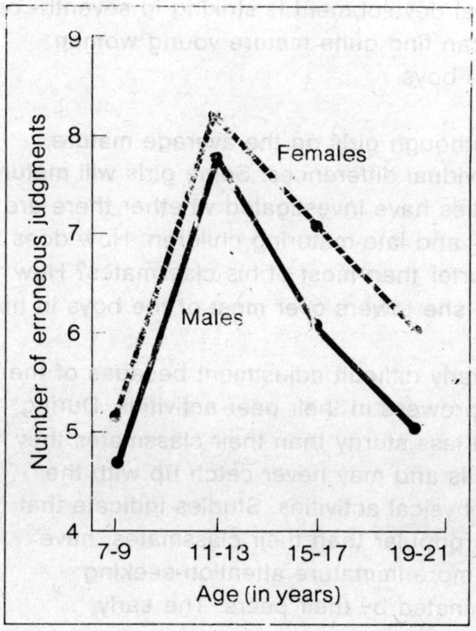

as many first-born as second- and third-born combined (Nichols, 1968).[2] First-born or only children have also been found to be more conscientious and less aggressive than later-born children (Altus, 1966). And, as can be seen in Figure 3-11, they are less likely to engage in dangerous sports.

Once a child enters school, his peers become important models for imitation and dispensers of reward and punishment. Although selfishness and dependency might have been accepted by doting parents, it may not be tolerated by peers. Whether the child maintains or modifies the attitudes and responses he has learned at home depends on peer reactions.

Studies indicate that conformity to peer opinions increases during the elementary school years, reaches its maximum at ages 11 to 13, and declines thereafter (see Figure 3-12). Conformity tests typically involve a situation where a person is asked to make a judgment (which of several lines matches a standard line in length, which of several answers to an arithmetic problem is correct) and is given false information as to the answers given by a group of his peers. The extent to which the individual's answers correspond to the false norms of the peer group, rather than the correct answers, provides a measure of conformity.

The preschool child is not much influenced by the opinions of his peers; Piaget describes him as *egocentric* in his social relationships. Middle childhood is the period of maximum sensitivity to peer values. During adolescence the youngster gains more confidence in his own judgment and shows an increasing tendency to resist pressure to conform to group norms.

Role of the Adolescent

Adolescence refers to the period of transition from childhood to adulthood. Its age limits are not clearly specified, but it extends roughly from age twelve to the late teens when physical growth is nearly complete. During this period the young person develops to sexual maturity, establishes his identity as an individual apart from his family, and faces the task of deciding how to earn a living.

A few generations ago, adolescence as we know it today was nonexistent. Many teen-agers worked fourteen hours a day and moved from childhood into the responsibilities of adulthood with little time for transition. With a decrease in the need for unskilled workers and an increase in the length of apprenticeship required to enter a profession, the interval between physical maturity and adult status has become longer. Such symbols of maturity as financial independence from parents and completion of school are accomplished at later ages. Young people are not given many adult privileges until late in their teens; in most states they cannot work full time, sign legal documents, drink alcoholic beverages, marry, or vote.

[2] How is the relationship between birth order and intelligence to be explained? It cannot be explained on genetic grounds for there is no known way in which genetic factors can be associated with birth order. It has been suggested that the relationship depends on social class and is only prevalent in the lower classes. However, this possibility has been ruled out by recent research showing the effect of birth order on intelligence at all class levels (Belmont and Marolla, 1973). A biological explanation cannot be completely discounted; mothers might become less effective producers with an increasing number of children but there is no direct medical evidence for this possibility. Perhaps the most tenable explanation is that parents pay increasingly less attention to each child as the family becomes larger. Data on the time between births and the attention parents give to each newborn would be useful in evaluating this explanation but so far none have been collected.

A gradual transition to adult status has some advantages; it gives the young person a longer period to develop his skills and prepare for the future. But it tends to produce a period of conflict and vacillation between dependence and independence. It is difficult to feel completely self-sufficient while living at home or receiving financial support from one's parents.

Not all young people want or can benefit from a long period of schooling, as evidenced by the number of high-school and college dropouts. A report by the President's Science Advisory Committee's Panel on Youth suggests that youth be allowed to assume more responsibilities. The panel recommended that schools provide more opportunity for outside work and public service, and that legal restrictions on work age be eased so that young people can alternate between school and work. Such a policy would permit the adolescent to assume independence while still allowing him time to find his future role.

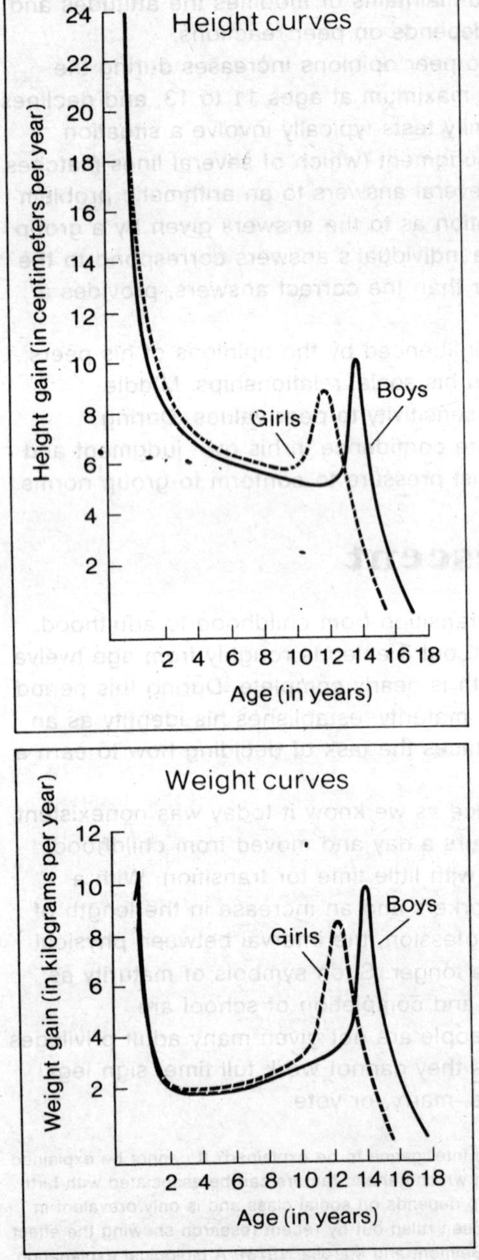

Fig. 3-13 Annual gains in height and weight

Note that the peak period comes earlier for girls than for boys. (After Tanner, Whitehouse, and Takaishi, 1966)

Sexual Development and the Adolescent Role

During the early adolescent years, most youngsters experience a period of very rapid growth (the *adolescent growth spurt*) accompanied by the gradual development of the reproductive organs and the *secondary sex characteristics* (breast development in girls, beard growth in boys, and the appearance of pubic hair in both sexes). These changes occur over a period of about two years and culminate in *puberty,* marked by menstruation in girls and by the appearance of live sperm cells in the urine of boys.

There is wide variation in the ages at which puberty is reached. Some girls may menstruate as early as 11 and or as late as 17, with the average age being 13. Boys show a similar range in the ages at which they reach sexual maturity, but on the average boys experience their growth spurt and mature two years later than girls (see Figure 3-13). Boys and girls average the same height and weight until around eleven when the girls suddenly spurt ahead in both dimensions. Girls maintain this difference for about two years, at which point the boys forge ahead and remain there for the rest of their lives. This difference in rate of physical development is striking in seventh- or eighth-grade classrooms where one can find quite mature young women seated alongside a group of immature boys.

EARLY AND LATE MATURERS. Although girls on the average mature earlier than boys, there are large individual differences. Some girls will mature *later* than some boys. Numerous studies have investigated whether there are personality differences between early- and late-maturing children. How does a late-maturing boy feel when he is shorter than most of his classmates? How does an early-maturing girl feel when she towers over most of the boys in her class?

Late-maturing boys face a particularly difficult adjustment because of the importance of strength and physical prowess in their peer activities. During the period when they are shorter and less sturdy than their classmates they may lose out on practice of game skills and may never catch up with the early maturers who take the lead in physical activities. Studies indicate that boys who mature late tend to be less popular than their classmates, have poorer self-concepts, and engage in more immature attention-seeking behavior. They feel rejected and dominated by their peers. The early maturers, on the other hand, tend to be more self-confident and independent. A few of these personality differences between early and late maturers persist into adulthood, long after the physical differences have disappeared (Mussen and Jones, 1958; Jones, 1957).

The effects of rate of maturation on personality are less striking for girls. Some early-maturing girls may be at a disadvantage because they are more grown-up than their peers in the late elementary grades, but by the junior high-school years the early maturers tend to have more prestige among classmates and to take leadership in school activities. At this stage, the late-maturing girls, like the boys, may have less adequate self-concepts and poorer relations with their parents and peers (Weatherly, 1964).

SEXUAL STANDARDS AND BEHAVIOR. The bodily changes that accompany sexual maturing are a source of both pride and embarrassment. How comfortable the adolescent feels with his new physique and the urges that accompany it depends to a large extent upon the attitudes toward sexual development conveyed by his parents and peers. Parental attitudes of secrecy or taboos concerning sex cannot fail to generate feelings of anxiety among teen-age offspring.

The past decade, however, has witnessed an almost revolutionary change in attitudes toward sexual activity. Views regarding premarital sex, homosexuality, extramarital sex, and specific sexual acts are more open and permissive today than at any time in history. Young people are exposed to sexual stimuli in magazines, television, and the movies to a greater extent than ever before. Satisfactory birth control methods and the availability of abortions have lessened fear of pregnancy. All of these changes give the newly matured individual more freedom today. These changes may produce more conflict too, since guidelines for "appropriate" behavior are less clear than in the past. In some families the divergence between adolescent and parental standards of sexual morality may be great.

Have more permissive attitudes toward sex been accompanied by changes in actual behavior? Some experts maintain that young people today are simply more open about activities their predecessors carried on in secret. But the data beginning to accumulate indicate definite changes in adolescent sexual behavior. A nationwide survey that interviewed 13–19 year olds found that 59 percent of the boys and 45 percent of the girls reported having experienced sexual intercourse at least once. And a sizable proportion of these nonvirgins had become so by the time they were 16 (see Table 3-5).

While strictly comparable data from earlier periods are not available, the studies conducted by Alfred Kinsey about 25 years ago found that only about 20 percent of the females and 40 percent of the males reported experiencing sexual intercourse by the time they were 20. Today's adolescents appear to be engaging in heterosexual activity at an earlier age than their parents.

The change in sex standards does not seem to be in the direction of greater promiscuity. While some of the boys said they had experienced intercourse with several partners, most of the girls reported they had limited their sexual relations to one boy with whom they were "in love" at the time. These young people feel that sex is a part of love and of intimate relationships, and that it need not necessarily be restricted to the context of marriage.

Today's adolescents tend to reject the "double standard," whereby men are allowed more sexual freedom than women. In the study referred to in

TABLE 3-5
Adolescent sexual experience*

	ALL TEEN-AGERS	BY SEX		BY AGE	
VIRGINS (All adolescents who have not had sexual intercourse)		BOYS	GIRLS	13–15	16–19
Sexually inexperienced (Virgins with no beginning sexual activities)	22%	20%	25%	39%	9%
Sexual beginners (Virgins who have actively or passively experienced sexual petting)	17%	14%	19%	12%	21%
Unclassified virgins (Virgins who for whatever reason could not be classified in the above groups)	9%	7%	11%	12%	6%
Total	**48%**	**41%**	**55%**	**63%**	**36%**
NONVIRGINS (All adolescents who have had sexual intercourse one or more times)					
Serial monogamists (Nonvirgins having a sexual relationship with one person)	21%	15%	28%	9%	31%
Sexual adventurers (Nonvirgins freely moving from one sexual-intercourse partner to another)	15%	24%	6%	10%	18%
Inactive nonvirgins (Nonvirgins who have not had sexual intercourse for more than one year)	12%	13%	10%	15%	10%
Unclassified nonvirgins (Nonvirgins who for whatever reason could not be classified in the above groups)	4%	7%	1%	3%	5%
Total	**52%**	**59%**	**45%**	**37%**	**64%**

Source: After Sorenson (1973).

***Based on interviews with 400 youngsters ages 13–19. The sample was carefully selected on the basis of the 1970 U.S. census to represent the adolescent population in terms of such variables as race, geographical location, family income and size, and urban-rural residence. Its results are similar to those of several studies using larger but less representative samples.**

Table 3-5, a majority of both boys and girls felt that what was moral for one sex was moral for the other. The majority of the adolescents in this study also felt that their sexual standards were quite different from their parents' and that, although they had a close relationship with their parents in many respects, sex was the area in which they were less likely to communicate. Many of today's parents seem willing to allow their offspring sexual freedom (as long as they are not directly confronted by the facts) but unwilling to discuss the topic with them.

Emancipation from Home

Emancipation from parental authority and from emotional dependence upon parents begins in childhood, but the process of emancipation is greatly accelerated during the early adolescent years. In order to function effectively as an adult, the adolescent must begin to detach himself from his family and develop independence in behavior, emotions, and values and beliefs. Clearly, the ease of transition to fuller independence in later adolescence depends to a great extent on the attitudes parents take during the preceding years. Some parents who have insisted upon close supervision of the child in his early years attempt to continue their control through his adolescence. As a result, the child is likely to continue his childish dependence and obedience through adolescence, and never fully mature as an adult.

Studies have shown that a "democratic family" (in which the child is allowed a fair degree of autonomy, is included in important decisions, and is controlled primarily by reasoning and verbal discipline) is more apt to produce a self-reliant and effective adolescent than an "authoritarian family" (in which rules are set without consulting the children, autonomy is limited, and discipline is predominantly physical). The child reared in the democratic atmosphere tends to have a warm relationship with his family, even though he feels free to disagree with them. The authoritarian product tends to be compliant on the surface but rebellious and impulsive underneath, willing to accept as "moral" anything he can get away with (Douvan and Adelson, 1966; Kandel and Lesser, 1972).

Although adolescence has traditionally been characterized as a time of intensified parent-child conflict (with the adolescent struggling for his freedom and the parent trying to restrict him), evidence indicates that this picture is not really accurate. Most adolescents report a harmonious relationship with their parents and are not too unhappy with the degree of freedom permitted. One study of middle-class adolescent boys found that in most instances the parents were satisfied with their son's sense of responsibility and maturity and felt that few restrictions were required (Bandura and Walters, 1959).

Problems of rebellion and resistance to parental control during adolescence are almost invariably a continuation of problems that began earlier in childhood. They become more visible at adolescence and have more serious consequences because the young person is now bigger, stronger, and more able to actively resist parental control or to escape it by taking off on his own.

Search for Identity

An important task confronting the adolescent is the development of a sense of his own *identity*—a conception of who he is and where he is going. To find out who he is, he must formulate standards of conduct for himself and for evaluating the behavior of others. He must know what he values as important and worth doing. And he needs a sense of his own worth and competence.

As we know, the child's values and moral standards are largely those of his parents; his feelings of self-esteem reflect primarily their view of him. Then as he moves away from the family during the high-school years, the values of his peer group and their appraisal of him become increasingly important. The adolescent tries to pull these appraisals together into a consistent picture. To the extent that parents, teachers, and peers reflect the same values, his search for identity is easier. When parental views and values differ markedly from those of his peers and other important figures, the possibility for conflict is great and the adolescent may experience what has been called role diffusion—he tries one role after another and has difficulty synthesizing the different roles into a single identity.

Reexamination of Beliefs

The adolescent is engaged in a reexamination of many of the beliefs he had previously considered to be immutable truths. New experiences and the new cognitive abilities that emerge during adolescence prompt him to challenge some of the values and beliefs he has incorporated from his parents. Prior assumptions about religion, sex, drugs, the value of hard work, and the omnipotence of one's parents are those most apt to be questioned. A girl who has accepted her parents' code of sexual conduct may discover that many of her high-school classmates do not consider virginity a virtue. An adolescent whose home and religious training has emphasized the dangers of drugs may find that some of his peers not only fail to share this view, but consider drug experiences an important avenue of self-awareness.

Questioning of previously accepted values is intensified during the early adolescent years for several reasons. For one thing, the youngster usually has progressed from a small neighborhood elementary school to a larger and more heterogeneous junior or senior high school, and is exposed to a wider peer group of different backgrounds. Second, the cognitive abilities of the

TABLE 3-6
Adolescent and parent values in two countries

VALUES	PERCENTAGE OF INDIVIDUALS WHO RANK EACH OF THE VALUES LISTED AT LEFT AS "EXTREMELY IMPORTANT"			
	UNITED STATES		DENMARK	
	ADOLESCENTS	MOTHERS	ADOLESCENTS	MOTHERS
FAMILY				
1. Doing things with the family	42%	65%	17%	42%
2. Helping at home	30	43	23	31
3. Respecting one's parents	87	96	60	76
4. Living up to one's religious ideals	9	15	2	4
5. Pleasing one's parents	34	11	52	20
PEER GROUP				
6. Being a leader in activities	20	11	4	1
7. Participating in sports	31	14	37	18
8. Going out on dates	40	6	35	2
9. Being popular in school	46	19	45	28
10. Earning money	56	36	30	17
11. Being accepted by other students	18	5	15	11
12. Being well liked	54	44	32	27
13. Having a good reputation	78	93	53	71
SCHOOL				
14. Preferred school image:				
Brilliant student	33	74	55	64
Athlete or leader in activities	34	21	10	7
Most popular	33	5	35	29
15. Learning much in school	39	69	31	64
16. Working hard on studies	54	83	32	54
17. Doing serious reading	28	54	21	51
18. Planning for the future	78	80	38	44

Source: Kandel and Lesser (1972).

teen-ager have developed to the point where he can think in more abstract and relative terms (see Piaget's formal operational stage of cognitive development, Table 3-1). He can envisage alternatives to the way things are. He begins to realize that morality is not absolute; whether an action is good or bad depends on a number of extenuating circumstances, including the culture in which one is raised. These new experiences and capabilities prompt a reexamining and adjusting of values. Some of the earlier beliefs may be reinstated; others may be left open to question or discarded.

The Generation Gap

"Go ahead, Melvin, tell your father you're sorry you gave him an ulcer."

According to some views, our society has been changing so rapidly that the values of today's parents are inappropriate to the problems and conditions faced by their teen-age children. Drugs, the pill, and a climate of increased sexual permissiveness create problems for young people that their parents did not have to face. Rapid scientific and technological advances have tended to make parental knowledge obsolete with reference to what their children are expected to know. These and other factors have led some experts to conclude that there is an almost unsurmountable gap between the values of today's parents and those of their adolescent sons and daughters. They view with alarm the lack of understanding and communication between the two generations (Mead, 1970; Coleman, 1961).

Recent research, however, leads to a much less pessimistic view. There is some distance between the attitudes of the two generations, to be sure, but it is not nearly as wide nor as different from that of past generations as the mass media would have us believe. Survey studies indicate that the values of parents and their children are quite similar.

Table 3-6 shows the results of a study on parent-adolescent values in two countries, the United States and Denmark. There is a close correspondence between mothers and their children regarding the activities and personal qualities rated as most important. The differences between the two countries are greater than those between parent and teen-ager. Americans emphasize hard work and achievement; the Danes stress a pleasant personality and the ability to get along with others (see Table 3-7).

Other studies find that most adolescents have a close and warm

TABLE 3-7
Responses to the question, "What is the best way to get ahead in life?"

	UNITED STATES		DENMARK	
	ADOLESCENTS	MOTHERS	ADOLESCENTS	MOTHERS
Work hard	52%	56%	13%	9%
Have a pleasant personality	22	17	43	50
Know the right people	4	2	12	10
Save your money	1	2	5	3
Get a higher education	18	22	23	27
Have a special talent	3	1	4	1
Total	**100%**	**100%**	**100%**	**100%**

Source: Kandel and Lesser (1972).

Note that mothers and adolescents hold similar values but there are national differences in the emphasis on hard work versus a pleasant personality.

relationship with their parents (Douvan and Adelson, 1966; Offer, 1969). In one nationwide survey the majority of 13–19 year olds interviewed said they respected their parents (88 percent) and their parents' opinions (80 percent); they enjoyed being with them (73 percent) and felt their relationship was warm and affectionate (78 percent). The area where there was least communality of viewpoint was sex; only about one-third of the adolescents felt they shared common attitudes with their parents on sexual values (Sorenson, 1973).

Peer Group Influences

Although the adolescent shares many of his parents' values and derives security from his relationship with them, the peer group serves an important role in his progress toward independence. His concerns over physical appearance, popularity, and the vicissitudes of relations with the opposite sex can be helped by discussions with others coping with similar problems. The adolescent needs the support and approval of peers, as well as parents, in attempting to crystallize his identity.

On important issues the peer values tend to be similar to those of the parents, because teen-agers usually pick friends with a common background in terms of race, social class, and educational goals. Thus peer values tend to support adult values in areas concerned with social and moral issues. Where peer values have their greatest influence and differ most from adult standards is in such matters as dress styles, tastes in music and entertainment, dating patterns, and use of language. It is in these more superficial characteristics that young people differ most from their parents; and the visible differences prompt the adults to conclude that adolescents are a new and foreign breed.

Instances where peer influences play a very dominant role in an adolescent's life may result from lack of attention and an unsatisfactory relationship at home. One study found that adolescents who are strongly peer oriented are more likely to have a negative view of themselves (and of their friends) and to report less affection, support, and discipline at home (Bronfenbrener, 1970).

Individuals vary in their need for conformity, whether it be to parental or peer standards. The more self-confident and assured the young person is, the less he will feel the need for blind adherence to anyone else's norms. He can evaluate for himself what is important among the various views proposed and arrive at his own conclusions. This is the essence of finding one's identity.

Development as a Lifelong Process

Development does not end with the attainment of physical maturity. Bodily changes occur throughout life, affecting the individual's attitudes, cognitive processes, and behavior. Such changes are particularly evident in the process of aging. Current research is concerned with whether some of the psychological changes that occur with old age result from physical changes or are primarily a function of the conditions of reduced stimulation and restricted mobility under which most elderly people live in our society.

Psychological development also continues throughout life. Identity problems do not end with adolescence. Many individuals in their twenties are still undecided about what they want to do in life. A study of college juniors and seniors found that more than one-half were still confused and unsure about their political ideology, religious beliefs, and occupational choice (Podd, 1969). This finding is not unexpected since college provides the young person with an opportunity to sample many ideas and potential life styles.

Commitment to an occupation and way of life begins to mold one's identity, as does assuming the role of a parent. But even in later years people need not be static; development of interests and abilities continue. And some individuals change their life style dramatically during middle age.

At each stage of life somewhat different problems must be dealt with (see Erikson's stages of psychosocial development, Table 3-2). The adolescent is busy forging his identity, developing independence, and building skills. The young adult is faced with decisions—what job to take, to marry or not, how many offspring to produce. Marriage, if chosen, involves further adjustments and problems. Despite such difficulties, most older people who have been married look back on their young adult years as the happiest in their lives. Older people who have never married tend to view childhood as the time of greatest happiness (Landis, 1942).

Middle age, the years from 45–65, brings new problems. Vocational status at this point is pretty well fixed; if the individual has not arrived at the station in life he had envisioned, chances are he will not. Children are beginning to leave home; the mother who has dedicated her life to their welfare may find existence very empty. The sharp increase in suicide rate in the 40–50 age group reflects some of these difficulties.

After age 65, there are other problems. For example, retired persons must adjust to their extra time. The person who has suffered a heart attack or other debilitating illness is often demoralized by the experience. Loneliness owing to death of family members, children's moving away, or the inability to travel have to be confronted. Since the proportion of older people in the population is progressively increasing (Figure 3-14) such problems require attention and research.

Fig. 3-14 The aged in the United States The percentage of the total population aged 65 or over has more than doubled in the last half-century, though the trend shows signs of slackening. (U.S. Bureau of the Census)

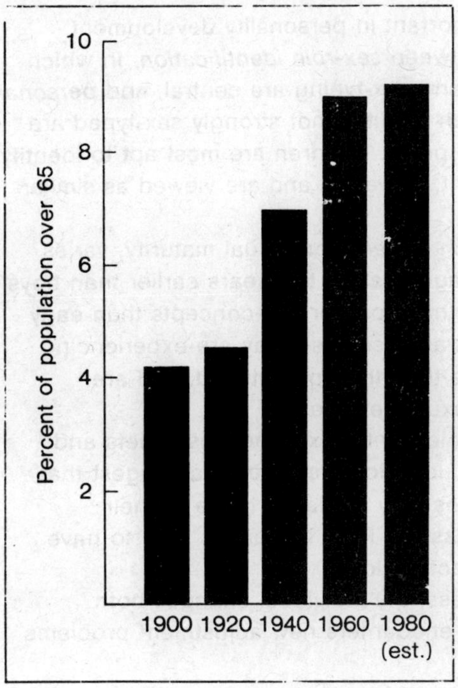

Summary

1. The course of development in man, as in other organisms, is shaped by *maturation* and *learning.* Maturation is an innately determined sequence of growth that proceeds at its own rate, relatively independent of the environment, although a minimum of environmental stimulation and support is needed. Some evidence suggests that there may be *critical periods* in development when the organism is most plastic and ready to acquire some of the behavior essential for optimal development later.
2. Conditions of severe deprivation or unusual stimulation can affect the rate of development. Animals deprived of stimulation at an early age are poorer learners as adults than normal animals; an enriched environment produces better learning ability as well as increased brain size. Studies with human infants, however, suggest that increased stimulation will not result in accelerated development unless the infant is maturationally ready.
3. An unresolved question is whether development is essentially *continuous* or consists of a series of definable *stages.* Piaget's theory describes stages in *cognitive,* or intellectual, growth, moving from the *sensorimotor*

stage through the *preoperational stage* and the *concrete operational stage* to the *formal operational stage.* The *psychosexual* stages of Freud and the *psychosocial* stages of Erikson are attempts to place personality development into the context of a stage theory. The concept of stages has been useful, but evidence indicates that development is probably more continuous than stage theories would imply.

4. Early social attachments form the basis for close interpersonal relations in adulthood. Insensitive mothering or repeated separations may undermine the child's trust and produce *anxious attachment.* Although consistent relationships between specific child-rearing methods and personality characteristics have not been found, an affectionate relationship with an adult in the early years appears to be crucial to normal personality development.
5. The process of *identification* is important in personality development. Some distinctions can be made between *sex-role identification,* in which modeling after the like-sex parent and sex-typing are central, and *personal (non-sex-role) identification* in which qualities not strongly sex-typed are learned from parents, siblings, and peers. Children are most apt to identify with adults who are warm, nurturant, powerful, and are viewed as similar to them in some way.
6. The age at which adolescents reach *puberty,* or sexual maturity, varies greatly, although girls, on the average, mature two years earlier than boys. Late maturers of either sex tend to have poorer self-concepts than early maturers. Survey data indicate that adolescents today are experiencing sexual intercourse at an earlier age than their parents did, and are rejecting the double standard of sexual behavior.
7. In searching for his identity the adolescent reexamines his beliefs and challenges many of his parents' values. However, the data suggest that most adolescents end up with values very similar to those of their parents—at least on the important issues. Peer influences tend to have more influence on superficial characteristics.
8. Development is a continuous process; the individual changes both physically and psychologically and encounters new adjustment problems throughout life.

Further Reading

Two authoritative textbooks on child development are Mussen, Conger, and Kagan, *Child development and personality* (4th ed., 1974), and Stone and Church, *Childhood and adolescence* (3rd ed., 1973). A book of readings covering many areas of child development is Lavatelli and Stendler, *Readings in child behavior and development* (3rd ed., 1972). For historical background see Kessen, *The child* (1965).

More advanced treatments may be found in Mussen (ed.), *Carmichael's manual of child psychology* (3rd ed., 1970), and Goslin (ed.), *Handbook of socialization: theory and research* (1969).

A short paperback covering Piaget's theories of intellectual development is Phillips, *The origins of intellect: Piaget's theory* (1969).

The problems of adolescence are dealt with in Conger, *Adolescence and youth* (1973).

part three

perception and awareness

4 sensory processes

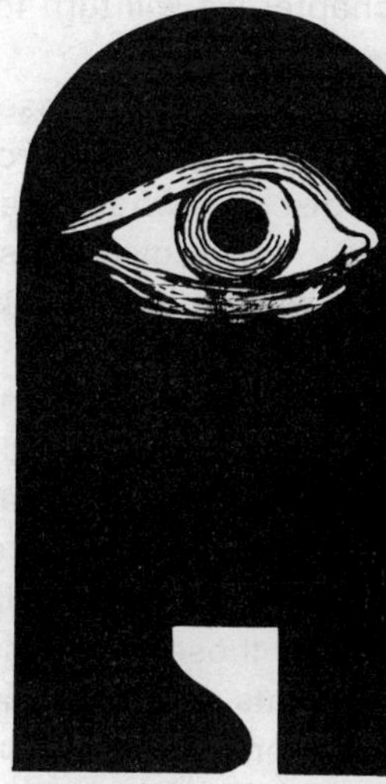

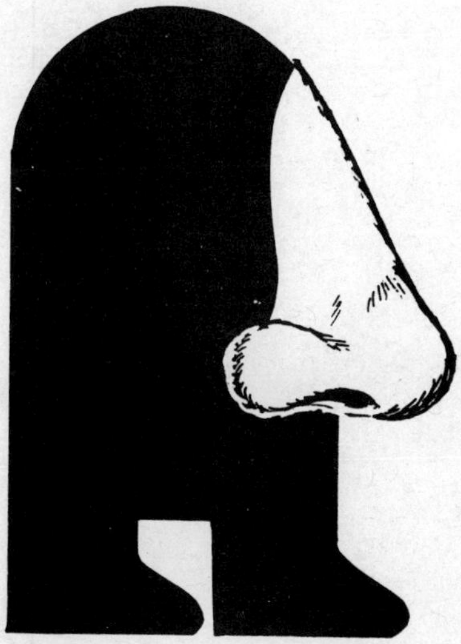

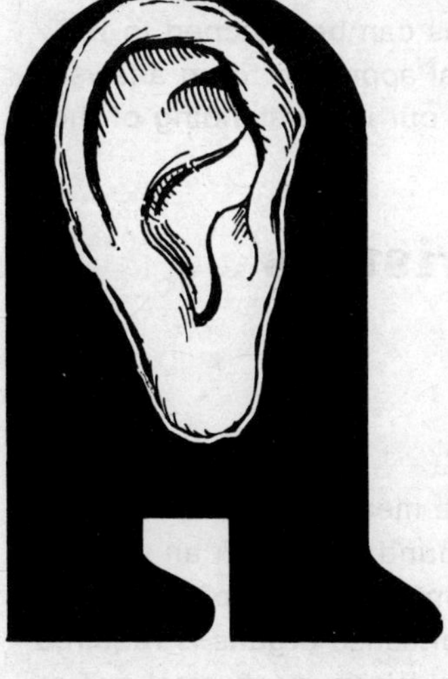

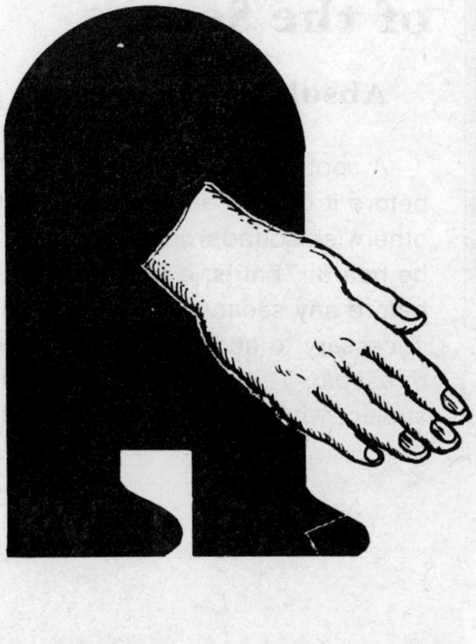

All of our information about the world comes to us by way of our senses. They warn us of impending danger and furnish the information we need to interpret events and anticipate the future. They also provide pleasure and pain. How do we distinguish colors, judge the quality of a vintage wine, or move to the rhythm of music? We need answers to these questions, for they form the basis for examining more complex psychological phenomena.

To understand behavior we need to know something of how the sensory mechanisms are constructed and how they mediate the sensations of light, sound, touch, taste, and the like. But perception goes beyond the discrimination of single stimuli; the human organism must be able to interpret and react to patterns of stimuli. He must be able to extract information from the changing array of stimulation provided by the environment. In this chapter we will consider the role of the specific sense organs in perceiving. In the next chapter we will turn to the factors involved in our perception of complex objects and events.

The study of sensory processes lends itself to two different, but closely related approaches: basic research and applied research. The aim of basic research is to discover what aspects of the environment the sense organs respond to, how they register this information, and how it is conveyed to the brain. Such knowledge is a first step in understanding the higher-order cognitive processes.

As our technology becomes increasingly complex it depends more and more upon accurate perceptual discriminations by human beings. Here is the need for applied research. The radar operator must be able to distinguish the brief visual blips on the radar screen that indicate the approach of aircraft. The sonar operator must discriminate between the echoes returning from a school of fish and those from a submarine. The pilot monitors an elaborate panel of instruments and makes appropriate adjustments. The astronaut must make countless complex discriminations under conditions of weightlessness and acceleration that alter his normal functioning. Through applied research on sensory processes scientists seek to determine man's ability to discriminate and interpret sensory stimuli so that his capabilities can be matched to the task requirements. Both the basic and the practical approach to an analysis of sensory mechanisms have contributed much to our understanding of these phenomena.

Some General Characteristics of the Senses

Absolute Thresholds

A spot of light in a dark room must reach some measurable intensity before it can be distinguished from darkness. A sound emitted in an otherwise soundproof room must reach a certain intensity level before it can be heard. That is, a certain minimum stimulation of sense organs is required before any sensory experience will be evoked. The minimum physical energy necessary to activate a given sensory system is known as the *absolute threshold.* The absolute threshold can be determined by presenting the subject with a stimulus of given intensity and asking whether or not he

Fig. 4-1 Psychophysical function

Plotted on the ordinate is the percentage of times the subject responds "Yes, I detect the stimulus"; on the abscissa is the measure of the physical energy of the signal. Psychophysical functions can be obtained for any sensory modality; when vision is involved the function is sometimes called the "frequency-of-seeing curve."

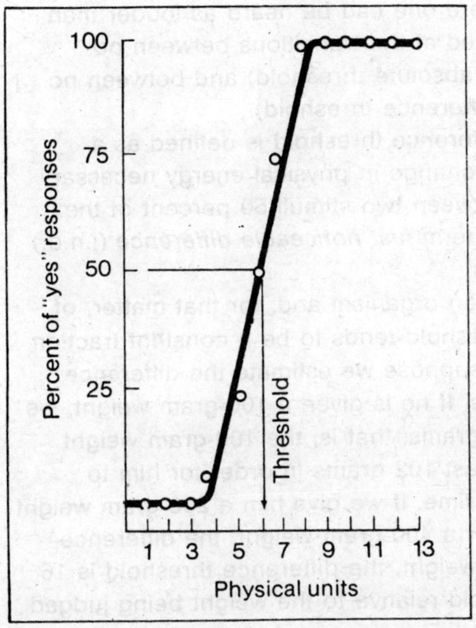

detects it; on the next trial a different stimulus intensity is used, and so on, through a wide range of intensities. With such a procedure, however, the term "absolute threshold" is somewhat inappropriate because the investigator does not arrive at a *single* intensity value below which the subject never detects the stimulus and above which he always reports detecting it. We find, instead, a range of intensities over which the physical energy of the stimulus gradually moves from having no effect to having a partial effect (that is, it is sometimes detected and sometimes not) to having a complete effect.

This region of partial effect is illustrated in Figure 4-1. The curve in the figure is called a *psychophysical function* because it expresses the relationship between a "psychological" variable (the experience of perceiving the stimulus) and a "physical" variable (the intensity of the stimulus). It plots the percentage of times the subject says, "Yes, I detect a stimulus," against a measure of the physical energy of the stimulus. In this case, the subject almost never reports the presence of a stimulus below an energy level equal to three units, whereas he almost always reports it above nine units. The relative frequency of reporting the presence of a stimulus gradually increases between three and nine units.

How do we define the threshold for a particular stimulus dimension when the performance can be characterized by a psychophysical function like that in Figure 4-1? Is it the point at which the subject's curve first appears to break away from zero (in this case at about three physical units) or at which it finally appears to reach 100 percent responding (in this case at about nine units)? Obviously, the definition of a threshold must be somewhat arbitrary. On the basis of certain theoretical considerations, psychologists have agreed to define the *absolute threshold* as that value at which the stimulus is perceived 50 percent of the time. Thus, for the data displayed in Figure 4-1, the absolute threshold would be six units.

Some estimates of absolute thresholds for various sense modalities in terms of physical measures that are intuitively meaningful are presented in Table 4-1. Of course, the absolute threshold varies considerably from one individual to the next. The threshold for a particular individual will also vary from time to time, depending on his physical condition, motivational state, and the conditions under which the observations are made.

TABLE 4-1
Some approximate values for absolute thresholds

SENSE MODALITY	THRESHOLD
Vision	A candle flame seen at 30 miles on a dark, clear night
Hearing	The tick of a watch under quiet conditions at 20 feet
Taste	One teaspoon of sugar in two gallons of water
Smell	One drop of perfume diffused into the entire volume of a six-room apartment
Touch	Wing of a fly falling on your cheek from a distance of 1 centimeter

Source: Galanter (1962).

Difference Thresholds

Just as there must be a certain minimum amount of stimulation to evoke a sensory experience, so there must also be a certain magnitude of difference between two stimuli before one can be distinguished from the other. The minimum amount of stimulation necessary to tell two stimuli apart is known as the *difference threshold.* Two reds must differ by some finite amount before they can be discriminated from each other; two tones must differ in intensity by a measurable amount before one can be heard as louder than the other. Thus, thresholds are identified at the transitions between no experience and some experience (the absolute threshold) and between no difference and some difference (the difference threshold).

Like the absolute threshold, the difference threshold is defined as a statistical quantity. It is the amount of change in physical energy necessary for a subject to detect a difference between two stimuli 50 percent of the time. Psychologists frequently use the term *just noticeable difference* (j.n.d.) to refer to this amount of change.

One remarkable feature of the human organism and, for that matter, of most animals is that the difference threshold tends to be a constant fraction of the stimulus intensity. To illustrate, suppose we estimate the difference threshold for a subject judging weights. If he is given a 100-gram weight, we note that his difference threshold is 2 grams; that is, the 100-gram weight must be compared to a weight of at least 102 grams in order for him to detect a j.n.d. about 50 percent of the time. If we give him a 200-gram weight the difference threshold is 4 grams. For a 400-gram weight, the difference threshold is 8 grams; for an 800-gram weight, the difference threshold is 16 grams. Note that the difference threshold relative to the weight being judged is constant:

$$\frac{2}{100} = \frac{4}{200} = \frac{8}{400} = \frac{16}{800} = .02$$

The above relationship is known as *Weber's law,* named after Ernst Weber. Stated mathematically, if I is the amount of stimulation taken as a referent, and ΔI is the increase in stimulation necessary for a j.n.d., then

$$\frac{\Delta I}{I} = k$$

where k is a constant that does not depend on I. The quantity k is called *Weber's constant.* In our example, $k = .02$.

Table 4-2 presents values of Weber's constant for various sense modalities. The tremendous range in values reflects the fact that some sensory systems are much more responsive to changes in the physical environment than others.

We may observe approximations of Weber's law operating in everyday experience. A twenty-minute increase in air-travel time from Los Angeles to San Francisco may be detected as a just noticeable difference, but a similar increase in travel time from San Francisco to London may not. An increase of five dollars in the cost of a shirt is quite noticeable, whereas a similar increase in the cost of a suit may be of little concern.

It is interesting to conjecture about the aspects of the sensory system that make Weber's law hold, and many theories have been proposed. We shall not discuss these theories here, but the research initiated by them has made it

TABLE 4-2
Weber's constant

Approximate values of Weber's constant for various sensory discriminations. The smaller the fraction, the greater the differential sensitivity.

SENSE MODALITY	WEBER'S CONSTANT
Pitch of a tone	$\frac{1}{333}$
Deep pressure, from skin and subcutaneous tissue	$\frac{1}{80}$
Visual brightness	$\frac{1}{60}$
Lifted weights	$\frac{1}{50}$
Loudness of a tone	$\frac{1}{10}$
Cutaneous pressure	$\frac{1}{7}$
Taste for saline solution	$\frac{1}{5}$

Source: Data are approximate, from various determinations.

clear that matters are more complex than indicated by Weber's law. Weber's law holds fairly well in the middle range of sensory dimensions but is somewhat in error at the extremes, particularly at very low levels of stimulation.

Although Weber's law was formulated for thresholds, Fechner (1860) soon extended it to develop scales for measuring sensory experiences. By summing successive j.n.d.'s, he developed a scale for measuring how far a given stimulus was above threshold; this procedure in turn permitted him to measure the psychological distance between any two stimuli. His formulation, commonly called the *Weber-Fechner law,* holds that the sensory experience bears a logarithmic relationship to the intensity of the physical stimulus. This logarithmic equation, although approximately correct, has been modified by modern workers to fit results from a wide variety of experiments. Equations relating sensory experience to the intensity of the physical stimulus have proved extremely helpful to engineers designing telephones, video displays, tape recorders, and other types of communication equipment. They tell the designer how intense a signal must be in order to be perceived accurately under varying conditions.

The Visual Sense

Each sense organ responds to a particular type of physical energy. The eye is sensitive to that portion of electromagnetic energy traveling through space that we call light. It is convenient to think of electromagnetic energy as traveling in waves, with wavelengths (the distance from one crest of a wave to the next) varying tremendously from the shortest cosmic rays (10 trillionths of an inch) to long radio waves that may measure many miles. The wavelengths that the human eye perceives as light extend only from about 380 nanometers (nm) to about 780 nm. Since a nanometer is one billionth millionth of a meter, it is clear that visible energy is but a very small section of the total electromagnetic spectrum.

More than three hundred years ago Sir Isaac Newton discovered that sunlight passing through a prism breaks into a band of varicolored light such as we see in a rainbow. The colors correspond to wavelengths, the red end of the rainbow being produced by the longer waves and the violet end by the short waves. The prism spreads the light waves out by bending the short wavelengths more than the long ones (see Figure 4-10).

The eye will respond to forms of stimulation other than light waves. Pressure on the eyeball or electrical stimulation of certain areas of the brain

CRITICAL DISCUSSION

ROC curves

The problem of establishing thresholds involves some complications that can be illustrated by the following experiment. Suppose we wanted to determine the likelihood that a subject will detect a particular weak auditory signal. An experiment could be set up involving a series of trials, each initiated with a warning light followed by the auditory signal. The subject would be asked to indicate on each trial whether he heard the signal. Suppose that on one hundred such trials the subject reported hearing the signal sixty-two times. How should this result be interpreted? On each trial precisely the same signal is presented, and the subject's responses presumably tell us something about his ability to detect it. But if the subject knows the same tone will be presented on each trial, what prevents him from always saying "yes"? Obviously nothing, but we assume that he is honest and trying to do as good a job as possible. The task of detecting very weak signals is difficult, however, and even a conscientious subject will often be uncertain whether to respond yes or no on a given trial. Further, motives and expectations can influence our judgments; even the most reliable subject may unconsciously tend toward yes answers to impress the experimenter with his acuity.

To deal with this problem, *catch trials,* on which there is no signal, can be introduced to see what the subject will do. The following results are typical of a subject's performance in an experiment involving several hundred trials, 10 percent of which are randomly selected as catch trials.

	YES	NO
Signal trial	.89 (HITS)	.11
Catch trial	.52 (FALSE ALARMS)	.48

Each entry in the table represents the proportion of times the subject answered yes or no when the signal was or was not presented. For example, on 89 percent of the trials on which a signal was presented, the subject said, "yes, there was a signal." We refer to these correct responses as *hits.* When the subject says "yes, there was a signal" on a trial when the signal was not presented, the response is called a *false alarm.* In the example, the probability of a hit was .89 and the probability of a false alarm was .52.

How can we interpret the fact that the subject falsely reported hearing the signal on 52 percent of the catch trials? We might conclude that the subject is careless or inattentive except for the fact that these results are typical of data obtained with dedicated, highly trained subjects. Even under the best conditions subjects make false alarms. The answer to the question of how to interpret false alarms appears when some additional observations are made. Suppose that the subject is tested for several days with the same signal, but with the percentage of catch trials varied from day to day. Results from such an experiment, in which the number of catch trials ranged from 10 percent to 90 percent, are given in the table in Figure 4-2. These data show that hits and false alarms both change as the proportion of catch trials to signal trials is manipulated. As the proportion of catch trials increases, the subject becomes aware of this fact (either consciously or unconsciously) and biases his judgments in favor of more "no" responses. Put another way, his *expectation* of a large number of catch trials causes him to inhibit "yes" responses, which leads to a decrease in both hits and false alarms.

Obviously, there is no fixed probability that the subject will detect a given intensity signal; the probability varies as the proportion of catch trials is manipulated. At first glance this is a discouraging picture, and one may question whether a simple measure can be devised to describe the subject's sensitivity level for a particular signal. Fortunately, recent developments have provided a clever answer. It involves plotting the hit and false alarm probabilities, as is done in the top graph in Figure 4-2. Note, for example, that the point farthest to the right is for data obtained when 10 per-

Fig. 4-2 ROC curves

The table presents data on the relationship between hits and false alarms as the percentage of catch trials is increased. The top figure plots these same data in the form of an ROC curve. The bottom figure presents ROC curves for several different values of d′. The more intense the signal, the higher the value of d′; the d′ value for the data in the table is 1.18.

Percentage of catch trials	Probability of a hit	Probability of a false alarm
10%	.89	.52
30	.83	.41
50	.76	.32
70	.62	.19
90	.28	.04

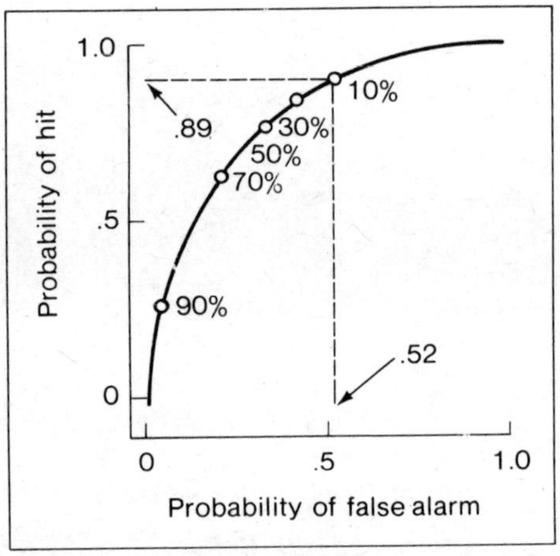

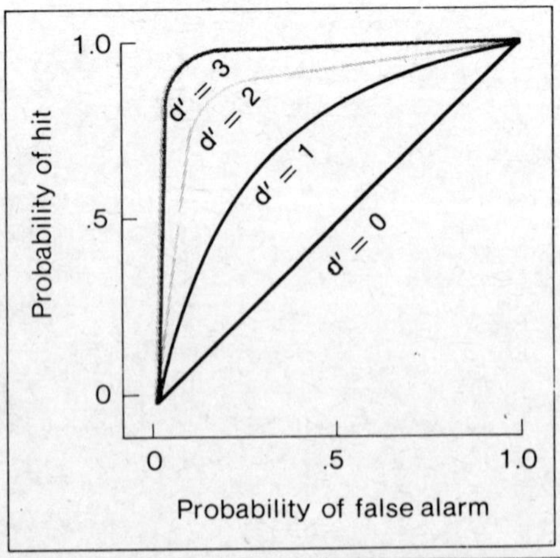

cent of the trials were catch trials; referring to the table, the hit rate plotted on the ordinate is .89, and the false alarm rate on the abscissa is .52. When all five points are plotted an orderly picture emerges. The points fall on a symmetric bow-shaped curve. If we ran still other experiments with the same signal but different percentages of catch trials, the hit and false alarm probabilities would differ from those in the table but would fall somewhere on the curve. This curve is called the *receiver-operating-characteristic curve,* or more simply the ROC curve. The term ROC describes the fact that the curve measures the operating, or sensitivity, characteristics of a person receiving signals.

The points that are plotted in the left figure are for a fixed signal intensity. When a stronger signal is used, the ROC curve arches higher; when the signal is weaker, the ROC curve is closer to the diagonal line. Thus, the degree of bowedness of the ROC curve is determined by the intensity of the signal. The measure used to define the bowedness of the ROC curve is called d′. The bottom graph in Figure 4-2 gives several ROC curves for d′, ranging from 0 through 3.

Thus, hit and false alarm rates can be converted into a d′ value that is a psychological dimension measuring the subject's sensitivity level for a particular signal. Manipulating the percentage of catch trials, or any of a number of other variables, will affect hits and false alarms for a fixed signal, but the proportions will always fall on an ROC curve defined by a particular d′ value. Theoretical work based on this method for measuring sensitivity is called *signal detectability theory* (Green and Swets, 1966). Even in a simple task like signal detection, performance is not just a function of the signal intensity but depends on the experience, motives, and expectations of the subject. Signal detectability theory permits one to separate out these factors and obtain a relatively pure measure of the sensory process. This measure, d′, characterizes the sensory capacities of a subject, independent of nonsensory variables that influence his judgments.

will produce the sensation of light. These observations point up the fact that the experience of light is a quality produced in the visual system. The visible portion of the electromagnetic spectrum is called *light* because it is what usually produces that sensation.

The Human Eye

The main parts of the human eye are shown in Figure 4-3. Light enters the eye through the transparent *cornea,* the amount of light being regulated by the *pupil;* the *lens* then focuses the light on the sensitive surface, the *retina.* Constriction and dilation of the pupil are controlled by the autonomic nervous system (see p. 55): the parasympathetic division controls the change in pupil size as a function of change in illumination (in much the same way as we increase the shutter opening of a camera to admit more light on a dark day and decrease the opening under conditions of bright illumination). The sympathetic division acts to dilate the pupil under conditions of strong emotion, either pleasant or unpleasant. Even conditions of mild emotional arousal or interest will result in systematic changes in pupil size (Figure 4-4).

The retina, the light-sensitive surface at the back of the eye, has three main layers: (1) the *rods* and *cones,* the photosensitive cells that convert light energy into nerve impulses; (2) the *bipolar cells,* which make synaptic connections with the rods and cones; and (3) the *ganglion cells,* the fibers of which form the optic nerve (Figure 4-5). Strangely enough, the rods and cones form the *rear* layer of the retina. The eye is a very imperfect optical system. The light waves not only have to pass through the lens and liquids that fill the eyeball, none of which is a perfect transmitter of light, but also have to penetrate the network of blood vessels and the bipolar and ganglion cells that lie on the inside of the eye before reaching the photoreceptors where light is converted into nervous impulses (note "direction of light" arrows at the top of Figure 4-5).

Fig. 4-3 A cross section of the left human eye

The size of the pupil is regulated by the iris, the diaphragm that gives the eye its color. The shape of the lens is regulated by the ciliary muscles. The external muscles that move the eye are not shown

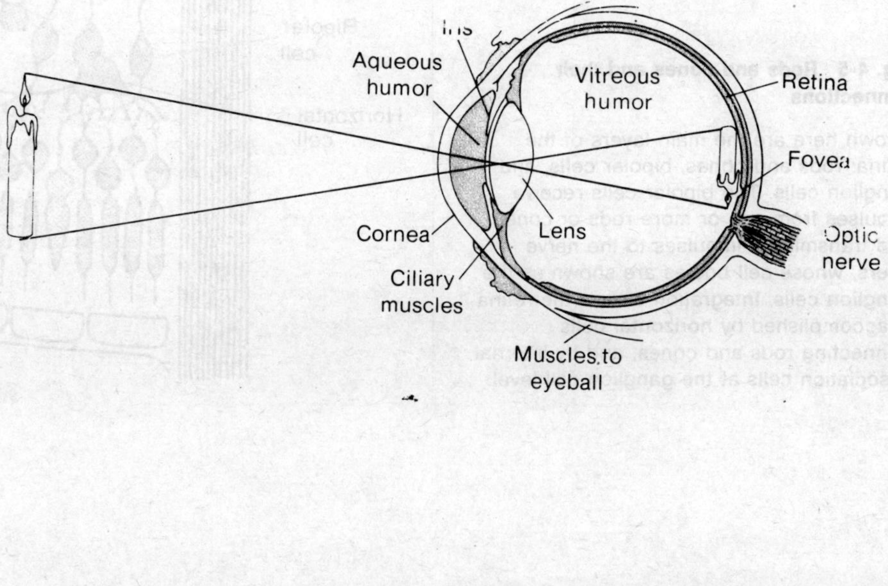

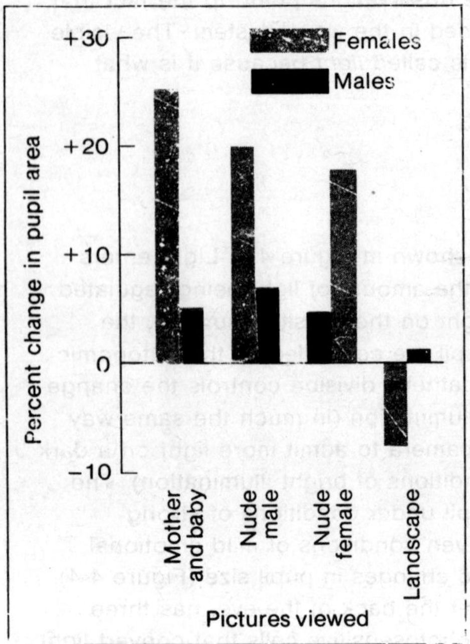

Fig. 4-4 Changes in pupil size as a response to pictures

Changes in pupil size were recorded on film and later measured. The figure shows the percentage of increase or decrease in pupil area in response to various pictures for both male and female subjects. The amount of light entering the eye was constant for all pictures. The sexes differ quite markedly with regard to the interest value of these particular pictures. A later study showed that homosexuals could be distinguished from normal males on the basis of pupillary responses to pictures of female pinups. (Data from Hess and Polt, 1960)

If you stare at a homogeneous background, such as a blue sky, you can see the movement of blood through the retinal blood vessels that lie in front of the rods and cones. The blood vessel walls can be seen as pairs of narrow lines in the periphery of our vision, and the disk-shaped objects that appear to move between these lines are the red blood cells flowing through the vessel.

The most sensitive portion of the eye in normal daylight vision is a part of the retina called the *fovea*. This area plays a major role in perception and yet it is so small that the projection (or image) of a thumbnail viewed at arms length will cover it. Not far from the fovea is an insensitive area, called the *blind spot,* where the nerve fibers from the ganglion cells of the retina come together to form the *optic nerve.* Although we are not normally aware of the blind spot, its existence can easily be demonstrated. Follow the instructions given in Figure 4-6.

Figure 4-7 shows the optic nerve fibers leading from each eye to the cortical areas where vision is represented (the *occipital lobes*). Notice that some of the fibers go from the right eye to the right cerebral hemisphere and from the left eye to the left hemisphere, whereas other fibers cross over at a junction called the *optic chiasma* and go to the opposite hemisphere. Fibers from the right sides of both eyes go to the right hemisphere of the cerebral cortex, and fibers from the left sides of both eyes go to the left hemisphere. Consequently, damage to the occipital lobe of one hemisphere (say, the left) will result in blind areas in *both* eyes (the left sides of both eyes). This fact is sometimes helpful in pinpointing the location of a cerebral tumor or injury.

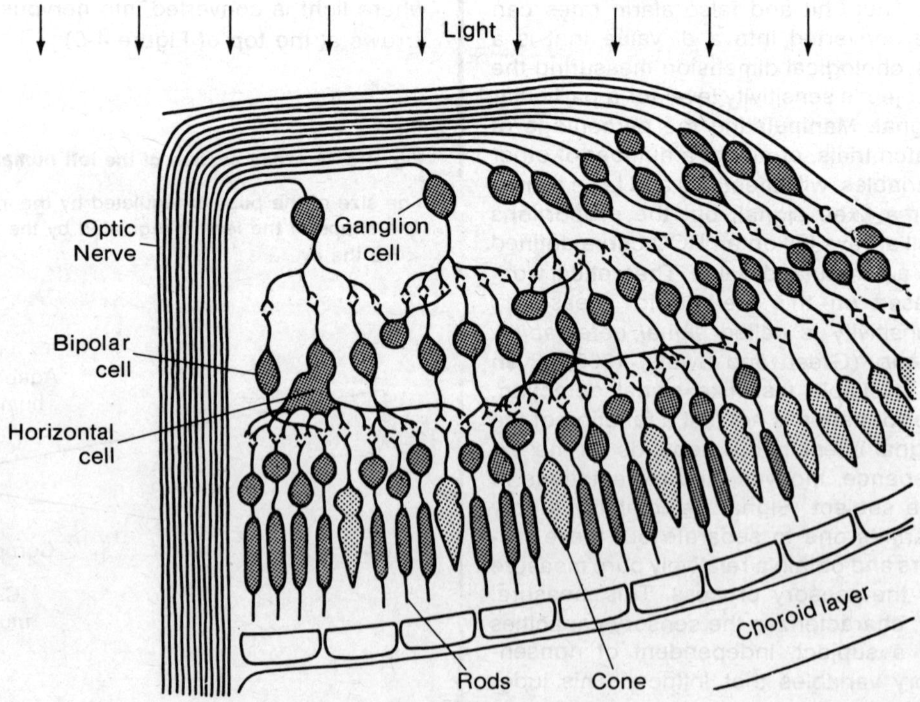

Fig. 4-5 Rods and cones and their connections

Shown here are the main layers of the retina: rods and cones, bipolar cells, and ganglion cells. The bipolar cells receive impulses from one or more rods or cones and transmit the impulses to the nerve fibers, whose cell bodies are shown as the ganglion cells. Integration across the retina is accomplished by horizontal cells connecting rods and cones, and by internal association cells at the ganglion cell level.

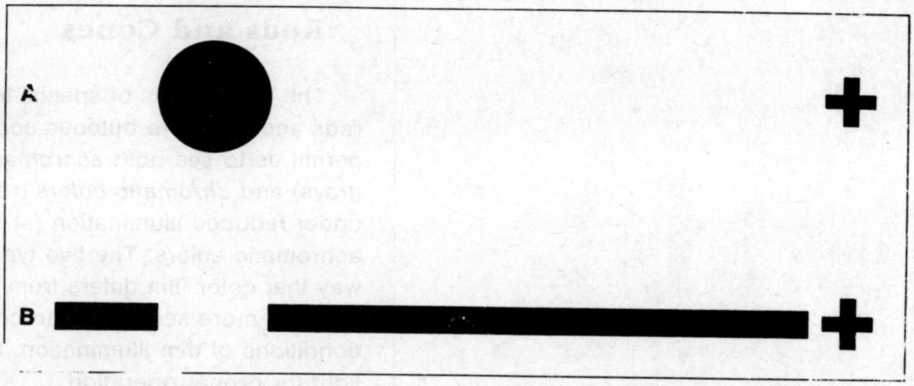

Fig. 4-6 Locating the blind spot

A. With the right eye closed, stare at the upper right cross. Move the book back and forth about 1 foot from the eye. When the black circle on the left disappears, it is projected on the blind spot.

B. With the right eye closed, stare at the lower right cross. Move the book back and forth again. When the white space falls in the blind spot, the black line appears to be continuous. This phenomenon helps us to understand why we are not ordinarily aware of the blind spot.

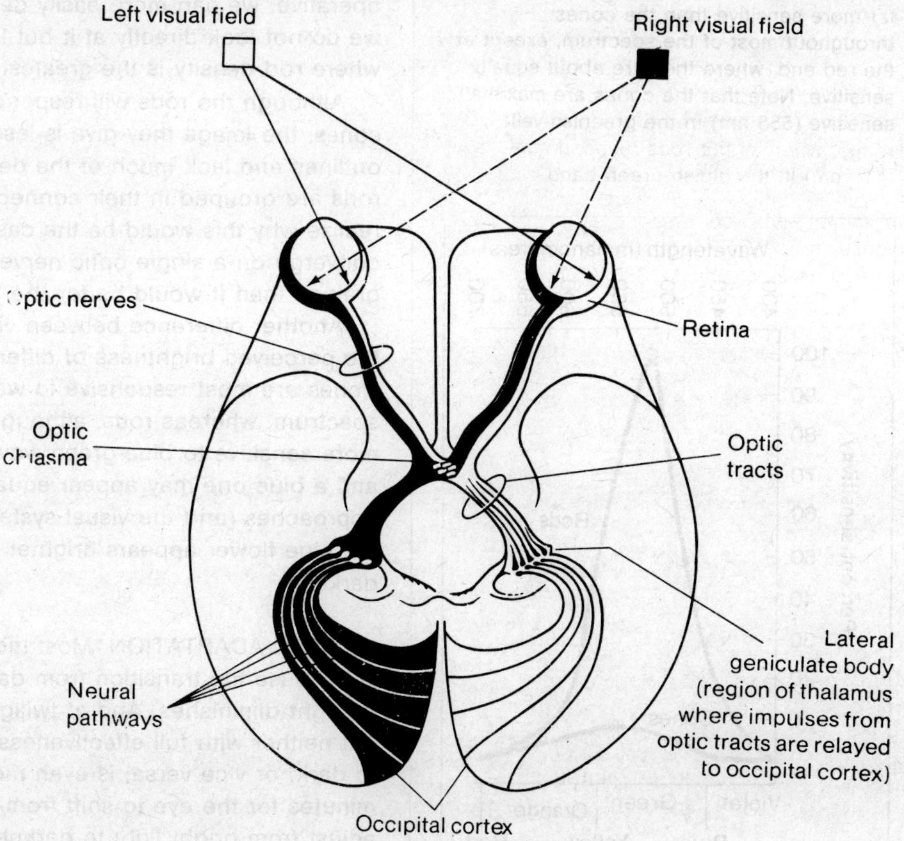

Fig. 4-7 Visual pathways

Light waves from objects in the right visual field fall on the left half of each retina; light waves from the left visual field impinge on the right half of each retina. The optic nerve bundles from each eye meet at the optic chiasma, where the nerve fibers from the inner, nasal half of the retina cross over and go to opposite sides of the brain. Thus stimuli impinging on the right side of each retina are transmitted to the occipital cortex of the right cerebral hemisphere, and stimuli impinging on the left side of each retina are transmitted to the left cerebral hemisphere. In terms of the visual field this means that objects in the right visual field are projected to the left cerebral hemisphere, while objects in the left visual field are projected to the right hemisphere.

Rods and Cones

The retinal cells of special interest are the photoreceptors: the cylindrical rods and the more bulbous cones. The cones, active only in daylight vision, permit us to see both *achromatic colors* (white, black, and the intermediate grays) and *chromatic colors* (red, green, blue, etc.) The rods function mainly under reduced illumination (at twilight or night) and permit us to see only achromatic colors. The two types of photoreceptors differ in much the same way that color film differs from black and white film. Black and white film (rods) is more sensitive than color film and can produce a picture even under conditions of dim illumination. Color film (cones) requires much more intense light for proper operation.

More than 6 million cones and 100 million rods are distributed, somewhat unevenly, throughout the retina. The fovea contains only cones—some 50,000 of them packed together in an area smaller than a square millimeter. Outside the fovea are both rods and cones, with the cones decreasing in number from the center of the retina to the periphery. The rods are connected in groups, and each group has one neuron running to the optic nerve. The cones in the periphery of the retina are grouped together in units along with the rods, but each of the cones in the fovea has its own "private wire" to the brain (see Figure 4-5). Our vision is more acute when light waves strike the fovea, because the nonconverging "private line" does not mix signals. For this reason we turn our head to look directly at an object when we want to see it clearly. Under dim illumination, however, when the cones are not operative, we can more easily detect a faint stimulus, such as a dim star, if we do not look directly at it but let its image fall just outside the foveal region, where rod density is the greatest.

Fig. 4-8 Visibility curves

There are two visibility functions, one for cones and the other for rods. The rods are far more sensitive than the cones throughout most of the spectrum, except at the red end, where they are about equally sensitive. Note that the cones are maximally sensitive (555 nm) in the greenish-yellow range, whereas the rods respond maximally (511 nm) in the bluish-green band.

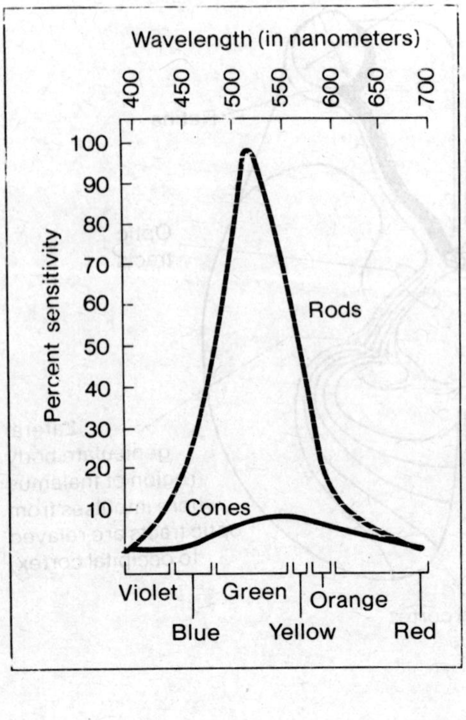

Although the rods will respond to a much dimmer stimulus than will the cones, the image they give is less clear. At night, objects have indistinct outlines and lack much of the detail seen in daylight. If we remember that rods are grouped in their connections to bipolar and ganglion cells, we can realize why this would be the case. Because signals from many rods converge on a single optic nerve fiber, interpretation by the brain is less fine grained than it would be for the "private wire" cone cells in the fovea.

Another difference between vision under high and low illumination is in the perceived brightness of different wavelengths at some fixed intensity. Cones are most responsive to wavelengths in the greenish-yellow part of the spectrum, whereas rods, although still giving only achromatic vision, are more sensitive to blue-green wavelengths (Figure 4-8). Thus a yellow flower and a blue one may appear equally bright in daylight, but as night approaches (and the visual system begins shifting from cone to rod vision) the blue flower appears brighter while the yellow one begins to appear darker.

DARK ADAPTATION. Most motorists find driving at dusk hazardous. This is because the transition from day to night vision takes place gradually as daylight diminishes. And at twilight both the cones and rods are operating but neither with full effectiveness. A sudden change from conditions of light to dark, or vice versa, is even more difficult to adjust to. It takes several minutes for the eye to shift from dim light to brightness, and even longer to adjust from bright light to darkness. We have all experienced the difficulty of finding our way to an empty seat when entering a dark theater. After a few

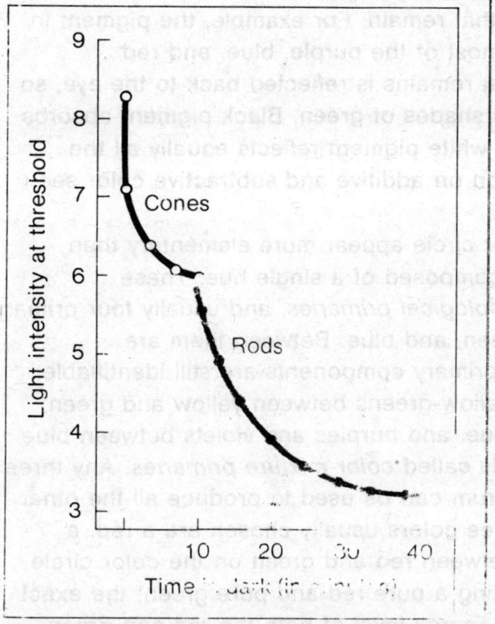

Fig. 4-9 The course of dark adaptation

The subject looks at a bright light until the retina has become light adapted. When he is then placed in darkness he becomes increasingly sensitive to fainter test flashes as the retina gradually becomes dark adapted. The curve shows the minimum light intensity for the test flash to be seen. The unfilled data points indicate at which points the color of the test flash was clearly visible; the filled data points indicate when the test flash appeared colorless. Note the sharp break in the curve at about 10 minutes, which is called the rod-cone break. By changing the color of the light flash or the area of the retina tested, it can be shown that the first part of the curve describes adaptation of the cones, and the second, adaptation of the rods. (Data are approximate, from various determinations)

minutes our eyes become accustomed to the dark, and we are able to see the people around us even though the lighting has not changed. We have undergone *dark adaptation.*

The course of dark adaptation provides further evidence for the difference in action between the rods and cones (see Figure 4-9). The first part of the curve shows that the cones gradually become sensitive to fainter lights, but after five minutes in the dark their sensitivity has increased as much as it will, as measured by the absolute threshold. The rods, however, continue to adapt and do not reach their maximum sensitivity for about a half-hour. The dark-adapted eye is much more sensitive to lights with wavelengths in the blue-green region than to the longer wavelengths in the red region. This fact has had an important practical implication for the individual who must work in a darkened room or shift quickly from conditions of light to dark, such as a photographer, or a ship's navigator on night duty. Wearing red goggles or working in a room illuminated by red light greatly reduces the time required for dark adaptation. Since red light stimulates the cones but not the rods, the rods remain in a state of dark adaptation. The person can see well enough to work under conditions of red light and still be almost completely dark adapted when it becomes necessary to go into the dark.

Color Vision

For the human subject the color spectrum fades into invisibility at the extreme ends, red and violet (Figure 4-10).[1] We are able to see, however, some vivid colors that do not exist in the spectrum at all; they do not correspond to any single wavelength but can be produced by mixing wavelengths. These are the purples redder than the violet end of the spectrum and the red that looks "purest" to most normal eyes.

An interesting relationship exists among colors. If the spectral colors are wrapped around the circumference of a circle, allowing room between the red and violet ends of the spectrum for the purples and reds not found on the spectrum, the colors opposite each other on the circle will be *complementary.* That is, if lights of these colors are mixed in proper proportions, they disappear to a neutral gray. Figure 4-11 presents such a color circle, with specimen complementary colors. For convenience in remembering the positions, we usually name the main complementary pairs as blue-yellow and red-green, although the yellow complementary to blue is slightly orange, and the green complementary to red is really a blue-green.

Those familiar with painting may object to naming yellow and blue as complementaries, because those pigments when mixed give green, not gray. But remember that we are talking here about mixing *lights,* not pigments. The principles of mixture in the two cases are not contradictory, though the explanation of the difference is somewhat involved. The mixture of lights is an *additive* mixture, whereas the mixture of pigments is a *subtractive* mixture because of the way in which pigments selectively absorb some of the light. Light is the source of all color, and pigments are simply reflectors and absorbers of color. They achieve their color by absorbing certain parts of the

[1] A useful mnemonic for remembering the order of colors on the spectrum involves the coined name "ROY G. BIV," which is a list of the first letters of the colors: *red, orange, yellow, green, blue, indigo,* and *violet.*

spectrum and reflecting the parts that remain. For example, the pigment in the chlorophyll of plants absorbs most of the purple, blue, and red wavelengths of light; the green that remains is reflected back to the eye, so we see most vegetation as various shades of green. Black pigment absorbs all wavelengths and reflects none; white pigment reflects equally all the colors of light. For more information on additive and subtractive color see Figure 4-12.

Some of the colors on the color circle appear more elementary than others; that is, they appear to be composed of a single hue. These elementary colors are called *psychological primaries,* and usually four primary colors are named—red, yellow, green, and blue. Between them are "secondary" colors, in which the primary components are still identifiable: orange between red and yellow, yellow-greens between yellow and green, blue-greens between green and blue, and purples and violets between blue and red. Another set of primaries is called *color-mixture primaries.* Any three widely spaced colors on the spectrum can be used to produce all the other colors by additive mixture. The three colors usually chosen are a red, a green, and a blue. Thus, colors between red and green on the color circle can be produced by additively mixing a pure red and pure green; the exact color obtained will depend on the energy level of both the red and green light sources. Similarly, colors between green and blue on the color circle can be obtained by their additive mixtures, and the same holds for blue and red. With additive mixing the entire color circle can be produced with just three colors.

PSYCHOLOGICAL DIMENSIONS OF COLOR. How do you describe a color? Light waves can be precisely described physically through the measurement of wavelengths and amplitude (the height of the wave). But a person trying to describe what he sees must resort to three psychological dimensions: hue, brightness, and saturation. *Hue* refers to what we ordinarily think of as the "name" of the color—for example, red, green, etc. The circumference of the color circle provides the scale along which the hues can be placed in order. There the hues follow the order of shortest to the longest visible wavelength.

Another dimension along which colors can be scaled is *brightness.* The physical basis of brightness is primarily the energy of the light source, which corresponds to the amplitude of the wave. But brightness also depends to some extent upon wavelength. Yellow, for example, appears slightly brighter than certain red and blue wavelengths, even when all three have equal amplitudes.

A third dimension along which colors can be scaled is *saturation,* which refers to the apparent purity of the color. Highly saturated colors appear to be pure hues, without any gray; colors of low saturation appear close to gray. The primary physical correlate of saturation is the complexity of the light wave. A light wave composed of only one or a few different wavelengths will produce the most highly saturated color. Light waves composed of many components result in colors of low saturation. However, as colors of a single wavelength become brighter (merge into white) or darker (merge into black) they begin to lose the apparent purity of their hues; the change in brightness is accompanied by a reduction in saturation.

THE COLOR SOLID. The relationship between the three dimensions of hue, brightness, and saturation will become clearer if we look at the color

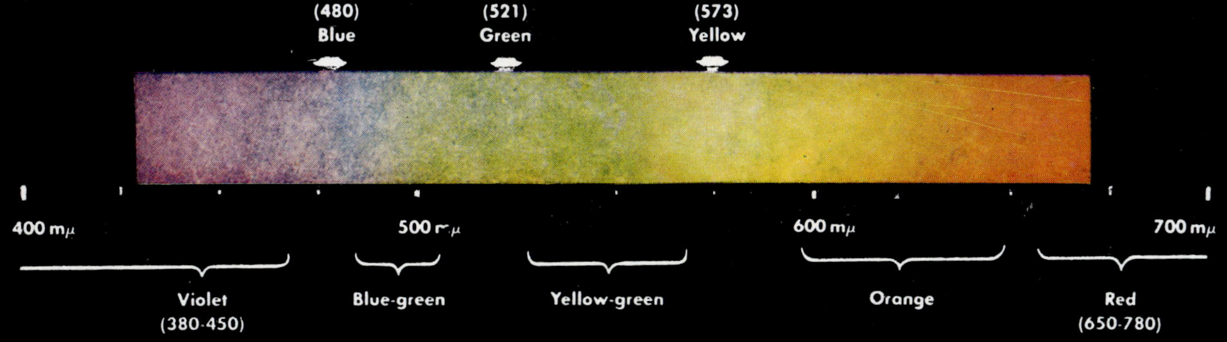

Fig. 4-10 The solar spectrum

The colors are in the order of the rainbow, as seen when sunlight is sent through a prism.

Fig. 4-11 A color circle showing complementary colors

The colors opposite each other, if in proper proportions, will mix on a color wheel to yield the neutral gray at the center. Wavelengths are indicated around the circle in nm. Note that the spectral colors lie in their natural order on the circle, but their spacing is not uniform by wavelength. The circle also includes the nonspectral reds and purples.

Fig. 4-12 Additive and subtractive color mixtures

Additive color mixture (illustrated by the left figure) takes place when lights are mixed. Red and green lights combine to give yellow, green and bluish-purple to give blue, and so on. The three colors overlap in the center to give white. Mixture of any two of the colors produces the complement of the third, as shown in the triangular portions.

Subtractive color mixture (illustrated by the right figure) takes place when pigments are mixed or when light is transmitted through colored filters placed one over another. Usually, blue-green and yellow will mix to give green, and complementary colors will reduce to black, as in the example given. Unlike an additive mixture, one cannot always tell from the color of the components what color will result. For example, blue and green will commonly yield blue-green by subtractive mixture, but with some filters they may yield red. Note that in the photograph the triangular portions are the original complementary colors used in the additive mixture, but here they appear as a result of subtractive mixture.

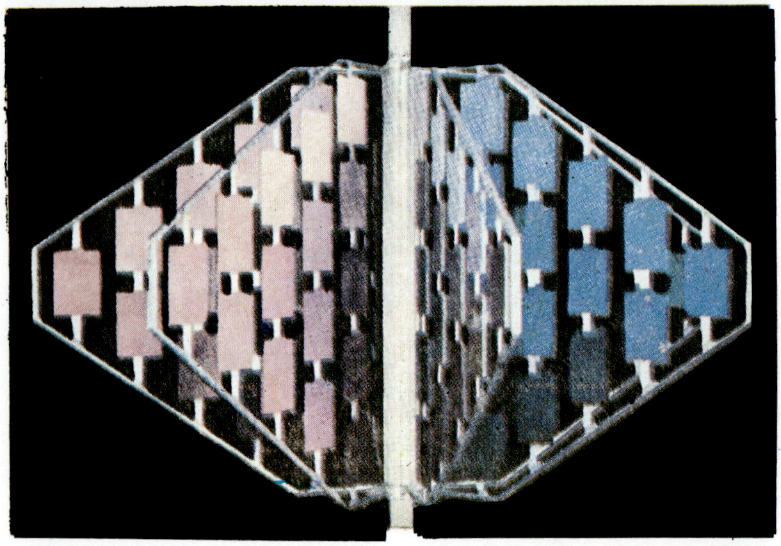

Fig. 4-13 The color solid

The three dimensions of color can be represented on a double cone. hue is represented by points around the circumference, saturation by points along the radius, and brightness by points on the vertical axis. A vertical slice from the color solid shows differences in saturation and brightness of a single hue.

Fig. 4-14 Tests for colorblindness

Two plates used in colorblindness tests. In the top plate, those with certain kinds of red-green blindness see only the number 5; others see only the 7; still others, no number at all. Those with normal vision see 57. Similarly, in the bottom plate, the person with normal vision sees the number 15, whereas those with red-green blindness see no number at all.

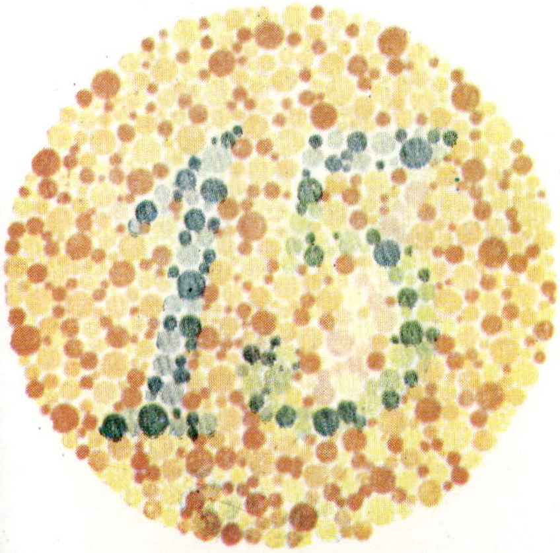

Upper left. A contemporary Persian miniature painting as it would look to a person with normal color vision. Upper right. Someone with red-green blindness sees this. Lower left. The yellow-blue blind person sees this. Lower right. The totally colorblind person sees this.

Fig. 4-15 Negative afterimages

Look steadily for about 20 seconds at the dot inside the blue circle; then transfer your gaze to the dot inside the gray rectangle. Now do the same with the dot inside the yellow circle. What do you see? (After Evans, 1948)

Fig. 4-16 Simultaneous contrast

Note the darkening effect on the gray patch when it is against white; the same patch of gray against black looks much lighter. A gray patch against a colored background tends to take on the complementary hue; the effect is much increased if a piece of thin tissue paper is placed over the colors. With colors that are approximately complementary (as in the red and green patches), there is an enhancement through contrast.

solid (Figure 4-13), which represents all three simultaneously. The dimension of hue is represented by points around the circumference; saturation, by points along the radius, going from a pure or highly saturated color on the outside to a gray or unsaturated color in the center; and brightness, by points along the vertical axis going toward black at the bottom and white at the top. (The color plate does not show the actual gradations of gray going from black to white along the central axis.) You can see that the reds and purples become pink as light gray is added; the oranges and yellows become variations of brown as they become less saturated. On any vertical half-slice taken through the center of the solid, all the colors are the same hue (wavelength) but vary in brightness and saturation.

The color solid helps in our understanding of the relationship between brightness and saturation. The most highly saturated colors are of medium brightness. The color solid tapers to a point at both top and bottom. Consequently, as colors increase or decrease in brightness from the medial circumference, they become less saturated, approaching at the extremes either black or white, which are by definition without hue and therefore of zero saturation.

COLORBLINDNESS. How can we explain colorblindness? We may conveniently think of the normal eye as discriminating three systems of color: light-dark, yellow-blue, and red-green. All other combinations can be derived from these. Colorblindness results from a deficiency in one or two of these systems, the light-dark system remaining intact if the person can see at all. The person with normal vision is called a *trichromat.* A person lacking one system but with use of the other two is called a *dichromat.* A dichromat is partially colorblind. Finally, the person with only the light-dark system is a *monochromat* and totally colorblind.

By far the most common form of colorblindness is red-green blindness, with the blue-yellow and light-dark systems intact. This deficiency affects some 7 percent of men but less than 1 percent of women. Total colorblindness, in which the person sees merely black, white, and gray, is extremely rare; yellow-blue blindness, in which red-green discrimination is preserved, is rarer still.

Many colorblind persons are unaware of their defect because they are able to make such skillful use of their remaining color discrimination, combining it with the learned colors and color names of familiar objects. Because our color vocabulary is not clear for unsaturated colors, the colorblind person can make some mistakes on these troublesome colors without being noticed.

Many tests are available for the detection of colorblindness. They usually require the subject to read a figure composed of colored dots on a background of other colored dots (Figure 4-14). The colors are chosen to confuse subjects who have the various forms of color deficiency.

AFTERIMAGES AND COLOR CONTRAST. If you stare at a *red* circle and then look at a plain gray surface, you are likely to see a *green* circle on it; that is, you experience a *negative afterimage.* It is negative because green is the complementary color of red. Not all afterimages are in the complementary color however. After staring at a very bright light you are likely to see a whole succession of colors, but seeing the complementary color is very common. Afterimages are illustrated in Figure 4-15.

The spreading effect The same red is used throughout the strip. But the red with black looks darker than the red with white. (After Evans, 1948)

CRITICAL DISCUSSION

Theories of Color Vision

Exactly how do the photoreceptors of the retina manage to send a different message to the brain for each of the many colors in the spectrum? Each attempt to explain how the eye sees color has taken as its starting point one of the three sets of facts about color that we have just discussed: color mixture, color contrast and afterimages, and colorblindness.

One of the earliest theories of color vision—proposed by Thomas Young, an English physicist, in 1802 and modified by the German physiologist Hermann von Helmholtz a half-century later—was based on the fact that three colors are sufficient to produce all the colors in the spectrum. The Young-Helmholtz theory proposes three different kinds of color receptors, each maximally sensitive to a different wavelength (one sensitive to red wavelengths, one to blue, and one to green). All other colors are somehow produced by a combined stimulation of these receptors. Yellow is produced when red and green receptors are stimulated simultaneously. White is produced when all three receptors are stimulated simultaneously. The modern form of this theory attempts to link three kinds of cones (or three kinds of cone substances) with the three colors.

However, the Young-Helmholtz theory has not been able to explain some of the facts of colorblindness. If yellow is produced by activity in red and green receptors, how is it that a person with red-green colorblindness has no difficulty seeing yellow? Another color theory, formulated by Ewald Hering in 1870, attempted to solve this problem. Hering felt that the Young-Helmholtz theory did not adequately reflect visual experience. He based his theory on the *psychological primaries* rather than the color-mixing primaries and argued that yellow is as basic a color as red, blue, or green. It does not appear to be a mixture of other colors, as orange appears to be a mixture of red and yellow, or purple a mixture of red and blue.

Hering was impressed with the facts of *color contrast* and *afterimages,* by the appearance of red-green and blue-yellow as pairs in so many circumstances. He proposed that there were three types of cones: one that responded to degrees of brightness, the black-white continuum; and two color cones, one provided the basis for red-green perception and the other for blue-yellow. Each receptor was assumed to function in two ways. One color of the pair was produced when the receptor was in a building-up phase (*anabolic*), and the other appeared when the receptor was in a tearing-down phase (*catabolic*). The two phases cannot occur at the same time in a given receptor; when a yellow-blue cone is stimulated it responds with either yellow or blue. It cannot react both ways simultaneously. That is why, according to the theory, we never see a red-green or a blue-yellow, whereas it is possible to see a reddish blue or greenish yellow. When stimulation is withdrawn, as in the afterimage experiment, the contrasting color appears because the anabolic-catabolic process is reversed. When we look at a blue circle and then transfer our gaze to a white sheet of paper, a yellow circle appears when the catabolic process takes over (see Figure 4-15). Hering's theory has become known as the *opponent-process theory.* In its modern form this theory assumes that the opponent processes take place not in the cones but in coding mechanisms closer to the brain in the optic system.

Recent developments suggest that both theories may be partially correct. MacNichol (1964), using a procedure called *microspectrophotometry,* was able to direct different wavelengths of light through single cones in the human retina and analyze the energy transmitted by means of a computer. He identified three kinds of light-sensitive pigments in the cones: one type primarily sensitive to wavelengths in the blue band, one sensitive to green, and a third sensitive to yellow. Although the third cone type had its peak sensitivity at 577 nm (which is yellow), these cones were also sensitive to the longer wavelengths (up to 650 nm) of the yellowish-red part of the spectrum. These measurements appear to support the Young-Heimholtz theory, although it is not clear whether the three cone types should be called blue, green, and yellow, or blue, green, and red.

At the same time, recordings taken with microelectrodes give evidence of an "on" and "off" type of process in bipolar cells and in cells of the lateral geniculate body—that portion of the thalamus where visual impulses are relayed to the visual cortex (refer to Figure 4-7). Some cells respond with a burst of impulses when stimulated by short wavelengths but are inhibited (respond as "off" cells) during illumination with long wavelengths, showing a burst of firing when stimulation ceases. Other cells are active when stimulated by long wavelengths and inhibited by short wavelengths. These results indicate an opponent-process operating not in the cones themselves, but further along in the pathway from the eye to the brain (DeValois and Jacobs, 1968).

At this point of scientific development it appears that color vision is a two-stage process: the retina contains pigments that respond differentially to the lights of three different colors; these responses are encoded into two-color, on-off signals by cells further along in the optic system for transmission to the higher visual centers. A final theory of color vision may be a modification of this two-stage theory, or it may be an entirely different formulation based on future research. The interesting feature is that two theories, those of Hering and Young-Helmholtz, proposed over a century ago, have had to wait until recent technological developments (microspectrophotometry and single-neuron recording) could provide verification of their propositions.

Complementary colors can also serve to enhance each other. When two complementary colors occur side by side, each color appears more highly saturated than it would when placed next to a noncomplementary color. This effect, termed *simultaneous contrast,* is one reason for making pennants of such complementary pairs as red and green and yellow and blue. Simultaneous contrast is illustrated in Figure 4-16.

Neural Processing of Visual Information

Research on neural activity during visual stimulation suggests that much of the information transmitted to the brain is concerned with differences and changes in the environment. Because the rods and cones of the human eye are so minute and difficult to isolate for study, much of this research has been done with lower organisms. The horseshoe crab is a particularly good subject because one of its eyes contains about 800 individual receptor cells, each with its own lens and nerve fiber going directly to the brain. An electrode can be placed on a single fiber and its response to light stimulation measured. It has been shown that different light intensities cause the fiber to fire at different frequencies, indicating that intensity information is conveyed to the brain by the rate of nerve firings.

If a light is projected onto a single receptor, causing its fiber to begin firing, and a neighboring receptor is then stimulated, the original fiber will begin to fire at a slower rate. The activation of the second receptor is inhibiting the first. This inhibitory effect is exerted mutually among the receptors so that each inhibits, and is inhibited by, its neighbor. The impulse from each receptor flows out its optic nerve, but part of the impulse is diverted into horizontal nerve cells and flows to neighboring retinal units to affect them negatively (Ratliff, 1965). This mechanism, called *recurrent inhibition,* has interesting consequences. Suppose that both receptor units A and B are stimulated with a light. Now if we also stimulate C, it will inhibit B; B will fire less frequently and consequently will have less of an inhibitory effect on A. Thus, even though the light intensity on B is the same, B will have less of an inhibitory effect on A if B itself is more inhibited by C. By extending this type of argument it can be shown that a system with recurrent inhibition will display a burst of neural impulses in the optic nerve when a light is first turned on; but after the light has been on for a while inhibition will gradually build up, and the nerve activity will drop back to approximately its resting level. When the light is turned off, the receptors will fire less rapidly, but the inhibitory effects still remain for a brief period; thus the neural activity in the optic fibers will drop far below the resting level and then gradually return to it as the inhibitory effects dissipate. In general, any change in intensity—either up or down—will have an effect on the activity of the fibers. An increase in intensity will result in a temporary increase in neural activity, after which it returns almost to its resting level; a decrease in intensity causes a temporary decrease in activity and a subsequent return to the resting level.

A system with recurrent inhibition has the ability to transmit information about changes in the environment while suppressing information about parts of the environment that are steady and unchanging. We can see that such system has adaptive value for the organism; attention to changing aspects its surroundings is important for survival. Recurrent inhibition can be demonstrated in the human visual system as indicated in Figure 4-17

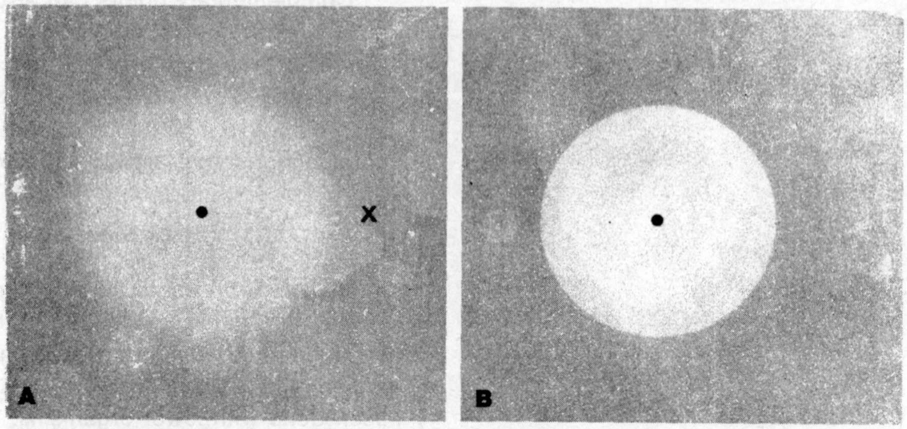

Fig. 4-17 Recurrent inhibition

Cover one eye and stare with the other at the dot in the middle of A. You will notice that the blurred, light-colored disc soon fades and disappears. Close the seeing eye for a few seconds and then open it; the disc will reappear and then fade again. If you stare at the dot until the disc fades and then shift your gaze to the X, you will find that the disc reappears, and it will reappear each time you shift your eyes between the dot and the X.

If you try doing the same thing with B, the disc will not disappear. Although you think you are staring at the dot steadily, your eyes are constantly making little oscillating movements. These minute oscillations, of which we are unaware although they occur continually, cause light from the stimulus to strike different retinal receptors from one moment to the next. When you are looking at the edge of something and the eye shifts from one side of the edge to the other, the receptors perceive a change in intensity. The intensity changes that occur with eye oscillations allow the receptors to continue firing at a high rate, and the disc remains visible. The same thing happens when you stare at the dot in A, but because the gradient of intensity of the blurred disc is more gradual, the eye movements produce a smaller change in intensity on the receptors viewing the edge of the blurred disc. The changes in intensity are so small that little neural excitation occurs in the receptors and the disc fades out. Closing and opening your eye causes marked changes in intensity and so does moving your eye to stare at the X. (After Cornsweet, 1970)

STABILIZED IMAGES. The concept of recurrent inhibition implies that retinal receptors respond only to changes in the environment; steady, unchanging stimulation will be ignored. Why then doesn't something we stare at over a period of time disappear? The reason is that the eyes continually make minute oscillatory movements that cause light from the stimulus to strike different retinal receptors from one moment to the next. What would happen if we could immobilize the eye so that these normal oscillations did not occur? It is impossible to hold the eye steady, but several devices have been developed to eliminate the movement of the image on the retina. One way is by means of a tiny slide projector mounted on a contact lens attached to the cornea, as diagramed in Figure 4-18. The slide is projected onto a screen, and the eye wearing the lens looks at the image. Since the lens and projector move with the eye, the image presented to the retina is stabilized; that is, the retinal image impinges on the same retinal receptors regardless of eye movements. When the projector is first turned on, the subject sees the projected figure with normal, or slightly better than normal, visual acuity. Within a few seconds, however, the image begins to fade and within a minute disappears altogether. This phenomenon is not an artifact caused by the attachment of the projector to the eye, because if the image that has disappeared is flickered, or moved on the retina, it immediately reappears.

From the research on recurrent inhibition and stabilized retinal images we can conclude that changes in illumination on receptors are necessary for us

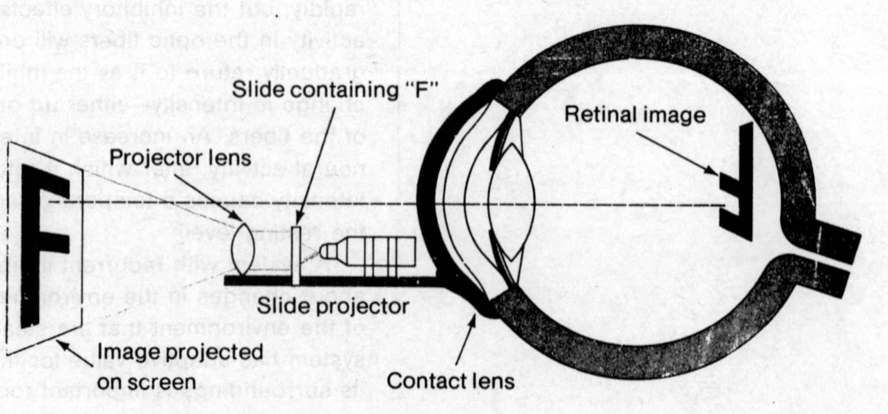

Fig. 4-18 Stabilized image

A set-up to demonstrate that without movement of the eye in relation to a scene, the scene disappears. A tiny projector mounted on a contact lens is worn over the subject's cornea. With each movement of the eyeball, the lens and projector also move so that the projected image always falls on the same area of the retina. After a few seconds the image will fade and then disappear. (After Cornsweet, 1970) to see things. Without changes in intensity everything disappears. Our ability to see stationary objects depends on a visual system that responds to changes in illumination and an eye that transforms a fixed image into changing stimulation on the retina.

The Auditory Sense

While the eye responds to electromagnetic energy, the ear is sensitive to mechanical energy—to *pressure changes* among the molecules in the atmosphere. A vibrating object, such as a tuning fork, causes successive waves of compression and expansion among the air molecules surrounding it. The sound waves generated by the vibration of molecules (in air, water, or some other medium) are the stimuli for hearing. Unlike light, sound cannot travel except through a medium; a ringing bell suspended in a vacuum jar cannot be heard when the air is pumped out.

Simple sound waves can be graphically represented as *sine functions.* Figure 4-19 shows how the cycles of the sine wave represent the successive compression and expansion of the air as the sound wave moves along. The two main characteristics of such a wave are its frequency and its amplitude. *Frequency* is measured in number of vibrations per second, that is, the number of times per second that the complete cycle is repeated. The unit Hertz (abbreviated Hz) is used to denote *cycles per second;* that is, one cycle per second is one Hz.[2] *Amplitude* refers to the amount of compression and expansion, as represented by the amount by which the curve is displaced above or below the baseline.

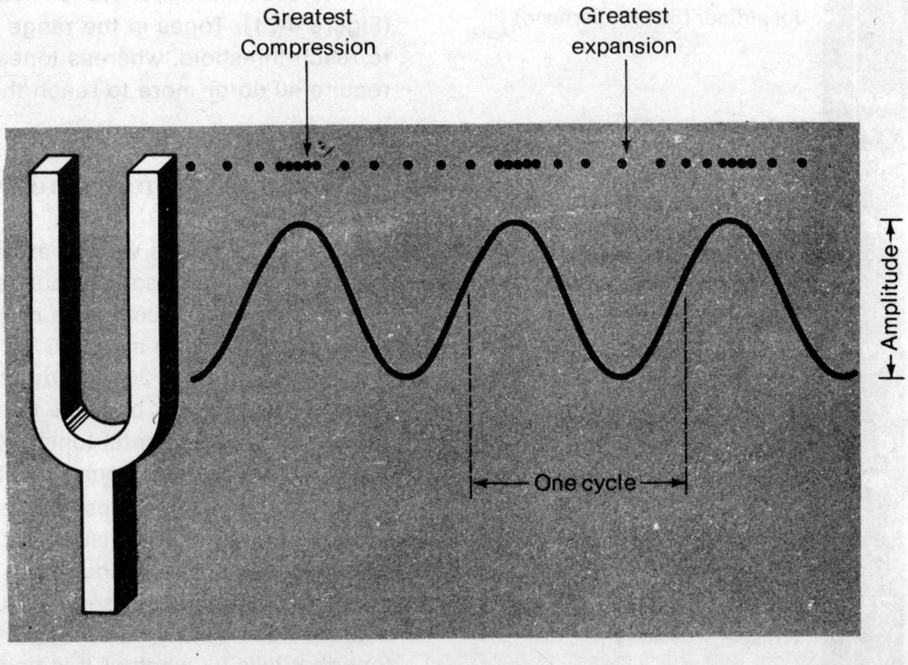

Fig. 4-19 Sound wave

As the tuning fork vibrates it produces successive waves of compression and expansion of the air that can be represented by a sine wave.

[2] The unit of frequency is named in honor of the German physicist Heinrich Hertz (1857–94). Note that light waves were specified in terms of the length of the wave, whereas sound waves are described on the basis of the number of waves per unit of time.

Fig. 4-20 Decibel scale

The loudness of various common sounds scaled in decibels. The takeoff blast of the Saturn V moon rocket, measured at the launching pad, is approximately 180 db. For laboratory rats, prolonged exposure to 150 db causes death.

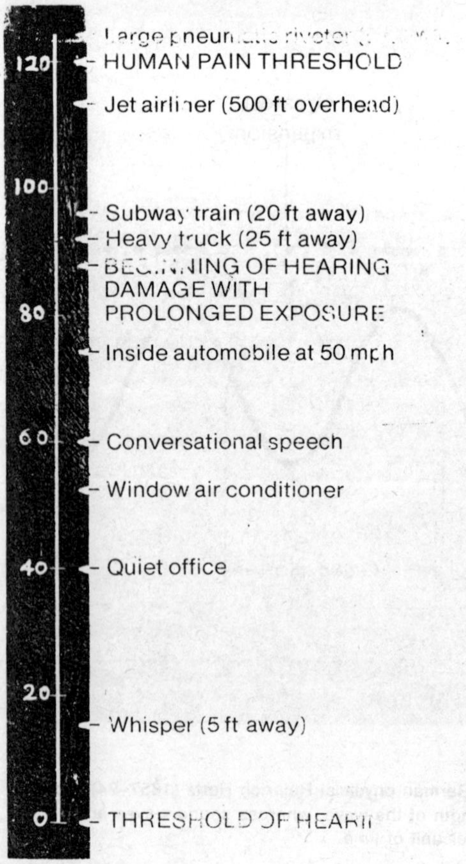

Pitch and Loudness

The psychological correlate of frequency is *pitch:* the higher the vibration frequency, the higher the perceived pitch. The amplitude of the sound wave determines the intensity with which sound pressure strikes the eardrum. The psychological correlate of intensity is *loudness:* the greater the intensity, the louder the tone (provided pitch remains constant).

We can hear frequencies that range from about 20 to 20,000 Hz. Reference points on this range are provided by the piano, which produces frequencies from roughly 27 to 4200 Hz. All organisms cannot hear the same range of frequencies; for example, dog-calling whistles make use of tones that are too high in frequency for us to hear.

We all know the difference between a loud and a soft sound, but assigning scale values to intensity is not so easy. Scientists from the Bell Telephone Laboratories have contributed to the measurement of sound intensity by formulating a convenient unit by which to convert the physical pressures at the eardrum into an understandable scale. The unit is called a *decibel* (one-tenth of a *bel,* named in honor of Alexander Graham Bell, and abbreviated db). A rough idea of what the decibel measures is given in the scale of familiar sounds shown in Figure 4-20. Zero decibels is arbitrarily set as the absolute threshold for hearing a 1000 Hz tone. At about 120 db, sound intensity becomes painful; the loudness of normal conversation is about midway between these extremes at 60 db. Exposure to sound intensities of 90 db or above for extended periods of time can result in permanent deafness. Some rock musicians, for example, have suffered serious hearing loss. Airport runway crews and pneumatic drill operators wear ear mufflers to guard against possible damage.

The absolute threshold for hearing varies with the frequency of the source (Figure 4-21). Tones in the range from 800–6000 Hz require less than 10 db to reach threshold, whereas tones less than 100 Hz or greater than 15,000 Hz require 40 db or more to reach threshold.

Complex Tones and Noise

Just as the colors we see are seldom pure hues produced by a single wavelength of light, so the sounds we hear are seldom pure tones represented by a sound wave of a single frequency. Even the musical note produced by striking middle C on the piano has, in addition to its fundamental tone of 262 Hz, *overtones,* which are multiples of that frequency. The overtones occur because the piano wire vibrates not only as a whole, producing a fundamental tone of 262 Hz, but also in halves, thirds, quarters, fifths, and so on, with each partial vibration producing its own frequency.

Why do the same notes sound different on the piano and the violin? The sounds of one musical instrument differ from those of another in the number of overtones produced and in the way in which the construction of the instrument enhances (resonates) certain overtones and deadens others. This characteristic quality of a musical tone is called *timbre.* It is the timbre of a tone that tells us whether it is being produced by a piano or a clarinet. If all overtones are eliminated by the use of sound filters, it is difficult to determine what instrument is being played. Instead of the regular sound wave pictured in Figure 4-19, a tone from a musical instrument has a complex wave

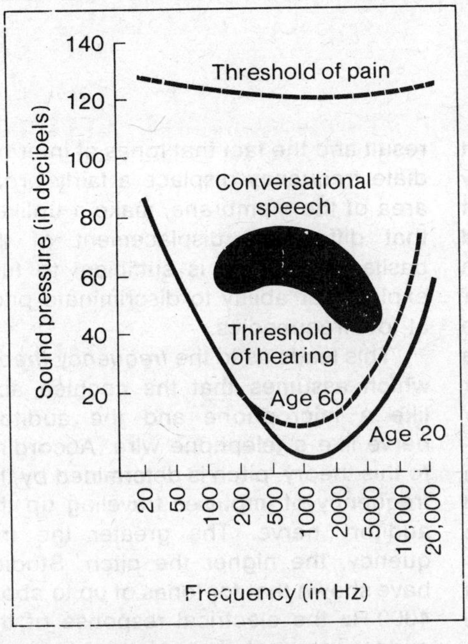

Fig. 4-21 Threshold of hearing

The curve across the top is the threshold of pain. The convex curves below are the thresholds of hearing for age 20 and age 60. Note that with increase in age, hearing is primarily affected in the range of frequencies above 500 Hz. (Data are approximate, from various determinations)

form, preserving only the peaks and troughs that define the fundamental pitch; the high and low points are the same but the wave is jagged or irregular rather than smooth.

If one compares the dimensions of tone with those of color, the followi correspondences hold approximately:

DIMENSIONS OF COLOR		DIMENSIONS OF TONE
Hue	⟷	Pitch
Brightness	⟷	Loudness
Saturation	⟷	Timbre

Hue and pitch are functions of wave frequency; brightness and loudness are functions of amplitude; saturation is a result of mixture, just as timbre is. But these are only analogies and are limited as all analogies are.

What happens when two tones are sounded together? They do not lose their identity as colors do when mixed, but they may lead to a fusion that is heard as *consonant* (pleasant) or as *dissonant* (unpleasant). The two tones create a third tone based on the difference in their frequencies. This *difference tone* may or may not harmonize with the fundamental tones sounded; for this reason some combinations of tones are preferred to others. Musical harmony depends in part on the interaction between fundamental tones, overtones, and difference tones, which combine to make up the complex tonal stimulus.

A *noise* is a sound composed of many frequencies not in harmonious relation to one another. Acoustical experts sometimes speak of *white noise* when referring to a noise composed of all frequencies in the sound spectrum at roughly the same energy level. White noise is analogous to white light, which is composed of all frequencies in the light spectrum. The sound of radio static or a bathroom shower approximates the sound of white noise.

A noise with energy concentrated in certain frequency bands may have a characteristic pitch. For example, we may legitimately use the musical term "bass" to characterize the sound of a drum, even though a drum is more noisy than tonal. Speech sounds make simultaneous use of tonal qualities and noise qualities: *vowels* are tonal, and *consonants* are noisy.

Photomicrograph sho[illegible] ells of the organ of Corti.

The Human Ear

The external ear connects with an auditory canal leading to the eardrum, a movable diaphragm activated by sound waves entering the ear (Figure 4-22). On the inner side of the diaphragm is a cavity housing the bony transmitters of the *middle ear* (three small bones called the hammer, anvil, and stirrup). The hammer is attached firmly to the eardrum, and the stirrup to another membrane, the *oval window.* The oval window conducts the sounds to the *cochlea,* the auditory portion of the *inner ear.* Because the oval window is much smaller than the eardrum, small movements at the eardrum are condensed into a magnified pressure on the oval window.

Pressure at the oval window sets into motion the fluid inside the cochlea (Figure 4-23). This pressure is relieved at the *round window* at the other end of the fluid-filled channel that runs through the cochlea. Pressure changes [illegible] the fluid displace the *basilar membrane* in the cochlea, upon which the or

CRITICAL DISCUSSION

Theories of Hearing

As we have noted, sound waves traveling through the fluid of the cochlea cause the basilar membrane to vibrate, thus activating the hair cells of the organ of Corti which are connected to fibers of the auditory nerve. But how does a structure as small as the organ of Corti (less than the size of a pea) enable us to differentiate thousands of different tones? What are the mechanisms that provide for discriminations in pitch and loudness?

Loudness appears to be determined by the total number of fibers firing and by the activation of certain high threshold fibers; that is, nerve fibers that require considerable bending of the hair cells in order to be stimulated. Pitch is a more complicated matter. The two major theories of pitch discrimination are the place theory and the frequency theory. The *place theory* assumes that the frequency of a tone is indicated by the region of the basilar membrane that is maximally displaced by the sound wave. Von Békésy tested this theory in a series of precise experiments for which he was awarded the Nobel Prize in 1961. He cut tiny holes in the cochlea of guinea pigs and observed the basilar membrane with a microscope as the ear was being stimulated by tones of different frequencies. He discovered that high frequency tones maximally displaced the narrow end of the basilar membrane near the oval window; tones of intermediate frequency caused displacement further toward the other end of the basilar membrane. Unfortunately for the consistency of the theory, however, low tones activated the entire membrane ith roughly equal displacement. This result and the fact that tones of intermediate frequency displace a fairly broad area of the membrane, make it unlikely that differential displacement of the basilar membrane is sufficient to fully explain our ability to discriminate pitch at low frequencies.

This leads us to the *frequency theory* which assumes that the cochlea acts like a microphone and the auditory nerve like a telephone wire. According to this theory, pitch is determined by the frequency of impulses traveling up the auditory nerve. The greater the frequency, the higher the pitch. Studies have shown that for tones of up to about 4000 Hz the electrical response of the auditory nerve does track the frequency of the tone. Thus a tone of 500 Hz produces 500 evoked responses per second in the nerve; a tone of 2000 Hz

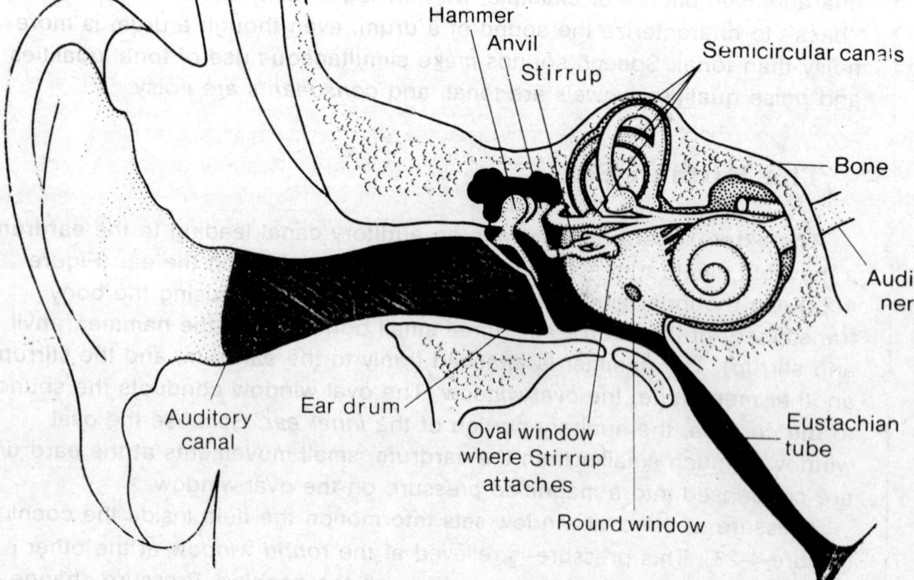

Fig. 4-22 A cross section of the ear

This drawing shows the general structure of the ear. For the detailed structure of the cochlea, see Figure 4-23.

produces 2000 responses; and so on. Since an individual neuron can conduct only about 1000 impulses per second, the ability of the auditory nerve to track frequencies above this point up to 4000 Hz has to be explained in terms of a *volley principle*. This principle assumes that the different groups of fibers fire in turn, in a sort of squad system. Different squads fire at each compression of the sound wave. One group may fire at the first compression, remain in a refractory phase while another group discharges, and then be ready to fire again at the third compression. Thus, although no one fiber responds at each compression, all respond synchronously with the frequency of the sound wave. For a 2000 Hz tone there would be a spurt of activity in the auditory nerve every five ten-thousandths of a second, with different groups of neurons firing each time. Pitch at intermediate frequencies depends upon the firing frequency of the volleys, not that of the individual nerve fibers.

As was the case with theories of color vision, an ultimate explanation of pitch discrimination will probably include some aspects of both theories. Both the *place* of excitation on the basilar membrane and the *frequency* of nerve response appear to be involved in transmitting information about the frequency of a tone. Place seems to be important for high frequencies (above 4000 Hz), whereas synchronous discharge in nerve fibers is important for the lower frequencies.

More precise coding of auditory information takes place in the auditory pathways closer to the brain and in the auditory cortex itself. An auditory nerve fiber makes synaptic connections with at least four other neurons on its way to the auditory cortex. At each of these levels, neurons can be found that fire at the onset of a tone, or decrease their firing when a tone is turned on, or discharge continuously to a maintained tone, or discharge only when a sound is presented to both ears. In addition, as we ascend from the auditory nerve to the auditory cortex, the range of frequencies to which a particular cell will respond becomes increasingly narrow. Thus coding of information becomes more precise as the cortex is approached. A general theory of hearing will also undoubtedly have to take into account neural codes based on different types of response patterns at each synaptic level of the auditory system.

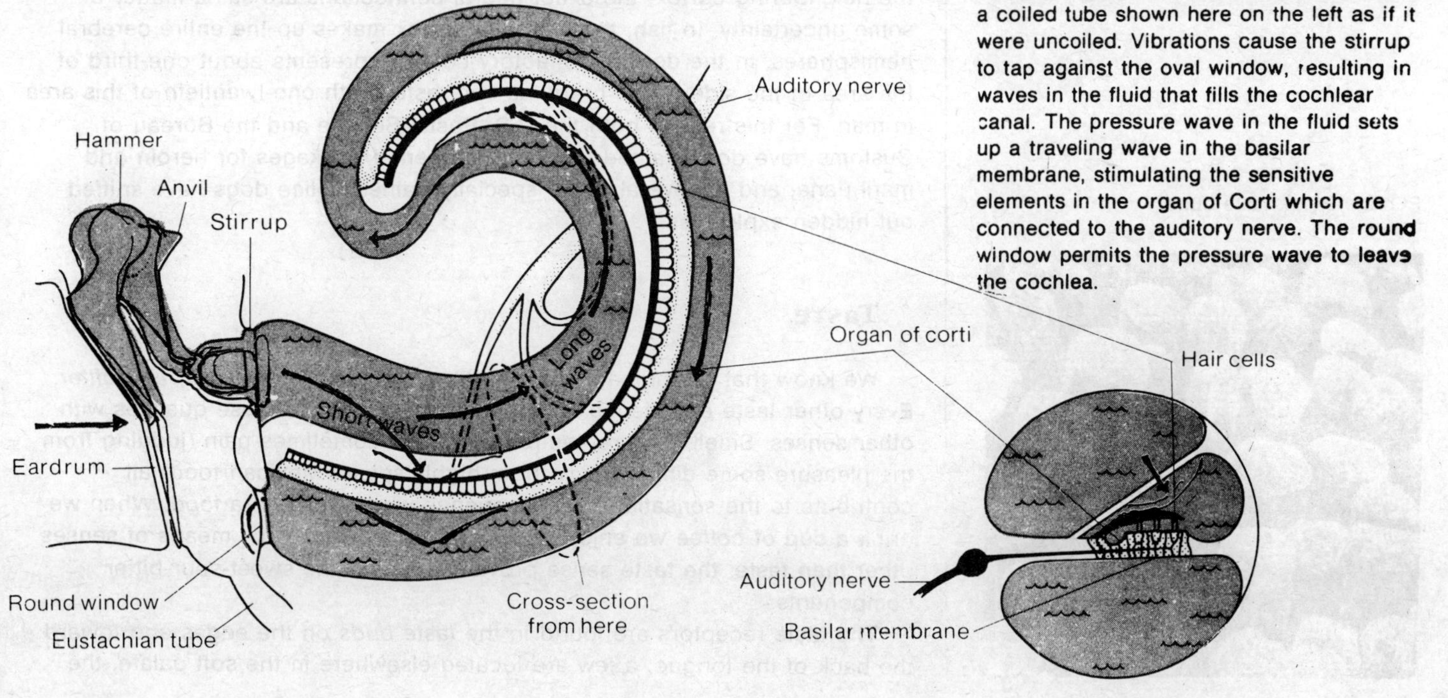

Fig. 4-23 Receptors for hearing

The figure to the lower right is a cross section through the snail-shaped cochlea, a coiled tube shown here on the left as if it were uncoiled. Vibrations cause the stirrup to tap against the oval window, resulting in waves in the fluid that fills the cochlear canal. The pressure wave in the fluid sets up a traveling wave in the basilar membrane, stimulating the sensitive elements in the organ of Corti which are connected to the auditory nerve. The round window permits the pressure wave to leave the cochlea.

of Corti rests, and this displacement stimulates the sensitive elements in the *hair cells* of the organ of Corti, which are connected with the auditory nerve.

The pathways of the auditory nerves resemble those of the optic nerves in that nerve fibers from each ear travel to both cerebral hemispheres (terminating in the temporal lobes). Thus, destruction of one temporal lobe will not cause complete deafness in either ear.

A [illegible] work for the [illegible] Service

Other Senses

Senses other than vision and audition are important for survival, but they lack the richness of patterning and organization that have led us to call sight and hearing the "higher senses." Our symbolic experiences are expressed largely in visual and auditory terms. Our spoken language is to be *heard;* our written language is to be *seen.* Musical notation permits music to be read or played on an instrument. Except for Braille (the raised form of printing that permits the blind to read) we do not have any comparable symbolic coding of odors, tastes, or touches.

Smell

From an evolutionary viewpoint, smell is one of the most primitive and most important of the senses. The sense organ for smell has a position of prominence in the head appropriate to a sense intended to guide behavior. Smell has a more direct route to the brain than any other sense. The receptors high in the nose, in the *olfactory epithelium* of each nasal cavity, are connected without synapse directly to the olfactory bulbs of the brain, lying just below the frontal lobes. The olfactory bulbs are in turn connected with the olfactory cortex on the inside of the temporal lobes and extend to the neighboring cortex; the exact neural connections are still a matter of some uncertainty. In fish, the olfactory cortex makes up the entire cerebral hemispheres. In the dog, the olfactory cortex represents about one-third of the area of the side of the brain, as contrasted with one-twentieth of this area in man. For this reason both the U.S. Postal Service and the Bureau of Customs have dogs trained to check unopened packages for heroin and marihuana, and in several cases specially trained police dogs have sniffed out hidden explosives.

Photograph of taste buds.

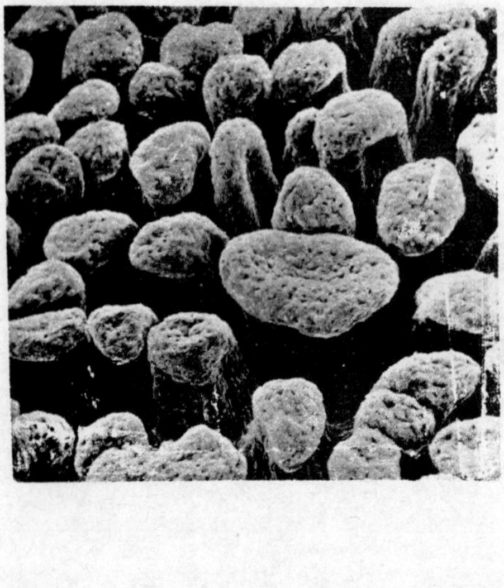

Taste

We know that the primary taste qualities are *sweet, sour, salt,* and *bitter.* Every other taste experience is composed of fusions of these qualities with other senses. Smell, texture, temperature, and sometimes pain (judging from the pleasure some diners derive from highly spiced Mexican food) all contribute to the sensations we experience when we taste a food. When we drink a cup of coffee we enjoy its aroma and its warmth by means of senses other than taste; the taste sense provides only for the sweet-sour-bitter components.

The taste receptors are found in the *taste buds* on the edges and toward the back of the tongue; a few are located elsewhere in the soft palate, the

Taste discrimination by experts

pharynx, and the larynx. it is known that the number of taste buds decreases with age, so that older people are less sensitive to taste than children. Some taste buds at the tip of the tongue react only to sweet, salt, or sour; others react to some or all of these in combination. In general, sensitivity to sweet is greatest at the tip of the tongue, to salt on the tip and the sides, to sour on the sides, and to bitter on the back.

Each of the approximately ten thousand taste buds in the human adult has 15–20 taste cells arranged in budlike form on its tip, much like the segments of an orange. These taste cells are continuously reproducing themselves at the rate of a complete turnover for each taste bud every seven days. Consequently, the taste cells we kill when we scald our tongue with a cup of hot coffee provide no cause for concern; they are quickly replenished. Recordings from microelectrodes implanted in single cells show that even the individual cells vary in their response to the four basic taste stimuli; that is, some cells may respond only to sugar and salt while others on the same taste bud may respond only to salt and acids, and so forth.

Measurement of impulses from the taste nerve fibers and behavioral evidence of discriminatory ability among taste substances show that other animals differ from man in the receptivity of their taste buds. Cats and chickens, for example, appear to have no taste receptors that respond to sweet, whereas dogs, rats, pigs, and most other vertebrates do. This helps explain the observation of pet owners that dogs are usually fond of desserts, while cats generally ignore them.

The Skin Sensations

The familiar sense of touch is not one sensation but at least four: *touch, pain, warm,* and *cold*—all of which are felt through distinct kinds of sensitive spots on the skin surface. All other skin sensations that we commonly describe, such as itch, tickle, quick-pricking pains, or dull, long-lasting pains, are variations of the four basic sensations. An itching sensation, for example, can be produced by stimulating pain spots by a light, repeated needle prick; tickle is experienced when adjacent touch spots on the skin are touched lightly in rapid succession.

The precise receptors for the various skin sensations have been the subject of much study and dispute. At one time, histologists identified a number of quite different nerve-end structures in the skin, each of which was thought to be the specific receptor for one of the four sensations. Subsequent studies, however, failed to substantiate such claims: when investigators "mapped" cold, warm, touch, and pain spots on their own skin, excised the underlying tissue, and examined it microscopically, there was no consistent relationship between the type of sensation experienced and the type of underlying nerve-end structures. Only two things can be stated with some degree of certainty:

1. Nerve fibers at the base of hair follicles serve as receptors for touch or light pressure (but they are not the only receptors, since the lips, which are hairless, are quite sensitive to pressure).
2. Free nerve-endings that terminate in the epidermis (as opposed to those nerves that end in certain encapsulated structures) are involved in pain reception.

If there are only warm and cold sensitive spots on the skin's surface, how can we experience the feeling of "hot"? The answer is that "hot" results from the simultaneous stimulation of warm and cold spots. This can be demonstrated with a device that allows two streams of water to be passed through intertwined coils (Figure 4-24). If cold water passes through both coils they of course feel cold when grasped with one hand. If warm water passes through both they feel warm. But when cold water circulates through one set of coils and warm water through the other, the coils feel *hot*. This is not the way the experience of "hot" is usually produced, but it is the way the receptors respond. Cold spots have two thresholds. They respond to stimuli of low temperature, do not respond to stimuli of intermediate temperature, but respond again to stimuli of high temperature. High temperatures, then, activate *both* warm and cold spots, and the felt experience of "hot" depends upon this double effect.

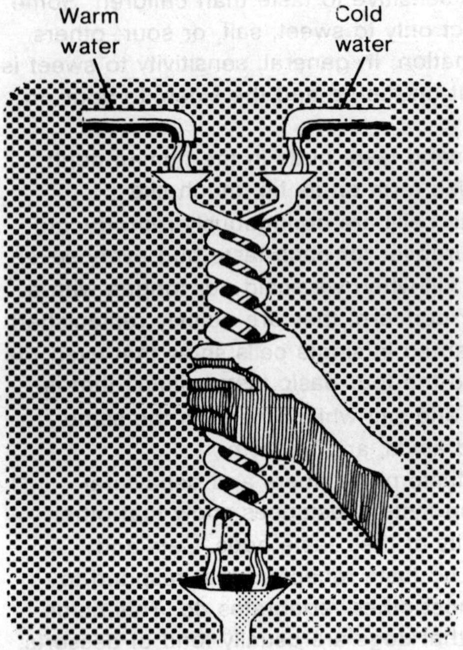

Fig. 4-24 "Hot" as simultaneous stimulation of warm and cold spots

When cold water (0–5°C) is circulated through one coil and warm water (40–44°C) through another intertwining coil, the subject experiences a hot, burning sensation on grasping the coils. This experiment demonstrates that the sensation of "hot" is produced by the simultaneous stimulation of warm and cold spots in the skin.

Kinesthesis and Equilibratory Senses

Our ordinary vocabulary lacks a word for the sensory system that informs us of the position and movement of parts of the body. In technical language this is *kinesthesis*—the muscle, tendon, and joint sense. Position and movement are detected by sense organs in the joints; sense organs in the muscles and tendons tell us whether a muscle is stretched or contracted and help to adjust muscular tension to the load upon it.

Without kinesthesis we would have great difficulty in maintaining posture, walking, climbing, and in controlling voluntary movements such as reaching, grasping, and manipulating. Whenever we act, we first make somewhat tentative movements and then adjust them according to their environmental effects. If something turns out to be heavier than expected, we brace ourselves and lift with greater effort. If we slip or stumble as we walk, we promptly make corrective movements. The kinesthetic sense gives us a feedback from the environment that keeps telling us how things are going. We take this sense for granted until a foot "goes to sleep" and we realize how strange it is to walk without any information as to the foot's contact with the floor.

Cooperating with kinesthesis are the *equilibratory senses,* which deal with total body position in relation to gravity and with motion of the body as a whole. The relation of bodily parts to one another and to external objects is the responsibility of kinesthesis; the orientation of the body in space is the responsibility of the equilibratory senses.

The sense organs for equilibrium, located in the inner ear, are a series of cavities extending from the cochlea. There are two systems: the *semicircular canals* and the *vestibular sacs.*

The three semicircular canals, each roughly perpendicular to the others, lie in three planes, so that bodily rotation in any one of the planes will have maximum effect on one of the canals and rotation at any angle to the planes will affect more than one. The canals are filled with a fluid that moves when the head rotates and exerts pressure on hair cells similar to those of the organ of Corti. Displacement of these hair cells by the movement of the fluid stimulates a nonauditory branch of the auditory nerve. When rotation is slow and of moderate amount, the chief consequence is information that we are moving. When it is more extreme we experience dizziness and nausea.

The vestibular sacs, between the base of the semicircular canals and the cochlea, provide for our perception of bodily position when the body is at rest. They respond to the tilt or position of the head and do not require rotation to be stimulated. The receptors again are hair cells that protrude into a gelatinous mass containing small crystals called *otoliths* (literally, "ear stones"). The normal pressure of the otoliths on the hair cells gives us the sense of upright position, and any distortion tells us that the head is tilted.

The equilibratory senses also signal accelerated motion in a straight line, but sometimes they produce illusions that distort the true path of motion. These illusions occur in flying, because of changes in speed and the banking and climbing of the plane. For example, when a plane is increasing its speed gradually, a blindfolded subject may feel sure that the plane is climbing; if its speed is decreasing gradually, he may feel equally sure that it is diving. Under conditions of poor visibility a pilot does better to trust his instruments than his equilibratory senses.

Summary

1. All sense experiences have their *thresholds* (both *absolute* and *difference* thresholds). Weber's law expresses the fact that difference thresholds tend to be a constant fraction of the stimulus intensity.
2. Some of the main features of the *visual sense:*
   a. The eye receives light waves by way of the *cornea, pupil, lens* and *retina*. The actual receptors are the *rods* and *cones* of the retina. The cones, concentrated in the *fovea* but scattered throughout the retina, mediate experiences of both black and white and hue (*chromatic* colors). The rods, in the periphery of the eye, mediate experiences only of black and white (the *achromatic* colors). In night vision, only the rods function.
   b. The distinctive roles of the rods and cones can be inferred from *dark adaptation,* in which the cones reach their maximum sensitivity in about five minutes, while the rods continue to become increasingly sensitive for about a half-hour.
   c. The *chromatic colors* can be arranged around a color circle (following the order of wavelengths) with space allowed for the nonspectral purples and reds. When properly spaced, the colors opposite each other are *complementaries.* When complementary colors are mixed as lights (additive mixture), they cancel each other and result in a neutral gray. Although four *psychological primaries* can be identified (red, yellow, green, blue), three *color primaries* (red, green, and blue) are enough to produce the range of hues by additive mixture. The chief dimensions of color are *hue, brightness,* and *saturation,* and can be represented on the color solid.
   d. *Afterimage* and *contrast effects* emphasize the pairing of colors, for the withdrawal of stimulation of one hue usually produces the complementary hue, and the contrast effect is maximum between complementaries.
   e. *Color theories* take these above facts as starting points and attempt to explain them. The Young-Helmholtz theory begins with color mixture; the Hering theory starts with afterimages and contrast. Recent research indicates that both theories are partially correct; color vision may be a

two-stage process involving three kinds of color responses from receptors in the retina that are encoded into two-color, on-off signals by cells further along in the optic system.

3. Some of the facts and principles arising from study of the *auditory sense:*
   a. The chief dimensions of auditory experience are *pitch,* correlated with the *frequency* of vibration of the sound waves that constitute the stimulus, and *loudness,* correlated with the *amplitude* of these waves. The absolute threshold for hearing depends on the frequency of the tone; very low- or very high-pitched tones must be more intense to be heard than tones in the middle range of frequencies.
   b. Most tones are not pure—that is, composed of only a single frequency. Musical instruments may be differentiated by the *timbre* of their tones, a quality that depends on the *overtones* and other impurities differing from one instrument to another. Complex sounds composed of many frequencies not in harmonious relation to one another are called *noise.*
   c. The auditory apparatus consists of the *external ear,* leading by way of the auditory canal to the *eardrum,* giving access to the *middle ear.* The bones of the middle ear transmit the sound waves to the *oval window,* leading to the *inner ear.* The *cochlea* houses the receptors of the inner ear, sensitive hair cells buried in the *basilar membrane.* Wave motion in the fluid of the inner ear agitates these hair cells, which in turn activate the auditory nerve.
   d. Theories attempting to give a physiological explanation of pitch are the *place theory,* which emphasizes the place on the basilar membrane where a particular frequency produces its maximum effect, and the *frequency theory,* which assumes that pitch is determined by the frequency of impulses traveling up the auditory nerve. Evidence indicates that the place theory applies to high frequencies, while synchronous discharge is important for the lower frequencies.
4. The other senses, important as they are, do not enter as much into man's symbolic behavior, so they are thought of as "lower senses." They include *smell, taste,* the four *skin sensations* (touch, pain, warm, cold), *kinesthesis* (muscle, tendon, and joint sense), and the *equilibratory senses.*

Further Reading

For a general introduction to the various senses, see Lindsay and Norman, *Human information processing* (1972). Also see Rock, *An introduction to perception* (1975); Haber and Hershenson, *The psychology of visual perception* (1973); and Cornsweet, *Visual perception* (1970). *Experimental psychology* (3rd ed., 1971), edited by Kling and Riggs, is a useful reference book with a number of chapters on sensory psychology. The multiple volume *Handbook of perception* (1974), edited by Carterette and Friedman, covers all aspects of perception.

A useful paperback is *Visual and auditory perception* (1973) by Murch. *Eye and brain* (1966) by Gregory, also in paperback, provides a delightful introduction to visual perception.

For mathematical theories of sensory psychology see Green and Swets, *Signal detection theory and psychophysics* (1966), and Krantz, Atkinson, Luce, and Suppes, *Contemporary developments in mathematical psychology* (1974).

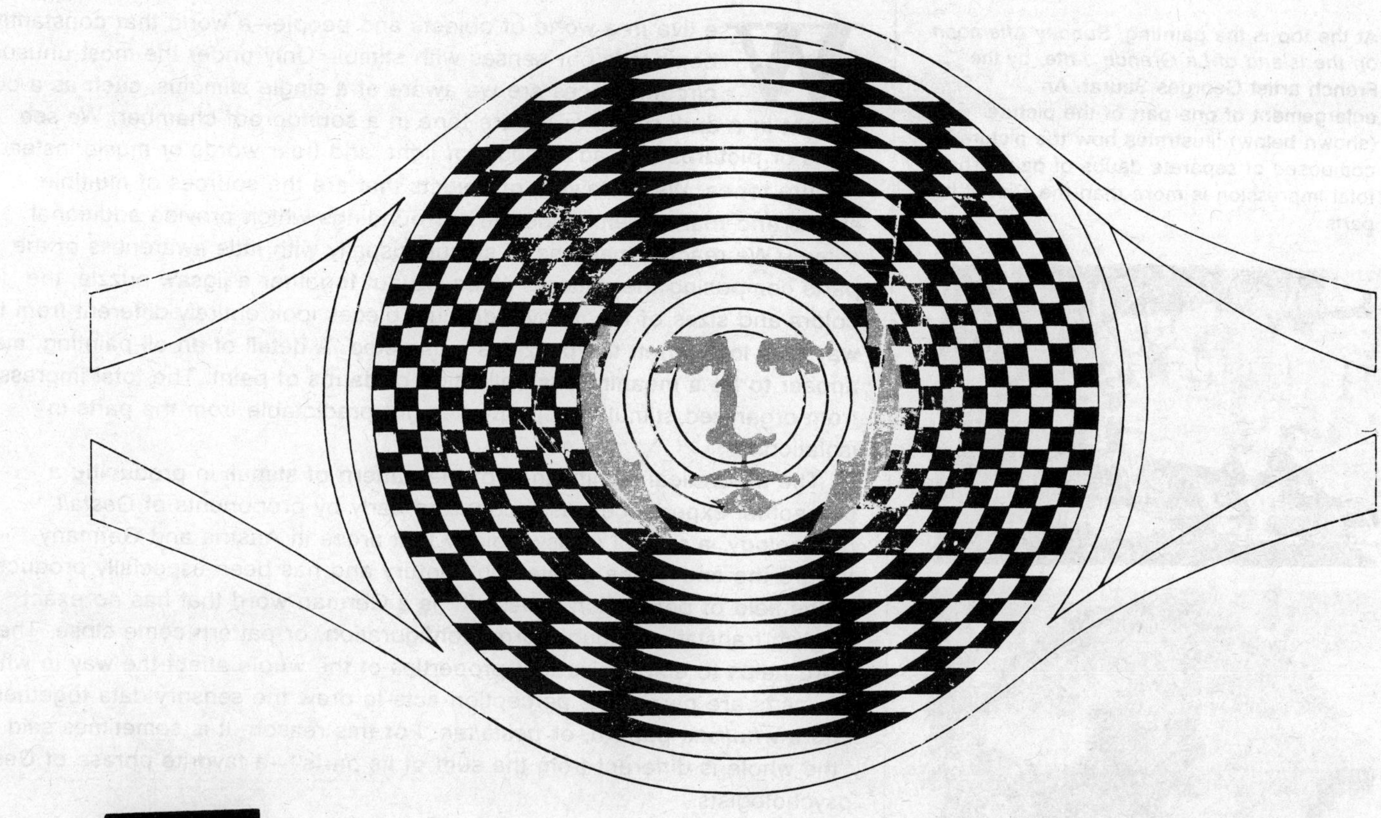

5 perception

At the top is the painting, *Sunday Afternoon on the Island of La Grande Jatte,* by the French artist Georges Seurat. An enlargement of one part of the picture (shown below) illustrates how the picture is composed of separate daubs of paint. The total impression is more than the sum of its parts

We live in a world of objects and people—a world that constantly bombards our senses with stimuli. Only under the most unusual circumstances are we aware of a single stimulus, such as a point of light in a dark room, or a pure tone in a soundproof chamber. We see signs or pictures instead of spots of light, and hear words or music instead of pure tones. We are aware of objects that are the sources of multiple stimuli and that are embedded in surroundings which provide additional stimuli. We react to patterns of stimuli, usually with little awareness of the parts composing the pattern. When we put together a jigsaw puzzle, the colors and sizes of the many individual pieces look entirely different from the way they look when the puzzle is completed. A detail of an oil painting, may appear to be a meaningless collection of daubs of paint. The total impression from organized stimuli has properties not predictable from the parts in isolation.

The theoretical significance of the pattern of stimuli in producing a perceptual experience was recognized early by proponents of *Gestalt psychology,* a school of psychology that arose in Austria and Germany toward the end of the nineteenth century and has been especially productive in the field of perception. "Gestalt" is a German word that has no exact English translation though form, configuration, or pattern come close. The word helps to emphasize that properties of the whole affect the way in which the parts are perceived; perception acts to draw the sensory data together into a *wholistic* pattern, or *gestalten.* For this reason, it is sometimes said that "the whole is different from the sum of its parts"—a favorite phrase of Gestalt psychologists.

The perception of objects and events takes place within a framework of space and time. Vision and audition provide the most complex patterns of these perceptual experiences. Vision is our preferred spatial sense, giving us variegated patterns of form and color in three dimensions, but it is also a good time sense because we see succession, movement, and change. Audition is a spatial sense too; we can be aware simultaneously of many sounds coming from different locations. But spatial patterns in audition are much more limited than those of vision; it is primarily a time sense, for its main patterns are those of succession, change, and rhythm. Because of vision's preeminence as a spatial sense, most of our discussion of perception will focus on visual processes. Of course many perceptual experiences depend on the operation of several senses at once; then the prominence of one sense over another becomes a matter for study.

Object Perception and Perceptual Constancies

If you look around the room and ask yourself what you see, your answer is likely to be, "a room full of objects" or "a room full of people and objects." You may pick out specific people or objects instead of making such a general statement, but you are not likely to report that you see a mosaic of light and shadow. Perception is oriented toward *things* rather than toward the *sensory features* that describe them. Detached sensory features ("blueness" "squareness" or "softness") can be perceived, but they are usually perceived as the qualities of objects. You are aware of the blue flowers or the square box or the soft pillow—not "blueness" "squareness" or "softness."

Our perceptual experiences are not isolated; they build a world of identifiable things. Objects endure, so that you meet the same object over and over again. When you turn your head away, you think of objects as remaining where you saw them. A well-known object is perceived as permanent and stable regardless of the illumination on it, the position from which it is viewed, or the distance at which it appears. The tendency to see the color of a familiar object as the same, regardless of the actual light conditions, is called *color constancy.* The tendency to see an object's shape as unchanging regardless of the viewing angle is called *shape constancy.* The tendency to see an object as the same size regardless of distance is called *size constancy.* Finally, the fact that an object appears to retain its "same" position, even as we move about, is known as *location constancy.* The word "constancy" is an exaggeration, but it dramatizes our relatively stable perception of objects.

Color Constancy

Familiar objects appear to retain their color under a variety of lighting conditions—even colored light—provided there are sufficient contrasts and shadows. The owner of a blue car sees it as blue whether looking at it in bright sunlight, in dim illumination, or under a yellow street light. He is relying on his memory of the car's color, which is one factor contributing to color constancy. Information about the nature of the illumination and the color of surrounding objects are also clues to color constancy. When these clues are eliminated, color constancy diminishes or disappears. If you look at a ripe tomato through a narrow tube so that you do not know the nature of the object or the source and kind of illumination, the tomato will appear to be blue or brown or any of a number of other colors, depending on the wavelength of the light being reflected from it. Without color constancy clues we see the color of objects according to the wavelength of light being reflected to the eye.

Shape and Size Constancy

When a door swings open toward us, its shape as projected on the retina goes through a series of distortions. The door's rectangular shape becomes a trapezoid, with the edge toward us looking wider than the hinged edge; then the trapezoid grows thinner, until all that is projected on the retina is a vertical line the thickness of the door. We can readily distinguish these changes, but the psychological experience is an unchanging door swinging on its hinges. The fact that the door does not seem to change its shape is an example of *shape constancy.* We see the top of a glass bottle as "circular" whether we view it from the side or from the top.

Size constancy refers to the fact that as an object is moved farther away we tend to see it as more or less invariant in size. Hold a quarter a foot in front of your eyes and then move it out to arm's length. Does it appear to get smaller? Not noticeably so. Yet the retinal image of the quarter 12 inches away is half the size of the image of the quarter when it is 24 inches from the eye (see Figure 5-1). It certainly does not appear to reduce to half its size as we move it to arm's length.

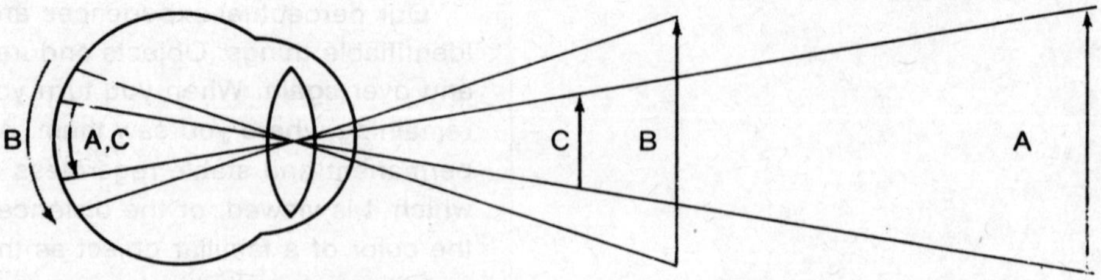

Fig. 5-1 Object size and retinal image

This figure illustrates the geometric relationship between the physical size of an object and the size of its retinal projection. Arrow A and arrow B represent objects of the same size, but one is twice as far from the eye's lens as the other. As a result the image projected on the retina by A is approximately half as large as that projected by B. The object represented by arrow C is smaller than A but closer to the eye; note that arrows A and C produce the same-size retinal image.

When we look at a distant object, we can judge its size in one of three ways:

1. *Perspective size.* We might judge it according to the geometry of perspective, seeing it as smaller the farther away it is. This size would correspond to the size of the image on the retina.
2. *Object size.* We might judge an object by its true size and hence see it as remaining constant in size regardless of its distance.
3. *Compromise between perspective size and object size.* We might compromise and see the object as smaller at a distance, but not as much smaller as the geometry of perspective indicates.

The last of the three alternatives is usually correct. Our size perceptions represent compromises between perspective size and object size. How well size constancy operates depends upon the presence of distance cues and *upon our familiarity with the object.* The more information available about the distance of the object, the more the perceived size approaches the actual size. As distance cues are eliminated, the perceived size approaches the size of the retinal image, unless the object is familiar. Familiarity with an object enables us to judge its appropriate size, even in the absence of depth cues.

Size constancy develops largely as the result of experience. Although research indicates that infants as young as eight weeks possess some degree of size constancy for objects 3–9 feet away (Bower, 1966), size constancy for more distant objects appears to develop with increasing age. Figure 5-2 shows the results of an experiment comparing the performance of eight year olds and adults in judging the size of objects at different distances. At 10 feet both children and adults show close to perfect size constancy; that is, their judgment of size agrees with the physical size of the object. At increasing distances, the children show increasingly less size constancy (their size estimates are closely related to the size of the retinal image), while the adults' judgments of size remain quite accurate.

These results are consistent with observations of the behavior of young children. A three year old watching cars on a roadway below a lookout point will see the cars as miniatures and often insist that they cannot be full size. He may even beg for them as toys. His size constancy is not yet developed for this new viewing angle. Adult size constancy commonly breaks down also when objects are viewed from a height, but the adult can make an intellectual correction that the young child cannot.

The effect of limited experience on the development of size constancy is further illustrated by an incident concerning a pygmy who was taken for the first time from his home in the forest into open country. When he spotted a herd of buffalo grazing several miles away the pygmy asked what kind of "insects" they were. He refused to accept the fact that they were buffalo, and actually larger in size than the forest buffalo with which he was familiar. As

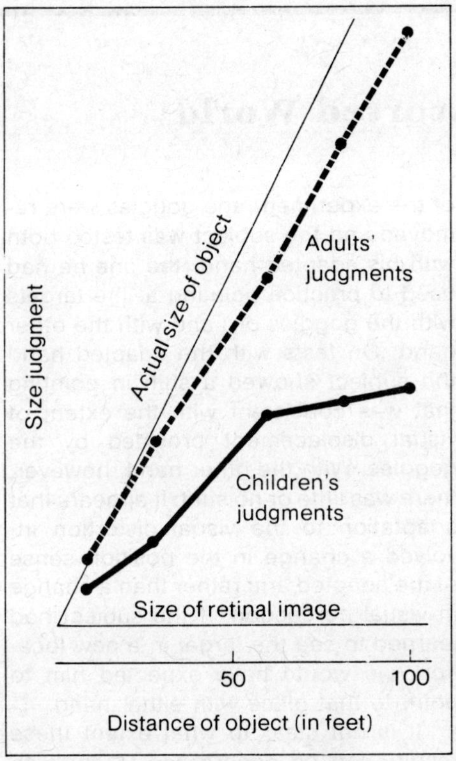

Fig. 5-2 Size perception and age

Adults and eight-year-old children viewed objects at distances ranging from 10 to 100 feet. The physical sizes of the objects were adjusted at the various distances so that the image projected on the retina was always the same size. The horizontal line indicates the size of the retinal image (which is constant for all distances), and the diagonal line the size of the physical object (which increases with distance). Note that adults make fairly accurate size judgments no matter how distant the object. The judgments of children, however, appear to be increasingly influenced by the size of the retinal image as the object is placed farther away. (Data from Zeigler and Leibowitz, 1957)

the car in which he was traveling approached the animals, the pygmy became alarmed because the animals appeared to be growing in size; he suspected that he was the victim of some sort of magic. Later he perceived a boat with several men in it sailing some distance from the shore of a lake as a scrap of wood floating on the water. Just as the small child's limited experience with viewing objects from a great height causes him to err in his perceptions, the pygmy's inexperience with distance viewing on a horizontal plane created similar misperceptions (Turnbull, 1961).

Location Constancy

Our world has perceptual stability for us because we perceive objects as enduring, as being the same as when we last looked. We also perceive these objects in a setting that remains essentially fixed, despite the fact that a myriad of changing impressions strike the retina as we move about. We take the stability of our perceptual world for granted, but unusual conditions demonstrate that it too depends upon past experience.

The role of learning in location constancy can be shown by experiments that use special glasses to rearrange the visual environment. In a classic study conducted more than 75 years ago, Stratton fitted himself with lenses that not only inverted the visual field so that he saw the world upside-down, but also reversed it so that objects perceived on the left were actually on the right and vice versa. Stratton reports that at first the world seemed to lose its stability:

> When I moved my head or body so that my sight swept over the scene, the movement was not felt to be solely in the observer, as in normal vision, but was referred both to the observer and to objects beyond . . . I did not feel as if I were visually ranging over a set of motionless objects, but the whole field of things swept and swung before my eyes (Stratton, 1897, p. 342).

After a few days this swinging or swirling sensation decreased, indicating some restoration of location constancy. Another sign of regained location constancy was that a fire was again heard to crackle in the fireplace where it was seen, a harmony of location that was at first lost because only the eyes, and not the ears, were perceiving in reverse. Although the distortion provided by the lenses made even the simplest task extremely difficult and laborious, Stratton found that as the experiment progressed he became more skillful in dealing with his mixed-up perceptual world. He bumped into objects less frequently and was able to perform such tasks as washing and eating, which initially had been very difficult. When the glasses were removed some adjustment was required before he regained his old visual-motor habits.

Experiments similar to Stratton's have been repeated with comparable results (Snyder and Pronko, 1952; Kohler, 1962). Human subjects show a remarkable ability to adjust to a visually rearranged world.

Organization and Perception

The perceptual constancies imply organization within perception. In a more analytical vein, let us identify some principles of perception that help to explain how objects and events are organized and perceived.

CRITICAL DISCUSSION

Factors in Adjusting to a Visually Distorted World

How does a person adjust when wearing distorting lenses? Does he learn to *see* the world differently? Or do his perceptions remain unchanged while he learns to *respond* differently to them?

An experiment by Rock and Harris (1967) helps answer these questions. The subject was asked to point under a table to one of five targets at the other end of the table (Figure 5-3). During the first part of the experiment, the glass surface of the table was covered with a black cloth so that the subject could see the targets but not his hand beneath the glass. Even so, he was able to point to the targets accurately. These data provided a baseline with which to compare later responses. During the next phase, the subject wore prism goggles that displaced his vision so that objects appeared to be four inches to the right of their actual location. The cloth was removed, and he practiced pointing to the center target. At first the prisms caused him to miss the target, but he quickly became quite accurate. In the third part of the experiment, the goggles were removed and the subject was tested both with his adapted hand (the one he had used to practice pointing at the targets with the goggles on) and with the other hand. On tests with the adapted hand the subject showed a shift in pointing that was consistent with the extent of visual displacement provided by the goggles. With the other hand, however, there was little or no shift. It appears that adaptation to the visual distortion involved a change in the position sense of the adapted arm rather than a change in visual perception. If the subject had learned to *see* the target in a new location, we would have expected him to point to that place with either hand.

Fig. 5-3 Visual displacement
An apparatus for testing displaced vision. There are five targets, and the goggles are selected so that the visual field is displaced to the right by about four inches (the distance between adjacent targets). A cover can be placed over the table top when desired, to prevent the subject from seeing where he is pointing. The biteboard ensures that the head remains steady throughout the experiment. The experimenter instructs the subject to point to targets one at a time and then measures the discrepancy between where the finger is pointing and the target. (After Rock and Harris, 1967)

It is not clear to what extent these results can be generalized to apply to Stratton's experiments, which involved more radical distortion of the visual scene and in which the subject could move about more freely than in the laboratory situation. Nevertheless, it seems likely that the adaptation that occurred as Stratton learned to coordinate his movements with the rearranged visual world was in part due to a change in the position sense of his limbs.

Figure and Ground

Geometrical patterns are always seen as figures against a background and thus appear to be like objects, with contours and boundaries. *Figure-ground* organization is basic to stimulus patterning. Patterns do not have to contain identifiable objects to be structured as figure and ground. Patterns of black and white and many wallpaper designs are perceived as figure-ground relationships, and very often figure and ground are reversible. In Figure 5-4 note that the part that is seen as *figure* seems more solid and well defined and tends to appear slightly in front of the background, even though you know it is printed on the surface of the page. You seem to look through the spaces in and around the figure to a uniform background behind, whether the background is in white (or a light color) or black (or a dark color). Figures 5-5, 5-6 and 5-7 show somewhat different kinds of reversible figure-ground effects.

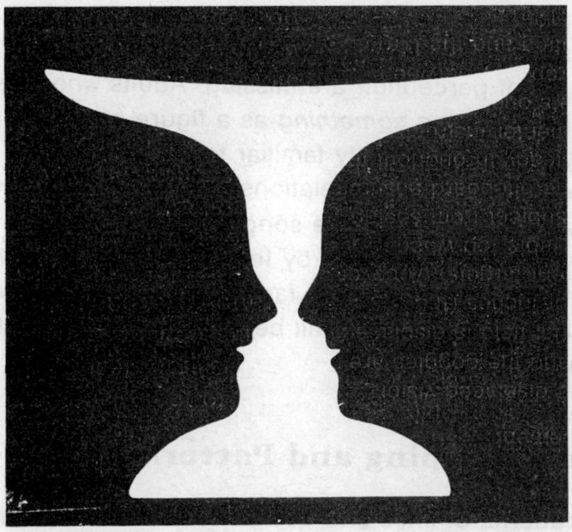

Fig. 5-4 Reversible figure and ground

Reversible goblet is a favorite demonstration of a figure-ground reversal. Note that either the light portion or the dark portion can be perceived as a figure against a background.

Fig. 5-5 Artistic use of reversible figure and ground

Circle Limit IV (Heaven and Hell), a woodcut by M. C. Escher. The angels and devils alternate but neither seems to dominate the other.

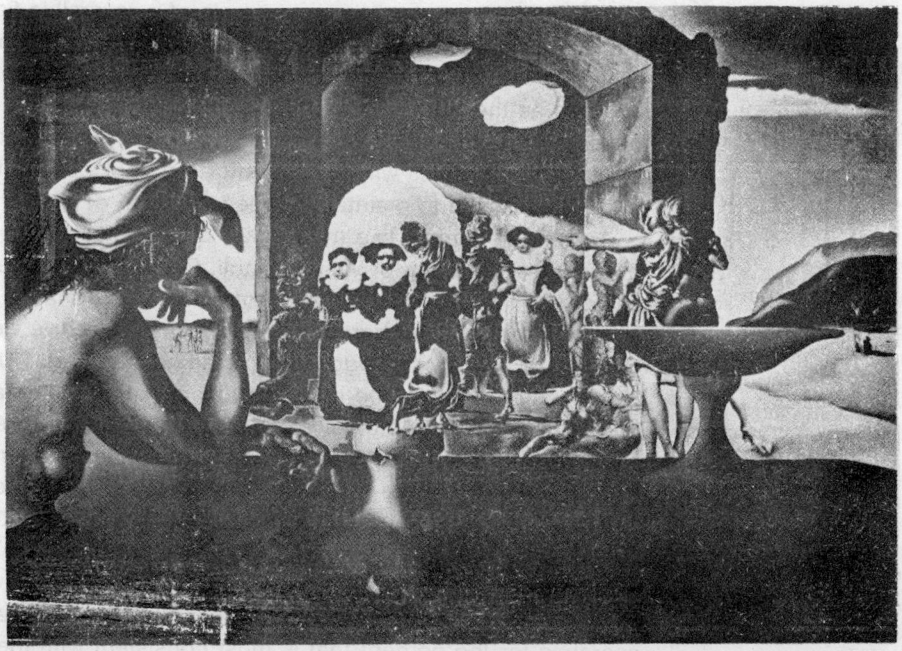

Fig. 5-6 The Slave Market with Disappearing Bust of Voltaire by Salvador Dali.

In the center of this painting is a reversible figure. Two nuns standing in an archway reverse to form a bust of Voltaire.

Fig. 5-7 Ambiguous figure-ground effects

An ambiguous drawing that can be seen either as an attractive young woman or as an old hag.

Studies of what people blind from birth see when their sight is restored through surgery show that the figure-ground organization is present even when other features of perception are missing. Adults who see for the first time have no difficulty seeing *something* as a figure on a background, although they are unable to identify familiar forms by sight.

We can perceive figure-ground relationships through senses other than vision. For example, we may hear the song of a bird against a background of outdoor noises or the melody played by the violin against the harmonies of the rest of the orchestra. Some of the factors that determine what is perceived as figure against ground will be considered later in the discussion of selective attention.

Perceptual Grouping and Patterning

Even simple patterns of lines and dots fall into ordered relationships when we look at them. In the top part of Figure 5-8 we tend to see three *pairs* of lines, with an *extra* line at the right. But notice that we could have seen three pairs beginning at the right with an extra line at the left. The slight modification shown in the lower part of the figure causes us to do just that. This tendency to *structure* what we see is very compelling; what we see in figures seems to be forced on us by the patterns of stimulation. The properties of wholes affect the ways in which parts are perceived. For that reason we may say—following the lead of Gestalt psychology—that the whole is different from the sum of its parts.

The proximity of the lines that appear to be in pairs leads us to see three pairs and an extra line at the right.

The same lines as above, but with extensions, lead to the opposite pairing: three broken squares and an extra line at the left.

Fig. 5-8 Patterning and perceptual structuring

Perceptual Hypotheses

Figure 5-9 shows a classic example of a reversible figure, the Necker cube. Study the figure and you will see that your perception of it changes. While looking at the cube you will find that the tinted surface sometimes appears as the front of the figure and sometimes as the back. Once you have observed the cube change perspective, it will jump back and forth between the two perspectives without any effort on your part. In fact you will probably find it impossible to maintain a steady fixation of only one aspect.

Reversible figures like the Necker cube indicate that our perceptions are not a static mirroring of visual stimuli. Perceiving can be thought of as a search for the best interpretation of sensory information, based on our knowledge of object characteristics. From a cognitive viewpoint, a perceived object is a *hypothesis* suggested by the sensory data. The pattern of the Necker cube contains no clue as to which of two alternative hypotheses is correct, so the perceptual system entertains first one then the other hypothesis and never settles on an answer. The problem arises because the Necker cube is a three-dimensional object represented on a two-dimensional surface. If we were to see it in three-dimensional form, there would be many cues to tell us which hypothesis to choose (Gregory, 1970).

The notion of *hypothesis testing* emphasizes the active nature of perception. The perceptual system does not passively sense inputs, but searches for the percept that is most consistent with the sensory data. In most situations there is only one reasonable interpretation of the sensory data, and the search for the correct percept proceeds so quickly and automatically that we are unaware of it. Only under unusual conditions, as

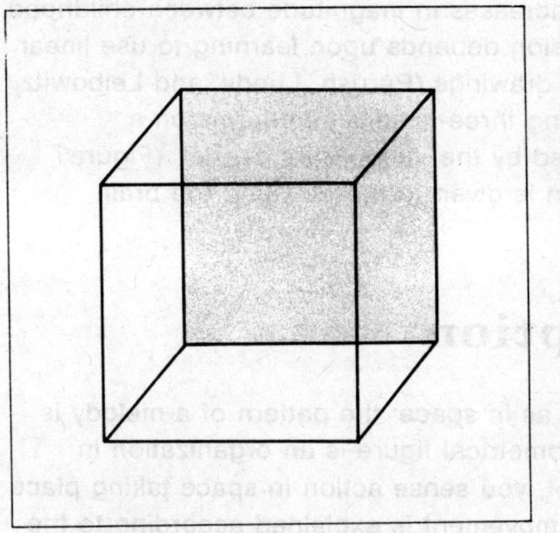

Fig. 5-9 Necker cube
An illusion devised in 1832 by the Swiss naturalist L. A. Necker. Note that the tinted surface can appear as either the front or the rear surface of a transparent cube.

when viewing ambiguous figures, does the hypothesis-testing nature of perception become apparent.

Visual Illusions

Sometimes we select a perceptual hypothesis that is actually incorrect; in this case we experience an illusion. Visual illusions have long intrigued psychologists; by studying stimulus situations where perceptions are misleading, they hoped to gain information about how perception works.

Geometrical illusions have been studied for many years, but their explanations are still not fully agreed upon. Some illusions are based on relative size in contrast with surroundings (Figure 5-10A). Others may be understood if we suppose the figures to be projected in the third dimension (Figure 5-10, B through D). If the lines in B and C were drawn on the surface of a solid double cone, or represented by a system of wires meeting at the horizon, they would have to be curved in order to be parallel as viewed. Because we tend to view these figures as though they were perspective drawings, we see the parallel lines as bent. In this case our tendency to "constancy" misleads us. Similarly, the backgrounds in illusions D and E can be viewed as three-dimensional (either concave or convex) thereby distorting the square and circle superimposed on them.

Figure 5-10F, the Ponzo illusion, can be better understood if we look at the photograph in Figure 5-11. The illusion can be thought of as a flat projection of three-dimensional space, with the vertical lines converging in the distance, as in the picture of the railroad tracks. We know from experience that the distant railroad ties are the same size as the nearest ones, even though the retinal image they give is much smaller. If real objects were lying between the tracks, the upper rectangle in the picture would be perceived as more distant. Because the brain tries to compensate for the expected shrinkage of images with distance (even though in this case there is no shrinkage for which to compensate), we see the upper rectangle as larger. Such an illusion is an inevitable result of size constancy mechanisms.

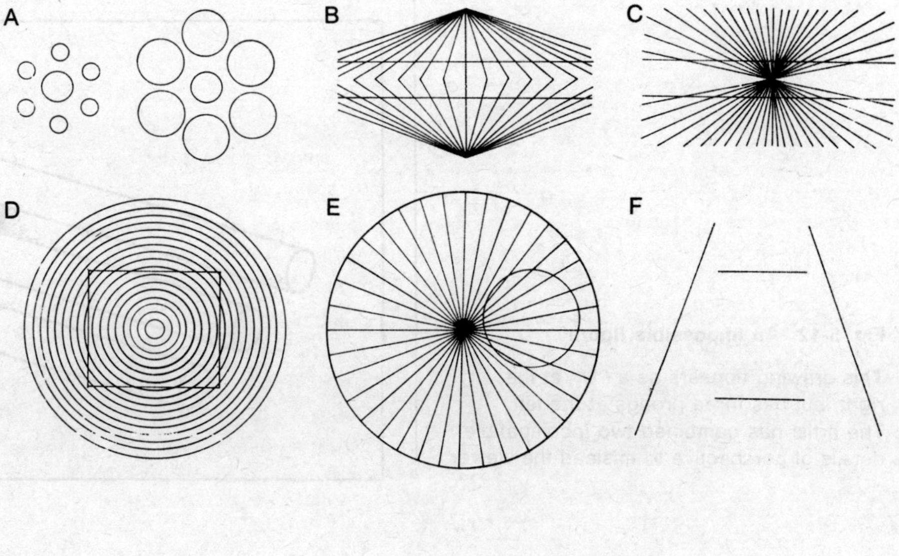

Fig. 5-10

A. Illusion based on relative size. The center circles are the same size, but the one to the left looks larger. **B,C,D,E. Illusions based on intersecting lines.** The horizontal lines in B and C are parallel. The inscribed figures in D and E are perfectly symmetrical. **F. Ponzo illusion.** The two horizontal lines are the same length, but the upper one appears longer.

Fig. 5-11 An illusion involving perspective

The two rectangles superimposed on the photograph are precisely the same size. However, because we know that the railroad ties are all the same length, the rectangle that is farthest away is unconsciously enlarged. In fact, if the rectangles were real objects lying between the tracks, we would correctly judge the more distant one to be larger.

The fact that the Ponzo illusion increases in magnitude between childhood and adulthood suggests that the illusion depends upon learning to use linear perspective cues in two-dimensional drawings (Parrish, Lundy, and Leibowitz, 1968). Some of the problems of seeing three-dimensional forms on a two-dimensional surface are illustrated by the "impossible figure" (Figure 5-12). Incompatible depth information is given to the eye, and the brain cannot decide how to interpret it.

Movement Perception

Events are organized in time as well as in space; the pattern of a melody is an organization in time, just as a geometrical figure is an organization in space. When you perceive movement, you sense action in space taking place over time. Usually the perception of movement is explained according to the stimulation of successive parts of the sensory surface. Trace a path on the skin and movement is felt as successive sensory receptors are stimulated. It seems reasonable to infer that a similar stimulation takes place on the retina. When an image moves across our line of vision it produces a pattern of successive stimulation of the rods and cones, and we perceive movement. The explanation is not this simple, however. It is possible for a pattern of successive stimulation to occur on the retina without any perception of motion. When you turn your head to look around the room, images move across the retina, yet objects in the room appear stationary. You are well aware that it is your head that is moving and not the room. The same sensation occurs when you hold your head steady and move your eyes; objects in the room do not appear to move. Some higher brain process apparently integrates the information from the retinal stimulation and the kinesthetic information from your head, neck, and eye muscles to tell you that your head or eyes are moving, not the room.

Apparent Motion

It is also possible to perceive motion without a successive pattern of stimulation. We will now consider some examples of this kind of *apparent motion.*

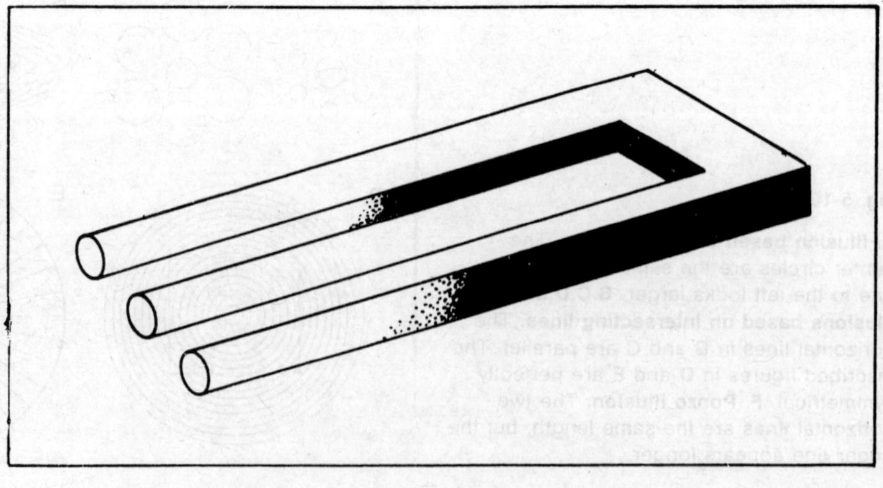

Fig. 5-12 An impossible figure

This drawing appears as a "U" at the right, but has three prongs at the left. The artist has combined two incompatible details of perspective to mislead the viewer.

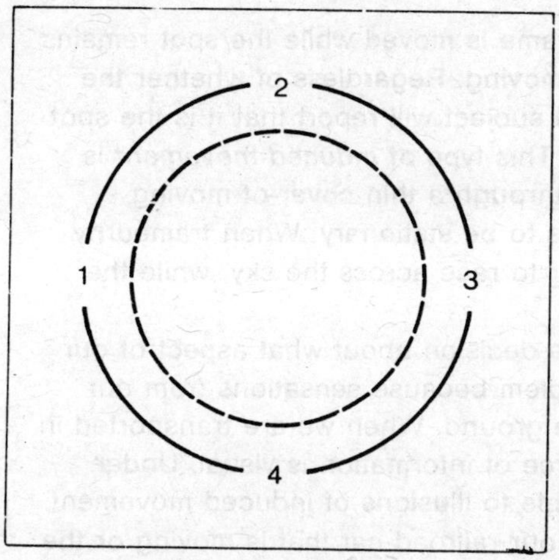

Fig. 5-13 The phi phenomenon

In a dark room if one of these four lights blinks on and off, followed shortly by another, there is the illusion of a single light moving from the first position to the second. When all four lights flash on and off in rapid sequence, it appears that a single light is traveling in a circle, but the perceived size of the circle is smaller (indicated by the dashed lines) than would be the case if the lights were actually rotating.

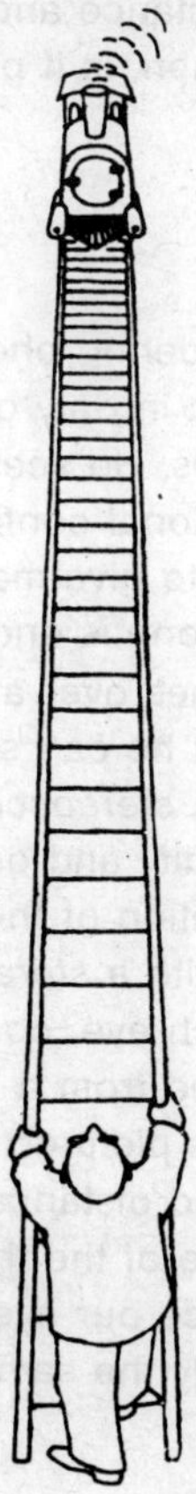

AUTOKINETIC EFFECT. If you stare for a few seconds at a single spot of light in a completely dark room, the light will appear to move about in an erratic manner—sometimes oscillating back and forth, sometimes swooping off in one direction. This apparent movement of a stationary light, known as the *autokinetic effect,* has been the subject of much experimentation, but there is still no certain explanation. What is clear though is that the autokinetic effect occurs only in a visually impoverished environment where there is no frame of reference against which to determine that the light spot is stationary. When other lights are introduced or the room is lightened, the effect disappears. Pilots during night flights are particularly susceptible to the autokinetic phenomenon; they sometimes line up a distant beacon with the edge of a windshield or some other frame of reference to minimize the effect.

STROBOSCOPIC MOTION. Another kind of apparent motion, familiar to us as the basis for films, is known as *stroboscopic motion.* This illusion of motion is created when separated stimuli, not in motion, are presented in succession. Each frame of a film is slightly different from the preceding one, but if the frames are presented rapidly enough, the pictures blend into smooth motion.

A simpler form of stroboscopic motion, known as the *phi phenomenon,* has been studied extensively in the laboratory. One arrangement is diagramed in Figure 5-13. The four lights can be turned on and off in any order. When one light blinks on and then off, followed shortly by another, there is the illusion of a single light moving from the position of the first to the position of the second, and so on. The apparent movement is seen as occurring through the empty space between the two lights. When the four lights of Figure 5-13 flash on and off in proper sequence, you see a rotating circle, but the apparent diameter of the circle is less than that of a circle that would actually pass through the four lights. Whatever "attracts" the light to the position of the next light operates also to "attract" it toward the center of the circle, thereby making the circle smaller. The two tendencies result in the compromise that is seen as a circle too small to pass through the actual position of the lights. Even though the phi phenomenon is illusory, it tends to preserve the perceptual structure that would be possible in real motion. For example, in Figure 5-14A the perceived motion is through an arc but in the plane of the paper; in Figure 5-14B the motion is seen in the third dimension, the figure turning over as it moves across.

Real Motion

These examples of apparent motion demonstrate that the perception of motion does not depend *solely* on real physical movement of stimuli in the environment. We can see apparent motion when there is no real motion at all. The perception of real motion is even more complex; it depends upon relations between objects within the visual field. Whenever there is movement, the perceptual system must decide what is moving and what is stationary with respect to some frame of reference.

Experiments have shown that when the only information we have about movement is visual, we tend to assume that large objects are stationary and smaller objects are moving. If a subject views a spot of light within a frame or against a screen background and the frame is moved while the spot remains stationary, he will perceive the spot as moving. Regardless of whether the spot or the frame is actually moved, the subject will report that it is the spot that is moving against the background. This type of *induced movement* is experienced when the moon is viewed through a thin cover of moving clouds. In a clear sky the moon appears to be stationary. When framed by the moving clouds the moon will appear to race across the sky, while the clouds appear stationary.

When we are walking or running, the decision about what aspect of our surroundings is moving is less of a problem because sensations from our limbs inform us of our motion along the ground. When we are transported in a car, train, or plane, our principle source of information is visual. Under these conditions, we are more susceptible to illusions of induced movement. We are not always certain whether it is our railroad car that is moving or the one on the next track. Illusions of this kind are so frequent in air travel (particularly during night flights when it is difficult to establish a frame of reference) that pilots tend to trust their instruments rather than their perceptions. An even greater problem is faced by astronauts attempting to land a spacecraft on the moon; in the unfamiliar conditions of space the size, distance, and velocity of objects may be misjudged when evaluated on the basis of man's perceptual experiences on earth.

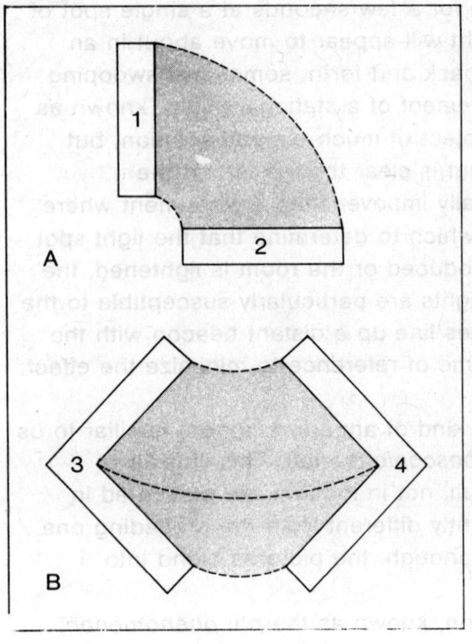

Fig. 5-14 Special cases of phi movement.

If a light is flashed on and off behind opening 1 in a screen and a moment later behind opening 2, then it appears as though a single bar of light is moving in an arc between the two positions in the plane of the paper. If a light is flashed on and off behind opening 3 and an instant later behind 4, then the motion is seen in the third dimension as if the figure were flipping over (like turning a page in a book) as it moves across.

Depth Perception

Our study of perception would be incomplete without considering the problems of perceiving the third dimension—that is, distance and depth. The retina is essentially a two-dimensional surface. How, then, is it possible to perceive things as filling a space of three dimensions?

Binocular Cues to Depth

Many of the facts of vision can be treated by considering phenomena that can be registered with one eye only. A man with vision in only one eye has most of the visual experiences of a man using two eyes. He sees colors, forms, and space relationships, including third-dimensional configurations. We might suppose that two eyes have evolved merely to give man a "spare" in case of injury, just as he has two kidneys although one is enough.

A man with vision in both eyes does have advantages over a man with vision in one eye: his total visual field is larger, so that he can see more at once, and he has the benefit of stereoscopic vision. In *stereoscopic vision* the two eyes cooperate to yield the experience of solidity and distance. That the experience does indeed depend upon the cooperation of the two eyes is clear enough from the effects that can be produced with a *stereoscope.* In this device two flat pictures, presented one before each eye, combine to yield an experience of depth very different from that received from a single flat picture. The depth appears real, as though the objects pictured were exactly set up on a stage or in their true relations of depth and distance.

Stereoscopic experience differs from the experience of the third dimension in single flat pictures because of *retinal disparity.*[1] Since our eyes are separated in our head, the left eye does not get exactly the same view as the

[1] Sometimes referred to as *binocular disparity.*

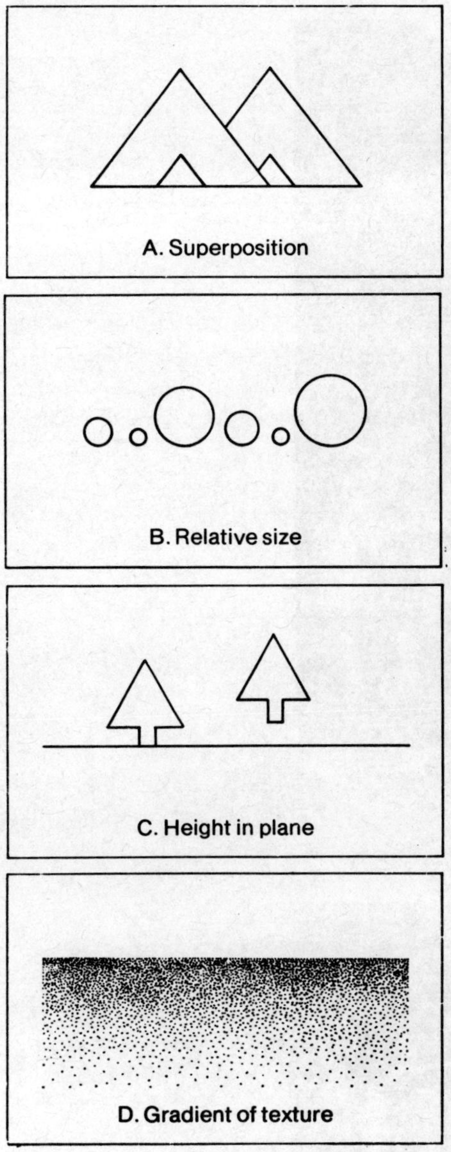

Fig. 5-15 Visual distance perception

Several types of cues used in the perception of distance are shown here.

right eye; the stereoscopic effect results from the combination of these slightly different pictures in one view. You can easily demonstrate retinal disparity for yourself. With one eye closed hold a pencil about a foot in front of you and line it up with some vertical edge on the opposite wall. Open that eye and close the other. The pencil will appear to have moved a considerable distance from its original alignment. If you line up the pencil with both eyes open and then close each eye alternately, you can determine which is your dominant eye; that is, if the pencil shifts when you close the right eye, your right eye is dominant (which is usually the case with right-handed individuals).

The facts of stereoscopic vision are clear enough, but just how the process works is not so clear. Because of the way in which the nerve fibers from the eyes are separated in passing to the brain (see Figure 4-7), the combination cannot take place in the eyes. Information from the two eyes must somehow be combined in the brain, probably at the level of the visual cortex (Barlow, 1972).

Monocular Cues to Depth

Although having two eyes helps us to perceive depth and distance, we are by no means restricted to binocular effects for this perception. Closing one eye causes the loss of some precision, but there is much left to go on. An artist is able to give depth to his picture because he can make use of the many *monocular cues* that tell us the distance of objects.

Figure 5-15 illustrates four types of cues that are used in the perception of depth. If one object appears to cut off the view of another, the presumption is strong that the first object is nearer (Figure 5-15A). If there is an array of like objects of different sizes then the smaller ones are perceived as being in the distance. Even a series of scattered circles of different sizes may be viewed as spheres of the same size at varying distances (Figure 5-15B). Another hint of perspective is height in the horizontal plane. As we look along a flat plane, objects farther away appear to be higher, so that we can create the impression of depth for objects of the same size by placing them at different heights (Figure 5-15C). Even for irregular surfaces, such as a rocky desert or the waving surface of the ocean, there is a gradient of texture with distance, so that the "grain" becomes finer as distance becomes greater (Figure 5-15D).

Just as the artist can make a picture appear to have depth, so also can he distort distance cues. The engraving in Figure 5-16 is such an example; the various cues for depth perception have been deliberately misused to produce an absurd figure. Another example is in Figure 5-17 which shows a waterfall continually running uphill.

Visual Coding and Pattern Recognition

Experiments using microelectrodes to record neural activity in the visual cortex have helped explain the complexities of perception. In the typical experiment, a microelectrode is implanted in the visual cortex of a cat or monkey. The microelectrode is extremely small and placed in such a way that recordings can be obtained from a single nerve cell while the animal's eyes

Fig. 5-16 Deliberate misuse of depth cues

Engraving entitled *False Perspective* by William Hogarth (1754). At first glance the picture appears sensible, but closer inspection indicates that the scene could not appear as depicted. Note the many ways in which the artist has misused depth cues to achieve unusual effects.

Fig. 5-17 Paradox of depth

Engraving by the Dutch artist M. C. Escher (*Waterfall*, 1961). The waterfall appears to be running uphill because of the artist's "false use" of depth cues.

are being stimulated by visual forms projected on a screen (see Figure 5-18). Unlike neurons in the retina and optic nerve, most cells in the visual cortex do not respond when the eye is stimulated by large or diffuse spots of light. Instead, these cortical cells are highly specific in terms of the stimuli to which they respond.

Fig. 5-18 Recording cortical activity

A partially anesthetized monkey is placed in a device that holds the head in a fixed position. A moving bar of light, whose direction and speed are varied, is projected on the screen. A microelectrode implanted in the visual cortex of the monkey samples activity from a single neuron, and this activity is amplified and displayed on an oscilloscope.

Feature Detectors

Hubel and Wiesel (1965), pioneers in microelectrode studies of the visual system, have identified two types of cortical neurons that they called *simple* and *complex cells.* Simple cells become active when the eye is exposed to a line stimulus like a bar of light or a straight edge (a straight line boundary between light and dark regions). Whether or not a particular simple cell responds depends on the orientations of the bar of light and its location in the animal's visual field. A bar shown vertically on the screen may activate a given cortical cell, whereas the same cell will fail to respond (but others will respond) if the bar is displaced to one side or moved appreciably out of the vertical. Apparently, some neurons respond only to a particular stimulus with specific orientation and location. A complex cell also responds to a line segment with a particular orientation (for example, vertical) but it responds no matter where in the visual field the line segment appears. Moreover, complex cells respond with sustained firing as the line segment moves across the visual field, so long as it maintains its proper orientation.

From what is now known, it appears that a complex cell receives inputs from a large number of simple cells all with the same field orientation. Thus a complex cell that responds to a vertical bar receives nerve fibers from those simple cells that respond to vertical bars. Each simple cell is activated only if the bar is at a particular location in the receptive field; the complex cell, on the other hand, is activated by any vertical bar no matter where it appears.

Hierarchical Feature Analyzers

This converging of a set of simple cells on one complex cell can be illustrated at a still higher level in the nervous system. Hubel and Wiesel recorded neural activity in the visual cortex by cells they named *hypercomplex cells.* These cells are active only if the stimulus line is in a particular orientation and of a specific length and width. Here again, the hypercomplex cell appears to be connected to an array of complex cells; the excitatory and inhibitory activity of each of the complex cells are such that the hypercomplex cell is activated only if the line segment is of a specific length.

Thus, we see that a stimulus can be coded in a hierarchical manner, with higher centers using the information coded at lower centers. When a straight line of a particular length is moved across the visual field it will activate a succession of simple cells, each responding to the particular orientation and locus of the line. These simple cells then activate a smaller set of complex cells that preserve the orientation information and add information about the movement of the line. Finally, the complex cells converge on a hypercomplex cell that specifies the exact length of the line and preserves information about its orientation and motion.

CRITICAL DISCUSSION

Pattern Recognition Models

If the nervous system has *feature detectors,* then in theory these detectors can be used for pattern recognition. How this might be done is illustrated by a model for recognizing hand-printed letters of the alphabet (Selfridge and Neisser, 1960). The model has been implemented on a computer and used with success in recognizing letters printed by different people and under different conditions. Although we would not claim that the model simulates the actual processes that a human uses in recognizing letters, it is suggestive of how the perceptual system might work.

Recognizing hand-printed letters is not a trivial task when one considers the tremendous variations in width, height, slant, etc., that may occur from one printing to the next (see Figure 5-19). The model assumes that letters can be described in terms of a *feature list,* where the features are much like those discussed above. For example, the letter H consists of two lines that are more vertical than horizontal and one line that is more horizontal than vertical; it also has a concavity (open space) at the top and at the bottom. These features taken together specify the letter H, but any of these features alone would not be enough. For example, A also has two more or less vertical lines, one horizontal line, and a concavity at the bottom; but it does not have a concavity on the top and that feature distinguishes it from H.

A *feature list* is stored in the computer's memory for each letter in the alphabet. When a test letter is presented its features are extracted and compared with each of the feature lists in memory until a match occurs. To illustrate the process we will consider a highly simplified program to distinguish among the letters A, H, V, and Y. With such a small set of letters the pattern recognition process can rely on the presence or absence of just three features: a con-

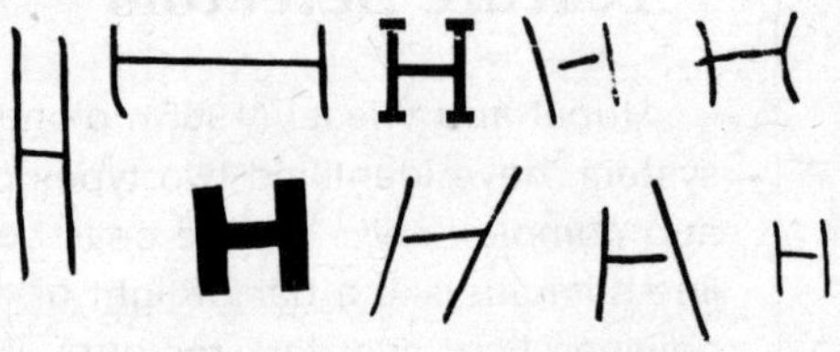

Fig. 5-19 Pattern recognition

An array of stimuli that are dissimilar in many respects, but should all be classified as the letter *H*. The recognition of hand-printed letters is a problem that has received a great deal of attention from psychologists and computer scientists, both for practical and theoretical reasons.

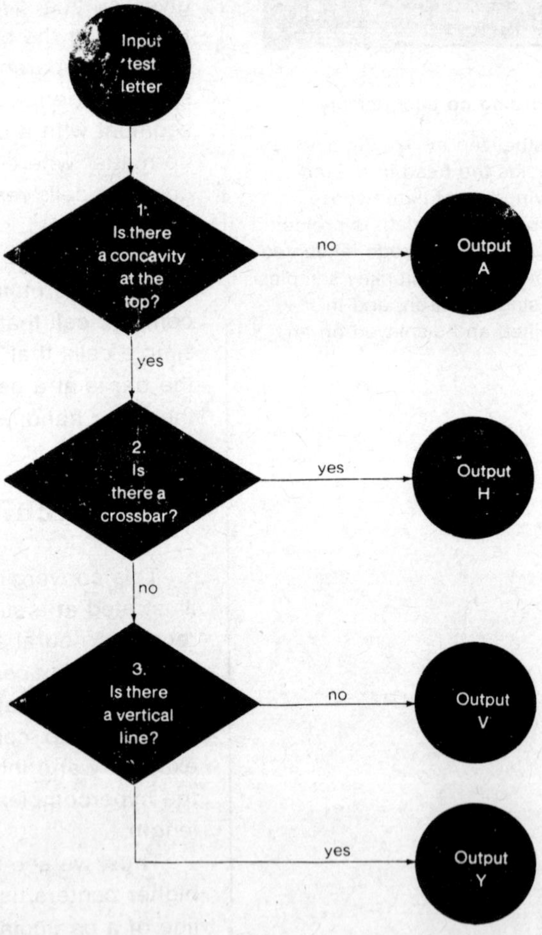

Fig. 5-20 Sorting tree

A pattern recognition program which employs three test features to categorize the hand-printed letters A, H, V, and Y. The tests are applied in order, with each outcome determining the next step. Each diamond indicates a decision point in the process that requires a yes or no answer.

cavity at the top of the letter, a cross bar, and a vertical bar. When a test letter is presented the computer first asks: "Is there a concavity at the top?" If the answer is no then the test letter is classified as an A. If yes, the computer would next ask: "Is there a cross bar?" If yes, the letter is H. If no, the next question would be "Is there a vertical line?" If yes, the letter is Y; if no, the letter is V. The scheme for checking features is illustrated in Figure 5-20 and is called a *sorting tree,* for as we move through the tree we sort inputs into appropriate output categories.

This program is extremely simple. Far more elegant ones are now in operation that are accurate in discriminating both hand-printed and handwritten letters. Although most of these programs are still in an experimental stage several have reached technological maturity; as an example, the Post Office has installed several ZIP-code readers that can discriminate hand-printed or typed digits. What is important for our purposes is to show how a set of feature detectors in conjunction with a sorting tree can recognize complex patterns. The human perceptual system may operate in a similar manner. Stored in your memory would be a feature list for "Aunt Sara"; it might include the width of her mouth, the slant of her nose, the color of her eyes, etc. When you encounter someone, the feature detectors are activated and if the extracted features match the list in your memory associated with Aunt Sara then you know who it is.

How man recognizes complex patterns, a problem occupying the attention of many psychologists, is just beginning to be understood. In wrestling with the problem, the psychologist's approach ranges from a concern with neurophysiological data to testing complex models by simulating them on a computer. It is just such diversity that gives promise of significant advances in the field.

At present we do not know how far a hierarchical analysis of this sort can be carried, but it is known that there are still other cells in the visual cortex that respond to specific patterns like curves and angles. And there is some evidence with monkeys that there are cells so finely tuned that they respond only to particular shapes, such as an object with many of the specific characteristics of a monkey's hand (Gross, Bender & Rocha-Miranda, 1972). Since everything we see is reducible ultimately to a series of minute lines at angles to each other, it may well be that these various types of cells, which act to detect particular features of a visual display, are the building blocks out of which complex perceptions are formed.

The Role of Learning in Perception

The phenomena of perceptual organization, movement, and depth perception, and the various perceptual constancies lend themselves to simple and convincing experimental demonstrations, so that by now there is general agreement over what the subject perceives. Disagreements remain, however, over how to *explain* what happens. One of the traditional problems of visual perception has been the question of whether our abilities to perceive the spatial aspects of our environment are learned or innate. This is the familiar nature-nurture problem, and its investigation with relation to perception goes back to the philosophers of the seventeenth and eighteenth centuries.

Nativist and Empiricist Viewpoints

One group, the *nativists* (Descartes, Kant), argued that we are born with the ability to perceive the way we do. In contrast, the *empiricists* (Berkeley, Locke) maintained that we learn our ways of perceiving through experience with objects in the world about us. Among the early sensory psychologists, Hering and Helmholtz (whose theories of color vision were discussed in Chapter 4) held opposing views. Hering pointed to retinal disparity as evidence for the view that our eyes are innately designed to perceive depth; he developed a theory of distance vision based on the fact that each eye registers a different image. Helmholtz argued that visual perceptions were too variable (for example, the reversible figure shown in Figure 5-9) to be explained on the basis of fixed receptor mechanisms and must therefore be learned.

Most contemporary psychologists believe that a fruitful integration of these two viewpoints is possible. No one today really doubts that practice and experience affect perception. The question is whether we are born with some ability to perceive objects and space in our environment or whether these abilities are completely learned. Let us examine some of the areas of research that yield information on the role of learning in perception.

Effects of Restored Vision

As far back as the seventeenth century, Locke quotes a letter he received from a colleague, in which the problem is posed:

> Suppose a man *born* blind, and now adult, taught by his *touch* to distinguish between a cube and a sphere of the same metal, and nighly of the same bigness, so as to tell, when he felt one and the other, which is the cube, which the sphere. Suppose that the cube and the sphere placed on a table, and the blind man be made to see . . . [could he] now distinguish and tell which is the globe, which the cube? (Locke, 1690)

Locke, supporting the empiricist viewpoint, concluded that he could not.

A partial answer to this question is provided by studies of individuals who were blind from birth with cataracts on both eyes and whose vision was restored by surgical means when they were adults (Senden, 1960). When the eye bandages are removed for the first time, the patient is confused by the bewildering array of visual stimuli. He is able, however, to distinguish figure from ground (apparently perceiving figure-ground relationships in much the same way as normally sighted people do), to fixate figures, scan them, and follow moving figures with his eyes. These abilities then appear to be innate. He cannot identify by sight alone objects very familiar from the sense of touch, such as faces, knives, and keys. He cannot distinguish a triangle from a square without counting the number of corners or tracing the outline with a finger. He also cannot tell which of two uneven sticks is longer without feeling them, although he may report that the two sticks look somehow different. Often it takes several weeks of training for such patients to learn to identify simple objects well from sight, and even after identification has been learned in a specific situation, the patient shows little evidence of generalization or perceptual constancy. A white triangle may not be recognized when it is turned over to its red side, or when viewed under altered illumination, or when turned upside down. His poor performance cannot be attributed to difficulty in discriminating colors; the restored-vision patient can distinguish between colors (although he does not at first know which name to attach to which color) long before he can distinguish between shapes.

These studies of previously blind adults who are suddenly able to see for the first time suggest that our perceptions develop gradually from primitive visual experiences in which figure-ground relationships and color predominate, becoming more accurate and more detailed with practice. They cannot, however, be taken as conclusive evidence of the innate visual ability of the infant. We do not know what deteriorative changes may have occurred over the years the adult subject was blind, nor do we know what compensating skills this adult may have developed to overcome his handicap.

Visual Deprivation with Animals

In an attempt to provide a more controlled situation similar to restored vision in humans, animals have been raised in various degrees of darkness and then tested for visual ability. Investigators who reared infant chimpanzees in total darkness until they were sixteen months old found serious perceptual deficiencies when the animals were tested upon first exposure to light. But these chimpanzees were later discovered to have defective retinas. Apparently a certain amount of light stimulation is necessary for normal anatomical development of the visual system. Without any light stimulation, nerve cells in the retina and the visual cortex begin to atrophy. This fact is

Fig. 5-21 An environment of diagonal line

A Cree Indian summer cook tent or *meechwop* at Wemindji, a small Indian village on the east coast of James Bay, Quebec. These structures, along with the Cree winter lodges or *matoocan*, presen contours in virtually all orientations.

interesting in itself, but it does not tell us much about the role of learning in perceptual development.

Later studies made use of translucent goggles so that the animals received light stimulation, but of a diffuse, unpatterned form. Studies have been carried out with monkeys, chimpanzees, and kittens wearing translucent goggles from birth to anywhere from one to three months of age. The result showed that although some simple perceptual abilities were unimpaired, more complex visual activity was seriously affected. The visually deprived animals did almost as well as normal animals in distinguishing differences in color, brightness, and size. But they could not perform such tasks as following a moving object with their eyes, discriminating forms (a circle from a square or triangle), perceiving depth, and distinguishing between a moving and a nonmoving stimulus (Riesen, 1965).

These findings are supported by more recent research using single-cell recording in the visual cortex. In one experiment, kittens were raised in an environment where they were exposed only to bright dots; they were never shown straight lines, contours, or edges. When these animals were subsequently tested using a procedure like the one shown in Figure 5-18, their visual cortex contained neurons of an abnormal type responding well to small spots of light and showing little of the customary preference for lines and edges. Even at the level of cells in the visual cortex, the effects of prior experience are evident (Barlow, 1972).

Similar studies have been run with kittens raised in a visual environment consisting solely of vertical or horizontal stripes. These animals behave as though they are blind to diagonal lines, and no neurons in their visual cortex appear to be tuned to this orientation. The same, it seems, may hold true for humans. Euro-Canadians raised in a "carpentered" environment, with its vertical and horizontal contours (straight sidewalks and rectangular buildings), were tested against Cree Indians from a more diverse environment. The Cree life style, for example, alternates between a summer cook tent and a winter lodge—both structures present line contours of virtually all orientations (see Figure 5-21). Visual acuity was tested with an apparatus that displayed a grating pattern in various orientations. The Euro-Canadians exhibited a much higher resolution for vertical and horizontal orientations than for diagonal orientations of the grating. The Crees, however, showed no differences; they were equally good at all orientations. There is no evidence to suggest genetically determined differences in the visual system of the two groups. Rather, it appears that the acuity of the Crees is the result of their visual experience (Annis and Frost, 1973).

Perception in Infants

If the human infant could tell us what the world looks like to him, many of our questions concerning the development of perception might be answered. Since he cannot, experimenters have had to stretch their ingenuity to try to measure the visual abilities of infants.

An infant's perception of height, a special case of depth perception, has been investigated. The apparatus shown in Figure 5-22 has been used with human and various animal infants in attempts to determine whether the ability to perceive and avoid a brink is innate or must be learned by the experience of falling off and getting hurt. Most parents, mindful of the caution they

Fig. 5-22 The "visual cliff"
Infants and young animals show an ability to perceive depth as soon as they can move about. The visual cliff consists of two surfaces, both displaying the same pattern, which are covered by a sheet of thick glass. One surface is directly under the glass; the other is dropped several feet. When placed on the center board shown in the photo, the infant refuses to cross the deep side, although he will readily move off the board onto the shallow side. (After Gibson and Walk, 1960)

exercise to keep their offspring from falling out of the crib or down the stairs, would assume that the ability to appreciate height is something the child must learn. But observation of the human infant's susceptibility to such accidents does not tell us whether he is unable to discriminate depth or whether he can indeed respond to depth cues but lacks the motor control to keep from falling.

Gibson and Walk (1960) tested the response of infants, ranging in age from 6–14 months, when placed on the center board of the visual cliff. The mother called to the child from the cliff side and the shallow side successively. Almost all the infants crawled off on the shallow side but refused to crawl on the deep side. Their dependence on vision was demonstrated by the fact that they frequently peered through the glass on the deep side and then backed away. Some of the infants patted the glass with their hands but still remained unassured that it was solid and refused to cross.

Since the infants could not be tested until they were old enough to crawl, the experiment does not prove that depth perception is present at birth. The results of studies with other organisms, however, indicate that depth perception is present at least as soon as the animal is able to locomote. Chickens tested when less than 24 hours old never made a mistake by stepping off on the deep side. Goats and lambs placed on the center board as soon as they could stand (some only one day old) always chose the shallow side. When placed on the deep side, such animals characteristically froze in a state of immobility.

Experiments designed to isolate the specific visual depth cues to which the organism responds on the visual cliff have yielded contradictory results; it seems, however, that monocular cues are sufficient. Infants who wore eye patches on one eye discriminated as well as those with binocular vision (Walk, 1968).

Attention and Perception

Our perceptions are selective. We do not react equally to all the stimuli impinging upon us; instead we focus upon a few. This perceptual focusing is called *attention.* Through attentive processes we keep in focus selected stimuli and resist distracting stimuli.

Selective Attention

Even as you sit reading this, stop for a moment, close your eyes, and attend to the various stimuli affecting you. Notice, for example, the tightness of the heel of your left shoe, the pressure of clothing on your neck or shoulders, the sounds coming from outside the room. We are constantly bombarded by stimuli to which we do not attend. In fact, our brains would be quite overloaded if we had to attend to every stimulus present in our environment. Somehow, our brain selects those stimuli that are pertinent and ignores the others until a change in a particular stimulus makes it important for us to notice it.

There is evidence, however, that stimuli to which we are not actively attending still register in some form in our perceptual system, even though

A goat cautiously approaching the deep side of a visual cliff.

we may not recognize them at the time. Consider what takes place during a cocktail party. Out of the complex volume of sound generated by the wavelengths of many voices taken together, you are able to listen to one voice. Although you may think you are not attending to the other voices, let someone in the far corner of the room mention your name and you are immediately aware of it; apparently the nervous system monitors the other voices for relevant stimuli without your being aware of such activity.

The cocktail party situation raises two interesting questions. How are we able to focus attention on one conversation out of the many that surround us? Of the conversations to which we are not attending how much do we register? Some of the cues that enable us to concentrate on one voice in a babel of many are the directions of sound, lip movements of the speaker, and the particular voice characteristics of the speaker (whether the voice is male or female, its speed, and intonation). Even if all these cues are eliminated, by recording two messages spoken by the same speaker and playing them on the same magnetic tape, it is still possible to distinguish the messages. The task is a difficult one requiring intense concentration, but most subjects can separate the two messages, apparently by relying on the grammatical and semantic content of the spoken material for cues. In the absence of appropriate grammatical cues, however, the task of separating two simultaneous messages by the same speaker becomes impossible.

Information about how much we register from conversations to which we are not attending is provided by an experimental situation similar to the cocktail party. Two different spoken messages are presented to the subject by means of earphones, one to the right ear and the other to the left. The subject has no difficulty in listening to either message at will; he can reject the unwanted one, or switch attention back and forth from one speech to the other. If we ask him to repeat aloud the speech presented to one ear he can do it fairly well even though the message is continuous. His words are slightly delayed behind those of the message to which he is listening, and his voice tends to have a monotonous noninflective quality, however. At the end of the passage he may have little idea of what it was all about, particularly if the material is difficult. What about the message to which he was not attending. How much information does the unattending ear assimilate? The answer depends on a number of factors including the difficulty of the two messages. If the attended message is a familiar nursery rhyme, the subject will recall a fair amount of the message to the unattended ear. With more difficult material, however, the subject usually can recall nothing of the verbal content of the unattended message and will not even be certain it was in English. He is aware of certain general characteristics: whether the message was speech rather than a pure tone, whether the voice was male or female, and, for many subjects, whether their own name was mentioned.

If the subject is interrupted during his repetition of the message to the attending ear and asked quickly what was just presented to the other ear, there does appear to be some temporary memory for the message not attended. This is similar to the situation in which someone to whom you are not listening asks you a question; your immediate response is "What did you say?" but before the question is repeated you suddenly realize what was asked.

Studies of this kind have led to the conclusion that the nervous system must have some kind of register where incoming sensory information is temporarily stored in a rather crude and unanalyzed form. Of all the stimuli that bombard our senses, only those that our higher mental processes tell us are relevant to the psychological processes going on at the moment are selected for attention. Some sort of attention mechanism selects for further processing those sensory inputs that seem most important or pertinent. Certain classes of sensory inputs, such as the sound of one's name, can be expected to have a permanently high level of pertinence, but most will fluctuate depending upon the ongoing events in the central nervous system (Norman, 1969).

Determinants of Stimulus Selection

What factors determine which of many competing stimuli will gain our attention? The characteristics of the stimulus are important, as are our own internal needs, expectancies, and past experience. The advertiser is concerned with discovering these factors so that he can direct attention to his product. Some physical properties of the stimulus that are important in gaining attention are *intensity, size, contrast,* and *movement.*

Certain internal variables, such as motives and expectations, are equally important in determining which stimulus attracts our attention. The advertiser counts on an appeal to the male sex drives when he uses pictures of scantily clad females to advertise anything from carpets to automobile tires. In a culture where hunger is a more generally unsatisfied drive than sex, pictures of food might prove to be a more powerful attention-getter.

Because of habitual or momentary interests, individuals vary greatly in their responses to the same stimuli. The naturalist will hear sounds in the woods that the ordinary picnicker would miss. A mother will hear her baby's cry above the conversation of a room full of people. These two illustrations represent abiding interests. Sometimes momentary interest controls attention. When you page through a book looking for a particular diagram, only pages with illustrations cause you to hesitate; others you ignore. Emotional states, especially moods, may also affect the ways in which attention is directed. In a hostile mood, personal comments are noticed that might go unremarked in a more friendly mood.

Physiological Correlates of Attention

When a stimulus attracts our attention, we usually perform certain body movements that enhance our reception of the stimulation. If it is a visual stimulus we turn our head in the proper direction, our eyes turn so that the image falls on the fovea, our pupils dilate momentarily to allow more light to enter the eye, and the lens muscles work to bring the image clearly into focus. If the stimulus is auditory we may cup our hands behind our ears or turn one ear in the direction of the sound, keeping the rest of our movements very still so as to enhance the reception of a faint auditory stimulus. These body movements are accompanied by certain characteristic internal physiological changes. The physiological reactions that occur in response to stimulation changes in the environment form such a consistent pattern that they have been called the *orienting reflex* and have been studied extensively by psychologists.

The orienting reflex occurs in both man and animals in response to even minimal changes in the stimulus environment. The physiological accompaniments of attention, in addition to the body movements mentioned above, include dilation of the blood vessels in the head, constriction of the peripheral blood vessels, certain changes in the gross electrical responses of the brain (EEG), and changes in muscle tone, heart rate, and respiration. These responses serve the dual function of (1) facilitating the reception of stimulation and (2) preparing the organism to respond quickly in case action is needed. We can see why such a reflex is extremely valuable for self-preservation.

The facilitating effect of the orienting reflex on sensory reception can be demonstrated in the laboratory. The arousal of the reflex by a loud tone will increase visual sensitivity, making it possible for the subject to see a light that was too faint to be detected before the arousal. The orienting reflex habituates over time, however. With repeated presentation of the sound the reflex gradually diminishes; the visual threshold is raised to its original level, and the same light intensity no longer evokes a response. Any change in the stimulus, or the introduction of a new stimulus, will reactivate the orienting reflex in its original strength (Sokolov, 1963).

Needs and Values

What a person perceives and how he perceives it may also be determined to some extent by his needs and personal values. The value an individual places on an object may affect such direct impressions as those of size. For example, it has been shown that children from poorer homes tend to overestimate the size of coins more than do children from well-to-do homes (Bruner and Goodman, 1947).

The following experiment attempted to subject this process to direct laboratory control; it involved an experimental and a control group of nursery school children. Children in the experimental group learned to turn a crank in order to receive a poker chip. When a child inserted the poker chip in a slot, he automatically received a piece of candy. The conjecture was that the candy would enhance the value of the poker chip and that this increased value would result in overestimation of size, as in the coin experiments. The size estimates were obtained by having each child adjust a variable spot of light so that it appeared equal to the poker chip when viewed from a few feet away. Both control and experimental subjects overestimated the size by 5 or 6 percent in a pretest, but after ten days of rewarded learning with poker chips the experimental group increased its overestimation to 13 percent. During the same period the overestimation of the control group did not increase significantly (Lambert, Solomon, and Watson, 1949).

Extrasensory Perception

If there are so many influences upon perception other than those coming from the presented stimuli, are there perhaps perceptions that require no sense organ stimulation whatsoever? The answer to this question is the source of a continuing controversy within psychology over the status of *extrasensory perception* (ESP). Although some psychologists believe that the evidence for the existence of certain forms of ESP is now incontrovertible (for example, Rhine and Brier, 1968; McConnell, 1969; Van de Castle, 1969), most remain unconvinced.

The phenomena under discussion are of two main kinds:

1. Extrasensory perception (ESP).
   a. Telepathy, or thought transference from one person to another.
   b. Clairvoyance, or the perception of objects or events not influencing the senses (such as stating the number and suit of a playing card that is in a sealed envelope).
   c. Precognition, or the perception of a future event.
2. Psychokinesis (PK), whereby a mental operation affects a material body or an energy system (for example, wishing for a number affects what number comes up in the throw of dice).

Experimenters investigating these problems work in accordance with the usual rules of science and generally disavow any connection between their work and spiritualism, supernaturalism, and other occult doctrines. Yet the phenomena with which they deal are so extraordinary and so similar to the superstitious beliefs of nonliterate people that many scientists reject even the legitimacy of their inquiries. Such a priori judgments are out of place in science; the real question is whether the empirical evidence is acceptable by ordinary scientific standards. Many psychologists who are not convinced are nevertheless ready to accept evidence that they find satisfactory. For example, the possibility of some sort of influence from one brain to another, other than by way of the sense organs, would not be inconceivable within the present framework of science were the facts of telepathy to be established in an orderly fashion. Some of the other phenomena, such as precognition, are more difficult to find believable, but if the evidence were firm, previous beliefs would have to yield to the facts.

Fig. 5-23 ESP cards

J. B. Rhine, an early worker in the area of parapsychology, and the ESP cards he used in his research.

The case for ESP is based largely on experiments with cards, in which, under various conditions, the subject attempts to guess the symbols on cards randomly arranged in packs that he cannot see. The usual ESP pack consists of 25 cards having 5 different symbols, so that a chance performance would be 5 hits per pack (see Figure 5-23). Even very successful subjects seldom reach as high a level as 7 hits, but they may score above 5 often enough to meet acceptable standards of statistical significance. If the experimenter, or "sender," thinks of the symbol at the time the subject makes his reponse, the experiment is one on telepathy; if the experimenter does not perceive the card at all (it may be face down on the table before him or sealed in an envelope), then the experiment is one on the subject's clairvoyance.

The kind of evidence used in support of the nonchance nature of the findings can be illustrated by the successive runs of one "sensitive" subject, Mrs. Gloria Stewart, studied in England over a long period (Table 5-1). If the evidence is viewed in the same spirit as that from any other experiment, it

TABLE 5-1
Results of telepathy and clairvoyance trials with one subject*

CHRONOLOGICAL ORDER OF SUCCESSIVE GROUPS OF 200 TRIALS	HITS PER 200 TRIALS (EXPECTED = 40)	
	TELEPATHY TRIALS	CLAIRVOYANCE TRIALS
1945	65	51
	58	42
	62	29
	58	47
	60	38
1947	54	35
	55	36
	65	31
1948	39	38
	56	43
1949	49	40
	51	37
	33	42
Total hits	707	509
Expected hits	520	520
Difference	+187	−11
Hits per 25 trials	6.8	4.9

*Each group of 200 trials consisted of alternating blocks of 50 telepathy and 50 clairvoyance trials.

Source: Soal and Bateman (1954).

would be clear that Mrs. Stewart responded above chance on the telepathy trials but not on the clairvoyance ones. This fact also meets certain objections about card arrangements sometimes voiced against such experiments, for her chance performance on the clairvoyance trials shows that above-chance scores are not an inevitable result possibly related to the method of shuffling the cards.

One of the chief reasons for skepticism about ESP is that no method has been found for reliably demonstrating the phenomena. Procedures that produce results for one experimenter do not for another. Even the same experimenter testing the same individuals over a period of time may obtain significant results on one occasion and yet be unable to repeat the effect later. Lack of replicability is a serious problem. In other scientific fields an experimental finding is not considered established until the experiment has been repeated by several different researchers with the same results. Until ESP experiments can be shown to be replicable, the authenticity of the phenomena is open to question.

A second complaint about ESP research is that the results do not seem to vary systematically with the introduction of different experimental manipulations. This objection, however, is not entirely fair. Some order effects are reported, in which early trials are more successful than later ones (McConnell, 1968), and there is evidence that an attitude favorable to ESP leads to positive results, while an unfavorable attitude leads to scoring below chance levels (Schmeidler and McConnell, 1958). It has also been reported that the emotional states of the sender and receiver are important; when the

CRITICAL DISCUSSION

Why Many Psychologists Find

We may expand a little upon the objections that psychologists have to the ESP and PK experiments and to *psi,* the special ability attributed to the "sensitive" subject.

1. *General skepticism about extraordinary phenomena.* Throughout history there have always been reports of strange happenings, ghosts, poltergeists (noisy spirits who engage in throwing things about), and dreams foretelling the future. The continuing appearance of these stories does not make them true. Painstaking investigation by the U.S. Air Force has yielded no "flying saucers"; no one has ever trapped the Loch Ness monster. A famous medium is a case in point. Eusapia Palladino was able to make a table move and produce other effects, such as tapping sounds, by the aid of "spirits." Investigated repeatedly between 1890 and 1910, she managed to convince many distinguished scientists of her powers. On several occasions, however, she was caught in deceptive trickery, and the results were published (Jastrow, 1935). Even so, believers continued to support her genuineness.

The above case is not unique. Almost every year strong claims are made for the powers of some newly-discovered psychic; careful examination reveals that the individual is using trickery and that his psychic feats can be duplicated by a skilled magician. Yet some researchers in parapsychology are so messianic about their field that they either do not see through the obvious trickery or they conclude that, while the individual may occasionally cheat, he still has paranormal powers. When those most convinced about ESP are also convinced about already disproven phenomena, their testimony carries less weight than if they were more critical.

2. *Problems of statistical inference.* A major contribution of ESP research to psychology may turn out to be the attention it has drawn to the circumstances that make a scientific finding believable. It is commonly supposed that tests of statistical significance are sufficient guarantees of objectivity, and hence a satisfactory statistical outcome should lead to acceptance of a hypothesis as plausible. This turns out not to be the case in ESP experiments, and it is probably not the case in other experiments either. Statistical tests merely tell us how well measurement seems to establish something that is already plausible; if it is not plausible, we search for some confounding variable that may have produced the nonchance result.

In this regard, let us consider an experiment performed by Rhine at Duke University (Rhine, 1942). He was trying to determine whether a subject might, through some combination of ESP and PK, influence the positions of cards in a mechanical shuffler. In all, 50 persons wrote down their predictions of the orders in which cards would come out of a mechanical shuffler ten days later. The experiment was carefully performed, and in a total of over 50,000 trials the results were at chance level—just 11 hits in excess of expectation. But was this plausible result accepted? No, so further statistical analyses were made. Two more of these, based on the division of the trials into segments, failed to yield nonchance results. Finally, a fourth analysis, based on a complex effect

sender is emotionally aroused and the receiver is reclining in a relaxed state, ESP is maximal (Moss and Gengerelli, 1968). Finally there are a number of studies that find ESP to be better when the receiver is dreaming or in a hypnotic state than in a normal waking state (Krippner, 1970, 1971; Van de Castle, 1969).

Empirical findings that meet ordinary statistical standards are offered in support of ESP and PK. Why, then, do the results not become a part of established psychological science? The many arguments used against the ESP and PK can be summarized as follows:

1. the fact that many claims of extraordinary phenomena in the past have turned out to be false when carefully investigated;
2. certain problems in statistical inference that arise when very large numbers

ESP Experiments Unconvincing

called a "covariance of salience ratio," gave a nonchance effect, with odds of 625 to 1 in its favor. When belief in bizarre effects is carried this far, it is no wonder that the unconvinced scientist begins to question the statistics, even though all the computations are accurate.

3. *Failure of improved methods to increase the yield.* In most scientific fields, the assay from the ore becomes richer as the methods become more refined. But the reverse trend is found in ESP experiments; it is almost a truism in research in the fields of telepathy and clairvoyance that the poorer the conditions, the better the results. In the early days of the Duke University experiments, subjects yielding high ESP scores were rather common. As the experiments have become better controlled, however, the number of high-scoring subjects has diminished. A similar decrease in significant results with improved experimental control has been found in PK studies (Girden, 1962).
4. *Lack of systematic consistency in the phenomena.* Sensitive subjects in Rhine's experiments appear to be equally successful at clairvoyance and telepathy, but subjects in a British laboratory appear to be good at telepathy and not at clairvoyance. Other peculiarities emerge. In a famous series of experiments in England, one subject gave no evidence of either telepathy or clairvoyance when scored in the usual way against the target card. Instead he was shown to be successful in *precognition telepathy,* that is, in guessing what was going to be on the experimenter's mind on the next trial. (Soal and Bateman, 1954). Why, the skeptic asks, does the direct telepathy fail with this subject in favor of something far more mysterious than the telepathic success of Mrs. Stewart?

Because the *psi* ability does not follow ordinary rules, explanations of it can be produced with the greatest of freedom. It need not be affected in any ordinary way by space or time, so that success over great distances is accepted as a sign of its extraordinary power rather than something to cause a search for artifacts. Similarly, the precognition experiments are merely evidence to the ESP proponents that it is as easy to read what is *about* to be on someone else's mind as what is on it now. The PK effects, which require the results of card sorting or dice rolling to be produced by mental effort ("mind over matter"), are nevertheless said to occur without any transfer of physical energy, thus presumably violating the conservation of energy. But in any experimental work *some* aspects of time and space have to be respected. Unless some restraint is shown, one might invent any number of hypotheses: the subject was perceiving the cards in reverse order, in a place-skipping order, and so on. With such hypotheses no test is possible.

The believer in *psi* is impatient with this kind of criticism. He says that more is asked of him than of other experimenters. In fact, we do ask more. To demonstrate something highly implausible requires better evidence than to demonstrate something plausible. Supporting evidence for the plausible finding comes from many directions, whereas the implausible one must hang upon a slender thread of evidence until systematic relationships are found that tie it firmly to what is known.

of trials are used to establish the significance of small differences;
3. the failure of improved methods to yield better results than crude methods;
4. a general lack of orderliness in the phenomena, without which formal theorizing cannot replace the current vague speculations about what may be taking place.

These arguments are not, in fact, decisive, and it is desirable to keep an open mind about issues that permit empirical demonstration, as ESP phenomena do. At the same time, it should be clear that the reservations of the majority of psychologists are based on more than stubborn prejudice. The critical discussion above is provided for those who want to look further into these issues.

Summary

1. We mainly perceive things, and we perceive these environmental objects as stable and enduring. This stability depends upon the various *constancies* of color, shape, size, and location. Size perception usually represents a compromise between perspective size and object size. The greater the number of distance cues available, the more the perceived size approaches object size. As environmental cues are reduced, perception approaches perspective size (that is, it corresponds to the size indicated by the retinal image).
2. The basic organization of visual perception appears to be that of *figure* and *ground,* so that we recognize patterns as figures against a background whether or not the patterns are familiar. Reversible figures illustrate the fact that perception involves an active search for the best interpretation of sensory information rather than a static mirroring of visual stimuli.
3. Visual illusions are incorrect perceptual hypotheses. Some are based on *size contrasts* with the surroundings, whereas others are created when we try to interpret figures on a two-dimensional surface as if they were three dimensional.
4. Movement perception depends upon the integration of signals from the *retina* with kinesthetic information from the head, neck, and eye muscles. Perception of *apparent motion,* as in the *autokinetic effect* and *phi phenomenon,* has not yet been adequately explained. Perception of real motion depends upon the relation between objects within the visual field. When vision alone is operating, we tend to assume that large objects are stationary while smaller ones are moving.
5. Visual depth is perceived binocularly with the help of *stereoscopic vision,* the fusion of the slightly unlike images of the two eyes. Depth is perceived monocularly with the aid of a number of cues: *superposition* of objects, *perspective* (whether geometric or given through relative size, height in the frontal plane, or gradients of texture), and *movement.*
6. Studies recording from the visual cortex of animals indicate that there are cells in the brain tuned to detect highly specific *features* such as straight lines and edges. Feature detectors in conjunction with a *sorting tree* provide the basis for *pattern recognition.*
7. Both learning and innate factors contribute to our abilities to perceive aspects of our environment. Perception of figure-ground relationships, color, and depth appears to be largely innate; form perception, although based upon an innate organization of cortical cells that respond selectively to specific features of the stimulus, must be mastered through experience.
8. Perception is *selective,* so that at any moment in time we *attend* to only part of the influx of sensory stimulation. Stimuli to which we are not actively attending may be registered temporarily in the nervous system, but they are not selected for attention unless deemed pertinent. Factors that favor attention to one stimulus in preference to another reside in its physical properties (intensity, size, contrast, and movement) and in the habitual and momentary interest of the individual. What an individual perceives and how he perceives it is determined to some extent by his needs and personal values.
9. The *orienting reflex* is a pattern of physiological reactions that correlates with attention. These reactions facilitate the reception of stimuli and prepare the organism for action.

10. *Extrasensory perception* (ESP) in its various forms (telepathy, clairvoyance, precognition) and *psychokinesis* (PK), the influencing of physical events by mental operations, are areas of controversy in psychology. There are many reasons for reserving judgment on these phenomena, but an a priori condemnation of the experiments is unjustified. The experiments raise interesting issues about the criteria by which scientific credibility is established.

Further Reading

Textbooks covering the topics dealt with in this chapter are Haber and Hershenson, *The psychology of visual perception* (1973); Cornsweet, *Visual perception* (1970); Lindsay and Norman, *Human information processing* (1972); Rock, *An introduction to perception* (1975); and Murch, *Visual and auditory perception* (1973). More detailed coverage may be found in the multiple volume. *Handbook of perception* (1974), edited by Carterette and Friedman.

Two entertaining paperbacks with emphasis on illusions, movement perception, and perspective are *Eye and brain* (1966), and *The intelligent eye* (1970), both by Gregory. The first of these books discusses some of the perceptual problems that may be experienced as man moves into outer space and explores alien planets.

Problems of attention, perceptual coding, and visual search are discussed in Neisser, *Cognitive psychology* (1967); Reed, *Psychological processes in pattern recognition* (1973); and Dodwell, *Perceptual processing: Stimulus equivalence and pattern recognition* (1971).

The development of visual perception in the young organism is covered in Gibson, *Principles of perceptual learning and development* (1969), and Bower, *Development in infancy* (1974).

For a review and criticism of extrasensory perception experiments, see Hansel, *ESP: A scientific evaluation* (1966). Reviews more favorable toward extrasensory perception are *ESP and credibility in science* (1969) by McConnell, and *Parapsychology today* (1968), edited by Rhine and Brier.

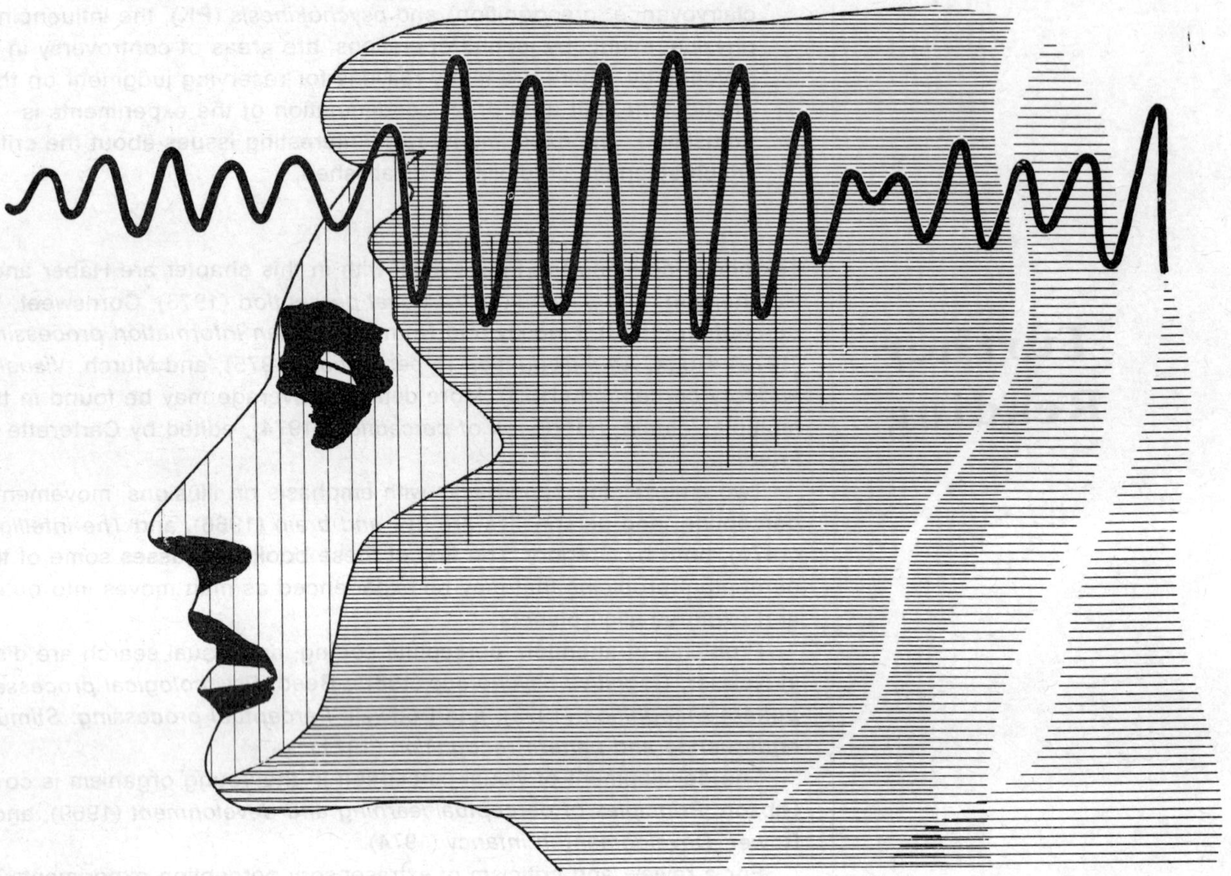

6 states of consciousness

In studying the perception of the world through our senses we have learned about the conditions of awareness in the normal waking state. But some problems of consciousness remain to be discussed, particularly the special problems connected with diminished, distorted, clouded, or even expanded awareness (ranging from sleep to ecstatic experiences).

Psychology was once thought to be the study of consciousness, and consciousness was accepted as open to immediate observation. If you drop a brick on your toe you know whether it hurts, and you can specify where you feel the pain. Similarly, if you look at a bright light and then close your eyes you will see a succession of colored images, and you can describe them as you see them. The question of whether there are "facts of consciousness" in this sense can be answered readily enough: of course there are.

An earlier behaviorism, in seeking to make psychology more like other sciences, rejected introspective reports (reflecting conscious experience). But the facts of consciousness are too pervasive and too important to be neglected. Persons can, of course, deceive their questioners and (in some instances) may deceive themselves. But this objection to listening to what is said can also apply to observing what is done; for example, a person can "fake" a stiff arm as well as he can "fake" a report that the arm feels painful. Actually, experimental subjects tend to be cooperative and honest, and "faking" is not at all prevalent. Increasingly, psychologists have adopted the convenience of a double language: the language of mental activities (private experiences, intentions, and so on) on the one hand, and the language of physics and physiology, on the other. Thus when one describes a dream according to its content, the one language is used; when dreaming is described according to brain waves or eye movements, the other language is used.

Once we become interested in exploring the facts of consciousness, or awareness, our attention is directed to different *states of consciousness.* We experience some of these fluctuations daily; they are so familiar that we do not see them as problematical. The sharpest distinction is between waking and sleeping, but many minor fluctuations occur in mood swings, or in the changes between excitement and quiescence, or between involved action and boredom. More extreme fluctuations are sometimes classified as "altered" states of consciousness; the person himself, or a qualified observer, detects a striking deviation from normal. The gradation from normal fluctuations to extreme alterations is not sharp. The more dramatically altered states arise under a variety of circumstances, usually characterized in one of the following ways. First, external stimulation may be either extremely enhanced or extremely reduced, along with the accompanying muscular activity; overstimulation or sensory bombardment will change a person's consciousness, and so will sensory deprivation. Second, a person may use subjective practices to decrease alertness or relax critical abilities, or heighten alertness and mental involvement. Finally, profound changes in the bodily condition, through disease or drugs or sleep loss, may also produce an altered state of consciousness (Ludwig, 1966).

These altered states are not mere curiosities of human functioning. Some are valued in religious practices or tribal ceremonies, where they serve socially useful purposes. Others, such as mental illness, are viewed as disturbing or destructive.

In this chapter we shall consider, first of all, the complications to be found within waking consciousness, including the unusual manifestations of fugue states and multiple personality only because they throw light on normal functioning. Sleeping and dreaming are the major alterations that take place each day, and recent work has enhanced our understanding of these states.

While postponing discussion of the more extreme changes associated with mental illness (Chapter 16), some attention is given to the more unusual states of hypnosis, meditation, and the psychoactive drugs.

Varieties of Waking States

The waking consciousness, in which we can report accurately what is happening in the environment about us, is a fluctuating state. Normal fluctuations include excitement, stillness, fatigue, emotion, and experiences which may reach ecstatic proportions. Most people believe that they know what the normal waking state consists of and find only the other states interesting or puzzling. In fact, the ordinary waking state may be the most puzzling of all.

The Complexity of Waking Consciousness

Waking consciousness is not itself a single, simple state. We may be attentive or inattentive; we may be looking, listening, talking, or planning—or perhaps all of these at once. While listening to someone else, we may also be preparing our reply; and even while replying we may be thinking of further arguments. We have long known, however, that when we try to do too many things at once they tend to interfere with one another. You may not find it difficult to talk while driving along a busy highway, but conversation may stop as the traffic gets snarled. We noted in the discussion of the "cocktail party phenomenon" (p. 149) our remarkable ability to focus on one conversation and to switch attention from one conversation to another. Although we can attend fully to only one message at a time, some information registers from a second message.

The planning function that goes on, even while we are talking, was commented upon by Miller, Galanter, and Pribram (1960). They noted that during our waking consciousness we tend to talk to ourselves about our plans—a kind of silent commentary on what is going on. ("How long shall I talk to Jim before calling Jane?" "Shall I take another helping?" "Is this worth noting?" "Will there be time to get to the library after class?") Plans to stop activities now engaged in, to enter others, to accept or refuse invitations, to drift or to schedule—this stream of self-talk, beyond listening and speaking, is part of waking consciousness. Writers of the stream-of-consciousness school, such as Gertrude Stein, James Joyce, and Virginia Woolf, have attempted to capture self-talk as a literary device.

Not all waking states are alert. Sometimes we find ourselves or others just staring—not examining anything, but looking rather blankly at nothing at all. We know the difference between our minds being very active and being almost free of thought. Hypnotized subjects often report that they can sit for a time with their minds practically blank, passively waiting for something to be suggested to them. Observation of newborn babies indicates that alert and inert states begin very early in life. Babies in the first five days of life tend to sleep, except when distressed or eating; in these states they pay little attention to sights and sounds about them. But during these first days they also have occasional quiet alert states, in which their eyes are wide open and their eyeballs are "bright" and appear to focus on objects. At this age these states are brief (the longest being seven minutes), and the total of the alert inactive periods does not exceed 30 minutes in a 24-hour period. Only during these alert inactive periods will the newborn baby turn his head and eyes to follow a visual object or turn toward a source of sound (Wolff, 1966).

The readiness for new stimuli, sometimes called a state of *vigilance,* can be tested in the adult by responses to the occasional appearance of a stimulus on a screen or to some change in a regularly appearing sound or other stimulus. Mackworth (1950) used a clock with a pointer that jumped regularly once a second, but at rare intervals gave a jump of double the length. The subject was to report these double jumps by pressing a key when they occurred. Mackworth found that a subject could do quite well for half an hour, but tended to make many more errors when set to work for a longer period. Errors could be reduced by reporting correct responses or errors to the subject or even by calling the subject up on the telephone and asking that he do better.

Studies of vigilance have shown that subjects can be kept alert by many techniques, and indeed we use such techniques on ourselves all the time. To keep from falling into states of vacant staring we keep orienting ourselves to our tasks, reminding ourselves where we are and what time it is; we squirm, scratch, adjust clothing, tap with our fingers, or chew a pencil. These are not mere nervous habits to discharge tension; they keep us from going to sleep, from becoming inattentive. Recent physiological studies suggest that these techniques serve to keep the reticular formation active (see p. 43).

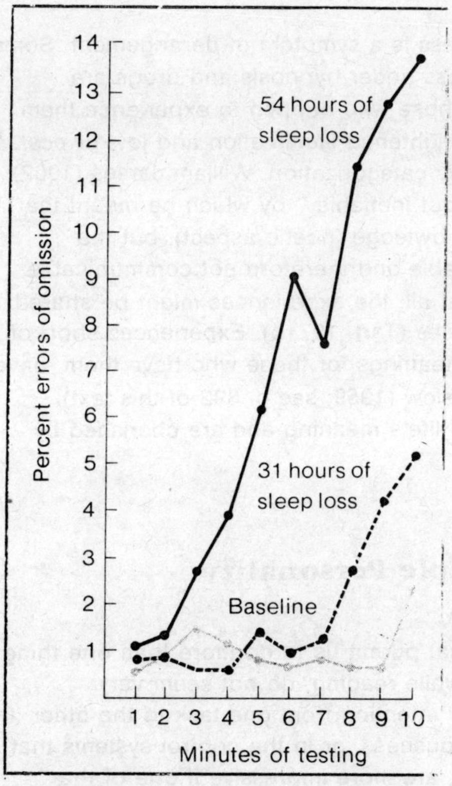

Fig. 6-1 Vigilance after loss of sleep

The subject can perform well for a short time after considerable sleep loss, but how long he can do well depends on how long he has been without sleep. The baseline represents errors in the task when there has been no sleep loss. (After Williams, Lubin, and Goodnow, 1959)

Modifications of Waking Consciousness

The familiar waking consciousness can be subjected to various degrees of alteration by excessive fatigue or sleep loss, by disease, or by drugs. Some changes, occurring outside the experimental laboratory, provide examples of these extremes.

FATIGUE AND EXHAUSTION. Hard muscular exertion produces a number of readily recognizable physiological changes, including waste products in the muscles and the blood stream accompanied by subjective experiences of weariness, pain, and desire to rest or sleep. The ability to continue at work is reduced, and the quality of work suffers. If the fatigue process has not gone too far, rest results in rapid recovery and the work can be resumed with satisfactory performance. More profound changes take place if exertion leads to exhaustion. In the cases of fatigue and exhaustion we are concerned with the results of actual physical work; many of the symptoms of listlessness may have psychosomatic or neurotic causes.

Experiments concerned with the debilitating effects of sleep loss have shown that the sleep-deprived subject can perform satisfactorily tasks of short duration, but a long-continued task suffers more interference. For instance, on one test little loss of vigilance was shown for the first seven minutes of testing after a 31-hour sleep loss, but then errors set in; after 54 hours of sleep loss, the good performance was sustained for only two minutes (Figure 6-1).

DISTORTIONS OF PERCEPTION AND THOUGHT. When a person is mistaken for someone else, or when an argument proceeds on the basis of false premises, slight inaccuracies of perception and thought have occurred. It is hard to draw a line between these normal aspects of functioning and the more extreme forms, but the extremes are given special names. A *delusion* is a thought system that is faulty, with the perceptual features accurate in themselves but misinterpreted as to context, for example, when a nurse is seen as planning to poison a patient, or visitors are believed to be enemy agents. An *illusion*, as we learned earlier, is a distortion of sense perception due to the arrangement of the stimulus components rather than to some characteristic of the perceiver. *Hallucinations*, by contrast, are more extreme in that they are the product primarily of the perceiver, for example, when a person sees someone in the room who is not there, and no shadow or other source of stimulation makes this qualify as an illusion. There may be minor stimulus supports, such as bloodshot eyes that make it easier for the alcoholic to perceive pink elephants as hallucinations. A *delirium* is a state of extreme confusion sometimes accompanied by agitated activity. These states are usually the result of some marked disturbance in the central nervous system such as a high fever or the presence of toxic substances.

ECSTASY. Not all altered awareness is a symptom of derangement. Some temporary distortions of consciousness under hypnosis and drugs are described as extremely pleasant by those who happen to experience them. Then there are the experiences of heightened illumination and joy, or *ecstasy* (as in religious mysticism), which defy categorization. William James (1902) called mystical experiences "noetic but ineffable," by which he meant that the mystic had a sense of gaining knowledge (noetic aspect), but the experience was essentially indescribable and therefore not communicable (ineffable aspect). If communicable at all, the experiences might be shared only with those with similar experiences (Tart, 1971b). Experiences short of ecstasy, but with somewhat similar meanings for those who have them, have been called *peak experiences* by Maslow (1959; see p. 392 of this text). These experiences are said to enrich life's meaning and are cherished by those who have them.

Fugue States and Multiple Personality

The divisions of consciousness that permit us to do more than one thing at a time, such as humming a tune while reading, do not seem very remarkable because we can shift our attention from one task to the other if we choose to do so. Splits in consciousness, or in the control systems that regulate what we do and experience, are more impressive if one of the control systems is out of awareness.

In rather rare cases of a split in consciousness known as a *fugue state*, a person may over an extended period of time engage in activities that are quite uncharacteristic, and after the fugue is over may deny having done these things because in fact they are totally forgotten. A famous case reported many years ago by William James (1890) is that of an itinerant preacher, the Reverend Ansel Bourne, who remembered nothing after drawing his money out of a Rhode Island bank in January until he suddenly recovered his identity in a strange environment in March, in Pennsylvania. In the meantime, under the name of A. J. Brown, he had rented a small store, stocked it with stationery, confectionery, fruit, and small articles, and carried on his trade without seeming at all odd or eccentric. After he recovered his identity he had such a horror of the idea of running a candy store that he refused to set foot in it again.

Fugue states may last for some time, as with Bourne, or they may be brief. The shorter states are somewhat like sleepwalking, in which the person leaves the bed, moves about, even converses with others, returns, and upon awakening in the morning is unaware of what happened.

Even more dramatic are cases of *multiple* or *alternating personalities* in which the person has more than one personality organization. These resemble fugue states, but are more extreme. In one condition the personality may be happy and carefree; in another it may be anxious and sullen. The personalities shift back and forth, but each retains its separate identity. Some amnesia is characteristic, so personality A is unaware of personality B, although in some instances personality B may be aware of personality A.

In earlier centuries these changes were commonly attributed to the invasion of the body by an outside spirit; the person was said to be "possessed," perhaps by a demon. In later years such cases have been viewed naturalistically as some sort of split or dissociation within the personality. Clear cases are rather uncommon, but several have appeared in recent years after almost none were reported in the previous several decades. Among the best known ones are the cases of Eve White, with her alternate personalities known as Eve Black and Jane (Thigpen and Cleckley, 1954), later made into a commercial motion picture, and, more recently, that of Sybil, with an incredible assortment of 16 multiple personalities (Schreiber, 1973).

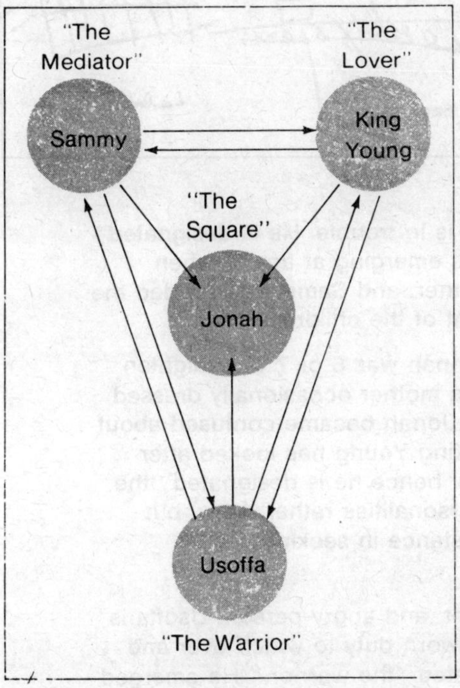

Fig. 6-2 The four component personalities, with their degrees of awareness of each other

The three personalities on the periphery have superficial knowledge of each other, but are intimately familiar with Jonah, who is totally lacking in knowledge of them. Another temporarily emerging personality, De Nova, is not shown. (From Ludwig and others, 1972)

A case that has been carefully studied from a psychological point of view is that of Jonah, a 27-year-old man who came to a hospital with complaints of severe headaches that were often followed by memory loss (Ludwig and others, 1972). Hospital attendants noticed striking changes in his personality on different days, and the psychiatrist in charge detected three distinct secondary personalities, prior to any attempt to explore the patient's problems with the help of hypnosis. Hypnosis was used in the effort to fuse the personalities, and the patient was discharged from the hospital. However, the result was unsuccessful, and on the patient's return the hospital staff was prepared to do a more thorough study of the personalities before attempting to fuse them again. Although we consider personality organization later (Chapter 13) we briefly discuss multiple personality here to point out the complexity of consciousness through an extreme example.

The relatively stable personality structures that emerged are diagramed in Figure 6-2. The four personalities may be characterized briefly:

Jonah. The primary personality. Shy, retiring, polite, passive, and highly conventional, he is designated "the square." Sometimes frightened and confused during interviews, Jonah is unaware of the other personalities.

Sammy. He has the most intact memories. He can coexist with Jonah, or set Jonah aside and take over. He claims to be ready

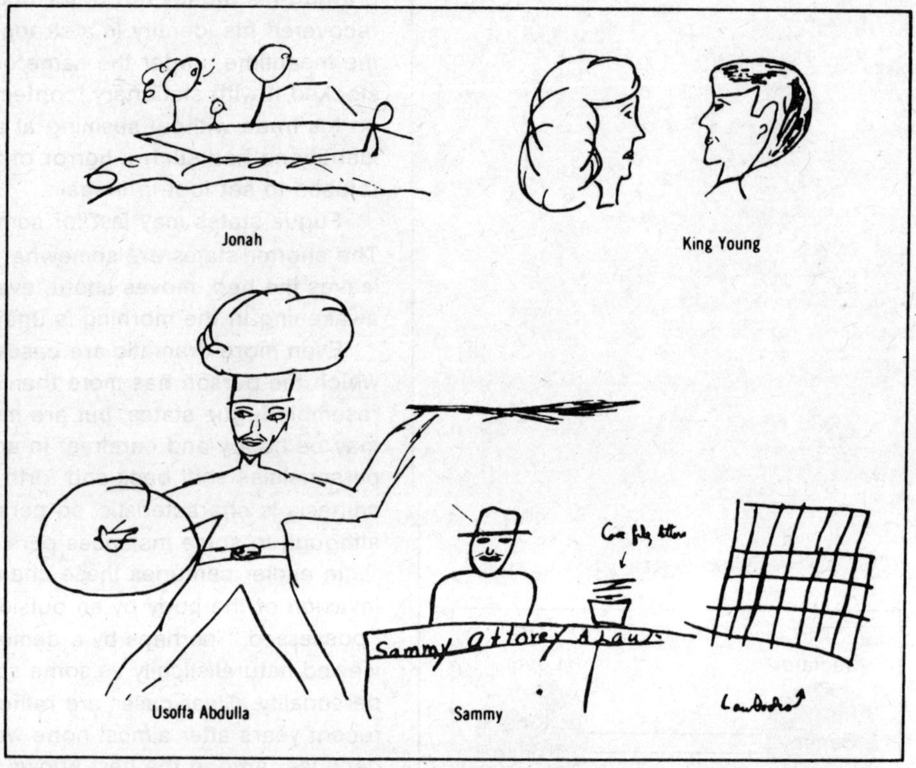

Fig. 6-3 Self-portraits of the four personalities

(From Ludwig and others, 1972)

when Jonah needs legal advice or is in trouble. He is designated "the mediator." Sammy remembers emerging at age 6, when Jonah's mother stabbed his stepfather, and Sammy persuaded the parents never to fight again in front of the children.

King Young. He emerged when Jonah was 6 or 7 to straighten out his sexual identity after Jonah's mother occasionally dressed him in girls' clothing at home, and Jonah became confused about boys' and girls' names at school. King Young has looked after Jonah's sexual interests ever since; hence he is designated "the lover." He is aware of the other personalities rather dimly, but takes over when Jonah needs assistance in seeking sexual gratification with a woman.

Usoffa Abdulla. A cold, belligerent, and angry person, Usoffa is capable of ignoring pain. It is his sworn duty to watch over and protect Jonah; hence he is designated "the warrior." He emerged at about age 9 or 10, when a gang of white boys beat up Jonah, who is black, without provocation. Jonah was helpless, but when Usoffa emerged he fought viciously and vehemently against the attackers. He is only dimly aware of the other personalities.

The fact that the personalities see themselves in these roles is evident from their self-portraits made during the course of the study (Figure 6-3). The psychological study showed that the four personalities tested very differently on all measures having to do with emotionally laden topics, but scored essentially alike on tests relatively free of emotion or interpersonal conflict, such as intelligence or vocabulary tests.

The outcome of the treatment, in which the four personalities were to be fused into one, has not been reported, although some early indications were that Jonah seemed "sicker" with all the strands of his personality out in the open than when the secondary personalities were in abeyance except when needed. The authors of the study conjectured that, for him, four heads were perhaps better than one!

Although much of such case material belongs in the study of psychological disturbances, there are occasional reports of creative activity carried out in dissociated states. The most famous concerns Coleridge, who composed parts of his poem *Kubla Khan* while under the influence of laudanum, an opium product.

Sleeping and Dreaming

The state most commonly contrasted with waking is sleeping, because it is a state of greatly lessened awareness and activity. Biologically, it is in part a restorative state. Like the waking state, however, it is *not simple.* Sleep does not come about just because the bodily processes resulting from waking activities require it; whatever the condition of the body, a person can choose either to sleep or to remain awake. Sleep is not altogether unconscious, for upon waking, dreams can be recalled. It is not entirely quiescent, because some people walk in their sleep. It is not entirely insensitive, because a mother can be awakened by the cry of her baby. It is not altogether planless, because some people can set themselves to wake up at a given time and do so. Still, sleep is the most obvious change in the conscious state; most of us experience the transitions between the two states (sleep and waking) at least twice a day.

Sleep Rhythms and Depth of Sleep

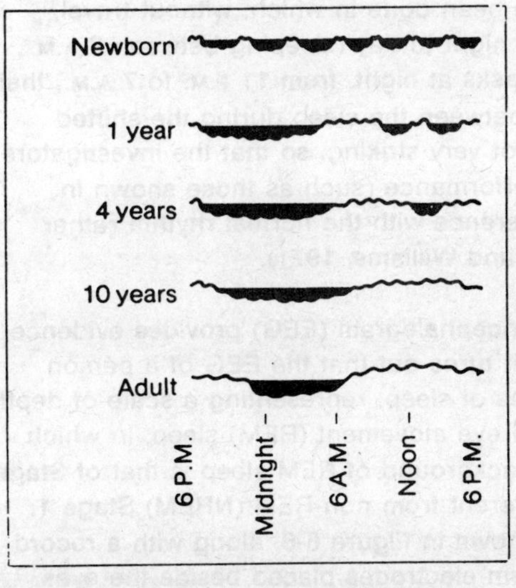

Fig. 6-4 Development of the sleep pattern

The shaded areas represent periods of sleep. Note that the newborn's frequent short periods of sleep gradually coalesce and eventually become the single night-day cycle of the adult. (After Kleitman, 1963)

The newborn baby tends to alternate rather frequently between sleeping and waking; gradually the sleep periods are consolidated, and eventually the night-day rhythm is established (Figure 6-4). In addition, the total time in sleeping tends to drop from 16 hours per day to 13 hours within the first six months.

BIOLOGICAL CLOCKS. The rhythms of sleep and waking and of other processes raise a number of questions about the extent to which control is external or internal. External control through changes in light and dark and temperature, including seasonal changes, can readily be demonstrated, but there are also internal controls, which are regulated by the hypothalamus in higher mammals.

People share a biological clock with the other mammals, controlling the daily rhythm known as the *circadian rhythm*. Experiments with human subjects, under rather free conditions, have shown a natural rhythm through the 24 hours, but if not regulated by external events the rhythm tends to have a 25-hour cycle. External events (alarm clocks, office hours, meal times) tend to obscure these rhythms in favor of the 24-hour one (Aschoff, 1965). If time is interpreted according to watches that are set to run an hour slow or fast per day (under conditions in which external light does not give time clues), bodily processes eventually follow the new rhythm, though some processes do so after a short time while others may take a week or more. Bodily temperature rhythms, for example, adjust more readily than water excretion (Lobban, 1965).

Because of their circadian rhythms, some travelers find it very hard to adapt to the new time schedules that jet travel can produce within a few hours. "Jet lag," as it has come to be called, may persist for several days. The problem is not only that of sleeping, but of the effect on many types of psychological functioning. For example, eight students between the ages of 21 and 26 participated in an experiment in which they were flown from their U.S. homes to Germany, where they remained for 18 days, and then were flown back. They were studied for three days before the outgoing flight, and for up to 13 days after the flight in both directions. Body temperature did not resume its normal daily rhythm for 14–15 days after the flight away from home, and for 11–12 days on return. Difficult psychomotor tasks took 12 days to recover after the outward flight and 10 days after the homeward flight. Even with easy tasks, differences could be noted for at least 6 days. The lesser time for recovery after the home flight has been checked for those whose homes are in Europe; it is not the east-west direction that matters (Klein, Wegmann, & Hunt, 1972). An example of the change in rhythm on the day after arriving in Europe is shown in Figure 6-5, which gives scores every three hours for a 24-hour period on a test that requires the subject to select different sized steel balls from a reservoir and to place them one at a time into the correct size hole in a revolving cylinder. There is a pronounced change in this ability during the normal day, with far greater success in the morning and afternoon hours. After the flight, with its six-hour time change, the daytime success is greatly interfered with, while the maximum success, at a reduced level, has moved with the clock from the afternoon to around midnight.

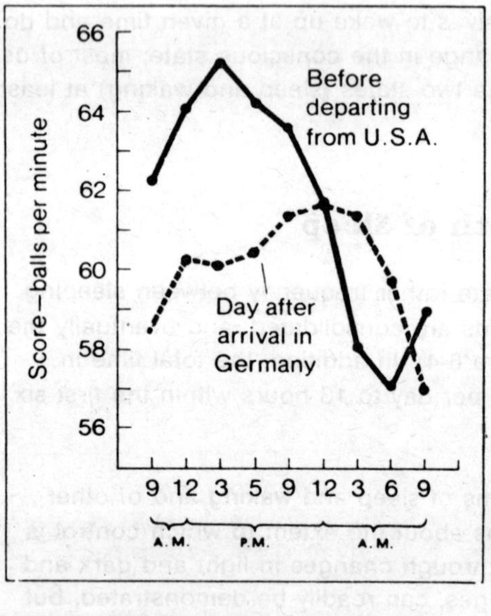

Fig. 6-5 Circadian rhythm of psychomotor performance as displaced by travel to a new time zone

Average results for eight subjects flying from the United States to Germany, with a six-hour time difference. The black line represents the scores on a test taken over three days prior to departure; the red line represents corresponding scores on the day after arrival in Germany. (After Klein, Wegmann, and Hunt, 1972)

The experiment described did not study sleep patterns as such because the requirements of the experiment produced some interference with sleep in any case. Related sleep studies have been done in which, without travel, young adults shifted their sleep from night to day (sleeping between 8 A.M and 4 P.M.) and doing performance tasks at night, from 11 P.M. to 7 A.M., their normal sleeping period. Differences between the sleep during the shifted period and the normal period were not very striking, so that the investigators concluded that the bad effects on performance (such as those shown in Figure 6-6) must be due to the interference with the normal rhythm rather than to loss of sleep (Webb, Agnew, and Williams, 1971).

STAGES OF SLEEP. The electroencephalogram (EEG) provides evidence of spontaneous activity of the brain. It turns out that the EEG of a person who is falling asleep shows five stages of sleep, representing a scale of depth from 1–4 and a stage known as rapid eye movement (REM) sleep, in which dreams commonly occur. The EEG background of REM sleep is that of Stage 1, but otherwise the state is quite different from non-REM (NREM) Stage 1. The five characteristic patterns are shown in Figure 6-6, along with a record of eye movements (REMs) derived from electrodes placed beside the eyes.

When an awake person closes his eyes and relaxes, his brain waves characteristically show a slow regular pattern of 8–13 vibrations (Hz) per second (known as *alpha waves*). As the individual drifts into Stage 1 sleep, the brain waves become less regular, and are reduced in amplitude, with

Fig. 6-6 Stages of sleep

Changes in EEG from waking through the stages of sleep are shown at the top of the chart, followed by Stage REM, in which the EEG is that of Stage 1, but the eye movements (REMs), essentially absent at the other stages, are clearly shown, alike for both eyes. (Adapted from Webb and Agnew, 1968)

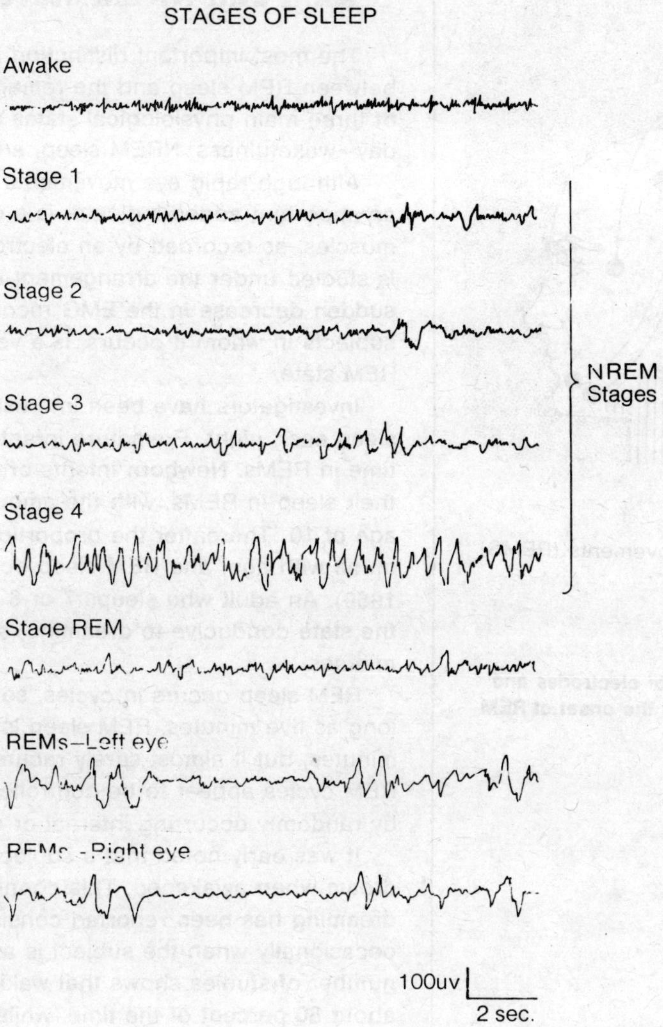

alpha intruding only occasionally. At Stage 2, there are a few quick bursts (see Figure 6-6) followed by the appearance of spindles. The still deeper stages, Stages 3 and 4, are characterized by slow waves known as *delta waves*. It becomes more and more difficult to awaken the person as he goes into deeper sleep, although a distinction has to be made between awakening by some impersonal method, such as a loud sound, and something personal, such as a familiar name, which can often arouse a person from a deep stage.

Another change occurs after the person has been asleep for an hour or so. The EEG record goes back to Stage 1, but the subject does not wake up. Instead, there are eye movements showing on the record, as indicated at the bottom of Figure 6-6. This stage is known as REM; the others are known as non-REM (or NREM). On arousal from Stage REM a person commonly reports a dream. Even though sleep at this stage is apparently light and the person is dreaming, it is as difficult to arouse him from the REM stage as from Stage 4.

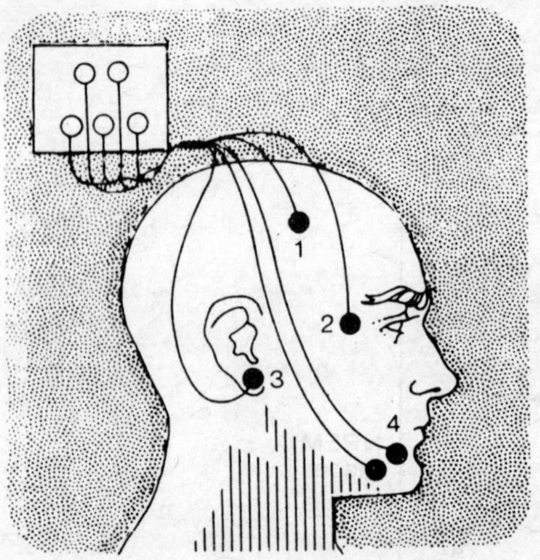

1 For recording EEG

2 For recording eye movements (REMS)

3 Neutral electrode

4 For recording EMG

Fig. 6-7 Arrangements of electrodes and characteristic records at the onset of REM sleep

REM and NREM States

The most important distinction in sleep analysis has come to be that between REM sleep and the remaining sleep. Researchers now think in terms of three main physiological states succeeding each other every day—wakefulness, NREM sleep, and REM sleep.

Although rapid eye movements were the original indicators of REM sleep, an important added indicator is a decrease in the tone of some striate muscles, as recorded by an electromyogram (EMG). In actual practice, sleep is studied under the arrangement indicated schematically in Figure 6-7. The sudden decrease in the EMG record as measured at the chin, for those subjects in whom it occurs, is a very precise indicator of the onset of the REM state.

Investigators have been interested in the amount of time spent in REM sleep each night. Premature infants spend about 75 percent of their sleeping time in REMs. Newborn infants of normal term spend about 50 percent of their sleep in REMs, with the amount of REM gradually decreasing until the age of 10. Thereafter the proportion of REM sleep does not change very much with age, and REM sleep occurs about 25 percent of the time, (Kales, 1969). An adult who sleeps 7 or 8 hours probably spends up to two hours in the state conducive to dreaming, so dreaming occurs roughly every 90 minutes.

REM sleep occurs in cycles, so that once NREM sleep interrupts for as long as five minutes, REM sleep is not likely to occur again for 30 to 60 minutes, but it almost surely recurs by 80 minutes (Dement, 1972). Hence REM cycles appear to be controlled by some internal pacemaker rather than by randomly occurring internal or external disturbances.

It was early noted that a subject in the REM state was likely to report a dream when awakened. This connection between the REM state and dreaming has been reported consistently, but dreams are also found occasionally when the subject is awakening from NREM sleep. Review of a number of studies shows that waking from the REM state yields dreams about 80 percent of the time, while waking from NREM sleep yields dreams about 14 percent of the time. Results vary because of different standards used in distinguishing between a "dream" and "just thoughts" (Dement, 1972).

The dreams reported following awakening from NREM sleep are often more like "thoughts" rather than dreams, but sharp distinctions are not to be expected because of the great variations in dreams themselves. Still, Monroe and others (1965) found that judges could distinguish between dream samples collected following REM and NREM awakenings. The judges determined successfully in better than 90 percent of the cases which dreams had been produced under REM conditions. It is somewhat surprising to find how active the brain is during sleep, whether it is producing just "thoughts" or more "dreamlike" products (Webb, 1973).

Dreams and Dreaming

Dreams are not alike in length, in content, in emotionality, or in vividness. Many dream diaries have been kept in order to determine what people dream about and whether dreams make any sense. Very few of the dreams collected from college students are very dramatic ("Alice-in-Wonderland") ones; most concern ordinary experiences. In one tabulation of 1,000 dreams (from 500 male and 500 female college students), it was found that the average dream concerned two or three persons and included mostly one or two objects. The objects were quite familiar ones for the most part; the most frequently mentioned objects were (in descending order): houses, automobiles, cities, rooms, homes, doors, and stairs (Hall and Van de Castle, 1966). Some of the events dreamed about were, of course, emotionally loaded, friendly, sexual, or aggressive.

An unusual type of dream occasionally reported is the *lucid* dream, so named by van Eeden (1913) on the basis of his own experience. He felt that he retained all his normal functions while dreaming, knew that he was dreaming, and yet did not have control of all that was happening. One of his "experiments" within a dream is reported as follows:

> I drew with my finger, moistened by saliva, a wet cross on the palm of my left hand, with the intention of seeing whether it would still be there on waking up. Then I *dreamt* that I woke up and felt the wet cross on my left hand by applying the palm to my cheek. And then a long time afterwards I woke up *really* and knew at once that the hand of my physical body had been lying in a closed position undisturbed on my chest all the while.

An allegorical painting depicting Frederick the Wise's dream of Luther posting his theses with a giant pen.

Apparently the state is not quite as "lucid" as van Eeden's statements sometimes make it sound. Others have reported similar experiences. One of the authors (E.R.H.) vowed to experiment the next time he had a dream that seemed almost too vivid to be a dream. An opportunity came when, in a dream, he was reading a billboard and finding the advertising copy so clear that it did not seem like a dream. At the same time something made him think that he was dreaming. To test whether he was dreaming, he lifted his legs to see if he could fly, and he did indeed fly off, forgetting about the experiment until upon awakening later he recalled what had happened.

The investigation of dreams and dreaming aided by the new psychophysiological methods has provided the answers to some age-old questions and raised many new ones. Some of these questions and relevant findings will be summarized below.

DO EYE MOVEMENTS REFLECT THE CONTENT OF THE DREAM? Occasionally eye movements correspond quite well to events reported in the dream (Figure 6-8), but this is not usually the case. It cannot be generally assumed that eye movements reflect what is being hallucinated in the dream. It is doubtful that the REM states of very young infants are accompanied by

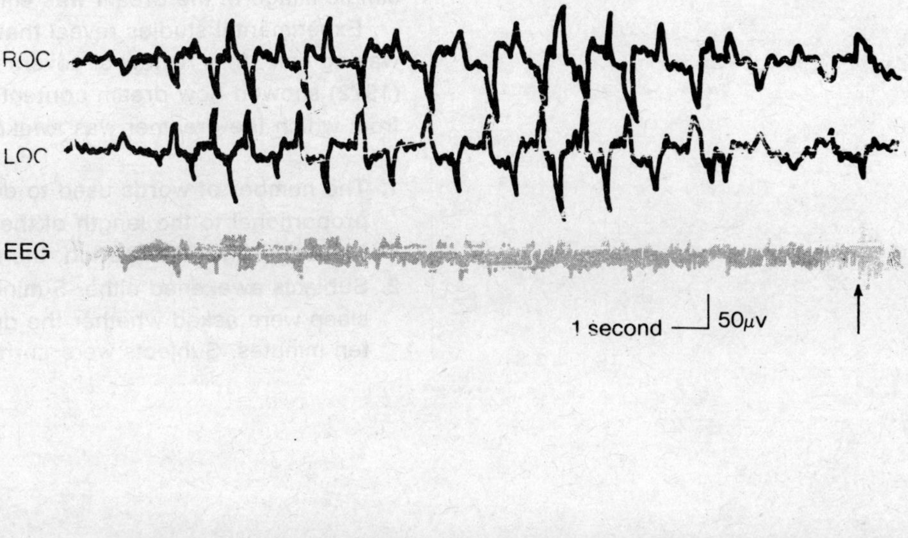

Fig. 6-8 Rapid eye movement and dream imagery correspondence

The eye movement records (ROC for right eye and LOC for left eye) showed a regular sequence of 26 eye movements alternating to the right and to the left. Following this sequence the subject was awakened (at the arrow at the lower right in the figure). He reported that just before being aroused he had dreamed that he was watching a ping-pong game between two friends. He had been standing at the side of the table so that he looked back and forth to follow the ball during a lengthy volley. (After Dement, 1967) dreams, for dreams, as we know them, depend upon remembered perceptions, even though they may be organized in novel or bizarre ways.

DOES EVERYONE DREAM? Although many people do not recall dreams in the morning, "recallers" and "nonrecallers" appear to dream equally often, if we accept the REM-sleep evidence (Goodenough and others, 1959).

Two hypotheses have been offered to account for the differential recall of dreams upon awakening in the morning. One is that non-recallers have an inherent difficulty in recalling dreams; those who do not recall dreams in everyday life recall fewer dreams in the laboratory, and their reports are shorter than those who do recall (Lewis and others, 1966). The other hypothesis is that some people awaken more readily in the midst of REM sleep, and those who do, report more dreams; in other words, the answer to the question: "Why do I remember dreaming?" is, according to this hypothesis, "You happened to wake up when you were dreaming" (Webb and Kersey, 1967). On the whole, regardless of the fate of these hypotheses, the evidence is that everyone dreams.

CAN THE SLEEPER REACT TO THE ENVIRONMENT WITHOUT AWAKENING? Williams, Morlock, and Morlock (1966) showed that subjects could discriminate auditory signals during sleep better during Stage 1 (sleep onset) and Stage 2 than during REM phases. Such results bear on the possibility of sleep learning, because material read to the learner while asleep (often from a tape recorder) must be responded to if it is to be learned. Many claims have been made for learning during sleep, but laboratory substantiation is lacking (Emmons and Simon, 1956; Hoskovec and Cooper, 1967). Signals that occur during REM sleep may be incorporated into the dream rather than awaken the dreamer. Berger (1963) showed that spoken names presented during REM sleep were incorporated into dream events. Subjects taught to respond posthypnotically to a verbal signal (for example, to scratch the nose, or to turn a pillow) carried out the instructions even though the signal was given during REM sleep (Cobb and others, 1965). The state of sleep is by no means a completely inert one.

HOW LONG DO DREAMS LAST? Occasionally it seems that dreams must be almost instantaneous because a person may wake up to a ringing alarm clock and recall that he had a complex dream of a fire breaking out and then of the fire truck coming with its clanging bell. It is possible that some dreams are almost instantaneous, but in such cases it is more likely either that a dream-memory was evoked by the external stimulus, or that a simple image in the dream was elaborated in the telling of the dream.

Experimental studies reveal that dream time is not very different from waking time. In a review of several studies in which he participated, Dement (1972) showed how dream content is related to the length of the REM period from which the dreamer was awakened:

1. The number of words used to describe the dream turns out to be directly proportional to the length of the REM period prior to awakening; that is, the longer the REM period, the more words needed for dream description.
2. Subjects awakened either 5 minutes or 10 minutes after the onset of REM sleep were asked whether the dream had probably lasted five minutes or ten minutes. Subjects were correct in 92 of 111 instances.

3. In order to produce a clear beginning time for a dream, a fine spray of cold water was ejected onto the dreaming subject. In 10 instances in which the subject did not wake up and incorporated the water identifiably into his dream the amount of activity reported in the dream between the water episode and the arousal was about right for the amount of activity that might have occurred in ordinary realistic time.

WHEN DO SLEEPTALKING AND SLEEPWALKING TAKE PLACE? Careful study has been made of sleeptalking in the laboratory by subjects who volunteered because they were known to be sleeptalkers. A total of 206 speeches recorded during the night from 13 subjects (averaging 3.9 speeches per subject per night) showed that 75–80 percent were from NREM sleep (Stages 2, 3, and 4), while 20–25 percent were associated with REM sleep (Arkin and others, 1970). Sleepwalking is also associated with NREM sleep; subjects usually forget what they did while sleepwalking, and the dreams they remember in the morning bear no resemblance to what they did while they were walking about (Jacobson and Kales, 1967).

"Macy's is closed!"

Although sleeptalking does not appear to be related to dreams under normal circumstances, it can be used as a method for studying dream content. Through posthypnotic suggestions planted in the waking state it is possible to instruct the subject to talk about his dream *while it is occurring,* without awakening, and to sleep comfortably and silently when the dream is over (Arkin, Hastey, and Reiser, 1966). The dream recalled in the morning may be a fragmentary version of the full dream reported while it was happening.

Dream Theories

People have long been puzzled by their dreams. Because a person does not feel responsible for his dreams, he is likely to think of them as informative, perhaps even prophetic, so dream interpretation has had a long history.

FREUD'S THEORY. The most influential theory of dreams in the last half-century has been that of Freud, the founder of psychoanalysis. Freud announced his theory in *The interpretation of dreams* (1900), a book he considered to be his most important work. He believed that unconscious impulses were responsible for the dream, and that the aim of the dream was the gratification of some drive (in the older terminology he used—the fulfillment of a wish). The real meaning of the dream, called its *latent content,* is not directly expressed, but is instead dramatized in disguised form. The remembered content of the dream, in this disguised form, is it *manifest content.* According to Freud, the dreamer constructs the dream by representing the impulse-provoked ideas in acceptable form, commonly as visual imagery. The manifest content derives from the thoughts of the previous day (the *day residues,* as Freud called them), combined with thoughts and emotions from the past.

Freud's theory holds that the work of dream construction occurs through the mechanisms of condensation, displacement, and symbolization. *Condensation* refers to the combining of ideas into more abbreviated form, so that a single word or figure may have multiple meanings in the dream. *Displacement* permits one thing to stand for another, as one part of the body may stand for a different part. *Symbolization* is the more general term for representing ideas or events by something else. These may be private symbols, related to the individual experience of the dreamer, or more universal symbols, of which sexual symbols are the most likely to be thought of in connection with Freud's ideas. Since to Freud much of the impulsive life centers around sexual wishes, and sex has certain taboos associated with it, the symbolization of the sexual organs is to be expected: the male organ is represented by a snake or other long or pointed object; the female organ is more often represented by some sort of container, such as a box, basket, or vessel.

Freud thought that the adaptive role of the dream was as the guardian of sleep: it did this by getting rid of unfulfilled impulses, which might otherwise disturb the sleep. The disguise was necessary so that the disturbing impulses would not be brought to the attention of the dreamer. If the raw meaning of the dream were open to the dreamer, the impulses would often be found to be intolerable, and he would wake up. The dream does often fail in its work; for instance, the dreamer sometimes awakens frightened, possibly because of anxiety aroused in the dream. In his later writings Freud acknowledged these failures of the dream work (Freud, 1933).

Many results from the physiological studies cast doubt on the Freudian theory. The prevalence of REM states in very young infants (including premature ones), and in animals low in the phyletic scale, makes it unlikely that the adaptive purpose of the REM state, whatever it may be, corresponds to the Freudian theory of the adaptive (sleep-protecting) nature of dreams.

ALTERNATIVE THEORIES ABOUT DREAMING. Freud's theory did not go unchallenged by other psychoanalysts. Erikson (1954) felt that the dream revealed much more than disguised wish fulfillment, and that its manifest content was worth taking seriously. French and Fromm (1963) showed that a series of dreams could be interpreted as repeated attempts by the dreamer to solve problems. Hall (1953) had earlier shown that sometimes the thoughts that appeared in "disguised" form also appeared in "plain" form in the same dream. This led him to suggest that the so-called dream disguise was no disguise at all, but merely a form of metaphor—a literary device within the dream.

Jung, an early disciple of Freud's, broke with his master and set up a system of his own, including his own theory of dream interpretation (Jung, 1944). Basic to his theory is the conception of archetypes—fundamental notions such as God, Mother, Wise Old Man—that exist in a universal unconscious which the individual shares. In dreams these archetypes emerge in interaction between the conscious and unconscious parts of the personality, often in a quaternary form in the dream (four people, representing parts of the personality, or various aspects of masculinity and femininity, good and evil, etc.) The whole theory is loosely structured and colored with religious and mystical overtones, so that, although it attracts a following, it is little assimilated within scientific psychology.

The dream interpretation controversies have a greater chance of being resolved now that new methods of investigation permit samples of dreams under controlled conditions and more detailed reports of the dreams themselves. It is to Freud's credit that he made dreams a subject of modern scientific inquiry; it remains for others to build new theories based on sounder knowledge than was available to him.

Hypnosis as an Altered State of Awareness

The word "hypnosis" is derived from the Greek word for sleep (*hypnos*); the metaphor of sleep is commonly used in inducing the hypnotic trance. Pavlov, the famous Russian physiologist, became interested in sleep and hypnosis during his later years; he conceived of hypnosis as a partial sleep. Now that EEG evidence is available, we can say with some assurance that hypnosis is not ordinary sleep, for the EEG of the hypnotic state is that of waking, not that of any of the recognized stages of sleep. Because it is possible to induce an alert hypnotic state without relaxation suggestions, the sleep metaphor appears to be increasingly inappropriate (Vingoe, 1973).

Hypnotic Induction

In order to hypnotize a willing and cooperative subject (the only kind who can be hypnotized under most circumstances), the hypnotist creates the conditions for entering hypnosis by any of a number of methods that relax the subject, exercise his imagination, and lead him to relinquish some control to the hypnotist and to accept some reality distortion. Often the hypnotist will ask the subject to fix his eyes upon some small target, such as a thumbtack on the wall, concentrate on the target, detach all thoughts from other things, and gradually become relaxed or sleepy. The suggestion of sleep is a convenient one because it is familiar as being a relaxed state, out of touch with ordinary environmental demands. But it is a metaphor, and the subject is in fact told that he will not really go to sleep. The subject continues to listen to the hypnotist and, if susceptible, finds it easy and congenial to do what the hypnotist suggests and to experience what he invites the subject to experience.

In its modern form, hypnosis does not involve authoritarian commands by the hypnotist; with a little training the subject can hypnotize himself, using what has been learned from the hypnotist. In other words, the subject enters the hypnotic state when the conditions are right; the hypnotist merely helps set these conditions. The transition from the waking state to the hypnotic state takes a little time, but with practice this time tends to be shortened. With special procedures, such as observing others being hypnotized, the subject can learn to go somewhat more deeply into hypnosis.

Characteristics of the Hypnotic State

The hypnotic state or trance recognized today is essentially as it was described in the nineteenth-century heyday of hypnosis. Some of its characteristics, as shown by subjects who illustrate a high degree of susceptibility, are the following:

1. *The subject ceases to make his own plans.* When deeply hypnotized, the subject does not like to initiate activity and would rather wait for the hypnotist to tell him what to do.
2. *Attention is redistributed.* While attention is always selective, under hypnosis it becomes more selective than usual. If the subject is told to

listen to the hypnotist's voice only, the subject will not pay attention to any other voices in the room.

3. *Reality testing is reduced and reality distortion accepted.* Ordinarily one checks up on things to see that he is awake, oriented in space and time, not suffering from illusions, and so on. Under hypnosis one may uncritically accept hallucinated experiences (petting the imaginary rabbit in his lap) or other distortions that would usually be rejected.
4. *Suggestibility is increased.* Of course one has to accept suggestions in order to be hypnotized at all, but the question is whether normal suggestibility is *increased* under hypnosis. This is a matter of some dispute, but careful studies do find an increase in suggestibility, though perhaps less than might be supposed from the common identification of hypnosis with heightened suggestibility (Ruch, Morgan, and Hilgard, 1973).
5. *The hypnotized subject readily enacts unusual roles.* When told to adopt a role, such as being someone other than himself, the hypnotized subject will commonly do so and will carry out complex activities related to that role. This includes re-enacting his own behavior at a much younger age (as in hypnotic age regression). There may be something of an actor in each of us, and the permissiveness of the hypnotic situation, in which ordinary restraints on behavior are set aside, makes this role behavior congenial. Impressed by this kind of behavior, Sarbin and Coe (1972) have formulated a role-enactment theory of hypnosis, affirming that those who become hypnotized have a high order of role-enactment ability and have attitudes appropriate to role-enactment.
6. *Posthypnotic amnesia is often present.* Some susceptible hypnotic subjects react to the suggestion that they will forget events within hypnosis after they are aroused from it, until a prearranged signal is given by the hypnotist. Following such instructions they will forget all or most of what transpired during the hypnotic session. When the release signal is given, the memories are restored. How the extent of forgetting varies from person to person in a college population is shown in Figure 6-9. Most subjects forget a few things they did under hypnosis, just as they forget what they have done in ordinary psychological experiments. But some are extremely forgetful following the suggestion that they will not "remember," and it is these we think of as demonstrating posthypnotic amnesia, particularly if they remember again when the release signal is given: "Now you can remember everything!"

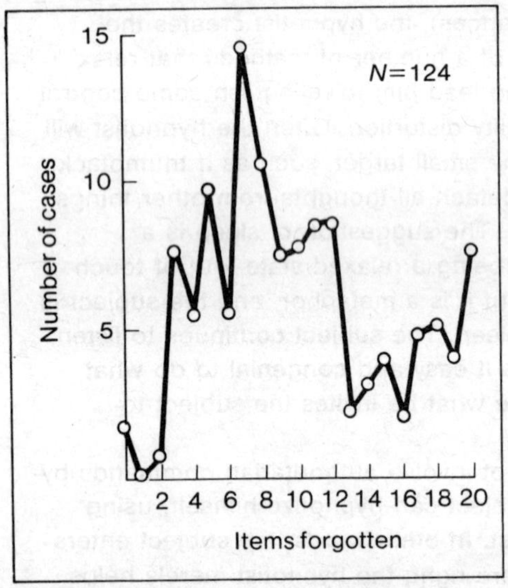

Fig. 6-9 Distribution of posthypnotic amnesia

The scores are plotted according to items forgotten after an amnesia suggestion given within hypnosis, with a possible of 20 items for total forgetting. Those who forgot 0–13 items may be illustrating ordinary forgetting, but those who forgot 14–20 may not only have been amnesic but they may have represented those to whom the concept of a change of state best applies. (After Hilgard and others, 1961)

While responsiveness to suggestions is the most characteristic aspect of hypnosis as it is usually witnessed, the possible alterations of consciousness within the hypnotic state are incompletely described by these typical behaviors. When subjects, hypnotized by ordinary relaxation procedures, are encouraged to go deeper into hypnosis, they eventually reach a state in which they are unresponsive to the hypnotist's suggestions (except for some prearranged signal at which they will return to a level at which they can communicate). In describing this state, they often use terms similar to those used in describing mystical experiences, such as a separation of mind from body, a feeling of oneness with the universe, a sense of gaining knowledge, but of a kind that is not communicable (Sherman, 1971). Hypnosis is not limited to such relaxed states, however, and it is possible to produce a hyperalert trance characterized by increased tension and alertness.

TABLE 6-1
Items of the Stanford hypnotic susceptibility scale, Form A

SUGGESTED BEHAVIOR	CRITERION OF PASSING (YIELDING SCORE OF +)
1. Postural sway	Falls without forcing
2. Eye closure	Closes eyes without forcing
3. Hand lowering (left)	Lowers at least six inches by end of 10 seconds
4. Immobilization (right arm)	Arm rises less than one inch in 10 seconds
5. Finger lock	Incomplete separation of fingers at end of 10 seconds
6. Arm rigidity (left arm)	Less than two inches of arm bending in 10 seconds
7. Hands moving together	Hands at least as close as six inches after 10 seconds
8. Verbal inhibition (name)	Name unspoken in 10 seconds
9. Hallucination (fly)	Any movement, grimacing, acknowledgment of effect
10. Eye catalepsy	Eyes remain closed at end of 10 seconds
11. Posthypnotic (changes chairs)	Any partial movement response
12. Amnesia test	Three or fewer items recalled

Source: Weitzenhoffer and Hilgard (1959).

Interestingly enough, the effect on responsiveness to ordinary hypnotic-like suggestions is very much the same in both the relaxed and the alert trance (Ludwig and Lyle, 1964).

Who Can Be Hypnotized?

There is no disagreement that some people can be hypnotized more readily than others, but there is uncertainty whether some persons can be hypnotized at all, even under the most favorable circumstances. Occasional reports have been given of heroic attempts in which the same person underwent hypnotic induction for hundreds of trials until hypnosis was finally achieved. The record, a case reported by Vogt in the 1800s, was six hundred trials. Under ordinary circumstances, a person's hypnotizability can be determined quite well from the first attempt at hypnosis.

The availability of scales for measuring susceptibility to hypnosis permits more precise statements about the distribution of hypnotizability than were formerly possible. The most satisfactory scales are based on the performances given by a subject following a standard form of hypnotic induction: the subject who responds most frequently like a hypnotized person is scored as most susceptible. The items of one such scale are listed in Table 6-1. The scores are reasonably stable—a retest 10 years later showed a correlation of .60 between earlier and later scores (Morgan, Johnson, and Hilgard, 1974). Furthermore, the greater similarity of scores for identical (monozygotic) twins compared with fraternal (dizygotic) twins suggests the possibility that the ability to be hypnotized may have a hereditary component (Morgan, 1973).

How are the special characteristics related to hypnotic susceptibility maintained or enhanced? Interviews with hundreds of subjects, before and after induction of hypnosis, have pointed to the importance of early childhood experiences. Experiences of a particular kind appear to either generate or maintain the abilities that enter into hypnotizability (J. R. Hilgard, 1970). A capacity to become deeply involved in imaginative experiences that are related to hypnosis derives from parents who are themselves deeply involved in such areas as reading, music, religion, or the esthetic appreciation of nature. Another experience leading to hypnotizability in some

CRITICAL DISCUSSION

Neo-Dissociation Theory and the "Hidden Observer" in Hypnosis

A familiar method of studying dissociation in hypnosis is to have a subject perform arithmetical operations and write out the computations and at the same time perform some other task, such as reading aloud. The subject is unaware of one part of his activity, say the mathematical computation, and completely aware of the other part. How can an intellectual task, such as arithmetic, and essentially voluntary behavior, such as writing, be carried on out of consciousness, while some other conscious task is being performed? At a subconscious level there may be a process that is very like consciousness but not available to the open consciousness. The expression "hidden observer" has been introduced as a metaphor to describe this concealed part that knows things that are not open to the ordinary consciousness of the person.

The nature of this "hidden observer" was brought out in some experiments in which pain was being controlled hypnotically. Subjects were asked to undergo a stress that is normally quite painful, such as placing the hand and forearm in circulating ice water, or of having the blood cut off from a forearm by a tourniquet placed above the elbow, followed by exercise of the occluded hand. If under hypnosis the subject receives the suggestion that he will feel no pain, he may indeed be entirely comfortable throughout the stress period, feeling nothing whatever if he is adequately susceptible to suggestion (e.g., Hilgard, 1969).

If, however, while one hand and arm are being stressed, the other is kept out of awareness owing to appropriate hypnotic suggestions, and the subject is told to report what is felt through automatic writing, the hidden part may report a rising pain, even while the hypnotized person verbally reports no pain at all. The subject may be continued in hypnosis after the stress is removed and he has had time for his arm to become completely normal, and then be told that when the experimenter places his hand on his shoulder a hidden part of himself (the "hidden observer") will tell what it remembers about the experience. The "hidden observer" recalls that the water was indeed very cold, or the bloodless arm was in pain, but usually reports that the pains were not as severe as in the normal nonhypnotic state, and were less distressing than a pain of the reported intensity would usually be (Hilgard, 1973a). Figure 6-10 shows a comparison of rising pain reports for one subject in the normal nonhypnotic state in the circulating ice water, the absent pain reported verbally after anesthesia has been suggested, and the somewhat reduced pain that is reported at the same time by the "hidden observer" through automatic writing.

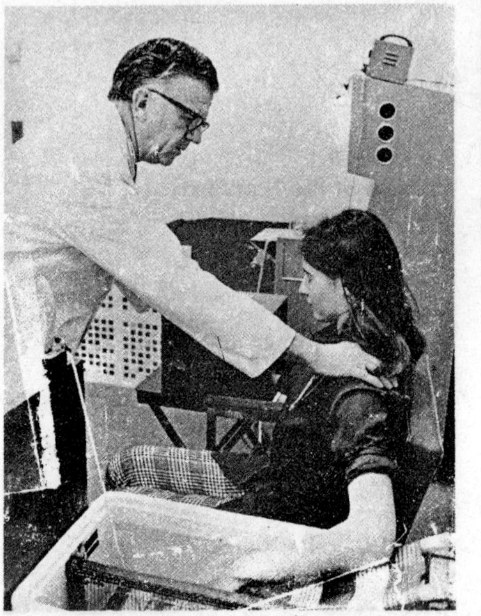

The hand in ice water may feel no pain following suggestions of hypnotic analgesia. With the hand on the shoulder, however, the experimenter can tap a hidden part of the person that reports that the pain is being felt at some level.

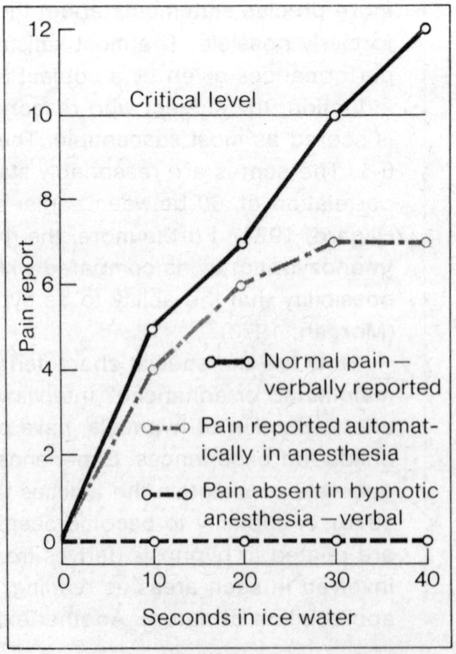

Fig. 6-10 Open and hidden reports of pain Pain as verbally reported normally, in hypnotic anesthesia, and as reported by the "hidden observer" in automatic writing. Data from a single subject. (Courtesy of Department of Psychology, Stanford University.)

In the same laboratory it has been shown that the "hidden observer" can report sounds heard while the subject was hynotically deaf, or can remember the number of fingers held before his face when he was hypnotically blind. It is as though under these circumstances the information received from the environment is registered, processed, stored in memory, and placed under some sort of barrier to recovery, before ever becoming openly conscious.

These are the kinds of facts a neo-dissociation theory is called upon to explain. Obviously merely labeling them is not enough, but an adequate theory could go far in accounting for the facts of not only hypnosis, but also multiple personality and other nonhypnotic phenomena.

persons is rather strict punishment in childhood. The conjecture is that a history of punishment by parents who care for their children may produce a tendency to escape harassment by moving off into a realm of imagination, thus practicing the kind of dissociations that are later to be used in hypnosis.

Theories of Hypnosis

The older theory that hypnosis was a form of sleep is now largely discredited by the physiological studies that show a difference between hypnosis and sleep and by the facts of hyperalert hypnosis. Another theory, derived from psychoanalysis, proposes that hypnosis is a state of partial regression, in which impulsiveness and fantasy are aroused in a state lacking the more mature controls of ordinary adult consciousness (Gill and Brenman, 1959). Still another theory follows the sociological and social-psychological theory of role behavior, in which the individual is seen as enacting different roles in ordinary behavior, so that adopting the role of hypnotized subject is not unlike adopting the role of mother, student, or musician, each of which has its own demands (Sarbin and Coe, 1972). An extremely skeptical view, associated with Barber (1969), accepts all the hypnotic phenomena but does not believe it useful to use the concept of hypnosis in reference to them, for fear that it will be used as an explanatory term rather than a descriptive one. An older interpretation, owing to Janet in the 1800s, treats hypnosis as a dissociative phenomenon, in which some aspect of mental functioning is separated from other functioning, as in the previously described cases of multiple personalities. This theory has recently been revised in modified form and called neo-dissociation theory (Hilgard, 1973b). Each of these theories calls attention to some significant features of hypnotic behavior, and they are not, in fact, contradictory in any important sense.

Meditation and Self-Induced Alterations of Consciousness

Because we can think and dream, we can transcend the everyday world and contemplate visions of ideal or unthought-of worlds. Through past ages people have isolated themselves on mountain tops, fasted, indulged in special exercises, or in other ways sought out experiences of novelty and depth; often this quest had religious significance, like the search of religious mystics for a reality that lies beyond the world as we know it. Many Western contemporaries, dissatisfied with what they see as a corruption of life through material interests and an ever-encroaching technology, have turned to some of the practices of the Eastern religions in the hope of finding a new set of values.

Experimental Meditation

It is possible to study what happens in meditation by inviting persons without any special background to participate in the kinds of exercises recommended by those practicing *yoga*, a system of thought based on Hindu philosophy, or *Zen,* which is derived from Chinese and Japanese Buddhism. The subjects' experiences are then studied in the same manner as any other experiences of psychological interest.

Meditative practices can be carried out under various instructions, but these instructions commonly fall into two main groups, first, an *opening-up meditation,* in which the subject clears his mind for receiving new experiences, and, second, a *concentrative meditation* in which the benefits are obtained through actively attending to some object, word, or idea (Naranjo and Ornstein, 1971). One illustration will be given of each of these approaches.

The exercises call for relaxation and controlled breathing, with the subject sitting or kneeling on the floor, perhaps partly supported by cushions; the position must be conducive to relaxation without inducing sleep. In yoga the eyes may be closed, but in Zen they are kept open. There are many variations on what the meditator is trying to do, but the following is a representative statement, classified as an opening-up meditation:

> The radical approach begins with the resolve to do nothing, to think nothing, to make no effort of one's own, to relax completely and let go one's mind and body . . . stepping out of the stream of ever-changing ideas and feelings which your mind is, watch the onrush of the stream. Refuse to be submerged in the current. Changing the metaphor, it may be said, watch your ideas, feelings and wishes fly across the firmament like a flock of birds. Let them fly freely. Just keep a watch. Don't allow the birds to carry you off into the clouds (Chaudhuri, 1965, pp. 30–31).

An experimental report can illustrate what happens during the early stages in practiced meditation. A subject sat in an armchair in a pleasantly carpeted room viewing a blue vase 10 inches high placed on a simple, brown table against the opposite wall, 8 feet before him. He was given the following instructions (quoted in part), illustrating concentrative meditation:

> The purpose of these sessions is to learn about concentration. Your aim is to concentrate on the blue vase. By concentration I do not mean analyzing the different parts of the vase, or associating ideas to the vase, but rather, trying to see the vase as it exists in itself, without any connections to other things. Exclude all other thoughts or feelings or sounds or body sensations. . . . (Deikman, 1963, p. 330).

After the session began, a number of sounds were presented by tape recorder in order to test the subject's ability to avoid being distracted by them. The meditation on the first day was 5 minutes, 10 minutes on the second day, and 15 minutes for each of the remaining sessions (a total of 12 spread over three weeks); a few sessions were spontaneously extended to as much as 33 minutes at the request of the subject. The most common effects were: (1) an altered, more intense perception of the vase; (2) some time-shortening, particularly in retrospect; (3) conflicting perceptions, as of the vase at once filling the visual field and not filling it; agitation, at once disturbing and pleasurable; (4) decreasing effectiveness of the external stimuli (both less distraction and eventually less conscious registration); and (5) a pleasurable state, the experience of which was reported as valuable and rewarding.

The most widely publicized meditation practice is called *transcendental meditation* (TM), as promoted by Maharishi Mahesh Yoga. It is difficult to judge the success of TM by its loyal adherents, for satisfied communicants are the rule in religious and quasi-religious movements. The total plan is quite ambitious, as defined by Maharishi in January 1972, in the seven goals of his world plan:

1. To develop the full potential of the individual.
2. To enhance governmental achievements.
3. To realize the highest ideal of education.
4. To solve the problems of crime, drug abuse and all behavior that brings unhappiness to the family of man.
5. To bring fulfillment to the economic aspirations of individuals and society.
6. To achieve the spiritual goals of mankind in this generation. (Forem, 1973, p. 10)

These ambitious objectives are said to be attainable: "The active cooperation of outstanding men and women in the world is all that is necessary now with this knowledge of the Science of Creative Intelligence" (Forem, p. 11). All of this comes about through a very simple process: that of meditation, which is the practical technique of the Science of Creative Intelligence.

The technique, while simple, is to be learned from a qualified instructor. A *mantra* is chosen for each subject at the time of instruction. This is a special sound which is repeated over and over to produce the deep rest and refined awareness that is said to characterize TM. "Because individuals differ in the quality of the vibrations which constitute their individual personalities, the right selection of a thought for a particular individual is of vital importance" (Maharishi, 1966, p. 56). The whole discussion is carried on at a dogmatic level; the evidence for the matching of mantras to vibrations is not given.

The scientific evidence that meditation does in fact have some effect on the meditator comes primarily from a widely cited study by Wallace and Benson (1972), which showed that experienced meditators do indeed achieve deeply relaxed states (see Figure 6-11). Their control studies with relaxation and hypnosis, however, are not at all comparable in terms of the amount of experience in practiced relaxation (using a method, for example, such as the progressive relaxation of Jacobson, 1970), or repeated hypnosis comparable to the time spent in meditation. Hence assertions that meditation and hypnosis have nothing in common have not yet been satisfactorily supported; subjects who have practiced both do indeed find many similarities.

Fig. 6-11 Effect of meditation on oxygen consumption of practiced subjects

Oxygen consumption (upper line) N = 20; carbon dioxide elimination (lower line) N = 15. (From Wallace and Benson, 1972)

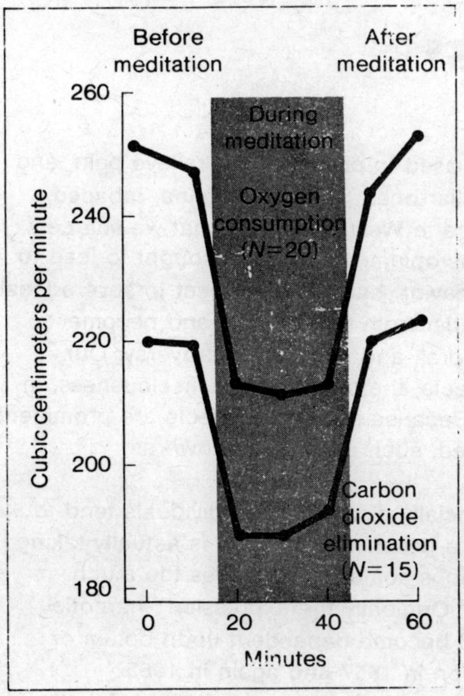

Biofeedback and the Voluntary Control of Normally Involuntary Processes

It is well known that some who practice yoga in India gain remarkable control over certain physiological processes not ordinarily under voluntary control, such as heart rate and smooth-muscle responses (Wenger and Bagchi, 1961; Wenger, Bagchi, and Anand, 1961). (See Figure 6-12.) Until recently it was assumed that such control resulted only from long-continued and disciplined exercise, but now laboratory methods have produced some of the effects in randomly selected subjects.

One type of control is that over the EEG alpha rhythm. The *alpha rhythm*

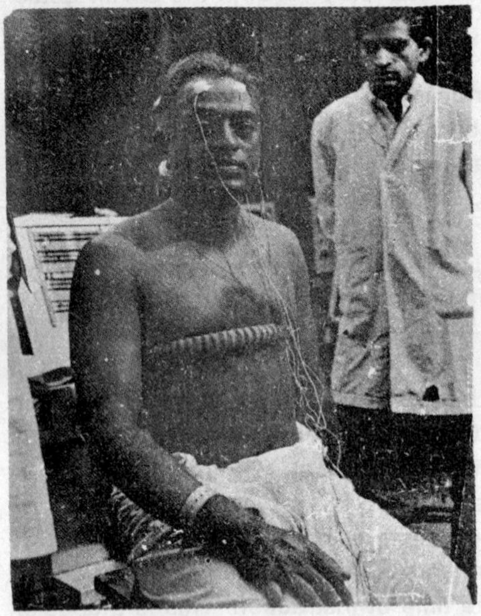

Fig. 6-12 The control of vital functions

Ramanand Yogi has transducers attached for the study of EEGs, heart rate, and breathing, as he prepares to reduce his oxygen needs while sealed in an airtight box. (From Calder, 1971)

is commonly displayed by a subject sitting quietly with eyes closed. The response becomes irregular (desynchronized) when the subject either opens his eyes or uses his mind alertly, as in mental arithmetic. By using special equipment attached to the EEG apparatus, it is possible to convert the presence of alpha to a tone that the subject can hear; when alpha is absent the tone is turned off. Thus the subject can tell, by listening for the tone, whether the alpha rhythm is being recorded from his scalp. He uses this information, or *biofeedback*, to "learn" to try to maintain the alpha with his eyes open, or to turn it off when it appears (Nowlis and Kamiya, 1970). The earlier reports were somewhat misleading in that changes in alpha were expressed as a difference in alpha under the instructions for "alpha-on" and "alpha-off." It is now known that it is relatively easy to turn alpha off, but extremely difficult to obtain a control that will increase alpha, despite the widely commercialized instruments and methods that claim to do this. Hence what appeared to be a learning to control alpha was more largely learning how to turn alpha off, which is not the end usually desired. Only if conditions are such as to suppress normal alpha (for example, dim illumination) will alpha enhancement through feedback be shown (Paskewitz and Orne, 1973). Whether or not feedback training is used, a high level of alpha may be associated with the calm and detached states meditators achieve.

Many of the various biofeedback experiments first done on animals (see page 206) have now been done on humans. For example, it is possible to change the blood distribution to the two hands so that the temperature in one hand is increased and the other decreased (Maslach, Marshall, and Zimbardo, 1972; Roberts, Kewman, and Macdonald, 1973). Hence the laboratory method has made it easier for many to achieve, without intensive practice, the kind of control achieved by a yogi in India, or in Western countries through other kinds of training, such as progressive relaxation (Jacobson, 1970) or autogenic training, a form of self-control closely related to hypnosis (Schultz and Luthe, 1969).

Psychoactive Drugs and Their Effects

Since ancient times drugs have been used to poison, cure, relieve pain, and produce sleep or hallucinations. Familiar ones, such as caffeine, tobacco, and alcohol, have become so accepted in Western culture that we scarcely think of them as drugs; others such as opium derivatives, thought to lead to socially undesirable or dangerous behavior, have been subject to severe legal restrictions. Many drugs become popular from time to time and become occasions for a great deal of legal, moral, and medical controversy. Our concern here is the psychological effects, the changes in consciousness, in feelings of well-being or depression. Because subjective effects are prominent when many of these drugs are ingested, such drugs are known as *psychoactive*.

The words used to characterize socially disapproved individuals tend to take on connotations that go beyond a description of what is actually taking place. As someone said, "An alcoholic is someone who uses too much alcohol and I don't like him anyhow." Originally the expression "narcotic addict" referred to someone who had become dependent upon opium or cocaine. The World Health Organization in 1957 and again in 1965 recommended against the use of the word *addiction,* especially in the form of *an addict* (Eddy and others, 1965). They pointed out that a person could be an habitual user of a psychoactive substance without conforming to the usual connotations of addiction. For example, the social drinker or regular smoker need not be "addicted" to alcohol or tobacco, even though some might find it very hard to give up the habit. For the word *addiction,* The National Commission on Marihuana and Drug Abuse prefers to substitute the more neutral expression *drug dependency,* recognizing that dependency may arise from social considerations, or as a consequence of repeated use, apart from the pharmacological characteristics of the drug that is taken.

The main classes of drugs that affect a person's mood or consciousness are listed in Table 6-2 along with some of their characteristics according to the amount of dependence they encourage, the degree of social impairment they create, and the consequence of discontinuing their use after it has become habitual. Any classification such as that presented in the table has to be made with reservations because of (1) wide individual differences in responsiveness to various drugs, (2) special effects when more than one drug are taken at a time, (3) characteristic responses that differ with amount and frequency of use, and (4) the social setting in which the use occurs.

Of the drugs most widely used for their psychological effects—caffeine, tobacco, and alcohol—we shall consider only alcohol because of the social consequences of its excessive use. We shall also discuss another depressant (heroin), a stimulant (amphetamines), and two hallucinogens (LSD and marihuana).

TABLE 6-2
A classification of some psychoactive substances, their prevalence and general effects

CLASSIFICATION	TENDENCY TO ENCOURAGE DEPENDENCE	PREVALENCE OF CHRONIC USE	IMPAIRMENT OF SOCIAL FUNCTIONING: ACUTE	IMPAIRMENT OF SOCIAL FUNCTIONING: CHRONIC	DISTURBANCE THROUGH ABSTINENCE AFTER CHRONIC USE
DEPRESSANTS					
Alcohol	High	High	High	High	High
Barbiturates (short-acting)	High	High	High	High	High
Mild tranquilizers (e.g., Meprobamate)	Moderate	Low	Moderate	Low	Low
Codeine	Low	Low	Low	Low	Low
Heroin	High	High	High	Moderate	High
Morphine	High	High	High	Moderate	High
Methadone					
(Parenteral)	High	High	High	Moderate	High
(Oral)	High	Moderate	Moderate	Moderate	High
STIMULANTS					
Amphetamines					
(Parenteral)	High	Low/Moderate	High	High	Low/Moderate
(Oral)	Moderate	High	Moderate	High	Low/Moderate
Caffeine	Low	High	None	None	None
Cocaine	High	Moderate	High	High	Low/Moderate
HALLUCINOGENS					
LSD	Low	Low	Low/Moderate	?	?
Mescaline	Low	Low	Low/Moderate	?	?
Marihuana	Low	Low	Low/Moderate	Moderate	Low
Synthetic THC	Moderate	Low	Low/Moderate	Moderate	Low

Source: After National Commission on Marihuana and Drug Abuse, 1973, pp. 116–118.

Alcohol

Alcohol in small quantities or in a social setting appears to be a stimulant, but such an interpretation is misleading because alcohol begins by inhibiting some of the restraints on social behavior. Although alcohol is primarily a depressant, the initial relaxation may turn to anger and aggression; later the depressing effects show again in drowsiness and sleep. The general symptoms of drunkenness are too well known to require detailed description. What is less well-known is how the responses to alcohol are specifically related to the blood alcohol concentration. At concentrations of .03 to .05 percent of alcohol in the blood symptoms begin with lightheadedness, relaxation, and release of inhibitions. At a concentration of 0.1 percent (say, after three cocktails or three bottles of beer) most sensory and motor functions have become severely impaired. The drinker is seriously incapacitated at a level of 0.2 percent, and a level above 0.4 percent may cause death. The legal definition of intoxication is usually a concentration of .10 to .15 percent.

One reason for the public disapproval of alcohol is the frequent involvement of intoxicated drivers in automobile accidents. Postmortem examinations of fatally injured drivers have shown some 60 percent to have had a blood alcohol concentration of more than .05 percent, and 35 percent a concentration of more than 0.15 percent (Midwest Research Institute, 1972).

Reactions slowed by alcohol

Laboratory technician drinks vodka and tomato juice while investigator prepares to measure reactions.

Why, in view of the well-known hazards, do people drink? Many social drinkers do not drink to excess; their drinking is a form of social participation, which might be as well served by nonalcoholic beverages if that were the custom. Others drink for some expected effect of the alcohol, often short of drunkenness. The common assumption is that alcohol is taken as a mild tranquilizer to reduce anxiety or tension. The motives must be more complex than this, however, for there is often a kind of bravado associated with drinking, in which the intoxicated person becomes domineering, angry, or combative. A careful 10-year study by psychologists attempted to assess the motivation for drinking of those who were not extreme alcoholics (McClelland and others, 1972). Through the use of story-telling pictures, a familiar method for studying motivation (see Chapter 13), it was found that one prominent motive for drinking is to overcome a sense of weakness, to feel stronger and more effective (although without concomitant feelings of responsibility). It is apparent that the motives are not simple, and taken together they must be strong or drinking would not occur so frequently in cultures that differ so much in other respects.

Heroin

Opium, its derivatives, and related substances—collectively known as *opiates* and classified as *narcotics*—are widely used both medically and illegally. Opium, derived from the juice of the opium poppy, has both *morphine* and *codeine* as its active ingredients. Codeine is very mild; morphine is about 10 times stronger; *heroin,* derived from morphine, is 20–25 times as potent. In fact, heroin is barred from medical use in the United States, and any use is illicit. Street heroin, usually only one to three percent

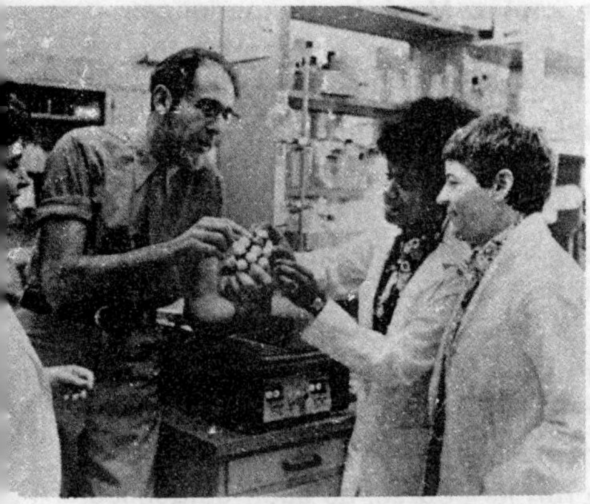

Advance in understanding action of opiat

Dr. Avram Goldstein of Stanford Medical School holds model of molecule identified as the chemical "receptor" in the brain fo morphine. His research team is pictured with him.

pure, is less powerful than morphine by weight. The drugs can be taken in various ways: opium is smoked or swallowed, morphine is taken intravenously, and heroin is either sniffed or injected. Slang names for heroin include H, horse, junk, smack, or stuff. Nasal use is called sniffing; subcutaneous injection, skin popping; and intravenous injection, mainlining.

The motives for heroin use, like any human motives, are complex. Heroin is first used for the positive sense of well-being that it can produce. Experienced adult users report a special "thrill" that occurs within a minute or two after an intravenous injection, which some describe as similar to an orgasm, except that the sensation seems to be centered in the abdomen, rather than in the genital region. This sensation is described as intensely pleasurable. Following this, the user feels "fixed," or gratified, with no hunger, pain, or sexual urges. He may "go on the nod" alternately waking and drowsing as he sits comfortably watching television or reading a book. The effect is very different from alcoholic or barbiturate intoxication, however, and a user can readily yield skilled responses to tests. Unlike the alcoholic, the heroin user is seldom aggressive or assaultive.

Youths who experience heroin for the first time through sniffing describe the pleasant effects of the initial experience somewhat differently:

> It gave me a sense of peace of mind. Nothing bothered me. It felt good.
>
> Felt above everyone else . . . great.
>
> I felt I always wanted to feel the same way as I felt then.
>
> I felt above everything. I felt I knew everything. I talked to people about interesting things.
>
> Felt like heat was coming through my body and head. It made me forget all things. Felt like nobody existed but me, like I was by myself. (From Chein, Gerard, Lee, and Rosenfeld, 1964, pp. 157–158)

The changes in consciousness are not very striking, in the sense that there are no exciting visual experiences or feelings of being transported elsewhere. Rather the changes are in mood, self-confidence, or anxiety reduction (either through being more comfortable with people, or escaping from them).

It must be true that the heroin experience satisfies motives, or its dangers would tell against its use, but the assertion that the only important motives are the good feelings produced would be in error. Not all the initial experiences are pleasant. To be sure, more of those whose initial experiences are favorable seek to repeat the experience very soon, but even those whose experiences are unfavorable return promptly for another try. Why? They know that it is dangerous to health and even to life; that it is costly and likely to lead to illegal activities to maintain a supply, once the person becomes dependent on the drug; and that it may lead to a general deterioration of character (Chein and others, 1964). Two facts of motivation are important here: (1) people like to experience danger, and they find it hard to believe that statistics apply to them and (2) social factors in motivation lead to behaviors that would not be entered into in isolation. The first point hardly needs elaboration. About half of those who participate in major automobile racing die on the track, and yet this does not prevent them from continuing to race even after they have demonstrated what they can do; less extreme are the dangers of mountain climbing, but the risk is part of the motivation. The social motives are more complex: Most drug experiences begin through the invitation of peers (not from "pushers"). Although the peer group may help to start the habit, it also tends to place some brakes upon addiction, so that easy assertions about the social influences are not appropriate.

A new cycle of motives begins after drug dependence becomes similar to appetite and eating: The drug experience is viewed as desirable, the abstinence symptoms are unpleasant, and the habit becomes somewhat self-perpetuating, even though, because of increasing tolerance of the drug, the particular experiences may no longer have the thrill that they once had.

Heroin use in the United States began to rise rapidly in the early 1960s, and in some areas reached nearly epidemic proportions. There are signs, however, that the epidemic has begun to run its course, as such epidemics historically have. A careful study in Washington, D.C., for example, of first users of heroin in a sample of 13,000 treated by the Narcotics Treatment Administration (including those coming voluntarily and those referred by the courts) showed first use to have peaked in 1969 and to have dropped thereafter (Figure 6-13). In the same study it was shown that property-related crimes (robbery, burglary, larceny) fell off coincidently with the drop in first heroin use, whereas person-related offenses (presumably not related to heroin use) remained at their same level. This strongly suggests (but does not prove) that the high cost of heroin may have been responsible for many of the crimes against property, for it is estimated that the person dependent on heroin may have to steal as much as $100 worth of goods per day to maintain an adequate supply.

The public is aroused by heroin use in part because of heroin-produced deaths. It is estimated that about 0.5 percent of users die of overdoses, that is, about 1 in 200 users. The total may be higher; in New York City, for example, there are about 1,000 deaths from heroin overdose per year, a number equal to the deaths from alcohol overdoses. These figures are tragic

Fig. 6-13 Rise and fall of initial heroin use in Washington, D.C.

The year of first heroin use is plotted from the reports of 13,000 patients treated in Washington, D.C. Each point represents the percentage of the total sample which began heroin use in a given year. (From DuPont and Greene, 1973)

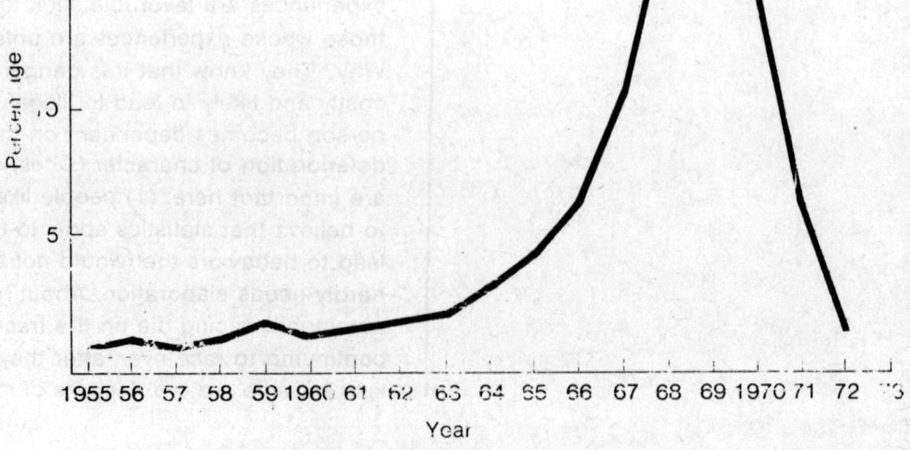

of course, but are not the inevitable outcome of heroin use, because many users do not become addicted.

The possibility of reversal of the heroin habit is not as bleak as earlier supposed. Modern clinics have used a long-acting, synthetic opiate called *methadone* for treatment. Although it, too, is dangerous, under careful supervision many habitual heroin users have been able to replace the heroin habit, but in so doing they acquire a methadone habit. Newer non-opium antagonists, such as cyclazocine and naltextrone, are also proving useful in helping the drug dependent to discontinue heroin use or any other opiate. Even so, however, a social problem remains because many post-addicts return to drug use in time of social conflict and stress, and treating the individual for present drug use may not solve problems of a particular social milieu.

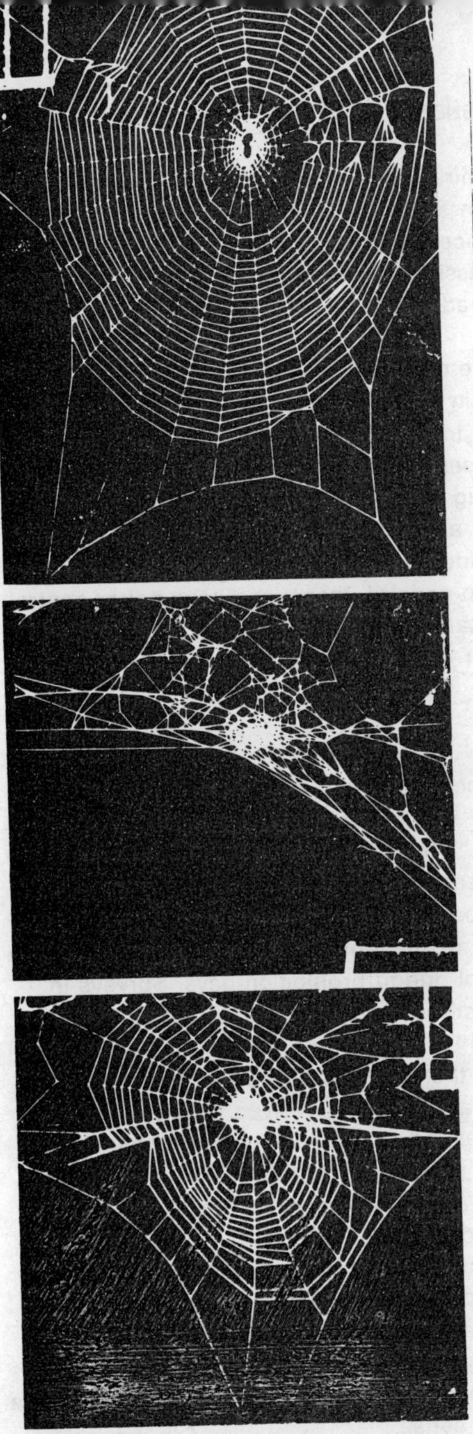

Web-building by a spider disturbed by amphetamine ("speed")

Three webs by an adult female cross spider, built on different days. The top web is a normal web. The middle web was built by the same spider about 12 hours after drinking water containing a small amount of dextro-amphetamine; it shows some remnants of a hub, a few irregular and frequently interrupted radii and some erratic strands of sticky spiral. The bottom web was spun after 24 hours of recovery; the web is not yet normal.

Amphetamines

Amphetamines are powerful stimulants, sold under trade names such as Benzedrine, Dexedrine, and Methedrine, and known colloquially by many names including "speed," "uppers," "bennies." The immediate effects are well known: an increase in alertness, wakefulness, and decreased feelings of fatigue or boredom. Strenuous activities calling for effort and endurance may be improved with their use (Weiss and Laties, 1962). As with other drugs these positive effects suffice as motivation for drug use.

We may distinguish three patterns of amphetamine use, initially serving somewhat different motives, but all affecting consciousness in one way or another (Tinklenberg, 1972).

Commonly one first uses low doses for limited periods to overcome fatigue, as in long nighttime driving, military maneuvers, or cramming for examinations. Were there no escalation in use, the effects might prove more beneficial than harmful, although there is some danger of impaired judgment and postamphetamine depression.

The second pattern—sustained oral doses, gradually increasing in amount--tends to be followed by those who attempt to control their weight or medicate themselves against fatigue and depression over long periods of time. Eventually undesirable consequences may ensue, including paranoid psychoses that involve unfounded suspiciousness, hostility, and persecutory delusions (Ellinwood, 1967).

The third, extreme pattern of large intravenous amounts commonly ends in a "run," in which the person injects himself every few hours over a period of several days. There is almost immediately a pleasant experience termed a "flash" or "rush," which is followed by irritability and discomfort thus necessitating an additional injection, and so on. Episode ends in a "crash," in which a deep sleep is followed by a period of lethargy and depression. One consequence of this "crash" is that the amphetamine user may seek relief from his discomfort by turning to a sedative, including heroin.

LSD

Although LSD was initially the most widely used psychedelic or "mind-manifesting" drug, the widespread knowledge of its dangers has apparently reduced its use. One problem with LSD (or "acid," as it is popularly called) is that its effects are highly individual and unpredictable. Some users have vivid hallucinatory experiences of colors and sounds, whereas others have mystical or semireligious experiences. An adverse reaction (or "bad trip") may occur in any user, even those who have had many pleasant LSD experiences. Since this disturbance is often severe enough for the person to seek professional help, psychiatrists and other mental health personnel have now had a great deal of experience with adverse LSD reactions.

A careful study of those who have used LSD shows that the drug is powerful enough to shift awareness in some respects for all of them, although the effects differ according to drug dosage and measurable personality characteristics of each user as well as expectations aroused through the context in which the drug is taken. Some difficulty in concentrating is commonly reported, although some features of the experience, such as visual imagery and fantasy, take on a "fascinating" quality that holds attentive interest. In general, those who have better control of themselves outside the drugged state maintain that control within the condition produced by the drug (Barr and others, 1972).

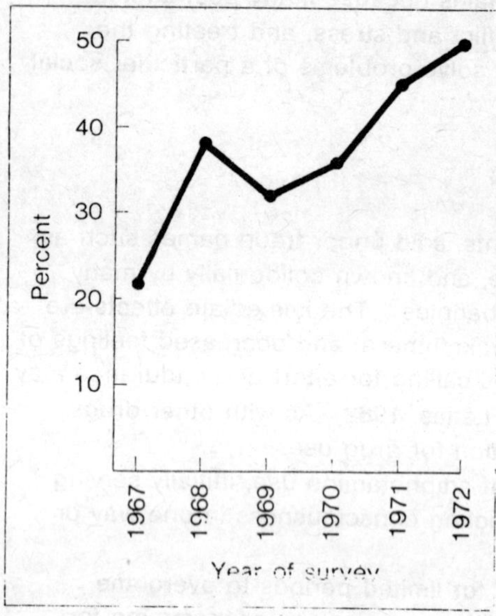

Fig. 6-14 Marihuana use by college students

The mean percentage of college students who report ever having used marihuana, by year of survey. (National Commission on Marihuana and Drug Abuse, 1973)

Marihuana

The most controversial of all the popular drugs is marihuana (*cannabis*) derived from hemp; another name for it is hashish, and popular slang in the United States calls it "pot" or "grass." The user smokes or eats the leaves of the marihuana plant to induce a general excitement or euphoria.

In the United States many young people have taken to marihuana as other generations took to alcohol; the legal restrictions today appear to be no more inhibiting than those outlawing alcohol during prohibition days. Surveys in successive years have reported an increasing number of college students who have used marihuana (Figure 6-14).

Because of the uncertain purity of the marihuana smoked, and the small amounts of the active ingredient that are typically involved, much of the research on the effects of the drug has led to uncertain conclusions. Better understanding has come since the active ingredient THC (tetrahydrocannabinol) was isolated. Taken orally in small doses (5–10 mg), a mild "high" of brief duration is produced; larger doses (30–70 mg) produce severe and longer reactions resembling those of other hallucinogenic drugs. As with alcohol, the reaction often occurs in two stages: a period of stimulation and euphoria followed by a period of sedation and tranquility, and, with higher doses, sleep. Although many of the alcohol and marihuana reactions are similar, especially with mild doses, a peculiarity of the marihuana experience is its distortion of the time sense.

The subjective experiences of marihuana users have been carefully studied (Tart, 1971a). By interviewing 150 regular users, all of whom had used marihuana at least a dozen times prior to the study, and most of whom used it once a week or more during the months of the study, Tart constructed a fairly adequate picture of the experienced changes from the user's viewpoint. Many sensory and perceptual changes were reported: some distortions of space and time, changes in social perception and experience, and a number of "out-of-body" experiences. Some users believed that they were able to communicate by telepathy. The more characteristic reports are summarized in Table 6-3.

A general euphoria and sense of well-being are commonly reported, although these states are accompanied by some distortions of reality.

TABLE 6-3
Characteristic effects at various levels of marihuana intoxication (Those effects in parentheses are less common.)

LEVEL OF MARIHUANA INTOXICATION	BEHAVIORAL AND EXPERIMENTAL EFFECTS
Mild	Less noisy at parties than when tipsy or drunk
	New, subtle quality to sounds
Fair	Taste sensations have new qualities
	Easy to get to sleep at bedtime
	Enjoy eating a lot
	(Hard to play ordinary social games)
	(Less need to feel in control of things)
	(Invariably feel good from turning on)
	(Understand words of songs better)
Fair to strong	Time passes more slowly
	Distance in walking changed
	More childlike, open to experience
	Physically relaxed
	(See patterns in normally ambiguous material)
	(Difficult to read)
	(Touch more exciting, sensual)
	(Greater spatial separation between musical instruments)
	(Visual imagery more intense)
Strong	(Easily sidetracked)
Strong to Very Strong	(Forget start of conversation)

Source: After Tart, 1971a, p. 245.

Musicians who believe that they play better under the influence of marihuana may find (when they listen to tapes of their performances) that their music is actually less satisfactory when performed in the intoxicated state.

Because the effects of marihuana as usually available are so mild, as compared, for example, to alcohol, serious doubts are raised from time to time about either the need for or the effectiveness of heavy penalties for its possession (Kaplan, 1970).

Why People use Psychoactive Drugs

With this brief survey of drug usage for psychological effects, we may summarize the considerations that lead to drug use. It is possible to list five major patterns of drug use, each of which differs from the other in the health risk to the individual and the risk to society (National Commission on Marihuana and Drug Abuse, 1973, pp. 92–98):

1. *Experimental use.* If the social environment encourages it, one can understand the experimental use of a drug motivated by curiosity or a desire to experience a new state of consciousness. Although there are some risks (depending on the drug or drug combination), the risks to the individual and society are ordinarily low.
2. *Social-recreational use.* If the use of drugs among friends remains under voluntary control and is not permitted to escalate, drug dependence need not result. The risks of escalation are greater for some drugs than for others, for example, for heroin than for marihuana.
3. *Circumstantial-situational use.* This use implies a specific purpose, such as self-medication to relieve some symptom, or to improve some performance.

"Lacking a sense of responsibility has, I believe, heightened all my other senses."

Examination preparation, athletic competition, long-distance trucking, or military combat may provide an occasion for drug use. The risk need not be great, except that when the drug succeeds in doing what it was expected to do reinforcement is provided for its further use, and intensified use may result. Impairment of function, as with amphetamines, may lead to accidents because a driver is unaware of any loss of discrimination.

4. *Intensified drug use.* By intensified drug use is meant habitual use at a minimum level of once daily. An individual who uses a drug this frequently comes to accept the drug through habit and is thus in some sense dependent; however, his behavior may remain socially and economically integrated into the life of the community. A person may regularly take barbiturates as a sleep inducer, or a mild tranquilizer to control anxiety and tension, or have cocktails daily, without any severe disruption. We are here at a borderline that depends on frequency, intensity, and amount of use.
5. *Compulsive drug use.* Compulsive use is characterized by a preoccupation with obtaining sufficient quantities of the drug to avoid abstinence symptoms; this is the only situation in which the noun "addiction" might appropriately be applied. The heavy and frequent use of powerful drugs at this level usually is accompanied by significantly reduced individual and social functioning. Not all those who fit this category are "down-and-outers"; there are hidden drug-dependent persons such as opiate-dependent physicians, barbiturate-dependent housewives, and alcohol-dependent white-collar workers.

It is quite evident that there is no one "drug problem," and the efforts to deal with the risks must take into account the kinds of motivation that are involved. The serious use of drugs in the hope of expanding consciousness and finding the deeper meanings of life through a quasi-mystical experience has to be given some consideration. The deep appeal of personal reorientation as a quick way to cut through personal and social problems has had a long history in America; one type of "positive thinking" has succeeded another through the decades (Meyer, 1965). But the promises have commonly been unfulfilled, just as the promises of enlightenment through drugs have often led to disillusionment and occasionally to tragedy.

Summary

1. Although there is considerable interest in the problems of altered states of consciousness, careful examination of the *waking consciousness* shows it to be problematical too. Our ability to register some information from two conversations heard at the same time indicates that waking consciousness is not a single, simple state. Another "split" in waking consciousness is the planning function, a sort of silent talking to oneself that goes on even as we are engaged in listening and overt talking. Attention tends to shift, and alert (vigilant) states may be followed by less alert ones. This process begins in early infancy; the newborn infant orients to sound or pursues with his head and eyes a visual object only in the alert state, which endures but a few minutes per day in the first few days of life. Later in life

we maintain alertness by all sorts of devices of fidgeting and irrelevant responding that prevent our drifting off into vacant staring or sleep.

2. Sleep, a familiar altered state of consciousness, is particularly interesting because of *dreaming.* Studies using the *electroencephalogram* (EEG) and the study of *rapid eye movements* (REMs) during sleep have now shown two main kinds of sleep: (1) REM sleep (with EEG at Stage 1) and (2) the remainder, occuring within all EEG stages of sleep, which may be called *nonrapid eye movement* (NREM) sleep. It is during REM sleep that the characteristic dreaming takes place. Numerous studies have been made using this method of detecting when the subject is dreaming to study the frequency and duration of dreams. Studies have also been made of the reactivity of the dreamer to outside influences and of such spontaneous behaviors as sleeptalking and sleepwalking, which seem not to be related directly to REM sleep.
3. Freud's dream theory holds that dreams express unfulfilled wishes in disguised form; the purpose of the dream (and of the disguise) is to protect sleep. The prevalence of REM sleep in animals and in newborn casts doubt on the generality of the psychoanalytic interpretation.
4. *Hypnosis,* though sometimes identified as a partial sleep, yields an EEG pattern unlike sleep. At present there are no clear physiological indicators by which to define the state.
5. People vary in their susceptibility to hypnosis; about one-fourth of college students are able to demonstrate relatively satisfactory hypnotic responsiveness upon their first hypnotic induction. Efforts to find out why some people are more readily hypnotizable than others have found that those capable of setting reality aside temporarily through imaginative involvements are most likely to prove hypnotizable. This ability may derive from childhood experiences, although some contribution from hereditary potential cannot be ruled out.
6. New interest in modifications of consciousness has led some in the Western world to adopt meditation practices associated with *yoga* or *Zen Buddhism.* These practices have been studied under conditions of experimental meditation, with many subjects reporting relaxation and a satisfying mental state as a result of the assigned exercises. Methods of controlling normally involuntary processes have been developed using a *biofeedback* method in which the subject's electrical responses are converted into auditory signals that he can learn to control. The consequence is that some of the physiological changes associated with meditative states can be achieved fairly quickly.
7. Drugs have long been used to affect consciousness. The psychoactive drugs include the *depressants,* such as the opiates and the barbiturates, the *stimulants,* such as caffeine and the amphetamines, and the *hallucinogens,* such as LSD and marihuana. Although dependency may become habitual, it need not reach the compulsive intensity implied by the word "addiction," and not all drugs produce intense withdrawal symptoms.
8. Drug use varies from brief experimentation and occasional social use through situational use (for specific purposes, usually in self-medication), to more frequent or habitual use, and, at the extreme, to compulsive use. The problems of public responsibility to reduce the risks of drug use to the individual and to society vary with the type of drug and the use to which it is put. Occasionally the use of a given drug reaches epidemic proportions, but, as with other epidemics, it eventually becomes controlled.

Further Reading

Three books of readings cover a number of the topics of this chapter: Ornstein (ed.), *The nature of human consciousness* (1973); Tart (ed.), *Altered states of consciousness* (1969); and Teyler, T. J. (ed.), *Altered states of awareness* (1971).

The literature on sleep and dreams is expanding rapidly. Some summaries for the nonspecialist include Dement, *Some must watch while others sleep* (1972); Luce and Segal, *Sleep* (1966); Webb, *Sleep: an experimental approach* (1968); and Webb and Agnew, *Sleep and dreams* (1973). For a thorough bibliography, see Chase, *The sleeping brain* (1972).

For night-day and other rhythms in man and animals and plants, see Bünning, *The physiological clock* (2nd ed., 1967); Colquhoun (ed.), *Biological rhythms and human performance* (1971); Luce, *Body time: physiological rhythms and social stress* (1971); and Richter, *Biological clocks in medicine and psychiatry* (1965).

Recent books on hypnosis include Barber, *Hypnosis, a scientific approach* (1969); Fromm and Shor (eds.), *Hypnosis: research developments and perspectives* (1972); E. R. Hilgard, *The experience of hypnosis* (1968); J. R. Hilgard, *Personality and hypnosis* (1970); and Sarbin and Coe, *Hypnosis: a social psychological analysis of influence communication* (1972).

For a general survey of meditation techniques, see Naranjo and Ornstein (1971). The book by Forem, *Transcendental meditation* (1973), is a thorough, but somewhat partisan, review of one of the more popular meditational sects.

Contemporary and historical drug problems are covered in a two-volume work: Blum and others, *Society and drugs*, vol. I, and *Students and drugs*, vol. II (1969). Other useful sources include Blum, Bovet, and Moore, *Controlling drugs: an international handbook for psychoactive drug classification* (1973); Brecher and the Editors of Consumer Reports, *Licit and illicit drugs* (1972); and Ray, *Drugs, society, and human behavior* (1972).

part four

learning and thinking

7 conditioning and learning

Learning is basic to human behavior. The psychological study of learning embraces much more than the learning of skills or academic subjects; it also bears upon the fundamental problems of emotional development, motivation, social behavior, and personality. We've already discussed many instances of learning—how, for example, children learn to perceive the world around them, to identify with the appropriate sex, and to control their behavior according to adult standards. We turn in this part of the book to a systematic study of learning. In this chapter we examine the methods used to study learning and some theoretical explanations of the process. In Chapter 8, we deal with memory, an essential element of learning. Chapter 9 treats some practical aspects of how to optimize learning. And, Chapter 10 discusses language and thought.

Learning may be defined as a *relatively permanent change in behavior that occurs as the result of prior experience.* This change may not be evident until a situation arises in which the new behavior can occur; learning is not always immediately reflected in performance. Not all changes can be explained as learning, so our definition has to be qualified to exclude them. The phrase *relatively permanent* excludes changes in behavior that result from temporary or transient conditions such as fatigue or the influence of drugs. By specifying that learning is the result of *experience* we exclude changes that are due to maturation, disease, or physical damage. Learning could be defined more simply as profiting from experience, were it not that some learning does not "profit" the learner: useless and harmful habits are learned just as are useful ones.

A number of controversies revolve about the process of learning. Some psychologists emphasize stimulus-response (S-R) relationships and interpret learning as an *associative process:* a new association, or connection, is formed between a stimulus and response. A child who says "kitty" when he sees the family cat has learned to associate a stimulus (the animal) with a verbal response ("kitty"). A person learning to catch a ball associates a series of motor responses with various stimuli arising from the ball and from his own movements. Some psychologists interpret *all* learned behavior as associative learning. According to this view, even the mastery of complex intellectual tasks can be broken down into a set of S-R associations.

Other psychologists argue that only simple forms of learning can be explained in terms of S-R associations. They are impressed by the role that perception and understanding play in more complex forms of learning. In their view, tasks involving memorizing, problem solving, and thinking can be most easily understood within the framework of cognitive psychology. As we noted earlier, a cognitive explanation of behavior postulates the existence of mental processes that operate on the stimulus in different ways—depending upon the context in which the stimulus occurs and the individual's past learning experiences—to arrive at a response. Such processes involve more than an automatic response elicited by a stimulus input. By means of *cognitive processes* we are able to follow a map over routes we have never taken before and reason our way through unfamiliar problems.

We will return to the cognitive versus S-R issue later. But regardless of how one explains learning, the kinds of tasks that psychologists use to study the phenomenon can be grouped into four categories:

1. Classical conditioning
2. Operant conditioning
3. Multiple-response learning
4. Cognitive learning

The first two categories emphasize tasks where identifiable stimulus-response associations are being acquired; the latter two deal with more complex situations where specific stimuli and responses are not clearly identifiable. Each of these categories will be discussed separately.

Classical Conditioning

Pavlov's Experiments

Ivan Pavlov (center) with assistants in his laboratory.

Associative learning can be studied in the *conditioned-response* experiment originated by the Russian physiologist and Nobel Prize winner Ivan Pavlov. While studying the relatively automatic reflexes associated with digestion, Pavlov noticed that a dog salivated not just when food was placed in its mouth but also at the mere sight of food. He interpreted the flow of saliva to food placed in the mouth as an unlearned response, or, as he called it, an *unconditioned response*. But surely, he thought, the response to the *sight* of food has to be a learned or *conditioned response*. Pavlov taught the dog to salivate to various signals, such as the onset of a light or tone, thereby proving to his satisfaction that a new stimulus-response association could be formed in the laboratory.

Under Pavlov's method, a dog is prepared for experimentation by having a minor operation performed on its cheek so that part of the salivary gland is exposed to the surface. A capsule attached to the cheek measures salivary flow. The dog is brought to the soundproof laboratory on several occasions and is placed in a harness on a table. This preliminary training is needed so the animal will stand quietly in the harness once the actual experiment gets underway. The laboratory is so arranged that meat powder can be delivered to a pan in front of the dog by remote control. Salivation is recorded automatically. The experimenter can view the animal through a one-way glass panel, but the dog is alone in the experimental room, isolated from extraneous sights and noises (see Figure 7-1).

Fig. 7-1 Classical-conditioning apparatus

Arrangements used by Pavlov in classical salivary conditioning. The apparatus permits a light (as the conditioned stimulus) to appear in the window, and the delivery of meat powder (as the unconditioned stimulus) to the food bowl. (After Yerkes and Morgulis, 1909)

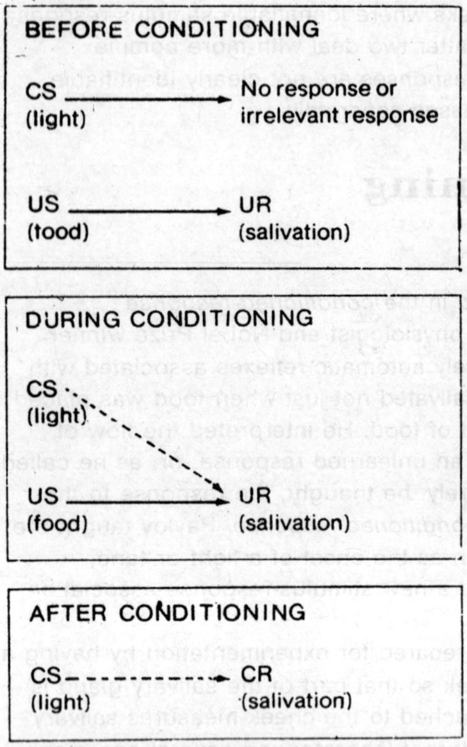

Fig. 7-2 A diagram of classical conditioning

The association between the unconditioned stimulus and the unconditioned response exists at the start of the experiment and does not have to be learned. The association between the conditioned stimulus and the conditioned response is learned. It arises through the pairing of the conditioned and unconditioned stimuli followed by the unconditioned response. The conditioned response resembles the unconditioned one but generally differs in some details.

A light (the *conditioned stimulus*) is turned on. The dog may move a bit, but it does not salivate. After a few seconds, the meat powder (the *unconditioned stimulus*) is delivered; the dog is hungry and eats. The recording device registers copious salivation. A few more trials are given in which the light is always followed by meat, and the meat, in turn, by salivation. This following of the conditioned stimulus (CS) by the unconditioned stimulus (US) is called *reinforcement.* After several reinforcements the dog salivates when the light is turned on, even though food may not follow. When this happens, a *conditioned response* has been established.

The usual order of events (conditioned stimulus—unconditioned stimulus—response) can best be remembered if the conditioned stimulus is thought of as a *signal* that the unconditioned stimulus is about to appear; in the foregoing example the light is a signal that food is coming. The conditioned response may be considered a simple habit because (1) an association is demonstrated to exist between a stimulus and a response, and (2) this association is learned.

We are ready now for a definition of *classical conditioning* as represented by Pavlov's experiment. (We shall presently describe another variety of conditioning, called *operant conditioning;* hence the adjective "classical" is applied to Pavlov's experiment.) Classical conditioning is the formation of an association between a conditioned stimulus and a response through the repeated presentation of the conditioned stimulus in a controlled relationship with an unconditioned stimulus that originally elicits that response. The original response to the unconditioned stimulus is called an *unconditioned response* (UR); the learned response to the conditioned stimulus is called a *conditioned response* (CR). The arrangement described in this definition is diagramed in Figure 7-2.

Laws of Classical Conditioning

Because classical conditioning represents an extremely simple form of learning, it has been regarded by many psychologists as an appropriate starting point for the investigation of the learning process. We will now consider some of the laws that characterize classical conditioning.

ACQUISITION. Each paired presentation of the CS and the US is called a *trial,* and the period during which the organism is learning the association between the CS and the US is the *acquisition* stage of conditioning. The time interval between the CS and the US may be varied. In *simultaneous conditioning,* the CS begins a fraction of a second or so before the onset of the US and continues along with it until the response occurs. In *delayed conditioning,* the CS begins several seconds or more before the onset of the US and then continues with it until the response occurs. And in *trace conditioning,* the CS is presented first and then removed before the US starts (only a "neural trace" of the CS remains to be conditioned). These three situations are illustrated in Figure 7-3.

In delayed and trace conditioning the investigator can look for the conditioned response on every trial because there is sufficient time for it to appear before the presentation of the US. Thus if salivation occurs before the delivery of food, we consider it a conditioned response to the light. In simultaneous conditioning the conditioned response does not have time to

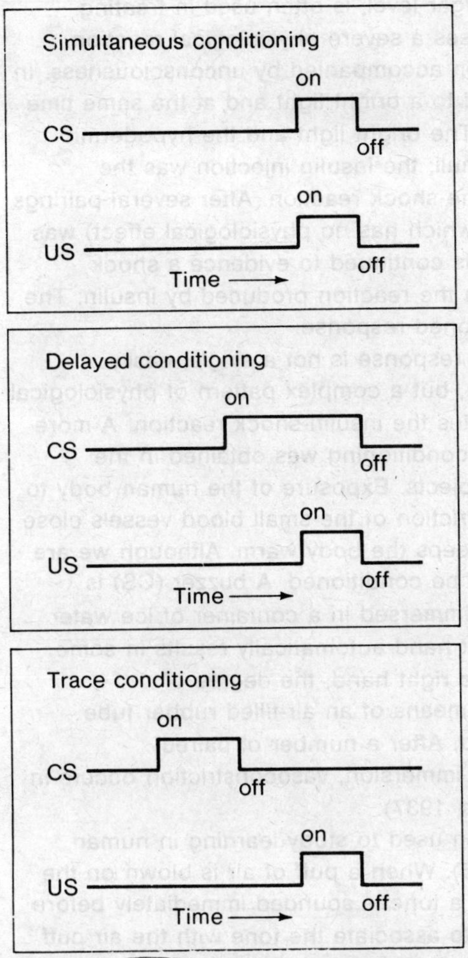

Fig. 7-3 Temporal relations in conditioning

Inflections stand for stimulus onsets; deflections represent terminations.

appear before the presentation of the US, and it is necessary to include test trials—trials on which the US is omitted—to determine whether conditioning has occurred. For example, if salivation occurs when the CS is presented alone, we consider that conditioning has occurred. Delayed-conditioning experiments indicate that learning is fastest if the CS is presented about 0.5 seconds before the US.

With repeated paired presentations of the CS and US, the conditioned response appears with increasingly greater strength and regularity. The procedure of pairing the CS and US is called *reinforcement* because any tendency for the CR to appear is facilitated by the presence of the US and the response to it. The left-hand panel of Figure 7-4 shows the dog's acquisition of the salivary response to the conditioned stimulus of a light.

By the third trial the animal is responding to the CS with seven drops of saliva. By the seventh trial saliva secretion has leveled off and continues (with minor fluctuations) at about the same strength for the next nine trials. This stable level of responding is called the *asymptote* of the learning curve; further acquisition trials will not produce any greater strength of response.

EXTINCTION. If the unconditioned stimulus is omitted repeatedly (no reinforcement), the conditioned response gradually diminishes. Repetition of the conditioned stimulus without reinforcement is called *extinction*. Its effect on the animal's performance is shown in the right-hand panel of Figure 7-4. Notice that on the fourth nonreinforced trial the amount of salivation has decreased to about three drops; by the ninth extinction trial the CS is eliciting no salivation at all.

Additional Examples of Classical Conditioning

Before continuing our discussion of classical conditioning let's consider a few more examples of the basic procedure. A wide variety of responses (ones we would not ordinarily consider learnable) have been successfully conditioned in both animal and human subjects. In one study an insulin reaction was conditioned in rats (Sawrey, Conger, and Turrell, 1956). Insulin,

Fig. 7-4 Acquisition and extinction of a conditioned response

The curve in the left panel depicts the acquisition phase of an experiment using the trace-conditioning procedure. Drops of salivation to the conditioned stimulus (prior to the onset of the US) is plotted on the ordinate, the number of trials on the abscissa. The CR gradually increases over trials and approaches an asymptotic level of about 11–12 drops of saliva. After 16 acquisition trials the experimenter switched to extinction; the results are presented in the right panel. Note that the CR gradually decreases when reinforcement is omitted. (Data from Pavlov, 1927)

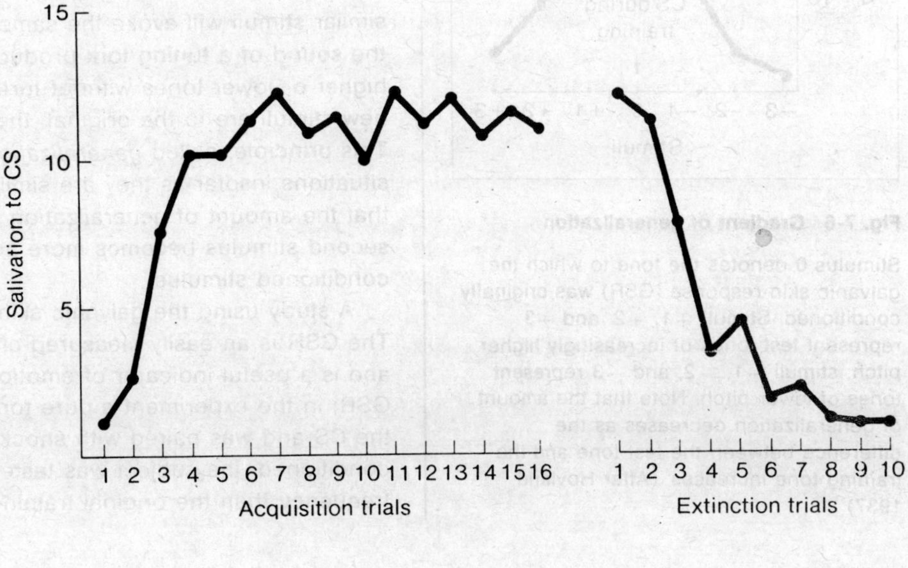

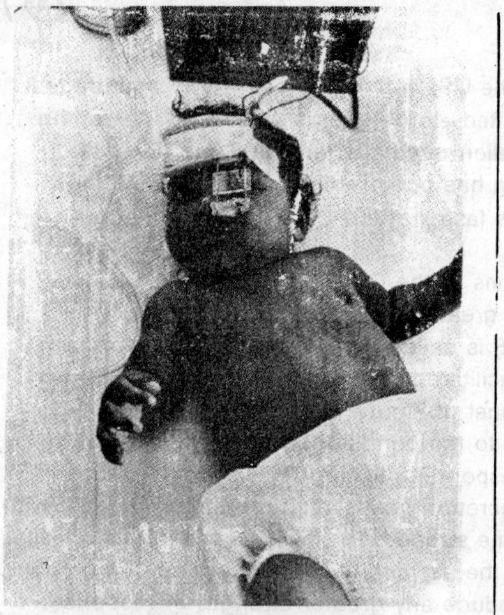

Fig. 7-5 Eye-blink conditioning with newborns

The CS is a tone and the US is a mild puff of air. The response is an eye-blink that is soon conditioned to the onset of the tone. (Courtesy of Lewis Lipsitt)

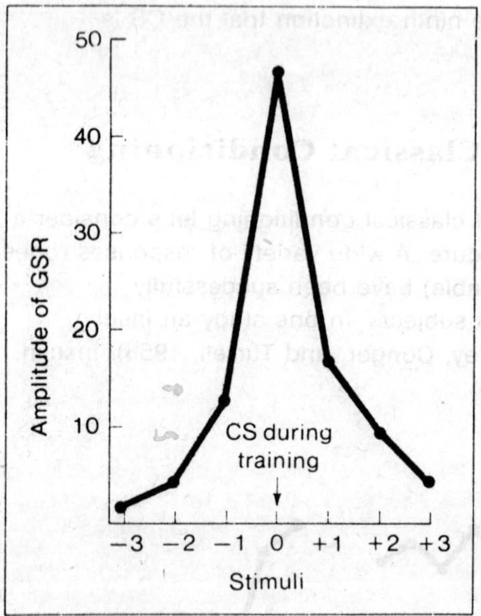

Fig. 7-6 Gradient of generalization

Stimulus 0 denotes the tone to which the galvanic skin response (GSR) was originally conditioned. Stimuli +1, +2, and +3 represent test tones of increasingly higher pitch; stimuli −1, −2, and −3 represent tones of lower pitch. Note that the amount of generalization decreases as the difference between the test tone and the training tone increases. (After Hovland, 1937)

a hormone that controls the blood-sugar level, is often used in treating diabetics. An overdose of insulin causes a severe physiological reaction known as *insulin shock,* which is often accompanied by unconsciousness. In the experiment the rats were exposed to a bright light and at the same time injected with an overdose of insulin. The bright light and the hypodermic needle served as the conditioned stimuli; the insulin injection was the unconditioned stimulus and elicited the shock reaction. After several pairings of the CS and US, a saline solution (which has no physiological effect) was substituted for the insulin. The animals continued to evidence a shock reaction almost indistinguishable from the reaction produced by insulin. The shock reaction had become a conditioned response.

In this experiment the conditioned response is not a single, easily measured response such as salivation, but a complex pattern of physiological and muscular responses that constitutes the insulin-shock reaction. A more quantitative physiological measure of conditioning was obtained in the following experiment using human subjects. Exposure of the human body to cold automatically results in the constriction of the small blood vessels close to the body surface—a reaction that keeps the body warm. Although we are totally unaware of this reaction, it can be conditioned. A buzzer (CS) is sounded as the subject's left hand is immersed in a container of ice water (US). Since vasoconstriction of the left hand automatically results in some constriction of the blood vessels in the right hand, the degree of vasoconstriction can be measured by means of an air-filled rubber tube placed around the subject's right hand. After a number of paired presentations of the buzzer and water immersion, vasoconstriction occurs in response to the buzzer alone (Menzies, 1937).

Classical conditioning has also been used to study learning in human newborns 5–7 days old (see Figure 7-5). When a puff of air is blown on the eye the natural response is to blink. If a tone is sounded immediately before the air puff, the newborn soon learns to associate the tone with the air puff and blinks on hearing the tone alone. Using this procedure, one can study learning in very young infants.

Generalization

When a conditioned response to a stimulus has been acquired, other similar stimuli will evoke the same response. A dog that learns to salivate to the sound of a tuning fork producing a tone of middle C will also salivate to higher or lower tones without further conditioning. The more nearly alike the new stimuli are to the original, the more completely they will substitute for it. This principle, called *generalization,* accounts for our ability to react to novel situations insofar as they are similar to familiar ones. Careful study shows that the amount of generalization falls off in a systematic manner as the second stimulus becomes more and more dissimilar to the original conditioned stimulus.

A study using the galvanic skin response (GSR) illustrates generalization. The GSR is an easily measured change in the electrical activity of the skin and is a useful indicator of emotional stress. A mild electric shock will elicit GSR; in the experiment a pure tone of a specified frequency (pitch) served as the CS and was paired with shock as the US. After the GSR had been conditioned, the subject was tested with tones of higher and lower frequency than the original training tone. Figure 7-6 shows the results plotted in terms of the amplitude of the GSR versus test tones of varying frequencies. The high point of the curve represents the amplitude of the GSR to the original CS; the points to the left show the GSR amplitudes to tones lower than the CS, and those to the right the amplitudes to tones higher than the CS. As you can see, the GSR amplitude decreases as the tones become progressively more dissimilar to the CS in frequency. This plotted relationship is called the *gradient of generalization*.

Stimulus generalization need not be confined to a single sense. For example, with human subjects a GSR conditioned to the sound of a bell may also appear (although in a lesser amount) to the sight of a bell or to the spoken word "bell." The conditioning of a response to the meaning of a word (as opposed to the configuration or sound of a word) is called *semantic conditioning*. An interesting example of semantic conditioning and generalization is provided by the work of a Russian psychologist (Volkova, 1953). She used a modification of Pavlov's salivary-conditioning method in an experiment with young children. The US was cranberry purée delivered to the subject's mouth via a chute; the response was salivation. The CS was the Russian word for "good" pronounced aloud by the experimenter. After conditioning had been established, the experimenter tested for generalization by pronouncing some Russian sentences that could be construed as possessing a "good" meaning and some that could not. She found, for example, that the children would salivate to sentences like "The pioneer helps his comrade" and "Leningrad is a wonderful city," but not to ones like "The pupil was rude to the teacher" and "My friend is seriously ill."

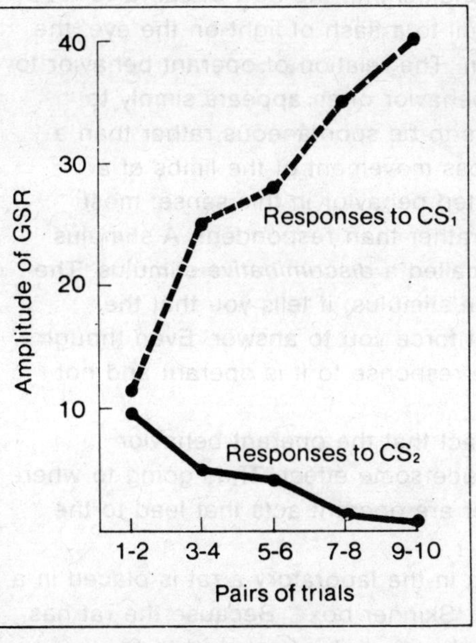

Fig. 7-7 The course of conditioned discrimination in man

The discriminative stimuli were two tones of clearly different pitch (CS_1 = 700 Hz and CS_2 = 3500 Hz). The unconditioned stimulus, an electric shock applied to the left forefinger, occurred only on trials when CS_1 was presented. The strength of the conditioned response, which in this case was the GSR, gradually increased following CS_1 and extinguished following CS_2. (After Baer and Fuhrer, 1968)

Discrimination

A process complementary to generalization is *discrimination*. Whereas generalization is reaction to similarities, discrimination is reaction to differences. Conditioned discrimination is brought about through selective reinforcement and extinction, as shown in Figure 7-7.

In the experiment illustrated, two clearly different tones, CS_1 and CS_2, served as the discriminative stimuli. On some trials CS_1 was presented, followed by a mild electric shock; on other trials CS_2 occurred, not followed by shock. The two tones were presented equally often but randomly. Initially the conditioned response (in this case, the GSR) occurred with about the same amplitude to the onset of both CS_1 and CS_2. During the course of the experiment, however, the amplitude of the conditioned response to CS_1 gradually increased, while the amplitude of the response to CS_2 decreased. Thus conditioned discrimination between CS_1 and CS_2 was demonstrated.

Generalization and discrimination appear in ordinary behavior. The young child who has learned to say "bow-wow" to a dog may understandably respond in like manner to a similar stimulus, such as a sheep. And a child on first learning the name "Daddy" may use it for all men. By differential reinforcement and extinction the response is finally narrowed to a single appropriate stimulus.

Operant Conditioning

Operant conditioning is another approach to the study of associative learning. When you teach a dog a trick, it is hard to specify the unconditioned stimuli that could produce such behavior before conditioning. Actually, you "got him to do it" as best you could and *afterward* rewarded him with either approval or food. The approval or food did not *produce* the behavior.

In Pavlov's experiment, the conditioned response resembles the response elicited by the unconditioned (reinforcing) stimulus; that is, salivation is a dog's normal response to food. But in operant training the reinforced behavior bears no resemblance to the behavior normally elicited by the reinforcing stimulus (for example, rolling over is not a dog's normal response to food). Still, the learning that takes place exhibits such principles as extinction, generalization, and discrimination.

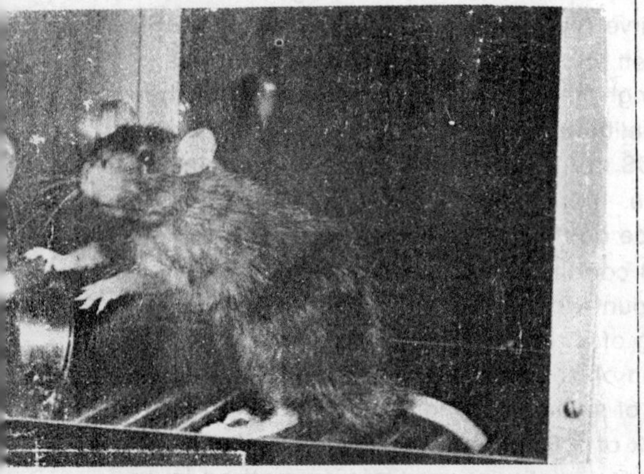

Fig. 7-8 Apparatus for operant conditioning

The photo shows the interior arrangement of the box used in the operant conditioning of a rat. This box has been named a Skinner box after its developer.

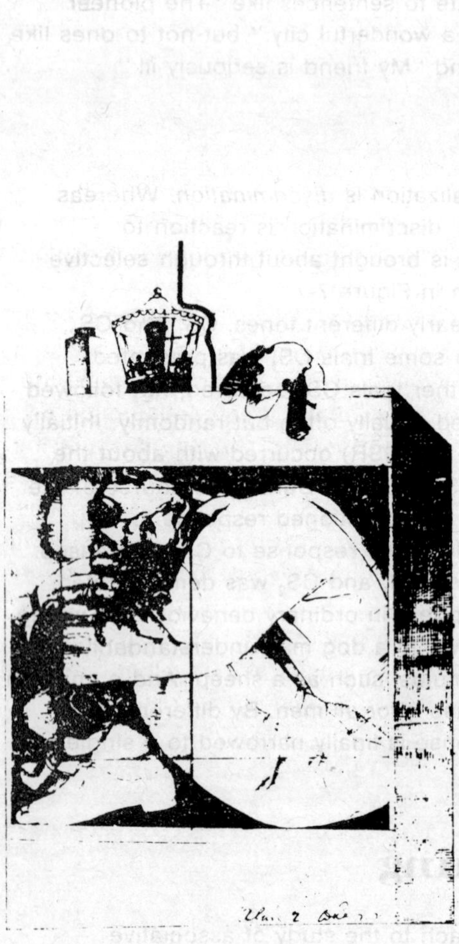

A "Skinner box" with its builder.

Skinner's Experiments

To describe this kind of conditioning, B. F. Skinner introduced the concept of *operant conditioning.* It shares many of the principles of classical conditioning. The arrangements for the experiments differ, however, as do some of the measures of the strength of conditioning.

To understand operant conditioning we need to distinguish between two kinds of behavior which Skinner called *respondent* and *operant* behavior. Respondent behavior is directly under the control of a stimulus, as in the unconditioned responses of classical conditioning: the flow of saliva to food in the mouth, the constriction of the pupil to a flash of light on the eye, the knee jerk to a tap on the patellar tendon. The relation of operant behavior to stimulation is somewhat different. The behavior often appears simply to happen, to be emitted; that is, it appears to be spontaneous rather than a response to a specific stimulus. The gross movement of the limbs of a newborn baby can be classified as emitted behavior in this sense; most so-called voluntary behavior is emitted rather than respondent. A stimulus that may influence operant behavior is called a *discriminative* stimulus. The ringing of a telephone is a discriminative stimulus; it tells you that the telephone is answerable, but it does not force you to answer. Even though the ringing telephone is compelling, the response to it is operant and not respondent behavior.

The word *operant* derives from the fact that the operant behavior "operates" on the environment to produce some effect. Thus going to where the telephone is and raising the receiver are operant acts that lead to the telephone conversation.

To demonstrate operant conditioning in the laboratory a rat is placed in a box like the one in Figure 7-8, called a "Skinner box." Because the rat has been deprived of food for some specified period, it is assumed to be motivated by a hunger drive. (By *drive* we refer to the aroused condition of an organism that results from deprivation of some sort. The concepts of drive and motivation are treated more fully in Chapter 11.) The inside of the Skinner box is bare, except for the protruding bar with the food dish beneath it. A small light bulb above the bar can be lighted at the experimenter's discretion.

Left alone in the box, the rat moves about restlessly and by chance occasionally presses the bar. The rate at which it first pushes on the bar defines its preconditioned *operant level* of bar pressing. After establishing the operant level, the experimenter attaches the food magazine, so that every time the rat presses the bar a pellet of food falls into the dish. The rat eats and soon presses the bar again. The food *reinforces* bar pressing, and the rate of pressing increases dramatically. If the food magazine is disconected, so that pressing the bar no longer delivers food, the rate of bar pressing will diminish. That is, the operant response undergoes *extinction* with nonreinforcement, just as a classical-conditioned response does.

The experimenter can set up a *discrimination* by presenting food if the bar is pressed while the light is on, and not giving reinforcement if the response is made in the dark. This selective reinforcement leads to the rat's pressing the bar only in the presence of the light. In this example, the light serves as a *discriminative stimulus* that controls the occurrence of the bar pressing response.

With this illustration before us, we are ready to consider the meaning of conditioned operant behavior. As indicated above, the behavior "operates" on the environment—the rat's bar pressing *produces* or *gains access* to the food. In classical conditioning, the animal is passive; it merely waits until the conditioned stimulus is presented and is followed by the unconditioned stimulus. In operant conditioning the animal is active; its behavior cannot be reinforced unless it first does something. There is no unconditioned stimulus that links the to-be-conditioned stimulus to the response.

Operant conditioning refers to increasing the probability of a response in a particular stimulus environment by following the response with *reinforcement.* Usually the reinforcement is something that can satisfy a basic drive, like food to satisfy hunger or water to satisfy thirst, but as we wiil see later it need not be.

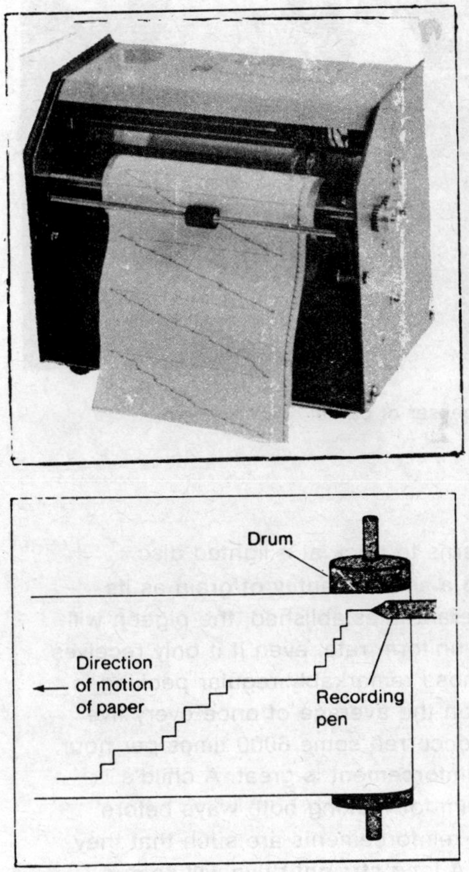

Fig. 7-9 Cumulative recorder

The axis of the drum is fixed, and as the drum rotates, the recording paper moves right to left under the head of a writing pen. The pen is rigged so that it can only move upward, never downward. Each time the animal makes a response, the pen steps upward a fixed amount. When no responses are being made, the pen moves in a straight line across the paper. Thus the height of each step is the same, but the length of the horizontal line varies as a function of the time between responses. Since the paper is moving at a fixed rate, the slope of the cumulative curve indicates the response rate. When the animal is responding at a high rate the slope of the cumulative curve will be quite steep; when the animal is responding very slowly there will be hardly any slope at all.

Measures of Operant Strength

Because the bar is always present in the Skinner box, the rat can respond to it as frequently or infrequently as it chooses. Hence *rate of response* is a useful measure of operant strength. The more frequently the response occurs during a given interval of time, the stronger it is.

The rate of response in operant conditioning is usually portrayed by a *cumulative curve* (Figure 7-9). The bar of the Skinner box is attached to a recording pen that rests on a slowly moving strip of paper. Each time the animal presses the bar the pen moves upward and then continues on its horizontal path. Because the paper moves at a fixed rate, the slope of the cumulative curve is a measure of response rate. A horizontal line indicates that the animal is not responding; a steep curve indicates a fast response rate. Figure 7-10A presents cumulative curves for two rats during acquisition of a bar pressing response. Rat A had been deprived of food for 30 hours and rat B for 10 hours. The hungrier rat responded much more rapidly.

Another measure of operant strength is the *total number of responses during extinction.* As Figure 7-10B shows, a single reinforcement can produce considerable strength according to this measure.

Partial Reinforcement

Operant conditioning shows a high degree of orderliness, or lawfulness. One illustration of orderliness is behavior controlled by *partial reinforcement*—that is, behavior taking place when the response is reinforced only a fraction of the time it occurs.

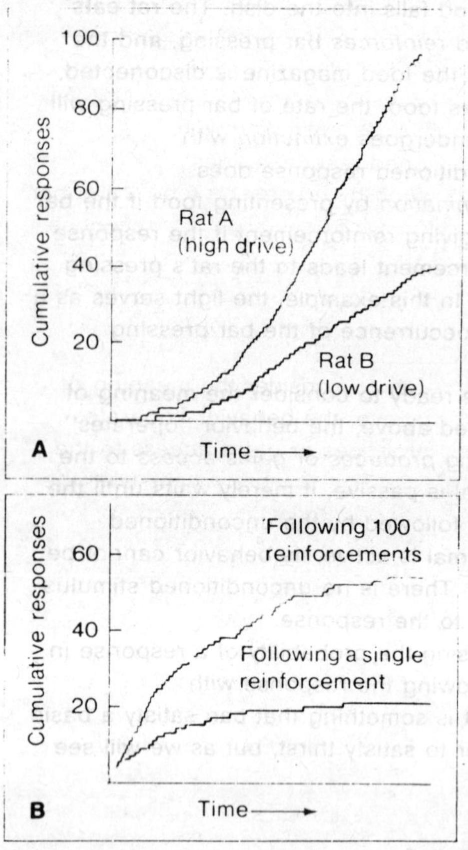

Fig. 7-10

A. Cumulative curves during acquisition

A comparison of the cumulative response curves for two rats during acquisition of a bar-pressing response. Rat A had been deprived of food for 30 hours and Rat B for 10 hours prior to the experiment. This difference in the drive level of the two rats is reflected in the rate of responding. (Data from Skinner, 1938)

B. Cumulative curves during extinction

Curves of extinction of operant responses in the rat are plotted following a single reinforcement and following 100 reinforcements. The plot shows the cumulative number of bar-pressing responses; every response raises the height of the curve, and the curve levels off when responses cease. (Data from Skinner, 1938)

The one-armed bandit (slot-machine) as a dispenser of partial reinforcement

In the typical experiment, a pigeon learns to peck at a lighted disc mounted on the wall and gains access to a small quantity of grain as its reinforcement. Once this conditioned operant is established, the pigeon will continue to peck at a high and relatively uniform rate, even if it only receives occasional reinforcement. The pigeon whose remarkably regular pecking is illustrated in Figure 7-11 was reinforced on the average of once every five minutes (12 times an hour), yet pecking occurred some 6000 times per hour.

The practical significance of partial reinforcement is great. A child's mother is not always present to reward him for looking both ways before crossing the street. But the influences of reinforcements are such that they persist against many nonreinforcements. A long straight drive will keep a golfer at the game despite many balls lost in the rough.

Fig. 7-11 Operant responses sustained by partial reinforcement

The curves record one pigeon's pecking responses, which were reinforced irregularly, but at an average interval of five minutes. The reinforcements are represented by horizontal dashes. Each of the sloping lines represents 1000 responses; the pen resets after each 1000.

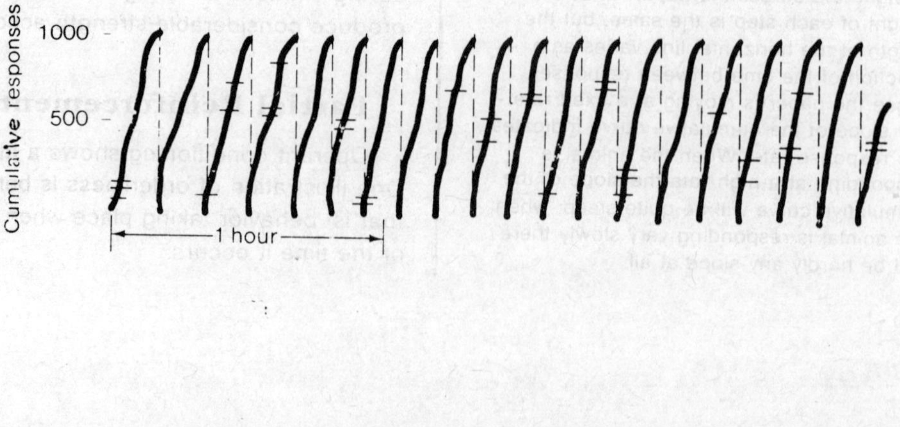

CRITICAL DISCUSSION

Reinforcement Schedules

Partial reinforcement procedures are of particular interest because they represent the type of reinforcement regime under which most organisms operate in nature. In addition, on partial reinforcement schedules an animal's response rate tends to be extremely sensitive to changes in the stimulus environment (both internal and external); these procedures thus provide a natural barometer for assessing the effects of radiation, drugs, fatigue, and other variables on performance. In the early exploration of space, scientists frequently housed rats, pigeons, and other animals in the space capsule and placed them on a partial reinforcement schedule. By observing changes in response rate during actual flight, they were able to determine the effects of acceleration, weightlessness, and the like, on performance.

Many different reinforcement schedules have been studied, but basically they all can be categorized according to two dimensions: (1) the period between successive reinforcements is determined either by the number of intervening nonreinforced responses or by the elapsed time and (2) the period between successive reinforcements is either regular or irregular. In terms of these two dimensions we can define the following four basic schedules.

1. *Fixed ratio* (FR). On this schedule reinforcement occurs after a fixed number of nonreinforced responses; if it occurs every 20 responses, for example, the ratio of nonreinforced to reinforced responses is 20 to 1.
2. *Fixed interval* (FI). Reinforcement follows the first response emitted after a fixed time period measured from the last reinforcement. For example, on a fixed-interval schedule of one minute, no further reinforcement will occur following a reinforced response until one minute has passed; once it has elapsed, the first response made will be reinforced.
3. *Variable ratio* (VR). Like the fixed-ratio schedule, reinforcement occurs after a specified number of nonreinforced responses. But for this schedule the number of reponses intervening between reinforcements varies from one reinforcement to the next. For example, a 20-to-1 variable-ratio schedule might be produced by requiring that the number of intervening responses be randomly selected from the numbers 0 to 40; this schedule averages an inter-reinforcement ratio of 20 responses, but it has a wide range of values.
4. *Variable interval* (VI). In this schedule reinforcement occurs after a specified period of time that varies from one reinforcement to the next. A simple variable-interval schedule of one minute might be generated by randomly setting the time period between reinforcements in a range of values from 0 to 120 seconds; this schedule yields an average time period of one minute, but a given interval can range anywhere from zero seconds to two minutes.

These four reinforcement schedules produce characteristic modes of responding. On an FI schedule the animal's pattern of responding suggests that it is keeping careful track of time. Immediately after a reinforcement its rate of responding drops to near zero and then increases at an accelerating pace as the end of the interval approaches. On VI schedules the response rate does not fluctuate as much between reinforcements. This is to be expected, since the animal does not know when the interval will terminate; the animal responds at a fairly steady rate in order to receive reinforcement promptly whenever it becomes available.

In contrast to the interval schedules, both the fixed- and variable-ratio schedules tend to produce extremely rapid rates of responding. If the ratio is small, responding begins immediately after a reinforcement; when the ratio is large there may be a brief pause after each reinforcement, followed by steady bursts of responding. On ratio schedules the animal responds as though it knows that the next reinforcement depends on its making a certain number of responses, and it bursts forth with them at as fast a rate as possible.

Secondary Reinforcement

Pavlov noted that once a dog had learned to respond to a conditioned stimulus in a highly dependable way, the conditioned stimulus could be used to reinforce a conditioned response to a new stimulus. Suppose the animal has learned to salivate to a tone as a conditioned stimulus. This is a *first-order* conditioned response. If a flashing light is then presented along with only the tone, the flashing light when presented alone will come to elicit the conditioned response. Pavlov called this process *second-order conditioning.* The conditioned stimulus of first-order conditioning (tone) has

Animals have been taught very complex responses by means of shaping techniques. At the Yerkes Primate Research Center in Atlanta, a chimpanzee named Lana has learned to answer questions and make requests by pressing symbols on a computer console. At bottom is an example of how the experiment works. A researcher outside the room asks Lana a question by pressing the symbols on his console for the words "What name-of this" and also holding up a candy. The chimp answered by pressing symbols for "M & M name-of this." Chapter 10 will provide additional examples of how chimpanzees have been taught to communicate with humans.

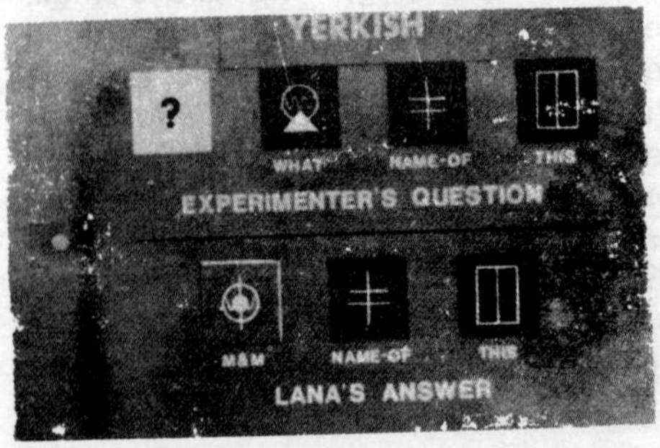

become a *secondary reinforcer.* Although second-order conditioning can be established with classical conditioning, it is more easily demonstrated with operant conditioning.

The introduction of a minor variation in the typical operant-conditioning situation will demonstrate how secondary reinforcement works. When a rat in a Skinner box presses a lever, a tone comes on momentarily, followed shortly by a food pellet. After the animal has been conditioned in this way, extinction is begun so that when the rat presses the lever, neither the tone nor the food appears. In time the animal virtually ceases to press the lever.

Now the tone is connected again, but without food. When the animal discovers that pressing the lever turns on the tone, the rate of pressing markedly increases, overcoming the extinction, even though no food follows. The tone has acquired secondary reinforcing qualities. The total number of responses made with only the tone connected to the bar depends upon the frequency of tone-food pairings during acquisition. Thus the strength of the tone as a secondary reinforcer increases as a function of the number of times it was associated with the primary reinforcer, food.

Secondary reinforcement has important practical implications because of its wide degree of generalization. The principle can be stated: *Once established, a secondary reinforcer can strengthen responses other than the response used during its original establishment and can do so with drives other than the one prevailing during the original training.* We know from ordinary observation that such reinforcers as social approval can be effective over a wide range of behavior, and experimental evidence supports the principle that secondary reinforcers have wide generality. In a study demonstrating this principle, the experimenter, using water-deprived rats, associated a tone with bar pressing reinforced by water. When the rats were later deprived of food rather than water, the same tone evoked bar pressing. If enough drive of any kind is present to instigate activity, a secondary reinforcer is effective, even though it derived its strength while another drive prevailed (Estes, 1949).

Secondary reinforcement greatly increases the range of possible conditioning. If everything we learned had to be followed by a primary reinforcer, the occasions for learning would be very much restricted. As it is, however, any habit once learned can have other habits built upon it. A verbal promise of food can reinforce behavior that would otherwise require food; mere praise (without the promise of a primary reinforcer) itself becomes reinforcing.

Shaping Behavior

In classical conditioning the conditioned stimulus substitutes for the unconditioned stimulus in evoking the response appropriate to the unconditioned stimulus. This substitution process fails, however, to account for *novelty* in behavior—for the learning of totally new responses. In contrast, operant conditioning plays an important role in the development of novel behavior.

The experimenter can produce novel behavior by taking advantage of random variations in the operant response and reinforcing only those

Fig. 7-12 Shaping behavior
By reinforcing only the desired responses, the experimenter taught the pigeon to tap the correct sign when light of a certain color was turned on.

responses that are in the desired direction. For example, a pigeon can be made to hold its head high as it walks around, by reinforcement with grain at first when its head is at average height, then when slightly above average, and finally only when its neck is stretched high. Or if the experimenter wants to train a dog to press a buzzer with its nose, he can give a food reinforcement each time the animal approaches the area of the buzzer, requiring closer and closer approximations to the desired spot for each reinforcement until finally the dog's nose is touching the buzzer. This technique is called *shaping* the animal's behavior, reinforcing only responses that meet the experimenter's specifications and extinguishing all others (see Figure 7-12).

Two psychologists developed a large-scale business teaching animals elaborate tricks and behavior routines by means of this shaping method. Using these relatively simple techniques, they and their staff have trained thousands of animals of many species for television shows and commercials, country fairs, and various tourist attractions, such as the famous whale and porpoise shows at "Marine Studios" in Florida and "Marineland of the Pacific" in California. One popular show featured a pig called "Priscilla, the Fastidious Pig." Priscilla turned on the TV set, ate breakfast at a table, picked up dirty clothes and put them in a hamper, vacuumed the floor, picked out her favorite food (from among foods competing with that of her sponsor!), and took part in a quiz program, answering questions from the audience by flashing lights indicating "Yes" or "No." She was not an unusually bright pig; in fact, because pigs grow so fast, a new "Priscilla" was trained every three to five months. The ingenuity was not the pig's but the experimenters', who used operant conditioning and shaped the behavior to produce the desired result (Breland and Breland, 1966).

In all these training techniques the behavior is shaped by means of reinforcement that is contingent upon the proper response. The importance of reinforcement in strengthening behavior is demonstrated by what happens when we introduce *noncontingent reinforcement*, that is, reinforcement not contingent upon a specific response. In one experiment Skinner placed hungry pigeons in separate Skinner boxes and at random intervals turned on a light that was immediately followed by a food reinforcement. The effect on the behavior of the pigeons was amazing. Each bird tended to select and repeat whatever it was doing when the reinforcement occurred. If one pigeon was pecking at its right wing just prior to reinforcement, this behavior tended to increase in frequency. The increased frequency made it more likely that this bit of behavior would occur about the time of the next food delivery, and so it would be reinforced again. Soon right-winged pecking dominated the bird's behavior. Thus for each bird some particular act or mannerism gained dominance because it occurred at the time of reinforcement, regardless of the fact that the act was in no way instrumental in producing the reinforcement.

Porpoises trained by shaping operant responses

The gambler who blows on the dice before throwing them and the baseball pitcher who habitually tugs at his cap and shakes his left foot before pitching are reinforced often enough by a successful performance that the behavior is strengthened and becomes part of their repertoire. They certainly are not successful every time. But, as we noted earlier, partial reinforcement is more resistant to extinction than continuous reinforcement.

CRITICAL DISCUSSION

Operant Conditioning

Classical conditioning has traditionally been viewed as a "lower" form of involuntary learning involving glandular and visceral responses, whereas operant conditioning has been regarded as a "higher" form of voluntary learning involving responses of the skeletal muscles. In fact, it has been assumed by some that responses mediated by the autonomic nervous system could be learned only by classical conditioning, while those mediated by the central nervous system could be acquired only operantly. This assumption has now been challenged by a series of studies indicating that it is possible to train animals to change their heart rate, blood pressure, and intestinal contractions by the proper application of operant techniques.

In one study rats were trained to modify two different visceral responses—heart rate and intestinal contraction. After a baseline of normal heart rate was established, one group of rats was rewarded for an increase in heart rate and another for a decrease. A shaping procedure was used so that initially any small increase or decrease above or below the baseline was rewarded; subsequently, progressively larger increases or decreases were needed to obtain reward. With this kind of training it was possible to slow a rat's heart rate, for example, from an initial 350 beats per minute to 230 within a relatively brief period of time. Similar procedures were used to train a third group of rats to increase intestinal contractions and a fourth group to decrease contractions.

Because visceral responses can be affected by tensing or moving skeletal muscles (for example, breathing slowly will decrease heart rate), it is possible that a subject, instead of learning a visceral response directly, may be learning a skeletal response that produces a visceral change. To control for this possibility the rats were given *curare,* a drug that temporarily paralyzes skeletal muscles but does not render the animal unconscious nor affect neural control of visceral responses. Since a paralyzed animal cannot be rewarded by food or drink, an unusual method of reward had to be used. This method consisted of electrical stimulation of certain "pleasure centers" in the rat's brain. Every time the rat produced a desired visceral change it received a brief electric current to a specific brain area where stimulation is known to have a reinforcing effect.

The results of this study are presented in Figure 7-13. One group of rats rewarded for increases in heart rate learned an increase, a second group rewarded for decreases learned a decrease, but neither of these groups showed a significant change in intestinal contractions. Conversely, a third group rewarded for increases in intestinal contraction showed an increase, and a fourth group rewarded for decreases in intestinal contraction showed a decrease, but neither of these groups showed a change in heart rate. These results suggest that visceral learning can be specific to an organ system; it is not the result of some general factor such as tensing or moving skeletal muscles.

Unfortunately, there have been difficulties replicating this experiment with curarized rats (Miller and Dworkin, 1973). So the question of whether autonomic responses can be operantly conditioned directly, without the mediation of vol-

Operant Conditioning of Human Behavior

In the following experiment (Verplanck, 1955) a college student was unaware that an experiment was being conducted, and the experimenter thereby avoided the artificiality of many conditioning experiments. The experimenter carried on what appeared to be an informal conversation with the subject, but actually behaved according to a plan. The experimenter determined in advance to reinforce all statements of opinion made by the subject, such as sentences beginning "I think," "I believe," "It seems to me," and the like. The *reinforcement* was the experimenter's saying "You're right," "I agree," "That's so" after each statement of opinion. *Extinction* was carried out in another portion of the experiment by mere nonreinforcement—silence--following a statement of opinion.

Following verbal reinforcement, statements of opinion showed a marked increase in frequency, following extinction, they decreased. The experimenter controlled verbal behavior in this situation in much the same way as he

of Autonomic Responses

Fig. 7-13 Operant conditioning of autonomic responses

Data from four groups of rats, each group rewarded for a different autonomic response. The left-hand figure plots rate of intestinal contractions for each group, and the right-hand figure plots heart rate. (After Miller and Banuazizi, 1968)

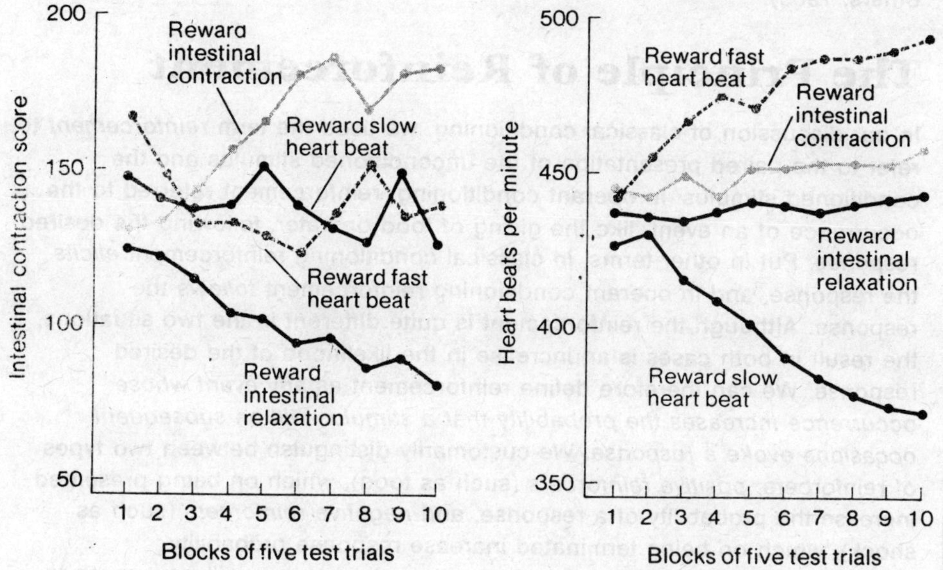

untary responses, is not yet resolved. The practical implications of this research, however, are important. Human subjects have been trained by operant methods to control such autonomic responses as heart rate, blood pressure, and the secretion of stomach acids that may produce ulcers. To control blood pressure, for example, the individual watches a machine that provides continuous visual feedback about his blood pressure. Whenever the blood pressure falls below a specified level a light flashes. The subject tries to analyze whatever he is thinking or doing when the blood pressure is low and to repeat that thought or emotion so as to keep it low.

The medical implications of such research are obvious. It would be better for people with high blood pressure to learn to control it themselves instead of depending on medications that are only partially successful and may have undesirable side-effects. Research on voluntary control of autonomic responses is still in the pioneer stage. The results so far indicate that some people are able to maintain control over heart rate or blood pressure when they leave the laboratory and return to their normal environment. But for many, the operantly conditioned response extinguishes rapidly without continued training. Conditioning apparatuses that the individual can carry with him or use at home are currently being developed and evaluated (Engel, 1972).

controlled bar pressing by a rat. In studies of this kind the subject may on some occasions begin to realize that the experimenter is actually manipulating his verbal behavior. There is evidence, however, that verbal conditioning can occur without the subject's being consciously aware of the fact that his statements are being controlled by the reinforcement schedule of the experimenter (Rosenfeld and Baer, 1969).

Operant-conditioning principles have also been used to modify problem behavior in children. In one case, nursery school teachers used social reinforcement to change the behavior of a shy, withdrawn three-year-old girl who spent most of her time crawling about the floor and resisted all attempts to encourage her to play or to join in group activities. On the assumption that getting the child to spend more time on her feet was the first step toward increasing participation in school activities, a reinforcement schedule was set up whereby the teachers gave attention to the child only when she was standing and ignored her completely the rest of the time. Careful recording of the child's minute-by-minute activity showed that she progressed from an initial rate of over 90 percent of the day on the floor to the point where, after two weeks, her behavior was indistinguishable from that of the other children in terms of talking, smiling, and using the school equipment.

To determine whether the reinforcement schedule was the causative factor, the procedure was reversed so that only on-the-floor activity was reinforced. Within two days the child was again spending the majority of her time on the floor. Interestingly enough, she did not revert to her earlier behavior in other respects, but managed to play happily while sitting or crawling and continued to initiate contacts with the other children. A second reversal procedure (that is, again giving the child steady attention when she was on her feet and none when she was on the floor) reinstated her vigorous on-the-feet participation in school activities within a few hours, and her behavior in the days that followed seemed adequate in every way (Harris and others, 1965).

The Principle of Reinforcement

In our discussion of classical conditioning, we used the term *reinforcement* to refer to the paired presentation of the unconditioned stimulus and the conditioned stimulus. In operant conditioning, reinforcement referred to the occurrence of an event, like the giving of food or water, following the desired response. Put in other terms, in classical conditioning reinforcement *elicits* the response, and in operant conditioning reinforcement *follows* the response. Although the reinforcement is quite different in the two situations, the result in both cases is an increase in the likelihood of the desired response. We can therefore define reinforcement as *any event whose occurrence increases the probability that a stimulus will on subsequent occasions evoke a response.* We customarily distinguish between two types of reinforcers: *positive reinforcers* (such as food), which on being presented increase the probability of a response, and *negative reinforcers* (such as shock), which on being terminated increase response probability.

In Chapters 11 and 12, which deal with motivation, we will have more to say about the nature of reinforcement, and what specifies a reinforcing event. Here we will only discuss some of the factors that determine the effectiveness of a reinforcer.

Fig. 7-14 T-maze

A maze used in the study of simple choice learning. The plexiglass covers on the start box and goal boxes are hinged so that the rat can be easily placed in or removed from the apparatus. The sliding doors (which usually are operated by a system of strings and pulleys from above) prevent the animal from retracing its path once it has made a choice. Note that the goal boxes are arranged so that the rat cannot see the food cup from the choice point.

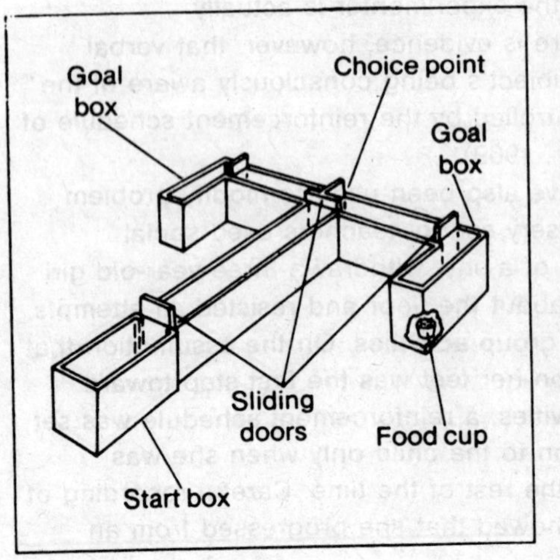

Variables Affecting Reinforcement

Psychologists have systematically investigated the effect of a number of reinforcement variables on the course of learning. Not surprisingly, the *amount of reinforcement* has been found to be an important parameter. Within limits the greater the amount of reinforcement, the more rapid the rate of learning. This relationship is illustrated in an experiment using a T-maze (Figure 7-14). After the rat was placed in the start box, it ran to the *choice point,* where it had to decide between a right or left turn to reach the food placed in one of the goal boxes. In this experiment there were three groups of rats, each group differing in the amount of food received for a correct turn: one group received four food pellets, another group two pellets, and a third group one pellet. Each rat ran four trials a day. The results in terms of proportion of correct responses per day are shown in Figure 7-15A. Note that the group with the largest amount of reinforcement learned at the fastest rate, while the other two groups learned more slowly. The curves start

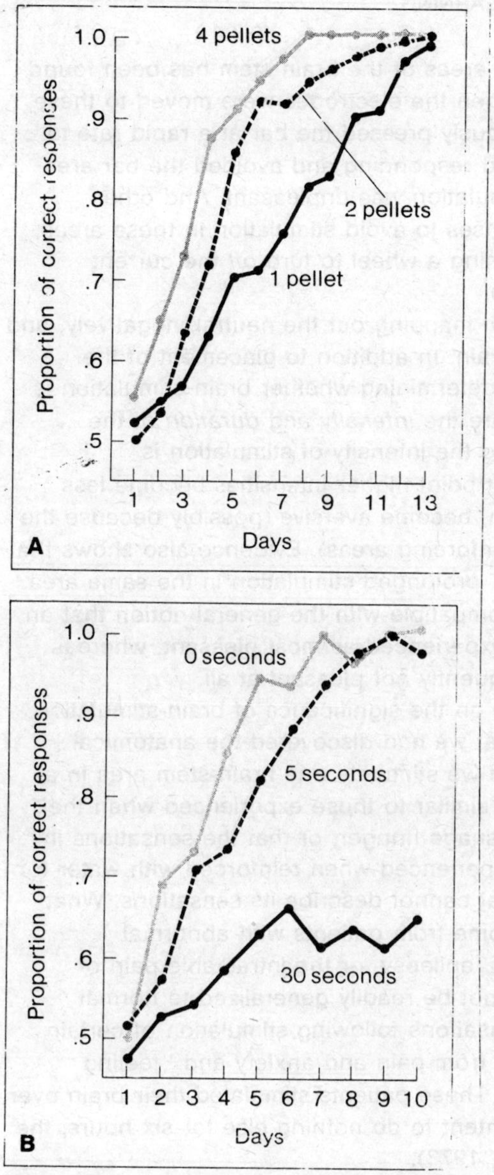

Fig. 7-15

A. Amount of reinforcement

Learning curves for three groups of rats run in a T-maze experiment. The groups were distinguished by the number of food pellets a rat received when it entered the correct goal box. Half the animals were trained with the left side of the maze designated as the correct response, half with the right side as the correct response. (After Clayton, 1964)

B. Delay of reward

The figure shows learning curves for three groups of rats. The groups were distinguished by the time interval between entering the correct goal box and receiving a pellet of food. (Unpublished data from Atkinson)

at about .5 since there are only two choices; the animal should make the correct turn 50 percent of the time by chance alone.

The *delay of reinforcement* is another important parameter of reinforcement. A common assumption in training animals or young children has been that it is most effective to reward or punish the organism immediately after it responds. The spanking given by father when he returns home from work is less effective (other variables being equal) in reducing a child's aggressive behavior toward baby brother than punishment delivered immediately following or during the act.

The effectiveness of immediate reinforcement in a laboratory learning situation is demonstrated by the following experiment. The apparatus used was a T-maze having goal boxes equipped with food dispensers that could be set to delay the presentation of food pellets. One group of rats received their food immediately upon entering the correct goal box (zero-second delay); another group was fed following a five-second delay; and a third group was delayed thirty seconds before receiving their food. Figure 7-15B shows the learning curves for each of the three groups. The zero-second group and the five-second group both reached near perfect responding by the ninth day, but the zero-second group learned at a faster rate. The thirty-second-delay group was markedly inferior and never achieved a very high level of performance.

Brain Stimulation and Reinforcement

An interesting area of research stems from the rather startling discovery that electrical stimulation of certain regions of the brain can be reinforcing. In 1953 Olds was investigating the reticular formation of the rat's brain (see p. 43) by means of microelectrodes. These tiny electrodes can be implanted permanently in specific brain areas without interfering with the rat's health or normal activity and, when connected with an electrical source, can supply stimulation of varying intensities. An electrode was implanted accidentally in an area near the hypothalamus, and Olds discovered that after he delivered a mild current through the electrodes the animal repeatedly returned to where it had been in the cage when stimulated. Further stimulations at the same cage location caused the animal to spend most of its time there. Later Olds found that this same animal could be drawn to any spot in a maze by giving electrical stimulation after each response in the appropriate direction. And other animals with electrodes implanted in the same brain region learned to press a bar in a Skinner box to produce their own electrical stimulation (see Figure 7-16); each bar-press closed a circuit that automatically provided a brief current. These animals were bar pressing at a phenomenal rate: a not unusual record would show an average of over 2000 responses an hour for 15 or 20 hours, until the animal finally dropped from exhaustion.

Since the initial brain-stimulation discovery, experiments with microelectrodes implanted in many different areas of the brain and brain stem have been carried out using rats, cats, and monkeys in a wide variety of tasks. The reinforcing effects of stimulation in certain areas (primarily the hypothalamus) are powerful: hungry rats will endure a more painful shock while crossing an electric grid to obtain brain stimulation than they will to obtain food (Olds and Sinclair, 1957); when given a choice between food or electric brain stimulation in a T-maze, rats that have been on a starvation diet for as long as ten days will choose the path leading to stimulation (Spies, 1965). On

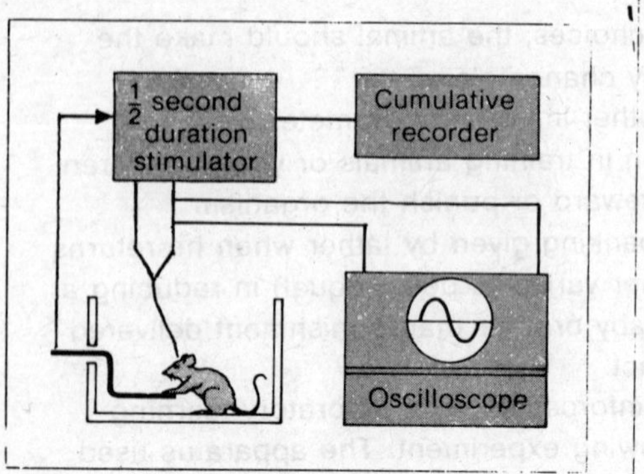

Fig. 7-16 Brain stimulation

The animal's bar press delivers a 60-cycle current for one-half second, after which the animal must release and press again for more current. The animal's response rate is recorded on the cumulative recorder, and the experimenter can monitor the delivery of the current by means of the oscilloscope. Rats respond with rates up to 100 per minute with electrodes in the medial-forebrain region of the hypothalamus. (After Olds and Olds, 1965)

the other hand, stimulation of some areas of the brain stem has been found to serve as a *negative* reinforcer; when the electrodes were moved to these different brain areas, rats that previously pressed the bar at a rapid rate to receive stimulation suddenly stopped responding and avoided the bar area entirely, indicating that the new stimulation was unpleasant. And other animals have learned various responses to avoid stimulation in these areas, for example, pressing a lever or turning a wheel to turn *off* the current (Delgado, Roberts, and Miller, 1954).

Much progress has been made in mapping out the neutral, negatively, and positively reinforcing areas of the brain. In addition to placement of the electrodes, two important variables determining whether brain stimulation is positively or negatively reinforcing are the *intensity* and *duration* of the stimulation. Up to a point, increasing the intensity of stimulation is increasingly reinforcing; beyond that point higher intensities become less effective and may, if intense enough, become aversive (possibly because the stimulation spreads to negatively reinforcing areas). Evidence also shows that while brief stimulation is reinforcing, prolonged stimulation in the same area becomes aversive. Both facts are compatible with the general notion that an intermediate level of stimulation is experienced as most pleasant, whereas deviations to either extreme are frequently not pleasant at all.

Psychologists are not yet agreed on the significance of brain-stimulation studies. It would be nice to think that we had discovered the anatomical location of reinforcement, that when we stimulate one brain-stem area in a rat, for example, the sensations are similar to those experienced when the animal is reinforced with food to assuage hunger, or that the sensations in another area are similar to those experienced when reinforced with water to alleviate thirst. Unfortunately, the rat cannot describe its sensations. What data we have on human subjects come from patients with abnormal conditions (suffering from psychosis, epilepsy, or the intractable pain of terminal cancer), so the results cannot be readily generalized to normal individuals. Among the reported sensations following stimulation of certain areas of the limbic system are relief from pain and anxiety and "feeling wonderful," "happy," and "drunk." These patients stimulated their brain over a 1000 times per hour and were content to do nothing else for six hours, the maximum period allowed (Campbell, 1973).

In some respects, learning with brain stimulation as reinforcement does not follow the same rules as learning with food or other external rewards. The extinction of the bar press response for brain stimulation is much more rapid than extinction for food or water rewards. If the current is turned off, the animal's responses stop quite abruptly, but it will start responding again at a rapid rate if it is given one or two stimulations. And while partial reinforcement can be used quite effectively with food or water reinforcement, it is much less effective when the reinforcement is brain stimulation. These and other data suggest that brain stimulation operates differently from other reinforcers; it seems to create a temporary sensation that does not increase in strength during deprivation.

Multiple-Response Learning

Thus far we have considered the strengthening or weakening of single identifiable responses. Although some of these responses are complex, they are still identifiable as unitary acts. But much of our learning consists of acquiring patterns or sequences of behaviors, as in learning athletic skills or in memorizing a poem. These patterns illustrate *multiple-response learning,* a kind of learning involving more than one identifiable act, with the order of events usually fixed by the demands of the situation. To study this kind of learning psychologists have designed such laboratory tasks as mirror drawing, target tracking, and rote memorization. The first two tasks are forms of sensorimotor skill, and the last is largely verbal. Tasks such as these approximate the learning of skills that are used in everyday life.

Sensorimotor Skills

By a *sensorimotor skill* we mean one in which muscular movement is prominent, but under sensory control. Riding a bicycle, turning a flip from a diving board, playing a piano, and typing are sensorimotor skills. They are not simply patterns of skilled movements. The bicycle rider has to watch the traffic and the bumps in the road and be guided by them; the diver must adjust his timing to the height of the platform; the musician reads notes and attempts to play with feeling; the typist must follow a manuscript and stay within specified boundaries. These considerations call attention to the *sensory control* of skill.

Psychologists have not limited themselves to laboratory tasks in studying skills. The pioneer study was, in fact, a practical one on learning to send and receive telegraphic messages, carried out by Bryan and Harter in 1897. Many of the best-established principles are first worked out on laboratory skills, however, and later validated in more complex practical situations. A convenient laboratory illustration is given by the mirror-drawing experiment. We learn something of the importance of eye-hand coordination in developing skills by studying what happens when our usual eye-hand coordinations are inappropriate and we have to reorient accordingly.

In a typical mirror-drawing experiment, the subject is required to trace a path around a geometric figure, such as a star, while viewing it in a mirror (Figure 7-17). The subject knows that the correct performance is a smoothly traced line within the path around the figure. The subject starts out by using familiar habits. These of course cause trouble. When using the visual cues from a mirror in the same way as cues in direct vision, the subject will find that the pencil will not go where it is supposed to go. The subject therefore attempts to correct movements and gradually approximates a good performance, although at first a very jagged line is drawn. Old habits may again interfere at the corners of the figure. With practice, however, the lines smooth out, and the subject can achieve a rapid tracing of the figure.

Fig. 7-17 Mirror drawing
The subject attempts to follow with her pencil the outline of a star, which she can see only as an image in the mirror. Because the usual right-left relationships are reversed in the mirror, she has to learn a new eye-hand coordination. This is a difficult task, but one that subjects find extremely interesting.

LEARNING CURVES FOR SKILL. Experimenters typically keep track of progress in skill learning by plotting a learning curve similar to those used to depict the course of classical conditioning. Two learning curves for mirror drawing are plotted in Figure 7-18, one representing *massed practice* (practice trials follow each other consecutively within one period) and the other depicting *spaced practice* (practice trials distributed one per day). Note that spaced practice is more efficient, which is generally the case although there are exceptions. This comparison shows how learning curves can be used to display a relationship between two variables.

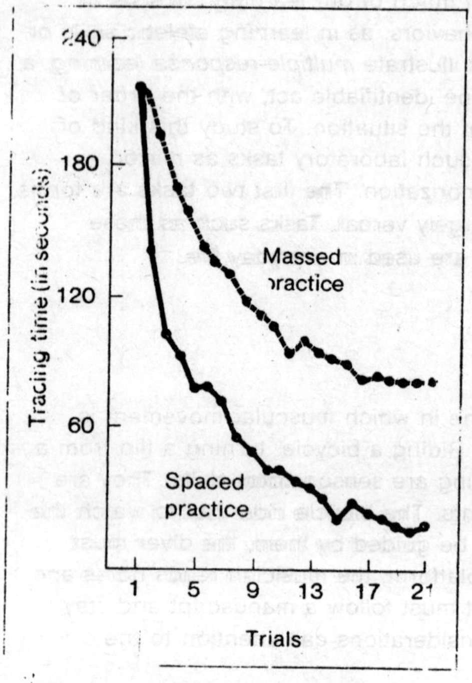

Fig. 7-18 Learning curves for mirror drawing

Proficiency is measured as the amount of time required to trace a figure seen in the mirror; thus time decreases over trials as the skill improves. The top curve is for massed practice, all trials occurring with in one session. The bottom curve is for spaced practice, with one trial per day. (Data from Lorge, 1930)

In Figure 7-18 the measure of proficiency is the time required to trace a figure seen in the mirror. Improvement shows a decrease in time required and yields a falling curve. If the measure of proficiency is a score that increases with practice, then the learning curve rises. Scores in a target-tracking task like the *pursuit rotor* are of this sort. The subject attempts to keep the tip of a hand-held stylus in contact with a small metal disc mounted near the edge of a revolving turntable much like that of an ordinary record player. When the stylus is in contact with the moving target, an electric circuit is completed through a clock. The subject's score is the amount of time on target. Proficiency gain will be represented in this case by a rising curve, for the longer the subject stays on target, the better the score (Figure 7-19).

Whether the curve falls or rises, its curvature can be described by the way the gains vary from trial to trial. Both Figure 7-18 and Figure 7-19 show curves of *decreasing gains.* By decreasing gain we mean that the change in performance from the current trial to the next is always less than the change that took place on the previous trial. These curves are common in studies of sensorimotor skill. They provide one reason why the learning of a skill is often discouraging to the learner; gains are visible and satisfying at first, but the slowing down of improvement after the first few trials may easily become disappointing.

QUALITATIVE CHANGES WITH PRACTICE. A learning curve presents performance over the course of an experiment as though the subject followed the same pattern of activity at the end as at the beginning and improved only in efficiency. But it is quite possible that in the course of improvement the subject's method changed. For example, in studying learning how to type, some investigators have detected a shift from a *letter habit* (learning the location of the individual keys associated with each letter) to a *word habit* (learning to write familiar words with a single burst of movement, embedding the letters in a total pattern). Occasionally these higher order and lower order learnings conflict, and there is a period of no improvement in the learning curve. This period is described as a *plateau* because it has been preceded by improvement and will be followed by more improvement when the higher order learning wins out.

Rote Memorization

By *rote memorization* we mean verbatim learning by repetition, as contrasted with substance memorization. Experiments on rote memorization take one of two chief forms, corresponding to the ways we learn things verbatim in ordinary experience. One form is *serial memorization,* as in memorizing poetry or lines of a play. In a laboratory experiment, a list of words is memorized from beginning to end, so that each word in the list is in some sense the stimulus for the word to follow. The second form is *paired-associate* learning, which is comparable to the method sometimes used in learning the words of a foreign language. The words are learned in stimulus-response pairs, such as *prepared-afraid, careless-vacant, hungry-quiet;* a stimulus word is presented, and the response word has to be learned. The pairs are not learned in any special order and depending on the experiment, may or may not be meaningfully related.

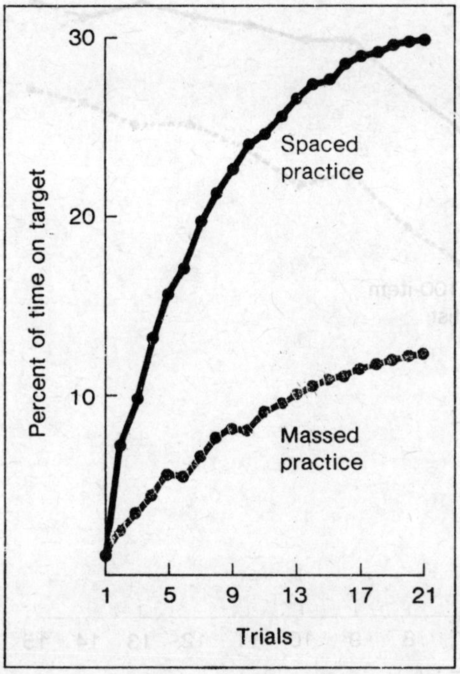

Fig. 7-19 Learning curves for pursuit rotor

Each trial lasts for 30 seconds, with some subjects having a 15-second rest period between trials (massed practice) and others a 45-second rest period (spaced practice). The dependent variable is percentage of time on target per trial. (Data from Bourne and Archer, 1956)

Fig. 7-20 A memory drum

The material to be memorized appears in the aperture as the drum revolves forward in discrete steps.

The experimenter usually presents the material to the subject by means of an exposure device called a *memory drum* (Figure 7-20). The items to be learned appear one at a time at fixed intervals in the aperture of the memory drum. After the initial presentation of each item, the subject tries to state in advance the next item to appear in the aperture. By keeping score of the subject's hits and misses throughout memorizing, the experimenter can plot a learning curve from his record.

The *anticipation method* for rote memorization requires that the subject try to state what lies immediately ahead. It can be used for either serial memorization or paired-associate memorization. In the serial method the item anticipated becomes the stimulus for the next anticipation when it (the item) appears in the aperture; it is both a response item and a stimulus item (Figure 7-21). In the paired-associate method the stimulus item is used only as a stimulus, not as a response. When the stimulus is presented in the aperture of the memory drum, the subject tries to anticipate the response item; then the stimulus-response pair appear together for a brief period of study prior to presentation of the next stimulus item.

To illustrate the paired-associate procedure in a practical situation, we shall briefly describe a study of second-language learning. The equipment used in this experiment was more elaborate than the typical memory drum, for reasons that will soon be obvious. The task was to learn the correct

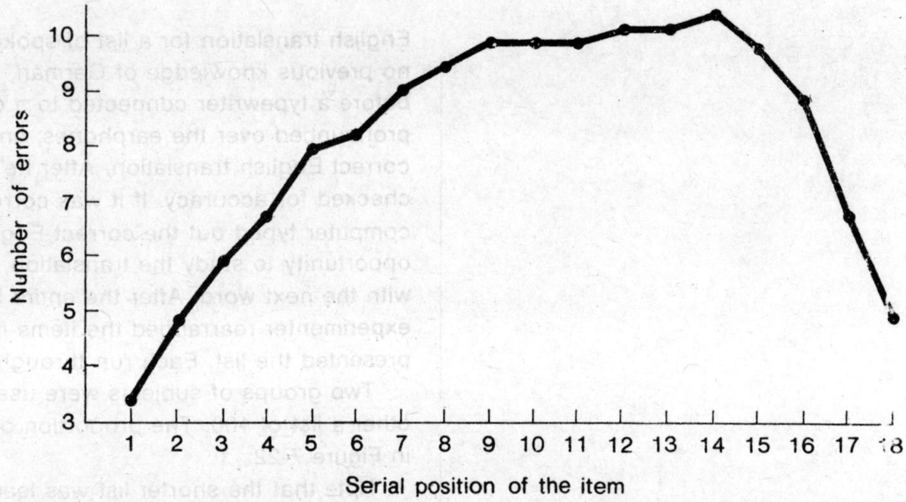

Fig. 7-21 Serial-anticipation method

Subjects were required to learn a list of 18 unrelated words by the method of serial anticipation. The words were presented one at a time in the window of a memory drum. When one word appeared, the subject tried to anticipate what the next word on the list would be. A moment later the next word appeared telling him whether he was correct and providing the cue for anticipating the next word, and so on. After each trial (a complete run through the list) there was a brief rest period before the start of the next trial. On the first trial the subject had no basis for making any correct anticipations because he had not seen the list before; he just studied each word as it appeared. On subsequent trials he began to make increasingly more correct anticipations. The curve plots the total number of failures to correctly anticipate the next word at each serial position during the course of mastering the list. Note that the initial words on the list were mastered most easily, the last words were next, and the middle words were the most difficult. The bow-shaped curve is typically obtained in learning lists by the serial-anticipation method. (After Atkinson, 1957)

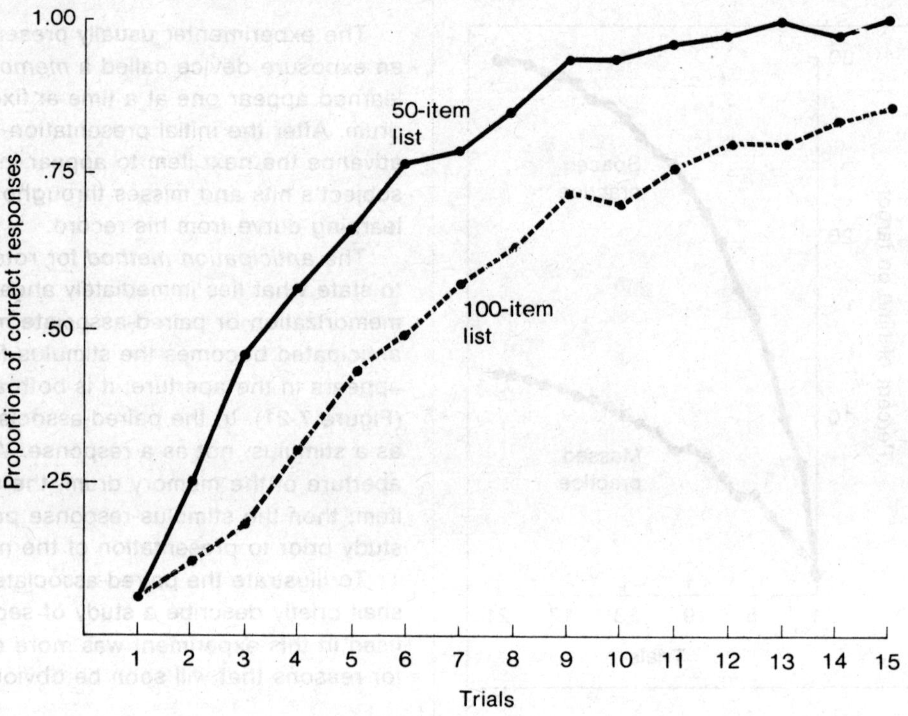

Fig. 7-22 Paired-associate learning curves
Proportion of correct anticipation responses over successive trials of a paired-associate learning experiment. The rate of learning is faster for the shorter list. (Data from Atkinson, 1972)

English translation for a list of spoken German words. The subject, who had no previous knowledge of German, wore a set of earphones while seated before a typewriter connected to a computer. A German word was pronounced over the earphones, and the subject's task was to type the correct English translation. After he made his response the computer checked for accuracy. If it was correct a "+" sign occurred; otherwise the computer typed out the correct English word. The subject had a brief opportunity to study the translation, and then the procedure was repeated with the next word. After the entire list of words had been run through, the experimenter rearranged the items in a new random order and again presented the list. Each run through the list constituted a new trial.

Two groups of subjects were used, one learning a list of 50 words and tne other a list of 100. The proportion of correct responses over trials is plotted in Figure 7-22.

Note that the shorter list was learned more rapidly. These results are expected; the more items that have to be mastered at one time, the slower the rate at which each individual item is learned.

Cognitive Learning

The kinds of learning that we have considered thus far all stress the organization of behavior into learned stimulus-response associations. In studying more complex forms of learning, attention must be given to the roles of perception and knowledge, or *cognitive processes.* There is the possibility that emphasis upon stimulus-response associations may lead to too much concern for piecemeal activities and too little attention to organized relationships and meaning. The teacher impressed by habit formation may use rote memorization and drill excessively, without caring enough about whether the child organizes and understands what is learned.

Those identified with the cognitive viewpoint argue that learning, particularly in humans, cannot be satisfactorily explained in terms of stimulus-response associations. They propose that the learner forms a *cognitive structure* in memory, which preserves and organizes information about the various events that occur in a learning situation. When a test is made to determine how much has been learned, the subject must *encode* the test stimulus and scan it against his memory to determine an appropriate action. What is done will depend upon the cognitive structure retrieved from memory, and the context in which the test occurs. Thus the subject's response is a *decision process* that varies with the nature of the test situation and the subject's memory for prior events. Even classical conditioning with animals is not interpreted by cognitive theorists as the formation of a new S-R association. The animal is assumed to store in memory a record of the events that occurred in the experiment; when tested this cognitive structure is retrieved, and the animal's response is determined by the information stored therein. The animal is not learning to salivate automatically to the conditioned stimulus; it is learning to anticipate food, and it is the anticipation that causes him to salivate. At the level of classical conditioning the cognitive approach may seem cumbersome, but in analyzing complex forms of learning it offers more flexibility in theorizing than a strict S-R approach.

Insight Experiments

Partly in protest against too much study of the kinds of learning that involve stimulus-response associations, Wolfgang Köhler, a German psychologist who emigrated to the United States, performed a series of dramatic experiments with chimpanzees. At some point in working on a problem, chimpanzees appeared to grasp its inner relationships through *insight;* that is, they solved the problem not through mere trial and error, but by perceiving the relationships essential to solution. The following experiment by Köhler is typical.

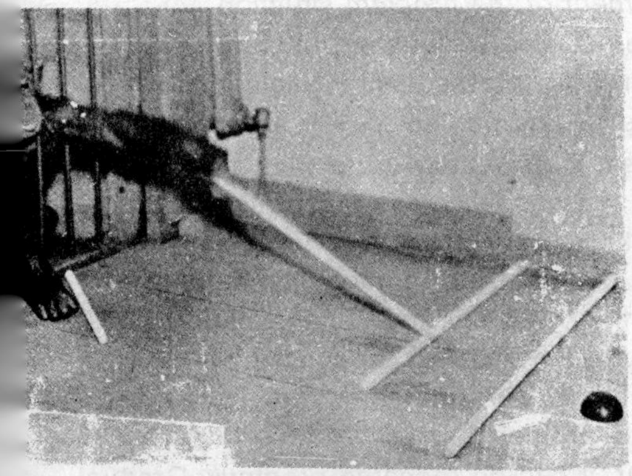

Fig. 7-23 A chimpanzee solving a multiple-stick problem

Using the shorter sticks, the chimpanzee pulls in a stick long enough to reach the piece of fruit. He has learned to solve this problem by understanding the relationship between the sticks and the piece of fruit.

Sultan [Köhler's most intelligent chimpanzee] is squatting at the bars but cannot reach the fruit which lies outside by means of his only available short stick. A longer stick is deposited outside the bars, about two meters on one side of the object and parallel with the grating. It cannot be grasped with the hand, but it can be pulled within reach by means of the small stick. [See Figure 7-23 for an illustration of a similar multiple-stick problem.] Sultan tries to reach the fruit with the smaller of the two sticks. Not succeeding, he tears at a piece of wire that projects from the netting of his cage, but that too, is in vain. Then he gazes about him (there are always in the course of these tests some long pauses, during which the animals scrutinize the whole visible area). He suddenly picks up the little stick once more, goes up to the bars directly opposite to the long stick, scratches it towards him with the "auxiliary," seizes it, and goes with it to the point opposite the objective (the fruit), which he secures. From the moment that his eyes fall upon the long stick, his procedure forms one consecutive whole, without hiatus, and although the angling of the bigger stick by means of the smaller is an action that could be complete and distinct in itself, yet observation shows that it follows, quite suddenly, on an interval of hesitation and doubt—staring

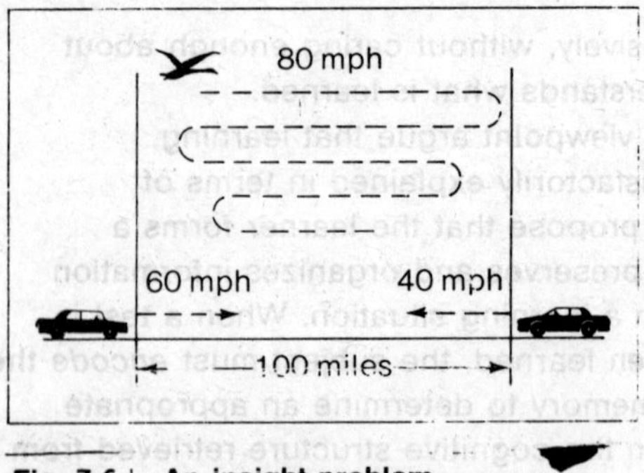

Fig. 7-24 An insight problem

Two cars, now 100 miles apart, are moving toward each other. The east-bound car is traveling at the rate of 60 mph. The west-bound one is traveling at the rate of 40 mph. An energetic bird, starting from the east-bound car, flies back and forth between the two cars without stopping or losing any speed on the turns. The bird flies at the uniform rate of 80 mph. Problem: How far does the bird fly from the start to the moment that the two cars meet? The problem can be solved without mathematical training (see text).

about—which undoubtedly has a relation to the final objective, and is immediately merged in the final action of the attainment of the end goal [Köhler, 1925, pp. 174–75].

A moderate degree of insight is so common in human learning that we tend to take it for granted. Occasionally insight comes dramatically, and then we have what has been appropriately called an "aha" experience. The solution of a problem becomes suddenly clear, as though a light had been turned on in the darkness. This experience usually comes with puzzles or riddles that make good party games, precisely because people enjoy the experience of insight when (and if) it comes. One illustration is furnished by the problem presented in Figure 7-24.

If we use the ordinary methods of problem solving to deal with the problem of Figure 7-24, we may set up some sort of algebraic equation to determine, step by step, how far the bird flies on each trip. For example, we know that on the first trip the bird flies east at 80 mph, while the car coming west toward it is traveling at 40 mph. It can be determined without too much difficulty that the bird will go twice as far as the car by the time they meet. Hence when they meet, the car will have gone $33\frac{1}{3}$ miles from its starting point, while the bird will have flown $66\frac{2}{3}$ miles. For the bird's return flight it will be necessary to take account of the movement of the first car during the time the bird flew the $66\frac{2}{3}$ miles. Then, knowing the rate of flight of the bird and of the car coming to meet it, the second trip can be computed just as the first one was. We continue these computations until the cars have met.

What is meant by solving this kind of problem with insight? Instead of trying to determine, first of all, how far the bird flies on each of its trips, we can take a different tack. The clue comes from the question: How long will the bird have been flying by the time the cars meet? When this question is answered, the rest of the solution comes quickly. If you now have the answer, having first been puzzled and then suddenly having "caught on," you know what the experience of insight is.

The variables that influence insight learning are not well understood but a few general remarks can be made.

1. *Insight depends upon the arrangement of the problem situation.* Appropriate past experience, while necessary, does not guarantee a solution. Insight will come easily only if the essentials for solution are arranged so that their relationships can be perceived. For example, a chimpanzee solves the stick problem more readily if the stick is on the same side of the cage as the food. He has more difficulty if he must turn away from the food to see the stick. Human beings can do much of their rearranging of a problem mentally; they can form a mental image of the situation and rearrange objects in that image in an attempt to find a solution. Mental manipulations may at times go on preconsciously, and only when a solution has been found does the person suddenly realize that he had been thinking about the problem.
2. *Once a solution occurs with insight, it can be repeated promptly.* Gradual solution appears to be the rule in trial-and-error learning. Sudden solution is the rule in insight. Once the chimpanzee has used a stick for pulling in a banana, he will seek out a stick on the next occasion.
3. *A solution achieved with insight can be applied in new situations.* What is learned in the insight experiment is not a specific S-R sequence, but a cognitive relationship between a means and an end. Hence one tool may

be substituted for another. In Figure 7-24 boats could replace cars without confusing the solver of the problem.

An effective learner is a resourceful, adaptable person, able to use what he knows in new situations and to discover for himself solutions to problems that he has never faced before. Emphasis upon insightful learning, rather than upon rote learning or mechanical skills, encourages such problem-solving behavior.

Sign Learning

Some learning classified as conditioned responses may actually involve learning the signs of "what leads to what." This was the contention of Edward C. Tolman, who believed that much learning is *sign learning* (Tolman, 1948). A rat running through a complex maze may be developing a kind of map, or *cognitive structure,* of the maze instead of learning merely a sequence of left and right turns. If a familiar path is blocked, the animal can adopt another route based on this understanding of spatial relationships.

Sign learning may be defined as *an acquired expectation that one stimulus will be followed by another in a particular context.* Note that what is acquired is an expectation rather than a chained sequence of responses. Although the expectation may lead the animal to make a specific response, the response need not be completely stereotyped. That is, one response may be readily substituted for another, provided both lead to the same end point where the expected stimulus will be encountered. Thus a rat that has learned to run a maze to obtain food in the goal box will, if the maze is flooded with water, swim without error to the goal. The rat appears to have learned the location of the goal rather than a chain of specific stimulus-response connections.

Because what is learned is a set of expectations or a cognitive map of the environment rather than specific responses, sign learning classifies as learning with understanding rather than as conditioning.

LATENT LEARNING. Experiments on latent learning support the concept of cognitive structures. *Latent learning,* broadly conceived, refers to any learning that is not evidenced by behavior at the time of the learning. Typically, such learning goes on under low levels of drive or in the absence of reward. When drive is heightened or appropriate reinforcement appears, there is a sudden use of what has been previously learned.

In one experiment three groups of rats were run daily in the maze diagrammed in Figure 7-25. One group was given a food reinforcement when it reached the goal box at the end of the maze. A second group was allowed to explore the maze, but when the rats reached the goal box they were removed with no reinforcement. A third group was treated in the same way as the second group for the first ten days, and then given reinforcement for the remaining seven days. As we can see in Figure 7-25, all groups showed some learning in that they made fewer errors in reaching the goal box as the number of trials increased. But the reinforced group clearly learned more rapidly than the two nonreinforced groups. With the introduction of food on the eleventh day, however, the error scores of the third group dropped markedly and it was soon performing as well as, and even better than, the reinforced group. Evidently the rats were learning something about the spatial

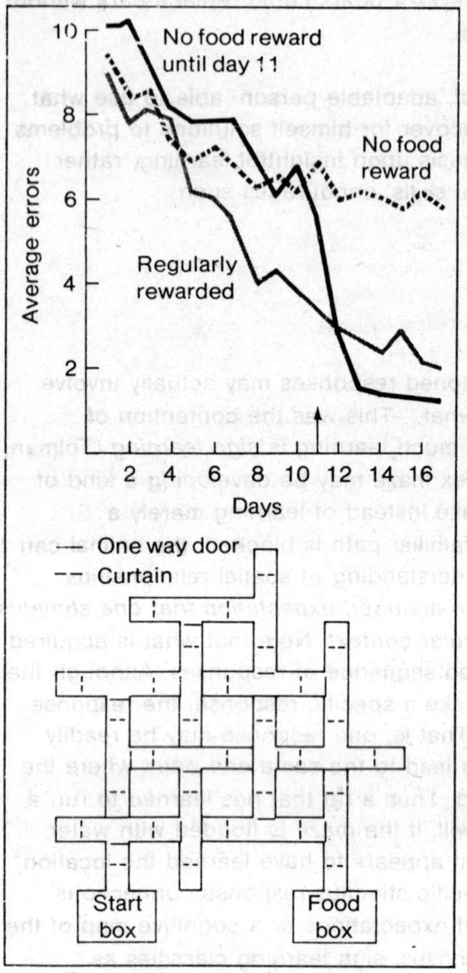

Fig. 7-25 Latent learning in rats

Note that after reward is introduced on the eleventh day, the rats represented by the black line perform as well as, and even a little better than, those regularly rewarded (gray line). Beneath the graph is a diagram of the maze used in this study. (After Tolman and Honzik, 1930)

orientation of the maze prior to the time that they were rewarded. Tolman would claim that in this experiment the rat formulated a schematic representation of the maze that included information about dead ends and incorrect pathways as well as about the path that leads to the goal.

In theorizing about how rewards and punishments influence behavior, Tolman distinguished between *learning* and *performance.* In the latent-learning study, the rat learned something about the spatial arrangement of the maze, but this learning was not evidenced in performance until reward motivated the animal to perform. Tolman would maintain that for learning, reward and punishment serve to convey information, to teach "what leads to what." They do not "stamp in" specific responses and eliminate others. In performance, on the other hand, rewards and punishments function (in conjunction with the schemata built up through past experience) to determine which of a repertoire of possible responses the subject decides to use. The response with the greatest expectation of reward will be made more quickly and efficiently.

Theoretical Interpretations

As noted at several points in this chapter, there has been a good deal of controversy among psychologists about how to explain learning. One approach views learning as the formation of S-R associations; the other emphasizes the cognitive nature of the process. When we examine classical or operant conditioning, the S-R approach has considerable appeal. It offers a simple and direct interpretation of the phenomena—an interpretation that does not require postulating mental events intervening between the stimulus input and the response output. Some psychologists argue that even the most complex forms of learning may be analyzed into component S-R associations; for them, the S-R association is the "behavioral atom" from which complex behaviors are constructed.

But the S-R approach has not proved satisfactory as an explanation for more complex forms of human learning. As we will see in the next three chapters, phenomena such as memory and problem solving are not readily interpretable in terms of S-R associations; such interpretations quickly become unwieldy and have proved unproductive in pointing to new avenues of research. Consequently psychologists have turned increasingly to a more cognitive approach to learning. This change in emphasis will be reflected in the discussions of memory, language, and thinking that follow.

For our purposes, it is possible to view associative learning and cognitive learning as complementary; neither in itself provides a complete explanation, but each helps to explain some features of learning that the other neglects or explains with greater difficulty.

It is possible to grade examples of learning on a crude scale, with the most automatic kind of learning (explained best as S-R associations) at one end and the most insightful and rational kind at the other (explained best according to cognitive principles). Those habits learned by classical conditioning, and without awareness, would be at one extreme of the scale. Perhaps learning to salivate when we see a delicious meal or becoming anxious when we encounter a situation that has proved dangerous in the past would be examples of such conditioning. Toward the middle of the scale would be tasks learned with full awareness but still somewhat automatically,

"Psst—want a map?"

as when we learn a foreign-language vocabulary or a skill like swimming. At the other end of the scale fall tasks that require reasoning about many facts in complex relationships. Most learning would probably fall somewhere in the middle range of the scale, a kind of mixture between simple association and understanding.

This kind of *mixture theory* is considered too eclectic for many psychologists who would rather commit themselves to one or the other position and attempt to "derive" the behavior that the opposing theorists raise as critical of the position adopted. However, for most practical applications it may be best to adopt a conservative position that pays attention to associative aspects of the learning process as well as to problems of cognitive organization. Thus in teaching a child to read, one needs to provide for drill in associating the printed word with its spoken form, as well as exercises designed to increase the child's understanding of phonetic regularities and the affects of context on meaning.

Summary

1. Pavlov's experiments on *classical conditioning* of the dog brought to light several principles useful in the understanding of habit formation. These include reinforcement, extinction, spontaneous recovery, generalization, and discrimination.
2. Skinner's experiments on *operant conditioning* have extended conditioning principles to kinds of responses that cannot be elicited by recognized unconditioned stimuli. Operant behavior acts upon the environment to produce or gain access to reinforcement and becomes strengthened by reinforcement.
3. Rate of responding is a useful measure of operant strength. *Partial reinforcement* illustrates the orderliness of operant behavior, since long and regular runs of responses can be sustained by occasional reinforcement. *Secondary reinforcement,* the fact that a stimulus associated with a reinforcing stimulus acquires reinforcing properties, increases the possible range of conditioning and explains the reward value of such incentives as social approval and money.
4. An animal trainer can *shape behavior* by reinforcing those variations in the operant response that meet his specifications and by extinguishing those that do not. Thus operant conditioning can account for the learning of novel behavior. Experiments have shown that some aspects of ordinary daily behavior can be brought under control through operant conditioning.
5. *Reinforcement* refers to any event the occurrence of which increases the probability that a stimulus will, on subsequent occasions, evoke a response. Amount, delay, and rate of reinforcement are important variables that affect learning.
6. Conditioning is most directly applicable to single identifiable responses, but much learning is more complex than this. These more complex instances are classified as *multiple-response learning.* Two examples are sensorimotor skills (such as mirror drawing and pursuit learning) and rote memorization (including serial learning and paired-associate learning).
7. The experimenter plots the results of multiple-response learning in the form of *learning curves,* indicating changes in proficiency with practice. These curves usually show *decreasing gains* over trials. Shifts from

lower-order to higher-order learning habits may result in a period of no improvement, called a *plateau.*

8. Emphasis within conditioning and multiple-response learning is upon the acquiring of specific responses or verbal habits. Some psychologists warn against an overemphasis upon the automatic nature of learning that comes from exclusive concern with stimulus-response associations. They stress instead situations in which understanding is prominent. Köhler's *insight* experiments pointed out how the arrangements of the problem make the solution easy or hard, and how a solution once achieved with insight can be repeated or applied to novel situations.
9. Tolman's *sign-learning* experiments also emphasize the role of understanding and the development of cognitive schemata. Results from an experiment on *latent learning* provide opposing evidence to theories that lay stress upon the acquisition of particular response sequences without taking into account the subject's *cognitive representation* of the relationships involved.
10. Something can be learned from each of these emphases. Learning goes on in part through *associative processes,* with little rational direction from the learner, and in part through *cognitive processes,* with which the learner perceives relationships and organizes knowledge.

Further Reading

Pavlov's *Conditioned reflexes* (1927) is the classic work on classical conditioning. Skinner's *The behavior of organisms* (1938) is the corresponding statement on operant conditioning. Cognitive theories also have their classics: Köhler's *The mentality of apes* (1925) describes the famous insight experiments with chimpanzees; Tolman's *Purposive behavior in animals and men* (1932) is the major statement of his cognitive (sign-learning) position.

The principal points of view toward learning, presented in their historical settings and with some typical experiments to which they have led, are summarized in Hilgard and Bower, *Theories of learning* (4th ed., 1975). Relevant material is also available in Glaser (ed.), *The nature of reinforcement* (1971), and McGuigan and Lumsden (eds.), *Contemporary approaches to conditioning and learning* (1973).

For substantive approaches, emphasizing the contributions of the learning laboratory, there are a number of textbooks on learning, such as Deese and Hulse, *The psychology of learning* (3rd ed., 1967); Rachlin, *Introduction to modern behaviorism* (1970); Hill, *Learning, a survey of psychological interpretations* (2nd ed., 1971); and Logan, *Fundamentals of learning and motivation* (1970). A more advanced but easily readable treatment is presented in Estes, *Learning theory and mental development* (1970).

Mathematical theories of the learning process are discussed in Atkinson, Bower, and Crothers, *An introduction to mathematical learning theory* (1965); Coombs, Dawes, and Tversky, *Mathematical psychology: An elementary introduction* (1970); and Krantz, Atkinson, Luce, and Suppes (eds.), *Contemporary developments in mathematical psychology* (1974).

8 memory and forgetting

All learning implies retaining, for if nothing were left from previous experience, nothing would be learned. We think and reason largely with remembered facts; the very continuity of our self-perceptions depends upon the continuity of our memories. We are able to deal with the concept of time as no other animal can, relating the present to the past and making predictions about the future, because of the endurance and availability of our memories.

One way of remembering is to recollect or *redintegrate* an event and the circumstances surrounding it. The word *recollect* is from ordinary vocabulary; *redintegrate* is a technical word meaning to reintegrate or to reestablish an earlier experience on the basis of partial cues. For example, you redintegrate your high-school graduation ceremony only if something "reminds" you of it. The stimuli to redintegration are in a literal sense souvenirs, remembrances, or reminders of total past experiences. In your recollection you may remember the orchestra playing the processional, the arrangement of the speaker's platform, the friends you spoke with, and possibly the emotions you experienced as the ceremony drew to a close. Such redintegrative memories are often quite detailed and complete, but they need not be.

Redintegration may also occur in the retrieval of factual information. Consider, for example, how you remember what you know about Cleopatra—memories not based on personal experience. First you recall one or two isolated facts; these lead you to explore other avenues until you piece together the knowledge you have on the topic. All the information is not immediately available once some part of it has been retrieved; rather a *search* of memory along many different dimensions gradually leads to the redintegration of knowledge about a given topic or experience. The memory search appears to be fairly orderly, following from one lead to the next as information is pieced together. However, every so often, something will "pop up" quite unrelated to what is currently in consciousness.

Many memories lack this redintegrative quality. For example, you may *recall* a poem in its entirety, not having to piece separate parts together—and this may occur even if you do not remember the circumstances under which you learned it. Since remembering through recall is easier to measure than the redintegration of knowledge or earlier experiences, it is the kind usually studied in the laboratory.

Another kind of remembering is the indication of memory merely by *recognizing* someone or something as familiar. "That tune is familiar. What is it?" "Someone I used to know had a copy of that picture on the wall, but I can't place it now." Finally, you may show that you once learned something by now *relearning* it more rapidly than you could if there were no retention of the earlier learning.

Redintegration, recall, recognition, and relearning all give evidence of memory, but each of these terms implies a different aspect of remembering.

Kinds of Remembering

Redintegrative Memory

Psychologists have paid relatively little attention to redintegrative memory, because it is difficult to check details of the recovery of events in the personal past of the subject. A few studies have used hypnosis; one of these, for example, has shown that memories of school experiences from ages seven to ten can be more accurately recovered by adults under hypnosis than in the waking state. These memories—of other pupils in the class or the teacher's name—were subject to confirmation (Reiff and Scheerer, 1959).

Studies of testimony are concerned with the reinstatement of scenes witnessed in the past. A class may unexpectedly be made witness to a staged crime and then be asked to report what happened. The reports are often distorted, even when a student insists his recollections are vivid and dependable. For example, one of the authors engaged in a staged argument with a workman who interrupted his lecture. The workman spoke with a German accent. Although the assistant who acted the part of the workman in this drama had blond hair and dark brown eyes, a substantial proportion of the students reported confidently that they had seen his *blue* eyes—the color falsely inferred from his Nordic appearance and German accent. Such experiments have bearing on the reliability of witnesses in courtrooms.

More studies of personal memories have been carried on by psychotherapists than by experimental psychologists. In psychoanalysis the recollection of childhood memories is one of the bases of treatment and cure. A curious problem, not fully understood, is posed by the paucity of very early memories, from that period in life when the child is having many exciting new experiences. This is the problem of "childhood amnesia" noted by Freud. One conjecture is that the child perceives the world so differently from an adult that the adult's effort to remember what registered for the child fails because of this difference. It may be too that the storage of memories depends upon language development.

Recall

The kind of remembering most easily tested in the laboratory is active recall of some performance learned in the past. You may show that you remember how to ride a bicycle by climbing on one and riding away. You may show that you know Hamlet's soliloquy on death by reciting it. You are demonstrating that present performance is different from what it would be if there were no residue from the past. You ride the bicycle. If there were no residue from the past, you could not ride it.

To get a quantitative measure of recall in the laboratory, the investigator allows time to elapse after a subject has memorized some material, often by the paired-associate method (p. 213). The elapsed time may be minutes, hours, days, or even months. Then the subject returns to the laboratory and attempts to recall the response previously paired with each stimulus as it is presented. The percentage correct is called the *recall score.*

Recognition

When we recognize something, we acknowledge that it is familiar, that we have met it before. Recognition is a common experience, but it is a complex and a somewhat mysterious process. The entire process takes place quite automatically. We meet someone and say, "I'm sure we have met before, though I cannot recall your name or just where or when it was."

We learn a little about recognition from faulty recognition, from a deceiving sense of familiarity. The French expression *déjà vu* ("previously seen") is often used to describe the sense of familiarity that is sometimes aroused in otherwise strange surroundings. So important and convincing was this experience that the Greek philosopher Plato made it part of the basis for his belief in a previous existence. What may happen is that a pattern of buildings along a street is actually somewhat like one seen in earlier experience, or that in a strangely familiar garden the scent of a flower permeating the air is one met on an earlier occasion but since forgotten. Then the present situation, though actually novel, seems vaguely familiar. This is a form of generalization from past experience.

To study recognition in the laboratory we have to distinguish between correct and faulty recognition. We do this by giving the subject a series of items, such as a set of 60 photographs. Later we test recognition by mixing the original 60 with 60 additional ones of the same general kind, and have the subject sort out those seen previously. We can obtain a score in the same manner as we do for a true-false examination corrected for guessing. The formula is:

$$\text{Recognition score} = \left[\frac{\text{Right} - \text{Wrong}}{\text{Total}}\right] \times 100$$

If all the original pictures are sorted into the "familiar" pile and all the new or misleading ones into the "unfamiliar" pile, the subject gets a score of 100 percent. If the subject sorts by chance, getting half right and half wrong, the score drops to zero percent.

Relearning

Another way to show that there is some residue from the past is to demonstrate that previously familiar material can be learned more rapidly than it could be learned if it were unfamiliar. Even though something may seem to be completely "forgotten," it may be easier to learn the second time because it was learned in the past. A dramatic illustration of how this may occur is given by a study in which a child was read selections from Greek and then learned those same selections years later.

For three months the experimenter read the same three Greek selections every day to a boy about one year old. Each selection consisted of 20 lines of iambic hexameter material. At the end of three months, another set of three selections was read for three more months. This procedure was continued until 21 selections had been read.

The residual influence of this early experience was studied through memorization experiments conducted when the boy was 8, 14, and 18 years old. He had not studied Greek in the meantime. At each of these ages he learned selected passages from the early experience along with equivalent but unfamiliar passages. At age 8 about 30 percent fewer repetitions were required to learn the familiar material than for equivalent new material. By age 14, however, the saving was only 8 percent, and by 18 no saving could be demonstrated. The main point is that there was demonstrable saving in learning more than five years after the original reading took place, even though the material was classical Greek, a language that was meaningless to the child (Burtt, 1941).

To use the relearning method in the laboratory, the experimenter proceeds as in the study of recall. After the initial learning a time period is allowed to

Hermann Ebbinghaus

elapse; then retention is tested in a second learning. The subject, having previously learned by one of the standard methods well enough to meet some *criterion of mastery* (for example, one perfect recitation), learns the material again *to the same criterion.* If the second learning requires fewer trials than the first, we may express this saving as a percentage by using the formula:

$$\text{Saving score} = \left[\frac{\text{Original trials} - \text{Relearning trials}}{\text{Original trials}}\right] \times 100$$

If on relearning, the criterion is reached on the first trial (that is, no relearning trials are necessary), the saving is 100 percent; if it takes as much time as original learning, there is zero percent saving.

A classic study by Ebbinghaus (1885) illustrates the use of the saving score. Using himself as a subject, Ebbinghaus learned seven lists of unrelated items until he could make two errorless repetitions. After learning the first list he waited 20 minutes and then relearned the list again to two errorless repetitions. After learning the other lists he waited for longer intervals—1 hour, 9 hours, 1 day, 2 days, 6 days, and 31 days, respectively—before relearning each list. Figure 8-1 shows the amount retained from each list as indicated by saving scores. This type of curve is called a *retention curve* because it shows the amount of learning retained as a function of time.

Varieties of Memory Processes

The processes underlying redintegration, recall, recognition, and relearning are not distinct. Each kind of memory, however, makes a somewhat different demand on the subject, so that retention of earlier learning might be detected by one method and not by another. For example, the retention of a past experience completely unavailable to redintegrative

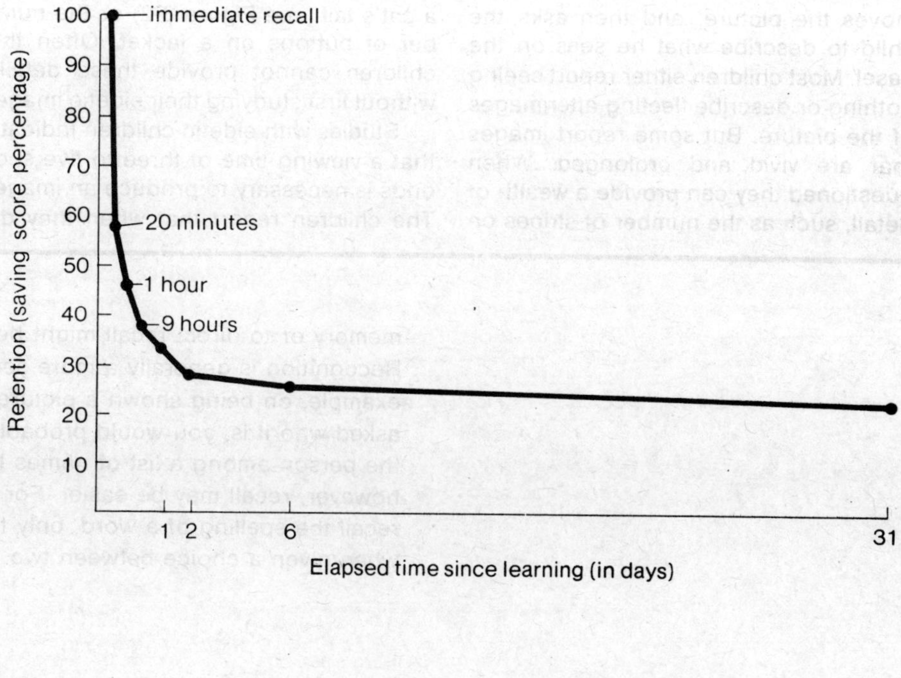

Fig. 8-1 Retention curve

Retention of lists of nonsense syllables was measured by relearning. The dependent variable is the saving score percentage. (After Ebbinghaus, 1885)

CRITICAL DISCUSSION

Eidetic Images

Although most of us can occasionally retain visual impressions of things that we have seen, such impressions usually are vague and lacking in detail. Some individuals, however, are able to retain visual images that are almost photographic in clarity. They can glance briefly at a picture and when it is removed still "see" its image located, not in their heads, but somewhere in space before their eyes. They can maintain the image for as long as several minutes, scan it as it remains stationary in space, and describe it in far more detail than would be possible from memory alone. Such people are said to have a "photographic memory," or, to use the psychologist's term, *eidetic imagery*.

Eidetic imagery is relatively uncommon. Studies with children indicate that only about 5 percent report visual images that last for more than a half-minute and possess sharp detail. The existing evidence suggests that after adolescence the occurrence of eidetic individuals is even less frequent. In a typical procedure for investigating eidetic imagery, the experimenter places a richly detailed picture agains an easel painted a neutral gray, gives the child 30 seconds to look at it, removes the picture, and then asks the child to describe what he sees on the easel. Most children either report seeing nothing or describe fleeting afterimages of the picture. But some report images that are vivid and prolonged. When questioned they can provide a wealth of detail, such as the number of stripes on a cat's tail (see Figure 8-2) or the number of buttons on a jacket. Often the children cannot provide these details without first studying their eidetic image.

Fig. 8-2 Testing for eidetic images

Test picture shown for half a minute to elementary school children. One boy saw in his eidetic image "about 16" stripes in the cat's tail. The picture, painted by Marjorie Torrey, appears in an edition of Lewis Carroll's *Alice in Wonderland* abridged by Josette Frank and is reproduced with the permission of Random House.

Studies with eidetic children indicate that a viewing time of three to five seconds is necessary to produce an image. The children report that when they do not look at the picture long enough, they do not have an image of parts of it, although they may remember what those parts contain. Exaggerated eye blinking or looking away from the easel usually makes the image disappear (Haber, 1969).

One theory assumed that eidetic imagery served to improve the transfer of visual stimuli into memory. But evidence suggests that this is not the case. Eidetic children seem to have no better long-term memories than other children. In fact, if while looking at a picture an eidetic child is asked to name parts of it (or otherwise actively attend to the parts), he is unable to form an image. It appears that eidetic children retain information either in the form of an image or in the form of the more typical verbal memory, but they are unable to do both at the same time.

Other evidence indicates that eidetic imagery is visual in nature and not a function of memory. For example, when the eidetic child tries to transfer the image from the easel to another surface, it disappears when it reaches the edge of the easel. At the same time, the eidetic image is not an exact photographic reproduction. The image usually contains additions, omissions, and distortions of the stimulus picture in the same way that memories contain distortions of the original event. The aspects of the picture that are of principal interest to the child are the ones that tend to be reproduced in greatest detail in the eidetic image.

memory or to direct recall might be detected by recognition or relearning. Recognition is generally a more sensitive measure of memory than recall. For example, on being shown a picture of a relatively well-known person and asked who it is, you would probably find it easier to *recognize* the name of the person among a list of names than to *recall* it. In special circumstances, however, recall may be easier. For example, we may on occasion correctly recall the spelling of a word, only to fail to recognize the correct spelling when given a choice between two alternatives.

There does seem to be an important difference between a memory dated in one's personal past and the kind of undated memory shown in, say, memory for a familiar vocabulary word. If one remembers having looked up an unusual word, then the memory is a recollection of a concrete experience, but most words are not tied in such a way to personal history. In cases of amnesia it is usually the personal memories that are lost; the amnesia victim is still able to speak his familiar language, buy a theater ticket, count his change, and do many other things that indicate that his undated or impersonal memories are not lost. Recognition has some features of redintegration (having been experienced before), whereas recall can be automatic, without any personal reference whatever.

"We're hoping that one day he'll remember his errand and go off as mysteriously as he came."

Retrieval Processes

In recent years there has been a move away from a *behavioristic* or stimulus-response approach to memory, partly because the approach has not proved fruitful in dealing with practical problems and also because certain newly discovered phenomena appear to be inconsistent with its basic assumptions. Psychologists have adopted a more cognitive view of memory in an attempt to isolate some of the processes that act between the input of a stimulus and the response output. The cognitive view divides memory into three stages: encoding, storage, and retrieval. *Encoding* implies transforming the sensory input into a form that can be processed by the memory system. If something is to be remembered, then *storage* must occur which requires transfer of the encoded information into memory. Finally, the process of *retrieval* involves locating the memorized information when needed. These three stages can be likened to an office filing system. A phone message is received and encoded into a typed document suitable for filing. The document is then stored in the files using possibly the date, the caller's name, or the topic of the conversation to determine where it is placed. When the information is needed at a later time it must be retrieved by searching the files. The failure to remember may involve faulty encoding, failure to have stored the information, or inability to retrieve it when needed.

Our ability to retrieve a word or name from memory is so efficient that we usually are not aware of the process involved. Sometimes an item cannot be retrieved immediately, although we feel certain that we know it. For example, you may not recall offhand the name of your third-grade teacher. But if you think for a while, trying out various possibilities, you probably will recall the name. In some cases the name may suddenly come to you, long after you stopped thinking about it. Events of this kind suggest that an active search of the memory store is going on even though consciously we may not be aware of it.

Tip-of-the-Tongue Phenomenon

The situation of feeling certain we know a specific name or word, yet being unable to recall it immediately, has been called the tip-of-the-tongue (TOT) state. The word seems to be on the tip of our tongue, and we may feel quite tormented until an active memory search (dredging up and then discarding words that are close but not quite right) reveals the correct word.

In an experimental investigation of the TOT state Brown and McNeill (1966)

William James writing in 1890 on the tip-of-the-tongue state

"Suppose we try to recall a forgotten name. The state of our consciousness is peculiar. There is a gap therein; but no mere gap. It is a gap that is intensely active. A sort of wraith of the name is in it beckoning us in a given direction, making us at moments tingle with the sense of our closeness and then letting us sink back without the longed-for term. If wrong names are proposed to us, this singularly definite gap acts immediately so as to negate them They do not fit into its mould. And the gap of one word does not feel like the gap of another, all empty of content as both might seem necessarily to be when described as gaps." (W. James, 1890, p. 251)

demonstrated that the words that come to mind when one is searching for a particular word (called the "target word") have certain characteristics in common with the target word. In their study, college students were read the definitions of words infrequently used in the English language—words like *cloaca, ambergris,* and *sampan,* some of which were in the recognition vocabulary of the subjects but not in their active vocabulary. A subject who felt that he knew the word being defined but was unable to recall it immediately (a TOT state) was asked a number of questions concerning the words being thought of in attempting to arrive at the correct word.

The study indicated that a subject in the TOT state has information about a number of characteristics of the target word, and the closer to successful recall the more accurate is the information. Although some of the words that came to mind could be classed as similar in *meaning* to the target word, the majority of words were similar in *sound.* For example, if the target word is *sampan,* then similar-sounding words would be *Saipan, Siam, Cheyenne, sarong,* and *sympoon,* whereas similar-meaning words would be *barge, houseboat,* and *junk.* An analysis of the similar-sounding words showed that the subject in a TOT state can specify with a high degree of accuracy the number of syllables in the target word and its initial letter. The final sound or suffix and the syllable that receives the primary stress are also frequently stated (although with less accuracy).

Thus retrieval is not a simple all-or-none process; we can forget certain characteristics of a word while retaining other relevant information. Studies of this type have led to interesting speculations (some of which we will consider later) about how information is stored in memory and subsequently retrieved.

Organization of Semantic Memory

The time that it takes to retrieve information from memory tells us something about the organization of memory. There can be little doubt that memory is not a grab bag of facts and episodes; information stored in memory must have some organization, otherwise our ability to reconstruct events and reason in terms of remembered facts would be hopelessly

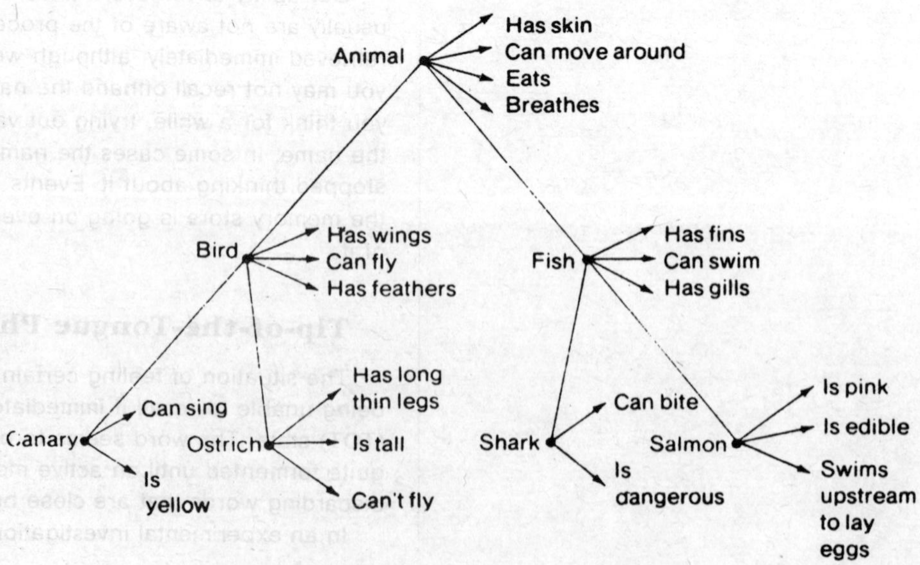

Fig. 8-3 Semantic network

Illustration of a hypothetical memory structure for a three-level hierarchy. (After Collins and Quillian, 1972)

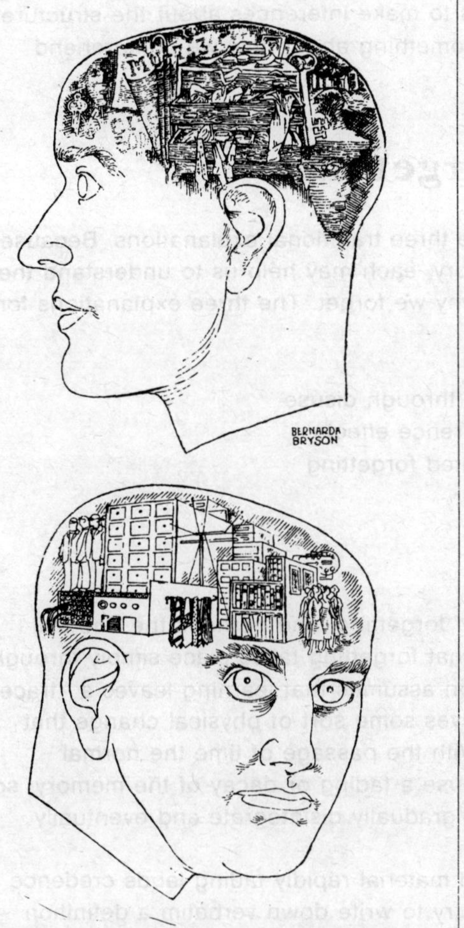

Fanciful heads drawn by Bernarda Bryson to depict René Descartes's *Rules for the Direction of the Mind*. The individual at the top has presumably not had the benefit of rules, whereas the man at the bottom has

haphazard. Of course, much of the organization of memory will be unique, depending on an individual's particular history of experiences. But certain information, particularly our knowledge of language and its usage, is common to individuals in a society and should have a somewhat similar organization from person to person. Memory necessary for the use of language is called *semantic memory* (Tulving, 1972).

Collins and Quillian (1972) have proposed that semantic memory might be organized as an interconnected network. A part of such a *semantic network* is illustrated in Figure 8-3. In the network, each word is stored with a set of pointers to other words in the network. The word concepts are the nodes, and the pointers are the connections in the network. Basic to this network is the assumption that information about a particular class of things is stored only at the level of the hierarchy for that class. Information generally true of birds (for example, wings, feathers) is not stored at the node for each separate type of bird. Rather, the fact that "A canary has wings" can be inferred by finding that a canary is a bird and that birds have wings. Storing information in this way economizes on the amount of space required to maintain necessary facts in memory. In the case of exceptions, such as an ostrich, the fact that it cannot fly is stored at the ostrich node (see Figure 8-3).

According to the model, a sentence is comprehended as being true if a path can be found through the semantic network that interrelates the words in the sentence. By referring to Figure 8-3, the sentence "A shark can move around" would be comprehended as true by finding the path: a shark is a fish, a fish is an animal, and an animal can move around.

To test the model, subjects were asked to judge sentences as true or false. The true sentences were of several forms. One form included sentences like "A canary is yellow"; for this type of sentence it is assumed that the descriptive property is stored with the instance itself. Other sentences were of the form "A canary can fly," where the property was assumed to be stored one level removed from the instance; and yet others like "A canary eats," where the property is assumed to be stored two levels above the instance. Mixed with the true sentences were false ones such as "A salmon has wings". The subject was to respond true or false as quickly as possible when a sentence was presented, and the time taken to respond was recorded by the experimenter.

If we assume that it requires time to move from one node in the hierarchy to the next, this time should be reflected in the speed with which the subject decides true or false. Figure 8-4 presents data on the time needed to make a true response. Points on the graph are labeled with an example of a typical sentence at each of three levels; the information to judge "A canary is yellow" is all at one level of the semantic network, whereas "A canary eats" required the subject to move from the canary node to the animal node, two levels away. As predicted, the time to decide that a sentence is true increases with the number of levels that have to be considered to answer the question. The experiment confirms the representation of semantic memory given in Figure 8-3. There is no absolute requirement that human memory should be organized in this way, but the experiment supports this hierarchical view.

Research of the sort described above contains many problems and possible confounding variables; thus the findings have to be evaluated with caution. Suffice it to say that current research supports the general conclusion that semantic information is organized in the form of a memory

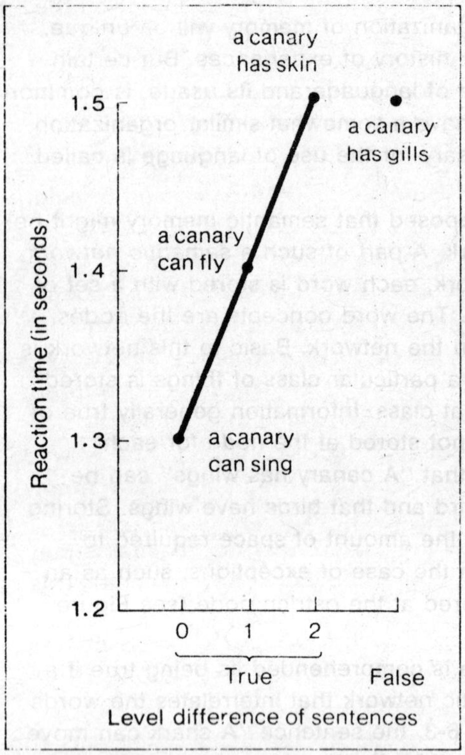

Fig. 8-4 Semantic memory and sentence comprehension

Time to process a sentence as a function of the number of levels involved in the semantic hierarchy. (After Collins and Quillian, 1972)

network. Work of this sort allows us to make inferences about the structure of semantic networks and tells us something about how we comprehend language.

The Nature of Forgetting

Why do we forget things? There are three traditional explanations. Because the explanations are not contradictory, each may help us to understand the nature of what we remember and why we forget. The three explanations for forgetting are

1. Decay through disuse
2. Interference effects
3. Motivated forgetting

Decay through Disuse

One of the oldest explanations of forgetting, and perhaps the one still most widely held by the layman, is that forgetting takes place simply through the passage of time. This explanation assumes that learning leaves a "trace" in the brain; the *memory trace* involves some sort of physical change that was not present prior to learning. With the passage of time the normal metabolic processes of the brain cause a fading or decay of the memory, so that traces of material once learned gradually disintegrate and eventually disappear altogether.

The experience of barely learned material rapidly fading lends credence to decay through disuse. Even as you try to write down verbatim a definition given in a lecture you may find it fading away. Forgetting pictures or stories also suggests a process of fading with the passage of time. When first perceived, a picture may reveal a wealth of detail But as time passes, the details are rapidly forgotten and only the main outlines are remembered.

Although plausible no direct evidence supports the decay theory, and much evidence suggests that it is a dubious or at least incomplete explanation. The form of the retention curve in Figure 8-1 can be accounted for on other grounds. In many instances learning is retained over long intervals of time with no intervening practice. Most motor skills, like swimming or driving a car, are not easily forgotten even though we may not have used these skills for many years. Some verbal material may be retained over long periods while other material is forgotten. We may be able to recall quite accurately a poem we memorized in sixth grade, yet be unable to remember a part we learned in a high-school play. Why should the decay process affect the second material but not the first?

Another argument against the decay theory rests on the recovery of memories supposedly lost. People approaching senility, who can barely remember the events of the day, often vividly recall events of their youth. Occasionally a delirious patient speaks a foreign language unused since childhood. Unavailable memories have not necessarily "decayed."

Although a great deal of evidence seems to argue against a theory of passive decay, it cannot be denied that some forgetting may occur through the organic changes taking place in the nervous system with the passage of time. We can only be sure that this explanation does not account for all the facts about forgetting.

Interference Effects

Another explanation maintains that it is not so much the passage of time that determines the course of forgetting but what we do in the interval between learning and recall; new learning may interfere with material previously learned. This theory of interference is illustrated by a story about Stanford University's first president, David Starr Jordan, who was an authority on fishes. As the president of a new university, Jordan began to call the students by name, but every time he learned the name of a student he forgot the name of a fish. Hence, it is said, he gave up learning the names of students. Although the story lacks foundation in fact, it illustrates how new learning may interfere with the recall of old learning. The theory that the new learning may interfere with the old is known as *retroactive inhibition.* A companion interference theory, based on the same principles, maintains that prior learning may interfere with the learning and recall of new material. This aspect of the theory is called *proactive inhibition.*

RETROACTIVE INHIBITION. Retroactive inhibition can easily be demonstrated by experiment. The subject learns a list of items such as nonsense syllables (list A), and then learns a second list (list B). After an interval an attempt is made to recall list A. If a control group (that has not learned list B) recalls list A significantly better than the experimental group that has learned the new list, we attribute the difference to *retroactive inhibition.* The *later* learning of B has interfered with the recall of the *earlier* learning of list A. The experimental arrangement can be diagrammed as follows:

Arrangement for testing retroactive inhibition

	Phase 1	Phase 2	Phase 3
Experimental group	Learn A	Learn B	Recall A
Control group	Learn A	Rest or unrelated activity	Recall A

If recall is tested after an interval of rest, without interpolated activity, some forgetting of course occurs. Can this, too, be accounted for by the theory of retroactive inhibition? Perhaps, but only if we think of the ordinary processes of waking life as corresponding in some respects to active learning between original learning and recall. This extension of the retroactive inhibition theory can be tested by comparing retention after periods of sleep and waking. If waking activity interferes with recall, then retention should be better after sleep, when less intervening activity has occurred. As Figure 8-5 shows, it has been found that we do forget more when awake than when

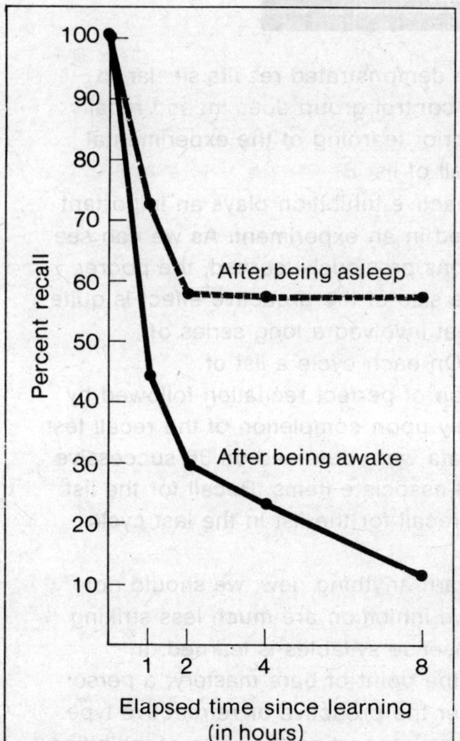

Fig. 8-5 Retroactive inhibition

The retention of information when the subject is either awake or asleep during the interval between initial learning and a subsequent test for recall. (Data from Jenkins and Dallenbach, 1924)

asleep. We lose a little during the first hour or two of sleep, but after that we forget very little more during the night.

We may therefore accept the hypothesis that retroactive inhibition occurs not only when formal learning takes place between initial learning and recall, but also when ordinary waking life intervenes. Retroactive inhibition has a secure place as one phenomenon of forgetting.

PROACTIVE INHIBITION. Another kind of interference occurs when material that we have previously learned interferes with the recall of something newly learned. The following experimental arrangement may be compared with that used in the study of retroactive inhibition:

Arrangement for testing proactive inhibition

	Phase 1	Phase 2	Phase 3
Experimental group	Learn A	Learn B	Recall B
Control group	Rest or unrelated activity	Learn B	Recall B

Experiments using the above design have demonstrated results similar to those found for retroactive inhibition; the control group does indeed recall better than the experimental group. The prior learning of the experimental group apparently interferes with their recall of list B.

Underwood (1957) has shown that proactive inhibition plays an important role when "experienced" subjects are used in an experiment. As we can see from Figure 8-6, the more lists a subject has previously learned, the poorer his retention of the newly learned list. The size of the proactive effect is quite remarkable as demonstrated in a study that involved a long series of successive cycles of learning and recall. On each cycle a list of paired-associates was learned to a criterion of perfect recitation followed by recall of the list two days later. Immediately upon completion of the recall test a new learning-recall cycle was begun. Data were obtained on 36 successive cycles, each involving a new list of paired-associate items. Recall for the list in the initial cycle was about 70 percent; recall for the list in the last cycle was virtually zero (Postman, 1969).

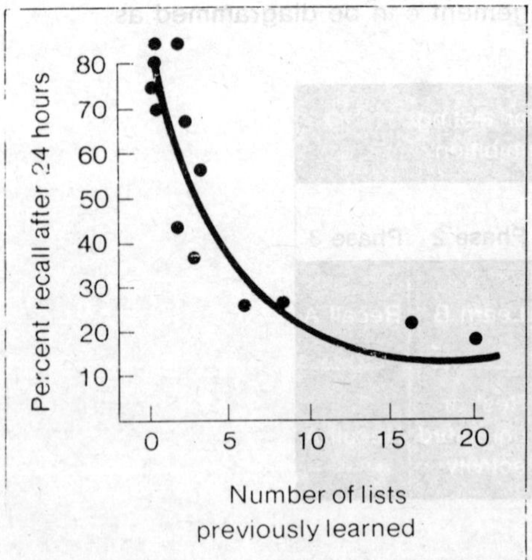

Fig. 8-6 Proactive inhibition. Each dot represents results from one experiment. For those experiments in which the subject had less previous experience in list-learning, the amount retained after an interval of a day was greater than in those in which the subject had learned many prior lists. (After Underwood, 1957)

Lest you decide that it is fruitless to learn anything new, we should note that the effects of proactive and retroactive inhibition are much less striking when meaningful material rather than nonsense syllables is learned. In addition, having learned material beyond the point of bare mastery, a person is less susceptible to interferences of either the proactive or retroactive type. Nevertheless, there is considerable evidence supporting the roles of inhibition in forgetting.

Motivated Forgetting

The preceding explanations of forgetting emphasize that it is a matter either of physiological processes affecting the memory trace or of interference between new and old material. Neither theory gives much attention to a person's motives in remembering and forgetting. This omission is a serious one, for a complete theory of forgetting cannot ignore what the person is trying to do—in both remembering and forgetting.

"I joined the Legion two or three weeks ago to try to forget a girl called Elsie or something."

REPRESSION. One aspect of motivated forgetting is the principle of repression, whereby some memories become inaccessible to recall because of the way in which they relate to our personal problems. The inaccessibility is due neither to faded traces nor to disruptive learnings, for the memories are still there and can be revealed under appropriate conditions. The theory of repression holds that the memories are not recalled because their retrieval would in some way be unacceptable to the person—possibly because of the anxiety they would produce or the guilt they might activate.

The nature of the forgetting that occurs in dramatic instances of amnesia aids in the understanding of repression. The amnesia victim does not forget everything, but has available a rich store of memories and habits to conduct current activities. Forgotten are items of personal reference—name, family, home address, and personal biography. The beginning of the amnesia can often be traced to some severe emotional shock that the individual suffered and from which the amnesia provides an escape.

Occasionally cases in psychotherapy give rather convincing evidence of repressed memories and recovery from the repression, of which the following is a striking, if unusual, illustration. [Case courtesy of Josephine R. Hilgard]

> A 40-year-old man came to a mental hospital with serious depression and haunting ideas about death. As a child he had lost his mother under traumatic circumstances. About the actual death he could remember only being awakened from sleep in order to be taken to the hospital some distance away. When he and his sisters arrived there, his mother was dead. The mother's death had been very disturbing to him, and it was evident to the therapist who treated him that some of his present symptoms dated from it. In order to help him recall specific events of that period, the therapist asked, among other questions, whether he recalled the time of night the events happened. He could not remember. That these memories were repressed is suggested by the information that came in a dream the night following this interview.
>
> The patient dreamt that he saw two clocks. One was running and one had stopped. The one that was running said twenty minutes to three, and the one that had stopped said twenty minutes to five. He was mystified by the dream.
>
> Because of the possibility that those clocks represented the repressed childhood memories, the man's older sister was located and asked about the circumstances of the mother's death. She said that they had been roused from sleep in their farmhouse about 2:30 A.M. and had driven to the distant hospital. When they arrived there about 4:30, their mother had just died.

Whichever version we accept, it is quite convincing that the times dreamed of were close to reality. Yet this memory was not consciously accessible to the patient, even when the therapist pressed him for it. But the probing by the supportive therapist in the midst of treatment may have facilitated the recall in the dream.

CRITICAL DISCUSSION

RNA and the

The use of the expression *memory trace* in the discussion on p. 230 requires a word of explanation. The memory trace is a *hypothetical construct;* it is not something known or something we can point to in the brain. It refers to whatever representation of an experience persists in the nervous system. When we say that a memory trace fades or that something else happens to it, all we are saying is that what emerges when we attempt recall is different from the experience that was originally registered.

The durability of memories implies that a stable change in brain structure may be involved. One hypothesis is that some sort of change takes place in the biochemical nature of the cell; more specifically it has been proposed that ribonucleic acid (RNA) might well be the complex molecule that serves as a chemical mediator for memory (Hydén, 1969).

It has been known for some time that deoxyribonucleic acid (DNA) is the substance primarily responsible for genetic inheritance; the genes are comprised chiefly of DNA, and the genetic code is literally written in a sequence of bases along the DNA molecule. In this rather unique package DNA crams the information needed to create a complete individual—an individual with blue eyes and freckles, with a heart that can beat and a brain that can think. The genetic instructions contained on a single DNA molecule, if spelled out in English, would require the space of several 24-volume sets of the *Encyclopaedia Britannica.*

DNA never leaves the cell's nucleus but directs the cell's activities by manufacturing its own assistants to which it then delegates responsibilities. These assistants are various forms of RNA, which (after being produced in the nucleus) move out to the cytoplasm where they control cellular functions. Hyden reasoned that if DNA, which is exceptionally stable, encodes "racial memory," then perhaps RNA, which is known to be more malleable, could act to encode the organism's individual memories.

Three types of studies tentatively support this idea. In the first, chemicals are injected to block the formation of RNA. For example, mice that had learned to avoid shock in a maze were injected with an antibiotic (puromycin) known to inhibit the synthesis of RNA. Their memory of the maze was com-

A number of experimental attempts have been made to determine whether or not repression can be demonstrated in the ordinary experiences of people who do not show dramatic symptoms of memory disturbance. Psychoanalytic studies of normal people suggest that repression is a very general phenomenon, but laboratory studies are not yet very satisfactory. Every so often a new study will be reported that claims to have demonstrated repression in a laboratory situation. Unfortunately, these experiments tend not to be replicable or the repression effect is so small that it is of questionable interest. If effective procedures were found to experimentally study repression, significant progress could be expected in a field of memory that now relies primarily on clinical observations.

Are Memories Permanent?

The explanations of forgetting that have been considered so far—decay of the memory trace, interference effects, and motivated forgetting—have different implications for the hypothesis that events once recorded in memory are never lost. The decay theory emphasizes actual erosion or physical loss of memories. The notion of motivated forgetting suggests that information is permanently stored in memory, but certain emotionally toned events have made it inaccessible for retrieval. The interference hypothesis can be interpreted as supporting either position; interfering materials could actually destroy the memory trace, or they could leave the memory trace intact while building up some sort of inhibition or barrier to prevent its retrieval.

Memory Trace

pletely destroyed (Flexner, 1967). The second type of study attempts to show that training produces a change in the RNA of specific nerve cells. For example, young rats were trained to balance on a thin, slanting wire in order to obtain food. Subsequently, the particular vestibular nerve cells involved in the act of balancing were analyzed microscopically. These nerve cells not only showed more RNA, but RNA of a significantly different composition than was found in the cells of control animals that had not received balance training. Thus a specific type of learning produced altered rates of RNA synthesis in the relevant cells (Hydén, 1967).

The third type of experiment implicating the role of RNA in memory is even more dramatic (McConnell and others, 1970). It involves training planaria (small flatworms), using classical-conditioning procedures. The planaria are housed in a trough of water; when a brief electrical current is passed through the water, the planaria respond with a vigorous muscular contraction. The onset of the shock is paired with the onset of a light. After repeated pairings, test trials with the light alone elicit the contraction response. The planaria, which had not previously responded to the light, now generate a muscular contraction when the light is turned on. A substance containing RNA is extracted from the bodies of the trained planaria and injected into untrained animals. The latter animals are then given the same classical-conditioning routine, along with a control group of untrained animals that are injected with RNA taken from untrained planaria. The results of these studies show that planaria injected with RNA extracted from previously trained planaria learn the conditioned response more rapidly than animals injected with RNA from untrained animals. Unfortunately, efforts to replicate this and related experiments have not always been successful, and conclusions regarding transfer effects must be quite tentative.

If subsequent research verifies the hypothesis that learning is coded on the RNA molecule and is capable of transfer from one organism to another, the speculations from a science-fiction viewpoint are intriguing. For example, students in the distant future may be able to avoid the rigorous study involved in learning calculus by receiving their knowledge through an injection of RNA extracted from their mathematics instructor!

These two types of forgetting (loss of information versus inability to retrieve information) have been called *trace-dependent* versus *cue-dependent* forgetting (Tulving and Madigan, 1970). Trace-dependent forgetting is caused by the actual decay of the memory trace. In cue-dependent forgetting, the information is stored in memory, but the critical cues that would allow it to be retrieved are lacking. The latter type of forgetting is most obvious in such instances as the tip-of-the-tongue state, when a cue permits sudden access to a name or word previously unrecalled.

In most situations failure to recall probably represents a combination of trace-dependent and cue-dependent forgetting. But the question of whether some memories are permanent has important theoretical as well as practical implications. Unfortunately, at this stage of investigation we have no conclusive answer. Evidence strongly suggests, however, that memories are much more permanently etched upon our brains than we might assume on the basis of everyday experience. When we make a concerted effort to remember a specific event, we frequently find that we can recall more than we had thought possible. The recovery of childhood memories under hypnosis is another example pointing to the permanent nature of memory.

Even more startling evidence comes from direct electrical stimulation of the brain of epileptic patients undergoing surgery. When epileptic seizures cannot be controlled by drugs, removal of brain tissue in the area where the epileptic disturbance is focused sometimes has beneficial effects. To be certain that the tissue removal will not interfere with important functions, the surgeon carefully "maps" the surrounding area by electrical stimulation while the patient is under local anesthesia. During this procedure, the patient is

A 16th century anatomist's attempt to draw a map of the brain.

conscious and can describe sensations as various points on the brain are electrically stimulated. Vivid memories can be elicited. The patient reports a sudden "flashback" of some previous event complete with all the sensations experienced at that earlier time. The experiences relived appear to be real events from the past, such as recollections of a childhood scene or of an orchestra playing a vaguely remembered tune. One man saw himself in his childhood home laughing and talking with his cousins. The scene and sounds were as clear to him as they would have been at the time the event occurred.

These recalled events are far more vivid than ordinary memories. It is as if the electrical current had started a film strip on which were registered the details of a past event that the patient had long since forgotten. As long as the electrode is held in place, the experience of the former day goes forward. When the electrode is removed, the experience stops abruptly (Penfield, 1969).

Interestingly enough, surgical removal of the area from which a recollection has been evoked does not destroy the individual's memory of that event. Perhaps the information is actually stored in some other area of the brain and the nerve activity initiated by the stimulating electrode activates this remote location. Or the brain may contain multiple representations or copies of a remembered event, and the removal of tissue in a specific area of the brain simply destroys one copy.

Electrical-stimulation studies of this type provide strong evidence for the hypothesis that many memories remain intact long after the ability to recall them has disappeared. What procedures other than electrical stimulation and hypnosis might be used to tap these hidden memories is an intriguing question.

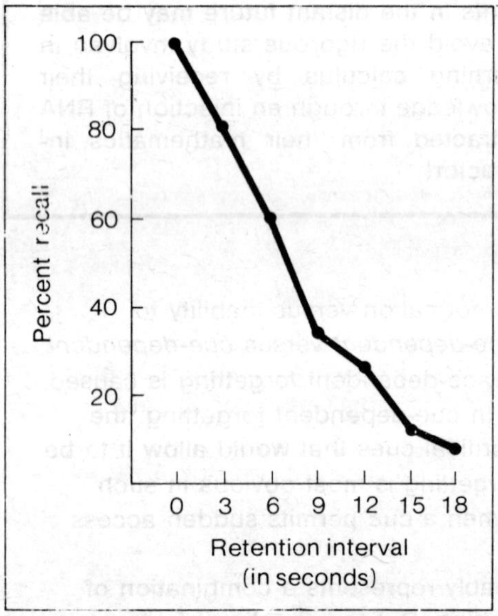

Fig. 8-7 Retention curve for short-term memory

The subjects attempted to recall a single trigram of three consonants (for example, XJR) after intervals of 3, 6, 9, 12, 15, or 18 seconds. The trigram was presented auditorily; during the next second a number was presented and the subject counted backward by 3's from that number until he received a signal to recall the trigram. This counting procedure prevented the subject from rehearsing the trigram. As the figure shows, recall after 18 seconds in this situation is practically zero. When rehearsal is prevented, recall of information in short-term memory decays rapidly. (Data from Peterson and Peterson, 1959)

Two-Process Theories of Memory

Because no single explanation provides an adequate account of forgetting, a number of psychologists have argued for a two-process theory of memory. They propose that one type of storage mechanism is involved in remembering events just recently experienced and that a different type is involved in the recall of information that has received repeated attention. These mechanisms have been labeled *short-term memory* (STM) and *long-term memory* (LTM). The difference between them is like the difference between recalling a telephone number you just looked up in the directory and recalling your own telephone number. Your own number is stored in LTM along with memories of such items as your name, the words and grammar of the language, addition and multiplication tables, and important events in your life. Except for occasional mental blocking on a word or the name of an acquaintance, these memories are relatively permanent. In contrast, the telephone number you have just looked up, the definition the instructor has just given in class, and the name of a stranger to whom you have just been introduced remain in STM only momentarily. Unless you make a conscious effort to focus your attention on the information, that is, to transfer it to LTM, it is quickly lost (see Figure 8-7).

Long- and Short-Term Memory

A number of current theories distinguish between LTM and STM. We will present a simplified version of one of them to illustrate the basic ideas

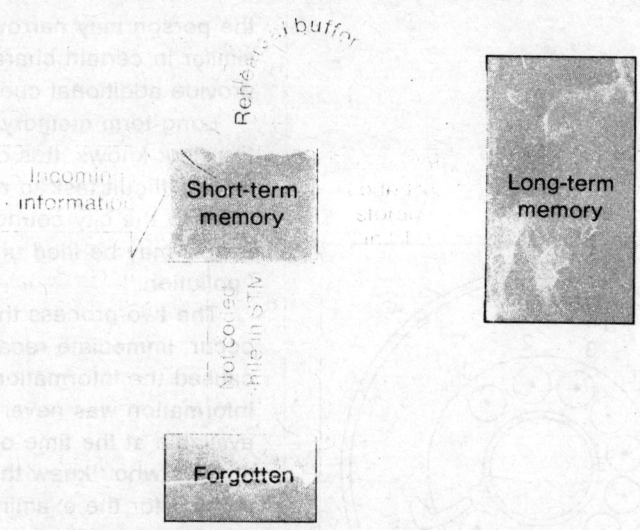

Fig. 8-8 Flow chart for a two-process theory of memory

Schematic representation of short-term and long-term storage mechanisms. Incoming sensory information enters STM, where it can be maintained by rehearsal and either successfully coded for storage in LTM or forgotten.

involved (Atkinson and Shiffrin, 1971). Two storage mechanisms are postulated, one for short-term memory and the other for long-term memory; the interaction between the two memories is characterized by the flow chart in Figure 8-8. The STM is viewed as a rapidly decaying system, whereas LTM is essentially a permanent store. In terms of our earlier distinction, we can characterize STM by trace-dependent forgetting. The memory trace of items entering STM is subject to rapid decay. In contrast, we characterize LTM by cue-dependent forgetting. The information is permanently recorded in LTM, but our ability to retrieve it depends upon having the appropriate cues.

Incoming information is fed into STM and, if not attended to, begins to fade away. It is possible, however, to maintain selected information in STM by means of rehearsal. By rehearsing the information, the trace in STM is prevented from decaying—at least for a short period of time. Each decaying trace is, so to speak, reset by rehearsal, at which point it begins to decay again. But the necessity for rehearsal imposes a limit upon the number of items that can be maintained simultaneously in STM; if an item is not rehearsed frequently enough, it will fade away. The set of traces being maintained in STM at any one time is referred to as the *rehearsal buffer.* We can think of the rehearsal buffer as resembling a box of fixed size that can hold only so many blocks. Each block represents a stimulus input. When new blocks are added to the box, old ones have to be removed to make room for them. The information coming into STM begins to decay rapidly unless the person regards it as particularly important, in which case it is entered into the rehearsal buffer. Information is maintained in the rehearsal buffer until the individual feels that he knows it or until his attention is drawn to new information. Thus information is temporarily stored in STM via rehearsal until incoming information replaces it. While information resides in STM it may be coded and transferred to long-term storage. Information that is allowed to decay in STM before such a transfer takes place is permanently lost.

In contrast, LTM is assumed to be virtually unlimited, so that any information transferred from STM to LTM will have a place for permanent storage. Even though the information is permanently stored, memory may fail because the cues needed to retrieve the information from LTM are incomplete. In the tip-of-the-tongue state an individual has inadequate cues to find the desired information. Unable to recall the information immediately, the person may narrow the area of search and retrieve some words that are similar in certain characteristics to the target word. These similar words may provide additional cues that lead eventually to the target word.

Long-term memory storage is analogous to a large filing cabinet. As any file clerk knows, it is one thing to toss items into various file drawers; it is a more difficult task to retrieve a desired item. For example, Mr. Johnson's letter to the city council complaining about possible pollution of the water supply may be filed under "Johnson," "complaints," "sanitation," or "pollution."

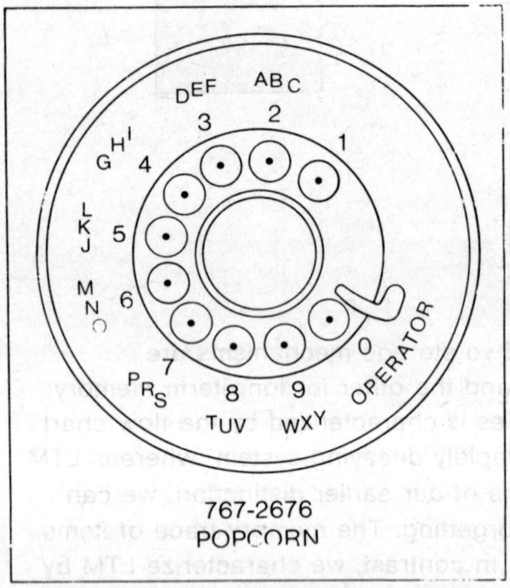

Mnemonic Aids

Recoding a phone number into its letter equivalent often can be an aid to memory. For example, in the San Francisco area the phone number for a crisis switchboard is 328-4357 which can be more easily remembered as 328-HELP. In many areas of the country the time of day can be obtained by dialing a number that recodes into the word POPCORN. Try dialing it in your area to see if it works.

The two-process theory provides several reasons why forgetting may occur. Immediate recall may fail because subsequent inputs to STM have caused the information to decay. Long-term recall may fail because the information was never transferred to LTM or because not enough cues are available at the time of attempted recall to locate the information in LTM. The student who "knew the material backwards and forwards" but could not recall it for the examination may simply have stared at the textbook with his mind on other things and never rehearsed the material so that it could be encoded into LTM. Or the material may be stored in LTM, but the examination questions did not provide sufficient cues to permit retrieval.

How do our earlier explanations of forgetting fit into this conceptual scheme? Although the information in STM is a fairly faithful representation of the stimulus input, some decay is possible in this state before the information is transferred to LTM. But once coded and stored in LTM, the code is assumed to be relatively fixed over time and not susceptible to decay. However, if other items of information with similar codes are stored in LTM, we have difficulty retrieving the correct item upon recall. The phenomena of retroactive and proactive inhibition can demonstrate their effects in this manner.

Frequently used items of information may be coded in such a way that many different cues lead to their recall. In terms of our file drawer analogy, they may be cross-indexed. Such items are thus readily available and require no searching. Or at times, when the recall of certain information is painful to us, we may instruct our "retrieval mechanism" to ignore the information; it is not lost, however, and can be retrieved once the need for repression is gone.

Physiological Evidence for a Two-Process Theory

Theories of the sort we have just described are frequently called *information-processing* models. Such models are highly schematized representations of the flow of information in the nervous system and do not venture into any of the physiological details. Clearly a large gap exists between the study of complex behavior and that of neurophysiology, and many psychologists feel that the use of simplified diagrams to describe the flow of information from the initial stimulus input to the response output forms a useful bridge between the two.

In the case of the two-process theory of memory, however, some neurological data from patients who have undergone surgery for relief of epileptic seizures provide striking evidence for the theory. If a lesion is made in a specific area deep in the temporal lobes (an area called the hippocampus), the patient then appears to be unable to successfully transfer new information from STM to LTM. Such patients have no trouble

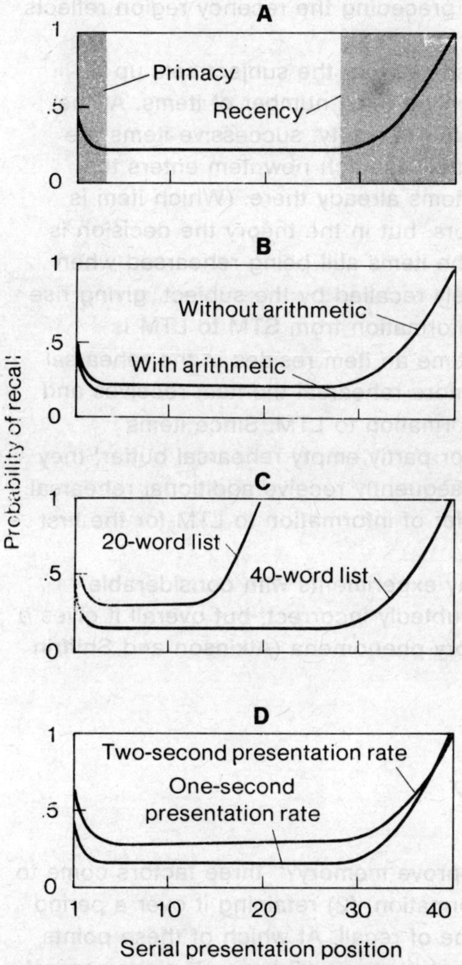

Fig. 8-9 Free-recall experiments

Probability of recall varies with an item's serial position in a list: a primacy effect and a recency effect are apparent (**A**). If an arithmetic task is interpolated between presentation and recall, the recency effect disappears (**B**). Words in long lists are recalled less well than words in short lists (**C**). Slower presentation also results in better recall (**D**). The curves are idealized ones based on experiments by James Deese, Bennet Murdock, Leo Postman, and Murray Glanzer.

remembering skills and information learned prior to the operation, but they have serious difficulty with new learning. For example, in one case, several months after the operation the patient's family moved to a new house a few blocks away on the same street. A year later the patient still could not remember his new address (although he recalled the old one perfectly) nor could he find his way to the new home alone. He could not remember where things he continually used were kept, and he would read the same magazines over and over without finding their contents familiar. Some patients with hippocampal lesions consistently fail to recognize or learn the names of people they have met following surgery even though they may have talked with them countless times. In fact, if a person to whom they are talking walks out of the room for a few minutes, they may fail to recognize him on his return (Milner, 1964).

The postoperative defect in these cases does not seem to be a deficiency in short-term memory per se. The patients can hold items, such as a series of digits, in memory if they concentrate upon repeating them. Such people can even carry out complicated mental arithmetic with speed and accuracy. But rehearsal does not produce permanent learning. Patients can walk to the store for a newspaper if they keep repeating verbally where and why they are going. When they stop rehearsing they quickly forget what they were supposed to do. The difficulty appears to lie in an inability to transfer new material from STM to LTM. The material can circulate in the short-term memory buffer but fails to be stamped into long-term memory.

Free-Recall Experiments

Evidence for a two-process theory also comes from an analysis of a memory task known as *free recall.* The free-recall task is similar to the one you face when asked to name all the people present at the last large party you attended. In the typical free-recall experiment, a list of unrelated words is presented to the subject one at a time. Later the subject attempts to recall as many words as possible in any order. The result of principal interest is the probability of recalling each item in a list as a function of its place in the list, or "serial presentation position." Plotting the function yields a U-shaped curve like that in Figure 8-9A. The increased probability of recall for the first few words in the list is called the *primacy effect;* the large increase for the last seven to ten words is called the *recency effect.* According to a two-process theory the recency effect is due to retrieval from STM, and the earlier portions of the serial position curve reflect retrieval from LTM only. In one experimental procedure the subject is required to carry out a difficult arithmetic task for 30 seconds immediately following presentation of the list, and is then asked to recall. One can assume that the arithmetic task causes the loss of all the words in STM, so that recall reflects retrieval from LTM only. The recency effect is eliminated when this experiment is performed; the earlier portions of the serial position curve are unaffected (Figure 8-9B). If variables that influence LTM but not STM are manipulated, the recency portion is relatively unaffected, but the earlier portions of the curve change. For example, one such variable is the number of words in the presented list. A word in a longer list is less likely to be recalled, but the recency effect is unaffected by list length (Figure 8-9C). Increases in the rate of presentation during study decrease the likelihood of recalling words preceding the recency region but leave the recency effect largely unchanged (Figure 8-9D).

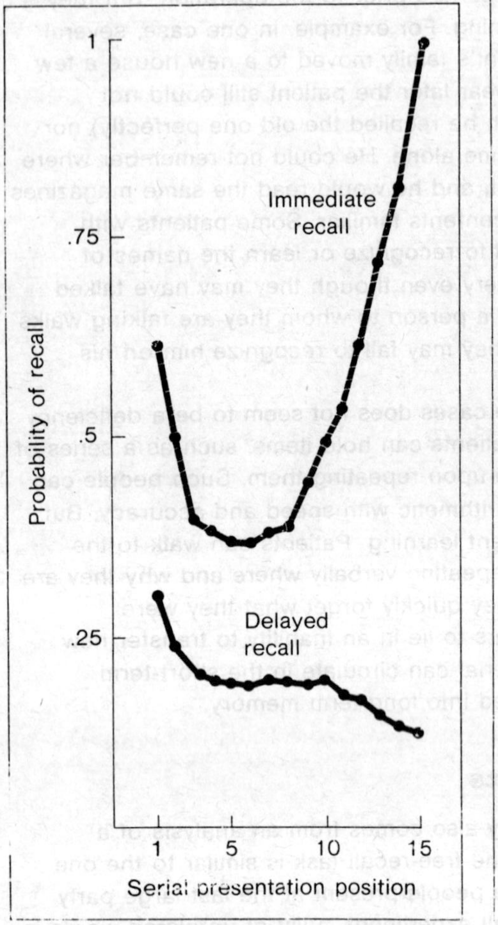

Fig. 8-10 Immediate versus delayed recall

Effect of delay is tested by asking subjects to recall at the end of a session all words from the entire session, and then plotting probability of recall against serial position within each list. The experiment compares immediate recall with delayed recall. The delayed recall curve emphasizes the transitory nature of the recency effect. (After F. Craik, 1970)

In free-recall experiments many lists are usually presented in a session. If the subject is asked at the end of the session to recall all the words presented during the session, we would expect recall to reflect retrieval from long-term storage only. The probability of recalling words as a function of their serial position within each list can be plotted for end-of-session recall and compared with the serial position curve for recall immediately following presentation (see Figure 8-10). As predicted, the primacy effect remains in the delayed recall curve, but the recency effect is eliminated. To summarize, the recency region of the serial position curve appears to reflect retrieval from both STM and LTM, whereas the curve preceding the recency region reflects retrieval from LTM only.

A two-process theory of memory assumes that the subject sets up a rehearsal buffer in STM that can hold only a fixed number of items. At the start of the presentation of a list the buffer is empty; successive items are entered until the buffer is filled. Thereafter, as each new item enters the rehearsal buffer it replaces one of the items already there. (Which item is replaced depends on a number of factors, but in the theory the decision is approximated by a random process.) The items still being rehearsed when the last item is presented are immediately recalled by the subject, giving rise to the recency effect. The transfer of information from STM to LTM is postulated to depend on the length of time an item resides in the rehearsal buffer; the longer the time period, the more rehearsal the item receives and therefore the greater the transfer of information to LTM. Since items presented first in a list enter an empty or partly empty rehearsal buffer, they remain longer than later items and consequently receive additional rehearsal This extra rehearsal causes more transfer of information to LTM for the first items, giving rise to the primacy effect.

The theory has been applied to many experiments with considerable success. Details of the theory are undoubtedly incorrect, but overall it gives a good account of a wide range of memory phenomena (Atkinson and Shiffrin 1971).

Improving Memory

When asking "What can be done to improve memory?" three factors come to mind: (1) encoding and storing the information, (2) retaining it over a period of disuse, and (3) retrieving it at the time of recall. At which of these points can we most easily effect an improvement in memory? Improving our general ability for retentivity seems the least likely possibility for major improvement—unless we want to indulge in long periods of sleep or inactivity between storage and recall, thereby reducing interference. But the circumstances surrounding storage and retrieval can certainly affect memory. Encoding can be improved to provide a richer and more integrated representation of the to-be-remembered material, and overlearning the material will increase the likelihood that the storage process is completed. Similarly, retrieval can be helped if the material is so organized that recall of any one part will lead to the recall of the entire memory structure. Also, providing *retrieval cues* at the time of study will facilitate the retrieval process. For example, noting the resemblance between fat Mr. Bier and a beer keg will provide a retrieval cue to his name when you next meet him.

CRITICAL DISCUSSION

Consolidation Theory and Retrograde Amnesia

There is increasing evidence that once new information is entered into LTM a period of time is required for it to consolidate and be firmly recorded in memory. This idea, which has been called *consolidation theory,* proposes that changes in the nervous system produced by learning are time dependent; that is, the memory trace must undergo a consolidation phase during which it is unstable and vulnerable to obliteration by interfering events. If the trace is in any way disrupted during this period, memory loss occurs. If no disruption takes place, then the trace consolidates and becomes a relatively permanent part of long-term memory, resistant to future destruction.

Some of the earliest evidence supporting the notion of consolidation comes from the observation that following a concussion or injury to the brain individuals usually have amnesia for events that occurred immediately prior to the accident. Depending upon the severity of the injury, the amnesia (called *retrograde amnesia* because it refers to memory loss before the accident) may cover a period from several minutes to more than an hour prior to the concussion. For example, it is not unusual for individuals who suffer head injuries in automobile accidents to have no recollection of the events that caused the accident. These facts are consistent with the theory that neural activity must have an opportunity to consolidate for a period of time following an experience if permanent storage is to take place.

Retrograde amnesia can be produced in the laboratory by using electroconvulsive shock (ECS). A typical experiment is roughly as follows. An animal is trained on some learning task and shortly thereafter is given an ECS that produces temporary unconsciousness. The animal is then tested several days later to measure retention of the learned response; the crucial variable is the time between initial learning and administration of ECS. In one study rats were given ECS at intervals of either zero seconds, 20 seconds, 30 minutes, or one hour following the termination of a learning task. When the animals were tested the next day, it was found that retention of the learned response increased with the length of the interval between training and the administration of ECS; the animals with a zero-second interval showed virtually no retention, whereas animals with a one-hour interval showed almost perfect retention (Hudspeth, McGaugh, and Thompson, 1964).

Retrograde amnesia has been studied in a wide variety of organisms and produced by methods other than ECS. Although alternative explanations have been offered to account for the results of these experiments, none of them have proved entirely satisfactory. It seems increasingly clear that a period of consolidation is necessary for permanent storage of the memory trace (McGaugh and Herz, 1970).

Support for the idea that the storage process is time dependent also comes from studies in which certain drugs (such as strychnine, nicotine, caffeine, and amphetamine) given immediately following a learning trial appear to speed up the consolidation process. Animals so treated require fewer trials to reach a given learning criterion and make fewer errors overall. The assumption is that these drugs somehow accelerate the neurological processes in memory consolidation, but the mechanism by which they do this, possibly by increasing RNA synthesis, is not yet clear (McGaugh, 1970).

Mental Imagery and Recall

In trying to memorize a poem or story, it often helps to visualize the action being described. It is difficult to define *mental imagery,* but most people will readily agree that they can form mental pictures, although they differ in the ease with which they can do this and in the vividness of the pictures and the amount of detail included. People with remarkable memories often deal with new material by forming visual images. The case history of a Russian newspaper reporter provides an example. When a sequence of digits was dictated to him, he would visualize the digits as written down on a piece of paper, usually in his own handwriting. To remember a long list of objects he would visualize the objects arranged in a row with their order preserved. He did this, for example, by taking an imaginary walk from Pushkin Square down Gorky Street and visualizing each object at some point along the route. To recall the sequence, he would repeat his imaginary walk, reading off the objects that had been positioned along the way. In brief, his technique was to translate the verbal material into imaged objects and maintain their order by locating them against the background of a well-known route. With this technique, called the *method of loci,* he could memorize lists of more than one hundred digits, mathematical formulas, or musical motifs and recall them years later (Luria, 1968).

The *method of loci* requires very little practice. Try to visualize a walk through the house or apartment in which you live. You enter the front hall, move next to the living room, then to the dining room, to the kitchen, to the bedroom, and so forth. If you were to use these loci to memorize a shopping list—e.g., bread, eggs, beer, milk, bacon, etc.—then you would try to form a series of mental images. A loaf of bread hanging from the hallway light fixture, an egg sitting as "humpty dumpty" on the living room fireplace, a spilled can of beer on the dining room table, a cow in the center of the kitchen, a pig sleeping in a bed, and so forth. When ready to recall the shopping list, you would take an imaginary walk trying to retrieve the image associated with each room (see Figure 8-11).

This kind of mental imagery is not the same as eidetic imagery (p. 226). An eidetic image is a literal projection before your eyes. Here the individual makes up an image to help in the recall of material that may not be pictorial.

The effects of mental imagery can be investigated in the laboratory. In a typical experiment the subject is presented with a deck of one hundred cards, one at a time; each card is printed with an arbitrary pair of unrelated concrete nouns such as *dog-bicycle.* The subject will later be shown the first word of each pair and asked to recall the second. One group of subjects is instructed to associate the two words on each card by imagining a visual scene in which they are interacting in some way. They are instructed to form bizarre or unusual images and include as many details as possible. (For example, picturing a *dog* dressed in a clown's outfit, pedaling an old-fashioned *bicycle.*) Another group of subjects is given exactly the same learning task but simply told to study and rehearse the word pairs so that when tested later the first member will cue the recall of the second. Both groups spend the same amount of time studying the material, but the group instructed to use imagery performs far better. In one experiment the imagery group showed 80 percent recall, whereas the control group remembered only 33 percent of the word pairs. The effectiveness of imagery may even be underestimated in this study, because interviews with the control subjects revealed some who were spontaneously using mental imagery to learn some of the pairs (Bower, 1972).

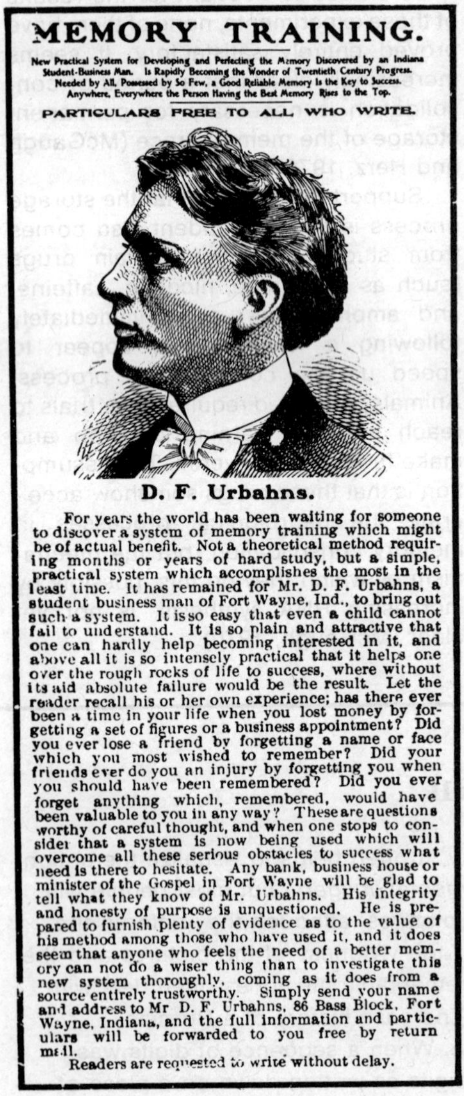

DUAL ENCODING SYSTEMS. Research of this sort suggests that encoding information in memory involves two separate processes. Information may be encoded in a pictorial form or as a verbal statement. We can refer to these two types of encoding systems as the *nonverbal imagery process* and the *verbal symbolic process* (Paivio, 1971). The nonverbal imagery process is best suited for representing concrete-spatial events and objects, whereas the verbal symbolic process is best for representing abstract verbal information. In a paired-associate study of the type just described, both processes are activated when the subject is given imagery instructions; in the absence of specific instructions to visualize, the subject relies primarily on the *verbal symbolic process.* The assumption of two separate encoding processes is in

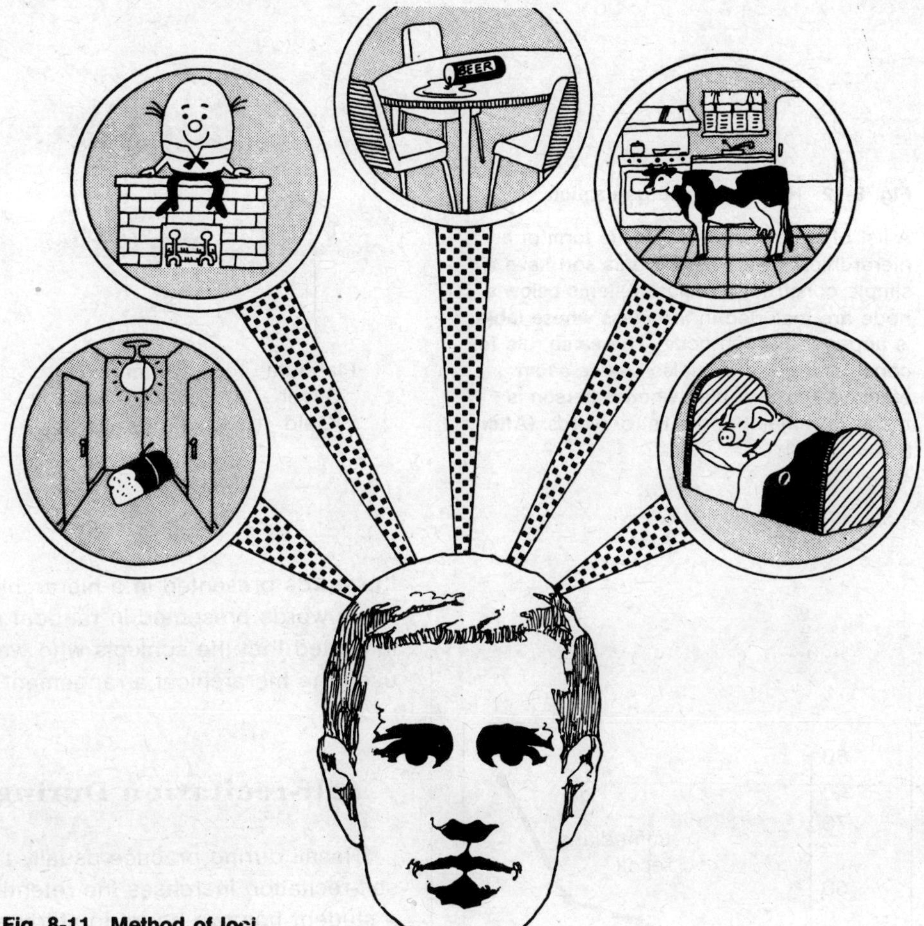

Fig. 8-11 Method of loci

A mental walk through the loci.

accord with the work on split-brain subjects discussed earlier (p. 51). The right cerebral hemisphere seems to play an important role in the imagery process; the left hemisphere predominates in the verbal symbolic process.

Organization and Memory

Memories are patterns of items, woven together by rules that impose varying degrees of *organization;* success in retrieval depends upon how much organization is present. When lists of words or other materials are studied, the greater the degree of organization that the learner can impose on the material, the better the subsequent recall (Mandler, 1974).

A dramatic illustration of the effect of organization on memory is provided in the following experiment. The subjects were required to memorize four separate lists of words. For some subjects each of the word lists was presented on a slide in the form of a hierarchical tree, much like the example shown in Figure 8-12. The other subjects studied each of the lists for the same length of time, but the items in each list were arranged randomly on the presentation slide. When tested later, subjects recalled 65 percent of

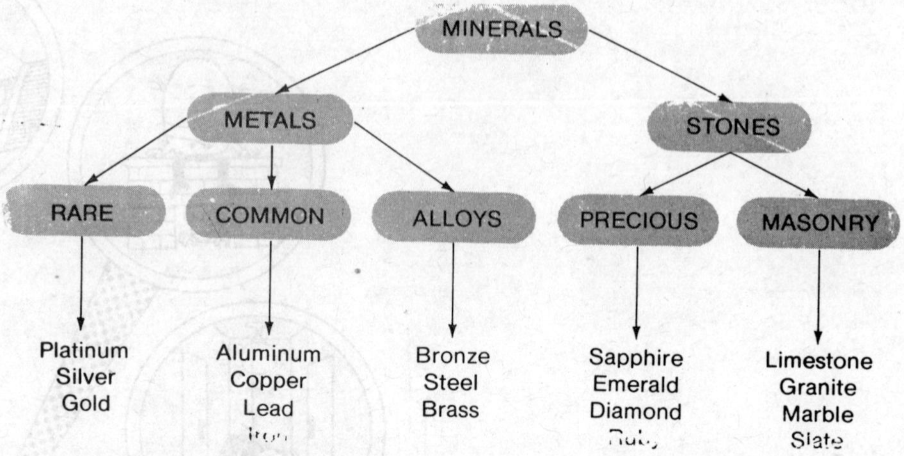

Fig. 8-12 Hierarchical organization

A list of words arranged in the form of a hierarchical tree. Trees of this sort have a simple construction rule; all items below a node are included in the class whose lable is appended to the node. The same rule for constructing the tree also serves as an effective retrieval plan when a person is trying to remember the list of words. (After Bower, 1970)

the words presented in a hierarchical organization, but only 19 percent of the same words presented in random arrangements. Further analysis of the data indicated that the subjects who were given the words in an organized form used the hierarchical arrangement as a retrieval scheme for generating recall.

Self-recitation During Practice

Recall during practice usually takes the form of reciting to oneself. Such self-recitation increases the retention of the material being studied. Suppose a student has two hours to study an assignment that can be read through in 30 minutes. Rereading the assignment four times is likely to be much less effective than reading it once and asking himself questions about the material he has read. He can then reread to clear up points that were unclear as he attempted to recall them. The generalization that it is efficient to spend a good fraction of study time in attempting recall is supported by experiments with laboratory learning as well as by experiments with school learning.

The percentage of study time that should be spent in self-recitation depends on the material and the type of test for which one is preparing. However, the percentage may be higher than our intuitions might suggest. A well-known laboratory experiment indicates that the greatest efficiency in recall of historical material occurs when as much as 80 percent of the study time is devoted to self-recitation. As shown in Figure 8-13, the amount recalled is an increasing function of the percentage of study time spent in self-recitation.

The self-recitation method in ordinary learning forces the learner to define and select what is to be remembered. In addition, recitation represents practice in the retrieval of information in the form likely to be demanded later on. That is, the learner tries to outline a history chapter or provide illustrations of operant conditioning in a fashion similar to what might be expected on an examination. The rule is to begin an active process of recall early in a study period. Time spent in active recall, with the book closed, is time well spent.

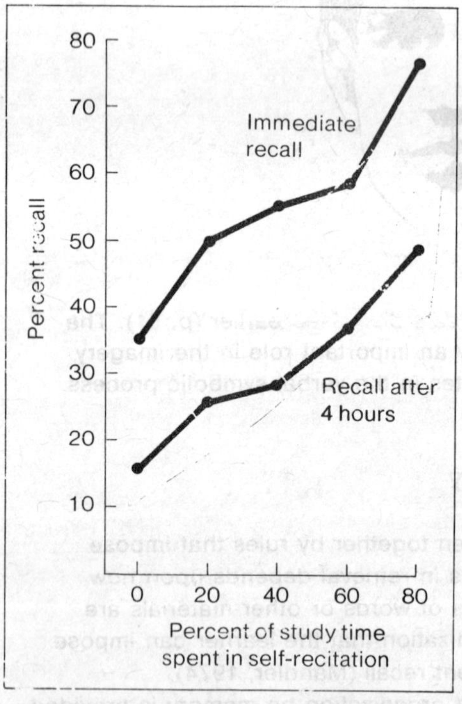

Fig. 8-13 Self-recitation during study

Effects on retention of spending various proportions of study time in self-recitation rather than in silent study. Results are shown for tests given immediately and four hours after completing study. (Data from Gates, 1917)

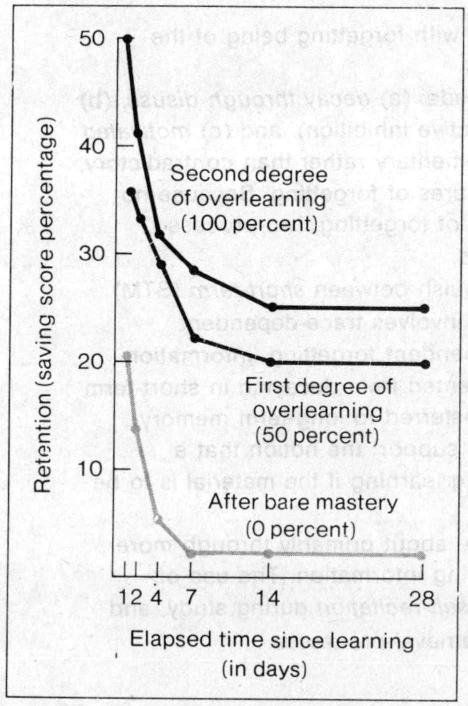

Fig. 8-14 Effects of overlearning on retention

Subjects learned a list of twelve nouns to three varying degrees of mastery and were then tested for retention at later points in time. Retention was measured as the saving score on subsequent relearning. (Data from Krueger, 1929)

Effects of Overlearning on Retention

Something to be long retained must be overlearned, that is, learned beyond the point of bare recall. Three groups of subjects were required to memorize a list of words by the serial-anticipation method (p. 213); each group learned to a different degree of overlearning. For subjects in the group of zero percent overlearning, practice was terminated at a criterion of one perfect recitation of the list. For the 50 percent overlearning group, practice was continued beyond the point of mastery for half as many trials as had been required to reach criterion; for the 100 percent overlearning group, the number of trials was doubled. The same list was then relearned from 1–28 days later. The results of the experiment are shown in Figure 8-14, in which the dependent variable is the *saving score* on relearning (p. 225). The curves indicate that the greater the degree of overlearning, the greater the retention at all time intervals.

The retention of skills learned in childhood, even after years of disuse, is not so surprising when we consider the amount of overlearning involved in such skills as swimming, skating, or riding a bicycle. The skill is not learned only to bare mastery, but is repeated far beyond the point of original learning. Overlearning may not suffice to account for all the difference in retention between skills and information, but it is assuredly a contributing influence.

Summary

1. When we remember something we may show the marks of earlier memory in several ways. *Redintegrative memory* reconstructs a past occasion not only according to its content but also its setting in time and place. Such rich memories have been studied very little in the psychological laboratory. Much easier to test are *recognition,* requiring only a sense of familiarity, and *recall,* requiring a reinstatement of something learned in the past. A *saving in relearning* material previously mastered is another measure of prior learning.
2. Memory can be viewed in terms of three stages: *encoding, storage,* and *retrieval.* Encoding refers to the transformation of sensory information into a form that can be processed by the memory system. Storage is the transfer of the encoded information into memory. And retrieval refers to the process by which information is located in memory when it is needed. Failures at any one of these stages will lead to a faulty memory.
3. *Cue-dependent forgetting* is most obvious in the *tip-of-the-tongue* (TOT) *state:* a word is stored in memory, but the appropriate cues that would allow retrieval are lacking. *Trace-dependent forgetting,* on the other hand, is the result of actual decay of the *memory trace.* Studies of electrical stimulation of the brain in epileptic patients support the hypothesis that

many memories are relatively permanent, with forgetting being of the cue-dependent type.

4. Traditional explanations of forgetting include: (a) *decay through disuse,* (b) *interference effects* (retroactive and proactive inhibition), and (c) *motivated forgetting.* These explanations are supplementary rather than contradictory, and each calls attention to important features of forgetting. Because no one of them can account for all the facts of forgetting, two-process theories of forgetting have been proposed.
5. *Two-process theories* of forgetting distinguish between *short-term* (STM) and *long-term memory* (LTM); the former involves trace-dependent forgetting, and the latter involves cue-dependent forgetting. Information maintained in the *rehearsal buffer* is prevented from decaying in short-term memory and thus is more likely to be transferred to long-term memory. The results of retrograde-amnesia studies support the notion that a *consolidation* period is necessary following learning if the material is to be retained in long-term memory.
6. Significant improvements in memory come about primarily through more effective methods of encoding and retrieving information. The use of *mental imagery, organizational schemes, self-recitation* during study, and *overlearning* aid both the encoding and retrieval processes.

Further Reading

The classic study that introduced the experimental analysis of memory is Ebbinghaus, *Memory* (1885; tr. 1913), now available in paperback (1964). A review of research on memory can be found in Murdock, *Human memory: theory and data* (1974); Norman, *Memory and attention* (1969); Kintsch, *Learning, memory and conceptual processes* (1970); Posner, *Cognition: An introduction* (1973); Lindsay and Norman, *Human information processing* (1972); and Howe, *Introduction to human memory* (1970).

More advanced topics in memory and cognition are treated in Norman (ed.), *Models of human memory* (1970); Tulving and Donaldson (eds.), *Organization of memory* (1972); Anderson and Bower, *Human associative memory* (1973); Gregg (ed.), *Cognition in learning and memory* (1972); Melton and Martin (eds.), *Coding processes in human memory* (1972); Norman and Rumelhart, *Explorations in cognition* (1975); and Krantz, Atkinson, Luce, and Suppes (eds.), *Contemporary developments in mathematical psychology* (1974).

For a review of research on the biological substrate of memory and learning see Deutsch, *The physiological basis of memory* (1973).

9 optimizing learning

Most research on learning and memory suggests practical applications, but it is seldom possible to move directly from research to applications. Usually it is necessary to take account of the setting, to try out the research findings in practical contexts, and adjust for special conditions. A drug may be found to kill the bacteria causing a given disease, but before this knowledge can be put to use, the proper dosage and method of administration must be determined and possible side effects evaluated. In this chapter we examine some laboratory findings that bear upon problems of efficient learning and yield suggestions for optimizing the learning process. We will be concerned with such issues as the structure of an individual's knowledge base and how best to add to it, the way in which learning one set of materials transfers to learning another, the importance of immediate information feedback, and motivational and emotional factors that affect learning efficiency.

Much of society's energy is devoted to the management of learning—to instruction in schools, to job training in industry, and to teaching health and safety procedures in the community. The aim of an applied psychology of learning is to produce the highest quality learning with the greatest possible efficiency. In recent years there have been many public discussions about which teaching methods are most effective; particular emphasis has been placed on the teaching of basic skills like reading and mathematics. All these discussions concern the appropriate applications of the principles of learning to the field of instruction.

A number of teaching aids have been developed to promote learning. Motion pictures, audio-visual tapes, and closed-circuit TV have become important adjuncts to instruction. Relative newcomers on the instruction scene are programmed texts and computer-assisted instruction. Although still in the developmental stage, such work is worth considering because of the way in which it illustrates learning principles.

Fig. 9-1 A Skinner-inspired machine

A statement with a fill-in blank is presented in the window at the left of the machine. The student writes the appropriate answer in the open space on the right-hand side. After being shown whether his response is correct he turns a knob on the left to proceed to the next item.

Programmed Learning and Automated Instruction

For centuries teachers have stood in front of classrooms and dispensed words of wisdom. Students passed or failed depending on how much of this knowledge they could recall at the time of an examination. This form of instruction has obvious limitations when compared to a tutorial arrangement — a one-to-one relationship between the student and teacher. But the cost of tutorial education makes it impractical on a large-scale basis. In the 1950s, under the guidance of B. F. Skinner at Harvard University, an effort was made to approximate some aspects of tutorial instruction in the form of a *teaching machine*. An example of this device is shown in Figure 9-1. The basic idea was to present information to the student in a series of *frames*. Each frame contains a new item of information and also poses a question which the student must answer. After writing the answer (usually in a word or brief phrase), the student turns a knob that uncovers the correct answer and exposes the next instructional frame. In this way the student goes step-wise through a course, gradually being introduced to each unit of instruction and being tested to see that he understands it.

With the advent of computers it became evident that teaching devices could be developed that would be far more flexible and responsive to the student than the Skinner-type teaching machine. As yet the use of computers in business, science, and engineering far exceeds applications in education. However, if potentials are properly realized, the nature of education during our lifetime will be radically changed by the computer. The most important feature of computerized instruction is that it permits a high degree of *individualization*; each student can proceed at his own pace following a path through the curriculum best suited to his particular interest and talents.

Computer-Assisted Instruction (CAI)

Because of its great speed of operation, a large computer can handle many students simultaneously—as many as several thousand students each at a different point in one of several hundred different curricula. Figure 9-2 displays one of the student terminals of a computer-assisted instruction (CAI) system used for research purposes at Stanford University. Located at each student's station is a cathode-ray tube, a microfilm-display device, earphones, and a typewriter keyboard. Each device is under computer control. The computer sends out instructions to the terminal to display a particular image on the microfilm projector—to write a message of text or construct a geometric figure on the cathode-ray tube—and simultaneously plays an auditory message. The student sees the visual display, hears the auditory message, and then may be required to respond. The student responds by operating the typewriter keyboard or by touching the surface of the cathode-ray tube with an electronic pencil. This response is fed back to the computer and evaluated.

If the student is correct the computer moves on to the next instructional item; if incorrect the computer evaluates the type of error made and then branches to appropriate remedial material. A complete record on each student is stored in the computer and is updated with each new response.

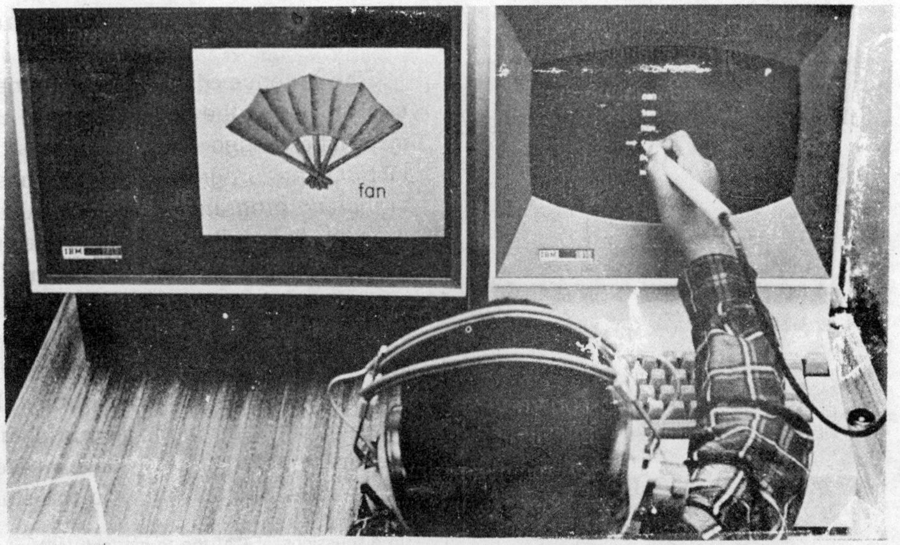

Fig. 9-2 Student station under computer control

An individual student's station in a CAI system. Shown here is a first-grade student learning word meanings as part of a course in reading. (After Atkinson, 1974)

The record is checked periodically to evaluate the student's rate of progress and to determine any particular difficulties. A student making exceptionally good progress may be moved ahead in the lesson sequence, or branched out to special materials designed to enrich his understanding of the curriculum. A student having difficulties may be branched back to review earlier materials or to a special remedial sequence. In a very real sense the CAI system simulates the human tutorial process.

Although CAI has had only limited development, experience and research support the claim that it will have wide application in the future. For example, CAI programs designed to teach reading in the early grades have proved remarkably successful. Children receiving computer-based instruction made significant gains over comparable groups taught by traditional classroom methods (Atkinson, 1974).

One interesting outcome of CAI concerns sex differences in reading. With traditional teaching methods girls generally learn to read more rapidly than boys. Several explanations have been offered for this difference. The environment of the primary classroom, which is often run by a female teacher, may be more oriented toward the needs of girls. The fact that first-grade girls tend to be more mature physically than boys of the same age may also be important. Whatever the explanation, this sex difference in reading performance disappears with the CAI reading program. Boys progress through the curriculum as rapidly as the girls, and do equally well on tests administered at the end of the school year.

Instruction under computer control has also been used successfully at the college level. More than fifty different courses at the University of Illinois are taught using CAI. At Stanford University students taught first-year Russian by computer provided an example of CAI's effectiveness when they performed significantly better on their final examinations than did a control group attending the regular Russian class. The CAI group had fewer dropouts, and more of its students elected to continue into the second year of Russian (Suppes and Morningstar, 1969).

Instructional Programs

The essence of teaching, whether in the classroom or under computer control, lies in the arrangement of the material to be learned. A body of material arranged so as to be most readily mastered is called a *program.*[1] Instructional programs have two basic formats: the *linear* program and the *branching* program. Figure 9-3 illustrates a linear program. With such a program the student progresses along a single track from one frame to the next; each time an item is answered the student moves on to the next regardless of whether the response was correct. Inspection of the linear program in Figure 9-3 indicates how new information is gradually introduced and elaborated, insuring the student's attention at each step by requiring a response. The branching program allows the learner to take any number of different paths through the curriculum. Each response is evaluated; that evaluation determines, in part, where the student goes next. An error in response is pointed out, and the student is given help to avoid making that

[1] In discussions of CAI the terms *instructional program* and *teaching program* are often used, rather than simply the term *program,* to distinguish them from the *computer program,* which is a sequence of commands that controls the computer.

Sentence to be completed	Word to be supplied
1. The important parts of a flashlight are the battery and the bulb. When we "turn on" a flashlight, we close a switch which connects the battery with the —.	bulb
2. When we turn on a flashlight, an electric current flows through the fine wire in the — and causes it to grow hot.	bulb
3. When the hot wire glows brightly, we say that it gives off or sends out heat and —.	light
4. The fine wire in the bulb is called a filament. The bulb "lights up" when the filament is heated by the passage of a(n) — current.	electric
5. When a weak battery produces little current, the fine wire, or —, does not get very hot.	filament
6. A filament which is *less* hot sends out or gives off — light.	less
7. "Emit" means "send out." The amount of light sent out, or "emitted," by a filament depends on how — the filament is.	hot
8. The higher the temperature of the filament the — the light emitted by it.	brighter
9. If a flashlight battery is weak, the — in the bulb may still glow, but with only a dull red color.	filament
10. The light from a very hot filament is colored yellow or white. The light from a filament which is not very hot is colored —.	red
11. A blacksmith or other metal worker sometimes makes sure that a bar of iron is heated to a "cherry red" before hammering it into shape. He uses the — of the light emitted by the bar to tell how hot it is.	color
12. Both the color and the amount of light depend on the — of the emitting filament or bar.	temperature
13. An object which emits light because it is hot is called incandescent. A flashlight bulb is an incandescent source of —.	light
14. A neon tube emits light but remains cool. It is, therefore, not an incandescent — of light.	source
15. A candle flame is hot. It is a(n) — source of light.	incandescent
16. The hot wick of a candle gives off small pieces or particles of carbon which burn in the flame. Before or while burning, the hot particles send out, or —, light.	emit
17. A long candlewick produces a flame in which oxygen does not reach all the carbon particles. Without oxygen the particles cannot burn. Particles which do not burn rise above the flame as —.	smoke
18. We can show that there are particles of carbon in a candle flame, even when it is not smoking, by holding a piece of metal in the flame. The metal cools some of the particles before they burn, and the unburned carbon — collect on the metal as soot.	particles
19. The particles of carbon in soot or smoke no longer emit light because they are — than when they were in the flame.	cooler, colder
20. The reddish part of a candle flame has the same color as the filament in a flashlight with a weak battery. We might guess that the yellow or white parts of a candle flame are — than the reddish part.	hotter
21. "Putting out" an incandescent electric light means turning off the current so that the filament grows too — to emit light.	cold, cool
22. Setting fire to the wick of an oil lamp is called — the lamp.	lighting
23. The sun is our principal — of light, as well as of heat.	source
24. The sun is not only very bright but very hot. It is a powerful — source of light.	incandescent
25. Light is a form of energy. In "emitting light" an object changes, or "converts," one form of — into another.	energy
26. The electric energy supplied by the battery in a flashlight is converted to — and —.	heat, light; light, heat
27. If we leave a flashlight on, all the energy stored in the battery will finally be changed or — into heat and light.	converted
28. The light from a candle flame comes from the — released by chemical changes as the candle burns.	energy
29. A nearly "dead" battery may make a flashlight bulb warm to the touch, but the filament may still not be hot enough to emit light—in other words, the filament will not be — at that temperature.	incandescent
30. Objects, such as a filament, carbon particles, or iron bars, become incandescent when heated to about 800 degrees Celsius. At that temperature they begin to — —.	emit light
31. When raised to any temperature above 800 degrees Celsius, an object such as an iron bar will emit light. Although the bar may melt or vaporize, its particles will be — no matter how hot they get.	incandescent
32. About 800 degrees Celsius is the lower limit of the temperature at which particles emit light. There is no upper limit of the — at which emission of light occurs.	temperature
33. Sunlight is — by very hot gases near the surface of the sun.	emitted
34. Complex changes similar to an atomic explosion generate the great heat which explains the — of light by the sun.	emission
35. Below about — degrees Celsius an object is not an incandescent source of light.	800

Fig. 9-3 Example of a linear program

This is part of a program in high school physics. The student covers the answer column with a slider, reads one frame at a time, writes his answer in the blank, and then moves the slider to uncover the correct answer. Several programming techniques are illustrated by this set of frames. For example, technical terms are introduced slowly. The more familiar term "fine wire" in frame 2 is followed by a definition of the technical term "filament" in frame 4; "filament" is then asked for as a synonym in frame 5 and without a synonym in frame 9. Initially the student may be prompted to give the correct answer. In frame 25, for example, the response "energy" is easily evoked by the words "form of ——" because the expression "form of energy" is used earlier in the frame. The word "energy" appears in the next two frames and is finally asked for without a *prompt* in frame 28. Beginning with fairly simple facts the student is gradually led to an understanding of the topic. (After Skinner, 1968) error again. The student who has done very well on a number of questions may be given an opportunity to jump ahead; the one who has made too many mistakes may retrace his steps or take an alternative route in an effort to resolve difficulties.

Learning programs in a linear format do not need to be presented and sequenced by an automated device; therefore, for reasons of economy, they are often printed in textbook form.[2] In the *programmed textbook* the answers to each frame usually are listed at the side of the page (see Figure 9-3). The student covers the answer column with a slider (strip of plastic) and reads one frame at a time. After reading the frame the student writes down his answer and then moves the slider down to uncover the appropriate answer. This procedure is followed throughout, each time checking the answer to one frame before going on to the next.

Some investigators have argued that all programs should be linear in form; others have argued for complex branching programs. Recent research suggests that the issue cannot be resolved in such a simple fashion. Some instructional materials can often be formulated quite nicely in a linear format, thus permitting them to be distributed very economically. However, other types of materials virtually require a branching scheme if the program is to be effective. Undoubtedly, the successful programs of the future will utilize both linear and branching segments, the particular format adopted depending upon the material being taught.

As yet, it is not possible to prescribe a definite set of rules for developing a successful program. The development of a good program is still very much an art in the same sense as is writing a good textbook or preparing an effective lecture. A person constructing a program must, however, have in mind the *organization of knowledge,* both its *logical* organization (what has to be known before something else can be understood) and its *psychological* organization (how attention can be directed to significant parts, generalizations made from prior information, and so on). Because these tasks are elusive, programmers conduct pilot tests of their programs.

The pilot testing is ordinarily done by trying the program out on a group of students, revising it to take care of the difficulties they experience, trying it on a second group, revising it again, and so continuing until it seems to be adequate. This process of successive revisions and improvement of a program is important. It focuses attention on the individual learning process and helps the programmer isolate for more careful analysis the parts that cause particular difficulties.

Effective Teaching Procedures

What are some of the features of programmed instruction and CAI that make them effective? At least three seem to be particularly important.

1 *Active participation.* The learner is actively interacting with the curriculum materials by responding, practicing, and testing each step of the material to be mastered. The old adage "learning by doing" is well exemplified, in contrast to the passive learning that takes place during a lecture.

[2] The study guide designed to accompany this textbook contains chapter reviews written in the form of a linear program.

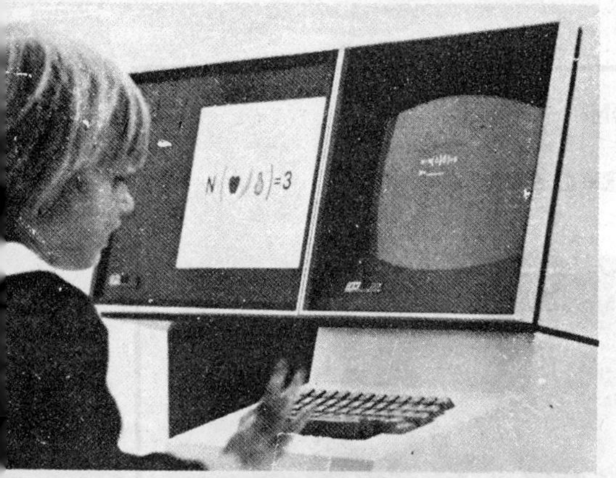

2. *Information feedback.* The learner finds out with minimal delay whether the response is correct; thus immediate correction of an error is permitted. This type of feedback has been shown to be important in a range of tasks—from operant conditioning with animals, in which immediate reinforcement produces faster learning, to verbal learning studies with human subjects, in which knowledge of results provides similar benefits.
3. *Individualization of instruction.* The learner moves ahead at his own rate. The rapid learner can progress quickly through the material, while the slower learner can move less rapidly (often being diverted to a remedial program) until he, too, has mastered the basic concepts. Branching programs are particularly important in this regard because the learner moves through the material on a path designed to fit his aptitudes and abilities.

The instructional procedures discussed in this section can be implemented with present technology and are economically feasible. It is not unreasonable to expect that in the not too distant future computers will be able to recognize spoken words and understand the meanings of questions asked by students. With this type of flexibility available, yet other approaches to instruction can be pursued that will permit a true dialogue between the student and the computer.

Some feel that computers in education pose a threat to human individuality. But in reality CAI provides the opportunity for greater development of individual potential. Just as books freed students from the tyranny of overly simple methods of oral recitation, so computers can free students from the drudgery of doing tasks not adjusted to their interests and needs.

Transfer of Learning

An important issue in optimizing learning is the extent to which the learning of one thing facilitates the learning of something else. If everything we learned was specific to the situation in which it was learned, the amount of learning that would have to be crammed into a lifetime would be phenomenal. Fortunately, most learning is readily transferable, with some modification, to a number of different situations.

The influence that learning one task may have on the subsequent learning of another is called *transfer of learning.* The term *positive transfer* is used when learning one task does facilitate learning another. If one is a good tennis player, it is easier to learn to play squash; this is positive transfer. But transfer is not always positive; when interference occurs, we have *negative transfer.*

There are numerous examples of negative transfer in everyday life. When driving a car with automatic transmission after having been accustomed to one with a stick shift, we may find ourselves depressing a nonexistent clutch pedal. When changing from a pedal-brake to a hand-brake bicycle, we may still try to press back on the pedal when we have to stop quickly. And the transition from driving on the right-hand side of the street to the British procedure of driving on the left is difficult for many American visitors to Great Britain. The original habit is so overlearned that even after driving successfully on the left for some time, an individual may revert to right-side driving when required to act quickly in an emergency.

CRITICAL DISCUSSION

Discovery Learning

A somewhat different approach to education is illustrated by a project under the direction of Seymour Papert at the Massachusetts Institute of Technology. A former assistant of child-development theorist Jean Piaget, Papert believes in so-called *discovery learning;* namely, that children learn best by doing, rather than by having knowledge directed at them. Papert's project involves grade-school children who learn about mathematics by programming a computer.

One of the primary attractions for the children is a "turtle"—a cluster of electronic innards mounted on wheels and wired to a computer keyboard (see Figure 9-4). Among other things, the turtle has a pen on its bottom side for drawing pictures on the floor upon command. Children have taught the turtle to play games, learn paths through mazes, and draw intricate patterns. Although they may look like space-age child's play, the computer exercises require complicated computations and painstaking planning. For example, to tell the turtle to draw a simple rectangle, a child types out instructions for the computer as follows: (1) pen down; (2) forward 10 [units of length]; (3) left 90 [degrees]; (4) forward 20; (5) left 90 . . . and so on until the rectangle is completed.

The purpose of the project is to establish a learning environment that allows pupils to discover, on their own, how to solve problems. Although no careful evaluation of this work has been made, many children are enthusiastic about the experience and some have produced truly creative programs. Papert believes that discovery through doing not only teaches, but can awaken original thinking.

Fig. 9-4 An electronic "turtle" in action

A learning environment that allows students to work things out on their own. The electronic gadget (called a "turtle") is connected to a computer; in order to operate it the student must learn some basic skills in computer programming.

Doctrine of Formal Discipline

The problem of transfer of learning has been historically of great concern to educators. For them it constitutes the very important practical question of how the school curricula should be arranged to ensure maximum positive transfer. Does learning algebra help in the learning of geometry? Which of the sciences should be taught first to ensure maximum transfer to other science courses?

One of the earliest notions of transfer of learning, prevalent among educators around the turn of the century, maintained that the mind was composed of faculties that could be strengthened through exercise, much as individual muscles can be strengthened. This notion, known as the *doctrine of formal discipline,* was advanced in support of keeping such studies as Latin and Greek in the high school curriculum. It was argued that the study of Latin, for example, trains a student's powers of self-discipline, reasoning, and observation.

The doctrine of formal discipline has been largely discredited by experiments. Some transfer does take place, but it depends much less on formal mental training than on learning for a specific purpose. For example, the study of Latin does indeed improve the understanding of English words, but only those with Latin roots. It does not improve the understanding of words of Anglo-Saxon origin. And the extent to which improvement occurs depends upon the way the Latin is taught: the gain in English vocabulary is much greater when the course is taught with emphasis on word derivation than when taught by more conventional methods.

Learning to Learn

A special example of transfer of training is a phenomenon that psychologists have labeled *learning to learn.* Subjects who learn successive lists of verbal materials over a period of days are able to increase the speed with which they learn subsequent lists. Positive transfer occurs even though the lists are not similar. The subjects apparently learn a technique or an approach to the task that facilitates their performance on later tasks of the same sort.

Another example of learning to learn is provided by an experiment in which monkeys are presented with a series of discrimination problems (see Figure 9-5). For each problem the animal is shown two objects—for example,

Fig. 9-5 Test apparatus for discrimination learning

When the experimenter changes the stimulus objects, the forward opaque screen is lowered, blocking the monkey's view of the stimulus tray. (After Davenport, Chamove, and Harlow, 1970)

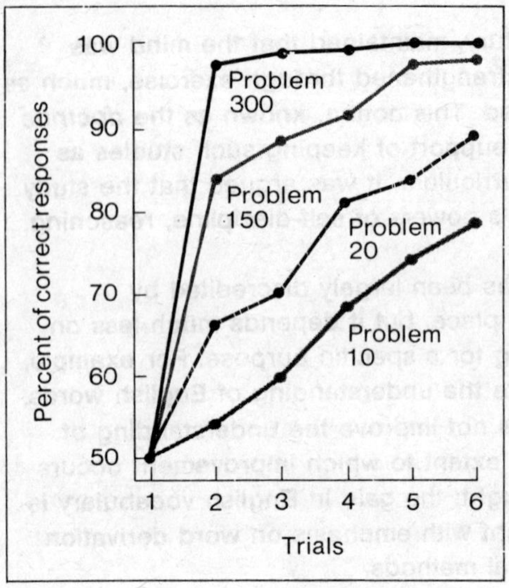

Fig. 9-6 Learning curves from the same subjects in a series of discrimination problems

Plotted here is the probability of a correct response over the first six trials on the 10th, 20th, 150th, and 300th discrimination problem. (After Harlow, 1949)

a red triangle and a green circle—and is reinforced with food if it selects the correct object, which might be the red triangle. Object position is alternated in a random order from trial to trial so that sometimes the triangle is on the right and sometimes on the left. The animal must learn to ignore positional cues in selecting the correct object. After the monkey has learned consistently to select the correct object, it is given a problem involving a different pair of objects.

In one experiment monkeys were given several hundred such problems, each problem using a completely new pair of stimulus objects. The learning curves for two problems that occurred early in the series of problems and two that occurred later are presented in Figure 9-6. All the curves begin at the 50-percent level, because on the first trial of each problem the objects are new and the animal has to guess. By the 10th problem the monkeys are making only about 54 percent correct choices on the second trial. By the 300th problem they were responding at the 98-percent level on the second trial. In the beginning the animals made little use of the information provided by the first trial, but by the 300th problem they utilized this information to obtain almost perfect performance on the second trial. The monkeys learned that if the object they select on the first trial is rewarded they should pick the same object on the second trial regardless of its position; if the first trial choice is not rewarded they should select the other object on the second trial. The monkeys have learned how to learn for this particular class of problems and can now proceed on the basis of *insight* as opposed to trial-and-error behavior.

Learning to learn has been extensively investigated not only with monkeys but also with young children. The findings indicate that the phenomenon is general and involves a number of different factors. One factor may be learning to relax in the experimental situation; another, to ignore distracting noises and other irrelevant stimuli. Most important is learning to identify the relevant cues in the situation; for example, in the experiment described above the monkey learns that the important cue is the quality (shape or color) of the object, not its position on the display board. In a sense this involves learning a principle. And as we shall see, learning principles rather than specific responses constitutes one of the chief ways in which learning transfers.

Transfer by Mastering Principles

One factor that makes transfer possible is the appropriate application to new situations of principles learned in old situations. The Wright brothers applied the principles they learned in flying kites to building an airplane. Principles of reasoning learned in logic are equally applicable in mathematics. The following experiment demonstrates the advantage of learning principles.

Two groups of boys shot with rifles at a target submerged under water. Prior to the target practice the experimental group studied an explanation of the theory of refraction of light so that they understood the apparent displacement of objects viewed under water. The control group received no explanation. The experimental group learned to hit the target in about the same number of trials as the control group; thus learning to hit the target was not influenced by whether or not the subject had studied the theory of light refraction. However, after the boys had become proficient at hitting the target, the depth of the target was changed. Both groups showed positive transfer from the first to the second task, but the experimental group evidenced the greatest amount of transfer. Their knowledge of the principle of refraction enabled them to master the new task in significantly fewer trials than the control group (Hendrickson and Schroeder, 1941).

Application to Education

We have talked about transfer in laboratory experiments, but studies on transfer have also been carried out in the classroom. What practical implications do they provide for the field of education?

The extent of transfer of an academic subject clearly depends on the teaching method. As we said earlier, Latin can be taught so as to improve understanding of English vocabulary. It is equally true that history can be taught in order to provide an understanding of current political and economic problems, and arithmetic in a way to provide positive transfer to the study of algebra. Teaching for transfer requires emphasizing the similarities between the current subject and the situations to which the new learning will transfer. If the two subject areas are similar in general principles or concepts, then transfer depends upon the extent to which the principles and their broad application are stressed. Studies have shown, too, that principles transfer more readily when the student (1) has practiced the basic problem to a high degree of mastery and (2) has experience with a variety of similar problems to ensure generalization of the principle. If a student is presented with a wide variety of problems without time to learn any one to a moderate degree of mastery, there will be little transfer.

Improvement in learning how to learn (in the sense of learning efficient study habits) provides another opportunity for transfer. One study demonstrated that college students who were taught certain principles of efficient memorization showed marked improvement in their ability to retain various memorized materials as compared with students who simply practiced memorizing without any specific instructions. Other studies have shown that introducing lessons on study skills in a high-school course (teaching such skills as learning to use reference books, interpret charts, summarize, and outline) results not only in substantial gains in that specific course but in a transfer of these gains to other courses (Gagné, 1970).

Imagery As an Aid to Learning

Mental imagery was discussed in the last chapter (p. 241) as a powerful aid to memory. One cannot help but think that such a remarkable method ought to have a practical application. And indeed it does. Recent experiments demonstrate that mental imagery may be applied with extraordinary effect to teaching foreign language vocabulary.

Subjects who did not know Spanish studied a list of Spanish words for a fixed time period; they would hear each Spanish word pronounced and simultaneously see its English translation on a screen. Later they took a test in which they gave the English translation as each Spanish word was pronounced. The experimental group, using mental imagery, averaged 88 percent correct as compared to 28 percent correct for the control group that used rote repetition (Raugh and Atkinson, 1975).

CRITICAL DISCUSSION

Structure of Knowledge

Psychologists know a great deal about effective methods for learning individual facts but not much about how facts are represented and interconnected in the mind to form a coherent body of knowledge. Earlier, in discussing cognitive psychology, we talked about such internal representations, calling them *cognitive structures,* but we were vague about their nature. Cognitive structures are difficult to define and are not well understood. But until psychology has a better understanding of mental organization, its contribution to the development of effective instructional methods will be limited.

Several recent theories have attempted to explain how information is organized in memory. We will discuss one proposed by Anderson and Bower (1973). They refer to their theory as HAM—an abbreviation for "human associative memory."

In HAM, memory is viewed as a large collection of *nodes,* where each node corresponds to an idea or concept that a person has acquired as a result of prior experience. When we are exposed to a new fact (i.e., see something happen, or read or hear about something) we represent that information as a *proposition* to be stored in memory. A proposition can be thought of as a tree structure where each branch of the tree links two memory nodes together in a particular relationship. Examples of tree structures are given in Figure 9-7. The bottom branches of each of these trees always terminate in a *node* that already exists in the subject's memory. Consequently, when a new input tree is formed and stored in memory it is necessarily linked into the existing memory structure, since each of the tree's terminal nodes already exists there. As more propositions are acquired, more trees are formed to represent them. Every time a statement about a particular topic, for example, Marily

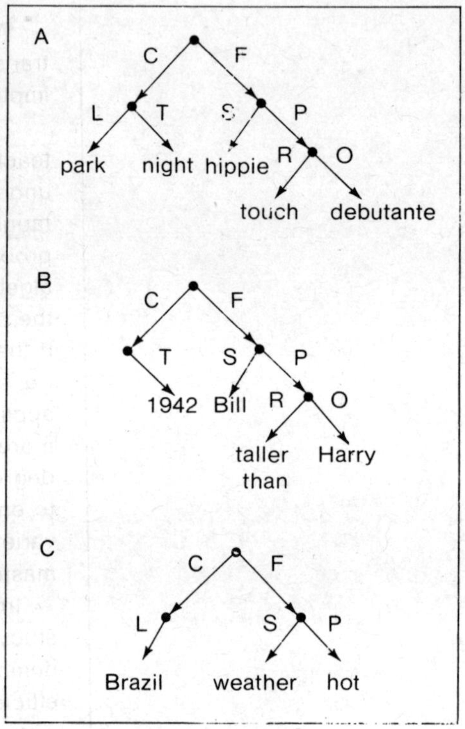

Fig. 9-7 Propositions in HAM

Tree structures are given for the following propositions: (a) During the night in the park the hippie touched the debutante. (b) Bill was taller than Harry in 1942. (c) In Brazil the weather is hot. Note that the top of each tree branches into two parts, one labeled C for "context" and the other F for "fact." A proposition involves a *fact* and the *context* within which it occurred. The C branch may specify location (L), or time (T), or both. Thus the fact "the hippie touched the debutante" occurred in location "L = park" at time "T = night." The fact side of a tree branches into a *subject* (S) and *predicate* (P). For example, the subject "S = Bill" has the property "P = taller than Harry." The P branch also divides into a branch specifying a particular *relation* (R) to the *object* (O); the predicate "taller than Harry" involves the relation "R = taller than" and the object "O = Harry."

Monroe, is input to the system a propositional tree is formed. If that proposition is successfully stored in memory, then one branch of its tree will be linked to the node for Marilyn Monroe. When the subject wants to recall all that he knows about Marilyn Monroe, he goes to that node in memory and traces out all branches leading from it. By doing this he can (if given enough time) retrieve all the propositions about Marilyn Monroe that are stored in memory.

Many experiments have been run to test the theory's predictions. We will consider one that illustrates the way HAM builds complex memory structures. At the start of the experiment subjects memorized a list of sentences, some of which are given in the top panel of Figure 9-8; each sentence is of the form subject-verb-object. Some of the sentences have no words in common with any of the other sentences, whereas other sentences involve different subject and object words but share a common verb. According to HAM, those sentences with no words in common should be represented in memory as completely separate trees. Those sentences with a verb in common would be represented as one large interlinked tree. The bottom panel of Figure 9-8 illustrates tree structures for the unique sentences and for the shared-verb sentences.

Fig. 9-8 Memory representations

The top panel presents examples of sentences used in the verification experiment. The lower panel illustrates the types of tree structures that would be set up in HAM for these sentences. (After Thorndike and Bower, 1974)

UNIQUE SENTENCES	The thief tackled the singer. The miner helped the judge. The addict scolded the infant.
SHARED-VERB SENTENCES	The gentleman watched the poet. The priest watched the officer. The father watched the miser.

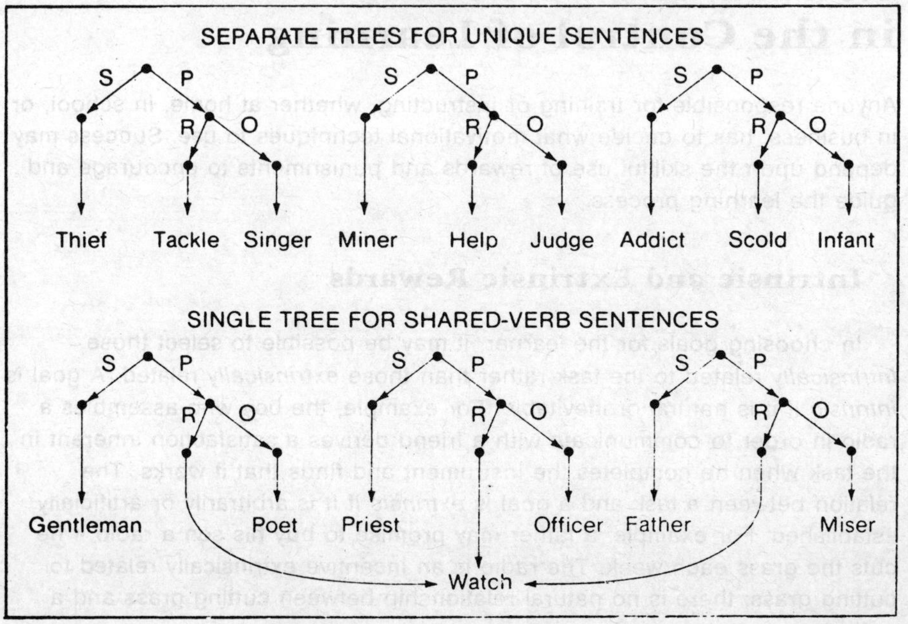

After the sentences had been memorized, the subjects were tested with a series of sentences. Some were from the memorized list; others were new but were formed by rearranging words from the memorized sentences. The subject was asked to respond as quickly as possible, saying "old" if the test sentence was from the memorized list and "new" if otherwise.

According to HAM, the time required to verify a test sentence depends upon how long it takes (1) to form its propositional tree and (2) to determine if that tree is stored in memory. In this experiment the time to form a propositional tree is the same for all test sentences; however, the time required to determine whether the tree is stored in memory will depend on the nature of the memory structure. If the memory tree corresponding to the input sentence has a simple structure, it will require less time to make a match than if the input sentence is part of a more complex tree. This prediction was confirmed; saying "old" to a unique sentence took about one-tenth of a second less time than the same response to sentences that shared a common verb (Thorndike and Bower, 1974).

The above is merely an outline of how HAM operates and the types of phenomena it can explain. But since this work has significant implications for optimizing learning, you should be acquainted with it. Psychology's ability to devise effective educational procedures will depend on the development of such theories.

TABLE 9-1
Examples of keywords used to link Spanish words to their English translations

SPANISH WORD:	KEY-WORD:	ENGLISH TRANSLATION:
caballo	[eye]	horse
charco	[charcoal]	puddle
muleta	[mule]	crutch
clavo	[claw]	nail
lagartija	[log]	lizard
cebolla	[boy]	onion
payaso	[pie]	clown
hilo	[eel]	thread
tenaza	[tennis]	pliars
jabon	[bone]	soap
carpa	[carp]	tent
pato	[pot]	duck

The image method required two steps in the study of a word. The first step was to recognize that the spoken Spanish word contained a sound similar to an English word. For example, subjects were told to observe that the word *caballo* (pronounced somewhat like "cob-eye-yo") had within it the sound of the English "eye." Such a similar sounding English word was presented with each Spanish word and was called a *keyword*. Thus, during study each Spanish word was presented with its keyword as well as its English translation. Table 9-1 shows some triplets used in the experiment. (The reader familiar with Spanish will realize that the key word may differ somewhat from the sound it relates to in the Spanish word.)

The second step was to invent a mental image in which the keyword interacted with the English translation in a graphic way. It was suggested that, in the case of *caballo* (meaning horse), one could picture something like an eye being flicked by the tail of a horse, or a Cyclopean eye winking in the forehead of a horse, or a horse kicking a giant eye. Subjects were instructed to seize the first image that came to mind and build it into a vivid picture, no matter how illogical it seemed.

The image method for learning a word may be described as a chain of two links connecting a Spanish word to its English equivalent through the *mediation* of a keyword. The paradigm can be presented schematically as in Figure 9-9, where the Spanish word is linked to the keyword by *acoustic properties,* and the keyword is in turn linked to the meaning by a subject-generated *mental image.*

It would be natural to suppose that such a complicated technique, involved as it is with spurious keywords and imagery, would be inefficient. But evaluation studies indicate that the method is very effective. And possibly because of the method's complexity, its usefulness appears to increase with practice, so that it is most effective when used regularly as an adjunct to a foreign language course (Atkinson and Raugh, 1975).

Fig. 9-9 Mental images and foreign language learning
Two illustrations of how mental images might be used to associate a spoken Spanish word with its English translation.

CABALLO → eye → HORSE

PATO → pot → DUCK

Reward and Punishment in the Control of Learning

Anyone responsible for training or instructing, whether at home, in school, or in business, has to decide what motivational techniques to use. Success may depend upon the skillful use of rewards and punishments to encourage and guide the learning process.

Intrinsic and Extrinsic Rewards

In choosing goals for the learner, it may be possible to select those *intrinsically* related to the task rather than those *extrinsically* related. A goal is *intrinsic* if it is natural or inevitable. For example, the boy who assembles a radio in order to communicate with a friend derives a satisfaction inherent in the task when he completes the instrument and finds that it works. The relation between a task and a goal is *extrinsic* if it is arbitrarily or artificially established. For example, a father may promise to buy his son a radio if he cuts the grass each week. The radio is an incentive extrinsically related to cutting grass; there is no natural relationship between cutting grass and a radio.

The distinction between intrinsic and extrinsic motivation is not clear-cut, and in most learning situations both types of motivation are involved. A child learning to ride a bicycle is usually intrinsically motivated by the pleasure derived from mastering this new skill. But fear of derision from his peers if he fails may also be a motivation, an extrinsic one.

Whenever possible, it is advantageous to use goals intrinsically related to the learning task. A child whose interest in music has been stimulated at an early age will persevere in practicing the piano longer than one whose motivation stems solely from promised rewards and threats of punishment. But even the intrinsically motivated child may require some extrinsic rewards when the drudgery involved in mastery outweighs the satisfaction of making music. In most cases, if the person who guides and controls the learning situation can capitalize on intrinsic motives, the battle is half won.

We know that rewards are effective, but extrinsic rewards—such as prizes for excellence—may have some objectionable byproducts:

1. A reward planned by an adult (parent or teacher) and arbitrarily related to the activity is like a bribe, and may lead to docility and deference to authority rather than to originality and self-initiated activity. It may engender in the child an attitude of "What do I get out of this?"—the activity becomes worthwhile only for the praise, attention, or financial gain it brings. Cheating on examinations sometimes occurs when desire for the external reward outweighs regard for the processes by which the reward is achieved.
2. Rewards are often competitive. One or a few learners may be encouraged by the reward, but many will be frustrated. If there is only one prize and many contestants, the problems of the losers must be considered. Is the gain to the winner worth the price in disappointment to the losers?

These remarks, however, should not be interpreted as justification for eliminating all extrinsic rewards in home or school situations. Evidence (to be discussed later with regard to behavior modification, Chapter 17) indicates that extrinsic rewards can be effective when properly administered, but the possibility of adverse effects also exists. In a study by Lepper, Greene, and Nisbett (1973) two groups of preschool children were asked to draw a picture with a special felt-tipped pen—an activity of initial intrinsic interest. In the Expect Award group, subjects agreed to engage in this activity in order to obtain an extrinsic reward (a "Good Player Award" certificate adorned with a gold seal and red ribbon). Subjects in the No Award group neither expected nor received the reward, but otherwise duplicated the experiences of the other subjects. Several weeks later, when observed unobtrusively in their classrooms, Expected Award subjects showed far less interest in the drawing activity than the No Award subjects. The provision of extrinsic rewards turned "play" (i.e., an activity that will be engaged in for its own sake) into "work" (i.e., an activity that will be engaged in only when extrinsic incentives are present). As Mark Twain noted long ago:

> If he [Tom Sawyer] had been a great and wise philosopher, like the writer of this book, he would have now comprehended that Work consists of whatever a body is obliged to do and that Play consists of whatever a body is not obliged to do. And this would help him to understand why constructing artificial flowers or performing on a treadmill is work, while rolling tenpins or climbing Mont Blanc is only amusement.

Threat of punishment as a controller of behavior.

Controlling Learning Through Punishment

Folklore leads us to believe that punishment is an effective way of controlling learning. "Spare the rod and spoil the child" is not an isolated epigram. Fines and imprisonment are forms of social control that are sanctioned by all governments. For many years arguments have continued over the relative advantages and disadvantages of benevolent treatment (emphasizing reward for good behavior) and stern treatment (emphasizing punishment for error). The preference has shifted slowly from punishment to reward.

Has this shift come about solely on humanitarian grounds or has punishment been found less effective than reward? Evidence from psychological experiments indicates two important conclusions: (1) punishment is often less effective than reward because it temporarily suppresses a response but does not weaken it and (2) when punishment is effective it accomplishes its purpose by forcing the individual to select an alternative response that may then be rewarded.

The temporary effects of punishment are illustrated in a series of studies reviewed by Estes (1970). In one experiment, two groups of rats learned to press a bar to obtain a food reward. After the response had been well learned, both groups were given extinction trials in which food was withheld. In the first few extinction trials the rats in one group received a strong electric shock every time they pressed the bar. During the remaining extinction trials no shock was administered; food was simply withheld. Results showed that the punished rats did make fewer responses during the first stage of extinction, but they later resumed their previous rate of bar pressing and by the end of the experiment had made as many responses as the unpunished animals. Punishment succeeded in temporarily suppressing the response but did not weaken it. As soon as punishment ceased, the response reappeared at full strength.

Other experiments have shown that the strength and duration of the suppression effect depend upon the intensity of the punishment and the degree of deprivation. Obviously, if the punishment is sufficiently severe and prolonged it may effectively stop a particular response, but the response has only been suppressed, not unlearned. The response may later reappear if motivation becomes strong enough to overcome the aversive qualities of the punishment. In addition, severe punishment of a strongly motivated response (for example, intense shock every time an acutely hungry rat presses a bar for food) creates such conflict in the organism that grossly maladaptive behavior may result. As we shall see in Chapter 16, some abnormal behavior may be due to the repressive nature of punishment, since response tendencies, though inhibited, may appear in indirect or disguised ways because they are not unlearned.

PROS AND CONS ON THE USE OF PUNISHMENT. In addition to its suppressive effect, punishment may unsatisfactorily control behavior for the following reasons:

1. The results of punishment, although they may include altered behavior, are not as predictable as the results of reward. Reward says: "Repeat what you have done." Punishment says: "Stop it!" Punishment by itself fails to

give you an alternative. As a result, an even more undesirable response may be substituted for the punished one.

2. Punishment under some circumstances tends to fix the behavior rather than eliminate it, perhaps as a consequence of the fear and anxiety induced by the punishment. Punishing a child for wetting the bed, for example, often increases the frequency of the behavior.
3. The byproducts of punishment may be unfortunate. Punishment often leads to dislike of the punishing person—whether parent, teacher, or employer—and to a dislike of the situation in which the punishment occurred.

These cautions about punishment do not mean that punishment is never serviceable in learning and teaching. In fact, it may be useful for several reasons:

1. Punishment can effectively eliminate an undesirable response if alternative responses are available that are not punished or, better yet, are rewarded. Rats who learned to take the shorter of two paths to reach food in a goal box will quickly switch to the longer path if they are shocked in the shorter one. In fact, they will learn the new response more quickly than animals whose response of taking the shorter path is blocked by a newly placed barrier. In this case, the temporary suppression produced by punishment provided the opportunity for the organism to learn a new response. Punishment was an effective means of redirecting behavior.
2. Punishment can be quite effective when all we want is that the organism respond to a signal to avoid punishment. For example, people learn to come inside when they hear thunder, or to seek shade when it is hot and additional sun may cause uncomfortable sunburn. Avoiding a threatened punishment can be rewarding. The policeman is seldom a punishing person; he is more usually a symbol of *threatened* punishment. How does a policeman control us if he has never struck us with his stick or placed us under arrest? Our anxiety explains his control over us. If we drive too fast and see a police car in the rearview mirror, we become anxious lest we get a ticket, and feel reassured when we have slowed down and the police officer has driven past without stopping us. Our reward comes from the reduction in anxiety we feel as a result of conforming to the law.
3. Punishment may be informative. A child who handles electrical appliances and gets shocked may learn which connections are safe, which hazardous. A teacher's corrections on a student's paper can be regarded as punishing; but they are also informative and can provide an occasion for learning. Informative punishment can redirect behavior so that the new behavior can be rewarded.

Parents are often puzzled about how much they should punish their children; yet most of them find that they resort to some sorts of deprivation if not to the actual inflicting of pain. The most effective use of punishment is the informative one, so that the child will know what is and is not allowed. Children occasionally "test the limits" to see what degree of unpermitted behavior they can get by with. When they do, it seems advisable to use discipline that is firm but not harsh, and to administer it promptly and consistently. Nagging a child to conform may in the end be less humane than an immediate spanking. A child who is threatened with a vague and postponed punishment ("What kind of person do you think you will grow up to be?") may suffer more severely than one who pays a consistent penalty for infringement but afterward is welcomed back into the family circle.

Anxiety and Learning

The apprehensiveness and uneasiness engendered by school tasks are familiar to most of us. Examinations are threatening, and often panic causes a student to do less well than was possible. Young children occasionally develop school phobias; they may become nauseated every school morning, yet escape all symptoms on Saturdays and Sundays. These cases are extreme, but most people carry some burden of anxiety. The following experiment gives some clues about the effect of an individual's general anxiety level on learning.

A large number of college students were given a questionnaire that asked about subjective experiences in testing situations: uneasiness, accelerated heartbeat, perspiration, and worry before and during a test session. On the basis of the answers high-anxious and low-anxious groups were chosen that were matched on intellectual ability.

The subjects received two types of instructions. Half of each group received "expected-to-finish" instructions: they were told the task would be easy enough to finish in the time allowed, and the instructions put pressure on them to finish. The other half of each group received "not-expected-to-finish" instructions: they were told that the task was too long to finish. (As it was, no one finished in the time allowed.) The "expected-to-finish" subjects fell behind what they thought they ought to be doing; the "not-expected-to-finish" subjects had no need to worry because they had been told that nobody could finish.

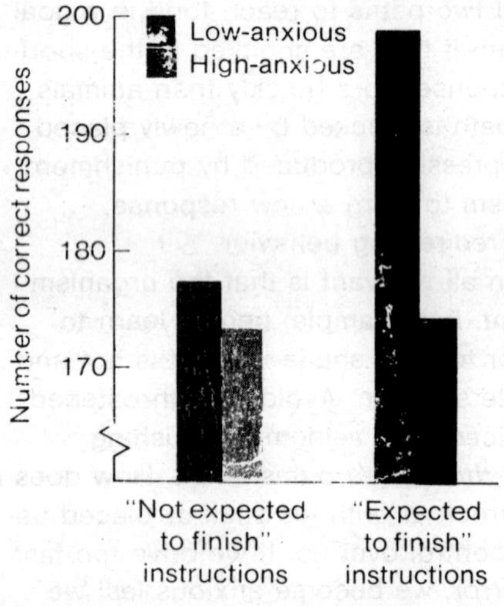

Fig. 9-10 Anxiety and learning

Digit-symbol learning for low-anxious and high-anxious subjects under two sets of instructions. (Data from Sarason, Mandler, and Craighill, 1952)

The results for one task, which required the subjects to learn a code for substituting digits in place of geometrical symbols, are plotted in Figure 9-10. The conclusions that can be drawn from this experiment are that (1) low-anxious subjects generally do better than high-anxious subjects, and (2) pressure to finish results in substantially improved scores for low-anxious but not for high-anxious subjects.

The study reported above is one of numerous experiments studying the relationship between anxiety level and learning. In general, the findings have shown that high-anxious subjects learn a simple classically conditioned response (for example, an eye blink to an air puff) more rapidly than low-anxious subjects; on more complex learning tasks high-anxious subjects usually do less well than low-anxious subjects, although there are some exceptions. Pressure of any kind—such as interrupting the task to report that the subject is doing poorly or giving ego-involving instructions implying that the task is an indication of intelligence—tends to depress the scores for high-anxious subjects but raises scores for low-anxious subjects.

Anxiety and Competing Responses

One explanation for the above results assumes that high anxiety does two things. It produces a high *drive level* that facilitates learning (see Chapter 11) and at the same time arouses a number of *competing responses* that may

interfere with learning—responses that are irrelevant to the task, such as autonomic responses or thoughts of worry and self-depreciation. Increasing the drive level in a classical-conditioning situation, in which a stimulus is associated with a single response, facilitates learning. In more complex situations, such as paired-associate learning, in which the stimuli may evoke a number of competing responses, increased drive level increases the strength of incorrect responses as well as that of the correct response, and hence usually leads to poorer learning for high-anxious subjects. Because in most instances the correct response initially is weaker than one or more of the competing incorrect responses, the higher the drive level, the poorer the performance.

It is possible, however, to devise a paired-associate learning task for which the correct response is stronger than the possible incorrect responses. For example, in one study using a list of paired-associates with high associative value (such as *tranquil-serene*) high-anxious subjects learned more rapidly than low-anxious subjects. However, when the stimulus words from the first list were paired with response words with no easy association (such as *tranquil-verbose*) low-anxious subjects learned more rapidly than high-anxious subjects (Standish and Champion, 1960). Thus, when the response to be learned is clearly the dominant one, high-anxious subjects perform better than low-anxious subjects. When the correct response is not dominant, low-anxious subjects have the advantage. It is not the complexity of the task per se that determines the effect of anxiety on performance, but the relative strength of the correct and incorrect responses.

When stress is introduced in the form of noxious stimuli, ego-involving instructions, or reports of failure, the performance of high-anxious subjects becomes worse while that of low-anxious subjects usually improves. It is hypothesized that stress, in addition to increasing drive level, also elicits task-irrelevant responses in high-anxious subjects. Instructions that stress the importance of "doing well" appear to trigger irrelevant responses in high-anxious subjects, while for low-anxious subjects the effect is merely to increase attention to the task and hence improve performance. In a sense, high-anxious subjects have a lower threshold for the arousal of anxiety than low-anxious subjects and tend to react to even mildly ego-involving instructions with a fear of failure that has a detrimental effect on performance (Spence and Spence, 1966).

Anxiety and Academic Performance

The effect of anxiety on the academic achievement of college students is illustrated by the following study. A group of high-anxious and a group of low-anxious freshmen were selected by means of a questionnaire. Both

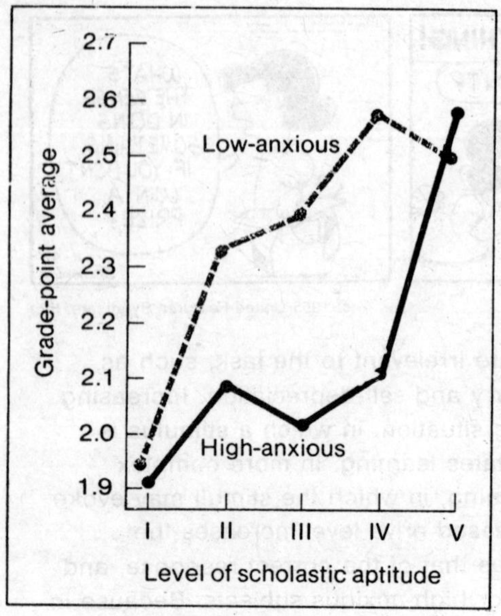

Fig. 9-11 Grade-point averages for high- and low-anxious college students

Students in the middle range of ability who score high on an anxiety questionnaire do less well scholastically than students of comparable ability who score low in anxiety. At the extremes of ability (Level I = lowest ability, V = highest ability), the degree of anxiety does not affect grade-point average Ability level is measured by college entrance examination scores. (After Spielberger, 1966)

groups were subdivided into five levels of scholastic ability on the basis of their college entrance examination scores. The investigator then evaluated the joint effects of anxiety and scholastic ability on the (1) grade-point average at the end of the freshman year and (2) dropout rate owing to academic failures by the end of the senior year. The grade-point averages for high- and low-anxious students of different ability levels are shown in Figure 9-11. In the broad middle range of ability, high-anxious students obtained poorer grades than low-anxious students. At the extremes of ability, anxiety had little effect on academic performance: the dull students did poorly regardless of their anxiety level; the most able students apparently were bright enough to overcome the detrimental effect of anxiety. In fact, at the highest level of ability. anxiety may facilitate performance by providing increased motivation.

Analysis of dropouts owing to academic failure gives further evidence of the destructive effect of anxiety on academic performance. More than 20 percent of the high-anxious students selected for this study left college because of academic failure; less than 5 percent of the low-anxious students left for the same reason. We conclude that some students who have the ability to obtain a college degree fail to do so because they are hampered by the effects of anxiety.

A follow-up study attempted to remedy this situation by providing group counseling for high-anxious students. All freshmen who scored high on the anxiety questionnaire were invited to participate in the experiment, and those who accepted were divided into two groups matched for college entrance examination scores and a number of other variables related to academic achievement. Students in one of the groups met with a counselor for a series of about ten sessions. Many topics were discussed during the counseling sessions, ranging from personal problems to efficient study habits. Counseling for the second group was postponed until the next semester. At the end of the first semester a comparison of the grade-point average of the counseled group with that of the group that had not yet received counseling indicated that the program was quite successful.

Emotional attitudes and anxieties can have a profound effect on our learning efficiency. Personal problems unrelated to the learning situation may interfere with concentration and sap the energy required for effective study. A certain level of anxiety may facilitate performance by increasing motivation, but excessive concern over grades and tests may be self-defeating. Although no one can deny that grades are important in this day of specialization, the student who studies because he wants to widen his fund of information will be less anxious in a test situation than one whose sole concern is an extrinsic reward, the test grade. The former has achieved something of value and has progressed regardless of the test grade; the latter feels that his efforts have been wasted if he does not get the desired grade.

Summary

1. *Computer-assisted instruction* (CAI) is proving to be a valuable aid to learning. Instructional programs designed for CAI may be in the form of *linear programs,* in which the student progresses along a single track from one frame to the next, or *branching programs,* in which the material to be presented next depends upon the student's response to previous frames. When a linear program is presented in book form it is called a *programmed text.*

2. Some of the features of programmed instruction and CAI that make them effective are: active participation by the learner, immediate feedback, and rate and path through the learning materials adjusted to individual differences.
3. The influence that learning one task has on the subsequent learning of another task is called *transfer of learning. Positive transfer* occurs when one task facilitates the learning of another; when there is interference we have *negative transfer.*
4. Factors that produce positive transfer include *learning to learn* (learning to relax in the situation, to ignore irrelevant stimuli, and to distinguish the relevant cues) and learning general *principles.*
5. In classroom situations transfer occurs best when there is a clearly designed effort on the teacher's part to emphasize similarities between the current subject and the situation to which the new learning will transfer, and to stress the application of principles.
6. In attempting to guide the learning of another person, *reward* is generally favored over *punishment.* Reward strengthens the rewarded behavior, whereas punishment may not lead to unlearning of the punished behavior; instead, the behavior may be merely suppressed, reappearing again when the threat of punishment is removed or perhaps appearing in disguised form.
7. Punishment may be effective, however, when it forces the individual to select an alternative response that can then be rewarded, or when it serves as an *informative cue* to avoid a certain response. Arbitrary rewards and punishments have some unfavorable consequences, in part because of the authoritarian control they often imply.
8. Subtle *emotional factors,* based on personal experiences of the individual, play a central role in learning. When college students are separated into *high-anxious* and *low-anxious* groups, the high-anxious subjects often perform better than the low-anxious ones in simple conditioning situations, but they do less well on complex tasks. Pressure on high-anxious students to do better may actually impede their performance, while such pressure spurs the low-anxious students to improve. High anxiety is also significantly related to lowered grade-point averages and dropout rates among college students.

Further Reading

Many of the standard experiments on economy in learning and transfer of learning are treated in Gagné, *The conditions of learning* (2nd ed., 1970); Biehler, *Psychology applied to teaching* (1971); and Ellis, *Fundamentals of human learning and cognition* (1972). The relation of learning theory to problems of education and instruction is discussed from many points of view in Hilgard (ed.), *Theories of learning and instruction* (1964); see also Hilgard and Bower, *Theories of learning* (4th ed., 1975).

Practical suggestions for the college student concerned with improving his study skills and exam-taking techniques may be found in Voeks, *On becoming an educated person* (3rd ed., 1970).

A survey of developments in programmed learning is provided in Skinner, *The technology of teaching* (1968). Progress in the area of computerized learning is reviewed by Atkinson and Wilson (eds.) in *Computer-assisted instruction* (1969).

Punishment and aversive behavior (1969) by Campbell and Church (eds.) reviews theories on the role of punishment in learning. A survey of research on anxiety in relation to learning is presented in Spielberger (ed.), *Anxiety: Current trends in theory and research* (vols. 1 and 2, 1972). Some interesting observations on obstacles to learning (chiefly in the age range of seven to sixteen, but with cases at college level as well) are reported in Harris, *Emotional blocks to learning* (1961).

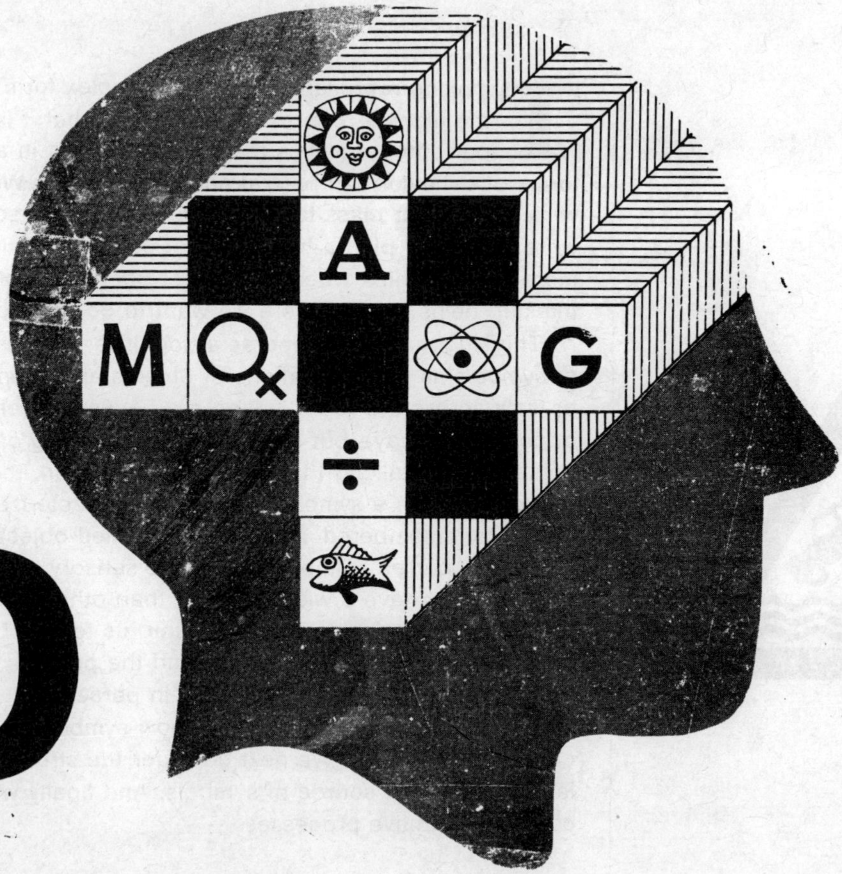

10 language and thought

Thinking represents the most complex form of human behavior, the highest form of mental activity, but it is not so different from our other activities that we must stand in awe of it. In fact, many forms of behavior can be classified as thinking. We think as we daydream while waiting for class to begin. We think as we solve a math problem or write a letter or plan a trip. Much of our thinking is highly practical; we are more likely to think when we cannot operate by old habits alone—when thinking helps us get where we want to go and do what we want to do.

Thinking may be viewed as a cognitive process characterized by the use of *symbols* as representations of objects and events. When we eat an apple or walk across the room, we do not necessarily engage in thought (although of course we may), but if we refer to the eating of something that is *not* present or to walking that is not now going on, then we must use a *symbolic* reference. Such a symbolic reference characterizes thought. Thought can deal with remembered, absent, or imagined objects and events, as well as with those currently impinging on the sensory system. Thought is symbolic and can thus have a wider content than other kinds of activity. It incorporates present perceptions and activities into its topics, but it deals with their *meanings* in a way that goes beyond the present; hence thought reflects upon and elaborates what is given in perception.

In this chapter we look first at how symbols acquire their meanings and can be manipulated. We next consider the structure and acquisition of language—a rich source of symbols. And finally we examine some other complex cognitive processes.

Symbols may show travelers the way.

Symbols and Concepts

Symbols and Meaning

A *symbol* is anything that stands for or refers to something other than itself. The word "book" stands for printed pages within a firm cover—the object called a book—but of course the symbol is not the book. We can think about the real books on the shelves and talk about them through the use of language symbols. Words are thus important components of our *symbol system.*

Symbols are not limited to the familiar language of words. There are other symbolic languages, such as the language of logic or of mathematics. Tangible symbols include such things as a stop sign, a cross on a church, a musical note, a red flag, or a paper dollar. Symbols always stand for something else. Of course we can talk about the symbols themselves. We can talk about the spelling of a word or the painting of a sign. When we do, we use symbols to refer to other symbols.

We think in symbols. Because verbal language is a rich symbolic process, much of our thinking goes on in terms of language. But it is possible to think without the aid of language. Some composers claim that they "hear" the music they are composing before they actually write it down or play it on an instrument. We could mentally visualize a dance routine, a series of tennis strokes, or some other athletic maneuver without resorting to language.

A symbol conveys *meaning.* It provides information about some object or event to which it refers and thereby suggests appropriate action to the person who perceives it. Symbolic stimuli produce reactions appropriate to some stimulus *other than themselves.* The sign POISON alerts one to danger,

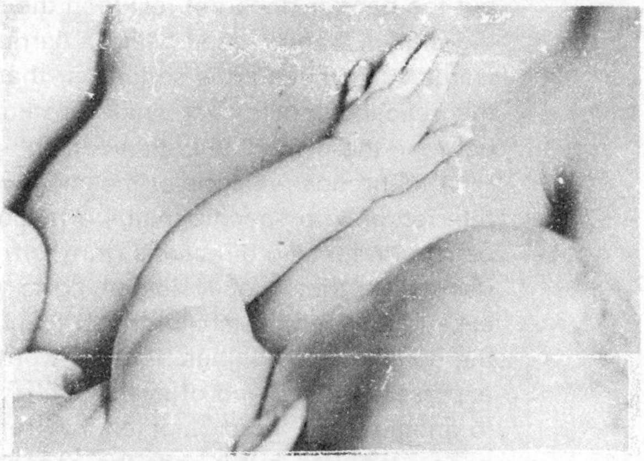

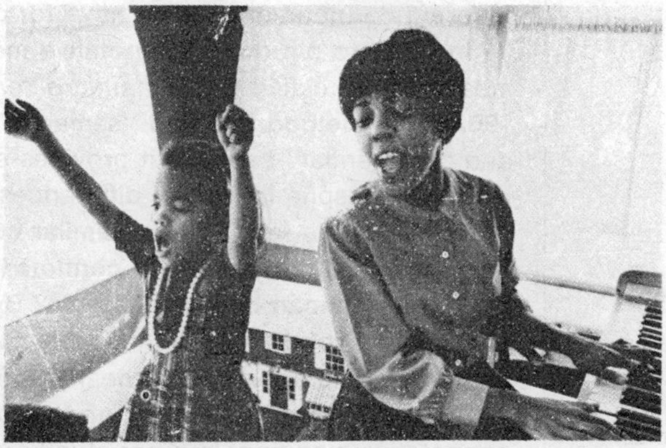

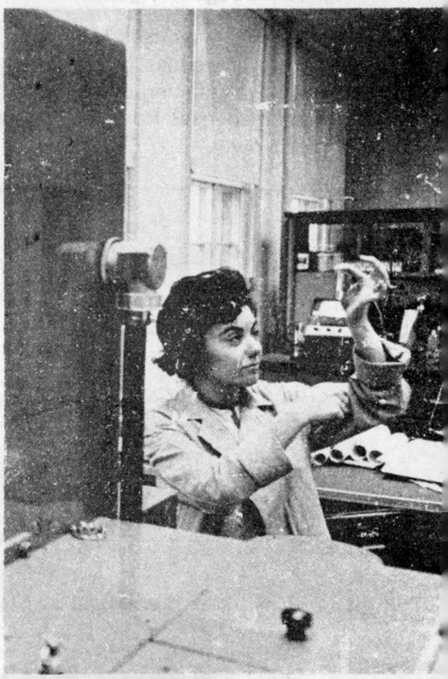

The word "woman" has numerous connotations. How many can you think of?

but the danger does not reside in the sign itself; a STOP sign arrests movement, without itself being a barricade or hazard. The fact that signs and words carry meaning is so familiar that it is a little surprising to find theoretical disputes over what constitutes meaning, and over the relationship between the symbol and its meaning.

A theoretical analysis of meaning would be less difficult if all symbols referred only to specific things or actions, such as names of objects (table, pencil) or specific directions (turn left, no parking). Such meanings are called *denotative;* they specify something to which you can point and basically are alike to all who can comprehend them. But *connotative* meanings accompany the denotative meanings of many words; connotations are emotional, usually expressing some kind of evaluation or preference, and vary from one person to another. The word "hippie" may refer to a specific group of nonconformists, but it adds the connotative meanings of being in tune with something ("hip") as well. Misunderstandings often arise because of the different connotations words have for different people.

In order to pin down connotative meanings more precisely, a method of measurement called the *semantic differential* has been developed (Osgood, 1962). The method is called "semantic" because it has to do with meaning, and "differential" because it provides several different dimensions of meaning. Despite individual differences in connotations, a fairly homogeneous group of people tend to have similar connotations for familiar words. For example, what distinctions in connotation do the words "good" and "nice" have for American college students? By using the semantic differential, it was found that "good" had slightly male overtones, and "nice" female ones. To express simple approval the nearly equivalent statements for the two sexes would be "He's a good man" and "She's a nice woman." As you can see, connotative meanings are not strictly rational.

Fig. 10-1 Osgood's semantic differential

Profiles of ratings used in arriving at a semantic differential for measuring the connotative meaning of the word "polite." Median responses from two groups of 20 subjects each.

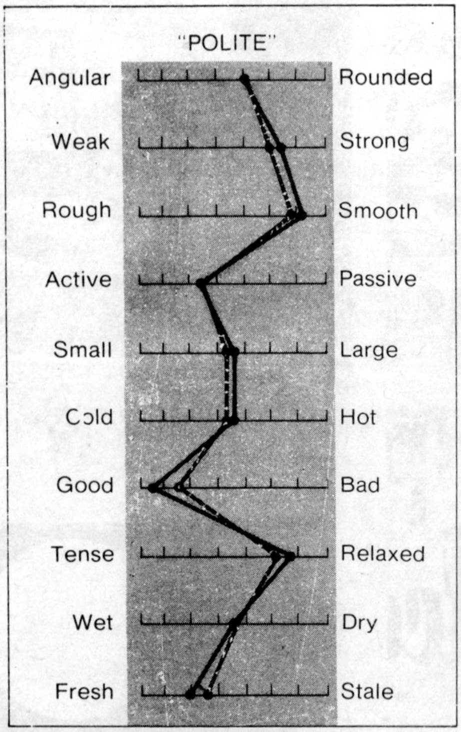

To determine the connotations of a word by the semantic differential method, the subject is asked to rate the word according to a number of bipolar adjective pairs; an example is the pair "strong-weak." With one member of an adjective pair at each end of a seven-point scale, the subject indicates the direction and intensity of his judgment by rating the word at some point on the scale. Figure 10-1 illustrates the scale values students assigned the word "polite." Note that the adjective pairs used have little to do with the denotative meaning of politeness.

Initially some 50 pairs of adjectives were used in determining the semantic differential for various words. But after analyzing many English words, it was found that the connotative meaning of most words could be expressed in terms of three basic dimensions: an *evaluative* dimension (such as good-bad, clean-dirty, sacred-profane), a *potency* dimension (strong-weak, powerless-powerful, light-heavy), and an *activity* dimension (fast-slow, active-passive, sharp-dull). These three dimensions account for a good share of connotative meanings, with the evaluative factor carrying the most weight. Subsequent studies have found that these same dimensions characterize connotative meaning in a wide variety of languages, including Japanese, Finnish, and the Kannada dialect of India (Osgood, 1967).

The semantic differential has also proved to be a promising method for distinguishing cultural groups. Figure 10-2 shows two examples of words rated by Hopi, Zuñi, and Navajo Indians. Although anthropologists regard these three tribes as distinct cultures, the Hopi and Zuñi cultures are more similar to each other (both being classified as Western Pueblo) than they are the Navajo. We can see this cultural similarity reflected in the semantic-differential profiles.

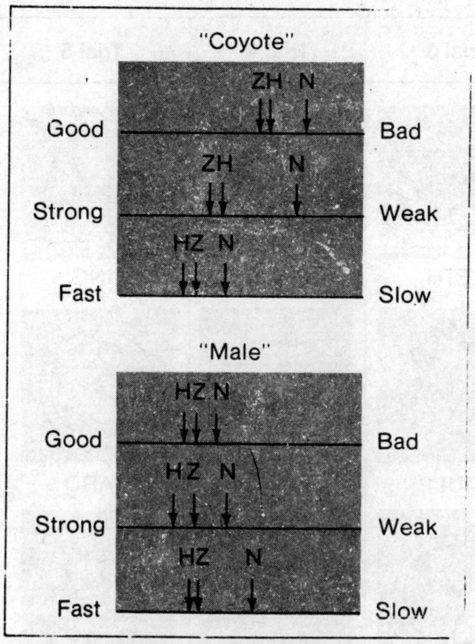

Fig. 10-2 Cultural differences reflected in the semantic differential

Two examples of word ratings made by Hopi (H), Zuñi (Z), and Navajo (N) Indians Note that the connotative meanings given by the Zuñi and Hopi are closer together than are those given by the Navajo. (After Maclay and Ware, 1961)

Concept Formation

When a symbol stands for a class of objects or events with common properties, we say that it refers to a concept. *Girl, holiday, vegetable,* and *round object* are examples of concepts based on common elements; *equality, longer,* and *smoother* are concepts based on common relations. We use concepts to order and classify our environment. Most words (with the exception of proper nouns) represent concepts in that they refer not to a single object or event but to a class. "The house on the corner of 10th and Market Streets" specifies a particular object; the word *house* alone refers to a class of buildings with common features. Concepts possess varying degrees of generality: the concept symbolized by the word *building* is more general than the concept of *house,* which in turn is more general than the concept of *cottage.*

Our superior position in the animal kingdom is based largely on our ability to use language and to learn concepts. But concepts can be learned without the use of language. Rats can learn the concept of triangularity—by being rewarded for selecting triangles of various shapes and sizes and not rewarded for responding to other geometrical forms, they can learn to respond consistently to triangles. Since the triangles vary in shape and size they are not responding to a specific object but to the concept of triangularity. Monkeys can learn the concept of "oddity" (see Figure 10-3). They can learn to select the odd stimulus object from a set of three objects, two of which are identical. The stimuli vary from trial to trial (for example, two circles and a square on one trial and two squares and a triangle on the next) so that the animal is not responding to a specific object but is learning to abstract the common property oddity.

Concept learning utilizes the psychological processes of generalization and discrimination (p. 198). In learning the concept of triangularity, a rat generalizes the response initially to other geometrical forms, but since these responses go unrewarded they are extinguished, and it eventually narrows the discrimination to triangles. A child learning the concept *dog* may generalize the term initially to include all small animals. But from parental corrections and personal observations the child learns to make finer discriminations until his concept approximates the conventional conception of *dog.* The child may refine the concept further and distinguish between

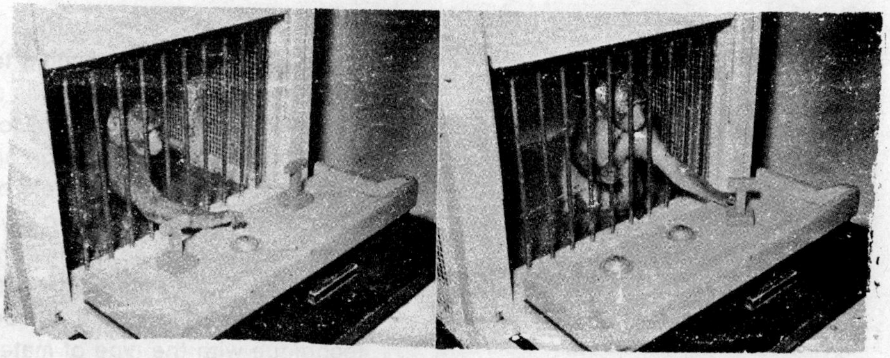

Fig. 10-3 Monkey solving the oddity problem

A monkey will learn to select the odd member of three objects if there is a bit of food or something else of interest in the well under it.

Fig. 10-4 Concept formation

Drawings similar to these were shown one at a time, starting on each trial from the top of the column and proceeding to the bottom. As each picture was shown, the subject tried to anticipate the nonsense word paired with it. After the subject responded the experimenter called out the correct nonsense word, which is listed below each picture. On the first trial the subject had no way of knowing what word was paired with a picture, but over the course of several trials he gradually learned to anticipate correctly on all pictures. Note that none of the pictures is repeated, so it is not learning a specific response to a specific stimulus, but rather learning a response to a concept. In this example the concept of face = RELK, building = LETH, tree = MULP, circle = FARD, the number two = LING, and the number five = DILT. (After Heidbreder, 1947)

friendly dogs, whose wagging tails indicate that approach is safe, and *unfriendly dogs,* whose growls signify that avoidance is the best response. Eventually the child will learn to distinguish among various breeds.

Because of their language ability, humans are able to deal with all sorts of concepts, from fairly concrete ones, such as *dog,* to highly abstract ones, such as *gravity, justice,* and *God.* But what kinds of concepts are attained most readily? Studies by Heidbreder (1947) indicated that concrete characteristics are generally easier to conceive than the more abstract relationships of form and number. These studies used a paired-associate technique with the type of material illustrated in Figure 10-4. On each trial several pictures were presented one at a time, and the subject was required to anticipate the response paired with each one. The experimenter arbitrarily assigned a different nonsense word as the response for each concept. Thus, MULP might refer to the object concept *tree,* FARD to the spatial concept of circular patterns, and DILT to the number concept of five objects. On the second trial *new* pictures representing the same concepts were paired with the original responses. For example, Figure 10-4 shows six pictures that might be presented on trial 1, a new set of six pictures for trial 2, and so on. The experiment continued until the subject responded correctly to all stimuli on a trial.

A series of such experiments showed that object concepts (*shoe, book, bird*) were the easiest to learn, spatial forms the next easiest, and then numbers. Our thinking apparently tends to run to *objects* rather than to *abstractions.* Piaget's stages of intellectual development (p. 75) indicate that the child first learns object concepts and develops more abstract concepts only as he grows older. Interestingly enough, with certain types of brain damage an individual may lose the ability to deal with abstract concepts and respond only in terms of concrete ideas. For example, he may be able to throw balls accurately into three boxes located at different distances from him but not be able to state which box is nearest and which farthest or explain his procedure in aiming. This inability to think abstractly is so marked in certain types of brain damage that performance on concept-learning tasks is sometimes used as a basis for diagnosis.

Forming number concept

Structure of Language

Language serves two major functions: (1) it allows us to communicate with one another—if the speaker and listener share a common meaning of words—and (2) it provides a system of symbols and rules that facilitates our thinking. The study of language involves both linguistics and psychology. Linguists are concerned with a formal description of the *structure of language,* including speech sounds, their meanings, and the grammar that relates sounds and meanings. Psychologists want to know how we acquire language and how such a system functions. But these enterprises cannot profitably be conducted in isolation; the field called *psycholinguistics* incorporates linguistic and psychological methods to study the mental processes underlying the acquisition and use of language.

Phonemes and Morphemes

All languages are based on a certain number of elementary sounds called *phonemes.* Some languages work with as few as 15 phonemes; others use as many as 85. The English language has about 45 phonemes, which correspond roughly to the different ways we pronounce the vowels and consonants of the alphabet. The smallest meaningful units in the structure of a language are called *morphemes.* Morphemes may be root words, prefixes, or suffixes and may consist of one or more phonemes. The words *talk, rug,* and *strange* are single morphemes. *Strangeness* consists of two morphemes, *strange* and *ness,* both of which have meaning (the suffix *ness* implies "being" or "having the quality of").

Although there are well over a hundred thousand morphemes in the English language, many more would be possible if each of the 45 phonemes were used in every possible combination. But every language has certain restrictions on how phonemes can be sequenced and combined. In English, for example, we seldom use more than two (and never more than three) consonants to begin a morpheme, and even then, only certain consonants can be combined in an initial cluster. We have words that start with *str* or *spl* but none beginning with *zb* or *vg* as in some Slavic languages. The restrictions a language places on phoneme sequencing help prevent errors of interpretation. If morphemes used all possible combinations of phonemes, then a change in a single phoneme would produce a new morpheme. A language based on such a system would be highly susceptible to communication errors. As it is, when we come across the typographical error *fwice* we know that an *fw* beginning is not permissible in English, so we guess at the nearest permissible morpheme (with help from the context of the sentence) and come up with *twice*.

Phrase Structure and Rule Learning

Just as rules govern the sequencing of phonemes, rules also specify (1) how words are formed from morphemes (for example, add *s* to form the plural of some nouns) and (2) how sentences are formed from words. A sentence can be analyzed at a number of levels. The speech sounds can be analyzed and classified as phonemes. The phonemes can then be grouped into meaningful units as morphemes and words. And the words can be

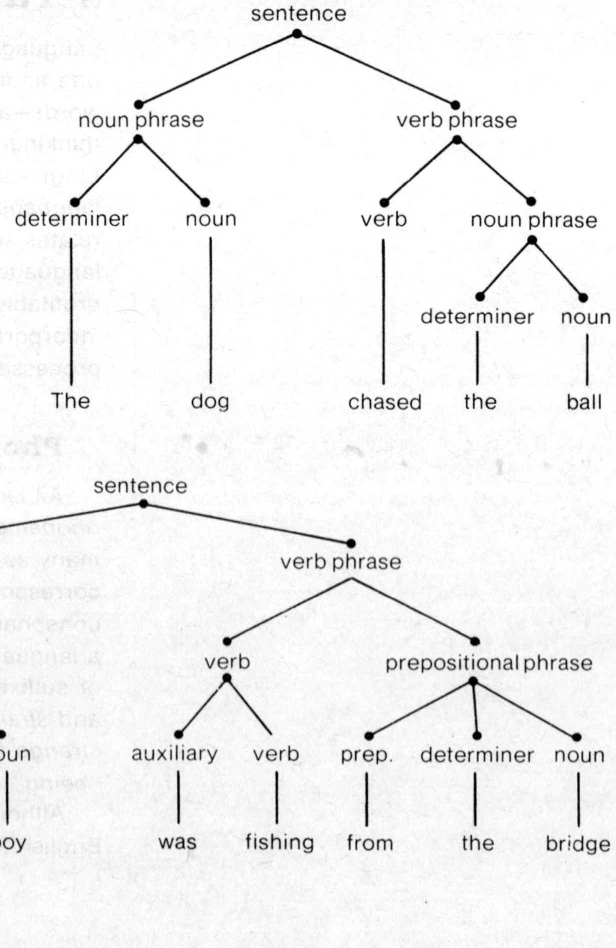

Fig. 10-5 Tree diagrams representing the phrase structure of two sentences

The phrase-marking shows how the words are related to one another and what role each plays in the sentence.

TABLE 10-1
Generative models of language

The notion of phrase-structure grammars originated with Noam Chomsky of Massachusetts Institute of Technology and has played an important role in psycholinguistics. Such a grammar involves *rewrite rules.* For example, the fact that a sentence (S) consists of a noun phrase (NP) followed by a verb phrase (VP) is represented in a rule of the form S ⟶ NP + VP. The arrow is an instruction to rewrite the left-hand symbol as the string of symbols on the right-hand side. The rewrite rule tells us that the symbol S can be replaced by NP + VP; other rules will similarly unpack NP and VP into their constituents. For example, a very simple grammar of a fragment of English might be as follows (Determiner = DET, Auxiliary = Aux):

1. S ⟶ NP + VP
2. NP ⟶ Det + N
3. VP ⟶ Aux + V + NP
4. N ⟶ (girl, man, paper, . . .)
5. V ⟶ (run, hit, took, . . .)
6. Aux ⟶ (will, can, may, . . .)
7. Det ⟶ (the, a, some, . . .)

We can use these rewrite rules to generate the sentence "The girl will read the book." The process can be represented by the following *tree diagram:*

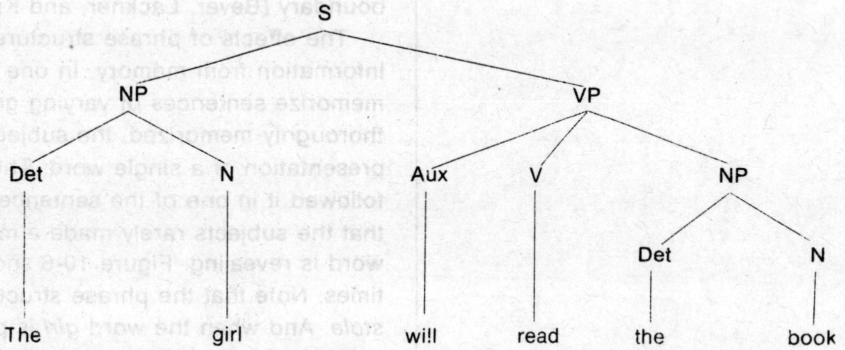

Rule 1 allows us to rewrite S as NP + VP. Rule 2 permits NP to be rewritten as Det + N. Rule 7 lets Det be rewritten as *the;* and Rule 4 lets N be rewritten as *girl.* In a similar way we can rewrite the VP side of the tree until the desired sentence is generated.

Because these rules center about phrases, they are called *phrase-structure rules.* A *transformational rule* is a rewrite rule that allows a complete sentence to be rewritten as a different sentence. For example, the simple active sentence *"John hit the ball"* is related to the passive sentence *"The ball was hit by John"* by a transformational rule that rewrites any active sentence into its passive form. These transformational grammars capture our intuitions about the similarity between active and passive forms of a sentence, since both are presumed to derive from the same underlying idea.

Transformations, at the level of relationships among words (phrase-structure rules) and relationships among sentences (transformational rules), are assumed by some psycholinguists to reflect universal properties of the mind. Research relevant to this proposition is reviewed in the text.

categorized into phrases to give structure to the sentence. Linguists have found it useful to describe a sentence by the organization of its various phrases. Such a description is called the *phrase structure* of the sentence (see Table 10-1).

Figure 10-5 shows the phrase structures of two sentences. The phrase-marking shows how the words are related to one another and what role each plays in the sentence. The location of pauses is also fixed by the phrase structure. In reading aloud the first sentence we normally would say (*the dog*) (*chased*) (*the ball*) rather than (*the*) (*dog chased*) (*the ball*) or (*the dog*) (*chased the*) (*ball*). In spontaneous speech only a fluent speaker consistently follows the pauses specified by the phrase structure of the sentence. Most of us in searching for the appropriate word with which to express our thoughts frequently pause in the middle of phrases. Evidence shows, however, that despite such fumbling, our listener tends to hear the pauses in the proper place. In an experiment in which a click sounded at various times while a sentence was being uttered, the click tended to be perceived at the boundaries of phrases rather than at the point where it actually occurred. Further, the clicks were not simply displaced to positions where there were pauses; rather, they were displaced only to those pauses that marked the boundary of phrases. These results suggest that the phrase structure of sentences function as natural units in the perception of speech—in normal conversation the listener does not perceive each word as a unit, but rather the phrase operates as a unit. These perceptual units tend to resist intrusions, and a click that occurs during a phrase is not processed as part of the unit, but is perceived as being displaced toward the phrase boundary (Bever, Lackner, and Kirk, 1969).

The effects of phrase structure are also evident in the retrieval of information from memory. In one experiment subjects were required to memorize sentences of varying grammatical form. Once the sentences were thoroughly memorized, the subject was given a series of tests involving the presentation of a single word. The subject's task was to give the word that followed it in one of the sentences; the sentences were so well memorized that the subjects rarely made a mistake but the time taken to supply the next word is revealing. Figure 10-6 shows a sample sentence with its response times. Note that the phrase structure involves a major break between *girl* and *stole*. And when the word *girl* is presented it takes longer to respond with *stole* than for any other pair of words in the sentence. These and other data from the experiment suggest that the sentences are stored with their phrase structures preserved. When a test occurs, the speed of response depends on the location of the test word in the phrase structure of the sentence.

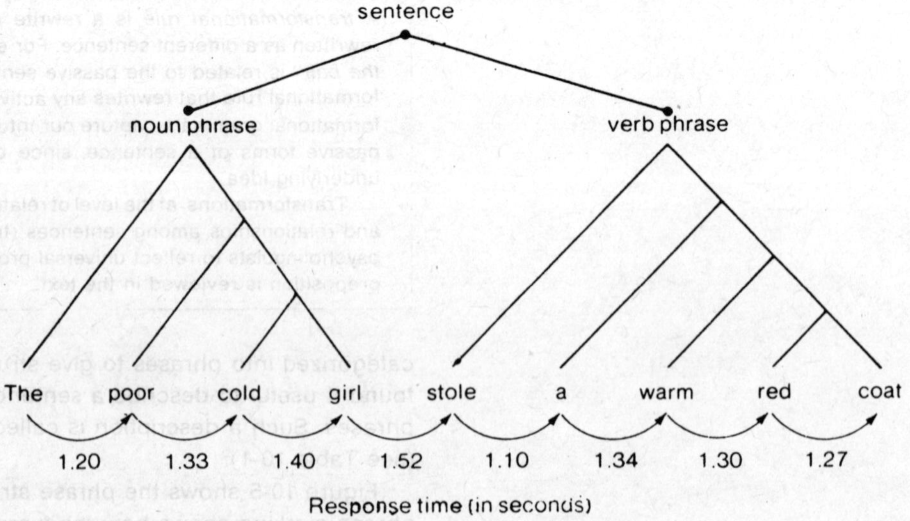

Fig. 10-6 Response latency and phrase structure

Listed at the bottom of the tree are the response times to the test words. For example, when *poor* is presented it took the subject 1.33 seconds to say *cold*. Note that the slowest response time occurs at the break between the noun phrase and the verb phrase. (Adapted from Wilkes and Kennedy, 1969)

Deep Structure and Surface Structure

Language is a system that relates sound to meaning. The same meaning can be expressed by different patterns of sound. The sentences *John read the book* and *The book was read by John* share the same meaning. Conversely, a single sound pattern can have more than one meaning. The sentence *They are eating apples* can be interpreted as stating that some people are eating apples or that those apples are good for eating (see Figure 10-7). Examples of this sort have led to the distinction between the *surface structure* and the *deep structure* of a sentence. The concept of deep structure is used to refer to the intent of a sentence—the thought behind it. The surface structure is the actual sound sequence—the production of the sentence.

It is assumed that the deep structure is transformed into the surface structure by a series of rules. In theory, these *transformational rules* specify the steps by which the thought is related to the actual sentence. A simple declarative sentence (*The boy fed the dog*) is assumed to be closely related to its deep structure, having undergone fewer transformations than a passive sentence (*The dog was fed by the boy*) or other more complex sentences such as negatives.

Recoding in Memory

Related to the issue of deep structure is the question of what information is coded in memory when we hear something. While we generally remember

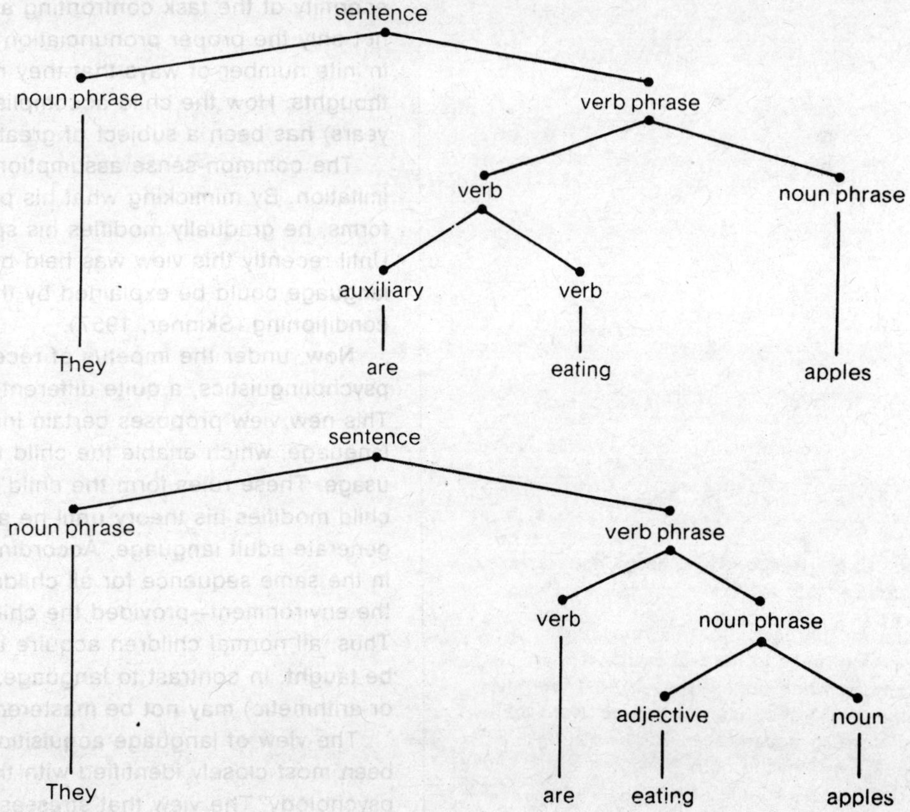

Fig. 10-7 An ambiguous sentence

Two phrase structures for the ambiguous sentence "They are eating apples."

what we have just heard, we often cannot repeat it word for word. It appears that the meaning of the message is remembered even when surface features of the sentence are forgotten. This phenomenon is illustrated by an experiment on memory for sentences. Subjects listened to recorded prose passages; at some point in the recording the message was unexpectedly interrupted and a test sentence was presented. These test sentences were either identical to a sentence presented in the passage, were altered so as to change the form of an earlier sentence without changing the meaning, or were altered to change the meaning. For example, if the sentence *The little girl hit the boy* appeared in the passage, then a change in form might yield the sentence *The boy was hit by the little girl,* whereas a change in meaning might yield *The boy hit the little girl.*

Subjects were very good at correctly identifying the original sentence or any change made in that sentence (whether involving form or meaning) if the test was given shortly after the sentence was read. However, when the test sentence was given after some intervening prose had been listened to, subjects could only recognize changes in meaning and not in form. Apparently, the original form of the sentence is held only long enough for comprehension; once a semantic interpretation has been made, the meaning alone is retained. The meaning of the sentence is coded in memory, but surface structure and stylistic details are soon forgotten (Sachs, 1967).

Development of Language

Our brief description of the structure of language should indicate the enormity of the task confronting a child learning to speak. He must master not only the proper pronunciation of words, but also their meaning and the infinite number of ways that they may be combined into sentences to express thoughts. How the child accomplishes this task in such a brief time (4–5 years) has been a subject of great interest to psychologists.

The common-sense assumption is that the child learns to speak by imitation. By mimicking what his parents say, and practicing these speech forms, he gradually modifies his speech until it approximates adult language. Until recently this view was held by many psychologists; the acquisition of language could be explained by the principles of classical and operant conditioning (Skinner, 1957).

Now, under the impetus of recent work in linguistics and psycholinguistics, a quite different picture of child language has emerged. This new view proposes certain innate, or built-in, mechanisms for processing language, which enable the child to construct his own "rules" for language usage. These rules form the child's "theory" of how language works; the child modifies his theory until he arrives at one that permits him to correctly generate adult language. According to this viewpoint, the same rules appear in the same sequence for all children and are little affected by conditions in the environment—provided the child receives some exposure to the language. Thus, all normal children acquire a native language; it is not a skill that must be taught. In contrast to language, some skills (such as swimming, reading, or arithmetic) may not be mastered despite considerable instruction.

The view of language acquisition that emphasizes the role of learning has been most closely identified with the behavioristic, or S-R, approach to psychology. The view that stresses the development of rules based on certain

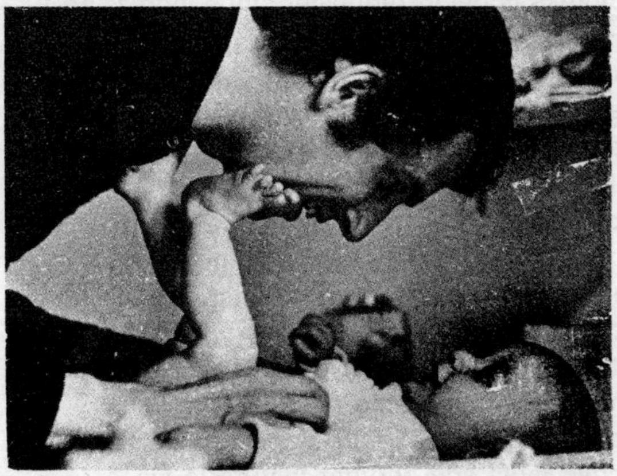

In babbling, infants produce the sounds that will later form the basis of language.

innate capacities is more closely associated with cognitive psychology. In this section we will examine the development of a child's language, noting evidence bearing on each of these views of language acquisition.

Babbling and Initial Words

During the first months of life vocalization is very limited, but at about six months infants begin to produce an immense variety of sounds in increasingly complex combinations. This repetition of the syllables resembling those used in adult speech is called *babbling.* During the early babbling stage infants are able to produce most of the sounds that form the basis of language—including sounds used in languages other than their own. Experiments have shown that the babbling of a Chinese baby cannot be distinguished from that of a Russian or English infant during this period (Atkinson, MacWhinney, and Stoel, 1970). By about nine months the range of babbled sounds narrows, and the infant begins to concentrate on those sounds that will appear in his first words. In a sense, the child stops experimenting with sounds and concentrates on those syllables that are to form the initial words.

Regardless of the child's native language, the first words consist of a front consonant, *p, m, b,* or *t* (produced with the tongue in the front of the mouth), and a back vowel, *e* or *a* (produced with the tongue in the back). This undoubtedly is the reason why the words for *mama* and *papa* are so similar in many languages. This is also why English children say *tut* before *cut;* Swedish children say *tata* before *kata;* and Japanese children say *ta* before *ka* (McNeill, 1970). Interestingly enough, back consonants such as *k* and *g,* which the child cannot yet use properly in words, may appear correctly in vocal play. There seems to be a difference between spontaneously producing a sound and producing it voluntarily. A child who uses only *p, m,* and *a* in speech will at the same time use many other sounds in nonspeech (Jakobson, 1968).

Words and Meaning

To produce a word sound is one accomplishment, but more is required before the word has meaning—before it stands as a symbol for something else. How do children learn to associate words with particular objects and events?

In the simplest case the parent repeatedly names an object with which the child is familiar, for example, saying *doll* every time he hands the child his doll. Through repeated pairing of the word with the object, the child learns to associate the two. An example that is more readily observable in the child's behavior is the parent's saying *no* and simultaneously slapping the child's hand when he reaches for a forbidden object. The hand-withdrawal response, which was originally elicited by the slap, is soon elicited by the word alone. An observer would say that the child had learned the meaning of the word *no.* You can recognize this situation as an example of classical conditioning (p. 195).

Operant conditioning may also play a role in the child's learning to associate word sounds and meaning. If the child produces a sound that approximates a word—for example, *muk* (milk) or *oukay* (cookie)—the parent may hasten to provide the food he thinks is being requested, thus increasing the likelihood that the child will produce a similar sound when hungry.

Although some of the child's early words may have an adult meaning, studies indicate that the child's use and interpretation of most of his early words differ considerably from those of an adult. When a child first uses a word, he tends to *overextend* it to include much more than the adult meaning. For example, the word *doggie* (first learned in reference to a dog) may subsequently be used to refer to all animals with four legs, or all small animals that move, or all objects that are furry. This is the problem we discussed in the section on concept formation.

Overextension occurs because the child is using only one or two features as a criterion. Gradually the child narrows his meaning by adding specific features. Thus, if the concept of *doggie* includes all four-legged animals and the next word learned is *cow,* the child must add another feature to his criterion. For *cow* he might add the feature of sound (moos), or size (large compared to dogs), or shape (horns, udder). At the same time he is probably adding more features to his concept of *doggie* (e.g., barks, relatively small, furry, etc.). As he learns more words that take over part of the domain he had reserved for dogs (e.g., cats are also relatively small and furry) he narrows his meaning of the word until it finally approaches the adult meaning.

By three or four years of age the child's overextensions of meaning are less obvious, but closely related words may still be confused. With word pairs such as *more-less, tall-short, same-different,* and *before-after,* the meaning of one of the words is initially extended to cover both. The average three year old does not differentiate *more* from *less;* rather they are treated as synonyms. He can correctly point to the tree that has *more* apples on it. When asked to point to the tree with *less* apples, he is apt to indicate the one that has more. He seems to know that *less* refers to quantity, but interprets it the same as *more.*

Studies have shown similar results with other word pairs that represent opposite ends of a dimension. Children at first respond to *same* and *different* as if they both meant *same,* and to *before* and *after* as if both meant *before.* Only as specific features are added to the meaning of each word in the pair do the two become differentiated (E. Clark, 1973).

Thus we see that children acquire the meaning of words by a gradual process of discrimination, proceeding from those more general features that characterize the word to specific ones.

Primitive Sentences

Associating vocal responses with objects and events is only a small part of the total process of learning a language. After the child has acquired a modest vocabulary he begins to form sentences. Eventually he must comprehend long, complicated sentences and produce such sentences on his own. This is a vastly more complicated problem than learning to use single words, and it seems unlikely that grammatical competency can be acquired by learning to associate one word sequence with another. There are too many possible combinations for each one to be learned via a process of operant or classical conditioning. It seems more likely that the child learns *rules* for generating acceptable sequences of words. Even as adults we may not be able to verbalize the exact form of these rules, but we know when an utterance is correct. We know, for example, that *ran handsome rapidly boys* is not a sentence because the words do not follow the sequence characteristic of English sentences. We find this sequence unacceptable, not because we have never heard it before, but because it does not match the rules we employ for generating sentences.

Another reason to doubt that simple learning principles can account for the child's acquisition of grammatical sequence lies in the fact that many of the child's earliest grammatical constructions are not imitations of adult sentences. In their spontaneous speech two year olds will say things like *all-gone shoe* and *go car Daddy,* which undoubtedly they have never heard an adult say. And a child imitating parental speech does not mimic the entire phrase but leaves out prepositions, articles, suffixes, prefixes, and auxiliary words as illustrated in the samples below.

PARENT SAYS	CHILD REPEATS
Where is Daddy's coat	Where Daddy coat
John will be unhappy	John unhappy
He is going out	He go out

Speech at this stage of development (at about two years) has been termed *telegraphic speech.* The child usually preserves the order of the parent's speech but leaves out the less important words or word parts.

The same telegraphic quality also is present in the child's spontaneous speech at this age. The words he selects to repeat or to use on his own are usually those that carry the most *meaning* as well as those that receive the most *stress* or emphasis. If you read aloud the parent's sentences given above, you will note that the stressed words are the ones repeated by the child. In most languages the stressed words are also the words that convey the meaning of the sentence. In English, for example, we seldom emphasize articles or prepositions in speaking; and the same is true for languages such as French, Russian, or Spanish. In German, however, more emphasis is placed on the articles *a* (ein) and *the* (das) and the possessive pronoun *my* (mein), and these words tend to be preserved by the German child in telegraphic speech (Park, 1970).

The dog is biting the cat.

The cat is biting the dog.

Fig. 10-8 Word order and meaning

One of a pair of pictures used with young children to test their understanding of the agent-object relationship expressed by word order. (Brown, 1973)

Thus in early speech (whether imitative or spontaneous) the child tends to preserve those elements of adult speech that are the most meaningful and the most salient or perceptually distinct. Proper word order is one of the cues to meaning that children appear to discriminate early. Two year olds, shown the pictures illustrated in Figure 10-8 and asked to point to the one where *The dog is biting the cat* (or *The cat is biting the dog*), will answer correctly 60 percent of the time, and three year olds give 85 percent correct responses (Brown, 1973).

Despite their brevity, the child's early utterances express most of the basic functions of language. Many of the first two-word sentences are devoted to naming objects (*see shoe*) and describing actions (*car go*). Quantitative and qualitative modifiers appear early (*pretty girl, big boat*), and some form of negation develops a little later (*no hungry, not wash*). Cross-cultural studies show a remarkable similarity in the functions served by early speech and the form and sequence in which they occur. Table 10-2 gives examples of some of the major functions served by the two-word sentences of children speaking different languages.

At this stage of language development the child comprehends much more

FUNCTION OF UTTERANCE	LANGUAGE ENGLISH	 GERMAN	 RUSSIAN	 SAMOAN
Locate, Name	there book that car see doggie	buch da [book there] gukuk wauwau [see doggie]	Tosya tam [Tosya there]	Keith lea [Keith there]
Demand, Desire	more milk give candy want gum	mehr milch [more milk] bitte apfel [please apple]	yeshchë moloko [more milk] day chasy [give watch]	mai pepe [give doll] fia moe [want sleep]
Negate	no wet no wash not hungry allgone milk	nicht blasen [not blow] kaffee nein [coffee no]	vody net [water no] gus' tyu-tyu [goose gone]	le 'ai [not eat] uma mea [allgone thing]
Describe Event or Situation	Bambi go mail come hit ball block fall baby highchair	puppe kommt [doll comes] tiktak hängt [clock hangs] sofa sitzen [sofa sit] messer schneiden [cut knife]	mama prua [mama walk] papa bay-bay [papa sleep] korka upala [crust fell] nashla yaichko [found egg] baba kreslo [grandma armchair]	pa'u pepe [fall doll] tapale 'oe [hit you] tu'u lalo [put down]
Indicate Possession	my shoe mama dress	mein ball [my ball] mamas hut [mama's hat]	mami chashka [mama's cup] pup moya [navel my]	lole a'u [candy my] polo 'oe [ball your] paluni mama [balloon mama]
Modify, Qualify	pretty dress big boat	milch heiss [milk hot] armer wauwau [poor dog]	mama khoroshaya [mama good] papa bol'shoy [papa big]	fa'ali'i pepe [headstrong baby]
Question	where ball	wo ball [where ball]	gde papa [where papa]	fea Punafu [where Punafu]

Source: Slobin (1971).

TABLE 10-2
Functions of two-word sentences in child speech, with examples from several languages

than he can express. Moreover, he intends to communicate more than his two-word sentences say on the surface; thus, the sentence *Mommy book* may mean *That is mommy's book* in one instance and *Mommy, give me the book* in another. It is clear from the context in which these utterances occur that the child understands the differences in meaning, but apparently is limited at this stage to sentences of two words in length. In order to speak so that someone other than mommy will understand, the child must learn to produce longer sentences with correct grammatical structures.

Complex Sentences

Children progress rapidly from two-word utterances to more complex sentences. By the time they are three many children are constructing sentences as complicated as those in Table 10-3. The progression, in terms of

TABLE 10-3
Representative examples of complex sentences taken from the records of one child between two and three years of age

AGE (YEAR–MONTH)	EXAMPLES
2–0	You lookit that book; I lookit this book.
2–6	I do pull it the way he hafta do that so he doesn't —so the big boy doesn't come out.
2–8	And that mouse is not scary; it's a library friend.
2–8	You play with this one and I play with this.
2–8	He was stuck and I got him out.
2–8	I can't put it on—too little.
2–8	He still has milk and spaghetti.
2–10	Here's a seat. It must be mine if it's a little one.
2–10	I went to the aquarium and saw the fish.
2–10	I want this doll because she's big.
2–10	When I was a little girl I could go "geek-geek" like that; but now I can go "this is a chair."

Source: Limber (1973).

morpheme usage and syntax, is quite predictable. For example, one of the first ways to expand a two-word sentence is to modify the noun phrase by a possessive; *want hat* becomes *want daddy hat.* The first complex constructions to appear in children's speech are object complements. These are noun-like versions of sentences serving as a subject within another sentence; *Watch me do it* or *I want to go home* are examples. The next step is the use of conjunctions to form complex sentences; for example, *You play with this one and I play with this* or *I want this doll because she's big.* The sequence of development is remarkably similar for all children.

While they are expanding the length of their utterances, children are also progressing from simple declarative sentences to sentences that have undergone grammatical transformations. An example can be seen in the formation of questions with *wh-words* (what, who, why, etc.). At first the child is able to carry out only one transformation in the same sentence. His wh-questions initially appear in the form *What the dog can eat?* or *Where I should put it?* The child has performed one grammatical operation—preposing the question word—but has failed to perform another—transposing the subject and auxiliary. Yet at this same stage, the child can correctly transpose in a yes-no question; he says *Can the dog eat?* It appears as if the child can perform either transformation singly, but is unable (because of some kind of performance limitation) to use both in the same sentence. Somewhat later he can generate a sentence requiring two transformations but cannot produce the appropriate adult sentence when three transformations are required (Bellugi-Klima, 1968).

The fact that children say things like *Where I should put it?* or *What the dog can eat?* also reveals that they are not simply imitating adult speech; they have never heard adults use that word order in a question. Children seem to be developing their own rule system in a gradual approach to the adult system. And they often filter adult speech through their system.

Adult: Say what I say: "Where should I put it?"
Child: Where I should put it?

Another example of the child's attempts to apply grammatical rules systematically is found in the use of certain verbs that have an irregular past tense (*come-came, run-ran, take-took*). These verbs are among the earliest acquired and are heard frequently in both the present and past tense, so the child has ample opportunity to learn both forms. Initially a child will use the past tense correctly—for example *Mommy came home* or *Daddy took the book.* Later, when he begins to acquire regular verbs and learns the rule that past tenses are formed by adding *-ed,* he will regularize the irregular verbs. He will say *Mommy comed home* or *Mommy camed home* and *Daddy tooked the book* or *Daddy taked the book.* Verb forms that have been practiced a great deal are replaced by forms that the child has not used before and may never have heard. The child appears to be striving for a general rule. Eventually he learns that verbs such as *come* and *take* are exceptions to the past-tense rule, and he returns to his initial correct form—saying *Mommy came home* and *Daddy took the book.* The same sort of learning procedure occurs with other exceptions to grammatical rules, such as the plural formation of *man;* the sequence followed by the child is *men, mans, men.* Children acquire general rules in learning a language and only through time and experience learn to modify these rules to accommodate exceptions.

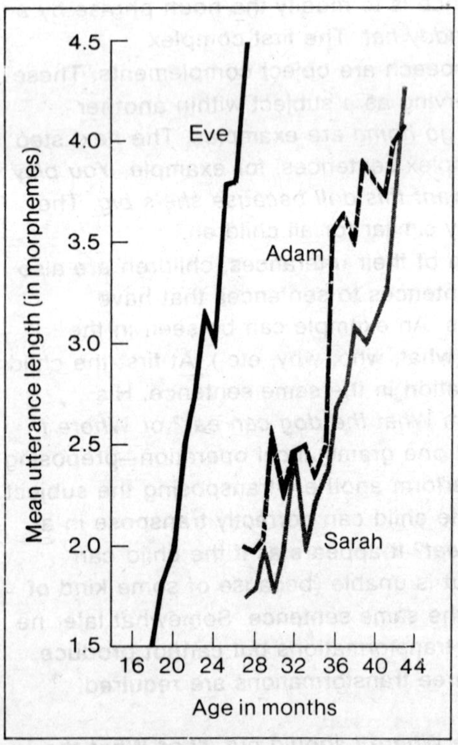

Fig. 10-9 Length of an utterance and age

Mean utterance lengths for three children plotted against their chronological age. Note that Eve has reached an utterance length of 4 by about 26 months of age, whereas Adam and Sarah do not reach this level until about 42 months. (Brown, 1973)

Invariance of Language Development

All children appear to master the various grammatical complexities in about the same order, although at different rates. One child, at two years of age, may use longer, more complex sentences than another child utters at four years (see Figure 10-9). The rate of language acquisition undoubtedly depends on a number of factors, including intelligence and the amount of verbal exchange within the home.

The *order* in which the child acquires his linguistic knowledge, however, seems to follow a fixed sequence that is only minimally related to the frequency with which the child hears specific utterances or certain types of grammatical constructions. And the same developmental sequence found among English-speaking children seems to occur, with only minor deviations, among children learning any language.

How do we explain the universality in the stages of language acquisition? One possibility is that the human brain is innately programmed to process linguistic input; the child operates on the language he hears and extracts grammatical rules of increasing complexity as various biological mechanisms mature. Some psychologists who hold to this view have suggested that there is a biologically-determined "critical period" for language development; if an individual is not exposed to language before age 14 or 15 (about the time the brain stops growing), he will be unable to acquire language (Lenneberg, 1967). Evidence bearing on this assumption is difficult to find. The few rare cases where attempts have been made to teach language to *feral children* (children who have been left as infants to grow up in the wild) have failed; but these results are confounded by such factors as possible mental retardation. Evidence does show that individuals who learn a second language in their teens or later do so with more difficulty and less "naturally" than a young child and usually retain something of an accent.

Another, more likely, possibility is that children acquire linguistic knowledge in an invariant order because the way they perceive and operate

Early exploration and manipulation help the child to learn "in" and "on."

on their environment progresses in a similar sequence. Linguistic development may mirror cognitive development. A child cannot use words correctly without understanding the concepts they represent. For example, all children have some understanding of position in space before they understand the concept of time. In their early explorations children move themselves and their toys into various positions; and one of their first manipulations is to place a toy *in* something. In language acquisition the first prepositions a child uses consistently are *in* and *on,* both of which specify spatial location. The prepositions *into* (which specifies location *plus* direction) and *over* and *under* (location *plus* relation) tend to occur later. The use of the preposition *in* to express temporal relations (*in a minute, in a week*) occurs still later (H. Clark, 1973). These observations illustrate how the acquisition of specific word forms depends upon the child's cognitive development.

Leaving aside the question of the innateness of linguistic ability, we can summarize by saying that language acquisition depends on learning the meaning of words and on developing general rules that permit one to comprehend and generate an infinite variety of sentences. The child starts out with his own rule system and gradually modifies the rules until they approximate adult rules and hence adult linguistic performance.

Language and Forms of Thought

Language in Children's Thinking

A child's ability to use language corresponds closely to his ability to deal with concepts and relationships. This correspondence is illustrated by an experiment in which preschool children were taught to select the smaller of a pair of squares, each mounted on the lid of a box. If the child chose the

CRITICAL DISCUSSION

Can Animals Learn a Language?

There is no doubt that some animals can communicate with one another. Many animals have "distress cries" that signal the approach of danger. By a sequence of "dance movements" honeybees communicate the direction and distance of food sources. When food is close by, the dance pattern is circular. More remote food sources are indicated by a dance in the form of a figure eight; the more rapid the dance, the farther away the food source (von Frisch, 1974). But communication is not the same as language. A single item of information can be communicated either verbally or nonverbally. Language, by using a system of arbitrary symbols, can convey an infinite variety of messages. It is this capacity that presumably sets man apart from the lower animals. Recent experiments with apes, however, suggest that language ability may not be uniquely human.

Psychologists have long been intrigued with the possibility of teaching language to an animal, and several unsuccessful attempts have been made. Over forty years ago a psychologist and his wife raised a female chimpanzee named Gua along with their son and

TABLE 10-4 Gesture-language signs used by a chimpanzee

MEANING OF SIGN	DESCRIPTION	CONTEXT
Come-gimme	Beckoning motion, with wrist or knuckles as pivot.	Sign made to persons or animals, also for objects out of reach. Often combined: "come tickle," "gimme sweet," etc.
More	Fingertips are brought together, usually overhead. (Correct ASL form: tips of the tapered hand touch repeatedly.)	When asking for continuation or repetition of activities such as swinging or tickling, for second helpings of food, etc. Also used to ask for repetition of some performance, such as a somersault.
Open	Flat hands are placed side by side, palms down, then drawn apart while rotated to palms up.	At door of house, room, car, refrigerator, or cupboard; with containers such as jars; and with faucets.
Hurry	Open hand is shaken at the wrist. (Correct ASL form: index and second fingers extended side by side as hand is shaken, but open hand is acceptable.)	Often follows signs such as "come-gimme," "out," "open," and "go," particularly if there is a delay before Washoe is obeyed. Also used while watching her meal being prepared.
Hear-listen	Index finger touches ear.	For loud or strange sounds: bells, car horns, sonic booms, etc. Also, for asking someone to hold a watch to her ear.
Hurt	Extended index fingers are jabbed toward each other. Can be used to indicate location of pain.	To indicate cuts and bruises on herself or on others. Can be elicited by red stains on a person's skin or by tears in clothing.
Sorry	Fisted hand clasps and unclasps at shoulder. (Correct ASL form: fisted hand is rubbed over heart with circular motion.)	After biting someone, or when someone has been hurt in another way (not necessarily by Washoe). When told to apologize for mischief.
Dog	Repeated slapping on thigh.	For dogs and for barking.
Baby	Arms crossed in front of body with hands grasping elbows; arms move in rocking motion.	For human infants, and for dolls and figurines, including animal dolls, such as a toy duck, and miniatures, such as a toy car.
Can't	Tip of index finger extended from closed hand. Index fingers touch, then move down and to side of body.	First used to signal inability to perform on potty chair. Later spontaneously transferred by Washoe to indicate inability to perform a difficult sign or to do something beyond her ability, such as breaking a metal rod.
Different	Tips of index fingers hooked and extended from closed hands. Hooked fingers are grasped and then drawn apart.	For two or more objects that differ in appearance, such as unmatched shoes or toy blocks, or a shoe and a toy block.
Help	Palm of flat hand is brought up repeatedly to contact closed fist of the other hand.	For assistance with tasks that are difficult, operating locks and keys, looping a rope around a rafter, etc.

Source: Gardner and Gardner (1972).

NOTE: These are only a few of the signs used by Washoe. ASL stands for American Sign Language.

compared the two developmentally. Although Gua showed considerable comprehension of English, responding appropriately to some 70 commands, she never learned to speak (Kellogg and Kellogg, 1933). A subsequent attempt, which focused more specifically on language training, was made by another couple, both psychologists. They adopted an infant chimpanzee, Vicki, and gave her intensive speech training, actually shaping her lips in an attempt to get her to produce various sounds. After three years Vicki could repeat only three sound patterns (*Mama, Papa,* and *cup*) that were recognizable approximations to English words (Hayes, 1951).

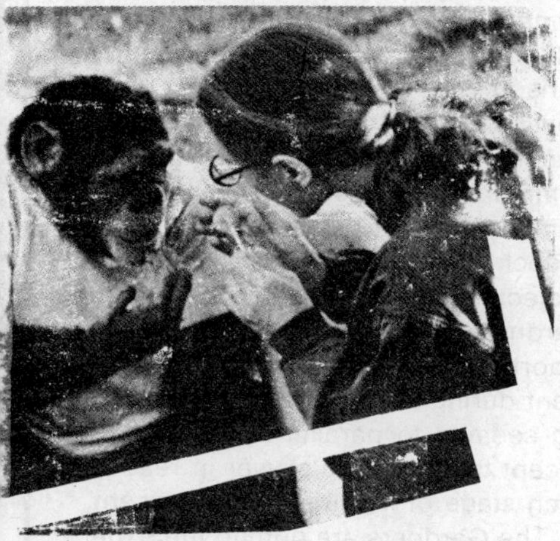
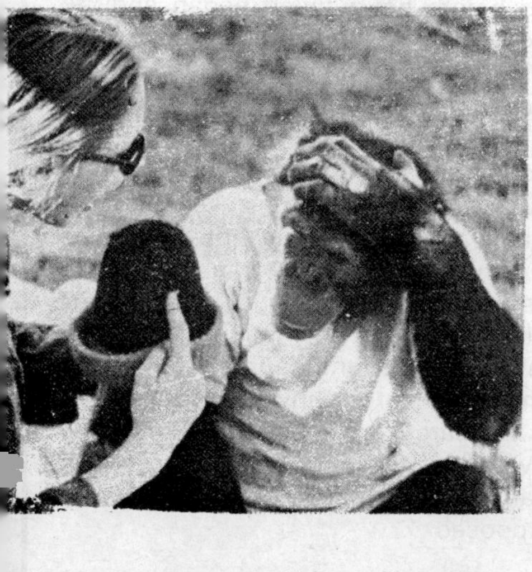

Washoe signing "hat" for woolen cap.

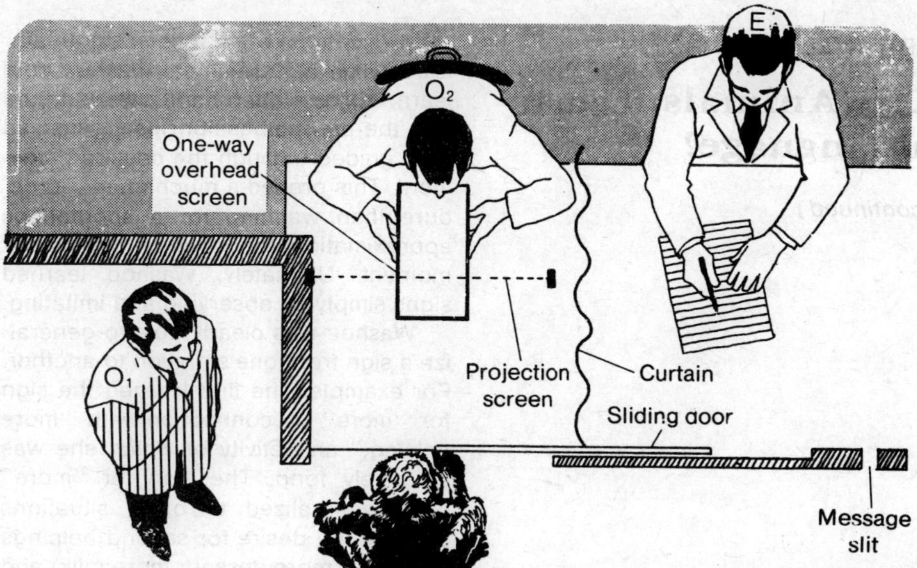

10-10 Apparatus used to test Washoe

Slides with pictures of objects were back-projected on a screen mounted inside a cabinet built into the wall between two rooms. An observer (O_1) standing beside the cabinet could observe Washoe's signing without seeing the pictures. Washoe began a trial herself by unlatching the sliding door of the cabinet. When she opened the door, O_1 asked her (in signs) what she saw, and wrote down her reply on a slip of paper which was passed to the experimenter (E) through a message slit in the wall. The experimenter operated a carousel projector, presenting the slides in a prearranged random order. A one-way vision screen placed above the projection screen allowed a second person (O_2) to observe Washoe and confirm the signs reported by O_1.

On the assumption that these earlier efforts failed because the chimpanzee's vocal apparatus is not adapted to produce human sounds, a more recent attempt has been made to teach a chimpanzee *American Sign Language*—a gesture language used by deaf persons in this country and Canada (Gardner and Gardner, 1971). Since chimpanzees are very facile with their fingers, this approach seemed promising. Training was begun with Washoe, a female chimpanzee, when she was about a year old and continued until age five. Washoe lived in a well-equipped house trailer with access to toys as well as extensive play areas. She heard no spoken words. Washoe's caretaker-companions communicated with her (and with each other while in her presence) by means of sign language. By the time she was three, Washoe used 34 signs appropriately, and spontaneously combined some of them into two- and three-word "sentences." By age five she understood several hundred signs and used over 130 of them reliably in many combinations. Examples of signs and the context in which they occurred are shown in Table 10-4.

Signs were first taught by shaping procedures (p. 204); the Gardners waited for Washoe to make a response that could be shaped into the sign they wished her to acquire. For example, when Washoe wanted to get through a door she would hold up both hands and pound on the door with her palms. This is the beginning position for the "open" sign. By waiting for Washoe to place her hands on the door and then lift them, the Gardners were able to shape a good

(*continued*)

CRITICAL DISCUSSION

Can Animals Learn a Language?

(*continued*)

approximation of the "open" sign. Later it became apparent that Washoe could learn signs if her hands were formed into the proper position for a sign and then guided through the desired movement. This proved a much faster procedure than waiting for a spontaneous approximation to occur at the proper moment. Ultimately, Washoe learned signs simply by observing and imitating.

Washoe was clearly able to generalize a sign from one situation to another. For example, she first learned the sign for "more" in connection with "more tickling," an activity of which she was extremely fond. The sign for "more" soon generalized to other situations such as the desire for second helpings of a food (more dessert, more milk) and then to the request that activities be continued (more swing, more write).

When shown pictures of objects she knew and asked "What's this?" Washoe was able to give the appropriate sign. And she enjoyed leafing through magazines by herself, signing the names of familiar objects as they appeared in the pictures. A careful record was kept of Washoe's daily "conversations;" a systematic program of testing was also administered using the apparatus shown in Figure 10-10.

Washoe combined a number of signs in sequences that seem similar to sentences of a two-year-old child. Examples are sign sequences that translated into English would mean *Hurry gimme toothbrush, Listen dog* (at the sound of barking), *You drink, Roger Washoe tickle, Come hug-love sorry sorry* (as appeasement for some wrongdoing). Washoe's sign order usually followed the proper grammatical sequence but did not always do so; for example, sometimes she would sign *Drink you* rather than *You drink.* However, two-year-old children often make the same mistake, and word order is less strict in sign language than in English. A study now in progress investigating the development of sign order in deaf children will provide a more appropriate comparison with Washoe's linguistic development (Brown, 1973). Until such data become available, Washoe's ability to communicate must be evaluated by comparison with studies of children's speech acquisition. The directors of Project Washoe, Allen and Beatrice Gardner at the University of Nevada, report that Washoe's linguistic development during the four years of her training seemed to parallel that of children except that she was slower in reaching each stage of language development.

The Gardners are putting the experience gained in training Washoe to use in a new project. This project has newborn chimps as subjects and deaf individuals as teachers. (Washoe was a year old before her training began and, although her companions were facile in American Sign Language, it was not their primary language.) The Gardners plan to train several chimps until intellectual maturity (12 to 16 years) and to study more explicitly the development of grammar. For example, the apparatus shown in Figure 10-10 can be used to test the understanding of agent-object relationships by determining whether a chimp can respond appropriately to the kinds of pictures shown in Figure 10-8.

Research projects of this kind may reveal that the linguistic gap between man and ape is narrower than previously supposed.

A project, similar to that of the Gardner's, is being conducted by Penny Patterson of Stanford University teaching a female gorilla named Koko sign language. Here Koko makes the sign for "sweater."

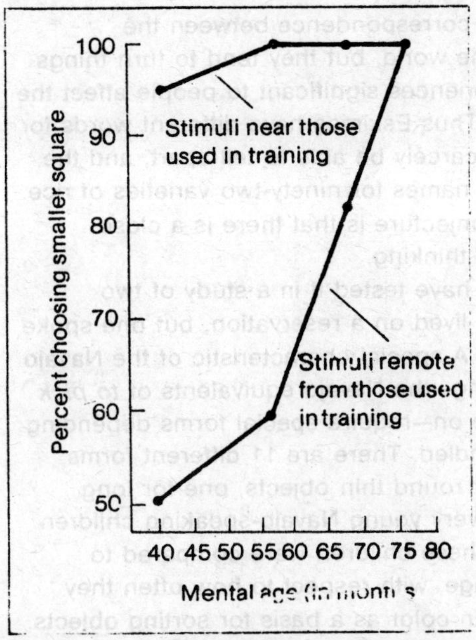

Fig. 10-11 Language and the perception of relationships

The older children (who were better able to state a test relationship in the form "The smaller one is always right") were able to transpose what they had learned from one pair to another remote pair, while the younger children could transpose the correct response only to pairs close in size to those used in training. (After Kuenne, 1946)

smaller square, he found the box open and an attractive toy inside. If he mistakenly chose the larger square, he found the box locked. The child began by learning to choose a six-inch square in preference to an eight-inch one. When he had learned to choose the six-inch square regularly, he was ready for the crucial tests with smaller squares.

He was now confronted with two test pairs, all pairs being smaller than the original ones. Of these smaller pairs, one (known as the "near pair") was close to the original squares in size (4.5 inches and 6 inches), the other (known as the "remote pair") was much smaller (1.4 and 1.9 inches). If the child had learned to "transpose," that is, to choose the smaller square regardless of absolute size, he should succeed in choosing the smaller square for both the near and the remote pairs. The results are plotted in Figure 10-11. Although all children did well on the near pair, they showed a striking increase in success with age on the remote pair.

The older children's success with the remote pair was clearly related to their use of language. If a child could say the equivalent of "The smaller one is always right," he could succeed with the remote pair. None of the children who failed to express in words the principle of correct choice during initial learning transposed the correct response on the test with the remote pair; 73 percent of the children who stated the correct solution in words, either spontaneously or upon questioning, successfully transposed what they had learned.

Of course, the older children were more developed as problem solvers, regardless of whether they relied upon language; the younger children were able to use language to some extent, but not well enough to serve as a tool for thinking in the transposition. We can recognize that language and thought are related, without assuming they are identical. Studies comparing the performances of deaf-mute children and those with normal hearing indicate that language may aid in solving problems of relationships and concept formation, but it is by no means essential for the development of such cognitive abilities (Robertson and Youniss, 1969).

Linguistic-Relativity Hypothesis

Most of us assume that reality, as we know it, exists independently of the ways in which we talk about it. We believe, for example, that any idea expressed in one language can be translated into another language. This statement seems so obvious that to question it is rather startling. But Whorf (1956), a student of American Indian languages, found such direct translation often impossible. One of the languages he studied makes no clear distinction between nouns and verbs; another blurs the distinctions of past, present, and future; a third uses the same name for the colors gray and brown. These differences led Whorf to two conclusions:

1. The world is conceived very differently by those whose languages are of completely unlike structure.
2. The structure of the language is a cause of these different ways of conceiving the world.

Whorf's thesis (known as the *linguistic-relativity hypothesis* because it proposes that thought is relative to the language in which it is conducted) has been the subject of much debate among psychologists and anthropologists. Most of them accept a correspondence between the language and the ways of conceiving the world, but they tend to turn things around and try to show that those experiences significant to people affect the way things are expressed in language. Thus Eskimos have different words for different kinds of snow that we would scarcely be able to tell apart, and the Hanunóo of the Philippine Islands have names for ninety-two varieties of rice. For us, the important part of Whorf's conjecture is that there is a close correspondence between language and thinking.

Researchers interested in his theory have tested it in a study of two groups of Navajo children. Both groups lived on a reservation, but one spoke only English and the other only Navajo. A special characteristic of the Navajo language is that certain verbs of handling—the Navajo equivalents of *to pick up, to drop, to hold in the hand,* and so on—require special forms depending upon the nature of the object being handled. There are 11 different forms, one for round spherical objects, one for round thin objects, one for long flexible objects, and so forth. Even the very young Navajo-speaking children knew and used these forms correctly. These children were compared to English-speaking Navajos of the same age, with respect to how often they used shape, form, or material rather than color as a basis for sorting objects. The objects given were those usually sorted by young children on the basis of color. The Navajo-speaking children tended to sort on the basis of form at significantly younger ages than did the English-speaking children. The fact that the Navajo language required attention to shapes, forms, and materials of objects presumably made the Navajo-speaking child pay more attention to this aspect of his environment (Carroll, 1964).[1]

Information-Processing Models of Thinking

People achieve the most complex use of language and concepts when engaged in problem solving. Whether the problem is as simple as multiplying nine times eighty-two or as difficult as proving a mathematical theorem, the thought processes are not easy to analyze. None of the traditional theories that attempt to explain thinking in terms of associations or S-R connections has proved adequate to the task. We saw that language acquisition involves more than associating strings of words. So too, there is more to solving a problem than simply following a chain of stimuli and responses from some initial cue to an eventual solution. We often sort through and reorganize a great deal of information according to various rules and procedures in order to arrive at a solution; the information processed may have been stored in memory or may have been immediately available in the environment. The nature of this problem-solving activity has many similarities to the way information is processed by a high-speed computer. These similarities have led to some interesting efforts to formulate models of human thinking based on the methods and procedures developed for programming and organizing computer systems.

Today computers are able to handle easily many tasks previously performed only by human beings. Computers balance bank accounts, figure payrolls, prepare tax returns, control manufacturing plants, translate

[1] For a critical review of this study and a more extensive discussion of the linguistic-relativity hypothesis, see Miller and McNeill (1969) and Slobin (1971).

foreign-language material, play reasonably good games of chess, and so forth. In fact, many of the tasks that 20 years ago we would have all agreed required thinking can now be done by computers. Does this mean that computers can indeed "think"? An immediate answer in the negative—that they can do only what they have been programmed to do—is too glib. Perhaps a human thinker can do only what he has been programmed to do also, either by inheritance or training. It is clear that a wide continuum of intellectual behavior describes human organisms; it is an open question just how far out on this continuum we can push the computer.

Computer Programs and Flow Charts

Before examining the role of the computer as a tool for studying cognitive processes, it will be useful to describe briefly the basic features of a computer program. The computer cannot figure out how to solve a problem by itself; it is helpless until it has been given a detailed set of instructions. These instructions make up what is called the *computer program.* To write a program it is first necessary to analyze the problem to be solved and to break it into its component parts. One of the best ways to do this is to construct a *flow chart,* which resembles the play diagram a football coach might draw on a blackboard. A flow chart shows component parts of the problem just as a coach's diagram indicates each player's assignment. The flow chart also shows how the various parts are to be fitted together. Once the problem has been mapped out, each part of the chart must be further broken into detailed instructions on how to handle each operation. One part of a flow chart might require a hundred or more individual steps in the program. Then the material can be fed into the computer.

Fig. 10-12 Flow chart

This chart illustrates a simple program for tallying distribution of word lengths. The output of this program is the count of the number of words in the text that have a length of one letter, a length of two letters, three letters, and so on.

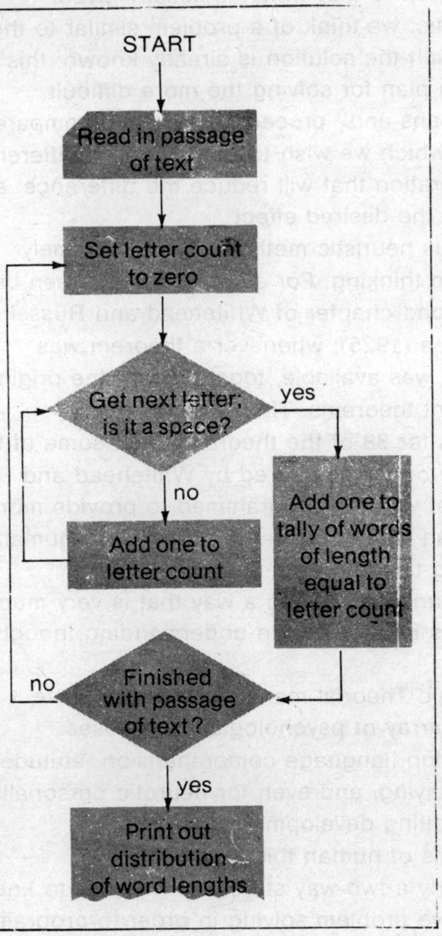

Figure 10-12 shows a flow chart of a very simple information-processing problem. The chart tells you the steps involved in finding the distribution of word lengths for a passage of English text. The input to the program is the text material, which has been punched on cards with numerical codes for the letters and space with all other punctuation ignored. The boxes in the flow chart represent work to be done, and the diamonds, decisions to be made. This flow chart by itself is not very impressive, but when many of them are cascaded one onto another into a hierarchy of operations the computer can indeed perform in a truly intelligent fashion.

The flow chart of a computer program is a convenient way of picturing the flow of information through a system. The human organism can be conceptualized as an information-processing system, and it is quite natural sometimes to use flow charts as models of psychological processes. Models based on flow charts have come to be called information-processing models.[2] Many psychologists feel that information-processing models are well suited for theorizing about psychological phenomena, particularly about complex cognitive processes.

Simulation Models

Computer programs used to mirror the cognitive activity of human beings are called *simulation models.* The first significant attempt to simulate complex

[2]Information-processing models for memory were discussed in Chapter 8 (p. 238).

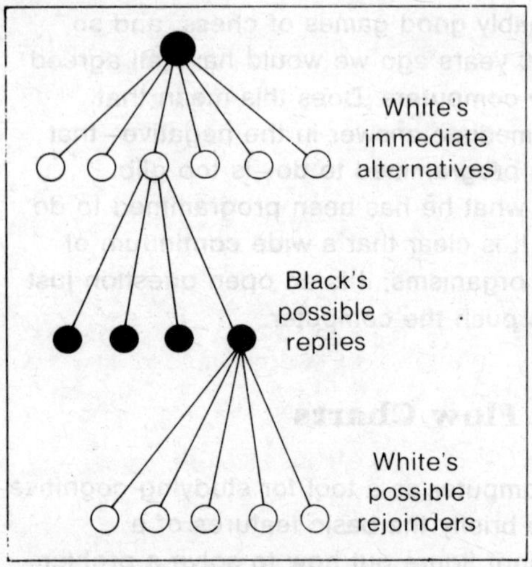

Fig. 10-13 Exhaustive vs. heuristic search
One method of problem solving in chess and related games is to enumerate exhaustively all possible sequences of moves, and then select one that is guaranteed to lead to a win. Part of the "tree of possibilities" for a chess game is illustrated in this figure: the complete tree would follow each branch out to a conclusion, and the end of each branch would be labeled win for white, win for black, or draw. The white player would then inspect the complete tree and select a move that would lead eventually to checkmate of black's king no matter how black played. In principle, the enumerative approach to chess could be programmed on a computer and would make the computer an unbeatable opponent. In actual practice, however, such an approach is not feasible, for it has been estimated that there are 10^{120} (give or take a few trillion) different paths through a complete chess tree. If this procedure of exhaustive search were employed it is unlikely that a single game could be completed within a lifetime, even if the enumeration were carried out at the speed of the fastest computer now in existence. Instead, to develop a chess-playing computer that simulates human players we must program it to behave intelligently—to make use of such heuristics as "try to control the center of the board," "protect your king." It must search the problem tree in a selective fashion, exploring paths of the tree that look promising and ignoring those that do not

cognitive processes was made by Newell and Simon (1956), who developed an information-processing model to prove theorems in symbolic logic. Their program, which was dubbed the *Logic Theorist,* did not try to prove theorems by searching all possible sequences of logical operations until one was found that yielded a proof. Rather, the approach taken in the Logic Theorist was to incorporate *heuristic* methods of the type used by human beings for proving theorems. A *heuristic* is a strategy, trick, simplification, gimmick, or any other procedure that drastically limits the search for solution in difficult problems. Heuristics do not guarantee that a solution will be found, but when they do work, they greatly reduce the search time required to obtain a solution. Human thinking obviously makes use of heuristic procedures. Good chess players solve their problems heuristically, since they cannot possibly foresee the consequences of every possible move (see Figure 10-13). In solving a geometrical problem we often add a line here or there, hoping that by forming a new diagram we may perceive relations that were previously not evident. This new construction may help, but there are no guarantees implied.

The use of heuristic procedures by humans is not well understood, but there can be little doubt that they play an important role in most problem-solving tasks. Several examples of heuristics particularly relevant to human thinking are worth describing. One of these is the heuristic of "working backwards": we begin with the result to be proved and then attempt to work backwards step by step to that which is initially given. Another is the "make-a-plan" heuristic: we think of a problem similar to the one we are trying to solve but to which the solution is already known; this method of solution is then used as a plan for solving the more difficult problem. A third heuristic is the "means-end" procedure: here we compare the current state of affairs with that which we wish to obtain, find a difference between the two states, seek an operation that will reduce the difference, and repeat the procedure until we obtain the desired effect.

The Logic Theorist, with its various heuristic methods, is an extremely impressive computer model of human thinking. For example, it has been used to derive the 52 theorems in the second chapter of Whitehead and Russell's famous treatise, *Principia mathematica* (1925); whenever a theorem was proved, it was stored in memory and was available, together with the original axioms, for use in proving subsequent theorems. The Logic Theorist succeeded in giving adequate proofs for 38 of the theorems, and some of the proofs were more elegant than those originally offered by Whitehead and Russell. Of course, the Logic Theorist was not programmed to provide more rapid or "better" proofs than a human would, but rather to simulate human behavior in an actual problem-solving task. When a computer can be programmed to perform such a task and behaves in a way that is very much like a human, then indeed progress is being made in understanding thought processes.

Since the development of the Logic Theorist many investigators have formulated simulation models for an array of psychological processes. There are models for concept formation, language comprehension, attitude change, music composition, chess playing, and even for neurotic personality processes—to name a few. These exciting developments are of great importance in unraveling the problems of human thinking. But the development of these models is clearly a two-way street, for one has to know something about the nature of creative problem solving in order to program

CRITICAL DISCUSSION

The General Problem Solver

The ability to simulate complex cognitive processes is a major accomplishment in itself. But what is more significant is that information-processing models developed for quite different problems (for example, a model to prove theorems in geometry versus a model to describe neurotic behavior) have many common component processes. This commonality of processes among models suggests that a general theory of complex cognitive processes may not be too far away. Simon and Newell (1964) were the first to isolate some of the components common to many information-processing models and pull them together into a single model, which they dubbed the General Problem Solver (GPS). They propose that we should be able to combine the special information of any particular task (chess playing, theorem proving, music composition) with GPS and come up with a composite program that can solve the task, using strategies and tactics of the type employed by human beings.

The GPS simulates in a formal manner what the individual is believed to do when attacking a problem. The programs are very complex and can be characterized here only in the barest outline. The actual program for GPS is built around two basic processes that follow each other in repeated cycles until the problem is solved, or abandoned as too difficult or insoluble. The first process, part of what is called the *problem-solving organization,* is to set subgoals that might be appropriate to the solution of the problem. These subgoals are then evaluated, and a promising one is selected for exploration. Note that this is a kind of "executive," or "decision-making," function, including both a search and an evaluation phase. A subgoal, for example, might be the solution of a simplified version of the more general problem. Once the executive routine selects a subgoal, the process known as the *means-end analysis* applies relevant heuristics to reach the subgoal. This requires that the information-processing mechanism begin with data that are given and follow permissible transformations as in ordinary problem solving. Because the heuristic approach does not guarantee a solution, if the initial approach fails, the executive routine then searches for subgoals that appear more productive.

The approach to complex cognitive processes exemplified by GPS is quite promising. If it turns out that information-processing models based on only a few basic methods of symbolic representation and a small number of elementary information processes can simulate complex human behavior, then we have truly advanced our understanding.

it on a computer. Because the computer will do only what it is instructed to do, the steps have to be clearly and completely specified in the computer program. If the psychologist who charts the computer program has made incorrect assumptions in interpreting the steps involved in problem solving, the program will not succeed or at least will not display outputs that accurately match the behavior of human subjects. The computer serves to check the adequacy of the theoretical assumptions that the psychologist believes will account for the psychological process under study. The chief advantages of the computer are its speed and its attention to all details of what it is programmed to do.

The development of information-processing models for psychological phenomena is still in an early stage, but the results have been encouraging. Newell and Simon (1972) have argued that there is already substantial evidence for explaining much of human thinking and problem solving in terms of a few basic processes, arranged into an appropriate hierarchy yielding outputs that appear incredibly complex. They suggest that the human information-processing system is primarily serial in its operation: It can process only a few symbols at a time, and the symbols being processed must be held in a limited short-term memory (see p. 236), the content of which can be rapidly reordered and changed. The major limitations on the subject's capacities to employ efficient strategies arise from the very small capacity of the short-term memory and from the relatively long time needed to transfer information from short-term to long-term memory.

Summary

1. Thinking is behavior that uses *symbols* as "representations" of objects and events. It thus can go beyond perceptual solution of problems, or solution through manipulation, by having reference to events not present—to remembered, absent, or imagined things.
2. A symbol *stands for* something else. Some symbols are concrete objects, such as a stop sign; because *words* are especially powerful symbols, language is an important agent in the thinking process. A symbol conveys *meaning;* but the precise relation between the symbol and the object it stands for (that is, its meaning) is a subject on which psychologists are not agreed.
3. A useful distinction can be made between *denotative* meanings, which are fixed and specific, and *connotative* meanings, which express evaluation or preference. One attempt to measure connotations is by means of the *semantic differential.*
4. When a symbol stands for a class of objects or events with common properties, we say that it refers to a *concept.* Studies of *concept formation* show that object concepts are usually attained more easily than abstract concepts, such as numbers.
5. Language provides a major source of symbols in thinking. The structure of language can be analyzed at several levels: *phonemes* are the basic units of sound; *morphemes* are the basic units of meaning; and *phrases* are the units from which sentences are constructed. Analysis in terms of *phrase structure* helps us to understand the meaning of a simple declarative sentence, but more complex sentences have usually undergone one or more *transformations* in their relationship to the *deep structure,* or underlying meaning of the sentence.
6. Classical and operant conditioning may play a role in the acquisition of word meanings as does a gradual process of discrimination between general and specific word referents. Grammatical learning involves more than simple stimulus-response associations; it requires learning *rules* for generating acceptable word sequences. The kinds of *meanings* expressed in the early sentences and the *order* in which grammatical constructions are acquired are similar for all children regardless of the language being learned. This invariance probably reflects a close dependence between linguistic and cognitive development.
7. Language and thought are intimately related. Thus children are able to solve some kinds of transposition problems only when they are old enough to state the solution in words. According to the linguistic-relativity hypothesis, the way man conceives the world is dependent upon the language forms he uses.
8. Information-processing models of thinking utilize *flow charts* that comprise the program (set of instructions) delivered to a computer to *simulate* the processes of human problem-solving. *Heuristic* methods (such as the means-end analysis) are valuable aids in reducing the search time required to solve a problem. The *General Problem Solver* incorporates heuristic methods common to a number of information-processing models in an attempt to devise a general theory of complex cognitive processes.

Further Reading

Very readable introductions to the psychology of language may be found in Slobin, *Psycholinguistics* (1971), and Foder, Bever, and Garrett, *The psychology of language* (1974). An account of early language development is given in Brown, *A first language: The early stages* (1973).

The transformational theory of grammar is expounded in Chomsky, *Language and mind* (1968). Books attempting to provide an integrated, theoretical account of language as it relates to the psychology of memory, learning, and perception are Anderson and Bower, *Human associative memory* (1973); Norman and Rumelhart, *Explorations in cognition* (1975); and Lindsay and Norman, *Human information processing* (1972).

Information-processing models of thinking and language are discussed in Newell and Simon, *Human problem solving* (1972); Schank and Colby (eds.), *Computer models of thought and language* (1973); and Dutton and Starbuck (eds.), *Computer simulation of human behavior* (1971). Various uses of computers in psychological research are presented in Apter and Westby (eds.), *The computer in psychology* (1973).

A more practical approach to problem solving is Wickelgren, *How to solve problems* (1974); it reviews heuristic procedures and presents useful suggestions for solving problems.

part five

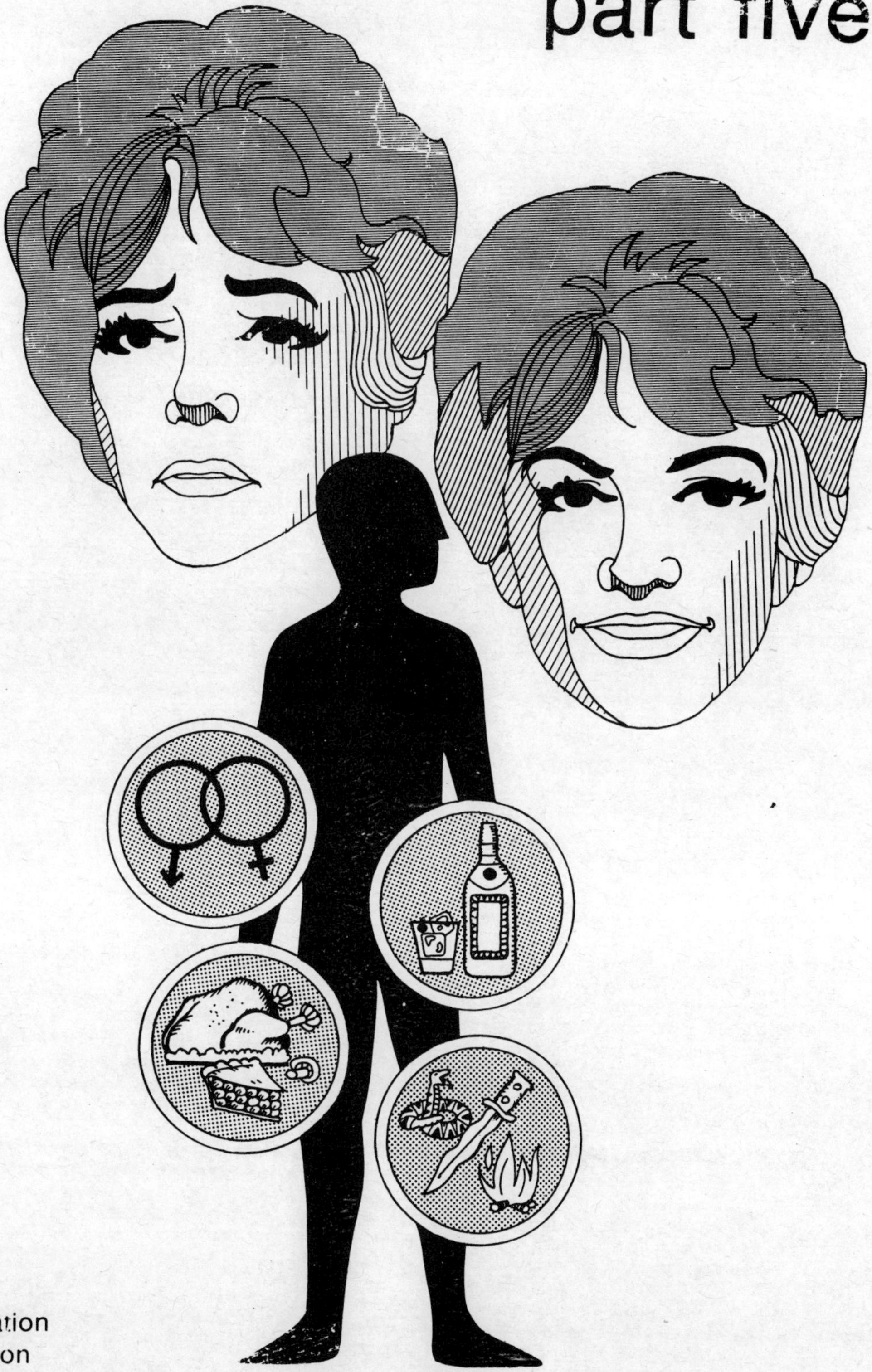

motivation and emotion

11 physiological basis of motivation

When we ask "What *motivates* a person to risk his life saving another or to work long hours to achieve a particular goal?" we usually mean "Why does he behave as he does?" The term motivation, as popularly used, refers to the *cause* or *why* of behavior. Used in this sense motivation would cover all of psychology, since psychology is the study of human behavior. But we know that many aspects of behavior can be explained as the result of maturation or learning. Psychologists, then, usually narrow the concept of motivation to those factors that *energize* behavior and give it *direction.* A motivated organism will engage in an activity more *vigorously* and more *efficiently* than an unmotivated one. In addition to a readiness for action, motivation also tends to focus behavior—the hungry person is ready to seek food and eat, the thirsty one to drink, the one in pain to escape the painful stimulus.

Although many psychologists would agree with the above usage of the term motivation, the status of the concept is not at all clear. Some psychologists feel that we need such a term only to account for the energizing aspects of behavior; other mechanisms (namely, learning and cognition) can account for the direction of behavior (Cofer, 1972). Some even argue that the concept is unnecessary and should be done away with altogether (Bolles, 1967). In order to help in understanding this controversy we briefly describe how the concept of motivation developed and the various forms it has taken since the beginning of this century. Then we consider the basic biological or physiological needs that humans share with lower organisms. In the next chapter we discuss more complex human motives.

Development of Motivational Concepts

The term motivation did not come into use until the beginning of the twentieth century. If people are viewed as rational beings whose intellects are free to choose goals and decide on courses of action, then a concept of motivation is unnecessary. Reason is the main determinant of what a person does. This conception of the human being, called *rationalism,* was the predominant view of philosophers and theologians for hundreds of years. A person was free to choose, and choices were good or bad depending upon one's intelligence and education. It was assumed that the good choice, if known, would automatically be selected. Within this viewpoint a person is very much responsible for his own behavior.

Seventeenth- and eighteenth-century philosophers (such as Descartes, Hobbes, Locke, and Hume) took a more *mechanistic view.* They suggested that some actions arise from internal or external forces over which we have no control. Hobbes, for example, held that we behave in such a way as to achieve pleasure and avoid pain. No matter what reasons we may give for our conduct, these two tendencies are the underlying causes of all behavior. This doctrine of *hedonism* is still very influential in some motivation theories.

Instincts

The extreme of the mechanistic view is the theory of *instincts.* An instinct is an innate biological force that predisposes the organism to act in a certain way. The behavior of animals had long been attributed to instincts, since they

Thomas Hobbes

had no soul or intellect and could not operate on the basis of reason. When Darwin suggested that there was no sharp distinction between humans and animals, the door was opened for the use of instincts in explaining human behavior. The strongest advocate of instinct theory was the psychologist William McDougall who maintained that *all* of our thoughts and behavior were the result of instincts. In his book *Social psychology*, published in 1908, McDougall mentioned the following instincts:

flight	self-assertion
repulsion	reproduction
curiosity	gregariousness
pugnacity	acquisition
self-abasement	construction

McDougall thought these instincts were inherited and compelling sources of conduct, but modifiable by learning and experience. He later expanded his list to 18 instincts, including some that related to specific bodily needs. By modifying and combining these instincts he attempted to explain all human behavior.

You can see that instinct theory is diametrically opposed to a rationalistic view of human beings. Instead of choosing goals and actions a person is at the mercy of innate forces, which determine or motivate his course of action.

Psychoanalytic theory, which we will discuss in the next chapter, also attributed behavior to powerful innate forces. Freud believed that behavior was determined by two basic energies: the *life instincts* which found expression in sexual behavior and the *death instincts* which underlie aggressive acts. These instincts, though unconscious, were powerful motivational forces. Both psychoanalytic theory and instinct theory were influential in turning interest away from a rationalistic conception of people toward a motivational view that saw behavior as the result of unconscious, irrational forces within the individual.

Needs and Drives

The problem with instincts as explanations of behavior was that there soon became too many of them and they did not explain anything. Added to the list were such human instincts as rivalry, secretiveness, modesty, cleanliness, imitation, hurting, sociability, and jealousy, until finally an instinct could be found for almost any imaginable behavior. But to call a particular action instinctive does not really explain much about it. To say that a man fought because he had an instinct of pugnacity does not offer much more than a description of his behavior; you saw him fight so you say he has a pugnacious instinct.

Anthropologists noted that many instincts were not found in all cultures. Pugnacity, for example, was not typical of all primitive societies. There were peaceful societies in which men found no need to fight.

Because of these and other difficulties, the notion of instincts was replaced during the 1920s by the concept of *drives*. A drive is an aroused state resulting from some bodily or tissue *need*, such as a need for food, water, oxygen, or avoidance of painful stimuli. This aroused condition motivates the organism to initiate behavior to remedy the need. For example, a lack of food produces certain chemical changes in the blood, indicating a need for food, which in turn create a drive state of arousal or tension. The organism seeks to reduce this drive by doing something (in this case, finding food) to satisfy the need.

Sometimes the terms *need* and *drive* are used interchangeably, but more often need refers to the physiological state of tissue deprivation, whereas drive refers to the psychological consequences of a need. Need and drive are parallel but not identical. Drive does not necessarily get stronger as need gets stronger. A starved organism may be so weakened by its great need for food that drive (the motivation to get it) is weakened. People who have fasted for long periods report that their feelings of hunger (drive level) come and go even though their need for food persists.

Like instinct, drive is a *hypothetical construct.* It is not something we can observe but is inferred from behavior. If we deprive an animal of food for a specified period of time, we note that it runs more rapidly down a runway to obtain food than a non-deprived animal and eats more than its counterpart. We infer from this behavior that the animal's hunger drive has been activated. Although drive is a hypothetical construct, it proved to be more amenable to experimental investigation than instinct. Needs could be defined objectively and conditions could be specified for creating and eliminating them. The period from 1920 through the 1950s saw a wealth of research that tied the concept of drive to such variables as length of deprivation, rate of learning, speed and efficiency of performing learned acts, and general activity level.

Homeostasis and Drive Theory

Basic to the drive concept is the principle of *homeostasis,* which refers to the body's tendency to maintain a constant internal environment. The healthy individual for example, maintains body temperature within a few degrees. Slight deviations from normal temperature set into operation mechanisms that restore the normal condition. Exposure to cold constricts blood vessels on the body's surface in order to retain the warmth of the blood, and we shiver which produces heat. In warm weather, peripheral blood vessels dilate to permit heat to escape, and perspiration has a cooling effect. These are automatic mechanisms designed to keep body temperature within normal range.

Numerous physiological states must be maintained within fairly narrow limits: the concentration of blood sugar, the levels of oxygen and carbon dioxide in the blood, water balance in the cells, to mention but a few. Various mechanisms within the body operate to keep these conditions stable. Presumably, sensors in the body detect changes from the optimal level and activate mechanisms designed to correct the imbalance. The principle is the same as a furnace thermostat, which turns the heat on when the temperature falls below a certain level and off when the temperature rises.

Hunger and thirst can be viewed as homeostatic mechanisms because they initiate behavior designed to restore the balance of certain substances in the blood. Within the framework of homeostasis, a need is any physiological imbalance or departure from the optimal state; its psychological counterpart is drive. When the physiological imbalance is restored, drive is reduced and motivated activity ceases. Many physiological imbalances can be corrected automatically. The pancreas releases sugar stored in the liver to maintain the proper balance of sugar in the blood. But when automatic mechanisms can no longer maintain a balanced state, the organism becomes aroused (drive is activated) and is motivated to restore the balance. A person goes in search of food on feeling the symptoms of low blood-sugar level. Figure 11-1 represents schematically the kind of control system that a homeostatic mechanism of this nature would require.

Psychologists have extended the principle of homeostasis to cover more than just tissue needs or physiological balances. In this broader sense any *physiological* or *psychological* imbalance will motivate behavior designed to restore equilibrium. A hungry, anxious, uncomfortable, or fearful person will be motivated to do something to reduce the tension. As we shall see later, there has been criticism of this view that motivation is solely tension arousal and ceases with tension reduction.

Incentive Theory as an Alternative to Drive Theory

During the 1950s, psychologists began to be disenchanted with the *drive-reduction theory* of motivation as an explanation of all types of behavior. It became apparent that external stimuli were being overlooked as instigators of behavior. The organism was not solely *pushed* into activity by internal drives. Certain objects in the environment (called *incentives*) were important in arousing behavior. Motivation could be better understood as an interaction between stimulus objects in the environment and a particular physiological state of the organism.

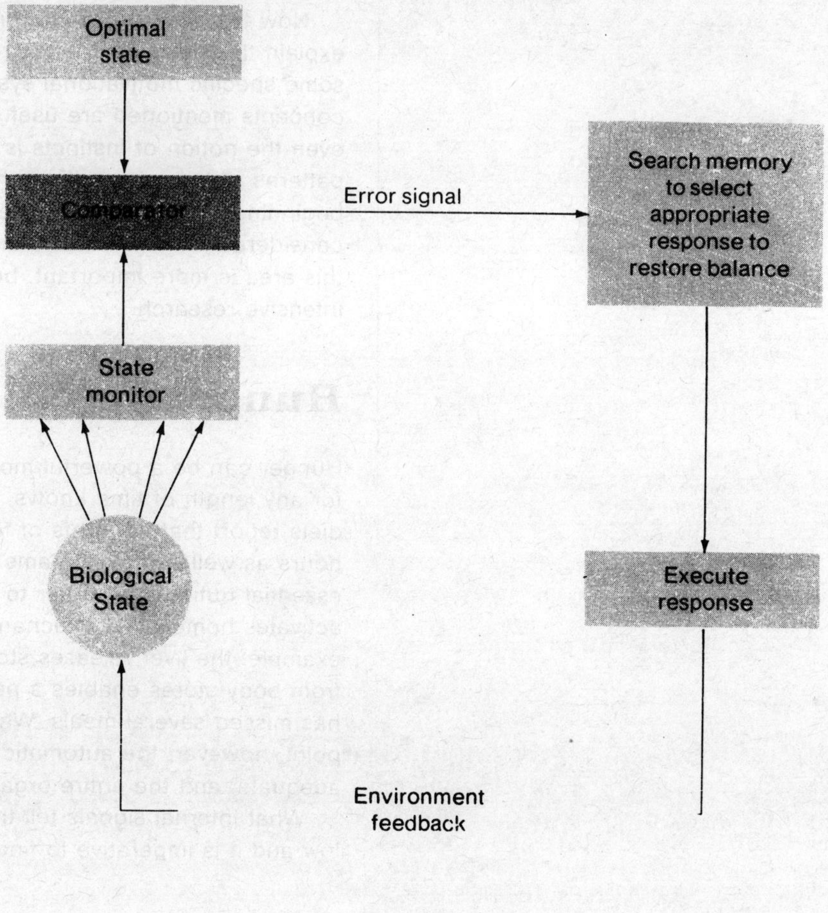

Fig. 11-1 Motivational control system

The state monitor continuously measures the internal condition of the organism. Whenever the comparitor notes a difference between the state monitor and some optimal level, it emits an error signal. The error signal activates cognitive processes that select behaviors designed to restore the balance between the state monitor and the optimal state. The behaviors will depend on the environmental situation—that is, they will not be stereotyped but more or less appropriate to the situation. These behaviors link the organism to its environment, producing feedback to the system that restores the imbalance between the optimal and current state. The system is organized so as to maintain the level of the state monitor nearly equal to the optimal level at all times.

Hunger can be aroused by external influences.

A person who is not hungry may have his hunger drive aroused by seeing some delicious pastries in a bakery window. In this case, the incentive (fresh pastries) can activate hunger as well as reduce it. An animal that has eaten until it is satiated will eat again if it sees another animal doing so. The goad to activity here is not an internal drive but an external event.

It became clear, too, that the homeostatic concept of drive as reducing tension and returning the organism to a quiescent state did not agree with all the evidence. Human beings often seek tension-arousing experiences such as roller-coaster rides, car racing, white-water canoeing, or horror movies. These activities certainly increase tension rather than reduce it.

More recent approaches to a theory of motivation have focused on the role of incentives. Incentives refer to objects or conditions in the environment. The organism will approach *positive incentives;* it will avoid *negative incentives.* For a thirsty animal water would be a positive incentive; for a sexually aroused animal, a mate. An object or situation that has caused pain would be a negative incentive. Incentives have two functions—they arouse the organism and they direct behavior either toward or away from themselves.

The dual function of incentives can be demonstrated experimentally. A hungry rat will run through a maze to a goal box that it knows contains food; the positive incentive directs behavior. If the rat is given a morsel of food at the start of the maze, it will run even faster toward the goal box; the incentive also serves to arouse behavior. As with drive theory, arousal is an important aspect of motivation, but here arousal is evoked by an external incentive rather than by conditions of deprivation.

Now that we have had a brief look at the way psychologists have tried to explain the energizing and directional aspects of behavior, we will examine some specific motivational systems in terms of empirical findings. All of the concepts mentioned are useful in explaining some aspects of behavior, and even the notion of instincts is currently being revisited in the study of certain patterns of behavior—although with a different emphasis than at the beginning of this century. The psychological aspects of hunger will be considered in more detail than the other motivational systems—not because this area is more important, but because it has been the subject of more intensive research.

Hunger

Hunger can be a powerful motivator, as anyone who has gone without food for any length of time knows. Those who have subsisted on semistarvation diets report that thoughts of food and eating occupy much of their waking hours as well as their dreams. The body needs an adequate supply of the essential nutrients in order to function efficiently. Depletion of these nutrients activates homeostatic mechanisms to release food stored in the body. For example, the liver releases stored sugar into the blood stream. Replenishment from body stores enables a person to continue functioning even though he has missed several meals. When the body stores are diminished to a certain point, however, the automatic homeostatic mechanisms are no longer adequate, and the entire organism becomes mobilized to seek food.

What internal signals tell the brain that the body's supply of nutrients is low and it is imperative to find food? The feelings most people describe as hunger—an empty or aching sensation in the region of the stomach, sometimes accompanied by a feeling of weakness—give us some clues. But this is only part of the story.

Stimuli outside the organism can influence feelings of hunger and eating behavior. You walk past a bakery only an hour after your last meal and find your mouth watering at the sight of a piece of cake in the window. Your signal for hunger in this case is not related to the depletion of nutrients in the body or to stomach pangs or a feeling of weakness. The odor or sight of food (external stimuli) can arouse hunger even when there is no physiological need.

Eating is influenced by social customs. Scene is the Great Hall of the People, Peking, on May Day Eve.

Habits and social customs can also influence eating behavior. You are accustomed to eating at certain times of day and may suddenly feel hungry when you notice that it is noon. You may consume more when having dinner with a group of friends who are all eating voraciously than you would when dining alone.

Eating behavior is influenced by a number of physiological, environmental, and social variables. We will look first at the physiological mechanisms that regulate food intake and then consider environmental and social factors when discussing some of the current research on obesity.

Regulatory Centers in the Hypothalamus

Regulation of food intake is so crucial to survival that nature has provided several homeostatic controls. If one or more sensory signals associated with eating is eliminated—by removing the sense of smell, or taste, or sensory information coming from the stomach—the organism is still able to regulate its food intake. The various control systems that regulate feeding are integrated in a region of the brain called the hypothalamus.

The hypothalamus, a small collection of cell nuclei located at the base of the brain (see Figure 2-7, p. 41), has numerous connections with other brain parts and with the pituitary gland. It also has a greater density of blood vessels than any other area of the brain, and thus can be readily influenced by the chemical state of the blood.

The hypothalamus plays an important role in the regulation of food intake. Physicians have observed that patients with tumors or injury in the region of the hypothalamus overeat (*hyperphagia*) and become obese. The development of precise instruments for exploring the brain has made it possible to specify more exactly the regulatory centers in the hypothalamus. We now know that two areas regulate food intake: the *lateral hypothalamus* (LH) initiates eating—it is a "start" or "feeding center"; the *ventromedial hypothalamus* (VMH) inhibits eating—it is a "stop" or "satiety center."

One way to study the function of a specific brain area is to insert a microelectrode and stimulate the spot with a weak electric current. Stimulation of LH cells causes a satiated animal to eat. Electrical stimulation of VMH cells inhibits eating; with a weak current the animal slows its feeding behavior, and with a stronger current it will stop entirely (Hoebel and Teitelbaum, 1962).

Another way to study the function of a brain area is to destroy cells in the region (also with a microelectrode but using direct instead of alternating current) and observe how the animal behaves when the area no longer exerts control. On destruction of cells in the LH the animal refuses to eat or drink and will die unless kept alive through artificial feeding and watering. Damage to cells in the VMH produces overeating and obesity in every species investigated, from rat and chicken to monkey and human (see Figure 11-2). No major metabolic disturbance has been found. The animals become fat simply because of overeating. If restricted to the same amount of food that a normal animal consumes, they do not gain weight.

Studies of the sort described above have made it clear that the VMH area (satiety center) and the LH area (feeding center) act in opposite ways to regulate food intake. Moreover, two kinds of control systems appear to be integrated in the hypothalamus. One system, responsive to the immediate nutritive needs of the organism, tells the brain when to start a meal and when to stop. A second, long-term control system, attempts to maintain a stable body weight over a period of time, regardless of how much the organism may or may not eat in any one meal.

Fig. 11-2 Hypothalamic overeating

Lesions in the ventromedial hypothalamus caused this rat to overeat and gain more than three times its normal weight.

SHORT-TERM CONTROL OF FOOD INTAKE. Three variables that influence hypothalamic control of immediate appetite have been identified: blood-sugar level, stomach fullness, and body temperature. A low sugar or glucose level in the blood makes us feel weak and hungry. Injections of insulin (which lower the blood-sugar level) increase food intake; injections of glucose (which raise the blood-sugar level) inhibit eating. Studies indicate that the hypothalamus contains "glucoreceptors," cells sensitive to the rate at which glucose passes through them. The glucoreceptors in the VMH respond differently to glucose level than do those in the LH.

Microelectrodes were implanted in the hypothalamus of dogs and cats so that the activity of single neurons in the VMH and LH could be recorded. Records of neural activity were obtained before and after injections of glucose or insulin. The results showed that after glucose injections, cells in the VMH (satiety center) become more active, whereas cells in the LH (feeding center) show decreased activity. The reverse is true after insulin injections. Cells in other parts of the brain monitored as controls showed no changes (Anand and others, 1964).[1]

But digestion is a slow process, and we stop eating long before the food we have consumed can be transformed into enough blood sugar to make up a deficit in the blood stream. A more immediate signal is needed to let the brain know that food is on its way. One such signal is provided by a full stomach. If food is injected directly into the stomach of a hungry animal (without passing through the mouth and throat) it eats much less than it would otherwise (Smith and Duffy, 1955). Experiments suggest that cells in the VMH respond to distention of the stomach to inhibit further eating (Sharm and others, 1953).

An empty stomach produces the periodic contractions of muscles in the stomach wall that we identify as "hunger pangs." This increased movement of the stomach wall has been shown to activate cells in the LH. Thus, an empty stomach signals the LH to start the organism eating; a full stomach signals the VMH that it is time to stop eating.

[1] The variable to which the glucoreceptors respond is hypothesized to be not the absolute blood-sugar level but the rate at which glucose is being utilized as reflected by the ratio of blood sugar in the arteries to blood sugar in the veins. As time since eating increases, the blood-sugar level in the two types of vessels becomes more nearly equal. When the glucose difference between venous and arterial blood is small, subjects show stomach contractions and report that they are hungry. When the arteries contain considerably more sugar than the veins, they do neither (Mayer, 1955).

A third short-term control mechanism is temperature. In a warm environment most animals and humans eat less than in a cold environment. Cooling the brain has a similar effect on food intake. The nature of these "thermoreceptors" is not clear, but evidence shows that the LH responds to decreased brain temperature and the VMH responds to increased brain temperature.

Thus, we have three mechanisms for short-term regulation of food intake. The LH responds to low blood-sugar level, increased motility of the stomach walls, and lowered brain temperature by initiating eating; the VMH, conversely, responds to high blood-sugar level, stomach distension, and increased brain temperature by stopping eating. But all of these short-term mechanisms are subject to a long-term mechanism which attempts to stabilize body weight over time.

LONG-TERM CONTROL OF FOOD INTAKE. Most wild animals maintain their weight at about the same level throughout their lifetime, despite the fact that food may be plentiful one week and scarce the next. Human beings have greater difficulty maintaining a constant weight because their eating behavior is more strongly influenced by emotional and social factors. Even so, most people stay at about the same weight from year to year. The hypothalamus appears to provide, in addition to its short-term controls of food intake, a delicate system for ensuring that the organism's weight remains at a stable level.

We noted that rats with damage to the VMH overeat and become obese. Originally, this gluttonous behavior was attributed to an increased appetite resulting from destruction of part of the short-term control system. But once the rat reaches a certain level of obesity (usually two or three times its normal weight), it no longer overeats. It reduces its food intake to only slightly more than normal and maintains itself at its new obese weight. If the animal's diet is restricted, it will drop to its original normal weight. If, once again, it is allowed to eat freely, it will overeat as before until it is back up to its obese state. It looks as if damage to the VMH disturbs the animal's long-term weight control system so that weight is regulated at a higher level. If obese rats are force-fed after their weight has leveled off, so that they become "super-obese," they reduce their food intake until their weight returns to its "normal-obese" level (see Figure 11-3). Some correlate of body weight must act on the VMH to influence food intake. Since autopsies have shown the surplus weight of animals with VMH lesions to be composed

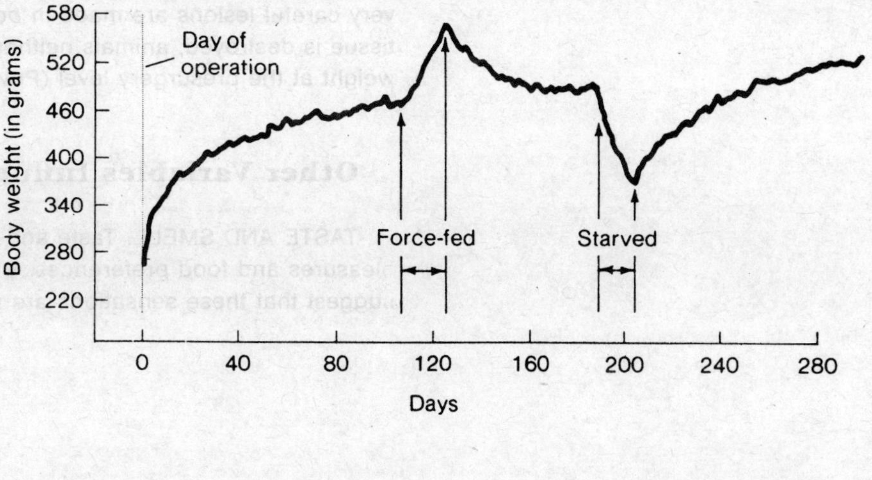

Fig. 11-3 Effects of forced feeding and starvation on body weight of rat with VMH lesions

Following VMH lesioning the rat overeats and gains weight until it stabilizes at a new obese level. Forced feeding or starvation alters the weight only temporarily; the rat returns to its stabilized level. (After Hoebel and Teitelbaum, 1966)

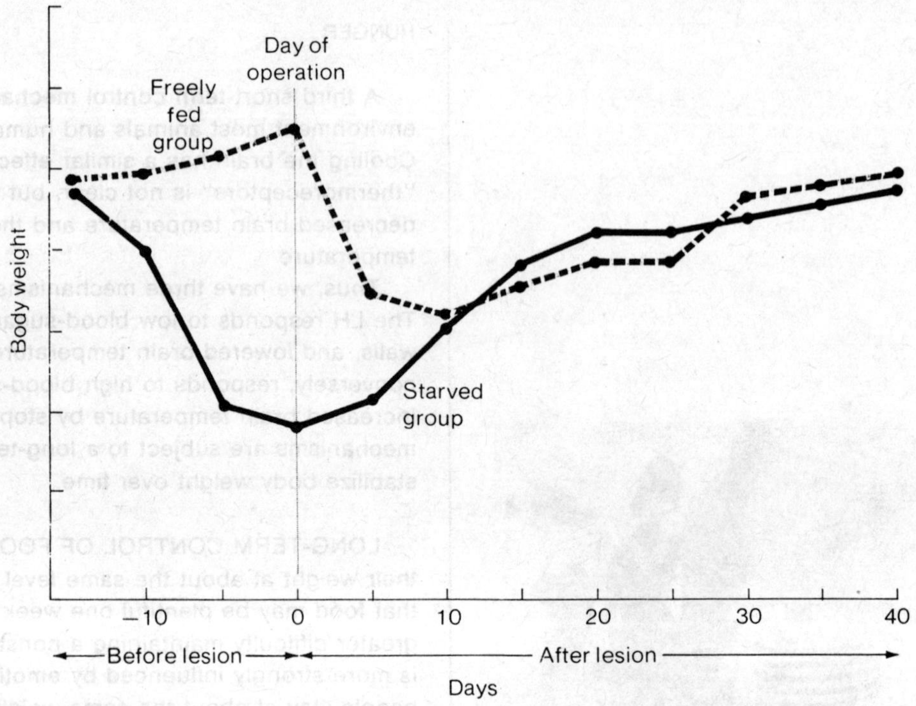

Fig. 11-4 Body weight and the lateral hypothalamus

Prior to LH lesioning one group of rats was starved while the other was allowed to feed freely. Following surgery, the starved animals increase their food intake and gain weight; the freely fed group loses weight. Both groups stabilize at the same level. (After Powley and Keesey, 1970)

almost entirely of fat, a likely candidate is the amount of free fatty acids in the blood stream.

A quite different reaction occurs in rats with lesions in the LH. These animals refuse all food and water for some time after the operation and will die unless artificially fed. Most animals eventually resume eating and drinking on their own, but they never regain their original weight. They stabilize at a new, lower weight level, just as VMH-damaged rats stabilize at a new, obese level. Again, it looks as if this behavior results from some impairment of a long-term weight control system rather than simple decreased appetite. Rats that are starved prior to LH lesioning (until their body weight is 80 percent of normal) do not act the same way after the operation. In fact, many overeat, but only until their weight reaches a new level (lower than their normal weight but higher than their starved, preoperational weight). These results are shown in Figure 11-4.

These findings indicate that the hypothalamus provides a fairly delicate system for maintaining the organism's weight at a stable level. The VMH and LH have reciprocal effects on the "set point" for body weight. If the VMH is damaged, the set point is raised; damage to the LH lowers the set point. If very careful lesions are made in *both* areas so that an equivalent amount of tissue is destroyed, animals neither overeat nor undereat but maintain their weight at the presurgery level (Powley, unpublished data).

Other Variables Influencing Food Intake

TASTE AND SMELL. Taste and smell play an important role in our eating pleasures and food preferences. But studies with both animals and humans suggest that these sensations are not essential to regulation of food intake.

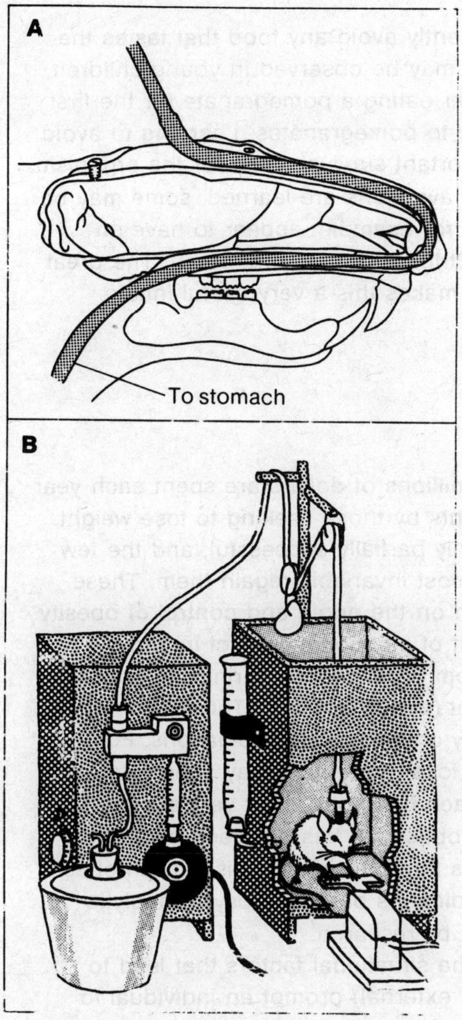

Fig. 11-5 Food regulation without taste or smell

Even without the benefit of taste and olfactory cues rats can regulate their food intake. **A.** The nasopharyngeal tube bypasses the taste and smell receptors. **B.** By pressing the bar, the rat activates the pipetting machine (center) and delivers a liquid diet from the reservoir (left foreground) through the nasopharyngeal tube directly into its own stomach.

The apparatus diagramed in Figure 11-5 was used so that rats could feed themselves without the accompanying sensations of taste, smell, or chewing. The animals were fitted with tubes that went through the nose to the stomach. A liquid food passing through the tube bypassed the taste and smell receptors. The animals could regulate their food intake by pressing a lever which delivered a predetermined amount of liquid to the stomach for each press.

The results of this study showed clearly that the rats could regulate their food intake under such conditions. If the amount or composition of liquid food per bar press was changed, the animals adjusted their rate of bar pressing to compensate for the change in caloric value. They were able to maintain a set intake of calories and a stable body weight without the help of taste and olfactory cues (Epstein and Teitelbaum, 1962).

In contrast to normal animals, food intake in rats with VMH lesions is markedly affected by the absence of taste and smell. When a rat that has been pressing the bar at a furious rate to receive large amounts of a liquid diet is outfitted with the nasal tube (so that now with each bar press the liquid flows directly into the stomach instead of into a food cup), its rate of bar pressing decreases markedly. Body weight and food intake drop drastically on this regime But if a drop of sweet saccharin solution is delivered to the animal's food cup at the same time that the liquid diet is delivered intragastrically, the rat will begin to increase its food intake and gain weight (McGinty and others, 1965).

Why is taste so important to the animal with VMH lesions? Probably because the impairment of its central control system forces it to rely on peripheral cues, taste and smell, to regulate food intake. For the normal rat, taste and smell may be powerful reinforcers, but they are not essential for the regulation of food intake.

SPECIFIC HUNGERS. Our understanding of the mechanisms that regulate hunger is complicated by the existence of *specific hungers* in addition to the need for a set amount of calories. Both people and animals show strong preferences for certain foods. Most of our food preferences can be traced to ethnic or cultural difference. We like what we are accustomed to and may find a strange diet not only unpalatable but indigestible. Many Japanese, for example, used to a diet consisting mainly of rice, fish, and vegetables, are unable to tolerate the richness of the typical American diet with its emphasis on animal fats, fried foods, and pastries.

Sometimes, however, specific hungers result from nutritional deficits. When rats on a fat-free diet are offered a choice among fat, sugar, and wheat, they show a marked preference for fat. Similarly, rats deprived of either sugar or wheat will prefer the food of which they have been deprived. What directs their behavior? Does the needed nutrient *taste* better than other foods? A series of experiments provides an explanation (Rozin and Kalat, 1971). Rats fed a diet deficient in thiamin (or calcium or magnesium) appear to develop an aversion to the deficient diet and will avidly accept a novel diet even though it may also be deficient. The animals will continue rejecting old diets and accepting new ones until they find a diet that relieves the illness caused by the deficiency. Once a satisfactory diet has been accepted, the old diet remains aversive even though it has been supplemented with the missing element.

Learning also plays a role in aversions to certain foods. If a rat gets sick after eating a novel food, it will subsequently avoid any food that tastes the same (Garcia, 1971). A similar response may be observed in young children. A child who gets stomach flu shortly after eating a pomegranate for the first time may subsequently have an aversion to pomegranates. Learning to avoid illness-associated foods would have important survival value for the organism.

Although most specific appetites and aversions are learned, some may be innate responses to certain tastes. Rats, for example, appear to have an innate preference for diets rich in salt (Stricker and Wilson, 1970). The great importance of salt in body fluid balance makes this a very useful innate appetite to have.

Obesity

Obesity is a major health problem, and millions of dollars are spent each year on special diets, drugs, or other treatments by those seeking to lose weight. Most attempts at weight reduction are only partially successful; and the few who do succeed in shedding pounds almost invariably regain them. These problems have stimulated much research on the origin and control of obesity. One approach views obesity as the result of emotional conflict in early childhood. Obesity is thought to stem from disturbances during the oral and anal stages of psychosexual development (see Chapter 3). The act of ingesting food is presumed to have many unconscious associations. For example, food may symbolize "mother's love"; or eating may substitute for sexual or aggressive activity. This approach has not proved very successful, however, in either explaining or treating obesity. It has not been possible to define any psychodynamic characteristics that consistently distinguish obese from nonobese individuals, nor have predictions based on psychoanalytic interpretations of obesity been borne out by research.

A second approach has focused on the situational factors that lead to overeating. What cues (both internal and external) prompt an individual to eat? How do obese individuals differ from those of normal weight in their response to these cues? It is this area of research that we will review.

Eating in Response to Internal Cues

Proceeding on the hypothesis that obese individuals may not be responding to the same hunger cues as nonobese, a study was made of the frequency with which both groups associated feelings of hunger with stomach contractions (Stunkard, 1959). Obese and nonobese subjects came to the laboratory in the morning without having had breakfast. Each subject swallowed a gastric balloon that was attached to a recording devise. By inflating the balloon with air so that it touched the stomach walls, it was possible to record gastric movements. Gastric motility was recorded continuously for four hours; every 15 minutes the subject was asked if he was hungry. The two groups did not differ significantly in the amount of gastric motility or the percentage of time they reported hunger when the stomach was not contracting. But they differed markedly in their reports during stomach contractions: self-reports of hunger for the nonobese coincided with stomach contractions about 71 percent of the time; for the obese the coincidence was only about 47 percent. Apparently, the cues for hunger are different for the obese and nonobese person.

More recent studies indicate that (1) obese individuals eat as much on a full stomach as they do on an empty one and (2) fear does not decrease their food consumption as it tends to do for individuals of normal weight (Schachter, Goldman, and Gordon, 1968). These findings suggest that the eating behavior of obese individuals is not governed by internal cues. If fat people do not eat in response to internal cues, what are the external conditions that determine their eating behavior?

Eating in Response to External Cues

One external cue for eating is the passage of time. Most of us assume that when four to six hours have passed it is time for the next meal. Do obese people differ from those of normal weight in their eating response to temporal cues? What happens when apparent elapsed time differs from actual elapsed time? If you believe that it is 6:30 but it is really only 4:30, would you feel hungry and ready for dinner?

In a laboratory study designed to answer these questions two clocks were rigged so that one ran at half the normal speed and the other ran at about twice normal speed. The subjects were college students, half with an average weight 31 percent above normal and half whose weight averaged only 2 percent above normal. Each subject arrived at the laboratory at 5:00 in the afternoon and remained alone in a windowless room for 30 minutes while certain physiological measures were recorded by means of attached electrodes. The study was described as an investigation of the relation between certain physiological measures (heart rate and GSR) and performance on psychological tests. The experimenter removed each subject's watch so electrodes could be placed on his wrist and left him in a room containing only the recording equipment and either a fast or slow clock. When the experimenter returned to the room 30 minutes later (5:30), the slow clock read 5:20 and the fast one read 6:05. The experimenter was nibbling from a box of crackers and he put the box down beside the subject, inviting him to help himself; he then left the subject alone with the box of crackers to complete a self-administered personality test. The only datum actually recorded was the weight of the box of crackers before and after the subject had a chance to eat from it.

Fig. 11-6 Eating behavior and perceived time

Actual time for all groups is 5:35. Obese subjects consume more when they believe it is close to supper time while normal subjects eat less. (After Schachter and Gross, 1968)

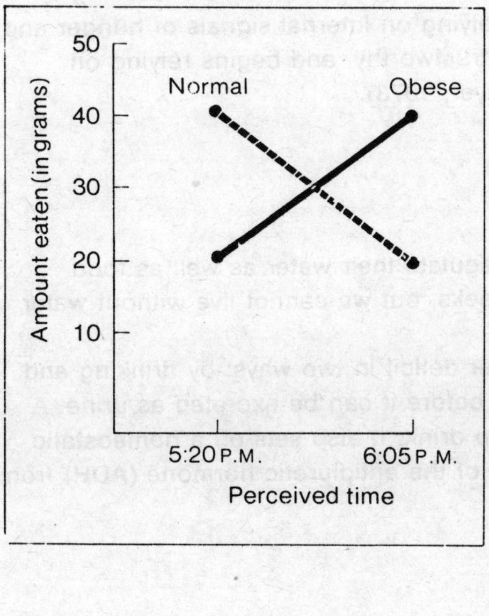

Figure 11-6 shows the amount of crackers eaten for obese and normal subjects for each time condition. It is clear that obese subjects eat almost twice as much when they think the time is 6:05 than when they believe it to be 5:20. For normal weight subjects the trend is reversed. This somewhat unexpected finding for the normal subjects is due primarily to several subjects who refused the crackers, saying, "No, thanks, I don't want to spoil my dinner." The eating behavior of both the obese and normal subjects is affected by time cues but in the opposite direction; the obese who thought it was time to eat ate significantly more than those who thought it was not yet dinner time. The normal subjects either did not increase their intake, or actually ate less when they believed it was close to their dinner hour.

An important source of external cues to eating arises from the food itself—its taste, smell, and appearance. A number of studies have shown that obese individuals are more responsive to these external cues than the nonobese. When allowed to help themselves to all they wanted of a nutritionally sound but rather bland tasting liquid diet, obese individuals diminished their intake over a period of three weeks until they were averaging

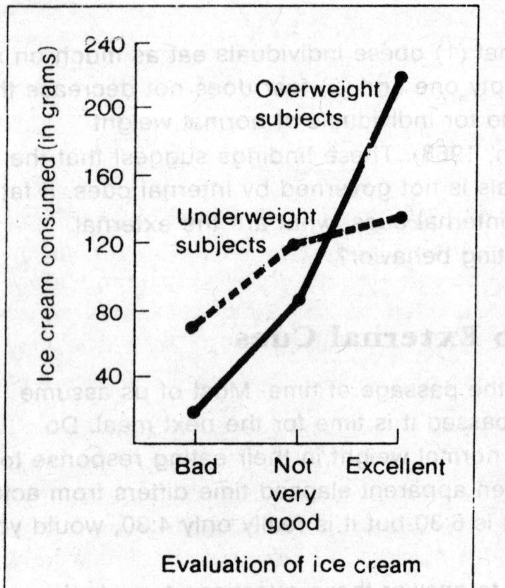

Fig. 11-7 Taste and obesity

Effects of food quality on amount eaten by overweight and underweight subjects. The subjects rated the quality of the ice cream and could eat as much as they desired. (After Nisbett, 1968b)

only 500 calories a day. Normal weight subjects showed a slight initial drop in calories consumed but thereafter returned to an average of 2300 calories per day (Hashim and Van Itallie, 1965). Of course, the obese were more motivated to lose weight than the normal subjects, but they had been unable to restrict their intake either at home or on a clinic diet of regular food.

Nisbett (1968b) examined the effects of taste on eating behavior for groups of underweight and overweight subjects. Each subject was allowed to eat as much vanilla ice cream as wanted. Half the subjects were given a creamy, expensive vanilla, while the other half were given cheap vanilla ice cream made somewhat bitter by the addition of quinine. After eating, the subjects were asked to rate the quality of the ice cream. Figure 11-7 plots the subject's ratings against amount eaten. When the ice cream is rated "very good," obese subjects eat the most. When the ice cream is rated "bad," the order is reversed; skinny subjects eat more than obese. Taste then seems to be particularly important for obese subjects.

The theme running through these different studies is that the obese individual responds less to internal hunger cues than to external cues having to do with the sight and taste of food or the time the next meal is due. For normal weight individuals the reverse is true; they rely more on internal cues of hunger. Schachter (1971) has proposed that the obese person is unable to discriminate between hunger and other states of physiological arousal, such as anxiety, fear, or anger. Such a person cannot identify internal hunger cues with certainty and must rely more on external cues.

The obese person's inability to correctly label the hunger state may stem from the way his needs were handled as an infant. The newborn infant cries when it is hungry, frightened, uncomfortable, or in pain. The mother who fails to recognize the cause of her child's crying and feeds him at every sign of distress may produce an individual who cannot discriminate between hunger and other states of emotional arousal. This individual may label all unpleasant internal states as hunger and eat whenever tense, anxious, angry, or hungry or may label no internal state as hunger and rely entirely on external cues (Bruch, 1961).

Other experts on obesity agree that the fat person is more sensitive to external food-related stimuli than the individual of normal weight, but they argue that this sensitivity is a *correlate* of obesity, not its cause. According to this view the cause of obesity, in most cases, is a disturbance of the long-term weight control mechanism in the hypothalamus. On reaching a state of obesity the individual stops relying on internal signals of hunger and satiety, because they have proven untrustworthy, and begins relying on sensory information (Thomas and Mayer, 1973).

Thirst

In order to survive, organisms must regulate their water as well as food intake. We can go without food for weeks, but we cannot live without water for more than a few days.

An organism can replenish its water deficit in two ways: by drinking and by recovering water from the kidneys before it can be excreted as urine. A water deficit motivates the organism to drink. It also sets off a homeostatic mechanism by stimulating the release of the antidiuretic hormone (ADH) from

CRITICAL DISCUSSION

Are Some People Naturally Fat?

Except for certain cases where glandular or hormone disorders are apparent, doctors have been unable to point to any physiological cause that accounts for an obese person's overeating. But the eating patterns of obese individuals and rats with VMH lesions are remarkably similar. Both eat more at a given meal and more rapidly than normal organisms; both are finicky eaters, highly responsive to food tastes; and the eating of both tends to be unrelated to internal signals of hunger. These parallels have led to the speculation that the hypothalamus of obese individuals sets a higher than normal baseline for fat tissue; these individuals are "biologically programmed to be fat" (Nisbett, 1972).

Body fat is stored in special fat cells called *adipocytes.* Obese individuals differ from nonobese both in the *size* and *number* of these fat cells, but the main difference is in the number of fat cells. In one sample, obese subjects were found to have three times as many fat cells as normal subjects (Knittle and Hirsch, 1968). This is an important finding because the number of fat cells an individual has is set at an early age and remains relatively fixed throughout life. Overeating increases the size of a person's fat cells but not their number (Sims and others, 1968); in turn, starvation decreases the size of fat cells, not the number (Hirsch and Knittle, 1970). After weight loss by dieting the formerly obese person has the same number of fat cells to be filled up again once he starts overeating. The individual with a large number of fat cells has a *higher baseline* of body fat than the individual with fewer fat cells. Evidence indicates that the number of fat cells is determined partly by heredity and partly by nutrition during the early months of life.

The individual's baseline of body fat is maintained by the hypothalamic centers which regulate food intake so as to keep fat stores at a certain set point or level. We have seen that rats with damage to the VMH (satiety center) regulate their weight at a new, higher level, whereas rats with lesions in the LH (the feeding center) regulate their weight at a new, lower level. The hypothalamus maintains fat tissue at a set point; and it is possible that the set point for an obese individual is different from that of a nonobese person of the same height and bone structure. If this is true, then obesity for some individuals is their "normal" weight which their hypothalamus tries to maintain. Attempts at weight reduction for such a person would hold him below his physiologically determined normal weight and would leave him in a state of energy deficit, feeling hungry all the time—just the same as a thin person who is on a starvation diet.

This theory is interesting but speculative and in need of further research. Obesity results from consuming more calories than the body utilizes. A higher than normal set point for fat tissue may be one reason for overconsumption, but there are undoubtedly many others. Most overweight people, unlike the VMH-damaged rats, do not become suddenly obese. Their fat accumulates over a period of months or years, a kind of "creeping obesity" that results from gradually consuming more calories than the body expends in energy.

Under normal conditions the physiological mechanisms that balance food intake and energy expenditure to keep weight stable function with remarkable precision. Body weight for most people does not vary more than two or three pounds from year to year, despite the fact that activity level and food intake vary widely from day to day. When you consider that an excess of intake over energy expended of only 100 calories a day would add 10 pounds in a year, this stability is remarkable. But research indicates that under conditions of extreme inactivity the hunger-satiety control mechanism fails to operate properly (Thomas and Mayer, 1973). Thus, people in very sedentary jobs may not get enough exercise to keep their weight-control mechanism functioning properly.

the pituitary gland. ADH acts on the kidneys so that water is reabsorbed into the blood stream and only very concentrated urine is formed. After a night's sleep you may notice that your urine is much more concentrated (darker color and stronger odor) than at other times of the day. The body has recovered water from the kidneys to compensate for the fact that you have not consumed fluids while sleeping. This homeostatic mechanism can maintain the body's water balance only up to a certain point. When the water deficit is too great, thirst becomes intense and the organism is impelled to find water.

What signals the organism that its body is in need of water?

CRITICAL DISCUSSION

Role of the Hypothalamus

The hypothalamus is involved in many types of motivated behavior. Electrical stimulation of the lateral hypothalamus elicits eating; stimulation of the preoptic region elicits drinking. But electrodes placed in the preoptic region also have produced "maternal behavior"—female rats start building nests—as well as behaviors associated with temperature regulation—opossums pant and groom their coats. Sexual behavior can be elicited by stimulation of the anterior or posterior hypothalamus in rats. And such emotional responses as rage or lethargy can be produced by hypothalamic stimulation or lesioning in many animals as well as humans. That such a tiny area can control so many different types of behavior is amazing. Psychologists disagree about the exact role the hypothalamus plays in motivated behavior. Is the hypothalamus just a connection center through which neural impulses pass on their way to other brain areas that may be more important in motivational control? Or does it contain distinct zones that control responses for each of the motivational systems—for example, eating, drinking, sex, or attack?

Some problems have arisen with the notion of the hypothalamus as a control center. For one thing, the response elicited by electrical stimulation of a single spot in the hypothalamus may change depending upon changes in the environment. If a rat eats in response to stimulation, and food is then removed from its cage, subsequent stimulation of the same spot will gradually elicit other forms of consumatory behavior, such as drinking or gnawing on wood. In addition, the behavior of animals who eat or drink in response to electrical stimulation of the hypothalamus differs in several respects from the behavior of animals who perform the same acts in response to deprivation of food or water. For example, a rat that is hungry because it has been deprived of food will switch to a second familiar food when its preferred food is removed. A rat eating in response to hypothalamic stimulation often will not switch to a different food, or even to the same food in a different form (as when food pellets are ground into powder). A rat drinking in response to hypothalamic stimulation will often continue to lap at the water tube even after the water has been removed, suggesting that the ingestion of water may not be as important as the consumatory act itself.

These and other considerations have led some psychologists to conclude that hypothalamic stimulation does not acti-

Peripheral Cues

Most people, when asked how it feels to be thirsty, describe sensations of dryness in the mouth and throat. But they are aware too that they continue drinking long after the throat has been wetted by the first swallow. Sucking on a piece of ice may provide some relief of thirst, but not for long.

Experiments with dogs provide fairly clear evidence of the role receptors in the mouth and throat play in the regulation of water intake. Dogs were fitted with a plastic tube leading from the esophagus to outside the body. They could drink normally, but the water drained out, never reaching the stomach. A thirsty dog equipped with this kind of esophagus bypass will drink its usual amount of water and then stop, apparently satisfied by fluid that never reaches the stomach. After about 10 minutes, however, it begins to drink again and consumes the same amount of water. This cycle continues with the dog gradually increasing its intake as the water deficit builds up (Adolph, 1941).

These results tell us two things. Receptors in the mouth and throat must somehow measure water intake, because the animal stops drinking after swallowing its usual amount. After a few minutes, however, the body realizes it has been duped and that although sufficient water entered the mouth, it never reached the stomach. There must be additional signals regulating water intake.

What happens if water is placed directly into a thirsty dog's stomach via a tube without passing through the mouth and throat? If it is allowed immediate

in Motivation

vate specific motivational states, such as hunger or thirst, but instead excites the neural circuits underlying well-established response patterns. According to this view, hypothalamic zones may involve broad response categories; for example, eating, drinking, and gnawing might be in one zone. The specific response elicited would be determined by such factors as prior experience and the availability of goal objects and would be independent of the precise area stimulated. Executing the particular response is reinforcing, not because it decreases a drive state, but because it discharges the neural circuits underlying the response. And once the response is executed, feedback associated with its execution is reinforcing in itself, increasing the probability that the response will be repeated (Valenstein, Cox, and Kakolewski, 1970).

Other investigators disagree with this interpretation of the role of the hypothalamus. They point out that electrical stimulation through an implanted electrode is a highly abnormal means of activating a hypothalamic control system. Such stimulation may set off responses that normally would never occur together. We know that hypothalamic areas for different motivational systems overlap to some extent, such as when the destruction of the lateral hypothalamus in rats results in cessation of both eating and drinking. And it may be that the neural mechanisms for different responses are so closely intertwined that it is difficult to stimulate one system without activating another (Bergquist, 1972). Studies using chemical stimulation lend support to this position. Norepinephrine, delivered through a tiny cannula to the lateral hypothalamus, elicits eating. Carbachol, a chemical similar to the neural transmitter acetylcholine, delivered through the same cannula elicits drinking (Grossman, 1962). This suggests that the cells that initiate drinking are cholinergic, that is, they use acetylcholine as their transmitter at the synapses, whereas the cells that initiate eating use adrenergic substances such as norepinephrine as their transmitter (see p. 58). The two systems, hunger and thirst, are closely intertwined but still involve different cells.

This controversy concerning the role of the hypothalamus in motivation is far from settled. Much remains to be learned before we have a clear understanding of the neurological basis of motivated behavior. However, progress in this area has been so dramatic in recent years that we may expect some major breakthroughs in the near future.

access to water, it will drink the usual amount. If there is a 5-, 10-, or 15-minute delay, the amount consumed decreases as the delay increases. After a 20-minute interval the dog does not drink at all (Adolph, 1941). These results indicate that a certain amount of water must be absorbed through the stomach wall into the blood stream before the mechanism that responds to water intake is activated.

Hypothalamic Regulation of Water Intake

Water deficit produces two changes in the blood and fluids surrounding the body cells: (1) decreases their volume and (2) increases the concentration of certain chemicals, primarily sodium. When the body fluids surrounding tissue cells become too concentrated, water passes out of the cells by osmosis, leaving them dehydrated. Current theories of thirst postulate two brain mechanisms for control of water intake: *osmoreceptors* that are sensitive to the chemical concentration of the body fluids and *volumetric receptors* that respond to the total volume of body fluids.

OSMORECEPTORS. Although cellular dehydration occurs in all body cells, certain nerve cells in the hypothalamus respond specifically to dehydration. Dehydration causes these cells to become slightly deformed or shriveled, and it is probably this mechanical change that triggers neural activity. The osmoreceptors are located in the hypothalamus just above the pituitary gland

and they stimulate the release of ADH from the pituitary. This hormone signals the kidneys to reabsorb water from urine into the bloodstream where it dilutes the chemical concentration of the blood and body fluids.

Dehydration of the osmoreceptors can be produced by depriving the organism of water or by injecting a salt solution directly into the brain. Even a minute amount of salt solution injected into the preoptic region of a goat's hypothalamus will cause the animal to drink several gallons of water (Anderson, 1971). A thirsty animal prefers a drink of cool water, but other fluids are accepted provided they are not more concentrated than normal body fluids. Lemonade is an acceptable thirst quencher; salty bouillon is not.

VOLUMETRIC RECEPTORS. Loss of blood volume produces thirst even in the absence of cellular dehydration. An injured person who has lost a lot of blood is intensely thirsty, although the concentration of the remaining blood is unchanged. An individual engaged in vigorous activity loses salt through perspiration, but still has the urge to drink a lot of water—which dilutes the salt concentration of the blood even further. There must be receptors sensitive to the total volume of blood and body fluids regardless of their concentration.

Evidence indicates that *renin* (a substance secreted by the kidneys into the bloodstream) is the cue for drinking in response to decreased volume of blood and body fluid. Renin causes constriction of the blood vessels, a homeostatic device to defend against further blood loss. It also effects the release of the hormone *angiotensin* from its bound form in the bloodstream; angiotensin acts upon specific receptors in the hypothalamus to produce thirst. If angiotensin is injected directly into the hypothalamus of rats, they drink copious amounts of water.

Thus, two physiological states stimulate the hypothalamus to elicit drinking: cellular dehydration and decreased blood volume (see Figure 11-8). Cellular dehydration acts directly on the hypothalamus to start the organism drinking and to stimulate the release of ADH from the pituitary, which tells the kidneys to reabsorb water into the bloodstream. Decreased blood volume causes the kidneys to secrete renin, which releases the hormone angiotensin in the bloodstream; when angiotensin reaches the hypothalamus it stimulates drinking.

When the body fluids become too concentrated, the brain signals the kidneys to retrieve water from the urine and send it back into the bloodstream; when the blood volume is low, the kidneys signal the brain to start the organism drinking. In both instances a hormone carries the message.

It is not certain what neural mechanisms tell the organism to stop drinking. Cellular hydration, the reverse of dehydration, cannot be the main stimulus for thirst satiation because the organism stops drinking long before fluid has time to enter the cells in any significant amount. Signals from the mouth, as it meters the amount of incoming water, and from the stomach, as it is distended by water, may operate to depress the activity of the hypothalamic cells responsible for drinking. But the exact process is far from clear.

Research on thirst mechanisms is complicated by the fact that in some animals (such as the rat) the hypothalamic areas for eating and drinking overlap. Areas outside of the hypothalamus are also involved in drinking, particularly the limbic system. Regulation of water intake may involve a complex neural integration of several brain areas.

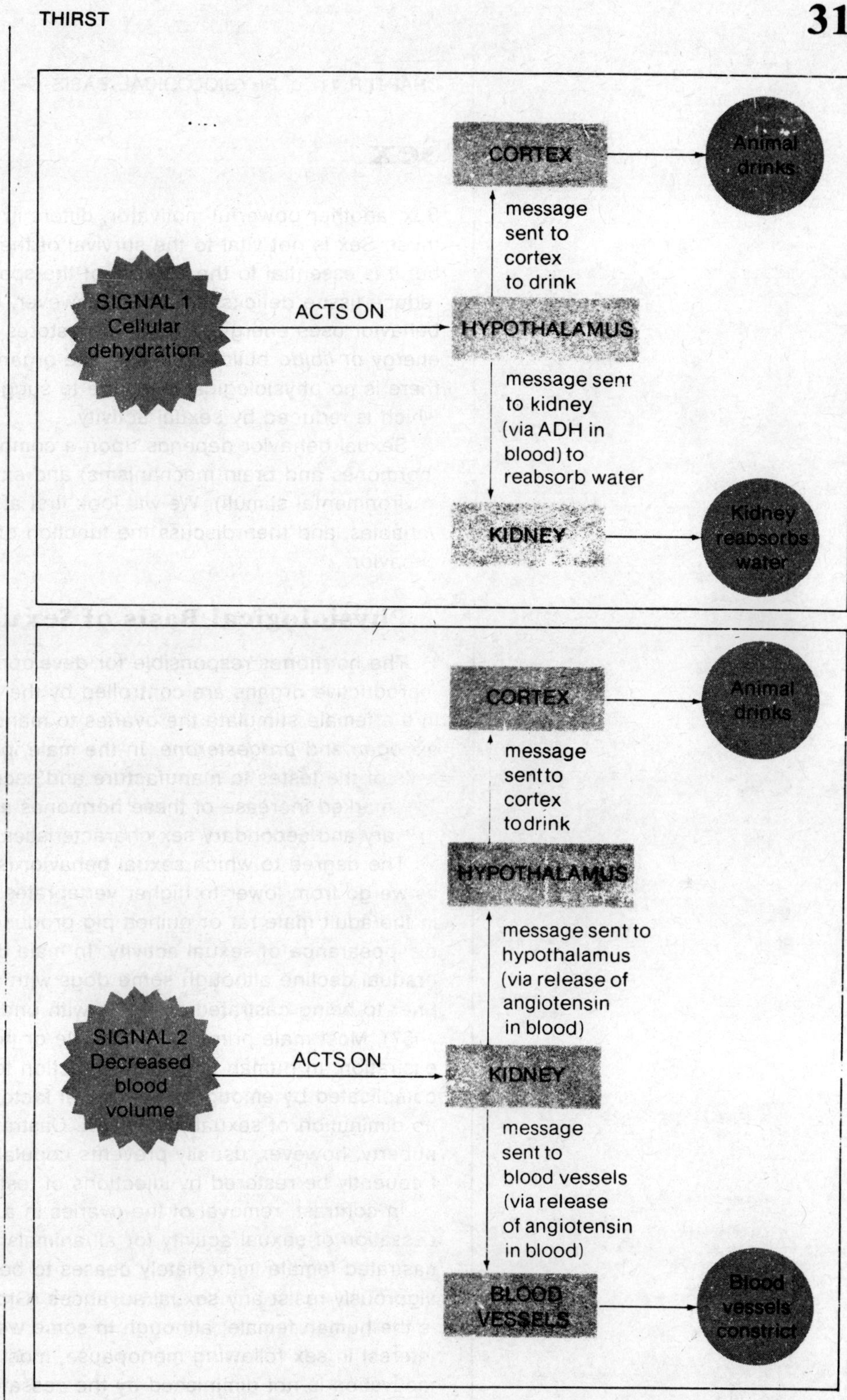

Fig. 11-8 Control mechanisms for regulation of water intake

The upper panel shows the effect of cellular dehydration on the hypothalamus. The lower panel shows the effect of decreased blood volume on the kidney and its indirect action on the hypothalamus.

Sex

Sex, another powerful motivator, differs in many respects from hunger and thirst. Sex is not vital to the survival of the organism, as are food and water, but it is essential to the survival of the species. Eating and drinking serve to reduce tissue deficits. With sex, however, there is no deficit, and sexual behavior uses energy rather than restores it. Freud proposed that sexual energy or *libido* builds up within the organism and must find some outlet. But there is no physiological evidence to suggest a buildup of some substance which is reduced by sexual activity.

Sexual behavior depends upon a combination of internal factors (hormones and brain mechanisms) and external ones (learned and unlearned environmental stimuli). We will look first at the internal or physiological variables, and then discuss the function of external variables in sexual behavior.

Physiological Basis of Sexual Behavior

The hormones responsible for development and functioning of the reproductive organs are controlled by the pituitary gland. Pituitary hormones in the female stimulate the ovaries to manufacture the sex hormones, *estrogen* and *progesterone*. In the male, pituitary hormones stimulate the cells of the testes to manufacture and secrete the sex hormone *testosterone*. The marked increase of these hormones at puberty produces changes in the primary and secondary sex characteristics at adolescence.

The degree to which sexual behavior is under hormonal control decreases as we go from lower to higher vertebrates. Castration (removal of the testes) in the adult male rat or guinea pig produces a rapid decline and disappearance of sexual activity. In male dogs, castration results in a more gradual decline although some dogs with considerable sexual experience prior to being castrated continue with undiminished sexual activity (Goldstein, 1957). Most male primates show little or no decline in sexual activity following castration. In human males, the reaction to removal of the testes is complicated by emotional and social factors. But most studies show little or no diminution of sexual motivation. Castration of any male organism *before* puberty, however, usually prevents copulation, although sexual activity can frequently be restored by injections of testosterone.

In contrast, removal of the ovaries in a female usually results in complete cessation of sexual activity for all animals from reptiles to monkeys. The castrated female immediately ceases to be receptive to the male and may vigorously resist any sexual advances (Grossman, 1967). The only exception is the human female; although in some women there may be decreased interest in sex following menopause, most reports indicate that sexual motivation is not diminished by the cessation of ovarian functioning. In fact, some women show an increased interest in sex after menopause, possibly because they need no longer be concerned about pregnancy.

Secretion of sex hormones is fairly constant in the male of most species, so that the level of sexual motivation is relatively stable. In the female, however, hormones fluctuate cyclically with accompanying changes in fertility. During the first part of the cycle, while the egg is being prepared for fertilization, the ovaries secrete estrogen which prepares the uterus for implantation and also tends to arouse sexual interest. After ovulation occurs, both progesterone and estrogen are secreted. Progesterone becomes important in preparing the mammary glands for nursing and is related to maternal behavior.

The fertility or *estrous* cycle (which varies from 36 days in the chimpanzee to 28 days in the human female to 5 days in the mouse) is accompanied by a consequent variation in sexual motivation in most species. Most female animals are receptive to sexual advances by a male only during the period of ovulation when the estrogen level is at a maximum (when they are "in heat"). Among primates, however, sexual activity is less influenced by the estrous cycle; monkeys, apes, and chimp females copulate during all phases of the cycle, although ovulation is still the period of most intense sexual activity. In the human female, sexual activity is so strongly influenced by social and emotional factors that hormonal influences are pretty much overridden.

Although hormones influence sexual motivation, they do not *elicit* specific patterns of sexual behavior. Rather, they produce *a state of readiness* to respond appropriately to certain classes of stimuli. Administration of hormones of the opposite sex has been shown to reverse sexual response patterns in a number of different species. Female dogs given testosterone show mounting behavior; male rats given estrogen show the typical female response pattern. But often the administration of hormones of the opposite sex produces *bisexual* behavior, the direction of which is largely controlled by environmental stimuli. Female rats treated with male hormones will show male sexual behavior in the presence of normal females, but will revert to the female pattern when confronted with a sexually aggressive male. Similarly, estrogen treated males will adjust their sex role in accordance with the sex of their partner (Cole and others, 1956; Beach, 1941). Hormones prime the animal to act, but the behavior displayed is largely determined by environmental stimuli.

NEURAL MECHANISMS. Neural control of sexual behavior is complex, and the mechanisms that influence sexual behavior vary considerably among different species. Some of the basic reflexes (such as erection, pelvic movements, and ejaculation in the male) are controlled at the level of the spinal cord and do not involve the brain. Men whose spinal cord has been severed from the brain by injury (paraplegics) are still capable of these movements. Much of the regulation of sexual arousal and behavior takes place in the hypothalamus, although the exact area varies across species. Electrical stimulation of the posterior hypothalamus of the rat produces not only copulation but the entire repertoire of sexual behavior. Male rats stimulated in the area do not mount indiscriminately but court the female by nibbling her ears and nipping the back of her neck until she responds. Intromission and ejaculation follow unless the electrical stimulation is terminated. Even a sexually satiated male rat will respond to stimulation by pressing a bar to open the door leading to the female, courting and mating her (Caggiula and Hoebel, 1966).

Very specific control of the rat's behavior can be obtained by implanting electrodes in both the lateral hypothalamus and the posterior hypothalamus and switching the current from one electrode to the other. With both food and a female available, the animal begins to copulate during posterior stimulation; when current is switched to the lateral electrode, it abandons the female and begins to eat. Resumption of posterior hypothalamic stimulation causes it to interrupt the meal and return to the female (Caggiula, 1967).

Such automatic determination of behavior does not occur with higher mammals. The cerebral cortex exerts control over sexual arousal and behavior, and the further up on the phylogenetic scale we go, the greater this control.

Role of Experience

Experience has little influence on patterns of mating behavior in the lower mammals. Inexperienced rats will copulate as efficiently as experienced rats. The behavior patterns are fairly specific and appear to be innate. As we go from the lower to higher mammals, however, experience and learning play increasingly important roles in sexual behavior.

Young monkeys raised together show in their play with each other many of the postural responses necessary for later copulation. In wrestling with their peers infant male monkeys display hindquarter grasping and thrusting responses that later become components of the adult sexual pattern. Infant female monkeys retreat when threatened by an aggressive male infant, and stand steadfastly in a posture that is a forerunner of the stance later required to support the weight of the male during copulation. These presexual responses appear as early as 60 days of age and increase in frequency and refinement as the monkeys mature. (See Figure 11-9.) Their early appearance suggests that they are innate responses to specific stimuli; the modification and refinement that occurs with experience indicates the role of learning in the development of the adult sexual pattern.

Monkeys raised in partial isolation—in separate wire cages where they can see other monkeys but have no contact with them—are usually unable to copulate at maturity. Male monkeys raised under such conditions are able to perform the mechanics of sex; they masturbate to ejaculation at about the same frequency as normal monkeys, but when confronted with a sexually receptive female, they seem to have no idea of how to go about the heterosexual procedure. They are aroused but proceed with aimless groping of the female or of their own bodies (Harlow, 1971).

The abnormal behavior displayed by the monkeys raised in isolation, however, extends beyond their inability to perform the specific sexual responses. Such monkeys usually are atypical in all of their social reactions and are unable to form any kind of affectional relationship. We saw in Chapter 3 that monkeys raised in isolation with wire mothers and without peer contact make poor mothers. They are also unable to relate to other adult monkeys, showing either fear and flight or extreme aggression. Harlow (1971) suggests that normal heterosexual behavior in primates (as well as humans) depends upon (1) the development of specific sexual responses, such as grasping the female and pelvic thrusting; (2) the influence of hormones; and (3) an affectional bond between two members of the opposite sex. The affectional bond is an outgrowth of interactions with the mother and with peers. Through these interactions the young monkey learns trust—it can expose its more delicate parts without fear of harm; it learns to accept and enjoy physical contact with another monkey; it develops the behavior pattern characteristic of its sex; and it becomes motivated to seek the company of other monkeys. According to Harlow, these experiences are necessary for normal heterosexual functioning. Abnormal sexual patterns usually result from disruption or disturbance of the mother-infant or peer affectional relationships.

Fig. 11-9 Infant play and adult sexual behavior

A. The first presexual step. **B.** Basic sexual posture. **C.** Inappropriate sexual response: female correct, male incorrect. **D.** Inappropriate sexual response: male correct, female incorrect.

Although these findings with monkeys cannot be extended to explain sexual development in humans, nor can we perform isolation experiments with human infants, clinical observation suggests certain parallels. Human infants first develop their feelings of trust and affection through a warm and loving relationship with the mother. (See Chapter 3 for a discussion of Erikson's concept of psychosocial stages and the development of basic trust.) This basic trust is necessary for satisfactory interactions with one's peers. And affectionate relationships with other youngsters of both sexes, prior to and during adolescence, lay the groundwork for the intimacy required for heterosexual relationships among young adults.

CULTURAL INFLUENCES. In contrast to other primates, human sexual behavior is strongly determined by cultural influences. Every society, even the most primitive, places some restrictions on sexual behavior. Incest (sexual relations within the immediate family) is prohibited by almost all cultures. Other aspects of sexual behavior—sexual activities among children, homosexuality, masturbation, and premarital sex—are viewed with varying degrees of tolerance by different societies. Among preliterate cultures studied by anthropologists the amount and type of sexual activity considered acceptable vary widely. Some very permissive societies encourage autoerotic activities and sex play among children of both sexes. The children may be instructed in sex or allowed to observe adult sexual activity. The Chewa of Africa, for example, believe that unless children exercise themselves sexually they will be unable to produce offspring later.

At the other extreme, very restrictive societies try to control preadolescent sexual behavior and keep children from learning about sexual matters. The Cuna of South America believe that children should be totally ignorant of sex until they are married; for example, they are not permitted to watch animals give birth. And among the Ashanti of Africa intercourse with a girl who has not undergone the puberty ceremony is punishable by death for both participants. Similar extremes are found in attitudes toward adult sexual behavior; homosexuality, for example, is viewed by some nonliterate societies as an essential part of growing up and by others as an offense punishable by death (Ford and Beach, 1951).

Until recently, the United States, along with most other western societies, would have been classified as restrictive. Traditionally, western society has tried to ignore or deny the existence of prepubertal sexuality and has considered marital coitus the only legitimate sexual outlet. Other forms of sexual expression—homosexual activities, oral-genital contacts, premarital and extramarital sex—have been generally condemned and in many instances prohibited by law. This is not to say that such activities were not engaged in by many members of these societies, but often with some feelings of shame.

Attitudes toward many sexual activities are much more permissive today than they were 25 years ago. Premarital sex, for example, is considered more acceptable and engaged in more frequently than in the past. Among college-educated individuals interviewed in the 1940s, 27 percent of the women and 49 percent of the men had had premarital coitus by the age of 21 (Kinsey and others, 1948, 1953). Several surveys of college students in the 1970s report considerably higher incidences, ranging from 43 to 56 percent for females and from 58 to 82 percent for males (Packard, 1970; Hunt, 1974).

The change in attitude toward premarital sex has been greatest for women, as can be seen from a recent survey of premarital experience among married individuals of different ages (see Table 11-1). The difference between women born before 1918 and those born after 1948 is striking. Other forms of

TABLE 11-1
Percentage of married individuals ever having had premarital coitus

AGE	UNDER 25	25–34	35–44	45–54	55–
Males	95	92	86	89	84
Females	81	65	41	36	31

Source: Hunt (1974).
Based on a national survey of 1400 individuals.

"Well, I'm sure Dr. Kinsey never spoke to anyone in Upper Montclair."

sexual behavior, such as masturbation and oral-genital stimulation, have also become increasingly more acceptable. Oral-genital practices reported by Kinsey for the 1940s compared with those reported by Hunt for the 1970s show a dramatic change.

Oral-Genital Foreplay Used Premaritally

	1940s	*1970s*
Fellatio	33%	72%
Cunnilingus	14%	69%

And homosexuality is viewed with greater tolerance than it was 25 years ago, although there is no indication that the proportion of homosexual individuals is increasing.

Although there is a trend toward greater sexual permissiveness among most developed nations, there are still cultural differences. For example, England, Sweden, and Denmark have more liberal standards of sexual behavior than Ireland and, at least for girls, Spain and Italy. Sexual behavior, while biologically motivated, can take many forms depending upon individual experiences as well as cultural conditioning.

Other Drives with Physiological Basis

Maternal Behavior

In many species care of offspring is a more powerful determiner of behavior than hunger, thirst, or sex. A mother rat will return its young to the nest if they are placed outside it. When separated from its young, a mother rat will overcome barriers and suffer pain in order to reach them. It will cross an electric grid to return to its nest more frequently than it will to obtain food when hungry or water when thirsty.

The physiological conditions that activate this maternal behavior are complex, but one influence is the hormone *prolactin,* which becomes dominant over the female sex hormones after the young are born and is associated with the production of milk. If this hormone is injected into virgin females or even into male rats, they begin to build nests and take care of the young as a mother rat does. In submammals, such as birds, prolactin is responsible for food gathering and feeding of the young.

Among primates, maternal behavior is largely under the influence of experience and learning. We saw in Chapter 3 that monkeys raised in isolation with cloth or wire mothers showed none of the normal maternal responses to their young when they became mothers for the first time. With subsequent pregnancies, however, they became more effective in their roles as mothers.

Although a "maternal instinct" has been posited as universal among human females, concern for one's offspring does not invariably follow from giving birth and secreting prolactin. Some women have been known to abandon their newborn infants or even kill them. And "battered children"—children deliberately injured by their own parents—are far more common than would be supposed. It is estimated that in the United States

CRITICAL DISCUSSION

Instinctive Tendencies as Explanations

The response patterns animals display in the care of their young provide a clear example of the type of behavior that has been called instinctive. Building nests, removing the amniotic sac so the newborn can breath, feeding the young and retrieving them when they stray from the nest, all involve complex patterns of behavior that appear without the opportunity to learn. The mother squirrel performs its maternal duties in the same manner as all other mothers of its species, whether it is the first litter or the fifth.

Interest in instinctive behavior, which declined during the early part of the century because it did not prove very helpful in understanding human behavior, has been revived by a group of European psychologists and zoologists who call themselves *ethologists.* These scientists are concerned with studying animals in their natural environment rather than in the laboratory where the artificiality of the situation often prevents behavior patterns from appearing in a natural form and in their entirety.

Ethologists prefer the term *species-specific* behavior to the more controversial term instinct. They study behavior that is specific to a certain species and that appears in the same form in all members of the species. And they attempt to determine the variables that govern this behavior.

One of the concepts introduced by ethologists is *imprinting,* which refers to a type of early learning that forms the basis for the young animal's attachment to its parents. A newly hatched duckling that has been incubated artificially without the presence of a mother duck will follow a human being, or a wooden decoy, or almost any other moving object that it first sees after birth. Following a wooden decoy for as little as 10 minutes is enough to "imprint" the duckling on the deccy so that it will remain attached to this object, following it even under adverse circumstances and preferring it to a live duck. (See Figure 11-10.) Imprinting takes place most readily at 14 hours after hatching but can occur any time during the first two days of life. After that, imprinting is difficult or impossible, probably because the duckling has acquired a fear of strange objects. This is an example of a *critical period* in development. If the behavior does not occur during a specific or critical period in the organism's life, it is unlikely to occur at all.

Imprinting has been found in a number of species—dogs, sheep, guinea pigs—but it is most clearly developed in birds that are able to walk or swim immediately after birth (as opposed to those that remain in a nest). An innate mechanism of this sort ensures that the young will follow and remain close to the mother

Austrian zoologist Konrad Lorenz demonstrates how young ducklings follow him instead of their mother because he was the first moving object they saw when they were hatched.

more than 700 children are killed by their parents each year, and an additional 40,000 are seriously beaten or tortured by parents, siblings, or relatives (Helfer and Kempe, 1968). The parents involved in these cases generally had received no love as children and frequently had been beaten by their own parents. There is a parallel here with Harlow's inadequate and cruel monkey mothers. In primates and in humans, experience far overrides whatever influence "maternal hormones" may have.

Avoidance of Pain

The need to avoid tissue damage is essential to the survival of any organism. Even a weak pain stimulus may dominate other stimuli in

# of Motivated Behavior

(normally the first moving object it sees) rather than wander off into a perilous world.

Studies with mallard ducks have identified the stimuli that are important for imprinting in birds and indicate that the phenomenon begins even before birth. Ducklings in the egg begin to make sounds a week before they break through their shells. Mallard mothers respond to these sounds and commence clucking signals, which increase in frequency about the time the duckling hatches. Auditory stimuli before and after hatching, together with tactile stimulation in the nest after birth, result in ducklings that are thoroughly imprinted on the female mallard present in the nest. The unhatched duckling who hears, instead of its mother's voice, a recording of a human voice saying "Come, come, come," will, after hatching, imprint to a decoy that utters "Come, come, come" as easily as to a decoy that utters normal mallard clucks. Ducklings that have been exposed to a mallard female's call prior to hatching are more likely to imprint to decoys that utter mallard clucks (Hess, 1972).

Another concept developed by the ethologists is that of a *releaser*, a particular environmental stimulus that sets off a kind of behavior characteristic of a species. Thus, a red or yellow spot on the mother's beak "releases" a pecking response in some young seagulls, causing the mother to regurgitate the food that the infant will eat. Varying the color and shape of the spot on cardboard models and observing whether or not the young gull pecks at it, makes it possible to determine the characteristics of the

Fig. 11-10 Imprinting in ducklings

The newly hatched duckling follows the model duck around a circular track. The duckling soon becomes imprinted on the model and will follow it in preference to a live duck of its own species. The more effort the duckling has to exert to follow the model (such as climbing a hurdle) the stronger the imprinting. (After Hess, 1958)

releaser to which the bird responds.

The swollen abdomen of the female stickleback fish initiates courtship behavior by the male. Owl-like figures initiate mobbing behavior—a kind of feigned attack—by birds for which the owl is a natural enemy. The bowing and cooing behavior of the male ring dove releases the entire sequence of reproductive behavior in the female (nest-building, egg laying, and incubating the eggs), and is responsible, directly or indirectly, for the hormonal and anatomical changes that go along with these activities (Lehrman, 1964).

The higher one goes up the phylogenetic scale, the fewer the species-specific behaviors and the more learning determines the kinds of actions used to satisfy needs. But even we have some built-in behavior patterns. The rooting reflex of the human infant is an example. Touching a nipple to the cheek of a newborn elicits head turning (both from side to side and up and down) with simultaneous opening of the mouth. If the mouth contacts the nipple, it closes on it and begins to suck. This behavior pattern is automatic and can occur even when the infant is sleeping. The rooting reflex disappears at about six months and voluntary motivated behavior takes over; the typical six-month old sees the bottle, reaches for it, and tries to bring it to his mouth.

controlling the direction of behavior. Pain will lead to any behavior that reduces the discomfort—removing one's hand from a hot stove, taking off a shoe that pinches, swallowing an aspirin to relieve a headache.

Pain involves two processes. It is a sensory event resulting from tissue damage and it is also a reaction of the central nervous system to the sensory message. The motivational aspects of pain depend upon normal growth experiences. We noted in Chapter 3 that dogs raised from birth with minimal sensory stimulation fail to show the normal avoidance reaction to painful stimuli; they do not respond to being pricked with a pin or having their tails stepped on and will repeatedly investigate a lighted match by putting their nose into the flame (Scott, 1968).

Some physiological conditions are aversive in the sense that they produce discomfort or pain and motivate the organism to do something to remedy the situation. Extremes of temperature, suffocation, the accumulation of excessive waste products in the body, and excessive fatigue all impel the organism to action. Sometimes the physiological basis of a drive is acquired. Drug dependency is an example. Initially, an individual has no physiological need for heroin, but continued usage creates an imperative need for it, and all actions become determined by this need. Deprived of heroin, the individual becomes restless and develops symptoms of acute illness that are relieved only by the drug.

Basic Motives with Unspecified Physiological Correlates

All the motives we have discussed—hunger, thirst, sex, maternal behavior, and pain avoidance—have had some basis in the physiological condition of the organism. As we noted in the beginning of this chapter, a *drive-reduction theory* of motivation explains all behavior as attempts to reduce drives stemming from bodily needs. Thus, food deprivation disturbs the balance of certain substances in the blood, thereby creating a need. The psychological counterpart of this need, the hunger drive, prompts the organism to seek whatever object will reduce the drive (in this case food) and return the body to its normal state. This homeostatic model provides a useful conception of motives based on deprivation and aversive stimulation (hunger, thirst, and pain), but seems less appropriate as a description of sexual and maternal behavior.

According to drive-reduction theory, an organism that has its biological needs satisfied should be in a quiescent state. But the evidence indicates that both people and animals are motivated to *seek* stimulation, to engage in active exploration of and interaction with their environment even when such activity satisfies no bodily need.

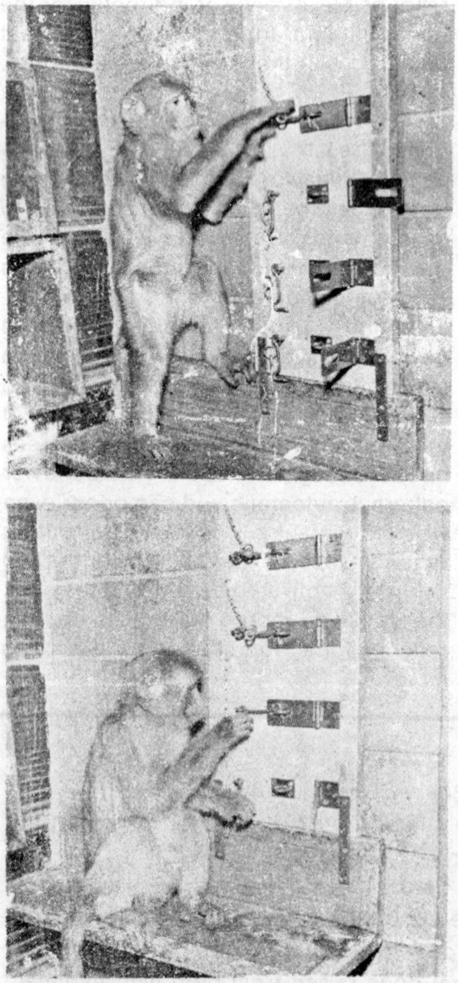

Fig. 11-11 Manipulation motive

The monkey takes the latches apart, even though there is no "reward" except that deriving from the manipulation itself.

Exploration and Manipulation

When placed in a new environment, animals tend to run about sniffing and inspecting—like a dog or cat in a new house. If a rat is placed in a T-shaped maze and turns to the right on the first trial, the probability is high that it will turn left on reaching the cross bar on the second trial. Its preference will be for the unexplored territory. The rat in this case is neither hungry nor thirsty and has not been rewarded with food or water in either goal box. We could call such behavior exploratory, or an indication of a motive to experience variety.

Another form of exploratory activity is the manipulation or investigation of objects. We give babies rattles, crib gymnasiums, and other toys because we know they like to hold, shake, and pull at them. Monkeys enjoy the same sort of activity; in fact, the word *monkey* is used as a verb to describe casual manipulation for whatever satisfaction it brings. A number of experiments have shown that monkeys do, indeed, like to "monkey." If various mechanical devices are placed in a monkey's cage (see Figure 11-11), it will begin to take them apart, becoming more skilled with practice, without any evident reward other than the satisfaction of manipulating them (Harlow,

Harlow, and Meyer, 1950). If the monkey is fed each time it takes the puzzle apart, its behavior changes: The interest in manipulation is reduced in favor of finding in the puzzle a means to food.

Sometimes manipulation has the quality of *investigation;* the organism picks up the object, looks at it, tears it apart, etc., in an apparent attempt to discover more about it. Piaget has made a number of observations bearing on such responses in the early life of the human infant. Within the first few months of life an infant learns to pull a string to activate a hanging rattle—a form of manipulation that might be considered merely entertaining. Between 5–7 months, the infant will remove a cloth from his face, anticipating the peekaboo game. At 8–10 months, the infant will begin to look for objects behind or beneath other objects; by 11 months, to "experiment" with objects, varying their placement or position (Piaget, 1952). This kind of inquisitive or investigative behavior is typical of the growing child. Perhaps we might call it curiosity or a need to develop competency over one's environment. In any event, it seems to develop as a motive apart from any physiological needs of the organism.

Need for Sensory Stimulation

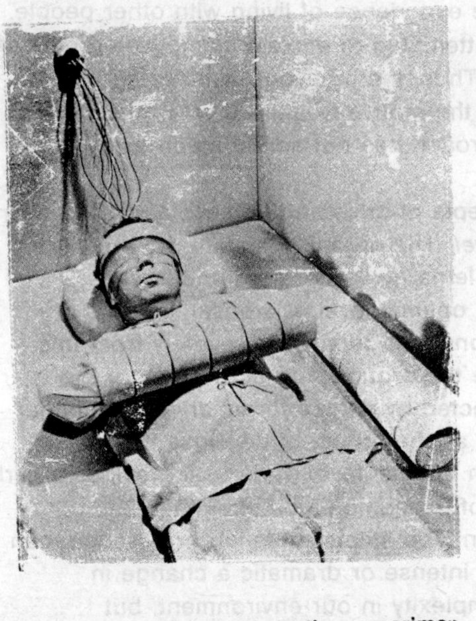

Fig. 11-12 Sensory deprivation experiment

Cardboard cuffs and translucent blindfold reduce stimulation

Exploration and manipulation provide new and changing sensory input. The need for such input has been demonstrated by studies in which the amount of sensory stimulation the organism receives is markedly reduced. We saw in Chapter 3 that sensory deprivation in the early months of life has a dramatic effect on later behavior. When a human adult is deprived of the normal amount of sensory stimulation, the results are equally dramatic. The first study of this type with humans was carried out at McGill University in Canada. College students were paid to lie on a cot in a lighted, partially sound-deadened room. They wore translucent goggles so that they could see diffuse light but no shapes or patterns. Gloves and cardboard cuffs reduced tactile stimulation. (See Figure 11-12.) The hum of an exhaust fan and an air conditioner provided a constant masking noise. Brief time-outs were allowed for meals and toilet needs, but, otherwise, the subject remained in a condition of very restricted stimulation compared to normal life. After two or three days, most of the subjects refused to continue the experiment; the situation was sufficiently intolerable to negate any financial gain.

Some of the subjects began to experience visual hallucinations, varying from light flashes and geometric patterns to dream-like scenes. They became disoriented in time and space, were unable to think clearly or concentrate for any length of time, and did poorly on problems given them to solve. In short, the condition of reduced stimulation had a detrimental effect on functioning and produced symptoms not unlike those experienced by some mental patients (Heron, Doane, and Scott, 1956).

A number of similar studies have since been carried out with some variations in procedure. In some studies the subject lay immersed to the neck in a tub of warm water for several days in an attempt to further reduce sensory stimulation. Results have differed somewhat depending upon differences in procedure, but in all instances the subjects found the condition of sensory deprivation aversive: they were bored, restless, irritable, and emotionally upset. People apparently need changes in stimulation and react adversely to its absence (Zubek, 1969).

Current Status of Motivational Concepts

Having examined a number of motivational systems that account for a wide range of actions in both humans and animals, what can we say about the theories that have attempted to explain motivated behavior? Each motivation theory has some grain of truth, but each is incomplete as an explanation of the full complexity of human behavior. Biological needs are powerful instigators to action, because their satisfaction is essential to the survival of the organism and/or the survival of the species. In our highly industrialized and affluent society, we tend to be less aware of biological motives. But the actions of someone who does not know where to find the next scrap of food or how to protect himself from the cold, will be dominated by physical needs. Only when our basic biological needs are satisfied can other, more distinctly human, motives become important. These include motives related to our feelings of self-esteem and competency, as well as social motives having to do with our relations with other people.

In Chapter 12 we will look at some of these psychological motives that are unrelated, as far as we know, to biological needs and are acquired as the result of experience—particularly, the experience of living with other people. Originally, drive-reduction theorists attempted to explain *all* motivated acts as the result of basic biological needs. Thus, the motive to achieve could be traced back to the hunger drive and the motive to affiliate with others was based on the sex drive. But this approach has not added much to our understanding of complex motives.

For many psychologists the concepts of drive and homeostasis have been replaced by the notion of *arousal level.* The organism's state of arousal or activation can range from sleep and lethargy to alertness and intense excitement. Theoretically, there is an optimal level of arousal in terms of internal and external stimuli. Conditions that depart too severely from this optimal state in either direction incite the organism to act to restore the equilibrium. Arousal level can be affected by such internal drives as hunger and thirst or by such external stimuli as the aroma of delicious food or the loud clang of a bell. The notion of an optimal level of arousal provides a fairly simple way of looking at the results of experiments on exploration, manipulation, and sensory deprivation. Too little stimulation or boredom can motivate the organism as well as too intense or dramatic a change in stimulation. We seek novelty and complexity in our environment, but situations that are too strange or too complex arouse anxiety. We will have more to say about arousal level when we consider emotion in the next chapter.

Summary

1. Motivation refers to the factors that *energize* and *direct* behavior. Attempts to explain motivated acts have had various emphases. (a) *Instinct theory* postulates innate predispositions to specific actions. (b) *Drive-reduction theory* bases motivation on bodily *needs* that create a state of tension or *drive* which the organism seeks to reduce by doing something to satisfy the need. Tissue needs prompt action because the body tends to maintain a constant internal environment or *homeostasis.* (c) *Incentive theory* emphasizes the importance of external conditions as a source of

motivation. These may be *positive incentives* which the organism will approach or *negative incentives* which he will avoid. Incentives can arouse behavior as well as direct it.

2. Important brain areas in the regulation of food intake are the lateral hypothalamus (LH), the "feeding center," and the ventromedial hypothalamus (VMH), the "satiety center," which acts reciprocally to maintain stable body weight. They also contain receptors that respond to stomach distension, blood glucose level, and temperature to effect short-term control of eating. Taste and olfactory cues are normally not essential for regulation of food intake but become so when the hypothalamic control centers are impaired.
3. Learning plays an important role in appetite for and aversion to specific foods. Research on obesity suggests that overweight individuals may respond more to external than to internal hunger cues, while for those of normal weight the reverse is true.
4. Hypothalamic regulation of water intake involves (a) *osmoreceptors* that respond to cellular dehydration by prompting the organism to drink and by stimulating the pituitary gland to secrete an anti-diuretic hormone into the blood which signals the kidneys to reabsorb water, and (b) *volumetric receptors* that are activated by angiotensin, a hormone released by the kidneys in the bloodstream in response to decreased blood volume.
5. Sexual behavior in lower animals is largely instinctive and controlled by hormones and stimuli emanating from the animal of the opposite sex. These factors, although important to sexual behavior in humans, are less influential than early experience with parents and peers and cultural norms.
6. Two more motives with a physiological basis are *maternal behavior* and *pain avoidance.* Maternal behavior in lower animals is largely instinctive; in primates and man, however, experience with one's own parents plays a major role. Even the motivational aspects of pain depend to some extent on normal growth experiences.
7. Motives with no known physiological basis are the needs to *explore* new environments and to *manipulate* objects. The organism requires a certain amount of stimulation; *sensory deprivation* can be very aversive.
8. Central to current approaches to motivation is the notion of *arousal level.* Internal or external stimulation that produces too severe a change from the optimal arousal level motivates the organism to do something to restore equilibrium.

Further Reading

Brief summaries of motivation may be found in Stein and Rosen, *Motivation and emotion* (1974), and Cofer, *Motivation and emotion* (1972).

More extensive accounts are Cofer and Appley, *Motivation: Theory and research* (1964), and Bolles, *Theory of motivation* (1967). Weiner, *Theories of motivation* (1972) compares four major theories of motivation.

Information on the biological bases of hunger, thirst, sex, and maternal behavior may be found in textbooks on physiological psychology, of which Morgan, *Physiological psychology* (1965) and Schwartz, *Physiological psychology* (1973) are representative.

An interesting paperback that summarizes some of the research on obesity and offers suggestions on diet and the behavioral control of eating is *Slim chance in a fat world* (1972) by Stuart and Davis.

12 human motivation and emotion

Why does a scientist spend long hours at work in the laboratory, forgoing all other activities and pleasures? An athlete endure months of painful training in preparation for Olympic competition? One person devote all efforts toward amassing a fortune; another give up a life of security and ease to work with impoverished peoples in a remote and primitive region? Obviously biological needs cannot begin to account for the diversity and complexity of human behavior.

It is true that an infant's early behavior is largely determined by basic biological needs—a child cries when hungry, cold, or in pain. But as the child grows, new motives appear that are learned by interacting with other people. We will call them *psychological motives* to distinguish them from motives based on physiological needs. Security, acceptance and approval from those around us, feelings of self-worth and competency, and the search for new experiences are important psychological motives, although the way in which they are satisfied varies with each individual and culture. The distinction between biological and psychological motives is not clear cut. In the last chapter we noted that biological motives can be aroused by external incentives, and that learning determines to some extent the way such needs as hunger and sex are satisfied. Psychological motives are influenced *primarily* by learning and the kind of society in which the individual is raised; they have no demonstrable basis in the physiological needs of the organism.

Abraham Maslow, a leader in the development of humanistic psychology (p. 9), proposed an interesting way of classifying human motives. He assumed a *hierarchy* of motives ascending from the basic biological needs present at birth to more complex psychological motives that become important only after the more basic needs have been satisfied. (See Figure 12-1.) The needs at one level must be at least partially satisfied before those at the next level become important determiners of action. When food and safety are difficult to obtain, the satisfaction of these needs will dominate a person's actions and the higher motives will have little significance. Only when the satisfaction of the basic needs is easy will the individual have the time and energy for aesthetic and intellectual interests. Artistic and scientific endeavors do not flourish in societies where people must struggle for food, shelter, and safety.

Maslow's scheme has not been supported by much data, but it provides an interesting way of looking at the relationships among motives and the opportunities afforded by the environment. We will have more to say about Maslow's highest motive, *self-actualization,* in discussing personality in the next chapter.

Many theories have been advanced to explain human motivation, but as yet there is little consensus. We will concentrate on two theories that adopt very different views concerning human nature: *psychoanalytic theory* and *social learning theory.* After summarizing these two theories, we will examine a specific area of motivated behavior—aggression—noting how each theory would explain aggressive behavior.

Obviously, motivation and emotion are closely related. Feelings determine our actions, and, conversely, our behavior often determines how we feel. Emotions can activate and direct behavior in the same way as biological drives. The last half of the chapter will be concerned with the way we experience and express emotion and the influence of emotion on behavior.

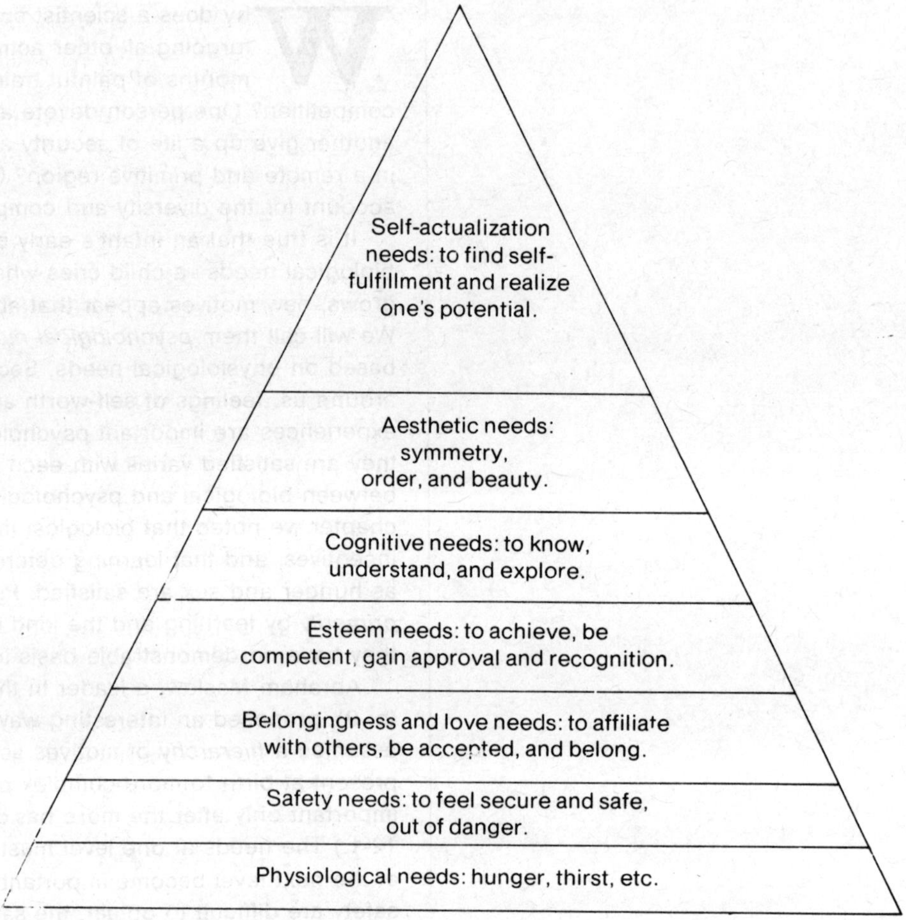

Fig. 12-1 Maslow's hierarchy of needs

The needs that are low in the hierarchy must be at least partially satisfied before those that are higher can become important sources of motivation. (Source: Maslow, 1954)

Theories of Motivation

According to Freud's psychoanalytic theory our actions are determined by inner forces and impulses, often operating below the level of consciousness. In contrast, social learning theory, as formulated by Albert Bandura at Stanford University, sees our behavior as learned through interaction with, and observation of, the environment.

Psychoanalytic Theory of Motivation

Apart from its methods for treating neurotic disorders (see Chapter 17), psychoanalysis is also a theory of human motivation. It began with Freud's *Interpretation of dreams* in 1900 and has evolved gradually. A complete exposition of psychoanalytic theory would require a lengthy discussion of its numerous changes. But for our purposes a broad outline of the theory will suffice.

INSTINCTUAL DRIVES. Freud believed that all behavior stemmed from two opposing groups of instincts: the life instincts (Eros) that enhance life and growth and the death instincts (Thanatos) that push toward destruction. The energy of the life instincts is *libido* which involves mainly sex and related activities. The death instincts can be directed inward in the form of suicide or self-destructive behavior or outward in the form of aggression toward others. For Freud, then, the two basic human motives are sex and aggression. He was not unaware of physiological needs, or of the role of fear, but they played little part in his theory.

Freud believed that the forerunners of sex and aggression are found early in a child's life: sex is expressed in the pleasure derived from stimulating the sensitive zones of the body (see p. 78) for the psychosexual stages of development); and aggression, in biting or hitting. When parental prohibitions place taboos on both sex and aggression, their free expression becomes *repressed* and, instead of finding full conscious expression, they remain active as *unconscious motives.* Sex undergoes more severe repression than aggression, but the expression of either motive may make the child anxious because of negative parental attitudes. Unconscious motives then find expression in disguised form. The concept of *unconscious motivation* is one of the cornerstones of psychoanalytic theory.

BEHAVIOR FROM WHICH UNCONSCIOUS MOTIVES ARE INFERRED. Although writers and philosophers had long recognized the existence of some unconscious controls over human conduct, it remained for Freud to call attention to the powerful role of unconscious motives in human behavior. He pointed to several forms of behavior through which unconscious motives are expressed:

1. In dreams we often express wishes and impulses of which we are unaware.
2. Unconscious mannerisms and slips of speech may "let the cat out of the bag" and reveal hidden motives.
3. Symptoms of illness (particularly the symptoms of mental illnesses) often can be shown to serve the unconscious needs of the person.

Many psychologists now accept the existence of unconscious motives (or at least motives that are unclear to the person), but they think more in terms of *degrees of awareness.* A person may be vaguely aware, for example, of the need to dominate others but may not realize the extent to which this need influences his behavior and relationships.

Interpreting dreams is a tricky business; very little is known about the content of dreams and what the content supposedly symbolizes. Slips of speech may reveal unconscious motives, but just as often they may give away motives of which the speaker is aware but wishes to keep hidden. Think, for example, of the person who says to an unwelcome visitor "I'm sad you came," when what was intended was "I'm glad you came." We can acknowledge that often we may not be fully aware of why we behave as we do without assuming that motives are always unconscious.

Social Learning Theory of Motivation

Social learning theory focuses not on instinctual drives but on patterns of behavior the individual learns in coping with the environment. The emphasis is on the reciprocal interaction between behavior and environment. We are

Vicarious learning

Self-reinforcement

neither driven by internal forces nor are we passive reactors to external stimulation. The type of behavior we exhibit partly determines the reward or punishment we receive, and these in turn influence our behavior.

Patterns of behavior can be acquired through direct experience or by observing the behavior of others. Some responses may be successful; others may produce unfavorable results. Through this process of differential reinforcement, the person eventually selects the successful behavior patterns and discards the others.

Social learning theory departs from a strict behaviorist position by stressing the importance of cognitive processes. Because we can think and represent situations symbolically, we are able to foresee the probable consequences of our actions and alter our behavior accordingly. Our actions are governed to a large extent by anticipated consequences. We don't wait until we've experienced frostbite to decide to wear warm gloves in subfreezing weather. Future consequences, represented symbolically in one's thoughts, can motivate behavior in much the same way as actual consequences.

Social learning theory also stresses the importance of *vicarious learning,* that is, learning by observation. Many patterns of behavior are learned by watching the behavior of others and observing its consequences for them. Emotions can also be learned vicariously by watching the emotional responses of others as they undergo painful or pleasant experiences. A young boy who observes the pained expressions of his older brother in the dentist's chair will probably be fearful when the time comes for his first dental appointment. Social learning theorists emphasize the role of *models* in transmitting both specific behaviors and emotional responses. And they have exerted much of their research efforts toward discovering how modeled behavior is transmitted—what types of model are most effective, and what factors determine whether the modeled behavior that is learned will actually be performed.

A third emphasis of social learning theory is the importance of *self-regulatory processes.* A specific behavior produces an external outcome, but it also produces a self-evaluative reaction. People set their own standards of conduct or performance and respond to their behavior in self-satisfied or self-critical ways, depending upon how the behavior relates to their standards. Thus, reinforcement has two sources: *external* and *self-evaluative.* Sometimes the two coincide, and sometimes they are contradictory. A person may be rewarded socially, or materially, for behavior that is not acceptable according to self-standards. Indeed, self-reproach is an important influence in motivating people to adhere to accepted standards of conduct in the face of opposing influences. One person is tempted to falsify information on an income tax return. The chances of getting caught (external punishment) are slim and the financial gain is substantial. But the anticipation of personal feelings of self-contempt prevent the individual from doing so: The behavior is not in accord with self-standards.

External reinforcement is most effective when it is consistent with self-reinforcement—when society approves actions that the individual values highly. An artist whose works are enthusiastically received by the public and the critics will probably be more motivated to continue than one whose creative endeavors are appreciated by neither group. It takes conviction in one's own standards to persevere when external reinforcement is lacking.

Social learning theorists have been active in developing procedures whereby people can control their own behavior by self-reinforcement or self-punishment. Successful methods have been developed to control abuse of alcohol or overeating by having individuals reward themselves with an activity they find pleasurable when they stick to a certain regimen of eating or drinking.

Both psychoanalytic theory and social learning theory will be explored further in Chapter 17 in terms of the methods they use in treating mental illness. The contrast between these two theoretical approaches will become clearer if we look at one area of motivated behavior and examine how each would handle it. Several motivational systems could be discussed, such as need for achievement or need for affiliation, but some of the most interesting work has been done in the area of aggression. The need to understand what instigates aggression and how it can be controlled is one of the most crucial problems facing society. In an age where powerful weapons are easily available, a single aggressive act can have disastrous consequences.

Hostile or instrumental aggression?

Motivational Factors in Aggression

Aggression is usually defined as behavior intended to injure another person (either physically or verbally) or to destroy property. The key word is *intent.* If I accidentally step on your toes in a crowded elevator and immediately apologize, you are not likely to label my behavior aggressive. If I walk up as you sit at your desk studying and stomp my foot down on yours, you are apt to respond with outrage at such a blatantly aggressive act. But it is also clear that even intentional aggressive acts can serve goals other than inflicting injury. (I may step on your foot in the elevator so that I can get out quickly and be first in line at the ticket office.)

Any specific act can satisfy a wide range of possible motives. Power, wealth, and status are only a few of the ends that can be attained by aggressive means. Some psychologists distinguish between (1) *hostile aggression,* the sole aim of which is to inflict injury, and (2) *instrumental aggression,* which is aimed at obtaining rewards other than the victim's suffering. Instrumental aggression would include such behavior as assault during a robbery, battling to defend the rights of an underdog, or fighting to prove one's strength and power. But the distinction is not clear cut. What looks like a case of hostile aggression may serve other ends: A gang member who brutally attacks an innocent passerby (on the surface, a case of hostile aggression) may be motivated by a need to gain status with his gang. A theory of aggression should be able to account for both hostile and instrumental aggression.

Aggression as a Drive

Freud viewed aggression as one of two basic instincts. The energy of the *death instinct* builds up within the organism until it must be discharged, either outwardly through overt aggression or inwardly in the form of self-destructive acts. Freud was pessimistic about the possibility of ever eliminating aggression. The best that society could do would be to modify its intensity by promoting positive emotional attachments between people and by providing substitute outlets (such as watching prize fights or engaging in sports).

Later theorists in the Freudian tradition rejected the idea that aggression was an innate drive or instinct and proposed that it was a frustration-produced drive. The *frustration-aggression hypothesis* assumes that thwarting a person's efforts to reach a goal induces an aggressive drive which, in turn, motivates behavior designed to injure the person or object causing the frustration (Dollard and others, 1939). The expression of aggression reduces the drive. Aggression is the dominant response to frustration, but other responses can occur if aggression has been punished in the past. By this formulation, aggression is not inborn; but, since frustration is a fairly universal condition, it is still a drive that must find an outlet.

Some support for a biologically based aggressive drive comes from studies showing that aggressive behavior can be elicited in animals by mild electrical stimulation of a specific region of the hypothalamus. When a cat's hypothalamus is stimulated via implanted electrodes, the animal hisses, its hair bristles, its pupils dilate, and it will strike out at a rat or other object placed in its cage. Stimulation of a slightly different area of the hypothalamus produces quite different behavior; the cat shows none of the above "rage" responses but, instead, will coldly stalk a rat and kill it.

Fig. 12-2 Brain stimulation and aggression

A mild electrical current is delivered to electrodes implanted in the monkey's hypothalamus via remote radio control. The animal's response (attack or flight) depends upon his position in the status hierarchy of the colony. (Courtesy Dr. Jose Delgado)

Aggressive behavior has been produced in monkeys and rats by similar techniques. A laboratory-bred rat that has never killed or seen a wild rat killing a mouse may live quite peaceably in the same cage with a mouse. But if the rat's hypothalamus is stimulated with neurochemicals, the animal will pounce upon its mouse cage-mate and kill it with exactly the same response pattern exhibited by a wild rat—a hard bite to the neck that severs the spinal cord. It is as if the stimulation triggers an innate killing response that had until this time remained dormant. On the other hand, a neurochemical blocker injected into the same brain site in rats that spontaneously kill mice on sight produces a temporary pacifism (Smith, King, and Hoebel, 1970).

In higher mammals such instinctive aggressive patterns are more under the control of the cortex and thus more influenced by experience. Monkeys living in groups establish a dominance hierarchy with one or two males as leaders and the others at various levels of subordination. Remote-control electrical stimulation of the hypothalamus of a monkey who assumes a dominant role in the group instigates attacks on subordinate males but not females. The same stimulation of a monkey low in rank elicits cowering and submissive behavior. (See Figure 12-2.) Thus, aggression is not automatically elicited by stimulation of the hypothalamus. The hypothalamus may send a message to the cortex indicating that its "aggression center" has been activated, but the cortex, in choosing the response it will initiate, considers what is going on in the environment and its memory of past experiences.

Like the lower animals, we have the neurological mechanisms that enable us to behave aggressively. But the activation of these mechanisms is under much more *cognitive control.* Some brain-damaged individuals may react aggressively to stimulation that normally would be ineffective; in these cases cortical control is impaired. One study reports a high incidence of neurological defects in persons who are repeatedly violent and assaultive (Mark and Ervin, 1970). But in normal individuals the frequency with which aggressive behavior is expressed, the forms it takes, and the situations in which it is displayed are determined largely by learning and social influences.

A wild bull charges Dr. Jose Delgado who is armed only with a cape and a radio transmitter (left photo). When he presses the transmitter the bull abruptly stops his attack (right photo). The radio transmitter sends a mild current to electrodes implant in specific areas of the bull's brain.

The idea of an aggressive drive is popular because we tend to view violence, particularly interpersonal violence, as a sudden, explosive, irrational type of behavior—as if some sort of aggressive energy had built up until it had to find an outlet. Newspaper and television accounts of crimes tend to encourage this view. Some of the most hideously brutal crimes have been committed by individuals who were reportedly very meek, quiet, and conforming until their outburst.

More often, however, the background of the assailant is not as innocent as the accounts would have us believe. Charles Whitman, for example, the University of Texas student who positioned himself in the campus bell tower and shot as many people as he could until he was finally gunned down, was described in newspaper reports as a model American youth—a former altar boy and Eagle Scout. Subsequent investigation revealed, however, that his life was replete with aggressive acts, including assaulting his wife and others, being court-martialed as a marine recruit for insubordination and fighting, and having a passion for collecting firearms. With the exception of some psychotic individuals who may be driven to violent acts because of delusional beliefs, most people who commit aggressive acts have a past history of aggressive behavior (Bandura, 1973).

Aggression as a Learned Response

Social learning theory rejects the notion of aggression as an instinct or frustration-produced drive and proposes that aggression is no different from any other learned response. It can be learned through observation or imitation, and the more often it is reinforced the more likely it is to occur. A person frustrated by being blocked from a goal or disturbed by some stressful event experiences unpleasant emotional arousal. This emotional arousal can elicit different responses depending on the kinds of responses the individual has learned for coping with stressful situations. The frustrated individual may seek help from others, aggress, withdraw, try even harder to surmount the obstacle, or anesthetize himself with drugs or alcohol. The response used will be the one that has been most successful in the past in relieving frustration. Figure 12-3 shows how social learning theory differs from psychoanalytic theory and drive theory (the frustration-aggression hypothesis) in conceptualizing the motivational components of aggression.

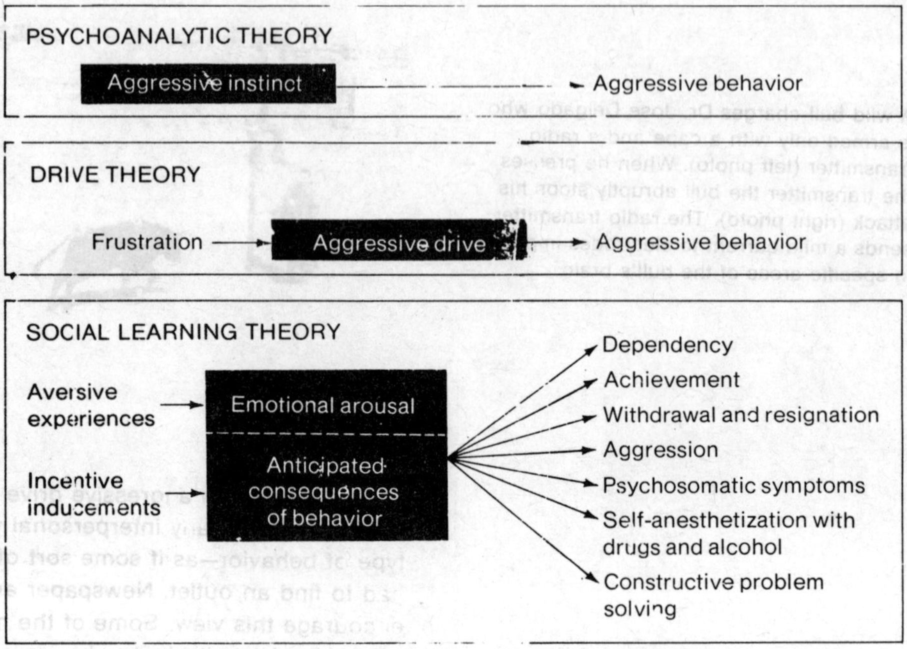

Fig. 12-3 Motivational determinants of aggression

The diagram represents schematically the motivational determinants of aggression as viewed by psychoanalytic theory, drive theory (the frustration-aggression hypothesis), and social learning theory. In the social learning view, the emotional arousal caused by unpleasant experiences can lead to any number of different behaviors depending upon the behavior that has been rewarded or has proved successful in the past. Cognitive factors, including knowledge of the results of past behavior and appraisal of positive and negative incentives operating in the current situation, enable the individual to anticipate the consequences of behavior and act accordingly. (Modified after Bandura, 1973)

A number of studies show that aggressive responses can be learned by being reinforced or through imitation (Bandura, 1973). Nursery school children who observed an adult express various forms of aggressive behavior toward a large, inflated Bobo doll subsequently imitated many of the adult's actions, including imitating unconventional and unusual aggressive behavior patterns. (See Figure 12-4.) When the experiment was expanded to include two filmed versions of aggressive modeling (one showed a live model aggressing toward the Bobo doll, and the other showed a cartoon character displaying the same aggressive behavior), the results were even more striking. Children who watched the two films produced more aggressive behavior toward the doll than children who had observed a live model displaying aggression. Figure 12-5 shows the total number of aggressive behavior episodes for each group as well as the number of episodes that actually imitated specific aggressive behaviors shown by the model. Observation of either live modeled or filmed aggression greatly increases the likelihood of aggression.

A subsequent study indicates that children do not soon forget aggressive responses they have seen modeled; they remember many of them even when tested eight months later (Hicks, 1968). Pertinent to this study is the fact that some individuals convicted of mass murders or brutal crimes report that they got the idea from newspaper accounts of similar crimes and remembered the details of these crimes long after the average reader would have forgotten them.

Expression of Aggression as Cathartic

Does the release of pent-up aggression decrease the person's need to aggress, or do such experiences actually increase the probability of future aggressive behavior? If aggression is a drive, either innate or frustration

Fig. 12-4 Children's imitation of adult aggression

Nursery school children observed a motion picture in which an adult expressed various forms of aggressive behavior toward an inflated Bobo doll. After watching the film, both boys and girls behaved aggressively toward the doll, using many of the detailed acts of aggression that the adult had displayed, including lifting and throwing, striking with a hammer, and kicking.

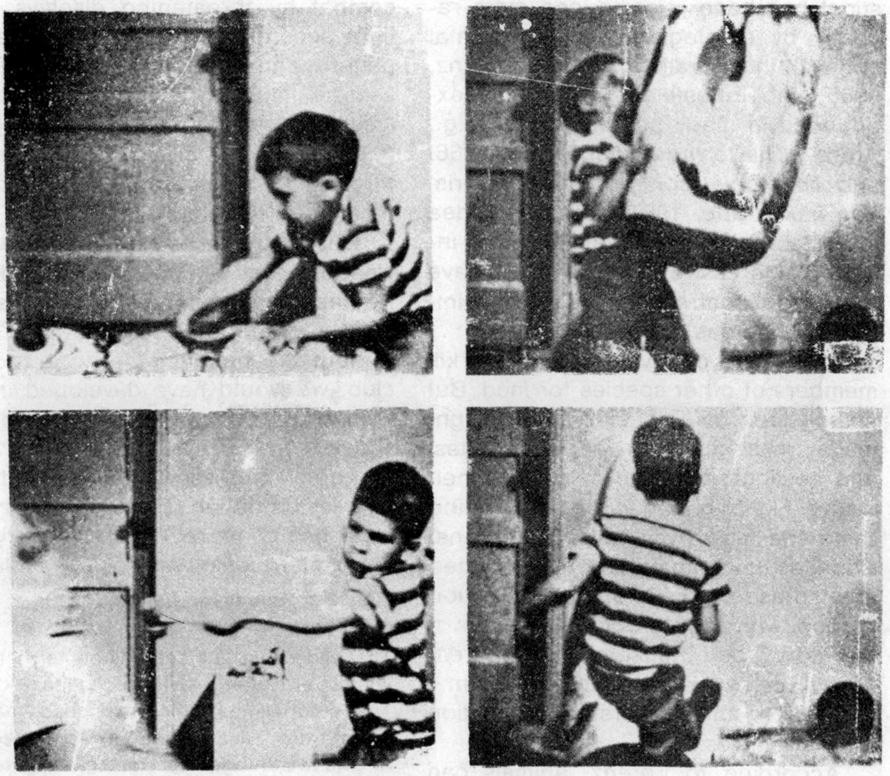

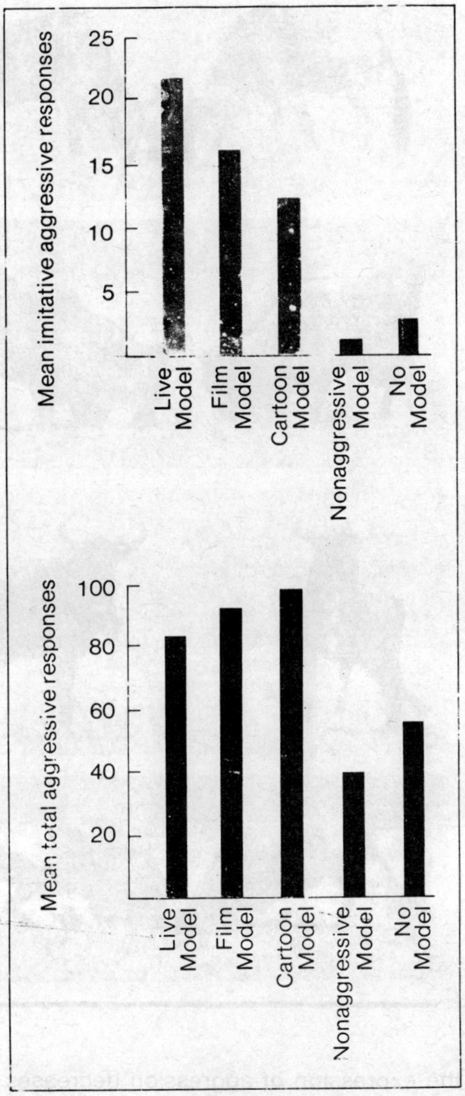

Fig. 12-5 Imitation of aggression

Observing aggressive models (either live or on film) greatly increases amount of aggressive behavior children display as compared to observing a nonaggressive model or no model at all. Note that observation of the live model produces more imitation of specific aggressive acts, whereas observation of filmed models (either real-life or cartoon) instigates more aggressive responses of all kinds. (After Bandura, 1973)

produced, then its expression should be *cathartic*, reducing the intensity of aggressive feelings. But the evidence suggests that this is not the case. Studies with children indicate that participating in aggressive activities either increases aggressive behavior or maintains it at the same level rather than reducing it (Nelsen, 1969). Experiments with adults have generally had similar results. When given repeated opportunities to shock another person (who can't retaliate), college students become more punitive the more they aggress (Buss, 1966a). And subjects who are angry show greater increases in punitiveness on successive attacks than subjects who are not angry (Loew, 1967). If catharsis were operating, the angry subjects should be reducing their aggressive drive by acting aggressively and should become less punitive the more they aggress.

These studies are relevant to real-life instances in which assailants become progressively more brutal and "overkill"—sometimes stabbing a victim as many as 50 times. Of course, there are many factors in such cases but there are indications that acting aggressively provides positive feedback for more aggression.

CRITICAL DISCUSSION

Man as an Aggressive Animal

Freud's view of aggression as an instinct has been reintroduced more recently by ethologists studying animal behavior in naturalistic settings (Lorenz, 1966; Eibl-Eibesfeldt, 1970) and expounded in many popular books (e.g., Ardrey, *The territorial imperative,* 1966, and *The social contract,* 1970; Morris, *The naked ape,* 1967). The basic idea is that both men and animals are innately aggressive, but animals have learned to control their aggressive impulses, whereas man has not.

Predatory, carnivorous animals kill members of other species for food. But among their own species animals fight mainly in competition for food, mates, and nesting sites, and to protect their young. Fighting among members of the same species serves several functions: it spaces the animals over the inhabited area so as to provide optimal utilization of food, with each group having its own "territory"; and it ensures that procreation will be by the strongest males, since they will be the winners in competition for the females.

According to Lorenz, animals can safely enjoy these benefits of aggression because, through the process of evolution, they have developed inhibitions that prevent them from destroying their own species. Many species have ritualistic patterns of threatening or fighting behavior that appear to be largely innate. (See Figure 12-6.) They ward off combat by threatening displays; they fight according to a stylized, ritualistic pattern; and the fight seldom results in serious injury or death because the loser can display submission signals (e.g., a wolf lies down and exposes its throat) that inhibit further aggression on the part of the victor.

But people have developed powerful weapons that can cause instant death. Perhaps, if all combat had remained on a hand-to-hand and tooth-to-flesh level, without the benefit of even a rock or club, we would have developed inhibitions to prevent the destruction of our species.

Lorenz thus believes, like Freud, that aggression is an innate instinct that must find some outlet. His prescription for a more peaceful society includes:

Fig. 12-6 Ritualistic patterns of fighting behavior

The wildebeest bull defends his territory against a rival in a stylized challenge duel. These skirmishes, which may occur many times a day, seldom result in bloodshed. **A.** The two antagonists stand grazing head to head, taking each other's measure. **B.** Suddenly they drop to their knees in the eyeball-to-eyeball combat attitude. **C.** Pretending to sense danger they raise their heads in mock alarm, apparently a means of easing tension. At this point the challenge may be called off or may progress to brief, horn-locked battle (D).

Obviously, in some circumstances the expression of aggression decreases its incidence. An aggressive threat may cause the antagonist to cease his provocative acts. And behaving aggressively may arouse feelings of anxiety in the aggressor, particularly if he observes the injurious consequences of his actions, thereby inhibiting further aggression. But in these instances the effect on aggressive behavior can be explained without resorting to the notion that an aggressive drive is being reduced.

What effect does expressing aggression vicariously through observing violence on television or in the movies have on aggressive behavior? Is it cathartic, providing fantasy outlets for aggressive tension? Or does it elicit aggression in viewers by its modelings of violent behavior? We have already seen that children will imitate live or filmed aggressive behavior in an safe outlets for aggression, such as competitive sports; broadening our view of "clan" and territory to include more people; and recognizing the stimuli that are "releasers" for aggression—a threatened in-group, a hated out-group, a persuasive leader, and the contagion of a group of angry people acting *en masse.*

Lorenz's views, though provocative, are highly speculative and have been criticized as lacking substantial basis in empirical data. Barnett (1967) points out that many animals do not have innate signals for stopping attacks, and the stereotyped signals they do use have variable effects on the responses of their foes. Other criticisms may be found in a book edited by Montagu (1968) that contains articles evaluating the validity of the views expressed in the popular books that relate human and animal aggression.

In contrast to Lorenz's prescriptions, social learning theory would stress minimizing the competitive and frustrating circumstances that lead to aggression, and making sure that aggressive behavior receives less reward than alternative forms of conduct. The debate between aggression as an innate force vs. aggression as learned behavior has important implications for the actions society should take in controlling aggressive behavior.

experimental setting. But what about in more natural settings? The amount of violence to which we are exposed through the mass media makes this an important question.

Some spokesmen for the television industry claim that watching violence on TV is beneficial—viewers discharge some of their own aggressive impulses through viewing, thus reducing the likelihood that they will perform aggressive acts. Freud would probably have agreed with this claim; an instinct or drive theory of aggression assumes that aggression builds up until it is discharged by some form of aggressive act, either actual or vicarious. Social learning theory, on the other hand, maintains that a state of arousal, or anger, can be reduced through behavior that is noninjurious as well as, or better than, through aggressive acts.

There have been several experimental studies where children's viewing of commercial TV was controlled: one group watched violent cartoons for a specified amount of time each day; another group watched nonviolent cartoons for the same amount of time. The amount of aggression the children showed in their daily activities during this period was carefully recorded. The results showed that repeated exposure to aggressive cartoons increased the children's assaultiveness in their interactions with their peers, whereas exposure to nonviolent cartoons produced no change in interpersonal aggressions (Steuer, Applefield, and Smith, 1971).

A number of correlational studies have shown a positive relationship between the amount of exposure to televised violence and the degree to which children use aggressive behavior as a means of solving interpersonal conflicts. Correlations, of course, do not imply causal relationships: it may be that children who are more aggressive prefer to watch violent TV programs. A longitudinal study which traced TV viewing habits over a ten-year period attempted to control for this possibility. A large number of children (more than 800) were studied when they were eight to nine years of age. Information was collected about each child's viewing time, the type of programs viewed, a number of family characteristics, and aggressiveness as rated by schoolmates. One of the major findings was that boys who preferred TV programs with a fair amount of violence were much more aggressive in their interpersonal relationships than those who preferred programs that were low in violence.

Ten years later, more than 400 of the original subjects (now age 18–19) were interviewed concerning their preferred TV programs, given a test that measured delinquency tendencies, and rated by their peers as to the aggressiveness of their behavior. As you can see from Figure 12-7, high exposure to violence on TV at age nine is positively related to aggressiveness in boys at age nineteen. The correlation remains significant even when statistical methods are used to control for the degree of childhood aggressiveness, thus reducing the possibility that initial level of aggression determines both childhood viewing preferences and adult aggressiveness.

Interestingly enough, no consistent relationship was found between the TV viewing habits of girls and their aggressive behavior at either age. This is in line with other studies showing that girls tend to imitate aggressive behavior much less than boys unless they are specifically reinforced for doing so. Girls in our society are seldom reinforced for behaving aggressively; quite the contrary. And since most of the aggressive roles on TV are male, the female is less likely to find aggressive models to imitate.

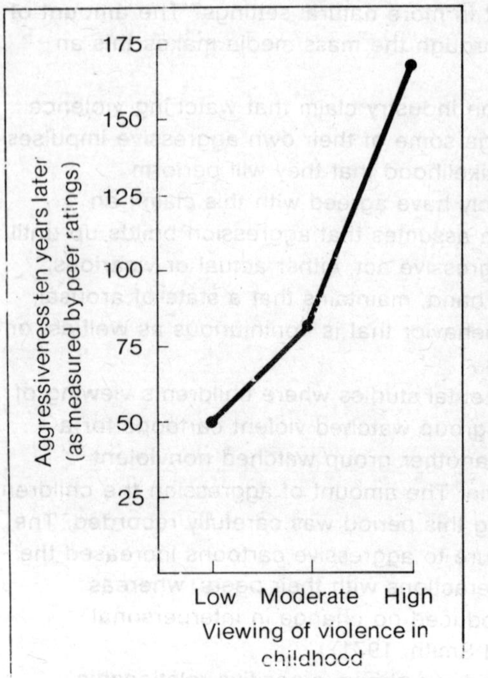

Fig. 12-7 Childhood viewing of violent television and adult aggression
Preference for viewing violent television programs by boys at age nine is positively correlated with aggressive behavior at age nineteen. (Plotted from data by Eron, Huesmann, Lefkowitz, and Walder, 1972)

The authors of this study conclude that there is a "critical period" in a boy's development when he is maximally susceptible to the influence of violent television, and that regular viewing of such programs during this period leads to the development of a more aggressive life style. The boy's preference for violent TV at age eight influences both his current aggressiveness and his aggressiveness ten years later. By the time he is nineteen, however, his TV preferences are *not* related to his aggressiveness. No correlation was found between preference for violent TV at age nineteen and current level of aggressiveness, nor between early and later television viewing habits (Eron and others, 1972).

Aggressive behavior has many causes, and the influence of TV models on behavior depends on whether the modes of behavior imitated prove effective in daily interactions. The child who is punished for imitating acts observed on TV, either by parents or peers, is apt to show no change in behavior or even a decrease in aggressiveness—although behavior that is prohibited in one setting may be displayed in another where there is less fear of punishment.

Since a very effective way of reducing aggressive acts in hyperaggressive boys is to have them observe models who behave in a restrained and nonaggressive manner in the face of provocation (Baron and Kepner, 1970), the television industry could perform a valuable service by including a few heroes who successfully overcome obstacles in a calm, firm, but nonviolent manner.

Clearly, many factors are involved in the instigation of aggression: conditions of poverty, overcrowding, the actions of authorities such as policemen, the values of one's subgroup within the society, to mention but a few. Some of these social influences will be considered in Chapters 18 and 19.

Emotion

The discussion of aggression makes it clear that motivation and emotion are closely related. Anger is frequently an instigator of aggressive behavior, although such behavior can also occur in the absence of anger. *Emotions can activate and direct behavior* in the same way as biological or psychological motives. *Emotions may also accompany motivated behavior;* sex is not only a powerful motive but also a source of intense pleasure. *Emotions can be a goal;* we engage in certain activities because we know they will bring pleasure.

The nature of the relationship between motivation and emotion, as well as the definition of emotion itself, is an unresolved issue in psychology. Most people would say that anger, fear, joy, and grief are emotions but would classify hunger, thirst, and fatigue as states of the organism that serve as motives. What is the difference? Why don't we call hunger an emotion?

There is no clear-cut distinction. The most common basis for differentiating between the two assumes that emotions are usually aroused by external stimuli and that emotional expression is directed toward the stimuli in the environment that arouses it. Motives, on the other hand, are more often aroused by internal stimuli and are "naturally" directed toward certain objects in the environment (e.g., food, water, a mate). However, you can think of a number of instances where this distinction does not hold. For example, an external incentive such as the sight or smell of delicious food

Children often imitate acts seen on TV

can arouse hunger in the absence of internal hunger cues. And internal stimuli, such as those caused by severe food deprivation, can arouse emotion.

Most motivated behavior has some affective or emotional accompaniment, although we may be too preoccupied in our striving toward the goal to focus on our feelings at the time. When we talk about motivation we usually focus on the goal-directed activity; in discussing emotion our attention is drawn to the subjective, affective experiences that accompany the behavior.

In the past psychologists devoted considerable effort to trying to classify emotions. They attempted to find dimensions along which to scale such emotions as sorrow, disgust, surprise, jealousy, envy, and ecstasy. But such attempts have not proved very worthwhile. For our purposes we will note that most emotions can be divided into those that are *pleasant* (joy, love) and those that are *unpleasant* (anger, fear)—a division that points up the importance of approach and avoidance as the basis of emotion. In addition, many of our emotional terms can be classified by *intensity.* Word pairs such as displeasure-rage, pain-agony, and sadness-grief convey differences of intensity. Some psychologists reserve the term *emotion* for the more intense states that are accompanied by widespread changes in body physiology and call the milder affective states *feelings.* But there are many intermediate states between mild experiences of pleasantness and unpleasantness and intense emotions. We will not attempt to pinpoint where on the intensity scale "emotions" begin but will be concerned instead with a variety of affective experiences.

Physiological Responses in Emotion

When we experience an intense emotion (such as fear or anger) we are aware of a number of bodily changes—rapid heart beat and breathing, dryness of the throat and mouth, increased muscle tension, perspiration, trembling of the extremities, a "sinking feeling" in the stomach. Table 12-1, which shows the symptoms of fear reported by fliers during the Second World War, illustrates the complexity of bodily changes in an emotional state.

Most of the physiological changes that occur during intense emotion result from activation of the sympathetic division of the autonomic nervous system as it prepares the body for emergency action (see Chapter 2, p. 55). The *sympathetic system* is responsible for the following changes:

1. Blood pressure and heart rate increase.
2. Respiration becomes more rapid.
3. The pupils of the eyes dilate.
4. Electrical resistance of the skin decreases.
5. Blood sugar level increases to provide more energy.
6. The blood becomes able to clot more quickly in case of wounds.
7. Motility of the gastrointestinal tract decreases or stops entirely; blood is diverted from the stomach and intestines and sent to the brain and skeletal muscles.
8. The hairs on the skin erect, causing "goose pimples."

The sympathetic system gears the organism for energy output. As the emotion subsides, the *parasympathetic system,* the energy-conserving system, takes over and returns the organism to its normal state.

TABLE 12-1
Symptoms of fear in combat flying

"DURING COMBAT MISSIONS DID YOU FEEL"	"OFTEN"	"SOMETIMES"	TOTAL
A pounding heart and rapid pulse	30%	56%	86%
That your muscles were very tense	30	53	83
Easily irritated, angry, or "sore"	22	58	80
Dryness of the throat or mouth	30	50	80
"Nervous perspiration" or "cold sweat"	26	53	79
"Butterflies" in the stomach	23	53	76
Sense of unreality, that this couldn't be happening to you	20	49	69
Need to urinate very frequently	25	40	65
Trembling	11	53	64
Confused or rattled	3	50	53
Weak or faint	4	37	41
Right after a mission, unable to remember details of what happened	5	34	39
Sick to the stomach	5	33	38
Unable to concentrate	3	32	35
That you had wet or soiled your pants	1	4	5

Source: Based on reports of 1985 flying officers and 2519 enlisted fliers during the Second World War. After Shaffer (1947).

These physiological changes accompanying intense emotions are the basis for use of the polygraph, commonly known as the "lie detector," in checking the reliability of an individual's statements. The term *lie detector* is actually incorrect. The polygraph does not detect lies; it simply measures some of the physiological accompaniments of emotion. The measures most frequently recorded are alternations in heart rate, blood pressure, respiration, and the galvanic skin response, or GSR (the GSR is a change in the electrical conductivity of the skin).

The standard procedure in operating a polygraph is to first take a recording while the subject is relaxed; this recording serves as a *base line* for evaluating subsequent responses. The examiner then asks a series of carefully worded questions that are answered "yes" or "no." "Critical questions" are interspersed among "neutral questions," and sufficient time is allowed between questions (usually a minute) for the measures to return to normal. Presumably, the subject's guilt is revealed by heightened physiological responses to the critical questions (Figure 12-8).

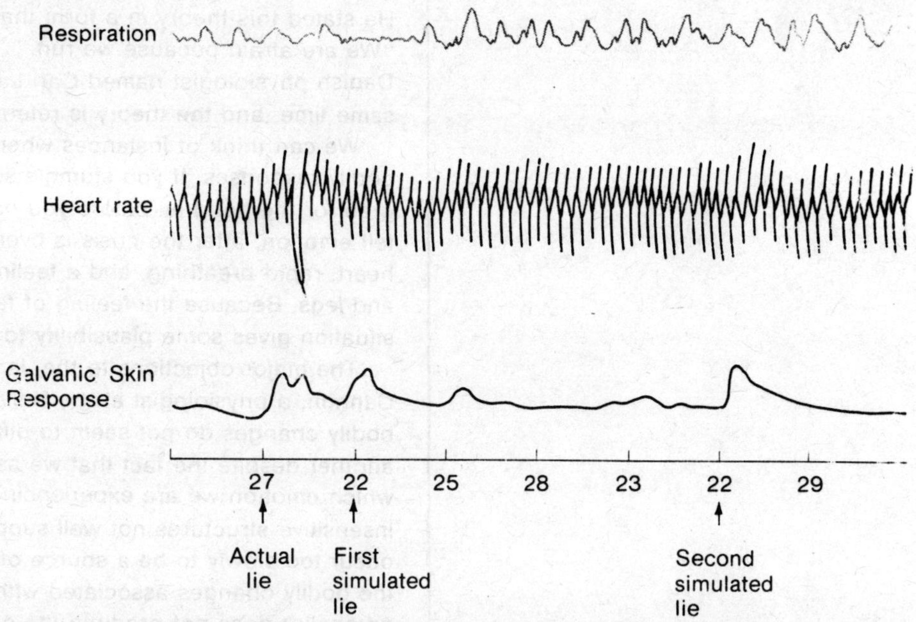

Fig. 12-8 The polygraph

The arm cuff measures blood pressure and heart rate, the pneumograph around the rib cage measures rate of breathing, and the finger electrodes measure GSR (Lafayette Instrument Co.). The right half of the figure shows the physiological responses of a subject as he lies and as he simulates lying. The respiratory trace (top line) shows that he held his breath as he prepared for the first simulation. He was able to produce sizable changes in heart rate and GSR at the second simulation. (After Kubis, 1962)

The problem with the use of the polygraph in detecting lies is that the method is not foolproof. An innocent subject may be very tense or may react emotionally to certain words in the questions and thus appear to be lying when telling the truth. On the other hand, a practiced liar may show little emotional response when lying. And a knowledgeable subject may be able to "beat" the machine by thinking about something exciting or by tensing muscles during neutral questions, thus creating a baseline comparable to reactions to the critical questions. The recording in the right half of Figure 12-8 shows the responses to an actual lie and a simulated lie. In this experiment the subject picked a number and then tried to conceal its identity from the examiner. The number was 27, and a marked change in heart rate and GSR can be seen where the subject denies number 27. The subject simulates lying to number 22 by tensing his toes, producing noticeable reactions in heart rate and GSR.

Because of these and other problems, lie detector results have been ruled inadmissible as court evidence. Such tests are frequently used, however, in preliminary criminal investigations and by prospective employers hiring personnel for trusted positions. The polygraph also serves as a research tool in studies measuring emotional responses to stress or observing the effects of drugs on physiological responses.

Theories of Emotion

We tend to think of bodily changes such as those in response to stress as being caused by emotion. But one of the earliest theories of emotion proposed that the perception of the physiological changes *is* the emotion. William James, a famous psychologist at Harvard during the late 1800s, believed that the important factor in our felt emotion is the feedback from the bodily changes that occur in response to a frightening or upsetting situation.

He stated this theory in a form that seems to put the cart before the horse: "We are afraid because we run." "We are angry because we strike." A Danish physiologist named Carl Lange arrived at a similar proposal about the same time, and the theory is referred to as the James-Lange theory.

We can think of instances where the recognition of emotion does follow bodily responses. If you stumble suddenly on the stairs, you automatically grab for the handrail before you have time to recognize a state of fear. Your felt emotion, after the crisis is over, includes the perception of a pounding heart, rapid breathing, and a feeling of weakness or trembling in the arms and legs. Because the feeling of fear follows the bodily responses, this situation gives some plausibility to the James-Lange theory.

The major objections to the James-Lange theory came from Walter Cannon, a physiologist at the University of Chicago, who pointed out that: (1) bodily changes do not seem to differ very much from one emotional state to another despite the fact that we as individuals are usually pretty clear about which emotion we are experiencing; (2) the internal organs are relatively insensitive structures not well supplied with nerves, and internal changes occur too slowly to be a source of emotional feeling; (3) artificially inducing the bodily changes associated with an emotion (e.g., injecting a person with adrenalin) does not produce the experience of the true emotion.

Cannon assigned the central role in emotion to the *thalamus.* He suggested that the thalamus responded to an emotion-producing stimulus by sending impulses *simultaneously* to the cerebral cortex and to other parts of the body; emotional feelings were the result of joint arousal of the cortex and the sympathetic nervous system. According to this view the bodily changes and the experience of emotion occur at the same time (Cannon, 1927). Figure 12-9 illustrates the differences between Cannon's theory of emotion and the James-Lange theory.

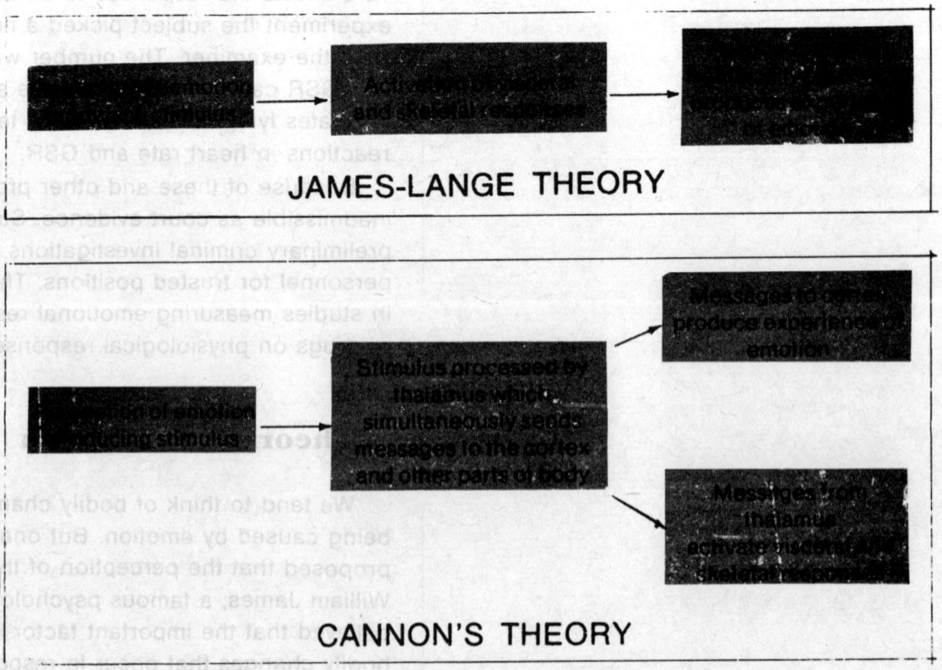

Fig. 12-9 Two theories of emotion

Illustrated is the sequence of events for two theories of emotion. According to the James-Lange theory feedback to the brain from bodily responses produces the conscious experience of emotion. According to Cannon's theory the emotional experience occurs as soon as the cortex receives the message from the thalamus; it does not depend upon feedback from internal organ and skeletal responses.

Subsequent investigation has made it clear that the *hypothalamus,* rather than the thalamus, is the important center for the integration of emotional impulses. (We noted earlier that electrical stimulation of the hypothalamus elicits fear or anger in many animals.) But whether the physiological responses precede or accompany the emotion is difficult to determine. Emotion is *not* a momentary event, but an experience that takes place over a period of time. An *emotional experience* may initially be activated by external inputs to the sensory system; we see or hear the emotion-arousing stimuli. But the autonomic nervous system is activated almost immediately, so that feedback from bodily changes adds to the emotional experience. Thus, our conscious experience of emotion involves the *integration* of information about the physiological state of the body and information about the emotion-arousing situation. Both types of information tend to be continuous in time, and their integration determines the intensity and nature of our felt emotional state.

In this framework the time distinctions made by the James-Lange and Cannon theories are not too meaningful. On some occasions, as in sudden danger, the first signs of emotional experience may be preceded by autonomic activity (in which case James and Lange are correct); on others, the awareness of an emotion clearly precedes autonomic activity (in which case Cannon is correct). The felt emotional state has a third source of information: *cognitive factors.* How an individual appraises the external situation in terms of memories of past experiences is a cognitive process that will influence emotion. The factors that contribute to the conscious experience of emotion are illustrated in Figure 12-10. We will have more to say about cognitive factors shortly. But first we will examine the role of physiological arousal in emotion.

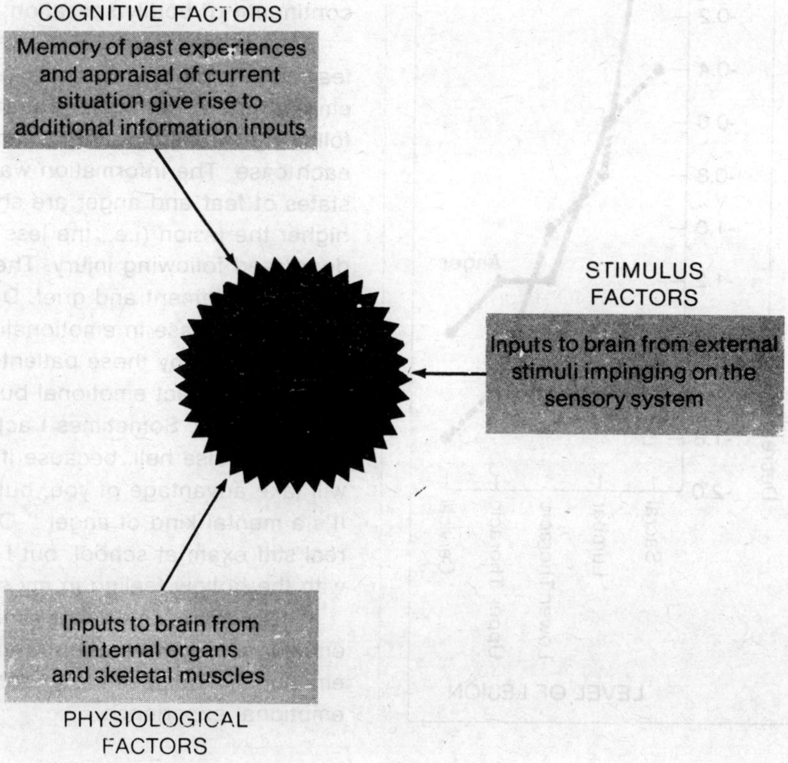

Fig. 12-10 Emotion as information integration

The conscious experience of emotion involves the integration of information from three sources. Feedback to the brain from the internal organs and other body parts activated by the sympathetic nervous system gives rise to an undifferentiated state of arousal and affect; but the emotion experienced is determined by the interpretation the subject assigns to the aroused state. Information stored in memory and the perception of what is taking place in the environment are used to interpret the current situation. This interpretation (based on cognitive and stimulus factors) interacts with feedback from bodily changes (physiological factors) to determine the emotional state.

Physiological Arousal in Emotion

Is it possible to distinguish between emotional states on the basis of what goes on inside the body? For example, can we distinguish between fear and anger on the basis of the types of physiological responses that occur? Most studies aimed at differentiating emotions on the basis of bodily changes have had little success. In this respect, Cannon was correct. The physiological changes that occur with fear (e.g., increased heart rate, respiration rate, and flushing *or* paling of the skin) also occur with anger. Those differences that have been found seem related to the way the emotion is *expressed* rather than to the subjective experience. For example, when anger is expressed outwardly in the form of aggressive activity, the adrenal glands increase their secretion of norepinephrine. Anger that is held in and not expressed is associated with increased adrenal secretion of epinephrine, as are fear and anxiety. The important variable seems to be the way the emotion is expressed rather than the subjective feelings of fear or anger.

Although bodily sensations may not be related to *specific* emotions, they are important to the *intensity* with which we experience emotions. The importance of bodily sensations is demonstrated by a study of the emotional life of individuals with spinal cord injuries. When the spinal cord is severed, sensations from below the point of injury are not communicated to the brain.

In this study army veterans with spinal-cord injuries were divided into five groups according to the level of the spinal cord at which the lesion occurred. Those in Group I had lesions near the neck, with only one branch of the parasympathetic nervous system intact and no innervation of the sympathetic system. Those in Group V had lesions near the base of the spine, with at least partial innervation of both sympathetic and parasympathetic nerves. The other groups fell between these two extremes. The five groups represent a continuum of bodily sensation; the higher the lesion, the less the sensation.

Each subject was interviewed to determine his feelings in situations of fear, anger, grief, and sexual excitement. The subject was asked to recall an emotion-arousing incident prior to his injury and a comparable incident following the injury, and to compare the intensity of emotional experience in each case. The information was coded as to degree of change. The data for states of fear and anger are shown in Figure 12-11. It is apparent that the higher the lesion (i.e., the less the bodily sensation), the more emotionality decreased following injury. The same relationship was true for states of sexual excitement and grief. Deprivation of body sensation *does* result in a marked decrease in emotionality.

Fig. 12-11 Spinal-cord lesions and emotionality

Subjects with spinal-cord lesions compared the intensity of their emotional experiences before and after injury. Their reports were coded according to degree of change—0 indicates no change; a mild change (e.g., "I feel it less, I guess.") is scored as −1 for a decrease or +1 for an increase; a strong change (e.g., "I feel it a helluva lot less.") is scored as −2 or +2. Note that the higher the lesion, the greater the decrease in emotionality following injury. (After Schachter, 1971, and adapted from Hohmann, 1966)

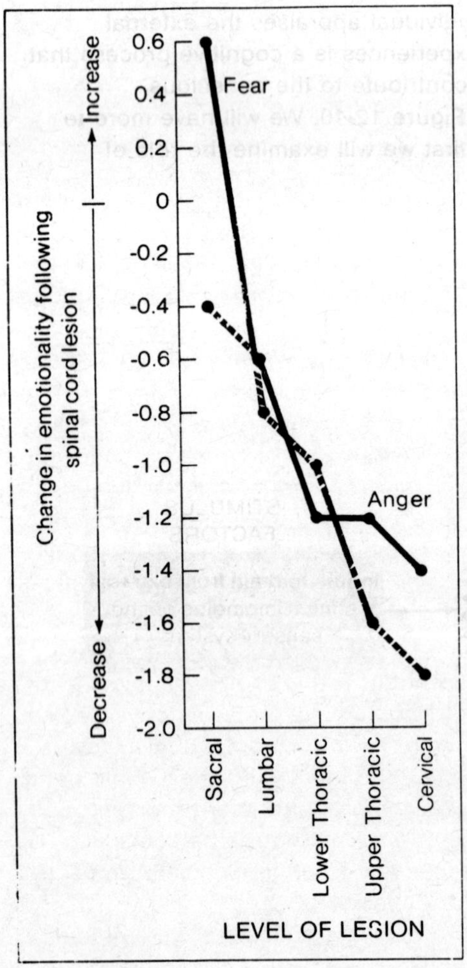

Comments by those patients with the highest spinal-cord lesions suggest that they can act emotional but do not feel emotional. For example, "It's sort of cold anger. Sometimes I act angry when I see some injustice. I yell and cuss and raise hell, because if you don't do it sometimes, I've learned people will take advantage of you, but it doesn't have the heat to it that it used to. It's a mental kind of anger." Or "I say I am afraid, like when I'm going into a real stiff exam at school, but I don't really feel afraid, not all tense and shaky, with the hollow feeling in my stomach, like I used to."

These men seem to be saying that they can make the appropriate emotional response when the situation calls for it, but they don't really feel emotional. The absence of autonomic arousal has a marked affect on emotional experience.

Cognitive Factors in Emotion

Bodily sensations, particularly the activity of the autonomic nervous system, are important to feelings of emotion, but different emotions show pretty much the same physiological patterns. People are usually aware that something is going on internally when they are angry, or excited, or afraid, but they do not discriminate their heart rate or blood pressure or what is happening in their stomach very well. When people are asked to describe their emotions, they usually begin by telling about the arousing circumstances, that is, what angered them, or pleased them, or frightened them. They go on to describe some of their bodily reactions and their difficulties in dealing with the situation. But they do not define the emotion solely in terms of their own internal feelings.

The individual's appraisal of the emotion-producing situation is an important factor in determining his emotional response. What happens if we artificially induce a state of physiological arousal by injecting a drug such as epinephrine (adrenalin), which produces many of the symptoms associated with discharge of the sympathetic nervous system? How would the individual label and describe his feelings?

Schachter (1959) proposed that emotional states are a function of the interaction of cognitive factors and a state of physiological arousal. He suggested that if a person were injected with epinephrine without his knowledge, he would be under pressure to understand his bodily feelings—and would do so in terms of his knowledge of the immediate situation. If he were with a beautiful woman, he might decide he was in love or sexually excited. If he were in a confrontation with his wife, he might explode in anger. If he were at a party where everyone around him was acting euphoric, he might decide he was very happy. If the situation provided him with no reasonable explanation for his bodily feelings, he might simply decide he was sick. In any event, Schachter proposed that an emotion depends both on the state of physiological arousal and on a cognition appropriate to the state of arousal; the cognition determines the label of the emotion. He designed an experiment to test this hypothesis.

To produce physiological arousal, he injected some subjects with epinephrine, telling them it was a vitamin injection and that he was studying the effects of vitamin C on vision. One group was informed correctly about the physiological reactions to be expected from the injection (accelerated heart rate and trembling of the limbs). A second group was not told about any possible symptoms. A third group was misinformed (they were told to expect numbness, itching, and headache). And a fourth group of subjects (the placebo group) received an injection of saline solution which did not produce any physiological arousal, nor were they told to expect any.

All subjects injected with epinephrine should have the same physiological reaction. The assumption was that the more misinformed the subjects were about the physiological reactions to expect, the more likely they would be to label their feelings according to what was going on in the environment around them. Subjects in the placebo group should not be particularly influenced by external events because they are not physiologically aroused and have no strange feelings in search of a label.

To manipulate the cognitive state, two opposite conditions were created by the use of a "stooge"—a trained companion-subject who had presumably

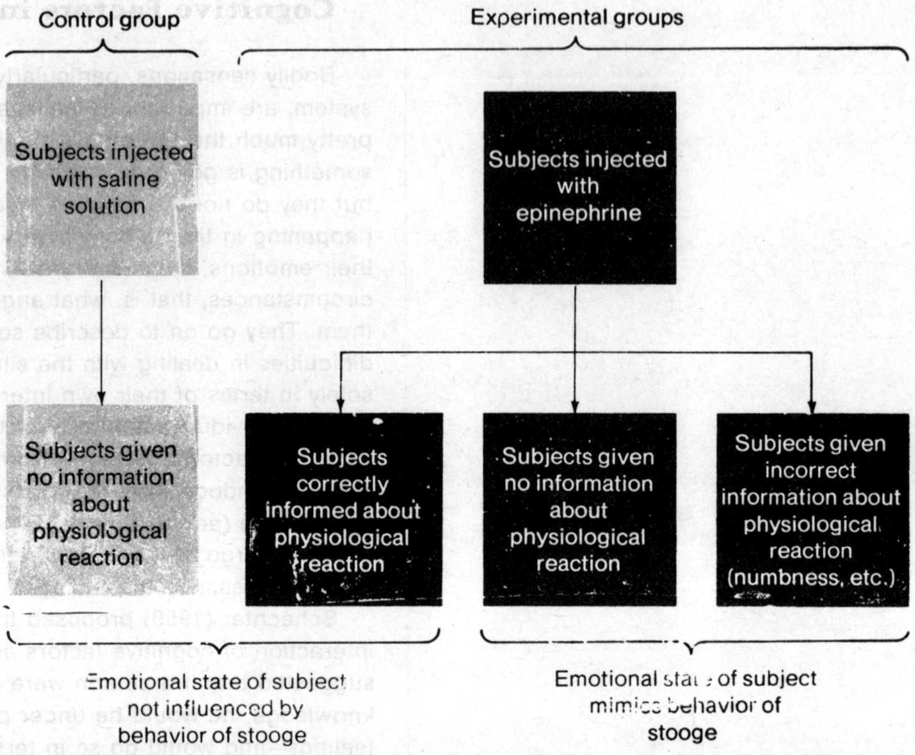

Fig. 12-12 Epinephrine injection study

Diagram illustrates the main experimental groups and summarizes the effect each condition had on the emotional state of the subject.

been given the same injection and who supposedly was participating in the experiment under the same circumstances as the untrained subjects. The stooge acted either "euphoric"—playfully doodling, making paper airplanes, playing "basketball" by throwing wads of paper into the wastebasket—or "angry"—complaining about the experiment, resenting a questionnaire that he and his partner had to fill out, and so on.

The design of the experiment and a summary of the results are given in Figure 12-12. The results showed that the subjects who had received epinephrine and were either misinformed or told nothing about its effects were most influenced by the behavior of the stooge. Compared to subjects in the other groups, they were more euphoric in the situation designed to create euphoria and angrier in the situation designed to produce anger. Since they had no ready explanation for their physiological reactions, they were more influenced by what was taking place around them.

Subjects who were told how they would feel following the epinephrine injection were affected very little by the behavior of the stooge in either situation. Similarly, the placebo group (which had not been physiologically aroused because no drug was given) was little affected by the behavior of the stooge. Thus, when the subject has an adequate explanation for his aroused physiological state (or when he is not aroused as in the case of the control group), his emotional state is less apt to be influenced by the behavior of a stooge. However, when he is physiologically aroused and has no explanation for his bodily feelings, he labels his emotion according to the emotion of those around him and behaves accordingly (Schachter and Singer, 1962).[1]

[1] A more recent study which attempted to replicate this experiment using only the euphoric condition found no differences between an epinephrine-misinformed group and a placebo group in terms of either behavioral measures or subjective reports (Marshall, 1974). It may be that emotions are not quite as malleable as the Schachter and Singer study suggests.

These results support what Schachter (1971) has labeled the *cognitive-physiological theory* of emotion: emotion is internal physiological arousal in interaction with cognitive processes. Feedback to the brain from physiological activity gives rise to an undifferentiated state of affect; but the felt emotion is determined by the "label" the subject assigns to that aroused state. The assignment of a label is a *cognitive process;* the subject uses information from past experiences and his perception of what is going on around him to arrive at an interpretation of his feelings. This interpretation will determine how he acts and the label that he uses to define his emotional state.

Learning to label bodily sensations in terms of emotional tone (i.e., as pleasant or unpleasant) is relevant to some of the differences observed between experienced and inexperienced users of alcohol, marihuana, and other drugs. First sensations are often unpleasant. Should the person experiencing such feelings consider himself "sick" or "high"? Much of the pleasure associated with the use of such drugs comes from cognitive and social factors. Initial users have to learn to label the physical sensations as enjoyable.

MODIFYING AROUSAL BY ALTERING COGNITIONS. If our state of emotional arousal is determined by our cognitive evaluation of the emotion-producing situation, then it should be possible to alter arousal level by changing one's cognitions. Indeed, you can think of instances where initial emotional responses to stimuli change as the situation is reappraised as threatening or benign. You are awakened by the telephone at midnight. Your initial fear reaction aroused by the thought that some catastrophe has happened to a loved one changes to relief as you discover it is a wrong number. A potentially emotion-producing situation has become neutral because of a change in your appraisal of it.

A number of studies have investigated various ways in which changing peoples' cognitions can change their emotional reactions. The general experimental procedure is to show the subjects a film that arouses emotion and measure autonomic arousal throughout the presentation. The subjects' cognitive activity is manipulated either by varying the sound track that accompanies the film or by varying what is told about the nature of the film before it starts. One film that has been used effectively in arousing stress shows the ceremony used by an aboriginal Australian tribe to initiate young boys into manhood. The ceremony includes, among other things, cutting into the penis of each initiate with a stone knife. The film shows six such operations, and subjects find these episodes extremely stressful.

Figure 12-13 shows emotional response, as measured by the galvanic skin response (GSR), for groups viewing the film under four different conditions: (1) no sound track; (2) a sound track that presents a detached, intellectualized view of the ceremony (e.g., "As you can see, the operation is formal, and the surgical technique, while crude, is very carefully followed."); (3) a sound track that tends to deny or minimize painfulness of the scene (e.g., ". . . the words of encouragement offered by the older men have their effect, and the boy begins to look forward to the happy conclusion of the ceremony."); (4) a sound track designed to increase emotional stress by emphasizing the cruelty and pain of the ceremony.

As you can see from the figure, the sound track designed to increase emotional reaction does so markedly; skin conductance is significantly higher

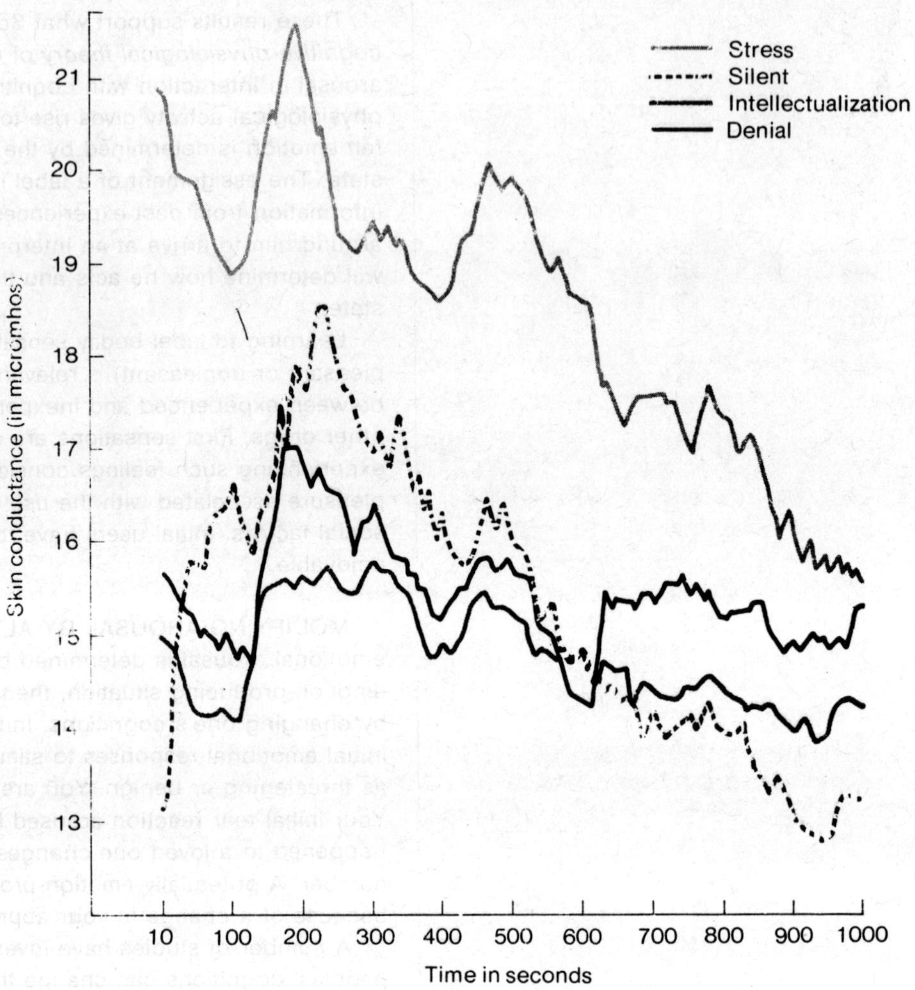

Fig. 12-13 Cognitive influences on emotion

The galvanic skin response (GSR) was measured for four different groups as they watched a stressful film. For one group, the sound track accompanying the film emphasized the cruelty of the scenes being viewed; the sound track for the second group denied the painfulness of the scenes, while that for the third group presented a detached, intellectualized description. The fourth group watched the film with no sound track. The stressful sound track clearly increased emotional reaction to the film, as measured by the GSR. The denial and intellectualization sound tracks reduced emotional reaction, compared to silent observation of the film, but the differences are not so marked. (After Speisman, Lazarus, Mordkoff, and Davison, 1964)

throughout the film for this group. The two sound tracks that attempt to make the experience less stressful by intellectualization or denial produce lower skin conductance than that of the group that watches the film silently (Speisman and others, 1964).

Subsequent studies showed that preparing the subjects before they watch the film (either with a detached intellectualized description of what they are about to see or with a description that attempts to deny the trauma) is even more effective than accompanying sound tracks in reducing emotional reaction (Lazarus and Alfert, 1964). Thus we see that emotional reactions are strongly influenced by one's cognitions concerning a perceived event.

ROLE OF LEARNING IN EMOTIONAL AROUSAL. Some situations appear to be innately emotion-producing in both animals and people. Anger tends to be provoked by restraint against the carrying out of a motivated sequence of behavior. Fear can be aroused by pain, a loud noise, or sudden loss of support in any young organism. The number of stimuli that arouse fear increases as we go from lower to higher mammals. It appears that the more intelligent the organism, the greater the number of stimuli that arouse fear. The fear-arousing element seems to be *strangeness,* and we can postulate that the important factor is the ability to discriminate the new from the

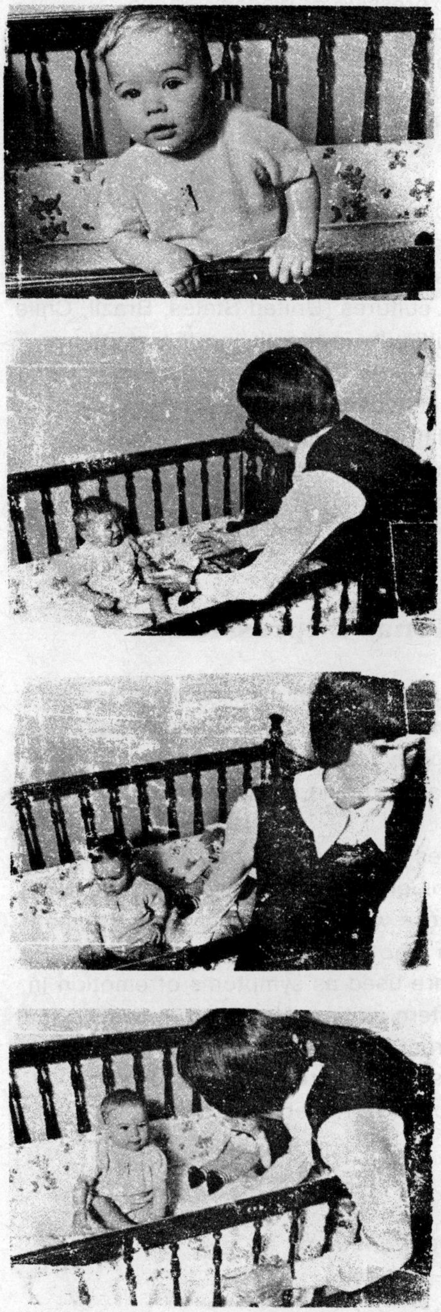

Fig. 12-14 Fear of strangers

A. Alone, but calm and attentive. **B.** Apprehension and crying at approach of stranger. **C.** Stranger turns away; crying subsides. **D.** Time and a more gradual approach elicit a positive reaction.

familiar. The more intelligent the animal, the more aware it is of differences in the environment.

Fear of something strange seems to be largely innate, but maturation and learning may be required as a background. At about eight months, human infants show an intense fear of strangers (see Figure 12-14). No matter how sociable the child has been prior to this time or how many different people he has been exposed to, the onset of "stranger shyness" is usually abrupt and intense. The most plausible interpretation is that maturation of perceptual abilities has enabled the child to discriminate familiar from strange adults.

Emotions may also be associated with new objects or situations by learning. In the classic experiment by J. B. Watson, the founder of Behaviorism, a boy named Albert was conditioned to fear a previously neutral object—a tame white rat. When eleven-month-old Albert was shown a white rat, he reached for it, evidencing no fear. But every time he touched the rat he was frightened by a loud sound. He soon became afraid of the rat. The originally neutral rat became a "conditioned stimulus" to fear. Albert also showed fear of his mother's fur neckpiece and of other furry objects. Albert's fear *generalized* to objects that were similar in some respect to the rat but not to toys, such as rubber balls or blocks, that were unratlike in appearance (Watson and Rayner, 1920).

It is probable that some irrational fears are acquired in this relatively automatic way. Because lightning precedes thunder, the child may come to fear the lightning as much as the thunder, although the loud sound of thunder is the primary reason for fright. But most fears are probably learned in a more complex way—some through actual contact with harmful objects, but more through imitation of parental fears.

Emotional Expression

Innate Emotional Expression

The basic ways of expressing emotion are innate; children all over the world cry when hurt or sad and laugh when happy. Studies of children blind and deaf from birth indicate that many of the facial expressions, postures, and gestures that we associate with different emotions develop through maturation; they appear at the appropriate age even when there is no opportunity to observe them in others.

Sir Charles Darwin was intrigued with the expression of emotion in blind children and in animals. In his book *The expression of emotions in man and animals,* published in 1872, he proposed an evolutionary theory of emotions. According to Darwin, many of man's ways of expressing emotion are inherited patterns that originally had some survival value. For example, the expression of disgust or rejection is based on the organism's attempt to rid itself of something unpleasant that has been ingested. To quote from Darwin:

> The term "disgust," in its simplest sense, means something offensive to the taste. But as disgust also causes annoyance, it is generally accompanied by a frown, and often by gestures as if to push away or to guard oneself against the offensive object. . . . Extreme disgust is expressed by movements around the mouth identical with those preparatory to the act of vomiting. The mouth is opened widely, with the upper lip strongly retracted. . . . The partial closure of the eyelids, or the turning away of the eyes or of

Drawing by E. Frascino; © 1973, The New Yorker Magazine.

"Your lips tell me 'No, no,' but—if you'll pardon my presumption, sir—there's 'Yes, yes' in your eyes."

the whole body, are likewise highly expressive of disdain. These actions seem to declare that the despised person is not worth looking at, or is disagreeable to behold. . . . Spitting seems an almost universal sign of contempt or disgust; and spitting obviously represents the rejection of anything offensive from the mouth.

Certain facial expressions do seem to have a universal meaning regardless of the culture in which the individual is raised. When photographs showing facial expressions of happiness, anger, sadness, disgust, fear, and surprise were shown to members of five different cultures (United States, Brazil, Chile, Argentina, and Japan), there was little difficulty in identifying the emotions that belonged to each expression. Even remote, preliterate tribes that had had virtually no contact with Western cultures (the Fore and Dani tribes in New Guinea) were able to judge the facial expressions correctly. And American college students were fairly accurate in identifying emotions expressed by Fore natives from videotapes, although fear and surprise were often confused with each other (Ekman, 1971).

Role of Learning in Emotional Expression

Although certain emotional expressions may be largely innate, many modifications occur through learning. Anger, for example, may be expressed by fighting, by using abusive language, or by leaving the room. Leaving the room is not an expression of emotion that is known at birth, and certainly the abusive language has to be learned.

Certain facial expressions and gestures are taught by one's culture as ways of expressing emotion. One psychologist reviewed several Chinese novels in order to determine how a Chinese writer portrayed various human emotions. Many of the bodily changes in emotion (flushing, paling, cold perspiration, trembling, goose pimples) are used as symptoms of emotion in Chinese fiction much as they are in Western writing. He found, however, that the Chinese have some other quite different ways of expressing emotion. The following quotations from Chinese novels would surely be misinterpreted by an American reader unfamiliar with the culture (Klineberg, 1938).

"Her eyes grew round and opened wide."
(She became angry.)

"They stretched out their tongues."
(They showed signs of surprise.)

"He clapped his hands."
(He was worried or disappointed.)

"He scratched his ears and cheeks."
(He was happy.)

Thus, superimposed upon basic expressions of emotion, which appear to be universal, are conventional or stereotyped forms of expression, which become a kind of "language of emotion" recognized by others within a culture. Skilled actors are able to convey to their audiences any intended emotion by using facial expressions, tone of voice, and gestures according to the patterns the audience recognizes. In simulating emotion, those of us who are less skilled actors can convey our intent by exaggerating the conventional expressions: gritting our teeth and clenching our fists to indicate anger, turning down the corners of our mouth to look sad, raising our eyebrows to express doubt or disapproval.

Emotions as Adaptive and Disruptive

What is the role of emotions in our lives? Are they beneficial? Do they help us to survive, or are they chiefly sources of disturbance and maladjustment? The answers to these questions depend upon the intensity of the emotions involved.

Arousal Level and Effectiveness of Performance

A mild level of emotional arousal tends to produce alertness and interest in the task at hand. When emotions become intense, however, whether they are pleasant or unpleasant, they usually result in some decrement in performance. The curve in Figure 12-15 represents the relation between the level of emotional arousal and the effectiveness of performance. At very low levels of arousal (for example, when one is just waking up), the nervous system may not be functioning fully and sensory messages may not get through. Performance is optimal at moderate levels of arousal. At high levels of arousal performance begins to decline. Presumably, the central nervous system is so responsive that it is responding to too many things at once, thus preventing the appropriate set of responses from dominating.

The optimum level of arousal and the shape of the curve differs for different tasks. A simple, well-learned habit would be much less susceptible to disruption by emotional arousal than a more complex response that depends upon the integration of several thought processes. In a moment of intense fear you would probably still be able to spell your name, but your ability to play a good game of chess would be seriously impaired.

Individuals differ in the extent to which their behavior is disrupted by emotional arousal. Observations of people during crises, such as fires or sudden floods, suggest that about 15 percent show organized, effective behavior. The majority, some 70 percent, show various degrees of disorganization but are still able to function with some effectiveness. The remaining 15 percent are so disorganized that they are unable to function at all; they may race around screaming or exhibit aimless and completely inappropriate behavior (Tyhurst, 1951). Studies of soldiers under stress of combat indicate that only 15 to 25 percent can be counted on to fire their weapons. The rest simply freeze on the spot and are unable to fire.

Emotions, when sufficiently intense, can seriously impair the processes that control organized behavior.

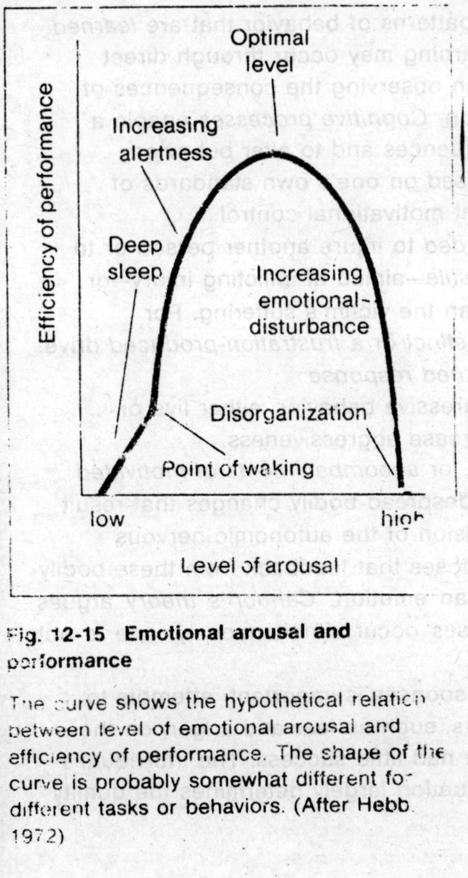

Fig. 12-15 Emotional arousal and performance

The curve shows the hypothetical relation between level of emotional arousal and efficiency of performance. The shape of the curve is probably somewhat different for different tasks or behaviors. (After Hebb. 1972)

Enduring Emotional States

Sometimes emotions are not quickly discharged but continue to remain unexpressed or unresolved. Perhaps the situation that makes one angry (e.g., prolonged conflict with one's employer) or that makes one fearful (e.g., worry over the chronic illness of a loved one) continues for a long period of time. The state of heightened arousal that results can take its toll of the individual's ability to function efficiently. Sometimes continual emotional tension can impair physical health. In a *psychophysiological disorder* (psychosomatic illness) the symptoms are physical, but the cause is primarily psychological. A number of different types of illness—e.g., ulcers, asthma, migraine headaches, high blood pressure, and skin eruptions—are related to emotional stress. We will have more to say about psychophysiological disorders in Chapter 16. At this point however, it should be noted that long-term emotional stress can impair a person's physical health as well as his mental efficiency.

Summary

1. *Psychological motives,* in contrast to *biological motives,* are determined primarily by learning. They appear later in development, and become important after basic needs are satisfied.
2. Two quite different theoretical approaches to human motivation are illustrated by *psychoanalytic theory* and *social learning theory.*
   a. The psychoanalytic theory of Freud emphasizes two basic drives: *sex* and *aggression.* These motives arise in infancy, but their expression is forbidden by parents, and *repression* occurs. A repressed tendency remains active, however, as an *unconscious motive* and finds expression in indirect or symbolic ways.
   b. Social learning theory focuses on patterns of behavior that are *learned* in coping with the environment; learning may occur through direct reinforcement or *vicariously* through observing the consequences of behavior *modeled* by another person. *Cognitive processes* enable a person to foresee probable consequences and to alter behavior accordingly. *Self-reinforcement,* based on one's own standards of conduct, also provides an important motivational control.
3. Aggression, defined as behavior *intended* to injure another person or to destroy property, may be primarily *hostile*—aimed at inflicting injury—or *instrumental*—aimed at goals other than the victim's suffering. For Freudian theorists aggression is an *instinct* or a *frustration-produced* drive; for social learning theorists it is a *learned response.*
4. Evidence indicates that observing aggressive behavior, either live or filmed, is not cathartic; it tends to increase aggressiveness.
5. Emotions can serve as *motives, goals,* or *accompaniments of motivated behavior.* Intense emotions involve widespread bodily changes that result from activation of the sympathetic division of the autonomic nervous system. The *James-Lange theory* proposes that feedback from these bodily responses determines the quality of an emotion. *Cannon's theory* argues that emotions and autonomic responses occur simultaneously; one is not the cause of the other.
6. Although feedback from autonomic responses is important, attempts to differentiate between different emotions, such as fear and anger, on the basis of physiological responses, have had little success. The individual's appraisal of the emotion-producing situation largely determines the quality of the emotion.

7. The *cognitive-physiological theory* proposes that emotional states are a function of the interaction of cognitive factors and physiological arousal. Experiments in which subjects were injected with epinephrine show the importance of cognitive factors in labeling emotional states.
8. Some forms of emotional expression appear to be inborn or to develop through maturation. But learning is important in modifying emotional expression to conform to the patterns approved by the culture.
9. Low levels of emotional arousal improve performance at a task, but intense arousal is usually disruptive; continual emotional tension can result in *psychophysiological illness.*

Further Reading

The most general coverage of human motivation and the most complete bibliography are found in Cofer and Appley, *Motivation: Theory and research* (1964), and Bolles, *Theory of motivation* (1967). Shorter treatments can be found in Stein and Rosen, *Motivation and emotion* (1974), and Cofer, *Motivation and emotion* (1972).

For a social learning approach to motivation, see McLaughlin, *Learning and social behavior* (1971), and Bandura, *Social learning theory* (1971). The psychoanalytic theory of motivation is presented in two books by Freud: *Beyond the pleasure principle* (1922), and *New introductory lectures on psychoanalysis* (1933).

Books on aggression (in addition to the popular ones mentioned in the text) include Berkowitz (ed.), *Roots of aggression* (1969) Daniels, Gilula, and Ochberg (eds.), *Violence and the struggle for existence* (1970); Johnson, *Aggression in man and animals* (1972); and Bandura, *Aggression: A social learning analysis* (1973).

For Maslow's views on motivation, see his *Motivation and personality* (2nd ed., 1970).

For an introduction to contemporary views on emotion see Strongman, *The psychology of emotion* (1973).

part six

personality and individuality

13

personality and its assessment

What do we mean when we say someone has a "lot of personality"? Usually we are referring to an individual's social effectiveness. We mean that people react positively to that person. Courses advertised to "improve your personality" attempt to teach social skills and enhance one's appearance or manner of speaking so as to elicit more favorable reactions from others.

Another common definition of personality is based on an individual's most striking characteristics. Thus, we may refer to someone as having an "aggressive personality" or a "shy personality."

When psychologists talk about personality, however, they are concerned primarily with *individual differences*—the characteristics that distinguish one individual from another. Psychologists do not agree on an exact definition of personality. But for our purposes we will define personality as the *characteristic patterns of behavior and modes of thinking that determine a person's adjustment to the environment.*

The term *characteristic* in the definition implies some consistency in behavior—that people have tendencies to act or think in certain ways regardless of the situation. For example, you can probably think of an acquaintance who seldom gets angry, no matter what the provocation, and another who flies off the handle at the slightest irritation. Behavior is the result of interaction between personality characteristics and the social and physical conditions of the situation. But, as we shall see later, personality theories differ in the extent to which they believe that behavior is consistent across situations rather than specific to a particular environmental context. Is "honesty" a trait displayed in most situations, or does it depend primarily on the specific situation?

A complete description of an individual's personality would include many factors: intellectual abilities, motives acquired in the process of growing up, emotional reactivity, attitudes, beliefs, and moral values. Some of these factors have been considered in earlier chapters. What concerns us here is the manner in which they are *organized within a particular individual* so as to differentiate that individual from other persons.

The Shaping of Personality

An infant is born with certain potentialities. The development of these potentialities depends upon maturation and upon experiences encountered in growing up. Although newborn infants in a hospital nursery look pretty much alike, the physical characteristics that will later make them readily distinguishable from each other are already determined by heredity. Intelligence and certain special abilities, such as musical talent, also have a large hereditary component, and some differences in emotional reactivity may be innate. One study found that reliable individual differences could be observed shortly after birth in such characteristics as activity level, attention span, adaptability to changes in the environment, and general mood. One infant might be characteristically active, easily distracted, and willing to accept new objects and people; another might be predominantly quiet, persistent in concentrating on an activity, and leery of anything new. These original characteristics of temperament tended to persist in many of the 100 or more children whose development was followed over a 14-year period (Thomas, Chess, and Birch, 1970).

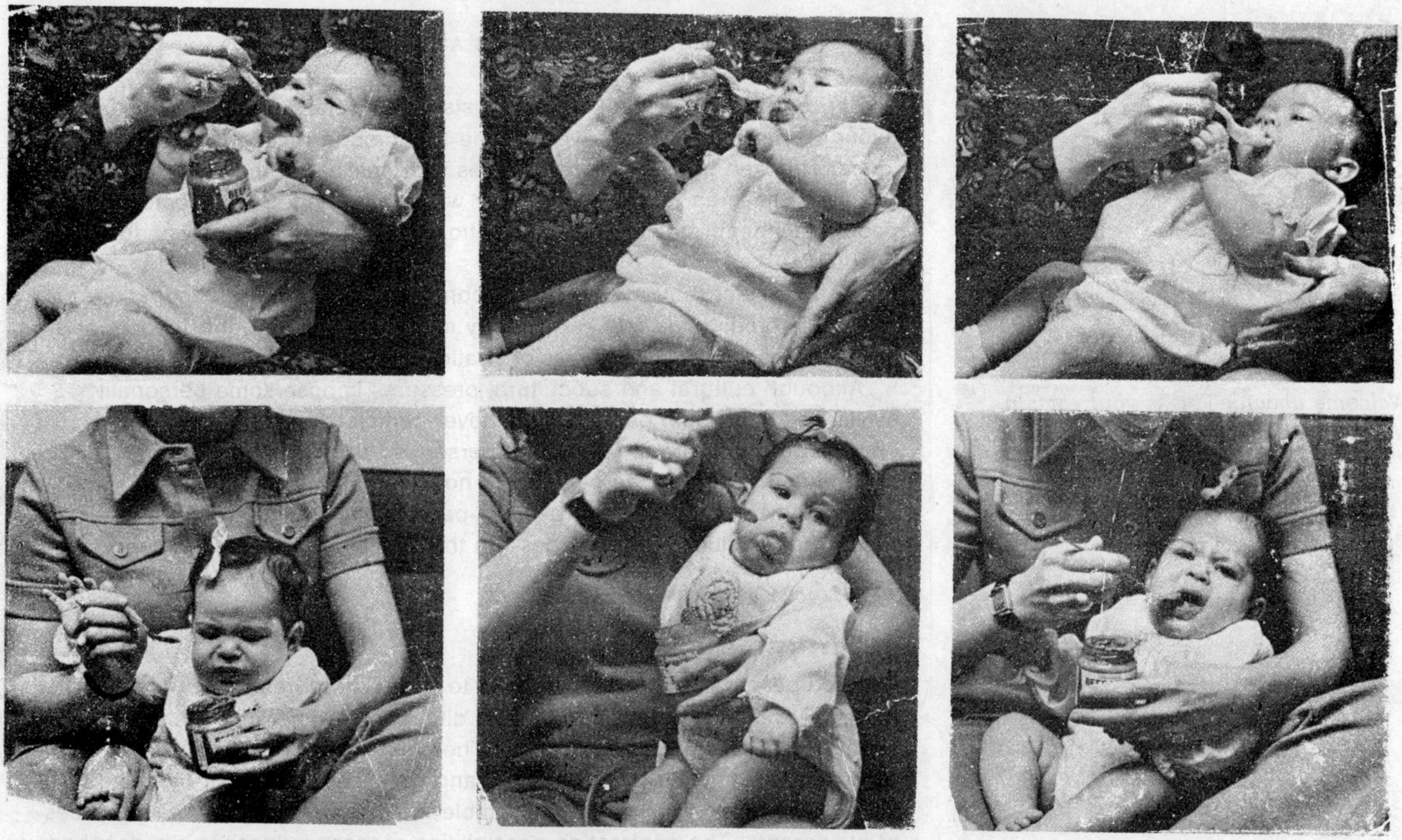

Fig. 13-1 Early individual differences in temperament

Two babies react quite differently to the same situation. One accepts a new food willingly (upper panel), while the other is obviously less enthusiastic. A baby's characteristic approach to something new may extend to many different situations.

Parents respond differently to babies with differing characteristics. In this way a reciprocal process starts that may exaggerate some of the personality characteristics present at birth. What happens to the potentialities with which the infant is born depends on his experiences while growing up. Although all experiences are individual, we may distinguish between two classes: the *common experience,* shared by most individuals growing up in a given culture or cultural subgroup, and the *unique experience,* not predictable from the roles that the culture assigns us.

Common Experiences

All families in a given culture share certain common beliefs, customs, and values. While growing up, the child learns to behave in ways expected by the culture. One of these expectations has to do with *sex roles.* Most cultures expect different behaviors from males than from females. Sex roles may vary from culture to culture, but it is considered "natural" in any culture for boys and girls to have predictable differences in personality merely because they belong to one or the other sex.

A culture as complex as that of the United States contains numerous subcultures, each with its own views about such things as moral values, standards of cleanliness, style of dress, and definitions of success. The cultural subgroup exerts its influence on the developing personality. All boys are expected to show certain personality characteristics (as compared with girls), but a poor boy raised in an urban slum is expected to behave differently in some respects than a well-to-do boy raised in a middle-class suburb.

Some roles, such as occupations, are of our own choosing. But such roles are also patterned by the culture. Different behaviors are expected of

"Welcome aboard. This is your captain, Margaret Williamson, speaking."

doctors, truck drivers, rock group artists, and opera singers. To be sure, occupational stereotypes have become less rigid in recent years; we are no longer shocked by business executives with hair below the ears, female telephone linemen, or the rock singer with a crew cut. But to some extent, people feel comfortable in an occupation if they behave as others do in that occupation.

To the extent that adult behavior conforms to social and occupational roles, it is predictable. We know pretty much what to expect of people at a formal reception, a political demonstration, a football game, or a funeral.

Although cultural and subcultural pressures impose some personality similarities, individual personality is never completely predictable from a knowledge of the group in which a person is raised, for two reasons. (1) The cultural impacts upon the person are not uniform, because they are transmitted by way of certain people—parents and others—who are not all alike in their values and practices; (2) the individual has some experiences that are unique.

Unique Experiences

Each person reacts in his own way to social pressures. Personal differences in behavior may result from biological differences—differences in physical strength, sensitivity, and endurance. They may result from the rewards and punishments imposed by the parents and the type of behavior modeled by them. Even though he may not resemble them, a child shows the influences of his parents. The contrasting possibilities of these influences are decribed by two brothers in Sinclair Lewis' novel *Work of Art*. Each of them ascribes his personality to his home surroundings.

> My father [said Oral] was a sloppy, lazy, booze-hoisting old bum, and my mother didn't know much besides cooking, and she was too busy to give me much attention, and the kids I knew were a bunch of foul-mouthed loafers that used to hang around the hoboes up near the water tank, and I never had a chance to get any formal schooling, and I got thrown on my own as just a brat. So naturally I've become a sort of vagabond that can't be bored by thinking about his "debts" to a lot of little shopkeeping lice, and I suppose I'm inclined to be lazy, and not too scrupulous about the dames and the liquor. But my early rearing did have one swell result. Brought up so unconventionally, I'll always be an Anti-Puritan. I'll never deny the joys of the flesh and the sanctity of beauty.
>
> My father [said Myron] was pretty easy-going and always did like drinking and swapping stories with the boys, and my mother was hard-driven taking care of us, and I heard a lot of filth from the hoboes up near the water tank. Maybe just sort of as a reaction I've become almost too much of a crank about paying debts, and fussing over my work, and being scared of liquor and women. But my rearing did have one swell result. Just by way of contrast, it made me a good, sound, old-fashioned New English Puritan.[1]

Although such extreme reactions to the same early environment are less likely to occur in real life, individuals do respond differently to similar circumstances.

[1] Sinclair Lewis, *Work of Art* (1934).

Beyond a unique biological inheritance and the specific ways in which the culture is transmitted, the individual is shaped by particular experiences. An illness with a long convalescence may provide satisfactions in being cared for and waited upon that profoundly affect the personality structure. Death of a parent may disrupt the usual identifications. Accidents, opportunities for heroism, winning a contest, moving to another part of the country—countless such experiences are relevant to development but are not predictable from the culture, although, of course, their effects are partly determined by the culture.

Approaches to Understanding Personality

The individual's common and unique experiences interact with inherited potential to shape personality. How this occurs, and how the resulting personality can best be described, has been the subject of many theories. Most personality theories can be grouped into one of four classes: *trait, psychoanalytic, social learning,* and *humanistic.* These theoretical approaches differ markedly in the constructs they propose as forming the structure of personality (e.g., traits, id-ego-superego, learned habits, or self-concept) and the way they relate these constructs to behavior. They also differ in the methods they use to assess or measure personality. In the remainder of this chapter we will summarize the main constructs of each theoretical approach, note how these constructs are related to behavior, and give examples of the methods used to assess personality. Personality cannot be studied scientifically unless there are satisfactory ways of measuring personality variables. We will see that one's theoretical conception of personality determines, to a large extent, the methods used to measure it.

The Trait Approach

Personality Types

Classification into *kinds* is the beginning of most sciences—kinds of rocks, kinds of clouds, kinds of plants, and so on. Thus it is not surprising that the first students of human nature tried to classify kinds of people. One of the earliest "personality theories" attempted to classify individuals into *personality types* on the basis of body build (Kretschmer, 1925; Sheldon, 1954). A short, plump person (*endomorph*) was said to be sociable, relaxed, and even-tempered; a tall, thin person (*ectomorph*) was characterized as restrained, self-conscious, and fond of solitude; a heavy-set, muscular individual (*mesomorph*) was described as noisy, callous, and fond of physical activity. Although a person's physique may well have some influence on personality, the relationship is much more subtle than this sort of classification implies, and research has shown little correlation between body build and specific personality characteristics (Tyler, 1956).

Personality type theories have also been based on purely psychological characteristics. One of Freud's pupils, the Swiss psychiatrist Carl Jung, divided all personalities into *introverts* and *extraverts.* The introvert tends to withdraw into himself, particularly in times of emotional stress and conflict; he tends to be shy and prefers to work alone. The introvert may take to the speaking platform in support of some movement to which he is strongly

[illegible] Garbo, an actress [illegible] [illegible] introversion

committed, but even then he is impelled from within. The extravert under stress seeks the company of others. He is likely to be very sociable, a "hail fellow well met," and tends to choose occupations that permit him to deal directly with people, such as sales or promotional work.

You probably know a "typical introvert" and a "typical extravert." But it is also likely that most of your friends fall somewhere between the two extremes (see Figure 13-2). This is one of the major problems of type theories. Most typologies, whether they are based on physical or psychological characteristics, involve a *continuum* of individual differences rather than discrete types. Type theories are appealing because they provide a simple way of looking at personality, but, in actuality, personality is far more complex.

Traits Versus Types

Instead of trying to sort people into types, trait theories assume that a personality can be described by its position on a number of continuous *dimensions* or *scales,* each of which represents a trait. Thus, we could rate an individual on a scale of intelligence, emotional stability, aggressiveness, creativeness, or any of a number of other dimensions. A *trait,* then, refers to any characteristic in which one individual differs from another in a relatively permanent and consistent way. When we informally describe ourselves and others by such adjectives as friendly, cautious, excitable, intelligent, or anxious, we are using trait terms. We abstract these terms from behavior. Observing a person behaving in an aggressive manner on several occasions, we may describe him as an aggressive individual. Using aggressiveness as a trait term is permissible as long as we remember that the term was derived from observations of behavior. The danger lies in using the trait term as a cause of behavior. To say that a person hit his roomate over the head because he has an aggressive trait explains nothing. We inferred the trait from behavior; we cannot then turn around and use it to explain behavior.

Psychologists working in the area of trait theory are concerned with (1) determining the basic traits that provide a meaningful description of personality and, (2) finding some way to measure them. What are the basic traits? Thousands of words in the English language refer to characteristics of behavior. How do we reduce them to a small number of meaningful traits? One approach uses *factor analysis.* Factor analysis is a complex statistical technique (to be discussed more fully in the next chapter) for reducing a large number of measures to a smaller number of independent dimensions. With this technique several hundred test responses might be reduced to a few underlying dimensions or *factors* that account for all of the response data.

For example, suppose you have a large number of word pairs describing personality characteristics in terms of polar opposites, such as *tidy-careless, calm-anxious, cooperative-negativistic.* You ask a group of people to rate their friends on each of these word pairs. An analysis of the ratings by the method of factor analysis would yield a fairly small number of dimensions, or *factors,* that account for most of the data obtained in rating a large number of individuals each on a large number of word pairs. The five trait dimensions listed in Table 13-1 were found in one study of this kind.

Factor analysis appears to provide a fairly straightforward way of arriving at a meaningful group of basic traits. But, unfortunately, because of

Fig. 13-2 Introversion-extraversion

Scores on a test of introversion-extraversion are shown for a group of college students and a group of adults. Note that the majority of the subjects range around the middle of the scale; introverts and extraverts represent only the extremes. (After Neymann and Yacorzynski, 1942)

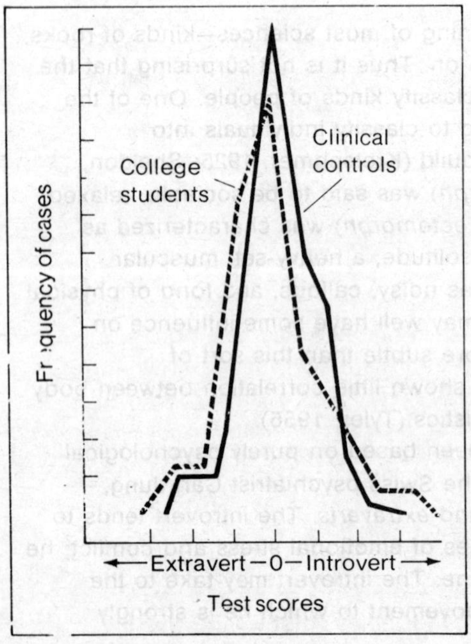

TABLE 13-1
Five trait dimensions and some of their components

TRAIT DIMENSION	DESCRIPTIVE ADJECTIVE PAIRS*
Extraversion	Talkative-Silent Open-Secretive Adventurous-Cautious
Agreeableness	Good natured-Irritable Gentle-Headstrong Cooperative-Negativistic
Conscientiousness	Tidy-Careless Responsible-Undependable Persevering-Quitting
Emotional Stability	Calm-Anxious Poised-Nervous Not Hypochondriacal-Hypochondriacal
Culture	Artistically Sensitive-Artistically Insensitive Refined-Boorish Intellectual-Unreflective

Adapted with modifications from Norman (1963).
*The adjectives describe the two ends of the scales that comprise the dimension.

differences in statistical techniques and in the type of data selected for analysis (e.g., self-ratings vs. ratings of one person by another), studies do not always find the same basic factors. A factor found in one study may not show up in another. While some investigators have found 5 factors that they believe to be the basic dimensions of personality, others have discovered as many as 20.

Despite the lack of agreement on basic traits, some overlap does occur. Two dimensions found fairly consistently in factor-analytic studies of personality are *introversion-extraversion* and *stability-instability.* Introversion-extraversion refers to the degree to which one's basic orientation is turned toward the self or outward toward the external world. It is essentially the same distinction made by Carl Jung. Stability-instability is a dimension of emotionality varying from calm, well-adjusted, reliable individuals at the stable end to those who are moody, anxious, temperamental, and unreliable at the other end. A British psychologist, Hans Eysenck, has developed a theory of personality based on these two dimensions. Figure 13-3 shows the dimensions as related to various personality traits.

Fig. 13-3 Eysenck's dimensions related to personality traits

Various traits studied by factor-analytic methods are shown in relation to the two basic dimensions of introversion-extraversion and stability-instability. (After Eysenck and Eysenck, 1963)

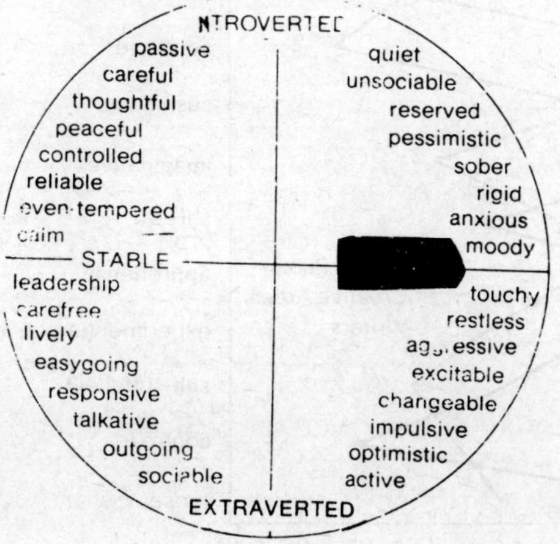

Assessing Personality Traits

Personality traits can be assessed by two methods: (1) the person describes himself by answering questions about his attitudes, feelings, and behaviors; (2) someone else evaluates the person's traits either from what he knows about the individual or from direct observations of behavior. With the first method a *personality inventory* is most often used, whereas the second usually involves a *rating scale.*

PERSONALITY INVENTORIES. A personality inventory is essentially a questionnaire in which the person reports reactions or feelings in certain situations. It resembles a very set or *standardized* kind of interview. A personality inventory asks the same questions of each person, and the answers are usually given in a form that can be easily scored—often by machine. A personality inventory may be designed to measure a single dimension of personality (such as introversion-extraversion) or it may measure several personality traits simultaneously, resulting in a *profile* of scores.

Different strategies have been used in constructing personality inventories. The Sixteen Factor Personality Questionnaire, whose results are shown in Figure 13-4 is based on factor analysis. By factor analyzing the trait descriptions of many individuals, the author of this questionnaire isolated 16 factors as the basic personality traits. He then devised questions to measure each of them. For example, answering "No" to the question "Do you tend to keep in the background on social occasions?" would earn you a point toward the dominant side of the E factor. Note that the factors themselves are nameless statistical quantities; they could just as well be called A, B, C, and so forth, which is the way they were initially labeled. The trait names that were given to the factors are simply the experimenter's best guess as to what a particular factor represents, based on the data that contribute to it and the real-life behavior with which it correlates.

Each factor in Figure 13-4 is given two names: one for a high score and another for a low score. By plotting an individual's test score for each of the factors, we arrive at a *personality profile*—a kind of shorthand description of the individual's personality. The black profile in Figure 13-4 shows the average test scores for a group of airline pilots, while the red and gray profiles give the average scores for a group of artists and a group of writers. We can see that artists and writers, as a group, differ significantly from pilots on a number of personality traits.

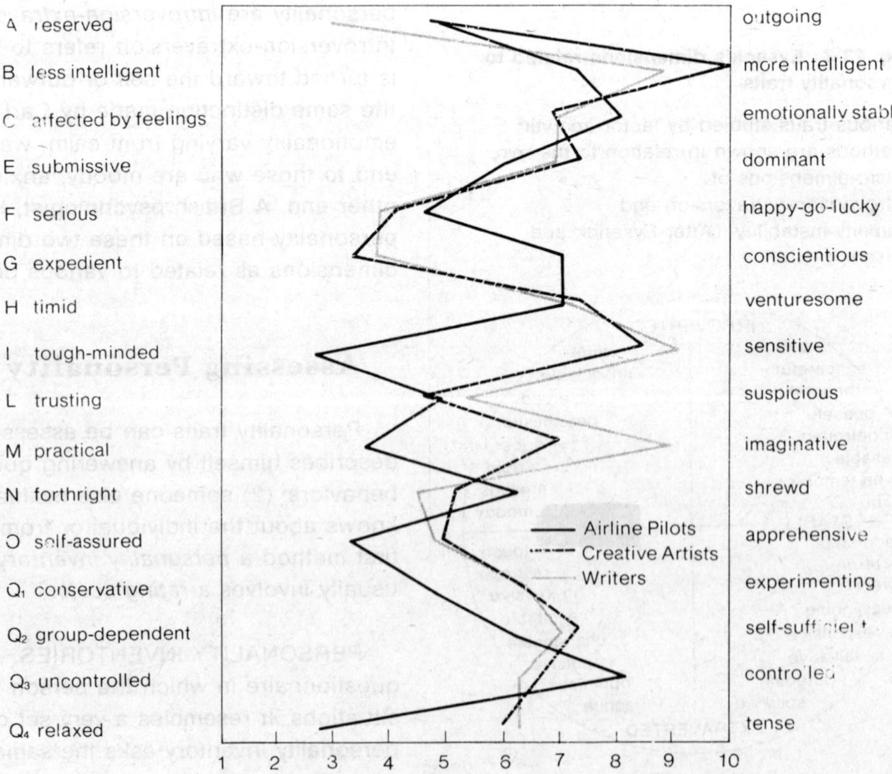

Fig. 13-4 Personality profiles

The trait names represent the 16 personality factors obtained by factor analysis of a large number of ratings. The factors are assigned two names: one for a high score and another for a low score. Factors A–O were obtained from factor analyses of ratings of one person by another; the four Q factors were found only in data from self-ratings. A personality test based on the 16 factors measures the level of each factor, and the scores can be graphed as a profile—either for an individual or a group. The black profile shows the *average* scores for a group of airline pilots; red and gray profiles are averages for a group of artists and a group of writers. Note that the writers and artists show similar traits which are somewhat different from those of the pilots. (After Cattell, 1973)

1. I like mechanics magazines.
2. I have a good appetite.
3. I wake up fresh and rested most mornings.
4. I think I would like the work of a librarian.
5. I am easily awakened by noise.
6. I like to read newspaper articles on crime.
7. My hands and feet are usually warm enough.
8. My daily life is full of things that keep me interested.
9. I am about as able to work as I ever was.
10. There seems to be a lump in my throat much of the time.
11. A person should try to understand his dreams and be guided by or take warning from them.
12. I enjoy detective or mystery stories.
13. I work under a great deal of tension.
14. I have diarrhea once a month or more.
15. Once in a while I think of things too bad to talk about.

[redacted]

Another personality inventory, the *Minnesota Multiphasic Personality Inventory* (referred to as the MMPI), is based on the method of *empirical construction* rather than factor analysis. Instead of assuming specific personality traits and designing questions to measure them, many items were given to well-defined groups of individuals who were known to differ from the norm on some external criterion. Only those questions that discriminated significantly between groups were retained to form the inventory. For example, to develop a scale of items that will distinguish between schizophrenic and normal individuals, the same series of questions are given to two groups: *the criterion group* consists of patients hospitalized with a diagnosis of schizophrenia; the *control group* is an equal number of individuals who have never been diagnosed as having psychiatric problems. Only those test items that discriminate significantly between the two groups are retained for use in a scale for measuring schizophrenia. Questions that at face value might seem to distinguish normals from schizophrenics (e.g., "I feel as if I am not a part of the world") may or may not do so when put to the test. The method of empirical construction contrasts the responses of two distinct groups to ensure that the test item bears an actual (empirical) relationship to the personality characteristic being measured.

Initially, the MMPI was developed to aid clinicians in the psychiatric diagnosis of abnormal personality types. The test is composed of some 550 statements (about attitudes, emotional reactions, physical and psychological symptoms, and past experiences) to which the subject answers "true," "false," or "cannot say." Some of the items are:

I have never done anything dangerous for the thrill of it.
I daydream very little.
My mother or father often made me obey even when I thought it was unreasonable.
At times my thoughts have raced ahead faster than I could speak them.

The responses are scored according to the correspondence between the answers given by the subject and those given by patients with different kinds of psychological disturbances.

Since the MMPI is derived from differences between criterion groups, it does not really matter whether what the person says about himself is true or not. The fact that he says it is important. If all schizophrenics answer true and all normal subjects false to the statement "My mother never loved me," their answers distinguish the two groups, regardless of how mother actually behaved. This is one of the advantages of a test based on the method of empirical construction as opposed to one where the test constructor assumes that certain answers indicate certain psychological disorders. Answering true to the statement "I think that most people would lie to get ahead" might be assumed to be a sign of paranoia. When this item was included in the MMPI it was found that patients diagnosed as paranoid were significantly *less* apt to respond true to this statement than normal individuals.

Although the original MMPI scales were derived from comparison groups suffering from personality disorders often severe enough to require hospitalization, they have been widely used in the study of other populations. One of these studies, illustrated in Figure 13-5, compares the scores of male delinquents and nondelinquents.

RATING SCALES. Unless the individual is motivated to answer honestly in

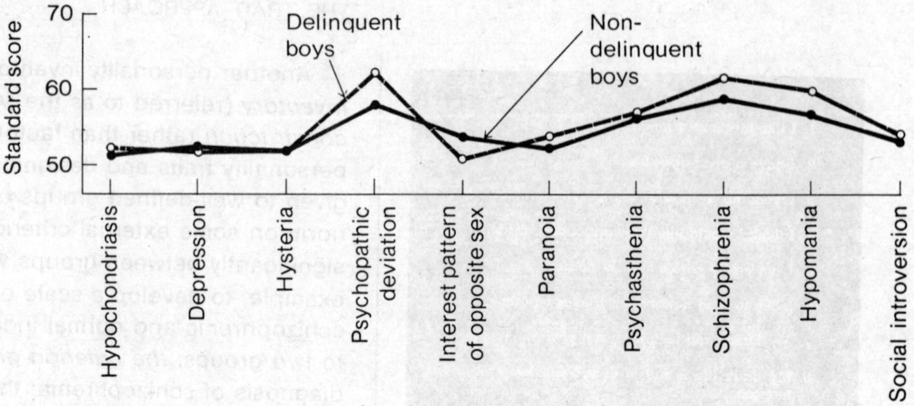

Fig. 13-5 Personality profiles of male delinquents and nondelinquents
The delinquents show three unusually high scores: on the psychopathic deviation, schizophrenia, and hypomania scales. Psychopathic deviation refers to the disregard of rules expected to characterize the delinquent; the schizophrenia scale, applied to the normally adjusted person, refers to negative or odd behavior, lack of social grace; hypomania refers to expansive behavior, not bound by custom. The scores on the scale of patterns of interest of the opposite sex are lower for delinquents than for nondelinquents, suggesting an excessively masculine type of response on the part of the delinquents. (Data from Hathaway and Monachesi. 1963)

a personality inventory, he can *bias* his responses so as to appear "sick" (e.g., if he wants to avoid military service or be eligible for a disability pension) or to appear more efficient and well adjusted than he really is (e.g., if he is applying for a job). And even the person who is trying to be as accurate as possible may have traits and tendencies of which he is unaware. Various devices have been incorporated into personality inventories to compensate for the individual's "test-taking attitude," but none have proved completely satisfactory.

One way to avoid this problem is to have someone else evaluate the individual, either on the basis of what they know or by observing him in certain situations. To put this kind of judgment into a standardized form, *rating scales* are used. A rating scale is a device for recording judgments about a trait. Some examples of rating scales are shown in Table 13-2.

In order for the rating to be meaningful, the rater must (1) understand the scale; (2) be sufficiently acquainted with the person being rated so that meaningful judgments can be made; and (3) avoid the *"halo effect"*—the tendency to rate a person in a favorable direction on all traits because of a good impression made on one or two (or, conversely, to rate unfavorably because of a poor impression made on one or two traits).

Unless the rater knows the person being rated fairly well, or the behavior being rated is very specific, ratings may be influenced by social stereotypes That is, the rater may base his ratings as much on how he *believes* a "suburban housewife," a "long-haired intellectual," or a "high school athlete" acts and thinks as on the actual behaviors of the subject being rated. Despite such problems, descriptions of a person provided by different raters in different situations often yield good agreement. In one study, for example, the aggressiveness of a group of school boys between the ages of eight and twelve was rated by their peers and by observers who watched them playing games in the school yard. There was close agreement between the two sets of ratings (Winder and Wiggins, 1964).

Evaluation of the Trait Approach

Despite decades of work devoted to the construction and refinement of tests designed to measure traits, none of the tests show much predictive power. Relationships between test scores and other measures of behavior are low—usually with a correlation coefficient of about .30. Thus, such tests may be useful as gross screening devices (e.g., to separate psychotics from

TABLE 13-2
Some examples of rating scales

How would you describe the individual's self-confidence?	Considers himself incapable of much success	Underestimates his own abilities	Knows just what he is capable of	Exaggerates his abilities	Judges himself capable of anything
Place a check at the point that describes the individual's poise.	Nervous and ill at ease	Somewhat tense; easily upset	Average poise and security	Sure of himself	Composed; adapts well to crises
How would you rate the subject's emotional control?	Very Low	Below Average	Average	Above Average	Very High
Does the individual antagonize others?	Never	Rarely	Sometimes	Often	Always
How would you rate the parent's behavior toward the child?	No control of emotion in response to child's behavior	Controlled more by emotion than reason in dealing with child	Emotion freely expressed but behavior controlled	Remains calm and objective toward child despite provocation	Never shows any signs of emotion; always controlled
Does the individual need constant prodding or proceed with his work without being told?	Needs much prodding in doing ordinary assignments	Needs occasional prodding	Does ordinary assignments of own accord	Completes suggested supplementary work	Seeks and sets for himself additional tasks

normal individuals), but they cannot be counted on to predict behavior in the individual case. If you want to estimate the likelihood that a patient will be readmitted to a mental hospital after discharge, you would be safer basing your prediction on the thickness of his hospital file (the thicker the file, the more likely that he will return) than on any of the existing personality inventories (Lasky and others, 1959). This simply means that past behavior is a good predictor of future behavior.

A number of factors contribute to the low predictive ability of personality tests. Many traits may not reflect fundamental attributes of a person but may be highly dependent on the situation. A youngster obtaining a high aggression score on a test may not display aggression under all provocations. He may aggress toward his school mates but not toward his parents and teachers; even with his peers he may behave aggressively on some occasions and docilely on others. Most personality inventories define traits in very broad terms. A scale measuring "anxiety" may be too abstract. To be useful for prediction, traits need to be defined in terms of environmental situations to which a person will respond consistently. A test that breaks down the concept of anxiety into more specific categories such as "anxiety related to achievement," "anxiety in peer relations," "anxiety in relation to authority figures," and so on, might prove to have more predictive power.

Variables such as age, sex, and intelligence may also influence the correlations found in trait studies. A test measure of "impulsivity" may correlate positively with "willingness to take risks" for boys but not for girls. Low-IQ children may show a positive correlation between two measures such as "aggressiveness" and "destructive behavior," while for children of high IQ the correlation may be negative. Variables that influence the correlations found in trait research have been called *moderator variables*—the effects of a particular trait are *moderated* by, are dependent upon, many other conditions. The age, sex, and intelligence of the subject and the characteristics of the test situation are all moderator variables that may influence test behavior, thereby diluting the predictive ability of the traits measured.

Another objection to some trait theories is that they tend to focus on isolated traits without specifying how these traits are organized within the personality. Without knowing which traits are most important and how they relate to other traits, we do not have an adequate description of the individual's personality. For example, a person who scores high on a measure of "compulsiveness" may engage in useless repetitive rituals, thereby interfering with the expression of other traits, or show dogged determination to stay with a productive task, thus taking advantage of other traits.

The Psychoanalytic Approach

Psychoanalytic theory approaches personality from a viewpoint that is very different from that of trait theory. Trait theorists try to find the stable dimensions of personality by studying groups of people, and much of their data is derived from self-reports—what the individual says about himself. In contrast, psychoanalytic theory is based on the in-depth study of individual personalities. And because motivation is believed to be *unconscious,* self-reports are not necessarily considered accurate. Instead, a person's verbalizations and overt behaviors are interpreted as disguised representations of underlying *unconscious processes.*

Freud's theories, developed over a 40-year period of clinical work, fill 24 volumes—from *The interpretation of dreams,* published in 1900, to *Outline of psychoanalysis,* published posthumously in 1940, a year after his death. We can present here only the barest outline of Freud's theory of personality; readers unfamiliar with Freudian theory may want to look at the suggested readings listed at the end of the chapter.

Freud compared the human mind to an iceberg; the small part that shows on the surface of the water represents *conscious experience,* while the much larger mass below water level represents the *unconscious*—a storehouse of impulses, passions, and primitive instincts that affect our thoughts and behavior. It was this unconscious portion of the mind that Freud sought to explore, and he did so by the method of *free association.* The method requires that the person talk about everything that comes into the conscious mind, no matter how ridiculous or trivial it might seem. By analyzing free associations, including the recall of dreams and early childhood memories, Freud sought to puzzle out the basic determinants of personality.

Personality Structure

Freud saw personality as composed of three major systems: the *id,* the *ego,* and the *superego.* Each of these systems has its own functions, but the three interact to govern behavior.

THE ID. The id is the original source of personality, present in the newborn infant, from which the ego and superego later develop. It consists of everything that is inherited, including the instinctual drives—sex and aggression. It is closely linked to the biological processes and provides the energy source (*libido*) for the operation of all three systems. Increases in energy level (from either internal or external stimulation) produce uncomfortable tension for the id, and the id seeks immediately to reduce this tension and return the organism to its normal state. Thus the id seeks immediate gratification of primitive, pleasure-seeking impulses. The id, like the newborn infant, operates on the *pleasure principle;* it endeavors to avoid pain and obtain pleasure regardless of any external considerations.

One process by which the id attempts to reduce tension is to form a mental image or hallucination of the object that will remove the tension. Thus, a starving man might form a mental image of a delicious meal. This is an example of *wish fulfillment.* Dreams, according to Freud, represent wish fulfillment; the objects and events we conjure up in our dreams represent attempts to fulfill some impulse of the id. The hallucinations of psychotic individuals are also considered by Freud to be examples of wish fulfillment. Freud called such attempts to satisfy needs irrationally, with no consideration of reality, *primary process thinking.*

THE EGO. Mental images do not satisfy needs. The starving man cannot reduce his hunger by eating visual images. Reality must be considered. And this is the role of the ego. The ego develops out of the id because of the necessity for dealing with the real world. The hungry man has to have food if the tension of hunger is to be reduced. He may not be able to immediately satisfy his hunger pangs if food is not present in the environment. Thus, the ego obeys the *reality principle,* which requires it to test reality and delay discharge of tension until the appropriate environmental conditions are found. The ego operates by *secondary process thinking,* which is realistic and logical and plans how to achieve satisfaction. The id seeks immediate tension reduction by such primary processes as direct gratification of impulses or wish-fulfilling imagery. The ego takes the real world into consideration. For example, it delays gratification of sexual impulses until conditions are appropriate. The ego is essentially the "executive" of the personality because it decides what actions are appropriate, which id instincts will be satisfied, and in what manner. The ego mediates between the demands of the id, the realities of the world, and the demands of the superego.

"Light on the id, heavy on the superego

THE SUPEREGO. The third part of the personality, the superego, is the internalized representation of the values and morals of society as taught to the child by the parents and others. The superego judges whether an action is right or wrong according to the standards of society. The id seeks pleasure, the ego tests reality, and the superego strives for perfection. The superego develops in response to parental rewards and punishments. It is composed of the *conscience,* which incorporates all the things the child is punished or reprimanded for doing, and the *ego-ideal,* which includes those actions the child is rewarded for doing. The conscience punishes by making the person feel guilty, and the ego-ideal rewards by making the individual feel proud of himself.

Initially, the parent controls the child's behavior directly through rewards and punishments. Through the incorporation of parental standards into the superego, behavior is brought under self-control. The child no longer needs anyone to tell him it is wrong to steal; his superego tells him.

The main functions of the superego are (1) to inhibit the impulses of the id, particularly those that society prohibits, such as sex and aggression, (2) to persuade the ego to substitute moralistic goals for realistic ones, and (3) to strive for perfection.

Sometimes the three components of personality are at odds: the ego postpones gratification that the id wants right away, and the superego battles with both the id and the ego because behavior often falls short of the moral code it represents. But more often in the normal person the three work as a team, producing integrated behavior.

ANXIETY AND ITS DEFENSES. Freud believed that the conflict between the id impulses—primarily sexual and aggressive instincts—and the restraining influences of the ego and superego constituted the motivating source of personality. Because society condemns free expression of aggression and sexual behavior, such impulses cannot be immediately and directly expressed. The child learns early that he may not hit his sibling or handle his genitals in public. He eventually internalizes parental restrictions on impulse satisfaction to form the superego. The more restraints a society (or its representatives, the parents) place on impulse expression, the greater the potential for conflict between the three parts of the personality.

The desires of the id are powerful forces that must be expressed in some way; prohibiting their expression does not abolish them. A person with an urge to do something for which he will be punished becomes anxious. Anxiety is a state of uncomfortable tension that the person is motivated to reduce. One way of reducing anxiety is to express the impulse in disguised form, thereby avoiding punishment by society and condemnation by the superego. For example, aggressive impulses may be displaced to sports car racing or to championing political causes.

Another method of reducing anxiety, called *repression,* is to push the impulse out of awareness into the unconscious. These methods of anxiety reduction, called *defense mechanisms,* are means of defending the personality against painful anxiety. They are never totally successful in relieving tension, and the residue spills over in the form of nervousness or restlessness, which, as Freud pointed out, is the price we must pay for being civilized. Presumably, a society that placed no restrictions on free expression of the id's instincts would produce people completely free of anxiety or tension. But such a society would probably not survive for long; all societies must place some restrictions on behavior for the well-being of the group.

Defense mechanisms form the basis of Freud's theory of neurotic and psychotic behavior and will be examined more fully in Chapter 15. At this point we will note only that individuals differ in the balance among id, ego, and superego systems and in the methods they use to defend against anxiety. The way in which a person approaches a problem situation reflects the manner in which he has learned to cope with the conflicting demands of the three parts of his personality.

Personality Development

Freud believed that the personality develops largely as the result of what occurs at certain fixed stages during the first five years of life. Individual differences in adult personality reflect the manner in which the person coped with the conflicts that may have arisen during the *stages of psychosexual development.* The id's energy, libido, attaches itself to different activities at each stage of development. Freud's psychosexual stages were discussed in

Chapter 3. To summarize them briefly, they include: (1) the *oral stage,* from birth to one year—pleasure is obtained through stimulation of the mouth as in nursing or thumb-sucking; (2) the *anal stage,* occurring during the second year of life, when the parent attempts to toilet train—gratification is obtained through holding or expelling feces; (3) the *phallic stage,* from about age three to six—pleasure is obtained through fondling the genitals; (4) a latency period follows the end of the phallic stage during which the child becomes less concerned with his own body and turns his attention toward skills needed for coping with the environment; (5) the *genital stage* during adolescence—the youth begins to love others for altruistic rather than self-gratification reasons. The experiences of the earlier stages become synthesized into the genital stage, the goal of which is adult sexual satisfactions leading to reproduction.

Problems encountered at any one stage, either of deprivation or overindulgence, may produce *fixation* at that stage. The individual's libido remains partially attached to the activities appropriate to that stage of psychosexual development. Thus, according to psychoanalytic theory, a person fixated at the oral stage when the infant is totally dependent upon others for the satisfaction of needs may, as an adult, be excessively dependent and overly fond of such oral pleasures as eating, drinking, or smoking. Such a person is called an ''oral'' personality.

The person fixated at the anal stage of psychosexual development, the ''anal'' personality, may be abnormally concerned with cleanliness and orderliness and is assumed to be obstinate and resistant to external pressure.

Evaluation of Psychoanalytic Theory

Psychoanalytic theory has had an enormous impact on psychological and philosophical conceptions of people. Freud's major contributions are his recognition that unconscious needs and conflicts motivate much of our behavior and his emphasis on the importance of early childhood experiences in personality development. His emphasis on sexual factors led to an awareness of their role in adjustmeht problems and paved the way for the scientific study of sexuality. But many critics think that Freud overemphasized the role of sex in human motivation. Freud made his observations during the Victorian period, when sexual standards were very strict, so it was understandable that many of his patients had conflicts centering around their sexual desires. Today, guilt feelings about sex are less frequent, yet the incidence of mental illness remains about the same. Sexual conflicts are not the only cause of personality disturbances—perhaps not even a major cause.

Some critics point out, too, that Freud's theory of personality is based almost entirely upon his observations of emotionally disturbed individuals. It may not represent an appropriate description of the normal, healthy personality.

Psychoanalysis, while acknowledged as a powerful influence, has been seriously questioned as a scientific theory. Freud's theory is largely untestable because his constructs are ambiguous and difficult to define. He does not tell us, for example, what behaviors indicate that an individual is fixated at the anal stage of psychosexual development, and what behaviors indicate he is not fixated. Research efforts to identify oral and anal personality types suggest that the parents' characteristic ways of handling the child (e.g., continual demands tor neatness and precision), or attempts to make the child

CRITICAL DISCUSSION

Modifications of Freud's Theory

Later psychoanalysts have proposed a number of modifications of Freud's theory. Carl Jung, one of Freud's students, started his own school of psychoanalysis, which became known as *analytical psychology* (Jung, 1968). Jung objected to Freud's emphasis on sexual impulses and believed that a number of other instincts were equally important. He stressed the importance of man's goals and aspirations.

Jung's theory of personality borders on the mystical. He went beyond Freud's idea of a personal unconscious and proposed a *collective unconscious,* which consists of all the memories and patterns of behavior inherited from man's ancestral past. All human beings have the same collective unconscious, which predisposes them to act in certain ways. The collective unconscious is the residue that accumulates as the result of repeated experiences over many generations; it is separate from the personal experiences of the individual. For example, since all human beings have a mother, infants are born with the tendency to perceive and react to their mother in certain predetermined ways. Because of our collective unconscious, we are born with predispositions for thinking and feeling according to certain patterns. Thus, we are predisposed to be afraid of the dark and of snakes because these were some of the dangers encountered by primitive people.

Jung felt that many symbols had uni-

13-6 The mandala

The mandala was considered by Jung to represent the universal symbol of the self. A mandala typically is in the form of a circle enclosing a square and often bears symmetrically arranged representations of deities. It is used in Hinduism and Buddhism as an aid to meditation. Because the mandala form was found in the art of so many cultures, Jung felt it was part of our collective unconscious.

Neo-Freudians

versal meaning because of their origin in the collective unconscious. For example, the mandala, or magic circle, is a symbolic representative of the self—of man's striving for unity and self-cohesiveness. Mandalas are found in the art and design of many cultures. (See Figure 13-6.)

As we noted earlier, Jung was also the first to distinguish between extraverts and introverts. Jung's writings have had much more influence in philosophy and religion than in psychology or psychiatry; analytical psychology is enjoying renewed popularity today among laymen, probably because of its optimistic and mystical flavor. Jung had a more positive view of man than Freud and was to some extent a predecessor of the humanistic psychologists.

Criticism of orthodox Freudian theory by other psychoanalysts has focused primarily on Freud's neglect of social influences. According to such *neo-Freudians* as Alfred Adler, Karen Horney, Erich Fromm, Harry Stack Sullivan, and Erik Erikson, Freud placed too much emphasis upon the instinctive and biological aspects of personality. He failed to recognize that people are largely products of the society in which they live. These later psychoanalysts see personality as shaped much more by the people, society, and culture that surround the individual than by instincts. And they place more emphasis on the ego and reality testing than they do on the id. Some feel that the ego develops independently of the id and has its own source of energy; part of its functioning is concerned with more positive goals than just avoiding conflict between the id and society's demands. By and large the neo-Freudians are more optimistic than Freud about the nature of man and his ability to change.

Alfred Adler

Photograph by Jill Krementz

Erich Fromm

Karen Horney

Harry Stack Sullivan

Fig. 13-7 A Rorschach inkblot

This inkblot is one of the standardized blots used in the Rorschach Test. The subject is asked to tell what is seen in the blot; it may be viewed from any angle.

excessively dependent) have more influence on later personality than the specific events that occur during particular psychosexual stages.

Psychoanalytic theory makes few predictions that can be empirically verified. Since very different behaviors, according to Freud, may be signs of the same underlying impulse or conflict, prediction is difficult. For example, a mother who feels resentful and rejecting of her child may be punitive and abusive, or she may deny her hostile impulses by behaving in a very concerned and overprotective manner toward the youngster (what Freud would call a *reaction formation*). Since very opposite behaviors are said to result from the same underlying motive, presence or absence of the motive is hard to confirm.

Assessment through Projective Techniques

The psychoanalytic approach to understanding an individual's personality requires finding out about his unconscious conflicts and motives. Since a large part of the personality is unconscious, the person cannot tell you about it. The psychoanalyst must interpret the symbolic meanings of the person's behavior to arrive at the underlying motives. *Projective tests* have been devised as one method for uncovering unconscious motives.

A projective test presents an ambiguous stimulus to which the individual may respond as he wishes. Theoretically, because the stimulus is ambiguous and does not demand a specific response, the individual *projects* his personality through his responses, just as a movie camera projects an image on the screen. Projective tests tap the subject's imagination, and through his imaginative productions it is assumed that he reveals something about himself. Two of the most widely used projective techniques are the *Rorschach Test* and the *Thematic Apperception Test.*

Psychologist administering the Rorschach Test

RORSCHACH. The Rorschach Test, developed by the Swiss psychiatrist Hermann Rorschach in the 1920s, consists of a series of 10 cards, each displaying a rather complex inkblot like the one shown in Figure 13-7. Some of the blots are colored and some are in black and white. The subject is instructed to look at the inkblots one at a time and report everything seen on the card—everything the inkblot could look like or resemble. After the subject has finished the 10 cards, the examiner usually goes back over each response, asking the subject to elaborate some responses and to tell what features of the blot gave a particular impression.

The subject's responses may be scored in terms of three categories: (1) location—does the response involve the entire inkblot or some small part; (2) determinants—is the subject responding to the shape of the blot, the color, or differences in texture and shading; (3) content—what does the response represent. Contrary to what most people think, content is considered the least important in revealing personality dynamics, except in certain fairly pathological cases.

Several elaborate scoring systems have been devised that take all three categories into consideration. But because these systems have not proved to have much predictive value, most psychologists base their interpretations on an impressionistic evaluation of the response record as well as the subject's general reaction to the test situation: for example, is the individual defensive, open, competitive, cooperative, and so on.

THEMATIC APPERCEPTION TEST. Another popular projective test is the Thematic Apperception Test (abbreviated TAT) developed at Harvard University by Henry Murray during the 1930s. This test is less ambiguous than the Rorschach because it involves pictures of actual scenes rather than inkblots. The subject is shown a series of pictures, similar to that in Figure 13-8, and asked to make up a story about each. He or she is encouraged to give free reign to imagination and to tell whatever story comes to mind. The test is intended to reveal the basic "themes" that recur in a person's imaginative productions. *Apperception* means a readiness to perceive in certain ways, based on prior individual experience. Hence, the test's name implies that people interpret ambiguous pictures according to their individual readiness to perceive, and that they elaborate stories in terms of preferred plots or themes that reflect personal fantasies. In taking the TAT, the subject tells stories about 20 pictures. If particular problems are bothering the subject, they may show up in a number of the stories.

When confronted with a picture similar to that in Figure 13-8, a 21-year-old male told the following story.

> She has prepared this room for someone's arrival and is opening the door for a last general look over the room. She is probably expecting her son home. She tries to place everything as it was when he left. She seems like a very tyrannical character. She led her son's life for him and is going to take over again as soon as he gets back. This is merely the beginning of her rule, and the son is definitely cowed by this overbearing attitude of hers and will slip back into her well-ordered way of life. He will go through life plodding down the tracks she has laid down for him. All this represents her complete domination of his life until she dies (Arnold, 1949, p. 100).

Although the original picture shows only a woman standing in an open door, the subject's readiness to respond with something about the relationship to his mother led to this story of a woman's domination of her son. The clinician whose patient told this story reports that facts obtained later confirmed the interpretation that the story reflected the subject's own problems.

In analyzing responses to the TAT cards the psychologist looks for recurrent themes that may reveal the individual's needs, motives, or characteristic way of handling interpersonal relations.

Fig. 13-8 A picture similar to one used in the Thematic Apperception Test

The pictures usually have elements of ambiguity in them so that the subject can "read into" them something from personal experience or fantasy.

CRITICISM OF PROJECTIVE TESTS. Many other projective tests have been devised. Such tests include giving the first response you can think of to a series of words, completing sentences that start "I often wish. . . ." "My mother. . . ." or "I feel like quitting when they. . . ." In fact, any stimulus to which a person can respond in an individualistic way could be considered the basis for a projective test. You could squeeze a lump of clay into an ambiguous shape and ask people what it looks like to them. You would probably get a wide range of responses; these responses might reflect something about the individual's personality, but it would be hard to say what—a momentary preoccupation, accuracy of perception, a deep-seated impulse? Most projective tests have not been subject to enough research to establish their usefulness in assessing personality.

The Rorschach and TAT, in contrast, have been intensively researched. But the results have not been promising, and the enthusiasm for projective tests has begun to dim. Test reliability of the Rorschach is poor because the interpretation of responses depends too much on the clinician's judgment. The same test protocol may often be evaluated quite differently by two trained examiners, possibly because each projects his own interpretations into the responses. Attempts to demonstrate the Rorschach's ability to predict behavior or discriminate between groups have been damaging to the test's reputation (Cronbach, 1970).

The TAT has fared a little better. When specific scoring systems are set up—for example, to measure achievement motives or aggressive themes—the inter-scorer reliability is fairly good. But the relation of TAT scores to overt behavior is complex. Preoccupations seen in the stories are not necessarily acted upon. A person who produces a number of stories with themes of aggression is often not very aggressive in actual behavior. Apparently the subject is compensating for inhibition of aggressive tendencies by expressing such impulses in fantasy. When inhibitions about expressing aggression and strength of aggressive tendencies are *both* estimated from the TAT stories, the relationship to behavior becomes more predictable. Among boys whose tests indicated they were not very inhibited, the correlation between amount of aggression in the stories and overt aggression was 0.55. Among boys showing a high degree of inhibition, the correlation between number of aggressive themes on the TAT and overt aggression was −0.50 (Olweus, 1969).

The TAT is a sample of behavior, and particular story themes are meaningful only when considered in the light of other TAT themes, as well as the subject's sex, educational level, and social class. The skilled clinician makes tentative interpretations about the individual's personality from the TAT stories, and verifies or discards them depending upon further information. The TAT stories alone may not provide very valid predictions, but they can be useful in suggesting possible areas of conflict to be explored during treatment.

The Social Learning Approach

Observational learning

As we noted in Chapter 12, the social learning approach to motivation focuses on the patterns of behavior the individual learns in coping with the environment. Within this viewpoint, individual differences in behavior result from variations in the conditions of learning that the person encounters in the course of growing up.[2]

Some behavior patterns are learned through direct experience; the individual behaves in a certain manner and is rewarded or punished. But responses can also be acquired without direct reinforcement. Because we can make use of complex symbolic processes to code and store our observations in memory, we can learn by observing the actions of others and by noting the consequences of those actions. Thus, for social learning

[2]The term social learning theory has been applied to several behavioral approaches to personality. Initially, it referred to attempts to reinterpret psychoanalytic concepts in terms of learning principles such as drive, stimulus, response, and reinforcement (e.g., Miller and Dollard, 1941). As used in this text, social learning theory refers to the current approach (e.g., Bandura, 1973; Mischel, 1973), which rejects Freudian concepts and stresses the importance of social and cognitive factors as well as the role of observational models in determining behavior.

theorists, reinforcement is not *necessary* for learning, although it may *facilitate* learning by focusing attention. Much of human learning is *observational* or *vicarious*.

Reinforcement may not be necessary for learning, but it is crucial for the *performance* of learned behavior. One of social learning theory's main assumptions is that people behave in ways likely to produce reinforcement. A person's repertoire of learned behaviors is extensive; the particular action chosen for a specific situation depends on the expected outcome. Most adolescent girls know how to fight, having watched their male classmates or TV characters aggress by kicking, hitting with the fists, and so on. But since this kind of behavior is seldom reinforced in girls, it is unlikely to occur except in unusual circumstances.

The reinforcement that controls the expression of learned behavior may be (1) *direct*—tangible rewards, social approval or disapproval, or alleviation of aversive conditions; (2) *vicarious*—observation of someone else receiving reward or punishment for similar behavior; or (3) *self-administered*—evaluation of one's own performance with self-praise or reproach. As we noted earlier, self-administered reinforcement plays an important role in social learning theory, and efforts have been devoted to discovering the conditions that facilitate regulation of behavior through self-reward and self-punishment.

Social Behavior as a Person-Situation Interaction

Trait theories assume that personality is consistent, so that a person can be characterized according to enduring traits. Social learning theorists regard the *situation* as an important determinant of behavior. A person's actions in a given situation depend upon the specific characteristics of the situation, the individual's appraisal of the situation, and past reinforcement for behavior in similar situations (or observations of others in similar situations). People behave consistently insofar as the situations they encounter and the roles they are expected to play remain relatively stable.

Most social behaviors, however, are not uniformly rewarded across different settings. The individual learns to discriminate those contexts in which certain behavior is appropriate and those in which it is not. To the extent that a person is rewarded for the same response in many different situations, *generalization* takes place, insuring that the same behavior will occur in a variety of settings. Thus, a boy whose father reinforces him for physical aggression at home as well as against his teachers and peers would probably develop a personality that is pervasively aggressive. But more often aggressive responses are differentially rewarded, and learned *discriminations* determine the situations in which the individual will display aggression.

Psychoanalytic theory assumes that basic personality motives endure, although overt responses may change. Thus, a woman who is hostile in some situations but not in others may be assumed to have a basically hostile personality concealed at times behind a facade of submissiveness and agreeableness. Or she may be described as a passive-dependent woman with a surface defense of aggressiveness.

Social learning theory, in contrast, assumes that diverse behaviors *do not* necessarily reflect variations on the same underlying motive; they often are discrete responses to different situations. As Mischel puts it, it is possible for such a woman to be

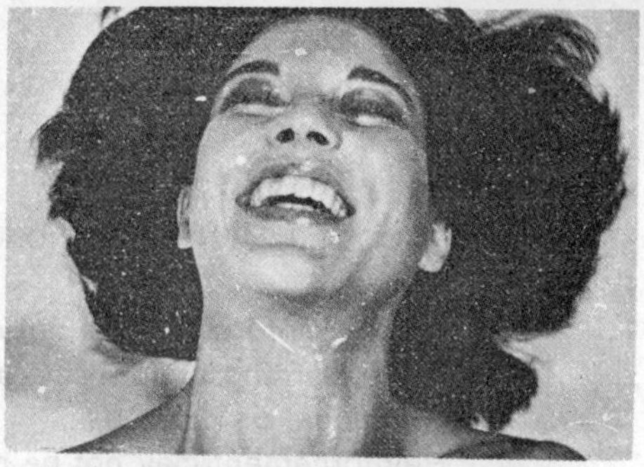

Many aspects of the same person.
". . . it is possible for such a woman to be . . ."

> . . . a hostile, fiercely independent, passive-dependent, feminine, aggressive, warm, castrating person all in one. Which of these she is at any particular moment would not be random and capricious; it would depend on discriminative stimuli—whom she is with, when, how, and much more. But each of these aspects of her self may be a quite genuine and real aspect of her total being (Mischel, 1971, p. 75).

Rather than study basic traits or underlying motives, social learning theory focuses on behavior patterns and cognitive activities in relation to the specific conditions that evoke, maintain, or modify them. The emphasis is not on what individuals *are like* but on what they *do* in relationship to the conditions in which they do it. Some of the *person variables* that determine what an individual will do in a particular situation include the following:

1. *Competencies*—intellectual abilities, social skills, and other abilities.
2. *Cognitive strategies*—habitual ways of selectively attending to information and organizing it into meaningful units.
3. *Outcome expectancies*—expectations about the consequences of different behaviors and the meaning of certain stimuli (e.g., "shifty eyes" may mean not trustworthy). Both types of expectancies depend upon inferences about the intentions motivating the behavior of others.
4. *Subjective value of outcome*—even if individuals have similar expectancies, they may choose to behave differently because of differences in the subjective values of the outcomes they expect. Two students may expect that a certain behavior will please the professor, but for one this outcome is important, while for the other it is not.
5. *Self-regulatory systems and plans*—individual differences in self-imposed goals, rules guiding behavior, self-imposed rewards for success or punishment for failure, and ability to plan and execute steps leading to a goal will lead to differences in behavior. (Paraphrased with modifications from Mischel, 1973)

All of the above variables interact with conditions of the particular situation to determine what an individual will do in that situation.

But we are not simply passive reactors to situational conditions. Our behavior influences the "situations" of life as well as being influenced by them; the relationship is reciprocal. By selectively attending to what is happening, we can prevent certain conditions from impinging on us. And by our actions we can partly create the conditions that do impinge; changes in behavior toward others are usually followed by reciprocal changes in the behavior of others.

Assessment and Behavior Change

Social learning theorists are interested in personality assessment mainly for the purpose of behavior change. They define a specific behavior pattern and attempt to discover the stimulus conditions that control that pattern. They are also interested in assessing the individual's response capabilities; a particular behavior may fail to appear not because the proper reinforcing stimuli are lacking but because that response is not in the individual's repertoire. In addition to assessing *stimulus conditions* and *response capabilities,* the social learning theorist may want to measure the *degree* and *type of self-reinforcement* the individual uses. All these variables are relevant to behavior and the possibilities for modifying that behavior.

BEHAVIORAL MEASUREMENT. Behavior can be observed directly in naturalistic settings. Children can be observed in a nursery school setting, and notes made on the number of aggressive responses displayed and the particular conditions that elicited the responses. A device has been developed to permit an observer to record categories of behavior automatically. A panel of buttons, each of which represents a category of behavior (e.g., talking, running, sitting alone), is attached to a recorder pen. By depressing the button whenever the child starts the behavior designated by that button and not releasing the button until that particular behavior is discontinued, an observer can obtain a continuous record of behavior. This apparatus has been used to study the behavior of disturbed children in an effort to determine the environmental conditions that elicit and maintain certain maladaptive behavior (Lovaas and others, 1965).

The strength of certain avoidance behaviors has been assessed by exposing the fearful individual to a series of real or symbolic fear-inducing stimuli. The strength of fear of heights can be measured by noting how far the individual will climb up a ladder; fear of snakes has been measured by noting how closely the individual will approach a live, but harmless snake—from simply looking at the snake in a glass cage to actually allowing the animal to crawl over one's body. This kind of direct behavior sampling is often used to measure strength of fear before and after receiving therapy aimed at relieving specific fears.

When it is not possible for the assessor to observe behavior directly, self-reports may be used. For example, a person might be given a list of situations that arouse anxiety and asked to rank the most disturbing ones. Or a subject might be asked to keep a daily log noting activities and the conditions under which certain anxieties or behaviors occur.

In one case a woman who suffered from severe asthma attacks was asked to keep a diary for 85 days including all her activities and detailed descriptions of any respiratory or other physical symptoms—what the symptoms were and under exactly what conditions they occurred. Subsequent analysis of the diary revealed that more than half of her acute

CRITICAL DISCUSSION

How Consistent Is Human Behavior?

In studying personality, psychologists try to discover regularities in behavior. An assumption basic to most personality theories is that people behave consistently. If an individual seems "honest," "friendly," and "conscientious" in one situation, then we assume that we can predict how he or she will act in a number of different situations. Indeed, the feeling of consistency within our own thoughts and behavior is essential to our emotional well-being; a loss of a sense of consistency is characteristic of personality disorganization.

But the empirical evidence for personality consistency is slim. Research over the years has failed to demonstrate much consistency in human behavior either over time or across situations. One of the earliest studies of "moral character" in children found very low correlations between different measures of honesty; a child might lie to a teacher but not to a parent, cheat in the classroom but not on the playground (Hartshorne and May, 1928; 1929). Studies of other personality traits (e.g., self-control, cooperativeness, submissiveness) have demonstrated little cross-situational consistency. Even such a clearly defined trait as punctuality appears to be more a function of the specific situation than a consistent personality characteristic. Knowing that a college student is usually late for an 8:30 class provides little basis for predicting punctuality in keeping appointments with professors or meeting friends for an evening at the movies (Dudycha, 1936). Subsequent studies have typically found low correlations (less than +.30) between a person's behavior across different situations or between behavior on a personality test and actions in real life.

How do we explain the discrepancy between the data and our intuitive assumption that personality is consistent? One possibility is that the consistency assumption is wrong. Behavior is largely situation specific, and we attribute more consistency to a person's behavior than actually exists. There are numerous reasons why we may do so (c.f. Bem and Allen, 1974). We will mention only three. (1) Our preconceived notions of how people behave may lead us to generalize beyond our actual observations. We may fill in the missing data according to our "implicit personality theories" of what traits and behaviors go together (Schneider, 1973). Stereotypes of how a "homosexual" or a "career woman" or an "athlete" behave may cause us to attribute greater consistency to a person's actions than observations warrant. (2) Our own presence can cause people to behave in certain ways. Thus, our acquaintances may appear to be behaviorally consistent because we are present as a stimulus during every observation we make. They may behave quite differently when we are not observing them. (3) Because the actions of another person are such a salient feature of any scene, we tend to overestimate the extent to which behavior is caused by personality characteristics or attitudes and underestimate the importance of situational forces that may cause the person to act as he does (Jones and Nisbett, 1971) Observing someone behaving aggressively, we assume that the person has an aggressive disposition and will behave similarly in other settings—even though the situational factors may be quite different.

But there is an alternative explanation for the discrepancy between the data and our intuitive assumption that personality is consistent. Most of the research assumes that every person can be described by every trait, that people differ from one another only in *how much* of the trait they possess. But our intuitions do not make this assumption. When we are asked to describe a friend, we pick out a few traits that strike us as pertinent. When asked to describe a different friend, we select a different set of traits. Other traits are ignored as irrelevant. It may be that for any given individual, we should expect to find consistency only on those traits that are central to his personality and to find little consistency on traits that are not particularly relevant for him.

This alternative explanation was tested in a study by Bem and Allen (1974). By asking college students to rate their own cross-situational variability on a set of traits, these investigators found that they could obtain higher cross-situational correlations for subjects who indicated that they did not vary much from one situation to another than for subjects who identified themselves as highly variable. For example, high-variable subjects showed a low cross-situational consistency (+.27) on the trait of friendliness, whereas the low-variable subjects showed much higher consistency across situations (+.57).

This study also pointed up the importance of describing traits in terms of specific behaviors. For example, the investigators assumed that personal neatness was one component of "conscientiousness." But the results showed otherwise. For most students the neatness of their room was *not* related to other measures of conscientiousness, such as completing assignments on time or arriving promptly for classes and appointments.

The results of past research suggest that a characterization of personality in terms of universal traits is not a useful predictor of behavior. However, it remains to be seen how useful the trait concept can be if developed on a more individualistic basis.

asthma attacks occurred following contact with her mother. Physical activity and other sources of stress, such as interviews, did not elicit attacks. Moreover, most of the days in which she was completely free of respiratory symptoms involved no contact with her mother (Metcalfe, 1956). This is an example of a procedure that can be used as the first step in identifying problem-producing stimuli.

CHANGING THE STIMULUS CONDITIONS. Once the conditions that control a certain behavior have been identified, the next step is to change the stimulus conditions and observe whether behavior changes correspondingly.

In the case of the asthmatic woman, the next step might be to control the number of contacts the woman had with her mother and note if the number of asthma attacks increased or decreased accordingly. Actual observations of mother-daughter interactions might reveal some of the specific actions of the mother that were related to the attacks. Perhaps the daughter responded with anxiety whenever her mother made critical remarks or dependent demands. The next step might then be to try to alter some of the mother's responses and note to what extent such changes alter the frequency or severity of the daughter's asthmatic symptoms.

As you can see, assessment methods for social learning theorists are closely linked to treatment procedures. In Chapter 17 we will consider social learning theory techniques for modifying maladaptive behavior in more detail. At this point we will give one more example to illustrate the interaction between behavioral assessment and modification procedures, and the use of reinforcement in changing behavior.

Nursery school teachers were concerned because four-year-old Ann had become somewhat of a social isolate and did not interact with the other children in play. As part of an initial assessment, two observers sampled Ann's behavior at regular ten-second intervals, recording her nearness to and interactions with adults and children during the school day. It became clear that the teachers were inadvertently reinforcing Ann's isolate behavior. She was a bright, attractive child, who was very skillful at gaining adult attention. But the activities she engaged in to attract adult attention were incompatible with relating to other children. And the more isolated she became from other children, the more attention she received from adults.

To break this cycle the teachers gave Ann attention only when she played with other children. Attention from adults became contingent upon playing with her peers. At first even approximations to social play, such as standing near another child, were rewarded by prompt attention from a teacher. Whenever Ann began to leave the group or tried to solicit solitary contact with adults, the teachers stopped attending to her.

As you can see from Figure 13-9, Ann began to spend much more time playing with the other children and much less time trying to interact individually with adults. To assess the effects of reinforcement more precisely, the teachers reversed their procedures on the twelfth day, rewarding Ann with attention for interacting with them and ignoring her interactions with other children. Under these conditions Ann's previous isolate behavior reappeared. When reinforcement for peer play was again instituted (on the seventeenth day), Ann increased contact with her peers until she was spending about 60 percent of the school day in play with her classmates.

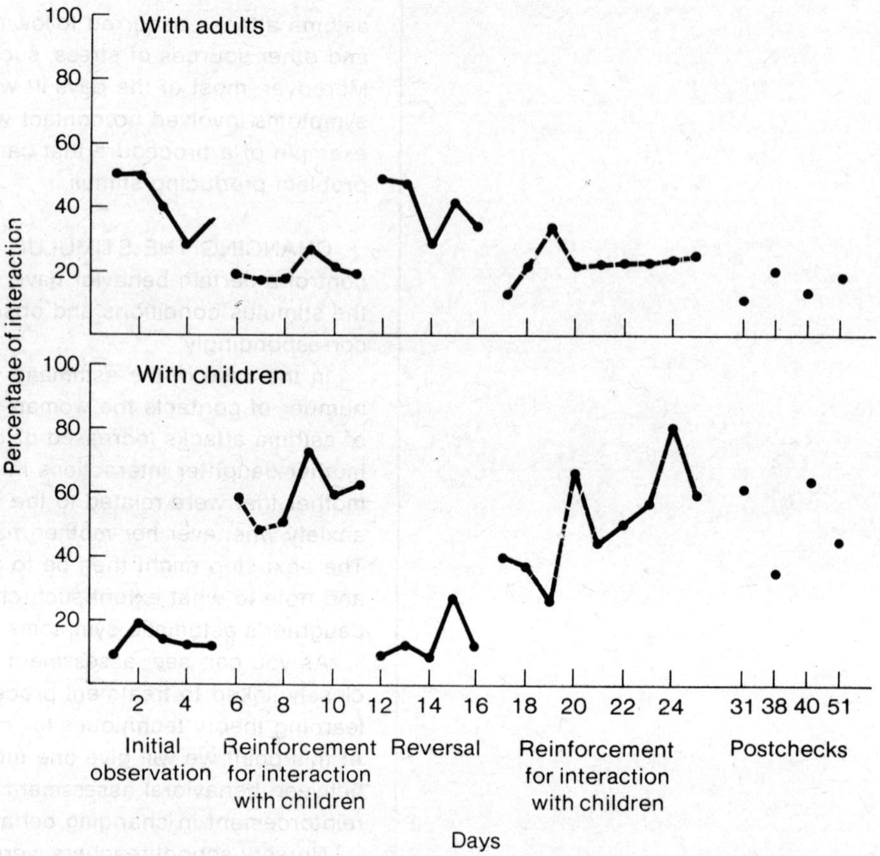

Fig. 13-9 Modifying social behavior

Percentage of time spent by Ann in social interaction with children and adults was recorded for two hours during each morning nursery school session. Reinforcement for playing with peers, introduced on day 6, produced a marked change in behavior. When the reinforcement conditions were reversed so that attempts to interact with adults gained attention (day 12), Ann reverted to her original behavior. Reintroduction of attention for peer play (day 17) reinstated interaction with classmates. Periodic checks after specific reinforcement was discontinued showed behavior at about the same level. (After Allen and others, 1964)

Periodic checks after the special reinforcement procedures ended indicated that the child's play behavior remained fairly stable at this level (Allen and others, 1964).

This case illustrates the use of behavior sampling to determine the conditions that are maintaining a specific problem behavior and the kinds of techniques that can be employed to substitute more satisfactory behavior.

Evaluation of Social Learning Theory

Social learning theory, through its emphasis on precision in the determination of environmental variables that elicit specific behaviors, has made a major contribution to both clinical psychology and personality theory. It has led us to look more closely at human actions as reactions to specific conditions rather than as symbolic manifestations of internal, unconscious forces. It has focused on the conditions that control our actions and the way changes in these conditions can be used to modify behavior. As we shall see in Chapter 17, the careful application of learning principles has proved very successful in changing maladaptive behavior.

Social learning theorists have been criticized for overemphasizing the importance of situational factors in behavior to the neglect of individual differences. They show little interest, for example, in innate differences that may predispose one person to be characteristically passive and slow to respond and another to be excitable and quick. Many personality theorists are not willing to concede the little stability to personality that social learning theory seems to imply. They point out that the experimental methods used by social learning theorists—measuring differences in behavior in different situations—are particularly sensitive to the impact of situational variables and are apt to emphasize behavior change. Correlational methods, on the other hand, which relate an individual's behavior in one situation (e.g., responses on a personality test) to behavior in another (e.g., real-life behavior) are more sensitive to individual differences and apt to emphasize behavioral stability (Bowers, 1973).

Statistical analyses of studies in which the behavior of individuals has been measured across different settings suggests that the variability in behavior accounted for by different situations is about the same as the variability accounted for by persisting individual differences. The largest proportion of the variability stems from the *interaction* between persons and situations. This implies that the way the person perceives the situation is the most important factor in determining behavior. Thus, the major determinant of behavior may lie in the particular "meaning" that a particular social situation has for a particular individual.

The Humanistic Approach

The humanistic approach to the study of personality includes a number of theories that, although different in some respects, share a common emphasis on man's potential for self-direction and freedom of choice. They are concerned with the "self" and the individual's subjective experiences.

Humanistic theories reject both the psychoanalytic and the behavioristic conceptions of human nature as too mechanistic, portraying people as creatures helplessly buffeted about by internal instincts or external stimuli. They are less concerned with motivational constructs as explanations of behavior than with the individual's perception of himself, immediate experiences, and his personal view of the world.

Carl Rogers

Most humanistic theories stress our positive nature—our push toward growth and self-actualization. Their emphasis is also on the "here and now" rather than on events in early childhood that may have shaped the individual's personality.

The main feature of the humanistic approach to personality will become clearer as we consider the ideas of two of its leading spokesmen, Carl Rogers (1970) and Abraham Maslow (1970).

Rogers' Self Theory

As was true of Freud, Rogers' theory of personality developed from his experiences with a specific therapeutic method for helping troubled individuals. His "nondirective," or "client-centered," therapy assumes that each person has the motivation and the ability to change; the therapist's task is simply to facilitate progress toward this change. As we shall see in Chapter 17, nondirective therapy was a startling departure in both theory and methods from psychoanalysis. In psychoanalysis therapy the therapist "analyzed" the patient's history to arrive at the problem. The assumption of nondirective therapy is that we are the best experts on ourselves. The patient, not the therapist, knows the factors that shape his personality and the best procedures for modifying them. The therapist's role is to act as a sounding board while the patient explores and analyzes problems.

SELF-CONCEPT. The most important concept in Rogers' theory of personality is the *self.* The self consists of all the ideas, perceptions, and values that characterize "I" or "me"; it includes the awareness of "what I am" and "what I can do." This perceived self (the self-concept) in turn influences both the person's perception of the world and his behavior. An individual with a strong, positive self-concept views the world quite differently from one whose self-concept is weak. The self-concept does not necessarily reflect reality; a person may be highly successful and respected yet view himself as a failure.

The individual evaluates every experience in relation to his self-concept. A person wants to behave in ways that are consistent with his self-image; experiences and feelings that are not consistent are threatening and may be denied admittance to consciousness (or, in Rogers' terms, remain *unsymbolized*). This is essentially Freud's notion of repression, although Rogers feels that such repression is neither necessarily inevitable in the course of growing up (depending on the parents' attitudes toward the child) nor permanent (during therapy the person can discover a real self and uncover all the repressed personality aspects). Freud would say that repression is inevitable and that some aspects of one's experiences always remain unconscious.

The more areas of experience one has to deny because they are inconsistent with one's self-concept, the wider the gulf becomes between the self and reality, and the greater the potential for anxiety. A person whose image is not congruent with personal feelings and experience must defend against the truth, because the truth will result in anxiety. If the incongruence becomes too great, the defenses may break down, resulting in severe anxiety or other forms of emotional disturbance. The well-adjusted person, in contrast, has a self-concept that is consistent with thought, experience, and behavior; the self is not rigid but flexible so that it can change as it assimilates new experiences and ideas.

There is another self in Rogers' theory, and that is the *ideal self.* We all have an ideal self, a conception of the kind of person we would like to be. This concept is similar to Freud's ego-ideal. The closer the ideal self is to the real self, the more fulfilled and happy the individual. A large discrepancy between the two results in an unhappy, dissatisfied individual.

Thus, two kinds of incongruence can develop: one between the self and the experiences of reality, and the other between the self and ideal self. Let us look at Rogers' view of how these incongruences may develop.

DEVELOPMENT OF THE SELF. Because the child's behavior is continuously being evaluated by parents and others (sometimes positively and sometimes negatively), he soon learns to discriminate between those thoughts and actions that are considered worthy and those that are not. The unworthy experiences become excluded from the self-concept, even though they may be quite valid or natural experiences. For example, relieving physiological tension in the bowel or bladder is experienced by the child as pleasurable. However, unless he urinates or defecates privately and in the proper place, parents usually condemn such activities as "bad" or "naughty." The child must then, because he needs to retain his parents' positive regard, deny his own experience. He must deny to himself that he receives satisfaction from defecating or urinating.

Feelings of competition and hostility toward a younger sibling who has usurped the center of attention are natural. But parents frown on hitting a little sister and usually punish such actions. The child must then revise his self-concept in some way so as to integrate this experience into his image of himself. He may decide he is bad and feel ashamed. He may decide his parents do not like him and feel rejected. Or he may deny his feelings and decide he does not want to hit his sister. Each of these attitudes contains a distortion of the truth. The third alternative is the easiest for the child to accept. But in so doing he denies his real feelings so that they become unconscious. He really does enjoy hitting his sister, but he can no longer admit it to himself. The more a person has to deny feelings and take on the values of others, the more uncomfortable he will feel about himself.

Obviously, there must be certain restrictions on behavior. Considerations of household efficiency and sanitation require some restraints on elimination. And children cannot be permitted to beat their siblings. Rogers suggests that the best approach is for the parents to recognize the child's feelings as valid, while explaining their feelings and the reasons for restraint.

SELF-ACTUALIZATION. Rogers feels that the basic force motivating the human organism is self-actualization; "a tendency toward fulfillment, toward actualization, toward the maintenance and enhancement of the organism." As the organism grows, it seeks to fulfill its potential within the limits of its heredity. A person may not always clearly perceive those actions that lead to growth and those that are regressive. But once he knows, he invariably chooses to grow rather than to regress. This innate motivation toward growth serves as the basis for Rogers' optimism about the outcome of therapy and the ability of the individual to change in a positive direction when aware of the choices. Rogers does not deny that there may be many needs, some of them biological, but they are all subservient to the organism's motivation to enhance and maintain itself.

The innate tendency toward self-actualization often runs into conflict with two learned needs: the need for *positive regard* and the need for *self-regard*. Rogers assumes that the need for positive regard is universal; we all want to be accepted and loved by others. Sometimes the regard we receive from others is *unconditional:* "I love you no matter how badly you may behave at times." But more often it is *conditional,* that is, it depends on specific behavior.

The need for self-regard develops later; it is essentially the internalization of those actions and values that others approve. In this sense it is similar to Freud's superego.

The need for self-actualization directs the individual to seek or to avoid activities depending upon whether the experience is seen as one that will enhance the person. The need for positive regard directs behavior according to whether the resulting experience will elicit favorable reactions from others—from those important in the individual's life. Obviously, there are situations where the two needs conflict.

Ideally, the more completely the individual is given positive regard—acceptance that is not conditional to specific behaviors—the more congruence there will be between his self-concept and his actual experiences, as well as between his self-concept and ideal self.

Maslow's Self-actualizers

The person who focused most on studying the characteristics of mature, competent, and self-fulfilled individuals was Abraham Maslow. We noted in Chapter 12 Maslow's hierarchy of needs progressing from the basic biological needs through the psychological needs and culminating in the need for self-actualization. By self-actualization Maslow meant the development of full individuality, with all parts of the personality in harmony.

He began his investigation in a somewhat unique manner. He selected from among eminent historical figures those whom he considered to be *self-actualizers*—men and women who had made extraordinary use of their full potential. Included in Maslow's group of self-actualizers were such persons as Abraham Lincoln, Thomas Jefferson, Jane Addams, Spinoza, Albert Einstein, Eleanor Roosevelt, and William James. After studying their lives he arrived at a composite picture of a self-actualizer. The distinguishing characteristics of self-actualized persons are listed in Table 13-3, along with some of the behaviors that Maslow believed could lead to self-actualization.

Albert Einstein

Abraham Lincoln

Maslow extended his study to a population of college students. Selecting those students who fitted his definition of self-actualizers, Maslow found this group to be in the healthiest one percent of the population—they showed no neurotic or psychotic symptoms and were making full use of their talents and capabilities (Maslow, 1970).

Many people experience transient moments of self-actualization. Maslow calls these *peak experiences.* A peak experience is one of happiness and fulfillment; an experience of *being*—a temporary, nonstriving, non-self-centered state of perfection and goal attainment. Peak experiences may occur with different degrees of intensity and in various contexts—creative activities, appreciation of nature, intimate relations with others, parental experiences, aesthetic perceptions, or athletic participation. After asking a large number of college students to describe any experience that came near to being a peak experience, Maslow attempted to categorize what they said. He derived a list of values found in such experiences; they included wholeness, perfection, aliveness, uniqueness, effortlessness, self-sufficiency, and the values of beauty, goodness, and truth.

Maslow's view is much more positive and optimistic than Freud's. None of our innate needs is antisocial. Aggression, for example, arises only when attempts to satisfy the basic needs are frustrated. The chief criticism of his approach lies in the lack of precision in his concepts. Self-actualization is not clearly defined, nor are the criteria he used in selecting his self-actualized persons. Someone else viewing the lives of the same famous people might not find the same characteristics. And some of the characteristics may even be somewhat negatively related. For example, some individuals who were most known for their social interest and concern for human welfare did not have very satisfying interpersonal relationships with their spouses or children. Eleanor Roosevelt and Abraham Lincoln are two examples.

Assessment in Humanistic Theory

The humanistic view of personality focuses on the person's world as he perceives it. It is the individual's perceptions and interpretations of experiences that determine behavior. To understand a person's behavior we need to know not only what the external situation is but how it looks to the individual. But to study the individual's experiences scientifically we need objective measurements of subjective experiences.

MEASURING SELF-CONCEPTS. Various methods have been used to measure a person's self-concept. One way is to have the individual select from a number of statements describing a person (e.g., "I am self-confident," "I am unusually fearful," "I work efficiently," etc.) those that apply to him. The self-concept arrived at by this method can be compared to the individual's ideal self by having him also select statements that describe the person he would like to be. Or his self-concept can be compared with the picture others have of him by asking friends and relatives to select statements that describe him. Thus, it is possible to determine congruences between self-concept and ideal self, and between self-concept and self as viewed by others.

Some interesting results have been obtained with methods of this type, but, as with other self-report tests (such as personality inventories), the individual's test-taking attitude may bias the results. He may not be willing to

TABLE 13-3
Self-actualization

CHARACTERISTICS OF SELF-ACTUALIZERS
Perceive reality efficiently and are able to tolerate uncertainty
Accept themselves and others for what they are
Spontaneous in thought and behavior
Problem-centered rather than self-centered
Have a good sense of humor
Highly creative
Resistant to enculturation, although not purposely unconventional
Concerned for the welfare of mankind
Capable of deep appreciation of the basic experiences of life
Establish deep, satisfying interpersonal relations with a few, rather than many, people
Able to look at life from an objective viewpoint
BEHAVIORS LEADING TO SELF-ACTUALIZATION
Experience life as a child does, with full absorption and concentration
Try something new rather than sticking to secure and safe ways
Listen to your own feelings in evaluating experiences rather than to the voice of tradition or authority or the majority
Be honest; avoid pretenses or "game playing"
Be prepared to be unpopular if your views don't coincide with those of most people
Assume responsibility
Work hard at whatever you decide to do
Try to identify your defenses and have the courage to give them up

Paraphrased with modifications from Maslow (1954, 1967).

admit he is as dissatisfied with himself as he really is. For example, a study of adolescent girls with behavior problems showed that some of the girls actually rated their self-concept higher than their ideal self (Cole and others, 1967). In view of the kinds of problems these girls were having, it seems unlikely that they were really that pleased with themselves.

MEASURING SELF-DISCLOSURE. An individual's willingness to expose his inner self to others has also been studied experimentally. The Self-Disclosure Questionnaire (Jourard, 1971) consists of 60 items of information about a person; some are concerned with attitudes and interests—for example, "My views on communism" or "My favorite ways of spending spare time"—while others are highly personal—"The facts of my sex life" or "How I feel about different parts of my body."

The subject indicates (on a four-point scale) the extent to which he has talked about each item to each of five different people—mother, father, male friend, female friend, and spouse. The summed ratings provide a measure of how much the subject reveals about himself and to whom.

Studies with the Self-Disclosure Questionnaire show that women generally disclose themselves more than men, both sexes reveal themselves more to people who are open and honest in return, and greater mutual disclosure takes place in marriage than in any other relationship (Jourard, 1971).

Portraying oneself accurately to others is often assumed to be characteristic of a healthy personality; the emotionally disturbed individual, in contrast, may not accept or know his "real" self and may be unable to reveal it to others. Research with the Self-Disclosure Questionnaire tends to support this assumption. For example, college students who applied for psychological help at a student counseling center tended to have lower self-disclosure scores than a matched group of students who did not seek help. But some of the applicants for counseling had unusually *high* disclosure scores, particularly in relation to their parents. This suggests that excessive self-disclosure may be as indicative of emotional immaturity as very low disclosure.

Overview of Personality Theories

Assessment and Theory

We have linked different ways of assessing personality with different theoretical conceptions of personality. This relationship, however, is a little forced. The various ways of looking at personality—trait, psychoanalytic, social learning, and humanistic theories—have led, because of the nature of their constructs, to different approaches to assessment. But methods developed by one group have been taken over and modified by other groups. Humanistic theorists, for example, may use projective techniques such as the Rorschach and TAT (designed originally to uncover hidden motives) to measure creative potential. The MMPI, a personality inventory that measures traits, has had widespread use in research guided by all four theoretical viewpoints.

There are many situations where personality assessment is necessary: decisions regarding job placement; educational or vocational choice; treatment for emotional problems; judgment of criminal responsibility and potential for rehabilitation. In any of these situations the assessor may use a

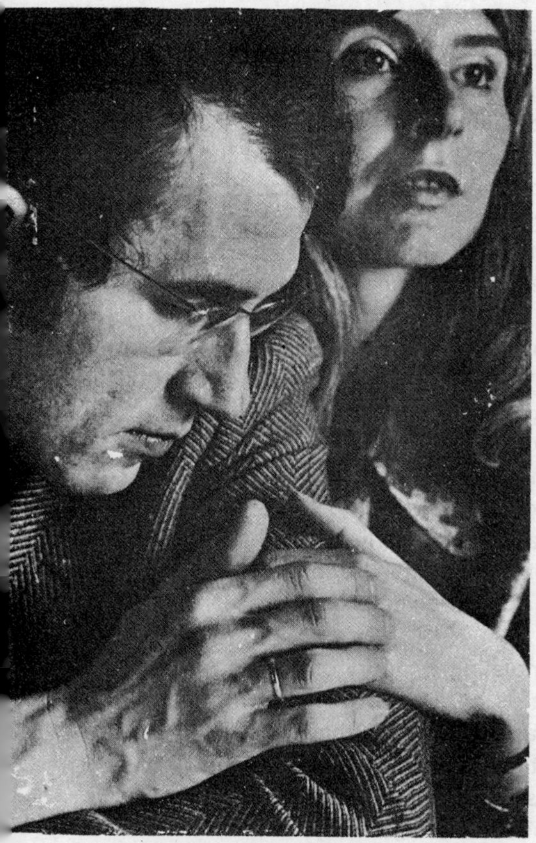

Nonverbal communication

number of methods for estimating personality variables in an attempt to arrive at a global picture of the personality. Any of the tests we have described might be used, as well as others we have not had space to discuss.

In addition to information from tests and what the person says about himself, a skilled assessor makes use of cues provided by the individual's expressive behavior. Voice quality, posture, gestures, and handwriting are all quite individualistic and may reveal aspects of personality. Communication is often nonverbal, and the experienced interviewer is alert to the possible meanings of facial expressions, gestures, body and eye movements.

Eye contact, for example, is an important means of nonverbal communication. When we wish to have nothing to do with another person we frequently avert our eyes. One study showed that when an interviewer evaluates subjects positively, they increase eye contact with him; when he evaluates them negatively, they decrease eye contact (Exline and Winters, 1965). A general lack of eye contact is usually considered indicative of serious emotional disturbance.

Comparison of Theories

We have considered four quite diverse ways of theorizing about personality. Each approach has certain advantages and disadvantages, which in part are related to the fact that they focus on different aspects of personality.

Trait theories have been concerned with the measurement of individual differences. Methods of assessment based on trait theories (such as personality inventories and rating scales) have been used primarily in situations where we have little information about a group of people and need to find out how the individuals rank on a certain characteristic, such as emotional stability or aggressiveness. This type of screening is important in selecting people for jobs or for service in the armed forces. One of the major impetuses for the development of personality inventories came during the Second World War, when it was necessary to eliminate from among millions of potential enlisted men and officers those who were apt to breakdown under the strain of military service.

Although personality inventories have proved valuable screening devices for evaluation of large groups in a limited amount of time, they have not been very effective in making specific predictions about individual behavior. In addition, the trait approach to personality has been criticized because it fails to provide much understanding of how the various traits are organized to form the coherent system that we know as personality.

Psychoanalytic theory grew out of the study of seriously disturbed individuals; it attempts to give therapists some explanation for the seemingly illogical behaviors of their patients. The theory has made significant contributions to the understanding of personality by emphasizing the importance of unconscious processes and early childhood experiences. But its value to the *science* of personality is limited by the fact that it makes few empirically testable predictions. Most psychoanalytic explanations of behavior are made "after the fact." Further, since psychoanalytic theory is based on clinical experiences with persons suffering adjustment problems, it tends to focus on maladaptive behavior and has less to say about the healthy personality.

Social learning theory emphasizes the conditions under which certain behaviors are learned and how they can be modified; it tries to predict what a given person will do in a specific situation. Because the assumptions are precisely stated and readily subject to experimental evaluation, the social learning approach has led to a great deal of research as well as to the formulation of effective procedures for modifying behavior. So far, however, it fails to provide a clear conception of how the various learned behaviors are integrated to form the total personality, although with further research the person variables (p. 384) proposed as integrating mechanisms may yield a more comprehensive picture.

Humanistic personality theories, in contrast, are concerned with the whole, healthy person. They stress the individual's private perception of the world, self-concept, and the importance of a single motivating force—self-actualization. They give a refreshingly optimistic view of people and the encouragement to view oneself in a positive light. Humanistic emphases on self-awareness, experiencing, and listening to one's inner voice have been helpful in certain kinds of therapy, particularly group therapy. But humanistic concepts, such as the concept of self-actualization, are too vaguely defined to be of much value in making precise predictions of behavior.

Thus, we see that the problems in formulating a theory of personality are not easily solved. Those theories that give us a framework for viewing the total personality (psychoanalytic and humanistic theories) are not very amenable to scientific validation, nor are they useful in predicting behavior; those theories that do employ rigorous research methods (trait and social learning theory) have other limitations. Social learning theory focuses on one individual's specific behavior without providing a total portrait of him; trait theory attempts a portrait but fails to consider the situation.

It is not clear how this problem can be solved, given the complexities of human behavior, but it seems likely that future efforts will focus on two areas of individual functioning that have only recently been considered an important part of the personality sphere. One of these is *cognitive processes*. People differ not only in intelligence and competence, but also in the way they perceive events and code them in memory as well as in the strategies they employ in solving problems. Traditionally, intellectual abilities have been considered separately from personality. And although they are treated in different chapters in this book, they are actually closely interrelated. Future research should define personality more broadly to include intellectual factors, particularly the cognitive processes an individual brings to bear in solving personal problems and in dealing with new situations.

The other area that is beginning to form an important part of personality theory has to do with the roles people play in social interactions—the impressions we make on other people and the qualities we attribute to them. Some of these developments will be discussed in Chapter 18.

Summary

1. *Personality* refers to the characteristic patterns of behavior and ways of thinking that determine a person's adjustment to his environment. Personality is shaped by *inborn potential* as modified by experiences common to the *culture* and *subcultural group* (such as sex roles) and by the *unique experiences* that affect the person as an individual.
2. The major theoretical approaches to an understanding of personality include *trait, psychoanalytic, social learning,* and *humanistic theories.*

3. *Trait theories* assume that a personality can be described by its position on a number of *continuous dimensions or scales.* The method of factor analysis has been used to discover the basic traits. Two dimensions found fairly consistently in factor-analytic studies of personality are *introversion-extraversion* and *stability-instability.*
4. Tests developed by trait theorists to measure personality traits include rating scales and personality inventories, such as the Minnesota Multiphasic Personality Inventory (MMPI).
5. *Psychoanalytic theory* assumes that much of human motivation is *unconscious* and must be inferred indirectly from behavior. Personality is composed of three systems, the *id, ego,* and *superego* that are interacting and are sometimes in conflict. The id is irrational and impulsive, seeking immediate gratification through such *primary process thinking* as *wish fulfillment.* The ego is realistic and logical, postponing gratification until it can be achieved in socially acceptable ways; the superego (conscience and ego-ideal) imposes a moral code.
6. The dynamic aspects of psychoanalytic theory assume that repressed id impulses cause *anxiety,* which can be reduced by *defense mechanisms.* The developmental aspects propose that some kinds of personality types (such as oral or anal) result from *fixation* (arrested development) at one of the psychosexual stages.
7. Psychoanalytic approaches to personality assessment include *projective tests,* such as the Rorschach and the Thematic Apperception Test (TAT). Because the test stimuli are ambiguous, the individual is assumed to project his personality through his responses.
8. *Social learning theory* assumes that personality differences result from variations in learning experiences. Responses may be learned through *observation* without reinforcement; but reinforcement is important in determining whether the learned responses will be *performed.* Emphasis is on *situation-specific* behavior rather than on broad characterizations of personality across diverse situations. People behave consistently insofar as the situations they encounter and the roles they are expected to play remain relatively stable.
9. Social learning theorists assess personality by discovering the kinds of situations in which specific behaviors occur (either through observation or self-reports) and noting the stimulus conditions that appear to covary with the behavior. By changing the stimulus conditions they attempt to modify behavior.
10. *Humanistic theories* of personality are concerned with the individual's personal view of the world, his *self-concept,* and his push toward growth or *self-actualization.* For Rogers, the most important aspect of personality is the *congruence* between the *self* and *reality,* as well as between the *self* and the *ideal self.* Rogers' basic motivating force, the innate tendency toward self-actualization, often runs into conflict with the learned needs for *positive regard* and *self-regard.* Maslow has helped to define the concept of self-actualization and has studied some of the characteristics of self-actualizing persons.
11. Humanistic approaches to assessment include techniques for measuring one's self-concept and degrees of self-disclosure.
12. None of the personality theories presented is completely satisfactory. Psychoanalytic and humanistic theories are not very amenable to scientific validation. Trait and social learning theories, while employing

rigorous research methods, do not provide a complete portrait of the individual. Future personality theories will probably pay more attention to cognitive processes and social role factors in the description of personality.

Further Reading

General books on personality include Mischel, *Introduction to personality* (1971), Hall and Lindzey, *Theories of personality* (2nd ed., 1970), and Maddi, *Personality theories: A comparative analysis* (1972). A useful paperback summarizing various personality theories is Geiwitz, *Non-Freudian personality theories* (1969). A text that treats personality from the viewpoint of development is Rappoport, *Personality development: The chronology of experience* (1972).

The trait approach to personality is described in Cattell, *The scientific analysis of personality* (1965), Guilford, *Personality* (1959), and Eysenck, *The biological basis of personality* (1967).

For a social learning approach to personality see Mischel, *Personality and assessment* (1968); Bandura, *Principles of behavior modification* (1969); and Rotter, Chance, and Phares, *Applications of a social learning theory of personality* (1972). See also Mischel, *Introduction to personality* (1971).

For psychoanalytic theories of personality, Blum, *Psychodynamics: The science of unconscious mental forces* (1966) and Holzman, *Psychoanalysis and psychopathy* (1970) are two paperback sources. See also Janis (ed.), *Personality: Dynamics, development, and assessment* (1969).

The humanistic viewpoint is represented in Maddi and Costa, *Humanism in personality* (1972), and Jourard, *Healthy personality: An approach from the viewpoint of humanistic psychology* (1974).

Cronbach, *Essentials of psychological testing* (3rd ed., 1970) has a number of chapters on personality appraisal. Other books devoted to personality appraisal include Mischel, *Personality and assessment* (1968) and Wiggins, *Personality and prediction: principles of personality assessment* (1973).

A guide to the MMPI, the most carefully researched of the personality inventories, is Butcher, *MMPI: Research developments and clinical applications* (1969). For projective techniques see Rabin, *Projective techniques in personality assessment* (1968).

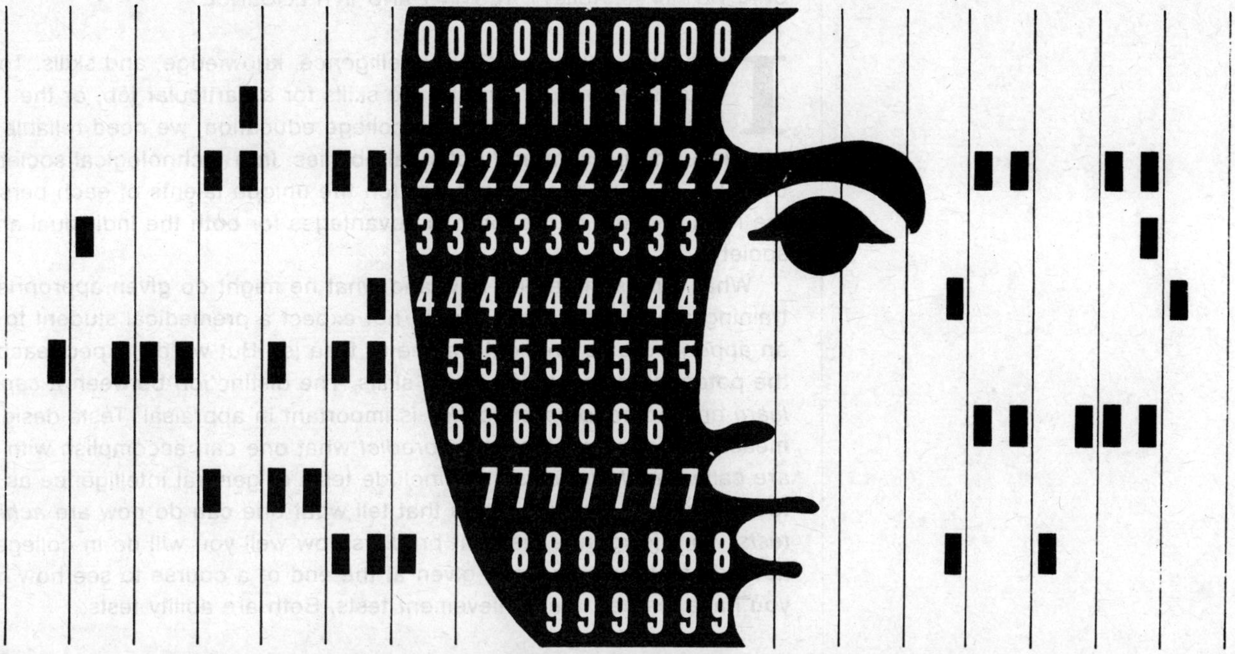

14 ability testing and intelligence

Individuals differ widely in intelligence, knowledge, and skills. To determine if a person has the skills for a particular job, or the intelligence to profit from a college education, we need reliable methods of measuring present *and* potential abilities. In a technological society as complex as ours, the ability to match the unique talents of each person to the requirements of the job has advantages for both the individual and society.

What a person can do now and what he might do given appropriate training are not the same. We do not expect a premedical student to remove an appendix, or a preflight trainee to fly a jet. But we do expect each to have the potential for acquiring these skills. The distinction between a *capacity to learn* and an *accomplished skill* is important in appraisal. Tests designed to measure capacities, that is, to *predict* what one can accomplish with training, are called *aptitude tests;* they include tests of general intelligence as well as tests of special abilities. Tests that tell what one can do now are *achievement tests*. An intelligence test that predicts how well you will do in college is an aptitude test; examinations given at the end of a course to see how much you have learned are achievement tests. Both are ability tests.

Testing Aptitudes and Achievements

Aptitude tests, by definition, predict performances not yet attained. But the *items*—the units of which a test is composed—must consist of samples of what can be accomplished *now*. How, then, is it possible to construct anything but achievement tests? This difficulty does not constitute an impasse, because it is possible to construct the tests from performances other than those being predicted. For example, one of the abilities contributing to success in flying is knowledge of mechanical principles. Thus, pilot *aptitude* tests may include a test of mechanical knowledge—even though from another point of view the mechanical knowledge test is an achievement test. The distinction between an aptitude test and an achievement test is not based on the content of the items, but upon the *purposes* of the two kinds of tests.

Aptitude Tests

Aptitude tests designed to predict performance over a broad range of abilities are called intelligence tests. Other aptitude tests measure more specific abilities: *mechanical aptitude* tests measure various types of eye-hand coordination; *musical aptitude* tests measure discrimination of pitch, rhythm, and other aspects of musical sensitivity that are predictive of musical performance with training; and *clerical aptitude* tests measure efficiency at number-checking and other skills that have been found to be predictive of an individual's later achievement as an office clerk. Many aptitude tests have been constructed to predict success in specific jobs or vocations. Since the Second World War the armed forces have devised tests to select pilots, radio technicians, submarine crews, and many other specialists.

Aptitude is usually measured by a combination of tests. Pilot aptitude tests include not only measures of mechanical knowledge but also tests of spatial orientation, eye-hand coordination, and other skills. A combination of tests used for prediction is known as a *test battery*. Scores from individual tests are weighted to get the best possible prediction. Scores on the tests that predict well count more than scores on tests that predict less well. If an eye-hand coordination test predicts pilot success better than a spatial orientation test, scores in eye-hand coordination will be weighted more heavily than scores in spatial orientation.

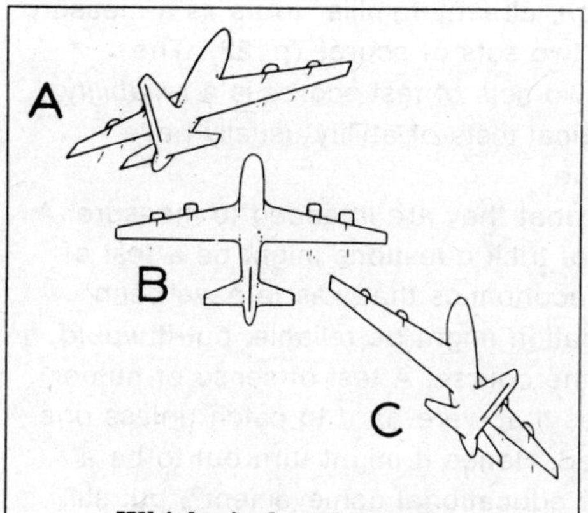

Which airplane is turning to the right?

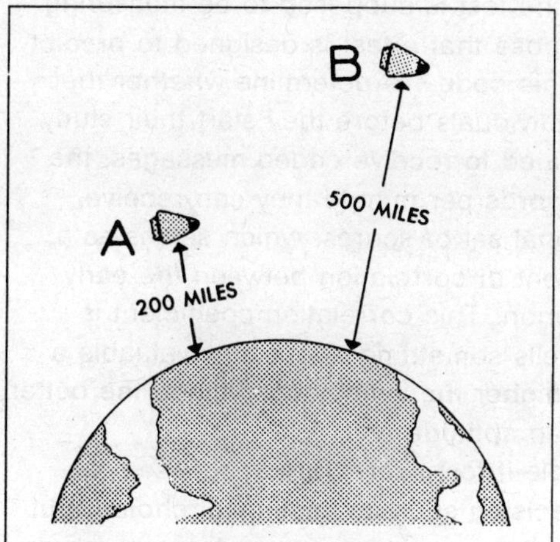

Which satellite must have a higher speed to stay in its orbit?

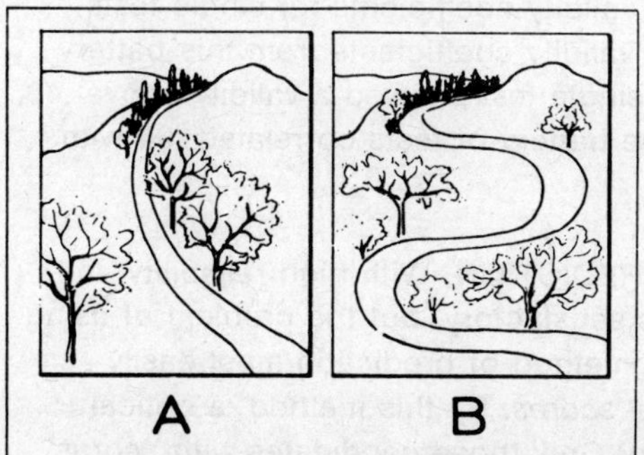

Which road is steeper?

Items from a test to measure mechanical comprehension

Achievement Tests

Although achievement tests are most commonly used in school and government examinations, they are also used to assess what has been learned in preparation for the practice of a specialty, such as law, medicine, or accounting. The consequences of these achievement tests are very important to the person who takes them. The successful candidate will receive a degree or a license to practice or an opportunity to enter a desired career; the one who fails may find many paths blocked. If the tests are in any way inappropriate, their use may lead to social injustice. It is crucial that examinations be well conceived so that they measure what they are intended to measure and their scores represent fairly the abilities of the candidate who takes the tests.

Psychologists are interested in the development of achievement tests for two reasons. First, there is much demand for such tests, especially in education and in government. Second, *achievement tests furnish a standard against which to judge the predictive effectiveness of aptitude tests.* To devise an aptitude test for pilot success, we first need a standard of excellent flying against which to measure the aptitude. Otherwise we have no way of checking predictions. If professors assigned college grades whimsically instead of on the basis of a student's achievement in the course, it would be futile to try to predict grades from an aptitude battery. Thus, achievement tests furnish a standard, or *criterion,* for the prediction of aptitudes. With improved achievement examinations, predictions can be made more efficiently. Of course, other criteria, such as success in a job, can be used. Then the measure of success serves as a measure of achievement.

Reliability and Validity

Test scores must be trustworthy if they are to be used for scientific purposes. To a psychologist this means that they must be both *reliable* and *valid.*

Test scores are *reliable* when they are dependable, reproducible, and consistent. Confusing or tricky tests may mean different things to a testee at different times. Tests may be too short to be reliable, or scoring may be too subjective. If a test is inconsistent in its results when measurements are repeated or when it is scored by two people, it is unreliable. A simple analogy is a rubber yardstick. If we did not know how much it stretched each time we took a measurement, the results would be unreliable, no matter how carefully we had marked the measurement. We need reliable tests if we are to use the results with confidence.

In order to evaluate reliability, we must secure two independent scores for the same individual on the same test—by treating halves of the test separately, by repeating the test, or by giving it in two different but equivalent

TABLE 14-1
Validity coefficients for prediction of success in pilot training

TESTS AMONG THOSE IN CLASSIFICATION BATTERY	VALIDITY COEFFICIENT
Printed tests with highest validity coefficients	
General information	.49
Instrument comprehension	.46
Mechanical principles	.42
Dial and table reading	.40
Spatial orientation II	.38
Apparatus tests with highest validity coefficients	
Complex coordination	.42
Discrimination reaction time	.41
Rudder control	.36
Two-hand pursuit	.35
Rotary pursuit	.31
Pilot stanine (a composite score)	.64

Source: DuBois (1947)

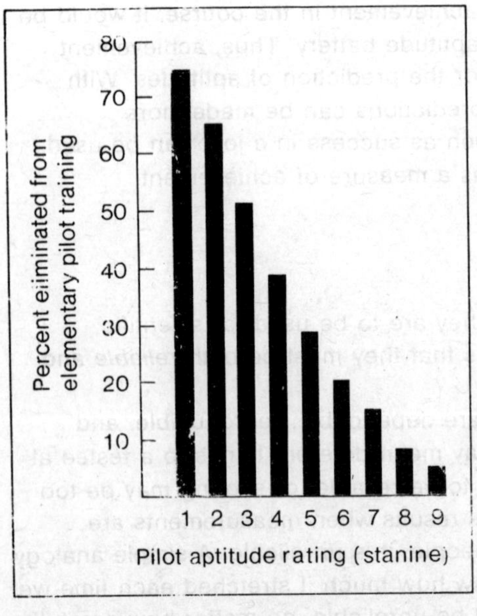

Fig. 14-1 The basis for a critical score

The graph shows the percentage of failures in pilot training at each stanine level. The Air Force established a stanine score of 5 as a requirement for pilot training. (After DuBois, 1947)

forms. If we have such a set of paired scores from a group of individuals, we can determine the test's reliability. If the same relative score levels are preserved on the two measurements, the test is reliable. Some differences are to be expected, owing to errors of measurement, so that an index of *degree of relationship* between the two sets of scores is needed. This relationship is provided by the *coefficient of correlation,* already familiar to us as a measure of degree of correspondence between two sets of scores (p. 22). The coefficient of correlation between the two sets of test scores is a *reliability coefficient.* Well-constructed psychological tests of ability usually have reliability coefficients of $r = .90$ or above.

Tests are *valid* when they measure what they are intended to measure. A college examination in economics full of trick questions might be a test of student intelligence rather than of the economics that was to have been learned in the course. Such an examination might be reliable, but it would not be a valid test of achievement for the course. A test of sense of humor, for example, might be made up of jokes that were hard to catch unless one were both very bright and very well read. Hence it might turn out to be a *reliable* test of something (intelligence? educational achievement?) but still not be *valid* as a test of sense of humor.

To measure validity, we must also have two scores for each person: the test score and some measure of what the test is supposed to be measuring. This measure is called a *criterion*. Suppose that a test is designed to predict success in learning to receive telegraphic code. To determine whether the test is valid, it is given to a group of individuals before they start their study of telegraphy. After they have been trained to receive coded messages, the students are tested on the number of words per minute they can receive. This later measure furnishes an additional set of scores, which serves as a criterion. Now we can obtain a coefficient of correlation between the early test scores and the scores on the criterion. This correlation coefficient is known as a *validity coefficient,* and it tells something about how valuable a given test is for a given purpose. The higher the validity coefficient, the better the prediction that can be made from an aptitude test.

High validity coefficients are desirable if test scores are to be used to help an individual with an important decision such as vocational choice. But even relatively low validity coefficients may prove useful when large numbers of people are tested. For example, a battery of tests used for the selection of air-crew specialists in the Second World War proved effective in predicting job success, even though some of the validity coefficients for single tests were of very moderate size. Illustrative validity coefficients from this battery are shown in Table 14-1. Although no single test showed a validity above .49, the "composite" score derived from the battery of tests correlated .64 with the criterion.

TEST SCORES AS A BASIS FOR PREDICTION. With high reliability and validity coefficients we know the test is satisfactory, but the problem of using the test in prediction still remains. The method of prediction most easily understood is the one based on *critical scores.* By this method, a critical point on the scale of scores is selected. Only those candidates with scores above the critical point are accepted—for pilot training, for admission to medical school, or for whatever purpose the testing may serve.

The pilot-selection program of the Air Force illustrates this use of critical scores. The composite scores (called *stanines*) give each candidate a

Sir Francis Galton

pilot-prediction rating from 1 to 9. Figure 14-1 shows that those with low stanines failed pilot training much more frequently than those with high stanines. After experience with the tests, the examiners eliminated those with stanines below 5 prior to training. Thus, a stanine of 5 is a critical score. Had this critical score been adopted before training the candidates represented in Figure 14-1, only 17 percent of those accepted would have failed to complete training. Those dropped would have been the group of low scorers, 54 percent of whom failed elementary pilot training.

Tests of General Intelligence

Sir Francis Galton, a cousin of Charles Darwin, developed the first tests designed to measure intelligence. Galton, a naturalist and mathematician, was interested in individual differences. He invented the correlation coefficient (which plays such an important role in psychology) and developed the ideas behind fingerprinting and eugenics. Galton administered a battery of tests—measuring such variables as head size, reaction time, visual acuity, memory for visual forms, breathing capacity, and strength of hand grip—to over 9000 visitors to the London Exhibition in 1884. His somewhat strange collection of tests reflected his belief that superior intelligence was accompanied by superior physical vigor. He undoubtedly was disappointed to discover that eminent British scientists could not be distinguished from ordinary citizens on the basis of their head size, and that strength of grip was not much related to other measures of intelligence. Galton's tests did not prove very useful.

The intelligence test as we know it today was formulated by the French psychologist Alfred Binet (1857–1911). The French government asked Binet to devise a test that would detect those children too slow intellectually to profit from regular schooling. He assumed that intelligence should be measured by tasks requiring reasoning and problem solving, rather than perceptual-motor skills. In collaboration with Theodore Simon (1873–1961), another French psychologist, Binet published a scale in 1905, which he revised in 1908 and again in 1911. These Binet scales are the direct predecessors of contemporary intelligence tests.

Alfred Binet

Binet's Method: A Mental-Age Scale

Binet assumed that a dull child was like a normal child but retarded in mental growth; he reasoned that the dull child would perform on tests like a normal child of younger age. Binet decided to scale intelligence as the kind of change that ordinarily comes with growing older. Accordingly, he devised a scale of units of *mental age*. Average mental-age (MA) scores correspond to *chronological age* (CA), that is, to the age determined from the date of birth. A bright child's MA is above his CA; a dull child has an MA below his CA. The mental-age scale is easily interpreted by teachers and others who deal with children differing in mental ability.

ITEM SELECTION. Because the intelligence test is designed to measure brightness rather than the results of special training, it must consist of items that do not assume any specific preparation. In other words, the intelligence

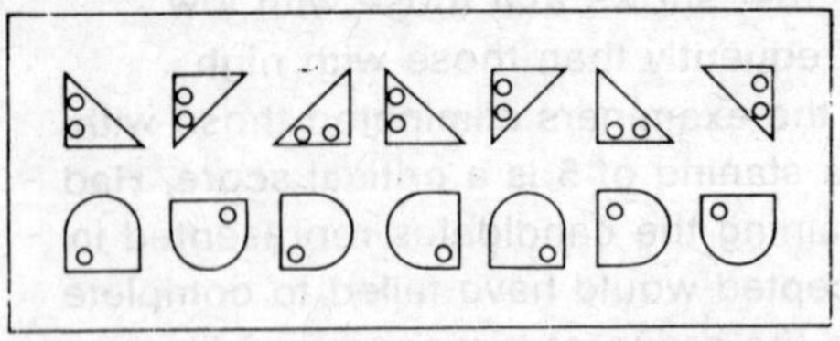

Fig. 14-2 Novel items used in intelligence tests

The following instructions accompany the test: "Here are some cards for you to mark. In each row mark every card that is like the first card in the row." (After Thurstone and Thurstone, 1941)

test is designed to be an *aptitude* test rather than an *achievement* test, and it must be constructed accordingly.

There are two chief ways to find items for which success is uninfluenced by special training. One way is to choose *novel items* with which an untaught child has as good a chance to succeed as one who has been taught at home or in school. Figure 14-2 illustrates novel items. In this particular case the child is asked to choose figures that are alike with the assumption that the designs are unfamiliar to all children. The second way is to choose *familiar items,* with the assumption that all those for whom the test is designed have had the requisite prior experience to deal with the items. The following problem provides an example of a supposedly familiar item:

Mark F if the sentence is foolish; mark S if it is sensible.

S F Mrs. Smith has had no children, and I understand that the same was true of her mother.[1]

This item is "fair" only for children who know the English language, who can read, and who understand all the words in the sentence. For such children, detection of the fallacy in the statement becomes a valid test of intellectual ability.

Many of the items on an intelligence test of the Binet type assume general familiarity. A vocabulary test, for example, appears in almost all the scales. Familiarity with the standard language of the test is necessarily assumed.

The intelligence test is in some respects a crude instrument, for its assumptions can never be strictly met. The language environment of one home is never exactly that of another, the reading matter available to the subjects differs, and the stress upon cognitive goals varies. Even the novel items depend upon perceptual discriminations that may be acquired in one culture or subculture and not in another. Despite the difficulties, items can be chosen that work reasonably well. The items included in contemporary intelligence tests are those that have survived in practice after many others have been tried and found defective. It should be remembered, however, that intelligence tests have been validated by success in predicting school performance within a particular culture.

ITEM TESTING. It is not enough to look at an item and to decide that it requires intelligence to answer it successfully. Some "tricky" or "clever" items turn out to be poor because of the successes or failures that occur through guessing. More pedestrian items, such as matters of common information, sometimes turn out to be most useful. These are "fair" items if all have had a chance to learn the answers.

How did Binet and those who came after him know when they had hit upon a good item? One method of testing an item is to study the *changes in proportions of children answering it correctly at different ages.* Unless older children are more successful than younger ones in answering the item, the item is unsatisfactory in a test based on the concept of mental growth.

A second method of testing an item is to find out whether the results for it *correspond to the results on the test as a whole.* This can be done by correlating success and failure on the item with the score made on the remaining items. If all items measure something in common, then every single item ought to contribute a score that correlates with the total score.

These two requirements for an acceptable item (increase in percentage passing with age and correlation with total score) reflect both validity and

[1] Thurstone and Thurstone (1941).

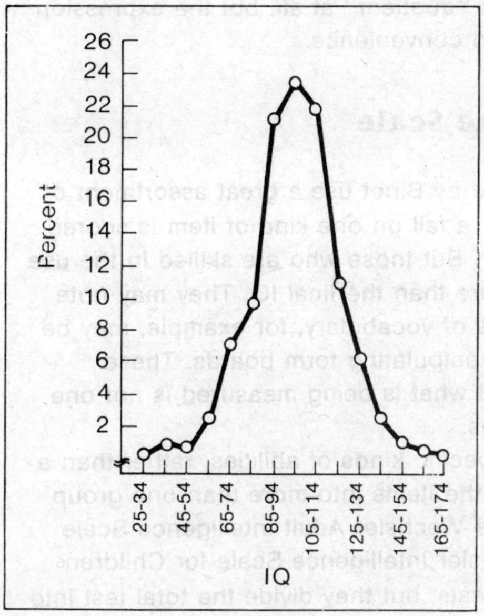

Fig. 14-3 A normal distribution curve of IQs

Distribution of IQs for 2904 children and youths, ages 2 to 18. This is the group upon which the Revised Stanford-Binet was standardized. (After Terman and Merrill, 1937)

reliability. The first requirement is an indirect way of guaranteeing validity, being based on the inference that what we mean by intelligence should distinguish an older child from a younger one; the second requirement is a guarantee of reliability through internal consistency of the measures.

CONTEMPORARY BINET TESTS. The tests originally developed by Binet underwent several revisions in this country, the first by Goddard in 1911. For many years the best-known and most widely used revision was that made by Terman at Stanford University in 1916, commonly referred to as the Stanford-Binet. The test was revised in 1937, 1960, and 1972.

In the Binet tests, an item is age-graded at the level at which a substantial majority of the children pass it. The present Stanford-Binet has six items of varied content assigned to each year, each item when passed earning a score of two months of mental age.

The procedure for testing is first to establish the child's *basal mental age,* the mental-age level at which he passes all items. Two months of mental age are then added for each item passed at higher age levels. Consider, for example, the child who passes all items at the mental-age level of six years. If the child then passes two items at the seven-year level, four months are added; passing an additional item at the eight-year level adds two more months. This particular child will have an earned mental age of six years and six months, regardless of chronological age. The test allows for some unevenness in development, so that two children can earn the same mental age by passing different items on the test.

Intelligence Quotient (IQ)

Terman adopted a convenient index of brightness that was suggested by the German psychologist William Stern (1871–1938). This index is the *intelligence quotient,* commonly known by its initials IQ. It expresses intelligence as a ratio of mental age to chronological age:

$$\text{IQ} = \frac{\text{Mental age (MA)}}{\text{Chronological age (CA)}} \times 100$$

The 100 is used as a multiplier to remove the decimal point and to make the IQ have a value of 100 when MA equals CA. It is evident that if the MA lags behind the CA, the resulting IQ will be less than 100; if the MA is above the CA, the IQ will be above 100.

How is the IQ to be interpreted? The distribution of IQs follows the form of curve found for many differences among individuals, such as differences in height; this is the bell-shaped "normal" distribution curve shown in Figure 14-3. In this curve most cases cluster around a midvalue, tapering off to a few at both extremes. The adjectives commonly used to describe the various IQ levels are given in Table 14-2.

TABLE 14-2
Interpretation of intelligence quotients on the Stanford-Binet

IQ	VERBAL DESCRIPTION	PERCENT IN EACH GROUP
Above 139	Very superior	1
120–139	Superior	11
110–119	High average	18
90–109	Average	46
80–89	Low average	15
70–79	Borderline	6
Below 70	Mentally retarded	3
		100%

In the 1960 and subsequent revisions of the Stanford-Binet, the authors introduced a method of computing the IQ from tables. The meaning of an IQ remains essentially the same as before, but the tables permit corrections to allow the IQ at any age to be interpreted somewhat more exactly. It is now arranged so that for each age the IQ averages 100 and has a standard deviation of 16.[2]

A modern IQ is merely a test score adjusted for the age of the person

[2] The concept of a standard deviation is explained in the Appendix.

being tested. It is therefore no longer a "quotient" at all, but the expression IQ persists because of its familiarity and convenience.

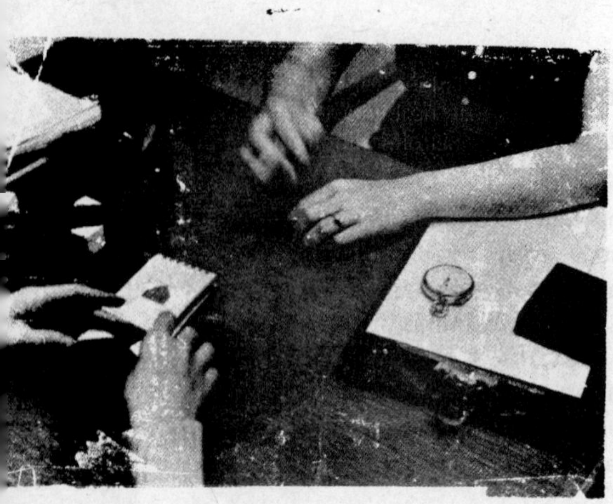

..lock design test from the Weschsler Scales

Subject attempts to match the pictured design with blocks.

Tests with More Than One Scale

Tests following the pattern originated by Binet use a great assortment of items to test intelligence, and a pass or a fail on one kind of item is scored the same as a pass or a fail on another. But those who are skilled in the use and scoring of the tests learn much more than the final IQ. They may note special strengths and weaknesses; tests of vocabulary, for example, may be passed at a higher level than tests of manipulating form boards. These observations lead to the conjecture that what is being measured is not one simple ability but a composite of abilities.

One way to obtain information on specific kinds of abilities, rather than a single mental-age score, is to separate the items into more than one group and to score the groups separately. The Wechsler Adult Intelligence Scale (described in Table 14-3) and the Wechsler Intelligence Scale for Children use items similar to those in the Binet tests, but they divide the total test into

TABLE 14-3
Tests comprising the Wechsler Adult Intelligence Scale

The tests comprising the Wechsler Intelligence Scale for Children are similar with some modifications.

TEST	DESCRIPTION
VERBAL SCALE	
Information	Questions tap general range of information; e.g., "How many weeks in a year?"
Comprehension	Tests practical information and ability to evaluate past experience; e.g., "How would you find your way out if lost in a forest?"
Arithmetic	Verbal problems testing arithmetic reasoning.
Similarities	Asks in what way certain objects or concepts (e.g., *egg* and *seed*) are similar; measures abstract thinking.
Digit Span	Series of digits presented auditorily (e.g., 7-5-6-3-8) are repeated in a forward or backward direction. Tests attention and rote memory.
Vocabulary	Tests word knowledge.
PERFORMANCE SCALE	
Digit Symbol	A timed coding task in which numbers must be associated with marks of various shapes; tests speed of learning and writing.
Picture Completion	The missing part of an incompletely drawn picture must be discovered and named; tests visual alertness and visual memory.
Block Design	Pictured designs must be copied with blocks (see above photo); tests ability to perceive and analyze patterns.
Picture Arrangement	A series of comic strip type pictures must be arranged in the right sequence to tell a story; tests understanding of social situations.
Object Assembly	Puzzle pieces must be assembled to form a complete object such as a human profile or elephant; tests ability to deal with part-whole relationships.

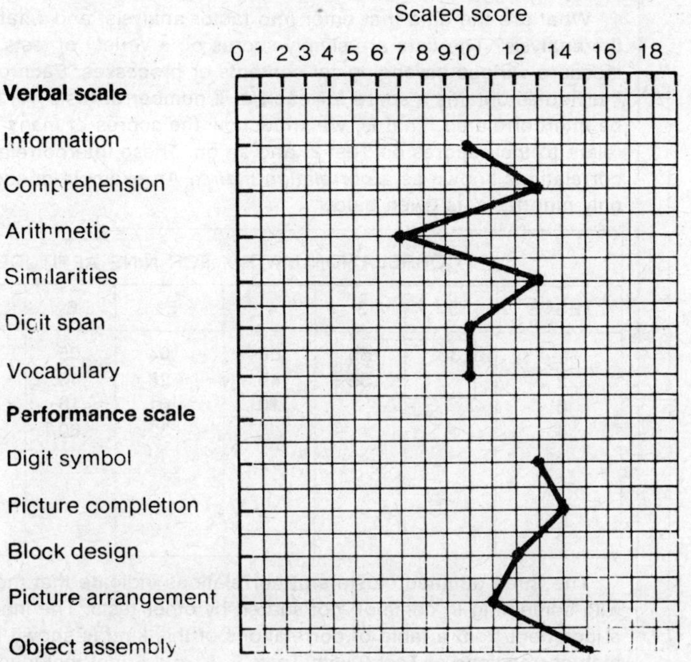

TEST	Scaled score	
Information	10	
Comprehension	13	
Arithmetic	7	
Similarities	13	
Digit span	10	
Vocabulary	10	
Verbal score	63	
Digit symbol	13	
Picture completion	14	
Block design	12	
Picture arrangement	11	
Object assembly	15	
Performance score	65	
Total score		
VERBAL SCORE 63	IQ 108	
PERFORMANCE SCORE 65	IQ 121	
FULL SCALE SCORE 128	IQ 115	

Fig. 14-4 Profile for Wechsler Adult Intelligence Scale (WAIS)

Test scores for a sixteen-year-old male. The table on the right shows these test scores combined to give a verbal, performance, and full-scale score. The manual that accompanies the test provides tables (adjusted for age) for converting these scores into IQs. Note that the testee has a performance IQ 13 points above his verbal IQ.

two parts—a *verbal* scale and a *performance* scale—according to the content of the items. A *performance* item is one that requires manipulation or arrangement of blocks, beads, pictures, or other materials in which both stimuli and responses are nonverbal. The separate scaling of the items within one test is convenient for diagnostic purposes. Figure 14-4 shows a test profile and how the test scores are summed to yield IQs.

In general, the full scale (verbal and performance) and the verbal scale of the Wechsler Scales yield scores corresponding closely to the scores of the Stanford-Binet. The verbal scale of the Wechsler correlates .77 with its performance scale.

Nature of Human Intelligence

Some psychologists view intelligence as a general capacity for comprehension and reasoning that manifests itself in various ways. This was Binet's assumption; although his test contained many different types of item, they were all assumed to tap general intelligence. Other psychologists see intelligence as an array of special abilities that tend to be positively correlated; they use the statistical method of *factor analysis* to provide more precise information about the abilities underlying intelligence. As noted in the previous chapter, factor analysis is a technique for determining the minimum number of dimensions, or factors, that account for the observed relations (correlations) among subjects' responses over a large number of different

TABLE 14-4
The method of factor analysis

What are the data that enter into factor analysis, and what are the major steps in the analysis? The data are simply scores on a variety of tests, which are designed to measure various psychological contents or processes. Each of a large number of individuals obtains a score for each of a number of tests. All these scores can then be intercorrelated. That is, we know how the scores of many individuals on Test 1 relate to their scores on Test 2, and so on. These intercorrelations yield a table of correlations known as a *correlation matrix*. An example of such a matrix, based on only nine tests, is given below.

CORRELATION MATRIX FOR NINE APTITUDE TESTS

TESTS	2	3	4	5	6	7	8	9
1	.38	.55	.06	−.04	.05	.07	.05	.09
2		.36	.40	.28	.40	.11	.15	.13
3			.10	.01	.18	.13	.12	.10
4				.32	.60	.04	.06	.13
5					.35	.08	.13	.11
6						.01	.06	.07
7							.45	.32
8								.32

The three outlined clusters of correlations indicate that these are groups of tests with something in common not shared by other tests. The inadequacy of making such a judgment from a table of correlations of this kind is shown by noting the additional high correlations of Test 2 with Tests 4, 5, and 6, not included in the outlined clusters. We can use factor analysis to tell us more precisely what underlies these correlations. If the correlation matrix contains a number of statistically significant correlations and a number of near-zero correlations, it is apparent that some tests measure similar abilities of one kind and others similar abilities of other kinds. The purpose of factor analysis is to be more precise about these underlying abilities.

Factor analysis then uses mathematical methods (assisted by high-speed computers) to compute the correlation of each of the tests with a few factors. Such correlations between test scores and factors are known as *factor loadings;* if a test correlates .05 on Factor I, .10 on Factor II, and .70 on Factor III, it is most heavily "loaded" on Factor III. For example, the nine tests with the above correlation matrix yield the *factor matrix* below.

FACTOR MATRIX FOR NINE APTITUDE TESTS AND THREE FACTORS

TESTS	FACTORS I	II	III
1	.75	−.01	.08
2	.44	.48	.16
3	.72	.07	.15
4	.08	.76	.08
5	−.01	.49	−.01
6	.16	.73	.02
7	−.03	.04	.64
8	.02	.05	.66
9	−.01	.10	.47

(Guilford, 1967)

The outlined loadings in the factor matrix show which tests are most highly correlated with each of the underlying factors. The clusters are the same as those found in the correlation matrix, but are now given greater precision. The problem of Test 2 remains, because it is loaded almost equally on Factor I and Factor II. It is obviously not a "factor pure" test. Having found the three factors that account for the intercorrelations of the nine tests, the factors can be interpreted by studying the content of the tests most highly weighted on each factor. The factor analysis itself is strictly a mathematical process, but the naming and interpretation of the factors depends upon a psychological analysis.

tests. The method is too intricate to describe in any detail here, but Table 14-4 gives some understanding of what factor analysis tries to accomplish.

The originator of factor analysis, Charles Spearman, proposed that all individuals possess a general intelligence factor (called *g*) in varying amounts. A person would be described as generally bright or generally dull depending upon the amount of *g*. According to Spearman, the *g* factor is the major determinant of performance on intelligence test items. In addition, special factors called *s*'s are specific to particular abilities or test items. For example, tests of arithmetic or spatial relations would each tap a separate *s*. An individual's tested intelligence reflects the amount of *g* plus the magnitude of the various *s* factors. Performance in mathematics would be a function of a person's general intelligence and mathematical aptitude.

Primary Abilities

A later investigator, Louis Thurstone (1938), objected to Spearman's emphasis on general intelligence; he felt that intelligence could be broken down into a number of primary abilities. To find these abilities he applied the method of factor analysis to results from a large number of tests employing many different types of items. One set of items was for verbal comprehension, another for arithmetical computation, and so on. He wished to find a more definitive way of grouping intelligence test items than the rather crude item-sorting used in the verbal and performance scales of the Stanford-Binet and Wechsler tests.

After intercorrelating the scores of all the tests, Thurstone applied factor analysis to arrive at the basic factors. Those test items that best represented each of the discovered factors were used to form new tests; these tests were then given to another group of subjects and the intercorrelations reanalyzed. After a number of studies of this kind, Thurstone identified the seven factors, shown in Table 14-5, as the *primary abilities* revealed by intelligence tests.

TABLE 14-5
Primary abilities

ABILITY	DESCRIPTION
Verbal comprehension	The ability to understand the meaning of words; vocabulary tests represent this factor.
Word fluency	The ability to think of words rapidly, as in solving anagrams or thinking of words that rhyme.
Number	The ability to work with numbers and perform computations.
Space	The ability to visualize space-form relationships, as in recognizing the same figure presented in different orientations.
Memory	The ability to recall verbal stimuli such as word pairs or sentences.
Perceptual speed	The ability to grasp visual details quickly and to see similarities and differences between pictured objects.
Reasoning	The ability to find a general rule on the basis of presented instances, as in determining how a number series is constructed after being presented with only a portion of that series.

Source: Thurstone and Thurstone (1963).

CRITICAL DISCUSSION

Culture-Fair Intelligence Tests

Serious efforts have been made to construct tests that will be less dependent on the subject's specific culture than are the more familiar tests of the Binet type. Among these efforts are the tests constructed by Cattell (1949), called a "culture-free" test, and by Davis and Eells (1953), called a "culture-fair" test. Both attempt to provide tests that will not penalize the subject from a culturally different background.

Consider the following item:

Pick out ONE WORD that does not belong with the others.

cello harp drum
violin guitar

This item was used by Eells and others (1951) to illustrate how experience can determine vocabulary. When the test was administered to a group of children, 85 percent of those from homes of high socioeconomic status chose "drum," the intended correct answer, whereas only 45 percent of the children from homes of low socioeconomic status answered with this word. The low-status children most commonly answered "cello," the word on the list least likely to be familiar to them and hence thought to be the word that did not belong. Children from homes of high socioeconomic status are more likely to be acquainted with cellos, or at least to have heard the word, than children from poorer homes.

Many other items in this study showed class differences for which the effects of differing experience would be hard to demonstrate. For example, the following item was also answered correctly more often by those from homes of higher socioeconomic status than by those from homes of lower status.

Find the THREE THINGS which are alike in this list.

store banana basket
apple seed plum

This item requires the child taking the test to note that banana, apple, and plum are fruits and that store, basket, and seed are nonfruits. It is hard to believe that nine- and ten-year-old children, even from underprivileged homes, would be unacquainted with the six words, or with the fruits, although we know little at present about the effects of severe environmental restriction upon the ability to categorize. Such an item may be "culture-fair," even though it shows class differences in its answer; the classes may actually differ in cognitive performance as measured by items that are "fair."

Although high hopes were expressed for culture-fair tests by those who developed them, the subsequent results have not been encouraging. In some cases class differences in scores have been reduced, but for the most part the class differences found with these tests are very similar to the differences found with the more usual tests. Moreover, as predictors of scholastic achievement, the newer tests are inferior to the more conventional ones. Perhaps a culture-fair test is impossible in principle; an individual's performance will always be affected by cultural background regardless of the nature of the test. Hence, with all their difficulties, the ordinary Binet-type tests serve their predictive purposes as well as

Thurstone devised a battery of tests to measure each of these abilities, called the *Test of Primary Mental Abilities,* which is still widely used. Its predictive power, however, is no greater than that provided by tests of general intelligence such as the Wechsler Scales. Thurstone's hope of discovering the basic elements of intelligence through factor analysis was not fully realized for several reasons. His primary abilities are not completely independent; there are significant intercorrelations among them providing some support for Spearman's idea of a general intelligence factor. In addition, the number of factors identified by factor analysis depends on the nature of the test items chosen. Other investigators using different test items have come up with a larger number of factors. Guilford (1967), for example, has suggested that there are at least 120 unique intellectual abilities.

Structure-of-Intellect Model

Guilford rejects the idea of a general intelligence factor and also broad factor groups like Thurstone's primary abilities. He believes that many aspects or better than these substitute tests that have not been extensively validated.

A study of children in a rural village in Nigeria illustrates how cultural experiences can influence performance on the Kohs block test, a task included in several intelligence scales. The test consists of sixteen painted blocks, each cube having two sides painted red, two white, and two divided diagonally into red and white. The child is shown a drawing of a design and asked to arrange the blocks to form the same design. When rural eight-year-old Nigerian children were shown the designs pictured in Figure 14-5, they succeeded very well with the first figure, moderately well with the second, but very poorly with the third. The average result would yield an IQ of 80 by American norms. However, when the instructor made the design with blocks, rather than with a drawing, the children learned promptly to match the design with their blocks. Having done this, they could match other drawings with blocks, as the original test required. The investigator concluded that these children were not inferior to American children in this performance once they had "caught on" to what was expected in an otherwise alien situation. In the villages where these children are raised there is almost total lack of familiarity with pictorial representation. Even adults are baffled by maps, or building designs, or (in some cases) the contents of ordinary photographs (D'Andrade, 1967).

Matters taken for granted in one culture cannot be taken for granted in another; this warning applies to different subcultures within countries as well.

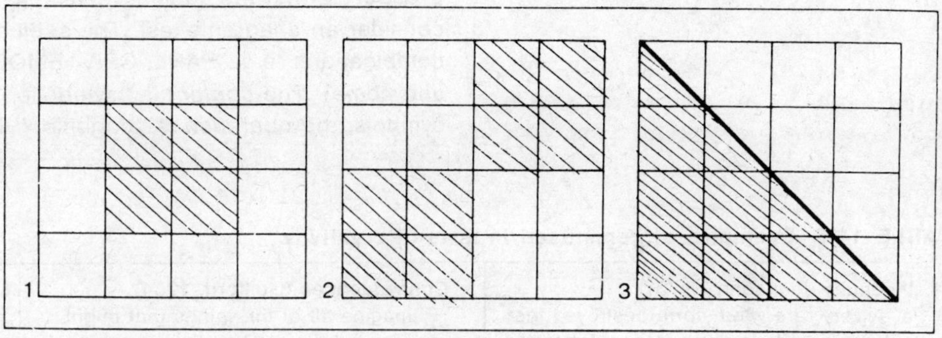

Fig. 14-5 Block designs used with rural Nigerian children

The third design proved very difficult for eight-year-old children to copy if presented as a drawing to be copied with blocks, but it was much easier when the design to be copied was itself made with blocks. Once having done it this way, the children could copy with their blocks other designs from drawings. (After D'Andrade, 1967)

of intelligence tend to be ignored when items are lumped together to form tests. An item used as a test of verbal ability is distinguished from one that is nonverbal on the basis of its content—words as opposed to pictorial material. But what one does with the content of the test item (e.g., memorizes it or uses it to engage in a reasoning process) will depend upon the nature of the task and may be relatively independent of the content. Suppose that you are shown a picture of a dozen different objects and told that you will be asked to recall the names of the objects at some later time. Does this task involve verbal or pictorial ability? To be sure, a picture is presented, but most subjects will name the objects and then rehearse the names rather than try to memorize the picture itself.

Guilford maintains that intelligence test items should not be distinguished in terms of content alone, but also in terms of the *operations* performed upon the *content* and the *product* that results. His structure-of-intellect model (Figure 14-6) shows the way in which 4 contents, 5 operations, and 6 products combine to yield 120 unique intellectual factors. The definitions of each type of content, product, and operation are too lengthy to present here. However, some examples may provide a feeling for the kinds of distinctions

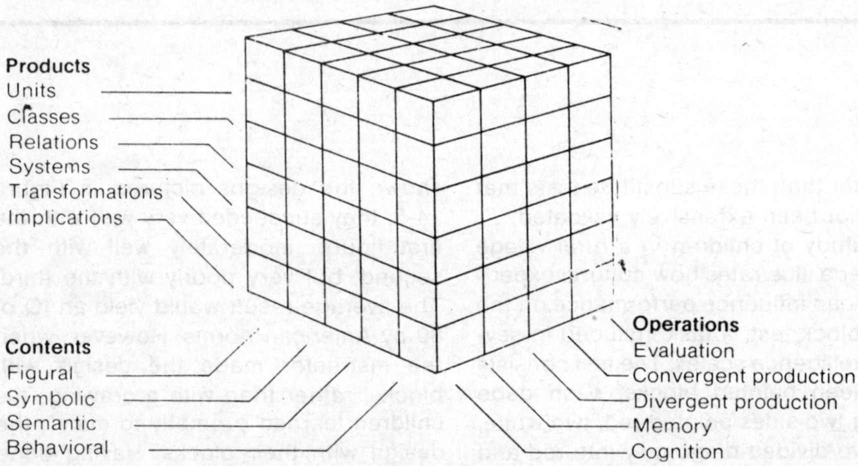

Fig. 14-6 Guilford's model of intelligence
Each of the small cubes in the solid represents a unique intellectual ability. An intelligence test item can be distinguished in terms of its *content*, the kind of *operation* the subject must perform on the item, and the *product* resulting from the particular operation applied to a specific content. According to Guilford, there are 4 types of content, 5 possible operations, and 6 products—yielding 120 identifiable abilities.

made. Assume that a subject is given a long list of unrelated words to study and is asked to recall the words at a later time. The *content* of this test is "semantic," since it involves words; the *operation* is "memory"; and the *product* is what the subject recalls, namely a list of words or "units." Or, consider an anagrams test. The subject is asked to rearrange four-letter combinations (e.g., PANL, CEIV, EMOC) to form familiar words (*plan, vice,* and *come*). The *content* is "symbolic," since the test involves a set of letter symbols; the *operation* is "cognition" because it requires recognition of

TABLE 14-6 Examples of items used in tests of creativity

1. **Ingenuity** (Flanagan, 1963) a. A very rare wind storm destroyed the transmission tower of a television station in a small town. The station was located in a town in a flat prairie with no tall buildings. Its former 300-foot tower enabled it to serve a large farming community, and the management wanted to restore service while a new tower was being erected. The problem was temporarily solved by using a ____. b. As part of a manufacturing process, the inside lip of a deep cup-shaped casting is machine threaded. The company found that metal chips produced by the threading operation were difficult to remove from the bottom of the casting without scratching the sides. A design engineer was able to solve this problem by having the operation performed ____. 2. **Unusual uses** (Guilford, 1954) Name as many uses as you can think of for: a. a toothpick b. a brick c. a paper clip	3. **Consequences** (Guilford, 1954) Imagine all of the things that might possibly happen if all national and local laws were suddenly abolished. 4. **Fable endings** (Getzels and Jackson, 1962) Write three endings for the following fable: a moralistic, a humorous, and a sad ending. THE MISCHIEVOUS DOG A rascally dog used to run quietly to the heels of every passerby and bite them without warning. So his master was obliged to tie a bell around the cur's neck that he might give notice wherever he went. This the dog thought very fine indeed, and he went about tinkling it in pride all over town. But an old hound said. . . . 5. **Product improvement** (Torrance, 1966) The subject is presented with a series of objects such as children's toys or instruments used in his particular occupation and asked to make suggestions for their improvement.	6. **Pattern meanings** (Wallach and Kogan, 1965) The subject is shown a series of patterns of geometric forms (like the samples shown below) and asked to imagine all the things each pattern could be. 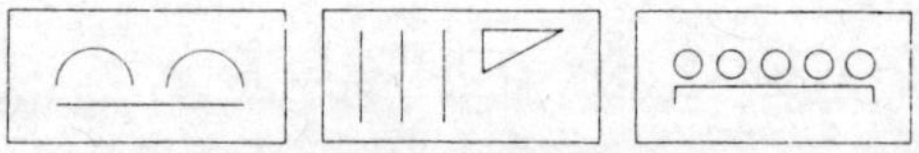 7. **Remote associations** (Mednick, 1962) Find a fourth word which is associated with each of these three words: a. rat—blue—cottage b. out—dog—cat c. wheel—electric—high d. surprise—line—birthday 8. **Word association** (Getzels and Jackson, 1962) Write as many meanings as you can for each of the following words: a. duck b. sack c. pitch d. fair

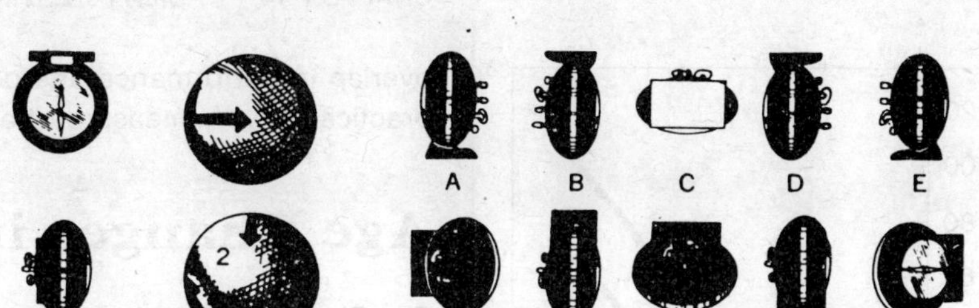

Fig. 14-7 Test of visualization

In each line imagine how the clock at the far left is turned in accordance with the arrow or arrows shown on the sphere. Which clock at the right shows how the clock would look after making the turn or turns? The first and second turns in Item II must be made in the 1–2 order. This test involves a "figural" content, a "cognitive" operation, and a "transformation" product. (Answers: B and C, respectively.)

information in disguised form; and the *product* is a word (i.e. "unit") response. For another example see Figure 14-7.

One reason for the large number of factors in Guilford's model is that he has broadened the concept of intelligence beyond that measured by standard IQ tests. Most intelligence tests measure *convergent thinking*—solving a problem that has a well-defined correct answer. Guilford also includes tests that measure *divergent thinking*—arriving at many possible solutions to a problem. An example would be a test item such as: "What uses can you think of for a brick?" The person who gives the most varied answers ("Heat to keep your bed warm," "As a weapon," "To hold the shelves of a bookcase") is the one who scores highest on divergent thinking. This kind of thinking is more closely related to creativity than convergent thinking and rightly belongs in the intellectual domain. Some illustrations of "creativity items," lacking in most intelligence tests, are presented in Table 14-6.

Experiments comparing results from conventional intelligence tests with tests designed to measure divergent thinking have tended to yield relationships such as those indicated in Figure 14-8. That is, highly creative persons tend frequently to be highly intelligent, but high intelligence (as measured by conventional tests) is no guarantee of creativity.

Fig. 14-8 Divergent production as related to IQ

An individual's IQ score and score for divergent thinking would be represented by a single point somewhere on this graph. Research indicates that individual points tend to be confined to the tinted area. More high scores for divergent production are associated with high IQ than with low IQ, but there are many moderately high scores on divergent thinking among those with average IQs, and a high IQ is no guarantee of a high score on divergent thinking. (After Guilford, 1967)

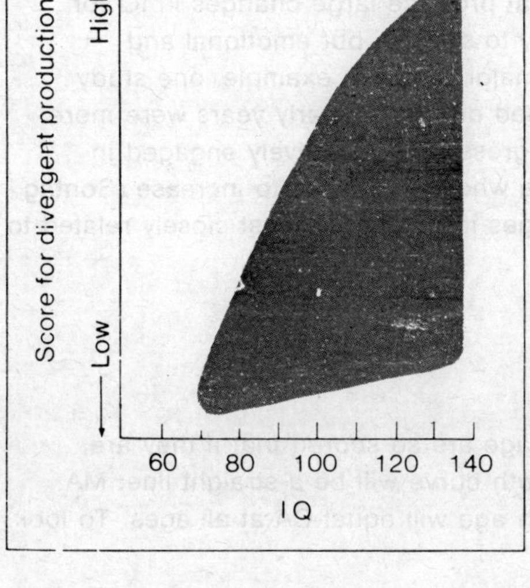

It appears unlikely that factor analysis will ever provide a clear picture of the number and nature of intellectual abilities. The number of abilities obtained through factor analysis depends on how specific the test items are. If you wanted to be really specific in measuring memory, you could devise separate tests for "auditory memory," "memory for printed words," "memory for geometric figures," and so forth. In some instances such specificity might be helpful, but for most practical purposes a fairly small number of broadly defined abilities (such as described by Thurstone) allows us to make predictions about success in particular types of jobs and to specify how different abilities vary with such factors as age, socioeconomic status, and cultural background.

Is intelligence a unitary general factor (*g*) or a number of correlated special abilities? On the basis of available evidence it seems reasonable to conclude that there is some sort of general intelligence in addition to specific abilities. An IQ difference of 10 or 15 points on a standard intelligence test is not very meaningful; the person with the lower IQ, but with some special abilities, may well outperform the individual with the higher IQ in many situations. But with an IQ difference of 30 points there will be virtually no

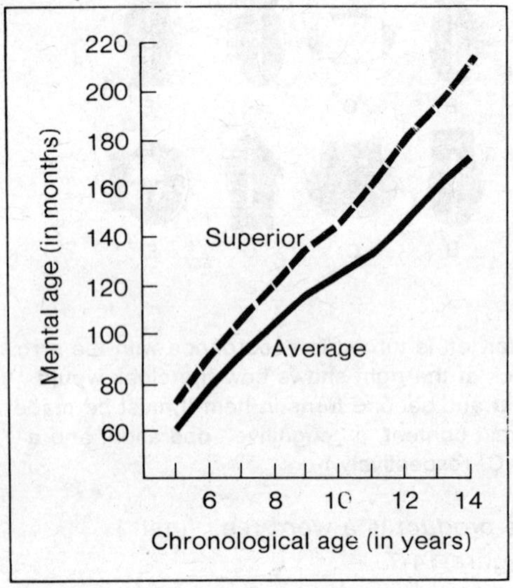

Figure 14-9 Consistency of mental age differences

Two groups of boys were selected at age five, one scoring high on intelligence tests, one average. The superior group gained in mental age more rapidly than the average one, thus approximating a constant IQ difference between the groups as they grew older. (After Baldwin and Stecher, 1922)

overlap in performance; the person with the higher IQ will do better on practically every measure of ability.

Age Changes in Intelligence

The Binet test was developed on the principle that the processes influencing intelligence test performance develop with the years, so that a mental-age score remains appropriate at least through childhood. The IQ was based on the presumption that the mental age for a bright child would grow more rapidly than for a dull one, so that some degree of constancy would be found for the ratio of MA to CA. Both of these conjectures were found to be approximately true (Figure 14-9), although later work has made a number of qualifications necessary.

Stability of IQ

The rate of intellectual growth is relatively stable for most people; once they reach school age their IQ does not change radically from test to retest even over fairly long time intervals. Table 14-7 presents correlations between IQs obtained from the same individuals at different ages. Inspecting this table we see that an IQ at age seven correlates .71 with one obtained at age eighteen. Stated otherwise, knowing the IQ at age seven provides a very accurate predictor of IQ at age eighteen. But the table also indicates that intelligence measures taken at age two or before do *not* correlate very highly with later measures. One reason is that the infant intelligence scales primarily measure visual-motor ability. Intelligence may also be much more plastic in the early years. However, by age seven the child's IQ score is on the average a fairly good predictor of later ability.

Although IQs are relatively stable for most people after about age seven, some individuals do show large shifts in IQ. If there are major changes in environmental conditions and in the opportunities for learning—either for better or worse—there may be marked changes in tested intelligence. One longitudinal study that tested a large number of individuals repeatedly from birth to age thirty-six found shifts in IQ of more than 15 points for some cases (Bayley, 1970). The variables that produce large changes in IQ for individual children are not always easy to specify, but emotional and motivational factors appear to play a major role. For example, one study found that children whose IQs increased during the early years were more vigorous, emotionally independent, aggressive, and actively engaged in exploring their environment than those whose IQs failed to increase (Sontag and others, 1958). In later years changes in IQ appear most closely related to strong motivation to achieve.

TABLE 14-7
Correlations among intelligence test scores at different ages

		RETEST AGE (IN YEARS)			
		7	10	14	18
TEST AGE (IN YEARS)	2	.46	.37	.28	.31
	7		.77	.75	.71
	10			.86	.73
	14				.76

Source: Jensen (1973).

Table entries give correlations between IQs obtained for the same individuals at different ages. An IQ obtained at age 7 correlates .77 with one obtained at age 10, and .71 with one obtained at age 18. Note that the size of the correlation decreases as years between testing increases.

Growth of Intelligence

Tests using the concept of mental age are so scored that if they are properly standardized an average growth curve will be a straight line: MA averaged over all individuals of a given age will equal CA at all ages. To look

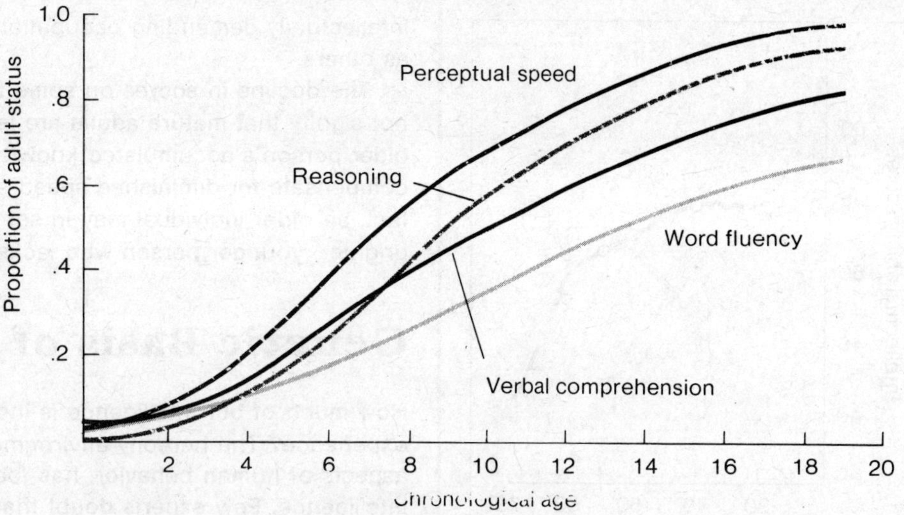

Fig. 14-10 Growth of four primary abilities

The scale adopted is that of 1.0 for adult status. Thus 80 percent of adult status is achieved for perceptual speed at age twelve, for reasoning at age fourteen, for verbal comprehension at age eighteen, and for word fluency later than twenty. (After Thurstone, 1955)

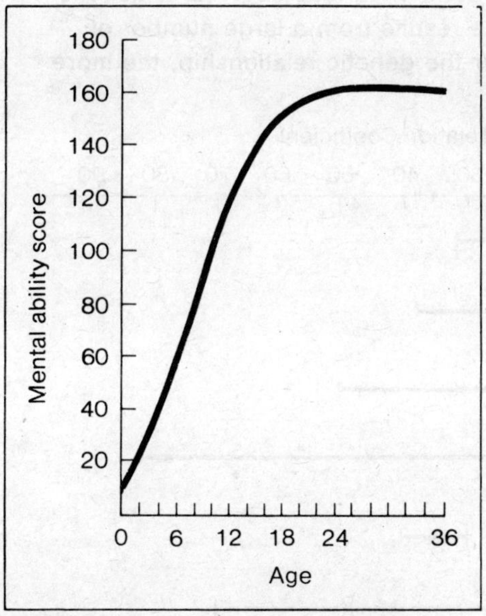

Fig. 14-11 Growth curve of intelligence

Theoretical curve of the growth of intelligence based on a large-scale longitudinal study. The intelligence scores are based on available age-appropriate tests, primarily Bayley infant scales, Stanford-Binet, and the Wechsler Adult tests, with the scores converted to an absolute scale of mental ability. (After Bayley, 1970)

at age changes in intellectual ability we need units for measuring mental growth that are not forced to correspond to age. Scores on Thurstone's primary abilities tests have been used for this purpose. Although the separate abilities grow at different rates, the gain is generally rapid in childhood and slows in the teens (Figure 14-10).

Figure 14-11 shows results from a large-scale longitudinal study that used Wechsler tests, with the scores converted to an absolute scale of mental ability. The same individuals were followed from birth to age thirty-six. Mental ability increased up to age twenty-six, after which it leveled off and remained unchanged through age thirty-six.

Remember that the curve in Figure 14-11 is an *average;* it masks the fact that some individuals may show an increase in IQ after age twenty-six, some a decrease. This confounding creates even more of a problem when we look at age changes in intellectual functioning after age forty. The typical study shows a steady decrease in intellectual ability after age forty with a percipitous drop after sixty (Figure 14-12). But analysis of the data indicates that whether ability declines during middle and old age depends both on the *person* and the *type of ability* tested. Individuals who remain physically well and continue to engage in stimulating activities show little decrease in intellectual ability up to age seventy. Physical disabilities, particularly those resulting from strokes or progressive reduction of blood circulated to the brain, usually result in dramatic decreases in intellectual ability. When data from these two types of individuals are combined, you get the somewhat deceptive average decline shown in Figure 14-12.

Mental abilities that require speed and extensive use of short-term memory tend to reach their peak between age thirty and forty and decline thereafter. Tests that tap general knowledge show little decline with age. The rate of decline of specific abilities is related to one's occupation; people in

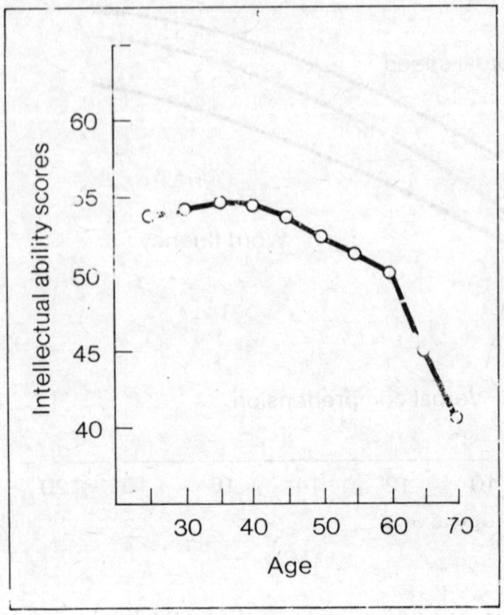

Fig. 14-12 Age changes in intellectual ability

The scores are based on a composite of five primary abilities tests, and weight heavily speeded tests such as word fluency. The height of ability appears at age thirty-five and declines fairly rapidly after age sixty (After Schaie and Strother, 1968)

intellectually demanding occupations do not decline in mental ability as early as others.

The decline in scores on some tests of intelligence in the later years does not signify that mature adults are less competent to play their roles in life. An older person's accumulated knowledge and experience may more than compensate for diminished speed and efficiency of intellectual functioning. In fact, an older individual may in some situations be more competent than a brighter, younger person who lacks experience.

Genetic Basis of Intelligence

How much of our intelligence is innate and how much is acquired through experience? The heredity-environment issue, debated in regard to many aspects of human behavior, has focused most intensely on the area of intelligence. Few experts doubt that there is some genetic basis for intelligence, but opinions differ as to the relative contributions of heredity and environment.

Genetic Relationships and Intelligence

Most of the evidence bearing on the inheritance of intelligence comes from studies correlating IQs between persons of various degrees of genetic relationship. Figure 14-13 summarizes the results from a large number of studies of this type. In general, the closer the genetic relationship, the more

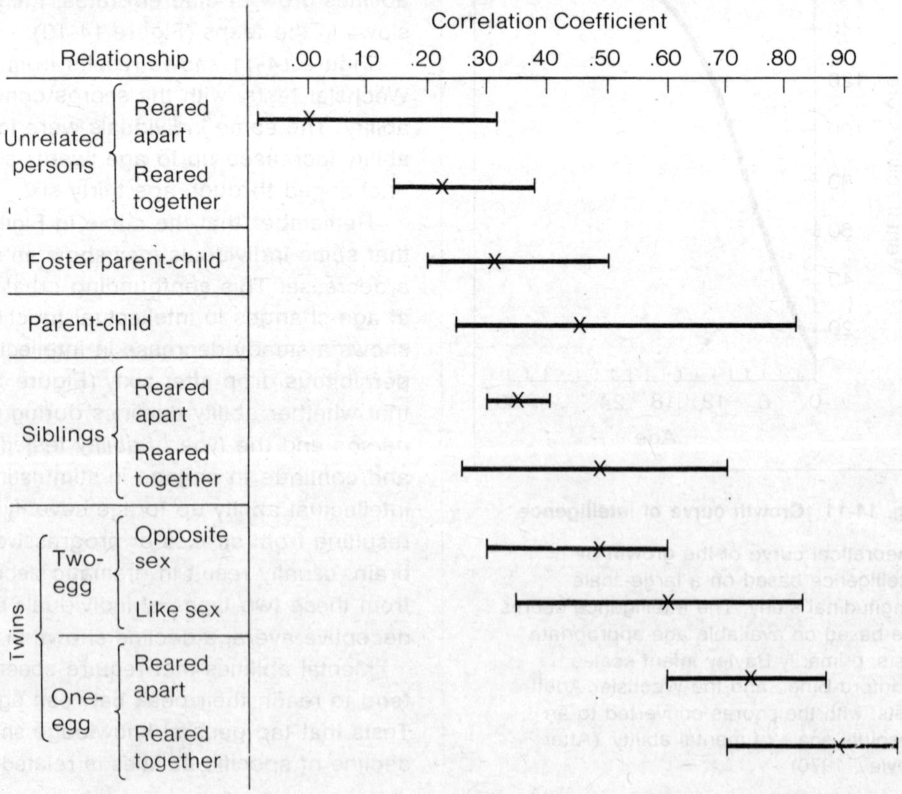

Fig. 14-13 Genetic relationships and IQ

The results of 52 studies of the correlation coefficients for "test intelligence" between persons of various relationships are summarized on the right. The horizontal lines give the range of the observed coefficients obtained in various studies and the X on each line marks the average. (After Erlenmeyer-Kimling and Jarvik, 1963) similar the tested intelligence. The average correlation between the IQs of parents and their natural children is .50; between parents and their adopted children the correlation is about .25. Identical twins, because they develop from a single egg, share precisely the same heredity; the correlation between their IQs is very high—about .90. The IQs of fraternal twins (who are genetically no more alike than ordinary siblings, since they develop from separate eggs) correlate about .55. Even when identical twins are reared apart in different homes their IQs correlate higher, .75, than those of fraternal twins reared together.

But, although genetic determinants of intelligence are strong, Figure 14-14 also points to the importance of environment. Note that being reared in the same home situation tends to increase IQ similarity, even for individuals who are unrelated. And, although adopted children resemble their natural parents more than their adopted parents in intellectual ability, their IQs are higher than would be predicted on the basis of their natural parents' ability (Skodak and Skeels, 1949). An improved environment makes a difference.

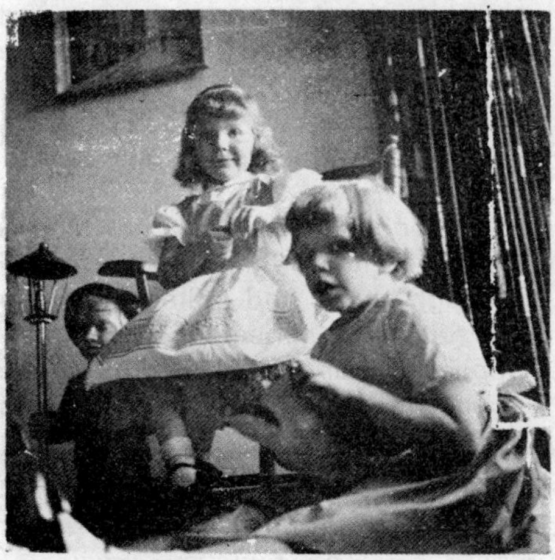

Phenylketonuria

Both of these sisters were afflicted with PKU, a genetically based metabolic disorder. The disorder was not identified in time to prevent retardation in the older girl, on the right. The younger girl was placed on a special diet immediately after birth, and her development was normal.

Estimates of Heritability

With any trait that varies widely within a population (e.g., intelligence or height) it is possible to estimate what portion of the variance is associated with differences in genes among that particular population. Starting with correlations like those in Figure 14-13, one can divide the observed variation in intelligence test scores into four components associated, respectively, with (1) environmental differences between different families, (2) genetic differences between families, (3) environmental differences between individuals within families, and (4) genetic differences between individuals within families. Carrying out the appropriate calculations reveals that about three-fourths of the total variance of IQ scores is associated with genetic factors and one fourth with environmental factors plus errors of measurement. For the data summarized in Figure 14-13 the estimate of *heritability* is .74. Heritability is a technical term referring to the proportion of the variation of a trait within a population that is attributable to genetic differences between individuals in that population.

Because of differences in the type of data analyzed and the exact method of calculation used, heritability estimates for intelligence have ranged from .45 to .87 (Jensen, 1973). The lower estimate is based on the assumption that a sizable portion of variation in IQ scores can be attributed to a genetic-environmental covariation. That is, parents of a certain gene type can influence their offspring both by direct genetic transmission and by the kind of environment they provide. Thus, brighter parents may provide not only "brighter genes" but also a more intellectually stimulating environment.

Regardless of the heritability estimate one accepts, it is clear that intelligence is influenced by genetic factors. But several important facts must be kept in mind. First, heritability estimates apply to populations under quite specific conditions and not to individuals. For example, the statement that the heritability of Stanford-Binet IQ scores for U.S. school children is .70 does not mean that the IQ of a particular child is 70 percent determined by heredity. Second, even though intelligence has a significant genetic component, environmental conditions can be crucially important. For

CRITICAL DISCUSSION

Racial Differences

Recently the issue of genetic contributions to intelligence has focused on the possibility of inherited racial differences in intelligence—more specifically the question of whether blacks are innately less intelligent than whites. In view of the heated controversy centered around this issue and its significance for social policy, it is important that we examine the available evidence.

On standard intelligence tests black Americans, as a group, score 10 to 15 IQ points lower than white Americans, as a group. This fact is not debated; the debate revolves around how to interpret the difference. Some possible explanations should be apparent from what we have already said about the nature of IQ tests and the influence of environmental factors on tested intelligence. For example, most intelligence tests have been standardized on white populations. Since blacks and whites generally grow up in quite different environments and have different experiences, the content of such tests may not be appropriate for blacks. And a black child may react differently to being tested (particularly if he or she is being tested by a white examiner) than a white child. Thus, the whole issue of estimating black intelligence is complicated by the question of whether the tests are appropriate and whether the data obtained by white testers represent an unbiased measure of IQ.

In the past, racial and ethnic minority groups have not had the same educational opportunities as white Americans. Since 1955, however, considerable effort has been devoted to providing equal funding and facilities for schools and to raising the achievement level of underprivileged groups by means of special educational programs. On the whole these special-education programs have not been very successful; group differences in academic performance remain about the same. An article by Arthur Jensen published in the *Harvard Educational Review* in 1969 came to the controversial conclusion that such programs have been ineffective because of innate differences in intelligence between the black and white populations in the United States. Jensen suggested that blacks fall below whites in abstract problem-solving ability, but are equal or superior in memorization. He recommended that educational programs be changed to take these innate differences into consideration (see also Jensen, 1973)

Jensen's article raised a storm of controversy, and numerous articles and debates have followed in its wake. Since the issues involved are exceedingly complex, the best we can do is to summarize a few of the main points.

1. The concept of race is largely demographic rather than biological. Although blacks and whites may differ in superficial appearance, the differences in their gene structures (where gene frequencies are known) are in

example, a genetically based metabolic disorder called *phenylketonuria* (PKU) will result in mental retardation if not detected soon after birth. The infant cannot properly metabolize the amino acid phenylalanine, and the accumulation of toxic products in the brain destroys brain tissue and prevents normal intellectual development. Fortunately, a simple urine test identifies the disorder, and a diet low in phenylalanine can be provided so that intelligence develops normally. A trait that is genetically determined can be critically influenced by environmental conditions.

An individual's mental abilities are a function of genetic potential in interaction with such prenatal and postnatal environmental conditions as

in Intelligence

most cases far less between races than within them.

2. Estimates of the heritability of intelligence differ, depending upon the assumptions one makes. Jensen estimates the heritability coefficient to be .81, but other investigators find heritability coefficients as low as .35; the lower estimates assume that more of the variance is attributable to a genetic-environment interaction.
3. Among black populations there is some tendency for lightness of skin color (presumably an indication of the degree of intermixture with whites) to correlate positively with IQ. But such correlations are very low (typically .15) and can be explained on the basis of environmental differences, a lighter skin color being associated with less discrimination and greater opportunity. A study of very high IQ black children in Chicago found no indication of greater Caucasian ancestry than for the black population as a whole (Witty and Jenkins, 1936).
4. Children born of interracial marriages have a higher IQ if the mother is white than if she is black (Willerman and others, 1970). This suggests a maternal environment effect (prenatal and/or postnatal) rather than a genetic effect. An alternative possibility—that there might be a difference in average parental intelligence in the two types of marriages—cannot be completely ruled out because the parents' IQs were not measured. But U.S. Census data indicate that the educational level of black husbands with white wives is about the same as that of white husbands with black wives.
5. A study of illegitimate children conceived as the result of liaisons between U.S. servicemen and German women during the occupation of Germany after the Second World War found no overall difference in average IQ between children whose fathers were black and those whose fathers were white. Since these children were reared in similar environmental circumstances (i.e., by a German mother under comparable conditions of social status and matched when possible with agemates in the same school classroom), the results provide strong support for environment as the major determinant of racial IQ differences (Eyferth and others, 1960).

The above are some of the major points examined in an extensive survey of the intelligence-race issue by Loehlin, Lindzey, and Spuhler (1975). The interested reader is referred to that monograph for a review of the controversy.

Many responses have been made to Jensen's original article. Some agree with his view that tested IQ differences between blacks and whites reflect innate differences in intelligence, although among this group there is considerable disagreement about the relative weight assigned to genetic versus environmental factors. Others argue that many of the studies cited by Jensen are methodologically and/or statistically faulty; examining the same data they conclude that there is no evidence for a genetic factor in IQ test differences (Kamin, 1974). A third conclusion seems more appropriate: it is not possible to draw valid inferences about innate racial differences in intelligence from available IQ data (Layzer, 1974). Cultural differences and differences in psychological environments between blacks and whites influence the development of cognitive abilities in complex ways, and no study has succeeded in either estimating or eliminating their effects. Culture-fair intelligence tests deal with this problem only on the most superficial level; using current methods it is impossible to separate those aspects of cognitive development that are influenced by cultural factors from those that are not. As long as systematic differences remain in the conditions under which blacks and whites are raised (and as long as the effects of these differences cannot be reliably estimated), no valid conclusions can be drawn concerning innate differences in intelligence between races.

We will have more to say about racial differences and intelligence testing in Chapter 19.

nutrition, health, enriched or impoverished stimulation, the emotional climate of the home, and the type of feedback provided for behavior. Given two children with the same gene structure at conception, the child with the best prenatal and postnatal nutrition, the most intellectually stimulating and emotionally secure home, and the most appropriate rewards for academic accomplishments will attain the higher intelligence score when tested in first grade. Studies have shown that IQ differences between children of low and high socioeconomic status become progressively greater between birth and entrance into school (Bayley, 1970). This suggests that environmental conditions accentuate whatever differences are present at birth.

Extremes of Intelligence

Mentally Subnormal

There is no sharp break between the mentally subnormal and the normal, and many borderline cases exist. The classification of a child as retarded tells us very little. The many kinds and degrees of retardation make calling retarded children by a common name such as "feeble-minded" misleading.

THE PREVALENCE OF SUBNORMALITY. It is estimated that about 3 percent of the population in the United States is mentally retarded (Isaacson, 1970); the percentage varies depending upon the criteria used. An IQ below 70 is generally considered retarded, but more important than a score on an intelligence test is the individual's social competence—what he is able to do for himself. The farm worker who was unable to finish school but lives independently as a hired hand is normal in his environment, even though he may be recognizably dull; the same man might find it difficult to live successfully in the city. Thus the distinction between dull-normal and subnormal rests upon the complexity of the social conditions under which independence must be maintained. By social criteria, individuals might change their classification by moving from one place to another, even though their tested intelligence does not change.

The majority of the retarded have IQs between 50 and 70 and are classified as *educable;* with the proper help they can learn to support themselves and find a place in the community. Their intellectual level as adults may be comparable to that of the average eight- to twelve-year-old child. A much smaller percentage of retarded individuals (three-tenths of one percent of the total population) have IQs between 30 and 50 and are classified as *trainable.* Although they will always be dependent upon others for support, they can learn to take care of their daily needs and can function in a sheltered environment. Their intellectual level as adults may be comparable to that of the average four- to seven-year-old child. Some of the brighter ones achieve a fair command of spoken language and may be taught to read and write a little. Individuals with IQs below 30 are severely handicapped and *totally dependent* upon others for care; this group constitutes less than one-tenth of one percent of the total population.

CAUSES OF SUBNORMALITY. In the majority of cases of subnormal intelligence no physical cause can be discovered. The child is essentially sound physically, and there is no history of disease or injury that might have produced brain damage. Retardation is usually minimal; the individual suffers from a general deficiency rather than an identifiable defect. Such individuals tend to come from families that are low in intelligence and living under impoverished conditions. This type of retardation has been called *familial-cultural;* the cause is assumed to be both genetic and environmental. Individuals of low intelligence cannot get jobs that pay well; they marry other low IQ persons and produce children whose intellectual potential is limited. Environmental circumstances—inadequate infant nutrition and medical care, lack of intellectual stimulation and parental concern—contribute to further intellectual impairment. Thus a vicious cycle continues.

In cases of more severe retardation some sort of physical cause can usually be identified—brain injury, disease, or accidents of development that preclude normal intellectual growth. The mental impairment in these cases is

Twins with Down's syndrome

Children afflicted by Down's syndrome have been called mongoloid because they tend to have slanting eye slits with small folds covering the inner corners of the eyes. Other characteristics often found are: short stature; small round head; irregularly spaced teeth; a thick, protruding tongue that is fissured; and square, stubby hands and feet. Their gait is often awkward. Postmortem studies of mongoloid brains show widespread areas of brain cells that have failed to grow.

usually related to brain damage, and gross structural defects are often apparent in the nervous system. It has been proposed that such children be called *mentally defective* rather than *mentally retarded,* since their intellectual impairment results from an identifiable defect. Mentally defective individuals may occur in any family or socioeconomic group regardless of genetic background.

Any condition that affects normal development of the brain can cause mental deficiency. Physical damage to the brain or lack of oxygen (anoxia) during birth can result in intellectual impairment. It is estimated that 1 baby in 1000 suffers from damage of this type sufficient to prevent the intelligence level from reaching that of a twelve-year-old (Isaacson, 1970). Infections of the mother during the early months of pregnancy, such as German measles or syphilis, can cause brain damage, as can certain drugs taken by the mother.

Some types of mental deficiency are caused by specific genetic defects that alter the body metabolism. PKU, which we discussed earlier (p. 418), is one such defect, but it is relatively rare. Somewhat more common is Down's syndrome (*mongolism*), a severe form of mental deficiency accompanied by physical abnormalities. The body cells of mongoloid children contain 47 chromosomes rather than the normal 46; the extra chromosome apparently comes from the mother as the result of faulty separation of a particular chromosome pair in the egg cell prior to ovulation. Mongoloid children are most frequently born to older mothers; a woman in her twenties has 1 chance in 2000 of producing a baby with Down's syndrome, while the risk for a woman in her forties is 1 in 50. The reason is not clear. Changes in the reproductive system of the older woman may be responsible for the genetic fault. It is also possible that the older the mother, the greater the probability of exposure to radiation that causes gene mutations. Although mongolism is a genetic disorder, it is not inherited.[3] The reproductive error produces a genetic makeup in the child that is unlike that of the parents. If the parents are young, they need not fear that subsequent offspring will be mongoloid (Lejeune, 1970).

Some children with Down's syndrome learn to speak a little and to master simple chores. For most, however, speech is absent or confined to a few hoarsely spoken sounds and skills beyond those basic to elementary self-care are seldom attained. Mongoloid children tend to be affectionate and docile compared to other retarded children. Because of their numerous physical deficiencies their health is poor; more than 60 percent die before the age of ten.

TREATMENT OF THE SUBNORMAL. From time to time reports appear of remarkable achievements in raising IQ scores of subnormal children. Headlines in newspapers and articles in magazines raise the hopes of countless parents who have retarded children. This publicity is unfortunately misleading because the overall evidence we have today is not encouraging. It gives little promise of dramatic improvement in the mentally subnormal, although this does not mean that the retarded or defective child cannot be helped.[4]

[3] One rare type of Down's syndrome that accounts for only 4 percent of all cases is inherited.

[4] The child who has special problems because he comes from a different cultural background, and who may be underachieving in school, can often be helped. The economically disadvantaged child should not be classified as mentally subnormal because he is behind academically. With appropriate help there is usually an improvement in school achievement, and there may even be an increase in IQ.

A great deal can be done for subnormal children. They can be taught social habits and can learn vocational skills appropriate to their intellectual level. Such instruction must not be confused, however, with raising the IQ. In many subnormal individuals a small increase in IQ comes with better social adjustment, but there is little reason to expect striking changes as a result of a bettered environment.

Many persons of low intelligence get along satisfactorily in the community. Several follow-up studies have been made of children whose IQs during school age rated them as mentally retarded. The investigators all found that a substantial proportion of these individuals were able to maintain themselves vocationally when they became adults.

Mentally Gifted

At the other end of the scale from the mentally subnormal are those who are intellectually gifted. With the development of intelligence tests it has become possible to select for study large groups of superior children and then to follow their careers. One of the best known of these studies, started by Terman and his associates in 1921, followed the progress of over 1500 gifted children from their early school years through the middle years of adult life. A 40-year follow-up has been published (Oden, 1968).

The group was chosen on the basis of IQs of 140 or above. About 1 out of every 100 children has an IQ that high; less than 1 out of every 1000 has an IQ above 160.

Terman's gifted children were better than average physical specimens. They averaged more than an inch taller than others of the same age in elementary school. Their birth weights were above normal. They talked early and walked early. When the tests started, seven out of eight were in grades ahead of their age group in school; none was below grade level. They read an unusually large number and variety of books, but reading did not interfere with their superiority in leadership and social adaptability.

These characteristics of the gifted children contradict the notion that the very bright child is a weakling and a social misfit. The evidence is all to the contrary. Superior intelligence in Terman's subjects was associated with good health, social adaptability, and leadership.

Lewis Terman

GIFTED CHILDREN AS YOUNG ADULTS. The extent to which early promise was fulfilled by Terman's gifted children can be estimated from their performances in adult life. Although on the whole they gave a superior account of themselves, not all the subjects had a history of success. Some failed in college, some were vocational misfits, some ran afoul of the law. But the least successful group differed little in their adult intelligence test scores from the most successful group. The average IQ difference between the most and least successful groups was only six points. The small difference in IQ scores cannot account for the differences in achievement. We must conclude that nonintellectual qualities are very important in success.

What do "successful" and "unsuccessful" mean in these comparisons? The subjects in Terman's study were classified into three success groups: A, the most successful; B, the intermediately successful; and C, the least successful. The criterion of success was primarily "the extent to which a subject made use of his intellectual ability." Listing in *Who's who in America* or *American men of science,* representation in literary or scholarly publications, holding responsible managerial positions, outstanding achievement in any intellectual or professional calling—all entered into the judgments.

Although the A and C groups did not differ very much in IQ, a study of their records showed that they differed in many other respects—chiefly in general social adjustment and in achievement motivation. These are personality and motivational traits rather than intellectual ones.

Have these intellectually able people passed on their abilities to the next generation? Tests given to their offspring showed an average IQ of 133, although, as expected, the scores ranged widely—from mentally subnormal to above 200 (Oden, 1968).

Present Status of Ability Tests

Among the various tests of ability, we have chosen to consider the intelligence test in greatest detail. Despite its limitations, the intelligence test is one of the most widely used tools that psychology has developed. The usefulness of such tests will continue, provided they are kept in perspective and neither overvalued as telling more about a person than they actually measure nor undervalued because of their obvious defects. In the discussion that follows, we shall try to view them in the perspective of other ability measures, and in relation to the social consequences of their use.

Blurred Distinction Between Aptitude and Achievement Tests

We pointed out earlier that aptitudes have to be assessed on the basis of prior achievements. It is a mistake to assign aptitude to innate potential and achievement entirely to training; both are complex results of innate potential, generalized experience, and specific training. Thus a scholastic aptitude test (the preferred name for an intelligence test that predicts school or college grades) includes learned material, although it does not demand that the student have taken a particular course in, say, mathematics or history. An achievement test in a particular subject does presuppose acquaintance with a specific body of material.

A useful illustration of the blurred distinction between the two types of tests is the National Merit Scholarship Qualifying Test taken annually by about 800,000 high-school students in the United States. This test is given to all interested students regardless of the school subjects they have studied, but it is still a test of *educational development,* not of aptitude alone; it is a measure of both the student's aptitude and the effectiveness of his schooling. The usefulness of the test in predicting success in college is quite high. For example, the first group of Merit Scholarship recipients entered college in 1956. In a study made approximately ten years later, it was found that 96 percent had graduated from college and that advanced degrees had been obtained by more than half of the men and by 40 percent of the women (Stalnaker, 1965). In terms of our definition of aptitude testing as designed for prediction, the National Merit Test reveals aptitude for college work, but of course various achievement tests and high school grades also predict college success.

For practical purposes of prediction, the fact that test content reflects both individual potential and the results of good schooling is immaterial. From the point of view of understanding the nature of intelligence it does matter, however, whether or not effective schooling actually raises intellectual potential.

Public Attacks on Testing

Attacks on psychological testing have focused on several objections: (1) the invasion of privacy, (2) the secrecy surrounding test scores, (3) the types of talent selected by tests, and (4) the unfairness of the tests to minority groups. All these problems must be taken seriously by those using tests, and we shall consider each in turn.

1. Because a test is personal, it is not necessarily an invasion of privacy. When the purpose of the test is benign, when it is used to help individuals plan their lives and avoid failure, it is no different, in principle, from the physical examination required for participation in athletics. (Children with heart ailments should not be advised to go out for long-distance running.)
2. The secrecy surrounding test scores was intended to guard against the possibility that parents might give too much credence to test scores indicating their child to be below average or handicapped in some way. Psychologists, aware of the many factors influencing test performance, prefer to give repeated tests and make allowances for poor performance. This generally good reason for withholding scores has backfired somewhat because it has made the test scores appear to be more important than they are. Since what intelligence tests do best is predict school grades, there should be no more damage in one's knowing that he has a low IQ than in knowing he is doing poorly in school. Results of attitude studies show that children who were given their test scores more often than not raised their estimates of their own intelligence (Brim, 1965). In other words, children have many indicators, beyond intelligence test scores, that they are brighter or duller than other children. The National Merit Scholarship Corporation gives full disclosure of its scores, with apparently beneficial results.
3. As Terman's study of gifted individuals showed, the intelligence test is a limited predictor of success; creativity, special talents, motivation, perseverance, and other personality variables are important. Psychologists have stressed that such nonintellectual variables should be considered in the selection policies of educational and business institutions. Used in conjunction with other information, intelligence test results can be valuable.
4. The fairness of the tests to underprivileged and minority groups is a complex problem to which psychologists have devoted considerable study (Loehlin and others, 1975). A point often overlooked is that ability tests provide objective criteria and, when properly used, may overcome some of the discrimination practiced against minority groups, thus increasing the opportunities for members of minority groups. This follows because the tests measure ability rather than social status. In one comparison of white and black adult respondents, it was found that lower-class blacks indeed favored the use of tests in job selection and promotion more than did the white respondents (Brim, 1965).

Summary

1. Ability tests include *aptitude tests* (which measure capacity to learn and predict what one can accomplish with training) and *achievement tests*, (which measure accomplished skills and indicate what one can do at present). Both tests may use similar types of items. The difference between them lies in their purposes.
2. In order to be useful for prediction, tests must meet certain specifications. Studies of *reliability* tell us whether the test scores are self-consistent. Studies of *validity* tell us how well the tests measure what they are supposed to measure—how well they predict according to an acceptable criterion.
3. One way of determining the accuracy of a test's predictions is to set a *critical score* so that those who score below this point are disqualified from the training or program under consideration. If the critical score separates those who will succeed in the program from those who will not, then the test is useful as a predictor.
4. The first successful intelligence tests were developed by Alfred Binet in France in 1905. We owe to him the concept of *mental age*, according to which dull children are regarded as slow in their development, their responses being like those of younger children. Conversely, bright children are advanced beyond their years. This concept has been followed in later revisions of Binet's scales, of which the most widely used has been the Stanford-Binet.
5. Louis Terman, who was responsible for the Stanford-Binet, adopted the *intelligence quotient* (IQ) as an index of mental development. The IQ originally expressed intelligence as a ratio of mental age (MA) to chronological age (CA). The IQ measure adopted in the most recent Stanford-Binet adjusts the obtained IQs so that at each chronological age they have a mean of 100 and a standard deviation of 16. Hence a contemporary IQ is no longer a ratio, but a score adjusted for the age of the person being tested.
6. A widely used intelligence test, the *Wechsler Intelligence Scales*, has both a verbal and a performance scale so that separate information can be obtained about each type of ability.
7. The method of factor analysis has been used to determine the kinds of abilities underlying intelligence. Spearman believed that intelligence consisted of a general factor (*g*) plus specific abilities (*s*'s); Thurstone identified seven primary mental abilities that he thought were the basic elements of intelligence; Guilford's structure-of-intellect model proposes 120 different intellectual abilities, many of which measure *divergent* rather than *convergent* thinking. Evidence indicates that both general intelligence and specific abilities are important.
8. After age six most people's IQs remain relatively stable, although some individuals may show large shifts in IQ as the result of favorable or unfavorable environmental conditions. Mental ability tends to increase up to age twenty-six, level off for the next ten years or so, and then decline after age forty. The rate of decline, however, depends upon the individual's health and occupation as well as the specific abilities tested.
9. Studies correlating IQs between persons with varying degrees of genetic relationships show that heredity plays a role in intelligence. Estimates of *heritability* vary, however, and such environmental factors as nutrition, intellectual stimulation, and the emotional climate of the home are important determiners of intelligence.

10. The extremes of intelligence are represented by the *mentally subnormal*, at one end of the scale, and the *intellectually gifted*, at the other. Social criteria are as important as intelligence scores in deciding whether a child is subnormal. In *familial-cultural* retardation (which results from the inheritance of low intelligence accentuated by impoverished living conditions) no physical defect is identifiable. A *mentally defective* child, in contrast, usually has some brain damage—resulting from maternal infections during pregnancy, birth trauma, genetic defects such as Down's syndrome, or other disorders. Subnormal children *can* learn; many can do socially useful work under supervision or even achieve a measure of independence.
11. As a group, the mentally gifted show superior attainments throughout childhood and adult life. Their histories belie the notion that highly intelligent people are maladjusted in some way. However, superior intelligence in itself is no assurance of success; some gifted children are misfits in adult life even though their intelligence scores remain high.
12. Public attacks upon testing are based on such objections as invasion of privacy, secrecy surrounding test scores, types of talent selected by tests, and unfairness of the tests to disadvantaged and minority groups. Psychologists have incomplete answers to these criticisms, but they do recognize that ability testing carries with it social responsibility.

Further Reading

For a general review of individual differences and psychological testing see Cronbach, *Essentials of psychological testing* (3rd ed., 1970). Among the books that specifically treat the problems of intelligence testing are Guilford and Hoepfner, *The analysis of intelligence* (1971); Butcher, *Human intelligence* (1968); and Vernon, *Intelligence and cultural environment* (1969).

Wechsler's measurement and appraisal of adult intelligence (5th ed., 1972) by Matarazzo includes a history of intelligence testing as well as current research on the Wechsler Scales.

The genetics of intelligence is discussed in McClearn and DeFries, *Introduction to behavioral genetics* (1973). On the issue of racial differences in intelligence see Loehlin, Lindzey, and Spuhler, *Race differences in intelligence* (1975).

part seven

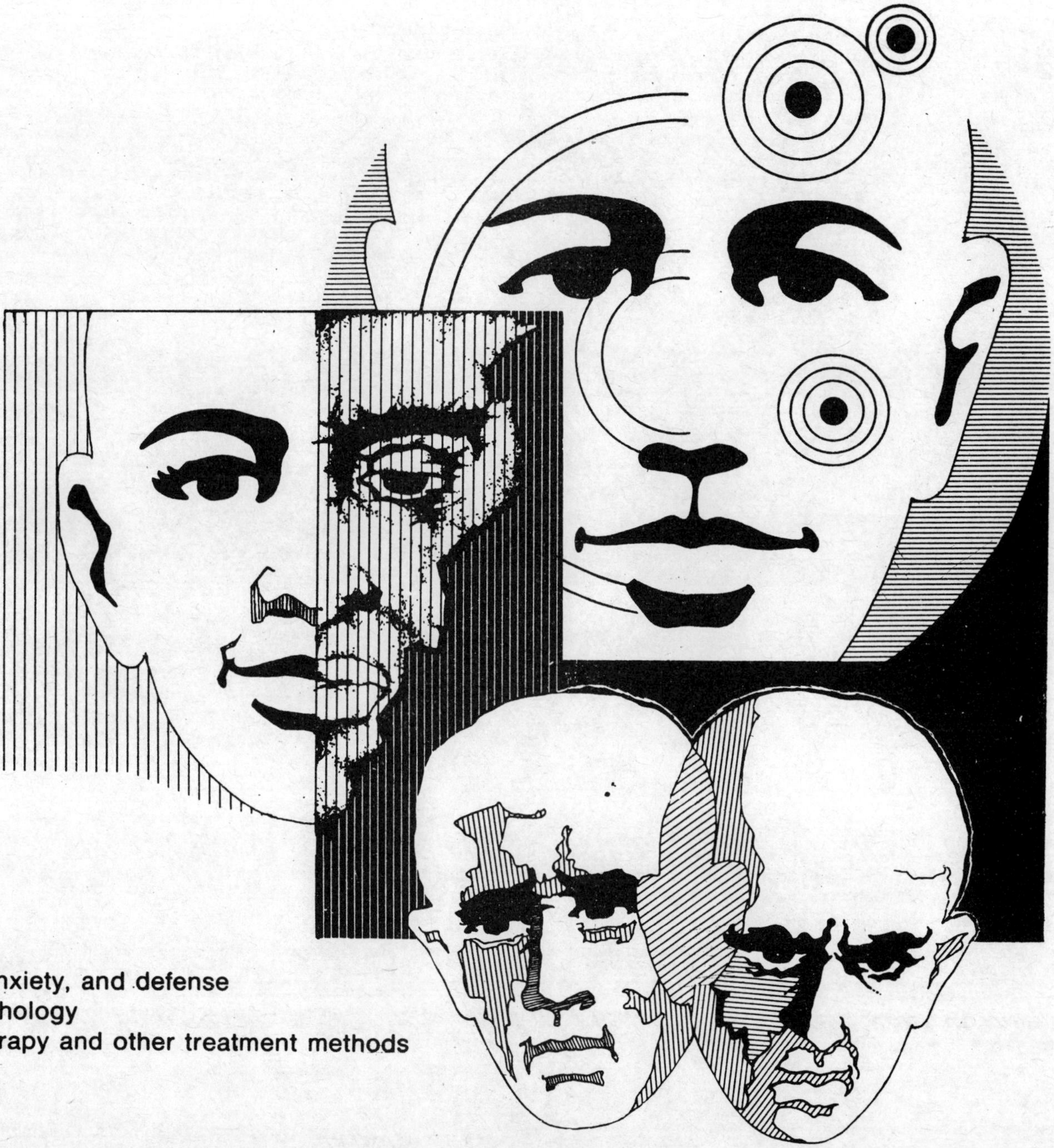

conflict, adjustment, and mental health

15 conflict, anxiety, and defense

No matter how resourceful we may be in coping with problems, the circumstances of life inevitably involve stress. Our motives are not always easily satisfied; obstacles must be overcome, choices made, and delays tolerated. Each of us develops characteristic ways of responding when our attempts to reach a desired goal are blocked. These responses to frustrating situations determine, to a large extent, the adequacy of our adjustment to life.

In this and the following two chapters we will look at the way people respond to frustration and stress, what happens when inadequate coping techniques pose a threat to mental health, and the methods used to treat abnormal behavior. Because this area of psychology is not as firmly based on experimental data as some of the topics covered in previous chapters, the material will be more discursive and case histories rather than experiments will be used at times to illustrate points.

Frustration

The term *frustration* has at least two different connotations in everyday speech. In one sense it refers to the blocking of motive satisfaction. When progress toward a desired goal is interfered with or delayed, we say that the person encounters frustration. But "frustration" is also used to describe the unpleasant emotional state that results from blocked goal-seeking, rather than the event itself. The individual whose car gets a flat tire as he hurries to catch a plane would probably say that he feels frustrated. Here frustration is equated with an internal state. For our purposes, however, we will hold to the meaning of frustration as the *thwarting circumstances*—the external events, rather than their internal consequences.

Environmental Obstacles and Personal Limitations

There are many barriers to the satisfaction of motives, to the attainment of a goal. The physical environment presents such obstacles as intemperate weather, droughts, and floods. The social environment presents obstacles through the restrictions imposed by other people and the customs of social living. Offspring are thwarted by parental denials and postponements: Mary must share her tricycle with her brother; John's father will not let him have the car for a camping trip; and Jane's parents insist that she is not old enough to live in her own apartment. The list is endless. Any society, no matter how simple, places restrictions on its members.

Sometimes the barriers to goal satisfaction lie within the individual's own deficiencies or limitations. Some people are handicapped by blindness, deafness, or paralysis. Not everyone can become a great musician or pass the examinations necessary to become a physician or lawyer. If goals are set beyond one's ability, then frustrations will inevitably result.

Conflict

A major source of frustration is conflict between two opposing motives. When two motives conflict, the satisfaction of one leads to the frustration of the other. For example, a student may not be able to gain recognition as an outstanding athlete and still earn the grades needed to enter law school.

Even when only one motive is involved, there may be various ways of approaching the goal, and conflict arises when the paths to the goal diverge. For example, you can get an education at any one of a number of colleges, but choosing which one to enter presents a conflict situation. Even though the goal will eventually be reached, progress toward it is disrupted by the necessity for making a choice.

Sometimes conflict arises between a motive and a person's internal standards, rather than between two external goals. For example, sexual desires may conflict with one's standards of what constitutes acceptable social behavior. A woman's motive for achievement may conflict with her standards for appropriate feminine behavior. Conflicts between motives and internal standards can often be more difficult to resolve than conflicts between external goals.

Most conflicts involve goals that are simultaneously desirable and undesirable—both positive and negative. Candy is delicious, but fattening. Going off for a weekend of skiing is fun, but the consequences of lost study time can be anxiety-producing. The attitude toward a goal at once wanted and not wanted, liked and disliked, is called an *ambivalent* attitude. Ambivalent attitudes are very common: a young woman leaves home to escape parental domination, only to come back to receive parental protection; her attitude toward her parents is ambivalent.

A person confronted by a goal that is at once attractive and dangerous vacillates while trying to decide what to do. The dangers seem less real when the goal is at a distance, so that its inviting aspects lead to approach reactions. But the sense of danger increases as the goal is approached, so that nearer to the incentive one has a tendency to withdraw (Figure 15-1). This simultaneous tendency "to" and "from" leads to vacillation at some point near enough to the goal for one to be aware of the dangers but distant enough to be safe from them. When a shy adolescent boy is about to call a girl for a date, he is drawn to the telephone by the possibility of success, but his anxiety about possible rebuff mounts as he approaches. As a result he may make several false starts before he either carries through his plan or abandons it.

Fig. 15-1 A case of ambivalence

The girl wants both to approach the duck and to back away from it. Such an approach-avoidance conflict results in vacillation; the attractiveness of the object keeps the child in the region of conflict but fear is increased as she gets closer.

This type of conflict—called *approach-avoidance conflict*—is illustrated by an experiment in which hungry rats were taught to run the length of an alley to obtain food in a goal box at the end of the alley; this training established approach reactions. Then the rats were given a brief electric shock while eating. The shock added avoidance tendencies to the approach tendencies and hence produced an approach-avoidance conflict. To test the resulting conflict behavior, the rats were placed at the start of the alley. The characteristic behavior corresponded to that predicted: the rat started in the direction of the goal box but came to a stop before reaching it. The place of stopping could be controlled by modifying the strength of either hunger or shock (Miller, 1959).

GRADIENTS OF APPROACH AND AVOIDANCE. The behavior of the rats in the preceding experiment can be better understood by using the concept of *gradients* of approach and avoidance. By a gradient we mean a change in response strength as a function of the distance from the goal-object. The pull of a magnet upon a piece of iron is an analogous gradient. The pull (or strength of the gradient) increases as the distance between the piece of iron and the magnet is shortened.

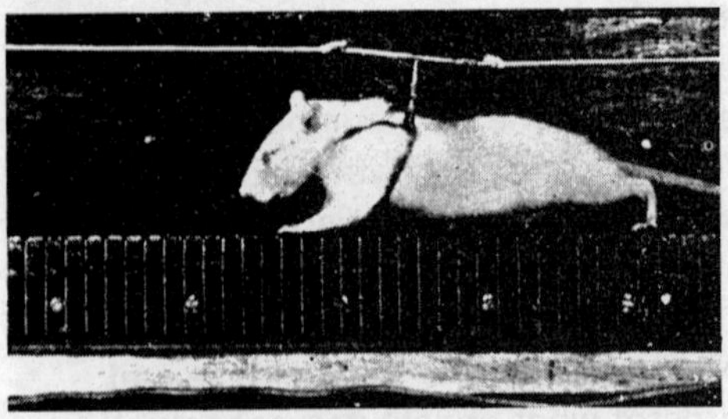

Fig. 15-2 Measuring approach and avoidance gradients

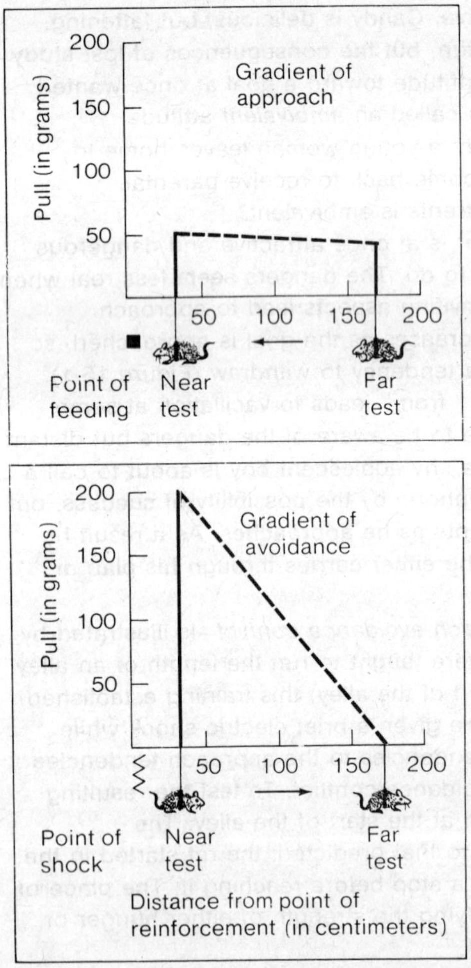

Fig. 15-3 Gradients of approach and avoidance
The strength of approach and avoidance is measured by the pull on the restraining harness on the rat. Note that the avoidance gradient (bottom) is steeper than the approach gradient (top). (After Brown, 1948)

There are experimental procedures to determine the gradients of approach and avoidance. In one such procedure a rat is placed in a straight alley with a goal box at the end. The rat is given food in the goal box and quickly learns to associate the box with the food reinforcement. The rat is then equipped with a light harness so that the experimenter can restrain it briefly at any point along the alley way to the goal box (Figure 15-2). When the animal is restrained, the amount of pull on the harness can be recorded, providing a measure of the approach tendency at that point. When restrained near the goal, the rat pulls harder than when restrained farther from the goal. This increase in pull is shown in the top panel of Figure 15-3 by the slight rise in the line representing the gradient of approach between the far and the near test.

Another rat receives a brief electric shock in the goal box. When later placed in the goal box without shock, it tends to run down the alley away from the place where the shock had been received. When restrained near to the goal box, the animal pulls harder than when restrained farther away from it. The difference between a test at a point near the goal box and that far from the goal box is shown in the gradient of avoidance in the bottom panel of Figure 15-3. Note that the slope of the two lines differs: the gradient for avoidance is much steeper than the one for approach.

How do the results of this experiment on gradients of approach and avoidance help us understand the results of the experiment on ambivalence? If we examine the two plotted gradients, the one for approach represents a pull on the harness toward the goal box, the one for avoidance represents a pull on the harness away from the goal box. When a rat has been both fed and shocked in the goal box, then both gradients are set up at once. If we imagine the two gradients superimposed, they would cross at a distance of about 135 centimeters from the goal box. At this point the two opposing tendencies would exactly balance. If the lines represent the true reaction tendencies, the rat in the experiment on ambivalence would be expected to stop at the point where the lines cross. This is approximately what happens. When the rat is placed in the alley at a point further from the goal box than 135 centimeters, it will tend to move toward the goal box; if placed at a point closer than 135 centimeters to the goal box, it will move away. This point of intersection can be moved either to the right or to the left by changing the strengths of either the approach or the avoidance tendencies. The effect of increasing the shock is to raise the avoidance gradient, thus placing the point of intersection farther from the place of shock. These predictions were made from the experiment on gradients and later were confirmed in the experiment on ambivalence.

The studies on gradients illustrate several principles important in the understanding of ambivalent behavior.

1. The tendency to approach a positive incentive is stronger the nearer the subject is to it.
2. The tendency to go away from a negative incentive is stronger the nearer the subject is to it.
3. In some situations the strength of avoidance increases more rapidly with proximity than does that of approach. In other words, the avoidance gradient tends to be steeper than the approach gradient.

The third principle helps explain how a person may be repeatedly drawn back into an old conflict situation. At a distance the positive aspects seem

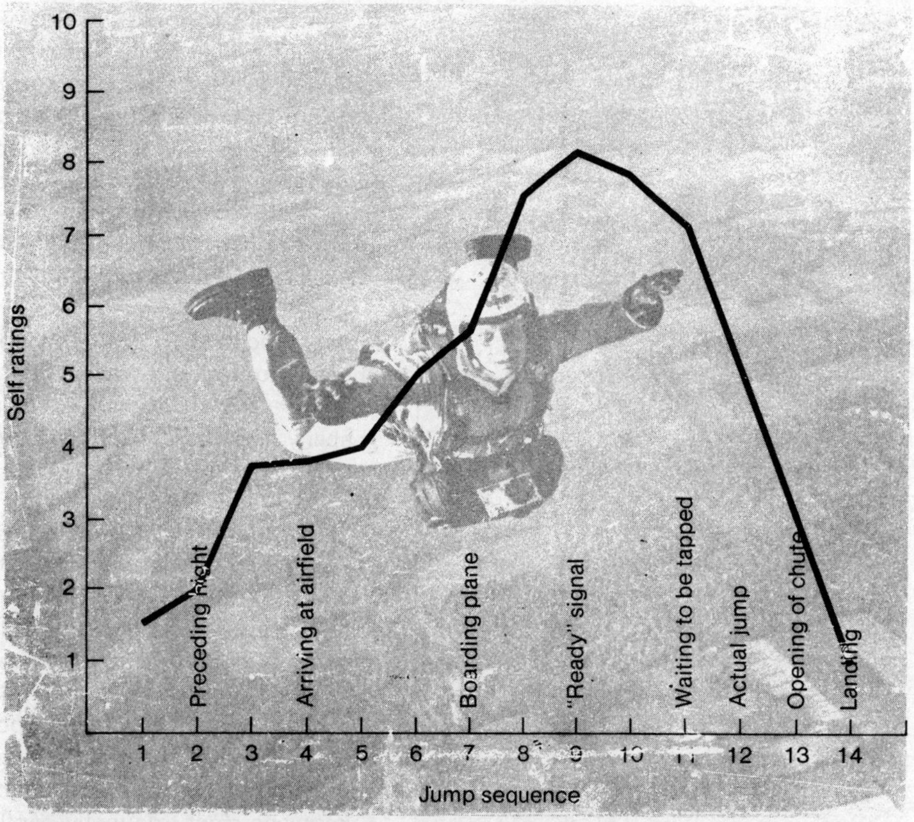

Fig. 15-4 Reactions of parachutists

Self-ratings by skydivers of feelings of avoidance (fear) at various times before and during their first parachute jump. (After Epstein and Fenz, 1965)

e inviting than the negative ones appear forbidding. Everyone knows of couples who go steady, break up, make up again, only to break up once more. Away from each other, their mutual attraction takes precedence because negative feelings are reduced; close to each other, the negative feelings drive them apart. To an outsider it appears irrational that people who get along so poorly attempt reconciliation. Once the ambivalence of their attitudes is recognized, however, their attempts at reconciliation become understandable—even if not reasonable.

Studies of the reactions of skydivers to their first parachute jump show how negative feelings (fear of death or injury) become stronger as the moment of danger becomes more imminent (Figure 15-4). The day before the jump positive feelings (the excitement and thrill of jumping) are predominant. But as the neophyte parachutist comes closer to the moment of jumping—arrives at the airfield, boards the plane, and waits for the ready signal—avoidance impulses increase rapidly, reaching a peak just before the signal is given. The would-be parachutist would probably back down at this point if it were possible to do so without losing face, since avoidance feelings far exceed approach tendencies. If the avoidance feelings had been this strong at some distance from the goal—for example, the week before while the jump was being planned—the individual might not have gotten into such a conflict situation.

Interestingly enough, the peak of fear occurs not at the moment of greatest danger (in the free fall before the parachute opens) but at the point of final commitment after which it would be difficult for the parachutist to change his mind. Once the decision is made, avoidance feelings begin to decrease.

The conflicts of real life, however, are usually more complicated than our discussion would imply. A conflict over alcohol, for example, usually involves more than a choice between its short-term relaxing aspects and its long-term aftereffects. The conflict can be affected by religious scruples, loss of self-control, search for companionship, escape from responsibility. Sometimes an approach-avoidance conflict is resolved by refusing to select either alternative or in some way evading the choice.

In our society the approach-avoidance conflicts that are most pervasive and difficult to resolve generally take place in the following areas:

1. *Independence versus dependence.* We may in times of stress want to resort to the dependency characteristic of childhood, to have someone take care of us and solve our problems for us. But we are taught that the ability to stand on our own and assume responsibilities is a mark of maturity.
2. *Cooperation versus competition.* In American life much emphasis is placed on competition and success. Competition begins in early childhood among siblings, continues through school and college, and culminates in business and professional rivalry. At the same time we are urged to cooperate and help others. The concept of "team spirit" is as American as the success story. Such contradictory expectations are potentially conflict-producing.
3. *Impulse expression versus moral standards.* All societies have to place some degree of regulation upon impulse control. We noted in Chapter 3 that much of childhood learning involves imposing cultural restrictions upon innate impulses. Sex and aggression are two areas in which our impulses most frequently conflict with moral standards, and violation of these standards may generate strong feelings of guilt.

These three areas present the greatest potential for serious conflict. As we shall see in the next chapter, failure to find a workable compromise may lead to severe psychological problems.

Reactions to Frustration

Frustration—whether it is the result of environmental obstacles, personal limitations, or conflict—has a number of possible consequences. A classic experiment with young children provides an illustration (Barker, Dembo, and Lewin, 1941). The experiment will be described in the present tense, as though we were observing it.

On the first day of the experiment, the children come one at a time into a room that contains several toys, parts of which are missing—a chair without a table, an ironing board with no iron, a dial unit without the rest of the telephone, a boat and other water toys but no water. Most of the children set about playing eagerly and happily. They make up for the missing parts imaginatively. They use paper as water on which to sail a boat, or they use their fist for a telephone.

On the second day of observation we see a group of children who behave quite differently. They seem unable to play constructively, unable to fit the toys into meaningful and satisfying activities. They play roughly with the toys, occasionally jumping on one and trying to break it. If they draw with the crayons, they scribble like younger children. They whine and nag at the adult who is present. One of them lies on the floor, stares at the ceiling, and recites nursery rhymes as if in a trance.

What accounts for the differences in behavior of these two sets of youngsters? Is the second group suffering from some sort of emotional disturbance? Have some of these children been mistreated at home? Actually, the children in the second group are the same as those in the first group; they are simply in a later stage of the experiment. They are showing the symptoms of frustration, which has been deliberately created in the following way.

After playing happily with the half-toys, as described earlier, the children were given an added experience. An opaque screen was removed, allowing them to see that they were in a larger room containing not only the half-toys but other more elaborate and attractive toys. This part of the room contained a table for the chair, a dial and bell for the telephone, a pond of real water for the boat. When we see the unhappy children in the later stage of the experiment, they are separated by a wire screen from the more desirable toys. The are denied the ''whole'' toys and can use only the ''part'' ones. They are frustrated.

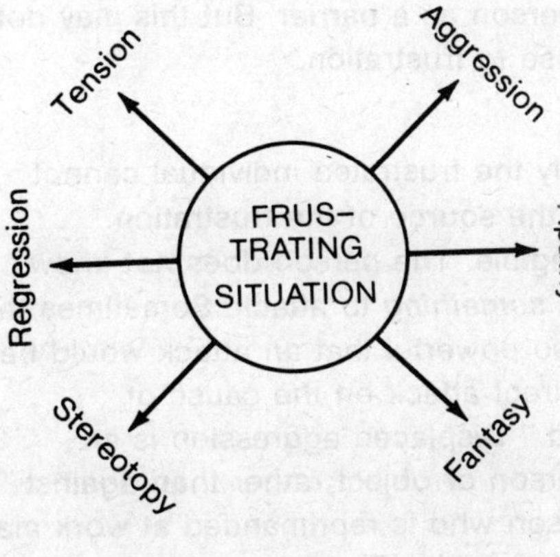

Fig. 15-5 Some reactions to frustration

Any individual can show one or more of these reactions

Why was the half-toy situation satisfying the first time and frustrating the second? The answer is easy to find. Goal-seeking behavior was satisfied the first time, as the children played happily with the available toys. In the second stage they knew of the existence of the more attractive toys, and so a new goal had been set up. The first day the goal was attainable; the second day it was not. To play now with the half-toys is to be stopped short of a richer experience, and hence is frustrating. Frustration is thus a relative matter; a person may be quite satisfied with a life situation until confronted with a friend who has achieved more.

This experiment illustrates a number of immediate responses to frustration (see Figure 15-5). In discussing some of these responses, we shall refer to additional details of the experiment and draw illustrations from other experiments and from the frustrating experiences of everyday life.

Restlessness and Tension

In the toy experiment one of the first evidences of frustration shown by the children was an excess of movement: fidgeting about and generally restless behavior. This restlessness was associated with many actions indicating unhappiness: whimpering, sighing, complaining. Unhappy actions were recorded for less than 20 percent of the children in the free-play situation but for over 85 percent in the frustrating situation.

An increase in tension and in the level of excitement also occurs when adults are blocked and thwarted. They blush or tremble or clench their fists. Children under tension fall back upon thumb-sucking and nail-biting; adults also turn to nail-biting, as well as to smoking and gum-chewing, as outlets for their restlessness and tensions.

Aggression

Closely related to increased tension and restless movements are feelings of anger that may lead to destructiveness and hostile attacks. In the toy experiment, kicking, knocking, breaking, and destroying were greatly increased following frustration. Only a few children did any kicking or knocking in the original free-play situation, but the majority did so after becoming frustrated.

DIRECT AGGRESSION. Sometimes aggression is expressed directly against the individual or object that is the source of the frustration. In ordinary play situations, when one small child takes a toy from another child, the second is likely to attack the first in an attempt to regain the toy. For adults, aggression may be verbal rather than physical—the victim of a slighting remark usually replies in kind. The anger engendered when one is blocked tends to find expression in some kind of direct attack.

Because the wire barrier was the source of the blocking in the toy experiment, the children's first attempt at problem-solving was to get by the barrier or remove it. Aggression of this kind need not be hostile; it may be a learned way of solving a problem. When the obstacle is another person, the first tendency is to attack, treating that person as a barrier. But this may not be the only form of aggression in response to frustration.

DISPLACED AGGRESSION. Frequently the frustrated individual cannot satisfactorily express aggression against the source of the frustration. Sometimes the source is vague and intangible. The person does not know what to attack, yet feels angry and seeks *something* to attack. Sometimes the person responsible for the frustration is so powerful that an attack would be dangerous. When circumstances block direct attack on the cause of frustration, aggression may be "displaced." Displaced aggression is an aggressive action against an innocent person or object rather than against the actual cause of the frustration. A person who is reprimanded at work may take out his unexpressed resentment on his family. The tongue-lashing Bill gives his roommate may be related to the poor grade Bill received on the midterm quiz. The child who is not getting along well with his playmates may pull the tail of his cat.

The practice of "scapegoating" is an example of displaced aggression. An innocent victim is blamed for one's troubles and becomes the object of aggression. Prejudice against minority groups has a large element of displaced aggression, or scapegoating. The fact that from 1882 to 1930 the price of cotton in certain regions of the South was negatively correlated with the number of lynchings in the same regions (the lower the price of cotton, the higher the number of lynchings) suggests that the mechanism of displaced aggression may have been involved. The greater the economic frustration, the greater the likelihood that aggression would be displaced against the blacks, a group serving as a scapegoat, since they were not responsible for the price of cotton.

An experiment with boys at a summer camp shows the relationship between frustration and scapegoating. The boys were required to participate in a lengthy and boring testing session which ran overtime so that they missed their weekly outing to the local movie. A survey measuring attitudes toward Japanese and Mexicans given before and after the testing session showed a significant increase in unfriendly feelings. The boys displaced their anger verbally toward remote peoples rather than expressing it directly toward the administrators of the tests (Miller and Bugelski, 1948).

Apathy

One of the factors complicating the study of human behavior is the tendency for different individuals to respond to similar situations in a variety of ways. Thus, although a common response to frustration is active aggression, another response is its opposite—apathy, indifference, withdrawal. We do not know why one person reacts with aggression and another with apathy to the same situation, but it seems likely that learning is an important factor; reactions to frustration can be learned in much the same manner as other behaviors. Children who strike out angrily when frustrated and find that their needs are then satisfied (either through their own efforts or because a parent rushes to placate them) will probably resort to the same behavior the next time their motives are thwarted. Children whose aggressive outbursts are never successful, who find they have no power to satisfy their needs by means of their own actions, may well resort to apathy and withdrawal when confronted with a frustrating situation.

LEARNED HELPLESSNESS. Studies with animals have demonstrated a reaction that has been called "learned helplessness." A dog placed in a shuttle box (an apparatus with two compartments separated by a barrier) quickly learns to jump to the opposite compartment to escape an electric shock delivered to its feet through a grid on the floor. If a light is turned on a few seconds before the grid is electrified, the dog can learn to avoid the shock entirely by jumping to the safe compartment on signal. However, if the dog has previously been placed in a situation where shocks are unavoidable and inescapable—where nothing it does terminates the shock—then it has great difficulty learning the avoidance response when appropriate. The animal simply sits and takes the shock, even though an easy jump to the opposite compartment would eliminate the discomfort. Some dogs never learn, even if the experimenter demonstrates the proper procedure by carrying them over the barrier. The dogs had previously learned that they were helpless to avoid the shock, and this *learned helplessness* was very difficult to overcome (Seligman, 1975).

Buchenwald, April 1945

A liberation-day picture shows prisoners staring dully at their rescuers, still unable to comprehend that freedom has come.

EXPERIENCES OF PRISONERS OF WAR. Studies of inmates in concentration or prisoner-of-war camps indicate that many prisoners develop attitudes of detachment and extreme indifference in the face of continual deprivation, torture, and threats of death. In fact, apathy may be a "normal" reaction to frustrating conditions of long duration from which there is no hope of escape. Interviews with American servicemen released from prison camps after the Korean War showed that almost all experienced, at some time during their imprisonment, a period characterized by listlessness, indifference to the immediate situation, and total lack of emotion. Since these men could respond appropriately when spoken to, and since their speech and behavior did not suggest psychosis, the reaction has been described as apathy. The most severe of such "apathy reactions" frequently resulted in death. Two remedies seemed capable of saving the man close to death; getting him on his feet and doing something, no matter how trivial, and getting him interested in some current or future problem. Usually the efforts and support of a friend helped the individual to snap out of a state of apathy (Strassman, Thaler, and Schein, 1956).

Concern over the reactions of American prisoners during the Korean War led the military to develop programs aimed at preparing servicemen to cope with the frustrations of imprisonment. Although detailed studies of American prisoners returned from Viet Nam have yet to be released, reports indicate that the programs were successful. Knowing how to keep physically and mentally active (e.g., by following a daily schedule that included calisthenics and classes taught by fellow prisoners) and how to organize themselves so as to delegate responsibility, provide mutual support, and plan for emergencies apparently did much to help the soldiers combat apathy and feelings of helplessness. These men, on the whole, returned from imprisonment in much better condition than did the U.S. Korean War prisoners who had not been taught explicit methods for coping.

Fantasy

When problems become too much for us, we sometimes seek the "solution" of escape into a dream world, a solution based in *fantasy* rather than reality. This was the solution of the child in the toy experiment, who lay on the floor reciting nursery rhymes and of other children in the experiment who in imagination crossed the barrier by talking about the whole toys on the other side. One girl fished through the wire, imagining the floor on the other side to be the pond that was actually out of reach.

Unrealistic solutions are not limited to children. The pin-up girls in soldiers' barracks symbolize a fantasy life that goes on when normal social life with women is frustrated. Experiments have shown that men on a starvation diet lose their interest in women and instead hang on their walls pictures of prepared food cut from magazines (Guetzkow and Bowman, 1946).

As we shall see in the next chapter, severe and continuous frustration may produce such complete escape into fantasy that the individual loses the ability to distinguish between fantasy and the real world.

Stereotypy

Another consequence of frustration is *stereotypy* in behavior—that is, a tendency to exhibit repetitive, fixated behavior. Ordinary problem-solving requires flexibility, striking out in new directions when the original path to the goal is blocked. When repeated frustration baffles a person, some flexibility appears to be lost, and the person will stupidly make the same effort again and again, though experience has shown its futility.

For example, a white rat can be taught to jump to one of a pair of stimulus cards attached to windows by so arranging the cards that the rat finds food behind the positive card but is punished if it jumps to the negative card. The positive card may be one with a black circle on a white background, the negative one a white circle on a black background. The cards are so arranged that the rat knocks over the positive card when it hits it, thus gaining access to a platform where there is a food reward. If the rat jumps against the negative card, the card does not give way. Instead, the rat bumps against the card and falls into a net. By varying the positions of the

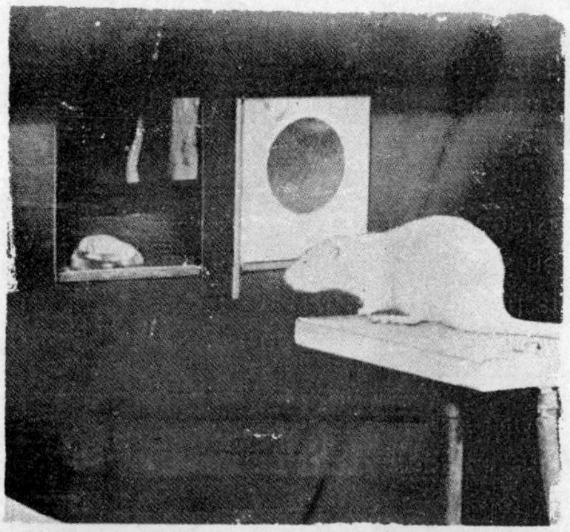

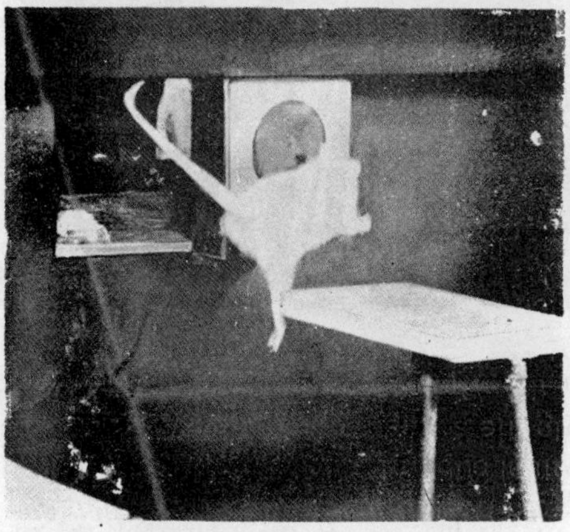

Fig. 15-6 Stereotypy

Shown here is the apparatus used in the experiment on stereotypy. Top: The left window is open, the food exposed, and the frustrated rat seems to pay attention to it. Bottom: The rat's jump remains fixated; that is, despite the open window, the rat continues to jump to the right and to bump its nose and fall into the net below. (After Maier, 1949)

cards, the experimenter can teach the rat to jump consistently to the positive card regardless of which side it is on. The rat jumps on every trail to avoid a blast of air aimed at it from behind the start platform.

This discrimination experiment is converted into a frustration experiment by making the problem insoluble. That is, by arranging it so that each of the two cards leads half the time to reward (positive reinforcement) and half the time to punishment (negative reinforcement), regardless of its position on the left or the right. Hence, whatever choice the animal makes is "correct" only half the time. The result is that the rat, forced to jump, tends to form a stereotyped habit of jumping regularly to one side (either to the right or to the left) and no longer pays attention to which card is exposed. The rat is still rewarded half the time and punished half the time after having adopted this stereotyped habit.

Once the stereotyped habit has been adopted, it is very resistant to change—so much so that it has been called an "abnormal fixation." For example, if the rat that has come to jump regularly to the right is now punished on every jump, it may continue to jump to the right for as many as 200 trials, even though the left window remains open as an easy and safe alternative (Figure 15-6). The behavior is so stereotyped that psychologically the alternative no longer exists for the rat.

Further studies must be made before we know just what analogies are permissible between human behavior and these experimental results. It is quite possible that some forms of persistent behavior, such as thumb-sucking in young children or stuttering, have become fixated because punishment and repeated frustration have intensified the undesirable responses. The persistence of difficulties in arithmetic and reading among some bright children also may be explained in part as a consequence of errors stereotyped by early frustration.

Regression

Regression is defined as a return to more primitive modes of behavior, that is, to modes of behavior characterizing a younger age. There are two interpretations of regression. One is that in the midst of insecurity the individual attempts to return to a period of past security. The older child seeks the love and affection bestowed upon him in childhood by behaving again as he did when younger: crying, seeking parental caresses, and so on. This type of regression is called *retrogressive behavior,* a return to behavior once engaged in.

The second interpretation of regression is that the childish behavior following frustration is simply a more primitive kind of behavior, not actually a return to earlier behavior. This kind of regression, in contrast to retrogression, is called *primitivation.* Thus the adult accustomed to the restraints of civilized behavior may become so upset by frustration as to lose control and start a fistfight, even though he did no fistfighting as a child.

Both forms of regression may, of course, occur together. In the toy experiment discussed earlier, regression was shown through decrease in the constructiveness of play. We consider that this decreased constructiveness is a form of primitivation rather than retrogression, because we do not ask whether the child returns to a mode of play characteristic of *him* at an earlier

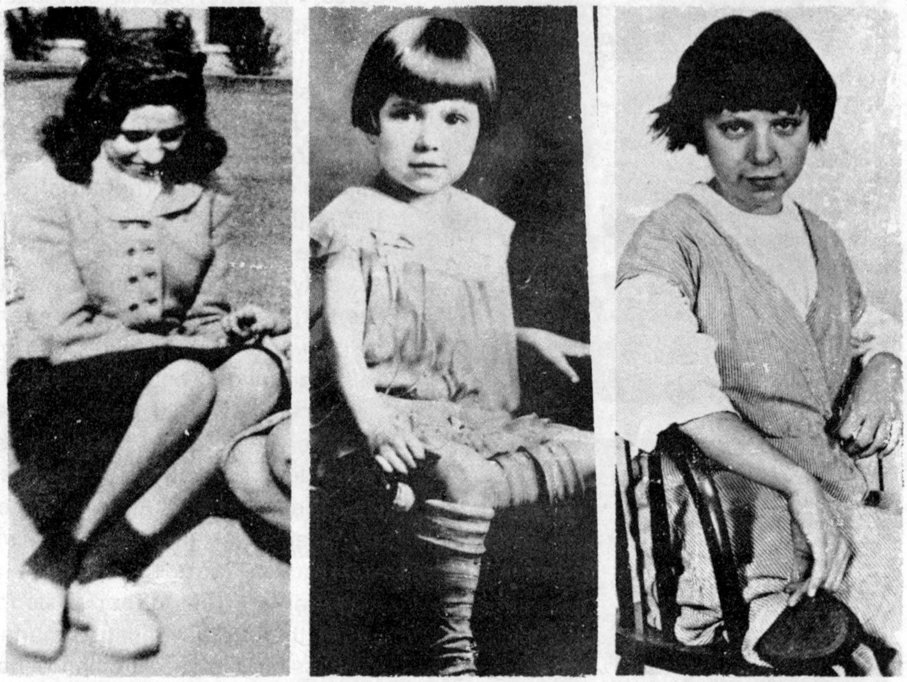

A case of extreme regression

The 17-year-old girl in the left picture found an old photograph of herself taken when she was five (center). She then cut her hair and tried to look as much as she could like the child in the photograph (right). She came from a very unstable home, and showed her first signs of disturbance at age 4 when her parents began to quarrel violently. When the girl was 7 her mother refused sexual relations with the father; the girl, however, slept in her father's bed until she was 13. The mother, suspecting that her daughter was being incestuously seduced, obtained legal custody and moved with her to a separate home. The girl resented the separation from her father, quarreled with her mother, and became a disciplinary problem at school. On the girl's insistence she and her mother visited the father after 3 years separation and found him living with a young girl. A violent scene ensued, and again the mother refused to let her daughter stay with the father. After this the girl became sullen and withdrawn and would not attend school. In one of her destructive rampages through the house she found the early picture of herself. She altered her appearance, became infantile and untidy, and no longer controlled her urine. She appeared to have regressed to a more desirable period in life that antedated conflicts and jealousies. (Adapted from Masserman, 1961, pp. 70–71, case of Dr John Romano)

age. Without careful case studies we have no way of being sure, however, that the behavior was not in fact retrogressive. It is a safe conjecture that it was in some instances. By means of a rating scale, each child's play in both the free and the frustrating situation was appraised as to its degree of constructiveness—that is, (1) according to its likeness to the well-thought-out and systematic play of older children, or (2) according to its similarity to the fragmentary play of younger children. As a consequence of frustration the play tended to deteriorate. Drawing became scribbling; instead of pretending to iron clothes on the ironing board, children would knock the board down. In this experiment the total loss in maturity shown amounted to about 18 months of mental age; that is, the play of these children became like that of children about a year and a half younger.

Anxiety

We have discussed a number of observable reactions to frustration. In order to explain these reactions (as well as reactions to other forms of stress), psychologists have introduced the concept of *anxiety*. Any situation that threatens the well-being of the organism is assumed to produce a state of anxiety. Conflicts and other types of frustration that block the individual's progress toward a goal provide one source of anxiety. Threat of physical harm, threats to one's self-esteem, and pressure to perform beyond one's capabilities also produce anxiety. By anxiety we mean the unpleasant emotion characterized by the terms "worry," "apprehension," "dread," and "fear" that we all experience at times in varying degrees. Since there is little agreement on a more precise definition, we will not attempt to provide one.

Freud, who was one of the first to focus on the importance of anxiety, differentiated between *objective anxiety* and *neurotic anxiety.* Objective anxiety was a realistic response to perceived danger in the environment;

ANXIETY

Freud viewed objective anxiety as synonymous with *fear.* Neurotic anxiety stemmed from an *unconscious* conflict within the individual; since the conflict was unconscious, the person was not aware of the reason for his anxiety. Many psychologists still find a distinction between fear and anxiety meaningful. But since it is not clear that the two emotions can be differentiated, either on the basis of physiological responses or the individual's descriptions of feelings, we will use the terms anxiety and fear interchangeably. Just as there are varying degrees of anxiety—ranging from mild apprehension to panic—there are probably varying degrees of awareness of the cause of one's discomfort. Often the individual who is suffering from an internal conflict has some idea why, even though unable to specify clearly all the factors involved.

Because anxiety involves a state of tension and discomfort, the individual is motivated to avoid or to reduce it. Over the course of a lifetime, a person develops various methods of coping with anxiety-producing situations and with feelings of anxiety. We will look at some of these *coping behaviors* shortly, but first let us examine the concept of anxiety in a little more detail.

Munch, Edvard. *Anxiety.* (1896). Lithograph, $16\frac{3}{8} \times 15\frac{3}{8}$″. Collection, The Museum of Modern Art, New York.

Theories of Anxiety

ANXIETY AS AN UNCONSCIOUS CONFLICT. Freud believed that neurotic anxiety was the result of an unconscious conflict between id impulses (mainly sexual and aggressive) and the constraints imposed by the ego and superego. Many of the id impulses pose a threat to the individua either because they are contradictory to personal values or because they are in opposition to what society will permit. For example, a young girl who has strong hostile feelings toward her mother may not consciously acknowledge these feelings because they conflict with her belief that one should love one's parents. To acknowledge her true feelings would produce anxiety because it would destroy her self-concept as a loving daughter and would place her in danger of losing her mother's love and support. Whenever she begins to feel angry toward her mother, anxiety is also aroused, serving as a *signal* of potential danger. She must then engage in certain defensive maneuvers to cope with the danger. These maneuvers, the *defense mechanisms* to be discussed in the next section, form an important part of Freud's theory of neurotic behavior. They are all methods for keeping anxiety-producing impulses out of conscious awareness.

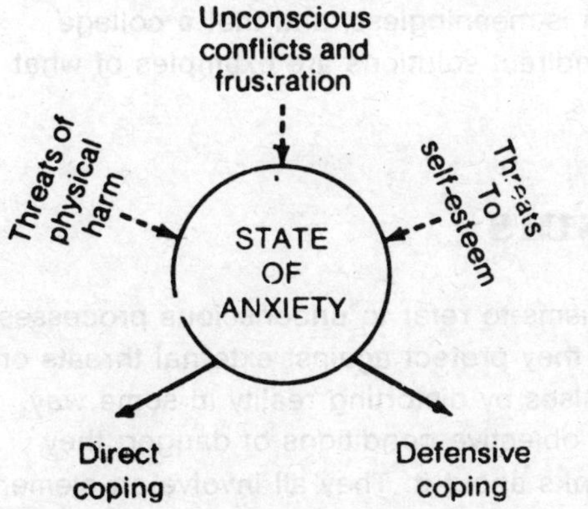

Fig. 15-7 Antecedent conditions and consequences of anxiety

Any threat to the well-being of the organism is assumed to arouse a state of anxiety. The organism responds by directly coping with the situation and/or trying to defend against anxious feelings by distorting perception of the situation.

ANXIETY AS A LEARNED RESPONSE. In contrast to psychoanalytic theory, the behaviorist or learning theory approach focuses not on internal conflicts but on ways in which anxiety becomes associated with certain situations via learning. In an earlier chapter (p. 355) we saw how a young child learned to be afraid of a rabbit because of its association with a fear-producing stimulus (a loud sound), and how this fear generalized to other furry objects. Sometimes fears learned in childhood are very difficult to extinguish. Because the first reaction is to avoid or escape the anxiety-producing situation, the child does not get a chance to find out that the situation is no longer dangerous. Avoidance responses are notoriously difficult to extinguish for this reason. An animal that has learned to jump the barrier in a shuttle box to avoid shock may continue to jump to the opposite compartment indefinitely, even though no shock has followed the signal since the first few trials of the experiment. It never gives itself a chance to learn that the shock has been turned off.

Similarly, the child who has had a bad encounter with a dog and thereafter runs on seeing a dog will not have the opportunity of discovering that most dogs are friendly. Since running away from a dog is reinforcing (because it reduces fear), the child is apt to continue this behavior. And avoiding the anxiety-producing situation gives the child no chance to reappraise the nature of the threat or to learn how to cope with the situation. Situations that were anxiety-producing in childhood may continue to be avoided in adulthood because the individual has never reappraised the threat or developed ways of coping with it.

Coping with Anxiety

Because anxiety is a very uncomfortable emotion that threatens our well-being, it cannot be tolerated for long. We are strongly motivated to do something to alleviate the discomfort. Sometimes we attempt to deal directly with the anxiety-producing situation by appraising the situation and then doing something to change or avoid it. These methods are called *direct coping.* Other methods focus on defending us against anxious feelings without trying to deal directly with the anxiety-producing situation; these are called *defensive coping.* They include various ways of distorting one's perception of the situation to make it less threatening, as well as deadening anxiety by means of drugs or alcohol. In any anxiety-producing situation an individual may employ a combination of direct and defensive coping methods.

As an illustration, consider the actions a student might take when confronted with a warning of failure in a course necessary for graduation. The student may be able to take direct action—confer with the professor to find out what can be done to raise the grade, devise a work schedule that will fulfill the requirements, and then start it. Or the student might defend against anxiety by refusing to acknowledge the possibility of failing the course or by deciding that graduation is meaningless, and that a college degree is really unnecessary. These indirect solutions are examples of what have been called *defense mechanisms.*

Defense Mechanisms

Freud used the term defense mechanisms to refer to unconscious processes that defend a person against anxiety; they protect against external threats or against internal anxiety-arousing impulses by distorting reality in some way. Defense mechanisms do not alter the objective conditions of danger; they simply change the way the person thinks about it. They all involve an element of *self-deception.*

Defense mechanisms differ in the extent of distortion or self-deception involved and in the source of danger they ward off. The most primitive defense against *external* threat is *denial of reality*—the individual tries to block out disturbing realities by refusing to acknowledge them. The mother of a child who is fatally ill may refuse to admit that there is anything wrong even though she is fully informed of the diagnosis and expected outcome. Because she cannot tolerate the pain that acknowledging reality would produce, she resorts to the defense mechanism of denial, at least for a while. Less extreme forms of denial may be seen in individuals who consistently ignore criticism or fail to perceive that others are angry with them.

The most primitive defense against *internal* threat is *repression*—impulses or memories that are too threatening are excluded from conscious awareness. Freud believed that repression of certain childhood impulses is universal. For example, he maintained that all young boys have feelings of sexual attraction toward the mother and feelings of rivalry and hostility toward the father (the Oedipus complex); these impulses are repressed to avoid the painful consequences of acting upon them. In later life feelings and memories that would cause anxiety because they are inconsistent with one's self-concept may be repressed. Feelings of hostility toward a loved one and experiences of failure may be banished from memory.

Freud viewed repression as the underlying process upon which the other defense mechanisms are built. All defense mechanisms attempt to keep thoughts or impulses out of awareness, but they employ additional means to make the inhibition more secure. For example, in the defense mechanism called *projection* one's own undesirable impulses are attributed to other people, thus making doubly certain they will not be recognized as our own.

A number of defense mechanisms have been proposed, but there is no agreement on a list of "basic" defense mechanisms or on the psychological processes involved. We will present some of those considered most important. In the discussion of defense mechanisms that follows, three precautions should be kept in mind.

1. Defense mechanisms are psychological constructs inferred from observations of the way people behave. They are useful ways of summarizing what we think is going on when we observe behavior. But although some of the mechanisms are supported by experimental evidence, others have little scientific verification.
2. Labeling a person's behavior (e.g., as projection, rationalization, or repression) may provide useful descriptive information, but it is not an explanation of the behavior. A full explanation requires understanding the needs that cause the person to rely on defense mechanisms in dealing with problems.
3. All the mechanisms are to be found in the everyday behavior of normal people. Used in moderation, they increase satisfaction in living and are therefore helpful modes of adjustment. It is only when the mechanisms become the dominant modes of problem-solving that they indicate personality maladjustment.

Rationalization

When the fox in Aesop's fable rejected the grapes he could not reach "because they were sour," he illustrated a defense mechanism known as *rationalization.* Rationalization does not mean "to act rationally"; it means assigning logical or socially desirable motives to what we do so that we *seem* to have acted rationally or properly. Rationalization serves two purposes: (1) it eases our disappointment when we fail to reach a goal—"I didn't want it anyway"—and (2) it provides us with acceptable motives for our behavior. If we act impulsively, or for motives that we do not wish to acknowledge even

to ourselves, we may interpret what we have done so as to place our behavior in a more favorable light.

In the search for the "good" reason rather than the "true" reason, a number of excuses can be put forth. These excuses are usually plausible, and the circumstances they justify may be true ones; they simply do not tell the whole story. A few illustrations may serve to show how common rationalization is.

1. Liking or disliking as an excuse: The girl who was not invited to a party said she would not have gone if asked because she did not like some of the people involved.
2. Blaming other people and circumstances as an excuse: "Mother failed to wake me." "I had too many other things to do." Both statements may be true, but they are not the real reason for failure to perform the behavior in question. If the individual had been really concerned, he could have set his alarm or found the time.
3. Necessity as an excuse: "I bought this new model because the old car would have had a lot of expensive repairs coming up soon."

While the foregoing examples show individuals fooling themselves instead of others, the excuses are of the sort that people might consciously use to put themselves in a favorable light. We therefore need a more convincing illustration to show us that rationalization may be used when individuals are completely unenlightened about the reasons for their conduct—when, in other words, rationalization is unconsciously motivated. Such an illustration is provided by the results of experiments on posthypnotic suggestion.

A subject under hypnosis is told that when he wakes from the trance he will watch the pocket of the hypnotist. When the hypnotist removes a handkerchief from the pocket, the subject will raise the window. The subject is told that he will not remember the hypnotist's telling him to do this. Aroused from the trance, the subject feels a little drowsy, but presently circulates among the people in the room and carries on a normal conversation, all the while furtively watching the hypnotist's pocket. When the hypnotist in a casual manner removes his handkerchief, the subject feels an impulse to open the window; he takes a step in that direction, but hesitates. Unconsciously, he mobilizes his wishes to be a reasonable person; so, seeking a reason for his impulse to open the window, he says "Isn't it a little stuffy in here?" Having found the needed excuse, he opens the window and feels more comfortable (Hilgard, 1965).

Projection

All of us have undesirable traits or qualities that we do not acknowledge even to ourselves. One unconscious mechanism that protects us from acknowledging them is called *projection.* In projection we protect ourselves from recognizing our own undesirable qualities by assigning them in exaggerated amount to other people. Suppose you have a tendency to be critical of or unkind to other people, but would dislike yourself if you were consciously aware of this tendency. If you are convinced that those around you are cruel or unkind, then any harsh treatment you give them is not based upon *your* bad qualities. You are simply giving them what they deserve. If you can assure yourself that everybody else cheats in college examinations, your unacknowledged tendency to take some academic shortcuts is not so bad. Projection is really a form of rationalization, but the tendency to projection is so pervasive in our culture that it merits discussion in its own right.

An experiment with fraternity members at a university highlights the pervasiveness of projection. The members of each fraternity were asked to rate the other members on such undesirable traits as stinginess, obstinacy, and disorderliness. Each student also was asked to rate himself on each of these traits. Of interest here are those students who possessed an undesirable trait to a high degree (as indicated by how others rated them) and yet were unaware of possessing it (as indicated by their rating of themselves). These individuals tended to assign that undesirable trait to other students to a far greater extent than did the rest of the students. The correlations on which these interpretations are based were all low, but they were consistently in the direction that would be expected if they were interpreted as indicating a projection mechanism (Sears, 1936).

Reaction Formation

It is sometimes possible to conceal a motive from oneself by giving strong expression to its opposite. Such a tendency is called *reaction formation*. The mother of an unwanted child may feel guilty about not welcoming her child, and so becomes overindulgent and overprotective of the child in order to assure the child of her love and also, perhaps, to assure herself that she is a good mother.

In one case, a mother who wished to do everything for her daughter could not understand why the child was so unappreciative. At great sacrifice she had the daughter take expensive piano lessons. She sat beside the girl to assist her in the daily practice sessions. While she thought she was being extremely kind to her child, she was actually very demanding and, in fact, hostile. She was unaware of her own hostility, but, when confronted with it, admitted that as a child she had hated piano lessons. Under the conscious guise of being kind, she was unconsciously being cruel to her daughter. The daughter, vaguely sensing what was going on, developed the symptoms that brought her to a child-guidance clinic.

There is always the possibility that reaction formation is active among some of those who engage in "anti" activities, such as censoring pornographic literature or preventing cruelty to animals. The censoring individuals may actually be fascinated by such literature. They wage a campaign against it in order to fight its fascination for them and to convince others of their "purity." Among the ardent antivivisectionists there undoubtedly are some who fear their own tendency toward cruelty so deeply that they become sentimental about protecting animals from the implied cruelty of others.

The existence of reaction formation in some people does not mean that motives can never be taken at their face values. Not all reformers are moved to action by veiled or hidden impulses. Real abuses need to be corrected, and concerned individuals will devote their efforts to such causes. But those who are defending against unacceptable impulses can usually be distinguished from the socially concerned reformers by the excessiveness with which they pursue their campaigns and by occasional slips that reveal their true motivation (see Figure 15-8).

> . . . I read [a magazine article] . . . on your work on alcoholism . . . I am surprised that anyone who is as well educated as you must be to hold the position that you do would stoop to such depths as to torture helpless little cats in the pursuit of a cure for alcoholics. . . . A drunkard does not want to be cured—a drunkard is just a weak minded idiot who belongs in the gutter and should be left there. Instead of torturing helpless little cats why not torture the drunks or better still exert your would-be noble effort toward getting a bill passed to *exterminate* the drunks. They are not any good to anyone or themselves and are just a drain on the public, having to pull them off the street, jail them, then they have to be fed while there and it's against the law to feed them arsenic so there they are. . . . If people are such weaklings the world is better off without them.
>
> . . . My greatest wish is that you have brought home to you a torture that will be a thousand fold greater than what you have, and are doing to the little animals. . . . If you are an example of what a noted psychiatrist should be I'm glad I am just an ordinary human being without a letter after my name. I'd rather be just myself with a clear conscience, *knowing I have not hurt any living creature,* and can sleep without seeing frightened, terrified dying cats—because I know they must die after you have finished with them. No punishment is too great for you and I hope I live to read about your mangled body and long suffering before you finally die—and I'll laugh long and loud.

Fig. 15-8 Reaction formation

Reaction formation can be illustrated with excerpts from a letter by an antivivisectionist sent to Dr. Masserman, who has done research on alcoholism using cats as experimental subjects. (After Masserman, 1961, p. 38)

Intellectualization

Intellectualization is an attempt to gain detachment from an emotionally threatening situation by dealing with it in abstract, intellectual terms. This kind of defense is frequently a necessity for people who must deal with life and death matters in their daily job. The doctor or nurse who is continually confronted with human suffering cannot afford to become emotionally involved with each patient. A certain amount of detachment may be essential for competent functioning. We saw in the chapter on emotion (p. 354) how adopting a defense of intellectualization can lessen distress when viewing a disturbing scene.

Adolescents, alarmed by the emotions accompanying newly intensified sexual impulses, sometimes go through a period when they scorn all emotion and try to make discussions as abstract and impersonal as possible. Intellectualization is a problem only when it becomes such a pervasive life-style that individuals cut themselves off from all emotional experiences.

Fig. 15-9 Undoing as a defense

Both children and adults may attempt to reduce anxiety by a magical, ritualistic protection against a worry or fear. The true basis for the anxiety is often unacknowledged, as indeed it is in the Milne poem. The child's fears are not really "the bears who wait at the corners." (From *When we were very young*, by A. A. Milne)

LINES AND SQUARES

Whenever I walk in a London street,
I'm ever so careful to watch my feet;
And I keep in the squares,
And the masses of bears,
Who wait at the corners all ready to eat
The sillies who tread on the lines of the street,
Go back to their lairs,
And I say to them, "Bears,
Just look how I'm walking
in all of the squares!"

Undoing

Undoing is an action that is designed to prevent or atone for some unacceptable thought or impulse. Such actions are usually repetitive and ritualistic—for example, avoiding stepping on the lines in the sidewalk or performing certain actions a fixed number of times (see Figure 15-9). Undoing is related to magical or superstitious thinking and has its roots in childhood. As children we are taught to apologize or make restitution when we have done something bad. If we say we are sorry and accept punishment, then our bad deed is negated and we can start again with a fresh conscience. Confession and acts of penance often forestall more serious punishment. From this sequence children may come to believe that certain acts have the power to atone for wrongdoing or to prevent something bad from happening (e.g., assembling your stuffed animals in a circle around your pillow and tucking yourself in just right will safeguard against the terrors of the night).

Adults have their superstitious rituals too. The baseball pitcher tugs at his cap and digs his left foot into the mound exactly three times before each pitch. The gambler blows on the dice before throwing. The actor on opening night must wear a certain article of clothing or piece of jewelry as a lucky charm. The individual associates these acts with past success and so continues them before each performance and may even feel anxious if a ritual is interfered with. They represent in a normal form the defense mechanism of undoing. In the next chapter we will see how undoing in an exaggerated form—time-consuming and elaborate rituals—shapes the behavior of the obsessive-compulsive neurotic.

Repression

Each defense mechanism is a method of protecting individuals from full awareness of impulses that they (perhaps unconsciously) would prefer to deny. If the anxiety-producing impulse is completely blocked from awareness, then we say that *repression* has occurred.

Repression must be distinguished from suppression. The process of suppression is one of deliberate self-control—keeping impulses, tendencies, or wishes in check and perhaps holding them privately while denying them publicly. In such instances, the individuals are aware of suppressed impulses. In the mechanism of repression, the individuals themselves are *unaware* of whatever it is that is repressed.

Repression, if completely successful, results in a total forgetting—a total absence of awareness of the personally unacceptable motive and a total absence of behavior resulting from such a motive. Usually, however, repression is not completely successful, and impulses find indirect expression. Many of the defense mechanisms already discussed serve repression, as they protect the individual from awareness of partially repressed impulses.

Cases of *amnesia* illustrate some aspects of repression. In one case, a man was found wandering the streets, not knowing his name or where he had come from. By means of hypnosis and other techniques it was possible to reconstruct his history and to restore most of his memory. Following domestic difficulties he had gone on a drunken spree completely out of keeping with his usual behavior, and he had subsequently suffered deep remorse. His amnesia was motivated by the desire to exclude from memory the embarrassing experiences that had occurred during this episode. He succeeded in forgetting all the events associated with the spree that might remind him of it. In this way amnesia spread, and he completely lost his sense of personal identity. When his memories returned, he could recall events before the drinking episode as well as subsequent happenings, but the deeper repression of the period of which he was most ashamed successfully protected him from recalling its disagreeable events.

Displacement

The last defense mechanism to be considered is the one that best succeeds in fulfilling its function (i.e., reducing anxiety) and yet still allows some gratification of the unacceptable motive. In *displacement* a motive whose gratification is blocked in one form is directed into a new channel. We saw an example of displacement when we talked about anger that could not be expressed toward the source of frustration and thus was directed toward a less threatening or more readily available object.

Freud felt that displacement was the most satisfactory way of handling aggressive and sexual impulses. The basic drives could not be changed, but the object toward which the drive is directed could. For example, sexual impulses toward the parents cannot be safely gratified, but such impulses can be displaced toward a more suitable love object. Erotic impulses that cannot be expressed directly may be expressed indirectly in creative activities such as art, poetry, and music. Hostile impulses may find socially acceptable expression through participation in physical contact sports.

It seems unlikely that displacement actually eliminates the frustrated impulses, but substitute activities do help to reduce tension when a basic drive is thwarted. For example, the activities of mothering, being mothered, or seeking companionship may help reduce the tension associated with unsatisfied sexual needs.

CRITICAL DISCUSSION

Adaptive Aspects of Defense Mechanisms

Our discussion has tended to emphasize the negative aspects of defense mechanisms. But some experts feel that not enough attention has been paid to the manner in which healthy, effective people handle their frustrations and conflicts. The behaviors we have been describing as defenses against anxiety can also be viewed as distorted adaptations of effective ways for coping with conflicts—that is, they are potentially adaptive processes that have gone astray.

Most mechanisms have a positive or *coping* aspect as well as a defensive aspect. Denial, the refusal to face painful thoughts or feelings, is a form of selective awareness or attention. Its positive aspect is *concentration,* the ability to temporarily set aside painful thoughts in order to stick to the task at hand. Projection is an exaggerated and erroneous sensitivity to another person's unexpressed feelings or thoughts. A positive form of sensitivity would be *empathy,* the ability to appreciate how another person feels. Table 15-1 lists some basic processes, or mechanisms, each followed by its defensive aspect and its coping aspect. For any given conflict situation an individual might use one or more of these mechanisms in its defensive form, its coping form, or a combination of both. One estimate of a person's mental health would be based on the extent to which he habitually uses these mechanisms in a coping manner rather than a defensive manner.

TABLE 15-1
Mechanisms and their manifestations

MECHANISM	AS A DEFENSE	AS A METHOD OF COPING
Discrimination: ability to separate ideas from feelings.	**Intellectualization:** severs ideas from their appropriate emotions.	**Objectivity:** separates ideas from feelings to achieve a rational evaluation or judgment when necessary.
Means-end symbolization: ability to analyze experience, to anticipate outcomes, to entertain alternatives.	**Rationalization:** offers apparently plausible explanation for behavior to conceal nature of underlying impulse.	**Logical analysis:** analyzes carefully the causal aspects of situations.
Selective awareness: ability to focus attention.	**Denial:** refuses to face painful thoughts or feelings.	**Concentration:** temporarily sets aside painful thoughts in order to stick to task at hand.
Sensitivity: apprehension of another's unexpressed feelings or ideas.	**Projection:** unrealistically attributes an objectionable tendency of his own to another person instead of recognizing it as part of himself.	**Empathy:** puts himself in the other person's place and appreciates how the other fellow feels.
Impulse diversion: ability to modify aim or object of an impulse.	**Displacement:** temporarily and unsuccessfully represses unacceptable impulses. May displace to an inappropriate object.	**Substitution:** finds alternate channels that are socially acceptable and satisfying for expression of primitive impulses.
Impulse restraint: ability to control an impulse by inhibiting expression.	**Repression:** totally inhibits feelings or ideas. Repressed material revealed only symbolically, as in dreams.	**Suppression:** holds impulses in abeyance until the proper time and place with the proper objects.

Source: Adapted with modifications from Kroeber (1963).

Defense Mechanisms and Adjustment

People are capable of rational problem-solving—they can face a problem squarely, weigh the alternatives according to their probable consequences, and take action guided by the results of deliberation. Our knowledge of defense mechanisms tells us, however, that some behavior that appears to be activated by conscious reasoning is in fact directed by unconscious motives.

Limitations upon Direct Problem-solving

It is possible to attack and solve a personal problem as we do any other kind of problem—such as one in mathematics or science—by asking clear questions, assembling evidence, judging the possible consequences, and trying to verify in practice what we have concluded from the evidence. But there are two chief reasons why we are often not able to solve our personal problems in this straightforward, rational manner.

1. A person's motives or emotions may be so strongly involved that they distort the evidence or the problem itself, so that the person is incapable of direct problem-solving. The self-deceptive mechanisms that we have been considering tend to set up such obstacles. For example, the engineering or premedical student who is failing cannot admit his inability to pursue certain courses at a chosen college; this student must therefore find a rationalization instead of solving the academic problem. Getting sick will convert an academic problem into a health problem; becoming a subject for disciplinary action will convert an intellectual problem into a disciplinary one. When defense mechanisms hold sway, the person sets up obstacles that stand in the way of a rational solution to problems.
2. Sometimes the equation has too many unknowns. The world in which we live is not sufficiently orderly to permit fully rational problem-solving. We have to take risks based on our best estimates about the future. But while the estimate of probabilities is the most rational solution, the uncertainty involved may not satisfy us, and we may relieve our anxiety by adopting a superstitious or fatalistic solution.

Because of these limitations—both internal and external—upon purely easonable conduct, we are often tempted to fall back on irrational mechanisms.

How Defense Mechanisms May Contribute to Satisfactory Adjustment

How successfully can a person use defense mechanisms to avoid or reduce anxiety and to maintain self-esteem? If defense mechanisms were not partially successful, they would not persist as they do. They may provide a protective armor while we are learning more mature and realistic ways of solving our problems. When we no longer need the defenses, their importance fades, and we increasingly face our problems according to the demands of the total situation. The defense mechanisms thus help toward satisfactory adjustment in several ways.

1. *They give us time to solve problems that might otherwise overwhelm us.* Being able to rationalize failures that would otherwise cause us to despair, or to find partial justification for conduct that would otherwise make us despise ourselves, sustains us until we can work out better solutions to our conflicts. These defense mechanisms provide palliatives comparable to those drugs that reduce symptoms without curing disease. Some of the antihistamines, for example, relieve the sneezing, itching, and tearing of hayfever victims until they take the pollen tests and allergy shots that will get at the cause of the hayfever. The temporary relief helps them to live

more comfortably until the basic treatment—desensitization against the offending pollens—can become effective. Similarly, defense mechanisms may provide relief against anxiety until more realistic ways of solving personal problems are worked out.

2. *The mechanisms may permit experimentation with new roles and hence teach new modes of adjustment.* Even when we adopt new roles for faulty reasons, as in reaction-formation, or when we misjudge people, as in projection, we expose ourselves to corrective experiences from which we may learn. We may judge some people to be unkind, but as we discover their genuine acts of kindness we may learn to correct our errors in judgment. What begins as self-deception may provide occasions for modifying the self.
3. *Rationalization, by starting a search for reasons, may lead to rational conduct in the future.* The tendency to justify behavior that we have found satisfying may lead to false reasons, but it may also lead to a more careful analysis of cause-and-effect relationships. If the latter occurs, a present rationalization may become a future reason.

Why Defense Mechanisms May Fail to Provide Satisfactory Adjustment

Nearly all the statements just made about the usefulness of defense mechanisms can also be reversed to point up their failures. The person who depends upon defense mechanisms for protection may never be forced to learn more mature ways of behaving. The roles adopted through the mechanisms may remain unrealistic, leading to withdrawal from social contacts rather than to improved relationships with people. Rationalizations may take the form of useless rituals instead of creative effort.

Even when behavior based on defense mechanisms is socially useful, it may not prove completely satisfying to the individual as long as the motives underlying the behavior remain. Actions based on such defense mechanisms never reach their goals; the drive continues, and the resulting behavior is not fully tension-reducing.

Summary

1. *Frustration* occurs whenever ongoing, goal-seeking activity is obstructed. Environmental obstacles, social restrictions, and personal limitations all produce frustration; but one of the major sources of frustration is motivational conflicts.
2. When two motives conflict, the satisfaction of one leads to the blocking of the other. Most conflicts involve goals that are simultaneously both positive and negative; one's attitude toward such goals is *ambivalent.*
3. Some of the immediate reactions to frustration are *restlessness* and *tension, aggression, apathy, fantasy, stereotypy,* and *regression.* Individuals show considerable variability in behavior when their goal-seeking behavior is blocked.
4. Threats to one's self-esteem and physical well-being, frustration and pressures to perform beyond one's capabilities all produce *anxiety.* Freud distinguished *objective anxiety* (fear of an external threat) from *neurotic anxiety,* which stems from an internal, unconscious conflict. But this text treats fear and anxiety as synonymous. The behaviorist approach

emphasizes the association of anxiety with specific situations via learning rather than internal conflicts.

5. *Direct methods* of *coping* with anxiety involve attempts to modify the anxiety-producing situation, while *defensive coping* is concerned with reducing feelings of anxiety. The *defense mechanisms* illustrate methods of defensive coping.
6. Two of the basic defense mechanisms are (a) *denial,* which distorts external reality so that it seems less threatening, and (b) *repression,* which attempts to keep painful impulses and emotions from conscious awareness. Among the defense mechanisms found in everyday behavior are *rationalization, projection, reaction formation, intellectualization, undoing,* and *displacement*.
7. Many personal problems can be solved rationally, that is, by taking into account the evidence, the alternatives, and the consequences of each of the alternatives. But logical decision making is difficult for two reasons: (a) the person's own emotions and unconscious conflicts often get in the way of such a choice; and (b) the future is uncertain, so that there are always unknowns and risks that have to be taken. Here defense mechanisms often enter. When defense mechanisms are employed in moderation and do not exclude more realistic solutions of problems, they may increase a person's sense of well-being and so serve a useful purpose, sometimes affording protection until the person can reach a realistic solution.

Further Reading

A classic account of the defense mechanisms is given in Freud, *The ego and the mechanisms of defense* (1946). More recent treatments may be found in Coleman, *Abnormal psychology and modern life* (4th ed., 1972), and Kleinmuntz, *Essentials of abnormal psychology* (1974). A useful paperback is Mahl, *Psychological conflict and defense* (1971).

16 psychopathology

Almost everyone has periods when they feel anxious, depressed, unreasonably angry, or inadequate in dealing with life's complexities. And each of us at times resorts to self-deceptive defense mechanisms when confronted with threatening situations. Only when such reactions become habitual do we consider them *psychopathological.* The term *psychopathology* includes a variety of disorders in addition to those most people think of as "mental illness." Alcoholism, drug addiction, compulsive lying, and physical symptoms caused by emotional problems are forms of psychopathology. Psychopathology deals with "abnormal" behavior. But how do you define abnormality? As we shall see, the dividing line between "normal" and "abnormal" behavior is not clear.

Abnormal Behavior

Concept of Abnormality

A number of criteria have been used to characterize abnormal behavior. The word itself, *ab-normal,* means "away from the norm." Many characteristics, such as height, weight, and intelligence, cover a range of values when measured over a large population. Most people fall within the middle range of height; a few are abnormally tall or abnormally short. So one definition of abnormality is based on *statistical frequency;* "abnormal behavior" is that which is statistically infrequent or deviant from the norm. But this definition would classify as abnormal the person who is extremely intelligent or extremely well-adjusted. In defining abnormal behavior we must consider more than statistical frequency.

The *society* in which one lives classifies certain behavior as abnormal according to that society's *standards.* Usually, but not always, such behavior is also statistically infrequent in that society. But behavior considered normal by one society may be considered abnormal by another. For example, some American Indian tribes find nothing unusual in "hearing voices" when no one is actually talking, or in "seeing visions"—but most societies consider such behavior abnormal. In addition, the concept of abnormality may change from time to time within the same society. Twenty years ago most Americans would have considered smoking marihuana, appearing nude at the beach, or publicly displaying physical affection for a person of the same sex abnormal. Now such behavior is viewed more often as an example of a different or atypical life style than as evidence of psychopathology. Thus, normality and abnormality differ from one society to another and from time to time within the same society. An individual's behavior must be evaluated in relation to the standards of his or her social group.

A third definition of abnormal behavior is based on *adaptiveness of behavior.* According to this definition, abnormal behavior is *maladaptive;* it has adverse effects for either the individual or society. By this criterion a man who is so fearful of crowds that he cannot ride the bus to work, a girl who attempts suicide, and a child who has violent aggressive outbursts would all be classified as abnormal.

A fourth criterion looks at abnormality in terms of the individual's subjective feelings—*personal distress*—rather than behavior. Most, but not all, people diagnosed as "mentally ill" feel acutely miserable; they are anxious, depressed, or agitated and may suffer from insomnia, loss of appetite, and numerous aches and pains. In the milder forms of psychopathology, the *neuroses,* personal distress may be the only symptom; the individual's behavior may appear normal or even highly effective to the casual observer. As we shall see, some forms of psychopathology (e.g., *conversion reactions* and *psychopathic personality*) do not appear to involve any subjective distress, but most are accompanied by severe discomfort.

None of the above definitions provides a completely satisfactory description of abnormal behavior. In most instances all four criteria—statistical, social, adaptiveness of behavior, and personal distress—are used in diagnosing psychopathology. The *legal* definition of abnormality, which declares a person *insane* largely on the basis of his or her inability to judge between right and wrong, is less satisfactory for diagnostic purposes then any of the above criteria. It should be emphasized that *insanity* is a legal term and not one used by psychologists in discussing psychopathology.

Difficulty in Characterizing Normality

Normality is even more difficult to define than abnormality, particularly in a rapidly changing and complex society such as ours. Traditionally, psychologists have focused on the individual's *adjustment* to the environment. Normal personality traits were those that helped individuals to *adjust* to the world as they found it—to get along well with others and find a niche in society. Many psychologists now feel that the term "adjustment," if it is equated with conformity to what others do and think, carries too many negative connotations to describe the healthy personality. They focus on more positive attributes, such as individuality, creativity, and the fulfillment of one's potential. Maslow, for example, considered *self-actualization* to be the highest of human motives. Most of his self-actualizing individuals (see p. 392) would be considered mentally healthy.

On the other hand, few people are able to exploit their potential to the degree that Maslow's self-actualizers (e.g., Martin Luther King Jr., Pablo Casals, Adlai Stevenson, and Eleanor Roosevelt) achieved. Most of us lead fairly routine lives, restricted by the innumerable demands of daily existence. Yet we would not be considered maladjusted or mentally unhealthy. The majority of people do not meet Maslow's criteria.

Despite a lack of consensus in defining the normal personality, most psychologists would agree on the following qualities as indicative of good mental health. These characteristics do not distinguish sharply between the mentally healthy and the mentally ill; they represent traits that the normal person possesses *to a greater degree* than the individual diagnosed as abnormal.

1. *Efficient perception of reality.* The normal individual is fairly realistic in his appraisal of his own reactions and abilities and of what is going on in the world around him. He does not consistently misperceive what others say and do, and he evaluates his capabilities in a fairly realistic manner—neither overevaluating his abilities and tackling more than he can accomplish nor shying away from a difficult task because he underestimates what he can do.
2. *Self-knowledge.* The well-adjusted person has some awareness of his own motives and feelings. Although no one fully understands his feelings or behavior, the normal person has more self-awareness than one who is

mentally ill. He is not trying to hide important feelings and motives from himself.

3. *Ability to exercise voluntary control over behavior.* The normal individual feels fairly confident that he can control and direct his own behavior. He may act on impulse on occasion, but he is able to restrain his sexual and aggressive urges when necessary. He may conform or fail to conform to social norms, but the decision is a voluntary one rather than the result of uncontrollable impulses.
4. *Self-esteem and acceptance.* The well-adjusted person has some appreciation of his own self-worth and feels accepted by those around him. He is comfortable with other people and is able to react spontaneously in social situations. At the same time, he does not always feel obligated to subjugate his opinions to those of the group. Feelings of worthlessness, alienation, and a lack of acceptance by others are prevalent among those diagnosed as mentally ill.
5. *Ability to form affectionate relationships.* The normal individual is able to form close and satisfying relationsnips with other people. He is sensitive to their needs and feelings and does not make excessive demands for the gratification of his own needs. Often the mentally ill person is so concerned with protecting his own security that he becomes extremely self-centered; he is preoccupied with his own feelings and strivings and can only seek affection, without being able to reciprocate.
6. *Productivity.* A mentally healthy person is able to use his abilities—whether meager or ample—in productive activity. He has a certain enthusiasm for living and does not have to drive himself to meet the demands of the day. A chronic lack of energy and excessive susceptibility to fatigue are common symptoms of psychological tension and unresolved conflicts.

Van Gogh

Gaaguin

It is sometimes argued that people who suffer from unresolved conflicts turn to creative work because of their suffering. Artists such as Van Gogh and Gauguin were emotionally disturbed, and one wonders if their creative powers would have been as great had they been "well-adjusted." The question is debatable, but it is clear from their lives that these artists achieved their artistic productions at the cost of great pain to themselves and those close to them. Although a few people manage to turn their troubles into advantages, most are unable to use their creative abilities because of emotional conflicts that inhibit their productivity.

Varieties of Psychopathology

Psychopathology can take innumerable forms, and classification systems have been devised to make some sense out of the many kinds of behavior diagnosed as abnormal. The most widely accepted classification system groups people according to the *behavioral symptoms* they display. Individuals who behave roughly the same way are given the same label. The major diagnostic categories under this classification system are *neuroses, psychoses, psychophysiological disorders,* and *personality disorders.* Each of these is further divided into subcategories. We will briefly describe the major categories here and examine some of the subcategories in the remainder of the chapter.

NEUROSES. A major distinction is made between neuroses and psychoses. The neuroses (plural form of *neurosis*) are a less severe form of psychological disorder. They are troublesome enough to call for expert help and may occasionally require hospitalization, but they do not involve personality disintegration or loss of contact with reality. Neurotic individuals can usually get along in society even though their anxiety prevents them from functioning at full capacity. The primary symptom of neurosis is anxiety, which may be experienced openly or defended against by one of the defense mechanisms.

PSYCHOSES. The psychoses (plural form of *psychosis*) are characterized by an impairment in mental functioning that seriously interferes with the individual's ability to meet the demands of daily life. There is gross distortion of reality, so that the person can no longer distinguish between fantasy and reality. These distortions may take the form of *delusions* or *hallucinations.*

A delusion is a false belief maintained despite contradictory evidence or experience. Psychotic delusions often center around ideas of *grandeur* (I am the King of the Universe or Napoleon or Jesus Christ), *persecution* (people are talking about me, trying to poison me), *external control* (my thoughts are being controlled by radio waves from Mars or by electrical impulses from the wall sockets), or *depersonalization* (I am not a real person anymore; everything inside me—my organs and brain—has rotted away).

Hallucinations are sense experiences occurring in the absence of the appropriate external stimuli. The person may hear voices, see images, experience strange odors or tastes when no such events are taking place. Often the hallucinations reinforce the delusional beliefs. If I hear voices calling me obscene names and smell strange odors (poison gas?), what more proof do I need that my enemies are out to get me?

The psychotic individual may also show profound changes of mood (from wild excitement to vegetablelike stupor) as well as defects in language and memory.

PSYCHOPHYSIOLOGICAL DISORDERS. Psychophysiological disorders (also called psychosomatic illnesses) are physical illnesses in which psychological factors play a major role. The illness is real—for example, asthma, skin rashes, ulcers, high blood pressure, migraine headaches—but psychological stress is presumed to be an important causative factor.

PERSONALITY DISORDERS. Personality disorders are usually long-standing patterns of socially maladaptive behavior. Extreme dependency, antisocial or sexually deviant behavior, alcoholism, and drug addiction are some of the disorders included in this category. Often the individual does not experience much anxiety and has little motivation to change. There is no gross distortion of reality or intellectual impairment (except when alcoholism or drug addiction has progressed to the point of brain damage, in which case the individual might show psychotic symptoms and be classified accordingly).

These four categories of abnormal behavior will seem more meaningful after we have looked at some examples of each. In actual practice the classification system is not as satisfactory as we would like. Although agreement is fairly good in broad distinctions (such as deciding whether or not a person is psychotic), psychologists often fail to agree on more specific diagnoses (such as type of neurosis or psychosis). Each person's set of symptoms, emotional background, and so on is unique and may not fit neatly into any single category.

Imperfect as it may be, however, a classification of mental disorders is useful. A diagnostic label helps communicate information among those working with disturbed individuals. Knowing that a person is classified as *paranoid schizophrenic* tells one quite a bit about the behavior to expect. And knowing that an individual's symptoms are similar to those of other patients (whose progress followed a particular course or who have benefited from a certain kind of treatment) is also helpful.

These advantages can become disadvantages, however, if we allow a diagnostic label to carry too much weight—that is, if we overlook the unique features of each case and expect the person to conform to the classification.

Neuroses

The term *neuroses* refers to a group of disorders in which the person has developed certain behavior patterns that avoid rather than cope with problems. We noted in the preceding chapter that unresolved approach-avoidance conflicts result in feelings of anxiety, tension, and helplessness. If a realistic solution cannot be achieved, the individual either remains in a state of severe anxiety or resorts to one or more of the defense mechanisms in an attempt to reduce anxiety. In the neurotic individual this defense is seldom satisfactory for two reasons: it usually alleviates only a small part of the total anxiety; and it interferes with the person's effective functioning, thereby creating further problems.

Anxiety, then, is assumed to be at the core of all neuroses. Sometimes the anxiety is very evident. The person appears strained and tense; insomnia, indigestion, diarrhea, inability to concentrate, or sexual impotence may be present. Sometimes the anxiety is not readily apparent, but we judge from the maladaptive behavior exhibited that the individual is defending against anxiety by the extreme use of one or more defense mechanisms.

Neurotic behavior has been described as a vicious cycle. The individual feels inadequate to cope with many everyday problems, so he avoids them by defensive maneuvers; he then feels guilty, unhappy, and even more inadequate because of his failure to deal directly with situations that others handle with apparent ease. Despite the self-defeating nature of this behavior, the neurotic individual clings rigidly to established behavior patterns and seems unable to recognize alternative courses of action. This rigid adherence to self-defeating behavior patterns is known as the "neurotic paradox." Why keep on doing something that makes one so unhappy? The answer seems to be that the neurotic behavior receives strong immediate reinforcement because it reduces or avoids anxiety; the immediate rewards override the long-term consequences.

In this section we will describe five of the more common neurotic reactions: *anxiety reactions, obsessive-compulsive reactions, phobias, conversion reactions,* and *neurotic depression.* Traditionally, neurotic disorders have been classified by symptoms, but such a classification is not completely satisfactory because frequently a neurotic individual has symptoms of more than one reaction type.

Anxiety Reactions

The most common neurotic disorder is an *anxiety reaction.* Although anxiety is the predominant characteristic of neurosis, in many neurotic

CRITICAL DISCUSSION

Models of Psychopathology

In our discussion of psychopathology we have used such terms as *mental illness, behavior disorders, maladaptive behavior, personal distress* almost interchangeably. This profusion of terminology results from the fact that abnormal behavior can be considered from several different viewpoints. Because much is still unknown about the causes and cures of most of the disorders included in our classification of psychopathology, quite diverse theoretical models have been proposed (see Figure 16-1).

MEDICAL MODEL. Terms such as *mental illness* and *mental health* reflect the *medical model* of abnormal behavior that draws an analogy between physical disease and mental illness. This model assumes that abnormal behavior is the symptom of an underlying disorder of the nervous system. The medical model evolved during the nineteenth century with the gradual discovery that damage to the brain could result in thought disturbances and bizarre behavior. The concept of psychopathology as a disease process was an improvement over earlier views that attributed abnormal behavior to possession by demons or to moral corruption. It provided for much more humane treatment. Individuals suffering from diseases were not responsible for their actions and could be treated in a hospital rather than being burned at the stake as witches or sent to prison.

Today, however, many psychologists question the appropriateness of the medical model (e.g., Szasz, 1961, 1970; Bandura, 1969; Krasner and Ullmann, 1973). They point out that most forms of psychopathology have *not* been traced to disorders of the nervous system. There is no evidence that the neuroses are based on a neurological disturbance. In addition, the medical model is misleading because it suggests a sharp division between normality and abnormality. Yet often behavior is considered normal or a symptom of some underlying disturbance depending on the sociocultural group to which the person belongs, the situation in which the behavior occurs (physical aggression is normal on the football field but not in the classroom), and the age of the individual (bed-wetting and temper tantrums may be normal for a two-year old but not for an adult). Labeling a person who displays unusual behavior as "sick" places the responsibility for "cure" on medical personnel rather than on the individual and may predispose him to act even "sicker" once he is so labeled.

PSYCHOANALYTIC MODEL. The *psychoanalytic model* sees abnormal

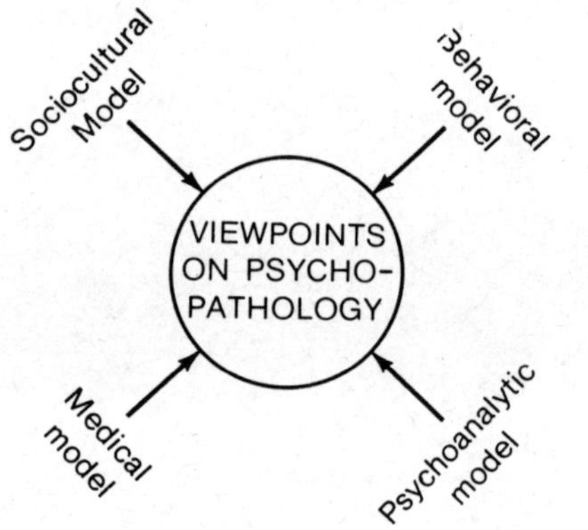

Fig. 16-1 Alternative viewpoints regarding psychopathology

reactions it is concealed by other symptoms. In anxiety reactions, however, it is very much in the open. The typical anxiety neurotic lives each day with a level of tension much greater than that of the normal individual. This chronic state of apprehension is often punctuated by *acute anxiety attacks* that may occur as often as several times a day or as infrequently as once a month. During acute attacks the individual has an overwhelming feeling that something dreadful is about to happen; this feeling is usually accompanied by such physiological symptoms as heart palpitations, rapid breathing, perspiration, muscle tension, faintness, and nausea. These physiological symptoms result from excitation of the sympathetic division of the autonomic nervous system (see p. 55) and are the same symptoms that one may experience when extremely frightened.[1]

[1] Several organic conditions, such as overactivity of the thyroid gland, heart disease, hypoglycemia, and some endocrine disorders, can produce the same symptoms as an anxiety attack. It is always wise to rule out such possibilities before assuming that the symptoms are of psychological origin.

behavior as the result of unconscious conflicts stemming from early childhood (e.g., Anna Freud, 1946; Hartmann, 1958; Rapaport, 1967). Freud believed that repressed aggressive and sexual impulses generate anxiety that is controlled by defense mechanisms. The neuroses represent an exaggerated use of defense mechanisms as the individual attempts to cope with anxiety. The psychoses represent a breakdown of the neurotic defense mechanisms, with the individual regressing to that period in his psychosexual development (see p. 78) at which his conflicts failed to be resolved (usually the oral stage). Treatment consists of uncovering the unconscious conflicts and learning to deal with the repressed impulses in more adaptive ways. The psychoanalytic model and the medical model share the assumption that abnormal behavior is a *symptom* of an underlying disturbance. It is the underlying conflict that must be dealt with, not the behavior itself.

BEHAVIORAL MODEL. The *behavioral model* views psychopathology as the result of faulty learning in the course of growing up (e.g., Lazarus, 1971; Bandura, 1969; Kanfer and Phillips, 1970). Abnormal or *maladaptive behavior* may be determined by the individual's past history of reinforcement in several ways. The person may have failed to learn the necessary behavior. For example, he may never have learned to relate to other people in a satisfactory way. Or he may have learned ineffective or maladaptive habits. If punished whenever he expressed sexual feelings as a child, the individual may have learned to respond with anxiety to sexually arousing stimuli. As an adult such responses would be maladaptive. The behavioral model assumes that abnormal behavior can be dealt with directly; there is no underlying conflict or illness. Change the behavior—either by changing the environment so that maladaptive behavior is no longer reinforced or by teaching new behavior—and you have "cured the illness."

SOCIOCULTURAL MODEL. A fourth model of psychopathology, one that is just beginning to have an impact, focuses on those factors in the *sociocultural environment* that contribute to abnormal behavior (e.g., Laing, 1967). The discovery that the incidence of serious mental disorders is markedly higher among the lower socioeconomic classes and in urban, as opposed to rural areas, has drawn attention to the effect of community conditions, such as poverty and overcrowding, on mental health. The *sociocultural model* looks beyond the individual and the family to the community and general sociocultural milieu in seeking the source and cure for problems. The emphasis is on developing a *healthy society* in which each person can develop his or her potential to the fullest. In this respect the *sociocultural model* shares the concerns of the humanistic conception of man.

Each model of psychopathology—medical, psychoanalytic, behavioral, and sociocultural—provides a different perspective from which to view abnormal behavior. In treating mental well-being as a function of the total organism in interaction with the environment, it is necessary to consider biological, psychological (whether in terms of inner conflicts or learned behavior), and sociocultural factors. As we shall see, these three determinants are involved in varying degrees in most instances of abnormal behavior, the relative importance of each depending upon the specific case.

The anxiety neurotic usually has no clear idea why he is frightened. This anxiety is sometimes termed "free-floating" because it is not associated with a particular stimulus or object but occurs in a variety of stiuations. It is less a function of external stimulus events than of feelings and conflicts within the individual. Anxiety evoked by specific situations (e.g., speaking before a group or going out on a blind date) is called "bound" anxiety because it is tied to a specific situation. Bound anxiety is less incapacitating than free-floating anxiety, but it can be troublesome enough to require professional help.

Most anxiety reactions lie between very diffuse, free-floating anxiety and highly specific fears. The mother who worries constantly about her child's safety is afraid of a number of possible accidents. A person who fears for his bodily safety is afraid of any one of a number of different possible mishaps. The general anxiety is diffuse, but at any point in time it may be specific (Levitt, 1967).

Most of us have felt anxious and tense in the face of threatening or stressful situations. Such feelings are normal reactions to stress; they are considered neurotic only when they become habitual ways of responding to situations that most people can handle with little difficulty.

Studies of individuals diagnosed as anxiety neurotic suggest that they have unrealistically high standards of performance. Typically, they come from families where the parents have high expectations for their offspring and make their love for the child contingent upon achieving their expectations. No matter how successful he may be, the anxiety neurotic cannot relax; he still feels apprehensive about his ability to meet the demands of the future (Jenkins, 1968).

Acute anxiety attacks may be precipitated by sudden stress in the life situation—a job promotion that requires more responsibility, the loss of a parent, failure to achieve some desired goal. The threatened breakthrough of unacceptable or "dangerous" impulses may also set off an anxiety attack. The person suffering from an anxiety neurosis feels inadequate and frustrated in his strivings to succeed and thus experiences a considerable amount of anger. But expressing this anger openly might lose the individual the support and acceptance of other people. Consequently, hostility must be repressed. The case study described in Figure 16-2 shows how the threatened breakthrough of hostile feelings was sufficient to trigger acute anxiety attacks.

Obsessive-compulsive Reactions

In *obsessive-compulsive* reactions the individual is compelled to think about things he would rather not think about, or to perform acts that he does not wish to carry out. Obsessions are persistent intrusions of unwelcome thoughts. Compulsions are irresistible urges to execute certain acts or rituals.

An eighteen-year-old male student developed severe anxiety attacks just before he went out on dates. In therapy it was revealed that he came from a very insecure home in which he was very much attached to an anxious, frustrated, and insecure mother. He was not particularly attractive and had considerable difficulty getting dates, particularly with the girls of his choice. The girl he had been recently dating, for example, would not make any arrangements to go out until after 6:00 P.M. of the same day after her chances for a more preferable date seemed remote. This had increased his already strong feelings of inferiority and insecurity and had led to the development of intense hostility toward the opposite sex, mostly on an unconscious level.

His repressed hostility began to appear in the form of obsessive thoughts of choking the girl to death when they were alone together. As he put it, "When we are alone in the car, I can't get my mind off her nice white throat and what it would be like to choke her to death." At first he put these thoughts out of his mind, but they returned on subsequent nights with increasing persistency. Then, to complicate the matter, he experienced his first acute anxiety attack. It occurred in his car on the way over to pick up his date and lasted only a few minutes, but the youth was panic stricken and thought that he was going to die. After that he experienced several additional attacks under the same conditions.

The relationship of the repressed hostility to the obsessive thoughts and anxiety attacks is clear in this case. Yet, it was not at all apparent to the young man. He was at a complete loss to explain either the obsessive thoughts or the attacks. (Coleman, 1972, p. 224)

A thirty-two-year-old mother of two small children sought help because of her distress over obsessively intrusive and repugnant thoughts related to injuring or murdering her children. On infrequent occasions her husband was also a "victim." These thoughts were so repugnant, made so little sense, and were so foreign to her conscious feelings that she had long been afraid and embarrassed to seek help. She had kept this problem to herself for nearly two years, despite considerable psychological pain, tension, and turmoil. Finally, the steadily increasing difficulty had reached an intolerable level.

These thoughts that were so terribly disturbing to her were really not too much different in quality from what every normal young woman may occasionally feel toward her children. Many a young parent less inhibited and more spontaneous than this one might on occasion say. "Oh, today I feel just like throwing Johnny out of the window! He makes me so mad!" She would not feel threatened by such a thought or feel very guilty about having had it. She would probably forget it rather quickly. Not so with this patient. She greatly feared and condemned such thoughts. To her the thought was nearly as threatening and as guilt-provoking as the act.

This woman had developed early in life a defensive need to deny the presence of all but positive feelings. To defend herself against the guilt occasioned by having such "terrible" thoughts, she endeavored to dissociate them from herself, to deny that they were hers. "It's just awful words that pop into my head. . . . They have nothing at all to do with the way I feel. They couldn't be my thoughts at all. . . ."

The patient had been raised by an anxious and insecure mother who was unable to permit herself or her children the slightest expression of negative feelings. The daughter soon realized that any feelings other than loving ones must be repressed or denied. The patient was the eldest of three siblings and had been assigned undue responsibility for their care. She felt deprived of her share of her parents' affection, was greatly resentful of her younger sister and brother, and fantasized what it would be like if they were not around. Her occasional murderous fantasies about them were accompanied by tremendous guilt and anxiety. As a result the fantasies and associated emotional feelings had been completely repressed from conscious awareness. These early conflicts were reactivated during her marriage when the needs of husband and children seemed to take precedence over her own. (Laughlin, 1967, pp. 324–25)

Obsessive thoughts may be linked with compulsive acts—for example, thoughts of lurking disease germs combined with the compulsion of excessive hand-washing.

All of us at times have persistently recurring thoughts ("Did I leave the gas turned on?") and urges toward ritualistic behavior (knocking on wood after boasting of good fortune). But for the obsessive-compulsive neurotic these obsessive thoughts and compulsive urges occupy so much time that they seriously interfere with his daily life. He recognizes the irrationality of his thoughts and behavior but is unable to control them. Often the attempt to stop produces anxiety.

Obsessive thoughts may cover a wide variety of topics, but most often they are concerned with the committing of immoral aggressive or sexual acts. A young man may have recurrent thoughts of exposing his genitals in public or shouting obscenities while in church. A mother may have persistent thoughts of drowning her infant in the bathtub. A man may be obsessed with the idea of poisoning his wife or bashing her over the head with a hammer. The possibility of these thoughts being carried out is virtually nil, but the individual feels no control over them. He is horrified by his obsessive thoughts, cannot understand why they persist, and fears not only that he will perform the act but that he is becoming insane.

Figure 16-3 reports the history of a young mother who was distressed by recurrent thoughts of murdering her two small children. The kind of

Compulsive behavior

This ball is composed of millions of pieces of string and rope collected by a farmer over many years.

prohibition her parents placed on any expression of negative feelings is fairly characteristic of the background of persons who develop obsessive-compulsive neuroses. When normal feelings of anger must be suppressed or denied, they become an "alien" part of the personality and find expression only in indirect ways.

Compulsive acts may range from the mild kind of superstitious behavior we discussed as examples of the defense mechanism of "undoing"—such as avoiding stepping on the cracks in sidewalks or carefully arranging one's desk and equipment in a certain order before starting on a difficult assignment—to the elaborate and time-consuming rituals described in the case reported in Figure 16-4.

Most of us find comfort in a certain amount of familiar routine or ritual, particularly in times of stress. But the obsessive-compulsive neurotic employs exaggerated rituals in the face of situations that would not disturb most people. These elaborate, time-consuming rituals seem to serve two main purposes. They establish order and control in a confusing and threatening world; a carefully organized, rigid pattern of behavior may prevent anything from going wrong. And they defend against anxiety by keeping threatening impulses out of awareness; a continually busy person has less opportunity for improper thoughts or actions.

Even when dangerous impulses do enter consciousness, they are dissociated from their normal emotion and appear in the form of obsessive thoughts that, although disturbing, are not felt by the individual to be really a part of himself. For example, the college student whose case was reported in Figure 16-2 was upset by his thoughts of choking his dates, but he would have been considerably more disturbed had he realized the extent of his hostile feelings and destructive impulses toward females.

Phobic Reactions

Phobic reactions are excessive fears of certain kinds of situations in the absence of real danger, or fears that are totally out of proportion to the amount of danger that a situation may involve. The person usually realizes that the fear is irrational but still feels anxiety (ranging from mild feelings of uneasiness to an acute anxiety attack), which is relieved only by avoiding the phobic situation. The list of objects or situations that can evoke phobic reactions is endless; some of the more common are fear of closed places (*claustrophobia*), fear of high places (*acrophobia*), fear of crowds (*ocholophobia*), fear of animals (*zoophobia*), and fear of the dark (*nyctophobia*). A scientific name can be constructed for any irrational fear simply by prefixing to the word "phobia" the Greek word for the object feared, and some of the earlier literature on phobias is replete with such terms.

Most of us have some minor irrational fears, but in phobic reactions the fears are so intense that they interfere with the person's daily living. Examples would be the person whose fear of closed places is intense enough to prevent him from traversing narrow hallways or entering small rooms, even though his daily activities require him to do so, or the individual whose fear of crowds prevents him from attending movies or walking down congested sidewalks. Occasionally a person may have one specific phobia and yet be normal in every other respect. But often a phobic individual shows other symptoms of neurotic disorder (see Figure 16-5).

Fig 16-4

A thirty-year-old woman had developed such an elaborate sequence of ritual acts that their consummation occupied most of her waking hours. She could not go to bed at night before she had checked each door and window three times to ensure that they were locked. The gas range and the pilot lights to the furnace and hot water heater had to be similarly checked to make certain that no gas was escaping. Bathing and dressing took up much of her time, since she often took three or four showers in succession—scrubbing her body thoroughly with a special antibacterial cleanser each time—before she was convinced that she was clean enough to put on her clothes. She wore only clothing that could be washed, not trusting the dry cleaner to remove all possible germs, and each article had to be washed and rinsed three times before she would wear it. Similar hygienic procedures were involved in food preparation; she scalded each dish and utensil with boiling water before and after using it, and would not eat a meal unless she had prepared it herself.

This woman had always been unusually neat and clean, but her "security operations" had intensified over the years until they reached pathological proportions. At times she realized the foolishness of her precautions, but she experienced intense anxiety whenever she attempted to cut short any of her procedures. (R. L. Atkinson, unpublished case report)

Fig. 16-5

An eighteen-year-old college freshman came for help at the student health center because each time he left his dormitory room and headed toward class he experienced a feeling of panic. "It would get so bad at times that I thought I would collapse on the way to class. It was a frightening feeling and I began to be afraid to leave the dorm." He could not understand these feelings, since he was reasonably well pleased with his classes and professors. Even after he returned to the dormitory, he would be unable to face anyone for hours or to concentrate on his homework. But if he remained in or near his room he felt reasonably comfortable.

During interviews with his therapist the youth reported other fears such as becoming contaminated by syphilis and growing prematurely bald. Occasionally these fears were sufficiently intense and persistent to cause him to compulsively scrub his hands, genitals, and head until these parts became red, and sometimes even bled. In addition, he touched doorknobs only reluctantly, never drank water from a public fountain, and only used the toilet in his home or dormitory. He realized that his fears were unfounded and exaggerated but also felt that many of his precautions and constant worrying were necessary to avoid even greater "mental anguish."

The student's past history revealed that he had serious concerns about his sexual identity and his adequacy as a male. As a youngster he had avoided playing with the other boys because he could not run as fast or hit a ball as far. His mother had strongly rewarded his tendency not to join others because she was convinced that he would get hurt if he participated in their "roughhousing." He was a late maturer and spent a traumatic summer at camp about the time most of his peers were reaching puberty. Discovering that he was sexually underdeveloped in comparison to the other boys, he worried about his deficiency, wondered whether he was destined to become a girl, and feared that the other boys might attack him sexually.

Although his puberty made a belated appearance, he continued to worry about his masculine identity and even fantasized on occasion that he was a girl. At these times he became extremely anxious and seriously considered suicide as a solution.

The therapist's immediate goal in treatment was to remove the student's irrational fear of leaving the dormitory, which was accomplished with the method of systematic desensitization (see p. 503). It was clear, however, that the phobias in this case were part of a deep-rooted problem of sexual identity which would require more extensive psychotherapy. (Kleinmuntz, 1974, pp. 168–69)

How do phobic reactions develop? When a person fears something that he knows is harmless, we assume that the phobic object is associated with (or symbolizes) something else that is dangerous. Some phobic reactions are simply conditioned fear reactions. We saw in Chapter 12 (p. 355) how the boy Albert was conditioned to fear a white rat when the appearance of the rat was paired with a noxious stimulus. This conditioned fear response then generalized to other furry objects. If in adult life Albert showed strong fear reactions to his wife's mink coat and had no awareness of the source of this fear (because he had forgotten the conditioning experience of his childhood), we would say he had a phobic reaction. Some phobias can be similarly traced to a traumatic childhood experience. Cameron and Magaret (1951) cite the case of a man who feared red skies at evening. After extensive analysis he was helped to recall that as a boy he had been terrified by the red flames of a tenement fire in which he erroneously thought his mother was being burned to death. The red sky of the sunset symbolized the red flames he feared would destroy his mother, upon whom he was very dependent. Frequently, as in this case, the fear is displaced from the originally feared object to another object or idea, so that the person is unaware of the source of the anxiety.

Phobic reactions of a more pervasive nature may develop as a means of defending the individual against impulses that he feels may become dangerous. For example, the student whose case is reported in Figure 16-5 could avoid the arousal of homosexual impulses by staying in his room, away from other men, and by not using public toilets. In one sense, phobias have an advantage over anxiety reactions or obsessive-compulsive reactions. In phobic reactions the fear is directed toward a specific object, and the person can reduce anxiety by avoiding the object. The obsessive-compulsive and the anxiety neurotic have no such easy way out.

Conversion Reactions

In *conversion reactions*[2] physical symptoms appear without any underlying organic cause. The symptoms may be (1) sensory—loss of sensation in some part of the body, blindness, or deafness; (2) motor—paralysis of a limb or entire side of the body, muscular tremors or tics, speech disturbances, and occasional convulsions or "fits" similar to epileptic convulsions; (3) visceral—including such symptoms as coughing or sneezing spells, persistent hiccuping, choking sensations, lump in the throat, and a variety of vague aches or pains.

Freud believed that reactions of this type represented the "conversion" of anxiety into physical symptoms. Although the term "conversion reaction" is retained, the physical symptoms are now usually interpreted as providing an unconscious means of avoiding a stressful situation. Conversion reactions occur most often among military personnel confronted with the extreme stress of combat. Paralysis of the legs or hands, blindness, or deafness prevent a person from returning to combat without being called a "coward."

Although no organic cause can be found, the individual with a conversion reaction is not faking; his disorder is quite real to him, and it usually is easy to distinguish him from a malingerer. In fact, in cases where there is loss of pain sensitivity (analgesia) in some part of the body, the patient reports no pain when stuck with a pin. (This situation is similar to that of a hypnotized

[2]Formerly called hysteria or conversion hysteria.

Fig. 16-6

A twenty-one-year-old soldier completed basic training without incident. Because of his superior physique and soldierly bearing, he was assigned to an "honor guard" unit. Upon completion of this tour he was ordered to overseas combat service. But before he could go he developed partial paralysis of the left leg, which he attributed to the aftermath of a minor physical injury. In response to his complaints, a physician indulgently placed a plaster splint on the leg for two weeks, hoping thus to "satisfy the patient." Upon removal of the splint the paralysis was complete, although medical evaluation made it clear that the difficulty was not physical in origin.

The soldier was a rather dependent and immature person who was extraordinarily proud of his physique and unusually concerned over any possible threat of injury thereto. Although his leg disability was severe enough to require him to use crutches, he appeared blandly indifferent to the serious implications of his handicap. This *belle indifférence* is considered diagnostic of conversion reactions. On several occasions the patient showed more concern over a minor skin irritation, demanding to see a dermatologist, than he did over his paralyzed leg.

This patient was unresponsive to any psychotherapeutic efforts; his paralysis gradually improved following the decision to discharge him from the service. (Laughlin, 1967, pp. 673–74)

subject who, under instructions that he will feel no pain, shows none when his skin is deeply pierced by a needle.) Even though real, the disorder may be selective: a pilot whose conversion reaction of night blindness prevents him from flying at night may be able to drive a car; a person whose symptom is total blindness may be able to see well enough to dodge an object thrown at him; a person reacting with deafness may be able to hear instructions shouted in an emergency.

Almost every conversion reaction can be traced to an attempt to avoid or solve a problem by means of illness (see Figure 16-6). Most of us have at times pleaded illness to avoid some particularly unpleasant situation. The neurotic carries this tendency to the extreme when faced with a serious conflict, so that he cannot function adequately in his daily life. In addition to avoiding the problem, the conversion symptom provides the secondary gain of eliciting sympathy and support from relatives and friends.

The more dramatic types of reactions, such as sudden paralysis or being struck blind or deaf, are becoming increasingly rare in civilian life, although they are still relatively common among servicemen during wartime. It may be that with the increasing medical sophistication of our population such dramatic afflictions are no longer viewed as medically feasible, and patients seem to be developing instead vague aches and pains that are more difficult to distinguish from organic disorders.

Neurotic Depression

In *neurotic depression* the individual reacts to a distressing event with more than the usual sadness and fails to recover within a reasonable length of time. Almost everyone feels depressed when faced with failure or loss. Among the situations that most often precipitate depression are failure at school or on the job, the loss of a loved one either through rejection or death, and the realization that illness or aging are depleting one's resources. Such depression is termed neurotic only when it is exaggerated out of proportion to the event and continues past the point where most people begin to recover.

The chief symptoms of depression are passivity and dejection. The individual experiences an overwhelming inertia; he feels unable to make decisions, to initiate activity, or to take an interest in anything or anyone. He broods over his inadequacies and worthlessness, has crying spells, and may contemplate suicide.

Psychoanalytic theory interprets depression as *anger turned inward* against the self. For example, a woman feels extremely hostile toward the employer who fired her, but because such feelings are unacceptable to her and would arouse anxiety if acknowledged, they are turned inward. Through the defense mechanism of projection, it is not she who is angry but others who are angry at her. And since they must have good reason for rejecting her, she assumes it is because she is incompetent and worthless. Similarly, prolonged depression following the death of a loved one is assumed by psychoanalysts to reflect *ambivalence* (simultaneous positive and negative feelings) toward the deceased. According to this view, a woman who has repressed feelings of resentment toward her husband would be more apt to experience prolonged depression upon his death than a woman whose feelings toward her spouse were primarily loving and positive. For the ambivalent wife normal grief is augmented by feelings of guilt as if the hostile feelings had somehow been responsible for her spouse's death.

The psychoanalytic theory of depression is difficult to prove or refute. Depressed persons do inhibit outward expression of aggression (as indeed they inhibit all active responses), and they do tend to blame themselves for their difficulties more than they blame other people. But such inhibition or inward direction of aggression may be the result, rather than the cause, of depression.

A behavioristic approach to the understanding of depression focuses on the similarity between depression and the phenomenon of *learned helplessness* discussed in the previous chapter. According to this view, depression occurs when a person believes that his actions make no difference in bringing about either pleasure or pain. Animals subjected to traumatic conditions that they are helpless to avoid (electric shock, loud noise, or confinement in small, dark quarters) develop some of the symptoms of depression. The most obvious symptom is *passivity;* when confronted with subsequent traumatic situations where escape *is* possible, they make little or no attempt to avoid the situation. If the animal that has developed learned helplessness *does* make a response that terminates an unpleasant situation (either by chance or with the help of the experimenter), it is slow to learn to make the response consistently when exposed to the situation over a series of trials. Other symptoms of learned helplessness in animals include apathy, decreased appetite, loss of sexual potency, and lack of normal aggressiveness (such animals do not fight back even when attacked). These symptoms (characteristic of human depression) are *not* found in animals subjected to traumatic conditions that can be avoided or terminated by an appropriate response (Seligman, 1975).

If we accept the analogy between learned helplessness and depression, these results suggest that it is not the traumatic event per se that produces depression, but the feeling that one has no control over the situation. Looking at the events described as frequently precipitating depression, we can see that they are the kinds of situations most apt to engender feelings of helplessness. For example, failure in school usually signifies that the person's efforts have been in vain; his responses have failed to bring about the desired gratification. When one loses the affection and support of a loved one, either through rejection or death, there is not much that one can do to regain this source of gratification. And physical disease or aging produce helplessness by their very nature.

The "learned helplessness" theory of depression suggests that people most prone to depression are those whose lives have been full of situations in which they were unable to obtain gratification or avoid pain by their own actions. Perhaps they never learned very effective ways of responding, or perhaps the difficulties they confronted were insurmountable. Individuals who are resistant to depression, or who recover from it very quickly, may have been more successful in controlling their sources of suffering and pleasure and may, as a result, be more optimistic about the future despite temporary setbacks. According to this view, a childhood of experience in which one's own actions are instrumental in bringing about gratifications and removing annoyances may be the most effective protection against depression. Animals that have had prior experience in avoiding or escaping trauma by means of their own responses do not develop learned helplessness when confronted with inescapable trauma. They return to adaptive responding once the unavoidable situation is over (Seligman, 1975).

Studies of learned helplessness in animals also have implications for the treatment of depression. For example, once a dog has learned to be helpless it is very difficult to get it to jump to the safe (nonelectrified) side of a shuttlebox. Coaxing and food placed in the safe compartment have little effect in overcoming its passivity. But if forced to make an adaptive response—by being pulled on a leash over the barrier to the safe compartment as many as 50 times—the dog gradually learns that there is a connection between relief from shock and its own action and begins to respond on its own. This kind of inertia must be overcome in depressed humans too. Successful treatment often depends on getting the individual to realize that his own responses can be instrumental in obtaining gratification. We will see an example of this kind of therapy for depression in the next chapter.

Causes of Neurotic Reactions

We have looked at five types of neurotic reactions. As we have said, the symptoms frequently overlap, and it is not always clear how to categorize a particular case. The case of the college student who had difficulty dating (see Figure 16-2) could be classified as an anxiety reaction or an obsessive-compulsive reaction, depending on which symptoms seemed the most prominent at the time he was evaluated. Actually, he was using obsessive thoughts as a defense against anxiety, but his defense was not very successful, and anxiety was breaking through in the form of acute panic reactions.

Phobic and obsessive-compulsive reactions often occur together; the individual may be obsessed with thoughts about his fears and may defend against them by means of compulsive rituals (see Figure 16-5).

All neurotic reactions can be viewed as attempts to cope with stress by means of avoidant behavior. In anxiety reactions the defense is not working well and anxiety is very apparent. The obsessive-compulsive tries to defend against anxiety by dissociating his thoughts from their true emotions or by occupying himself with rituals that atone for or keep him from thinking about dangerous impulses. The phobic individual focuses his fear on particular objects or situations—by avoiding them he can reduce anxiety. The person with a conversion reaction avoids stressful situations by resorting to physical illness. The neurotic depressive has essentially given up—anxiety has been replaced by feelings of complete hopelessness and helplessness.

Neurotic reactions are exaggerated forms of normal defense mechanisms; neurotic symptoms are responses that the individual uses to defend against anxiety and to increase feelings of security. Because these responses may be fairly successful in reducing anxiety initially, they are reinforced and strengthened. Under conditions of increased stress, however, the individual redoubles his defensive efforts so that they reach maladaptive proportions and are only partially successful in reducing anxiety. He is thus stuck with a pattern of responding that not only fails to relieve anxiety but creates additional adjustment problems for him.

Since feelings of inadequacy and anxiety underlie all the neurotic reactions, we may well ask what determines the particular symptoms an individual develops. Why is one person plagued by obsessive thoughts while another develops paralysis of the arm in response to stress? We do not know the complete answer. The most plausible explanation is that neurotic symptoms are extreme forms of the reaction patterns a child learns in early attempts to cope with stress. Often such reaction patterns are appropriate in the situation in which they were learned but maladaptive when applied to other situations.

A study of conversion reactions among student naval aviators found certain background conditions that predisposed a student to develop physical symptoms (ranging from paralysis of the arms or legs to difficulties in seeing or hearing) as an unconscious means of avoiding stress without admitting failure. Most of the men came from achievement-oriented families and had been athletes in high school and college. In athletics (as in the military) physical illness is an acceptable means of avoiding difficult situations while quitting is not. And in many cases the parents of these students had had significant illnesses affecting the particular organ system utilized in the students' conversion reaction. These earlier experiences undoubtedly influenced the "choice" of neurotic reaction in later life (Mucha and Reinhart, 1970).

Psychoses

A *psychotic* individual is more severely disturbed than one suffering from a neurotic reaction. The psychotic's personality is disorganized, and normal social functioning is greatly impaired. Whether psychoses represent an extreme form of the kind of processes underlying neuroses or whether the two types of disorder are distinctly different remains an unresolved controversy. Some experts believe that there is a continuity from normality through neurosis and psychosis, the differences being largely a matter of severity of the symptoms. Others believe that the psychoses are qualitatively different from the neuroses, involving physiological changes in the nervous system that are possibly genetically based. We will examine the evidence for these two viewpoints as we go along.

TABLE 16-1
Characteristics of psychotics compared with those who are neurotic or psychophysiologically ill

NEUROTIC AND PSYCHOPHYSIOLOGICALLY ILL	PSYCHOTIC
He frequently talks about his symptoms and does not accept his condition. Talks about how healthy he used to be and anticipates the day that he will return to his normal self.	The psychotic often denies that there is anything wrong with him and tends to accept his illness as inevitable. If someone calls attention to his unusual behavior, he will defend it. He lives his psychosis.
This person does not lose contact with reality. If reality testing is at all impaired, it is in the direction of overactivity—he can't seem to ignore reality.	In sharp contrast, the psychotic has lost contact with or has a tenuous reality and substitutes fantasy for it.
Orientation for person, place, and time is intact.	Orientation is poor or entirely gone.
Although he complains that he is "falling apart," he rarely does.	The psychotic's total personality may be disorganized by his illness and his life style is chaotic.
He continues to function socially and on the job.	The psychotic may harm himself or others. Consequently he often requires close care or hospitalization. His close relatives are among the first to insist that he seek help because they are often the victims of his strange behavior.
The prognosis for recovery of acceptable functioning is favorable.	Although many psychotics benefit from treatment (sometimes recovery is spontaneous), most benefits consist of temporary cures of particular symptoms or of behavior.

Source: Kleinmuntz (1974).

The most apparent distinction is that the neurotic is trying desperately to function in the world, whereas the psychotic has to some extent given up the struggle and *lost contact with reality.* He may withdraw into his own fantasy world and fail to respond to things going on around him. Or he may respond with exaggerated emotions and actions that are inappropriate to the situation. Frequently the thought processes are disturbed to the extent that the psychotic experiences delusions or hallucinations. For these reasons the psychotic individual is more likely to require hospitalization and protective care than the neurotic. Table 16-1 lists some of the differences between psychotic individuals and those who are neurotic or psychophysiologically ill.

It is customary to distinguish between two general categories of psychoses: *organic* and *functional. Organic psychoses* refer to psychotic symptoms resulting from damage to the central nervous system. Head injuries, brain tumors or infections (e.g., syphilis and encephalitis), hardening of the arteries, poisoning by such toxic substances as lead, carbon monoxide, and drugs are some of the conditions that can produce psychotic symptoms. Psychedelic drugs such as LSD can produce hallucinations and feelings of unreality not unlike those experienced by psychotics (see p. 185). *Functional psychoses* are disorders that are presumed to be primarily psychological in origin, although genetic and other biological factors may play a significant role.

The distinction between organic and functional psychoses is not clear cut, however. The human organism functions as a whole, and behavior results from the complex interaction of biological and environmental factors. An unstable person might become confused, delusional, and out of control following brain injury or drug poisoning, whereas a better-adjusted individual might show little change. In addition, some of the psychoses now classed as functional may ultimately be traced to disturbances of the central nervous system. *General paresis* (a disorder characterized by progressive deterioration of behavior and mental ability) was classed as functional until it was discovered to be the result of brain tissue destruction by the syphillis spirochete. Although only about 10 percent of untreated syphilitics develop general paresis, those that do show a wide variety of psychotic symptoms.

Nevertheless, it is practical to distinguish between those psychoses in which nervous system disturbances have been identified (the organic psychoses) and those in which physiological factors are unknown and environmental conditions are assumed to play a major role (the functional psychoses). Two of the most prevalent functional psychoses are *manic-depressive psychoses* and *schizophrenia*.

Manic-depressive Psychoses

Manic-depressive psychoses are characterized by recurrent and exaggerated shifts of mood from normal to either a *manic state* (strong excitement and elation) or a *depressed state* (extreme fatigue, despondency, and sadness). Some patients exhibit the whole cycle, but most vary between the normal mood state and one of the extreme phases, depression being the most common.

Sorrow (November 1882) by Van Gogh
Collection The Museum of Modern Art, N.Y.

MANIC STATES. In the milder form of mania (*hypomania*) the patient shows great energy and enthusiasm. He talks continually, has unbounded confidence in his ability, rushes from one activity to another with little need of sleep, and makes grandiose plans with little attention to their practicality (but seldom puts these plans into action or completes them if he does). His behavior is similar in some respects to an individual who is mildly intoxicated (see Figure 16-7).

In the more severe form of mania (*hypermania*) the person behaves more like the popular notion of the raving maniac. He may be continually pacing about, singing, shouting obscene phrases, screaming. He is confused and disoriented and may experience hallucinations and delusions. Some hypermanic individuals abandon all moral inhibitions and may exhibit unrestrained sexual behavior or violent assaultive behavior. The intense excitement of the hypermanic state can be reduced by the use of sedatives and hydrotherapy, so the visitor to a neuropsychiatric ward seldom sees the violent ravings and uncontrolled behavior commonly seen thirty years ago.

DEPRESSED STATES. The depressed individual's behavior is essentially the opposite of that of someone in the manic phase. Instead of being overactive, his mental and physical activity is much slower than normal. Instead of feeling overconfident and boastful, his self-esteem is at its lowest ebb. He feels rejected and discouraged; life seems hopeless and not worth living. Feelings of worthlessness and guilt predominate, and it is not infrequent for patients in this condition to attempt suicide. In the most intense state of depression the patient is bedridden and indifferent to all that goes on

Fig. 16-7

Robert B., fifty-six years old, was a dentist who for most of his twenty-five years of dental practice provided rather well for his wife and three daughters. Mrs. B. reported that there had been times when Robert displayed behavior similar to that which preceded his hospitalization, but that this was the worst she had ever seen.

About two weeks prior to hospitalization, the patient awoke one morning with the idea that he was the most gifted dental surgeon in his tri-state area; his mission then was to provide services for as many persons as possible so that they could benefit from his talents. Consequently, he decided to enlarge his two-chair practice to a twenty-chair one, and his plan was to reconstruct his two dental offices into twenty booths so that he could simultaneously attend to as many patients. That very day he drew up the plans for this arrangement and telephoned a number of remodelers and invited them to submit bids for the work. He also ordered the additional necessary dental equipment.

Toward the end of that day he became irritated with the "interminable delays" and, after he attended to his last patient, rolled up his sleeves and began to knock down the walls of his dental offices. When he discovered that he couldn't manage this chore with the sledge hammer he had purchased for this purpose earlier, he became frustrated and proceeded to smash his more destructible tools, washbasins, and X-ray equipment. He justified this behavior in his own mind by saying, "This junk is not suitable for the likes of me; it'll have to be replaced anyway."

He did not tell any of his family about these goings-on for about a week, and his wife started to get frantic telephone calls from patients whom he had turned away from his office. During this time, also, his wife realized something was "upsetting him" because he looked "haggard, wild-eyed, and run-down." He was in perpetual motion, and his speech was "overexcited." That evening Robert's wife mentioned the phone calls and his condition and she was subjected to a fifteen-minute tirade of "ranting and raving." She said later that the only reason he stopped shouting was because he became hoarse and barely audible.

After several more days of "mad goings-on," according to Mrs. B., she telephoned two of her married daughters for help and told them that their father was completely unreasonable and that he was beyond her ability to reach him. Her daughters, who lived within several minutes' drive, then visited their parents one evening and brought along their husbands. It turned out that bringing their spouses along was a fortunate happenstance because the father, after bragging about his sexual prowess, made aggressive advances toward his daughters. When his sons-in-law attempted to curtail this behavior, Robert assaulted them with a chair and had to be physically subdued. The police were then called and he was admitted to the hospital several hours later.

During the interview with Robert it was apparent that he was hyperactive and overwrought. He could not sit in his chair; instead he paced the office floor like a caged animal. Throughout his pacing he talked constantly about his frustrated plans and how his wife and two favorite daughters double-crossed him. It was also learned, both from him and subsequently from Mrs. B., that this was not the first episode of this sort and that he had a history of three prior hospitalizations.

He responded well to lithium treatment (see p. 518) and was discharged within several weeks of admission to the hospital. (Kleinmuntz, 1974, p. 234)

around him. He refuses to speak or to eat, and he has to be fed intravenously and completely cared for by others.

The depressed state of the manic-depressive psychosis differs from other depressions in that (1) there is no apparent precipitating stress, (2) the depression usually lifts spontaneously after a period of time, and (3) subsequent periods of depression almost invariably occur. The cyclical nature of the mood changes suggests some sort of disturbance or defect in the neurohormonal mechanisms that control emotion.[3]

[3] Neurotic depressive reactions to stressful events, when they reach psychotic proportions with severe thought disturbances and loss of reality contact, are classified under another category. A different category is reserved also for the kind of depression that sometimes occurs during menopause in women (and more rarely in men at about the same age) which is called *involutional melancholia*. Involutional melancholia is associated with hormone changes and other life stresses that occur with aging and often does not improve without treatment.

Most people diagnosed as manic-depressive experience either mania or depression, with periodic recovery to normal behavior, but some develop a cycle of alternating between manic and depressed states. The factors that initiate the switch from one state to the other are not clear, but the two states are assumed to be psychologically related. The elation and frantic activity of the manic state appear to be a last-ditch attempt to defend against the underlying feelings of inadequacy and worthlessness that precipitate depression. Such a reaction is not unlike that of a normal person who participates in a round of gay and busy activities in an attempt to forget his problems. Unlike some forms of psychosis, manic-depressive psychosis does not result in progressive degeneration of social behavior and mental ability. Between psychotic episodes the individual may function quite normally.

There is much we do not know about the causes of manic-depressive psychoses. The fact that this type of reaction occurs much more frequently among the offspring of manic-depressives than in the general population suggests the possibility of a genetic predisposition to the disorder.

Many of the paintings of the 16th century Dutch painter Hieronymous Bosch resemble psychotic art—the minute detail, the sexual symbolism and mutilated figures, and the attempt to include so many elements in one picture are characteristic of disordered thought processes

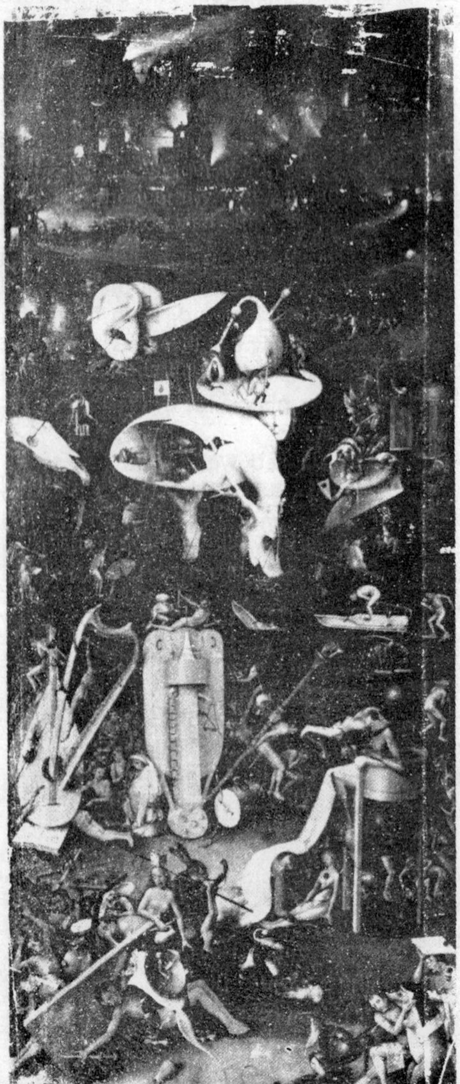

Schizophrenia

Schizophrenia is by far the most common of the psychotic disorders. It has been estimated that 50 percent of all neuropsychiatric hospital beds are occupied by patients diagnosed as schizophrenic. The word *schizophrenic* is derived from the Greek words *schizein* ("to split") and *phren* ("mind"). The split does not refer to multiple personalities, as in the case of Jonah (see p. 163), or as in the famous fictional account of Dr. Jekyll and Mr. Hyde, but rather to a splitting of the thought processes from the emotions. One of the symptoms of schizophrenia is a blunting or dulling of emotional expression or the display of an emotion that is inappropriate to the situation or the thought being expressed. Schizophrenia is actually a label for a group of psychotic disorders. The symptoms are many and varied, but the primary characteristics can be summarized under the following six headings (although not every schizophrenic will show all of the symptoms):

1. *Disturbances of affect.* The schizophrenic does not show emotion in a normal way. He usually appears dull and apathetic, or he may display inappropriate emotions (e.g., speaking of tragic events without any display of emotion or while actually smiling).
2. *Withdrawal from active interchange with the realistic environment.* The schizophrenic loses interest in the people and events around him. In extreme cases the individual may remain silent and immobile for days (in what is called a *catatonic stupor*) and may have to be cared for as an infant.
3. *Autism.* Withdrawal from reality is usually accompanied by absorption in an inner fantasy life. This state of self-absorption is known as *autism* (from the Greek *autos,* meaning "self"). Inappropriate emotional behavior can sometimes be explained by the fact that the schizophrenic may be reacting to what is going on in his private world rather than to external events. The schizophrenic may be so enmeshed in his fantasy world that he is disoriented in time and space; that is, he may not know what day or month it is or where he is.
4. *Delusions and hallucinations.* The most common delusions of the schizophrenic are the beliefs that external forces are trying to control his

Schizophrenic drawing showing what is believed to be a self-portrait (left) cringing before a dominating female form.

thoughts and actions (delusions of influence) or that certain people or groups are persecuting him (delusions of persecution). Auditory hallucinations are much more common than visual ones—the schizophrenic frequently hears voices. When persecutory delusions or hallucinations are predominant, the person is called *paranoid.* He may become suspicious of friends and relatives, fear that they are poisoning him, complain that he is being watched, followed, and talked about. Paranoid delusions can be understood as extreme forms of the defense mechanism of projection. Rather than face the anxiety generated by recognition of his own hostile impulses, the paranoid schizophrenic projects his hostility onto others; it is they who are unjustly trying to harm him.

5. *''Bizarre'' behavior.* The schizophrenic's behavior may include peculiar gestures, movements, and repetitive acts that make no sense to the observer but are usually closely related to the schizophrenic's fantasy world.

6. *Disturbances of thought.* Disturbed thought processes constitute the most fundamental symptom of schizophrenia, and some of the other symptoms (e.g., delusions, hallucinations, and bizarre behavior) can be interpreted as manifestations of the schizophrenic's thought disorder. Whereas the manic-depressive psychoses are characterized by disturbances of *mood,* in schizophrenia *thought* disorders predominate.

The following excerpt from a patient's writings illustrates how difficult it often is to understand a schizophrenic's thought processes.

> If things turn by rotation of agriculture or levels in regards and timed to everything; I am re-fering to a previous document when I made some remarks that were facts also tested and there is another that concerns my daughter she has a lobed bottom right ear, her name being Mary Lou. . . . Much of abstraction has been left unsaid and undone in this product/milk syrup, and others, due to economics, differentials, subsidies, bankruptcy, tools, buildings, bonds, national stocks, foundation craps, weather, trades, government in levels of breakages and fuses in electronics too all formerly stated not necessarily *factuated.* (Maher, 1966, p. 395)

The words and phrases in themselves make sense, except for the italicized word (factuated) which is a *neologism,* an invented word. But they are meaningless in relation to each other. The juxtaposition of unrelated words and phrases and idiosyncratic word associations are characteristic of schizophrenic writing and speech.

The thought disorder in schizophrenia appears to reflect a general difficulty in ''filtering out'' irrelevant stimuli. A normal person is able to selectively focus his attention. From the mass of incoming sensory information, he attends to those stimuli relevant to the task at hand and ignores the rest (see p. 148). If irrelevant stimuli were not ''inhibited'' or ''filtered out,'' we would not be able to function efficiently—the system would be overloaded. The schizophrenic appears unable to screen out irrelevant stimuli or to distinguish relevant inputs. He is perceptually receptive to many stimuli at the same time and has trouble making sense out of the profusion of inputs bombarding him, as the following statement by a schizophrenic illustrates.

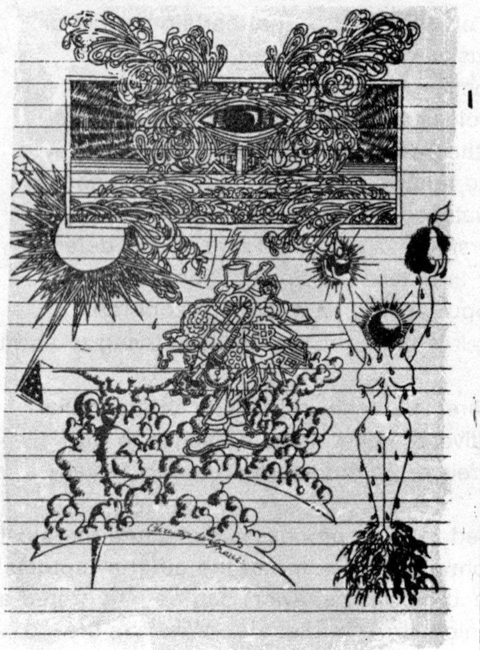

An example of schizophrenic art

This painting is one of many created by a young man in his twenties while hospitalized for schizophrenia. It is an attempt by the artist to communicate his feelings. He describes his picture as "my way of being in a safe place at the time of judgment." In the center are symbols of the materialistic world—money, computer, the hydrogen bomb, and so on. They are "being retracted from the earth's surface." The face at lower left is the patient's own; the woman at the right represents the marihuana plant—"to smoke the plant is like drinking mama's milk"; the eye at the top represents God.

> I can't concentrate. It's diversion of attention that troubles me. I am picking up different conversations. It's like being a transmitter. The sounds are coming through to me, but I feel my mind cannot cope with everything. It's difficult to concentrate on any one sound. (McGhie and Chapman, 1961, p. 104)

The inability to inhibit irrelevant stimuli shows up in many aspects of the schizophrenic's thinking. The disjointed nature of schizophrenic speech is partly due to the intrusion of irrelevant associations. And often one word will set off a string of associations, as the following sentence written by a schizophrenic patient illustrates.

> I may be a "Blue Baby" but "Social" Baby not, but yet a blue heart baby could be in the Blue Book published before the war.

This patient had suffered from heart trouble and may have started out to say "I was a blue baby." The association of "blue baby" with "blue blood" in the sense of social status may have prompted the interruption of "Social Baby not." And the last phrase shows the interplay between the two meanings: "yet a blue heart baby could have been in the [Society] Blue Book" (Maher, 1966, p. 413).

Normal adults inhibit associative sequences of this sort; their speech is determined primarily by the requirements of grammar and meaning. Schizophrenics, often unable to restrain the direction of their associations, may string together phrase after phrase that seem to have no logical connection as far as the listener is concerned.

Schizophrenia usually occurs during young adulthood, the peak of incidence being between ages 25 and 35. In some cases the schizophrenic symptoms appear suddenly, following a period of stress. But more often they are the result of a gradual process of increasingly unsatisfactory interpersonal relationships, inability to cope with the world, and withdrawal from social contacts (see Figure 16-8).

Schizophrenia has been found in all cultures, even those remote from the stresses of modern civilization. Table 16-2 lists the symptoms agreed upon as most diagnostic of schizophrenia in an international study of the disorder sponsored by the World Health Organization.

Attempts to Classify Schizophrenic Reactions

Because schizophrenics exhibit such a wide range of symptoms, attempts have been made to classify different types on the basis of the predominant clinical symptoms. The four categories most often used are listed in Table 16-3. One purpose of classification is to provide a basis for collecting further information. Once we classify schizophrenics according to one set of criteria (their predominant symptoms), we can examine each group further to discover additional variables that distinguish between them. It is hoped that such a procedure will add to our knowledge about causative factors and beneficial treatments.

Unfortunately, the traditional classification based on symptoms has not proved very satisfactory. The symptoms overlap from one category to the next, and the diagnosis for a single patient may change during the course of his illness. For example, patients remaining in the hospital a long time without improving frequently end up diagnosed as simple or hebephrenic.

TABLE 16-2
Signs and symptoms of schizophrenia

SIGN OR SYMPTOM	DIAGNOSTIC OBSERVATION OR QUESTION
Restricted affect	Blank, expressionless face. Very little or no emotion shown when delusion or normal material is discussed which would usually bring out emotion.
Poor insight	Overall rating of insight.
Thoughts aloud	Do you feel your thoughts are being broadcast, transmitted, so that everyone knows what you are thinking? Do you ever seem to hear your thoughts spoken aloud? (Almost as if someone standing nearby could hear them?)
Waking early (−)	Have you been waking earlier in the morning and remaining awake? (Rate positive if 1 to 3 hours earlier than usual.)
Poor rapport	Did the interviewer find it possible to establish good rapport with patient during interview? Other difficulties in rapport.
Depressed facies (−)	Facial expression sad, depressed.
Elation (−)	Elated, joyous mood.
Widespread delusions	How widespread are patient's delusions? How many areas in patient's life are interpreted delusionally?
Incoherent speech	Free and spontaneous flow of incoherent speech.
Unreliable information	Was the information obtained in this interview credible or not?
Bizarre delusions	Are the delusions comprehensible?
Nihilistic delusions	Do you feel that your body is decaying, rotting? Do you feel that some part of your body is missing, for example, head, brain, or arms? Do you ever have the feeling that you do not exist at all, that you are dead, dissolved?

Source: Carpenter, Strauss, and Bartko (1973).

The twelve signs and symptoms listed in the table were derived by National Institute of Mental Health investigators working in an international study of schizophrenia sponsored by the World Health Organization. The signs are those found to be most reliable in discriminating between schizophrenia and other forms of psychopathology in nine countries. A minus sign (−) indicates that the absence of the criterion favors a diagnosis of schizophrenia.

Fig. 16-8

A. J. was always extremely shy and as a small child would run away and hide when visitors came to the house. He had one or two boy friends, but as a teenager he never associated with girls and did not enjoy school parties or social functions. He had few interests and did not engage in sports. His school record was mediocre, and he left high school at the end of his sophomore year. The principal felt that he "could have done better" and remarked about his "queer" and seclusive behavior. Shortly before leaving school his shyness increased considerably. He expressed fears that he was different from other boys and complained that the other children called him names. He became untidy, refusing to wash or wear clean clothes.

After leaving school, A. J. worked at a number of odd jobs but was irregular in performing his duties and never held any one job longer than a few weeks. He finally became unemployable and stayed home, becoming more and more seclusive and withdrawn from community and family life. He would sit with his head bowed most of the time, refused to eat with the family, and when visitors came would hide under the bed. He further neglected his appearance, refusing to bathe or get a haircut. He occasionally made "strange" remarks and frequently covered his face with his hands because he felt he looked "funny."

The psychiatrist who interviewed the boy when he was brought to a local mental hygiene clinic at the age of seventeen noted frequent grimacing and silly and inappropriate smiling but found that he was correctly oriented in terms of time and place and could answer questions coherently in a flat tone of voice. He complained of having recurring thoughts but denied any hallucinations or delusions. He expressed a wish for help so that he could go back to work.

A. J. was admitted to the state neuropsychiatric hospital with a diagnosis of schizophrenia. Testing with the Wechsler Adult Intelligence Scale showed that he had average intelligence (full scale IQ 96) but indicated the beginnings of some intellectual impairment. The results of the Rorschach test reinforced the schizophrenic diagnosis. (Rabin, 1947, pp. 23–30)

TABLE 16-3
Types of schizophrenia

TYPE	GENERAL DESCRIPTION
Simple	Gradual development of social withdrawal, loss of interest, and emotional apathy that usually begins at adolescence. Less bizarre behavior than other types; hallucinations and delusions rare. Many maintain marginal adjustment without hospitalization, working in solitary occupations or becoming prostitutes or vagrants. The case reported in Figure 16-8 would be diagnosed simple schizophrenia.
Hebephrenic	Reactions resemble common stereotype of the psychotic with sudden fits of laughing or crying, silly grins or grotesque facial expressions, hallucinations, and bizarre delusions. Often talk to themselves or to fantasied companions. In advanced stages may regress to infantile behavior, including soiling and wetting, rocking to and fro, and head banging.
Catatonic	In addition to some of the other symptoms of schizophrenia, has extreme mood fluctuations from stuporous, immobile state to wild excitement. While in stupor may assume a rigid posture for hours; remains mute, apparently oblivious to surroundings, and may have to be fed intravenously.
Paranoid	Characterized by delusions of persecution or grandeur and auditory hallucinations. Is overly sensitive and suspicious; frequently hostile and belligerent. Less severe personality disorganization than other types, presumably because patient is *projecting* onto others qualities he cannot accept in himself.

Rigidly held position of a catatonic patient during the stuperous phase of catatonic schizophrenia

More recently a two-dimensional classification has been proposed, based not on the schizophrenic's present symptoms, but on his premorbid (pre-illness) adjustment and the prognosis for recovery. A *process schizophrenic* has a history of long-term, progressive deterioration in adjustment, with little chance of recovery. A *reactive schizophrenic* has had a fairly adequate premorbid social development, the illness being precipitated by some sudden stress, such as the death of a loved one or loss of a job; the prognosis for recovery is good. Rating scales have been developed that attempt to evaluate the patient's premorbid personality and the nature of the onset of illness and to classify him accordingly. Some of these scales have shown good ability to predict a patient's speed of recovery. But it appears that there is no clear-cut dichotomy between the two groups; rather, there is a continuum of personality organization from the most process to the most reactive schizophrenic (Higgins and Peterson, 1966).

Initially some experts thought that the two groups might be distinguished on a neurological basis. They hypothesized that process schizophrenia, which starts comparatively early in life, might be caused by some sort of brain damage or deficit. Consequently, process schizophrenics might respond on certain tests in a manner similar to patients with diagnosed brain damage, whereas the reactive schizophrenics would not. Such studies have generally had negative results. Little empirical evidence supports the notion that process schizophrenia has an organic origin and reactive does not (Buss, 1966b). However, it has been possible to differentiate between process and reactive schizophrenics on some physiological and psychological measures. Reactive schizophrenics are more responsive physiologically (in terms of blood pressure response to a chemical stimulant) than process schizophrenics and more responsive emotionally to anxiety-producing stimuli (Stephens, Astrup, and Mangrum, 1967). These results support the conclusion that the withdrawal of the process schizophrenic is of long duration, whereas the withdrawal of the reactive schizophrenic is in response to more recent environmental stress. The positive correlation of the severity of the schizophrenic disorder (as measured by length of hospitalization) with the degree of withdrawal from interpersonal contacts during adolescence is indicated in Table 16-4.

Research on the Causes of Schizophrenia

In seeking the causes of schizophrenia, as with other forms of psychopathology, research has been focused in several directions. We will look at some studies that have sought to determine if there are genetic, biochemical, or psychological differences between schizophrenics and normals.

Heredity

There is little doubt that schizophrenia has a genetic component, although experts differ as to its importance. Table 16-5 summarizes the results of a number of twin studies. If one member of a twin pair is diagnosed as schizophrenic, what are the chances that the other twin will also be schizophrenic? If there is a hereditary component to the disorder, then twins

TABLE 16-4
Adolescent peer interaction and length of hospitalization as an adult schizophrenic

LENGTH OF HOSPITALIZATION	NUMBER OF CASES IN EACH INTERACTION CATEGORY		
	HIGH INTERACTION	MEDIUM INTERACTION	LOW INTERACTION
Short term (6 months)	8	2	1
Relapsing (at least 2 separate admissions and total hospitalization 1–3 years)	1	4	6
Long term (3 years or more)	0	2	9

Source: Modified from Pitt and Hage (1964).

Adult hospitalized schizophrenics were categorized (on the basis of intensive interviews) as to amount of weekly interaction they had with their peers during mid-adolescence (ages 15–17). Clearly, those schizophrenics who withdraw from social interaction earlier in life are likely to remain hospitalized longer. This result lends support to the distinction between slow-onset (process) schizophrenia and crisis-onset (reactive) schizophrenia.

who develop from the same egg (*monozygotic twins*) will be more apt to *both* turn out to be schizophrenic than twins who develop from different eggs (*dizygotic twins*) and are no more alike genetically than ordinary siblings. As you can see from Table 16-5, the *concordance rate*—the percent of pairs in which the second twin is diagnosed schizophrenic when the first twin is so diagnosed—is higher for monozygotic (MZ) than for dizygotic (DZ) twins. The concordance rate for MZ twins varies from 35 to 69 in the studies reported. But eight of the eleven studies show a concordance of 50 percent or above

TABLE 16-5
Studies of schizophrenia in twins

INVESTIGATOR	COUNTRY	PERCENT CONCORDANCE	
		MZ TWINS	DZ TWINS (SAME SEX)
Early Studies			
Luxenburger (1928)	Germany	58	0
Rosanoff and others (1934)	USA	61	13
Essen-Moller (1941)	Sweden	64	15
Kallmann (1946)	USA	69	11
Slater (1953)	UK	65	14
Inouye (1961)	Japan	60	18
Later Studies			
Kringlen (1967)	Norway	45	15
Fischer and others (1969)	Denmark	56	26
Tienari (1971)	Finland	35	13
Allen and others (1972)	USA	43	9
Gottesman and Shields (1972)	UK	58	12

Source: Gottesman and Shields (1973).

The number of twin sets varied from 19 MZ and 13 DZ in the Essen-Moller study to 174 MZ and 296 DZ in the Kallman study. Concordant pairs are those in which both members are schizophrenic. The later studies, reported in the lower half of the table, used a more carefully controlled method for diagnosing schizophrenia, which probably accounts for their slightly lower concordance rates for MZ twins.

for MZ pairs; none of the studies shows a rate this high for DZ pairs. All the studies show a higher rate for MZ pairs than for DZ pairs.

The MZ twin of a schizophrenic may not be diagnosed as schizophrenic, but there is a high probability that he or she will be abnormal in certain respects. A review of a number of studies suggests that only about 13 percent of the MZ twins of schizophrenics can be regarded as normal (Heston, 1970). The presence of schizophrenic-like disabilities among the relatives of schizophrenics is so striking that the term *schizoid* has been coined to refer to those who resemble the schizophrenic in many traits but whose pathology is not severe enough to warrant the diagnosis of schizophrenia. The characteristics included under this still ill-defined label are many: social isolation, suspiciousness, extreme anxiety in social situations, rigidity of thinking, and blunting of affect are some of the more prevalent features. When the presence of both schizophrenia and schizoidia in families is studied (on the assumption that they are manifestations of the same disorder), the evidence in favor of a genetic basis is even more striking. Table 16-6 shows the incidence of schizophrenia and schizoidia among the immediate relatives of schizophrenics. Note that the child of a schizophrenic has a 49 percent chance of being either schizophrenic or schizoid; if both parents are schizophrenic, the probability increases to 66 percent.

It can be argued, of course, that the clustering of schizophrenia and schizoidia in families may result solely from environmental factors. The schizophrenic parent may transmit the disorder to the offspring by means of faulty child-rearing practices rather than faulty genes. And two schizophrenic parents would surely provide a more abnormal environment than one. A study of children born to schizophrenic mothers and raised in foster homes, however, provides additional support for the genetic hypothesis. These children were permanently separated from their parents shortly after birth. They were assessed in adulthood (by means of interviews and records of their past history) and compared with a control group born to normal parents and reared in foster homes. The incidence of schizophrenia and schizoidia was much higher among those individuals whose biological mothers were schizophrenic (Heston, 1970).

Although the evidence favors a hereditary factor in the origin of schizophrenia, we do not know how this susceptibility is transmitted. And it is clear that environmental factors play a significant role. The fact that the MZ twin of a schizophrenic is as likely to be schizoid as schizophrenic points up the influence of environment.

TABLE 16-6
Percentages of first-degree relatives of schizophrenics found to be schizophrenic or schizoid

RELATIONSHIP	SCHIZOPHRENIA	SCHIZOID	TOTAL: SCHIZOID AND SCHIZOPHRENIC
Relatives of Schizophrenics			
Children	16.4%	32.6%	49.0%
Siblings	14.3	31.5	45.8
Parents	9.2	34.8	44.0
Both Parents Schizophrenic			
Children	33.9	32.2	66.1

Source: Heston (1970), summarizing other studies.

The incidence of schizophrenia and schizophrenic-like disabilities among relatives of schizophrenics provides evidence of familial influences both genetic and environmental

At present researchers are identifying "high risk" children (children with a schizophrenic parent) before birth and following the course of their development through adulthood. They hope to determine those factors that distinguish the "high risk" children who ultimately develop schizophrenia from normals or from "high risk" children who do not develop psychopathology. So far only early results have been reported from long-term studies of this type. But the accumulated findings of high risk studies, tracing the course of schizophrenia from gestation to the onset of the disorder, should be of major value in the development of preventative programs.

Psychosocial Factors

Research on the psychosocial factors in the origins of schizophrenia has focused on early child rearing practices and interpersonal relationships in the home. Investigators have looked for factors in the parent-child relationship that would account for the social withdrawal, poor reality contact, and insecurity characteristic of the schizophrenic. Numerous studies in which parents of schizophrenics were interviewed or patients were questioned about their early home life have yielded conflicting results. Mothers have been found to be both overprotective and rejecting, neglectful and overly involved with their offspring, too restrictive and too permissive. Fathers of schizophrenics have tended to be characterized as weak and ineffectual, or aloof and uninvolved with their children.

Most studies that attempt to relate early child-care practices with the development of schizophrenia fail to provide a control group of parents whose children did not become schizophrenic. Hence, it is not clear whether the behavior of the parents of schizophrenics actually differs from that of other parents. In those few studies with adequate controls it is difficult to determine whether the parents' attitudes caused the schizophrenia or whether the child was deviant to begin with and the parents' behavior was in response to this abnormality. The tendency for the mother to be overcontrolling, for example, may be a reaction to deviance in her child. When mothers of schizophrenic, brain-injured, and retarded children were questioned about their child-rearing practices, all three groups were found to be more possessive and overcontrolling than mothers of normal children (Klebanoff, 1959). This finding suggests that mothers tend to develop similar attitudes when confronted by abnormal behavior regardless of the nature of the behavior. Hence, maternal attitudes toward preschizophrenic children may be an effect and not a cause of the disorder.

Despite these qualifications, disturbed home life and early trauma are found much more often in the background of schizophrenics than of normals. The early death of one or both parents, emotionally disturbed parents who use psychotic-like defense patterns in dealing with problems, and a homelife characterized by discord and strife between the parents are all factors found with greater than normal frequency in the background of schizophrenics. The home environments are often marked by intense conflict, with both parents trying to dominate and devaluate the other, or a very skewed marital relationship, in which the more disturbed parent dominates the family life (Lidz and others, 1965). One of the findings coming from a study of monozygotic twins (only one member of which developed schizophrenia despite the fact that they were raised in the same family) was that the schizophrenic twin identified more strongly with the parent who was psychologically less healthy (Mosher and others, 1971).

Research efforts over the past fifty years have failed to reveal any single pattern of family interaction that leads to schizophrenia. Stressful childhoods of various kinds may contribute to the disorder. It should be noted too that most families with serious pathological qualities do not produce schizophrenic children. There is undoubtedly an interaction between genetic predisposition and family environment. Some families may be so healthy that a genetically susceptible child grows up to be normal. In contrast, some families may be so destructive that not even a child with "super-healthy" genes could escape unscathed.

Biochemical Factors

It may be that as a result of a hereditary defect, prenatal deficiency, or some other factor schizophrenics metabolize products that cause their mental symptoms. Investigators concerned with this possibility have searched for products in the blood or urine that differentiate schizophrenics from other persons. This search was given added impetus by the discovery that drugs such as LSD, mescaline, and psilocybin produce hallucinatory experiences and disorganized thought processes similar to those found in schizophrenia. Such drugs have been called *psychotomimetic* because they produce symptoms that mimic psychoses. It was speculated that the chemical basis of schizophrenia and the drug-induced psychoses might be similar.

Unfortunately, schizophrenia and drug-induced symptoms have been found to differ significantly (Hollister, 1962; Himwich, 1970). And many experimental discoveries that seemed very promising either have not been consistently replicated or have been found to be related to some condition of the schizophrenic patient other than his illness. One study that generated considerable enthusiasm found that schizophrenics had increased levels of ceruloplasmin in their blood (Akerfeldt, 1957). But subsequent studies showed this condition to be due to a deficiency of vitamin C—the result of either poor appetite and/or poor hospital diet. This type of result points up one of the problems in searching for a biochemical explanation of schizophrenia. Numerous substances have been found in the blood or urine of schizophrenics that distinguish them from normals. But it is difficult to be sure that the substance is a *cause* rather than a *result* of the disorder. For example, the weeks of intense panic and agitation that usually precede a schizophrenic's first admission to a hospital undoubtedly produce a number of abnormal bodily changes. And some of the conditions of prolonged hospitalization—diet, reduced activity, and various kinds of medication—might well do the same thing for a chronic schizophrenic. The discovery of abnormal amounts of a certain chemical in either of these cases would not say anything about the origins of schizophrenia unless it could be shown that (1) the substance was present prior to the schizophrenic break, (2) the amount of the substance changed with the severity of the symptoms, (3) injecting it into a normal person produced schizophrenic symptoms, and (4) chemical antidotes to that substance alleviated the symptoms.

Several biochemical explanations of schizophrenia are currently being investigated, but to date there is no conclusive evidence that the disorder is caused by a biochemical abnormality.

All the developments we have discussed are promising, all are controversial, and no two are mutually exclusive. It is highly probable that there is a hereditary component to schizophrenia; most likely it takes the form of an inherited defect in the metabolism of certain chemical transmitters involved in neural activity, which predisposes the individual to a schizophrenic reaction when under stress. But it seems unlikely that heredity alone can account for schizophrenia. The situation may be similar to the case of allergies; there is an inherited predisposition to allergic sensitivities, but certain environmental events are necessary to trigger the reaction. The controversial issue is whether schizophrenia can result from faulty learning in childhood in the absence of an inherited predisposition. Those who advocate an extreme hereditary viewpoint maintain that all schizophrenics have an inherited predisposition that will eventually lead to the disorder regardless of the nature of the early family environment. A stressful childhood will lead to an early and more severe illness (corresponding to process schizophrenia). Those raised in a favorable family situation will not develop the disorder until they encounter stress later in life; their illness will be less severe and more easily reversible (reactive schizophrenia). Research workers who emphasize the role of the environment point to the variety and complexity of schizophrenia symptoms as evidence that we are dealing not with a single disorder but with a group of disorders, which have some symptoms in common. Consequently, there may be a number of causative agents. In some cases inherited physiological or biochemical weaknesses are primarily responsible for the schizophrenic symptoms; in others, environmental factors play the major role.

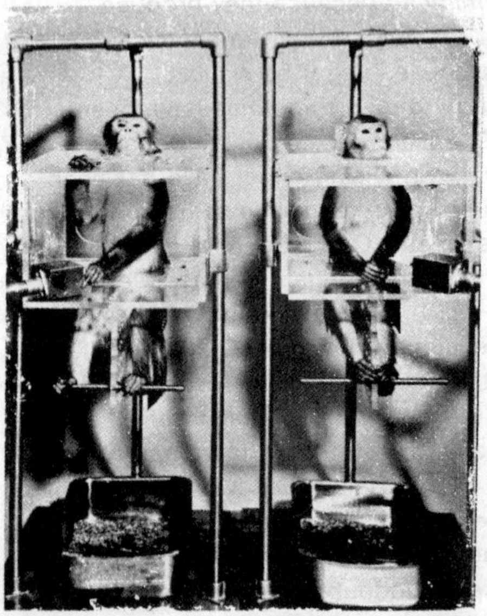

Fig. 16-9 Ulcers in "executive" monkeys

Both animals receive brief electric shocks at 20 second intervals. The one at the left (the "executive") has learned to press its lever, which prevents shocks to both animals provided it is pressed at least once every 20 seconds; the lever for the monkey at the right is a dummy. Although both monkeys receive the same number of shocks, only the "executive" monkey develops the ulcers. (Brady and others 1958)

Psychophysiological Disorders

Sometimes the effects of emotional stress manifest themselves in impaired physical health. A *psychophysiological disorder* (psychosomatic illness) is a physical illness that has psychological causes. Unlike a conversion reaction, where no physical cause can be found, a person with a psychosomatic disorder is actually ill. But it is assumed that psychological stress plays an important role in the illness.

Experimentally Induced Ulcers

A classic experiment with monkeys shows the kind of stress situation that can produce duodenal ulcers. The monkeys participated in the experiment in pairs, each monkey being confined in a restraining device (Figure 16-9). An electric shock was delivered at intervals. One of the monkeys (whimsically called the "executive" monkey) had a lever that could be used to turn off or prevent the shock. When the "executive" pressed the lever, the shock was turned off for *both* monkeys. Thus both monkeys suffered identical shocks; if their physiological damage were due to shocks, it would affect both equally. What happened was that only the "executive" monkey developed the ulcers; apparently the constant alertness required to turn off or prevent the shock produced a continuing state of tension that resulted in the ulcers. The helpless monkey, which could only take the shocks as they came, was somehow less reactive and less disturbed (Brady and others, 1958).

It may occur to you that, although the helpless monkey did not develop ulcers, it should have become depressed. We noted earlier that unavoidable shock produces a state of conditioned helplessness similar in many respects to depression. But actually the executive monkey was responding so effectively that its helpless companion received very few shocks.

Subsequent research indicates that there is more to developing ulcers than the responsibility of having to make decisions. In a series of experiments with rats it was found that the ability to make an *effective response* and receiving *immediate feedback* are important in preventing ulcers. In fact, in one situation results were obtained that seemed to contradict those found with monkeys. The rat that could avoid shock by turning a wheel in response to a warning signal (see Figure 16-10) developed *less* ulceration than its yoked companion that was helpless to avoid the shocks. The experimenter suggests several reasons for the difference between his results and those obtained in the studies with monkeys. The executive monkey was responding at a very high rate and had no immediate feedback indicating that its response was successful (until sometime later when it received or failed to receive the shock). The stress in this situation was evidently much greater than for the executive rat that was required to make an avoidance response at well-spaced intervals and knew immediately that the response would prevent shock (Weiss, 1972).

Physical Health and Mental State

Initially it was believed that each psychosomatic disorder was related to a particular kind of conflict or personality type. Thus, an asthmatic was described as a very dependent person whose asthmatic attacks represented a

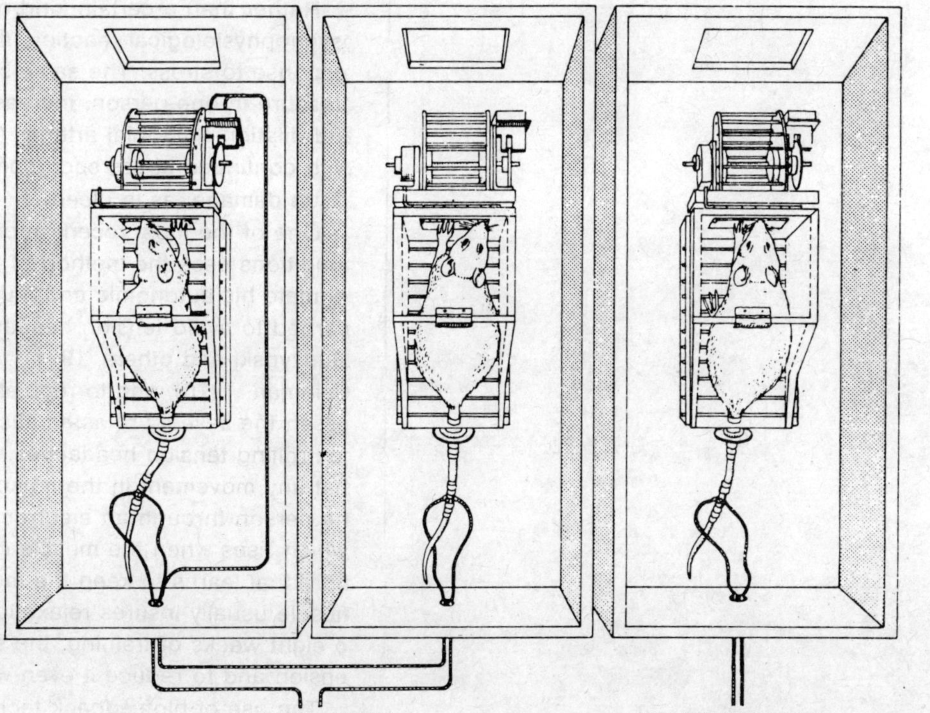

Fig. 16-10 Ulcers in rats
The rat on the left is the avoidance-escape subject; it can terminate the programmed shock by turning the wheel. Moreover, turning the wheel between shocks will postpone the shock. The rat in the center is electrically wired in series to the first rat, so that when the first rat receives a shock, the yoked rat simultaneously receives a shock of the same intensity and duration. The actions of the yoked rat do not affect the shock sequence. The electrodes on the tail of the control rat on the right are not connected, and this rat does not receive shocks at any time. At the end of the experimental session the rats are sacrificed and the length of their gastric lesions is measured. (After Weiss, 1972)

"cry for help." High blood pressure was assumed to result from the inhibition of angry feelings. Ulcers tended to develop in people who were hard driving and competitive but basically wanted to be dependent. Research, however, has generally failed to show a relationship between specific personality characteristics and specific illnesses. When such relationships have been indicated, it is difficult to separate cause from effect. For example, asthmatics do tend to be unusually dependent; but it is quite possible that the asthma produces the dependency, rather than the other way around. An asthma attack is a terrifying experience, particularly for children; struggling for each breath, they often fear they are going to die. Such experiences undoubtedly encourage dependency.

Current psychophysiological research takes a different approach. The focus is on determining the effect of people's mental state on their general health, and vice versa. Any illness, whether physical or mental, is a disorder of the whole person. Just as fatigue or illness can lower one's tolerance for psychological stress, so emotional stress can lower resistance to disease. A study of college students compared the general happiness of those who sought medical help for respiratory infections with the mental state of a group that did not. The ill students were significantly more likely than the healthy to view the year preceding their illness as one of failure and disappointment. A follow-up study revealed that these students tended to have recurrent illnesses, whereas the healthy group stayed pretty healthy. The implications are that maladaptive adjustment leads to physical illness; such illness creates further anxiety and depression which, in turn, make one more susceptible to physical illness (Jacobs and others, 1970; 1971). It had long been noted that psychiatric patients suffer more from physical illnesses of all kinds than do normals. There is also evidence from animal research that stress (acting through the central nervous system and changing hormonal balances) affects the body's immune response (Solomon, 1974).

Rather than a certain kind of conflict producing a specific psychophysiological reaction, it appears that each individual has his own response to stress. The same stressful event may produce elevated blood pressure in one person, increased secretion of digestive juices in another, and dilation of cranial arteries (which causes migraine headaches) in a third. With continued stress such conditions may become chronic or may result in tissue damage, as in ulcers.

One of the most recent approaches to the control of stress-related conditions uses the method of *biofeedback* to try to train the patient to regulate his autonomic and muscular responses (see p. 179). Individuals have learned to avoid tension headaches by relaxing the forehead muscle (Budzynski and others, 1971), to lower their blood pressure (Brener and Kleinman, 1970), and to regulate airway resistance in the lungs so as to lessen the severity of asthmatic attacks (Knapp, 1967). In the procedure for controlling tension headaches, electrodes are attached to the forehead so that any movement in the muscle can be detected, amplified, and fed back to the person through an electromyograph (EMG) machine. By controlling a tone (which rises when the muscle contracts and falls when it relaxes) the individual learns to keep the muscle relaxed. Relaxation of the forehead muscle usually insures relaxation of scalp and neck muscles also. After four to eight weeks of training, the subject learns to recognize the onset of tension and to reduce it even without feedback from the machine.

The use of biofeedback techniques in controlling bodily responses is still very much in the experimental stage. The results are promising, but it is too early to tell how beneficial such techniques will ultimately be.

Personality Disorders

Personality disorders include a group of behavior patterns that are pathological more from society's viewpoint than in terms of the individual's own discomfort or unhappiness. The person fails to behave in socially approved ways because he lacks either the motivation or the skills necessary to do so. Personality disorders are distinguished from neuroses and psychoses in that they are more often long-standing patterns of maladaptive behavior rather than reactions to conflict or stress. But this distinction is largely a matter of degree, as is true of most attempts to separate individuals into categories.

Included among the personality disorders are alcoholism, drug dependence, sexual deviations, "immature" or dependent personalities, and psychopathic personalities. We will restrict our discussion to the *psychopathic personality,* one of the most baffling types with which clinical psychologists have to deal.

Psychopathic Personality

Psychopathic personalities are people who have no sense of responsibility or morality and no concern or affection for others; their behavior is determined almost entirely by their own needs. In other words, they lack a *conscience.* Whereas the average child realizes at an early age that there are some restrictions on behavior and that at times pleasures must be postponed in consideration of the needs of others, the psychopath seldom learns to consider any but his own desires. He behaves impulsively, seeks immediate gratification of his needs, and cannot tolerate frustration. The term *antisocial personality* is sometimes used to describe such persons, but since most people who commit antisocial acts do not meet the characteristics described above, we prefer the term psychopathic personality (or more simply *psychopath*). Antisocial behavior can result from a number of causes (e.g., membership in a delinquent gang or criminal subculture, neurotic needs for attention and status, loss of reality contact and inability to control impulses). And most juvenile delinquents or adult criminals have some concern for others (for family or gang members) and some code of moral conduct (e.g., you don't squeal on a friend). The psychopath, in contrast, has little feeling for anyone but himself and seems to experience little guilt or remorse no matter how much suffering his behavior may cause others.

Other characteristics of the psychopathic personality include great facility in lying, a need for thrills and excitement with little concern for possible injury, and an inability to alter behavior as a consequence of punishment. Those who work with psychopaths are impressed by the fact that they are often attractive, intelligent, and charming people who are quite facile in manipulating others—in other words, good "con artists." Their facade of competence and sincerity wins them promising job opportunities, but they have little staying power. Their restlessness and impulsivity soon lead them into an escapade that reveals their true nature—accumulating debts, deserting their families, squandering company money, or more serious criminal acts. When caught, the psychopath's declarations of repentance and protestations that "next time I'll go straight" are so convincing that often he escapes punishment and is given another chance. He seldom lives up to these expectations; what he says has little relation to what he does (see Figure 16-11).

The two characteristics considered most diagnostic of a psychopathic personality disorder are "lovelessness" (the inability to feel any empathy for or loyalty to another person) and "guiltlessness" (the inability to feel any remorse for his actions no matter how reprehensible).

Causative Factors in Psychopathic Personality

What factors contribute to the development of the psychopathic personality? We might expect such individuals to come from homes in which they received no discipline or training in moral behavior. But the answer is not that simple. Although some psychopaths do come from neighborhoods where antisocial behavior may actually be reinforced and where adult criminals may serve as models for personality development, many more come from "good" homes and their parents are prominent and respected members of the community.

There is no well-supported theory of psychopathy; many factors are involved that may vary from case to case. Current research focuses on biological determinants and on the qualities of the parent-child relationships that reinforce psychopathic styles of coping.

BIOLOGICAL FACTORS. The clinical impression that the psychopathic individual experiences little anxiety about future discomforts or punishments has been supported by experimental studies. In one study, galvanic skin response (GSR) measurements (p. 346) were taken on two groups of adolescent delinquents selected from the detention unit of a juvenile court: one group had been diagnosed psychopathic personality disorder and the other "adjustment reaction of adolescence." The measurements were taken from each subject during successive periods of rest, auditory and visual stimulation, and stress.

During the stress period dummy electrodes were attached to the subject's leg, and he was told that in ten minutes he would be given a very strong but not harmful shock. (A large clock was visible so that the subject knew precisely when the shock was supposed to occur; no shock was actually administered.) The results showed no difference between the two groups in GSR measures during rest or in response to auditory or visual stimulation. However, during the ten minutes of shock anticipation the nonpsychopathic group showed significantly more tension than the psychopathic group, and, at the moment when the clock indicated shock was due, most of the nonpsychopathic delinquents showed an abrupt drop in skin resistance (indicating a sharp increase in anxiety); *none* of the psychopaths showed this reaction (Lippert and Senter, 1966).

Other studies have shown that psychopaths do not learn as quickly as normals or neurotics in an avoidance conditioning situation where a buzzer is followed by shock, and they do not evidence as much autonomic nervous system activity (as measured by GSR, heart and respiration rate, and vasoconstriction) as other prisoners under a variety of conditions (Lykken,

Fig. 16-11

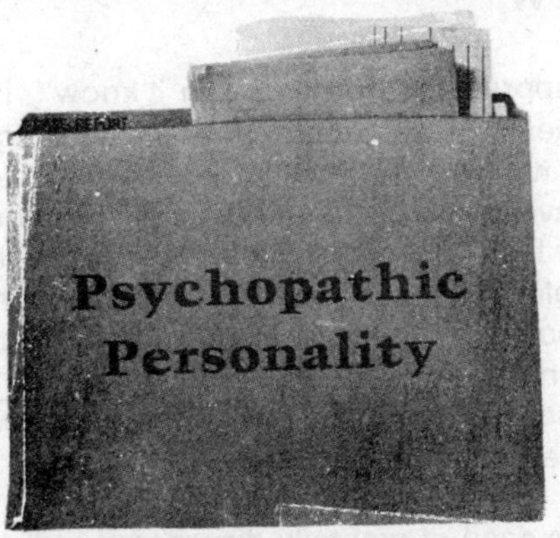

A forty-year-old man was convicted of check forgery and embezzlement. He was arrested with a young woman, age eighteen, whom he had married bigamously some months before the arrest. She was unaware of the existence of any previous marriage. The subject in this case had already been convicted for two previous bigamous marriages and for forty other cases of passing fraudulent checks.

The circumstances of his arrest illustrate the impulsivity and lack of insight characteristic of many psychopaths. He had gotten a job managing a small restaurant; the absentee owner who lived in a neighboring town arranged to call at the end of each week to check on progress and collect the income. The subject was provided with living quarters over the restaurant, a small salary, and percentage of the cash register receipts. At the end of the first week the subject took all the money (having avoided banking it nightly as he had been instructed) and departed shortly before the employer arrived; he left a series of vulgar messages scribbled on the walls saying he had taken the money because the salary was "too low." He found lodgings with "his wife" a few blocks from the restaurant and made no effort to escape detection. He was arrested a few days later.

During the inquiry it emerged that he had spent the past few months cashing checks in department stores at various cities. He would make out the check and send his wife in to cash it; he commented that her genuine innocence of the fact that he had no bank account made her very effective in not arousing suspicion. He did not trouble to use a false name when signing checks or when making the bigamous marriage, yet seemed surprised at the speed with which the police discovered him.

Inquiry into the man's past history revealed that he had been well educated (mostly in private schools) and his parents were financially well off. They had planned for him to go to college but his academic record was not good enough (although on examination he proved to have superior intelligence). Failing to get into college he started work as an insurance salesman trainee and proceeded to do very well. He was a distinguished-looking young man and an exceptionally fluent speaker.

Just as it appeared that he could anticipate a successful career in the insurance business, he ran into trouble because he failed to turn in the checks that customers had given him to pay their initial premiums. He admitted to having cashed these checks, spending the money mostly on clothes and liquor. It apparently did not occur to him that the company's accounting system would quickly discern embezzlement of this kind. In fact, he expressed amused indignation at the company's failure to realize that he intended to pay back the money from his salary. No legal action was taken, but he was requested to resign, and his parents made good the missing money.

At this point he enlisted in the Army and was sent to Officer Candidate School, graduating as a second lieutenant. He was assigned to an infantry unit where he soon got into trouble, progressing from minor infractions (drunk on duty, smuggling women into his quarters) to cashing fraudulent checks. He was court-martialed and given a dishonorable discharge. From then on his life followed a pattern of finding a woman to support him (with or without marriage), and running off with her money to the next woman when life became tedious.

At his trial, where he was sentenced to five years imprisonment, he gave a long and articulate speech, pleading clemency for the young woman who was being tried with him, expressing repentance for having ruined her life, and stating that he was glad to have the opportunity to repay society for his crimes. (Maher, 1966, pp. 214–15)

1957; Hare, 1970). These findings have led to the hypothesis that psychopathic individuals may have been born with an *underreactive autonomic nervous system;* this would explain why they require so much excitement and why they fail to respond normally to the threats of danger that deter most people from antisocial acts. Interpretations must be made with caution, however. It is possible that psychopaths view experimental situations as something of a game, and they may try to play it "extracool" by attempting to control their responses.

PARENTAL INFLUENCES. Psychoanalytic theory assumes that the development of a conscience or superego depends upon an affectionate relationship with an adult during the early childhood years. The normal child

CRITICAL DISCUSSION

Mental Disorders and the Law

What should our laws be with regard to treatment of a mentally disturbed person who commits a criminal act? This is a question that is of great concern to social scientists, members of the legal profession, and to anyone who works with criminal offenders. The psychopath can be one of the most dangerous types of criminals; nevertheless, by legal definition he is not insane and, consequently, cannot be committed to a neuropsychiatric hospital for treatment.

The idea that a person is not responsible for an act that is due to a mental disorder was first introduced into law in 1724, when an English court maintained that a man was irresponsible if "he doth not know what he is doing, no more than . . . a wild beast." Most standards of legal responsibility, however, have been based on the M'Naghten decision of 1843. M'Naghten, a Scotsman, suffered the paranoid delusion that he was being persecuted by the English prime minister, Sir Robert Peel. In an attempt to kill Peel he mistakenly shot Peel's secretary. All involved in the trial were convinced by M'Naghten's senseless ramblings that he was insane. He was judged not responsible by reasons of insanity and sent to a mental hospital, where he remained until his death. The reigning monarch at the time, Queen Victoria, was not pleased by the verdict—apparently feeling that political assassinations should not be taken lightly—and called upon the House of Lords to review the decision. The decision was upheld and the rules were put into writing regarding the legal definition of insanity. The M'Naghten Rules state that a defendant may be found "not guilty" by reasons of insanity only if he were so severely disturbed at the time of his act that he did not know what he was doing or, if he did know, did not know that it was wrong.

The distinction of knowing right from wrong is still the basis of most decisions of legal insanity. But many psychologists and psychiatrists who are called upon for expert testimony in such trials feel that the M'Naghten Rules are much too narrow. Frequently individuals who are clearly psychotic can still respond correctly when asked if a particular act is morally right or wrong. A kleptomaniac knows that it is wrong to steal, but the compulsion to do so is so intense that such knowledge is not a deterrent. Some states, recognizing this situation, have added to their statutes the doctrine of "irresistible impulse"; in such states a defendant may be declared legally insane, even if he knew what he was doing and knew right from wrong, if the jury decides he was driven to his crime by a compulsion too strong to be resisted.

A more reasonable legal definition of insanity was adopted by the U.S. Court of Appeals for the Second Circuit in 1966. The definition of criminal responsibility had been proposed by the American Law Institute after a careful ten-year study. It is: "A person is not responsible for criminal conduct if at the time of such conduct as a result of mental disease or defect he lacks substantial capacity either to appreciate the wrongfulness of his conduct or to conform his conduct to the requirements of the law." The word "substantial" suggests that "any" incapacity is not enough to avoid criminal responsibility, but "total" incapacity is not required either. The word "appreciate" rather than "know" implies that intellectual awareness of right or wrong is not enough; the person must have some understanding of the moral or legal consequences of his behavior before he can be held criminally responsible. The new rule is mandatory in a number of federal and state courts, and it is assumed that most courts will eventually adopt it.

The problem of legal responsibility in the case of mentally disordered individuals is indeed complex. A revolutionary approach toward criminal law has been proposed by Glueck (1962). His proposal would separate two functions of the law: determination of guilt and imposition of the sentence. The jury hearing a criminal case in which the defendant's sanity is in question would be asked only to determine whether the defendant is guilty of the crime with which he is charged. If he is convicted, the determination of treatment would be made by a tribunal of criminologists, psychologists, and psychiatrists who would evaluate the nature and causes of his behavior and decide whether the needs of society and the individual's chances for rehabilitation would be best served by treating him in a neuropsychiatric hospital or punishing him in a prison. The convicted individual's progress could be evaluated periodically and a decision made as to when he had made a sufficiently satisfactory adjustment so that he could be released. This procedure would be superior to a system under which the judge must prescribe at the time of sentencing the length of time the individual should be hospitalized.

internalizes his parents' values (which generally reflect the values of his society) because he wants to be like them and fears the loss of their love if he does not behave in accordance with their values. When a child receives no love from either parent, he does not fear its loss. He does not identify with the rejecting parents and does not internalize their rules. This explanation seems reasonable, but it does not fit all of the data. Many rejected children do not become psychopathic personalities, and some psychopaths reveal a background of childhood indulgence.

An alternative suggestion focuses on the kind of models the parents provide and the kind of behavior they reward. According to this view a child may develop into a psychopath if he learns that he can avoid punishment by being charming, lovable, and repentant. If a child is never punished for any wrongdoing, if he is consistently allowed to avoid the consequences of his transgressions by saying he is sorry and promising never to do it again, he may learn that it is not the deed that counts but one's charm and ability to act repentant. And if the same child is indulged in other respects—by never having to wait or work for a reward—he does not learn to tolerate frustration. Lack of frustration tolerance and conviction that one can get by on one's charm are two of the characteristics of the psychopath. In addition, a child that is always protected from frustration or distress may have no ability to empathize with the distress of others (Maher, 1966).

Studies of the parents of male psychopaths indicate that it is the mother who overindulges the son while the father remains aloof and uninvolved. He is not around enough for the son to identify with him. Typically, the parents are concerned with maintaining status in the community—concealing all difficulties behind the facade of a happy, successful family. Thus, the children learn that appearance is more important than reality.

Undoubtedly a number of family interaction patterns foster psychopathy. Other patterns that have been suggested are parents who are inconsistent in supplying affection, rewards, and punishments as well as inconsistent in their own role behavior so that the child does not have a reliable model on which to base his own identity (Buss, 1966b).

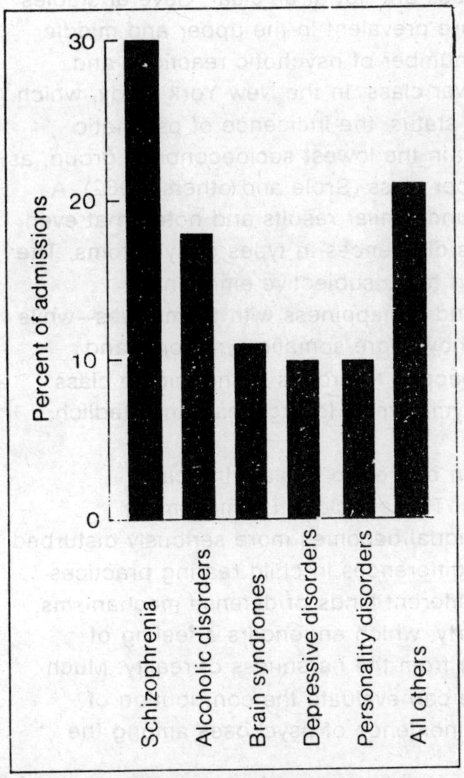

Fig. 16-12 First admissions to U.S. state and county mental hospitals.

In this figure, brain syndromes include senile disorders related to cerebral arteriosclerosis and other physiological conditions of aging; alcoholic disorders include brain syndromes related to alcohol and the category alcoholism from the personality disorders; personality disorders include all such disorders except alcoholism; depressive disorders include affective reactions and neurotic depressive reactions. (Data from National Institute of Mental Health, 1974)

Prevalence of Mental Disorders

Severe mental illness is an important social problem. At any given moment approximately 750,000 patients are being cared for in the mental hospitals of the United States, and they occupy more than half of all hospital beds.[4] This means that more people are presently hospitalized for mental illness than for cancer, heart disease, tuberculosis, and all other diseases combined. Estimates indicate that one out of every ten babies born today will be hospitalized for mental illness at some time during his life. If these statistics sound too depressing, we should hasten to add that half the patients admitted to mental hospitals are eventually discharged as improved or recovered, most of these within the first year of entering the hospital. The percentage is higher for patients in well-staffed hospitals that use modern treatment methods.

The approximate distribution of mental hospital admissions according to type of disorder is shown in Figure 16-12. The most prevalent diagnosis is schizophrenia; about 30 percent of first admissions to public mental hospitals are individuals classed as having this disorder. Because schizophrenic patients tend to be young and their death rate is comparatively low, those who are not discharged accumulate over the years to make up half the

[4]This somewhat astonishing figure results from the fact that many mental patients are hospitalized for several months or even years, while general medical patients require an average hospitalization of only two weeks.

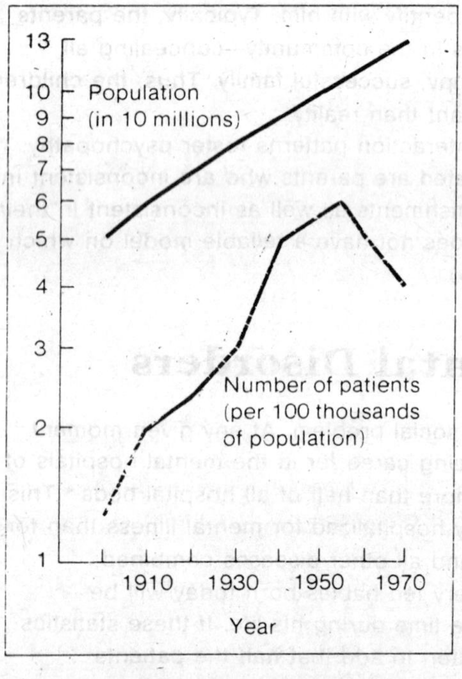

Fig. 16-13 Patients in mental hospitals
This figure compares the number of patients in mental hospitals with the total population (age 15 and over) of the United States from 1900 to 1970. The black curve measures the total population in units of 10 million. The color curve measures the number of hospitalized mental patients per 100,000 persons in the population. Note that the number of patients increased more rapidly than the population until the 1950s and then dropped off. (Data from the U.S Department of Health, Education, and Welfare)

resident population of mental hospitals. The admission rate for depressive disorders is lower because many depressed individuals are treated in the psychiatric wards of general medical hospitals or in outpatient clinics.

The incidence of the neuroses in the population is difficult to estimate because many neurotic individuals do not seek help or are treated by their family physicians. The data suggest that neurotic disorders are far more prevalent than one might expect. Two community studies, one in New York City and another in a small town in Nova Scotia, give some measure of the extent of symptoms of disturbed mental health. The New York study estimates that 30 percent of the population have clinical symptoms sufficient to disturb their everyday lives. That this high figure is not due solely to the strains of urban life is indicated by the figure of 32 percent for the small town (Srole and others, 1962; Leighton and others, 1963).

Community surveys provide some interesting information concerning the distribution of the various disorders in different socioeconomic groups, although the reasons for the differences are not at all clear. Several studies have found that the neuroses are more prevalent in the upper and middle classes, whereas a disproportionate number of psychotic reactions and personality disorders occur in the lower class. In the New York study, which covered all ranges of socioeconomic status, the incidence of psychotic disorders was found to be 13 percent in the lowest socioeconomic group, as compared with 3.6 percent in the upper class (Srole and others, 1962). A study in New Haven, Connecticut, found similar results and noted that even among the neurotics there were class differences in types of symptoms. The upper-class neurotics tended to report more subjective emotional discomfort—anxiety, dissatisfaction, and unhappiness with themselves—while the lower-class neurotics tended to show more somatic symptoms and unhappiness and friction with other people. Neurotics in the middle class were characterized by both sorts of symptoms (Hollingshead and Redlich, 1958; Myers and Bean, 1968).

A number of hypotheses have been offered to explain the class differences in incidence of psychoses. These include (1) movement downward in class status as the individual becomes more seriously disturbed and less able to hold a job, (2) class differences in child rearing practices that may predispose the children to different kinds of defense mechanisms, and (3) the devastating effect of poverty, which engenders a feeling of helplessness and a desire to withdraw from the harshness of reality. Much more information is needed before we can evaluate the contribution of these and other factors to the higher incidence of psychoses among the lower class.

Have the stresses of modern life increased the amount of mental illness? This is an extremely difficult, if not impossible, question to answer. But the evidence suggests that a simple and uncomplicated way of life does not provide immunity against mental disorders. The incidence of psychoses in preindustrial societies (certain isolated groups in Africa, Australia, and Taiwan) is about the same as it is in modern urban communities (Dohrenwend and Dohrenwend, 1974). Although mental-hospital admission rates in the United States have increased more rapidly than the increase in population within the past eighty years, the difference can be largely explained by increased hospital facilities, a more enlightened attitude toward mental illness, and a major increase in the number of senile patients being cared for in hospitals.

The past two decades have seen a significant decline in the number of patients in mental hospitals. Despite an increasing population there were about 200,000 fewer patients in United States mental hospitals in 1971 than there were in 1955 (see Figure 16-13). This encouraging trend can be attributed in part to improved techniques of treatment (including the use of tranquilizing drugs), and in part to the current emphasis on returning patients as soon as possible to the community, where they can be treated as outpatients rather than prolonging hospitalization. These developments will be discussed in the next chapter.

Summary

1. The diagnosis of abnormal behavior is based on *statistical frequency, social standards, adaptiveness of behavior,* and *personal distress.* Characteristics that are considered indicative of good mental health include an efficient perception of reality, self-knowledge, an ability to exercise voluntary control over behavior, self-esteem, an ability to form affectionate relationships, and productivity. These qualities do not distinguish sharply between the mentally healthy and the mentally ill, but represent traits that the normal person possesses *to a greater degree.*
2. The major categories of psychopathology (based on behavior symptoms) are *neuroses, psychoses, psychophysiological disorders,* and *personality disorders. Neuroses,* a less severe form of psychological disorder than psychoses, are behavior patterns that avoid rather than cope with problems; they are often extreme forms of normal defense mechanisms used in an attempt to reduce anxiety. They include *anxiety reactions, obsessive-compulsive reactions, phobias, conversion reactions,* and *neurotic depression.*
3. *Psychoses* reflect a more serious disintegration of behavior, disturbance of thought processes, and distortion of reality—as evidenced by delusions (false beliefs) and hallucinations (false perceptions). Two common *functional psychoses* (those with no clear organic basis) are *manic-depressive reactions* and *schizophrenia.* The manic-depressive reaction is characterized by exaggerated shifts of mood; schizophrenia is primarily a thought disorder characterized by an inability to "filter out" irrelevant stimuli, autism, withdrawal, and inappropriate affect. Schizophrenics can be classified, on the basis of premorbid adjustment and prognosis for recovery, as *process schizophrenics* (long-term maladjustment and little chance of recovery) and *reactive schizophrenics* (illness precipitated by sudden stress and good prognosis for recovery).
4. Research on the causative factors in schizophrenia has been concerned with evidence for a hereditary predisposition to the disorder, pathology of the schizophrenic's early home life, and the possibility that biochemical defects may cause schizophrenic symptoms.
5. *Psychophysiological disorders* are physical illnesses that are assumed to have psychological causes. Although there appears to be no clear relationship between specific illnesses (such as asthma and ulcers) and specific personality types, emotional stress can have a significant affect on one's physical health. Biofeedback techniques have been used to train people to control bodily responses.
6. *Personality disorders* are longstanding patterns of *socially* maladaptive behavior such as *drug dependence, alcoholism,* and *psychopathic personality.* Individuals classified as psychopathic personalities are

impulsive, concerned only with their own needs, unable to form close relationships, free from anxiety or guilt, and frequently in trouble with the law. An underreactive autonomic nervous system and inconsistent parental rewards and punishments may be factors that prevent the psychopath from developing a mature conscience.

7. Mental disorders constitute a serious social problem. It is estimated that one out of every ten babies born today will spend some time in a mental hospital; community studies have shown that as many as 30 percent of the population have clinical symptoms of personality disturbance sufficient to interfere with their daily efficiency.

Further Reading

General textbooks in psychopathology include Coleman, *Abnormal psychology and modern life* (4th ed., 1972); Kleinmuntz, *Essentials of abnormal psychology* (1974); and White and Watt, *The abnormal personality* (4th ed., 1973). Emphasizing a learning theory approach to abnormal behavior are Buss, *Psychopathology* (1966); Maher, *Principles of psychopathology: An experimental approach* (1966); Sarason, *Abnormal psychology* (1972); and Davison and Neale, *Abnormal psychology* (1974).

The hereditary aspects of mental illness are reviewed in McClearn and DeFries, *Introduction to behavioral genetics* (1973), and Gottesman and Shields, *Schizophrenia and genetics* (1972).

The world of psychosis from the patient's viewpoint is graphically portrayed in Green, *I never promised you a rose garden* (1971), and Kesey, *One flew over the cuckcoo's nest* (1962).

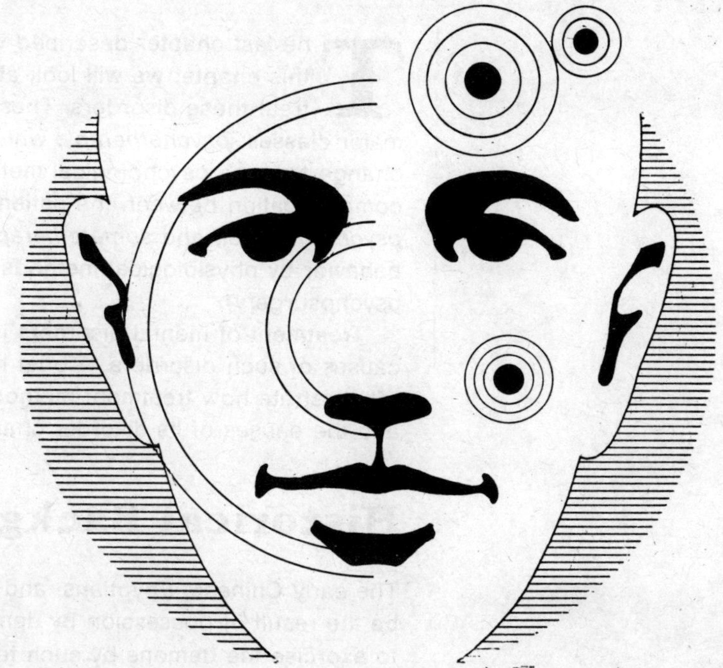

17 psychotherapy and other treatment methods

The last chapter described various types of psychopathology. In this chapter we will look at some therapeutic techniques used to treat these disorders. These techniques can be divided into two major classes: *psychotherapy,* which attempts to bring about behavior change through psychological methods, most frequently processes of communication between the patient and another person called the *psychotherapist;* and *somatotherapy,* which attempts to change a person's behavior by physiological methods (drugs, shock treatment, or psychosurgery).

Treatment of mental disorders is closely linked to theories about the causes of such disorders. A brief history of the treatment of the mentally ill will illustrate how treatment methods change as theories about human nature and the causes of its disorder change.

Historical Background

Archeological evidence of *trephining,* a primitive form of treatment for mental disorders in which holes were burred in the skull of the patient. Evidently it was believed that these holes permitted the evil spirits and demons to leave.

The early Chinese, Egyptians, and Hebrews thought disordered behavior to be the result of possession by demons or evil spirits. The treatment then was to exorcise the demons by such techniques as prayer, incantation, magic, and the use of purgatives concocted from herbs. If such treatment brought no improvement, more extreme measures were taken to ensure that the body would be an unpleasant dwelling place for the evil spirit. Flogging, starving, burning, even stoning to death were not infrequent forms of "treatment." The Old Testament makes several references to demonology. In Leviticus (20:28) it is stated, "A man also or woman that hath a familiar spirit, or that is a wizard, shall surely be put to death: they shall stone them with their stones: their blood shall be upon them." Although in most cases possession was thought to be by evil spirits, behavior of a mystical or religious nature was believed to result from possession by a good or holy spirit. Such people were therefore respected and worshipped. During this period treatment of the mentally ill was in the hands of the priests, who had the power to perform the exorcism.

The first progress in the understanding of mental disorders came with the Greek physician Hippocrates (c. 460–377 B.C.). Hippocrates rejected the idea of demonology and maintained that mental disorders were the result of a disturbance in the balance of body fluids. He and the Greek and Roman physicians who followed him argued for a more humane treatment of the mentally ill. They stressed the importance of pleasant surroundings, exercise, proper diet, massage, soothing baths, and some less desirable methods such as bleeding, purging, and mechanical restraints. Although there were no institutions as such for the mentally ill, many were cared for with great kindness by physicians in temples dedicated to the Greek and Roman gods.

Such progress did not continue, however. The Middle Ages saw a growing revival of primitive superstition and demonology. The mentally ill were thought to be in league with Satan and to possess supernatural powers by which they could cause floods, pestilence, and injuries to others. Those living in medieval times believed that by treating an insane person cruelly one was punishing the devil and so justified such measures as beating, starving, and branding with hot irons (see Figure 17-1). This type of cruelty culminated in the witchcraft trials that sentenced to death thousands of people (many of them mentally ill) during the fifteenth through the seventeenth centuries.

During the late nineteenth century, treatment consisted of swinging a patient while he was hanging in a harness. Presumably such swinging calmed the patient's nerves.

An early method of treatment called for the branding of the patient's head with hot irons to bring him to his senses.

As late as the early nineteenth century, English asylums used rotating devices of this sort, in which the patients were whirled around at high speeds.

Fig. 17-1 Early methods for treating the mentally ill

Early Asylums

To cope with the mentally ill who roamed the streets in the latter part of the Middle Ages, asylums were created. These were not treatment centers but simply prisons; the inmates were chained in dark and filthy cells and treated more like animals than human beings. It was not until 1792, when Philippe Pinel was put in charge of an asylum in Paris, that some improvement was made in the treatment of these unfortunate people. Pinel was allowed, as an experiment, to remove the chains from the inmates. Much to the amazement of the skeptics who thought he was mad to unchain such "animals," Pinel's experiment was a success. With release from restraint, placement in clean and sunny rooms instead of dungeons, and kind treatment, many who had been considered hopelessly mad for years improved sufficiently to leave the asylum.

The turn of this century brought great forward strides in medicine and psychology. The discovery of the syphilis spirochete in 1905 demonstrated that there was a physical cause for the mental disorder general paresis and encouraged physicians who held that mental illness was organic in origin. The work of Sigmund Freud and his followers laid the groundwork for an understanding of mental illness as a function of environmental factors. And Pavlov's laboratory experiments demonstrated that a state similar to an acute neurosis could be produced in animals by requiring them to make discriminations beyond their capacities.

Despite these scientific advances, the general public in the early 1900s still had no understanding of mental illness and viewed mental hospitals and their inmates as objects of fear and horror. The education of the public in the principles of mental health was begun through the efforts of Clifford Beers. As a young man Beers developed a manic-depressive psychosis and was hospitalized for three years in several private and state hospitals. Although chains and other methods of torture had long since been abandoned, the

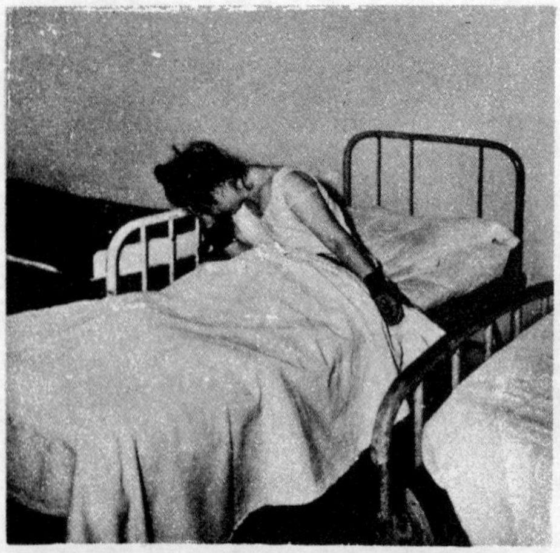

Conditions in an Ohio insane asylum during the 1950s

strait-jacket was still widely used to restrain excited patients. Lack of funds made the average state mental hospital—with its overcrowded wards, poor food, and unsympathetic and frequently sadistic attendants—a far from pleasant place to live. After his recovery Beers published his experiences in a now famous book entitled *A mind that found itself* (1908). This book did much to arouse public interest. Beers worked ceaselessly to educate the public in an understanding of mental illness and helped to organize the National Committee for Mental Hygiene. In 1950 this organization joined with two related groups to form what is now the National Association for Mental Health. The mental-hygiene movement played an invaluable role in educating the public and in stimulating the organization of child-guidance clinics and community mental-health centers, which could aid in the prevention as well as the treatment of mental disorders.

Modern Treatment Facilities

The past thirty years have seen a great improvement in treatment facilities for the mentally ill. The neuropsychiatric hospitals established by the Veterans Administration after the Second World War were generally superior to the average state-supported hospital and served as an impetus for the improvement of state hospitals. Although some state hospitals are primarily custodial institutions where inmates lead an idle and futile existence in rundown, over-crowded wards, most mental hospitals today are attractive, well kept, and busy places where trained personnel guide the patients through a wide range of activities. Daily schedules are planned to meet each patient's particular needs and may include time with an individual therapist, in group psychotherapy, or in occupational therapy designed to teach skills as well as provide relaxation. Treatment may also include physical recreation to help relieve tensions and educational therapy to prepare the patient for a job on release from the hospital. Patients who are well enough may work part time in the various hospital departments as patient-employees, which enables them to earn some money and to feel that they are contributing to the welfare of the hospital community.

Many mental hospitals are located near universities and medical schools so that research and training programs can be undertaken jointly. Such hospitals serve as training centers for interns in psychology, psychiatry, and social work as well as for students in psychiatric nursing and occupational therapy. Many general medical hospitals also provide treatment centers for the mentally ill. At present, more patients are treated in the psychiatric wards of general hospitals than are admitted to state or federal neuropsychiatric hospitals.

During the past ten years emphasis has shifted from hospital treatment to treating patients within their home community whenever possible. Hospitalization, no matter how excellent the facilities, has inherent disadvantages. It cuts the patient off from family and friends. It tends to make the patient feel "sick" and unable to cope with the outside world; it encourages dependency and may discourage active problem-solving. The Community Mental Health Centers Act of 1963 made federal funds available for the establishment of community treatment centers. More than 400 community mental health centers have been built. These centers provide a number of services, including (1) treatment of emotionally disturbed individuals before their condition becomes serious, (2) short-term

Improved conditions in an institution in 19,4

hospitalization, and (3) partial hospitalization. With partial hospitalization a person may spend the day receiving treatment at the center and return home in the evening, or work during the day and spend nights at the center. Such a program has great flexibility.

Because current methods of treatment have proved far from satisfactory in ameliorating mental disorders, early detection and prevention have become all the more important. To this end greater emphasis is being placed on psychological services in the early school years. Studies have shown that children identified as having emotional problems in the elementary-school grades do not outgrow such problems as a matter of development but instead function even more ineffectively by the time that they enter high school.

Professions Involved in Psychotherapy

Regardless of where treatment takes place—in a hospital, community mental health center, private clinic or office—several different professions are involved. A psychiatrist, clinical psychologist, and psychiatric social worker may work together on a given case, or they may function independently. A *psychiatrist* is a physician whose experience covers cases both in mental hospitals and in outpatient clinics. The psychiatrist takes medical responsibility for the patient in addition to playing a psychotherapeutic role. A *psychoanalyst* is a specialist within psychiatry who uses methods and theories derived from those of Sigmund Freud. The psychoanalyst has spent several years enrolled in a psychoanalytic institute learning the specific techniques of psychoanalysis. A psychoanalyst is almost always a psychiatrist,[1] but a psychiatrist is most often not a psychoanalyst.

A *clinical psychologist* has had graduate training in psychology, has usually earned a Ph.D., and has served special internships in the fields of testing and diagnosis, psychotherapy, and research. The clinical psychologist administers and interprets psychological tests, conducts psychotherapy, and is also active in research.

A *psychiatric social worker* usually has an M.A. from a graduate school of social work and special training in interviewing in the home and in carrying treatment procedures into the home and community. Because of this special training, the social worker is likely to be called upon to collect information about the home and to interview relatives, in addition to participating in the therapeutic procedures with the patient.

In mental hospitals a fourth professional joins the team: the *psychiatric nurse.* Psychiatric nursing is a specialty within the nursing profession and calls for special training in the handling of mental patients—both those severely disturbed and those on the way to recovery.

In our discussion of psychotherapeutic techniques we will not specify the profession of the psychotherapists; we assume they are trained and competent members of any one of these professions.

Techniques of Psychotherapy

The term *psychotherapy* embraces a wide variety of techniques, all of which have the goal of helping emotionally disturbed individuals modify their behavior so that they can more satisfactorily adjust to the environment. As we

[1] There are a few "lay" psychoanalysts, that is, analysts without an M.D. degree.

shall see, some psychotherapists believe that modification of behavior is dependent upon the individual's understanding of his unconscious motives and conflicts, whereas others feel that people can learn to cope with their problems without necessarily exploring the factors that have led to their development. Despite differences in techniques, all methods of psychotherapy have certain basic features in common. They involve communication between two individuals, the patient or client and the therapist. The patient is encouraged to express freely his most intimate fears, emotions, and experiences without fear of being judged or condemned by the therapist. The therapist, in turn, while being sympathetic and understanding of the patient's problems, does not become emotionally involved (as would a friend or relative) but maintains an objectivity that enables him to view the patient's difficulties more clearly.

The techniques of psychotherapy have been used most successfully with the milder forms of psychopathology, the neuroses, although some therapists have reported success with psychotics. Neurotics are usually aware of their problems, anxious for help, and able to communicate with the therapist. Psychotics, on the other hand, are frequently so involved in a fantasy world and so unaware of reality that it is extremely difficult to communicate with them. The process of establishing contact (developing what is called *rapport*) with the psychotic is a lengthy one that must be undertaken before psychotherapy can begin. Fortunately, some new drugs being used with psychotic patients make them more amenable to treatment by psychotherapy.

Psychoanalysis

Couch used by Freud's patients

The most familiar psychotherapeutic technique is psychoanalysis, a method of treatment based on the concepts of Sigmund Freud. Psychoanalysis is not a large profession; in 1974 there were 1369 active members of the American Psychoanalytic Association, the recognized organization for fully accredited psychoanalysts in this country. But the influence of psychoanalysis is much more pervasive than the small number of practitioners would suggest.

Along with a method of treatment, Freud proposed a body of psychological theory that has, in one form or another, influenced much of modern thinking—in literature as well as in psychology, medicine, and social science. We shall be concerned chiefly with the nature of psychoanalytic therapy, but it should be kept in mind that the observations made within this technique represent the basic data upon which Freud's theories rest.

FREE ASSOCIATION. The psychoanalyst ordinarily sees a patient for fifty-minute visits several times a week for periods of from one to several years. Psychoanalytic therapy, in its original form, is thus not only intensive but extensive. In the introductory sessions the patient describes symptoms and recounts relevant facts from his personal biography. He is then prepared to enter upon *free association*, one of the foundations of the psychoanalytic method. The purpose of free association is to bring to awareness and to put into words thoughts and feelings of which the patient is unaware or that ordinarily go unacknowledged if they come to awareness.

In free association the patient is taught the "basic rule": Say everything that enters your mind, without selection, without editing. This rule is a very difficult one to follow. The patient's lifetime has been spent in learning

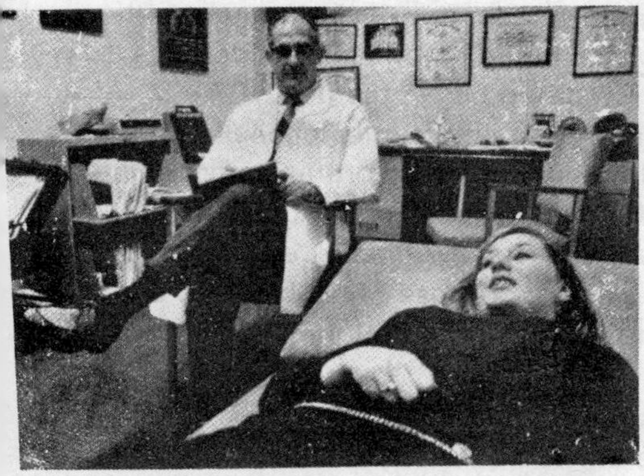

Modern psychoanalytic couch

self-control, in learning to hold his tongue, in learning to think before speaking. Even the patient who tries conscientiously to follow the rule will fail to tell many things. Some passing thoughts seem to be too unimportant to mention, some too stupid, others too indiscreet.

Suppose, for example, that a person's freedom is being hampered by having to care for an invalid. Under such circumstances he may unconsciously wish for the relief that the invalid's death might bring. But he would disapprove of such a death wish because it would be a violation of his loyalty to the sick person. Actually, a death wish of this kind may be very near to awareness, but the habits of a lifetime make the patient deny the wish even to himself. He may show in his fantasies or in other ways a preoccupation with death; possibly he hums tunes that are played at funerals. By acknowledging these fleeting thoughts instead of repressing them, he becomes aware of previously unrecognized ideas and feelings close to awareness. With practice, he gradually brings to consciousness ideas and feelings that have been deeply repressed.

A person unconsciously represses or resists the recall of certain thoughts and feelings because he fears that to acknowledge them will threaten or degrade him. The therapist aids the patient in overcoming this resistance. Sometimes a patient has a free flow of associations until something blocks him. Then his mind seems to go blank, and he can think of nothing to say. This blankness is judged to be resistance to the recall of something effectively repressed. Sometimes, after a particularly revealing session, the patient may forget his next appointment, another indication of resistance to revealing what is hidden.

INTERPRETATION. The psychoanalyst attempts to overcome the patient's resistance and to lead him to fuller self-understanding through *interpretation*. The interpretation is likely to take two forms. First, the analyst calls the attention of the patient to his resistances. The patient often learns something about himself when he discovers that a train of associations is suddenly blocked, that he forgets his appointment, that he wants to change the subject, and so on. Second, the analyst may privately deduce the general nature of what lies behind the patient's statements and by imparting a hint may facilitate further associations. The patient may say something that seems trivial to him and half apologize for its unimportance. Here the analyst may point out that what seems trivial may in fact allude to something important. This hint may lead, if the interpretation is appropriately timed, to significant associations. It should be noted that the analyst is careful not to suggest *just what it is* that is important to the patient; this the patient must discover for himself.

The analyst gives somewhat different interpretations in the early and late stages of analysis. Early in the analysis the interpretations are to help the patient understand resistance. The analyst may encourage association by pointing out the importance of the seemingly trivial or by noting connections in the patient's associations between thoughts that at first seemed totally unrelated. But, as the analysis moves on, the analyst gives more complex interpretations of the content of the patient's associations.

TRANSFERENCE. Any psychotherapeutic relationship is social, involving as it does an interaction between the patient and therapist. In psychoanalytical treatment the attitudes of the patient toward the analyst

"Mr. Prentice is __*not*__ *your father. Alex Binster is* __*not*__ *your brother. The anxiety you feel is* __*not*__ *genuine. Dr. Froelich will return from vacation September 15th. Hang on."*

become important in determining his progress. Sooner or later in analysis the patient develops strong emotional responses to the psychoanalyst, perhaps admiring him greatly in one session but despising him in the next. This tendency of the patient to make the therapist the object of emotional response is known as *transference,* and the interpretation of transference, although a controversial topic, is one of the foundations of psychoanalytic therapy. According to the theory, the patient sees the therapist as possessing attitudes and attributes like those of his parents or those of his brothers and sisters, even though the therapist may be very unlike any of the people for whom he substitutes.

To cite one example: A young woman being treated by a woman psychoanalyst remarked one day as she entered the analyst's office, "I'm glad you're not wearing those lace collars you wore the last several times I was here. I don't like them on you." During the hour, the analyst was able to point out that she had not in fact worn any lace collars. During the preceding sessions the patient had assigned to the analyst the role of the patient's mother and had falsely pictured the analyst as dressing as the patient's mother had dressed when the patient was a child undergoing the emotionally disturbing experiences being discussed with the analyst. The patient, while surprised, accepted the interpretation and thereby gained understanding of transference.

Transference is not always manifested in false perceptions; often the patient simply expresses feelings toward the analyst that he had felt toward figures important earlier in his life. On the basis of these expressed feelings, the analyst is able to interpret the nature of the impulses that have been displaced in his direction. For example, a patient who has always admired an older brother detects something in the analyst's attitude that reminds him of the brother. An angry attack upon the analyst may lead to the uncovering of hostile feelings toward his brother that the patient heretofore had never acknowledged. By studying how the patient feels toward him, the analyst helps the patient to better understand his conduct in relation to others.

ABREACTION, INSIGHT, AND WORKING THROUGH. The course of improvement during psychoanalytic therapy is commonly attributed to three main experiences: *abreaction,* gradual *insight* into one's difficulties, and the repeated *working through* of conflicts and one's reactions to them.

A patient experiences *abreaction* when he freely expresses a repressed emotion or relives an intense emotional experience. The process is also called "catharsis," as though it were a kind of emotional cleansing. Such free expression may bring some relief, but by itself does not eliminate the causes of conflict.

A patient has *insight* when he understands the roots of the conflict. Sometimes insight comes upon the recovery of the memory of a repressed experience, but the popular notion that a psychoanalytic cure typically results from the sudden recall of a single dramatic episode is mistaken. The patient's troubles seldom have a single source, and insight comes through a gradual increase in self-knowledge. Insight and abreaction must work together: the patient must understand his feelings and feel what he understands. The reorientation is never simply intellectual.

As analysis progresses the patient goes through a lengthy process of reeducation known as *working through.* By examining the same conflicts over and over again as they have appeared in a variety of situations, the patient learns to face rather than to deny reality and to react in more mature and effective ways. By working through, the patient becomes strong enough to face the threat of the original conflict situation and to react to it without undue anxiety.

The end result claimed for a successful psychoanalysis is a deep-seated modification of the personality that makes it possible for the patient to cope with his problems on a realistic basis, without the recurrence of the symptoms that brought him to treatment, and that will lead to a more comfortable and richer life.

Psychoanalysis is a lengthy process and generally very expensive. It is most successful with individuals who are highly motivated to solve their problems and who can verbalize their feelings with some ease.

Client-centered Psychotherapy

Client-centered or *nondirective* psychotherapy is a method of treatment developed by Carl Rogers and his associates (Rogers, 1951; 1967; 1970). It is *client-centered* because its purpose is to have the client or patient arrive at the insights and make the interpretations rather than the therapist. It is *nondirective* because the therapist does not try to direct the patient's attention to specific topics (such as his relationship with his wife or his early childhood experiences). Unlike psychoanalysis, client-centered therapy does not attempt to relate the patient's problems to experiences in his early history. It is concerned with the patient's *present* attitudes and behavior. For this reason the client-centered therapist does not believe it necessary to obtain a case history or to spend the initial interviews gathering biographical material.

Client-centered therapy can be described rather simply, but in practice it requires great skill and is much more subtle than it first appears. The therapist begins by explaining the nature of the interviews: the responsibility for working out his problems is the client's; the client is free to leave at any time, and to choose whether or not to return; the relationship is a private and confidential one; the client is free to speak of intimate matters without fear of reproof or of having information revealed to others. Once the situation is structured, the client does most of the talking. Usually he has a good deal to "get off his chest." The therapist is a patient but alert listener. When the client stops, as though expecting the therapist to say something, the therapist usually acknowledges and accepts the feelings the client has been expressing. For example, if the client has been telling about how he is nagged by his mother, the therapist may say: "You feel that your mother tries to control you." His object is to *clarify* the feelings the client has been expressing, not to judge them or to elaborate on them.

What usually happens is that the client begins with a rather low evaluation of himself, but in the course of facing up to his problems and bringing his own resources to bear on them he becomes more positive. For example, one reported case began with statements such as the following:

> Everything is wrong with me. I feel abnormal. I don't do even the ordinary things of life. I'm sure I will fail on anything I undertake. I'm inferior. When I try to imitate successful people, I'm only acting. I can't go on like this (case reported by Snyder and others, 1947).

By the time of the final interview the client expressed the following attitudes, contrasting strikingly with those of the first interview:

> I am taking a new course of my own choosing. I am really changing. I have always tried to live up to others' standards that were beyond my abilities. I've come to realize that I'm not so bright, but I can get along anyway. I no longer think so much about myself. I'm much more comfortable with people. I'm getting a feeling of success out of my job. I don't feel quite steady yet, and would like to feel that I can come for more help if I need it.

To determine whether this kind of progress is typical, experimenters have carefully analyzed recorded interviews. When the client's statements are classified and plotted, the course of therapy turns out to be fairly predictable. For example, in the early interviews the client spends a good deal of time talking about his difficulties, stating his problems, and describing his symptoms. In the course of therapy he increasingly makes statements showing that he understands the implications for his personality of the topics being discussed. By classifying all the client's remarks as either problem restatements or statements of understanding and insight, one can see the progressive increase in insight as therapy proceeds (Figure 17-2).

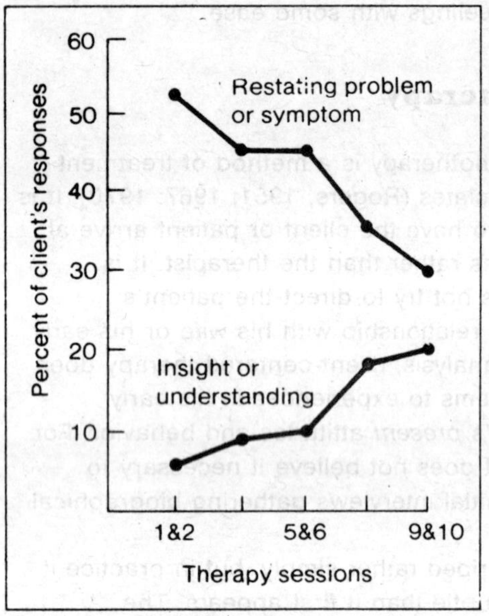

Fig. 17-2 Changes during client-centered therapy

Recital of the problem on the part of the client gradually gives way during the course of therapy to increased frequency of statements indicating understanding. (Data from Seeman, 1949)

What does the therapist do to bring about these changes? First of all, he creates an atmosphere in which the client feels his own worth and significance. The atmosphere arises not as a consequence of technique but out of the therapist's conviction that every person has the capacity to deal constructively with his psychological situation and with those aspects of his life that can come into conscious awareness.

In accepting this viewpoint the therapist is not merely a passive listener; if he were, the client might feel that the therapist was not interested in him. The therapist listens intently and tries to show in what he says that he can see things as the client sees them. When Rogers originated client-centered therapy, he laid great emphasis upon having the therapist try to clarify the feelings expressed by the client. Rogers now believes that method to be too intellectualistic. Currently he places the emphasis upon the therapist's trying to adopt the client's own frame of reference, upon his trying to see the problems as the client sees them but without becoming emotionally involved in them. To have therapeutic value, the change in the client must be a change in feeling, a change in attitude—not merely a change in intellectual understanding.

For Rogers the most important element of a therapeutic relationship is a therapist who is a "genuine or self-congruent person," that is, one who is not playing a role or operating behind a professional front but is open and honest in his relationship with the patient. People tend not to reveal themselves to those who seem to be saying things they do not feel and who are not completely genuine in their relationship with others.

A great deal has been learned from those who advocate and practice client-centered therapy. It is difficult to know with certainty what its range of usefulness is and wherein its limitations lie. It does appear that this method (as is true of psychoanalysis) can function successfully only with individuals who are fairly verbal and motivated to discuss their problems. With persons who do not voluntarily seek help and with psychotics who are too withdrawn to be able to discuss their feelings, more directive methods are usually necessary. The techniques of client-centered therapy have been used successfully, however, in counseling with neurotic patients, in play therapy with children, and in group therapy.

Behavior Therapy

Both psychoanalysis and client-centered therapy are "insight" therapies; their goal is to help patients achieve a better understanding of their feelings and motives so that they can better cope with problems. Psychoanalysis is concerned with understanding how *past* conflicts influence present behavior; client-centered therapy aims at insight into *current* problems and modes of interacting. A more recent approach to psychotherapy focuses not on insight but on the problem behavior itself. The aim is to change the behavior, using techniques derived from *learning theory,* without worrying about the underlying dynamics. The assumption is that maladaptive behavior is learned and that techniques developed in experimental work on learning can be employed to substitute new and more appropriate responses for the maladaptive ones. Psychotherapy based on this approach is called *behavior therapy* or *behavior modification* because it is concerned with modifying the *behavior* of the patient rather than developing insight or resolving unconscious conflicts (Lazarus, 1971; Wolpe, 1969; Ullmann and Krasner, 1969; Bandura, 1969).

Behavior therapists point out that while insight or self-knowledge is a worthwhile goal, it does not insure behavior change. Often we understand why we behave as we do in a certain situation without being able to change the behavior. If you are unusually timid about speaking up in class, you may be able to trace this fear to a number of past events—your father criticized your opinions whenever you tried to express them, your mother made a point of correcting your grammar, you had little experience in public speaking during high school because you were afraid to compete with your older brother who was captain of the debate team. Understanding the reasons behind your fear probably will not make it easier for you to contribute to class discussion.

Behavior therapists maintain that insight is neither necessary nor sufficient for behavior change. They use a number of different techniques (based on the principles of classical and operant conditioning) to modify behavior.

SYSTEMATIC DESENSITIZATION. One technique used by behavior therapists employs the principle of *counter-conditioning:* a maladaptive response can be weakened or eliminated by strengthening an incompatible or antagonistic response. Wolpe (1958), who originated this method of changing behavior, provides an experimental example; he created a "neurosis" in cats and then cured it by counter-conditioning. Cats that received electric shocks in their feeding cages eventually refused to eat not only in their cages but anywhere in the experimental room. The normal eating response was inhibited by anxiety, and the anxiety generalized from the place of shock to the entire room. Wolpe likens this result to the generalization of anxiety in a neurotic individual. To cure the cats' neuroses so that normal eating can occur, the anxiety response must be extinguished. Wolpe found that he could reduce anxiety by a gradual process of feeding the animal elsewhere in the laboratory, at some distance from the room in which the shock had been administered. Although there might be some incipient fear reactions, these were overcome (inhibited) by the successful act of eating. Gradually the feeding was brought closer to the original place, but never at a pace too rapid to upset the eating. When the cat was able to eat in the room where it had become disturbed, it was soon also ready to eat in the cage where it had originally been shocked. Thus it was "cured" of its neurosis.

In extending this process to the treatment of human patients, the behavior therapist begins by discovering in interviews with the patient what situations are anxiety producing. He then compiles a list of situations or stimuli to which the patient responds with anxiety; the stimuli are ranked in order from the least anxiety producing to the most fearful (known as an *anxiety hierarchy*). On the assumption that relaxation is antagonistic to anxiety, the therapist trains the patient to relax (using a method of progressive muscle relaxation, sometimes accompanied by hypnotic suggestion or tranquilizing drugs) and instructs him to visualize the least anxiety-producing situation. (This would correspond to feeding the cat in a remote room in the laboratory.) If visualizing this mild scene does not disturb the relaxation, the patient then goes on to imagine the next item on the list. If the patient still reports anxiety, relaxation is again induced and the same scene is again visualized until all anxiety is neutralized. This process continues through a series of sessions until the situation that originally provoked the most anxiety now elicits only relaxation. Thus the patient has been conditioned to respond with relaxation to situations that initially produced anxiety. He has been systematically desensitized to the anxiety-provoking situation through the strengthening of an antagonistic or incompatible response—relaxation.

Table 17-1 presents two anxiety hierarchies that were used in treating a young woman who was so nervous and "afraid of everything" that she had no appetite, vomited frequently, and had lost twenty pounds. Over a period of about a year she was gradually desensitized to several of her greatest fears, including finding her way about the city alone and worrying about what other people thought of her. General improvement in her feelings of self-confidence and her social behavior resulted.

Sometimes the method of systematic desensitization is used in the presence of the actual fear-producing stimuli rather than visually imagined scenes. The patient is taught to relax in a series of situations that gradually approach the situation that elicits the most intense fear. This procedure has been used successfully to treat cases of impotence and frigidity, as well as phobias, such as fear of heights or snakes. For example, in treating impotence the man is first trained in progressive relaxation and then instructed to practice relaxing while in bed with a woman, confining his sexual activities to preliminary foreplay with no intention of proceeding to intercourse. Only after the anxieties associated with sexual performance have been reduced and sexual responsiveness has increased over a number of sessions is he encouraged to proceed to intromission and actual coitus. Similar procedures have been used in the treatment of frigidity in women (Masters and Johnson, 1970; Madsen and Ullmann, 1967).

ASSERTIVE TRAINING. The procedure of counter-conditioning may also be used with other responses that are antagonistic to anxiety, such as *assertive* or *approach* responses. Some people feel inadequate in interpersonal situations because their anxieties prevent them from "speaking up" for what they feel is right or from "saying no" when others take

TABLE 17-1
Anxiety hierarchies used in systematically desensitizing a young woman who was fearful of traveling alone and easily upset by criticism

TRAVEL

1. You take a streetcar to downtown Cleveland in order to shop.
2. You drive to the dressmaker's, accompanied by your sister, Florence.
3. You take the train to Columbus, accompanied by friends, to attend a nurses' convention.
4. You travel by bus to Columbus accompanied by a friend.
5. You take the streetcar downtown for an appointment with the dentist (first appointment).
6. You take the streetcar to Parkside to attend the cinema (first time that you have gone to this theater).
7. You travel to a suburb of Cleveland alone on the bus.
8. You are driving alone from Stanton to Cleveland.
9. You drive alone to the dressmaker's house.
10. You are flying to Cincinnati with some friends.
11. Taking the train to Columbus to visit Bill.

CRITICISM

1. Your mother reminds you that you have not yet sent a thank-you letter to a relative from whom you received a gift.
2. Your uncle wonders out loud why you don't visit him more often.
3. Your mother notes that you haven't been to church with her in quite a while.
4. Your mother comments that it has been a long time since you have visited your grandmother.
5. Your mother criticizes a friend: she just makes herself at home!
6. Your stepfather says that he can't understand how anyone could be so stupid as to be a Catholic.
7. You return an overdue book to the library. The librarian looks at you critically.
8. A physician making rounds discovers a baby in convulsions. He comments to a colleague: "You see what I mean about having to make rounds."
9. Bill looks over your shoulder as you are writing, and comments that it doesn't look very neat.
10. Bill comments that you are too heavy in the waist and should exercise.
11. Bill criticizes you for being quiet on a double date.
12. You are at a party given by one of Bill's friends. You mispronounce a word and Bill corrects you.
13. Your mother comes into a room and finds you smoking.

Source: Lang (1965).

advantage of them. By practicing *assertive responses*—first in role playing with the therapist and then in real-life situations—the individual not only reduces anxiety but also develops more effective coping techniques. The therapist might start out by finding out the kinds of situations in which the patient is passive, and then help him think of and practice some assertive responses that might be effective in those situations. The following situations are some that might be worked through during therapy sessions.

Someone steps in front of you in line.
A friend asks you to do something you don't want to do.
Your boss criticizes you unjustly.
You return defective merchandise to a store.
You are annoyed by the continual conversation of people behind you in the movies.
The mechanic did an unsatisfactory job of repairing your car.

Most people do not enjoy dealing with such situations, but some individuals are so fearful of asserting themselves that they say nothing and build up feelings of resentment and inadequacy instead. Assertive training involves rehearsing with the therapist effective responses that could be made in such situations and gradually trying them out in real life.

Aversive conditioning as a method of breaking the cigarette habit

The smoker gets a faceful of stale cigarette smoke blown at her by the machine every time she takes a puff. This treatment, combined with other techniques such as inhaling faster than usual to the tick of a metronome, has proved successful in reducing smoking.

AVERSIVE CONDITIONING. Although the method of counter-conditioning has been used principally in dealing with anxiety or fear reactions, it can also be used to eliminate maladaptive behavior that involves *approaching* a situation rather than avoiding it.

By pairing nausea-producing drugs with the intake of alcohol, or by giving electric shock to an alcoholic every time he lifts his glass, an avoidance response can be conditioned to a stimulus (alcohol) that previously elicited an approach response. Aversive conditioning has also been used in the treatment of male homosexuals by pairing electric shock with the viewing of pictures showing nude males (Feldman and MacCulloch, 1971). Such methods have been effective, although it is generally concluded that suppressing a response through punishment does not completely solve the problem. The person must also be taught to emit an appropriate response to the situation. Thus, the treatment of homosexuality is more effective if alternate behaviors, such as learning to be more relaxed in intimate situations with women, are encouraged. And aversive conditioning with alcoholics is more long-lasting if it is followed by teaching ways of dealing with anxiety other than seeking relief through alcohol (Krasner and Ullmann, 1973).

CONTROLLING REINFORCEMENT CONTINGENCIES. Systematic desensitization and aversive conditioning are examples of *classical* (Pavlovian) *conditioning* (p. 195). In both methods a new response becomes associated with an old stimulus. With systematic desensitization, either relaxation or assertiveness becomes associated with a stimulus that previously elicited anxiety or avoidance. In aversive conditioning, avoidance is elicited by a stimulus that previously signaled approach.

Other behavior modification techniques are based on the principles of *operant conditioning* (p. 199). The therapist tries to eliminate those factors in the patient's environment that are reinforcing maladaptive behavior and also to provide positive reinforcement for learning new, more adaptive behavior. Some examples of this method of changing behavior were given in an earlier chapter when we discussed the *social learning approach* to personality assessment. We saw how a child's tendency to remain socially isolated from her peers was being inadvertently reinforced by the nursery school teachers and what procedures they instituted to change this behavior (see p. 387).

Sometimes the behavior the therapist wants to reinforce occurs infrequently or is totally absent, such as talking in a mute child or schizophrenic. In this case a technique similar to Skinner's *shaping* of behavior (see p. 204) is used: responses that approximate or move in the direction of the desired behavior are reinforced, with the therapist gradually requiring closer and closer approximation until the desired behavior occurs. For example, with one very withdrawn schizophrenic (who had remained mute for 19 years) chewing gum proved to be an effective reinforcement for shaping speech. At first the therapist rewarded the patient with a stick of gum simply for looking at it when it was held in front of his face, then for moving his lips, then for making any verbalization if only a croak, then for saying the

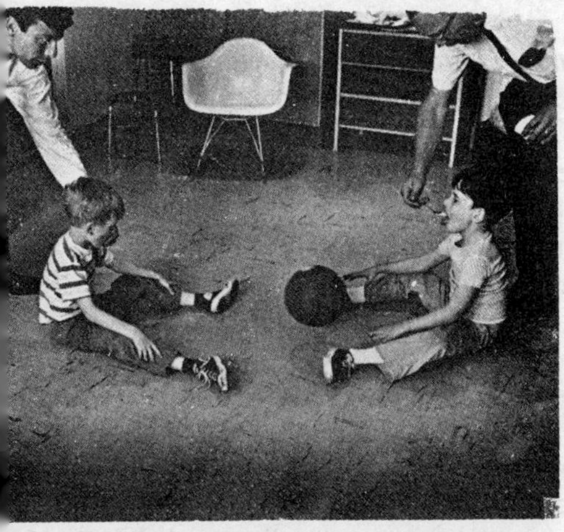

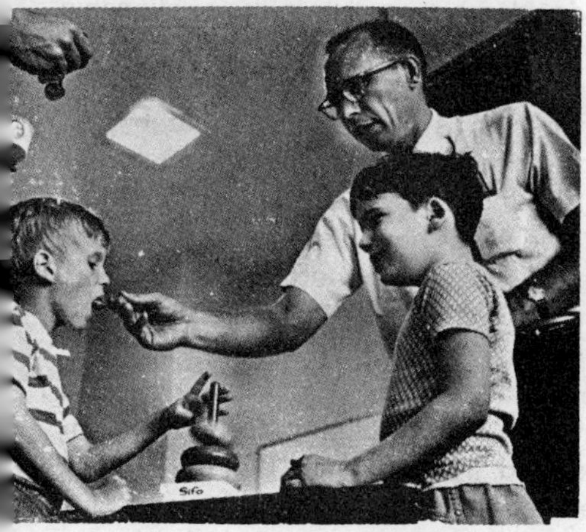

Fig. 17-3 Behavior-contingent reinforcement

These two autistic children were enrolled in an intensive behavior therapy program at the UCLA Neuropsychiatric Institute. Here they are shown receiving immediate reinforcement, in the form of food, for interacting with each other. Other techniques used included punishment (electric shock) for self-destructive behavior or uncontrollable tantrums, and modeling of the appropriate behavior. The boy on the right, mute and self-destructive when he entered the program, was able to return home in less than a year and two years later was doing first-grade work in a special school.

word "gum." All this took place over a period of weeks. Once the patient reached the point where he said "gum please," he began to respond to questions by the therapist. The ward personnel were then asked to respond to the patient's requests only if they were verbalized. For example, if he brought his coat to the nurse as an indication that he wanted to go for a walk, she was not to acquiesce unless he expressed his desire in speech. Other kinds of reinforcement gradually took the place of chewing gum, and the formerly mute schizophrenic became more and more verbal (Isaacs and others, 1965).

Similar procedures have proved effective in teaching seriously disturbed children to talk, interact with other children, sit quietly at a desk, and respond appropriately to questions (see Figure 17-3). These children were not given regular breakfasts or lunches but were provided instead with bits of food for responses that approximated the desired behaviors. Although such procedures may seem cruel, they proved an effective means of establishing normal behavior where all other attempts had failed. Once the child begins to respond to primary forms of reward (such as food), social rewards (praise, attention, and special privileges) become effective reinforcers.

A number of mental hospitals have instituted "token economies" on wards with very regressed, chronic patients as a means of inducing socially appropriate behavior. Tokens (which can later be exchanged for food, cigarettes, and privileges such as watching TV) are given for dressing properly, interacting with other patients, eliminating "psychotic talk," helping on the wards, and so on. Such programs have proved successful in improving both the patients' behavior and the general functioning of the ward.

MODELING. Another effective means of changing behavior is *modeling* (see p. 340). Modeling was used along with several other behavior modification techniques in a study designed to eliminate fear of snakes (Bandura and others, 1969). The subjects were young adults whose snake phobias were severe enough to restrict their activities in various ways—for example, some could not participate in gardening or hiking for fear of encountering snakes. After being tested initially to determine how closely they would approach a live but harmless king snake, the subjects were rated according to their degree of fearfulness and divided into four matched groups. One group watched a film in which child and adult models interacted with a large king snake. The models gave every indication of enjoying interactions that most people would find progressively more fear-arousing. The subjects in this group had been trained in relaxation and were instructed to stop the film whenever a particular scene provoked anxiety, reverse the film to the beginning of the sequence that bothered them, and reinduce relaxation. This procedure was termed "symbolic modeling." A second group imitated the behavior of a live model as the model performed progressively more fearful activities with the snake (see Figure 17-4). Gradually the subjects were guided in such activities as touching the snake with a gloved hand, then with a bare hand, holding the snake, letting it coil around their arm, and finally letting the snake loose in the room, retrieving it, and letting it crawl over their bodies. The procedure was termed "live modeling with participation." Subjects assigned to the third group received the standard desensitization procedure described above, in which deep relaxation was successively paired with imagined scenes of snakes until the subject's anxiety

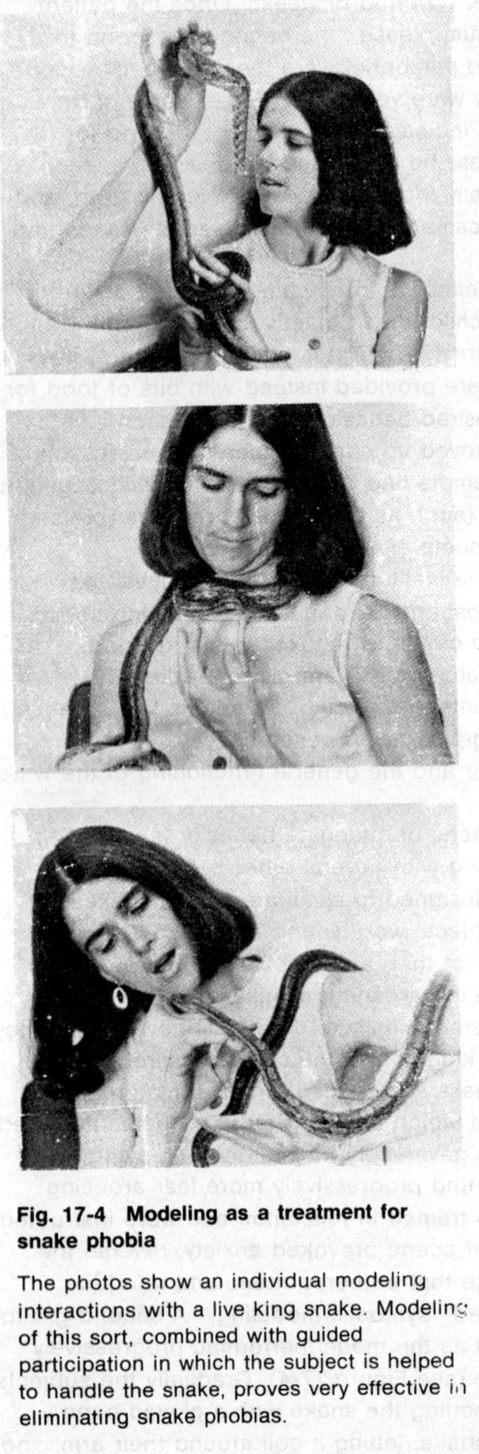

Fig. 17-4 Modeling as a treatment for snake phobia

The photos show an individual modeling interactions with a live king snake. Modeling of this sort, combined with guided participation in which the subject is helped to handle the snake, proves very effective in eliminating snake phobias.

disappeared. The fourth group served as a control and received no special training.

Figure 17-5 shows the number of snake-approach responses performed by the subjects before and after receiving the different treatments. All three treatment groups showed improvement as compared with the control group, but the group that had live modeling combined with guided participation showed the greatest gain. Almost all the subjects in this group completely overcame their fear of snakes. Interestingly enough, the fear of these subjects in relation to a variety of other situations was also reduced. A follow-up investigation some time later indicated that the subjects' snake phobias did not reoccur.

Systematic desensitization, assertive training, aversive conditioning, extinction of maladaptive behaviors along with positive reinforcement of adaptive ones, and modeling have been used successfully by behavior therapists in treating a wide variety of problems. Although these procedures may sound rather cold and unfeeling, in actual practice the therapist shows concern for the patient's welfare and considerable warmth in the relationship. These qualities appear to be necessary in any type of therapy—when they are lacking, behavior modification techniques are not very successful.

Behavior therapy differs from other types of psychotherapy in that it focuses on behavior rather than feelings, understanding, or insight. Behavior can be modified directly by the use of learning principles. And once certain "undesirable" aspects of an individual's behavior have been changed, other persons react to him in a more positive way, stimulating further behavior modification. At this point extrinsic reinforcers are no longer necessary to maintain the improved behavior.

More traditional therapists and psychoanalysts have criticized behavior therapy as a superficial method of treatment, claiming that it deals only with symptoms and leaves the conflict unresolved. They maintain that the beneficial results obtained with this method are a function of the relationship between the therapist and patient (the interest and attention given by the therapist, with the possibility of transference taking place) and not the specific techniques employed. The behavior therapists have rebutted these criticisms by claiming that the success of traditional psychotherapy is based upon the unwitting use of learning principles in the therapy sessions. When a patient discusses behavior or impulses about which he feels guilt and the therapist does not reinforce these feelings with disapproval, the guilt feelings tend to *extinguish.* Such claims and counterclaims can be answered only by further research, including studies designed to compare the effectiveness of behavior therapy and of traditional therapies in treating psychopathology. In the meantime it is clear that behavior theory has provided a challenge to some of the older concepts of therapeutic interaction and has opened up new possibilities in the practice of psychotherapy.

Group Therapy

A majority of emotional problems are caused by an individual's difficulties in relating to others—feelings of isolation, rejection, and loneliness; an inability to interact satisfactorily with others or to form meaningful friendships. In addition to dealing with anxieties and conflicts, the psychotherapist attempts to help the patient achieve more satisfactory interpersonal relations.

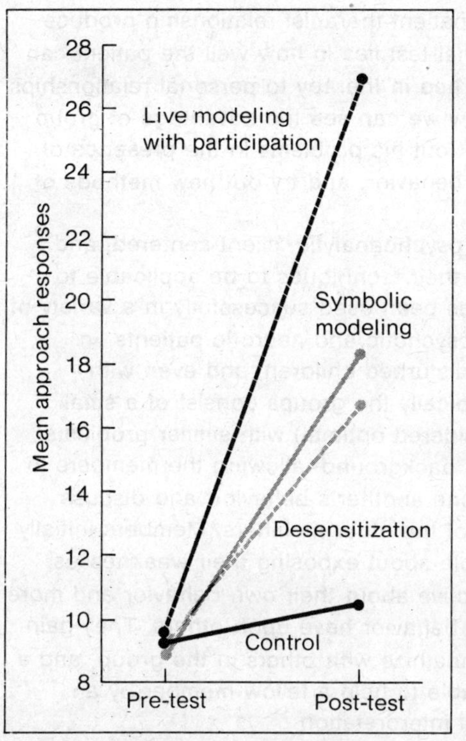

Fig. 17-5 Treatment of snake phobia

The mean number of snake-approach responses made by subjects both before and after receiving different behavior therapy treatments. (After Bandura, Blanchard, and Ritter, 1969)

CRITICAL DISCUSSION

"Mental Illness" versus "Maladaptive Habits"

A person shows certain abnormal behavior; for example, a phobic fear of crowds, compulsive rituals, or mute unresponsiveness. Are these "maladaptive habits" or "symptoms of an underlying disorder?" This is an issue on which *behavior therapists* and *insight therapists* disagree. Behavior therapists say "change the behavior and you have cured the disorder." Psychoanalysts and other more traditional therapists maintain that maladaptive behavior is only a symptom of an underlying "disease." They view mental disorders as analogous to physical disorders and consider it futile to treat the symptoms without removing the underlying pathology. (The physician confronted with a case of syphilis does not simply apply an ointment to the rash but destroys the syphilis spirochete by antibiotics.) According to this view, a phobia or other neurotic symptom is only the surface expression of more complex emotional difficulties; removal of the phobia without treatment of the underlying problem may result in *symptom substitution.* Symptom substitution refers to the development of *new* symptoms (new neurotic defenses against the anxiety caused by internal conflict) if the therapist eliminates the patient's original symptom without curing the underlying conflict. Behavior therapy is criticized by some as a superficial method of treatment that removes the symptoms without dealing with the inner conflicts, thereby leaving the patient vulnerable to symptom substitution.

Behavior therapists, of course, disagree. They maintain that there need be no underlying conflict. A neurosis is a set of maladaptive habits formed through the process of conditioning; once the habits (symptoms) are extinguished and replaced by more adaptive ones, the "illness is cured." The symptom *is* the problem, and eliminating the symptom eliminates the problem.

The debate is not easily settled for a number of reasons, but the evidence suggests that symptom substitution does not occur very often. Several reviews of post treatment evaluation studies found few instances of new symptoms up to two years after successful treatment by behavior modification methods (Grossberg, 1964; Paul and Bernstein, 1973). Instead, the removal of a disturbing "symptom" usually creates better emotional health; the person's self-esteem is increased by this accomplishment, and others respond more favorably once the patient's behavior has changed.

The broader issue of whether psychopathology is best considered "mental illness" or "maladaptive behavior" is more difficult to resolve. There does seem to be some advantage in minimizing the disease concept, at least as far as neuroses are concerned, and focusing instead on the very practical problem of how people can change their behavior to cope more satisfactorily with the problems of life. As one psychiatrist sums up the issue: "Our adversaries are not demons, witches, fate, or mental illness. We have no enemy whom we can fight, exorcise, or dispel by 'cure.' What we do have are problems *in living*—whether these be biologic, economic, political, or sociopsychological" (Szasz, 1961, p. 118).

On the other hand, to completely deny that any illness is involved in serious mental disorders does not seem fully justified. Current research makes the complex interplay between "physical" and "mental" functioning increasingly clear. To view psychotic disorders as solely a problem of reeducation is a misleading oversimplification. To deny any illness connotations to personality disturbance would be to deprive sufferers of hospital facilities, even though the person suffering from an emotional panic may be quite as "ill" as someone with a serious disease.

Group therapy

The patients and therapist usually sit in a circle or around a table within view of one another. Initially the group members tend to be defensive and self-conscious when discussing problems, but over time they become more objective about themselves and more aware of the effect their attitudes and actions have upon others.

Although a number of aspects of the patient-therapist relationship produce progress toward the latter goal, the final test lies in how well the patient can apply the attitudes and responses learned in therapy to personal relationships in everyday life. From this point of view we can see the advantage of *group therapy,* in which the patient can work out his problems in the presence of others, observe how they react to his behavior, and try out new methods of responding when old ones fail.

Therapists of various orientations (psychoanalytic, client-centered, and even behavior therapy) have modified their techniques to be applicable to therapy groups. And group therapy has been used successfully in a variety of settings—in hospital wards with both psychotic and neurotic patients, in mental-health clinics, with parents of disturbed children, and even with troubled business executives. Most typically the groups consist of a small number of individuals (6 to 12 is considered optimal) with similar problems. The therapist generally remains in the background, allowing the members to exchange experiences, comment on one another's behavior, and discuss their own symptoms as well as those of the other members. Members initially tend to be defensive and uncomfortable about exposing their weaknesses, but they gradually become more objective about their own behavior and more aware of the effect their attitudes and behavior have upon others. They gain an increased ability to identify and empathize with others in the group, and a feeling of self-esteem when they are able to help a fellow member by an understanding remark or a meaningful interpretation.

Group therapy has several advantages over individual therapy: (1) the method saves time, because one therapist can help several people at once; (2) the patient becomes aware that he is not alone in his problem, that others have similar feelings of guilt, anxiety, or hostility; (3) the patient has the opportunity to explore his attitudes and reactions by interacting with a variety of people, not just with the therapist. Individuals frequently avail themselves of both group and individual therapy so that they can benefit from the advantages of both.

ENCOUNTER GROUPS. The past decade has seen the expansion of group therapy from a method for resolving emotional problems to a popular means of learning how to relate to others. In this age of isolation and alienation, people have become increasingly concerned with learning how to relate openly and honestly to one another. Encounter groups, also known as *T-groups* (training groups) or *sensitivity groups,* consist of 12 to 20 individuals who may meet together for only an intensive weekend session or over a period of several months in an attempt to better understand why they behave as they do in their interpersonal interactions. The emphasis is upon expressing attitudes and feelings not usually displayed in public. The group leader (or *facilitator,* as he is sometimes called because his job is not really to lead) encourages the participants to explore their own feelings and motives as well as those of other group members. The objective is to stimulate an exchange that is not inhibited by defensiveness and that achieves a maximum of openness and honesty.

Carl Rogers, who has studied various types of encounter groups, describes a fairly consistent pattern of change as the sessions progress (Rogers, 1970). Initially there tends to be confusion and some frustration when the facilitator makes it clear that he will not take the responsibility for directing the group. There is also resistance to expressing feelings; if one

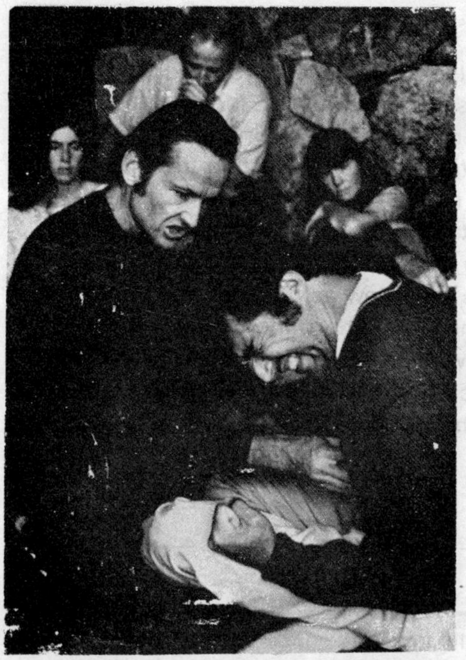

Some methods used in an encounter gro
to explore feelings and release tensio s

member describes some personal feeling other members may try to turn him off, questioning whether it is appropriate to express such feelings in the group. At the next stage the participants gradually begin to talk about feelings and problems they have encountered outside the group. They then move toward discussing relationships within the group; often the first feeling expressed is a negative attitude toward oneself or toward another group member. When the individual finds that the feelings he has expressed are accepted, a climate of trust begins to develop. By the final sessions the group members have become impatient with defensiveness; they attempt to destroy facades, insisting that the individual be himself. The tact and polite cover-up that are acceptable outside the group are not tolerated within it.

In theory, the feedback the individual gains about how his behavior affects others and the feelings of acceptance engendered by the sympathy and helpfulness of the group members lead to increased self-awareness and to behavior change both within and outside the group. Studies of the effects of encounter group participation, however, raise doubts about the extent of behavior change that actually occurs. One study of more than 200 college students who participated in encounter groups with well-trained leaders found that only a third of the students showed positive changes following their experience (based on self-reports and ratings by close friends). One-third showed no change, and a third displayed negative changes—either dropping out of the group because they found it disturbing or feeling afterwards that the experience aggravated personal problems without resolving them (Lieberman, Yalom, and Miles, 1973).

Although encounter groups provide an opportunity for psychologically healthy people to learn something about themselves from the open reactions of others, they are less effective than individual psychotherapy in producing behavior change, and they may prove damaging to those whose self-esteem is too tenuous to withstand group criticism and pressure. Encounter group casualties, including those who become psychotic or commit suicide as a result of the experience, can be minimized by carefully screening participants and by insuring that the leaders are well qualified for their job.

FAMILY THERAPY. A special form of group therapy that has recently received increased attention is *family therapy.* Here the therapy group includes one or two therapists (usually one male and one female), the patient, and the patient's immediate family. The family group may consist of husband and wife or parents and children. On the assumption that the patient's problems reflect a more general maladjustment of the family, the therapy is directed toward helping the family members clarify and express their feelings toward one another, develop greater mutual understanding, and work out more effective ways of relating to one another and solving their common problems.

Sometimes videotape recordings are used to make the family members aware of how they interact with each other. Sometimes the therapist visits the family in the home to observe the conflicts and verbal exchanges as they occur in their natural setting. Traditional therapists focus on resolving family conflicts; behavior therapists try to modify the reinforcing conditions within the family that serve to maintain maladaptive behavior. Parents with a problem child may be taught to carefully observe their own and their child's behavior to determine the reinforcement contingencies and then plan ways of altering them. Temper tantrums and abusive behavior on the part of the child may be inadvertently reinforced by the attention they elicit.

An Eclectic Approach

There are many variations of psychotherapeutic methods in addition to those we have discussed. Several are listed in Table 17-2 Most psychotherapists, however, do not adhere strictly to any *one* particular method. Instead they maintain an *eclectic approach,* selecting from the different techniques those they feel are most appropriate for the individual patient. Although their theoretical orientation may be toward a particular method or "school" (for example, more psychoanalytic than client-centered), they feel free to discard those concepts they view as not especially helpful and to select techniques from other schools. In short, they are flexible in their approach to treatment. In dealing with an anxiety neurotic, for instance, a psychotherapist who takes an eclectic approach might first use tranquilizers and relaxation training to help reduce the patient's level of anxiety. (A

TABLE 17-2
Some approaches to psychotherapy

NAME	FOCUS	METHODS
Gestalt Therapy	To become aware of the "whole" personality by working through unresolved conflicts and discovering those aspects of one's being that are blocked from awareness. Emphasis is on becoming intensely aware of how one is feeling and behaving at the moment.	Treatment in group setting but therapist works with one individual at a time. Acting out fantasies, dreams, or the two sides to one's conflict are methods used to increase awareness. Combines psychoanalytic emphasis on resolving internal conflicts with behaviorist emphasis on awareness of one's behavior and humanistic concern for self-actualization.
Reality Therapy	To clarify one's values and evaluate current behavior and future plans in relation to these values.	Therapist helps person perceive the consequences of possible courses of action and decide on a realistic solution or goal. A "contract" may be signed once a plan of action is chosen in which patient agrees that he will follow through.
Rational-Emotive Therapy	To get rid of certain "irrational" ideas, e.g., "It is essential to be loved and admired by everyone all the time," "One should be competent in all respects," "People have little control over their sorrow and unhappiness." Assumes that cognitive change will produce emotional change.	Therapist attacks and contradicts patient's ideas in an attempt to persuade him to take a more "rational" view of the situation.
Transactional Analysis	To become aware of the intent behind one's communications; to eliminate subterfuge and deceit in order to see one's behavior for what it really is.	Treatment in group setting. Communications between married couples or group members are analyzed in terms of the part of the personality that is speaking—"Parent," "Child," or "Adult" (similar to Freud's superego, id, and ego)—and the intent of the message. Destructive social interactions or "games" are exposed for what they are.
Primal Therapy	To eradicate the *Primal Pains* produced by the early denial of one of the *Primal Needs* (hunger, warmth, privacy, to be held, to develop according to one's natural abilities). The tension and pain generated by unfulfilled Primal Needs must find free expression before the neurosis can be cured. In contrast with Reality and Rational-Emotive Therapies, the emphasis is on "feeling" rather than understanding.	The patient's defenses are weakened by a preparatory period of isolation and sleeplessness so that when he meets the therapist in an intensive encounter his feelings will no longer be inhibited but will be expressed in their primitive intensity.

psychoanalyst would not, because he considers anxiety necessary to motivate the patient to explore his conflicts.) To help him understand the origins of his problems, he might discuss certain aspects of the patient's history (a client-centered therapist does no delving into the past) but might feel it unnecessary to explore childhood experiences to the extent that a psychoanalyst does. He might use educational techniques: for example, he might provide information about sex and reproduction to help relieve the anxieties of an adolescent who has been badly misinformed and feels guilty regarding his sexual impulses; or he might explain the functioning of the autonomic nervous system to reassure an anxiety neurotic that some of his symptoms, such as heart palpitations and hand tremors, are not indications of a disease.

Another technique the psychotherapist might use, and one not mentioned so far in our discussion of psychotherapy, would be to change the patient's environment. The psychotherapist might feel, for example, that a young man who has serious conflicts in his relationships with his parents can make little progress in overcoming his difficulties while remaining in the home environment. In this instance he might recommend that the youth attend a preparatory school or college away from home or seek employment in another community. Occasionally, with a younger child, the home environment may be so seriously detrimental to the child's mental health that the therapist, with the help of welfare agencies and courts, may see that he is placed in a foster home.

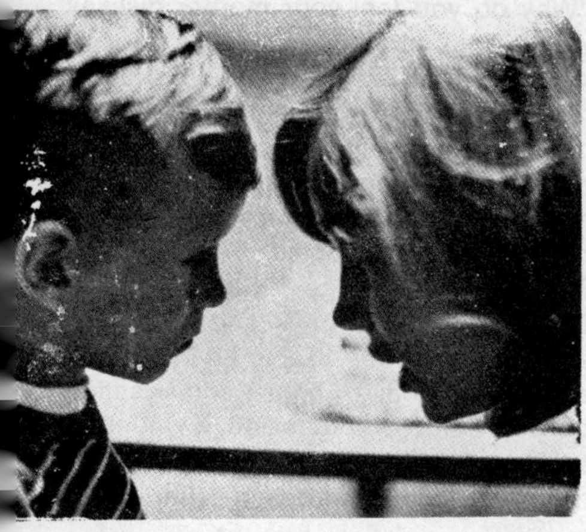

Nonprofessionals as therapists

College students and other volunteers can do much to augment treatment programs in hospitals and mental health centers, whether trained in special therapeutic techniques or simply providing conversation and companionship.

Nonprofessionals as Therapists

Because the need for psychological services has outstripped the supply of available therapists, there has been a trend toward training nonprofessionals to work in the field of mental health. College students have served as companions for hospitalized psychotics (Matarazzo, 1971); older women who have successfully raised a family have been trained as "mental-health counselors" to work with adolescents in community clinics, to counsel mothers of youngsters with behavior problems, and to work with schizophrenic children (Rioch, 1967; Donahue, 1967); former mental patients, drug addicts, or prison inmates have been trained to treat those with similar problems.

An example of the use of nonprofessionals in therapy is a project in which male college students served as "companion-therapists" for young boys with behavior problems. Fifty pairs of boys, matched according to age, socioeconomic status, and several other variables, were selected. One member of each pair was assigned to a student companion-therapist; the other served as a control, receiving no treatment. Each student-therapist met with his boy for several hours two or three times a week throughout the school year, engaging in whatever activities seemed to interest the boy. The training received by the student-therapists consisted of (1) two initial half-day workshops that focused on "helping relationships" and (2) weekly group discussions with professional leaders throughout the year. The results of the project indicated that boys who had problems of isolation and withdrawal gained most from the relationships, although more aggressive boys improved too. The student-therapists themselves felt that they had improved in their ability to work with children and to relate to their own friends (Goodman, 1970). The use of nonprofessionals in this type of relationship is still in an exploratory stage, but initial reports have generated considerable enthusiasm.

CRITICAL DISCUSSION

Computer Simulation of Psychotherapy

TABLE 17-3
Excerpt from a "therapeutic" dialogue between a computer and a subject

PROGRAM	I would like to know more about your background, especially about your family life.
PERSON	My father and mother did not get along well.
PROGRAM	Tell me something else you think is important about your father.
PERSON	He was hard to live with because he was so domineering.
PROGRAM	Are you like your father?
PERSON	No, I am not.
PROGRAM	In some way though you must be like your father.
PERSON	He liked to fish and I do too.
PROGRAM	Did you admire him when you were young?
PERSON	I don't think so.
PROGRAM	Why not?
PERSON	Because he was too weak a person.
PROGRAM	I see. Now tell me something else about him.
PERSON	Well he was very opinionated.
PROGRAM	Was there much friction between you and him when you were growing up?
PERSON	Yes. We fought all the time.
PROGRAM	Perhaps you were afraid of him.
PERSON	I certainly was. He used to really blow up.
PROGRAM	Perhaps you are still fearful of older men.
PERSON	Let's talk about something else.
PROGRAM	O.K. Go ahead. I will try to follow what you have to say about it.

Source: Colby and Enea (1967).

A rather revolutionary approach to psychotherapy programs a computer to act as a therapist (Colby and Enea, 1967). The subject sits at a teletype connected to the computer and types out anything he wishes to say. The computer sends back a typewritten reply.

The rules for coding the program are complex; essentially they operate according to the following process. The computer is programmed to recognize several hundred key words or phrases, such as "I hate," "I worry," "my mother," and to select a response from a group of replies designated as appropriate for that key word or phrase. The response selected may require the addition of certain appropriate words to the input sentence. For example: PERSON: "My mother dislikes me." PROGRAM: "Why do you feel your mother dislikes you?" The computer also keeps track of key topics for use in formulating future responses. If the input sentence does not contain any key words, the computer is programmed to steer the person away from non-key topics or to return him to previous topics. For example: PERSON: "It is a nice day today." PROGRAM: "Let's go back and talk more about your mother." Table 17-3 presents an excerpt from an actual conversation between the computer and a volunteer subject. The conversation is not unlike the information-gathering type of in-

Evaluation of Psychotherapies

With so many types of psychotherapy available, you may well wonder "Which method is best?" or "Who can help me with my problem?." Unfortunately, there are no clear-cut answers to such questions. Research into the effectiveness of psychotherapy is hampered by several major difficulties. How do we define "cure"? How do we know which treatment variables were responsible? What about the "placebo effect"?

terview a therapist conducts in his first few sessions with a patient. Indeed, experienced therapists who were asked to evaluate a group of computer protocols without being told their source judged them to be quite adequate initial interviews.

So far the computer's responses are limited to questioning, clarifying, rephrasing, and only occasionally interpreting. Colby and his fellow investigators are also attempting to develop a program that can make causal interpretations based on an understanding of the patient's problems. If such a program can be developed satisfactorily, computer simulation of psychotherapy could serve a number of highly useful purposes. It could provide a unique research opportunity; for example, certain rules for responding could be changed and the effect on the subject observed. If it proved beneficial in the treatment of individuals with behavior disorders, it would provide a very efficient means of overcoming the shortage of therapists in hospitals, for one computer system could then handle several hundred patients an hour. And the program need not be completely automatic; it could be designed so that a human therapist could monitor the system, adding his own responses when he thought it appropriate or directing the computer to certain problem areas.

Criteria of Cure

How do we know that a person is cured? We cannot always rely on the patient's statement. Sometimes patients report that they are feeling better simply to please the therapist or to convince themselves that the money was well spent. The *hello-goodbye effect* has long been recognized by therapists. When the patient says "hello" at the beginning of therapy he tends to exaggerate his unhappiness and problems as if to convince the therapist that he really needs help. After a course of treatment the patient tends to exaggerate his good health as he says "goodbye," either to express appreciation to the therapist for his efforts or to convince himself that his time and money were not wasted. These phenomena must always be considered when evaluating the patient's view of his progress.

The therapist's evaluation of the treatment as "successful" cannot always be taken as an objective criterion either. The therapist has a vested interest in proclaiming that the patient is better. And sometimes the changes that the patient shows during the therapy hour do not carry over into real-life situations.

Objective measures of improvement—performing more effectively on the job, getting along better with family and friends, drinking less, and so on—are more valid but are difficult to obtain in long-term studies of psychotherapeutic effectiveness.

Interaction of Treatment Variables

It is not always clear that the techniques the therapist consciously employs are the ones that effect the observed changes in the patient's behavior; other variables, of which the therapist could have been unaware, may have been more important. In addition, no two therapists who use the same method have the same personality, and no two patients bring the same attitudes, problems, and methods of coping with their difficulties to the therapeutic session. *Therapist variables* and *patient variables* interact with treatment methods to make it difficult to assess which are related to a successful outcome. For example, it has been shown that some therapists are more effective with certain types of patients than with others and that experienced therapists are more effective than inexperienced therapists regardless of the treatment method used (Whitehorn and Betz, 1960).

To complicate the picture, some psychotics get well spontaneously without any specific treatment, and some patients improve if they think they are receiving effective treatment even if it is only a sugar pill. The *placebo effect* has to be acknowledged when any form of treatment is given.

Despite these difficulties the general consensus seems to be that (1) psychotherapy does help and (2) with the exception of phobias and specific anxieties, which are best treated by behavior therapy techniques, there is little evidence that one form of therapy produces better results than another. Regardless of diagnosis or type of treatment, most patients who come to psychotherapy show progressive improvement over time. It has been suggested that all people who seek treatment, regardless of their specific symptoms, are unhappy and demoralized; they feel unable to cope with their life situation. And all psychotherapies, regardless of their superficial diversity, share certain features in common: (1) a warm, confiding relationship between the patient and a help-giving individual or group; (2) a special setting that provides promise of healing; and (3) a set of activities that both the therapist and patient believe will provide help. It may be these features that ease the patient's despair and give him hope that he can master his inner feelings and the demands of the external world (Frank, 1974).

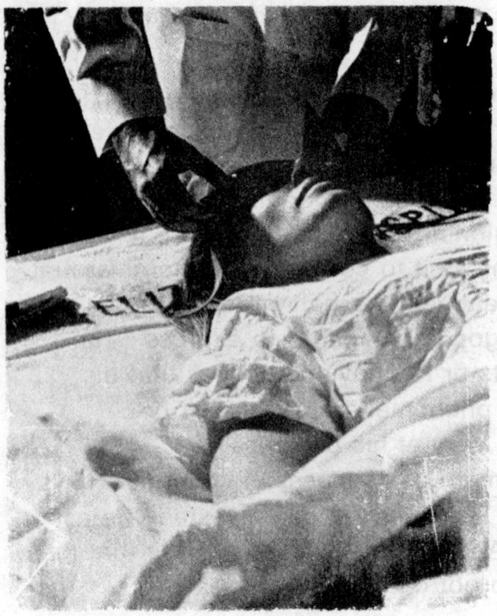

Electroshock therapy being administered to patient

Somatotherapy

The medical model assumes that psychopathology, particularly the psychoses, is caused by neurophysiological malfunctioning and can be best cured by treating the *soma* (body) rather than the *psyche*. Indeed, some notable successes have been achieved with somatotherapy. Vitamin treatment has reduced the prevalence of mental disturbances associated with pellagra; antibiotics for the cure of syphilis have reduced the once prevalent organic psychosis known as general paresis; barbiturates have alleviated the symptoms of epilepsy.

The somatotherapies developed for treatment of the functional psychoses have proved less successful than anticipated, however. The use of electric shock to produce convulsive seizures and unconsciousness was a popular method of treatment thirty years ago. But it was not found to be successful in curing most disorders (including schizophrenia) and is used today only with severely depressed patients who have failed to respond to other forms of treatment. The patient is injected with a muscle-relaxant type of sedative, placed on a bed, and given an electric shock across electrodes placed on the temples. The shock is of sufficient intensity to produce a convulsion, which is followed by a brief period of unconsciousness (up to 30 minutes). The patient cannot remember anything about the shock or convulsion. No one knows how the shock produces its therapeutic effect, but it does seem to snap some patients out of a severe depression. Unfortunately, it does not prevent future depressions.

Psychosurgery, in which the nerve fibers connecting the hypothalamus with the frontal lobes are severed to reduce uncontrolled emotional behavior, has proved unsatisfactory. The patients become more relaxed and cheerful and are no longer violent, but they cannot function very efficiently. They have irreversible brain damage and in some cases lead a vegetablelike existence.

The method of somatotherapeutic treatment that appears to hold the most promise of success is *chemotherapy*, the use of tranquilizers and other types of drugs to modify behavior.

Chemotherapy

Chemicals have been used to influence behavior for centuries. Narcotics were found to reduce pain, alcohol and sedatives to lessen anxiety and induce sleep, stimulants such as caffeine to relieve depression. However, only within the past fifteen years, with the introduction of the two major tranquilizers, *reserpine* and *chlorpromazine*, have chemicals been used extensively in the treatment of mental disorders.

Both of these tranquilizers have the amazing capacity to calm and relax the individual without inducing sleep, although they may produce some degree of drowsiness and lethargy. They have been particularly effective in the treatment of schizophrenics. In addition to calming the intensely agitated schizophrenic, these drugs gradually alleviate or abolish hallucinations and,

CRITICAL DISCUSSION

The Double-blind Procedure in Drug Studies

The initial enthusiasm for a new treatment method is almost always dampened by evidence from more carefully controlled research. This has been particularly true in the area of chemotherapy. The results of a drug study may be affected by a number of variables other than the therapeutic properties of the drug itself. One such variable is the hope and confidence the patient places in a new treatment. For example, the giving of a *placebo* (an inert substance that has no pharmacological properties and cannot affect the patient physiologically) can frequently bring about marked improvement in a patient's condition, thus demonstrating that improvement was the result of attitude. Another variable is the confidence of the doctors and nurses in a new treatment method, which can also inadvertently affect their judgment of the results. And the extra attention focused on the patient as the subject of a research project can have beneficial effects. To control the first two variables the more stringent studies use what is called the *double-blind* procedure. Half the patients receive a placebo, the others receive the actual drug. Neither the patients nor the doctors and nurses who must judge the results of the treatment know who received the drug; thus in the ideally controlled study both patients and judges are "blind"—hence the term "double-blind."

The importance of a well-controlled research design has been shown by a survey of a large number of studies dealing with the effect of chlorpromazine on hospitalized schizophrenics. Each study was classified according to the extent that awareness of medication was controlled: (1) double-blind, neither patient nor judges aware; or (2) single-blind, only judges aware. The group of studies taken as a whole showed a median of 52 percent of the patients judged as "improved." The double-blind studies showed a median of 37 percent judged as improved; the single-blind studies showed a median of 60 percent improved. The more carefully controlled studies report considerably less improvement following treatment with chlorpromazine than do the studies that are less well controlled (Glick and Margolis, 1962).

Although it seems probable that differences in adequacy of experimental control were partly responsible for the differences in results, the double-blind studies differed from the single-blind in another major respect: the average period of drug treatment was significantly longer for patients in the single-blind studies than for those in the double-blind. Hence the higher improvement rate for the single-blind studies may have resulted from the fact that the patients in these studies had a more extended period of treatment. The more control one requires in a study, the more difficult it is to sustain the procedures for a long period of time.

to a lesser extent, delusions; even more important, they frequently decrease the extent of emotional withdrawal so that the patient can be reached by psychotherapy. The introduction of tranquilizing drugs produced a marked decrease in the total number of patients in neuropsychiatric hospitals.

Minor tranquilizers such as Valium (diazepam), Miltown (meprobamate), and Librium (chlordiazepoxide hydrochloride) have proved effective in reducing tension in normal individuals as well as treating neuroses and psychophysiological disorders.

Another group of drugs, the *antidepressants,* help to elevate the mood of depressed individuals. They energize rather than tranquilize. They apparently affect the amount of certain neurotransmitters within the brain, thereby accelerating synaptic transmission. Phenelzine (Nardil) and isocarboxazid (Marplan) are two of the most widely used antidepressants.

The most recent discovery has been the use of *lithium* for treating manic disorders. Initial reports are encouraging, but it is too early to tell how effective its use will be in the long run.

Chemotherapy has successfully reduced the seriousness of many types of pathology, particularly the psychoses. Many individuals who would otherwise require hospitalization can function within the community with the help of some of the above-mentioned drugs. On the other hand, there are limitations. All of these drugs can have undesirable side effects. In addition, many psychologists feel that they alleviate symptoms without bringing the individual to grips with the problems that are creating maladaptive behaviors. They point out that the attitudes and response patterns that have developed gradually over a lifetime cannot be suddenly changed by the administration of a drug.

Enhancing Mental Health

Rather than spending so much time and effort on the treatment of mental disorders, it would be better to provide for normal emotional development by creating conditions that promote healthful living. We do not know what all of these conditions are, but we have some clues.

Useful Work

Absorption in useful work keeps individuals in touch with reality and enhances self-esteem, provided that they accept the work as dignified and suited to their abilities and interests.

The depression of the early 1930s showed the demoralizing effects of idleness and unemployment. Initially the unemployed were placed on a dole, because it was the cheapest kind of relief to administer. But experience taught the importance of work relief instead, for without work the individual tended to disintegrate. Work is not only a matter of livelihood; it provides satisfaction in itself and is usually essential to self-esteem.

Activities that enhance the feeling of being a useful and creative person—volunteer work, crafts, gardening, community activities—are beneficial even if they are not remunerative.

Social Participation

We are social animals and suffer when isolated from our fellows. The circumstances of modern life tend to produce loneliness for many people. As people move—and they move about a great deal these days—they lose contact with friends and relatives. Apartment dwellers today seldom know those who live across the hall; the urban child often has difficulty finding playmates. Social correctives have to be introduced, not as newfangled ideas but as a return to earlier social arrangements. For example, the nursery school substitutes for the large family and for association with neighborhood children; the community center takes the place of the neighborhood barn dance. Such substitutes must be found for people of all ages.

Self-understanding

To what extent may people better their own mental health through self-understanding? This is a difficult question, because preoccupation with personal problems may be worse than ignoring them and going about the business of living. A few helpful suggestions, nevertheless, emerge from the experiences of therapists.

1. *A person can learn to accept his feelings as something natural and normal.* Sometimes the desire to face situations unemotionally leads to a false kind of detachment and imperturbability that has destructive consequences. The person begins to suspect emotion and loses the ability to accept as valid the joys and sorrows of interplay with other people. In many emotion-arousing situations the disturbing emotion is in part a result of his feeling that he does not come up to expectations or that he falls short of his ideal. Even to experience such emotions is frightening, so he tries to escape them by denial.

   Actually, there are many situations in which one can accept unpleasant emotion as perfectly normal and not belittling. It is not necessary to be ashamed of being homesick, or of being afraid of a spirited horse one does not know how to ride, or of being angry at someone who has been a disappointment. These emotions are natural; civilized life permits them, and it is more wholesome to give them free play than to deny them. Anxiety about one's emotions often results in a vicious circle. The person becomes afraid that he will be afraid. He then discovers that he is in fact mildly afraid. The discovery confirms his suspicion about himself and then exaggerates the fear. It is better to be willing to accept the naturalness of emotions as they arise.

2. *If blocked by circumstances from free emotional expression, a person can seek permissible outlets.* Civilized life puts restraints upon free emotional expression. It may be inadvisable for a person to tell his boss or his mother just what his feelings are, but he may accept his own feelings as justified while withholding their direct expression. But on the principle that such unexpressed feelings tend to persist as tensions, some indirect outlet is desirable. Sometimes an outlet can be found in vigorous exercise—who hasn't taken a rapid walk and eventually found both his pace and his emotion slowing down? Sometimes it helps to acknowledge felt emotion to a sympathetic person not involved in the crisis situation. As long as a person accepts his right to feel emotion, he may give expression to it in indirect or substituted ways when the direct channels of expression are blocked.

3. *By discovering the occasions that provoke emotional overreaction, a person can learn to guard against it.* Most people find some kinds of situations in which they tend to be more emotional than do other people. It may be that small failures cause them undue chagrin; it may be that they find certain people excessively annoying. Once they are able to detect the situations that lead to emotional distortion, they sometimes learn to see the situations in new ways so that this undue emotion no longer arises. Sometimes our exaggerated awareness of some shortcoming makes us unduly sensitive to criticism. This is one form that projection takes. If a lawyer's work is so heavy that he has to return to the office at night, he may get the feeling that he is neglecting his wife or family. If, however, his

wife so much as mentions his return to the office, he may get angry—sure that she is accusing him of neglect. Then he will insist that his family makes too many demands upon him. If he could recognize his wife's remark for what it is, an expression of sympathy because he is so busy, then he should feel no anger.

Limitations of Self-help

The person overwrought by emotional problems does well to seek the counsel of a clinical psychologist, a psychiatrist, or other trained therapist. The mechanisms of self-deception are so pervasive that it is difficult to solve a long-standing personal problem without help. The willingness to seek help is a sign of emotional maturity, not of weakness. The therapist should not be thought of only as the court of last appeal. We do not wait until our teeth are falling out before we go to a dentist. Obtaining psychological help when needed should become as accepted a practice as going to a dentist.

Summary

1. The history of treatment of the mentally ill has progressed from the ancient notion that disordered behavior resulted from possession by evil spirits and should be punished accordingly, through custodial care in ill-kept and isolated asylums, to our modern mental hospitals and community mental-health centers, which employ a wide variety of activities designed to help the patient understand and modify his behavior.
2. *Psychotherapy* is the treatment of behavior disorders by psychological means. An extended type of psychotherapy is *psychoanalysis,* which is based on concepts developed by Freud. Through the method of *free association* repressed thoughts and feelings are brought to awareness. By *interpreting* the patient's associations, the analyst helps him to see the roots of his disturbance. Through the process of *transference* the patient substitutes the analyst for another person who is the object of many of his neurotic reactions. The analyst, in turn, attempts through the understanding of transference to use it as an aid to therapy. Through the processes of *abreaction, insight,* and *working through,* the disorder may eventually be cured.
3. Another psychotherapeutic approach is Carl Rogers' *client-centered psychotherapy,* which tries to help the individual gain insight into his current problems and methods of interacting with others rather than focusing on those events in the past that caused the disturbance. The therapist provides a warm, empathic atmosphere and maintains a *nondirective approach,* letting the patient determine the topics to be discussed and the goals to be accomplished.
4. *Behavior therapy* applies learning principles to *modify* the individual's *behavior.* Behavior therapy methods based on the principle of counter-conditioning include *systematic desensitization, assertive training,* and *aversive conditioning;* with these methods a new response becomes associated with the stimulus or situation that previously elicited a maladaptive response. Operant conditioning principles are used in *shaping behavior* and *controlling reinforcement contingencies. Modeling* provides another effective means of changing behavior.
5. *Group therapy* provides an opportunity for the disturbed individual to explore his attitudes and behavior in interaction with others who have

similar problems. *Encounter groups* and *family therapy* are special forms of group therapy.

6. The effectiveness of psychotherapy is difficult to evaluate because of problems in defining "cure," separating out those variables that were responsible for improvement, and controlling for the *placebo effect.*
7. In the treatment of behavior disorders by physical methods (*somatotherapy*) the greatest advances have been made by *chemotherapy,* the use of drugs to modify behavior. Tranquilizers have proved effective in the treatment of schizophrenia, antidepressants help to elevate the mood of depressed patients, and the chemical lithium shows promise in treating manic disorders.
8. Mental illness is a serious and widespread problem in our society, and it is important that we focus on its *prevention* as well as its treatment. Some of the conditions that promote mental health include useful employment and satisfactory social participation. We can also help ourselves through appropriate self-evaluation: by accepting our emotions as natural, by finding channels for emotional expression, and by gaining such understanding as we can on occasions when we overreact. There are limitations to self-help, however, and it is not a sign of weakness to seek professional help.

Further Reading

Material on the history of treatment of the mentally ill may be found in Zilboorg and Henry, *A history of medical psychology* (1941); Veith, *Hysteria: The history of a disease* (1965); and Roback, *History of psychology and psychiatry* (1961). A paperback by Szasz, *The manufacture of madness* (1970), traces the historical origins of the current concept of "mental illness."

An analysis of different systems of psychotherapy is provided by Martin, *Introduction to psychotherapy* (1971). Problems and issues in mental health are discussed in Cowen, Gardner, and Zax, *Emergent approaches to mental health problems* (1967); Braginsky, Braginsky, and Ring, *Methods of madness: The mental hospital as a last resort* (1969); and Zax and Cowen, *Abnormal psychology: Changing conceptions* (1972).

For an introduction to psychoanalytic methods see Menninger and Holzman, *Theory of psychoanalytic technique* (1973). On client-centered therapy, see Rogers, *On becoming a person: A therapist's view of psychotherapy* (1970). The principles of behavior therapy are presented in Wolpe and Lazarus, *Behavior therapy techniques* (1966); Bandura, *Principles of behavior modification* (1969); and Kanfer and Phillips, *Learning foundations of behavior therapy* (1970). For suggestions of how to modify your own behavior by self-use of behavior modification techniques see Watson and Tharp, *Self-directed behavior: Self-modification for personal adjustment* (1972).

A comprehensive overview and evaluation of group therapy is presented in Yalom, *The theory and practice of group psychotherapy* (1970). On encounter groups see Lieberman, Yalom, and Miles, *Encounter groups: First facts* (1973).

Social and cultural influences on psychopathology are discussed in Dohrenwend and Dohrenwend, *Social status and psychological disorder* (1969).

part eight

social behavior

18

social psychology

Social psychology studies the ways in which a person's thoughts, feelings, and behaviors are influenced by other persons. When will individuals conform to the opinions of a group? What factors influence our first impressions of others? Under what conditions will people come to the aid of a stranger in distress? How can racial prejudice be reduced? What kinds of people will be attracted to one another? These questions—and many others—are being investigated by social psychologists; in fact, complete books have been written about each of them.

A chapter like this, then, must necessarily be selective if it is to devote more than a few sentences to any given topic. Accordingly, we have chosen sets of interrelated topics from four of the major areas of social psychology. First, we will look at some of the factors involved in our perception of other people. How do we form impressions of people? What leads us to like some people more than others? How do we assess each other's personalities? Closely related is a second group of questions concerning the way motives are inferred from behavior. What implicit rules do we employ in attributing causes to another person's actions? Do we use the same rules in explaining our own acts? Next, we will look at some of the processes of social influence How does the simple physical presence of others affect our behavior? And finally, we will examine the social forces that lead to attitude and behavior change. If you force people to comply, will they change their attitudes? What are some of the techniques of persuasive communication, and how can they be resisted? Although these topics do not begin to exhaust the possibilities, they will enable us to touch on several concerns of major interest to contemporary social psychologists and give us some of the flavor of this active subfield of psychology.

Social influences on behavior have been considered in earlier chapters. We saw, for example, how the child's development is affected by early experiences with other people and how personal motives are influenced by social interactions. Indeed, since most of our lives are spent in the presence of others, we might conclude that almost all of psychology is "social." The social psychologist, however, tends to look at social influence from a somewhat different perspective than either the personality or the developmental psychologist. First of all, he is more apt to focus on the *current or ongoing situational influences* on human behavior than on developmental or personality factors. For example, when a person goes out of his way to help a stranger in distress, the developmental or personality psychologist is likely to inquire into the kinds of past life experiences that caused this person to act as he did (that is, to have an "altruistic" personality). In contrast, the social psychologist is more likely to be interested in the kinds of surrounding circumstances that encouraged the individual to intervene in this particular situation. Were other bystanders present? Was physical danger involved? Would someone have intervened if the same situation had arisen in a New York subway? And so forth.

The second distinguishing feature of the social-psychological approach is its emphasis on the individual's *"phenomenology,"* that is, on the *individual's own point of view or subjective definition of the situation* rather than on some "objective" measure of the circumstances. Thus, if a person acts in certain ways because he believes that others are hostile to him—even if objectively it is untrue—this perceived hostility *is* a cause of the individual's behavior as far as the social psychologist is concerned. (Social psychologists did not invent the phenomenological approach. One of William Shakespeare's favorite devices was to have events and actions set in motion by a character's erroneous belief that something or other was true when in fact it was not. Thus did Romeo take poison in the incorrect belief that Juliet had done so, and events in *Richard III* are constructed almost entirely around the mistaken phenomenologies of the characters.) In this chapter, we shall see recurrent examples of both the situational and phenomenological emphases that characterize the social-psychological perspective.

Perception of Others

You meet someone for the first time and observe or talk with him or her for a few minutes. Chances are that even in this short space of time you make judgments about a number of characteristics. People tend to form impressions quickly on the basis of very little information.

First Impressions: Primacy and Recency Effects

What kind of impression do you have of Jim from the following observations of his behavior?

> Jim left the house to get some stationery. He walked out into the sun-filled street with two of his friends, basking in the sun as he walked. Jim entered the stationery store, which was full of people. Jim talked with an acquaintance while he waited to catch the clerk's eye. On his way out, he stopped to chat with a school friend who was just coming into the store. Leaving the store, he walked toward school. On his way he met the girl to whom he had been introduced the night before. They talked for a short while, and then Jim left for school. After school Jim left the classroom alone. Leaving the school, he started on his long walk home. The street was brilliantly filled with sunshine. Jim walked down the street on the shady side. Coming down the street toward him, he saw the pretty girl whom he had met on the previous evening. Jim crossed the street and entered a candy store. The store was crowded with students, and he noticed a few familiar faces. Jim waited quietly until he caught the counterman's eye and then gave his order. Taking his drink, he sat down at a side table. When he had finished his drink he went home. (Luchins, 1957a, pp. 34–35)

What do you think Jim is like? Do you think of him as a friendly, outgoing sort of person? Or do you have the impression that he is rather shy and introverted? If you think Jim is better described as friendly than unfriendly, you are in agreement with most people (78 percent) who read this description. But now examine the description more closely; it is actually composed of two very different portraits. Up to the sentence that begins "After school, Jim left . . . ," Jim is portrayed in several situations as a fairly friendly guy; after that point, however, a nearly identical set of situations shows him to be much more of a loner. In fact, 95 percent of people who are shown only the first half of the description rate Jim to be friendly, whereas only 3 percent of people who are shown only the second half do so. Thus, in the combined description that you read, it is Jim's "friendliness" that seems to win out over his unfriendliness in the final impression. Why might

TABLE 18-1
Primacy effects in impression formation

CONDITIONS	PERCENTAGE RATING JIM AS FRIENDLY
Friendly description only	95%
Friendly first—unfriendly last	78%
Unfriendly first—friendly last	18%
Unfriendly description only	3%

this be so? Is it something about the trait of friendliness or does it hinge on the sequence of description, on the fact that Jim is described as friendly first and unfriendly second? To find out, Abraham Luchins, the psychologist who designed this study, had a number of individuals read the same description but with the second half of the paragraph (the "unfriendly" half) appearing first. Table 18-1 shows that only 18 percent found Jim to be friendly under this condition; that is, now Jim's unfriendly behaviors left the major impression. In other words, apparently the first information we receive has the greatest impact on our overall impressions. This is known as the *primacy effect*.

The primacy effect in impression formation has also been found in studies where an actual rather than a hypothetical person was observed and where traits other than friendliness were examined. For example, in a group of related studies, subjects watched a student attempt to solve a series of difficult multiple-choice problems of the sort found on the College Board Examinations and then were asked to assess his or her intelligence (Jones and others, 1968). The experiment was arranged so that the observed student always solved exactly 15 of the 30 problems correctly. Some subjects watched a student whose 15 successes were bunched mostly at the beginning of the series; other subjects observed a student who was more successful near the end of the series. The experimenters began these studies with the initial common-sense expectation that greater ability would be attributed to the individual who showed systematic improvement (that is, whose successes came at the end) than to the one whose performance got worse.

But this is not what happened. In five different studies with several variations in procedure, a strong primacy effect was observed. The individual who had done better at the beginning of the series was judged to be the more intelligent. Moreover, the subjects' memories were distorted in the same direction. When asked to recall how many problems the student had solved correctly, subjects who had seen the 15 successes bunched at the beginning recalled on the average that the student had solved 20.6 of the 30 problems, whereas subjects who had seen the successes bunched at the end of the series recalled seeing only 12.5 successes on the average.

What causes the primacy effect? This is still a matter of some controversy, but the evidence to date seems to favor the hypothesis that people pay more attention to information presented when they are first attempting to form some judgment about a person; after having formed an initial impression, they pay less attention to subsequent information (Anderson, 1974). There is evidence, too, that when later information is discrepant with earlier information, people tend to regard the first information as revealing the "real" person and to explain away or to dismiss the later information as not really representative. For example, when asked how they reconcile the apparent contradictions in Jim's behavior, subjects sometimes say that Jim is "really" friendly but was probably tired by the end of the day (Luchins, 1957a).

This tendency to discount later information has important implications for the recognition and reward of talent. For example, graduate students are selected partly on the basis of high scores on the Graduate Record Examination. Those who later do poorly in graduate school may be retained despite their poor performance because it is attributed to temporary motivational or neurotic factors. "Late blooming" students, on the other hand, may never get the recognition they deserve; others may consider their later successes as instances of high motivation or luck rather than ability (Jones and others, 1968).

Is it possible to counteract the primacy effect? Luchins (1957b) reasoned that if the primacy effect is due to decreased attention paid the later information, then it should be possible to destroy the effect by warning the subjects about the dangers of making snap judgments and telling them to take all information into account before arriving at their judgments. This warning worked. No primacy effect was observed under these conditions. The warning was particularly effective if it came not at the beginning of the experiment, but *between* the presentation of the two inconsistent blocks of information about Jim. In another variation of the experiment, Luchins did not warn the subjects but simply had them work mathematics problems or listen to a history lecture between exposures to the two halves of the description of Jim. This condition not only destroyed the primacy effect, but reversed it. That is, when an irrelevant task was interpolated between the two blocks of information, the *later* information had the greater impact. This is called the *recency effect,* because it is the more recent information that carries the weight. Luchins also discovered that the longer the time interval between the first and second blocks of information, the greater the recency effect. This suggests that the earlier information probably dims in memory. The two blocks of information do not "add" together, but instead the earlier block of information gets replaced in the observer's memory by the later one.

In summary, it appears that when we receive conflicting information about a person all in one block, we tend to give greater weight to the information that comes first—to form a first impression and then attempt to reconcile the later conflicting information, either by ignoring it or by reinterpreting it as a sort of accidental deviation from the person's "real" personality. We should thus expect primacy effects to be important in situations like job interviews, first dates, political canvassing, and other situations where the success of the first impression determines whether there will even be a subsequent encounter. In these situations, the charm school ads are correct: First impressions count. On the other hand, recency effects will be more important in continuing relationships, where real life provides the "interpolated tasks" and permits new information to have the opportunity to correct erroneous first impressions. One of the favorite pastimes of friends and lovers is looking back with amusement upon their disastrous first encounters and laughing about the warped first impressions they formed of each other. One does not, of course, ponder the far greater number of similar disastrous first encounters that—because they were disastrous—were never followed up. Just think of the potential friends and lovers that never materialized because of the primacy effect!

This is not the end of our discussion of primacy and recency effects. We will encounter them again in discussing social influence when we consider whether it is best to present your side of an argument first or last in situations such as debates or courtroom trials.

Interpersonal Attraction

Two questions usually concern us whenever we meet new people: Will they like us and will we like them? Research has uncovered a number of factors that promote interpersonal attraction; although none of these factors will surprise you, each contains at least one unexpected twist.

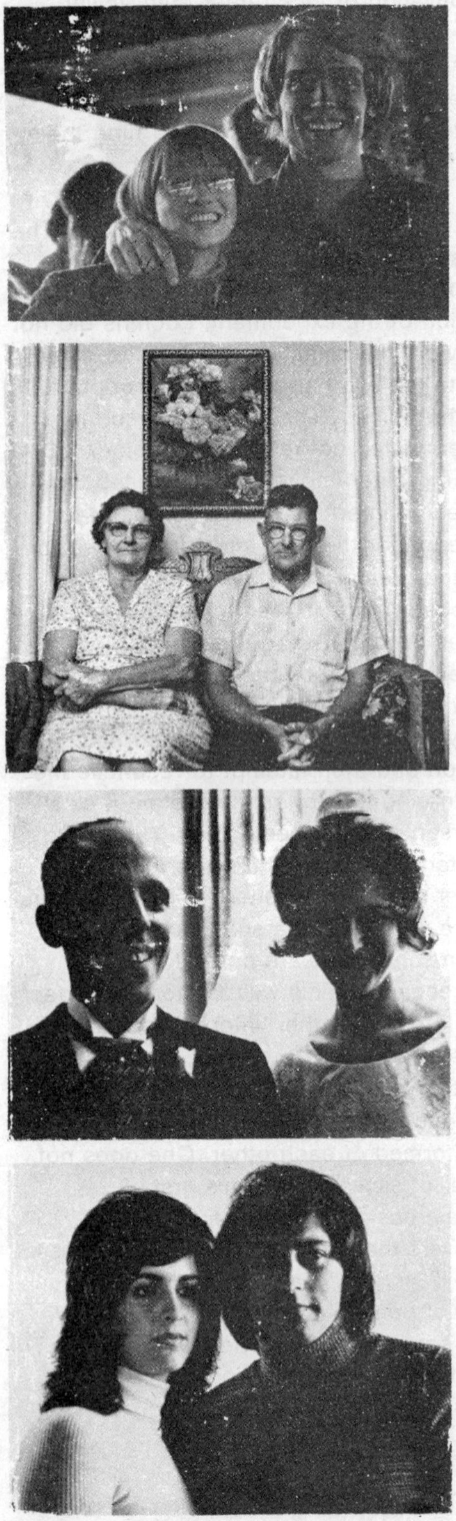

People tend to find partners who closely match them in physical attractiveness.

PHYSICAL APPEARANCE. To most of us, there is something mildly undemocratic about the possibility that a person's physical appearance is a determiner of how others respond to him. Unlike character, niceness, and other personal attributes, physical appearance is a factor over which we have little control. Hence, it seems "unfair" to use it as a criterion for liking someone. And, in fact, surveys have shown that people do not rank physical attractiveness as very important in their liking of other people. Thus, in 1921, men stated that physical attractiveness of others was a less important determinant of their attraction for them than such things as sincerity, individuality, and affectionate disposition (Perrin, 1921). A half-century later, both male and female college students still downplay "good looks" as a criterion for date and mate selection, rating it below such qualities as personality, character, and emotional stability (Miller and Rivenbark, 1970; Tesser and Brodie, 1971); in one study, the highest ranking "good looks" received was eleventh (Hudson and Henze, 1969).

But research on actual behavior shows otherwise. For example, a group of psychologists set up a "computer dance" for freshmen at the University of Minnesota in which each person was randomly paired with a partner (Walster and others, 1966). At the intermission of the dance each person filled out an anonymous questionnaire evaluating his or her date. In addition, the experimenters had several personality test scores for each person as well as an independent estimate of his or her physical attractiveness. The results showed that only physical attractiveness mattered. The more physically attractive the date, the more he or she was liked by the partner. Similarly, the physical attractiveness of the woman was the only factor that predicted whether the man actually asked her out for subsequent dates. None of the measures of intelligence, social skills, or "personality," were related to the partners' liking for one another.

Subsequent studies have confirmed these results in the heterosexual dating situation. For example, Brislin and Lewis (1968) found a correlation of .89 between the perceived physical attractiveness of a computer-dance date and a desire to date the partner again; Tesser and Brodie (1971) found a correlation of .69 between these two variables. In both of these studies, the perceived physical attractiveness of the date correlated higher with the "desire to date again" than did any other perceived characteristics of the partner, including perception of similar interests, character, and so on. However, within this overall relationship between physical attractiveness and liking, there is also a "matching" phenomenon. After all, not everyone can date and mate only the most attractive persons; and it has been found that in actual pairing off, people tend to end up with partners who closely match them in physical attractiveness (Berscheid and Walster, 1974). In one study, photographs were taken of each partner of 99 couples who were engaged or going steady, and judges rated each photograph for physicial attractiveness without knowing who was paired with whom. The physical-attractiveness ratings of the couples matched each other significantly more closely than did the ratings of photographs that were randomly paired into "couples" (Murstein, 1972).

The importance of physical appearance is not confined just to the heterosexual dating and mating patterns. For example, physically attractive boys and girls (ages 5 to 6 years) are more popular with their peers than are less attractive children; for boys, this effect was observed as early as $4\frac{1}{2}$ years of age (Dion and Berscheid, 1972). Even adults are affected by a child's physical attractiveness. Dion (1972) had women read a description of an aggressive act committed by a 7-year-old child. The description was accompanied by a photograph of either an attractive or an unattractive child, and each woman was then asked to describe the child who committed the act. It was found that attractive children are seen as less likely than unattractive children to commit a similar aggressive act in the future. When the women were asked to describe how they thought the child usually behaved on a typical day, the attractive children were viewed as generally less antisocial than the unattractive children. For example, in describing an attractive child who had committed the aggressive act, one woman said

> She appears to be a perfectly charming little girl, well-mannered, basically unselfish. It seems that she can adapt well among children her age and make a good impression . . . she plays with everyone, but like anyone else, a bad day can occur. Her cruelty . . . need not be taken too seriously.

When the same act was committed by a physically unattractive child, another woman wrote

> I think the child would be quite bratty and would be a problem to teachers . . . she would probably try to pick a fight with other children her own age . . . she would be a brat at home . . . all in all, she would be a real problem. (Berscheid and Walster, 1974, p. 192)

Kennedy was actually only a few inches taller than Nixon.

What makes someone physically attractive? There appears to be no single answer to this question, and different cultures have different criteria. In our society, for example, the height of a male appears to be an important determinant, with short males being at a disadvantage (Berscheid and Walster, 1974). A recent survey published in the *Wall Street Journal* showed that taller college graduates (6′2″ and over) received average starting salaries 12.4 percent higher than graduates under 6 feet, and every American president elected between 1900 and 1968 was taller than his major opponent (Feldman, 1971). Of course, the cause and effect are not clear here. It is possible that taller men have other characteristics that make them more desirable than shorter men. And, in fact, our *perception* of a person's height is itself correlated with our liking for the person. Thus, two-thirds of a sample of Californians who planned to vote for John F. Kennedy in 1960 perceived him as being taller than Richard Nixon, whereas a majority of those who planned to vote for Nixon perceived him to be at least as tall as Kennedy (Kassarjian, 1963). Another study found a significant correlation between students' liking for President Johnson and their estimates of his height (Ward, 1967). These last findings illustrate why social psychologists are often more interested in the individual's phenomenology (his *perception* of people and events) than with just the objective measurements of the stimuli.

In summary, physical appearance turns out to be more important than we might have anticipated. Although we might have expected adolescent dating preferences to hinge on this variable, the number of other situations and contexts in which being beautiful predisposes people to respond positively to us is surprising. Fortunately, other variables also help to determine who likes whom.

COMPETENCE. If we cannot all be beautiful, some of us might be able to get by on our competence. The evidence, however, is mixed. In problem-solving groups, people with the best ideas are not generally the best liked. And a Gallup poll taken just after President Kennedy's blunder in Cuba (the "Bay of Pigs fiasco") showed that his personal popularity went up rather than down (Aronson, 1972). It may be that some people are just "too perfect" for us and that when they commit some blunder they become more human in our eyes, and hence more likable.

An experiment to test this hypothesis had subjects listen to a tape of a college student trying out for the "College Quiz Bowl" (Aronson, Willerman, and Floyd, 1966). Some of the subjects heard a highly competent individual. He answered 92 percent of the very difficult quiz questions, modestly admitted that he had been an honor student, editor of the yearbook, and a member of the track team. Other subjects heard an individual of average ability, one who answered 30 percent of the questions, received average grades, had been a proofreader on the yearbook staff, and tried out for the track team but failed to make it. On half of the tapes, the individual was heard committing an embarrassing blunder near the end of the interview. There was a clatter, the scraping of a chair, and the individual saying, "Oh, my goodness, I've spilled coffee all over my new suit." After hearing the tape, each subject was asked to rate the person heard. The results showed first that, blunder or no blunder, the superior person was liked better than the average one. But the superior person who committed a blunder was rated as more attractive than the superior person who did not. In other words, the blunder did make the superior individual more likable. The average person's image, however, was hurt by the blunder. He was rated as less attractive when he spilled coffee than when he did not.

The hypothesis in this study was that the blunder makes a superior person more human, more like us, and thus more attractive. But what if we think of ourselves as very superior? Then the blunder may not endear the superior person to us because it makes him *less* like ourselves (or our image of ourselves), and hence less likable. Or consider the opposite possibility: we have very low self-esteem and are attracted to someone who can serve as an ideal hero for ourselves. Under this condition, the blunder gives our potential idol feet of clay and, hence, he again becomes less likable.

To test these possibilities, the blunder experiment was extended (Helmreich, Aronson, and LeFan, 1970). Spilling the coffee again enhanced the attractiveness of the superior person, but only for subjects who had an average amount of self-esteem. For those subjects with very high or very low self-esteem, the superior individual was less liked after his blunder (see Figure 18-1). Thus, if you are perfect, you can expect to impress either other gods like yourself or those inferiors who are looking for someone to provide the admirable qualities they themselves lack. But if you want to impress the rest of us, a little bit of "klutziness" is advised.

SIMILARITY. The coffee-spilling experiments raise another question about attraction: Do we like people who are similar to ourselves or do "opposites attract"? The evidence is mixed because it appears to depend on the dimensions of similarity being compared. Thus, there is a great deal of evidence that we prefer people who share our beliefs, attitudes, and values (Byrne, 1971; Newcomb, 1961). We tend to forget that some of our friends whom we consider very different from ourselves are often quite similar to us in terms of such variables as age, religion, education, and socioeconomic class. Hundreds of statistical studies dating all the way back to 1870 show that husbands and wives are significantly similar to each other not only on

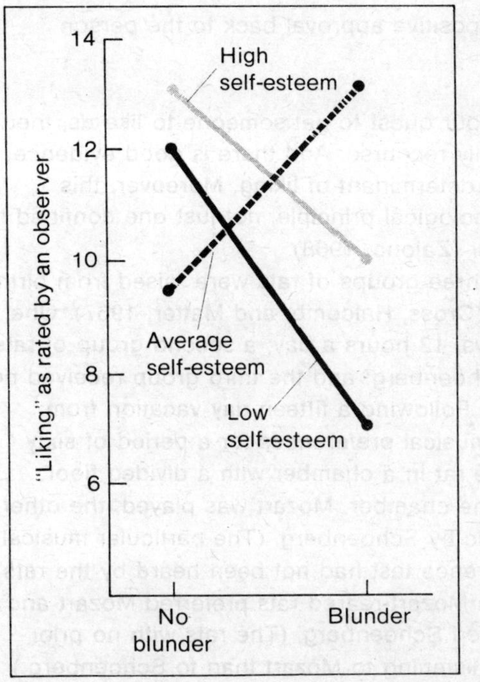

Fig. 18-1 Attraction as a function of a blunder

Subjects of high, average, and low self-esteem rated their liking for a highly competent individual after observing a situation in which that individual either did or did not commit a blunder. High scores indicate greater liking. (After Helmreich, Aronson, and LeFan, 1970)

these sociological characteristics but also with respect to physical characteristics like height and eye color and psychological characteristics like intelligence (Rubin, 1973). Thus, most evidence indicates that liking is positively correlated with similarity on most dimensions.

The saying that "opposites attract" seems to be applicable mainly to "need systems." That is, members of a couple often complement each other in terms of what they bring to the relationship (Winch, 1952; Winch, Ktsanes, and Ktsanes, 1954). To take the most obvious case, one partner may be quite dominant and thus require someone who is relatively more submissive. A person with strong preferences may do best with someone who is very flexible or even "wishy-washy." Note, however, that even in the case of complementary need systems an underlying similarity of attitudes can often be discerned. For example, the marital relationship in which the man is dominant and the wife submissive will be smooth only if both are in agreement on the appropriateness of the traditional sex roles. In other words, successful complementarity presupposes similar attitudes toward the appropriateness of the dissimilarity.

Kerckhoff and Davis (1962) interviewed, tested, and later retested college couples who were seriously considering marriage. They found that couples who had been going together less than 18 months reported greater movement toward a permanent relationship when they had more similarity in values; the presence of complementary needs did not lead to feelings of more permanency. But among long-term couples, possession of similar values no longer seemed to facilitate a move toward marriage; instead, complementarity of needs began to be important. Kerckhoff and Davis proposed that each relationship passes through a sequence of "filters." The first filter favors similarity on the basis of sociological variables such as socioeconomic status and religion; the second filter, coming after the couple has dated a little longer, requires consensus on values; and the third filter, coming only after a longer period, confers advantage on a complementarity of needs. It should be noted, however, that a subsequent attempt to confirm the Kerckhoff-Davis results did not find that need complementarity became an important variable (Levinger, Senn, and Jorgensen, 1970). This adds further emphasis to the general conclusion that similarity is the truly potent variable in determining who likes whom.

RECIPROCAL LIKING. One of the more compelling reasons for liking someone is their liking for us. We tend to like people who like us and to reject those who reject us. And research shows that this tends to be especially true at those times when we have a greater need to be liked and appreciated. In one study, college women were approached by a good-looking male while they waited, one at a time, in a reception room to be in an experiment. After some conversation, he asked the woman for a date for the following evening. In the subsequent experimental session each woman was given information about herself, that would make her feel either positively or negatively about her personality. After the experiment, she was asked to rate a number of people, including that "fellow whom you were waiting with."

It was found that women who had been led to feel negatively about themselves liked their male admirer significantly more than those women who had received favorable information about themselves in the experiment. In other words, those who had been temporarily put into the position of needing some positive approval gave more positive approval back to the person providing it (Walster, 1965).[1]

FAMILIARITY. If all else fails in our quest to get someone to like us, then simple persistence might be our only recourse. And there is good evidence that sheer familiarity is a pervasive determinant of liking. Moreover, this appears to be a very general psychological principle, not just one confined to the liking of one person for another (Zajonc, 1968).

To take a nonhuman example, three groups of rats were raised from birth with different musical experiences (Cross, Halcomb, and Matter, 1967). One group listened to Mozart for 52 days, 12 hours a day; a second group of rats listened to a 52-day program of Schoenberg; and the third group received no musical-appreciation training at all. Following a fifteen-day vacation from music, each rat was tested for its musical preferences for a period of sixty days. This was done by placing the rat in a chamber with a divided floor. When the rat was on one side of the chamber, Mozart was played; the other side of the chamber activated music by Schoenberg. (The particular musical selections played during this preference test had not been heard by the rats before.) The results were clear: the Mozart-reared rats preferred Mozart and the Schoenberg-reared rats preferred Schoenberg. (The rats with no prior musical exposure spent more time listening to Mozart than to Schoenberg.) Several other experiments with both human and nonhuman subjects confirm the general nature of these results: Repeated exposure to a stimulus leads to greater liking for it.

This principle has also been tested in an interpersonal liking context (Saegert, Swap, and Zajonc, 1973). Unacquainted female subjects were shuttled from one booth to another under the guise of tasting different kinds of liquids. The shuttling was arranged in such a way that each woman was "incidentally" exposed to five other women differing numbers of times. No talking or other interaction was permitted. Subsequent ratings of liking were found to be dramatically affected by the number of exposures between each pair of subjects. Subjects expressed greatest liking for the woman to whom they had been exposed ten times, next most for the woman to whom they had been exposed five times, and least liking for the women to whom they had been exposed only once or not at all.

An even stronger test of the familiarity variable was provided by Newcomb (1961), who rented a boarding house at the University of Michigan and provided free room and board to male students transferring to the University in exchange for their participation in his study of the acquaintance process. In the first year of the study, Newcomb simply assigned people to rooms at random; he verified that similarity among people is a strong determinant of liking. In the second year of the study (with a different set of participants) he actually assigned each man a roommate, seeing to it that half of the paired students were as different as possible from one another on a host of beliefs, attitudes, and values. The other half of the assignments paired students who were highly similar. It was Newcomb's expectation that the similarity variable would again operate to produce greater liking among those who were paired with others highly similar to themselves. But this is not how things turned out. The variable of familiarity swamped everything. In nearly all cases, regardless

[1] A study like this raises ethical questions, and the experimenter spent close to an hour with each woman, carefully explaining the study and the need for the deception employed. We will have more to say about this kind of "debriefing" later, however.

of whether low or high similarity had been produced by room assignments, roommates came to be very attracted to one another.

We can conclude this discussion of interpersonal attraction with the comforting thought that if you aren't beautiful, competent, or similar to the one you wish to attract, be persistent. If nothing else is in your favor, familiarity will help; with enough exposure, even rats can come to love Schoenberg. (An exception to the "familiarity breeds attraction" principle is noted in the next section.)

Stereotypes

Some stereotypes are based on physical appearance. What personality traits and attitudes—friendly, conscientious, liberal—would you attribute to the students in each of the above photographs?

In one of the many studies on physical attractiveness, subjects were given photographs of attractive and unattractive individuals and asked to rate the pictured individuals on a number of personality traits (Dion, Berscheid, and Walster, 1972). Perhaps this seems like an impossible task since the photograph was the only information given to the subjects; but it turns out that this kind of "guessing" task is not so hard. In fact, we do it all the time: After seeing or meeting a person for a very short period of time, we are often willing to "go beyond the data given" and draw some inferences about other, unobserved aspects of the person. In this particular study, the attractive person was judged (in contrast to the unattractive person) to be more friendly, have a better character, be a more exciting date, have higher occupational status, be a better marital partner, be generally happier, and, interestingly, to be a *less* good parent. Except for this last item, then, the attractive individual was judged to be a more desirable person than the unattractive individual—not an unexpected finding in light of the results we discussed earlier. These subjects carried around a *stereotype,* a cluster of interrelated traits and attributes assumed to be characteristic of certain kinds of individuals— in this case, attractive or unattractive individuals.

Most of us have learned that stereotypes can be misleading, if not dangerous. Stereotypes often have no basis in fact. Sometimes they are formed to rationalize our prejudices or to justify shabby treatment of individuals on the basis of some assumed group characteristics that neither they nor the group actually possess. But the process by which stereotypes arise is not evil in itself. Going beyond the data and generalizing tentatively about an individual until additional data are obtained is not only a common "cognitive" act but a necessary one. It is simply not possible to deal with every person as if he were unique or as if we knew nothing about him until all the data are in hand. Social interaction requires that we be able to predict to some extent that new individuals will behave as others like them have behaved in the past; the formation of "working stereotypes" is inevitable, until further experiences either refine or discredit them.

The danger, however, is that if our subsequent experiences are too narrow they may reinforce rather than extinguish our stereotypes. Stereotypes will not vanish if we continue to see the members of the stereotyped category in the same situations that originally gave rise to the stereotypes. For example, it is often suggested that increased contact between ethnic groups will automatically lead to the disappearance of negative stereotypes and thence to decreased racial prejudice. But nobody has more interracial contact than black ghetto residents and white policemen. Yet these frequent interracial contacts are not particularly noted for producing interracial tolerance. The reason is that the two groups continue to play the same stereotyped roles, with the white policeman cast in the role of the authority figure dealing primarily with the black resident in the role of victim or "trouble maker." As Gordon Allport (1954) noted in his famous book on prejudice, interracial contacts lead to decreased prejudice only when the participants are of equal status; only under these conditions can the participants begin to see each other as sharing common beliefs, attributes, and goals.

Note that this case is an exception to the general principle, discussed in the previous section, that familiarity or simple frequent exposure leads automatically to increased liking. When people who hold negative stereotypes about one another have repeated contact in the same stereotype-producing situations, the negative feelings on both sides are reinforced. Note, too, that the kind of broadening familiarity that does serve to diminish the stereotypes is the kind that produces perceived similarity between the participants. Thus, the principles discussed in the previous section on interpersonal attraction continue to be valid, but one must examine each situation carefully to see which principles will be more potent in a given case.

Implicit Personality Theories

A stereotype can be thought of as a miniature theory of personality. It is an implicit set of assumptions about the traits and attributes possessed by certain classes of people. In fact, stereotypes are special cases of a more general set of assumptions that psychologists call *implicit personality theories*—preconceived notions we all have about which traits and behaviors go with what other traits and behaviors. For example, when we hear that a person is "warm," we are also likely to assume that he is an extravert even though this is not logically necessary. An implicit personality theory, then, is like a set of correlations we carry around in our heads, correlations that enable us to go beyond the information we are given about a person and to "fill in" the missing data. Implicit personality theories are often wrong, of course, but it is hard to do without them just as it is hard to do without "working stereotypes."

The power of implicit personality theories is shown by a study in which students were given descriptions of a guest lecturer before he spoke. For half the students the guest lecturer was described as intelligent, skillful, industrious, warm, determined, practical, and cautious; the other students were given the same list of traits, but the word *cold* was substituted for the word *warm* in the list. The lecturer then came into the class and led a twenty-minute discussion, after which the students were asked to give their impressions of him. Although all the students had seen and heard the same person at the same time, students who were told he was warm formed very different impressions from those who were told he was cold. The "cold" group found him to be more self-centered, unsociable, unpopular, formal, irritable, humorless, and ruthless than did the "warm" group. Moreover, the students who expected him to be warm tended to interact with him more freely in the discussion, a difference in their behavior that in itself probably influenced their perceptions (Kelley, 1950).

It is important to note that an implicit personality theory may have some basis in fact: A person who is cold may actually tend to be more self-centered and irritable than a person who is warm. Our implicit personality theories do not arise in a vacuum. On the other hand, the study just described shows clearly that we go far beyond whatever validity our implicit personality theories might have to unwarranted inferences about the observed person.

Our implicit personality theories also lead us to see people as more consistent than they actually are; we tend to "see" positive correlations among their behaviors that are not really there. For example, in a very early study of extraversion and introversion, a daily record was kept of the behavior of a group of boys at a summer camp (Newcomb, 1929). The correlations between behaviors selected to indicate extraversion or introversion were very low; most of the boys were simply not consistent one way or the other. But when the camp counselors were asked to rate each boy's behavior, the correlations among the reported behaviors were quite high. In other words, the counselors "saw" more consistency in the boys' behaviors than was actually present. In one case the correlation between two behaviors measured by the counselors' rating was as high as +.75, whereas the actual correlation computed from the daily behavior record was only +.23. (See also Chapman and Chapman, 1969.)

This study suggests that our implicit personality theories may be one of the causes of the primacy effect discussed earlier. At an initial encounter with another person, we compose a more-or-less complete personality portrait of him or her on the basis of the few cues given, using our implicit personality theories to fill in the gaps. This leads us to see later information about the person as more consistent than it deserves to be; we tend either to ignore contradictory information or to reinterpret it in such a way that we can "assimilate" it to our initial impression. Our implicit personality theories lead us to believe that we have gained much more knowledge about a new acquaintance than we really have in our first meeting, and we are thus inclined to treat later data as redundant rather than as a source of potentially new information.

Attribution Processes

Fritz Heider

Suppose you see a well-known personality endorse a commercial product on television. Why does he do it? Is it for the money? Maybe he craves public exposure. Perhaps he simply believes in the product and wants to share his enthusiasm with us. A woman kisses her male companion at the end of a date. Does she love him? Perhaps most women do this in similar circumstances? Maybe this woman just happens to kiss everyone she knows? You give a $5 donation to the United Fund? Why? You are altruistic? You were under social pressure? You need a tax write-off? You particularly believe in the United Fund?

In all of these cases, you, as an observer of the action, are attempting to solve the "attribution problem." You are confronted with a person's behavior—perhaps your own—and must decide to which of the many possible causes the action should be attributed. The study of the attribution problem has become one of the central concerns in social psychology. The basic thrust of *attribution theory,* as it is called, is to make explicit the rules we all use in attempting to infer the causes of behavior and to discover the biases and errors that plague our attempts to do so.

The first major attempt to formulate these implicit rules was made by Fritz Heider (1958), but active interest in the topic really began in the mid-sixties when a number of important papers began to appear that built on Heider's earlier contribution (e.g., Jones and Davis, 1965; Kelley, 1967). Not surprisingly, the research has found that we are pretty good at being amateur psychologists. Considering how few clues we often have, we manage to bring a good deal of logic and common sense to the task. For example, if the observed action is very common (a man gives a dollar to the United Fund), we are much less likely to draw an inference about the person's attitudes or personality (called his *dispositions*) from the behavior than if the act is uncommon (he gives $500 or takes a dollar from the collection box). Similarly, we like to see how the behavior varies over time and situations before making a "dispositional" inference about the person. For instance, before concluding that the woman in our example loves the man, we usually seek to ascertain that (1) she will kiss him in more unusual circumstances (in class, for example); (2) she does not kiss all men indiscriminately; and (3) all women do not kiss this particular man. We use rules such as these automatically and unconsciously in everyday interaction, and they go a long way in helping us understand other people even when complete information about their actions is not available. (See Jones and Davis, 1965; Kelley, 1967, 1971, 1972, for more formal statements of the several rules.)

But we also show some systematic biases in our attributions. As Heider (1958) pointed out in his original analysis, the behavior of another person is such a prominent feature of what we observe that we are inclined to weight it too heavily, to take it too much at face value, and underestimate the situational forces that led the person to behave as he did. Thus, in one attribution study (Jones and Harris, 1967), subjects heard an individual give a speech either favoring or opposing racial segregation. They were also informed that the individual was merely participating in an experiment and *had been told* which side of the issue he had to argue and which arguments to use. That is, the subjects knew that the individual they were hearing had no choice about what to say—as in a debate where the sides are drawn by lot. And yet despite this knowledge, subjects were still willing to infer that the individual believed to some degree the point of view he was arguing. Apparently, a person's behavior is so compelling that we cannot ignore it in making attributions about his attitudes or personality even when we know that the actions are irrelevant to him. We make "dispositional attributions" when the evidence says we should be making "situational attributions"; that is, we should be inferring that situational features (not dispositional factors) caused the behavior. This bias toward dispositional attributions has a number of important implications, as we shall see later.

Self-perception

When making inferences about someone's attitudes and feelings we rely heavily on our observations of his behavior. If we want to know about another person's inner state we look to see how he acts. To some extent this is true of our own self-perceptions. Sometimes we infer our attitudes from observing our behavior. Bem has proposed a self-perception theory that states that weak or ambiguous internal cues force an individual into the role of an outside observer; he must look at his own behavior and the surrounding circumstances to help him decide what his feelings are (Bem, 1970, 1972). Although this proposal might seem surprising, it is exactly what

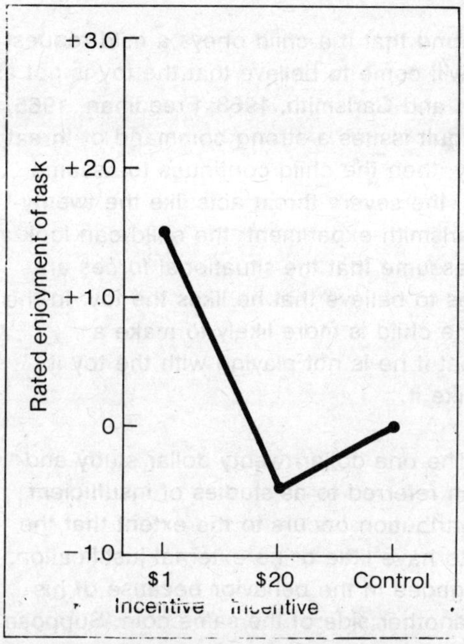

Fig. 18-2 Attitude change and incentive

The more positive the enjoyment rating, the greater the attitude change toward liking the task. (After Festinger and Carlsmith, 1959)

is suggested by such common remarks as "This is my second sandwich; I guess I was hungrier than I thought" or "I've been biting my nails all day; something must be bugging me." In both of these cases, the individual observes his own behavior to help him decide on his inner state in exactly the same way an outside observer would ("You've been biting your nails all day; something must be bugging you"). This simple proposition, that self-perception is in many ways a special case of interpersonal perception, has a number of far-reaching implications.

Several years before self-perception theory was formulated, Festinger and Carlsmith (1959) performed an experiment designed to test Festinger's theory of *cognitive dissonance*, a theory we will discuss later in this chapter. In their study, college students were brought one at a time to a small room to work for half an hour on two very dull and repetitive tasks (stacking spools and turning pegs). After completing the tasks, some of the students were offered one dollar to go into the waiting room and tell the next subject that the tasks had been fun and interesting. Other students in the study were offered twenty dollars to do the same thing. After accepting the offer, the student went into the waiting room and attempted to convince the next subject that the tasks were enjoyable. Later, all of the students were asked for their actual opinions of the tasks: How interesting did they really think the tasks were?

The students who had been paid only one dollar stated that they had, in fact, enjoyed the tasks. But students who had been paid twenty dollars did not; they found them as dull as did a control group of subjects who were never asked to talk to the next subject (see Figure 18-2). In other words, the small sum of money (but not the large sum) led individuals to believe what they had heard themselves say.

We can make sense of these results by assuming for the moment that the subjects in this study had to solve an attribution problem about their own behavior the same way an outside observer would. Such a hypothetical observer sees the individual saying that the tasks were fun and interesting and must decide whether to make a dispositional attribution (he did it because he believes it) or a situational attribution (he did it for the money). When the individual is paid twenty dollars, the observer is most likely to assume that anyone would have done it for such a sum; that is, he makes a situational attribution and assumes that the behavior tells him little or nothing about the individual's true attitudes. Accordingly, the observer will assume the individual thought the tasks were actually dull in spite of what he had said. On the other hand; if the individual had been paid only one dollar, the observer is more likely to decide that the individual to some extent really does believe that the tasks were interesting (a dispositional attribution) because the situational force (the one-dollar inducement) is insufficient to explain why the individual was willing to say so ("He must believe it to some extent or he wouldn't be willing to say it for only one dollar"). If we assume that the individual looks at his own behavior, asks "What must my attitude be if I am willing to say these things under these circumstances?" and follows the same attribution rules as the outside observer, then the results of the Festinger-Carlsmith experiment follow directly. Twenty-dollar subjects look at their behavior, infer that it was due to situational factors, and decide they did not really find the tasks interesting. But one-dollar subjects look at their behavior and arrive at a dispositional attribution: "I must think the tasks are interesting; otherwise, I would not have said so."

The results of many other studies can be interpreted in the same way. Fo example, several experiments have found that if a child obeys a mild request not to play with an attractive toy, he will come to believe that the toy is not as attractive as he first thought (Aronson and Carlsmith, 1963; Freedman, 1965). But if, instead of a mild request, an adult issues a strong command ot threat of punishment for playing with the toy, then the child continues to assume that he does like the toy. In this case, the severe threat acts like the twenty-dollar inducement in the Festinger-Carlsmith experiment; the child can look at his behavior of avoiding the toy and assume that the situational forces are responsible. Accordingly, he continues to believe that he likes the toy. In the absence of such a threat, however, the child is more likely to make a dispositional attribution, to assume that if he is not playing with the toy it must be because he does not really like it.

Rewarding an intrinsically interesting activity may make it less appealing.

OVERJUSTIFICATION EFFECTS. The one dollar-twenty dollar study and the forbidden toy experiment are often referred to as studies of insufficient justification because a dispositional attribution occurs to the extent that the individual's behavior appears to him to have little or no external justification. He then comes to assume that he engaged in the behavior because of his true beliefs or attitudes. But there is another side of the same coin. Suppose that you paid a person a large sum of money for doing something that he would normally do without any inducement. Self-perception theory suggests that he might then decide (from observing his behavior) that he was engaging in the activity primarily because of the payoff and not because he really enjoyed the activity for its own sake. In other words, by overjustifying the behavior, it might be possible to undermine an individual's initial interest in the activity itself.

There is evidence that this is true. We saw in Chapter 9 (p. 261) that children who were rewarded for drawing pictures with magic markers subsequently spent less time drawing with the markers than children who were not rewarded (Lepper, Greene, and Nisbett, 1973). Rewarding an intrinsically interesting activity actually makes it less interesting. These findings have some important practical implications. Many parents reward schoolwork with money or other rewards. Similarly, many school systems are now employing "token economies" in which children are paid in tokens of privileges for completing a unit of work. The existence of overjustification effects should caution us that the use of such rewards may have undesirable side effects. Although external rewards may motivate the person to perform at the time, they may simultaneously be undermining the person's future interest in performing the activity for its own sake. This suggests that external rewards should not be used for children who are already motivated and that such rewards should be phased out for the unmotivated child soon after he begins to engage in the activity. It should be mentioned, however, that other studies suggest that verbally praising children probably does not have the same destructive effect on intrinsic motivation that tangible physical rewards do (Deci, 1971). Further research is needed before it is possible to give parents and school systems firm guidance on just how tangible rewards can be used to motivate performance without creating the undesirable self-perception in the person that he is performing only for extrinsic rewards. But it is clear that our tendency to draw attributions about ourselves from observations of our own behavior is not always a good thing. And, as we shall see below, there are additional problems with self-attributions.

The Irreversibility of Dispositional Attributions

Earlier we noted a systematic bias in interpersonal attributions: Even when the situational forces are clear, unambiguous, and fully sufficient to account for an observed behavior, observers are still inclined to draw some dispositional inferences about the individual. We saw, for example, how individuals tend to think that debaters believe the positions they argue even when they know the positions are randomly assigned. There is also a bias toward dispositional attributions in the self-attribution studies discussed in the previous section. We, the experimenters, know, for example, that the one-dollar inducement was, in fact, sufficient to get all subjects to comply with the request to say that the tasks were interesting; we, the experimenters, know that the mild request is sufficient to get all of the children to refrain from playing with the forbidden toy. In other words, we, the investigators, know that the behaviors were caused by situational forces. Accordingly, it is not really "logical" or "rational" for the subjects in these experiments to make dispositional inferences about themselves at all, since even the weaker situational forces are fully sufficient to get *everyone* to comply. Thus, when the subject, who is willing to say the tasks were interesting for only one dollar, implicitly asks himself "Why did I do this?" strictly speaking, he should answer "because one dollar is sufficient to get me to do so." But he does not. Instead, he makes the dispositional attribution "because I must find the tasks somewhat interesting."

In other words, the very fact that these experiments "work" as predicted is evidence for the fact that individuals underestimate the degree to which situational forces control their behavior. If individuals truly appreciated the control of situational forces, they would not draw dispositional inferences about themselves—even in the low-paying or weak-situational-forces conditions. Like interpersonal attribution processes, then, self-attribution processes seem to be biased toward dispositional answers rather than situational ones—at least in these situations.

There is also some evidence that dispositional attributions, once they are made, are difficult to reverse. For example, in a variation of the forbidden toy study, some children were told that all of the children obey and refrain from playing with the forbidden toy. When this was told to the children before they entered the toy room, it destroyed the attitude change effect. These children did not decrease their liking for the toy. It is as if they said to themselves, "If all children obey in such circumstances then, the fact that I obey must be due to the situational forces (the mild request of the experimenter) rather than my feelings." But if the children were told that everyone obeys *after* they had complied, the effect was still there. Despite being told that all children obey, these children still held to the conclusion that they must have obeyed because they do not like the toy. Apparently, the dispositional attribution, "I don't like the toy," is made while they are in the toy room; and once it is made, knowing that all other children also obey, does not reverse the attribution as it logically should (Lepper, Zanna, and Abelson, 1970).

This irreversibility of dispositional attributions was demonstrated even more strongly in a recent series of studies (Ross, Lepper, and Hubbard, 1974). High school and college women were led to believe that they had done either quite well or quite poorly on a novel problem-solving task. They were then "debriefed." That is, each woman was told that her scores had

CRITICAL DISCUSSION

Some Implications of Our Bias Toward

As we have seen, we tend to underestimate situational forces, we are overeager to make dispositional attributions, and we are sometimes unwilling to discard dispositional attributions when they are discredited. All of these attributional biases have implications that extend well beyond the psychology laboratory. For example, these biases imply that many people will continue to hold negative stereotypes about disadvantaged ethnic groups even if they can be persuaded to appreciate the external societal circumstances that have produced the disadvantage. Moreover, these same biases can affect the members of the disadvantaged groups themselves. If you have been unsuccessful in life, it will not automatically restore your self-esteem or give you a positive self-image if you are persuaded that it was discrimination or lack of opportunity that impeded you. Instead, self-perception theory implies that you must actually have success experiences, must actually see yourself succeed before new dispositional attributions can fully replace the older, discredited ones.

There is, moreover, a special kind of attributional error that occurs whenever a person is labeled with a disposition that is perceived as highly deviant (e.g., schizophrenic, homosexual). Once such a label is attached to an individual, any behavior he displays that seems to require explanation is automatically attributed to his "deviance." Situational factors that would normally be taken into account for other individuals displaying the same behavior are ignored. Thus, observers of mental hospitals (e.g., Goffman, 1961; Rosenhan, 1973) have noticed that many of the behaviors observed in the hospital wards can be accounted for by the unusual situational factors present. For example, in order to get any attention from the nurses or aides in understaffed institutions, one must do something out of the ordinary or become especially persistent; simple questions and quiet requests are typically ignored as if the patient were a nonperson. Similarly, because there is little to do on the ward, pacing back and forth is at least one way to relieve the boredom and get some exercise. But such behaviors as demanding attention or pacing are almost always interpreted by the staff as "part of the illness."

In one study (Rosenhan, 1973), the investigators themselves entered the hospitals as patients, behaving as normally as possible during their stay. Although some of the other patients suspected that the investigators were not really patients, the staff did not. In fact, an examination of the staff records showed that the most innocuous behaviors by the investigators were inter-

really been falsified (that they had been predetermined and entered on the scoresheet before she even came into the room), and that the feedback she had been given about her performance contained absolutely no information about how well she had done. But when these subjects were later asked to (1) rate their ability at the problem-solving task, (2) estimate how many of the 25 problems they had actually gotten correct, and (3) predict how well they would do in the future on such a task, it was found that the debriefing had failed to destroy the initial attributions (see Table 18-2). Subjects who originally believed they had done well continued to rate their ability higher, to believe that they had actually solved more of the original problems, and to predict they would solve more problems in the future than did subjects who had originally believed that they had done poorly.

TABLE 18-2
Post-debriefing perceptions.

The subjects' estimates of their abilities and performance after debriefing as a function of false success and failure information.

	SUCCESS INFORMATION	FAILURE INFORMATION
Rated ability at task (1 = low, 7 = high)	5.28	3.90
Estimated number of correct problems (out of 25)	17.05	12.75
Predicted number correct on future series of problems	16.67	13.48

Source: Ross, Lepper, and Hubbard (1974).

Dispositional Attributions

preted as part of the "schizophrenic syndrome." One investigator, who took observational notes during his stay, was ominously described in a staff report as "patient engages in writing behavior." Thus, once the label of "mental patient" or "schizophrenic" is attached to a person, observers act as if all attribution problems are automatically solved. Any behavior that is not completely ordinary is simply attributed to the "illness." The label becomes a scapegoat.

This attribution error due to labeling is also well-known to any college student whose parents regard his or her marihuana smoking as a form of deviance. Did the student get a bad grade on an examination? It must be, the parents are certain, because he smokes marihuana. Is he or she having trouble falling asleep the week before finals? The obvious effect of marihuana. Has he or she rejected the parental attitude against premarital sex? Marihuana must have ruined the student's morals, and so it goes. The label of "marihuana smoker" collects the blame.

And finally, we should note that the individual himself is vulnerable to this attributional trap. For example, many college students complain that their social lives do not always go smoothly, that they think about sex a lot, that problems with their love lives sometimes interfere with school work, and that they wish they were more outgoing and less preoccupied with themselves. And most students come to appreciate that such problems are a consequence of a whole host of situational factors endemic to the unmarried college life. Now because of these same situational factors, gay (i.e., homosexual) men and women on the campus also share these common complaints. But gay students are much more vulnerable to the trap of attributing all of these same problems to their sexual orientation. (Of course, they also do have a number of complaints that arise from following a sexual orientation that society disapproves of, but these, too, are situationally caused problems.) Because the gay sexual orientation is such a prominent feature of their phenomenologies in current society, it becomes the scapegoat for any behavior that seems to require explanation. If he gets a bad grade on an examination, the nongay student assumes that he did not study hard enough, the exam was unfair, he does not understand chemistry, he stayed up too late the night before, or whatever. The gay student, however, may be tempted to assume he flunked the exam because he is gay. The "disposition" becomes the explanation for all things. Such is the power of "deviant" labels in leading our attributional processes astray.

In one variation of this study, investigators had a second subject serve as an observer of each of the experimental subjects. Thus, in each session an observer saw the entire process (including the debriefing) along with the subject herself. When the observers were later asked to rate the subjects' actual ability, they showed the same irreversibility as the subjects. Observers who watched a "successful" subject *and* also heard that the success was falsified, still rated the observed individual as higher in ability than did obervers who watched "unsuccessful" subjects. Dispositional attributions, whether made by interpersonal or self-observers, are hard to disconfirm once they are made.

Perhaps you have noticed a similarity between the primacy effect discussed earlier and the irreversibility phenomenon. In both cases, the initial information is taken more seriously than later information. But the irreversibility phenomenon is even more startling. In the primacy effect, the earlier information is sometimes contradicted by later information, but the individual is not told that the later information is any more valid than the earlier information. In the irreversibility effect, the original information is actually shown to be invalid, and yet it still carries some weight.

The Social-Psychological Perspective

In the introduction to this chapter we noted that the social psychologist tends to stress situational causes of behavior and the individual's phenomenology. We can now see that in his emphasis on situational explanations of behavior the social psychologist is doing precisely the opposite of what our intuitions lead us to do as everyday amateur psychologists. As we have seen, the more common tendency is to favor dispositional rather than situational explanations when we attempt to explain behavior. In this sense, then, the approach of social psychology serves to counterbalance our normal bias and remind us of the power of situational forces.

As for the social psychologist's emphasis on phenomenology, the individual's own subjective view of the world, it should now be apparent that the study of social perception is, almost by definition, the study of phenomenology. It exemplifies better than almost any other topic the perspectives and preoccupations of contemporary social psychology. Indeed, if social perception has any rival in claiming the attention of social psychologists, it is the topic of social influence, the topic to which we now turn.

Social Influence

Of the many influences on human behavior, social influences are the most pervasive. The main influence on people is people. When we hear the term social influence, most of us think of deliberate attempts of someone to persuade us to alter our actions or change our opinions. The television commercial comes to mind. But many of the most important forms of social influence are unintentional, and some of the effects we humans have upon one another occur by virtue of the simple fact that we are in each other's physical presence.

Coaction and audience effects

Each of these runners will probably make better time in competition before an audience than when running alone against the clock.

The Physical Presence of Others: Coaction and Audience Effects

In 1898 a psychologist named Triplett made an interesting observation. In looking over speed records of bicycle racers, he noticed that better speed records were obtained when cyclists raced against each other than when they raced against the clock. This observation led Triplett to perform the first controlled laboratory experiment ever conducted in social psychology. He instructed children to turn a fishing reel as fast as possible for a fixed period of time. Sometimes two children worked at the same time in the same room, each with his own reel; at other times, they worked alone. The results confirmed the effect he sought: Children worked faster in *coaction,* that is, when another child doing the same task was present, than when they worked alone.

Since this first experiment, many studies have demonstrated the facilitating effects of coaction both with human and infrahuman subjects. For example, chickens, puppies, rats, rhesus monkeys, armadillos, and opossums will all eat more if other members of their species are present (Harlow, 1932; James, 1953; Platt and James, 1966; Platt, Yaksh, and Darby, 1967; Stamm, 1961; Tolman, 1969); and, Harvard students will complete more multiplication problems in coaction than when alone (Allport, 1920, 1924).

Soon after Triplett's experiment on coaction, it was discovered that the mere presence of a passive spectator (an audience rather than a coactor) was sufficient to facilitate performance. This was discovered accidentally in an experiment on muscular effort and fatigue by Meumann (1904), who found that subjects lifted a finger weight faster and further whenever the experimenter was in the room. Later experiments have confirmed this audience effect. For example, a follow-up study to the one that examined Harvard students' performance on multiplication problems showed that the mere presence of an audience had the same facilitation effects as coactors had had in the earlier study (Dashiell, 1930). Coaction and audience effects have been labeled social facilitation effects.

Even in this simplest case of social influence, matters turn out to be less than simple. For example, in the study of Harvard students cited above, it was found that more errors on the multiplication problems were made in coaction or with an audience than when subjects performed alone (Dashiell, 1930). In other words, the quality of performance declined even though quantity increased in the presence of coactors or an audience. But in still other studies, the quality of performance also improved with coactors or audiences present (e.g., Dashiell, 1935; Cottrell, 1972). How can these contradictions be reconciled?

In looking over the results of all these studies, Robert Zajonc noted that the behaviors showing social facilitation were usually so well-learned, well-practiced, or instinctive (like eating) that the correct response is the most likely or most dominant response the individual would make. On the other hand, the behaviors impaired in the presence of coactors or audiences were those in which the most likely or dominant response of the individual would be wrong (like a complex mathematical problem where there are many wrong responses but only one correct one). This pattern of results led Zajonc to remember a principle of motivation that states that a higher level of drive or arousal tends to energize the dominant responses of an organism. If the mere presence of another member of the species raises the general arousal or drive level of an organism, then this would predict that simple or well-learned behavior should show social facilitation—since these behaviors involve the dominant response in the situation—whereas more complex behavior or behavior just being learned (in which the dominant or most likely response is more apt to be incorrect) would be impaired.

Zajonc and others have tested this theory in a number of ingenious experiments both with human and infrahuman subjects. For example, it is known that cockroaches will run away from a bright light, and so a study was conducted in which cockroaches were prompted to run away from a light into a darkened "goal" box (Zajonc, Heingartner, and Herman, 1969). Figure 18-3 shows the four boxes used in this study. All the boxes were housed in 20-inch cubes of transparent plexiglass; two "runway" boxes contained a straight runway leading from the light to the goal, whereas the two "maze" boxes required the roach to make a right turn to get to the goal. Since the dominant response of a roach is to run straight ahead, the mazes required the roach to execute a nondominant response to get to the goal.

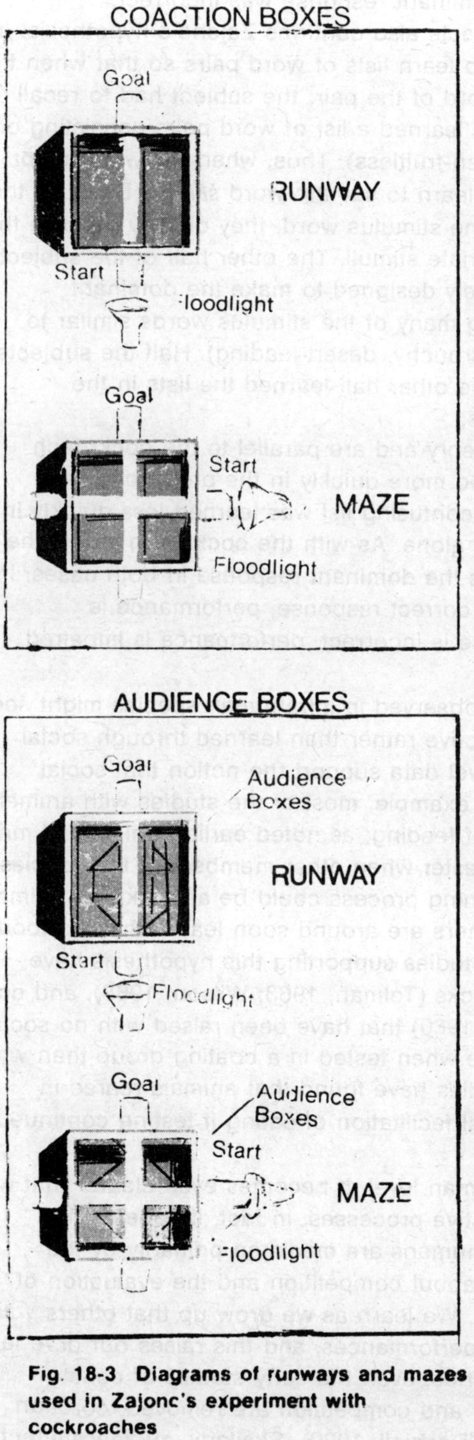

Fig. 18-3 Diagrams of runways and mazes used in Zajonc's experiment with cockroaches

Cockroaches were tested in the coaction runway box, half of them alone and half of them in coacting pairs; other roaches were tested in the coaction box with the maze. As Zajonc's theory predicted, the presence of coactors *reduced* the time to get to the goal in the runway (social facilitation) but *increased* the time it took to get to the goal through the maze (impaired performance). This experiment was repeated with more cockroaches, all of which ran alone in the audience apparatus, half of the roaches having an audience of four other roaches that watched from small plexiglass boxes alongside the runways. Again, it was found that the presence of other roaches—even if they were just spectators—facilitated performance when the dominant response (running down the straight runway) was correct and impaired performance when the dominant response was incorrect.

An experiment with human subjects also confirms Zajonc's hypothesis. In this study subjects were required to learn lists of word pairs so that when the experimenter presented the first word of the pair, the subject had to recall the second word. Half the subjects learned a list of word pairs consisting of synonyms (e.g., adept-skillful, barren-fruitless). Thus, when the word *adept* was presented, the subject had to learn to say the word *skillful*. Because the response words are synonyms of the stimulus word, they quickly become the dominant responses to the appropriate stimuli. The other half of the subjects learned a list of word pairs purposely designed to make the dominant response the wrong one by making many of the stimulus words similar to each other in meaning (e.g., arid-grouchy, desert-leading). Half the subjects learned the word lists alone and the other half learned the lists in the presence of two passive spectators.

The results support Zajonc's theory and are parallel to the cockroach study. The synonym list was learned more quickly in the presence of the audience than alone, whereas the confusing list was learned less quickly in the presence of the audience than alone. As with the cockroach study, the presence of an audience facilitates the dominant response in both cases. If the dominant response is also the correct response, performance is facilitated; if the dominant response is incorrect, performance is impaired (Cottrell, Rittle, and Wack, 1967).

The fact that these effects are observed in infrahuman species might seem to suggest that they may be instinctive rather than learned through social contact. But even at the animal level data support the notion that social learning produces the effects. For example, most of the studies with animals have examined social facilitation of feeding; as noted earlier, animals of many species eat more food and eat it faster when other members of the species are around. Certainly a social learning process could be at work: the animal that does not eat quickly when others are around soon learns that the food disappears and he goes hungry. Studies supporting this hypothesis have found that rats (Harlow, 1932), chicks (Tolman, 1963; Wilson, 1968), and dogs (James and Gilbert, 1955; James, 1960) that have been raised with no social contact from birth do not eat more when tested in a coating group than when tested alone. Moreover, some studies have found that animals reared in isolation eventually show the social facilitation of eating if testing continued over an extended period of time.

When we move back to the human level, it becomes even clearer that we are not dealing with simple instinctive processes. In fact, it appears that coaction and audience effects in humans are mediated primarily by the individual's "cognitive" concerns about competition and the evaluation of performance that others will make. We learn as we grow up that others praise or criticize, reward or punish our performances, and this raises our drive level when we perform before others. Thus, even the early studies of coaction found that if all elements of rivalry and competition are removed, coaction effects are reduced or eliminated (Dashiell, 1930). Similarly, audience effects are a function of the subject's "interpretation" of how much he is being evaluated. Audience effects are enhanced if it is an "expert" who is watching and diminished if the audience is composed merely of "undergraduates who want to watch a psychology experiment" (Henchy and Glass, 1968; Paulus and Murdoch, 1971). And finally, it has been shown that members of an audience produced no enhancement of dominant responses when they wore blindfolds and, hence, could not watch or evaluate the individual's performance (Cottrell and others, 1968).

The Social Presence of Others: Bystander Intervention

We began the previous section by inquiring into the effects upon an individual of having others present in the environment. But as we saw, such effects often depend on the person's definition or interpretation of what those other individuals were doing or thinking. Are they competitors? Is the audience evaluating the performance? Thus, even in the simple case of coaction and audience effects, the "social" presence of others rather than their mere physical presence appears to be the critical variable. We turn now to social influence effects where the role of others in defining the nature of the situation for the individual is even more crucial.

In 1964 Kitty Genovese was murdered near her home in New York City at 3:30 in the morning. Because she attempted to resist and escape from her assailant, it took him over half an hour to murder her, during which time approximately 40 of her neighbors heard her screams for help. And yet nobody came to her aid. No one even called the police (Rosenthal, 1964).

This incident horrified the American public and led social psychologists to begin investigating "bystander apathy." As it turns out, this is not really a very accurate term, for it is not simple indifference to the fate of the victim that prevents bystanders from intervening in emergency situations; rather, there is a whole host of realistic deterrents to intervention. First, for example there is sometimes real physical danger; second, "getting involved" often means a lengthy period in which one's life is disrupted with court appearances and/or other entanglements that extend well beyond the incident itself. Third, emergencies arise quickly without warning, are very different from one another, require quick unplanned action, and are sufficiently rare that few of us are prepared for them. And, finally, one runs the risk of making a fool of oneself by misinterpreting a situation as an emergency when it is not (such as a family quarrel) and intervening inappropriately. Indeed, the two psychologists who have been the most active in researching this problem have commented, ". . . the bystander to an emergency situation is in an unenviable position. It is perhaps surprising that anyone should intervene at all" (Latané and Darley, 1970, p. 247).

But what remains surprising is that an individual is so unlikely to intervene in an incident like the Kitty Genovese murder, when so many other bystanders are present and when a simple phone call to the police is all that is required. One might suppose that the presence of other people would embolden the individual to overcome these several deterrents to intervention and prompt him to act despite these risks of "getting involved." But ironically, research demonstrates that it is the very presence of other people that serves to decrease rather than increase the probability that any given individual will intervene. Specifically, the presence of others serves to (1) define the situation as a nonemergency and (2) diffuse the responsibility for acting.

DEFINING THE SITUATION. Most emergencies begin rather ambiguously. Is the man who is staggering about ill or simply drunk? Is the woman's life really being threatened or is it a family quarrel? Is that smoke from a fire pouring out a window or just steam or water vapor? Should one intervene or not? One common way to deal with such a dilemma is to postpone action, act as if nothing is wrong, and look around to see how others are reacting. And what are you likely to see? A number of other people who, for the same reasons, are also acting as if nothing is wrong. What arises, then, is a state of "pluralistic ignorance," in which everybody in the group misleads everybody else by defining the situation as a nonemergency. We have all heard about cases in which a crowd can cause a panic because each person leads everybody else to overreact. It may be that the reverse is even more common, the case in which a crowd lulls its members into inaction. Several ingenious experiments demonstrate this effect.

In one such study college students were invited to an interview. As they sat in a small waiting room filling out a preliminary questionnaire, a stream of smoke began to come into the room through a wall vent. Some subjects were alone in the waiting room when this occurred, whereas other subjects were tested in groups of three. The experimenters observed the waiting room through a one-way window and waited six minutes after the subjects had noticed the smoke to see if they would report it. The results show that the average subject who was tested alone came out of the waiting room and reported the smoke within two minutes of first noticing it; in all, 75 percent of subjects tested alone reported the smoke. In contrast, fewer than 13 percent of the people tested in groups reported the smoke within the entire six-minute period, and only one person reported the smoke before the room was completely filled with unpleasant smoke. Interviews with the subjects confirmed that those who had not reported the smoke had decided that it must have been steam, air conditioning vapors, smog, "truth gas," or practically anything but a real fire or emergency. In other words, bystanders serve to define situations as nonemergencies for each other (Latané and Darley, 1968).

To ensure that the results of this study were not due simply to subjects' not wanting to appear "chicken" in the face of possible personal danger, a similar study was conducted in which the "emergency" was provided by the female tester who was working in her office next to the testing room. She was heard to climb up on a chair to reach a bookcase, fall to the floor with a crash, and then yell "Oh my god, my foot . . . I . . . I . . . can't move . . . it. Oh . . . my ankle, . . . I can't get this . . . thing off me." She continued to moan for about a minute longer. The entire incident took about two minutes. Subjects were present in the adjacent testing room either alone or in pairs, and only a curtain separated the testing room from the woman's office. The results confirmed the findings of the smoke study. Seventy percent of the subjects in the alone condition came to the woman's aid, whereas in only 40 percent of the two-person groups did even one person offer help. The victim was actually helped more quickly when only one person heard her fall than when two did. And again, those who had not intervened claimed later that they were unsure what had happened but had decided that it was not too serious (Latané and Rodin, 1969). It seems clear that the group members in these experiments managed to produce a pluralistic ignorance; each person, observing the calmness of other group members, resolved the ambiguity of the situation by deciding there was no emergency.

Diffusion of responsibility

Although each of these passers-by has undoubtedly noticed the man lying on the sidewalk, no one has stopped to help—to find out if he is asleep, sick, drunk, or dead If others were not present, someone would be more likely to come to his aid.

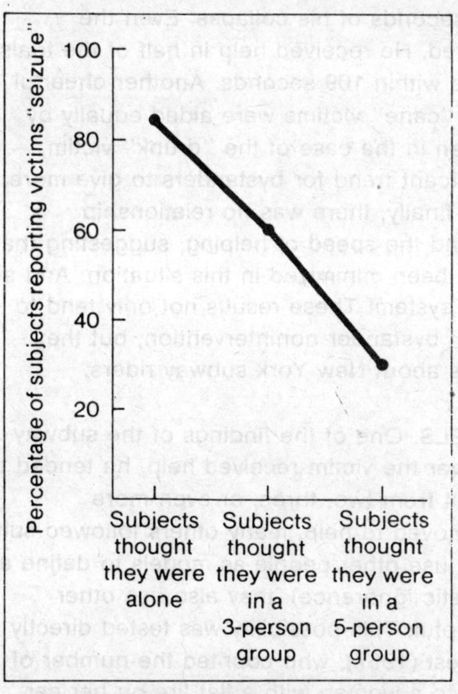

Fig. 18-4 Diffusion of responsibility

Percentage of subjects who reported a victim's apparent seizure as a function of how many other people the subject believed were in his discussion group. (After Darley and Latané, 1968)

DIFFUSION OF RESPONSIBILITY. Clearly "pluralistic ignorance" can lead individuals to define an emergency as a nonemergency because they observe other individuals not reacting. But this process still does not explain incidents like the Genovese murder in which the situation ceases rather quickly to be ambiguous; the fact that it is an emergency is abundantly clear. Moreover, the neighbors who failed to intervene in the Genovese murder could not observe one another and hence could not really tell whether or not others were calm or were reacting with panic behind their curtained windows. The crucial process that appears to be at work here is a "diffusion of responsibility." Because each individual knows that many others are present, the burden of responsibility for doing something about the situation does not fall solely on him. He can think to himself that "certainly someone else must have called the police by now; someone else will intervene."

To test this hypothesis, an experiment was run in which each subject was brought into the laboratory and placed in an individual booth. The subject was told that he would participate in a group discussion about personal problems faced by college students but that, to avoid embarrassment about discussing personal matters with strangers, the discussion would be held via an intercom that connected several such booths. He was further told that the discussion would begin by having each person speak for two minutes about his problems, that the microphone would be turned on only in the booth of the person speaking at that time, and that the experimenter himself would not be listening to the discussion. Actually the voices of all participants except the subject were on tape. On the first round of discussion one of the "taped" participants mentioned that he had problems with seizures, and on the second round of the discussion the subject heard this individual actually start to have a seizure. The experimenters then waited to see if the subject would emerge from his booth to report the emergency and how long it would take him. Note that (1) the emergency is not at all ambiguous, (2) the subject cannot tell how the other "bystanders" he believes are in the other booths are reacting, and (3) he knows the experimenter cannot hear the emergency. Some subjects were led to believe that the discussion group consisted only of themselves and the victim of the seizure. Others were told it was a three-person group consisting of themselves, the victim, and one other person. Finally, some subjects thought they were in a group consisting of themselves, the victim, and four other persons.

The results show that 85 percent of the subjects who thought that they alone knew of the victim's seizure reported it; 62 percent of those who thought they were in a three-person group reported the seizure; and only 31 percent of those who thought four other bystanders were present did so (see Figure 18-4). Interviews with the subjects showed that all of them perceived the situation to be a real emergency—no pluralistic ignorance was observed in this study—and most of them were very emotional about the conflict between the two negative alternatives of letting the victim continue to suffer or rushing, perhaps foolishly and unnecessarily, to help. In fact, subjects who did not report the seizure seemed far more upset than those who did. Clearly, it was not appropriate to interpret their nonintervention as "bystander apathy." Instead, what happened in this study was that the presence of others lifted some of the burden for acting; the presence of others "diffused the responsibility" (Darley and Latané, 1968).

We have suggested that pluralistic ignorance and diffusion of responsibility are the major factors that prevent individuals from intervening in emergencies. This implies that it should be possible to obtain significantly higher rates of helping if both of these processes could be minimized in an emergency situation. To see if this could be done, three psychologists (Piliavin, Rodin, and Piliavin, 1969) converted the New York City subway system into their laboratory to provide a real-world test of this possibility. Two male and two female experimenters would board a subway train through different doors; the female experimenters would take seats and record the results while the two men remained standing. As the train moved along, one of the men staggered forward and collapsed, remaining prone and looking at the ceiling until he received help. If no help was forthcoming, the other man would finally help him to his feet. Several variations of the study were tried in which the victim was either carrying a cane (and hence would appear ill) or smelled of alcohol (and hence would appear drunk). Sometimes the victim was white; other times he was black.

Note that there should be no pluralistic ignorance in this situation. The emergency and the bystanders are all in one "room," and it is clear that help is needed. Diffusion of responsibility should be minimized because one cannot keep assuming that "someone else will intervene" if, in fact, nobody does after a few seconds. Although it might still be true that the presence of others will lower the probability that any given person will intervene, the overall probability that *someone* will help should still be much higher in this situation than in the laboratory studies described above. In other words, people should help.

The results support this optimistic expectation. The victim with the cane received spontaneous help on over 95 percent of the trials; moreover, on the average this help arrived within five seconds of his collapse. Even the "drunk" victim was not entirely ignored. He received help in half of the trials and, on the average, this help arrived within 109 seconds. Another cheerful result was that both black and white "cane" victims were aided equally by both black and white bystanders. Even in the case of the "drunk" victim, there was only a slight and nonsignificant trend for bystanders to give more aid to victims of their own race. And finally, there was no relationship between the number of bystanders and the speed of helping, suggesting that diffusion of responsibility had indeed been minimized in this situation. And all of this on the New York City subway system! These results not only tend to support the proposed explanations of bystander nonintervention, but they should help us revise our stereotypes about New York subway riders.

THE ROLE OF "HELPING" MODELS. One of the findings of the subway study just described was that whenever the victim received help, he tended to receive help not from one person, but from two, three, or even more individuals. As soon as one person moved to help, many others followed suit. This suggests that just as individuals use other people as models to define a situation as a nonemergency (pluralistic ignorance), they also use other people as models for when to be helpful. This possibility was tested directly in a real-world study by Bryan and Test (1967), who counted the number of drivers who would stop to offer help to a woman with a flat tire on her car. During some of the test periods, another car with a flat tire (the "model" car) was planted alongside the highway one-quarter mile ahead of the test car. The model car was raised by a jack under the bumper and a female was watching a male change the flat tire. Of 4,000 passing cars, 93 stopped to help. Thirty-five stopped without the model car and 58 with the model car, a statistically significant difference. This experiment (along with several others in a wide variety of situations) indicates that not only do others define when *not* to act in an emergency, but they also serve as models to show us how and when to be good Samaritans.

PHENOMENOLOGY REVISITED. Before leaving this discussion of bystander intervention, it is pertinent to note that "defining the situation" and "diffusion of responsibility," the two factors that inhibit bystanders from intervening, refer to phenomenological variables; they refer to the emergency situation as the individual perceives and understands it subjectively. Once again we see why social psychology emphasizes seeking the causes of human behavior within the phenomenological world of the individual rather than within the objective world.

"Well, heck! If all you smart cookies agree, who am I to dissent?"

Compliance and Attitude Change

Up to this point we have been considering the kind of social influences that are more accidental than planned. Coactors and audiences do not intend to facilitate or hinder performance, and bystanders do not purposely mislead one another about emergencies. We turn now to deliberate attempts to produce behavior or attitude change.

We have long known that we could use strong rewards and threats of punishment to induce or coerce individuals to comply with our wishes. Here we are concerned with more psychological questions: What kinds of social pressures can achieve the same result? How can an influence agent go beyond mere compliance and cause the individual to change his beliefs and attitudes as well? And finally, what kinds of counter-techniques can be developed to immunize the individual against undesirable influence attempts? We begin with socially induced compliance.

Studies of Compliance

In a now-classic series of studies, Asch (1951, 1956, 1958) set out to demonstrate that individuals could stand up to social pressures and maintain relative independence even when other people disagreed with them. In Asch's standard procedure, a subject is seated at a table with a group of other subjects (in actuality, confederates of the experimenter) and asked to make a series of perceptual judgments. On each trial the group is shown a display with three vertical lines of differing lengths; members of the group are asked to judge which line is the same length as a standard line drawn on another display (see Figure 18-5). Each individual announces his decision in turn, and the situation is arranged so that the actual subject always announces his judgment next to last. The judgments are quite easy to make and on most trials everyone gives the same response. But on some trials, the confederates are instructed beforehand to give the wrong answer. The question is, will the individual conform to the majority response or stand by the evidence of his senses on these critical trials?

The results of these studies did not support Asch's expectations. Despite the fact that the correct answer was always obvious, Asch found that about 32 percent of the time the incorrect, conforming response was given by his

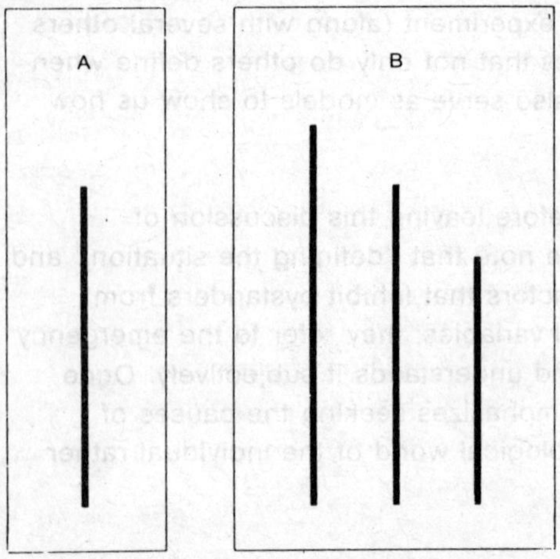

Fig. 18-5 Representative stimulus in Asch's study

After viewing display A, the subjects must pick the line from display B that matches.

subjects; a more pertinent statistic is that about 74 percent of the subjects conformed on at least one of the critical trials.

The Asch studies attracted immediate attention, and many other investigators have conducted variations on them. One of the most striking findings is that if even one of the confederates breaks with the majority on a critical trial the amount of subject compliance drops from 32 percent to about 6 percent. The presence of another "deviant" emboldens the individual to stick with his judgment. Interestingly, the other deviant individual does not even have to give the right answer. In one study (Allen and Levin, 1971), when the majority of the group gave the wrong answer, the planted "deviant" gave an answer that was even more incorrect than the majority. But the presence of even an incorrect deviant still had a powerful effect on the subject; he was more likely to give his own, correct judgment, and the amount of conformity obtained under these conditions was greatly reduced.

A more recent and controversial series of studies on compliance has been reported by Milgram (1963, 1964a, 1965). In these studies, the experimenter required each subject to deliver a series of increasingly powerful electric shocks to another subject (the "learner") whenever the latter made an error while engaged in a learning task. The learner (who in fact was a confederate of the experimenter and did not actually receive any shocks) was strapped in a chair in an adjacent room and could be heard protesting as the "shocks" became more intense. As they got stronger, he began to shout and curse; at 300 volts he began to kick the wall; and at the next shock level (marked "extreme intensity shock" on the subject's apparatus panel) the learner no longer answered nor made any noise at all. The last shock in the series was marked 450 volts. As you would expect, subjects began to protest to the experimenter during this excruciating procedure, pleading with him to call a halt. But the experimenter continued to push by saying things like "please go on" or "the experiment requires that you continue."

In the basic experiment, 65 percent of the subjects continued to obey throughout the experiment, continuing to the end of the shock series (see Figure 18-6). No subject stopped prior to administering 300 volts—the point at which the learner began kicking the wall. Milgram concludes that obedience to authority is a strong force in our society, since the majority of his subjects obeyed the experimenter even though they thought they were hurting another person.

Variations on the Milgram experiment show that the obedience rate drops significantly if (1) the subject is brought closer to the learner or put into the same room with him when the shocks are administered, (2) the experiment is conducted in a run-down suite of offices not connected to a prestigious university as in the original experiment, and (3) the subject is made to feel

A B C

Conflict caused by resistance to yielding

A. All of the group members except the man sixth from left are confederates previously instructed to give uniformly wrong answers on 12 of the 18 trials; number six, who has been told he is participating in an experiment in visual judgment, thus finds himself a lone dissenter when he gives the correct answers.

B. The subject, showing the strain of repeated disagreement with the majority, leans forward anxiously to look at the pair of cards.

C. This particular subject persists in his opinion, saying that "he has to call them as he sees them."

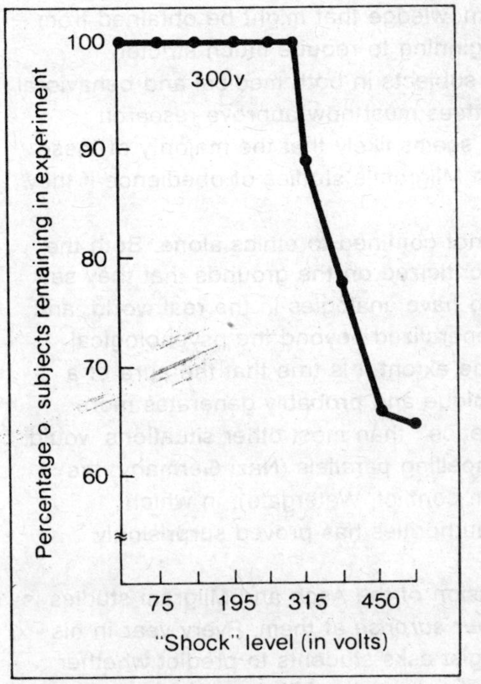

Fig. 18-6 Compliance to authority

Percentage of subjects willing to administer a punishing shock as a function of the intensity level of the shock. Note that for shocks of 300 volts or less all subjects administered the shock. (After Milgram, 1963)

more personally responsible for his behavior. The last factor is important. Because the original experiment was conducted by an official-looking "scientist" at a prestigious university, the subjects were probably able to feel absolved of any ultimate responsibility for their actions. And finally, if the experimenter is out of the room and issues his orders by telephone instead of looking over the shoulder of the subject, obedience drops dramatically from 65 percent to below 25 percent. Moreover, several of the subjects who did continue under these conditions "cheated"; they administered shocks of lower intensity than they were supposed to and did not inform the experimenter of that fact. None of these findings, however, diminishes the fact that compliance rates in these studies remain frighteningly high.

This series of experiments raises a number of very serious ethical questions about the conduct of psychological research (e.g., Baumrind, 1964; Milgram, 1964b, 1968). A subject comes out of a Milgram experiment quite shaken up. Just as we are disturbed and surprised by the amount of compliance obtained in the studies, so too the subjects are often aghast at what they have done. Milgram has defended such charges by noting that he completely "debriefs" the subjects afterward, and that interviews by psychiatrists and follow-up questionnaires indicate no long-term negative effects. Milgram's critics are not convinced. Moreover, it is not irrelevant to recall our earlier discussion of the "irreversibility" effect in self-attributions; as we noted there, "debriefing" a subject cannot be counted upon to erase the dispositional attributions he may have been led to draw about himself during the course of an experiment.

The debate over the ethics of the Milgram studies is part of a recent reexamination of the ethics of research. As you may have noted throughout this chapter, social psychological experiments often mislead subjects about the nature of the experiment and their participation in it, and social psychologists (e.g., Kelman, 1967) are searching for ways to minimize the potential harm in the investigations and to weigh such practices against the

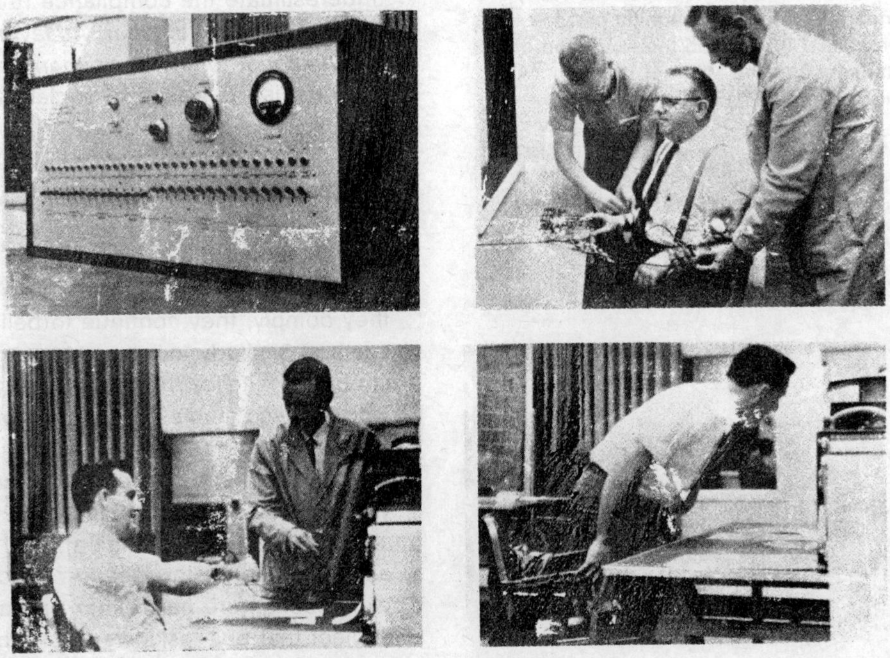

Top left photo shows the "shock generator" used in Milgram's experiment on obedience. Top right, the victim is being strapped in the "electric chair." Bottom left, a subject is receiving the sample shock before starting the "teaching session." Bottom right, a subject is refusing to go on with the experiment. Most subjects became deeply disturbed by the role they were being asked to play whether they continued in the experiment to the end or refused at some point to go on any longer. (From the film *Obedience*, distributed by New York University Film Library; copyright © 1965, by Stanley Milgram)

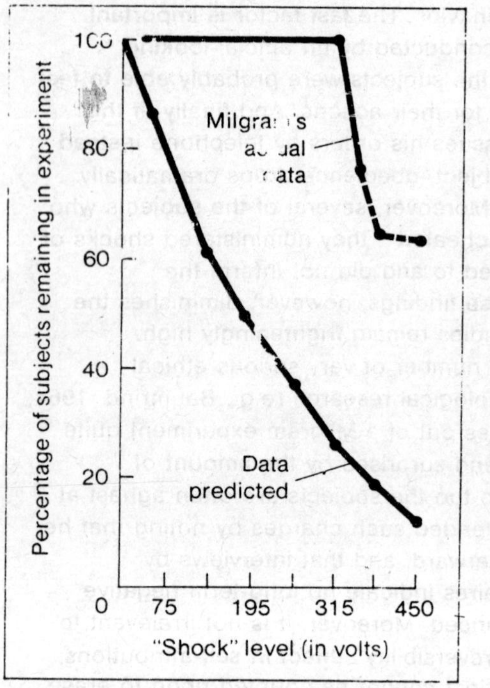

Fig. 18-7 Predicted and actual compliance

The upper curve presents the Milgram data and shows the percentage of subjects who remained obedient in the situation, continuing to administer shocks as the voltage increased. The lower curve is from a study where observers witnessed a reenactment of the Milgram experiment and attempted to predict what percentage of the subjects would continue to be obedient as shock increased. The observers vastly underestimated the magnitude of the situational forces and the likelihood of obedience in the Milgram situation. (After Bierbrauer, 1973)

importance and potential benefits of knowledge that might be obtained from the study. The government, too, is beginning to require much stricter standards for the treatment of human subjects in both medical and behavioral research, and university ethics committees must now approve research projects before they are conducted. It seems likely that the majority of these committees would not give approval to Milgram's studies of obedience if they were proposed today.

Criticism of the Milgram studies is not confined to ethics alone. Both the Asch and Milgram studies have been criticized on the grounds that they set up highly unusual situations unlikely to have analogies in the real world, and consequently the results cannot be generalized beyond the psychological laboratory (Wrightsman, 1972). To some extent it is true that the aura of a "psychological experiment" is itself unique and probably generates more compliance from a desire to "help science" than most other situations would. But history itself contains enough compelling parallels (Nazi Germany, the massacre at My Lai during the Vietnam conflict, Watergate), in which compliance to group pressures or to authorities has proved surprisingly pervasive and easy to obtain.

But perhaps the most important lession of the Asch and Milgram studies is not to be found in the results, but in *our surprise* at them. Every year in his social psychology class, one psychologist asks students to predict whether they would continue to administer the shocks in the Milgram situation after the "learner" begins to pound on the wall. About 99 percent of the students say they would not (Aronson, 1972). Milgram himself surveyed psychiatrists at a leading medical school; they predicted that most subjects would refuse to go on after reaching 150 volts, that only about 4 percent would go beyond 300 volts, and that fewer than 1 percent would go all the way to 450 volts. And in a recent study (Bierbrauer, 1973), subjects were asked to "walk through" the entire Milgram procedure complete with shock apparatus and a tape recording of the protesting "learner." Whether they role-played the part of the subject or the part of an observer, all subjects continued to vastly underestimate the compliance rates actually obtained by Milgram (see Figure 18-7). The moral is clear: *As laymen we underestimate the extent and power of situational forces on human behavior.* This, more than any specific set of findings, is the lesson of social psychology.

From Compliance to Attitude Change

Very few of the subjects in the Asch conformity experiments believe that the majority opinion on the critical trials is the correct opinion; even when they comply, they continue to believe privately that they, not the group, are correct. Similarly, none of Milgram's subjects believes that giving lethal shocks to a fellow human being is the correct or ethical thing to do. In other words, these studies produce compliance, not belief or attitude change. But there are circumstances in which inducing a person to engage in some behavior he does not really believe in will lead him to change his attitude. What are those circumstances?

If you think for a moment, you will realize that you have already seen the answer earlier in this chapter. Recall the experiment in which subjects in an experiment were paid either one dollar or twenty dollars to tell a waiting subject that dull tasks were fun and interesting. All subjects complied with

Leon Festinger

the request, but in addition, the one-dollar subjects showed attitude change as well. They came to believe that the tasks *were* fun and interesting. Recall, too, that all the children in the forbidden toy studies comply with the request not to play with the toy; but, in addition, the children who received the mild request show attitude change as well. They come to believe that the toy is no longer as attractive.

Perhaps you can discern the general principle here: Compliance will lead to attitude change to the extent that the behavior can be induced with the *minimum* amount of inducement. Greater rewards or more severe threats of punishment are generally more successful in obtaining compliance, but they are less successful in getting the individual to believe in what he is induced to do.

Earlier in this chapter we interpreted these results in terms of attribution and self-perception theory. But it is now time to give credit where credit is due. These studies and the resulting general principle emerged originally from the formulation and testing of Leon Festinger's *theory of cognitive dissonance* (1957), one of the most influential theories of attitude change in social psychology.

Festinger's theory states, among other things, that whenever a person engages in some behavior he does not believe in, he will be uncomfortable because his behavior is inconsistent with his beliefs. Festinger termed this feeling of inconsistency *cognitive dissonance* and proposed that individuals will be motivated to reduce this state of dissonance however they can. One way of doing this is for individuals to persuade themselves that they really do believe in the behavior; that is, they can change their beliefs or attitudes to be consistent with their behavior, thus resolving the "dissonance."

Now reconsider the student who has engaged in a series of dull tasks and who then states to another person that the tasks were fun and interesting. Normally this should produce cognitive dissonance because the behavior is obviously inconsistent with the individual's true beliefs. But if he is offered a large sum of money for making the statements (like twenty dollars), things are very different; the money gives him a very consistent reason for making the statements. He can justify the behavior to himself, and, accordingly, there is no longer any "dissonance pressure" on him to alter his opinion of the tasks. Not so for the individual who is paid very little for making the statements. He can find no "good reason," no consistent rationalization for having done so. Accordingly, he will continue to suffer from the pressure of cognitive dissonance until he changes his opinions to be consistent with his behavior. He will become more favorable toward the tasks. Thus, cognitive dissonance theory predicts the results that were actually found: the smaller the compensation received, the greater the attitude change observed.

These general results have also been found in other experiments in different kinds of settings (Brehm and Cohen, 1962). It is also true, however, that some studies have failed to confirm the result, and it is now clear that these effects are influenced by many other variables in the situation besides the amount of justification offered (Aronson, 1968).

Predictions for the forbidden toy study also can be derived from the theory of cognitive dissonance. The child who refrains from playing with the toy under severe threat of punishment does not experience dissonance because he has a perfectly "consonant" reason for complying; the child who refrains under mild threat, however, still experiences the dissonance because of the prominent inconsistency between his avoidance of the toy and the

CRITICAL DISCUSSION

When Two Theories Compete

If both dissonance theory and self-perception theory can predict the results of the one dollar-twenty dollar experiment and the forbidden toy studies, which theory is really true? As is often the case in science, this question is not easy to answer. First of all, the results of some studies can be predicted by dissonance theory but not by self-perception theory (e.g., Waterman, 1969; Pallak and Pittman, 1972). And the results of other studies are predicted by self-perception theory but not by dissonance theory (e.g., Kiesler, Nisbett, and Zanna, 1969, plus some of the studies discussed earlier in the self-perception section). But what about a "crucial" experiment, a situation in which the two theories make opposing predictions? At least three such experiments have been tried (Green, 1974; Ross and Shulman, 1973; Snyder and Ebbesen, 1972). But the results from these "crucial" confrontations were a standoff. For example, the Ross-Shulman study favored dissonance theory, but the Snyder-Ebbesen favored self-perception theory, despite the fact that the two studies were quite similar in conception and design. More recently, Greenwald (in press) has argued that no crucial test is possible.

This outcome is not unusual, and historically science rarely abandons one theory and adopts another because a crucial experiment decides between them. Sometimes a theory is favored because it appears more "elegant," more "fertile," or more general than another: it requires fewer assumptions, or more predictions can be derived from it than from its rival. But most often scientists adopt a new theory and discard an older one because they are more interested in the problems that can be explored with the new one and simply abandon for a time the problems dealt with by the older "paradigm" (Kuhn, 1962).

This is what has happened with dissonance theory and self-perception theory. Problems of attitude change were worked on very intensively during the 1960s, and cognitive dissonance theory was a very fruitful theory, suggesting many new leads and phenomena. But after most of the original ideas were explored, attention shifted to attribution phenomena. In this area of problems, self-perception theory provides a more convenient vocabulary and suggests more interesting leads to be followed than does dissonance theory. Thus, self-perception theory has "won," but only in the sense that it arrived with a set of fresh problems currently of interest to social psychologists (Bem, 1972). The controversy between the two theories has now simply faded away; it has ended with a whimper (and a sigh of relief) instead of a bang. Disappointing, perhaps, but by far the more common outcome in the history of science.

belief that he likes it. Accordingly, he comes to believe that he no longer does like it. And, as we have noted, these are the results.

Cognitive dissonance theory predicts a number of other things as well, and, in general, the theory has had a fairly good batting average in having its predictions confirmed. The unintuitive nature of many of its predictions brought it widespread attention during the 1960s. There were a number of other theories developed in the late 1950s and early 1960s concerning consistency and inconsistency in an individual's beliefs, attitudes, and behaviors (for a review, see Abelson and others, 1968). Collectively, these theories generated most of the research on attitude change during the past fifteen years.

Persuasion

Obtaining attitude change through the induced compliance of behavior is a rather exotic technique. By far the more familiar method by which most of us try to change the opinions of others is simple persuasion. Accordingly, the topic of persuasion is a familiar one to social psychologists as well.

Intensive laboratory study of persuasion began during the 1950s at Yale University (Hovland, Janis, and Kelley, 1953). The Yale investigators examined such things as the prestige and credibility of the persuader, the most effective order in which to present arguments, whether it is more effective to present only one side of the argument, whether certain personality types are more persuasible than others, and many other questions related to the effectiveness of communication and persuasion. Because none of the answers turned out to be simple, several of these questions are still being investigated. Accordingly, it will not be our purpose in this section to list all the findings. Instead, we will illustrate some of the reasons for the complexity of the answers by selecting but one of the questions: What is the most effective order in which to present the arguments? Should your side be presented first? Or should you go last?

PRIMACY AND RECENCY EFFECTS REVISITED. At the beginning of this chapter we noted that *primacy effects* seem to be the rule in impression formation; the first information tends to be given greater weight than later information in determining our perceptions of persons. It was noted that *recency effects* (greater weight given to later information) tended to occur only if the earlier information had a chance to be forgotten before new information was introduced. Similar, but not identical, factors affect the persuasive impact of arguments heard in debates and courtroom trials, where primacy and recency effects can be of significant importance to society.

Unlike first impressions, our reactions to persuasive arguments rely much more heavily on factors of learning and memory. It is known, for example, that it is more difficult to learn new material if one has just attempted to learn very similar material (see p. 232). This suggests that if the opposing sides of an argument are heard one right after another, the primacy effect will occur. It will be more difficult to learn the later information because the earlier information interferes. On the other hand, if the later arguments *could* be learned as well as the first ones, they should be retained better merely because they are closer in time to the "test," whether that is an examination or an election.

Notice that the important variable here is *time*. The first side will have the advantage if the second side has to follow immediately. Primacy effects will prevail. But when the target individual must act immediately after hearing the second communication, recency effects should occur. These predictions were tested in a study by Miller and Campbell (1959). These investigators set up a simulated jury situation in which subjects were presented with a condensed version of the transcript of an actual jury trial involving a damage suit. The arguments were arranged, however, so that all of the plaintiff's arguments were heard in a block and all of the defendant's arguments were also heard in a block. The study varied the time that intervened between the blocks of arguments and also the time that intervened between the reading of the last argument and when the subject was required to give a verdict. The results confirm the theoretical analysis (see Table 18-3). A primacy effect was obtained when there was a small time interval between the first and second arguments and a large interval between the second argument and the verdict. A recency effect was obtained when there was a large time interval between the arguments but a small gap between the final argument and the verdict. This study thus illustrates that there is no simple answer to a question like "which argument should come first?" And timing is but one of the variables that can affect the learning, retention, and acceptance of arguments. This study also illustrates that questions like those concerning primacy and recency effects are not just academic exerices but have important practical implications as well.

TABLE 18-3
Primacy and recency in attitude formation

A positive entry indicates that the first communication had more effect on the final verdict (primacy effect); a negative figure indicates that the second communication had more effect (recency effect).

CONDITION	SIZE OF EFFECT	DIRECTION OF EFFECT
Communication 1, communication 2, test	−.06	Not significant
Communication 1, communication 2, one week delay, test	2.11	Primacy effect
Communication 1, one week delay, communication 2, test	−1.67	Recency effect
Communication 1, one week delay, communication 2, one week delay, test	.11	Not significant

Source: Miller and Campbell (1959).

IMMUNIZING THE INDIVIDUAL AGAINST PERSUASION. Since we have spent considerable time discussing the ways in which people can be manipulated, induced, and persuaded, it may be appropriate to end this chapter by asking how we might help an individual build up his defenses against persuasion. Of course, every time an experiment discovers the ways in which some method of influence operates, it automatically suggests ways of countering the method. But it is possible to make a more direct approach to immunization as well.

How might we build up an individual's defenses against smallpox? One way is to bolster the individual's general health. Give him vitamins, exercise, and so forth. The more usual method is to immunize him by giving him a mild case of smallpox through vaccination. The inoculation stimulates the body to produce antibodies against the disease.

William McGuire and his colleagues have attempted to employ this medical analogy in the area of persuasion (McGuire and Papageorgis, 1961). As a first step, they had to find some beliefs that were relatively "germ-free," that is, beliefs that most of us accept without thinking and that have never been attacked. What they used were cultural truisms from the field of health. For example, most people accept the belief that it is good to have regular medical checkups or to brush one's teeth twice a day. Someone holding these views is analogous to the individual who has never been exposed to the smallpox germ. He has never been forced to defend himself from attack so he has never built up any defenses against attack.

Subjects in the experiment were divided into three groups. The first group received arguments supporting the truisms. They were given some actual reasons why it is good to have regular medical checkups, for example. This treatment is analogous to giving a person vitamins to bolster his general health. The second group had their position attacked rather weakly, and then the attack was refuted (the inoculation condition). The third group, the control group, received neither of these procedures. Afterward, all groups were subjected to a strong attack on their beliefs.

The results show that giving individuals some supporting arguments for their beliefs does help them resist the attack. But, more importantly, the group that received the "inoculation" was significantly more resistant to attack than either the "support" group or the control group (see Table 18-4). The investigators, continuing the medical analogy, suggest that this occurs because the earlier weak attack stimulates the individual to bolster his defenses on his own—preparing arguments supporting his position,

TABLE 18-4
Resistance to persuasion

CONDITION	AMOUNT OF ATTITUDE CHANGE
Support	5.87
Inoculation	2.94
Neither	6.62

Source: McGuire and Papageorgis (1961).

constructing counter-arguments against opposing views, belittling the possible source of opposing views, and so forth. This prepares him well for future attack.

An alternative explanation may be that the earlier attack demonstrates that the opposing point of view—even though not fairly represented in the weak attack—is not a viable position; only stupid people would argue against the truism. This may lead the individual to reject out of hand any future arguments against his position, even if he cannot really refute them. Note that this is exactly what many persuaders attempt to do: they set up their opposition as a straw man, putting forth a distorted and weak form of the opposition arguments. They then proceed to knock it down. The opposition has been made to look stupid and noncredible before being given a fair chance. But whichever explanation is correct—and the chances are that both processes are at work—inoculation does provide immunity against persuasion.

Perhaps there is a lesson here for parents who are concerned about harmful influences on their offspring when they leave home for the wider world of college or a job. Many try to protect their teenage children from the germs of religious agnosticism, premarital sex, and drug usage by treating the traditional positions on these issues as truisms and never discussing them (the control group of the above experiment). Other parents try the "support" method, bolstering the traditional positions with arguments for them. Perhaps a more effective way of preserving parental values in one's children would be to try the immunization approach: offer arguments against religion, chastity, and drug inexperience—and then refute the arguments, or, better yet, let one's offspring do so. However, there is a risk in this procedure. Parents may find their own belief systems being altered in the attempt.

Summary

1. Social psychology studies the ways in which an individual's thoughts, feelings, and behaviors are influenced by other persons. It focuses on the *situational causes* of behavior (as opposed to developmental or personality factors) and on the individual's *phenomenology,* or subjective view of the situation.
2. First impressions of people are important because we are biased toward *primacy effects;* we tend to give too much weight to initial information and too little to later information that may be contradictory. However, if a long time interval intervenes between two sets of information, *recency effects* begin to emerge; the earlier information fades in memory and is replaced by the more recent information.
3. A number of factors influence the degree to which people will like or be attracted to another. *Physical appearance,* for example, plays a more important role than generally acknowledged. Other factors are *competence, similarity* of the people to one another, *reciprocal liking,* and *familiarity.*
4. *Stereotypes* are clusters of interrelated traits and attributes that we assume to be characteristic of certain kinds of individuals. Although stereotypes are often false, they arise from the normal process of generalizing beyond the data at hand until further information is available.

False stereotypes on both sides of a relationship can sometimes be corrected if the individuals meet in a situation where they have equal status and where they can see themselves as sharing common attributes, values, and goals.

5. Stereotypes are a special case of *implicit personality theories,* preconceived notions that we have about which traits and behaviors go with other traits and behaviors. Implicit personality theories lead us to see people as more consistent than they really are and may be one cause of the primacy effect.
6. Some systematic biases are found in our *attribution processes*—the implicit rules we use to infer causes of behavior. For example, we tend to overestimate the importance of personality traits and attitudes in determining behavior and to underestimate the power of situational factors.
7. *Self-perception* may at times be a special case of person perception. The individual often relies upon observations of his own behavior to infer his emotions, attitudes, and personality traits in the same way an outside observer would.
8. *Dispositional attributions*—attributing behavior to personality traits or attitudes—tend to persist. It is difficult for new information to disconfirm such attributions in the observer's mind even when later information invalidates earlier information. This is true for both interpersonal perception and self-perception.
9. The physical presence of others can facilitate or hinder our performance. Simple or well-learned responses are generally facilitated, whereas more complex responses are hindered by the presence of others.
10. Bystanders often fail to intervene in emergency situations for several reasons. By attempting to appear calm, they may *define the situation as a nonemergency* for each other. The presence of other people also *diffuses responsibility* so that no one person feels the necessity to act. Bystanders are more likely to intervene when these factors are changed, particularly if at least one person serves as a "model" for helping behavior.
11. Studies of conformity, obedience, and compliance show that situational factors can produce compliance to a much greater extent than most of us realize. We tend to underestimate situational forces on behavior.
12. Inducing an individual to behave in ways contrary to his beliefs can lead him to change his beliefs if compliance is obtained with a *minimum* amount of inducement. *Cognitive dissonance theory* and *self-perception theory* provide different explanations for this fact.
13. *Primacy and recency effects* are also found in the area of persuasion. The first side of the argument has the advantage (the primacy effect) if the second side must follow immediately because the initial information interferes with the learning of the second information. The second side has the advantage (recency effect) if a long time interval separates the two sides and the individual must act immediately after hearing the second side.
14. An effective way to immunize an individual's beliefs against persuasion is to *inoculate* him by attacking his beliefs with weak arguments and then refuting them. Like a smallpox vaccination, which stimulates the individual's body to build up antibodies, the weak attack stimulates the individual to build up his resistance to later, stronger attacks on his beliefs.

Further Reading

A number of stimulating paperback books deal in more depth with the topics discussed in this chapter. Particularly recommended are: Rubin, *Liking and loving* (1973); Aronson, *The social animal* (1972); Bem, *Beliefs, attitudes, and human affairs* (1970); Zajonc, *Social psychology: An experimental approach* (1966); and Hastorf, Schneider, and Polefka, *Person perception* (1970). A comprehensive textbook in this area is *Social psychology* by Freedman, Carlsmith, and Sears (2nd edition, 1974); see also *Handbook of social psychology,* vols. 1–5, edited by Lindzey and Aronson.

Because social psychologists are often concerned with real-world social problems as well as with laboratory experimentation, all of the readings suggested at the end of Chapter 19 are also relevant.

19

psychology and society

Over the years our society has come to adopt as an article of faith the notion that science and technology can solve any problem no matter how small or large it may be. There are, of course, a few skeptics, a few doubters who believe that science and technology are sometimes more a part of the problem than they are a part of the solution. But despite these dissident voices, it appears that science and technology will continue to be society's major resource for problem solutions.

The science and technology of psychology are no exception, for they too have been enlisted in the service of problem-solving. As previous chapters in this book have demonstrated, practical problems of every sort fall within the domain of psychology. What color should interstate highway signs be for maximum day and night visibility? The psychology of perception provides the answer. How can methods of teaching be made both more efficient *and* more individualized at the same time? The psychology of learning has a number of suggestions. How can we alleviate problems of behavior pathology and emotional distress? Psychology has been addressing these problems both theoretically and therapeutically from the very beginning. As psychology's participation in practical problem-solving has increased, so too has public awareness of psychology's role in these several areas.

What is less well known, however, is the degree to which behavioral scientists, including psychologists, increasingly affect the formulation and implementation of public policy. Therefore, this will be the focus of the present chapter. As we shall see, the influence of behavioral science on public policy is older than most people suspect.

Behavioral Science and Public Policy

White teenagers protesting racial integration march on City Hall in Baltimore, Maryland, October, 1954

In 1954, the United States Supreme Court declared that legally enforced racial segregation in the public schools was unconstitutional (*Brown* v. *Board of Education*). In supporting its decision, the Court cited seven social science documents it had considered during its deliberations, and, in speaking for the Court, Chief Justice Earl Warren concluded that "to separate [black children] from others of similar age and qualification solely because of their race generates a feeling of inferiority as to their status in the community that may affect their hearts and minds in a way unlikely ever to be undone."

Many people believed then, and continue to believe today, that the 1954 Court had departed radically from tradition by considering psychological and sociological factors in reaching its decision. Opponents of the 1954 decision were particularly vocal in expressing their dismay that the Court had strayed from its obligation to render purely legal decisions. Thus, the editor of a newspaper in Virginia complained in an editorial that the subsequent violence in integrating some Southern schools would not have occurred if "nine justices had not consulted sociologists and psychologists, instead of lawyers, in 1954, and attempted to legislate through judicial decrees" (Dabney, 1957, p. 14; quoted by Pettigrew, 1964). Even people who welcomed the 1954 decision appeared to agree that the Court had done something very different from tradition. Not so. The 1954 Court was simply more scholarly and intellectually honest than previous Courts in acknowledging its psychological and sociological sources explicitly.

Consider, for example, an 1896 decision of the Court, *Plessy* v. *Ferguson*. This is the very decision that the Court overturned in 1954, for it was in 1896 that the Supreme Court first gave judicial sanction to the "separate but equal" doctrine of race relations by ruling that legalized racial segregation was not a violation of constitutional rights. The 1896 Court arrived at its conclusion, in part, by noting that "legislation is powerless to eradicate racial instincts" and it upheld the view that "stateways cannot change folkways." Look at these statements carefully, for they reveal that the 1896 decision was just as "psychological and sociological" as the 1954 decision. Thus, the notion that there are "racial instincts" and the belief that legislative or judicial action does not produce attitude change in a society are psychological assumptions that require empirical evidence for or against them. They are neither self-evident truths nor historic legal principles. In fact, they are false. Nobody has ever produced evidence of "racial instincts," and psychological research shows that enforced compliance to legislative and judicial decrees may produce attitude change in a society (Bem, 1970).

But the 1896 Court did not fabricate its psychological assumptions out of whole cloth. These assumptions simply mirrored the sociological thinking of the day. Even the language used by the 1896 Court in justifying its decision reads as if it were taken from the writings of William Graham Sumner, the influential sociologist of the day who maintained that "stateways cannot change folkways." The notion of "racial instincts" also fits very nicely into the sociology of the time.

Thus, the difference between the 1896 and 1954 Supreme Court decisions does not reside in the fact that the later decision was less "legally pure" and more "psychological," but rather it resides in the difference between nineteenth- and twentieth-century psychological knowledge. As noted above, the 1954 Court was simply more scholarly than the 1896 Court in documenting its psychological and sociological sources explicitly.

The moral of this bit of history is that legislation and court decisions are *always* influenced by psychological and sociological assumptions. It is an inescapable fact of life. Rulings concerning the conditions under which an individual can be held responsible for his acts, beliefs about the deterrent effects of capital punishment, and decisions concerning what is or is not obscene all involve "psychological" assumptions. Those who formulate and implement public policy cannot avoid such assumptions. They have only the choice of dealing with them knowingly and explicitly, as the 1954 Court did, or allowing their psychological assumptions to enter unwittingly through the back door, as the 1896 Court did.

Thus, the influence on public policy of assumptions and conclusions in the domain of behavioral science has been with us a long time. Now that the influence is explicitly recognized, behavioral scientists are increasingly called from their laboratories and classrooms to Congress, the courtroom, and administrative agencies to provide information about the nature of human behavior. It is our purpose in this chapter to look carefully and critically at what gifts they bear, and to note that those gifts often contain hidden surprises. The time has long passed when we could assume that the application of scientific knowledge to public policy constitutes a "value-free" undertaking. As we shall see, even the behavioral scientist's purely methodological contributions to public policy (i.e., his techniques of inquiry) often have subtle political consequences of which neither the scientist nor the public is fully aware. And, as we shall see in the last sections of this chapter, the ideologies, prejudices, and stereotypes held by the society can, in turn, infiltrate the "objectivity" of the scientific enterprise itself.

The Methodological Contributions of Behavioral Science

It is commonly assumed that the psychologist's major contribution to the solution of a societal problem is either psychological theory or specific information obtained from research. In some cases this is true. For example, the optimal color of highway signs is known directly from both the theory and findings of experimental psychology. In a quite different realm, Dr. Spock's (1968) advice on the rearing of children is more heavily based upon Freudian psychoanalytic theory than most parents realize. And even when a theory or set of findings cannot be directly applied to the problem at hand, they can often serve as a guide to help the psychologist formulate potential solutions.

But this kind of specific contribution is less frequent than most people suppose. More often the behavioral scientist draws on his methodological skills. When a school system wants to know the optimal length of a computer-programmed sequence for teaching geometry to eighth graders, the psychologist does not usually provide a ready answer. Instead, he brings a methodology, a set of techniques for formulating the question experimentally, testing it out, and evaluating the results. Similarly, the psychologist does not have a theory that tells him which presidential candidate will win an election. But he does have a set of survey and polling techniques that will help him answer the question empirically. Methodology, then, is the most frequent contribution of the behavioral scientist. Accordingly, we turn now to an examination of some of the methodological techniques that have entered the domain of public policy. We begin with the psychologist's favorite and most powerful tool: experimentation.

Experimentation

Social problems are typically "big." They involve large numbers of people and massive expenditures for their solution. And as we shall see in later sections, the research needed to investigate such problems frequently must be large in scale, but not always. Even a small-scale experiment can help to determine if a change in some practice will affect the members of that society and, if so, in what way. As an illustration we will consider a study of sex bias in advertising practices (Bem and Bem, 1973).

Title VII of the 1964 Civil Rights Act forbids discrimination in employment on the basis of race, color, religion, national origin, or sex. According to the Equal Employment Opportunities Commission (EEOC), the federal agency charged with enforcing the act, the number of sex discrimination complaints filed each year has increased steadily since the act was passed. Title VII extends as well to practices that aid and abet discrimination. For example, the act forbids job advertisements from indicating a preference for one sex or the other unless sex is a bona fide occupational qualification for employment. In interpreting this provision, the EEOC has ruled that even the practice of labeling help-wanted columns as "Male" or "Female" should be considered a violation of the law.

Figure 19-1 Sex bias in advertising

Advertisements for the job of telephone operator were written in three formats: **A.** sex-biased; **B.** sex-unbiased; **C.** sex-reversed. The format of the advertisement had a marked effect on the proportion of males and females that showed an interest in the job. (After Bem and Bem, 1973)

Telephone Operator:

WHO SAYS IT'S A MAN'S WORLD?

Behind every man's telephone call, there is a woman. She's a smart woman. She's efficient. She has to be. She places the complex long distance calls people cannot place themselves or helps them locate telephone numbers.

Hers is a demanding job. But we make it worth her while. We can make it worth your while too. Not only do we pay a good salary to start, but also offer group life insurance, group medical coverage, good vacations with pay and free pensions.

A stepping stone to management positions.

Pacific Telephone

A. An Equal Opportunity Employer m/f

Telephone Operator:

We need calm, coolheaded men and women with clear friendly voices to do that important job of helping our customers. They must be capable of handling emergency calls quickly and competently. They also place the complex long distance calls people cannot place themselves or help them locate hard-to-find telephone numbers.

Theirs is a demanding job. But we make it worth their while. We can make it worth your while too. Not only do we pay a good salary to start, but also offer group life insurance, group medical coverage, good vacations with pay and free pensions.

A stepping stone to management positions.

Pacific Telephone

B. An Equal Opportunity Employer m/f

Telephone Operator:

We need calm, coolheaded men with clear masculine voices to do that important job of helping our customers. He must be capable of handling emergency calls quickly and competently. He also places the complex long distance calls people cannot place themselves or helps them locate hard-to-find telephone numbers.

His is a demanding job. But we make it worth his while. We can make it worth your while too. Not only do we pay a good salary to start, but also offer group life insurance, group medical coverage, good vacations with pay and free pensions.

Pacific Telephone

C. An Equal Opportunity Employer m/f

A switchboard operator, bored with her job became one of the first line workers in 1972

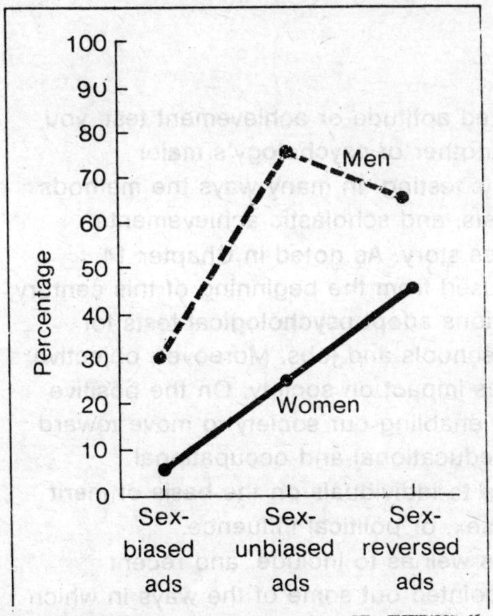

Fig. 19-2 Interest in "opposite-sex" jobs

Graph shows the percentage of men and women applying for opposite-sex jobs as a function of the advertising format. Women were applying for jobs as linemen or framemen; men, for jobs as operators or service representatives. (After Bem and Bem, 1973)

Nevertheless, a large number of employers continue to write advertisements that specify a sex preference, and many more write advertising copy clearly intended to appeal to one sex only. Moreover, some newspapers continue to divide their help-wanted advertisements into sex-segregated columns.

As part of an investigation into sex and race discrimination at the American Telephone and Telegraph Company (AT&T), the EEOC discovered a pervasive sex bias in the company's job advertisements and recruiting brochures. For example, advertisements for the jobs of lineman and frameman were clearly written to appeal only to men, whereas advertisements for the jobs of operator and service representative were written to appeal only to women. The EEOC wanted to determine whether this sex bias discouraged applicants of the opposite sex and, if so, whether rewriting the ads, so that they were either neutral with respect to sex or actually attempted to recruit members of the "other" sex, would encourage more men and women to apply for "opposite-sex" jobs with the company.

Because none of the advertised jobs required more than a high-school education, graduating high-school seniors were recruited as participants in the study. Each participant was shown 12 job advertisements and asked to indicate how interested he or she would be in applying for each job. The 12 advertisements included the 4 telephone jobs mentioned above and 8 nontelephone jobs. For one-third of the participants, the telephone company ads were in the sex-biased format actually used by the company; for one-third of the participants, the ads were unbiased, both in overall tone and with all sex-related job titles and pronouns altered to sex-neutral forms. And finally, one-third of the participants saw sex-reversed "affirmative action" advertisements. An example of one job advertisement in its three formats is shown in Figure 19-1.

The results of this study, shown in Figure 19-2, demonstrate that sex-biased job advertisements do indeed discourage men and women from applying for "opposite-sex" jobs. Consider first the results for women. When the jobs of lineman and frameman were advertised in the sex-biased format used by the Telephone Company, no more than 5 percent of the women were interested in applying for either of them. When these same jobs were advertised in a sex-unbiased format, 25 percent of the women were interested. And when the ads for lineman and frameman were specifically written to appeal to women, nearly half (45 percent) of the women were interested in applying for one or the other of the two jobs. The results for men show a similar but not identical pattern. As can be seen in Figure 19-2, men are generally more interested in the jobs of operator and service representative than women are in the jobs of lineman and frameman. Even so, the percentage of men interested in applying for one or the other of these two jobs jumps from 30 percent to 75 percent when the sex bias is removed. Wording these ads in sex-reversed "affirmative-action" format does not further increase the percentage of men who are interested (the slight decline is not statistically significant).

The EEOC submitted the results from this study as part of its overall complaint against AT&T. The case has now been settled, and AT&T has directed that all of its advertising and recruiting materials be rewritten to remove sex bias. In addition, a nationwide advertising campaign was launched featuring sex-reversed "affirmative-action" ads very similar to those designed for the study itself. Finally, AT&T agreed to recruit and promote women until they hold at least 38 percent of the inside craft jobs (like frameworker) and 19 percent of the outside craft jobs (like lineworker). Men will be recruited and hired into at least 10 percent of the operator jobs and 25 percent of the other clerical jobs. In the long run, this means that about 100,000 or more persons will be in jobs traditionally held by the opposite sex. The chairman of the EEOC has stated that the agreement with AT&T was a milestone in the history of civil rights.

In a similar case, the National Organization for Women filed a complaint against a Pittsburgh, Pennsylvania newspaper for sex-segregating its classified advertising columns. Again, an experiment showed that segregated advertising columns discourage women from applying for "opposite-sex" jobs for which they might well be qualified (Bem and Bem, 1973). The National Organization for Women won the case, and the newspaper appealed the decision up to the United States Supreme Court, which ruled against the newspaper on June 21, 1973. Most newspapers have now "desegregated" their want-ad columns.

Public service advertising campaign prepared by the National Organization for Women (NOW)

It is relevant to note that neither of these studies involved psychological theory or previous findings about advertising or sex bias. Instead, they illustrate that it is the psychologist's methodological training (his knowledge of how to design and evaluate an empirical study) that frequently contributes to the formulation and implementation of public policy. And these cases are merely illustrative. Psychologists across the country increasingly find themselves teaching the rudiments of experimentation in courtrooms as well as in the classroom.

Testing

If you have ever taken a standardized aptitude or achievement test, you have already come into contact with another of psychology's major methodological contributions to society: testing. In many ways the methods of assessing abilities, aptitudes, interests, and scholastic achievements constitute psychology's biggest success story. As noted in Chapter 14, techniques of assessment have been used from the beginning of this century, and every year more and more institutions adopt psychological tests for selecting and guiding individuals into schools and jobs. Moreover, objective testing methods have had an enormous impact on society. On the positive side they have been a primary tool for enabling our society to move toward implementing its egalitarian ideal that educational and occupational opportunities should be made available to individuals on the basis of merit rather than wealth, social class, race, sex, or political influence.

But tests can be used to exclude as well as to include, and recent criticisms of testing procedures have pointed out some of the ways in which tests can fail in their mission to remove discrimination from selection procedures. For example, we noted in Chapter 14 that it is not easy to construct a test that is equally "fair" to all members of a society, a test that does not give unfair advantage to those who have already benefited disproportionately from opportunities in the society. Tests are also often used inappropriately so that they exclude individuals on the basis of factors irrelevant to the job for which they are being selected. For example, a court in San Francisco recently ruled that the fire department could not use a

Why does a fireman wear red suspenders?

A. ☐ The red goes well with the blue uniform.

B. ☐ They can be used to repair a leaky hose.

C. ☐ To hold up his pants.

particular test to select firemen because there was no evidence that it was a valid test of the individual's ability to actually perform the duties of a fireman (*Waco* v. *Alioto*). What the test actually appeared to do was assess the individual's ability to rephrase information in the Fire Department Manual. This is a very common misuse of tests. Thus, many aptitude or intelligence tests have some validity in predicting how quickly an individual will complete an employer's training program, but they are of little value in predicting how well an individual will do on the job after completing the training program. This is a fairly subtle point, and it is only recently that the courts have required employers to furnish evidence that their selection tests are a valid predictor of on-the-job performance. The San Francisco Fire Department case is illustrative of several recent court decisions.

The psychological profession is increasingly attentive to the shortcomings of current tests, particularly to those shortcomings that serve unfairly to discriminate against members of minority groups, and the courts are increasingly attentive to the misuse of tests in selection procedures. These are hopeful trends, for, despite their flaws, objective assessments of an individual's abilities remain one of society's major instruments for assuring equal access to educational and occupational opportunities. And indeed, in a comparison of white and black adult respondents, controlled for social class, it was found that lower-class blacks favored the use of tests in job selection and promotion more than did the white respondents (Brim, 1965).

The Hidden Conservatism of Testing

As we have just noted, psychologists are aware of the shortcomings of tests, and steps are being taken to correct these failings. But the concern with test deficiencies is likely to obscure a subtle effect of tests upon our society that stems not from their failures but from their successes: A successful test can help to freeze the status quo. For example, the Scholastic Aptitude Test (SAT), widely used by American colleges and universities for selecting students, has been quite effective over the years in matching the right students with the right colleges. Because grading standards vary from one high school to another, the SAT provides a needed national yardstick for assessing scholastic aptitude and achievement. Its use has not only helped capable students from poor families or undistinguished high schools to get into the best colleges, but the very existence of a national yardstick has spurred many schools to improve the quality of their instruction. However, the narrow range of abilities measured by the SAT has now become an end in itself. High schools across the nation offer college preparatory courses that are little more than thinly veiled cram courses for the SAT itself. High school students who may have extraordinary talent in drama, music, or science know that they must not spend too much time on these things if they hope to get into the best colleges, for it is their SAT performances that will count. And the colleges themselves do so well in picking "successful" students on the basis of SAT scores that they are not motivated to ask if they should redefine "success" to include more than a high grade point average and successful graduation. In other words, the very success of the SAT poses the societal danger; it has led to a self-perpetuating satisfaction with the status quo. If the SAT did not work, high schools and colleges would probably be trying out

Artistic ability cannot be measured by the SAT.

other kinds of educational experiences and selection criteria. Instead, the educational world now tends to revolve around the test; it has become the master instead of the slave.

These points have been demonstrated in two studies by a psychologist and a college admissions officer. In the first study (Wallach and Wing, 1969) 500 freshmen students in a highly selective university were assessed in terms of extracurricular accomplishments in high school. These included prize-winning accomplishments in leadership, art, social service, literature, drama, music, and science. The investigators found that the SAT scores of these students were of little use in identifying any of these talents. In other words, many of the very talents that colleges and universities hope to produce for society are simply not predicted by the SAT. The second study (Wing and Wallach, 1971) showed that college admission decisions are made almost exclusively on the basis of SAT scores and high-school grade point averages. Even when admission committees think that they are giving weight to extracurricular talents and accomplishments, SAT scores still play the major role.

These studies indicate that high-school students who feel that they should curtail their extracurricular accomplishments so that they can spend more time preparing for the SAT and getting higher grades are being realistic about the factors that will currently gain them admission to the colleges of their choice. Once again, it is important to emphasize that this failure to question the status quo comes about not because objective aptitude testing has failed in its mission, but because it has succeeded.

Aptitude tests are not the only successful tests that produce societal conservatism. So do the interest tests used for vocational and educational guidance. For example, the Strong Vocational Interest Blank (SVIB) is a widely used questionnaire that tells an individual whether or not he shares the interests and attitudes of members of various occupational groups (Campbell, 1971). Thus, the individual who scores high on the "psychologist" scale of the SVIB shares many of the interests and attitudes of successful practicing psychologists; presumably he would feel comfortable among them. This test has been carefully developed, evaluated, and revised over the years, and it is widely used with apparent success to counsel young people into various occupational paths.

But it is important to note that the SVIB thus acts to perpetuate the status quo by guiding into each occupation those individuals who most closely resemble current members of that occupation. Thus, if a particular occupation is currently represented by individuals who are aggressive, masculine, and interested primarily in economic values, the SVIB helps to ensure that aggressive, masculine, and economically motivated individuals will continue to be fed into that occupation, even if the society would benefit by having a different group of individuals redefine the nature of that occupation. It is not accidental that until its most recent revision, the SVIB had separate forms for men and women. Unless a woman insisted on taking the male form of the test, she could not even be scored for traditionally male-only occupations such as accountant. And this is because there were few or no women in those particular "male" occupational groups upon which the SVIB was constructed. If it were not for the recent woman's movement, this conservatism might never have been questioned. And again, it is the success, not the failure, of the test that creates this hidden danger and permits it to function as an obstacle to social change.

CRITICAL DISCUSSION

Racial Differences and Intelligence Testing Revisited

In Chapter 14, we took note of the controversy over the possibility that genetic factors might be involved in producing racial differences in IQ test performances. It was appropriate in that chapter to discuss the technical arguments on both sides of the issue and to point out some of the biases in such tests that might discriminate against ethnic minorities. Here, however, it is pertinent to raise a broader issue, to question the assumption often made by adversaries on both sides of the controversy that intelligence as measured by such tests is the only or even the most important index of human merit and accomplishment.

For example, as the research discussed in this section shows, the SAT overlooks many students who have already revealed talented achievement outside of their classroom work, and studies of postcollege accomplishment yield similar findings. Thus, in a study by Bloom (1963), a group of chemists and mathematicians who had been chosen as outstandingly creative by panels of their peers were compared to a matched control group of scientists who had not been chosen. Both groups were given a battery of 27 different tests of intelligence and perceptual-cognitive functioning. The results show that only two of the tests yielded significant differences between the groups and these two differences were in the direction *opposite* to that predicted. Another study of over 500 scientists showed that scientific excellence on the job was not predictable from either intelligence tests or from earlier academic work, and again, some of the correlations were actually negative (Harmon, 1963). Finally, a review of several studies by Hoyt (1965, 1966) concluded that there was very little relationship between grades in college and accomplishment in occupations undertaken after formal education.

It is true, of course, that one has to have a certain minimal level of intelligence to enter college or most of the occupations examined in these studies, but beyond that minimal level, further distinctions based upon grades or measures of intelligence are apparently of little value. As noted earlier, intelligence tests sometimes predict how fast individuals will complete a training program but fail to predict their performance on the job itself. Similarly, intelligence tests may predict college grades to some degree but not talented accomplishments after college. Thus, on the basis of empirical findings alone, a shift from exclusive preoccupation with intelligence tests would seem warranted.

There is a second reason for questioning the exclusive reliance on intelligence measures: a shift toward a broader range of considerations can help achieve goals of racial equality without raising the abrasive questions about "sacrificing quality" or "lowering standards" that often arise. The study by Wing and Wallach (1971) on college admission decisions showed that if the university in which they conducted their study had selected a freshman class on the basis of demonstrated extracurricular talent and accomplishment in high school, it would have automatically admitted nonwhite applicants in almost exact proportion to their numbers in the applicant pool and would still have ended up with a class with very high SAT scores. In contrast, had the university relied exclusively on SAT scores, nearly all of the most talented nonwhite applicants—those already displaying many of the accomplishments college presumably hopes to stimulate—would have been refused admission.

It should be clear that the implicit assumption that intelligence tests provide the final word on an individual's merit is far more dangerous to the egalitarian principles of our society than the belief that genetic factors may contribute to racial differences in IQ test performance.

"Twenty-eight per cent said yes, 19 per cent said no, and 53 per cent were offended by the question."

Opinion Surveys

The testing methods discussed above are familiar to most Americans, particularly to college students, who have probably had more than their share of exposure to tests. But in a contest of familiarity, it is probably the public opinion survey that takes first place among the methodological contributions of the behavioral sciences. At least once a week, Americans are told the results of one or another survey showing that a certain percentage of their fellow citizens have lost confidence in the President or that some other percentage think that marihuana should be legalized or that inflation is the major worry of the public.

Moreover, surveys are no longer mere passive recorders of opinion. Increasingly they help to shape the very public opinion they attempt to describe; policy makers rely upon them for deciding upon the wisdom and timing of their decisions, and politicians base their stands on survey results, particularly at election time. Clearly, the reliability, validity, and objectivity of the surveys have become crucially important, and most of the major survey organizations take great care to see that they use the most sophisticated statistical methods of sampling and analysis.

The goal of most surveys is to ascertain what percentage of the population under investigation subscribes to a particular viewpoint at a particular time. But it is also possible to use survey techniques to obtain more long-lasting information about the nature of opinion formation and change. For example, Lloyd Free, a pollster and political analyst, and Hadley Cantril, a social psychologist, conducted a large-scale study of political liberalism and conservatism in America (1967). Using the resources of the Gallup polling organization, they interviewed over 3,000 Americans in 1964 to see what percentage of the public supported several of the government social-welfare programs then in effect. They found that 65 percent of the public were "liberals" in the sense that they supported all or nearly all of the programs mentioned by the interviewers; only 14 percent of the public were "conservatives" in the sense that they opposed all or nearly all of the programs. In other words, about two-thirds of the American public qualified as "liberal" with respect to favoring specific government welfare programs. These results are consistent with previous polls that show that the American public has been liberal in this sense at least since the days of the New Deal under Franklin Roosevelt.

But Free and Cantril went further. In addition to asking about specific programs, they also asked people whether they agreed or disagreed with statements like "Social problems here in this country could be solved more effectively if the government would only keep its hands off and let people in local communities handle their own problems in their own ways," and "We should rely more on individual initiative and ability and not so much on governmental welfare programs." If the questions about specific programs can be conceived of as tapping "operational" liberalism and conservatism, then these more general questions can be thought of as inquiring about "ideological" liberalism and conservatism. And the results are quite different.

Compared to 65 percent of Americans who are "operational" liberals, the survey showed that only 16 percent of the public are "ideological" liberals; compared to 14 percent of Americans who are "operational" conservatives, 50 percent are "ideological" conservatives. Clearly, somebody is inconsistent.

TABLE 19-1
Percentage of ideological liberals and conservatives classified as liberal, middle-of-the-road, or conservative on the operational scale

		IDEOLOGICAL SCALE	
		LIBERAL GROUP	CONSERVATIVE GROUP
Operational Scale	Liberal	90%	46%
	Middle-of-the-road	9	28
	Conservative	1	26
		100%	100%

(Adapted from Free and Cantril, 1967, p. 37).

Table 19-1 shows us who. As you can see, 90 percent of the ideological liberals are consistent in that they are also liberals on the operational scale, but almost half of the ideological conservatives (46 percent) proved to be operational liberals. Another way of stating this result is to say that nearly one out of every four Americans is an ideological conservative and at the same time an operational liberal. They oppose federal welfare programs in general, but approve of all or nearly all of the federal welfare programs currently in operation.

Information like this has not been lost upon political leaders. Thus, in the 1964 Presidential election, the conservative Republican candidate Barry Goldwater (who lost) attacked both federal welfare programs in general *and* specific programs in particular. But in 1968, Richard Nixon (who won) made many campaign statements attacking federal welfare programs in general—just like the statements on the ideological scale of the Free and Cantril survey—while simultaneously proposing such things as increased Social Security benefits. Whether you approve of this tactic or not probably depends upon your politics, but in either case, it should be clear that opinion surveys are increasingly affecting public policy.

Large-Scale Methodology and Interdisciplinary Approaches

Social problems typically have two characteristics: they are large, and they are complex. Thus, social problems are often nationwide if not worldwide in scope, and comprise a tangled web of psychological, sociological, economic, political, and sometimes even religious factors. In contrast, attempts to solve social problems have too often been limited in scope, with several isolated groups of researchers attacking the problems from within their own specialties and having little or no contact with others who are working on the same problem. There is now a heightened awareness that this piecemeal approach is no longer sufficient, that large-scale problems require large-scale (and expensive) approaches and that complex "system" problems require parallel systems of coordinated and interlocking interdisciplinary efforts for their solution. We are just now beginning to see the emergence of such coordinated large-scale efforts.

POPULATION CONTROL. The field of family planning and population control provides a good example of the above points. Overpopulation is a pressing worldwide problem that involves a host of intertangled factors,

A birth control lecture in an Indian village

including cultural and religious variables. By and large, however, only the demographers and the sociologists have tried in a systematic way to bring behavioral science to bear upon this problem (Fawcett, 1970). A few psychologists, particularly those with psychoanalytic orientation, have concerned themselves with motivational and attitudinal factors affecting family size (see Rainwater, 1965; Pohlman, 1969; Wyatt, 1967), and there have been several psychological studies examining the use of different contraceptive methods (Fawcett, 1970). But none of these studies is really an integrated part of a large-scale coordinated effort among behavioral scientists to approach the problem in a systematic way.

A start toward more systematic inquiry in the population field has evolved from what have become known as KAP surveys. These surveys, usually conducted in connection with family planning programs in developing countries, seek three kinds of information: *Knowledge* possessed by the population about the physiology of reproduction and methods of contraception; *Attitudes* and values related to family size, pregnancy, family limitation in general, and specific contraceptive methods in particular; and *Practice* of birth control. More than 400 KAP surveys have been conducted in virtually all of the world's major geographic and cultural areas. They have been similar enough in form and content to provide a significant collection of comparative international data (Mauldin and others, 1970; Fawcett, 1970). Moreover, substantial efforts have been made to develop standard instruments and procedures for KAP surveys (see The Population Council, 1967, 1970).

Even this small step toward more systematic inquiry has paid off in numerous ways. For example, KAP data have shown that women desire smaller families than they are likely to have; that they are willing to discuss sex, procreation, and contraception; that they know little about contraception but are eager to learn; and that they consider it proper for the government to provide family planning advice and services. Results like these have persuaded many policy makers in developing countries to revise their views concerning the political acceptability of family planning programs. KAP surveys have also been used to evaluate the effectiveness of ongoing programs. For example, it has been found that there is a genuine desire for information and that, although the information about physiology tends to be forgotten, details about contraceptive techniques are not.

But even the KAP surveys do not begin to tap the opportunities open to behavioral scientists to help solve the population problem. As we have seen in previous sections, behavioral science has many theories and techniques at its disposal. For example, the area of family planning and population control provides an excellent setting for trying out theories and techniques of persuasive communication. Several studies utilizing this approach have been conducted (Fawcett, 1970). The best-known and by far the most ambitious is the Taichung Study, conducted in the third largest city in Taiwan (Freedman and Takeshita, 1969). The Taichung Family Planning Program was a large-scale experimental effort to make family planning available to the entire population of an Asian city and to observe the effects systematically. It is probably the largest behavioral science study yet conducted under some approximation to an actual experiment.

The main part of the Taichung experiment consisted of a preprogram survey, an intensive communications and service program, and a postprogram survey, all of which took place in a one-year period. The major dependent variable was the increase in practice of family planning during the experiment and for two subsequent years following the program. The communications program itself consisted of personal visits by health workers, mailings, and group meetings. The 2,400 neighborhood units in the city of Taichung were assigned randomly to one of four treatments: (a) visits, mailings and group meetings for both husbands and wives; (b) visits, mailings, and meetings for wives only; (c) mailings only; and (d) control (no visits, mailings, or meetings). In addition, the city was divided into different sectors which received different "densities" of treatment. For example, in one sector 50 percent of the neighborhood units received the program, whereas in another only 20 percent of the units did.

The results of this experiment showed that group meetings that were rated as "effective" by the group leader had a greater influence on birth control practices than did home visits or mailings, especially for family acceptance of the IUD. It was also found that educational efforts directed toward wives were as effective as the much more costly programs aimed at both husbands and wives. Acceptance rates of family planning were relatively high even in neighborhoods in which only a few of the family units received the program; acceptance rates were higher among those who believed that their friends, neighbors, and relatives were beginning to practice contraception. These are just some of the important and useful findings from this experiment. The Taichung Study stands as a model of what behavioral scientists can accomplish when the scope of their methodology begins to match the scope of the problem.

SOCIAL INDICATORS. For a number of years, the American public has become accustomed to hearing the government justify some change in economic policy on the grounds that the President's Council of Economic Advisors has recommended it after looking at the balance of payments, the gross national product, the unemployment rate, the prime interest rate, the consumer price index, and so forth. These several indicators of the nation's economic status are now routinely collected, and economists continue to research ways in which such indices can be developed and utilized in planning the nation's economic future. In recent years, it has been proposed that a parallel set of indicators be developed that would perform a similar function for formulating and evaluating social policies and programs. Such *social indicators* would help us to monitor the social aspects of national life such as health, education, recreation, and public safety on a continuing basis. And it has been proposed that eventually a Council of Social Advisers might be formed to translate these indicators into proposals for government policy in the same way that the Council of Economic Advisors now does.

In 1969, the United States Department of Health, Education, and Welfare issued a publication entitled *Toward a Social Report,* which spelled out many of the variables that might be useful in composing social indicators. Many of these are already familiar statistics: crime rates, life expectancies, availability of health services in different geographical areas, air pollution measures, personal incomes, and so forth. But many of the proposed indicators are more psychological than these. For example, it might be useful to have a measure to assess the degree to which a city or town has a "sense of community." Similarly, it might be useful to know how effective or powerless members of a community feel in controlling decisions that affect them. It should be clear that behavioral scientists of all kinds would have to be involved in the development of a complete catalogue of social indicators.

FUTURE FORECASTING. Social indicators, like economic indicators, would be enormously useful in describing the present state of the nation. But such indicators are also essential in forecasting the future. How many schools will the nation require in the year 2000? Should mass transit systems be built in the expectation that fewer people will own cars in 1990? How will mass transit systems affect the geographical distribution of job opportunities in 1980? Will the two-party political system still exist in America in 1995? What will be the psychological effects of having all financial transactions conducted by computerized credit card systems with nobody carrying cash? These are but a few of the questions that future forecasters attempt to answer now on the basis of current social trends and educated guesses about new inventions and technologies that might be developed.

Some questions like these can be answered by simply looking at current trends and extrapolating them into the future. For example, the present birth rate can give us a pretty good idea of how many elementary school teachers we will need seven or eight years from now. But often simple "trend analysis" can be disrupted by the development of a new technology or the sudden appearance of a new social trend. For example, the recent emergence of the women's movement is affecting a number of predictions concerning the birth rate, the job market, the marriage and divorce statistics, the need for child care facilities, and the distribution of family income. In order to anticipate these sharp breaks in current trends, future forecasting has gone beyond simple trend analysis to more exotic methods. For example, the *Delphi method* (named after the ancient and celebrated oracle of Apollo at Delphi) is a formal procedure for pooling the judgments of experts about events likely to take place in the years ahead that are not fully reflected in available trend analyses. Thus, in estimating the number of doctoral degrees in psychology to be produced in the 1970s, the experts would have had to have anticipated such developments as the end of the military draft, the reduction in federal expenditures for fellowships and research assistantships in the post-Vietnam War era, the current high interest in social problems, and so forth.

A step beyond the Delphi method is the *cross-impact matrix method* (Gordon and Hayward, 1968). Forecasted events are not independent but necessarily interact; the concept of "cross-impact" takes this into account. Suppose, for example, we want to predict the state of weather forecasting in 1980. We would need to know: (1) the future state of the art of weather forecasting predicted by simply extrapolating present methods of meteorology; (2) the likely influences of new technologies based upon the use of satellites, computer simulation, and more massive world data; (3) the chances that artificial control of the weather will become a day-to-day reality; and (4) the political obstacles that will stand in the way of adopting available methods. Panels of experts can provide independent Delphi estimates for each of these questions, and then the estimates can be combined to produce the most likely overall estimate of the state of weather forecasting in 1980.

The challenge of developing social indicators and predicting the future has excited many behavioral scientists. A recent bibliography contains over 1,000 separate listings of books and articles concerned with social indicators and societal monitoring, including future forecasting (Wilcox and others, 1972); the government is sponsoring numerous studies on social indicators throughout the country. It is clearly an idea whose time has come.

THE NEED FOR PROBLEM-ORIENTED INSTITUTIONS. This discussion of social indicators makes it clear that behavioral scientists interested in social problems can no longer work in isolation from one another just because they are in different disciplines. Similarly, behavioral scientists must now be prepared to collaborate with specialists like engineers, architects, and others; and finally, all of these specialists must be able to communicate with the policy makers themselves.

But this task of collaboration is itself a minor social problem. In a large university, for example, members of the psychology department often do not even know the names of sociologists and political scientists on campus, let alone the engineers or architects. And panels and agencies that have reported on this problem (National Academy of Sciences/Social Science Research Council, 1969; National Science Board, 1969) have asserted that the departmental structure of universities, built around disciplinary specialties, is unfavorable to social research and application. They have recommended the establishment of multidisciplinary institutes inside or outside of universities, or a school of applied behavioral science modeled after a school of engineering or a school of medicine. These suggestions are now being adopted in some places, and new organizations that fit such descriptions are coming into being.

There is, however, a great deal of resistance to change within universities, and in some cases psychology departments have found it more feasible to retain their departmental structure while extending their teaching and research into community psychology, or into specialties concerned with public affairs. Because psychology covers a broad spectrum (from the biological to the social sciences) and because psychology departments have usually been congenial to both basic and applied research, many of them find it easier to extend their own degree programs than to establish new degree-granting schools within their universities. These programs usually include seminars taught by scholars from other departments.

But the fact remains that the hand that created social problems did not fashion university departments. The boundaries of social problems simply do not fit the neat disciplinary lines found in college course catalogues or in the typical graduate training curricula of behavioral scientists. Before the behavioral sciences are in a position to contribute to the solutions of social problems on a large scale, they will have to go even further toward remaking the boundaries of the organizational units in which they work to approximate more closely the contours of the problems themselves. We are now seeing only the beginning of such reorganization.

Societal Ideology and Behavioral Science

At the beginning of this chapter we contrasted the 1896 Supreme Court decision that upheld legalized racial segregation and the 1954 decision that overturned it. We pointed out that both decisions were products, in part, of the psychological and sociological thinking of their respective times. We thus implied that the perspectives and assumptions of behavioral scientists affect the thinking of society. But influence is a two-way street: The perspectives and assumptions of the society affect the thinking of behavioral scientists. Once again, a bit of history is instructive.

Political Bias: An Historical Example

In the first three decades of this century, many Americans were alarmed by the increasing flow of immigrants from southeastern Europe, particularly by the influx of Italians, Poles, Russians, and Jews. There was a strong belief that these "new immigrants" were genetically inferior to native-born Americans and that their increasing presence in America would "pollute" the country's genetic potential. This feeling culminated in the passage of the immigration law of 1924, which set up our country's first "national origin quotas" on immigration, thereby severely restricting the immigration of the "undesirable" elements.

Tagging immigrants in a railroad waiting room, Ellis Island, 1926

Many psychologists who were prominent in the intelligence testing movement at the time were persuaded that differences between ethnic groups in intelligence test performance were primarily genetic in character. They gave little consideration to the many cultural and situational factors that we now know can lower test performances. Thus, the U.S. Public Health Service invited Henry Goddard to Ellis Island to apply the new mental tests to the arriving European immigrants. Goddard (1913) reported that, based upon his examination of the great mass of average immigrants, "83 percent of Jews, 80 percent of Hungarians, 79 percent of Italians, and 87 percent of Russians were feeble-minded'." He was also able to report later (Goddard, 1917) that the use of mental tests "for the detection of feeble-minded aliens" had vastly increased the number of aliens deported.

The most direct psychological contribution to the 1924 immigration law, however, was a book by Carl Brigham entitled *A Study of American Intelligence* (1923). In this book, Brigham analyzed intelligence test data collected by the army during the First World War. He found that immigrants who had been in the country 16 to 20 years before being tested were as bright as native-born Americans, whereas immigrants who had been in America only 0 to 5 years when tested were virtually feeble-minded. How would you explain these findings? Perhaps you would be prompted to conclude something about the difficulties of giving a fair intelligence test to non-English-speaking immigrants who have just arrived in an unfamiliar culture. But this was not Brigham's interpretation of the findings. "We must assume," he wrote, "that we are measuring native or inborn intelligence." He then noted that the immigrants who had arrived 16 to 20 years ago came primarily from England, Scandinavia, and Germany, but that more recent immigration had come from southeastern Europe. The decline of immigrant intelligence, Brigham noted, paralleled precisely the decrease in the amount of "Nordic blood," and the increase in the amount of "Alpine" and "Mediterranean" blood in the immigrant stream.

Brigham's book concludes that ". . . we are incorporating the negro into our racial stock, while all of Europe is comparatively free from this taint. . . . The steps that should be taken . . . must of course be dictated by science and not by political expediency. . . . The really important steps are those looking toward the prevention of the continued propagation of defective strains in the present population." This book was widely quoted in Congress as "scientific" support for the 1924 immigration law.[1]

Brigham's idea that "the really important steps" to be taken would involve preventing the continued propagation of "defective strains" was also shared by other psychologists. For example, one eminent psychologist of the period felt that Indian, Mexican, and Negro children ". . . should be segregated in special classes. . . . They cannot master abstractions, but they can often be made efficient workers. . . . There is no possibility at present of convincing society that they should not be allowed to produce. . . . They constitute a grave problem because of their unusually prolific breeding (Terman, 1916)."

When one notes the flawed data and fallacious reasoning upon which such arguments rested, it becomes clear that these behavioral scientists were using their "science" to bolster the prejudices and presuppositions that they shared with many of their less eminent countrymen. But unlike their less eminent countrymen, their "scientific" conclusions were taken seriously in formulating public policy. Thus does behavioral science become part of the problem.

Political Bias: Contemporary Variations

Blessed with the wisdom of hindsight, it is easy to recognize the biases of behavioral scientists of an earlier era. Moreover, several decades of added experience in the behavioral sciences have made us more sophisticated methodologically and have taught us to guard against unconscious biases in the interpretation of data. The "objectivity" of behavioral science is probably more secure now than it was in an earlier time. But biases can still enter the behavioral sciences in subtle ways. First of all, an investigator's biases, perspectives, and orientations enter into his decision about which questions to pursue and how to formulate those questions. It is unlikely that a very liberal or radical psychologist would spend time and effort investigating the genetic bases of racial differences in intelligence. White psychologists have often studied the black ghetto family, using the nuclear white family as their implicit ideal model. Accordingly, the investigator sees only weakness, decay, and "pathology" in the ghetto family and fails to see alternate forms of strength (e.g., how the existence of an extended family structure in many black families provides some advantages not found in many highly mobile, white, middle-class families) (Billingsley, 1968). Notice that the methods of investigation themselves can be completely "objective"; but the bias has already entered in the way the question has been formulated.

The second kind of bias that creeps into behavioral science research is simple neglect. For example, an important line of research in psychology has focused on the motivation to achieve (McClelland and others, 1953). An individual's motivation to achieve excellence is typically assessed in this research by asking him to write a story about a picture the experimenter shows him. The stories are then rated or scored for the amount of achievement motivation they reflect. It was found very early in this research that the procedure "worked" only for male subjects, and, accordingly, almost all the subsequent research used only male subjects. Because they had not shown any evidence of an enhanced motive to achieve under the predicted

[1] It is to Brigham's credit that he later reexamined the data and the generalizations he had drawn from them, concluded that he was wrong, and said so publicly (see Brigham, 1930).

CRITICAL DISCUSSION

The Politics of Contemporary Behavioral Scientists

The racial beliefs of the psychologists quoted in this section were not necessarily representative of all psychologists in the early part of this century. Even then, many behavioral scientists were spending their time investigating the environmental causes of behavior. And despite its problems with racism, America itself has always subscribed to a strong environmentalism, a belief that a good environment and equal opportunities can enable anybody to succeed in the society. Accordingly, most behavioral scientists in America today share this bias toward environmental explanations of behavior. In fact, because the discovery of the "causes" of behavior is the occupational preoccupation of many behavioral scientists, they are even more sensitized than most Americans to the kinds of environmental variables that can block opportunity and create unfair disadvantage. Thus, a survey of behavioral scientists in academic institutions showed that the majority of them are found on the "liberal" side of the political spectrum; they are active supporters of governmental programs for social change and are clearly to the "left" of most Americans politically (McClintock, Spaulding, and Turner, 1965). To cite one statistic, at the time of the survey about 42 percent of the American public affiliated itself with the Democratic party, the party traditionally identified with the more "liberal" platform. But 70 percent of the psychologists, 74 percent of the political scientists, and 78 percent of the sociologists considered themselves Democrats—a marked difference from the national average.

It may also be that the direction of cause and effect is different from that implied in the preceding paragraph. Psychologists may be liberal not primarily because they study the environmental causes of behavior, but because liberal individuals choose careers in one of the behavioral sciences. They may regard such a career as an effective means of contributing to society in ways compatible with their political views. Thus, differential recruitment of individuals with particular political views is probably one way in which thinking in the behavioral sciences is affected by ideological trends in the society itself. The current "liberalizing" influence of the behavioral sciences on society may come about in part because liberals become behavioral scientists.

experimental conditions, women were dropped from the experiments. Not until several years later was it found that achieving women do, in fact, write stories reflecting achievement motivation, but only if they are shown pictures containing female figures. In fact, women who wrote stories about achievement to pictures containing men, but not to pictures containing women, were underachievers (Lesser and others, 1963).

But it was too late; the damage had already been done. The pictures that had been adopted for conducting most of the research contained no female figures; moreover, after the first failures to obtain the expected results with female subjects, investigators stopped including them in their studies. And finally, many writers have forgotten over the years that the results obtained in most studies applied only to men; they continue to cite the results as if they applied to everyone. We do not know to this day which research results would replicate with women and which would not.

It is important to emphasize that the extensive research on achievement motivation is of high quality. It is carefully executed; the procedures ensure that the stories are scored in "objective" fashion without bias; and the results are publicly reported. Moreover, the results have been used in practical training programs in the developing countries (McClelland and Winter, 1969). But there is one problem: Half of the population has been systematically excluded from the research because the original set of stimulus materials contained a "male" bias.

Where Is the "Objectivity" of Science?

After this extended discussion of the ways in which the process of behavioral science can be influenced by the prevailing ideological biases and prejudices of the society in which the science is practiced, it is natural to wonder how behavioral scientists can even claim to be "doing science" at all. Where is the vaunted "objectivity" that distinguishes science from other forms of inquiry?

The answer to this question lies in the methodology and dissemination practices of science. The scientific aim is to make research findings public, truthfully reported, and responsive to checking by competently trained people. The best guardians of the integrity of any one scientist are other scientists who can criticize the work, repeat it if necessary to verify it, disconfirm it, or demonstrate its limitations. All of the sciences rest their claim to objectivity on their public information-seeking and information-testing methods. Nothing we have said in this chapter implies that the behavioral sciences have been amiss in following this proven model of inquiry. Indeed, because they are involved in advising on public policy, many behavioral scientists have devoted enormous time and effort to disseminating the knowledge gained from the behavioral sciences to the general public, where it can be scrutinized, evaluated, and criticized by those citizens whom this knowledge might affect. At the time of this writing, psychology is the favorite undergraduate major of college students throughout the country; thus, nearly every college graduate has received some amount of training in how to evaluate the validity of research evidence in the behavioral sciences. This, too, keeps behavioral science "honest."

In conclusion, the human mind has not yet devised a more objective method of gaining knowledge than the scientific method of open, repeatable inquiry, and it is this self-correcting feature of the scientific method that guarantees its "objectivity" in the long run. We have nothing that can compete with its reliability, validity, and objectivity. But precisely because it is human minds that are at work, nonobjective elements will always creep into the process. In the final analysis psychology, too, is a human enterprise. And that is why it has the potential for being part of the problem as well as part of the solution.

Summary

1. The findings and theories of the behavioral sciences have influenced the formulation and implementation of public policy for many years, although it is only recently that this influence has been explicitly acknowledged and actively sought by policy makers.

2. The major contributions of behavioral science to public policy have been methodological contributions. These include experimentation, testing, opinion surveys, and, more recently, large-scale projects and interdisciplinary attacks upon social problems.
3. An example of an experiment that played a role in changing public policy is a study showing that sex-biased advertising discourages men and women from applying for jobs normally reserved for the opposite sex.
4. Standardized tests have contributed to the American ideal that opportunities should be made available to individuals on the basis of merit rather than wealth, social class, race, sex, or political influence. A number of shortcomings in current tests are being corrected, but in many ways it is the success of testing, not its failure that poses a subtle danger to society. Because of its ability to predict an individual's performance in some area (e.g., college grades), a successful test does not stimulate questions or criticisms of the criterion itself. Thus, the widely used Scholastic Aptitude Test (SAT) is so successful at picking "good" students that performance on the test has become an end in itself.
5. Opinion surveys can be used not only to discover what proportion of the public holds a certain view but also to discover longer-lasting information about the nature of beliefs and attitudes. For example, a survey study found that many Americans oppose social welfare progams in general while simultaneously endorsing nearly all of the specific programs already in operation.
6. The behavioral sciences are finding it necessary to develop large-scale methods of research in order to contribute effectively to the solution of large-scale problems. Moreover, the amount of interdisciplinary collaboration among behavioral scientists, between behavioral scientists and other specialists, and between all specialists and the policy makers will have to increase. Universities are not well organized for interdisciplinary work, and alternative, problem-oriented institutions may be needed.
7. The field of population control and family planning provides an example of a problem requiring both large-scale methods and interdisciplinary work from the behavioral sciences. The developing interest in social indicators and future forecasting also requires extensive interdisciplinary collaboration.
8. The perspectives, assumptions, and prejudices of the society in which the behavioral scientist works can affect and subvert the objectivity of the scientific enterprise. Historically, this can be seen in some of the statements of behavioral scientists, statements that reflected the societal prejudices and idelology of the time and had little or no scientific basis. Contemporary societal prejudices influence behavioral science in more subtle ways: first, by influencing the ways in which research questions are chosen and formulated; and second, by causing certain questions to be neglected.
9. Despite the influences that can subvert the objectivity of the research enterprise, the behavioral sciences, like all sciences, rest their claims of objectivity upon the open, public methods of gathering and reporting their results and the self-correcting character of the process. But in the final analysis, science is a human enterprise and, hence, it has the potential for being part of the problem as well as part of the solution.

Further Reading

A number of books seek to apply psychological principles systematically to the solution of social problems. One of the more general works is Varela, *Psychological solutions to social problems* (1971). Among books devoted to more specialized topics are Stagner, *Psychological aspects of international conflict* (1967), and Proshansky, Ittelson, and Rivlin (eds.), *Environmental psychology: Man and his physical setting* (1970).

Two psychological journals specialize in the application of psychology to social problems: *Journal of Applied Social Psychology* and the *Journal of Social Issues*. Both are edited for the nonspecialist, and the *Journal of Social Issues* devotes each issue to a single topic such as poverty, women's roles, race relations, psychology and the law, and pornography. *The American Psychologist* usually carries one or two articles relevant to social problems in each monthly issue.

Further reading on topics specifically discussed in this chapter may be found in the listed reference. In particular, see Wallach and Wing, *The talented student* (1969), and Wing and Wallach, *College admissions and the psychology of talent* (1971), for the discussion of the limitations on intelligence tests for identifying talent. A review of research on population and family planning is provided by Fawcett, *Psychology and population* (1970); and a complete annotated bibliography of research and theory in the area of social indicators and future forecasting is found in Wilcox, Brooks, Beal, and Klonglan, *Social indicators and societal monitoring* (1972).

Advances in the behavioral sciences raise a number of fundamental issues concerning freedom and the control of human behavior. Some of these are discussed in Andrews and Karlins, *Requiem for democracy?* (1971); Delgado, *Physical control of the mind* (1969); London, *Behavior control* (1969); and *Beyond freedom and dignity* by B. F. Skinner (1971).

appendix

statistical methods and measurement

Much of the work of psychologists, like that of other scientists, calls for making measurements either in the laboratory or under field conditions. This work may involve measuring eye movements of infants when first exposed to a novel stimulus, recording the galvanic skin response of people under extreme stress, counting the number of trials required to condition a monkey with a prefrontal lobotomy, determining achievement test scores for students using computer-assisted instruction, or counting the number of patients who show improvement following a particular type of psychotherapy. In all these examples the *measurement operation* yields numbers, and the psychologist has the problem of interpreting them and arriving at some general conclusions. Basic to this task is *statistics*—the discipline that deals with collecting and handling numerical data and with making inferences from such data. The purpose of this Appendix is to review certain statistical methods that play an important role in psychology.

The Appendix is written on the assumption that the problems of statistics are essentially problems of logic, that is, problems of clear thinking about data, and that an introductory acquaintance with statistics is *not* beyond the scope of anyone who understands enough algebra to use plus and minus signs and to substitute numbers for letters in equations.

Even an introductory acquaintance with statistics, however, requires practice in applying what has been learned. The treatment that follows states the essential relationships first in words and then with simple numerical examples that require little computation. These examples use a minimum of data, artificially selected to make the operations clear even to the student who is mathematically unskilled. Because of the scantiness and artificiality of the data, these specimen computations violate an important principle in the use of statistics, namely, that a formula should be used only with appropriate data. But this violation can be justified here, because our purpose is to provide examples that are easy to master so the process can be understood.

Descriptive Statistics

Statistics serves, first of all, to provide a shorthand description of large amounts of data. Suppose that we want to study the college entrance examination scores of 5000 students, recorded on cards in the registrar's office. These scores are the raw data. Thumbing through the cards, we will get some impressions of the students' scores, but it will be impossible to keep all of them in mind. So we make some kind of summary of the data, possibly averaging all the scores or finding the highest and lowest scores. These statistical summaries make it easier to remember and think about the data. Such simplified or summarizing statements are called *descriptive statistics*.

Frequency Distributions

Items of raw data become comprehensible when they are ranked in numerical order or grouped in a *frequency distribution*. To group these items of data, we must first divide the scale along which they are measured into intervals and then count the number of cases that fall into each interval. An interval in which scores are grouped is called a *class interval* and represents a portion of the measurement scale. The decision of how many class intervals the data are to be grouped into is not fixed by any rules, but based upon the judgment of the investigator. It will depend to some extent upon what he intends to do with the grouped data, but also upon the range of values to be covered and the actual number of scores to be grouped.

Table 1 provides a sample of raw data, representing college entrance examination scores for fifteen students. The scores are listed in the order in which the students were tested (the first student tested had a score of 84, the second 61, and so on). Table 2 shows these data in a frequency distribution for which the class interval has been set at 10. One student has a score that falls in the interval from 50–59, three scores fall in the interval from 60–69, and so forth. Note that more scores are in the interval from 70–79, and that none are below the 50–59 interval or above the 90–99 interval.

TABLE 1
Raw scores

84	75	91
61	75	67
72	87	79
75	79	83
77	51	69

College entrance examination scores for 15 students, listed in the order in which they were tested.

TABLE 2
Frequency distribution

CLASS INTERVAL	NUMBER OF PERSONS IN CLASS
50-59	1
60-69	3
70-79	7
80-89	3
90-99	1

Scores of Table 1 accumulated with class intervals of 10.

A frequency distribution can often be better understood in a graphic presentation. The most widely used graph form is the *frequency histogram;* an example is shown in the top panel of Figure 1. Histograms are constructed by drawing bars, the bases of which are given by the class intervals and the heights of which are determined by the corresponding class frequencies. An alternative way of presenting frequency distributions in graph form is to use a *frequency polygon,* an example of which is shown in the bottom panel of Figure 1. Frequency polygons are constructed by plotting the class frequencies at the center of the class interval and connecting by straight lines the points thus obtained. In order to complete the picture one extra class is usually added at each end of the distribution, and since these classes have zero frequencies, both ends of the figure will come down to the horizontal axis. The frequency polygon gives the same information as the frequency histogram, but by means of lines rather than bars.

In practice one would want far more cases than those plotted in Figure 1, but all our illustrations use a minimum of data so that the reader can easily check the steps in tabulating and plotting.

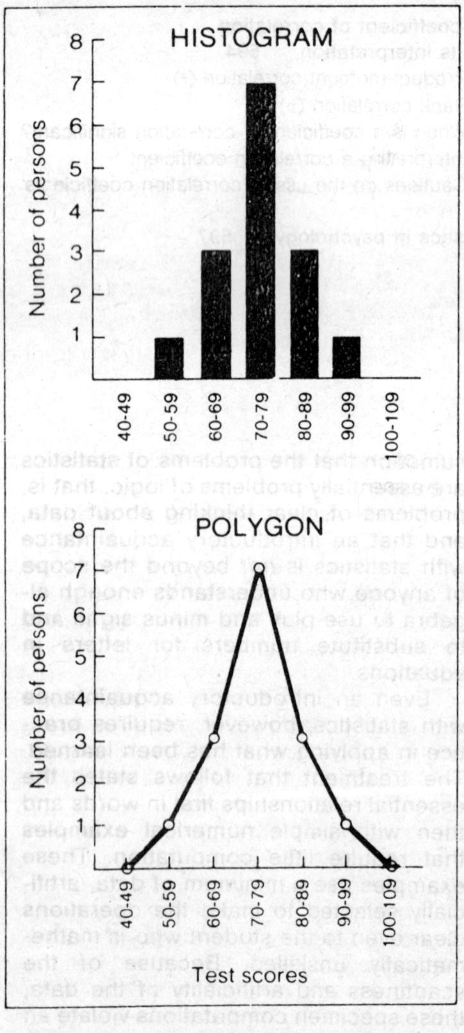

Fig. 1 Frequency diagrams

The data plotted are those from Table 2. A frequency histogram is on the top, and a frequency polygon on the bottom.

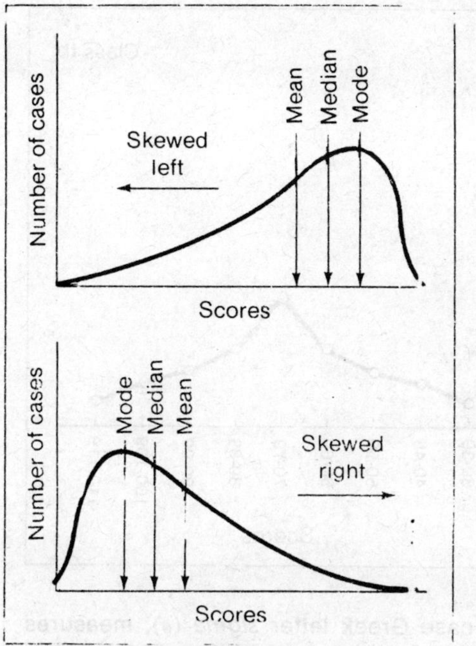

Fig. 2 Skewed distribution curves

Note that skewed distributions are named by the direction in which the tail falls. Also note that the mean, median, and mode are not identical for a skewed distribution; the median commonly falls between the mode and the mean.

Measures of Central Tendency

A *measure of central tendency* is simply some representative point on our scale, a central point with scores scattering on either side. Three such measures are in common use: the *mean*, the *median*, and the *mode*.

The *mean* is the familiar arithmetic average obtained by adding the scores and dividing by the number of scores. The sum of the raw scores of Table 1 is 1125. Divide this by 15 (the number of students' scores), and the mean turns out to be 75.

The *median* is the score of the middle case, obtained by arranging the scores in order and then counting in to the middle from either end. When the 15 scores in Table 1 are placed in order from highest to lowest, the eighth from either end turns out to be 75. If the number of cases is even, one may simply average the two cases on either side of the middle. For instance, with 10 cases, the median can be taken as the arithmetic average of the fifth and sixth cases.

The *mode* is the most frequent score in a given distribution. In Table 1 the most frequent score is 75; hence the mode of the distribution is 75.

In a *symmetrical distribution,* in which the scores distribute evenly on either side of the middle (as in Figure 1), the mean, median, and mode all fall together. This is not true for distributions that are *skewed,* that is, unbalanced. Suppose we were analyzing the starting times of a morning train. The train is usually on time in leaving; occasionally it starts late, but it never starts early. For a train with a scheduled starting time of 8:00 A.M., one week's record might be:

M	8:00	Mean starting time: 8:07
Tu	8:04	Median starting time: 8:02
W	8:02	Modal starting time: 8:00
Th	8:19	
F	8:22	
Sat	8:00	
Sun	8:00	

The distribution of starting times in this example is skewed because of the two late departures; they raise the mean departure time but do not have much effect on either the median or the mode. Skewed distributions are either "skewed left" or "skewed right," according to the direction in which the *tail* of the distribution falls—the direction of the most extreme scores (see Figure 2). The skew in our train example is toward the late departure, and so is skewed right.

Skewness is important because unless it is understood the differences between the median and mean may sometimes prove misleading. Suppose that two political parties are arguing about the prosperity of the country. It is quite possible (though not common) for the mean and median incomes to move in opposite directions. Suppose, for example, that a round of wage increases was combined with a reduction in extremely high incomes. The median income might go up while the mean went down. The party wanting to show that incomes were getting higher would choose the median; the one that wishes to show that incomes were getting lower would choose the mean.

The mean is the most widely used of the measures of central tendency, but there are times when the mode or median is more appropriate.

Measures of Variation

Usually more information is needed about a distribution than can be obtained from a measure of central tendency. For example, we need a measure to tell us whether scores cluster closely around their average or whether they scatter widely. A measure of the spread, or dispersion, of scores around the average is called a *measure of variation.*

Measures of variation are useful in at least two ways. First, they tell us how representative the average is. If the variation is small, we know that individual cases are close to it. If the variation is large, we can make use of the mean as a representative value with less assurance. Suppose, for example, that clothing is being designed for a group of people without the benefit of precise measurements. Knowing their average size would be helpful; but it would be very important to also know the spread of sizes. The second measure provides a "yardstick" by which we can decide on how much variability there is among the sizes.

To illustrate, consider the data in Figure 3, which shows frequency distributions of entrance examination scores for two classes of thirty students. Both classes have the same mean of 75,

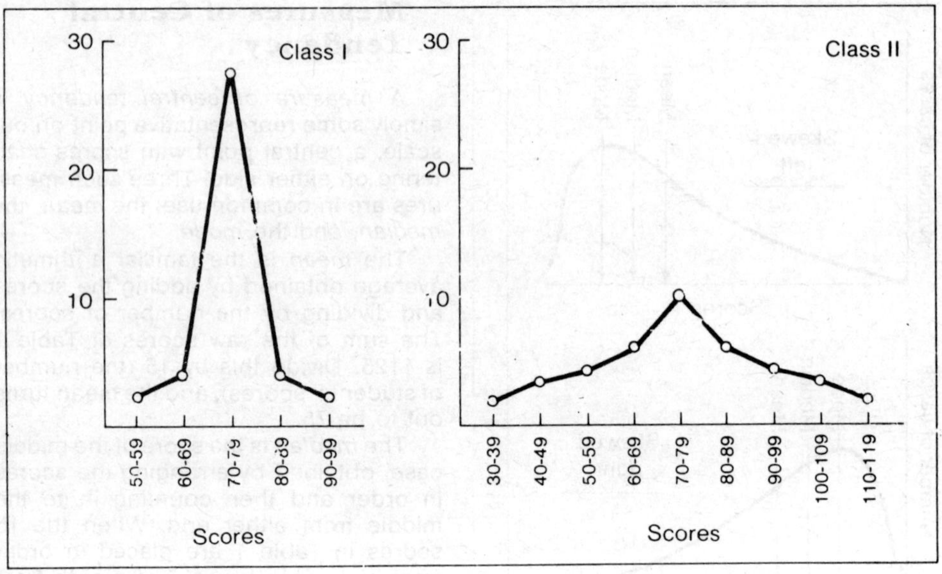

Fig. 3 Distributions differing in variation

It is easy to see that the scores for Class I cluster closer to the mean than those for Class II, even though the means of the two classes are identical (75). For Class I all the scores fall between 60 and 89, with the large majority of them in the interval from 70 through 79; for Class II the scores are distributed fairly uniformly over a wide range from 40 through 109. This difference in variability between the two distributions can be measured using the standard deviation, which would be much smaller for Class I than for Class II.

TABLE 3
Computation of standard deviation

CLASS I SCORES (MEAN = 75)	d (DEVIATION FROM MEAN)	d^2 (DEVIATION SQUARED)
77 − 75 =	2	4
76 − 75 =	1	1
75 − 75 =	0	0
74 − 75 =	−1	1
73 − 75 =	−2	4
		10

Sum of $d^2 = 10$
Mean of $d^2 = \frac{10}{5} = 2.0$
Standard deviation (σ) = $\sqrt{2.0} = 1.4$

CLASS II SCORES (MEAN = 75)	d (DEVIATION FROM MEAN)	d^2 (DEVIATION SQUARED)
90 − 75 =	15	225
85 − 75 =	10	100
75 − 75 =	0	0
65 − 75 =	−10	100
60 − 75 =	−15	225
		650

Sum of $d^2 = 650$
Mean of $d^2 = \frac{650}{5} = 130$
Standard deviation (σ) = $\sqrt{130} = 11.4$

but they exhibit clearly different degrees of variation. All the students of Class I have scores clustered close to the mean, whereas the scores of Class II are spread over a wide range. Some measure is required to specify more exactly how these two distributions differ. Two measures of variation frequently used by psychologists are the *range* and the *standard deviation*.

In order to simplify our example for ease in arithmetic computation, let us suppose that five students from each of these classes seek entrance to college, and their entrance examination scores are as follows:

Student scores from Class I:
73, 74, 75, 76, 77 (mean = 75)

Student scores from Class II:
60, 65, 75, 85, 90 (mean = 75)

Let us now compute the measures of variation for these two small samples, one from Class I, the other from Class II.

The *range* is the spread between the highest and the lowest score. The range for the five students from Class I is 4 (from 73 to 77); for those from Class II it is 30 (from 60 to 90).

The range is very easy to compute, but the *standard deviation* is more frequently used because it has certain properties that make it the preferred measure. One such property is that it is an extremely sensitive measure of variation because it takes account of every score, not just extreme values as does the range. The standard deviation, which we will abbreviate with the lower-case Greek letter *sigma* (σ), measures how far the scores making up a distribution depart from that distribution's mean.[1] The deviation, *d*, of each score from the mean is computed and squared; then the average of these squared values is obtained. The standard deviation is the square root of this average. Written as a formula

$$\sigma = \sqrt{\frac{\text{Sum of } d^2}{N}}.$$

Specimen computation of the standard deviation. The scores for the samples from the two classes are arranged in Table 3 for separate computation of the standard deviation. The first step involves subtracting the mean from each score (the mean is 75 for both classes). This operation yields positive *d* values for scores above the mean, and negative ones for scores below the mean. The minus signs disappear when the *d*'s are squared in the next column. The squared deviations are then added and divided by *N*, the number of cases in the sample; in our example $N = 5$. Taking the square root of this average yields the standard deviation. In this

[1] For this introductory treatment we shall use *sigma* (σ) throughout. However, in scientific literature the lower-case letter *s* is used to denote the standard deviation of a sample, whereas σ is used for the standard deviation of the population. Moreover, in computing the standard deviation of a sample, *s*, the sum of d^2 is divided by $N - 1$ rather than *N*. For reasonably large samples, however, the actual value of the standard deviation is little affected whether we divide by $N - 1$ or *N*. To simplify this presentation we will not distinguish between the standard deviation of a sample and that of a population, but instead will use the same formula to compute both. For a more detailed discussion of this point, see Horowitz (1974).

example the two standard deviations tell much the same story as the ranges, although they are not equivalent.

Statistical Inference

Now that we have become familiar with statistics as ways of describing data, we are ready to turn to the processes of interpretation, to the making of inferences from data.

Populations and Samples

First it is necessary to distinguish between a *population* and a *sample* drawn from that population. The U.S. Census Bureau attempts to describe the whole population by obtaining descriptive material on age, marital status, and so on, from everyone in the country. The word "population" is appropriate to the Census, because it represents *all* the people living in the United States.

The word "population" in statistics is not limited to people or animals or things. The population may be all the temperatures registered on a thermometer during the last decade, all the words in the English language, or all of any other specified supply of data.[2] Often we do not have access to the total population, and so we try to represent it by a sample drawn in a *random* (unbiased) fashion. We may ask some questions of a random fraction of the people, as the U.S. Census Bureau has done as part of recent censuses; we may derive average temperatures by reading the thermometer at specified times, without taking a continuous record; we may estimate the words in the encyclopedia by counting the words on a random number of pages. These illustrations all represent the selection of a *sample* from a larger population. If any of these processes are repeated, we will come out with slightly different results, owing to the fact that a sample does not fully represent the whole population and hence has within it *errors of sampling.*

[2] Sometimes the supply of data (the total population) is not so easily specified, as when we sample a subject's speed of reaction by taking 100 measurements among all those he might possibly yield if we continued the experiment endlessly. As long as the total supply of data is many times that of the sample—whether finite (all college students studying Latin) or indeterminate (all possible reaction times)—statistical theory can be used in treating the results.

This is where statistical considerations enter.

A sample of data is collected from a population in order to make inferences about that population. A sample of census data may be examined to see whether the population is getting older or whether the trend of migration to the suburbs is continuing. Similarly, experimental results are studied to find out what effects experimental manipulations have had upon behavior—whether the threshold for pitch is affected by loudness, whether child-rearing practices have detectable effects later in life. In order to make *statistical inferences* we have to evaluate carefully the relationships revealed by our sample of data. These inferences are always made under circumstances in which there is some degree of uncertainty because of sampling errors. If the statistical tests indicate that the magnitude of the effect found in the sample is fairly large relative to the estimate of the sampling error, then we can have confidence that the effect that was observed in the sample also holds for the population at large.

Thus, statistical inference deals with the problem of making an inference or judgment about some feature of a population based solely on information obtained from a sample of that population. As an introduction to statistical inference let us first consider the normal distribution and its use in interpreting standard deviations. Then we shall turn to problems of sampling errors and the significance of differences.

The Normal Distribution

When large amounts of data are collected, tabulated, and plotted on a graph, they often fall into a symmetrical distribution of roughly bell shape, known as the *normal distribution* and plotted as the *normal curve.* Most cases fall near the mean, thus giving the high point of the bell, and the bell tapers off sharply at very high and very low scores. This form of curve is of special interest because it also arises when the outcome of a process is based on a large number of *chance* events all occurring independently.

What do we mean by "chance" events? We mean only that the causal factors are complex and numerous, yielding results of the sort found when we toss dice or spin a roulette wheel. The demonstration device displayed in Figure 4 illustrates how a sequence of

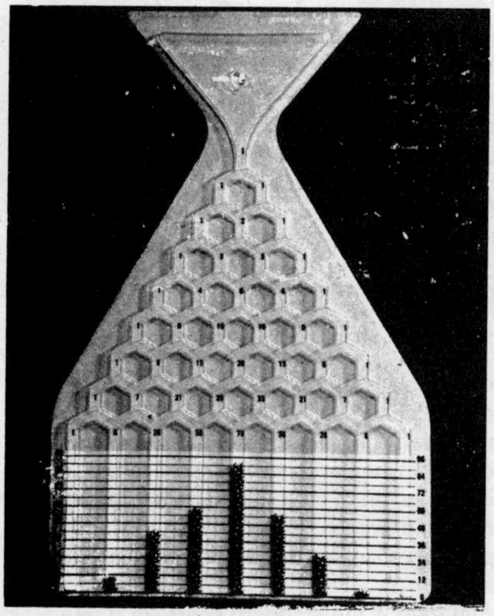

Fig. 4 A device to demonstrate a chance distribution

To observe chance factor at work one first holds the board upside-down until all the steel balls fall into the reservoir. Then he turns the board over and holds it vertically until the balls fall into the nine columns at the bottom (as shown in figure). The precise number of balls falling into each column will vary from one demonstration to the next. On the average, however, the heights of the columns of balls approximate a normal distribution, with the greatest height in the center column and gradually decreasing heights in the outer columns. (Hexstat Probability Demonstrator, Harcourt Brace Jovanovich, Inc.)

chance events gives rise to a normal distribution. The chance factor of whether a steel ball will fall left or right each time it encounters a point where the channel branches results in a symmetrical distribution; more balls fall straight down the middle, but an occasional one reaches the end compartments. This is a useful way of visualizing what is meant by a chance distribution closely approximating the "normal" curve.

The normal curve (Figure 5) can be defined mathematically to represent the idealized distribution approximated by the device shown in Figure 4. It gives the likelihood that cases within a normally distributed population will depart from the mean by any stated amount. Roughly two-thirds of the cases (68 percent) will tend to fall between plus and minus one standard deviation of the mean ($\pm 1\sigma$); 95 percent of the cases within plus and minus 2σ; and virtually all cases (99.7 percent) within plus and minus 3σ. Thus, if we understand the properties of the normal curve, we can interpret any statistic expressed in units of the standard deviation, provided the cases upon which the statistic is based are normally distributed. The percentages shown in Figure 5 represent the *percentage of the area* lying under the curve between the indicated scale values, with the total area representing the whole population. A more detailed listing of areas under portions of the normal curve is given in Table 4.

Using Table 4, let us trace where the 68-percent and 95-percent values of Figure 5 come from. We find from column 3 of Table 4 that between -1σ and the mean there lies .341 of the total area, and between $+1\sigma$ and the mean also lies .341 of the area. Adding these, we get .682, which has been expressed in Figure 5 as 68 percent. Similarly, we can find the area between -2σ and $+2\sigma$ to be $2 \times .477 = .954$, which has been expressed as 95 percent.

We shall have two uses for these percentages in the Appendix. One of them is in connection with the interpretation of standard scores, to which we turn next. The other is in connection with tests of the significance of the differences between means and other statistical measures.

Fig. 5 The normal curve

The normal distribution curve can be constructed provided the mean and standard deviation are known. For all practical purposes the area under the curve below -3σ and above $+3\sigma$ is negligible.

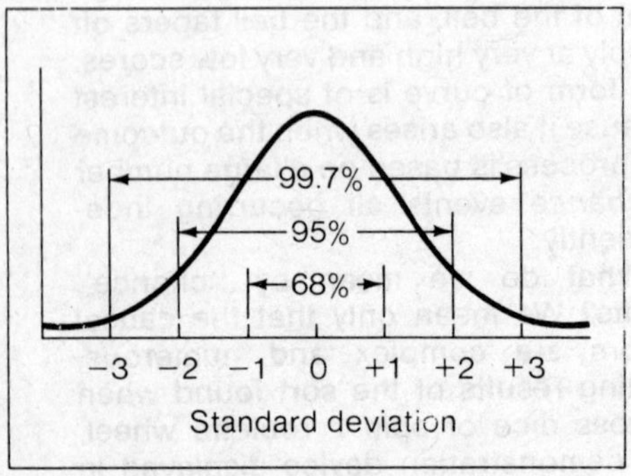

Scaling of Data

In order to interpret a score we often want to know whether it is high or low in relation to other scores. If a person takes a driver's test and finds that he needs 0.500 seconds to put his foot on the brake after a danger signal, how can he tell whether his performance is fast or slow? If he gets a 60 on a physics examination, does he pass the course? To answer questions of this kind we have to derive some sort of *scale* against which the scores can be compared.

RANKED DATA. By placing scores in rank order from high to low we derive one kind of scale. An individual score is interpreted by telling where it ranks among the group of scores. For example, the graduates of West Point know where they stand in their class—perhaps 35th or 125th among a class of 400.

STANDARD SCORES. The standard deviation is a very convenient unit for scaling, because we know how to interpret how far away 1σ or 2σ is from the mean (Table 4). A score based on some multiple of the standard deviation is known as a *standard score*. Many scales used in psychological measurement are based on the principle of standard scores, with modifications often being made to eliminate negative signs and decimals. Some of these scales derived from standard scores are given in Table 5.

Specimen computations of standard scores and transformation to arbitrary scales. Table 1 presented college entrance scores for fifteen students. Without more information we do not know whether these are representative of the population of all college applicants. Let us assume, however, that on this examination the population mean is 75 and its standard deviation is 10.

What then is the *standard score* for a student who made 90 on the examination? We must express how far this score lies above the mean in multiples of the standard deviation.

$$\text{Standard score for grade of 90} = \frac{90 - 75}{10} = \frac{15}{10} = 1.5\sigma$$

As a second example consider a student with a score of 53.

$$\text{Standard score for grade of 53} = \frac{53 - 75}{10} = \frac{-22}{10} = -2.2\sigma$$

TABLE 4
Area under normal curve as proportion of total area

STANDARD DEVIATION	(1) AREA TO THE LEFT OF THIS VALUE	(2) AREA TO THE RIGHT OF THIS MEAN	(3) AREA BETWEEN THIS VALUE AND MEAN
-3.0σ	.001	.999	.499
-2.5σ	.006	.994	.494
-2.0σ	.023	.977	.477
-1.5σ	.067	.933	.433
-1.0σ	.159	.841	.341
-0.5σ	.309	.691	.191
0.0σ	.500	.500	.000
$+0.5\sigma$	.691	.309	.191
$+1.0\sigma$	.841	.159	.341
$+1.5\sigma$	.933	.067	.433
$+2.0\sigma$	.977	.023	.477
$+2.5\sigma$	.994	.006	.494
$+3.0\sigma$	.999	.001	.499

In this case the minus sign tells us that the student is below the mean, and by 2.2 standard deviations. Thus the sign of the standard score (+ or −) indicates whether the score is above or below the mean, and its value indicates how far in standard deviations.

Suppose we wish to compare the first standard score computed above to a score on the scale used in the Navy General Classification Test, as shown in Table 5. This scale has a mean of 50 and a standard deviation of 10. Therefore the standard score of 1.5σ becomes $50 + (10 \times 1.5) = 50 + 15 = 65$.

Using column 1 of Table 4, we find beside the value for a standard score of $+1.5\sigma$ the number .933. This means that 93 percent of the scores of a normal distribution will lie *below* a person whose standard score is $+1.5\sigma$. Thus a score of 65 on the Navy General Classification Test, 650 on a Graduate Record Examination, or 8 on the Air Force Stanine (all equivalent as standard scores) is above that achieved by 93 percent of those on whom the test was calibrated. Scores representing any other multiple of the standard deviation can be similarly interpreted.

How Representative Is a Mean?

When we ask about the representativeness of a mean, we are really implying two questions. First, what are the *errors of measurement*? Second, what are the *errors of sampling*? Two people measuring the same length with a rule or timing an event with a stopwatch may not get exactly the same results. These differences are errors of measurement, which usually can be assumed to be small if care is taken in making the measurement. The second kind of error, the sampling error, interests us now. Suppose we were to select two random samples from the same population, make the necessary measurements, and compute the mean for each sample. What differences between the first and the second mean could be expected by chance?

Successive random samples drawn from the same population will have different means, forming a distribution of *sample means* around the *true mean* of the population. These sample means are themselves numbers for which one can compute their own standard deviations. We call this standard deviation the *standard error of the mean,* or σ_M, and can make an estimate of it on the basis of the following formula:

$$\sigma_M = \frac{\sigma}{\sqrt{N}}$$

where σ is the standard deviation for the sample and N is the number of cases from which each sample mean is computed.

According to the formula, the size of the standard error of the mean decreases with increase in the sample size; thus, a mean based on a large sample is more trustworthy (more likely to be close to the actual population mean) than one based on a smaller sample. Common sense would lead us to expect this. Computations of the standard error of the mean permit us to make clear assertions about the degree of uncertainty in our computed mean. The more

TABLE 5
Some representative scales derived from standard scores

	STANDARD SCORE	GRADUATE RECORD EXAMINATION	ARMY GENERAL CLASSIFICATION TEST	NAVY GENERAL CLASSIFICATION TEST	AIR FORCE STANINE*
	-3σ	200	40	20	—
	-2σ	300	60	30	1
	-1σ	400	80	40	3
	0σ	500	100	50	5
	$+1\sigma$	600	120	60	7
	$+2\sigma$	700	140	70	9
	$+3\sigma$	800	160	80	—
Mean	0	500	100	50	5
Standard deviation	1.0	100	20	10	2

* The word "stanine" was coined by the Air Force to refer to a scale with scores ranging from 1 to 9, known originally as "standard nine," a type of standard score with a mean of 5 and a standard deviation of 2.

cases in the sample, the more uncertainty has been reduced.

Specimen computation of the standard error of the mean. In order to estimate the standard error of the mean, we need the number of cases in the sample and the standard deviation of the sample. Suppose we take the mean and standard deviation computed in Table 3 for Class II but assume that the sample was larger. The sample mean is 75, and the standard deviation is 11.4. Let us assume sample sizes of 25, 100, and 900 cases; the standard errors of the mean would be, respectively:

$$N = 25: \quad \sigma_M = \frac{11.4}{\sqrt{25}} = \frac{11.4}{5} = 2.28$$

$$N = 100: \quad \sigma_M = \frac{11.4}{\sqrt{100}} = \frac{11.4}{10} = 1.14$$

$$N = 900: \quad \sigma_M = \frac{11.4}{\sqrt{900}} = \frac{11.4}{30} = 0.38$$

Now we may ask, how much variation can be expected among means if we draw samples of 25, 100, and 900? We know from Table 4 that 68 percent of the cases in a normal distribution lie between -1σ and $+1\sigma$ of the mean. The sample mean of 75 is the best estimate of the population mean. We know the size of σ_M, so we may infer that the chances are .68 that the population mean lies between the following limits:

$N = 25$:
75 ± 2.88, or between 72.72 and 77.28

$N = 100$:
75 ± 1.14, or between 73.86 and 76.14

$N = 900$:
75 ± 0.38, or between 74.62 and 75.38

Thus, on the basis of sample data it is possible to specify the probability that the mean for the entire population will lie in a certain interval. Note from the above computations that the estimated interval decreases as the size of the sample increases. The larger the sample, the more precise is the estimate of the true population mean.

Significance of a Difference Between Sample Means

Many psychological experiments collect data on two groups of subjects, one group exposed to certain specified experimental conditions and the other serving as a control. The question then is whether there is a difference in the mean performance of the two groups, and if such a difference is observed, whether it holds for the population from which these groups of subjects are a sample. Basically, we are asking whether a difference between two sample means reflects a true difference, or whether this difference is simply the result of sampling error.

As an example, let us consider scores on a reading test for a sample of first-grade boys, compared with the scores for a sample of first-grade girls. The boys score lower than the girls, as far as mean performances are concerned; but there is a great deal of overlap, some boys doing extremely well and some girls doing very poorly. Hence, we cannot accept the obtained difference in means without making a test of its *statistical significance.* Only then can we decide whether the observed differences in sample means reflect true differences in the population, or arose because of sampling error. The difference could be due to sampling error if by sheer luck we happened to get some of the brighter girls and some of the duller boys in the samples.

As a second example, suppose that in an experiment to determine whether right-handed men are stronger than left-handed men the results shown in the first table (this column) had been obtained. Our sample of five right-handed men averaged eight kilograms stronger than our sample of five left-handed men. What can be inferred about left-handed and right-handed men in general? Can we argue from the sample data that right-handed men are stronger than left-handed men? Obviously not, for the averages derived from most of the right-

	STRENGTH OF GRIP IN KILOGRAMS, RIGHT-HANDED MEN		STRENGTH OF GRIP IN KILOGRAMS, LEFT-HANDED MEN
	40		40
	45		45
	50		50
	55		55
	100		60
Sum	290	Sum	250
Mean	58	Mean	50

handed men would not differ from averages derived from the left-handed men; the one very deviant case (score of 100) tells us we are dealing with an uncertain situation.

Suppose that, instead, the results had been those shown in the second table. Again the same mean difference

STRENGTH OF GRIP IN KILOGRAMS, RIGHT-HANDED MEN		STRENGTH OF GRIP IN KILOGRAMS, LEFT-HANDED MEN	
	56		48
	57		49
	58		50
	59		51
	60		52
Sum	290	Sum	250
Mean	58	Mean	50

of eight kilograms is found, but we are now inclined to have greater confidence in the results, because the left-handed men scored consistently lower than the right-handed men. What we ask of statistics is that it provide a precise way of taking into account the reliability of the mean differences, so that we do not have to depend solely on intuition that one difference is more reliable than another.

The above examples suggest that the significance of a difference will depend both upon the size of the obtained difference and upon the variability of the means being compared. We shall find below that from the standard error of the means we can compute a *standard error of the difference between two means* (σ_{D_M}). We can then evaluate the obtained difference by using a *critical ratio,* which is the ratio of the obtained difference between the means (D_M) to the standard error of the difference between the means:

$$\text{Critical ratio} = \frac{D_M}{\sigma_{D_M}}$$

This ratio helps us to evaluate the significance of the difference between the two means.[3] As a rule of thumb, a critical ratio should be 2.0 or larger in order for the difference between means to be accepted as significant. Throughout this book statements that the difference between means is "statistically significant" mean that the critical ratio is at least that large.

Why is a critical ratio of 2.0 selected as statistically significant? Simply because a value this large or larger can occur by chance only 5 in 100 times. Where do we get the 5 in 100? We can treat the critical ratio as a standard score, for it is merely the difference between two means, expressed as a multiple of its standard error. Referring to column 2 in Table 4, we note that the likelihood of a standard deviation as high as or higher than +2.0 occurring by chance is .023. Because the chance of deviating in the opposite direction is also .023, the total probability is .046. This means that 46 times in 1000, or about 5 in 100, a critical ratio as large as 2.0 would be found by chance if the population means were identical.

The rule of thumb that says a critical ratio should be at least 2.0 is just that—an arbitrary but convenient rule that defines the "5-percent level of significance." Following this rule we will make less than 5 errors in 100 decisions by concluding on the basis of sample data that a difference in means exists when in fact there is none. The 5-percent level need not always be used; a higher or lower level of significance may be appropriate in certain experiments depending upon how willing we are to make an occasional error in inference.

Specimen computation of the critical ratio. The computation of the critical ratio calls for finding the *standard error of the difference between two means,* which is given by the following formula:

$$\sigma_{DM} = \sqrt{(\sigma_{M_1})^2 + (\sigma_{M_2})^2}$$

In this formula, σ_{M_1} and σ_{M_2} are the standard errors of the two means being compared.

As an illustration, suppose we wanted to compare reading achievement test scores for first-grade boys and girls in the United States. A random sample of boys and girls would be identified and given the test. Suppose for the boys the mean score was 70 with .40 as the standard error of the mean, and for the girls a mean of 72 and a standard error of .30. We want to decide, on the basis of these samples, whether there is a real difference between boys and girls in the population as a whole. The sample data suggest that girls are better than boys, but can we infer that this would have been the case if we had tested all the

[3] Care must be taken in interpreting a critical ratio when the computations are based on small samples. With small samples the ratio should be interpreted as a *t*-test, but for large samples *t* and the critical ratio are equivalent. For an explanation of this see Horowitz (1974).

girls and all the boys in the United States? The critical ratio helps us make this decision.

$$\sigma_{D_M} = \sqrt{(\sigma_{M_1})^2 + (\sigma_{M_2})^2}$$

$$= \sqrt{.16 + .09} = \sqrt{.25}$$

$$= .5$$

$$\text{Critical ratio} = \frac{D_M}{\sigma_{D_M}} = \frac{72 - 70}{.5} = \frac{2.0}{.5} = 4.0$$

Because the critical ratio is well above 2.0, we may assert that the observed mean difference is statistically significant at the 5-percent level. Thus we conclude that there is a reliable difference between boys and girls in performance on the reading test.

The Coefficient of Correlation and Its Interpretation

Correlation refers to the concomitant variation of paired measures, so that when one member of the pair rises, so does the other, or (in negative correlation) as one rises, the other falls. Correlation is often used in psychology. Suppose that a test is designed to predict success in college. If it is a good test, high scores on it will be related to high performance in college, and low scores will be related to poorer performance. The *coefficient of correlation* gives us a way of stating more precisely the degree of relationship.[4]

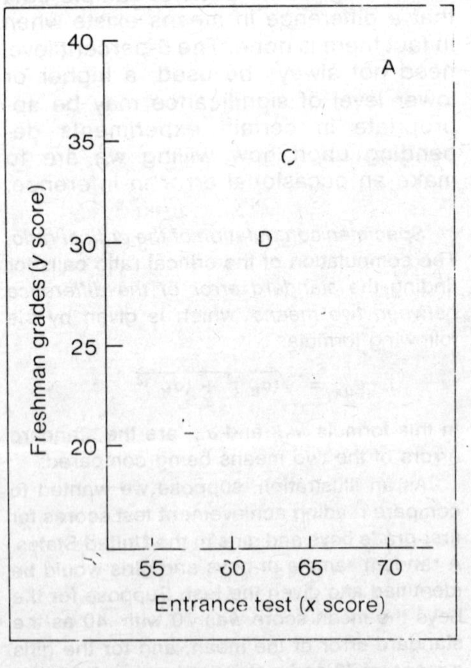

Fig. 6 Scatter diagram for hypothetical data

Each point represents the x- and y-scores for a particular student. The letters appended to the points identify the students in the data table (A = Adam, B = Bill, etc.).

Product-Moment Correlation (r)

The most frequently used method of determining the coefficient of correlation is the *product-moment method,* which yields the index conventionally designated r. The product-moment coefficient r varies between perfect positive correlation ($r = +1.00$) and perfect negative correlation ($r = -1.00$). Lack of relationship is designated $r = .00$.

The formula for computing the product-moment correlation is

$$r = \frac{\text{Sum } (dx)(dy)}{N\sigma_x\sigma_y}$$

Here one of the paired measures has been labeled the x-score and the other the y-score. The dx and dy refer to the deviations of each score from its mean, N is the number of paired measures, and σ_x and σ_y are the standard deviations of the x-scores and the y-scores.

The computation of the coefficient of correlation requires the determination of the sum of the products of the deviation of each of the two scores (x and y) from its respective mean, that is, the sum of the $(dx)(dy)$ products for all of the subjects entering into the correlation. This sum, in addition to the computed standard deviations for the x-scores and y-scores, can then be entered into the formula.

Specimen computation of product-moment correlation. Suppose that we had the following pairs of scores, the first being a score on a college entrance test (to be labeled arbitrarily as the x-score) and the second being freshman grades (the y-score).

NAMES OF STUDENTS	ENTRANCE TEST (x)	FRESHMAN GRADES (y)
Adam	71	39
Bill	67	27
Charles	65	33
David	63	30
Edward	59	21

Figure 6 shows a *scatter diagram* of these data. Each point simultaneously represents the x-score and y-score for a given subject; for example, the uppermost right-hand point is for Adam (labeled A). Looking at these data, we can easily detect that there is some positive correlation between the x-scores and the y-scores. Adam makes the highest score on the entrance test and also the highest freshman grades; Edward makes the lowest score on both. The others are a little irregular, so we know that the correlation is not perfect; hence r is less than 1.00.

We shall compute the correlation to illustrate the method, though no researcher would consent, in practice, to determining a correlation with so few cases. The details are given in Table 6. Following the procedure outlined in Table 3, we compute the standard deviation of the x-scores and then the standard deviation of the y-scores; it is 4 for the x-scores, and 6 for the y-scores. Next we compute the $(dx)(dy)$ products for each subject and total the five cases. Entering these results in our equation yields an r of $+.85$.

Rank Correlation (ρ)

When computers or desk calculators are not available and computations must

[4] This topic was discussed in Chapter 1 (pp. 22–23). The reader may find it helpful to review that material.

TABLE 6
Computation of a product-moment correlation

SUBJECT	ENTRANCE TEST (*x*-score)	FRESHMAN GRADES (*y*-score)	(*dx*)	(*dy*)	(*dx*)(*dy*)
Adam	71	39	6	9	+54
Bill	67	27	2	−3	−6
Charles	65	33	0	3	0
David	63	30	−2	0	0
Edward	59	21	−6	−9	+54
Sum	325	150	0	0	+102
Mean	65	30			

$$\sigma_x = 4 \qquad \sigma_y = 6 \qquad r = \frac{\text{Sum } (dx)(dy)}{N\sigma_x\sigma_y} = \frac{+102}{5 \times 4 \times 6} = +.85$$

be done by hand, a simpler method for determining correlations makes use of ranked scores. The resulting correlation is not an exact equivalent of *r*, but rather it is an estimate of *r*. The coefficient obtained by the rank method is designated by the lower-case Greek letter *rho* (ρ). The formula for the rank-correlation coefficient is

$$\rho = 1 - \frac{6(\text{Sum } D^2)}{N(N^2 - 1)}$$

where *D* is the difference in ranks for the scores of any one subject, and *N* is the number of subjects whose scores are being correlated.

Specimen computation of rank-correlation coefficient. We shall use the same data employed in the preceding example. All the details are given in Table 7. The procedure is to rank both sets of scores from highest to lowest, obtain the differences in ranks for each subject on the two tests, square and sum the differences, and enter them into the formula. The value of ρ for our example turns out to be +.70. As indicated above, ρ may be viewed as an estimate of *r*. The fact that in our example the values of *r* and ρ are not closer together is due to the small number of cases ($N = 5$). When reasonably large samples are taken, ρ and *r* will closely approximate each other.

When is a Coefficient of Correlation Significant?

A coefficient of correlation, like other statistical measures, has a standard error. That is, if a second sample were taken from a particular population, the correlation computed from it would not be exactly the same as that obtained from the first sample. The *standard error of r* (denoted as σ_r) can be used to determine whether an *r* based on a sample of data is significantly different from zero. The formula for computing the standard error of *r* is

$$\sigma_r = \frac{1}{\sqrt{N - 1}}$$

where *N* is the number of pairs entering into the correlation.

TABLE 7
Computation of a rank-correlation coefficient

SUBJECT	ENTRANCE TEST	FRESHMAN GRADES	RANK, ENTRANCE TEST	RANK, FRESHMAN GRADES	DIFFERENCE IN RANK (*D*)	SQUARED DIFFERENCE (D^2)
Adam	71	39	1	1	0	0
Bill	67	27	2	4	−2	4
Charles	65	33	3	2	+1	1
David	63	30	4	3	+1	1
Edward	59	21	5	5	0	0
						Sum D^2 = 6

$$\rho = 1 - \frac{6(\text{Sum } D^2)}{N(N^2 - 1)} = 1 - \frac{6 \times 6}{5 \times 24} = 1 - \frac{36}{120} = +.70$$

If r is divided by σ_r, we get a critical ratio that can be interpreted just like the critical ratios discussed before. If the value of r/σ_r is greater than 2.0, we may be fairly confident that the "true" value of r for the population as a whole is significantly greater than zero; stated otherwise, that there is a real correlation between the scores in the population from which the sample was drawn.

Interpreting a Correlation Coefficient

It is not always enough to know that a correlation is significantly greater than zero. Sometimes we want to make use of correlations in prediction. For example, if we know from past experience that a certain entrance test correlates with freshman grades, we can predict the freshman grades for beginning college students who have taken the test. If the correlation were perfect, we would predict their grades without error. But r is usually less than 1.00, so we will make some errors in prediction; the closer r is to zero, the greater the sizes of the errors in prediction.

While we cannot go into the technical problems of predicting freshman grades from entrance examinations or of making other similar predictions, we can consider the meanings of correlation coefficients of different sizes. It is evident that with a correlation of zero between x and y, knowledge of x will not help to predict y. If weight is unrelated to intelligence, it does us no good to know weight when we are trying to predict intelligence. At the other extreme, a perfect correlation would mean 100 percent predictive efficiency—knowing x we can predict y. What of intermediate values of r?

Because correlation coefficients vary from between zero and ± 1.00, there is a temptation to interpret the correlation as a percent, which would imply that a correlation of .50 is twice as large as one of .25. This is not correct; a more appropriate interpretation is based on the square of the correlation. The squared correlation (r^2) multiplied by 100 provides an estimate of the percentage of the variance that the distribution of x-scores and y-scores have in common. If $r = .50$, then $100 \times (.50)^2$ or 25 percent of the variation of the y's is accounted for by differences in x; similarly, if $r = .40$, 16 percent of the variation of the y's is accounted for by the relation with x. In the sense of "percentage of variance accounted for" we can say that a correlation of $r = .70$ is twice as strong as a correlation of $r = .50$, and that a correlation of $r = .50$ is twenty-five times as strong as a correlation of $r = .10$.

Some appreciation of the meaning of correlations of various sizes can be gained by examining the scatter diagrams in Figure 7. Each dot represents the score of two tests for the same individual. If the correlation is $+1.00$, then all the points in the scatter diagram fall on a straight line. When the correlation is zero, the points in the scatter diagram are uniformly distributed and do not line up in any particular direction.

In the preceding discussion we did not emphasize the sign of the correlation coefficient, since this has no bearing on the strength of a relationship. The only distinction between a correlation of $r = +.70$ and $r = -.70$ is that for the former increases in x are accompanied by increases in y, and for the latter increases in x are accompanied by decreases in y.

Cautions on the Use of Correlation Coefficients

While the correlation coefficient is one of the most widely used statistics in psychology, it is also one of the most widely misused procedures. First, those who use it sometimes overlook the fact that r measures only the strength of a linear (straight-line) relationship between x and y. Second, they often fail to recognize that r does not necessarily imply a cause-and-effect relation between x and y.

CORRELATION MEASURES LINEAR RELATIONSHIPS. If r is calculated for the data plotted in Figure 8, a value close to zero will be obtained, but this does not mean that the two variables are not related. The curve of Figure 8 provides an excellent fit even though a straight line does not; knowing the value of x we could predict very precisely what y would be by plotting it on the curve. Let us therefore emphasize that the correlation coefficient measures only the strength of a linear (straight-line) relationship between two variables. If there is reason to believe that a *nonlinear* relation holds, then other statistical procedures need to be used.

Fig. 7 Scatter diagrams illustrating correlations of various sizes

Each dot represents one individual's score on two tests, *x* and *y*. In A all cases fall on the diagonal and the correlation is perfect ($r = +1.00$); if we know a subject's score on *x*, we know that it will be the same on *y*. In B the correlation is zero; knowing a subject's score on *x*, we cannot predict whether it will be at, above, or below the mean on *y*. For example, of the four subjects who score at the mean of *x* ($dx = 0$), one makes a very high score on *y* ($dy = +2$), one a very low score ($dy = -2$), and two remain average. In both C and D there is a diagonal trend to the scores, so that a high score on *x* is associated with a high score on *y*, and a low score on *x* with a low score on *y*, but the relation is imperfect. The interested student will discover that it is possible to check the value of the correlations by using the formulas given in the text for the coefficient of correlation. The computation has been very much simplified by presenting the scores in the deviation form that permits entering them directly into the formulas. The fact that the axes do not have conventional scales does not change the interpretation. For example, if we assigned the values 1 through 5 to the *x* and *y* coordinates and then computed *r* for these new values, the correlation coefficients would be the same.

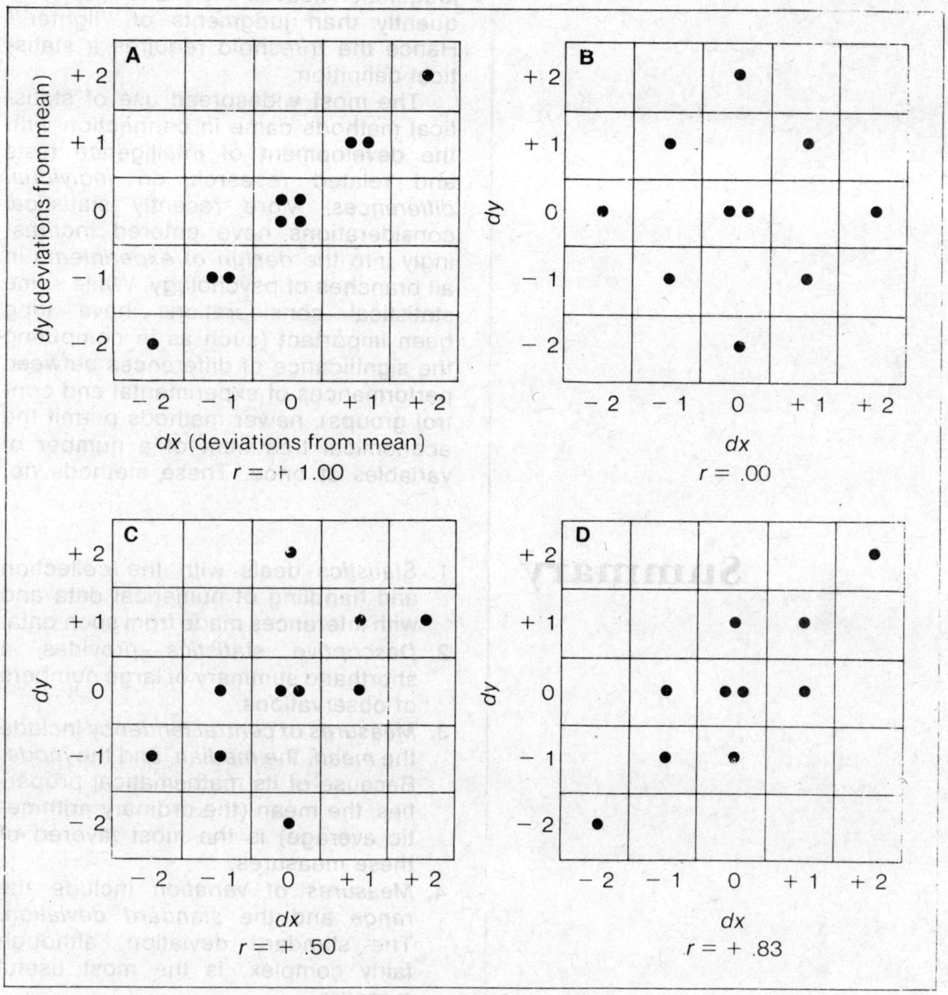

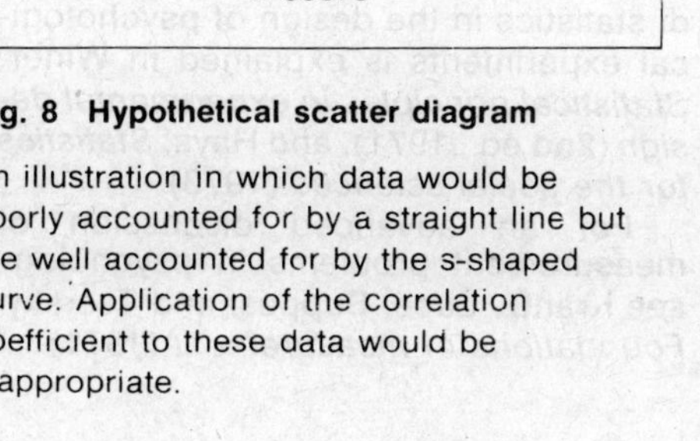

Fig. 8 Hypothetical scatter diagram

An illustration in which data would be poorly accounted for by a straight line but are well accounted for by the s-shaped curve. Application of the correlation coefficient to these data would be inappropriate.

CORRELATION DOES NOT YIELD CAUSE. When two sets of scores are correlated, we may suspect that they have some causal factors in common, but we cannot conclude that one of them causes the other (see Chapter 1, p. 22).

Correlations sometimes appear paradoxical. For example, the correlation between study time and college grades has been found to be slightly negative (about −.10). If a causal interpretation were assumed, one might suppose that the best way to raise grades would be to stop studying. The negative correlation arises because some students have advantages over others in grade-making (possibly because of native ability or better college preparation), so that often those who study the hardest are those who have difficulty earning the best grades.

This example provides sufficient warning against giving a causal interpretation to a coefficient of correlation. It is possible, however, that when two variables are correlated one may be the cause of the other. The search for causes is a logical one, and correlations can help by providing leads to experiments that can verify cause-and-effect relations.

Statistics in Psychology

Statistical methods are becoming increasingly important in all sciences, but particularly so in psychology because of the complexity and variability of the phenomena it studies.

The earliest demand upon statistics was made when psychologists began to use psychophysical methods for *thresh old measurement*. A weight that is slightly heavier than another is not always judged as heavier, even though the judgment "heavier" is made more frequently than judgments of "lighter." Hence the threshold requires a statistical definition.

The most widespread use of statistical methods came in connection with the development of intelligence tests and related research on *individual differences.* More recently statistical considerations have entered increasingly into the *design of experiments* in all branches of psychology. While some statistical considerations have long been important (such as in computing the significance of differences between performances of experimental and control groups), newer methods permit the economical treatment of a number of variables at once. These methods not only save in the time and costs of experimentation but yield information that earlier experimental comparisons could not.

Another field, that of *attitude and opinion surveys* (of which election polls are one illustration), relies heavily upon sampling methods to determine how many and which people to interview. The results must meet acceptable statistical standards if they are to be appropriately interpreted.

Modern computational aids, including high-speed computers and automatic test-scoring machines, permit the rapid handling of masses of data. The procedures of modern psychology, as we know them, would be impossible without these developments.

Summary

1. *Statistics* deals with the collection and handling of numerical data and with inferences made from such data.
2. *Descriptive statistics* provides a shorthand summary of large numbers of observations.
3. *Measures of central tendency* include the *mean,* the *median,* and the *mode.* Because of its mathematical properties, the mean (the ordinary arithmetic average) is the most favored of these measures.
4. *Measures of variation* include the *range* and the *standard deviation.* The standard deviation, although fairly complex, is the most useful measure.
5. *Statistical inference* deals with the problem of making an inference or judgment about some feature of a population when the inference must be based solely upon information obtained from a sample of the population. The accuracy of such inferences depends upon two factors: the size of the sample and the faithfulness with which the sample represents the population. *Random-sampling* procedures are most frequently used in order to ensure a representative sample.
6. In the *scaling* of data, raw scores may be converted into *ranks* or *standard scores.* Standard scores have many advantages and are widely used; they are based on distance from the mean expressed as multiples of the standard deviation.
7. It is possible to compute a *standard error of the difference between two means* from the *standard error* of each mean. The *critical ratio* expresses the obtained difference between two means in multiples of the standard error of the difference between the means. If the critical ratio is 2.0 or above, we have confidence that a true difference between the means exists, and is not likely to be the result of chance factors.
8. The *coefficient of correlation* is a convenient method for expressing the degree of relationship between two variables. The *product-moment correlation* is the one favored in psychological research. A convenient approximation is provided by the *rank-correlation coefficient.*

Further Reading

A number of textbooks on statistics are available to students of psychology, of which Horowitz, *Elements of statistics for psychology and education* (1974), Phillips, *Statistical thinking* (1974), Edwards, *Statistical methods* (3rd ed., 1973), and Mendenhall, Ott, and Larson, *Statistics: A tool for the social sciences* (1974) are excellent examples. The role of statistics in the design of psychological experiments is explained in Winer, *Statistical principles in experimental design* (2nd ed., 1971), and Hays, *Statistics for the social sciences* (1973).

For an advanced discussion of measurement problems in psychology see Krantz, Luce, Suppes, and Tversky *Foundations of measurement* (1971).

glossary

The glossary defines technical words appearing in the text and some common words when they are used in psychology with special meanings. No attempt is made to give the range of variations of meaning beyond those used in the text. For fuller definitions and other shades of meaning, consult any standard dictionary of psychology.

ability. Demonstrable knowledge or skill. Ability includes aptitude and achievement (cf. ***aptitude, achievement***).

abnormal fixation. A stereotyped habit very resistant to change (cf. ***stereotypy***).

abreaction. In psychoanalysis, the process of reducing emotional tension by reliving (in speech or action or both) the experience that caused the tension (syn. *catharsis*).

absolute threshold. The intensity or frequency at which a stimulus becomes effective or ceases to become effective, as measured under experimental conditions (cf. ***threshold, difference threshold***).

achievement. Acquired ability, e.g., school attainment in spelling (cf. ***aptitude***).

achievement motive. The social motive to accomplish something of value or importance, to meet standards of excellence in what one does.

achromatic colors. Black, white, and gray (cf. ***chromatic colors***).

acquisition. The stage during which a new response is learned and gradually strengthened.

adaptive behavior. Behavior that brings the organism into adjustment with its variable environment (cf. ***behavior***).

additive mixture. The mixture of lights; two spotlights focused on the same spot yield additive mixture; colored sectors of paper rotated on a color wheel also yield additive mixture (cf. ***subtractive mixture***).

ADH. Cf. ***antidiuretic hormone.***

adolescence. In human beings, the period from puberty to maturity, roughly the early teens to the early twenties (cf. ***puberty***).

adrenal gland. One of a pair of endocrine glands located above the kidneys. The medulla of the gland secretes the hormones epinephrine and norepinephrine. The cortex of the gland secretes a number of hormones, collectively called the adrenocortical hormones, which include cortisone (cf. ***endocrine gland***).

adrenalin. Cf. ***epinephrine.***

affective experience. An emotional experience, whether pleasant or unpleasant, mild or intense (cf. ***emotional state***).

afferent nerve. A bundle of nerve fibers transmitting impulses into the central nervous system from the periphery. Receptors connect directly with afferent nerves (usually synonymous with *sensory nerve;* cf. ***efferent nerve***).

affiliative motive. The tendency to depend upon another person or persons, to associate with them, to form friendships or other attachments.

afterimage. The sensory experience that remains when a stimulus is withdrawn. Usually refers to visual experience, e.g., the negative afterimage of a picture, or the train of colored images that results after staring at the sun.

aggression. Behavior intended to harm another person (cf. ***hostile aggression, instrumental aggression***).

agoraphobia. Fear of open places (cf. ***phobic reaction***).

algorithm. A fixed routine for finding a mathematical solution, an exact procedure, as in extracting a square root. A computer commonly uses algorithmic methods, but may use other methods (cf. ***heuristic method***).

ambivalence. Simultaneous liking and disliking of an object or person; the conflict caused by an incentive that is at once positive and negative (cf. ***conflict***).

amnesia. The partial or total loss of memory for past experiences. The memories lost in amnesia have not been completely destroyed, for the forgotten events may again be remembered without relearning when the person recovers from his amnesia (cf. ***repression***).

amphetamines. Central nervous system stimulants that produce restlessness, irritability, anxiety, and rapid heart rate. Dexedrine sulfate ("speed") and methamphetamine ("meth") are two types of amphetamines.

anal stage. The second stage according to the psychoanalytic theory of psychosexual development, following the oral stage. The sources of gratification and conflict have to do with the expulsion and retention of feces (cf. ***psychosexual development***).

androgen. The collective name for male sex hormones, of which testosterone, secreted by the testes, is best known (cf. ***sex glands, estrogen***).

anthropology. The science that studies chiefly preliterate ("primitive") societies. Its main divisions are archaeology (the study of the physical monuments and remains from earlier civilizations), physical anthropology (concerned with the anatomical differences among men and their evolutionary origins), linguistic anthropology, and social anthropology (concerned with social institutions and behavior) (cf. ***behavioral sciences***).

anticipation method. A method of rote memorization, appropriate to either serial memorization or paired-associate learning, in which the subject learns to respond to a stimulus item with the response item next to appear in the aperture of the memory drum. The method permits the scoring of successes and failures throughout memorization.

antidepressant. Drug used to elevate the mood of depressed individuals: imipramine (Tofranil), isocarboxazid (Marplan), and tranylcypromine (Parnate) are examples.

antidiuretic hormone (ADH). Hormone secreted by pituitary gland that signals the kidney to reabsorb water into the blood stream instead of excreting it as urine.

antisocial personality. Cf. ***psychopathic personality.***

anxiety. A state of apprehension or uneasiness, related to fear. The object of anxiety (e.g., a vague danger or foreboding) is ordinarily less specific than the object of fear (e.g., a vicious animal).

anxiety hierarchy. A list of situations or stimuli to which a person responds with anxiety ranked in order from the least anxiety-producing to the most fearful. Used by behavior therapists in systematically desensitizing patients to feared stimuli by associating deep relaxation with the situations rather than anxiety (cf. ***behavior therapy, systematic desensitization***).

anxiety reaction. A form of neurotic reaction characterized by a diffuse dread, often accompanied by tenseness, palpitation, sweating, nausea (cf. ***neurotic reaction***).

apathy. Listlessness, indifference; one of the consequences of frustration (cf. ***frustration***).

aphagia. Inability to eat (cf. ***hyperphagia***).

aphasia. Impairment or loss of ability to articulate words or to comprehend speech.

appetitive behavior. Seeking behavior (cf. ***aversive behavior***).

applied science. Research whose aim is a finding of practical value (cf. ***basic science***).

aptitude. The capacity to learn, e.g., typing aptitude prior to practice on a typewriter. Aptitude tests are designed to predict the outcome of training, hence to predict future ability on the basis of present ability (cf. ***achievement***).

artificial intelligence. The performance by a computer of tasks that have hitherto required the application of human intelligence.

assertive training. A form of counter-conditioning in which assertive or approach responses are reinforced in an attempt to extinguish passivity or anxiety in certain situations (cf. ***behavior therapy, counter-conditioning***).

association areas. Portions of the cerebral hemispheres other than the projection areas. Because their function is unknown, the assumption is made that these areas serve some sort of integrative ("association") function.

association psychology. A pre-experimental psychology, whose basic explanatory principle was the association of ideas.

asymptote. The stable level to which a variable tends over the course of time; e.g., in learning, the final response strength after an extended period of acquisition. The asymptote is the point at which the learning curve levels out.

attention. The focusing of perception leading to heightened awareness of a limited range of stimuli.

attitude scale. A scale for the quantitative appraisal of attitudes.

attribution theory. A theory concerned with the psychological processes by which individuals attribute causes to behavior.

authoritarian personality. A personality syndrome said to be common to those whose attitudes are authoritarian instead of democratic. The syndrome is characterized by highly conventional behavior, concern over sex, superstitiousness, destructiveness, and cynicism.

autistic thinking. A form of associative thinking, controlled more by the thinker's needs or desires than by reality; wishful thinking (cf. ***daydreaming, rationalization***).

autism. Absorption in fantasy to the exclusion of interest in reality; a symptom of schizophrenia.

autokinetic effect. The apparent movement of a stationary spot of light when viewed in a totally dark room.

autonomic nervous system. A system of nerve cells and nerve fibers regulating smooth muscle and glandular activities. While the system is closely integrated with the brain and spinal cord, it has some cell bodies and synapses lying outside the brain and spinal cord (syn. *vegetative nervous system;* cf. ***parasympathetic division, sympathetic division***).

average. Cf. ***measure of central tendency.***

aversive behavior. Avoidance behavior (cf. ***appetitive behavior***).

aversive conditioning. A form of conditioning in which an undesirable response is extinguished through association with punishment; has been used in behavior therapy to treat alcoholism, smoking, and sexual problems (cf. ***behavior therapy, counter-conditioning***).

avoidance learning. A form of learning controlled by the threat of punishment. The learning is motivated by the anxiety raised by the threat and the reduction of anxiety when the punishment is avoided (cf. ***escape learning***).

axon. That portion of a neuron that transmits impulses to other neurons (cf. ***neuron, dendrite***).

basal mental age. In individual tests of the Binet type, the highest age level at which, and below which, all tests are passed (cf. ***mental age***).

basic science. Research whose aim is to further knowledge regardless of whether or not its findings have practical value (cf. ***applied science***).

basilar membrane. A membrane of the ear within the coils of the cochlea, supporting the organ of Corti. Movements of the basilar membrane stimulate the hair cells of the organ of Corti, producing the neural effects of auditory stimulation (cf. ***cochlea, organ of Corti***).

behavior. Those activities of an organism that can be observed by another organism or by an experimenter's instruments. Included within behavior are verbal reports made about subjective, conscious experiences (cf. ***conscious processes***).

behavior genetics. The study of the inheritance of behavioral characteristics.

behavior modification. Cf. ***behavior therapy.***

behavior therapy. A method of psychotherapy based on learning principles. It uses such techniques as counter-conditioning, reinforcement, and shaping to modify behavior (syn. *behavior modification*).

behavioral sciences. The sciences concerned in one way or another with the behavior of man and lower organisms; especially social anthropology, psychology, and sociology, but including some aspects of biology, economics, political science, history, philosophy, and other fields of study (cf. ***anthropology, psychology, sociology***).

behaviorism. A school or system of psychology associated with the name of John B. Watson; it defined psychology as the study of behavior and limited the data of psychology to observable activities. In its classical form it was more restrictive than the contemporary objective (behavioral) viewpoint in psychology (cf. ***school of psychology***).

bimodal distribution. A frequency distribution with two points at which there are a high number of cases, hence two modes (cf. ***mode***).

binocular cues. Cf. ***distance cues.***

binocular disparity. Cf. ***retinal disparity.***

biofeedback. Voluntary regulation of bodily processes (e.g., heart rate, blood pressure, brain waves) through the feedback of information from internal organs.

blind spot. An insensitive area of the retina where the nerve fibers from the ganglion cells join together to form the optic nerve.

blood pressure. The pressure of the blood against the walls of the blood vessels. Changes in blood pressure following stimulation serve as one indicator of emotion.

body-sense area. A projection area of the cerebral cortex lying behind the central fissure. Electrical stimulation of the area commonly results in the report of sensory experiences, e.g., "It feels as though I am moving my finger" (syn. *somesthetic area;* cf. ***motor area***).

brain stem. The structures lying near the core of the brain; essentially all of the brain with the exception of the cerebral cortex and the cerebellum and their dependent parts.

brainwashing. Cf. ***coercive persuasion.***

branching program. A teaching program often

implemented by a computer in which the student's path through the instructional materials varies as a function of his performance. The student may branch rapidly through the material if his responses are generally correct, or go off to remedial loops if he encounters difficulties (cf. ***linear program***).

brightness. The dimension of color that describes its nearness in brilliance to white (as contrasted with black). A bright color reflects more light than a dark one (cf. ***hue, saturation***).

brightness constancy. The tendency to see a familiar object as of the same brightness, regardless of light and shadow that change its stimulus properties (cf. ***color constancy, object constancy***).

Broca's speech area. A portion of the left cerebral hemisphere said to control motor speech.

CAI. A common abbreviation for computer-assisted instruction, i.e., instruction carried out under computer control.

Cannon's theory. A classical theory of emotion proposed by Walter Cannon; also known as the Cannon-Bard theory. The theory states that an emotion-producing stimulus activates the cortex and bodily responses at the same time; bodily changes and the experience of emotion occur simultaneously (cf. ***James-Lange theory, cognitive-physiological theory***).

cardiac muscle. A special kind of muscle found only in the heart (cf. ***smooth muscle, striate muscle***).

case history. A biography obtained for scientific purposes; the material is sometimes supplied by interview, sometimes collected over the years.

castration. Surgical removal of the gonads; in the male, removal of the testes; in the female, removal of the ovaries.

catharsis. Reduction of an impulse or emotion through direct or indirect expression, particularly verbal and fantasy expression.

central fissure. A fissure of each cerebral hemisphere that separates the frontal and parietal lobes (syn. *fissure of Rolando*).

central nervous system. In vertebrates, the brain and spinal cord, as distinct from the nerve trunks and their peripheral connections (cf. ***autonomic nervous system, peripheral nervous system***).

cerebral cortex. The surface layer of the cerebral hemispheres in higher animals, including man. It is commonly called gray matter because its many cell bodies give it a gray appearance in cross section, in contrast with the nerve fibers that make up the white matter.

cerebral hemispheres. Two large masses of nerve cells and fibers constituting the bulk of the brain in man and other higher animals. The hemispheres are separated by a deep fissure, but connected by a broad band of fibers, the corpus callosum (syn. *cerebrum;* cf. ***cerebral cortex***).

cerebrum. Cf. ***cerebral hemispheres.***

chemotherapy. The use of drugs in the treatment of mental disorders (cf. ***somatotherapy***).

chlorpromazine. Cf. ***tranquilizer.***

chromatic colors. All colors other than black, white, and gray, e.g., red, yellow, blue (cf. ***achromatic colors***).

chromosome. Small particles found in pairs in all the cells of the body, carrying the genetic determiners (genes) that are transmitted from parent to offspring. A human cell has 46 chromosomes, arranged in 23 pairs, one member of each pair deriving from the mother, one from the father (cf. ***gene***).

chronological age (CA). Age from birth; calendar age (cf. ***mental age***).

circadian rhythm. A biological cycle or rhythm that is roughly 24 hours long. Sleep-wakefulness, body temperature, and water excretion follow a circadian rhythm as do a number of behavioral and physiological variables.

clairvoyance. A form of extrasensory perception in which the perceiver is said to identify a stimulus that is influencing neither his own sense organs nor those of another person (cf. ***extrasensory perception, telepathy, precognition***).

class interval. In statistics, a small section of a scale according to which scores of a frequency distribution are grouped, e.g., heights grouped into class intervals of a half inch (cf. ***frequency distribution***).

classical conditioning. Conditioned-response experiments conforming to the pattern of Pavlov's experiment. The main feature is that the originally neutral conditioned stimulus, through repeated pairing with the unconditioned one, acquires the response originally given to the unconditioned stimulus (syn. *stimulus substitution;* cf. ***operant conditioning***).

claustrophobia. Fear of closed places (cf. ***phobic reaction***).

client. A synonym for *patient,* the term used by counselors who wish to avoid the medical connotations of the patient-physician relationship (cf. ***client-centered therapy***).

client-centered therapy. A method of psychotherapy designed to let the client learn to take responsibility for his own actions and to use his own resourcefulness in solving his problems (syn. *nondirective counseling*).

clinical psychologist. A psychologist, usually with a Ph.D. degree, whose training includes hospital and clinic experience. His techniques include testing, diagnosis, interviewing, psychotherapy, and conducting research (cf. ***counseling psychologist, psychiatrist***).

cochlea. The portion of the inner ear containing the receptors for hearing (cf. ***basilar membrane, organ of Corti***).

coefficient of correlation. A numerical index used to indicate the degree of correspondence between two sets of paired measurements. The most common kind is the product-moment coefficient designated by *r*.

coercive persuasion. Influencing the thought patterns of prisoners whose lives are completely under the control of those seeking to influence them, thereby permitting kinds of influence not ordinarily possible (syn. *brainwashing*).

cognition. An individual's thoughts, knowledge, interpretations, understandings, or ideas about himself and his environment (cf. ***cognitive processes***).

cognitive dissonance. The condition in which one has beliefs or knowledge that disagree with each other or with behavioral tendencies; when such cognitive dissonance arises, the subject is motivated to reduce the dissonance through changes in behavior or cognition (Festinger).

cognitive-physiological theory. A theory of emotion proposed by Schachter; emotion is bodily arousal in interaction with cognitive processes. Emotion is determined by the label a person gives to his state of bodily arousal (cf. ***James-Lange theory, Cannon's theory***).

cognitive processes. Mental processes hypothesized to occur during perception, learning, and thinking.

cognitive psychology. A point of view contrasted with stimulus-response (S-R) theory, more concerned with "knowing" and "perceiving" than with "movement-responses" (cf. ***stimulus-response psychology***).

color blindness. Defective discrimination of chromatic colors (cf. ***monochromatism, dichromatism, red-green color blindness***).

color circle. An arrangement of chromatic colors around the circumference of a circle in the order in which they appear in the spectrum, but with the addition of nonspectral reds and purples. The colors are so arranged that those opposite each other are complementaries in additive mixture.

color constancy. The tendency to see a familiar object as of the same color, regardless of changes in illumination on it that alter its stimulus properties (cf. ***object constancy***)

color-mixing primaries. Three hues chosen to

produce the total range of hues by their additive mixture. A spectral red, green, and blue are usually selected (cf. ***psychological primaries***).

comparative psychology. The study of the behavior of lower organisms in their interrelationships with one another and with man.

compensation. A form of defense mechanism by which one attempts to cover up or balance failure in, or lack of talent for, one activity by a strenuous effort to excel in either a different or an allied activity (cf. ***substitution, sublimation***).

complementary colors. Two colors that in additive mixture yield either a gray or an unsaturated color of the hue of the stronger component.

compulsive movements. Repetitive actions that a person feels driven to make and that he is unable to resist; ritualistic behavior.

compulsive personality. A personality syndrome characterized by cleanliness, orderliness, and obstinacy. In the extreme, behavior becomes repetitive and ritualistic (syn. *anal character*).

concept. The properties or relationships common to a class of objects or ideas. Concepts may be of concrete things, e.g., the concept "poodle" referring to a given variety of dog, or of abstract ideas, e.g., equality, justice, number, implying relationships common to many different kinds of objects or ideas.

conditioned emotion. An emotional response acquired by conditioning, i.e., one aroused by a stimulus that did not originally evoke it (cf. ***conditioning***).

conditioned response. The learned or acquired response to a conditioned stimulus, i.e., to a stimulus that did not evoke the response originally (cf. ***classical conditioning, unconditioned response***).

conditioning. The process by which conditioned responses are learned (cf. ***classical conditioning, operant conditioning***).

cone. In the eye, a specialized cell of the retina found predominantly in the fovea and more sparsely throughout the retina. The cones mediate both chromatic and achromatic sensations (cf. ***retina, rod, fovea***).

confidence limits. In statistics, upper and lower limits derived from a sample, used in making inferences about a population; e.g., from the mean of a sample and its standard error one can determine limits which permit a statement that the probability is 95 in 100 that the population mean falls within these limits (cf. ***statistical inference, statistical significance***).

conflict. The simultaneous presence of opposing or mutually exclusive impulses, desires or tendencies.

connotative meaning. The suggestions and emotional meanings of a word or symbol, beyond its denotative meaning. Thus naked and nude both refer to an unclothed body (denotative meaning), but they have somewhat different connotations (cf. ***denotative meaning, semantic differential***).

conscience. An internal recognition of standards of right and wrong by which the individual judges his own conduct (cf. ***superego***).

conscious processes. Events such as perceptions, afterimages, private thoughts, and dreams, of which only the person himself is aware. They are accessible to others through verbal report or by way of inference from other behavior (syn. *experience, awareness;* cf. ***unconscious processes***).

conservation. Piaget's term for the ability of the child to recognize that certain properties of objects (e.g., mass, volume, number) do not change despite transformations in the appearance of the objects.

consolidation theory. The assumption that changes in the nervous system produced by learning are time dependent, and particularly vulnerable to obliteration during this consolidation period.

consummatory behavior. The activity in the presence of the incentive that reduces the drive or in other ways completes the motivated sequence of behavior.

control group. In an experimental design contrasting two groups, that group not given the treatment whose effect is under study (cf. ***experimental group***).

controlled association. The process in word-association experiments in which the subject is instructed to give a specific kind of associated word, e.g., one opposite to that of the stimulus word (cf. ***free association***).

convergent thinking. In tests of intellect, producing a specified "correct" response in accordance with truth and fact (cf. ***divergent thinking***).

conversion reaction. A form of neurotic reaction in which the symptoms are paralysis of the limbs, insensitive areas of the body (anesthesias), uncontrolled emotional outbursts, or related bodily symptoms. The presumption is that anxiety has been "converted" into a tangible symptom (syn. *hysteria;* cf. ***neurotic reaction***).

coping. A method of direct problem-solving in dealing with personal problems, contrasted with defense mechanisms (q.v.).

corpus callosum. A large band of fibers (white matter) connecting the two cerebral hemispheres.

correlation. Cf. ***coefficient of correlation.***

counseling psychologist. A trained psychologist, usually with a Ph.D. or Ed.D. degree, dealing with personal problems not classified as illness, such as academic, social, or vocational problems of students. His skills are similar to those of the clinical psychologist, but his work is usually in a nonmedical setting (cf. ***clinical psychologist***).

counter-conditioning. The replacement of a particular response to a stimulus by the establishment of another (usually incompatible) response.

criterion. (1) A set of scores or other records against which the success of a predictive test is verified. (2) A standard selected as the goal to be achieved in a learning task, e.g., the number of runs through a maze to be made without error as an indication that the maze has been mastered.

critical flicker frequency. If the rate of alternation between light and dark phases of stimuli is increased, there comes a point at which flicker disappears and a steady light is perceived; this fusion rate is known as the critical flicker frequency (syn. *critical fusion frequency*).

critical period. A stage in development during which the organism is optimally ready to learn certain response patterns. It is closely related to the concept of maturational readiness.

critical ratio. A mean, mean difference, or coefficient of correlation, divided by its standard error. Used in tests of significance (cf. ***statistical significance, t-test***).

critical scores. Scores based on experience with tests used for a given purpose, so that persons scoring below the critical level are rejected as unlikely to succeed; e.g., a critical score on a scholastic aptitude test for college students is one below which no candidate is accepted for admission.

cross-impact matrix method. A method of predicting possible future events by synthesizing the predictions made by a number of experts to take into account their interdependencies; a refinement of the Delphi method (cf. ***trend analysis, Delphi method***).

cue-dependent forgetting. The proposition that forgetting is not due to the loss of information in memory, but rather that the retrieval cues necessary to locate the information in memory are lacking. Information not recalled at one time may become accessible later when appropriate retrieval cues become available (cf. ***trace-dependent forgetting***).

cues to distance. Cf. ***distance cues.***

culture-fair test. A type of intelligence test that has been so constructed as to minimize bias due to the differing experiences of children raised in a rural rather than an urban culture or in a lower-class rather than in a middle-class or upper-class culture (syn. *culture-free test*).

cumulative curve. A graphic record of the

responses emitted during an operant conditioning session. The slope of the cumulative curve indicates the rate of response.

dark adaptation. The increased sensitivity to light when the subject has been continuously in the dark or under conditions of reduced illumination (cf. ***light adaptation***).

daydreaming. Reverie; free play of thought or imagination. Because of self-reference, usually a form of autistic thinking (cf. ***autistic thinking***).

db. Cf. ***decibel.***

decibel (db). A unit for measuring sound intensity.

deep structure. A term used in linguistics and psychology to refer to the intended meaning of a sentence (cf. ***surface structure***).

defense mechanism. An adjustment made, often unconsciously, either through action or the avoidance of action in order to escape recognition by oneself of personal qualities or motives that might lower self-esteem or heighten anxiety.

deindividuation. The process whereby social restraints are weakened and impulsive, aggressive, and regressive tendencies released as the person loses his individual identity, usually as the result of being part of a large group or having his identity concealed in some way, as by a mask.

delayed conditioning. A classical conditioning procedure in which the CS begins several seconds or more before the onset of the US and continues with it until the response occurs (cf. ***simultaneous conditioning, trace conditioning***).

delayed-response experiment. An experiment used with both animals and man as a test of memory. The subject observes the experimenter place an incentive under one of two or more containers. Then a shield is placed between the subject and the containers for a period of delay before the subject chooses the proper container. Accuracy of his choice tests his memory for the placing of the incentive.

Delphi method. A procedure for pooling the judgments of experts about new events that are likely to occur in the future in an effort to improve predictions based on trend analyses (cf. ***trend analysis, cross-impact matrix method***).

delusion. False beliefs characteristic of some forms of psychotic disorder. They often take the form of delusions of grandeur or delusions of persecution (cf. ***paranoid schizophrenia***).

dendrite. The specialized portion of the neuron that (together with the cell body) receives impulses from other neurons (cf. ***axon***).

denial. Cf. ***self-deception.***

denotative meaning. The primary meaning of a symbol, something specific to which the symbol refers or points; e.g., my street address is denotative; whether or not I live in a desirable neighborhood is a connotative meaning secondary to the address itself (cf. ***connotative meaning***).

deoxyribonucleic acid (DNA). Large molecules found in the cell nucleus and primarily responsible for genetic inheritance. These molecules manufacture various forms of RNA, which are thought by some to be the chemical basis of memory (cf. ***ribonucleic acid***).

dependent variable. The variable whose measured changes are attributed to (or correspond to) changes in the independent variable. In psychological experiments, the dependent variable is often a response to a measured stimulus (cf. ***independent variable***).

depth perception. The perception of the distance of an object from the observer or the distance from front to back of a solid object (cf. ***distance cues***).

descriptive statistics. Simplifying or summarizing statements about measurements made on a population. Strictly speaking, descriptive statistics should apply solely to populations, rather than to samples, but the term is used loosely for summarizing statements about samples when they are treated as populations (cf. ***statistical inference***).

developmental psychologist. A psychologist whose research interest lies in studying the changes that occur as a function of the growth and development of the organism, in particular the relationship between early and later behavior.

deviation IQ. An intelligence quotient (IQ) computed as a standard score with a mean of 100 and a standard deviation of 15 (Wechsler) or 16 (Stanford-Binet), to correspond approximately to traditional intelligence quotient (cf. ***intelligence quotient***).

dichromatism. Color blindness in which either the red-green or the blue-yellow system is lacking. The red-green form is relatively common; the blue-yellow form is the rarest of all forms of color blindness (cf. ***monochromatism, red-green color blindness***).

difference threshold. The minimum difference between a pair of stimuli that can be perceived under experimental conditions (cf. ***threshold, absolute threshold, just noticeable-difference***).

diffusion of responsibility. The tendency for persons in a group situation to fail to take action (as in an emergency) because others are present, thus diffusing the responsibility for acting. A major factor in bystander apathy.

digital computer. A computer that performs mathematical and logical operations with information, numerical or otherwise, represented in digital form.

discrimination. (1) In perception, the detection of differences between two stimuli. (2) In conditioning, the differential response to the positive (reinforced) stimulus and to the negative (nonreinforced) stimulus (cf. ***generalization***). (3) In social psychology, prejudicial treatment, as in racial discrimination.

discriminative stimulus. A stimulus that becomes an occasion for an operant response, e.g., the knock that leads one to open the door. The stimulus does not elicit the operant response in the same sense that stimulus elicits respondent behavior (cf. ***operant behavior***).

displaced aggression. Aggression against a person or object other than that which was (or is) the source of frustration.

displacement. A defense mechanism whereby a motive that may not be directly expressed (e.g., sex, aggression) appears in a more acceptable form (cf. ***defense mechanism***).

dispositional attribution. Attributing a person's actions to internal dispositions (attitudes, traits, motives), as opposed to situational factors (cf. ***situational attribution***).

dissonance. (1) In music, an inharmonious combination of sounds; contrasted with consonance. (2) In social psychology, Festinger's term for a perceived inconsistency between one's own attitudes and one's behavior (cf. ***cognitive dissonance***).

distance cues. (1) In vision, the monocular cues according to which the distance of objects is perceived—such as superposition of objects, perspective, light and shadow, and relative movement—and the binocular cues used in stereoscopic vision (cf. ***stereoscopic vision***). (2) In audition, the corresponding cues governing perception of distance and direction, such as intensity and time differences of sound reaching the two ears (cf. ***stereophonic hearing***).

divergent thinking. In tests of intellect (or creativity), producing one or more "possible" answers rather than a single "correct" one (cf. ***convergent thinking***).

dizygotic twins. Twins developed from separate eggs. They are no more alike genetically than ordinary brothers and sisters and can be of the same or different sexes (syn. *fraternal twins;* cf. ***monozygotic twins***).

DNA. Cf. ***deoxyribonucleic acid.***

dominance. The higher status position when social rank is organized according to a dominance-submission hierarchy; commonly found in human societies and in certain animal groups.

dominant gene. A member of a gene pair, which, if present, determines that the individual will show the trait controlled by the gene, regardless of whether the other member of the pair is the same or different, that is, recessive (cf. ***recessive gene***).

double blind. An experimental design, often used in drug research, in which neither the investigator nor the patients know which subjects are in the treatment and which in the nontreatment condition until the experiment has been completed.

Down's syndrome. A form of mental deficiency produced by a genetic abnormality (an extra chromosome on pair 21). Characteristics include a thick tongue, extra eyelid folds, and short, stubby fingers (also known as mongolism).

drive. (1) An aroused condition of the organism based upon deprivation or noxious stimulation, including tissue needs, drug or hormonal conditions, and specified internal or external stimuli, as in pain (text usage). (2) Loosely, any motive (cf. ***motive***).

drive-reduction theory. The theory that a motivated sequence of behavior can be best explained as moving from an aversive state of heightened tension (i.e., drive) to a goal state in which the drive is reduced. The goal of the sequence, in other words, is drive reduction.

dualism. The assumption that psychic (mental) and physical (body; brain) phenomena are both real but fundamentally different in nature.

duct gland. A gland, such as the tear gland or salivary gland, that secretes its product on the surface of the body or into the body cavities but not directly into the blood stream (cf. ***endocrine gland***).

eardrum. The membrane at the inner end of the auditory canal, leading to the middle ear (cf. ***middle ear***).

ectomorphic component. The third of the three components of physique in Sheldon's type theory. It comprises delicacy of skin, fine hair, and ultrasensitive nervous system (cf. ***endomorphic component, mesomorphic component, type theory***).

educational psychologist. A psychologist whose research interest lies in the application of psychological principles to the education of children and adults in schools (cf. ***school psychologist***).

EEG. Cf. ***electroencephalogram.***

effector. A bodily organ activated by motor nerves; a muscle or gland (cf. ***receptor***).

efferent nerve. A bundle of nerve fibers transmitting impulses from the central nervous system in the direction of the peripheral organs. Efferent nerve tracts commonly end in muscles or glands (usually synonymous with *motor nerve;* cf. ***afferent nerve***).

ego. In Freud's tripartite division of the personality, that part corresponding most nearly to the perceived self, the controlling self that holds back the impulsiveness of the id in the effort to delay gratification until it can be found in socially approved ways (cf. ***id, superego***).

ego theory. The theory in psychoanalysis that stresses functions of the ego, as against almost exclusive preoccupation with libido (cf. ***ego***).

eidetic imagery. The ability to retain visual images of pictures that are almost photographic in clarity. Such images can be described in far greater detail than would be possible from memory alone.

electroconvulsive shock therapy. A form of shock treatment for mental illness in which high-voltage current is passed briefly through the head, producing temporary unconsciousness and convulsions, with the intention of alleviating depression or other symptoms (cf. ***shock therapy***).

electroencephalogram (EEG). A record obtained by attaching electrodes to the scalp (or occasionally to the exposed brain) and amplifying the spontaneous electrical activity of the brain. The EEG is useful in studying some forms of mental disturbance (e.g., epilepsy) and in research on brain function.

emotional state. The condition of the organism during affectively toned experience, whether mild or intense (cf. ***affective experience***).

empiricism. The view that behavior is learned as a result of experience (cf. ***nativism***).

encoding. Transforming a sensory input into a form that can be processed by the memory system.

encounter group. A general term for various types of groups in which people meet together to learn more about themselves in relation to other people (syn. *sensitivity group, T group*).

endocrine gland. A ductless gland, or gland of internal secretion, that discharges its products directly into the blood stream. The hormones secreted by the endocrine glands are important chemical integrators of bodily activity (cf. ***duct gland, hormones***).

endomorphic component. The first of three components of physique in Sheldon's type theory. It comprises prominence of intestines and other visceral organs, including a prominent abdomen, as in the obese individual (cf. ***mesomorphic component, ectomorphic component, type theory***).

epinephrine. One of the hormones secreted by the adrenal medulla, active in emotional excitement (syn. *adrenalin;* cf. ***norepinephrine***).

equilibratory senses. The senses that give discrimination of the position of the body in space and of the movement of the body as a whole (cf. ***kinesthesis, semicircular canals, vestibular sacs***).

errors of measurement. That part of the variation in a distribution of scores, or in statistics derived from them, attributable to the fallibility of the measuring instrument, errors in observation, etc. (cf. ***sampling errors***).

escape learning. A form of learning controlled by actual painful stimulation. Escape from the punishment brings an end to the unpleasant or painful situation and is therefore rewarding (cf. ***avoidance learning***).

ESP. Cf. ***estrasensory perception.***

estrogen. A female sex hormone manufactured and secreted by the ovaries; it is partially responsible for the growth of the female secondary sex characteristics and influences the sex drive.

estrus. The sexually receptive state in female mammals. It is a cyclical state, related to menstruation in the primates and man (syn. *heat;* cf. ***menstruation***).

ethologist. One group of zoologists and naturalists particularly interested in kinds of behavior that are specific to a species. More of their work has been on insects, birds, and fishes than on mammals (cf. ***instinct***).

evoked potential. An electrical discharge in some part of the nervous system produced by stimulation elsewhere. The measured potential is commonly based upon response averaging by a computer.

existentialism. A philosophical viewpoint emphasizing that man is not a ready-made machine, but rather that he has the freedom to make vital choices and to assume responsibility for his own existence. It emphasizes subjective experience as a sufficient criterion of truth.

existential therapy. Derived from the existentialist philosophical belief that each individual has to choose his values and decide the meaning of his life. The therapist tries to achieve an authentic, spontaneous relationship with the patient in order to help him discover his free will and make his choices.

expectation. An anticipation or prediction of future events based on past experience and present stimuli (cf. ***sign learning***).

expectation-value theory. A theory of motivation and decision-making that accounts for choices on the basis of values (or utility) and the risks involved, e.g., the probability that such values will be attained.

experimental design. A plan for collecting and treating the data of a proposed experiment. The design is evolved after preliminary exploration, with the aims of economy, precision, and control, so that appropriate inferences and decisions can be made from the data.

experimental group. In an experimental design contrasting two groups, that group of subjects given the treatment whose effect is under investigation (cf. ***control group***).

experimental psychologist. A psychologist whose research interest is in the laboratory study of general psychological principles as revealed in the behavior of lower organisms and man.

extinction. (1) The experimental procedure, following either classical or operant conditioning, of presenting the conditioned stimulus without the usual reinforcement. (2) The reduction in response that results from this procedure (cf. ***reinforcement***).

extrasensory perception (ESP). A controversial category of experience consisting of perception not mediated by sense-organ stimulation (cf. ***clairvoyance, precognition, telepathy, psychokinesis***).

extravert. One of the psychological types proposed by Jung. The extravert is more preoccupied with social life and the external world than with his inward experience (cf. ***introvert***).

extrinsic motivation. The motivational control of behavior through the possibility of reward or punishment external to whatever satisfactions or annoyances reside in the behavior itself, e.g., working for a prize rather than the satisfactions in the task (cf. ***intrinsic motivation***).

factor analysis. A statistical method used in test construction and in interpreting scores from batteries of tests. The method enables the investigator to compute the minimum number of determiners (factors) required to account for the intercorrelations among the scores on the tests making up the battery.

family therapy. Psychotherapy with the family members as a group rather than treatment of the patient alone (cf. ***group therapy***).

fantasy. Daydreaming, "wool gathering," imagination; sometimes a consequence of frustration. It is used as a personality indicator in projective tests (cf. ***projective tests***).

figure-ground perception. Perceiving a pattern as foreground against a background. Patterns are commonly perceived this way even when the stimuli are ambiguous and the foreground-background relationships are reversible.

fixation. In psychoanalysis, arrested development through failure to pass beyond one of the earlier stages or to change the objects of attachment (e.g., fixated at the oral stage, or fixated upon the mother).

flow chart. A diagrammatic representation of the sequence of choices and actions in an activity.

forebrain. The portion of the brain evolved from the foremost of the three enlargements of the neural tube, consisting of the cerebrum, thalamus, hypothalamus, and related structures (cf. ***hindbrain, midbrain***).

formal discipline. An older interpretation of transfer of learning, justifying the study of a subject not for its own sake but for the training it supposedly gives the mental faculties, e.g., studying Latin not to learn Latin but to improve judgment and reasoning (cf. ***transfer of learning***).

formal operational state. The fourth stage of Piaget's theory of cognitive development in which the child becomes able to use abstract rules. Usually age 12 years and up.

fovea. In the eye, a small area in the central part of the retina, packed with cones; in daylight, the most sensitive part of the retina for detail vision and color vision (cf. ***retina, cone***).

fraternal twins. Cf. ***dizygotic twins.***

free association. (1) The form of word-association experiment in which the subject gives any word he thinks of in response to the stimulus word (cf. ***controlled association***). (2) In psychoanalysis, the effort to report without modification everything that comes into awareness.

frequency distribution. A set of scores assembled according to size and grouped into class intervals (cf. ***class interval, normal distribution***).

frequency theory. A theory of hearing that assumes that neural impulses arising in the organ of Corti are activated by the basilar membrane of the ear in accordance with the frequency of its vibration rather than with the place of movement (cf. ***place theory, traveling wave theory, volley theory***).

frontal lobe. A portion of each cerebral hemisphere, in front of the central fissure (cf. ***occipital lobe, parietal lobe, temporal lobe***).

frustration. (1) As an event, the thwarting circumstances that block or interfere with goal-directed activity. (This is the usage in the text.) (2) As a state, the annoyance, confusion, or anger engendered by being thwarted, disappointed, defeated.

frustration-aggression hypothesis. The hypothesis that frustration (thwarting a person's goal-directed efforts) induces an aggressive drive, which, in turn, motivates aggressive behavior.

fugue state. An unusual condition in which a person has no memory for his actions over a period of time; the fugue state may last for several minutes or months.

functional autonomy. The theory that motives may become independent of their origins, e.g., the miser may come to value money for its own sake rather than for the motive-satisfying things that originally gave it reinforcing value.

functional psychosis. A psychotic disorder of psychogenic origin without clearly defined structural change (cf. ***organic psychosis***).

galvanic skin response (GSR). Changes in electrical conductivity of, or activity in, the skin, detected by a sensitive galvanometer. The reactions are commonly used as an emotional indicator.

ganglion (pl. **ganglia**). A collection of nerve cell bodies and synapses, constituting a center lying outside the brain and spinal cord, as in the sympathetic ganglia.

gastrointestinal motility. Movements of parts of the digestive tract caused by contraction of smooth muscle; one form of emotional indicator.

gene. The unit of hereditary transmission, localized within the chromosomes. Each chromosome contains many genes. Genes are typically in pairs, one member of the pair being found in the chromosome from the father, the other in the corresponding chromosome from the mother (cf. ***chromosome, dominant gene, recessive gene***).

generalization. (1) In concept formation, problem-solving, and transfer of learning, the detection by the learner of a characteristic or principle common to a class of objects, events, or problems. (2) In conditioning, the principle that once a conditioned response has been established to a give stimulus, similar stimuli will also evoke that response (cf. ***gradient of generalization, discrimination***).

general factor. (1) A general ability underlying test scores, especially in tests of intelligence, as distinct from special abilites unique to each test (Spearman). (2) A general ability with which each of the primary factors correlates (Thurstone) (cf. ***factor analysis***).

genetics. That branch of biology concerned with heredity and the means by which hereditary characteristics are transmitted.

genital stage. In classical psychoanalysis, the final stage of psychosexual development, culminating in sexual union with a member of the opposite sex (cf. ***psychosexual development***).

genotype. In genetics, the characteristics that an individual has inherited and will transmit to his descendants, whether or not he manifests these characteristics (cf. ***phenotype***).

Gestalt psychology. A system of psychological theory emphasizing pattern, organization, wholes, and field properties. It permits a form of introspection known as phenomenology (cf. ***behaviorism***).

glia cells. Supporting cells (not neurons) composing a substantial portion of brain tissue; recent speculation suggests that they may play a role in the storage of memory.

goal. (1) An end state or condition toward which the motivated behavior sequence is directed and by which the sequence is completed. (2) Loosely, the incentive (cf. ***incentive***).

gradient of texture. If a surface is perceived visually as having substantial texture (hard, soft, smooth, rough, etc.) and if the texture has a noticeable grain, it becomes finer as the surface recedes from the viewing person, producing a gradient of texture that is important in judgments of slant and of distance (cf. ***distance cues***).

grammar. The system of rules that links the deep structure of a sentence to its surface structure (cf. ***surface structure, deep structure***).

group test. A test administered to several people at once by a single tester. A college examination is usually a group test.

group therapy. A group discussion or other group activity with a therapeutic purpose participated in by more than one client or patient at a time (cf. ***psychotherapy***).

GSR. Cf. ***galvanic skin response.***

habit. A learned stimulus-response sequence (cf. ***conditioned response, sensorimotor task***).

hallucination. A sense experience in the absence of appropriate external stimuli; a misinterpretation of imaginary experiences as actual perceptions (cf. ***illusion, schizophrenia***).

hedonism. The theory that man seeks pleasure and avoids pain; an extreme form of the theory (in philosophy) is that pleasure or happiness is the highest good.

heritability. The proportion of the total variability of a trait in a given population that is attributable to genetic differences among individuals within that population.

hertz (Hz). The wave frequency of a sound source measured in cycles per second.

heterosexuality. Interest in or attachment to a member of the opposite sex; the normal adult outcome of psychosexual development.

heuristic method. A nonrigorous method for discovering the correct solution to a problem through obtaining approximations to the correct answer, through using analogies and other methods of search, without the painstaking exploration of all possibilities. Computing machines can be programed to use such methods (cf. ***algorithm***).

hindbrain. The portion of the brain evolved from the final one of the three enlargements of the primitive neural tube, consisting of the cerebellum, the medulla, and related structures (cf. ***forebrain, midbrain***).

homeostasis. An optimal level of organic function, maintained by regulatory mechanisms known as homeostatic mechanisms, e.g., the mechanisms maintaining a uniform body temperature (cf. ***homeostat***).

homeostat. A particular portion of the brain that regulates the equilibrium point of some bodily system, analogous to the regulation of temperature by a thermostat (cf. ***homeostasis***).

homosexuality. A behavior pattern characterized by a sexual preference for or relations with members of the same sex.

hormones. The internal secretions of the endocrine glands that are distributed via the blood stream and affect behavior (cf. ***chemical integration, endocrine gland***).

hostile aggression. Aggression whose primary aim is to inflict injury (cf. ***instrumental aggression***).

hue. The dimension of color from which the major color names are derived (red, yellow, green, etc.), corresponding to wavelength of light (cf. ***brightness, saturation***).

human factors research. An applied science participated in jointly by engineers and psychologists, concerned with the design of equipment and the arrangement of work conditions to provide the most effective combination of man and machine (syn. *human engineering*).

humanistic psychology. A psychological approach that emphasizes the uniqueness of human beings; it is concerned with subjective experience and human values. Often referred to as a third force in psychology in contrast to behaviorism and psychoanalysis.

hunger drive. A drive based on food deprivation (cf. ***drive, specific hunger***).

hyperphagia. Pathological overeating (cf. ***aphagia***).

hypnotic trance. The dreamlike state of heightened suggestibility induced in a subject by a hypnotist (cf. ***post-hypnotic suggestion***).

hypnotism. The process of inducing the hypnotic trance (syn. *hypnosis*).

hypothalamus. One of the structures at the base of the brain, portions of which are significant in sleep and in emotional and motivational behavior.

hypothetical construct. One form of inferred intermediate mechanism. The construct is conceived of as having properties of its own, other than those specifically required for the explanation, e.g., the memory trace, which is inferred to explain the retention curve, is assumed to have electrochemical properties, localization in the nervous system, etc. (cf. ***intervening variable***).

Hz. Cf. ***hertz.***

id. In Freud's tripartite division of the personality, that part reflecting unorganized, instinctual impulses. If unbridled, it seeks immediate gratification of primitive needs (cf. ***ego, superego***).

identical twins. Cf. ***monozygotic twins.***

identification. (1) The normal process of acquiring appropriate social roles in childhood through copying, in part unconsciously, the behavior of significant adults, e.g., the child's identification with his like-sexed parent (cf. ***imitation***). (2) Close affiliation with others of like interest, e.g., identifying with a group.

identification figures. Adult models (especially parents) copied, partly unconsciously, by the child (cf. ***identification***).

identity formation. The process of achieving adult personality integration, as an outgrowth of earlier identifications and other influences (cf. ***identification, role diffusion***).

illusion. In perception, a misinterpretation of the relationships among presented stimuli, so that what is perceived does not correspond to physical reality; especially, but not exclusively, an optical or visual illusion (cf. ***delusion, hallucination***).

imitation. Behavior that is modeled upon or copies that of another (cf. ***identification***).

immediate memory span. The number of items (digits, letters, words, etc.) that can be repeated after a single presentation.

immunization against persuasion. A technique for developing resistance to persuasion by exposing individuals to fairly weak counterarguments against their own beliefs with refutations of these opposing views. Also known as innoculation against persuasion.

implicit personality theory. A set of assumptions or preconceived notions a person has about which traits and behaviors are correlated with certain other traits and behaviors. A stereotype is a special kind of implicit personality theory.

imprinting. A term used by ethologists for a species-specific type of learning that occurs within a limited period of time early in the life of the organism and is relatively unmodifiable thereafter; e.g., young ducklings learn to follow one adult female (usually the mother) within 11 to 18 hours after birth. But whatever object they are given to follow at this time they will thereafter continue to follow (cf. ***ethologist***).

incentive. (1) A tangible goal object that provides the stimuli that lead to goal activity. (2) Loosely, any goal (cf. ***goal***).

incentive theory. A theory of motivation that emphasizes the importance of negative and positive incentives in determining behavior; internal drives are not the sole instigators of activity (cf. ***drive-reduction theory***).

independent variable. The variable under experimental control with which the changes studied in the experiment are correlated. In psychological experiments, the independent variable is often a stimulus, responses to which are the dependent variables under investigation (cf. ***dependent variable***).

individual differences. Relatively persistent unlikenesses in structure or behavior between persons or members of the same species.

infancy. The period of helplessness and dependency in man and other organisms; in humans, roughly the first two years (cf. ***adolescence***).

information-processing model. A model based on assumptions regarding the flow of information through a system; usually best realized by a computer program.

inner ear. The internal portion of the ear containing, in addition to the cochlea, the vestibular sacs and the semicircular canals (cf. ***cochlea, semicircular canals, vestibular sacs***).

insight. (1) In problem-solving experiments, the perception of relationships leading to solution. Such a solution can be repeated promptly when the problem is again confronted. (2) In psychotherapy, the discovery by the subject of dynamic connections between earlier and later events, so that he comes to recognize the roots of his conflicts.

instinct. The name given to unlearned, patterned, goal-directed behavior, which is species-specific, as illustrated by nest-building in birds or by the migration of salmon.

instrumental aggression. Aggression aimed at obtaining rewards other than the victim's suffering (cf. ***hostile aggression***).

insulin. The hormone secreted by the pancreas (cf. ***hormones, insulin shock***).

insulin shock. A state of coma resulting from reduced blood sugar when insulin is present in excessive amounts. Insulin shock is used as one form of shock therapy in treating mental illness (cf. ***shock therapy***).

intellectualization. A defense mechanism whereby a person tries to gain detachment from an emotionally threatening situation by dealing with it in abstract, intellectual terms (cf. ***defense mechanism***).

intelligence. (1) That which a properly standardized intelligence test measures. (2) According to Binet, the characteristics of an individual's thought processes that enable him to take and maintain a direction without becoming distracted, to adapt means to ends, and to criticize his own attempts at problem solution (cf. ***mental age***).

intelligence quotient (IQ). A scale unit used in reporting intelligence test scores, based on the ratio between mental age and chronological age. The decimal point is omitted, so that the average IQ for children of any one chronological age is set at 100 (cf. ***chronological age, mental age, deviation IQ***).

intermittent reinforcement. Cf. ***partial reinforcement.***

interpretation. In psychoanalysis, the analyst's calling attention to the patient's resistances in order to facilitate the flow of associations; also his explanation of symbols, as in dream interpretation (cf. ***resistance***).

intervening variable. A process inferred to occur between stimulus and response, thus accounting for one response rather than another to the same stimulus. The intervening variable may be inferred without further specification, or it may be given concrete properties and become an object of investigation.

interview. A conversation between an investigator (the interviewer) and a subject (the respondent) used for gathering pertinent data either for the subject's benefit (as in the psychotherapeutic interview) or for information-gathering (as in a sample survey).

intrinsic motivation. Motivation in which the action and the ends served by the action are organically or inherently related, as distinct from action motivated by promise of reward or threat of punishment, e.g., assembling a model airplane in order to fly it, composing a sonnet to give expression to a mood (cf. ***extrinsic motivation***).

introspection. (1) A specified form of introspection (trained introspection) describing mental content only, without the intrusion of meanings or interpretations. (2) Any form of reporting on subjective (conscious) events or experiences (cf. ***phenomenology***).

introvert. One of the psychological types proposed by Jung, referring to the individual who, especially in time of emotional stress, tends to withdraw into himself and to avoid other people (cf. ***extravert***).

item. Any single unit of test or experimental materials, e.g., a single question in a test composed of many questions or a single nonsense syllable in a list of syllables to be memorized (cf. ***test, test battery***).

James-Lange theory. A classical theory of emotion, named for the two men who independently proposed it. The theory states that the stimulus first leads to bodily responses, and then the awareness of these responses constitutes the experience of emotion (cf. ***Cannon's theory, cognitive-physiological theory***).

j.n.d. Cf. ***just noticeable difference.***

just noticeable difference (j.n.d.). A barely perceptible physical change in a stimulus; a measure of the difference threshold. The term is used also as a unit for scaling the steps of sensation corresponding to increase in the magnitude of stimulation (cf. ***difference threshold***).

kinesthesis. The muscle, tendon, and joint senses, yielding discrimination of position and movement of parts of the body (cf. ***equilibratory senses***).

Klinefelter's syndrome. An abnormal condition of the sex chromosomes (XXY instead of XX or XY); the individual is physically a male with penis and testicles but has marked feminine characteristics.

latency. (1) A temporal measure of response, referring to the time delay between the occurrence of the stimulus and the onset of the response. (2) In psychoanalysis, a period in middle childhood, roughly the years from six to twelve, when both sexual and aggressive impulses are said to be in a somewhat subdued state, so that the child's attention is directed outward, and his curiosity about the environment makes him ready to learn (cf. ***psychosexual development***).

latent content. The underlying significance of a dream, e.g., the motives or wishes being expressed by it, as interpreted from the manifest content (cf. ***interpretation, manifest content***).

latent-learning experiment. A type of experiment in which opportunity for learning spatial relationships is given under conditions of inappropriate drive or absent incentive; e.g., a rat is permitted to explore a maze without food in the goal box. The learning is later tested under changed drive-incentive conditions. The experiment, when successful, is used to support the sign learning theory (cf. ***sign learning***).

lateral fissure. A deep fissure at the side of each cerebral hemisphere, below which lies the temporal lobe (syn. *fissure of Sylvius*).

lateral hypothalamus. Area of the hypothalamus important to the regulation of food intake. Electrical stimulation of this area will make an experimental animal start to eat; destruction of brain tissue here causes an animal to stop eating (cf. ***hypothalamus, ventromedial hypothalamus***).

law of effect. Thorndike's principle that the consequences of an activity determine whether or not it will be learned. In its later forms stress was placed on the influence of reward. Hence learning under the law of effect is virtually synonymous with operant conditioning (q.v.).

learning. A relatively permanent change in behavior that occurs as the result of practice. Behavior changes due to maturation or temporary conditions of the organism (e.g., fatigue, the influence of drugs, adaptation) are not included.

learning curve. A graph plotting the course of learning, in which the vertical axis (ordinate) plots a measure of proficiency (amount per unit time, time per unit amount, errors made, etc.), while the horizontal axis (abscissa) represents some measure of practice (trials, time, etc.).

learning set. A case in which an animal's rate of learning gradually improves over a series of problems of the same general type; in essence, the phenomenon of learning to learn.

libido theory. The theory within psychoanalysis that human development and motivation are best understood by studying the manifestations of the libido—the energy of the sexual instinct—which throughout life becomes attached to new objects and expressed through various types of motivated behavior (cf. ***ego theory***).

lie detector. An apparatus using one or more of the emotional indicators in order to determine guilt of a subject through his emotional responses while answering questions in a false or unintentionally revealing manner (syn. *polygraph*).

light adaptation. The decreased sensitivity of the eye to light when the subject has been continuously exposed to high levels of illumination (cf. ***dark adaptation***).

limbic system. A set of structures in and around the midbrain, forming a functional unit regulating motivational-emotional types of behavior, such as waking and sleeping, excitement and quiescence, feeding, and mating.

linear program. A teaching program in which the student progresses along a fixed track from one instructional frame to the next. After responding to a frame he moves to the next frame regardless of whether his answer is correct (cf. ***branching program***).

linguistic-relativity hypothesis. The proposition that one's thought processes, the way one perceives the world, are related to one's language.

lithium. A chemical element, related to sodium. Has shown some success in relieving the symptoms of manic behavior.

localized functions. Behavior controlled by known areas of the brain; e.g., vision is localized in the occipital lobes (cf. ***projection area***).

location constancy. The tendency to perceive the place at which a resting object is located as remaining the same even though the relationship to the observer has changed (cf. ***object constancy***).

longitudinal study. A research method that studies an individual through time, taking measurements at periodic intervals.

long-term memory (LTM). The relatively permanent component of the memory system, as opposed to short-term memory (q.v.).

loudness. An intensity dimension of hearing correlated with the amplitude of the sound waves that constitute the stimulus. Greater amplitudes yield greater loudnesses (cf. ***pitch, timbre***).

LSD-25. Cf. ***lysergic acid derivatives.***

LTM. Cf. ***long-term memory.***

lysergic acid derivatives. Chemical substances derived from lysergic acid, the most important of which is LSD-25. When taken by a normal person, it produces symptoms similar in some respects to those of the schizophrenic reaction (cf. ***schizophrenic reaction***).

manic-depressive psychosis. A psychotic reaction characterized by mood swings from the normal in the direction either of excitement and elation (manic phase) or of fatigue, despondency, and sadness (depressive phase). Many patients do not show the whole cycle.

manifest content. The remembered content of a dream, the characters and their actions, as distinguished from the inferred latent content (cf. ***latent content***).

mantra. Cf. ***transcendental meditation.***

marihuana. The dried leaves of the hemp plant; also known as hashish, "pot," or "grass." Intake may enhance sensory experiences and produce a state of euphoria.

masochism. A pathological desire to inflict pain upon oneself or to suffer pain at the hands of others (cf. ***sadism***).

massed practice. Practice in which trials are continuous or closely spaced (cf. ***spaced practice***).

maternal drive. The drive, particularly in animals, induced in the female through bearing and nursing young, leading to nest-building, retrieving, and other forms of care (cf. ***drive***).

mathematical model. A model of a phenomenon formulated in mathematical terms (cf. ***model***).

maturation. Growth processes in the individual that result in orderly changes in behavior, whose timing and patterning are relatively independent of exercise or experience though they may require a normal environment.

maze. A device commonly used in the study of animal and human learning, consisting of a correct path and blind alleys.

mean. The arithmetical average; the sum of all scores divided by their number (cf. ***measure of central tendency***).

measure of central tendency. A value representative of a frequency distribution, around which other values are dispersed, e.g., the mean, median, or mode of a distribution of scores (syn. *average*).

measure of variation. A measure of the dispersion or spread of scores in a frequency distribution, e.g., the range, the mean deviation, the standard deviation (q.v.).

median. The score of the middle case when cases are arranged in order of size of score (cf. ***measure of central tendency***).

memory drum. A mechanical device used to present verbal materials in rote-learning experiments.

memory trace. The inferred change in the nervous system that persists between the time that something is learned and the time that it is recalled.

menarche. The first menstrual period, indicative of sexual maturation in a girl (cf. ***menstruation***).

menstruation. The approximately monthly discharge from the uterus (cf. ***menarche***).

mental age (MA). A scale unit proposed by Binet for use in intelligence testing. If an intelligence test is properly standardized, a representative group of children of age six should earn an average mental age of six, those of age seven, a mental age of seven, etc. A child whose MA is above his chronological age (CA) is advanced; one whose MA lags behind is retarded (cf. ***chronological age, intelligence quotient***).

mental imagery. Mental pictures used as an aid to memory. *Not* the same as eidetic imagery.

mentally defective. A descriptive term applied to a mentally subnormal individual whose deficiency is based on some sort of brain damage or organic defect (cf. ***mentally retarded***).

mentally gifted. An individual with an unusually high level of intelligence, commonly an IQ of 140 or above.

mentally retarded. A mentally subnormal individual whose problems lie in a learning disability with no evident organic damage (cf. ***mentally defective***).

mentally subnormal. An individual whose intelligence is below that necessary for adjustment to ordinary schooling; the more intelligent among the subnormal are classified as *educable* in special classes, the next level as *trainable,* while the lowest group classifies as more severely retarded (syn., but now obsolete, *feeble-minded;* cf. ***mentally defective, mentally retarded***).

mesomorphic component. The second of three components of physique in Sheldon's type theory. Refers to the prominence of bone and muscle, as in the typical athlete (cf. ***endomorphic component, ectomorphic component, type theory***).

method of loci. An aid to serial memory. Verbal material is transformed into mental images which are then located at successive positions along a visualized route, such as an imaged walk through the house or down a familiar street.

midbrain. The second of the three enlargements of the neural tube, upon which later structures of the brain have evolved. The midbrain in the fish consists chiefly of the optic lobes ("eye brain"); in man this portion has not been greatly increased in relative size, the most pronounced evolutionary changes having taken place in the forebrain (cf. ***forebrain, hindbrain***).

middle ear. The portion of the ear containing the hammer, anvil, and stirrup bones, which connect the eardrum to the oval window of the inner ear.

mirror drawing. A laboratory learning task in which the skill under study is that of tracing the contour of a star or other figure while viewing it in a mirror.

mnemonics. A system for improving memory often involving a set of symbols that can substitute for the material to be remembered. For example, in attempting to remember a number sequence one may translate the sequence into letters of the alphabet that in turn approximate words that are easily remembered.

modality. A separate sense or sensory department, e.g., vision, audition. Experiences within a single modality can be arranged along continuous dimensions, with intermediate values. There is no simple way of moving across from one modality to another, e.g., to find the experience lying midway between a given odor and a given color.

mode. The most frequent score in a distribution, or the class interval in which the greatest number of cases fall (cf. ***measure of central tendency***).

model. (1) Miniature systems are often constructed according to a logical, mathematical, or physical model. That is, the principles according to which data are organized and made understandable parallel those of the model; e.g., the piano keyboard is a model for understanding the basilar membrane; the speed-regulating governor is a model for the feedback principle of cybernetics. (2) In behavior therapy a person who *models* or performs behaviors that the therapist wishes the patient to imitate.

moderator variable. A variable such as age, sex, or intelligence that moderates or influences the correlations found in personality trait research.

mongolism. See Down's syndrome.

monochromatism. Total color blindness, the visual system being achromatic. A rare disorder (cf. ***dichromatism***).

monocular cues. Cf. ***distance cues.***

monozygotic twins. Twins developed from a single egg. They are always of the same sex and commonly much alike in appearance, although some characteristics may be in mirror-image, e.g., one right-handed, the other left-handed (syn. *identical twins;* cf. ***dizygotic twins***).

morpheme. The smallest meaningful unit in the structure of a language, whether a word, base, or affix; examples—*man, strange, ing, pro* (cf. ***phoneme***).

motivated forgetting. The theory that forgetting can be explained according to the motives of the learner (cf. ***repression***).

motivation. A general term referring to the regulation of need-satisfying and goal-seeking behavior (cf. ***motive***).

motive. Any condition of the organism that affects its readiness to start upon or continue in a sequence of behavior (cf. ***physiological motive, social motive***).

motor area. A projection area in the brain lying in front of the central fissure. Electrical stimulation commonly results in motor responses (cf. ***body-sense area***).

multimodal distribution. A distribution curve with more than one mode (cf. ***mode***).

multiple personality. An extreme form of dissociation in which the individual's personality is split into separate personalities often alternating with each other. The memories of one of the split-off personalities commonly are not accessible to the other.

multiple-response learning. The acquiring of patterns or sequences of responses in mastering a task, e.g., in learning a skill or memorizing a poem (cf. ***sensorimotor task, rote memorization***).

myelin. The fatty sheath surrounding certain nerve fibers known as myelinated fibers. Impulses travel faster and with less energy expenditure in myelinated fibers than in unmyelinated fibers.

narcissism. Self-love; in psychoanalytic theory, the normal expression of pregenital development (cf. ***pregenital stages***).

nativism. The view that behavior is innately determined (cf. ***empiricism.***).

naturalistic observation. Cf. ***field observation.***

nature-nurture issue. The problem of determining the relative importance of the hereditary component (nature) and the result of up-bringing in the particular environment (nurture) upon mature ability; such a determination is especially important in relation to intelligence.

need. A physical state involving any lack or deficit within the organism. (cf. ***motive, drive***).

negative incentive. An object or circumstance away from which behavior is directed when the object or circumstance is perceived or anticipated (syn. *negative reinforcer;* cf. ***positive incentive***).

negativism. A type of defiant behavior in which there is active refusal to carry out requests. Common in early childhood but met occasionally at all ages (syn. *negativistic behavior*).

nerve cell. Cf. ***neuron.***

neural quantum theory. A theory of psychophysical phenomena that views the sensory system as a discrete, step-wise process.

neuron. The nerve cell; the unit of a synaptic nervous system.

neurosis. A form of maladjustment in which the individual is unable to cope with his anxieties and conflicts and develops abnormal symptoms. The disturbance is not so severe as to produce a profound personality derangement, as with the psychotic reactions (syn. *psychoneurosis;* cf. ***anxiety reaction, conversion reaction, phobic reaction, obsessive-compulsive reaction neurotic depression***).

neurotic depression. A neurotic reaction characterized by continuing sadness and dejection that is out of proportion to any precipitating event; distinguished from psychotic depression in that reality perception is not grossly impaired.

noncontingent reinforcement. Reinforcement not contingent upon a specific response.

nonsense syllable. An item used in rote memorization experiments, usually consisting of two consonants with a vowel between, e.g., PUV, GEB. The combination of letters must not form a word in familiar languages.

noradrenalin. Cf. ***norepinephrine.***

norepinephrine. One of the hormones secreted by the adrenal medulla. Its action is in some, but not all respects, similar to that of epinephrine (syn. *noradrenalin;* cf. ***epinephrine***).

norm. An average, common, or standard performance under specified conditions, e.g the average achievement test score of nine-year-old children or the average birth weight of male children (cf. ***test standardization***).

normal curve. The plotted form of the normal distribution (q.v.).

normal distribution. The standard symmetrical bell-shaped frequency distribution, whose properties are commonly used in making statistical inferences from measures derived from samples (cf. ***normal curve***).

null hypothesis. A statistical hypothesis that any difference observed among treatment conditions occurs by chance and does not reflect a true difference. Rejection of the null hypothesis means that we believe the treatment conditions are actually having an effect.

object constancy. The tendency to see objects as relatively unchanged under widely altered conditions of illumination, distance, and position (cf. ***color constancy, location constancy, shape constancy, size constancy***).

object permanence. A term used by Piaget to refer to the child's realization that an object continues to exist even though it is hidden from view.

object size. The size of an object as determined from measurement at its surface. When size constancy holds, the observer perceives a distant object as being near its object size (cf. ***perspective size, size constancy***).

objective scoring. Scoring done according to a code so that all competent scorers arrive at the same score for the same test, e.g., the scoring of fixed-alternative (multiple-choice) questions (cf. ***subjective scoring***).

observational method. Studying events as they occur in nature, without experimental control of variables; e.g., studying the nest-building of birds or observing children's behavior in a play situation.

obsessive-compulsive reaction. A neurotic reaction taking one of three forms: (1) recurrent thoughts, often disturbing and unwelcome (obsessions); (2) irresistible urges to repeat stereotyped or ritualistic acts (compulsions); (3) both of these in combination (cf. ***neurotic reaction***).

occipital lobe. A portion of the cerebral hemisphere, behind the parietal and temporal lobes (cf. ***frontal lobe, parietal lobe, temporal lobe***).

occupational therapy. A form of help to a patient suffering from personality maladjustment or mental illness, whereby he is kept busy in constructive work.

Oedipal stage. In psychoanalysis, an alternative designation of the phallic stage of psychosexual development, because it is at this stage that the Oedipus complex arises (cf. ***psychosexual development, Oedipus complex***).

Oedipus complex. In psychoanalytic theory, sexual attachment to the parent of the opposite sex, originating as the normal culmination of the infantile period of development.

operant behavior. Behavior defined by the stimulus to which it leads rather than by the stimulus that elicits it; e.g., behavior leading to reward (syn. *emitted behavior, instrumental behavior;* cf. ***respondent behavior***).

operant conditioning. The strengthening of an operant response by presenting a reinforcing stimulus if, and only if, the response occurs (syn. *instrumental conditioning, reward learning;* cf. ***classical conditioning***).

opponent-process theory. The theory that human color vision depends upon three pairs of opposing processes: white-black, yellow-blue, and red-green.

oral behavior. Behavior deriving from the infant's need to suck or, more generally, to be fed through the mouth.

oral stage. In psychoanalysis, the first of the stages of psychosexual development, in which pleasure is derived from the lips and mouth, as in sucking at the mother's breast (cf. ***psychosexual development***).

organ of Corti. In the ear, the actual receptor for hearing, lying on the basilar membrane in the cochlea and containing the hair cells where the fibers of the auditory nerve originate (cf. ***basilar membrane, cochlea***).

organic psychosis. A psychotic disorder caused by disease, injury, drugs, or other definable structural change (cf. ***functional psychosis, psychotic disorder***).

organism. In biology, any form of plant or animal life. In psychology, the word is used to refer to the living individual animal, whether human or subhuman.

orienting reflex. (1) A nonspecific response to change in stimulation involving depression of cortical alpha rhythm, galvanic skin response, pupillary dilation, and complex vasomotor responses (a term introduced by Russian psychologists). (2) Head or body movements that orient the organism's receptors to those parts of the environment in which stimulus changes are occurring.

osmoreceptors. Hypothesized cells in the hypothalamus that respond to dehydration by stimulating the release of ADH by the pituitary gland which, in turn, signals the kidneys to reabsorb water back into the blood stream (cf. ***antidiuretic hormone, volumetric receptors***).

otoliths. "Ear stones" (cf. ***vestibular sacs***).

ovarian hormones. Cf. ***estrogen.***

overlearning. Any learning beyond bare mastery.

overtone. A higher frequency tone, a multiple of the fundamental frequency, which occurs when a tone is sounded by a musical instrument (cf. ***timbre***).

paired-associate learning. The learning of stimulus-response pairs, as in the acquisition of a foreign language vocabulary. When the first member of a pair (the stimulus) is presented, the subject's task is to give the second member (the response).

pancreas. A bodily organ situated near the stomach. As a duct gland it secretes pancreatic juice into the intestines, but some specialized cells function as an endocrine gland, secreting the hormone insulin into the blood stream (cf. ***endocrine gland***).

parameter. Any of the constants in a function that defines the form of the curve. It ordinarily differs when experimental conditions or subjects are changed.

paranoid schizophrenia. A schizophrenic reaction in which the patient has delusions of persecution (cf. ***schizophrenia***).

parasympathetic division. A division of the autonomic nervous system, nerve fibers of which originate in the cranial and sacral portions of the spinal cord. Active in relaxed or quiescent states of the body, and to some extent antagonistic to the sympathetic division (q.v.).

parathyroid glands. Endocrine glands adjacent to the thyroid gland in the neck, whose hormones regulate calcium metabolism, thus maintaining the normal excitability of the nervous system. Parathyroid inadequacy leads to tetany (cf. ***endocrine gland***).

parietal lobe. A portion of the cerebral hemisphere, behind the central fissure and between the frontal and occipital lobes (cf. ***frontal lobe, occipital lobe, temporal lobe***).

partial reinforcement. Reinforcing a given response only some proportion of the times it occurs (syn. *intermittent reinforcement*).

passive decay. A theory of forgetting that implies that the memory trace fades with disuse (cf. ***memory trace***).

perception. The process of becoming aware of objects, qualities, or relations by way of the sense organs. While sensory content is always present in perception, what is perceived is influenced by set and prior experience, so that perception is more than a passive registration of stimuli impinging on the sense organs.

perceptual patterning. The tendency to perceive stimuli according to principles such as proximity, similarity, continuity, and closure. Emphasized by Gestalt psychologists (cf. ***figure-ground perception***).

performance. Overt behavior, as distinguished from knowledge or information not translated into action. The distinction is important in theories of learning.

peripheral nervous system. That part of the nervous system outside the brain and spinal cord; it includes the autonomic nervous system and the nerves that connect the central nervous system with the receptors and muscles (cf. ***autonomic nervous system***).

personality. The individual characteristics and ways of behaving that, in their organization or patterning, account for an individual's unique adjustments to his total environment (syn. *individuality*).

personality assessment. (1) Generally, appraisal of personality by any method. (2) More specifically, personality appraisal through complex observations and judgments, usually based in part upon behavior in contrived social situations.

personality disorders. Ingrained, habitual, and rigid patterns of behavior or character that severely limit the individual's adaptive potential; often society sees the behavior as maladaptive while the individual does not (syn. *character disorders*).

personality dynamics. Theories of personality that stress personality dynamics are concerned with the interactive aspects of behavior (as in conflict resolution), with value hierarchies, with the permeability of boundaries between differentiated aspects of personality, etc. Contrasted with developmental theories, though not incompatible with them.

personality inventory. An inventory for self-appraisal, consisting of many statements or questions about personal characteristics and behavior that the person judges to apply or not to apply to him (cf. ***projective test***).

perspective size. The size of an object according to the geometry of perspective, i.e., its size diminishes directly in proportion to its distance (cf. ***object size, size constancy***).

phallic stage. In psychoanalysis, that stage of psychosexual development in which gratification is associated with sex organ stimulation and the sexual attachment is to the parent of the opposite sex (cf. ***Oedipal stage, psychosexual development***).

phenomenology. Naive report on conscious experience, as by a child, as contrasted with trained introspection; the study of unanalyzed experience (cf. ***Gestalt psychology***).

phenotype. In genetics, the characteristics that are displayed by the individual organism, e.g., eye color, intelligence, as distinct from those traits that he may carry genetically but not display (cf. ***genotype***).

phi phenomenon. Stroboscopic motion in its simpler form. Commonly produced by successively turning on and off two separated stationary light sources; as the first is turned off and the second turned on, the subject perceives a spot of light moving from the position of the first to that of the second (cf. ***stroboscopic motion***).

phobic reaction. Excessive fear in the absence of real danger (cf. ***agoraphobia, claustrophobia, neurotic reaction***).

phoneme. The smallest unit in the sound system of a language; it serves to distinguish utterances from one another (cf. ***morpheme***).

phrase structure. The analysis of a sentence in terms of its component phrases, e.g., noun phrase, verb phrase, article (cf. ***deep structure, surface structure***).

physiological motive. A motive based upon an evident bodily need, such as the need for food or water (syn. *organic motive;* cf. ***social motive***).

physiological psychology. That branch of experimental psychology concerned with the relationship between physiological functions and behavior.

physiology. That branch of biology concerned primarily with the functioning of organ systems within the body.

pilomotor response. The response of muscles in the skin in which the hairs stand on end, giving a roughened appearance to the skin known as "goose flesh" or "goose pimples." May result either from cold or as part of an emotional state.

pitch. A qualitative dimension of hearing correlated with the frequency of the sound waves that constitute the stimulus. Higher frequencies yield higher pitches (cf. ***loudness, timbre***).

pituitary gland. An endocrine gland located centrally in the head. It consists of two parts, the anterior pituitary and the posterior pituitary. The anterior pituitary is the more important part because of its regulation of growth and of other endocrine glands. One of its hormones, ACTH (adrenocorticotropic hormone), has become medically important (syn. *hypophysis;* cf. ***endocrine gland***).

place-learning experiment. A variety of animal maze experiments designed to test whether what is learned is the location of the goal in space rather than the movements required to reach the goal (cf. ***sign learning***).

place theory. A theory of hearing that associates pitch with the place on the basilar membrane where activation occurs (cf. ***frequency theory, traveling wave theory, volley theory***).

placebo. An inert substance used in place of an active drug; given to the control group in an experimental test.

plateau. In a learning curve a period of no improvement, preceded and followed by improvement (cf. ***learning curve***).

pluralistic ignorance. The tendency in a group situation to define an emergency as a non-emergency because others are remaining calm and are not taking action.

polygenic traits. Characteristics determined by many sets of genes, e.g., intelligence, height, emotional stability.

population. The total universe of all possible cases from which a sample is selected. The usual statistical formulas for making inferences from samples apply when the population is appreciably larger than the sample, e.g., five to ten times larger than the sample (cf. ***sample***).

positive incentive. An object or circumstance toward which behavior is directed when the object or circumstance is perceived or anticipated (cf. ***negative incentive***).

post-hypnotic suggestion. A suggestion made to a hypnotized subject that he will perform in a prescribed way after coming out of the trance. The activity is usually carried out without the subject's awareness of its origin in a specific suggestion (cf. ***hypnotism***).

precognition. A claimed form of extrasensory perception in which a future event is perceived (cf. ***extrasensory perception, clairvoyance, telepathy***).

prejudice. An attitude that is firmly fixed, not open to free and rational discussion, and resistant to change.

preliterate society. A society or culture without written records, formerly called a primitive society (cf. ***anthropology***).

preparatory set. Cf. ***set.***

primacy effect. (1) In memory experiments, the tendency for initial words in a list to be recalled more readily than later words. (2) In studies of impression formation or attitude change, the tendency for initial information to carry more weight than information received later (cf. ***recency effect***).

primary abilities. The abilities, discovered by factor analysis, that underlie intelligence test performance (cf. ***factor analysis***).

primary colors. Cf. ***color-mixing primaries, psychological primaries.***

primary sex characteristics. The structural or physiological characteristics that make possible sexual union and reproduction (cf. ***secondary sex characteristics***).

proactive inhibition. The interference of earlier learning with the learning and recall of new material (cf. ***retroactive inhibition, transfer of learning***).

probability value. A probability statement associated with a statistical inference, e.g. "The probability is .05 that a difference of this size between the sample means would have occurred even though the population means were the same" (cf. ***statistical inference, statistical significance***).

product-moment correlation. Cf. ***coefficient of correlation.***

progesterone. A female sex hormone produced by the ovaries; it helps prepare the uterus for pregnancy and the breasts for lactation.

program. (1) A plan for the solution of a problem; often used interchangeably with "routine" to specify the precise sequence of instructions enabling a computer to solve a problem. (2) In connection with teaching, a set of materials arranged in sequences of units, called frames, so that learning can proceed with a minimum of error. The program can be presented in book form as well as in a form suitable for use with a teaching machine (cf. ***teaching machine***).

projection. A defense mechanism by which a person protects himself from awareness of his own undesirable traits by attributing those traits excessively to others (cf. ***defense mechanism***).

projection area. A place in the cerebral cortex where a function is localized; e.g., the visual projection area is in the occipital lobes.

projective test. A personality test in which the subject reveals ("projects") himself through his imaginative productions. The projective test gives much freer possibilities of response than the fixed-alternative personality inventory. Examples of projective tests are the Rorschach Test (ink blots to be interpreted) and the Thematic Apperception Test (pictures that elicit stories) (cf. ***personality inventory***).

prolactin. A pituitary hormone associated with the secretion of milk (cf. ***hormones***).

psi. The special ability said to be possessed by the subject who performs successfully in experiments on extrasensory perception and psychokinesis (cf. ***extrasensory perception, psychokinesis***).

psychedelic drugs. An alternate name for "consciousness-expanding" drugs (cf. ***psychotomimetic drugs, LSD-25***).

psychiatric nurse. A nurse specially trained to deal with patients suffering from mental disorders.

psychiatric social worker. A social worker trained to work with patients and their families on problems of mental health and illness, usually in close relationship with psychiatrists and clinical psychologists (cf. ***psychiatrist, clinical psychologist***).

psychiatrist. A medical doctor specializing in the treatment and prevention of mental disorders both mild and severe (cf. ***psychoanalyst, clinical psychologist***).

psychiatry. A branch of medicine concerned with mental health and mental illness (cf. ***psychiatrist, psychoanalyst***).

psychoactive drugs. Drugs that affect man's behavior and consciousness (cf. ***tranquilizers, psychedelic drugs, psychotomimetic drugs, LSD-25***).

psychoanalysis. (1) The method developed by Freud and extended by his followers for treating neuroses. (2) The system of psychological theory growing out of experiences with the psychoanalytic method.

psychoanalyst. A psychotherapist, now usually trained as a psychiatrist, who uses methods related to those originally proposed by Freud for treating neuroses and other mental disorders (cf. ***psychiatrist, clinical psychologist***).

psychodrama. A form of spontaneous play acting used in psychotherapy.

psychogenic. Caused by psychological factors (e.g., emotional conflict, faulty habits) rather than by disease, injury, or other somatic cause; functional rather than organic.

psychograph. Cf. ***trait profile.***

psychokinesis (PK). A claimed form of mental operation said to affect a material body or an energy system without any evidence of more usual contact or energy transfer, e.g., affecting the number that comes up in the throw of dice by a machine through wishing for that number (cf. ***extrasensory perception***).

psycholinguistics. The study of the psychological aspects of language and its acquisition.

psychological motive. A motive that is primarily learned rather than based on biological needs.

psychological primaries. Hues that appear to be pure, i.e., not composed of other hues. Most authorities choose a particular red, yellow, green, and blue. (The red-green and blue-yellow pairs chosen in this way are not complementary colors.) (cf. ***color-mixing primaries***).

psychology. The science that studies behavior and mental processes.

psychopathic personality. A type of character disorder marked by impulsivity, inability to abide by the customs and laws of society, and lack of anxiety or guilt regarding behavior (syn. *antisocial personality*).

psychopharmacology. The study of the effects of drugs on behavior.

psychophysical function. A curve relating the likelihood of a response to the intensity of the presented stimulus.

psychophysical methods. Experimental and statistical methods for determining absolute thresholds, difference thresholds, and scale values for stimuli that can be arranged along a physical continuum (cf. ***threshold***).

psychophysics. A name used by Fechner for the science of the relationship between mental processes and the physical world. Now usually restricted to the study of the sensory consequences of controlled physical stimulation (cf. ***psychophysical methods***).

psychophysiological disorder. A physical illness that has psychological causes (syn. *psychosomatic disorder*).

psychosexual development. In psychoanalysis, the theory that development takes place through stages (oral, anal, phallic, latent, genital), each stage characterized by a zone of pleasurable stimulation and appropriate objects of sexual attachment, culminating in normal heterosexual mating (cf. ***oral stage, anal stage, phallic stage, latency, genital stage, psychosocial crises***).

psychosocial crises. A modification by Erikson of the psychoanalytic theory of psychosexual development, giving more attention to the social and environmental problems associated with the various stages of development, and adding some adult stages beyond genital maturing (cf. ***psychosexual development***).

psychosomatic disorders. Cf. ***psychophysiological disorder.***

psychotherapy. Treatment of personality maladjustment or mental illness by psychological means, usually, but not exclusively, through personal consultation (cf. ***somatotherapy***).

psychosis. Mental illness in which the patient shows severe change or disorganization of personality, often accompanied by agitation or depression, delusions, hallucinations; commonly requires hospitalization (syn. *psychosis,* pl. *psychoses;* cf. ***functional psychosis, organic psychosis***).

psychotomimetic drugs. Drugs that produce psychotic symptoms (cf. ***LSD-25***).

puberty. The climax of pubescence, marked by menstruation in girls and the appearance of live sperm cells in the urine of boys (cf. ***adolescence***).

punishment. A negative incentive, capable of producing pain or annoyance (cf. ***reward***).

pupillary response. The constriction or dilation of the pupil of the eye, brought about either by changes in illumination or as an emotional accompaniment.

pursuit learning. A laboratory task in which the subject learns to keep the point of a hinged stylus in contact with a small metal target mounted on a rotating turntable.

range. The variation of scores in a frequency distribution from the lowest to the highest. A value that grows larger as the number of cases increases, hence to be used with extreme caution (cf. ***measure of variation***).

rank correlation (ρ). A correlation computed from ranked data. The coefficient is designated by the small Greek letter rho (ρ) to distinguish it from the product-moment correlation (r), of which it is an approximation (cf. ***coefficient of correlation***).

rapid eye movements (REMs). Eye movements that usually occur during dreaming and that can be measured by attaching small electrodes laterally to and above the subject's eye. These register changes in electrical activity associated with movements of the eyeball in its socket.

rapport. (1) A comfortable relationship between the subject and the tester, ensuring cooperation in replying to test questions. (2) A similar relationship between therapist and patient. (3) A special relationship of hypnotic subject to hypnotist.

rating scale. A device by which a rater can record his judgment of another person (or of himself) on the traits defined by the scale.

rationalization. A defense mechanism in which self-esteem is maintained by assigning plausible and acceptable reasons for conduct entered upon impulsively or for less acceptable reasons (cf. ***defense mechanism***).

reaction-formation. A defense mechanism in which a subject denies a disapproved motive through giving strong expression to its opposite (cf. ***defense mechanism***).

reaction time. The time between the presentation of a stimulus and the occurrence of a response (cf. ***latency***).

recall. The form of remembering in which the subject demonstrates retention by repeating what was earlier learned, e.g., demonstrating recall of a poem by reciting it (cf. ***recognition, redintegrative memory, relearning***).

receiver-operating-characteristic curve (ROC curve). The function relating the probability of hits and false alarms for a fixed signal level in a detection task. Factors influencing response bias may cause hits and false alarms to vary, but their variation is constrained to the ROC curve (cf. ***signal detection task***).

recency effect. (1) In memory experiments, the tendency for the last words in a list to be recalled more readily than other list words. (2) In studies of impression formation or attitude change, the tendency for later information to carry more weight than earlier information (cf. ***primacy effect***).

receptor. A specialized portion of the body sensitive to particular kinds of stimuli and connected with sensory nerves, e.g., the retina of the eye. Used more loosely, the organ containing these sensitive portions, e.g., the eye or the ear (cf. ***effector***).

recessive gene. A member of a gene pair that determines the characteristic trait or appearance of the individual only if the other member of the pair is recessive. If the other member of the pair is dominant, the effect of the recessive gene is masked (cf. ***dominant gene***).

recognition. That form of remembering indicated by a feeling of familiarity when something previously encountered is again perceived (cf. ***recall, redintegrative memory, relearning***).

recurrent inhibition. A process whereby some receptors in the visual system when stimulated by nerve impulses inhibit the firing of other visual receptors, thus making the visual system responsive to changes in illumination.

red-green color blindness. The commonest form of color blindness, a variety of dichromatism. In the two sub-varieties, red-blindness and green-blindness, both red and green vision are lacking, but achromatic bands are seen at different parts of the spectrum (cf. ***color blindness, dichromatism***).

redintegrative memory. Remembering the whole of an earlier experience on the basis of partial cues; recollection of events in the personal history of the subject, with their attendant circumstances (cf. ***recall, recognition, relearning***).

reference group. Any group to which an individual refers for comparing, judging, and deciding on his opinions and behaviors.

reflex action. A relatively simple response largely under the control of a specific stimulus, occurring rather mechanically, such as the pupillary response to light or the knee-jerk from a tap on the tendon below the knee. Other examples of reflex action are sneezing, perspiring, and the beating of the heart (cf. ***respondent behavior***).

refractory phase. The period of temporary inactivity in a neuron after it has once fired.

regression. A return to more primitive or infantile modes of response, either (1) retrogression to behavior engaged in when younger, or (2) primitivation, i.e., more infantile or childlike behavior, but not necessarily that which occurred in the individual's earlier life.

rehearsal buffer. The array of information that is undergoing rehearsal and consequently being continuously regenerated in short-term memory. The process facilitates the short-term recall of information and its transfer to long-term memory.

reinforcement. (1) In classical conditioning, the experimental procedure of following the conditioned stimulus by the unconditioned stimulus. (2) In operant conditioning, the analogous procedure of following the occurrence of the operant response by the reinforcing stimulus. (3) The process that increases the strength of conditioning as a result of these arrangements (cf. ***classical conditioning, operant conditioning, extinction***).

reinforcing stimulus. (1) In classical conditioning, the unconditioned stimulus. (2) In operant conditioning, the stimulus that reinforces the operant (typically, a reward).

relearning. That form of remembering in which the subject demonstrates memory for something previously learned through the saving in time or trials required for learning the material again (cf. ***recall, recognition, redintegrative memory***).

releaser. A term used by ethologists for a stimulus that sets off a cycle of instinctive behavior (cf. ***ethologist, instinct***).

reliability. The self-consistency of a test as a measuring instrument. Reliability is measured by a coefficient of correlation between scores on two halves of a test, alternate forms of the test, or retests with the same test, a high correlation signifying high consistency of scores for the population tested (cf. ***validity***).

REMs. Cf. ***rapid eye movements.***

repression. (1) A defense mechanism in which an impulse or memory that might provoke feelings of guilt is denied by its disappearance from awareness (cf. ***defense mechanism, suppression***). (2) A theory of forgetting (cf. ***motivated forgetting***).

reserpine. Cf. ***tranquilizer.***

resistance. In psychoanalysis, a blocking of free association; a psychological barrier against bringing unconscious impulses to the level of awareness. Resistance is part of the process of maintaining repression (cf. ***repression, interpretation***).

respondent. (1) One who responds; used chiefly to refer to those interviewed in public opinion surveys. (2) A class of responses (cf. ***respondent behavior***).

respondent behavior. A type of behavior corresponding to reflex action, in that it is largely under the control of, and predictable from, the stimulus (syn. *elicited behavior;* cf. ***operant behavior***).

response. (1) The behavioral result of stimulation in the form of a movement or glandular secretion. (2) Sometimes, any activity of the organism, including central responses (such as an image or fantasy), regardless of whether the stimulus is identified and whether identifiable movements occur. (3) Products of the organism's activity, such as words typed per minute.

retention curve. A curve plotted with some measure of remembering on the vertical axis and the elapsed time since learning on the horizontal axis. The curve tends to fall rapidly at first, then more slowly, though this is not invariable.

reticular activating system (RAS). A system of ill-defined nerve paths and connections within the brain stem, lying outside the well-defined nerve pathways, and important as an arousal mechanism.

retina. The portion of the eye sensitive to light, containing the rods and the cones (cf. ***rod, cone***).

retinal disparity. The fact that an object projects slightly different images on the two retinas due to the different positions of the right and left eyes (syn. *binocular disparity*).

retrieval. Locating information in memory.
retroactive inhibition. (1) The interference in recall of something earlier learned by something subsequently learned. (2) The theory of forgetting which proposes that much, or most, forgetting is due to the interference by new learning with the recall of the old (cf. ***proactive inhibition, transfer of learning***).
retrograde amnesia. The inability to recall events that occurred during a period of time immediately prior to a shock or functional disturbance, although the memory for earlier events remains relatively unimpaired.
retrogression. Cf. ***regression.***
reward. A positive incentive capable of arousing pleasure or satisfying a drive; a reinforcing stimulus (cf. ***punishment***).
rhodopsin. A light-sensitive substance contained in the rods of the eye (syn. *visual purple*).
ribonucleic acid (RNA). Complex molecules that control cellular functions; theorized by some to be the chemical mediator of memory.
RNA. Cf. ***ribonucleic acid.***
ROC. Cf. ***receiver-operating-characteristic curve.***
rod. In the eye, an element of the retina mediating achromatic sensation only; particularly important in peripheral vision and night vision (cf. ***retina, cone***).
role. By analogy with an actor's role, the kind of behavior expected of an individual because of his place within social arrangements, e.g., the male role, the mother's role, the lawyer's role. Any one person fulfills or adopts numerous roles on varied occasions.
role diffusion. A stage of development said by Erikson to characterize many adolescents (and others) in which various identifications with others have not been harmonized and integrated (cf. ***identification, identity formation***).
role playing. A method for teaching principles affecting interpersonal relations by having the subject assume a part in a spontaneous play, whether in psychotherapy or in leadership training (cf. ***psychodrama***).
rote memorization. Verbatim learning, as in learning a poem "by heart" (cf. ***paired-associate learning, serial memorization***).

saccule. Cf. ***vestibular sacs.***
sadism. A pathological motive that leads to inflicting pain upon another person (cf. ***masochism***).
sample. A selection of scores from a total set of scores known as the "population." If selection is random, an unbiased sample results; if selection is nonrandom, the sample is biased and unrepresentative (cf. ***population***).
sampling errors. The variation in a distribution of scores, or of statistics derived from them, to be attributed to the fact that measurements are made on a variable sample from a larger population. Thus sampling errors persist even though all measurements are accurate (cf. ***errors of measurement, sample***).
saturation. The dimension of color that describes its purity; if highly saturated it appears to be pure hue and free of gray, but if of low saturation it appears to have a great deal of gray mixed with it (cf. ***brightness, hue***).
saving score. A measure of retention: a percentage showing the amount of time saved in relearning material to the original criterion.
scale. A set of ascending or descending values used to designate a position or an interval along a dimension. Thus a ruler may have a scale in inches, a test a scale in I.Q. units.
scaling. Converting raw data into types of scores more readily interpreted, e.g., into ranks, centiles, standard scores (cf. ***attitude scale***).
scapegoating. A form of displaced aggression in which an innocent but helpless victim is blamed or punished as the source of the scapegoater's frustration (cf. ***displaced aggression***).
schedule of reinforcement. A well-defined procedure for reinforcing a given response only some proportion of the time it occurs (cf. ***partial reinforcement***).
schizophrenia. A functional psychotic disorder in which there is a lack of harmony or split between aspects of personality functioning, especially between emotion and behavior. Symptoms may include autism, hallucinations, and delusions (cf. ***psychosis***).
school of psychology. An all-embracing system designed to encompass the data of psychology according to a limited set of principles and procedures. Such schools are not as prominent today as they once were (syn. *system of psychology;* cf. ***behaviorism, Gestalt psychology, psychoanalysis, S-R psychology***).
school psychologist. A professional psychologist employed by a school or school system, with responsibility for testing, guidance, research, etc. (cf. ***educational psychologist***).
secondary reinforcer. A stimulus that has become reinforcing through prior association with a reinforcing stimulus (cf. ***reinforcing stimulus***).
secondary sex characteristics. The physical features distinguishing the mature male from the mature female, apart from the reproductive organs. In man, the deeper voice of the male and the growth of the beard are illustrative (cf. ***primary sex characteristics***).
second-order conditioning. Conditioning in which what was previously the conditioned stimulus now serves as the unconditioned or reinforcing stimulus (cf. ***secondary reinforcer***).
selective breeding. A method of studying genetic influences by mating animals that display certain traits and selecting for breeding from among their offspring those that express the trait. If the trait is primarily determined by heredity, continued selection for a number of generations will produce a strain that breeds true for that trait.
selectivity. The perceptual response to parts of incoming stimuli and the ignoring of others (cf. ***attention***).
self-actualization. A person's fundamental tendency toward maximal realization of his potentials; a basic concept in humanistic theories of personality such as those developed by Maslow and Rogers.
self-concept. The composite of ideas, feelings, and attitudes a person has about himself.
self-consciousness. A form of heightened self-awareness when an individual is especially concerned about reactions of others to him.
self-deception. Behavior, the motives of which are unconscious or inadequately perceived by the person himself because of (1) denial of the true motives, or (2) disguise of these motives (cf. ***defense mechanism***).
self-perception. The individual's awareness of himself; differs from self-consciousness because it may take the form of objective self-appraisal (cf. ***self-consciousness***).
self-perception theory. The theory that attitudes and beliefs are influenced by observations of one's own behavior; sometimes we judge how we feel by observing how we act (Bem).
self-persuasion. The process by which an individual changes his opinion so that it is consistent with his behavior.
semantic differential. A method developed by Osgood for using rating scales and factor analysis in studying the connotative meanings of words (cf. ***connotative meaning***).
semantic memory. Memory necessary for the use of language.
semicircular canals. Three curved tubular canals, in three planes, which form part of the labyrinth of the inner ear and are concerned with equilibrium and motion.

sensorimotor task. A multiple-response task in which muscular movement is prominent, e.g., riding a bicycle, playing a piano. Laboratory sensorimotor tasks include mazes, mirror drawing, pursuit learning, etc. (cf. ***multiple-response learning***).

sensory adaptation. The reduction in sensitivity that occurs with prolonged stimulation and the increase in sensitivity that occurs with lack of stimulation; most noted in vision, smell, taste, and temperature sensitivity (cf. ***dark adaptation, light adaptation***).

septal area. A portion of the brain deep in the central part, between the lateral ventricles, which when stimulated electrically (in the rat, at least) appears to yield a state akin to pleasure.

serial memorization. That form of rote memorization in which a list of items, or a passage of prose or poetry, is learned in sequence from begeinning to end, so that each item or word is a cue to the one that follows it (cf. ***paired-associate learning***).

serial position effect. The difficulty in memorization and recall resulting from position of items within a list to be learned and remembered. The point of maximum difficulty is just after the middle of the list.

set. (1) A preparatory adjustment or readiness for a particular kind of action or experience, usually as a result of instructions, e.g., the set to respond with a word opposite in meaning to the stimulus word in an experiment on controlled association. (2) A habitual tendency to respond in a particular manner.

sex gland. As duct glands, the sex glands are active in mating behavior, but as endocrine glands their hormones affect secondary sex characteristics as well as maintaining functional sexual activity. The male hormones are known as androgens, the female hormones as estrogens (syn. *gonads;* cf. ***endocrine gland***).

sex-linked trait. A trait determined by a gene transmitted with the same chromosomes that determine sex, e.g., red-green color blindness (cf. ***X-, Y-chromosome***).

sex-role standards. Behavior that a society considers appropriate for the individual because of his sex.

shape constancy. The tendency to see a familiar object as of the same shape regardless of the viewing angle (cf. ***object constancy***).

shaping of behavior. Modifying operant behavior by reinforcing only those variations in response that deviate in a direction desired by the experimenter; the whole population of responses thus reinforced then drifts in the desired direction (Skinner) (syn. *method of approximations*).

shock therapy. A form of treatment of mental illness, especially in the relief of depression (cf: ***electroconvulsive shock therapy, insulin shock***).

short-term memory (STM). The assumption that certain components of the memory system have limited capacity and will maintain information for only a brief period of time. The precise definition varies somewhat from theory to theory (cf. ***long-term memory***).

sibling. A brother or a sister.

sibling rivalry. Jealousy between siblings, often based on their competition for parental affection.

signal detection task. A procedure whereby the subject must judge on each trial whether or not a weak signal was embedded in a noise background. Saying "yes" when a signal was presented is called a hit and saying "yes" when the signal was not presented is called a false alarm (cf. ***receiver-operating-characteristic curve***).

signal detectability theory. A theory of the sensory and decision processes involved in psychophysical judgments, with special reference to the problem of detecting weak signals in noise (cf. ***signal detection task***).

sign learning. An acquired expectation that one stimulus (the sign) will be followed by another (the significate) provided a familiar behavior route is followed. This interpretation of learning, by Tolman, is considered by him an alternative to the interpretation of learning as habit formation (cf. ***latent-learning experiment, place-learning experiment***).

simulation. The representation of the essential elements of some phenomenon, system, or environment to facilitate its study (often by or involving an automatic computer).

simultaneous conditioning. a classical conditioning procedure in which the CS begins a fraction of a second before the onset of the US and continues with it until the response occurs (cf. ***delayed conditioning, trace conditioning***).

sine wave. A cyclical wave that when plotted corresponds to the plot of the trigonometric sine function. The sound waves of pure tones yield this function when plotted.

situational attribution. Attributing a person's actions to factors in the situation or environment, as opposed to internal attitudes and motives (cf. ***dispositional attribution***).

size constancy. The tendency to see a familiar object as of its actual size regardless of its distance (cf. ***object constancy***).

skewed distribution. A frequency distribution that is not symmetrical. It is named for the direction in which the tail lies; e.g., if there are many small incomes and a few large ones, the distribution is skewed in the direction of the large incomes (cf. ***frequency distribution, symmetrical distribution***).

smooth muscle. The type of muscle found in the digestive organs, blood vessels, and other internal organs. Controlled via the autonomic nervous system (cf. ***cardiac muscle, striate muscle***).

social facilitation. The enhancement of individual performance brought about by the social presence of other persons.

social indicators. Measures that help evaluate the social aspects of a nation's life, including such areas as health, education, and public safety. Crime rate, incidence of mental disorders, and literacy rate would be examples.

social learning theory. The application of learning theory to the problems of personal and social behavior (syn. *social behavior theory*).

social norms. A society's unwritten rules that govern its members' behavior, attitudes, and beliefs.

social psychologist. A psychologist whose research interest lies in the behavior of the individual as he influences and is influenced by other individuals in a social environment.

socialization. The shaping of individual characteristics and behavior through the training that the social environment provides.

sociology. The behavioral or social science dealing with group life and social organization in literate societies (cf. ***behavioral sciences***).

somatotherapy. Treatment of personality maladjustment or mental illness by drugs, electric shock, or other methods directly affecting bodily processes (cf. ***psychotherapy, chemotherapy***).

spaced practice. An arrangement of learning trials in which there is a time interval between trials, as opposed to immediately consecutive trials (syn. *distributed practice;* cf. ***massed practice***).

spastic paralysis. A condition of excessive isotonic muscular contraction, commonly due to a brain injury at birth (syn. *cerebral palsy*).

specific hunger. Hunger for a specific food incentive, such as a craving for sweets (cf. ***hunger drive***).

split-brain preparation. A deep vertical incision through the corpus callosum in an animal's brain that separates most of the two hemispheres. It is used to study the bilateral transfer of training (cf. ***corpus callosum***).

spontaneous recovery. The return in strength of a conditioned response after a lapse of time following extinction (cf. ***extinction***).

S-R psychology. Cf. ***stimulus-response psychology.***

stabilized retinal image. The image of an object on the retina when special techniques are used to counteract the minute movements of the eyeball that occur in normal vision. When an image is thus stabilized it quickly disappears, suggesting that the changes in stimulation of retinal cells provided by eye movements are necessary for vision.

stages of development. Developmental periods, usually following a progressive sequence, that appear to represent qualitative changes in either the structure or the function of the organism (e.g., Freud's psychosexual stages, Piaget's cognitive stages).

standard deviation. The square root of the mean of the squares of the amount by which each case departs from the mean of all the cases (syn. *root mean square deviation;* cf. ***measure of variation, standard error, standard score***).

standard error. The standard deviation of the sampling distribution of a mean and of certain other derived statistics. It can be interpreted as any other standard deviation (cf. ***standard deviation***).

standard error of estimate. The standard error of the differences between predicted values and true values of some measure; used, for example, in interpreting a coefficient of correlation.

standard score. (1) A score that has been converted to a scale of measurement with a mean of zero and a standard deviation of 1.0, based on a distribution of scores used in calibration. (2) A score based on standard scores but converted to another scale for convenience, e.g., with a mean of 50 and a standard deviation of 10.

stanine score. A U.S. Air Force type of standard score (originally, "standard nine"), with a mean of five and standard deviation of two. Scores range from one through nine (cf. ***standard score***).

statistical inference. A statement about a population or populations based on statistical measures derived from samples (cf. ***descriptive statistics***).

statistical significance. The trustworthiness of an obtained statistical measure as a statement about reality, e.g., the probability that the population mean falls within the limits determined from a sample. The expression refers to the reliability of the statistical finding and not to its importance.

stereophonic hearing. The binaural perception of the distance and direction of a sound source owing to the difference in reception by the two ears.

stereoscopic vision. (1) The binocular perception of depth and distance of an object owing to the overlapping fields of the two eyes. (2) The equivalent effect when slightly unlike pictures are presented individually to each eye in a stereoscope (cf. ***distance cues***).

stereotype. A biased generalization, usually about a social or national group, according to which individuals are falsely assigned traits they do not possess. Thus a person may have a stereotyped conception of the Italians or Scots that distorts his perception of any individual Italian or Scot.

stereotypy. The continued repetition of behavior that appears to serve no realistic purpose and may, in fact, be punished: inflexible behavior, which may be a consequence of frustration (cf. ***frustration***).

steroids. Complex chemical substances, some of which are prominent in the secretions of the adrenal cortex and may be related to some forms of mental illness (cf. ***adrenal gland***).

stimulus (pl. **stimuli**). (1) Some specific physical energy impinging upon a receptor sensitive to that kind of energy. (2) Any objectively describable situation or event (whether outside or inside the organism) that is the occasion for an organism's response (cf. ***response***).

stimulus-response psychology. A psychological view that all behavior is in response to stimuli and that the appropriate tasks of psychological science are those identifying stimuli, the responses correlated with them, and the processes intervening between stimulus and response. There are several varieties of stimulus-response (S-R) theory, depending on the kind of intervening processes inferred (cf. ***intervening variables***).

stimulus substitution. Cf. ***classical conditioning.***

STM. Cf. ***short-term memory.***

striate area. Cf. ***visual area.***

striate muscle. Striped muscle; the characteristic muscles controlling the skeleton, as in the arms and legs. Activated by the somatic, as opposed to the autonomic, nervous system (cf. ***cardiac muscle, smooth muscle***).

stroboscopic motion. An illusion of motion resulting from the successive presentation of discrete stimulus patterns arranged in a progression corresponding to movement, e.g., motion pictures (cf. ***phi phenomenon***).

subjective scoring. Test scoring requiring complex judgments by the scorer, as in the grading of essay examinations (cf. ***objective scoring***).

sublimation. A form of the defense mechanism of substitution, whereby socially unacceptable motives find expression in socially acceptable forms; most commonly applied to the sublimation of sexual desires (cf. ***substitution, compensation***).

substitution. A defense mechanism whereby the person maintains self-esteem by substituting approved goals for unapproved ones and activities that can be carried out successfully for activities doomed to failure (cf. ***sublimation, compensation***).

subtractive mixture. Color mixture in which absorption occurs, so that results differ from additive mixture obtained by rotating colors on a color wheel or by mixing projected lights. Subtractive mixture occurs when transparent colored filters are placed one in front of the other, and when pigments are mixed (cf. ***additive mixture***).

superego. In Freud's tripartite division of the personality, that part corresponding most nearly to conscience, controlling through moral scruples rather than by way of social expediency. The superego is said to be an uncompromising and punishing conscience (cf. ***id, ego***).

suppression. A process of self-control in which impulses, tendencies to action, wishes to perform disapproved acts, etc., are in awareness, but not overtly revealed (cf. ***repression***).

surface structure. In linguistics the sound sequence of a sentence (cf. ***deep structure***).

survey method. A method of obtaining information by questioning a large sample of people.

symbol. Anything that stands for or refers to something other than itself.

symmetrical distribution. A frequency distribution in which cases fall equally in the class intervals on either side of the middle; hence the mean, median, and mode fall together (cf. ***frequency distribution, skewed distribution***).

sympathetic division. A division of the autonomic nervous system, characterized by a chain of ganglia on either side of the spinal cord, with nerve fibers originating in the thoracic and lumbar portions of the spinal cord. Active in emotional excitement and to some extent antagonistic to the parasympathetic division (q.v.).

synapse. Cf. ***synaptic nervous system.***

synaptic nervous system. A nervous system characteristic of all higher organisms, in which nerve cells are distinct and conduction is polarized, that is, occurs only in one direction across the junction between nerve cells called a synapse.

systematic desensitization. A behavior therapy technique in which hierarchies of anxiety-producing situations are imagined (or sometimes confronted in reality) while the person is in a state of deep relaxation. Gradually the situations become dissociated from the anxiety response (cf. ***behavior therapy, counter-conditioning***).

tachistoscope. An instrument for the brief exposure of words, symbols, pictures, or other visually presented material; sometimes called a T-scope.

teaching machine. A device to provide self-instruction by means of a program proceeding in steps following each other at a rate determined by the learner; the machine is arranged to provide knowledge about the correctness or incorrectness of each reply.

telegraphic speech. A stage in the development of speech where the child preserves only the most meaningful and perceptually salient elements of adult speech. He tends to omit prepositions, articles, prefixes, suffixes, and auxiliary words.

telepathy. The claimed form of extrasensory perception in which what is perceived depends upon thought transference from one person to another (cf. ***extrasensory perception, clairvoyance, precognition***).

temperament. That aspect of personality revealed in the tendency to experience moods or mood changes in characteristic ways; general level of reactivity and energy.

temporal lobe. A portion of the cerebral hemisphere, at the side below the lateral fissure and in front of the occipital lobe (cf. ***frontal lobe, occipital lobe, parietal lobe***).

test. A collection of items (questions, tasks, etc.) so arranged that replies or performances can be scored and the scores used in appraising individual differences.

test battery. A collection of tests whose composite scores are used to appraise individual differences.

test method. A method of psychological investigation. Its advantages are that it allows the psychologist to collect large quantities of useful data from many people, with a minimum of disturbance of their routines of existence and with a minimum of laboratory equipment.

testosterone. The male sex hormone produced by the testes; it is important for the growth of the male sex organs and the development of the secondary male sex characteristics. It influences the sex drive.

test profile. A chart plotting scores from a number of tests given to the same individual (or group of individuals) in parallel rows on a common scale, with the scores connected by lines, so that high and low scores can be readily perceived (cf. ***trait profile***).

test standardization. The establishment of norms for interpreting scores by giving a test to a representative population and by making appropriate studies of its reliability and validity (cf. ***norm, reliability, validity***).

theory. A set of assumptions (axioms) advanced to explain existing data and predict new events; usually applicable to a wide array of phenomena and experimental situations.

thinking. Behavior carried on in terms of ideas (representational or symbolic processes); ideational problem-solving as distinguished from solution through overt manipulation.

threshold. The transitional point at which an increasing stimulus or an increasing difference not previously perceived becomes perceptible (or at which a decreasing stimulus or previously perceived difference becomes imperceptible). The value obtained depends in part upon the methods used in determining it (cf. ***absolute threshold, difference threshold, psychophysical methods***).

thyroid gland. An endocrine gland located in the neck, whose hormone thyroxin is important in determining metabolic rate (cf. ***endocrine gland***).

thyroxin. The hormone of the thyroid gland (cf. ***thyroid gland***).

timbre. The quality distinguishing a tone of a given pitch sounded by one instrument from that sounded by another. The differences are due to overtones and other impurities (cf. ***overtone***).

tip-of-the-tongue phenomenon. The experience of failing to recall a word or name when we are quite certain we know it.

T-maze. An apparatus in which an animal is presented with two alternative paths, one of which leads to a goal box. It is usually used with rats and lower organisms (cf. ***maze***).

token learning. An arrangement within operant conditioning in which a token (e.g., a poker chip) as a secondary reinforcer can be exchanged for a primary reinforcing stimulus (e.g., food).

trace conditioning. A classical conditioning procedure in which the CS terminates before the onset of the US (cf. ***simultaneous conditioning, delayed conditioning***).

trace-dependent forgetting. The proposition that information stored in memory decays over time; the rate of decay may depend on both the elapsed time and the intervening activity (cf. ***cue-dependent forgetting***).

trait. A persisting characteristic or dimension of personality according to which individuals can be rated or measured (cf. ***trait profile***).

trait profile. A chart plotting the ratings of a number of traits of the same individual on a common scale in parallel rows, so that the pattern of traits can be visually perceived (syn. *psychograph;* cf. ***trait, test profile***).

trait theory. The theory that human personality is most profitably characterized by the scores that an individual makes on a number of scales, each of which represents a trait or dimension of his personality.

transcendental meditation. A form of meditation practiced by some who follow Hindu yoga. The meditative state is induced by repeating a particular sound or phrase, called a mantra, over and over again. Each individual has his own mantra selected as most appropriate for him.

tranquilizer. A drug such as chlorpromazine or reserpine used to reduce anxiety and relieve depression; hence useful in the therapy of mental disorders.

transfer of learning. The effect of prior learning on present learning. If learning a new task is facilitated, transfer is positive; if the new learning is interfered with, transfer is negative (cf. ***formal discipline***).

transfer through principles. A theory of transfer of learning that proposes that new learning is facilitated by detecting the applicability of principles or generalizations discovered in prior learning (cf. ***transfer of learning***).

transference. In psychoanalysis, the patient's unconsciously making the therapist the object of emotional response, thus transferring to him responses appropriate to other persons important in the life history of the patient.

traveling wave theory. A modification by Békésy of the place theory of hearing. The theory states that when a sound of given frequency enters the ear, a wave travels along the basilar membrane and displaces it a maximum amount at a certain point, the point depending on its frequency (cf. ***basilar membrane, frequency theory, place theory, volley theory***).

trend analysis. A method of forecasting the future based on past events, e.g., predicting the number of people that will be killed in automobile accidents this year on the basis of the number killed in previous years and the expected increase in the number of drivers (cf. ***Delphi method, cross-impact matrix method***).

trial-and-error learning. An expression characterizing multiple-response learning, in which the proper response is selected out of varied behavior through the influence of reward and punishment. Variously described as approximation and correction, fumble and success, etc. (cf. ***multiple-response learning, operant conditioning***).

trichromatism. Normal color vision, based on the classification of color vision according to three color systems: black-white, blue-yellow, and red-green. The normal eye sees all three; the colorblind eye is defective in one or two of the three systems (cf. ***dichromatism, monochromatism***).

t-test. A preferred measure for interpreting the significance of differences with small samples; for large samples, equivalent to critical ratio (cf. ***critical ratio, statistical significance***).

Turner's syndrome. An abnormal condition of the sex chromosomes in which a female is born with one X chromosome instead of the usual XX.

type theory. The theory that human subjects can profitably be classified into a small number of classes or types, each class or type having characteristics in common that set its members apart from other classes or types (cf. ***trait theory***).

unconditioned response. The response given originally to the unconditioned stimulus used as the basis for establishing a conditioned response to a previously neutral stimulus (cf. ***conditioned response***).

unconscious motive. A motive of which the subject is unaware, or aware of in distorted form. Because there is no sharp dividing line between conscious and unconscious, many motives have both conscious and unconscious aspects.

unconscious processes. (1) Processes, such as wishes or fears, that might be conscious but of which the subject is unaware. (2) Less commonly, physiological processes of the body (circulation, metabolism, etc.) that go on outside of awareness (cf. ***conscious processes***).

undoing. A defense mechanism whereby a person wards off anxiety by ritualistic action designed to prevent or atone for some unacceptable thought or impulse; similar to superstitious acts (cf. ***defense mechanism***).

validity. The predictive significance of a test for its intended purposes. Validity can be measured by a coefficient of correlation between scores on the test and the scores that the test seeks to predict, i.e., scores on some criterion (cf. ***criterion, reliability***).

variable. One of the conditions measured or controlled in an experiment (cf. ***dependent variable, independent variable***).

variance. The square of a standard deviation.

ventromedial hypothalamus. Area of the hypothalamus important to the regulation of food intake. Electrical stimulation of this area will make an experimental animal stop eating; destruction of brain tissue here produces voracious eating, eventually leading to obesity (cf. ***hypothalamus, lateral hypothalamus***).

vestibular sacs. Two sacs in the labyrinth of the inner ear, called the saccule and utricle, which contain the otoliths ("ear stones"). Pressure of the otoliths on the hair cells in the gelatinous material of the utricle and saccule gives us the sense of upright position or departure from it (cf. ***equilibratory senses***).

vicarious learning. Learning by observing the behavior of others and noting the consequences of that behavior.

visual area. A projection area lying in the occipital lobe. In man, partial damage to this area produces blindness in portions of the visual field corresponding to the amount and location of the damage (syn. ***striate area***).

visual field. The total visual stimuli acting upon the eye when it is directed toward a fixation point.

visual purple. Cf. ***rhodopsin.***

volley theory. A modified frequency theory of hearing proposed by Wever and Bray suggesting that the frequency of the stimulus may be represented in bundles of fibers in the auditory nerve responding somewhat independently, so that the frequency is represented by the composite volley, even though no single fiber carries impulses at that rate (cf. ***frequency theory, place theory, traveling wave theory***).

volumetric receptors. Hypothesized receptors that regulate water intake by responding to the volume of blood and body fluids. Renin, a substance secreted by the kidneys into the bloodstream, may be one volumetric receptor; it constricts the blood vessels and stimulates the release of the hormone, angiotensin, which acts on cells in the hypothalamus to produce thirst (cf. ***osmoreceptors***).

Weber's law. A law stating that the difference threshold is proportional to the stimulus magnitude at which it is measured. It is known to be accurate only over limited stimulus ranges (cf. ***difference threshold***).

word-association experiment. An experiment designed for studying associative processes in which the subject responds to a stimulus word by saying as promptly as possible the first word that he thinks of (cf. ***free association, controlled association***).

working through. In psychoanalytic therapy, the process of reeducation by having the patient face the same conflicts over and over again in the consultation room, until he can independently face and master the conflicts in ordinary life.

X-chromosome. A chromosome that, if paired with another X-chromosome, determines that the individual will be a female. If it is combined with a Y-chromosome, the individual will be a male. The X-chromosome transmits sex-linked traits (cf. ***chromosome, sex-linked trait, Y-chromosome***).

XYY syndrome. An abnormal condition in which a male has an extra Y sex chromosome; reputedly associated with unusual aggressiveness, although the evidence is not conclusive.

Y-chromosome. The chromosome that, combined with an X-chromosome, determines maleness (cf. ***chromosome, sex-linked trait, X-chromosome***).

Young-Helmholtz theory. A theory of color perception that postulates three basic color receptors, a "red" receptor, a "green" receptor, and a "blue" receptor.

references and index to authors of works cited

The numbers in *bold face* following each reference give the text pages on which the paper or book is cited. Citations in the text are made by author and date of publication.

ABELSON, R. P., ARONSON, E., MCGUIRE, W. J., NEWCOMB, T. M., ROSENBERG, M. J., and TANNENBAUM, P. H. (eds.) (1968) *Theories of cognitive consistency: A sourcebook.* Chicago: Rand McNally. **556**

ABELSON, R. P., see LEPPER, ZANNA, and ABELSON (1970).

ABRAHAMS, D., see WALSTER, ARONSON, ABRAHAMS, and ROTTMANN (1966).

ADELSON, J., see DOUVAN and ADELSON (1966).

ADLER, C., see BUDZYNSKI, STOYVA, and ADLER (1970).

ADOLPH, E. F. (1941) The internal environment and behavior: Water content. *American Journal of Psychiatry,* 97:1365–73. **316, 317**

AGNEW, H. W., Jr., see WEBB and AGNEW (1968); see WEBB and AGNEW (1973); see WEBB, AGNEW, and WILLIAMS (1971).

AINSWORTH, M. D. S. (1973) Anxious attachment and defensive reactions in a strange situation and their relationship to behavior at home. Paper presented at meeting of the Society for Research in Child Development, Philadelphia, March 30, 1973. **83**

AKERFELDT, S. (1957) Oxidation of N, N-dimethyl-p-phenylenediamine by serum from patients with mental disease. *Science,* 125:117–19. **481**

ALFERT, E., see LAZARUS and ALFERT (1964).

ALLEN, A., see BEM and ALLEN (1974).

ALLEN, K. E., HART, B. M., BUELL, J. S., HARRIS, F. R., and WOLF, M. M. (1964) Effects of social reinforcement on isolate behavior of a nursery school child. *Child Development,* 35:511–18. **388**

ALLEN, V. L., and LEVIN, J. M. (1971) Social support and conformity: The role of independent assessment of reality. *Journal of Experimental Social Psychology,* 7:48–58. **552**

ALLPORT, F. H. (1920) The influence of the group upon association and thought. *Journal of Experimental Psychology,* 3:159–82. **544**

ALLPORT, F. H. (1924) *Social psychology.* Boston: Houghton Mifflin. **544**

ALLPORT, G. W. (1954) *The nature of prejudice.* Reading, Mass.: Addison-Wesley. **536**

ALTUS, W. C. (1966) Birth order and its sequelae. *Science,* 151:44–49. **91**

AMERICAN PSYCHOLOGICAL ASSOCIATION (1970) *A career in psychology.* Washington, D.C.: American Psychological Association. **27**

ANAND, B. K., SHARMA, K. W., and DUA, S. (1964) Activity of single neurons in the hypothalamic feeding centers: Effect of glucose. *American Journal of Physiology,* 207:1146–54. **308**

ANAND, B. see WENGER, BAGCHI and ANAND (1961).

ANDERSON, B. (1971) Thirst—and brain control of water balance. *American Scientist,* 59:408. **318**

ANDERSON, J. R., and BOWER, G. H. (1973) *Human associative memory.* Washington, D.C.: Winston. **246, 258, 297**

ANDERSON, L. S., see JACOBS, SPILKEN, NORMAN, and ANDERSON (1970); see JACOBS, SPILKEN, NORMAN, and ANDERSON (1971).

ANDERSON, N. H. (1974) Cognitive algebra: Integration theory applied to social attribution. In Berkowitz, L. (ed.) *Advances in experimental social psychology,* Vol. 7. N.Y.: Academic Press. **528**

ANDREWS, L. M., and KARLINS, M. (1971) *Requiem for democracy?.* N.Y.: Holt, Rinehart and Winston. **583**

ANGELL, J. R. (1910) *Psychology.* N.Y.: Henry Holt. **12**

ANNIS, R. C., and FROST, B. (1973) Human visual ecology and orientation antistropies in acuity. *Science,* 182:729–31. **147**

APPLEFIELD, J. M., see STEUER, APPLEFIELD, and SMITH (1971).

APPLEY, M. H., see COFER and APPLEY (1964).

APTER, M. J., and WESTBY, G. (eds.) (1973) *The computer in psychology.* N.Y.: Wiley. **297**

ARAKAKI, K., see KOBASIGAWA, ARAKAKI, and AWIGUNI (1966).

ARCHER, E. J., see BOURNE and ARCHER (1956).

ARDREY, R. (1966) *The territorial imperative.* N.Y.: Atheneum. **342**

ARDREY, R. (1970) *The social contract.* N.Y.: Delta Books. **342**

ARKIN, A. M., HASTEY, J. M., and REISER, M. F. (1966) Post-hypnotically stimulated sleep-talking. *Journal of Nervous and Mental Disease,* 142:293–309. **171**

ARKIN, A. M., TOTH, M. F., BAKER, J., and HASTEY, J. M. (1970) The frequency of sleep talking in the laboratory among chronic sleep talkers and good dream recallers. *Journal of Nervous and Mental Disease,* 151:369–74. **171**

ARNOLD, M. (1949) A demonstrational analysis of the TAT in a clinical setting. *Journal of Abnormal and Social Psychology,* 44:97–111. **381**

ARONSON, E. (1968) Dissonance theory: Progress and problems. In Abelson, R. P., Aronson, E., McGuire, W. J., Newcomb, T. M., Rosenberg, M. J., and Tannenbaum, P. H. (eds.) *Theories of cognitive consistency: A sourcebook.* Chicago: Rand McNally. **555**

ARONSON, E. (1972) *The social animal.* San Francisco: Freeman. **532, 554, 561**

ARONSON, E. WILLERMAN, B., and FLOYD, J. (1966) The effect of a pratfall on increasing interpersonal attractiveness. *Psychonomic Science,* 4:157–58. **531**

ARONSON, E., and CARLSMITH, J. M. (1963) The effect of the severity of threat on the devaluation of forbidden behavior. *Journal of Abnormal and Social Psychology,* 66:584–88. **540**

ARONSON, E., see ABELSON, ARONSON, MCGUIRE, NEWCOMB, ROSENBERG, and TANNENBAUM (1968); see HELMREICH, ARONSON, and LEFAN (1970); see LINDZEY and ARONSON (1970).

ARONSON, V., see WALSTER, ARONSON, ABRAHAMS, and ROTTMANN (1966).

ASCH, S. E. (1951) Effects of group pressure upon the modification and distortion of judgments. In Guetzkow, H. (ed.) *Groups, leadership, and men.* Pittsburgh: Carnegie Press. **551**

ASCH, S. E. (1956) Studies of independence and conformity: A minority of one against a unanimous majority. *Psychological Monographs,* 70, Whole No. 416. **551**

ASCH, S. E. (1958) Effects of group pressure upon modification and distortion of judgments. In Maccoby, E. E., Newcomb, T. M., and Hartley, E. L. (eds.) *Readings in social psychology* (3rd ed.). N.Y.: Holt, Rinehart and Winston. **551**

ASCHOFF, J. (1965) Circadian rhythm in man. *Science,* 148:1427. **165**

ASTRUP, C., see STEPHENS, ASTRUP, and MANGRUM (1967).

ATKINSON, J. W., see MCCLELLAND, ATKINSON, CLARK, and LOWELL (1953).

ATKINSON, K., MACWHINNEY, B., and STOEL, C. (1970) An experiment on recognition of babbling. *Papers and reports on child language development.* Stanford, Calif.: Stanford Univ. Press. **281**

ATKINSON, R. C. (1957) A stochastic model for rote serial learning. *Psychometrika,* 22:87–95. **213**

ATKINSON, R. C. (1972) Ingredients for a theory of instruction. *American Psychologist,* 27:921–31. **214**

ATKINSON, R. C. (1974) Teaching children to read using a computer. *American Psychologist,* 29:169–78. **21, 249, 250**

ATKINSON, R. C., BOWER, G. H., and CROTHERS, E. J. (1965) *An introduction to mathematical learning theory.* N.Y.: Wiley. **220**

ATKINSON, R. C., and RAUGH, M. R. (1975) An application of the mnemonic keyword method to the acquisition of a Russian vocabulary. *Journal of Experimental Psychology: Human Learning and Memory,* in press. **260**

ATKINSON, R. C., and SHIFFRIN, R. M. (1971) The control of short-term memory. *Scientific American,* 224:82–90. **237, 240**

ATKINSON, R. C., and WILSON, H. A. (eds.) (1969) *Computer-assisted instruction.* N.Y.: Academic Press. **267**

ATKINSON, R. C., see DARLEY, TINKLENBERG, ROTH, HOLLISTER, and ATKINSON (1973); see KRANTZ, ATKINSON, LUCE, and SUPPES (1974); see RAUGH and ATKINSON (1975).

AWIGUNI, A., see KOBASIGAWA, ARAKAKI, and AWIGUNI (1966).

BACK, K. (1972) Beyond words: The story of sensitivity training and the encounter movement. N.Y.: Russell Sage. **521**

BAER, D., see ROSENFELD and BAER (1969).

BAER, P. E., and FUHRER, M. J. (1968) Cognitive processes during differential trace and delayed conditioning of the G.S.R. *Journal of Experimental Psychology,* 78:81–88. **199**

BAGCHI, B., see WENGER and BAGCHI (1961); see WENGER, BAGCHI, and ANAND (1961).

BAKER, C. T., see SONTAG, BAKER, and NELSON (1958).

BAKER, J., see ARKIN, TOTH, BAKER, and HASTEY (1970).

BALDWIN, B. T., and STECHER, L. I. (1922) Mental growth curves of normal and superior children. *University of Iowa Studies in Child Welfare,* 2, No. 1. **414**

BALL, E. S., see BOSSARD and BALL (1955).

BANDURA, A. L. (1969) *Principles of behavior modification.* N.Y.: Holt, Rinehart and Winston. **398, 458, 459, 503, 521**

BANDURA, A. L. (1971) *Social learning theory.* N.Y.: General Learning Press. **359**

BANDURA, A. L. (1973) *Aggression: A social learning analysis.* Englewood Cliffs, N.J.: Prentice-Hall. **339, 340, 341, 359, 382**

BANDURA, A. L., BLANCHARD, E. B., and RITTER, B. (1969) The relative efficacy of desensitization and modeling approaches for inducing behavioral, affective, and attitudinal changes. *Journal of Personality and Social Psychology,* 13:173–99. **507, 509**

BANDURA, A., and WALTERS, R. H. (1959) *Adolescent aggression.* N.Y.: Ronald. **95**

BANDURA, A., and WALTERS, R. H. (1963) *Social learning and personality development.* N.Y.: Holt, Rinehart and Winston. **87**

BANUAZIZI, A., see MILLER and BANUAZIZI (1968).

BARBER, T. S. (1969) *Hypnosis: A scientific approach.* N.Y.: Van Nostrand Reinhold. **177, 190**

BARKER, R. G., DEMBO, T., and LEWIN, K. (1941) Frustration and regression: An experiment with young children. *University of Iowa Studies in Child Welfare,* 18, No. 386. **434**

BARLOW, H. B. (1972) Single units and sensation: A neuron doctrine for perceptual psychology? *Perception,* 1:371–94. **141, 147**

BARNETT, S. A. (1967) Attack and defense in animal societies. In Clemente, C. D., and Lindsley, D. B. (eds.) *Aggression and defence.* Los Angeles: Univ. of California Press. **343**

BARON, R. A., and KEPNER, C. R. (1970) Model's attraction toward the model as determinants of adult agressive behavior. *Journal of Abnormal and Social Psychology,* 14:335–44. **344**

BARR, H. L., LANGS, R. J., HOLT, R. R., GOLDBERGER, L., and KLEIN, G. S. (1972) *LSD: Personality and experience.* N.Y.: Wiley. **186**

BARTKO, J. J., see CARPENTER, STRAUSS, and BARTKO (1973).

BATEMAN, F., see SOAL and BATEMAN (1954).

BAUMRIND, D. (1964) Some thoughts on the ethics of research: After reading Milgram's "Behavioral study of obedience." *American Psychologist,* 19:4211–23. **553**

BAYLEY, N. (1970) Development of mental abilities. In Mussen, P. (ed.) *Carmichael's manual of child psychology.* N.Y.: Wiley, 1:1163–1209. **414, 415, 419**

BEACH, F. A. (1941) Female mating behavior shown by male rats after administration of testosterone propionate. *Endocrinology,* 29:409–12. **321**

BEACH, F. A., see FORD and BEACH (1951).

BEAL, G. M., see WILCOX, BROOKS, BEAL, and KLONGLAN (1972).

BEAN, L. L., see MYERS and BEAN (1968).

BEERS, C. W. (1908) *A mind that found itself.* N.Y.: Doubleday. **496**

BELLUGI-KLIMA, U. (1968) Linguistics mechanisms underlying child speech. In Zale, E. M., (ed.) *Proceedings of the conference on language and language behavior.* N.Y.: Appleton-Century-Crofts. **285**

BELMONT, L., and MAROLLA, F. A. (1973) Birth order, family size, and intelligence. *Science,* 182:1096–1101. **91**

BEM, D. J. (1970) *Beliefs, attitudes and human affairs.* Belmont, Calif.: Brooks-Cole. **538, 561, 564**

BEM, D. J. (1972) Self-perception theory. *Advances in Experimental Social Psychology.* N.Y.: Academic Press, 6:1–62. **583, 556**

BEM, D. J., and ALLEN, A. (1974) On predicting some of the people some of the time: The search for cross-situational consistencies in behavior. *Psychological Review,* in press. **189, 386**

BEM, D. J., see BEM and BEM (1973).

BEM, S. L., and BEM, D. J. (1973) Does sex-biased job advertising "aid and abet" sex discrimination? *Journal of Applied Social Psychology,* 3:6–18. **565, 567, 568**

BENDER, D. B., see GROSS, BENDER, and ROCHA-MIRANDA (1972).

BENDFELDT, F., see LUDWIG, BRANDSMA, WILBUR, BENDFELDT, and JAMESON (1972).

BENNETT, E. L., see ROSENZWEIG and BENNETT (1969); see ROSENZWEIG, BENNETT, and DIAMOND (1972).

BENSON, H., see WALLACE and BENSON (1972).

BERGER, R. J. (1963) Experimental modification of dream content by meaningful verbal stimuli. *British Journal of Psychiatry,* 109:722–40. **170**

BERGQUIST, E. H. (1972) Role of the hypothalamus in motivation: An examination of Valenstein's reexamination. *Psychological Review,* 79:542–46. **317**

BERKOWITZ, L. (ed.) (1969) *Roots of aggression.* N.Y.: Atherton Press. **359**

BERNSTEIN, D. R., see PAUL and BERNSTEIN (1973).

BERSCHEID, E., and WALSTER, E. (1974) Physical attractiveness. In Berkowitz, L. (ed.) *Advances in experimental social psychology.* N.Y.: Academic Press. **530, 531**

BERSCHEID, E., see DION and BERSCHEID (1972); see DION, BERSCHEID, and WALSTER (1972).
BETZ, B. J., see WHITEHORN and BETZ (1960).
BEVER, T. G., LACKNER, J. R., and KIRK, R. (1969) The underlying structures of sentences are the primary units of immediate speech processing. *Perception and Psychophysics,* 5:225–31. **278**
BEVER, T. G., see FODER, BEVER, and GARRETT (1974).
BIEHLER, R. F. (1971) *Psychology applied to teaching.* N.Y.: Houghton Mifflin. **267**
BIERBRAUER, G. A. (1973) *Attribution and perspective: Effects of time, set, and role on interpersonal inference.* Unpublished doctoral dissertation, Stanford University, Stanford, Calif. **554**
BILLINGSLEY, A. (1968) *Black families in white America.* Englewood Cliffs, N.J.: Prentice-Hall. **579**
BIRCH, H. G., see THOMAS, CHESS, and BIRCH (1970).
BLANCHARD, E. B., see BANDURA, BLANCHARD, and RITTER (1969).
BLEHAR, M. P. (1973) Anxious attachment and defensive reactions associated with day care. Paper presented at meeting of the Society for Research in Child Development, Philadelphia, March, 1973. **84**
BLOOM, B. S. (1963) Report on creativity research by the examiner's office of the University of Chicago. In Taylor, C. W., and Barron, F. (eds.) *Scientific creativity: Its recognition and development.* N.Y.: Wiley. **571**
BLUM, G. S. (1966) *Psychodynamics: The science of unconscious mental forces.* Belmont, Calif.: Wadsworth. **398**
BLUM, R. H., and associates (1969) *Drugs: Vol. I. Society and drugs: Vol. II. Students and drugs.* San Francisco: Jossey-Bass. **190**
BLUM, R. H., BOVET, D., and MOORE, J. (1973) *Controlling drugs: An international handbook for psychoactive drug classification.* San Francisco: Jossey-Bass. **190**
BOLLES, R. C. (1967) *Theory of motivation.* N.Y.: Harper and Row. **302, 331, 359**
BORING, E. G. (1939) *Introduction to Psychology.* N.Y.: Wiley. **12**
BORING, E. G. (1950) *A history of experimental psychology* (2nd ed.). N.Y.: Appleton-Century-Crofts. **27**
BORING, E. G., see HERRNSTEIN and BORING (1965).
BOSSARD, J. H. S., and BALL, E. S. (1955) Personality roles in the family. *Child Development,* 26:71–78. **90**
BOURNE, L. E., Jr., and ARCHER, E. J. (1956) Time continuously on target as a function of distribution of practice. *Journal of Experimental Psychology,* 51:25–33. **213**
BOVET, D., see BLUM, BOVET, AND MOORE (1973).
BOWER, G. H. (1970) Organizational factors in memory. *Cognitive Psychology,* 1:18–41. **244**
BOWER, G. H. (1972) Mental imagery and associative learning. In Gregg, L. (ed.) *Cognition in learning and memory.* N.Y.: Wiley. **242**
BOWER, G. H., see ANDERSON and BOWER (1973); see ATKINSON, BOWER, and CROTHERS (1965); see HILGARD and BOWER (1974); THORNDYKE and BOWER (1974).
BOWER, T. G. R. (1966) The visual work of infants. *Scientific American,* 215:80–92. **132**
BOWER, T. G. R. (1974) *Development in infancy.* San Francisco: Freeman. **157**
BOWERS, K. (1973) Situationism in psychology: On making reality disappear. *Psychological Review,* in press. **389**
BOWLBY, J. (1969) *Attachment.* N.Y.: Basic Books. **70, 82**
BOWMAN, P. H., see GUETZKOW and BOWMAN (1946).
BRADY, J. V., PORTER, R. W., CONRAD, D. G., and MASON, J. W. (1958) Avoidance behavior and the development of gastroduodenal ulcers. *Journal of the Experimental Analysis of Behavior,* 1:69–73. **482**
BRAGINSKY, B. M., BRAGINSKY, D., and RING, K. (1969) *Methods of madness: The mental hospital as a last resort.* N.Y.: Holt Rinehart and Winston. **521**
BRAGINSKY, D., see BRAGINSKY, BRAGINSKY, and RING (1969).
BRANDSMA, J. M., see LUDWIG, BRANDSMA, WILBUR, BENDFELDT, and JAMESON (1972).
BRANDT, U., see EYFERTH, BRANDT, and WOLFGANG (1960).
BRECHER, E., and the editors of *Consumer Reports* (1972) *Licit and illicit drugs.* Mt. Vernon, N.Y.: Consumers Union. **190**
BREHM, J. W., and COHEN, A. R. (1962) *Explorations in cognitive dissonance.* N.Y.: Wiley. **555**
BRELAND, K., and BRELAND, M. (1966) *Animal behavior.* N.Y.: Macmillan. **205**
BRELAND, M., see BRELAND and BRELAND (1966).
BRENER, J., and KLEINMAN, R. (1970) Learned control of decreases in systolic blood pressure. *Nature,* 226:1063–64. **484**
BRENMAN, M., see GILL and BRENMAN (1959).
BRIER, R., see RHINE and BRIER (1968).
BRIGHAM, C. C. (1923) *A study of American intelligence.* Princeton, N.J.: Princeton Univ. Press. **578**
BRIGHAM, C. C. (1930) Intelligence of immigrant groups. *Psychological Review,* 37:158–65. **579**
BRIM, O. G., JR. (1965) American attitudes toward intelligence tests. *American Psychologist,* 20:125–30. **424, 569**
BRISLIN, R. W., and LEWIS, S. A. (1968) Dating and physical attractiveness: Replication. *Psychological Reports,* 22:976. **530**
BRITTAIN, R. P., see JACOBS, BRUNTON, MELVILLE, BRITTAIN and MCCLEMONT (1965); see JACOBS, PRICE, COURT BROWN, BRITTAIN and WHATMORE (1968).
BRODIE, M., see TESSER and BRODIE (1971).
BRONFENBRENER, U. (1970) *Two worlds of childhood.* N.Y.: Russell Sage. **98**
BROOKS, R. M., see WILCOX, BROOKS, BEAL, and KLONGLAN (1972).
BROWN, J. S. (1948) Gradients of approach and avoidance responses and their relation to motivation. *Journal of Comparative and Physiological Psychology,* 41:450–65. **432**
BROWN, M. E., see SCHWARTZ, FELDMAN, BROWN, and HEINGARTNER (1969).
BROWN, R. (1973) *A first language: The early stages.* Cambridge, Mass.: Harvard Univ. Press. **283, 286, 290, 297**
BROWN, R. W., and MCNEILL, D. (1966) The "tip-of-the-tongue" phenomenon. *Journal of Verbal Learning and Verbal Behavior,* 5:325–37. **227**
BRUCH, H. (1961) Transformation of oral impulses in eating disorders: A conceptual approach. *Psychiatry Quarterly,* 35:458–81. **314**
BRUNER, J. S., and GOODMAN, C. C. (1947) Value and need as organizing factors in perception. *Journal of Abnormal and Social Psychology,* 42:33–44. **151**
BRUNTON, M., see JACOBS, BRUNTON, MELVILLE, BRITTAIN, and MCCLEMONT (1965).
BRYAN, J. H., and TEST, M. A. (1967) Models and helping: Naturalistic studies in aiding behavior. *Journal of Personality and Social Psychology,* 6:400–07. **550**
BUDZYNSKI, T., STOYVA, J., and ADLER, C. (1971) Feedback-induced muscle relaxation. In Barber, T., DiCara, L., Kamiya, J., Miller, N., Shapiro, D., and Stoyva, J. (eds.) *Biofeedback and self-control.* Chicago: Aldine-Atherton. **484**
BUELL, J. S., see ALLEN, HART, BUELL, HARRIS, and WOLF (1964).
BUGELSKI, R., see MILLER and BUGELSKI (1948).
BUNNING, E. (1967) *The physiological clock* (2nd ed.). N.Y.: Springer-Verlag. **190**
BURTT, H. E. (1941) An experimental study of early childhood memory. *Journal of Genetic Psychology,* 58:435–39. **224**
BUSS, A. H. (1966a) Instrumentality of aggression, feedback, and frustration as determinants of physical aggression. *Journal of Personality and Social Psychology,* 3:153–62. **341**
BUSS, A. H. (1966b) *Psychopathology.* N.Y.: Wiley. **341, 477, 489, 492**
BUTCHER, H. J. (1968) *Human intelligence: Its nature and assessment.* London: Methuen. **426**
BUTCHER, J. N. (ed.) (1969) *MMPI: Research developments and clinical applications.* N.Y.: McGraw-Hill. **398**
BYRNE, D. (1971) *The attraction paradigm.* N.Y.: Academic Press. **532**
CAGGIULA, A. R. (1967) Specificity of copulation reward systems in the posterior hypothalamus. Proc. 75th Convention, American Psychological Association, 125–26, **321**
CAGGIULA, A. R., and HOEBEL, B. G. (1966) A "copulation-reward site" in the posterior hypothalamus. *Science,* 153:1284–85. **321**

CALDER, N. (1971) *The mind of man.* N.Y.: Viking Press. **180**

CAMERON, N., and MAGARET, A. (1951) *Behavior pathology.* Boston: Houghton Mifflin. **464**

CAMPBELL, B. A., and CHURCH, R. M. (eds.) (1969) *Punishment and aversive behavior.* N.Y.: Appleton-Century-Crofts. **268**

CAMPBELL, D. P. (1971) *Handbook for the strong vocational interest blank.* Stanford, Calif.: Stanford Univ. Press. **570, 571**

CAMPBELL, D. T., see MILLER and CAMPBELL (1959).

CAMPBELL, H. J. (1973) *The pleasure areas.* London: Eyre Methuen. **210**

CANNON, W. B. (1927) The James-Lange theory of emotions: A critical examination and an alternative theory. *American Journal of Psychology,* 39:106–24. **348**

CANTRIL, H., see FREE and CANTRIL (1967).

CARLSMITH, J. M., see ARONSON and CARLSMITH (1963); see FESTINGER and CARLSMITH (1959); see FREEDMAN, CARLSMITH, and SEARS (1974).

CARPENTER, W. T., STRAUSS, J. S., and BARTKO, J. J. (1973) Flexible system for the diagnosis of schizophrenia: Report from the WHO International Pilot Study of Schizophrenia. *Science,* 182:1275–77. **475**

CARROLL, J. B. (1964) *Language and thought.* Englewood Cliffs, N.J.: Prentice-Hall. **292**

CARTERETTE, E. C., and FRIEDMAN, M. P. (eds.) (1974) *Handbook of perception.* N.Y.: Academic Press. **128, 157**

CATES, J. (1970) Psychology's manpower; Report on the national register of scientific and technical personnel. *American Psychologist,* 25:254–63. **13**

CATTELL, R. B. (1949) *The culture free intelligence test.* Champaign, Ill.: Institute for Personality and Ability Testing. **410**

CATTELL, R. B. (1965) *The scientific analysis of personality.* Baltimore, Md.: Penguin Books. **398**

CATTELL, R. B. (1973) Personality pinned down. *Psychology Today,* 7:40–46. **370**

CHAMOVE, A. S., see DAVENPORT, CHAMOVE, and HARLOW (1970).

CHAMPION, R. A., see STANDISH and CHAMPION (1960).

CHANCE, J. E., see ROTTER, CHANCE, and PHARES (1972).

CHAPMAN, J., see MCGHIE and CHAPMAN (1961).

CHAPMAN, J. P., see CHAPMAN and CHAPMAN (1969).

CHAPMAN, L. M., and CHAPMAN, J. P. (1969) Illusory correlations as an obstacle to the use of valid psycho-diagnostic signs. *Journal of Abnormal Psychology,* 74:271–80. **537**

CHASE, M. H. (ed.) (1972) *The sleeping brain.* Los Angeles: Brain Research Institute, Univ. of California. **190**

CHAUDHURI, H. (1965) *Philosophy of meditation.* N.Y.: Philosophical Library. **178**

CHEIN, I., GERARD, D. L., LEE, R. S., and ROSENFELD, E. (1964) *The road to H.* N.Y.: Basic Books. **183**

CHESS, S., see THOMAS, CHESS and BIRCH (1970).

CHOMSKY, N. (1968) *Language and mind.* N.Y.: Harcourt Brace Jovanovich. **297**

CHURCH, J., see STONE and CHURCH (1973).

CHURCH, R. M., see CAMPBELL and CHURCH (1969).

CLARK, E. V. (1973) What's in a word? On the child's acquisition of semantics in his first language. In Moore, T. E. (ed.) *Cognitive development and the acquisition of language.* N.Y.: Academic Press. **282**

CLARK, H. (1973) Space, time, semantics, and the child. In Moore, T. E. (ed.) *Cognitive development and the acquisition of language.* N.Y.: Academic Press. **287**

CLARK, K. E., and MILLER, G. A. (eds.) (1970) *Psychology.* Englewood Cliffs, N.J.: Prentice Hall. **12, 27**

CLARK, R. A., see MCCLELLAND, ATKINSON, CLARK, and LOWELL (1953).

CLAYTON, K. N. (1964) T-maze choice-learning as a joint function of the reward magnitudes of the alternatives. *Journal of Comparative and Physiological Psychology,* 58:333–38. **209**

CLECKLEY, H. M., see THIGPEN and CLECKLEY (1954).

COBB, J. C., EVANS, F. J., GUSTAFSON, L. A., O'CONNELL, D. N., ORNE, M. T., and SHOR, R. E. (1965) Specific motor response during sleep to sleep administered meaningful suggestion: An exploratory investigation. *Perceptual and Motor Skills,* 20:629–36. **170**

COE, W. C., see SARBIN and COE (1972).

COFER, C. N. (1972) *Motivation and emotion.* Glenview, Ill.: Scott, Foresman. **302, 331, 359**

COFER, C. N., and APPLEY, M. H. (1964) *Motivation: Theory and research.* N.Y.: Wiley. **331, 359**

COHEN, A. R., see BREHM and COHEN (1962).

COLBY, K. M., and ENEA, H. (1967) Heuristic methods for computer understanding of natural language in the context-restricted on-line dialogue. *Mathematical Biosciences,* 1:1–25. **514**

COLBY, K. M., see SCHANK and COLBY (1973).

COLE, C. W., OETTING, E. R., and HINKLE, J. E. (1967) Non-linearity of self-concept discrepancy: The value dimension. *Psychological Reports,* 21:58–60. **394**

COLE, H. H., HART, G. H., and MILLER, R. F. (1956) Studies on the hormonal control of estrous phenomena in the anestrous ewe. *Endocrinology,* 36:370–80. **321**

COLEMAN, J. (1972) *Abnormal psychology and modern life* (4th ed.). N.Y.: Scott, Foresman. **451, 460, 492**

COLEMAN, J. S. (1961) *The adolescent society.* N.Y.: Free Press. **97**

COLLINS, A. M., and QUILLIAN, M. R. (1972) How to make a language user. In Tulving, E., and Donaldson, W. (eds.) *Organization of memory.* N.Y.: Academic Press. **228, 229, 230**

COLQUHOUN, W. P. (ed.) (1971) *Biological rhythms and human performance.* N.Y.: Academic Press. **190**

CONGER, J. J. (1973) *Adolescence and youth: Psychological development in a changing world.* N.Y.: Harper and Row. **100**

CONGER, J. J., see MUSSEN, CONGER, and KAGAN (1974); see SAWREY, CONGER, and TURRELL (1956).

CONRAD, D. G., see BRADY, PORTER, CONRAD, and MASON (1958).

COOMBS, C. H., DAWES, R. M., and TVERSKY, A. (1970) *Mathematical psychology: An elementary introduction.* Englewood Cliffs, N.J.: Prentice-Hall. **220**

COOPER, L. M., see HOSKOVEC and COOPER (1967).

CORNELISON, A. R., see LIDZ, FLECK, and CORNELISON (1965).

CORNSWEET, T. N. (1970) *Visual perception.* N.Y.: Academic Press. **118, 128, 157**

COSTA, P. T., see MADDI and COSTA (1972).

COSTANZO, P. R., and SHAW, M. E. (1966) Conformity as a function of age level. *Child Development,* 37:967–75. **91**

COTTRELL, N. B. (1972) Social facilitation. In McClintock, C. G. (ed.) *Experimental social psychology.* N.Y.: Holt. **545**

COTTRELL, N. B., RITTLE, R. H., and WACK, D. L. (1967) Presence of an audience and list type (competitional or noncompetitional) as joint determinants of performance in paired-associates learning. *Journal of Personality,* 35:217–26. **546**

COTTRELL, N. B. WACK, D. L., SEKERAK, G. J., and RITTLE, R. H. (1968) Social facilitation of dominant responses by the presence of an audience and the mere presence of others. *Journal of Personality and Social Psychology,* 9:245–50. **547**

COURT BROWN, W. M., see JACOBS, PRICE, COURT BROWN, BRITTAIN, and WHATMORE (1968).

COWEN, E. L., see ZAX and COWEN (1972).

COWEN, E. L., GARDNER, E. A., and ZAX, M. (1967) *Emergent approaches to mental health problems.* N.Y.: Appleton. **521**

COX, V. C., see VALENSTEIN, COX, and KAKOLEWSKI (1970).

CRAIGHILL, P. G., see SARASON, MANDLER, and CRAIGHILL (1952).

CRAIK, R. I. M. (1970) The fate of primary memory items in free recall. *J. Verbal Learning and Verbal Behavior,* 9:143–48. **240**

CRONBACH, L. J. (1970) *Essentials of psychological testing* (3rd ed.). N.Y.: Harper and Row. **382, 398, 426**

CROSS, H. A., HALCOMB, C. G., and MATTER, W. W. (1967) Imprinting or exposure learning in rats given early auditory stimulation. *Psychonomic Sci.,* 7:233–34. **534**

CROTHERS, E. J., see ATKINSON, BOWER, and CROTHERS (1965).

DABNEY, V. (1957) The violence at Little Rock. *Richmond Times-Dispatch,* Sept. 24, 1957. **563**

DALLENBACH, K. M., see JENKINS and DALLENBACH (1924).

D'ANDRADE, R. C. (1967) *Report on some*

testing and training procedures at Bassawa Primary School, Zaria, Nigeria. Unpublished manuscript. **411**

DANIELS, D. N., GILULA, M. F., and OCHBERG, F. M. (eds.) (1970) *Violence and the struggle for existence.* Boston: Little, Brown. **359**

DARBY, C. L., see PLATT, YAKSH, and DARBY (1967).

DARLEY, C. F., TINKLENBERG, J. R., ROTH, W. T., HOLLISTER, L. E., and ATKINSON, R. C. (1973) *Memory and cognition,* 1:196–200. **17**

DARLEY, J. M., and LATANÉ, B. (1968) Bystander intervention in emergencies: Diffusion of responsibility. *Journal of Personality and Social Psychology,* 8:377–83. **549**

DARLEY, J. M., see LATANÉ and DARLEY (1968); see LATANÉ and DARLEY (1970).

DARWIN, C. (1872) *The expression of emotions in man and animals.* N.Y.: Philosophical Library. **355**

DASHIELL, J. F. (1930) An experimental analysis of some group effects. *Journal of Abnormal and Social Psychology,* 25:190–99. **545, 546**

DASHIELL, J. F. (1935) Experimental studies of the influence of social situations on the behavior of individual human adults. In Murchison, C. (ed.) *Handbook of social psychology.* Worcester, Mass.: Clark University. **545**

DAVENPORT, J. W., CHAMOVE, A. S., and HARLOW, H. F. (1970) The semi-automatic Wisconsin general test apparatus. *Behavioral Research Methods and Instrumentation,* 2:135–38. **255**

DAVIS, A., and EELLS, K. (1953) *Davis-Eells games.* Yonkers, N.Y.: Wold Book. **410**

DAVIS, A., see EELLS, DAVIS, HAVIGHURST, HERRICK, and TYLER (1951).

DAVIS, B., see STUART and DAVIS (1972).

DAVIS, K. E., see JONES and DAVIS (1965); see KERCKHOFF and DAVIS (1962).

DAVIS, W. N., see MCCLELLAND, DAVIS, KALIN, and WANNER (1972).

DAVISON, G. C., and NEALE, J. M. (1974) *Abnormal psychology.* N.Y.: Wiley. **492**

DAVISON, L., see SPEISMAN, LAZARUS, MORDKOFF, and DAVISON (1964).

DAWES, R. M., see COOMBS, DAWES and TVERSKY (1970).

DECI, E. L. (1971) Effects of externally mediated rewards on intrinsic motivation. *Journal of Personality and Social Psychology,* 18:105–15. **540**

DEESE, J. (1972) *Psychology as science and art.* N.Y.: Harcourt Brace Jovanovich. **27**

DEESE, J. E., and HULSE, S. (1967) *Psychology of learning* (3rd ed.) N.Y.: McGraw-Hill. **220**

DEFRIES, J. C., see MCCLEARN and DEFRIES (1973).

DEIKMAN, A. J. (1963) Experimental meditation. *Journal of Nervous and Mental Disease,* 136:329–73. **178**

DELGADO, J. M. R. (1969) *Physical control of the mind.* N.Y.: Harper and Row. **583**

DELGADO, J. M. R., ROBERTS, W. W., and MILLER, N. E. (1954) Learning motivated by electrical stimulation of the brain. *American Journal of Physiology,* 179:587–93. **210**

DE LUCIA, L. A. (1963) The toy preference test: A measure of sex-role identification. *Child Development,* 34:107–17. **89**

DEMBO, T., see BARKER, DEMBO, and LEWIN (1941).

DEMENT, W. C. (1967) Discussion. In Kety, S. S., Evarts, E. V., and Williams, H. L. (eds.) *Sleep and altered states of consciousness.* Baltimore, Md.: Williams and Wilkins. **169**

DEMENT, W. C. (1972) *Some must watch while some must sleep.* Stanford, Calif.: Stanford Alumni Association. **168, 170, 190**

DENNIS, W. (1960) Causes of retardation among institutional children: Iran. *Journal of genetic psychology,* 96:47–59. **71**

DEUTSCH, J. A. (1973) *The physiological basis of memory.* N.Y.: Academic Press. **246**

DEVALOIS, R. L., and JACOBS, G. H. (1968) Primate color vision. *Science,* 162:533–40. **116**

DIAMOND, M. C., see ROSENZWEIG, BENNETT, and DIAMOND (1972).

DION, K. K. (1972) Physical attractiveness and evaluations of children's transgressions. *Journal of Personality and Social Psychology,* 24:207–13. **531**

DION, K. K., BERSCHEID, E., and WALSTER, E. (1972) What is beautiful is good. *Journal of Personality and Social Psychology,* 24:285–90. **535**

DION, K. K., and BERSCHEID, E. (1972) Physical attractiveness and social perception of peers in preschool children. Unpublished manuscript Univ. of Minnesota, Minneapolis, Minn. **530**

DOANE, B. K., see HERON, DOANE, and SCOTT (1956).

DOBELLE, W. H., MLADEJOVSKY, M. G., and GIRVIN, J. P. (1974) Artificial vision for the blind: Electrical stimulation of visual cortex offers hope for a functional prothesis. *Science,* 183:440–44. **47**

DODDS, J. B., see FRANKENBURG and DODDS (1967).

DODWELL, P. C. (1971) *Perceptual processing: Stimulus equivalence and pattern recognition.* N.Y.: Appleton-Century-Crofts. **157**

DOHRENWEND, B. P., and DOHRENWEND, B. S. (1969) *Social status and psychological disorder: A casual inquiry.* N.Y.: Wiley. **521**

DOHRENWEND, B. P., and DOHRENWEND, B. S. (1974) Social and cultural influences on psychopathology. *Annual Review of Psychology,* 25:417–52. **490**

DOHRENWEND, B. S., see DOHRENWEND and DOHRENWEND (1969); see DOHRENWEND and DOHRENWEND (1974).

DOLLARD, J., DOOB, L. W., MILLER, N. E., MOWRER, O. H., and SEARS, R. R. (1939) *Frustration and aggression.* New Haven, Conn.: Yale Univ. Press. **338**

DOLLARD, J., see MILLER and DOLLARD (1941).

DONAHUE, G. (1967) A school district program for schizophrenic children. In Cowen, E., and Zax, M. (eds.) *Emergent approaches to mental health problems.* N.Y. Appleton-Century-Crofts. **513**

DONALDSON, W., see TULVING and DONALDSON (1972).

DOOB, L. W., see DOLLARD, DOOB, MILLER, MOWRER, and SEARS (1939).

DOUVAN, E., and ADELSON, J. (1966) *The adolescent experience.* N.Y.: Wiley. **95, 98**

DUA, S., see ANAND, SHARMA, and DUA (1964).

DUBOIS, P. H. (ed.) (1947) The classification program. *AAF Aviation Psychology Program Research Report,* No. 2. **402**

DUDYCHA, G. J. (1936) An objective study of punctuality in relation to personality and achievement. *Archives of Psychology,* 204:1–319. **189, 386**

DUFFY, M., see SMITH and DUFFY (1955).

DUPONT, R. L., and GREENE, M. H. (1973) The dynamics of a heroin addiction epidemic. *Science,* 181:716–22. **184**

DUTTON, J. M., and STARBUCK, W. H. (eds.) (1971) *Computer simulation of human behavior.* N.Y.: Wiley. **297**

DWORKIN, B. R., see MILLER and DWORKIN (1973).

DYE, H. B., see SKEELS and DYE (1939).

EBBESEN, E. B., see SNYDER and EBBESEN (1972).

EBBINGHAUS, H. (1885) *Memory* (Trans. by H. A. Ruger and C. E. Bussenius). N.Y.: Teachers College (1913). **225, 246**

ECCLES, J. C. (1958) The physiology of imagination. *Scientific American,* 199:135–46. **39**

ECCLES, J. C. (1973) *The understanding of the brain.* N.Y.: McGraw-Hill. **54**

ECHERMAN, C. O., see RHEINGOLD and ECHERMAN (1970).

EDDY, N. B., HALBACH, H., ISBELL, H., and SEEVERS, M. H. (1965) Drug dependence: Its significance and characteristics. *Bulletin of the World Health Organization,* 32:721–33. **181**

EELLS, K., DAVIS, A., HAVIGHURST, R. J., HERRICK, V. E., and TYLER, R. W. (1951) *Intelligence and cultural differences.* Chicago: Univ. of Chicago Press. **410**

EELLS, K., see DAVIS and EELLS (1953).

EIBL-EIBESFELDT, I. (1970) *Ethology.* N.Y.: Holt, Rinehart and Winston. **342**

EKMAN, P. (1971) Universals and cultural differences in facial expressions of emotion. In Cole, J. K. (ed.) *Nebraska Symposium on Motivation.* **356**

ELLINWOOD, E. H. (1967) Amphetamine psychosis: Description of the individuals and process. *Journal of Nervous and Mental Disease,* 144:273–83. **185**

ELLIS, H. C. (1972) *Fundamentals of human learning and cognition.* Dubuque, Ia.: Brown. **267**

EMERSON, P. E., see SCHAFFER and EMERSON (1964).

EMMONS, W. W., and SIMON, C. W. (1956) The non-recall of material presented during sleep. *American Journal of Psychology,* 69:76–81. **170**

ENEA, H., see COLBY and ENEA (1967).

ENGEL, B. T. (1972) Operant conditioning of cardiac function: A status report. *Psychophysiology,* 9:161–77. **207**

EPSTEIN, A. W., see MCGINTY, EPSTEIN, and TEITELBAUM (1965).

EPSTEIN, A. W., and TEITELBAUM, P. (1962) Regulation of food intake in the absence of taste, smell, and other oro-pharyngeal sensations. *Journal of Comparative and Physiological Psychology,* 55:753–59. **311**

EPSTEIN, S., and FENZ, W. D. (1965) Steepness of approach and avoidance gradients in humans as a function of experience. *Journal of Experimental Psychology,* 70:1–12. **433**

ERIKSON, E. H. (1954) The dream specimen of psychoanalysis. *Journal of the American Psychoanalytic Association,* 2:5–56. **172**

ERIKSON, E. H. (1963) *Childhood and society* (2nd ed.). N.Y.: Norton. **79**

ERIKSSON, K. (1972) Behavior and physiological differences among rat strains specially selected for their alcohol consumption. *Annals of the New York Academy of Science,* 197:32–41. **62**

ERLENMEYER-KIMLING, L., and JARVIK, L. F. (1963) Genetics and intelligence: A review. *Science,* 142:1477–79. **416**

ERON, L. D., HUESMANN, L. R., LEFKOWITZ, M. M., and WALDER, L. O. (1972) Does television violence cause aggression? *American Psychologist,* 27:253–63. **344**

ERVIN, F. R., see MARK and ERVIN (1970).

ESTES, W. K. (1949) A study of motivating conditions necessary for secondary reinforcement. *Journal of Experimental Psychology,* 39:306–10. **204**

ESTES, W. K. (1970) *Learning theory and mental development.* N.Y.: Academic Press. **220, 262**

EVANS, F. J., see COBB, EVANS, GUSTAFSON, O'CONNELL, ORNE, and SHOR (1965).

EVANS, R. M. (1948) *An introduction to color.* N.Y.: Wiley. **115**

EXLINE, R., and WINTERS, L. C. (1965) Affective relations and mutual glances in dyads. In Tomkins, S., and Izard, C. (eds.) *Affect, cognition, and personality.* N.Y.: Springer. **395**

EYFERTH, K., BRANDT, U., and WOLFGANG, H. (1960) *Farbige Kinder in Deutschland.* Munich, Germany: Juventa. **419**

EYSENCK, H. J. (1967) *The biological basis of personality.* Springfield, Ill.: Thomas. **398**

EYSENCK, H. J., and EYSENCK, S. B. G. (1963) *The Eysenck Personality Inventory.* San Diego, Calif.: Educational and Industrial Testing Service; London: Univ. of London Press. **369**

EYSENCK, S. B. G., see EYSENCK and EYSENCK (1963).

FAWCETT, J. T. (1970) *Psychology and population.* N.Y.: The Population Council. **574, 583**

FECHNER, G. (1860) *Elements of psychophysics* (Trans. by H. E. Adler). N.Y.: Holt, Rinehart and Winston, 1966. **107**

FELDMAN, K. A., see SCHWARTZ, FELDMAN, BROWN, and HEINGARTNER (1969).

FELDMAN, M. P., and MACCULLOCH, M. J. (1971) *Homosexual behavior: Therapy and assessment.* Oxford, England: Pergamon Press. **506**

FELDMAN, S. D. (1971) The presentation of shortness in everyday life—height and heightism in American society: Toward a sociology of stature. Paper presented to the American Sociological Association meetings. **531**

FELDMAN, S. S., see MACCOBY and FELDMAN (1972).

FENZ, W. D., see EPSTEIN and FENZ (1965).

FESTINGER, L. (1957) *A theory of cognitive dissonance.* Stanford, Calif.: Stanford University Press. 18–57. **555**

FESTINGER, L., and CARLSMITH, J. M. (1959) Cognitive consequences of forced compliance. *Journal of Abnormal and Social Psychology,* 58:203–10. **539**

FLANAGAN, J. C. (1963) The definition and measurement of ingenuity. In Taylor, C. W., and Barron, F. (eds.) *Scientific creativity: Its recognition and development.* N.Y.: Wiley. **412**

FLECK, S., see LIDZ, FLECK, and CORNELISON (1965).

FLEXNER, L. (1967) Dissection of memory in mice with antibiotics. *Proceedings of the American Philosophical Society,* 111:343–46. **235**

FLOYD, J., see ARONSON, WILLERMAN, and FLOYD (1966).

FODER, J. A., BEVER, T. G., and GARRETT, M. F. (1974) *The psychology of language.* N.Y.: McGraw-Hill. **297**

FORD, C. S., and BEACH, F. A. (1951) *Patterns of Sexual Behavior.* N.Y.: Harper & Row. **324**

FOREM, J. (1973) *Transcendental meditation: Maharishi Mahesh Yogi and the science of creative intelligence.* N.Y.: Dutton. **179, 190**

FOULKES, D., see MONROE, RECHTSCHAFFEN, FOULKES, and JENSEN (1965).

FRANK, J. D. (1974) Psychotherapy: The restoration of morale. *American Journal of Psychiatry,* 131:271–74. **516**

FRANKENBURG, W. K., and DODDS, J. B. (1967) The Denver developmental screening test. *Journal of Pediatrics,* 71:181–91. **71**

FRANKIE, G., see HETHERINGTON and FRANKIE (1967).

FREE, L. A., and CANTRIL, H., (1967) *The political beliefs of America.* New Brunswick, N.J.: Rutgers Univ. Press. **572, 573**

FREEDMAN, J. L. (1965) Long-term behavioral effects of cognitive dissonance. *Journal of Experimental Social Psychology,* 1:145–55. **540**

FREEDMAN, J. L., CARLSMITH, J. M., and SEARS, D. O. (1974) *Social Psychology* (2nd ed.). Englewood Cliffs, N.J.: Prentice-Hall. **561**

FREEDMAN, R., and TAKESHITA, J. (1969) *Family planning in Taiwan: An experiment in social change.* Princeton, N.J.: Princeton Univ. Press. **574**

FREITAG, G., see LOVAAS, FREITAG, GOLD, and KASSORLA (1965).

FRENCH, G. M., and HARLOW, H. F. (1962) Variability of delayed-reaction performance in normal and brain-damaged rhesus monkeys. *Journal of Neurophysiology,* 25:585–99. **49**

FRENCH, T. M., and FROMM, E. (1963) *Dream interpretation: A new approach.* N.Y.: Basic Books. **172**

FREUD, A. (1946) *The ego and the mechanisms of defense.* London: Hogarth Press. **451, 459**

FREUD, S. (1900) *The interpretation of dreams* (Standard ed., 1953), vols. IV, V. London: Hogarth Press. **171, 374**

FREUD, S. (1922) *Beyond the pleasure principle.* London: International Psychoanalytic Press. **359**

FREUD, S. (1933) *New introductory lectures on psychoanalysis.* N.Y.: Norton. **172, 359**

FREUD, S. (1940) *Outline of psychoanalysis.* (Standard ed., 1964). vol. XXIII. London: Hogarth Press. **374**

FRIEDMAN, M. P., see CARTERETTE and FRIEDMAN (1974).

FROMM, E., and SHOR, R. E. (eds.) (1972) *Hypnosis: Research developments and perspectives.* Chicago: Aldine-Atherton. **190**

FROMM, E., see FRENCH and FROMM (1963).

FROST, B., see ANNIS and FROST (1973).

FUHRER, M. J., see BAER and FUHRER (1968).

FULLER, J. L., see SCOTT and FULLER (1965).

GAGNÉ, R. M. (1970) *The conditions of learning* (2nd ed.). N.Y.: Holt, Rinehart and Winston. **257, 267**

GALANTER, E. (1962) Contemporary psychophysics. In Brown, R., and others (eds.) *New directions in psychology.* N.Y.: Holt, Rinehart and Winston. **105**

GALANTER, E., see MILLER, GALANTER, and PRIBRAM (1960).

GARCIA, J. (1971) The faddy rat and us. *New Scientist and Science Journal,* Feb. 4, 1971. **312**

GARDNER, B. T., and GARDNER, R. A. (1971) Two-way communication with an infant chimpanzee. In Schrier, A., and Stollnitz, F. (eds.) *Behavior of non-human primates,* vol. IV. N.Y.: Academic Press. **289**

GARDNER, R. A., see GARDNER and GARDNER (1971).

GARDNER, B. T., see GARDNER and GARDNER (1972).

GARDNER, R. A., and GARDNER, B. T. (1972) Communication with a young chimpanzee: Washoe's vocabulary. In Chauvin, R. (ed.) *Edition du Centre National de La Recherche Scientific.* Paris, France. **288**

GARRETT, M. F., see FODER, BEVER, and GARRETT (1974).

GATES, A. I. (1917) Recitation as a factor in memorizing. *Archives of Psychology,* No. 40. **244**

GATES, A. I. (1931) *Elementary Psychology.* N.Y.: Macmillan. **12**

GAZZANIGA, M. S. (1970) *The bisected brain.* N.Y.: Appleton-Century. **53, 66**

GAZZANIGA, M. S. (1972) One brain—two minds? *American Scientist,* 60:311–17. **54**

GEBHARD, P. H., see KINSEY, POMEROY, MARTIN, and GEBHARD (1953).

GEIWITZ, P. J. (1969) *Non-Freudian personality theories.* Belmont, Calif.: Brooks-Cole. **398**

GENGERELLI, J. A., see MOSS and GENGERELLI (1968).

GERARD, D. L., see CHEIN, GERARD, LEE, and ROSENFELD (1964).

GETZELS, J. W., and JACKSON, P. W. (1962) *Creativity and intelligence: Explorations with gifted students.* N.Y.: Wiley. **412**

GIBSON, E. J. (1969) *Principles of perceptual learning and development.* N.Y.: Appleton-Century-Crofts. **157**

GIBSON, E. J., and WALK, R. D. (1960) The "visual cliff." *Scientific American,* 202:64–71. **148**

GILBERT, T. F., see JAMES and GILBERT (1955).

GILL, M. M., and BRENMAN, M. (1959) *Hypnosis and related states.* N.Y.: International Universities Press. **177**

GILULA, M. F., see DANIELS, GILULA, and OCHBERG (1970).

GIRDEN, E. (1962) A review of psychokinesis. *Psychological Bulletins,* 59:353–88. **155**

GIRVIN, J. P., see DOBELLE, MLADEJOVSKY, and GIRVIN (1974).

GLASER, R. (ed.) (1971) *The nature of reinforcement.* Columbus, Ohio: Merrill. **220**

GLASER, R., and RESNICK, L. B. (1972) Instructional psychology. *Annual Review of Psychology,* 23:207–76. **78**

GLASS, D. C., see HENCHY and GLASS (1968).

GLICK, B. S., and MARGOLIS, R. (1962) A study on the influence of experimental design on clinical outcome in drug research. *American Journal of Psychiatry,* 118:1087–96. **517**

GLUCK, C. M., see SIMS, KELLEHER, HORTON, GLUCK, GOODMAN, and ROWE (1968).

GLUECK, S. (1962) *Law and psychiatry.* Baltimore, Md.: Johns Hopkins Press. **488**

GODDARD, H. H. (1913) The Binet tests in relation to immigration. *Journal of Psychoasthenics,* 18:105–07. **578**

GODDARD, H. H. (1917) Mental tests and the immigrant. *Journal of Delinquency,* 2:243–77. **578**

GOETHALS, G. R., see JONES, ROCK, SHAVEN, GOETHALS, and WARD (1968).

GOFFMAN, E. (1961) *Asylums.* Garden City, N.Y.: Doubleday. **542**

GOLD, V. J., see LOVAAS, FREITAG, GOLD, and KASSORLA (1965).

GOLDBERGER, L., see BARR, LANGS, HOLT, GOLDBERGER, and KLEIN (1972).

GOLDIAMOND, I., see ISAACS, THOMAS, and GOLDIAMOND (1965).

GOLDMAN, R., see SCHACHTER, GOLDMAN, and GORDON (1968).

GOLDSTEIN, A. C. (1957) *Hormones, brain function, and behavior.* Hoagland, H. H. (ed.) N.Y.: Academic Press. **320**

GOODENOUGH, D. R., see LEWIS, GOODENOUGH, SHAPIRO, and SLESER (1966).

GOODENOUGH, D. R., SHAPIRO, A., HOLDEN, M., and STEINSCHRIBER, L. (1959) A comparison of dreamers and nondreamers: Eye movements, electroencephalograms and the recall of dreams. *Journal of Abnormal and Social Psychology,* 59:295–302. **170**

GOODMAN, C. C., see BRUNER and GOODMAN (1947).

GOODMAN, J. (1970) Companions as therapy: The use of nonprofessional talent. In Hart, J. T., and Tomlinson, T. M. *New directions in client-centered therapy.* Boston: Houghton Mifflin. **513**

GOODMAN, R. F., see SIMS, KELLEHER, HORTON, GLUCK, GOODMAN, and ROWE (1968).

GOODNOW, J. J., see WILLIAMS, LUBIN, and GOODNOW (1959).

GORDON, A., see SCHACHTER, GOLDMAN, and GORDON (1968).

GORDON, T. J., and HAYWARD, H. (1968) Initial experiments with the cross-impact matrix method of forecasting. *Futures,* 1:100–17. **576**

GOSLIN, D. A. (ed.) (1969) *Handbook for socialization: Theory and research.* Chicago: Rand McNally. **100**

GOTTESMAN, I. I., and SHIELDS, J. (1972) *Schizophrenia and genetics: A twin study vantage point.* N.Y.: Academic Press. **492**

GOTTESMAN, I. I., and SHIELDS, J. (1973) Genetic theorizing and schizophrenia. *British Journal of Psychiatry,* 122:15–30. **478**

GREEN, D. (1974) Dissonance and self-perception analyses of "forced compliance": When two theories make competing predictions. *Journal of Personality and Social Psychology,* 29:819–28. **556**

GREEN, D. M., and SWETS, J. A. (1966) *Signal detection theory and psychophysics.* N.Y.: Wiley. **109, 128**

GREEN, H. (1971) *I never promised you a rose garden.* N.Y.: New American Library. **492**

GREENE, D., see LEPPER, GREENE, and NISBETT (1973).

GREENE, M. H., see DUPONT and GREENE (1973).

GREENWALD, A. G. On the inconclusiveness of "crucial" cognitive tests of dissonance versus self-perception theories. *Journal of Experimental Social Psychology,* in press. **556**

GREGG, L. W. (ed.) (1972) *Cognition in learning and memory.* N.Y.: Wiley. **246**

GREGORY, R. L. (1966) *Eye and brain: The psychology of seeing.* N.Y.: McGraw-Hill. **128, 157**

GREGORY, R. L. (1970) *The intelligent eye.* N.Y.: McGraw-Hill. **136, 157**

GROSS, C. G., BENDER, D. B., and ROCHA-MIRANDA, C. E. (1972) Visual receptive fields of neurons in inferotemporal cortex of the monkey. *Science,* 166:1303–06. **145**

GROSS, L. P., see SCHACHTER and GROSS (1968).

GROSSBERG, J. M. (1964) Behavior therapy: A review. *Psych. Bulletin,* 62:73–85. **509**

GROSSEN, N. E., see MYERS and GROSSEN (1974).

GROSSMAN, S. P. (1962) Direct adrenergic and cholinergic stimulation of hypothalamic mechanisms. *American Journal of Physiology,* 202:872–82. **317**

GROSSMAN, S. P. (1967) *A textbook of physiological psychology.* N.Y.: Wiley. **320**

GUETZKOW, H., and BOWMAN, P. H. (1946) *Men and hunger.* Elgin, Ill.: Brethren Publishing House. **438**

GUILFORD, J. P. (1954) A factor analytic study across the domains of reasoning, creativity, and evaluation I: Hypothesis and description of tests. *Reports from the psychology laboratory.* Los Angeles, Calif.: Univ. of Southern California. **412**

GUILFORD, J. P. (1959) *Personality.* N.Y.: McGraw-Hill. **398**

GUILFORD, J. P. (1967) *The nature of human intelligence.* N.Y.: McGraw-Hill. **410, 413**

GUILFORD, J. P., and HOEPFNER, R. (1971) *The analysis of intelligence.* N.Y.: McGraw-Hill. **426**

GUSTAFSON, L. A., see COBB, EVANS, GUSTAFSON, O'CONNELL, ORNE, and SHOR (1965).

HABER, R. N. (1969) Eidetic images. *Scientific American,* 220:36–55. **226**

HABER, R. N. (ed.) (1969) *Information-processing approaches to visual perception.* N.Y.: Holt. **226**

HABER, R. N., and HERSHENSON, M. (1973) *The psychology of visual perception.* N.Y.: Holt, Rinehart and Winston. **128, 157**

HAGE, J., see PITT and HAGE (1964).

HALBACH, H., see EDDY, HALBACH, ISBELL, and SEEVERS (1965).

HALCOMB, C. G., see CROSS, HALCOMB, and MATTER (1967).

HALL, C. S. (1953) *The meaning of dreams.* N.Y.: Harper and Row. **172**

HALL, C. S., and LINDZEY, G. (eds.) (1970) *Theories of personality* (2nd ed.). N.Y.: Wiley. **398**

HALL, C. S., and VAN DE CASTLE, R. L. (1966) *The content analysis of dreams.* N.Y.: Appleton-Century-Crofts. **169**

HAMPSON, J. G., see MONEY, HAMPSON, and HAMPSON (1957).

HAMPSON, J. L., see MONEY, HAMPSON, and HAMPSON (1957).

HANSEL, C. E. M. (1966) *ESP: A scientific evaluation.* N.Y.: Scribners. **157**

HARDING, J. S., see LEIGHTON, HARDING, MACKLIN, MACMILLAN, and LEIGHTON (1963).

HARE, R. D. (1970) *Psychopathy: Theory and Research.* N.Y.: Wiley. **487**

HARLOW, H. F. (1932) Social facilitation of feeding in the albino rat. *Journal of Genetic Psychology,* 41:211–21. **544, 546**

HARLOW, H. F. (1949) The formation of learning sets. *Psychological Review,* 56:51–65. **256**

HARLOW, H. F. (1971) *Learning to love.* San Francisco: Albion. **322**

HARLOW, H. F., HARLOW, M. K., and MEYER, D. R. (1950) Learning motivated by

a manipulation drive. *Journal of experimental psychology,* 40:228–34. **328**
HARLOW, H. F., and HARLOW, M. K. (1966) Learning to love. *American Scientist,* 54:244–72. **81**
HARLOW, H. F., and SUOMI, S. J. (1970) Nature of love—simplified. *American Psychologist,* 25:161–68. **81**
HARLOW, H. F., see DAVENPORT, CHAMOVE, and HARLOW (1970); see FRENCH and HARLOW (1962).
HARLOW, M. K., see HARLOW and HARLOW (1966); see HARLOW, HARLOW, and MEYER (1950).
HARMON, L. R. (1963) The development of a criterion of scientific competence. In Taylor, C. W., and Barron, F. (eds.) *Scientific creativity: Its recognition and development.* N.Y.: Wiley. **571**
HARRIS, C. S., see ROCK and HARRIS (1967).
HARRIS, F. R., JOHNSTON, M. K., KELLEY, C. S., and WOLF, M. M. (1965) Effects of positive social reinforcement on regressed crawling of a nursery school child. In Ullmann, L., and Krasner, L. (eds.) *Case studies in behavior modification.* N.Y.: Holt, Rinehart and Winston. **208**
HARRIS, F. R., see ALLEN, HART, BUELL, HARRIS, and WOLF (1964).
HARRIS, I. D. (1961) *Emotional blocks to learning.* N.Y.: Free Press. **268**
HARRIS, V. A., see JONES and HARRIS (1967).
HART, B. M., see ALLEN, HART, BUELL, HARRIS, and WOLF (1964).
HART, G. H., see COLE, HART, and MILLER (1956).
HARTMAN, H. (1958) *Ego psychology and the problems of adaptation.* N.Y.: International Universities Press. **459**
HARTSHORNE, H., and MAY, M. A. (1928, 1929) *Studies in the nature of character:* Vol. 1, *Studies in deceit;* Vol. 2, *Studies in self-control.* N.Y.: Macmillan. **386**
HASHIM, S. A., and VAN ITALLIE, T. B. (1965) Studies in normal and obese subjects with a monitored food dispensary device. *Annals of the New York Academy of Science,* 131:654–61. **314**
HASTEY, J. M., see ARKIN, HASTEY, and REISER (1966); see ARKIN, TOTH, BAKER, and HASTEY (1970).
HASTORF, A. H., SCHNEIDER, D. J., and POLEFKA, J. (1970) *Person perception.* Reading, Mass.: Addison-Wesley. **561**
HATHAWAY, S. R., and MONACHESI, E. D. (eds.) (1963) *Analyzing and predicting juvenile delinquency with the MMPI.* Minneapolis: Univ. of Minnesota Press. **372**
HAVIGHURST, R. J., see EELLS, DAVIS, HAVIGHURST, HERRICK, and TYLER (1951).
HAYES, C. (1951) *The ape in our house.* N.Y.: Harper and Row. **289**
HAYS, W. L. (1973) *Statistics for the social sciences.* N.Y.: Holt, Rinehart and Winston. **598**
HAYWARD, H., see GORDON and HAYWARD (1968).
HEBB, D. O. (1972) *Textbook of Psychology* (3rd ed.). Philadelphia: Saunders. **357**
HEIDBREDER, E. (1947) The attainment of concepts: III. The problem. *Journal of Psychology,* 24:93–138. **274**
HEIDER, F. (1958) *The psychology of interpersonal relations.* N.Y.: Wiley. **537, 538**
HEINGARTNER, A., see SCHWARTZ, FELDMAN, BROWN, and HEINGARTNER (1969); see ZAJONC, HEINGARTNER, and HERMAN (1969).
HELFER, R. E., and KEMPE, C. H. (1968) *The battered child.* Chicago: Univ. of Chicago Press. **326**
HELMREICH, R., ARONSON, E., and LEFAN, J. (1970) To err is humanizing—sometimes: Effects of self-esteem, competence, and a pratfall on interpersonal attraction. *Journal of Personality and Social Psychology,* 16:259–64. **531, 533**
HENCHY, T., and GLASS, D. C. (1968) Evaluation apprehension and the social facilitation of dominant and subordinate responses. *Journal of Personality and Social Psychology,* 10:446–54. **547**
HENDRICKSON, G., and SCHROEDER, W. H. (1941) Transfer of training in learning to hit a submerged target. *Journal of Educational Psychology,* 32:205–13. **257**
HENRY, G. W., see ZILBOORG and HENRY (1941).
HENZE, L. F., see HUDSON and HENZE (1969).
HERMAN, E. M., see ZAJONC, HEINGARTNER, and HERMAN (1969).
HERON, W., DOANE, B. K., and SCOTT, T. H. (1956) Visual disturbances after prolonged perceptual isolation. *Canadian Journal of Psychology,* 10:13–16. **329**
HERRICK, V. E., see EELLS, DAVIS, HAVIGHURST, HERRICK, and TYLER (1951).
HERRNSTEIN, R. J., and BORING, E. G. (1965) *A source book in the history of psychology.* Cambridge, Mass.: Harvard Univ. Press. **27**
HERSHENSON, M., see HABER and HERSHENSON (1973).
HERZ, M. J., see MCGAUGH and HERZ (1970).
HESS, E. H. (1958) "Imprinting" in animals, *Scientific American,* 198:81–90. **327**
HESS, E. H. (1972) "Imprinting" in a natural laboratory. *Scientific American,* 227:24–31. **327**
HESS, E. H., and POLT, J. M. (1960) Pupil size as related to the interest value of visual stimuli. *Science,* 132:349–50. **110**
HESTON, L. (1970) The genetics of schizophrenia and schizoid disease. *Science,* 167:249–56. **479**
HETHERINGTON, E. M., and FRANKIE, G. (1967) Effects of parental dominance, warmth, and conflict on imitation in children. *Journal of Personality and Social Psychology,* 6:119–25. **90**
HICKS, D. J. (1968) Short and long-term retention of affectively varied modeled behavior. *Psychonomic Science,* 11:369–70. **340**
HIGGINS, J., and PETERSON, J. C. (1966) Concept of process-reactive schizophrenia: A critique. *Psychological Bulletin,* 66:201–06. **477**
HILGARD, E. R. (1961) Hypnosis and experimental psychodynamics. In Brosen, H. (ed.) *Lectures on experimental psychiatry.* Pittsburgh: Univ. **23**
HILGARD, E. R. (1965) *Hypnotic susceptibility.* N.Y.: Harcourt Brace Jovanovich. **444**
HILGARD, E. R. (1968) *The experience of hypnosis.* N.Y.: Harcourt Brace Jovanovich. **190**
HILGARD, E. R. (1969) Pain: A puzzle for psychology and physiology. *American Psychologist,* 24:103–113. **176**
HILGARD, E. R. (1973a) A neodissociation interpretation of pain reduction in hypnosis. *Psychological Review,* 80:396–411. **176**
HILGARD, E. R. (1973b) The domain of hypnosis, with some comments on alternative paradigms. *American Psychologist,* 28:972–82. **177**
HILGARD, E. R. (ed.) (1964) *Theories of learning and instruction.* 63rd Yearbook, Part I, National Society for the Study of Education. Chicago: Univ. of Chicago Press. **267**
HILGARD, E. R., WEITZENHOFFER, A. M., LANDES, J., and MOORE, R. K. (1961) The distribution of susceptibility to hypnosis in a student population: A study using the Stanford Hypnotic Susceptibility Scale. *Psychological Monographs,* 75, No. 512. **174**
HILGARD, E. R., and BOWER, G. H. (1975) *Theories of learning* (4th ed.). Englewood, N.J.: Prentice-Hall. **220, 267**
HILGARD, E. R., see MORGAN, JOHNSON, and HILGARD (1974); see RUCH, MORGAN, and HILGARD (1973); see WEITZENHOFFER and HILGARD (1959).
HILGARD, J. R. (1970) *Personality and hypnosis: A study of imaginative involvement.* Chicago: Univ. of Chicago Press. **89, 90, 175, 190**
HILL, W. F. (1971) *Learning, a survey of psychological interpretations* (2nd ed.). San Francisco: Chandler. **220**
HIMWICH, H. E. (1970) Study backs biochemical etiology in schizophrenia. *Psychiatric News,* 5–15. **481**
HINKLE, J. E., see COLE, OETTING, and HINKLE (1967).
HIRSCH, J., and KNITTLE, J. L. (1970) Cellularity of obese and nonobese human adipose tissue. *Federation Proceedings,* 29:1516–21. **315**
HIRSCH, J., see KNITTLE and HIRSCH (1968).
HOEBEL, B. G., and TEITELBAUM, P. (1962) Hypothalamic control of feeding and self-stimulation. *Science,* 135:375–77. **307**
HOEBEL, B. G., and TEITELBAUM, P. (1966) Effects of force-feeding and starvation on food intake and body weight of a rat with ventromedial hypothalamic lesions. *Journal of Comparative and Physiological Psychology.* 61:189–93. **309**
HOEBEL, B. G., see CAGGIULA and HOEBEL (1966); see SMITH, KING, and HOEBEL (1970).

HOEPFNER, R., see GUILFORD and HOEPFNER (1971).

HOFFMAN, M. L. (1970) Moral development. In Mussen, P. (ed.), *Carmichael's manual of child psychology.* N.Y.: Wiley. **87**

HOHMANN, G. W. (1966) Some effects of spinal cord lesions on experienced emotional feelings. *Psychophysiology,* 3:143–56. **350**

HOLDEN, M., see GOODENOUGH, SHAPIRO, HOLDEN, and STEINSCHRIBER (1959).

HOLLINGSHEAD, A. B., and REDLICH, F. C. (1958) *Social class and mental illness: A community study.* N.Y.: Wiley. **490**

HOLLISTER, L. E. (1962) Drug induced psychoses and schizophrenic reactions: A critical comparison. *Annals of New York Academy of Science,* 96:80–92. **481**

HOLLISTER, L. E., see DARLEY, TINKLENBERG, ROTH, HOLLISTER, and ATKINSON (1973).

HOLT, R. R., see BARR, LANGS, HOLT, GOLDBERGER, and KLEIN (1972).

HOLZMAN, P. S. (1970) *Psychoanalysis and psychopathology.* N.Y.: McGraw-Hill. **398**

HOLZMAN, P. S., see MENNINGER and HOLZMAN (1973).

HONZIK, C. H., see TOLMAN and HONZIK (1930).

HOROWITZ, L. M. (1974) *Elements of statistics for psychology and education.* N.Y.: McGraw-Hill. **588, 593, 598**

HORTON, E. S., see SIMS, KELLEHER, HORTON, GLUCK, GOODMAN, and ROWE (1968).

HOSKOVEC, J., and COOPER, L. M. (1967) Comparison of recent experimental trends concerning sleep learning in the U.S.A. and the Soviet Union. *Activitas Nervosa* Prague), 9:93–96. **170**

HOVLAND, C. I. (1937) The generalization of conditioned responses: I. The sensory generalization of conditioned responses with varying frequencies of tone. *Journal of General Psychology,* 17:125–48. **198**

HOVLAND, C. I., JANIS, I. L., and KELLEY, H. H. (1953) *Communication and persuasion.* New Haven, Conn.: Yale Univ. Press. **556**

HOWE, M. J. A. (1970) *Introduction to human memory.* N.Y.: Harper and Row. **246**

HOYT, D. P. (1965) The relationship between college grades and adult achievement: A review of the literature. *American College Testing Program Research Reports,* No. 7. **571**

HOYT, D. P. (1966) College grades and adult accomplishment: A review of research. *The Educational Record,* (Winter) 70–75. **571**

HUBBARD, M., see ROSS, LEPPER, and HUBBARD (1974).

HUBEL, D. H., and WIESEL, T. N. (1965) Receptive fields and functional architecture in two non-striate visual areas (18 and 19) of the cat. *Journal of Neurophysiology,* 28:229–89. **47, 143**

HUDSON, J. W., and HENZE, L. F. (1969) Campus values in mate selection: A replication. *Journal of Marriage and the Family,* 31:772–75. **530**

HUDSPETH, W. J., MCGAUGH, J. L., and THOMPSON, C. W. (1964) Aversive and amnesic effects of electroconvulsive shock. *Journal of Comparative and Physiological Psychology,* 57:61–64. **241**

HUESMANN, L. R., see ERON, HUESMANN, LEFKOWITZ, and WALDER (1972).

HULSE, S., see DEESE and HULSE (1967).

HUNT, B. M., see KLEIN. WEGMANN, and HUNT (1972).

HUNT, M. (1974) *Sexual behavior in the 1970's.* Chicago: Playboy Press. **324**

HYDEN, H. (1967) Biochemical and molecular aspects of learning and memory. *Proceedings of the American Philosophical Society,* 111:347–51. **235**

HYDEN, H. (1969) Biochemical aspects of learning and memory. In Pribram, K. (ed.) *On the biology of learning.* N.Y.: Harcourt Brace Jovanovich. **234**

HYMAN, R. (1964) *The nature of psychological inquiry.* Englewood Cliffs, N.J.: Prentice-Hall. **27**

ISAACS, W., THOMAS, J., and GOLDIAMOND, I. (1965) Application of operant conditioning to reinstate verbal behavior in psychotics. In Ullmann, L. P., and Krasner, L. (eds.) *Case studies in behavior modification.* N.Y.: Holt, Rinehart, and Winston. **507**

ISAACSON, R. L. (1970) When brains are damaged. *Psychology Today,* 3:38–42. **420, 421**

ISBELL, H., see EDDY, HALBACH, ISBELL, and SEEVERS (1965).

ITTELSON, W. H., see PROSHANSKY, ITTELSON, and RIVLIN (1970).

JACKSON, P. W., see GETZELS and JACKSON (1962).

JACOBS, G. H., see DEVALOIS and JACOBS (1968).

JACOBS, M. A., SPILKEN, A. Z., NORMAN, M. M., and ANDERSON, L. S. (1970) Life stress and respiratory illness. *Psychosomatic Medicine,* 32:233. **484**

JACOBS, M. A., SPILKEN, A. Z., NORMAN, M. M., and ANDERSON, L. S. (1971) Patterns of maladaptive and respiratory illness. *Journal of Psychosomatic Research,* 15:63–72. **484**

JACOBS, P. A., BRUNTON, M., MELVILLE, M. M., BRITTAIN, R. P., and MCCLEMONT, W. F. (1965) Aggressive behavior, mental subnormality and the XYY male. *Nature,* 208:1351–52. **60**

JACOBS, P. A., PRICE, W. H., COURT BROWN, W. M., BRITTAIN, R. P., and WHATMORE, P. B. (1968) Chromosome studies of men in a maximum security hospital. *Annals of Human Genetics,* 31:339–58. **60**

JACOBSON, A., and KALES, A. (1967) Somnambulism: All-night EEG and related studies. In Kety, S. S., Evarts, E. V., and Williams, H. L. (eds.) *Sleep and altered states of consciousness.* Baltimore, Md.: Williams and Wilkins. **171**

JACOBSON, E. (1970) *Modern treatment of tense patients.* Springfield, Ill.: Thomas. **179, 180**

JAKOBSON, R. (1968) *Child language, aphasia, and general sound laws* (Trans. by A Keiler). The Hague, Netherlands: Mouton. **281**

JAMES, W. (1890) *The principles of psychology.* N.Y.: Holt. **12, 162, 228**

JAMES, W. (1902) *The varieties of religious experience.* N.Y.: Longmans, Green. **162**

JAMES, W. T. (1953) Social facilitation of eating behavior in puppies after satiation. *Journal of Comparative and Physiological Psychology,* 46:427–28. **544**

JAMES, W. T. (1960) The development of social facilitation of eating in puppies. *Journal of Genetic Psychology,* 96:123–27. **546**

JAMES, W. T., and GILBERT, T. F. (1955) The effect of social facilitation on food intake of puppies fed separately and together for the first niney days of life. *British Journal of Animal Behavior,* 3:131–33. **546**

JAMES, W. T., see PLATT and JAMES (1966).

JAMESON, D. H., see LUDWIG, BRANDSMA, WILBUR, BENDFELDT, and JAMESON (1972).

JANIS, I. L. (ed.) (1969) *Personality: Dynamics, development, and assessment.* N.Y.: Harcourt Brace Jovanovich. **398**

JANIS, I. L., see HOVLAND, JANIS, and KELLEY (1953).

JARVIK, L. F., see ERLENMEYER-KIMLING and JARVIK (1963).

JASTROW, J. (1935) *Wish and wisdom.* N.Y.: Appleton-Century-Crofts. **154**

JENKINS, J. G., and DALLENBACH, K. M. (1924) Oblivescence during sleep and walking. *American Journal of Psychology,* 35:605–12. **231**

JENKINS, M. A., see WITTY and JENKINS (1936).

JENKINS, R. L. (1968) The varieties of children's behavioral problems and family dynamics. *American Journal of Psychiatry,* 124:1440–45. **460**

JENSEN, A. R. (1969) How much can we boost I.Q. and scholastic achievement? *Harvard Educational Review,* 39:1–123. **418**

JENSEN, A. R. (1973) *Educability and group differences.* N.Y.: Harper and Row. **414, 417, 418**

JENSEN, J., see MONROE, RECHTSCHAFFEN, FOULKES, and JENSEN (1965).

JOHNSON, D. L., see MORGAN, JOHNSON, and HILGARD (1974).

JOHNSON, J. I., see WELKER, JOHNSON, and PUBOLS (1964).

JOHNSON, R. N. (1972) *Aggression in man and animals.* Philadelphia: Saunders. **359**

JOHNSON, V. E., see MASTERS and JOHNSON (1966); see MASTERS and JOHNSON (1970).

JOHNSTON, M. K., see HARRIS, JOHNSTON, KELLEY, and WOLF (1965).

JONES, E. E., ROCK, L., SHAVEN, K. G., GOETHALS, G. R., and WARD, L. M. (1968) Pattern of performance and ability attribution: An unexpected primacy effect. *Journal of Personality and Social Psychology,* 9:133–41. **528, 529**

JONES, E. E., and DAVIS, K. E. (1965) From acts to dispositions. In Berkowitz, L. (ed.)

Advances in experimental social psychology, 2:219–66. N.Y.: Academic Press. **538**

JONES, E. E., and HARRIS, V. A. (1967) The attribution of attitudes. *Journal of Experimental Social Psychology,* 3:1–24. **538**

JONES, E. E., and NISBETT, R. E. (1971) *The actor and observer: Divergent perceptions of the causes of behavior.* N.Y.: General Learning Press. **386**

JONES, M. C. (1957) The later careers of boys who were early- or late-maturing. *Child Development,* 93:87–111. **93**

JONES, M. C., see MUSSEN and JONES (1958).

JORGENSEN, B. W., see LEVINGER, SENN, and JORGENSEN (1970).

JOURARD, S. M. (1971) *The transparent self* (2nd ed.). N.Y.: Van Nostrand. **394**

JOURARD, S. M. (1974) *Healthy personality: An approach from the humanistic viewpoint.* N.Y.: Macmillan. **398**

JUNG, C. G. (1944) *Psychology and alchemy.* N.Y.: Pantheon. **172**

JUNG, C. G. (1968) *Analytical psychology.* N.Y.: Pantheon. **378**

KAGAN, J., see MUSSEN, CONGER, and KAGAN (1974).

KAKOLEWSKI, J. W., see VALENSTEIN, COX, and KAKOLEWSKI (1970).

KALAT, J. W., see ROZIN and KALAT (1971).

KALES, A. (ed.) (1969) *Sleep: Physiology and pathology.* Philadelphia: Lippincott. **168**

KALES, A., see JACOBSON and KALES (1967).

KALIN, R., see MCCLELLAND, DAVIS, KALIN, and WANNER (1972).

KAMIN, L. J. (1974) *The science and politics of IQ.* Potomac, Md.: Erlbaum Assoc. **149**

KAMIYA, J., see NOWLIS and KAMIYA (1970).

KANDEL, D. B., and LESSER, G. S. (1972) *Youth in two worlds.* San Francisco: Jossey-Bass. **95, 96, 97**

KANFER, F. H., and PHILLIPS, J. S. (1970) *Learning foundations of behavior therapy.* N.Y.: Wiley. **459, 521**

KAPLAN, J. (1970) *Marijuana: The new prohibition.* N.Y.: World Publishing. **187**

KARLINS, M., see ANDREWS and KARLINS (1971).

KASSARJIAN, H. H. (1963) Voting intentions and political perception. *Journal of Psychology,* 56:85–88. **531**

KASSORLA, I. C., see LOVAAS, FREITAG, GOLD, and KASSORLA (1965).

KEESEY, R. E., see POWLEY and KEESEY (1970).

KELLEHER, P. E., see SIMS, KELLEHER, HORTON, GLUCK, GOODMAN, and ROWE (1968).

KELLEY, C. S., see HARRIS, JOHNSTON, KELLEY, and WOLF (1965).

KELLEY, H. H. (1950) The warm-cold variable in first impressions of persons. *Journal of Personality,* 18:431–39. **536**

KELLEY, H. H. (1967) Attribution theory in social psychology. In Levine, D. (ed.) *Nebraska symposium on motivation,* vol. 15. Lincoln, Nebr.: Univ. of Nebraska Press. **538**

KELLEY, H. H. (1971) Attribution in social interaction. In Jones, E. E., Kanouse, D. E., Kelley, H. H., Nisbett, R. E., Valins, S., and Weiner, B. (eds.) *Attribution: Perceiving the causes of behavior.* Morristown, N.J.: General Learning Press. **538**

KELLEY, H. H. (1972) Causal schemata and the attribution process. In Jones, S., E. E., Kanouse, D. E., Kelley, H. H., Nisbett, R. E., Valins, S., and Weiner, B. (eds.) *Attribution: Perceiving the causes of behavior.* Morristown, N.J.: General Learning Press. **538**

KELLEY, H. H., see HOVLAND, JANIS, and KELLEY (1953).

KELLOGG, L. A., see KELLOGG and KELLOGG (1933).

KELLOGG, W. N., and KELLOGG, L. A. (1933) *The ape and the child.* N.Y.: McGraw-Hill. **289**

KELMAN, H. C. (1967) Human use of human subjects: The problem of deception in social psychological experiments. *Psychological Bulletin,* 67:1–11. **553**

KEMPE, C. H., see HELFER and KEMPE (1968).

KENNEDY, R. A., see WILKES and KENNEDY (1969).

KEPNER, C. R., see BARON and KEPNER (1970).

KERCKHOFF, A. C., and DAVIS, K. E. (1962) Value consensus and need complementarity in mate selection. *American Sociological Review,* 17:295–303. **533**

KERSEY, J., see WEBB and KERSEY (1967).

KESEY, K. (1962) *One flew over the cuckoo's nest.* N.Y.: Viking Press. **492**

KESSEN, W. (1965) *The child.* N.Y.: Wiley. **100**

KESSLER, S., and MOOS, R. H. (1970) The XYY karyotype and criminality: A review. *Journal of Psychiatric Research,* 7:153–70. **60**

KEWMAN, D. G., see ROBERTS, KEWMAN, and MACDONALD (1973).

KIESLER, C. A., NISBETT, R. E., and ZANNA, M. P. (1969) On inferring one's beliefs from one's behavior. *Journal of Personality and Social Psychology,* 4:321–27. **556**

KING, M., see SMITH, KING, and HOEBEL (1970).

KINSEY, A. C., POMEROY, W. B., MARTIN, C. E. (1948) *Sexual behavior in the human male.* Philadelphia: Saunders. **19, 324**

KINSEY, A. C., POMEROY, W. B., MARTIN, C. E., and GEBHARD, P. H. (1953) *Sexual behavior in the human female.* Philadelphia: Saunders. **19, 324**

KINTSCH, W. (1970) *Learning, memory, and conceptual processes.* N.Y.: Wiley. **246**

KIRK, R., see BEVER, LACKNER, and KIRK (1969).

KLEBANOFF, L. B. (1959) Parental attitudes of mothers of schizophrenics, brain-injured and retarded, and normal children. *American Journal of Orthopsychiatry.* 29:445–54. **480**

KLEIN, G. S., see BARR, LANGS, HOLT, GOLDBERGER, and KLEIN (1972).

KLEIN, K. E., WEGMANN, H. M., and HUNT, B. M. (1972) Desynchronization of body temperature and performance circadian rhythm as a result of outgoing and homegoing transmeridian flights. *Aerospace Medicine,* 43:119–32. **166**

KLEINMAN, R., see BRENER and KLEINMAN (1970).

KLEINMUNTZ, B. (1974) *Essentials of abnormal psychology.* N.Y.: Harper and Row. **451, 463, 469, 471, 492**

KLEITMAN, N. (1963) *Sleep and wakefulness* (2nd ed.) Chicago: Univ. of Chicago Press. **165**

KLINEBERG, O. (1938) Emotional expression in Chinese literature. *Journal of Abnormal and Social Psychology,* 33:517–20. **356**

KLING, J. W., and RIGGS, L. A. (1971) *Experimental psychology* (3rd ed.). N.Y.: Holt, Rinehart and Winston. **27, 128**

KLONGLAN, G. E., see WILCOX, BROOKS, BEAL, and KLONGLAN (1972).

KNAPP, P. (1967) Airway resistance and emotional state in bronchial asthma. *Psychosomatic Medicine,* 29:450–51. **484**

KNITTLE, J. L., and HIRSCH, J. (1968) Effect of early nutrition on the development of rat epididymal fat pads: Cellularity and metabolism. *Journal of Clinical Investigation,* 47:2091. **315**

KNITTLE, J. L., see HIRSCH and KNITTLE (1970).

KOBASIGAWA, A., ARAKAKI, K., and AWIGUNI, A. (1966) Avoidance of feminine toys by kindergarten boys: The effects of adult presence or absence, and an adult's attitudes toward sex-typing. *Japanese Journal of Psychology,* 37:96–103. **89**

KOFFKA, K. (1925) *The growth of the mind* (trans. Ogden, R. M.). N.Y.: Harcourt Brace Jovanovich. **12**

KOGAN, N., see WALLACH and KOGAN (1965).

KOHEN-RAZ, R. (1968) Mental and motor development of Kibbutz, institutionalized, and home-reared infants in Israel. *Child Development,* 39:489–504. **84**

KOHLBERG, L. (1967) Moral and religious education and the public schools: A developmental view. In Sizer, T. (ed.) *Religion and public education.* Boston: Houghton Mifflin. **80**

KOHLBERG, L. (1969) Stage and sequence: The cognitive-developmental approach to socialization. In Goslin, D. A. (ed.), *Handbook of socialization theory and research.* Chicago: Rand McNally. **80**

KOHLBERG, L. (1973) Implications of developmental psychology for education: Examples from moral development. *Educational Psychologist,* 10:2–14. **81**

KOHLER, I. (1962) Experiments with goggles. *Scientific American,* 206:62–72. **133**

KOHLER, W. (1925) *The mentality of apes.* N.Y.: Harcourt Brace Jovanovich. **216, 220**

KOVACH, J., see MURPHY and KOVACH (1972).

KRANTZ, D. L., ATKINSON, R. C., LUCE, R. D., and SUPPES, P. (eds.) (1974) *Contemporary developments in mathematical psychology.* San Francisco: Freeman. **128, 220, 246**

KRANTZ, D. L., LUCE, R. D., SUPPES, P., and TVERSKY, A. (1971) *Foundations of measurement.* N.Y.: Academic Press. **598**

KRASNER, L., and ULLMAN, L. P. (1973) *Behavior influence and personality.* N.Y.: Holt, Rinehart and Winston. **506, 458**

KRASNER, L., see ULLMAN and KRASNER (1969).

KRAWITZ, R. N., see LESSER, KRAWITZ, and PACKARD (1963).

KRETSCHMER, E. (1925) *Physique and character.* London: Kegan Paul. **367**

KRIPPNER, S. (1970) Electrophysiological studies of ESP in dreams: Sex differences in seventy-four telepathy sessions. *Journal of the American Society for Psychical Research,* 64:277–85. **154**

KRIPPNER, S. (1971) "Clairvoyant" perception of art prints in altered consciousness states. *Proceedings of the Annual Convention of the American Psychological Association,* 6:423–24. **154**

KROEBER, T. C. (1963) The coping functions of the ego mechanisms. In White, R. W. (ed.) *The study of lives.* N.Y.: Atherton Press, 178–98. **448**

KRUEGER, W. C. F. (1929) The effect of overlearning on retention. *Journal of Experimental Psychology,* 12:71–78. **245**

KTSANES, T., see WINCH, KTSANES, and KTSANES (1954).

KTSANES, V., see WINCH, KTSANES, and KTSANES (1954).

KUBIS, J. F. (1962). Cited in Smith, B. M., The polygraph. In Atkinson, R. C. (ed.) *Contemporary Psychology.* San Francisco: Freeman. **347**

KUENNE, M. R. (1946) Experimental investigation of the relation of language to transposition behavior in young children. *Journal of Experimental Psychology.* 36:471–90. **291**

KUHN, T. S. (1962) *The structure of scientific revolutions.* Chicago: Univ. of Chicago Press. **556**

LACKNER, J. R., see BEVER, LACKNER, and KIRK (1969).

LAING, R. D. (1967) *The politics of experience.* N.Y.: Ballantine. **459**

LAMBERT, W. W., SOLOMON, R. L., and WATSON, P. D. (1949) Reinforcement and extinction as factors in size estimation. *Journal of Experimental Psychology,* 39:637–41. **151**

LANDES, J., see HILGARD, WEITZENHOFFER, LANDES, and MOORE (1961).

LANDIS, J. T. (1942) What is the happiest period of life? *School and Society,* 55:643–45. **99**

LANG, P. J. (1965) Behavior therapy with a case of nervous anorexia. In Ullman, L., and Krasner, L. (eds.) *Case studies in behavior modification.* N.Y.: Holt, Rinehart and Winston. **505**

LANGNER, T. S., see SROLE, LANGNER, MICHAEL, OPLER, and RENNIE (1962).

LANGS, R. J., see BARR, LANGS, HOLT, GOLDBERGER, and KLEIN (1972).

LARSON, R. F., see MENDENHALL, OTT, and LARSON (1974).

LASKY, J. J., and others (1959) Post-hospital adjustment as predicted by psychiatric patients and their staffs. *Journal of Consulting Psychology,* 23:213–18. **373**

LATANÉ, B., and DARLEY, J. M. (1968) Group inhibition of bystander intervention in emergencies. *Journal of Personality and Social Psychology,* 10:215–21. **548, 549**

LATANÉ, B., and DARLEY, J. M. (1970) *The unresponsive bystander: Why doesn't he help?* N.Y.: Appleton-Century-Crofts. **547**

LATANÉ, B., and RODIN, J. (1969) A lady in distress: Inhibiting effects of friends and strangers on bystander intervention. *Journal of Experimental and Social Psychology,* 5:189–202. **548**

LATANÉ, B., see DARLEY and LATANÉ (1968).

LATIES, V. G., see WEISS and LATIES (1962).

LAUGHLIN, H. P. (1967) *The neuroses.* Washington, D.C.: Butterworths. **461, 465**

LAVATELLI, C. S., and STENDLER, F. (1972) *Readings in child behavior and development.* (3rd ed.) N.Y.: Harcourt Brace Jovanovich. **100**

LAYZER, D. (1974) Heritability analyses of IQ scores: Science or numerology? *Science,* 183:1259–66. **419**

LAZARUS, A. A. (1971) *Behavior therapy and beyond.* N.Y.: McGraw-Hill. **459, 503**

LAZARUS, A. A., see WOLPE and LAZARUS (1966).

LAZARUS, R. S., and ALFERT, E. (1964) Short-circuiting of threat by experimentally altering cognitive appraisal. *Journal of Abnormal and Social Psychology,* 69:195–205. **354**

LAZARUS, R. S., see SPEISMAN, LAZARUS, MORDKOFF, and DAVISON (1964).

LEE, R. S., see CHEIN, GERARD, LEE, and ROSENFELD (1964).

LEFAN, J., see HELMREICH, ARONSON, and LEFAN (1970).

LEFKOWITZ, M. M., see ERON, HUESMANN, LEFKOWITZ, and WALDER (1972).

LEHRMAN, D. S. (1964) Control of behavior cycles in reproduction. In Etkin, W. (ed.) *Social behavior and organization among vertebrates.* Chicago: Univ. of Chicago Press. **327**

LEIBOWITZ, H., see ZIEGLER and LEIBOWITZ (1957).

LEIBOWITZ, H. W., see PARRISH, LUNDY, and LEIBOWITZ (1968).

LEIGHTON, A. H., see LEIGHTON, HARDING, MACKLIN, MACMILLAN, and LEIGHTON (1963).

LEIGHTON, D. C., HARDING, J. S., MACKLIN, D. B., MACMILLAN, A. M., and LEIGHTON, A. H. (1963) *The character of danger: Psychiatric symptoms in selected communities.* N.Y.: Basic Books. **490**

LEJEUNE, J. (1970) Down's syndrome explained as an error in meiotic process. *Roche Reports,* 7:1–2. **421**

LENNEBERG, E. H. (1967) *Biological foundations of language.* N.Y.: Wiley. **286**

LEPPER, M. R., GREENE, D., and NISBETT, R. E. (1973) Undermining children's intrinsic interest with extrinsic reward: A test of the "overjustification" hypothesis. *Journal of Personality and Social Psychology,* 28:129–37. **261, 540**

LEPPER, M. R., ZANNA, M. P., and ABELSON, R. P. (1970) Cognitive irreversibility in a dissonance reduction situation. *Journal of Personality and Social Psychology.* **541**

LEPPER, M. R., see ROSS, LEPPER, and HUBBARD (1974).

LESSER, G. S., KRAWITZ, R. N., and PACKARD, R. (1963) Experimental arousal of achievement motivation in adolescent girls. *Journal of Abnormal and Social Psychology,* 66:59–66. **580**

LESSER, G. S., see KANDEL and LESSER (1972).

LEVIN, H., see SEARS, MACCOBY, and LEVIN (1957).

LEVIN, J. M., see ALLEN and LEVIN (1971).

LEVINGER, G., SENN, D. J., and JORGENSEN, B. W. (1970) Progress toward permanence in courtship: A test of the Kerckhoff-Davis hypotheses. *Sociometry,* 33:427–43. **533**

LEVITT, E. E. (1967) *The psychology of anxiety.* Indianapolis, Ind.: Bobbs-Merrill. **459**

LEWIN, K., see BARKER, DEMBO, and LEWIN (1941).

LEWIS, H. B., GOODENOUGH, D. R., SHAPIRO, A., and SLESER, I. (1966) Individual differences in dream recall. *Journal of Abnormal Psychology,* 71:52–59. **170**

LEWIS, S. (1934) *Work of art.* Garden City, N.Y.: Doubleday. **366**

LEWIS, S. A., see BRISLIN and LEWIS (1968).

LIDZ, T., FLECK, S., and CORNELISON, A. R. (1965) *Schizophrenia and the family.* N.Y.: International Universities Press. **488**

LIEBERMAN, M. A., YALOM, I. D., and MILES, M. B. (1973) *Encounter groups: First facts.* N.Y.: Basic Books. **511**

LIMBER, J. (1973) The genesis of complex sentences. In Moore, T. E. (ed.) *Cognitive development and the acquisition of language.* N.Y.: Academic Press. **285**

LINDSAY, P. H., and NORMAN, D. A. (1972) *Human information processing.* N.Y.: Academic Press. **128, 157, 246, 297**

LINDZEY, G., and ARONSON, E. (eds.) (1970) *The handbook of social psychology* (2nd ed.) Vol. 1–5. Reading, Mass.: Addison-Wesley. **561**

LINDZEY, G., see HALL and LINDZEY (1970); see LOEHLIN, LINDZEY, and SPUHLER (1975).

LIPPERT, W. W., and SENTER, R. J. (1966) Electrodermal responses in the sociopath. *Psychonomic Science,* 4:25–26. **486**

LOBBAN, M. C. (1965) Dissociation in human rhythmic functions. In Aschoff, J. (ed.) *Circadian clocks.* Amsterdam, Netherlands: North-Holland, 219–27. **166**

LOEHLIN, J. C., LINDZEY, G., and SPUHLER, J. N. (1975) *Race differences in intelligence.* San Francisco: Freeman. **419, 424, 426**

LOEW, C. A. (1967) Acquisition of a hostile attitude and its relationship to aggressive behavior. *Journal of Personality and Social Psychology,* 5:335–341. **341**

LOGAN, F. A. (1970) *Fundamentals of learning and motivation.* Dubuque, Iowa: Brown. **220**

LONDON, P. (1969) *Behavior control.* N.Y.: Harper and Row. **583**

LORENZ, K. (1966) *On aggression.* N.Y.: Harcourt Brace Jovanovich. **342**

LORGE, I. (1930) Influence of regularly interpolated time intervals on subsequent learning. *Teachers College Contributions to Education,* No. 438. **212**

LOVAAS, O. I., FREITAG, G., GOLD, V. J., and KASSORLA, I. C. (1965) Recording apparatus for observation of behaviors of children in free play settings. *Journal of Experimental Child Psychology,* 2:108–20. **385**

LOWELL, E. L., see MCCLELLAND, ATKINSON, CLARK, and LOWELL (1953).

LUBIN, A., see WILLIAMS, LUBIN, and GOODNOW (1959).

LUCE, G. G. (1971) *Body time: Physiological rhythms and social stress.* N.Y.: Pantheon. **190**

LUCE, G. G., and SEGAL, J. (1966) *Sleep.* N.Y.: Coward-McCann. **190**

LUCE, R. D., see KRANTZ, ATKINSON, LUCE, and SUPPES (1974); see KRANTZ, LUCE, SUPPES, and TVERSKY (1971).

LUCHINS, A. (1957a) Primacy-recency in impression formation. In Hovland, C. I. (ed.) *The order of presentation in persuasion.* New Haven, Conn.: Yale; Univ. Press. **528**

LUCHINS, A. (1957b) Experimental attempts to minimize the impact of first impressions. In Hovland, C. I. (ed.) *The order of presentation in persuasion.* New Haven, Conn.: Yale Univ. Press. **527, 529**

LUDWIG, A. M. (1966) Altered states of consciousness. *Archives of General Psychiatry,* 15:225–34. **159**

LUDWIG, A. M., BRANDSMA, J. M., WILBUR, C. B., BENDFELDT, F., and JAMESON, D. H. (1972) The objective study of a multiple personality. *Archives of General Psychiatry,* 26:298–310. **163, 164**

LUDWIG, A. M., and LYLE, W. H. (1964) Tension induction and the hyperalert trance. *Journal of Abnormal and Social Psychology.* 69:70–76. **175**

LUMSDEN, D. B., see MCGUIGAN and LUMSDEN (1973).

LUNDY, R. M., see PARRISH, LUNDY, and LEIBOWITZ (1968).

LURIA, A. R. (1968) *The mind of a mnemonist.* N.Y.: Basic Books. **242**

LUTHE, W., see SCHULTZ and LUTHE (1969).

LYKKEN, D. T. (1957) A study of anxiety in the sociopathic personality. *Journal of Abnormal and Social Psychology,* 55:6–10. **486**

LYLE, W. H., see LUDWIG and LYLE (1964).

MACCOBY, E. E., and FELDMAN, S. S. (1972) Mother attachment and stranger reactions in the third year of life. *Monograph of the Society for Research in Child Development,* No. 1, 37:1–86. **83, 84**

MACCOBY, E. E., see SEARS, MACCOBY, and LEVIN (1957).

MACCULLOCH, M. J., see FELDMAN and MACCULLOCH (1971).

MACDONALD, H., see ROBERTS, KEWMAN, and MACDONALD (1973).

MACKLIN, D. B., see LEIGHTON, HARDING, MACKLIN, MACMILLAN, and LEIGHTON (1963).

MACKWORTH, N. H. (1950) Researches in the measurement of human performance. *Medical Research Council Special Report Series,* No. 268. London: H. M. Stationery Office. **161**

MACLAY, H., and WARE, E. E. (1961) Cross-cultural use of the semantic differential. *Behavioral Science,* 6:185–90. **273**

MACMILLAN, A. M., see LEIGHTON, HARDING, MACKLIN, MACMILLAN, and LEIGHTON (1963).

MACNICHOL, E. F., JR. (1964) Three-pigment color vision. *Scientific American,* 211:48–56. **116**

MACWHINNEY, B., see ATKINSON, MACWHINNEY, and STOEL (1970).

MADDI, S. (1972) *Personality theories: A comparative analysis.* Homewood, Ill.: Dorsey. **398**

MADDI, S., and COSTA, P. T. (1972) *Humanism in personality.* Chicago: Aldine-Atherton. **398**

MADIGAN, S. A., see TULVING and MADIGAN (1970).

MADSEN, C. H., and ULLMAN, L. P. (1967) Innovations in the desensitization of frigidity. *Behavior Research and Therapy,* 5:67–68. **504**

MAGARET, A., see CAMERON and MAGARET (1951).

MAHARISHI MAHESH YOGI (1963) *The science of being and art of living.* N.Y.: Signet Books. **179**

MAHER, B. A. (1966) *Principles of psychotherapy: An experimental approach.* N.Y.: McGraw-Hill. **473, 474, 487, 489, 492**

MAHL, G. F. (1971) *Psychological conflict and defense.* N.Y.: Harcourt, Brace, Jovanovich. **451**

MAIER, N. R. F. (1949) *Frustration: A study of behavior without a goal.* N.Y.: McGraw-Hill. **439**

MANDLER, G. (1974) Organization and recognition. In Tulving, E., and Donaldson, W. (eds.) *Organization of memory.* N.Y.: Academic Press. **243**

MANDLER, G., see SARASON, MANDLER, and CRAIGHILL (1952).

MANGRUM, J. C., see STEPHENS, ASTRUP, and MANGRUM (1967).

Manual for the Wechsler Intelligence Scale for Children (1974) N.Y.: Harcourt Brace Jovanovich, **406**

MARGOLIS, R., see GLICK and MARGOLIS (1962).

MARK, V. H., and ERVIN, F. R. (1970) *Violence and the brain.* N.Y.: Harper and Row. **338**

MAROLLA, F. A., see BELMONT and MAROLLA (1973).

MARSHALL, G. (1974) *Cognitive, social and physiological determinants of emotional states: A replication and extension.* Unpublished Ph.D. dissertation, Stanford University, Stanford, Calif. **352**

MARSHALL, G., see MASLACH, MARSHALL, and ZIMBARDO (1972).

MARTIN, C. E., see KINSEY, POMEROY, and MARTIN (1948); see KINSEY, POMEROY, MARTIN, and GEBHARD (1953).

MARTIN, D. G. (1971) *Introduction to psychotherapy.* Monterey, Calif.: Brooks-Cole. **521**

MARTIN, E., see MELTON and MARTIN (1972).

MASLACH, C., MARSHALL, G., and ZIMBARDO, P. (1972) Hypnotic control of peripheral skin temperature: A case report. *Psychophysiology,* 9:600–05. **180**

MASLOW, A. H. (1954) *Motivation and personality.* N.Y.: Harper and Row. **334, 393**

MASLOW, A. H. (1959) Cognition of being in the peak experiences. *Journal of Genetic Psychology,* 94:43–66. **162**

MASLOW, A. H. (1967) Self-actualization and beyond. In Bugental J. F. T. (ed.) *Challenges of humanistic psychology.* N.Y.: McGraw-Hill. **393**

MASLOW, A. H. (1970) *Motivation and personality* (2nd ed.). N.Y.: Harper and Row. **359, 389, 392**

MASON, J. W., see BRADY, PORTER, CONRAD, and MASON (1958).

MASSERMAN, J. H. (1961) *Principles of dynamic psychiatry.* (2nd ed.). Philadelphia: Saunders. **440, 445**

MASTERS, W. H., and JOHNSON, V. E. (1966) *Human sexual response.* Boston: Little, Brown. **18**

MASTERS, W. H., and JOHNSON, V. E. (1970) *Human sexual inadequacy.* Boston: Little, Brown. **504**

MATARAZZO, J. D. (1971) Some national developments in the utilization of nontraditional mental health manpower. *American Psychologist,* 26:363–72. **513**

MATARAZZO, J. E. (1972) *Wechsler's measurement and appraisal of adult intelligence* (5th ed.). Baltimore, Md.: Williams, and Wilkins. **426**

MATTER, W. W., see CROSS, HALCOMB, and MATTER (1967).

MAULDIN, W. P., WATSON, W. B., and NOE, L. F. (1970) *KAP surveys and evaluation of family planning programs.* N.Y.: The Population Council. **574**

MAY, M. A., see HARTSHORNE and MAY (1928, 1929).

MAYER, J. (1955) Regulation of energy intake and the body weight: The glucostatic theory and the lipostatic theory. *Annals of the New York Academy of Science,* 63:15–43. **308**

MAYER, J., see THOMAS and MAYER (1973).

MCCLEARN, G. E., and DEFRIES, J. C. (1973) *Introduction to behavioral genetics.* San Francisco: Freeman. **62, 66, 426, 492**

MCCLELLAND, D. C., ATKINSON, J. W., CLARK, R. A., and LOWELL, E. L. (1953) *The achievement motive.* N.Y.: Appleton-Century-Crofts. **579**

MCCLELLAND, D. C., DAVIS, W. N., KALIN,

R., and WANNER, E. (1972) *The drinking man.* N.Y.: Free Press. **182**

MCCLELLAND, D. C., and WINTER, D. G. (1969) *Motivating economic achievement.* N.Y.: Free Press. **581**

MCCLEMONT, W. F., see JACOBS, BRUNTON, MELVILLE, BRITTAIN, and MCCLEMONT (1965).

MCCLINTOCK, C. G., SPAULDING, C. B., and TURNER, H. A. (1965) Political orientations of academically affiliated psychologists. *American Psychologist,* 20:211–21. **580**

MCCONNELL, J. V., SHIGEHISA, T., and SALIVE, H. (1970) In Pribram, K. H., and Broadbent, D. E. (eds.) *Biology of memory.* N.Y.: Academic Press. **235**

MCCONNELL, R. A. (1968) ESP without cards. *The Science Teacher.* 35:29–33. **153**

MCCONNELL, R. A. (1969) ESP and credibility in science. *American Psychologist,* 24:531–38. **151, 157**

MCCONNELL, R. A., see SCHMEIDLER and MCCONNELL (1958).

MCGAUGH, J. L. (1970) Time-dependent processes in memory storage. In McGaugh, J. L., and Herz, M. J. (eds.) *Controversial issues in consolidation of the memory trace.* N.Y.: Atherton Press. **241**

MCGAUGH, J. L., and HERZ, M. J. (eds.) (1970) *Controversial issues in consolidation of the memory trace.* N.Y.: Atherton Press. **241**

MCGAUGH, J. L., see HUDSPETH, MCGAUGH, and THOMPSON (1964).

MCGHIE, A., and CHAPMAN, J. (1961) Disorders of attention and perception in early schizophrenia. *British Journal of Medical Psychology,* 34:103–16. **474**

MCGINTY, D., EPSTEIN, A. W., and TEITELBAUM, P. (1965) The contribution of oropharyngeal sensations to hypothalamic hyperphagia. *Animal Behavior.* 13:413–18. **311**

MCGUIGAN, F. J., and LUMSDEN, D. B. (eds.) (1973) *Contemporary approaches to conditioning and learning.* Washington, D.C.: Winston. **220**

MCGUIRE, W. J., and PAPAGEORGIS, D. (1961) The relative efficacy of various types of prior belief-defense in producing immunity against persuasion. *Journal of Abnormal and Social Psychology,* 62:327–37. **558**

MCGUIRE, W. J., see ABELSON, ARONSEN, MCGUIRE, NEWCOMB, ROSENBERG, and TANNENBAUM (1968).

MCLAUGHLIN, B. (1971) *Learning and social behavior.* N.Y.: Free Press. **359**

MCNEILL, D. (1970) *The acquisition of language: The study of developmental psycholinguistics.* N.Y.: Harper and Row. **281**

MCNEILL, D. V., see BROWN and MCNEILL (1966); MILLER and MCNEILL (1969).

MEAD, M. (1970) *Culture and commitment.* N.Y.: Natural History Press, Doubleday. **97**

MEDNICK, S. A. (1962) The associative basis of the creative process. *Psychological Review,* 69:220–32. **412**

MELTON, A. W., and MARTIN, E. (eds.) (1972) *Coding processes in human memory.* Washington, D.C.: Winston. **246**

MELVILLE, M. M., see JACOBS, BRUNTON, MELVILLE, BRITTAIN, and MCCLEMONT (1965).

MENDENHALL, W., OTT, L., and LARSON, R. F. (1974) *Statistics: A tool for the social sciences.* Belmont, Calif.: Duxbury Press. **598**

MENNINGER, K., and HOLZMAN, P. S. (1973) *Theory of psychoanalytic technique* (2nd ed.). N.Y.: Basic Books. **521**

MENZIES, R. (1937) Conditioned vasomotor responses in human subjects. *Journal of Psychology,* 4:75–120. **198**

MERRILL, M. A., see TERMAN and MERRILL (1937).

METCALFE, M. (1956) Demonstration of a psychosomatic relationship. *British Journal of Medical Psychology,* 29:63–66. **387**

MEUMANN, E. (1904) Haus- und Schularbeit: Experimente an Kindern der Volkschule. *Die Deutsche Schule,* 8:278–303. **545**

MEYER, D. (1965) *The positive thinkers: A study of the American quest for health, wealth and personal power from Mary Baker Eddy to Norman Vincent Peale.* Garden City, N.Y.: Doubleday. **188**

MEYER, D. R., see HARLOW, HARLOW, and MEYER (1950).

MICHAEL, S. T., see SROLE, LANGNER, MICHAEL, OPLER, and RENNIE (1962).

MIDWEST RESEARCH INSTITUTE (1972) *The incidence of drugs in fatally injured drivers.* Washington, D.C.: U.S. Dept of Transportation. **182**

MILES, M. B., see LIEBERMAN, YALOM, and MILES (1973).

MILGRAM, S. (1963) Behavioral study of obedience. *Journal of Abnormal and Social Psychology,* 67:371–78. **552, 553**

MILGRAM, S. (1964a) Group pressure and action against a person. *Journal of Abnormal and Social Psychology,* 69:137–43. **552**

MILGRAM, S. (1964b) Issues in the study of obedience: A reply to Baumrind. *American Psychologist,* 19:848–52. **553**

MILGRAM, S. (1965) Some conditions of obedience and disobedience to authority. *Human Relations,* 18:57–76. **552**

MILGRAM, S. (1968) Reply to the critics. *International Journal of Psychiatry,* 6:294–95. **553**

MILGRAM, S. (1974) *Obedience to authority: An experimental view.* N.Y.: Harper and Row. **553**

MILLER, G. A., GALANTER, E., and PRIBRAM, K. H. (1960) *Plans and the structure of behavior.* N.Y.: Holt. **160**

MILLER, G. A., and MCNEILL, D. V. (1969) Psycholinguistics. In Lindzey. G., and Aronson, E. (eds.) *The handbook of social psychology* (2nd ed.), vol. III. Reading, Mass.: Addison-Wesley, 666–794. **292**

MILLER, G. A., see CLARK and MILLER (1970).

MILLER, H. L., and RIVENBANK, W. H. (1970) III. Sexual differences in physical attractiveness as a determinant of heterosexual likings. *Psychological Reports,* 27:701–02. **530**

MILLER, J. M., MOODY, D. B., and STEBBINS, W. C. (1969) Evoked potentials and auditory reaction time in monkeys. *Science,* 163:592–94. **48**

MILLER, N. E. (1959) Liberalization of basic S-R concepts: Extensions to conflict behavior, motivation, and social learning. In Koch, S. (ed.) *Psychology: A study of a science,* vol. II. N.Y.: McGraw-Hill. **431**

MILLER, N. E., and BANUAZIZI, A. (1968) Instrumental learning by curarized rats of a specific visceral response, intestinal, or cardiac. *Journal of Comparative and Physiological Psychology,* 65:1–7. **207**

MILLER, N. E., and BUGELSKI, R. (1948) Minor studies of aggression: II. The influence of frustrations imposed by the in-group on attitudes expressed toward out-groups. *The Journal of Psychology,* 25:437–42. **436**

MILLER, N. E., and DOLLARD, J. (1941) *Social learning and imitation.* New Haven, Conn.: Yale Univ. Press. **382**

MILLER, N. E., and DWORKIN, B. R. (1973) Visceral learning: Recent difficulties with curarized rats and significant programs for human research. In Obrist, P. A., et al. (eds.) *Contemporary Trends in Cardiovascular Psychophysiology.* Chicago: Aldine-Atherton. **206**

MILLER, N. E., see DOLLARD, DOOB, MILLER, MOWRER, and SEARS (1939).

MILLER, N., and CAMPBELL, D. T. (1959) Recency and primacy in persuasion as a function of the timing of speeches and measurements. *Journal of Abnormal and Social Psychology,* 59:1–9. **557, 558**

MILLER, N. E., see DELGADO, ROBERTS, and MILLER (1954).

MILLER, R. F., see COLE, HART, and MILLER (1956).

MILNER, B. (1962) Literality effects in audition. In Mountcastle, V. B., (ed.) *Interhemispheric relations and cerebral dominance.* Baltimore, Md.: The Johns Hopkins Press. **53**

MILNER, B. (1964) Some effects of frontal lobectomy in man. In Warren, J. M., and Akert, K. (eds.) *The frontal granular cortex and behavior.* N.Y.: McGraw-Hill. **49**

MILNER, P. M. (1970) *Physiological psychology.* N.Y.: Holt, Rinehart, and Winston. **65, 239**

MISCHEL, H. N., see MISCHEL and MISCHEL (1974).

MISCHEL, W. (1968) *Personality and assessment.* N.Y.: Wiley. **398**

MISCHEL, W. (1971) *Introduction to personality.* N.Y.: Holt, Rinehart and Winston. **384, 398**

MISCHEL, W. (1973) Toward a cognitive social learning reconceptualization of personality. *Psychological Review,* 80:252–83. **382, 384**

MISCHEL, W., and MISCHEL, H. N. (1974) A cognitive social learning approach to morality and self-regulation. In Lickona, T.

(ed.) *Men and morality.* N.Y.: Holt, Rinehart and Winston. **81**

MLADEJOVSKY, M. G., see DOBELLE, MLADEJOVSKY, and GIRVIN (1974).

MONACHESI, E. D., see HATHAWAY and MONACHESI (1963).

MONEY, J., HAMPSON, J. G., and HAMPSON, J. L. (1957) Imprinting and the establishment of gender role. *Archives of Neurological Psychiatry,* 77:333–36. **70**

MONROE, L. J., RECHTSCHAFFEN, A., FOULKES, D., and JENSEN, J. (1965) The discriminability of REM and NREM reports. *Journal of Personality and Social Psychology,* 2:456–60. **168**

MONTAGU, M. F. A. (1968) *Man and aggression.* N.Y.: Oxford Univ. Press. **343**

MOODY, D. B., see MILLER, MOODY, and STEBBINS (1969).

MOORE, J., see BLUM, BOVET, and MOORE (1973).

MOORE, R. K., see HILGARD, WEITZENHOFFER, LANDES, and MOORE (1961).

MOOS, R. H., see KESSLER and MOOS (1970).

MORDKOFF, A. M., see SPEISMAN, LAZARUS, MORDKOFF, and DAVISON (1964).

MORGAN, A. H. (1973) The heritability of hypnotic susceptibility in twins. *Journal of Abnormal Psychology,* 82:55–61. **175**

MORGAN, A. H., JOHNSON, D. L., and HILGARD, E. R. (1974) The stability of hypnotic susceptibility: A longitudinal study. *International Journal of Clinical and Experimental Hypnosis,* 22:249–57. **175**

MORGAN, A. H., see RUCH, MORGAN, and HILGARD (1973).

MORGAN, C. T. (1965) *Physiological psychology* (3rd ed.) N.Y.: McGraw-Hill. **65, 331**

MORGULIS, S., see YERKES and MORGULIS (1909).

MORLOCK, H. C., see WILLIAMS, MORLOCK, and MORLOCK (1966).

MORLOCK, J. V., see WILLIAMS, MORLOCK, and MORLOCK (1966).

MORNINGSTAR, M., see SUPPES and MORNINGSTAR (1969).

MORRIS, D. (1967) *The naked ape.* N.Y.: McGraw-Hill. **342**

MOSHER, L. R., POLLIN, W., and STABENAU, J. R. (1971) Families with identical twins discordant for schizophrenia: Some relationships between identification thinking styles, psychopathology and dominance-submissiveness. *British Journal of Psychiatry,* 118:29–42. **481**

MOSS, T., and GENGERELLI, J. A. (1968) ESP effects generated by affective states. *The Journal of Parapsychology,* 32:90–100. **154**

MOWRER, O. H., see DOLLARD, DOOB, MILLER, MOWRER, and SEARS (1939).

MUCHA, T. F., and REINHART, R. F. (1970) Conversion reactions in student aviators. *American Journal of Psychiatry,* 127:493–97. **468**

MUNN, N. L. (1951) *Psychology: The fundamentals of human adjustment.* Boston: Houghton Mifflin. **12**

MURCH, G. M. (1973) *Visual and auditory perception.* N.Y.: Bobbs-Merrill. **128, 157**

MURDOCH, P., see PAULUS and MURDOCH (1971).

MURDOCK, B. B. (1974) *Human memory: Theory and data.* Potomac, Md.: Lawrence Erlbaum. **246**

MURPHY, G., and KOVACH, J. (1972) *Historical introduction to modern psychology* (3rd ed.). N.Y.: Harcourt Brace Jovanovich. **27**

MURSTEIN, B. I. (1972) Physical attractiveness and marital choice. *Journal of Personality and Social Psychology,* 22:8–12. **530**

MUSSEN, P. H. (ed.) (1970) *Carmichael's manual of child psychology* (3rd ed.), vols. I, II. N.Y.: Wiley. **100**

MUSSEN, P. H., CONGER, J. J., and KAGAN, J. (1974) *Child development and personality* (4th ed.). N.Y.: Harper and Row. **100**

MUSSEN, P. H., and JONES, M. C. (1958) The behavior-inferred motivations of late- and early-maturing boys. *Child Development,* 29:61–67. **93**

MUSSEN, P., and RUTHERFORD, E. (1963) Parent-child relations and parental personality in relation to young children's sex-role preferences. *Child development,* 34:589–607. **90**

MYERS, J. K., and BEAN, L. L. (1968) *Social class and mental illness.* N.Y.: **490**

MYERS, L. S., and GROSSEN, N. E. (1974) *Behavioral research: Theory, procedure, and design.* **27**

MYRIANTHOPOULOS, N. C., see WILLERMAN, NAYLOR, and MYRIANTHOPOULOS (1970).

NARANJO, C., and ORNSTEIN, R. E. (1971) *On the psychology of meditation.* N.Y.: Viking Press. **178, 190**

NATIONAL ACADEMY OF SCIENCES /SOCIAL SCIENCE RESEARCH COUNCIL (1969) *The behavioral and social sciences: Outlook and needs.* Englewood Cliffs, N.J.: Prentice-Hall. **27, 577**

NATIONAL COMMISSION ON MARIHUANA AND DRUG ABUSE (1973) *Drug use in America: Problem in perspective.* Washington, D.C.: U.S. Government Printing Office. **181, 186, 187**

NATIONAL SCIENCE BOARD (1969) *Knowledge into action: Improving the nation's use of the social sciences.* Report of the Special Commission on the Social Sciences. Washington, D.C.: U.S. Government Printing Office. **577**

NAYLOR, A. F., see WILLERMAN, NAYLOR, and MYRIANTHOPOULOS (1970).

NEALE, J. M., see DAVISON and NEALE (1974).

NEBES, R. D., and SPERRY, R. W. (1971) Cerebral dominance in perception. *Neuropsychologia,* 9:247. **52**

NEISSER, U. (1967) *Cognitive psychology.* N.Y.: Appleton-Century-Crofts. **7, 157**

NEISSER, U., see SELFRIDGE and NEISSER (1960).

NELSEN, E. A. (1969) Social reinforcement for expression vs. suppression of aggression. *Merill-Palmer Quarterly,* 15:259–78. **341**

NELSON, V. L., see SONTAG, BAKER, and NELSON (1958).

NEWCOMB, T. M. (1929) *Consistency of certain extrovert-introvert behavior patterns in 51 problem boys.* N.Y.: Columbia Univ. Teachers College Bureau of Publications. **537**

NEWCOMB, T. M. (1961) *The acquaintance process.* N.Y.: Holt, Rinehart, and Winston. **532, 534**

NEWCOMB, T. M., see ABELSON, ARONSON, MCGUIRE, NEWCOMB, ROSENBERG, and TANNENBAUM (1968).

NEWELL, A., and SIMON, H. A. (1956) The logic theory machine: A complex information processing system. *Transactions on Information Theory.* Institute of Radio Engineers, IT-2, No. 3, 61–79. **294**

NEWELL, A., and SIMON, H. A. (1972) *Human problem solving.* Englewood Cliffs, N.J.: Prentice-Hall. **295, 297**

NEWELL, A., see SIMON and NEWELL (1964).

NEYMANN, C., and YACORZYNSKI, G. (1942) Studies of introversion-extraversion and conflict of motives in the psychoses. *Journal of General Psychology,* 27:241–55. **368**

NICHOLS, R. C. (1968) Nature and nurture in adolescence. In Adams, J. F. (ed.) *Understanding adolescence.* Boston: Allyn and Bacon. **91**

NISBETT, R. E. (1968a) Birth order and participation in dangerous sports. *Journal of Personality and Social Psychology,* 8:351–53. **91**

NISBETT, R. E. (1968b) Taste, deprivation, and weight determinants of eating behavior. *Journal of Personality and Social Psychology,* 10:107–16. **314**

NISBETT, R. E. (1972) Hunger, obesity, and the ventromedial hypothalamus. *Psychological Review,* 79:433–53. **315**

NISBETT, R. E., see JONES and NISBETT (1971); see KIESLER, NISBETT, and ZANNA (1969); see LEPPER, GREENE, and NISBETT (1973).

NOE, L. F., see MAULDIN, WATSON, and NOE (1970).

NORMAN, D. A. (1969) *Memory and attention.* N.Y.: Wiley. **150, 246**

NORMAN, D. A. (ed.) (1970) *Models of human memory.* N.Y.: Academic Press. **246**

NORMAN, D. A., and RUMELHART, D. E. (1975) *Explorations in Cognition.* San Francisco: Freeman, in press. **246, 297**

NORMAN, D. A., see LINDSAY and NORMAN (1972).

NORMAN, M. M., see JACOBS, SPILKEN, NORMAN, and ANDERSON (1970); see JACOBS, SPILKEN, NORMAN, and ANDERSON (1971).

NORMAN, W. T. (1963) Toward an adequate taxonomy of personality attributes: Replicated factor structure in peer nomination

personality ratings. *Journal of Abnormal and Social Psychology,* 66:574–83. **369**
NOWLIS, D. P. and KAMIYA, J. (1970) The control of EEG alpha rhythms through auditory feedback and the associated mental activity. *Psychophysiology,* 6:476–84. **180**
O'CONNELL, D. N., see COBB, EVANS, GUSTAFSON, O'CONNELL, ORNE, and SHOR (1965).
OCHBERG, F. M., see DANIELS, GILULA, and OCHBERG (1970).
ODEN, M. H. (1968) The fulfillment of promise: 40-year follow-up of the Terman gifted group. *Genetic Psychology monographs,* 77:3–93. **422, 423**
OETTING, E. R., see COLE, OETTING, and HINKLE (1967).
OFFER, D. (1969) *The psychological world of the teen-ager: A study of normal adolescent boys.* N.Y.: **98**
OLDS, J., and OLDS, M. E. (1965) Drives, rewards, and the brain. In Barron, F., and others. *New directions in psychology II.* N.Y.: Holt, Rinehart and Winston. **210**
OLDS, J., and SINCLAIR, J. (1957) Self-stimulation in the obstruction box. *American Psychologist,* 12:464. **209**
OLDS, M. E., see OLDS and OLDS (1965).
OLWEUS, D. (1969) *Prediction of aggression.* Scandinavian Test Corporation. **382**
OPLER, M. K., see SROLE, LANGNER, MICHAEL, OPLER, and RENNIE (1962)
ORNE, M. T., see COBB, EVANS, GUSTAFSON, O'CONNEL, ORNE, and SHOR (1965); see PASKEWITZ and ORNE (1973).
ORNSTEIN, R. E. (1972) *The psychology of consciousness.* San Francisco: Freeman. **54**
ORNSTEIN, R. E. (ed.) (1973) *The nature of human consciousness.* San Francisco: Freeman. **190**
ORNSTEIN, R. E., see NARANJO and ORNSTEIN (1971).
OSGOOD, C. E. (1962) Studies on the generality of affect meaning systems. *American Psychologist,* 17:10–18. **272**
OSGOOD, C. E. (1967) Semantic differential technique in the comparative study of cultures. In Jakobovits, L. A., and Miron, M. S. (eds.) *Readings in the psychology of language.* Englewood Cliffs, N.J.: Prentice-Hall, 371–97. **272**
OTT, L., see MENDENHALL, OTT, and LARSON (1974).
OWEN, D. R. (1972) The 47, XYY male: A review. *Psychological Review.* 78:209–33. **60**
PACKARD, R., see LESSER, KRAWITZ, and PACKARD (1963).
PACKARD, V. (1970) *The sexual wilderness: The contemporary upheaval in male-female relationships.* N.Y.: Pocket Books. **324**
PAIVIO, A. (1971) *Imagery and verbal processes.* N.Y.: Holt, Rinehart and Winston. **242**
PALIAVIN, J. A., see PILIAVIN, RODIN, and PALIAVIN (1969).
PALLAK, M. S., and PITTMAN, T. S. (1972) General motivational effects of dissonance arousal. *Journal of Personality and Social Psychology,* 32:349–58. **556**
PAPAGEORGIS, D., see MCGUIRE and PAPAGEORGIS (1961).
PARK, T. Z. (1970) The acquisition of German syntax. Unpublished paper. Univ. of Bern, Switzerland: Psychological Institute. **283**
PARRISH, M., LUNDY, R. M., and LEIBOWITZ, H. W. (1968) Hypnotic age-regression and magnitudes of the Ponzo and Poggendorff illusions. *Science,* 159:1375–76. **138**
PASKEWITZ, D. A., and ORNE, M. T. (1973) Visual effects on alpha feedback training. *Science,* 181:360–63. **180**
PAUL, G. L., and BERNSTEIN, D. R. (1973) *Anxiety and clinical problems: Systematic desensitization and related techniques.* Morristown, N.J.: General Learning Press. **509**
PAULUS, P. B., and MURDOCH, P. (1971) Anticipated evaluation and audience presence in the enhancement of dominant responses. *Journal of Experimental Social Psychology,* 7:280–91. **547**
PAVLOV, I. P. (1927) *Conditioned reflexes.* N.Y.: Oxford Univ. Press. **197, 220**
PENFIELD, W. (1969) Consciousness, memory, and man's conditioned reflexes. In Pribram, K. (ed.) *On the biology of learning.* N.Y.: Harcourt Brace Jovanovich. **49, 236**
PENFIELD, W., and RASMUSSEN, T. (1950) *The cerebral cortex of man.* N.Y.: Macmillan. **46**
PERRIN, F. A. C. (1921) Physical attractiveness and repulsiveness. *Journal of Experimental Psychology,* 4:203–17. **530**
PETERSON, J. C., see HIGGINS and PETERSON (1966).
PETERSON, L. R., and PETERSON, M. J. (1959) Short-term retention of individual verbal items. *Journal of Experimental Psychology,* 30:93–113. **236**
PETERSON, M. J., see PETERSON and PETERSON (1959).
PETTIGREW, T. F. (1964) *A profile of the Negro American.* Princeton, N.J.: Van Nostrand. **563**
PHARES, E. J., see ROTTER, CHANCE, and PHARES (1972).
PHILLIPS, J. L. (1969) *The origins of intellect: Piaget's theory.* San Francisco: Freeman. **100**
PHILLIPS, J. L. (1974) *Statistical thinking.* San Francisco: Freeman. **598**
PHILLIPS, J. S., see KANFER and PHILLIPS (1970).
PIAGET, J. (1932) *The moral judgment of the child.* London: Kegan Paul. **80**
PIAGET, J. (1952) *The origins of intelligence in children.* N.Y.: International Universities Press. **329**
PILIAVIN, I. M., RODIN, J., and PILIAVIN, J. A. (1969) Good Samaritanism: An underground phenomenon? *Journal of Personality and Social Psychology,* 13:289–99. **550**
PITT, R., and HAGE, J. (1964) Patterns of peer interaction during adolescence as prognostic indicators in schizophrenia. *American Journal of Psychiatry,* 120:1089–96. **478**
PITTMAN, T. S., see PALLAK and PITTMAN (1972).
PLATT, J. J., YAKSH, T., and DARBY, C. L. (1967) Social facilitation of eating behavior in armadillos. *Psychological Reports,* 20:1136. **544**
PLATT, J. J., and JAMES, W. T. (1966) Social facilitation of eating behavior in young opossums. I. Group vs. solitary feeding. *Psychonomic Science,* 6:421–22. **544**
POHLMAN, E. (1969) *The psychology of birth planning.* Cambridge, Mass.: Schenkman. **574**
POLEFKA, J., see HASTORF, SCHNEIDER, and POLEFKA (1970).
POLLIN, W., see MOSHER, POLLIN, and STABENAU (1971).
POLT, J. M., see HESS and POLT (1960).
POMEROY, W. B., see KINSEY, POMEROY, and MARTIN (1948); see KINSEY, POMEROY, MARTIN, and GEBHARD (1953).
POPULATION COUNCIL (1967) *Selected questionnaires on knowledge, attitudes, and practice of family planning.* N.Y.: The Population Council. **574**
POPULATION COUNCIL (1970) *A manual for surveys of fertility and family planning: Knowledge, attitudes, and practice.* N.Y.: The Population Council. **574**
PORTER, R. W., see BRADY, PORTER, CONRAD, and MASON (1958).
POSNER, M. I. (1973) *Cognition: An introduction.* Glenview, Ill.: Scott, Foresman. **246**
POSTMAN, L. (1969) Experimental analysis of learning to learn. In Bower, G. H., and Spence, J. T. (eds.) *The psychology of learning and motivation.* N.Y.: Academic Press. **232**
POWLEY, T. L., and KEESEY, R. E. (1970) Relationship of body weight to the lateral hypothalamic feeding syndrome. *Journal of Comparative and Physiological Psychology,* 70:25–36. **310**
PRIBRAM, K. H. (1969) The neurophysiology of remembering. *Scientific American,* 220:73–86. **49**
PRIBRAM, K. H., see MILLER, GALANTER, and PRIBRAM (1960).
PRICE, W. H., see JACOBS, PRICE, COURT BROWN, BRITTAIN, and WHATMORE (1968).
PRONKO, N. H., see SNYDER and PRONKO (1952).
PROSHANSKY, H. M., ITTELSON, W. H., and RIVLIN, L. G. (eds.) (1970) *Environmental psychology: Man and his physical setting.* N.Y.: Holt, Rinehart and Winston. **583**
PUBOLS, B. H., see WELKER, JOHNSON, and PUBOLS (1964).
QUILLIAN, M. R., see COLLINS and QUILLIAN (1972).
RABIN, A. I. (1947) A case history of a simple schizophrenic. In Burton, A., and Harris, R. E. (eds.) *Case histories in clinical and abnormal psychology.* N.Y.: Harper and Row. **476**

RABIN, A. I. (1965) *Growing up in the Kibbutz.* N.Y.: Springer. **84**

RABIN, A. I. (1968a) Some sex differences in the attitudes of Kibbutz adolescents. *The Israel Annals of Psychiatry,* 6:63–69. **85**

RABIN, A. I. (ed.) (1968b) *Projective techniques in personality assessment.* N.Y.: Springer. **398**

RABKIN, K., see RABKIN and RABKIN (1969).

RABKIN, Y., and RABKIN, K. (1969) Children of the Kibbutz. *Psychology Today,* 3:40–46. **84**

RACHLIN, H. (1970) *Introduction to modern behaviorism.* San Francisco: Freeman. **220**

RAINWATER, L. (1965) *Family design.* Chicago: Aldine. **574**

RAPAPORT, D. (1967) *Collected papers.* Gill, M. M. (ed.). N.Y.: Basic Books. **459**

RAPPOPORT, L. (1972) *Personality development: The chronology of experience.* Glenview, Ill.: Scott, Foresman. **398**

RASMUSSEN, T., see PENFIELD and RASMUSSEN (1950).

RATLIFF, F. (1965) *Mach bands: Quantitative studies on neural networks in the retina.* San Francisco: Holden-Day. **117**

RAUGH, M. R., and ATKINSON, R. C. (1975) A mnemonic method for the learning of a second-language vocabulary. *Journal of Educational Psychology,* in press. **257**

RAUGH, M. R., see ATKINSON and RAUGH (1975).

RAY, O. S. (1972) *Drugs, society, and human behavior.* St. Louis: Mosby. **190**

RAYNER, R., see WATSON and RAYNER (1920).

RECHTSCHAFFEN, A., see MONROE, RECHTSCHAFFEN, FOULKES, and JENSEN (1965).

REDLICH, F. C., see HOLLINGSHEAD and REDLICH (1958).

REED, S. K. (1973) *Psychological process in pattern recognition.* N.Y.: Academic Press. **157**

REIFF, R., and SCHEERER, M. (1959) *Memory and hypnotic age regression.* N.Y.: International Universities Press. **223**

REINHART, R. F., see MUCHA and REINHART (1970).

REISER, M. F., see ARKIN, HASTEY, and REISER (1966).

RENNIE, T. A. C., see SROLE, LANGNER, MICHAEL, OPLER, and RENNIE (1962).

RESNICK, L. B., see GLASER and RESNICK (1972).

RHEINGOLD, H. L., and ECHERMAN, C. O. (1970) The infant separates himself from his mother. *Science.* 168:78–83. **82**

RHINE, J. B. (1942) Evidence of precognition in the covariation of salience ratios. *Journal of Parapsychology,* 6:111–43. **154**

RHINE, J. B., and BRIER, R. (eds.) (1968) *Parapsychology today.* N.Y.: Citadel Press. **151, 157**

RICHTER, C. P. (1965) *Biological clocks in medicine and psychiatry.* Springfield, Ill.: Thomas. **190**

RIESEN, A. H. (1965) Effects of early deprivation of photic stimulation. In Osler, S., and Cooke, R. (eds.) *The biosocial basis of mental retardation.* Baltimore, Md.: Johns Hopkins Press. **72, 147**

RIGGS, L. A., see KLING and RIGGS (1971).

RING, K., see BRAGINSKY, BRAGINSKY, and RING (1969).

RIOCH, M. J. (1967) Pilot projects in training mental health counselors. In Cowen, E. L., Gardner, E. A., and Zax, M. (eds.) *Emergent approaches to mental health problems.* N.Y.: Appleton-Century-Crofts. **513**

RITTER, B., see BANDURA, BLANCHARD, and RITTER (1969).

RITTLE, R. H., see COTTRELL, RITTLE, and WACK (1967); see COTTRELL, WACK, SEKERAK, and RITTLE (1968).

RIVENBARK, W. H., see MILLER and RIVENBARK (1970).

RIVLIN, L. G., see PROSHANSKY, ITTELSON, and RIVLIN (1970).

ROBACK, A. A. (1961) *History of psychology and psychiatry.* N.Y.: Philosophical Library. **521**

ROBERTS, A. H., KEWMAN, D. G., and MACDONALD, H. (1973) Voluntary control of skin temperature: Unilateral changes using hypnosis and feedback. *Journal of Abnormal Psychology,* 82:163–68. **180**

ROBERTS, W. W., see DELGADO, ROBERTS, and MILLER (1954).

ROBERTSON, A., and YOUNISS, J. (1969) Anticipatory visual imagery in deaf and hearing children. *Child development,* 40:123–35. **291**

ROCHA-MIRANDA, C. E., see GROSS, BENDER, and ROCHA-MIRANDA (1972).

ROCK, I. (1975) *An Introduction to perception.* N.Y.: MacMillan. **128, 157**

ROCK, I., and HARRIS, C. S. (1967) Vision and touch. *Scientific American,* 216:96–104. **134**

ROCK, L., see JONES, ROCK, SHAVEN, GOETHALS, and WARD (1968).

RODIN, J., see LATANÉ, and RODIN (1969); see PILIAVIN, RODIN, and PALIAVIN (1969).

ROGERS, C. R. (1951) *Client-centered therapy.* Boston: Houghton Mifflin. **501**

ROGERS, C. R. (1970) *On becoming a person: A therapist's view of psychotherapy.* Boston: Houghton Mifflin-Sentry Edition. **389, 501, 510, 521**

ROGERS, C. R. (ed.) (1967) *The therapeutic relationship and its impact: A study of psychotherapy with schizophrenics.* Madison, Wis.: Univ. of Wisconsin Press. **501**

ROSEN, J. J., see STEIN and ROSEN (1974).

ROSENBERG, M. J., see ABELSON, ARONSON, MCGUIRE, NEWCOMB, ROSENBERG, and TANNENBAUM (1968).

ROSENFELD, E., see CHEIN, GERARD, LEE, and ROSENFELD (1964).

ROSENFELD, H., and BAER, D. (1969) Unnoticed verbal conditioning of an aware experimenter by a more aware subject: The double-agent effect. *Psychological Review,* 76:425–32. **207**

ROSENHAN, D. L. (1973) On being sane in insane places. *Science,* 179:250–58. **542**

ROSENTHAL, R. (1964) Experimental outcome-orientation and the results of the psychological experiment. *Psychological Bulletin,* 61:405–12. **547**

ROSENZWEIG, M. R. (1969) Effects of heredity and environment on brain chemistry, brain anatomy, and learning ability in the rat. In Manosovitz, M., Lindzey, G., and Thiessen. D. D. (eds.) *Behavioral genetics.* N.Y.: Appleton-Century-Crofts. **61**

ROSENZWEIG, M. R., and BENNETT, E. L. (1969) Effects of differential environments on brain weights and enzyme activities in gerbils, rats, and mice. *Developmental Psychology,* 2:87–95. **73**

ROSENZWEIG, M. R., BENNETT, E. L., and DIAMOND, M. C. (1972) Brain changes in response to experience. *Scientific American,* 226:22–29. **44**

ROSS, L., LEPPER, M. R., and HUBBARD, M. (1974) Perseverance in self-perception and social perception: Biased attributional processes in the debriefing paradigm. Unpublished manuscript, Stanford University, Stanford, Calif. **541, 542**

ROSS, M., and SHULMAN, R. F. (1973) Increasing the salience of initial attitudes: Dissonance versus self-perception theory. *Journal of Personality and Social Psychology,* 28:138–44. **556**

ROTH, W. T., see DARLEY, TINKLENBERG, ROTH, HOLLISTER, and ATKINSON (1973).

ROTTER, J. B., CHANCE, J. E., and PHARES, E. J. (1972) *Applications of a social learning theory of personality.* N.Y.: Holt, Rinehart, and Winston. **398**

ROTTMANN, L., see WALSTER, ARONSON, ABRAHAMS, and ROTTMANN (1966).

ROWE, D. A., see SIMS, KELLEHER, HORTON, GLUCK, GOODMAN, and ROWE (1968).

ROZIN, P., and KALAT, J. W. (1971) Specific hungers and poison avoidance as adaptive specializations of learning. *Psychological Review,* 78:459–86. **311**

RUBIN, Z. (1973) *Liking and loving.* N.Y.: Holt, Rinehart, and Winston. **533, 561**

RUCH, J. C., MORGAN, A. H., and HILGARD, E. R. (1973) Behavioral predictions from hypnotic responsiveness scores when obtained with and without prior induction procedures. *Journal of Abnormal Psychology,* 82:543–46. **174**

RUMELHART, D. E., see NORMAN and RUMELHART (1975).

RUSSELL, B., see WHITEHEAD and RUSSELL (1925).

RUTHERFORD, E., see MUSSEN and RUTHERFORD (1963).

SACHS, J. S. (1967) Recognition memory for syntactic and semantic aspects of connected discourse. *Perception and Psychophysics,* 2:437–42. **280**

SACKETT, G. P. (1967) Some persistent effects of different rearing conditions on preadult social behavior of monkeys. *Journal of Comparative Physiological Psychology,* 64:363–65. **82**

SAEGERT, S., SWAP, W., and ZAJONC, R. B. (1973) Exposure, context, and interpersonal attraction. *Journal of Personality and Social Psychology,* 15:234–42. **534**

SALIVE, H., see MCCONNELL, SHIGEHISA, and SALIVE (1970).

SANDIFORD, P. (1938) *Foundations of educational psychology.* N.Y.: Longmans, Green. **63**

SARASON, I. G. (1972) *Abnormal psychology.* N.Y.: Appleton-Century-Crofts. **492**

SARASON, S. B., MANDLER, G., and CRAIGHILL, P. G. (1952) The effect of differential instructions on anxiety and learning. *Journal of Abnormal and Social Psychology,* 47:561–65. **264**

SARBIN, T. R., and COE, W. C. (1972) *Hypnosis: A social psychological analysis of influence communication.* N.Y.: Holt, Rinehart and Winston. **174, 177, 190**

SAWREY, W. L., CONGER, J. J., and TURRELL, E. S. (1956) An experimental investigation of the role of psychological factors in the production of gastric ulcers of rats. *Journal of Comparative and Physiological Psychology,* 49:457–61. **197**

SCHACHTER, S. (1959) *Psychology of affiliation.* Stanford, Calif.: Stanford Univ. Press. **341**

SCHACHTER, S. (1971) *Emotion, obesity, and crime.* N.Y.: Academic Press. **314, 350, 353**

SCHACHTER, S., GOLDMAN, R., and GORDON, A. (1968) The effects of fear, food deprivation, and obesity on eating. *Journal of Personality and Social Psychology,* 10:107–16. **313**

SCHACHTER, S., and GROSS, L. P. (1968) Manipulated time and eating behavior. *Journal of Personality and Social Psychology,* 10:98–106. **313**

SCHACHTER, S., and SINGER, J. E. (1962) Cognitive, social and physiological determinants of emotional state. *Psychological Review,* 69:379–99. **352**

SCHAFFER, H. R., and EMERSON, P. E. (1964) The development of social attachments in infancy. *Monographs of the Society for Research in Child Development,* 29, Serial No. 94. **81**

SCHAIE, K. W., and STROTHER, C. R. (1968) A cross-sequential study of age changes in cognitive behavior. *Psychological Bulletin,* 70:671–80. **416**

SCHANK, R. C., and COLBY, K. M. (eds.) (1973) *Computer models of thought and language.* San Francisco, Calif.: Freeman. **297**

SCHEERER, M., see REIFF and SCHEERER (1959).

SCHEIN, E. H., see STRASSMAN, THALER, and SCHEIN (1956).

SCHMEIDLER, G. R., and MCCONNELL, R. A. (1958) *ESP and personality patterns.* New Haven, Conn.: Yale Univ. Press. **153**

SCHNEIDER, D. J. (1973) Implicit personality theory: A review. *Psychological Bulletin,* 79:294–309. **386**

SCHNEIDER, D. J., see HASTORF, SCHNEIDER, and POLEFKA (1970).

SCHREIBER, F. R. (1973) *Sybil.* Chicago: Regnery. **163**

SCHROEDER, W. H., see HENDRICKSON and SCHROEDER (1941).

SCHULTZ, J. H., and LUTHE, W. (1969) *Autogenic therapy: I. Autogenic methods.* N.Y.: Grune and Stratton. **180**

SCHWARTZ, M. D. (1973) *Physiological psychology.* Englewood Cliffs, N.J.: Prentice-Hall. **65, 331**

SCHWARTZ, S. H., FELDMAN, K. A., BROWN, M. E., and HEINGARTNER, A. (1969) Some personality correlates of conduct in two situations of moral conflict. *Journal of Personality,* 37:41–57. **81**

SCOTT, J. P. (1968) *Early experience and the organization of behavior.* Belmont, Calif.: Brooks-Cole. **72, 327**

SCOTT, J. P., and FULLER, J. L. (1965) *Genetics and the social behavior of the dog.* Chicago: Univ. of Chicago Press. **62**

SCOTT, T. H., see HERON, DOANE, and SCOTT (1956).

SEARS, D. O., see FREEDMAN, CARLSMITH, and SEARS (1974).

SEARS, R. R. (1936) Experimental studies of projection: I. Attribution of traits. *Journal of Social Psychology,* 7:151–63. **445**

SEARS, R. R., MACCOBY, E. E., and LEVIN, H. (1957) *Patterns of child rearing.* Evanston, Ill.: Row, Peterson. **86**

SEARS, R. R., see DOLLARD, DOOB, MILLER, MOWRER, and SEARS (1939).

SEEMAN, J. (1949) A study of the process of nondirective therapy. *Journal of Consulting Psychology,* 13:157–68. **502**

SEEVERS, M. H., see EDDY, HALBACH, ISBELL, and SEEVERS (1965).

SEGAL, J., see LUCE and SEGAL (1966).

SEKERAK, G. J., see COTTRELL, WACK, SEKERAK, and RITTLE (1968).

SELFRIDGE, O., and NEISSER, U. (1960) Pattern recognition by machine. *Scientific American,* 203:60–80. **144**

SELIGMAN, M. E. P. (1975) *Helplessness.* San Francisco: Freeman. **437, 466, 467**

SENDEN, M. V. (1960) *Space and sight* (Trans. by P. Heath). N.Y.: Free Press. **146**

SENN, D. J., see LEVINGER, SENN, and JORGENSEN (1970).

SENTER, R. J., see LIPPERT and SENTER (1966).

SHAFFER, L. F. (1947) Fear and courage in aerial combat. *Journal of Consulting Psychology,* 11:137–43. **346**

SHAPIRO, A., see GOODENOUGH, SHAPIRO, HOLDEN, and STEINSCHRIBER (1959).

SHAPIRO, A., see LEWIS, GOODENOUGH, SHAPIRO, and SLESER (1966).

SHARMA, K. W., see ANAND, SHARMA, and DUA (1964).

SHAVEN, K. G., see JONES, ROCK, SHAVEN, GOETHALS, and WARD (1968).

SHAW, M. E., see COSTANZO and SHAW (1966).

SHELDON, W. H. (1954) *Atlas of men: A guide for somatotyping the adult male at all ages.* N.Y.: Harper and Row. **367**

SHERMAN, A. R. (1973) *Behavior modification: Theory and practice.* Belmont, Calif.: Brooks-Cole. **521**

SHERMAN, S. E. (1971) Very deep hypnosis: An experimental and electroencephalographic investigation. Unpublished Ph.D. dissertation, Stanford University, Stanford, Calif. **174**

SHIELDS, J., see GOTTESMAN and SHIELDS (1972); see GOTTESMAN and SHIELDS (1973).

SHIFFRIN, R. M., see ATKINSON and SHIFFRIN (1971).

SHIGEHISA, T., see MCCONNELL, SHIGEHISA, and SALIVE (1970).

SHOR, R. E., see COBB, EVANS, GUSTAFSON, O'CONNELL, ORNE, and SHOR (1965); see FROMM and SHOR (1972).

SHULMAN, R. F., see ROSS and SHULMAN (1973).

SIMON, C. W., see EMMONS and SIMON (1956).

SIMON, H. A., and NEWELL, A. (1964) Information processing in computer and man. *American Scientist,* 52:281–300. **295**

SIMON, H. A., see NEWELL and SIMON (1956); see NEWELL and SIMON (1972).

SIMS, E. A., KELLEHER, P. E., HORTON, E. S., GLUCK, C. M., GOODMAN, R. F., and ROWE, D. A. (1968) Experimental obesity in man. *Excerpta Medica Monograph.* **315**

SINCLAIR, J., see OLDS and SINCLAIR (1957).

SINGER, J. E., see SCHACHTER and SINGER (1962).

SKEELS, H. M. (1966) Adult status of children with contrasting early life experiences: A follow-up study. *Monographs of the Society for Research in Child Development,* 31, Serial No. 105. **74**

SKEELS, H. M., and DYE, H. B. (1939) A study of the effects of differential stimulation on mentally retarded children. *Proceedings of the American Association for Mental Deficiency,* 44:114–36. **74**

SKEELS, H. M., see SKODAK and SKEELS (1949).

SKINNER, B. F. (1938) *The behavior of organisms.* N.Y.: Appleton-Century-Crofts. **202, 220**

SKINNER, B. F. (1957) *Verbal behavior.* N.Y.: Appleton-Century-Crofts. **280**

SKINNER, B. F. (1968) *The technology of teaching.* N.Y.: Appleton-Century-Crofts. **251, 267**

SKINNER, B. F. (1971) *Beyond freedom and dignity.* N.Y.: Knopf. **583**

SKODAK, M., and SKEELS, H. M. (1949) A final follow-up of one hundred adopted children. *Journal of Genetic Psychology,* 75:3–19. **417**

SLESER, I., see LEWIS, GOODENOUGH, SHAPIRO, and SLESER (1966).

SLOBIN, D. I. (1971) *Psycholinguistics.* Glenview, Ill.: Scott, Foresman, **284, 292, 297**

SMITH, D., KING, M., and HOEBEL, B. G. (1970) Lateral hypothalamic control of killing: Evidence for a cholinoceptive mechanism. *Science,* 167:900–01. **338**

SMITH, M. B. (1973) Is psychology relevant to new priorities? *American Psychologist,* 6:463–71. **10**

SMITH, M. P., and DUFFY, M. (1955) The effects of intragastric injection of various substances on subsequent bar pressing. *Journal of Comparative and Physiological Psychology,* 48:387–91. **308**

SMITH, R., see STEUER, APPLEFIELD, and SMITH (1971).

SNYDER, F. W., and PRONKO, N. H. (1952) *Vision with spatial inversion.* Wichita, Kans.: McCormick-Armstrong. **133**

SNYDER, M., and EBBESEN, E. B. (1972) Dissonance awareness: A test of dissonance theory versus self-perception theory. *Journal of Experimental Social Psychology,* 8:502–17. **556**

SNYDER, W. U., and others (1947) *Casebook of nondirective counseling.* Boston: Houghton Mifflin. **501**

SOAL, S. G., and BATEMAN, F. (1954) *Modern experiments in telepathy.* New Haven, Conn.: Yale Univ. Press. **153, 155**

SOKOLOV, E. N. (1963) Higher nervous functions: The orienting reflex. *Annual Review of Physiology.* 25:545–80. **151**

SOLOMON, G. F. (1974) Emotions, stress, and immunity. Unpublished manuscript, Stanford University Medical School, Stanford, Calif. **484**

SOLOMON, R. L., see LAMBERT, SOLOMON, and WATSON (1949).

SONTAG, L. W., BAKER, C. T., and NELSON, V. L. (1958) Mental growth and development: A longitudinal study. *Monographs of the Society for Research in Child Development,* **23,** Serial No. 68. **414**

SORENSON, R. C. (1973) *Adolescent sexuality in contemporary America.* N.Y.: World Publishing. **94, 98**

SPAULDING, C. B., see MCCLINTOCK, SPAULDING, and TURNER (1965).

SPEISMAN, J. C., LAZARUS, R. S., MORDKOFF, A. M., and DAVISON, L. (1964) Experimental reduction of stress based on ego-defense theory. *Journal of Abnormal and Social Psychology,* 68:367–80. **354**

SPENCE, J. T., and SPENCE, K. W. (1966) The motivational components of manifest anxiety: Drive and drive stimuli. In Spielberger, C. D. (ed.) *Anxiety and behavior.* N.Y.: Academic Press. **265**

SPENCE, K. W., see SPENCE and SPENCE (1966).

SPERRY, R. W. (1970) Perception in the absence of neocortical commissures. In *Perception and Its Disorders,* Res. Publ. A.R.N.M.D., vol. 48, The Association for Research in Nervous and Mental Disease. **50, 51, 52**

SPERRY, R. W., see NEBES and SPERRY (1971).

SPIELBERGER, C. D. (ed.) (1966) *Anxiety and behavior.* N.Y.: Academic Press. **266**

SPIELBERGER, C. D. (ed.) (1972) *Anxiety: Current trends in theory and research* (vols. 1 and 2, 1972). N.Y.: Academic Press. **268**

SPIES, G. (1965) Food versus intracranial self-stimulation reinforcement in food-deprived rats. *Journal of Comparative Physiological Psychology,* 60:153–57. **209**

SPILKEN, A. Z., see JACOBS, SPILKEN, NORMAN, and ANDERSON (1970); see JACOBS, SPILKEN, NORMAN, and ANDERSON (1971).

SPOCK, B. (1968) *Baby and child care.* N.Y.: Pocket Books. **565**

SPUHLER, J. N., see LOEHLIN, LINDZEY, and SPUHLER (1975).

SROLE, L., LANGNER, T. S., MICHAEL, S. T., OPLER, M. K., and RENNIE, T. A. C. (1962) *Mental health in the metropolis: The Midtown Manhattan study.* N.Y.: McGraw-Hill. **490**

STABENAU, J. R., see MOSHER, POLLIN, and STABENAU (1971).

STAGNER, R. (1967) *Psychological aspects of international conflict.* Belmont, Calif.: Brooks-Cole. **583**

STALNAKER, J. M. (1965) Psychological tests and public responsibility. *American Psychologist,* 20:131–35. **423**

STAMM, J. S. (1961) Social facilitation in monkeys. *Psychological Reports.* 8:479–84. **544**

STANDISH, R. R., and CHAMPION, R. A. (1960) Task difficulty and drive in verbal learning. *Journal of Experimental Psychology,* 59:361–65. **265**

STARBUCK, W. H., see DUTTON and STARBUCK (1971).

STAYTON, D. J. (1973) Infant responses to brief everyday separations: distress, following, and greeting. Paper presented at meeting of the Society for Research in Child Development, March, 1973. **83**

STEBBINS, W. C., see MILLER, MOODY, and STEBBINS (1969).

STECHER, L. I., see BALDWIN and STECHER (1922).

STEIN, D. G., and ROSEN, J. J. (1974) *Motivation and emotion.* N.Y.: Macmillan, **331, 359**

STEINSCHRIBER, L., see GOODENOUGH, SHAPIRO, HOLDEN, and STEINSCHRIBER (1959)

STENDLER, F., see LAVATELLI and STENDLER (1972).

STEPHENS, J. J., ASTRUP, C., and MANGRUM, J. C. (1967) Prognosis in schizophrenia. *Archives of General Psychiatry,* 16:693–98. **477**

STEUER, F. B. APPLEFIELD, J. M., and SMITH, R. (1971) Televised aggression and the interpersonal aggression of preschool children. *Journal of Experimental Child Psychology,* 11:422–47. **343**

STEVENS, L. A. (1971) *Explorers of the brain.* N.Y.: Knopf. **66**

STOEL, C., see ATKINSON, MACWHINNEY, and STOEL (1970).

STONE, L. J., and CHURCH, J. (1973) *Childhood and adolescence* (3rd ed.). N.Y.: Random House. **100**

STOYVA, J., see BUDZYNSKI, STOYVA, and ADLER (1970).

STRASSMAN, H. D., THALER, M. B., and SCHEIN, E. H. (1956) A prisoner of war syndrome: Apathy as a reaction to severe stress. *American Journal of Psychiatry,* 112:998–1003. **437**

STRATTON, G. M. (1897) Vision without inversion of the retinal image. *Psychological Review,* 4:341–60. **133**

STRAUSS, J. S., see CARPENTER, STRAUSS, and BARTKO (1973).

STRICKER, E. M., and WILSON, N. E. (1970) Salt-seeking behavior in rats following acute sodium deficiency. **312**

STRONGMAN, K. T. (1973) *The psychology of emotion.* N.Y.: Wiley. **359**

STROTHER, C. R., see SCHAIE and STROTHER (1968).

STUART, R. B., and DAVIS, B. (1972) *Slim chance in a fat world.* Champaign, Ill.: Research Press. **331**

STUNKARD, A. (1959) Obesity and denial of hunger. *Psychosomatic Medicine,* 21:281–89. **312**

SUOMI, S. J., see HARLOW and SUOMI (1970).

SUPPES, P. and MORNINGSTAR, M. (1969) Computer-assisted instruction. *Science,* 166:343–50. **250**

SUPPES, P., see KRANTZ, ATKINSON, LUCE, and SUPPES (1974); see KRANTZ, LUCE, SUPPES, and TVERSKY (1971).

SWAP, W., see SAEGERT, SWAP, and ZAJONC (1973).

SWETS, J. A., see GREEN and SWETS (1966).

SZASZ, T. S. (1961) *The myth of mental illness: Foundations of a theory of personal conduct.* N.Y.: Harper and Row. **509, 458**

SZASZ, T. S. (1970) *The manufacture of madness.* N.Y.: Dell. **52, 458, 521**

TAKAISHI, M., see TANNER, WHITEHOUSE, and TAKAISHI (1966).

TAKESHITA, J., see FREEMAN and TAKESHITA (1969).

TANNENBAUM, P. H., see ABELSON, ARONSON, MCGUIRE, NEWCOMB, ROSENBERG, and TANNENBAUM (1968).

TANNER, J. M., WHITEHOUSE, R. H., and TAKAISHI, M. (1966) Standards from birth to maturity for height, weight, height velocity and weight velocity: British children 1965. *Archives of Diseases of Childhood,* 41:613–35. **92**

TART, C. T. (1971a) *On being stoned: A psychological study of marijuana intoxication.* Palo Alto, Calif.: Science and Behavior Books. **186**

TART, C. T. (1971b) Scientific foundations for the study of altered states of consciousness. *Journal of Transpersonal Psychology,* 3:93–124. **162**

TART, C. T. (ed.) (1969) *Altered states of consciousness.* N.Y.: Wiley. **190**

TEITELBAUM, P. (1967) *Physiological psychology.* Englewood Cliffs, N.J.: Prentice-Hall. **65**

TEITELBAUM, P., see EPSTEIN and TEITELBAUM (1962); see HOEBEL and TEITELBAUM (1962); see HOEBEL and TEITEL-

BAUM (1966); see MCGINTY, EPSTEIN, and TEITELBAUM (1965).

TERMAN, L. M. (1916) *The measurement of intelligence.* Boston: Houghton Mifflin. **579**

TERMAN, L. M., and MERRILL, M. A. (1937) *Measuring intelligence.* Boston: Houghton Mifflin. **405**

TESSER, A., and BRODIE, M. (1971) A note on the evaluation of a "computer date." *Psychonomic Science.* 23:300. **530**

TEST, M. A., see BRYAN and TEST (1967).

TEYLER, T. J. (ed.) (1971) *Altered states of awareness: Readings from Scientific American.* San Francisco: Freeman. **190**

THALER, M. B., see STRASSMAN, THALER, and SCHEIN (1956).

THARP, R. G., see WATSON AND THARP (1972).

THIGPEN, C. H., and CLECKLEY, H. M. (1954) A case of multiple personality. *Journal of Abnormal and Social Psychology,* 49:135–51. **163**

THOMAS, A., CHESS, S., and BIRCH, H. G. (1970) The origin of personality. In Atkinson, R. C. (ed.) *Contemporary Psychology: Readings from Scientific American.* **364**

THOMAS, D. W., and MAYER, J. (1973) The search for the secret of fat. *Psychology Today,* 7:74–79. **314, 315**

THOMAS, J., see ISAACS, THOMAS, and GOLDIAMOND (1965).

THOMPSON, C. W., see HUDSPETH, MCGAUGH, and THOMPSON (1964).

THOMPSON, R. F. (1967) *Foundations of physiological psychology.* N.Y.: Harper and Row. **35, 65**

THOMPSON, W. R. (1954) The inheritance and development of intelligence. *Proceedings of the Association for Research on Nervous and Mental Disease,* 33:209–31. **62**

THORNDYKE, P., and BOWER, G. (1974) Storage and retreival processes in sentence memory. *Cognitive Psychology,* in press. **259**

THURSTONE, L. L. (1938) Primary mental abilities. *Psychometric Monographs,* No. 1. Chicago: Univ. of Chicago Press. **409**

THURSTONE, L. L. (1955) *The differential growth of mental abilities.* Chapel Hill, N.C.: Psychometric Laboratory, Univ. of North Carolina. **415**

THURSTONE, L. L., and THURSTONE, T. G. (1941) Factorial studies of intelligence. *Psychometric Monographs,* No. 2. Chicago: Univ. of Chicago Press. **404**

THURSTONE, L. L., and THURSTONE, T. G. (1963) *SRA primary abilities.* Chicago: Science Research Associates. **409**

THURSTONE, T. G., see THURSTONE and THURSTONE (1941); see THURSTONE and THURSTONE (1963).

TINKLENBERG, J. R. (1972) A current view of the amphetamines. In Blachly, P. H. (ed.) *Progress in drug abuse.* Springfield, Ill.: Thomas. **185**

TINKLENBERG, J. R., see DARLEY, TINKLENBERG, ROTH, HOLLISTER, and ATKINSON (1973).

TOLMAN, C. W. (1963) A possible relationship between the imprinting critical period and arousal. *Psychological Review.* 13:181–85. **546**

TOLMAN, C. W. (1969) Social feeding in domestic chicks: Effects of food deprivation of non-feeding companions. *Psychonomic Science,* 15:234. **544**

TOLMAN, E. C. (1932) *Purposive behavior in animals and men.* N.Y.: Appleton-Century-Crofts. **220**

TOLMAN, E. C. (1948) Cognitive maps in rats and men. *Psychological Review,* 55:189–208. **217**

TOLMAN, E. C., and HONZIK, C. H. (1930) Introduction and removal of reward, and maze performance in rats. *University of California Publications in Psychology,* 4:257–75. **218**

TORRANCE, E. P. (1966) *Torrance Tests of Creative Thinking,* Verbal Forms A and B. Princeton, N.J.: Personnel Press. **412**

TOTH, M. F., see ARKIN, TOTH, BAKER, and HASTEY (1970).

TRIPLETT, N. (1898) The dynamogenic factors in pacemaking and competition. *American Journal of Psychology.* 9:507–533. **544**

TULVING, E. (1972) Episodic and semantic memory. In Tulving, E., and Donaldson, W. (eds.) *Organization of memory.* N.Y.: Academic Press. **229**

TULVING, E., and DONALDSON, W. (eds.) (1972) *Organization of memory.* N.Y.: Academic Press. **246**

TULVING, E. and MADIGAN, S. A. (1970) Memory and verbal learning. *Annual Review of Psychology,* 21:437–84. **235**

TURNBULL, C. M. (1961) Some observations regarding the experiences and behavior of the Ba Mbuti Pygmies. *American Journal of Psychology,* 74:304–08. **133**

TURNER, H. A., see MCCLINTOCK, SPAULDING, and TURNER (1965).

TURRELL, E. S., see SAWREY, CONGER, and TURRELL (1956).

TVERSKY, A., see COOMBS, DAWES and TVERSKY (1970) see KRANTZ, LUCE, SUPPES, and TVERSKY (1971).

TYHURST, J. S. (1951) Individual reactions to community disaster. *American Journal of Psychiatry.* 10:746–69. **357**

TYLER' L. E. (1956) *The psychology of human differences.* N.Y.: Appleton-Century-Crofts, **367**

TYLER, R. W., see EELLS, DAVIS, HAVIGHURST, HERRICK, and TYLER (1951).

ULLMANN, L. P., and KRASNER, L. (1969) *A psychological approach to abnormal behavior.* Englewood Cliffs, N.J.: Prentice-Hall. **503**

ULLMANN, L. P., see KRASNER and ULLMANN (1973); see MADSEN and ULLMANN (1967).

UNDERWOOD, B. J. (1957) Interference and forgetting. *Psychological Review,* 64:49–60. **232**

U.S. DEPARTMENT OF HEALTH, EDUCATION, and WELFARE (1969) *Toward a social report.* Washington, D.C.: U.S. Government Printing Office. **230**

VALENSTEIN, E. S., COX, V. C., and KAKOLEWSKI, J. W. (1970) Reexamination of the role of the hypothalamus in motivation. *Psychological Review,* 77:16–31. **317**

VAN DE CASTLE, R. L. (1969) The facilitation of ESP through hypnosis. *American Journal of Clinical Hypnosis,* 12:37–56. **151, 154**

VAN DE CASTLE, R. L., see HALL and VAN DE CASTLE (1966).

VAN EEDEN, F. V. (1913) A study of dreams. *Proceedings of the Society for Psychical Research,* 26:431–61. **169**

VAN ITALLIE, T. B., see HASHIM and VAN ITALLIE (1965).

VARELA, J. A. (1971) *Psychological solutions to social problems.* N.Y.: Academic Press. **583**

VEITH, I. (1965) *Hysteria: The history of a disease.* Chicago: Univ. of Chicago Press. **521**

VERNON, P. E. (1969) *Intelligence and cultural environment.* London: Methuen. **420**

VERPLANCK, W. S. (1955) The control of the content of conversation: Reinforcement of statements of opinion. *Journal of Abnormal and Social Psychology,* 51:668–76. **206**

VINGOE, F. J. (1973) Comparison of the Harvard group scale of hypnotic susceptibility, Form A, and the group alert trance scale in a university population. *International Journal of Clinical and Experimental Hypnosis,* 21:169–78. **173**

VOEKS, V. (1970) *On becoming an educated person* (3rd ed.) Philadelphia: Saunders **267**

VOLKOVA, V. D. (1953) On certain characteristics of conditioned reflexes to speech stimuli in children. *Fiziologicheskii Zhurnal SSSR,* 39:540–48. **199**

VON FRISCH, K. (1974) Decoding the language of the bee. *Science,* 185:663–68. **288**

WACK, D. L., see COTTRELL, RITTLE, and WACK (1967); see COTTRELL, WACK, SEKERAK, and RITTLE (1968).

WALDER, L. O., see ERON, HUESMANN, LEFKOWITZ, and WALDER (1972).

WALK, R. D. (1968) Monocular compared to binocular depth perception in human infants. *Science,* 162:473–75. **148**

WALK, R. D., see GIBSON and WALK (1960).

WALLACE, R. K., and BENSON, H. (1972) The physiology of meditation. *Scientific American,* 226:85–90. **179**

WALLACH, M. A., and KOGAN, N. (1965) *Modes of thinking in young children.* N.Y.: Holt, Rinehart and Winston. **412**

WALLACH, M. A., and WING, C. W., JR. (1969) *The talented student.* N.Y.: Holt, Rinehart and Winston. **570, 583**

WALLACH, M. A., see WING and WALLACH (1971).

WALSTER, E. (1965) The effect of self-esteem on romantic liking. *Journal of Experimental Social Psychology.* 1:184–97. **533**

WALSTER, E., ARONSON, V., ABRAHAMS, D., and ROTTMANN, L. (1966) Importance

of physical attractiveness in dating behavior. *Journal of Personality and Social Psychology.* 4:508–16. **530**
WALSTER, E., see BERSCHEID and WALSTER (1974); see DION, BERSCHEID, and WALSTER (1972).
WALTERS, R. H., see BANDURA and WALTERS (1959); see BANDURA and WALTERS (1963).
WANNER, E., see MCCLELLAND, DAVIS, KALIN, and WANNER (1972).
WARD, C. D. (1967) Own height, sex, and liking in the judgment of the heights of others. *Journal of Personality.* 35:381–401. **531**
WARD, L. M., see JONES, ROCK, SHAVEN, GOETHALS, and WARD (1968).
WARE, E. E., see MACLAY and WARE (1961).
WATERMAN, C. K. (1969) The facilitating and interfering effects of cognitive dissonance on simple and complex paired associates learning tasks. *Journal of Experimental Social Psychology,* 5:31–42. **556**
WATSON, D. L., and THARP, R. G. (1972) *Self-directed behavior: Self modification for personal adjustment.* Belmont, Calif.: Wadsworth. **521**
WATSON, J. B. (1919) *Psychology from the standpoint of a behaviorist* (2nd ed.). Philadelphia: J. B. Lippincott. **12**
WATSON, J. B. (1928) *Psychological care of infant and child.* N.Y.: Norton. **86**
WATSON, J. B., and RAYNER, R. (1920) Conditioned emotional reactions. *Journal of Experimental Psychology,* 3:1–14. **355**
WATSON, P. D., see LAMBERT, SOLOMON, and WATSON (1949).
WATSON, R. I. (1971) *The great psychologists: From Aristotle to Freud* (3rd ed.). Philadelphia: Lippincott. **27**
WATSON, W. B., see MAULDIN, WATSON, and NOE (1970).
WATT, N. F., see WHITE and WATT (1973).
WEATHERLY, D. (1964) Self-perceived rate of physical maturation and personality in late adolescence. *Child Development,* 35:1197–1210. **93**
WEBB, W. B. (1968) *Sleep: An experimental approach.* N.Y.: Macmillan. **190**
WEBB, W. B. (ed.) (1973) *Sleep: An active process.* Glenview, Ill.: Scott, Foresman. **168**
WEBB, W. B., and AGNEW, H. W., JR. (1968) Measurement and characteristics of nocturnal sleep. In Abt, L. E., and Riess, B. F. (eds.) *Progress in clinical psychology,* Vol. VIII. N.Y.: Grune and Stratton. **167**
WEBB, W. B., and AGNEW, H. W., JR. (1973) *Sleep and dreams.* Dubuque, Ia.: Brown. **190**
WEBB, W. B., AGNEW, J. W., JR. and WILLIAMS, R. L. (1971) Effect on sleep of a sleep period time displacement. *Aerospace Medicine,* 42:152–55. **166**
WEBB, W. B., and KERSEY, J. (1967) Recall of dreams and the probability of Stage 1—REM sleep. *Perceptual and Motor Skills,* 24:627–30. **170**
WEGMANN, H. M., see KLEIN, WEGMANN, and HUNT (1972).
WEINER, B. (1972) *Theories of motivation.* Chicago: Markham. **331**
WEISS, B., and LATIES, V. G. (1962) Enhancement of human performance by caffeine and amphetamines. *Pharmacological Review,* 14:1–37. **185**
WEISS, J. M. (1972) Psychological factors in stress and disease. *Scientific American,* 226:106. **483**
WEITZENHOFFER, A. M., and HILGARD, E. R. (1959) *Stanford Hypnotic Susceptibility Scales, Forms A and B.* Palo Alto, Calif.: Consulting Psychologists Press. **175**
WEITZENHOFFER, A. M., see HILGARD, WEITZENHOFFER, LANDES, and MOORE (1961).
WELKER, W. L., JOHNSON, J. I., and PUBOLS, B. H. (1964) Some morphological and physiological characteristics of the somatic sensory system in raccoons. *American Zoologist,* 4:75–94. **46**
WENGER, M., BAGCHI, B., and ANAND, B. (1961) Experiments in India on "voluntary" control of the heart and pulse. *Circulation,* 24:1319–25. **179**
WENGER, M., and BAGCHI, B. (1961) Studies of autonomic function in practitioners of yoga in India. *Behavioral Science,* 6:312–23. **179**
WERTHEIMER, M. (1970) *A brief history of psychology.* N.Y.: Holt, Rinehart and Winston. **27**
WESTBY, G., see APTER and WESTBY (1973).
WHATMORE, P. B., see JACOBS, PRICE, COURT BROWN, BRITTAIN, and WHATMORE (1968).
WHITE, P. L. (1971) *Human infants: Experience and psychological development.* Englewood Cliffs, N.J.: Prentice-Hall. **72, 74**
WHITE, R. W., and WATT, N. F. (1973) *The abnormal personality* (4th ed.). N.Y.: Ronald. **492**
WHITEHEAD, A. N., and RUSSELL, B. (1925) *Principia mathematica* (2nd ed.). (original date, 1910–13). Cambridge, England: Cambridge Univ. Press. **294**
WHITEHORN, J. C., and BETZ, B. J. (1960) Further studies of the doctor as a crucial variable in the outcome of treatment with schizophrenic patients. *American Journal of Psychiatry,* 117:215–23. **515**
WHITEHOUSE, R. H., see TANNER, WHITEHOUSE, and TAKAISHI (1966).
WHORF, B. L. (1956) *Language, thought, and reality.* In Carroll, J. B. (ed.). N.Y.: Wiley. **291**
WICKELGREN, W. A. (1974) *How to solve problems: elements of a theory of problems and problem solving.* San Francisco: Freeman. **297**
WIESEL, T. N., see HUBEL and WIESEL (1965).
WIGGINS, J. S. (1973) *Personality and prediction: Principles of personality assessment.* Reading, Mass.: Addison-Wesley. **398**
WIGGINS, J. S., see WINDER and WIGGINS (1964).
WILBUR, C. B., see LUDWIG, BRANDSMA, WILBUR, BENDFELDT, and JAMESON (1972).
WILCOX, L. D., BROOKS, R. M., BEAL, G. M., and KLONGLAN, G. E. (1972) *Social indicators and societal monitoring: An annotated bibliography.* Amsterdam: Elsevier Scientific Publishers. **583**
WILKES, A. L., and KENNEDY, R. A. (1969) Relationship between pausing and retrieval latency in sentences of varying grammatical form. *Journal of Experimental Psychology,* 79:241–45. **278**
WILLERMAN, B., see ARONSON, WILLERMAN, and FLOYD (1966).
WILLERMAN, L., NAYLOR, A. F., and MYRIANTHOPOULOS, N. C. (1970) Intellectual development of children from interracial matings. *Science,* 170:1329–31. **419**
WILLIAMS, H. L., LUBIN, A., and GOODNOW, J. J. (1959) Impaired performance with acute sleep loss. *Psychological Monographs,* 73, Whole No. 484. **161**
WILLIAMS, H. L., MORLOCK, H. C., and MORLOCK, J. V. (1966) Instrumental behavior during sleep. *Psychophysiology,* 2:208–15. **170**
WILLIAMS, R. L., see WEBB, AGNEW, and WILLIAMS (1971).
WILSON, G. F. (1968) Early experience and facilitation of feeding in domestic chicks. *Journal of Comparative and Physiological Psychology,* 66:800–02. **546**
WILSON, H. A., see ATKINSON and WILSON (1969).
WILSON, N. E., see STRICKER and WILSON (1970).
WINCH, R. F. (1952) *The modern family.* N.Y.: Holt, Rinehart, and Winston. **533**
WINCH, R. F., KTSANES, T., and KTSANES, V. (1954) The theory of complementary needs in mate selection: An analytic and descriptive study. *American Sociological Review,* 29:241–49. **533**
WINDER, C. L., and WIGGINS, J. S. (1964) Social reputation and social behavior: A further validation of the peer nomination inventory. *Journal of Abnormal and Social Psychology,* 68:681–85. **372**
WINER, B. J. (1971) *Statistical principles in experimental design* (2nd ed). N.Y.: McGraw-Hill. **598**
WING, C. W., JR., and WALLACH, M. A. (1971) *College admissions and the psychology of talent.* N.Y.: Holt, Rinehart and Winston. **571, 583**
WING, C. W., JR., see WALLACH and WING (1969).
WINTER, D. G., see MCCLELLAND and WINTER (1969).
WINTERS, L. C., see EXLINE and WINTERS (1965).
WITTY, P. A., and JENKINS, M. A. (1936) Intra-race testing and Negro intelligence. *Journal of Psychology,* 1:179–92. **419**
WOLF, M. M., see ALLEN, HART, BUELL

HARRIS, and WOLF (1964); see HARRIS, JOHNSTON, KELLEY, and WOLF (1965).
WOLFF, P. H. (1966) The causes, controls, and organization of behavior in the neonate. *Psychological Issues,* 5, Monograph 17. **161**
WOLFGANG, H., see EYFERTH, BRANDT, and WOLFGANG (1960).
WOLPE, J. (1958) *Psychotherapy by reciprocal inhibition.* Stanford, Calif.: Stanford Univ. Press. **503**
WOLPE, J. (1969) *The practice of behavior therapy.* N.Y.: Pergamon Press. **503**
WOLPE, J., and LAZARUS, A. A. (1966) *Behavior therapy techniques: A guide to the treatment of neuroses.* N.Y.: Pergamon Press. **521**
WOOLDRIDGE, D. E. (1968) *Mechanical man: The physical basis of intelligent life.* N.Y.: McGraw-Hill. **43**
WRIGHTSMAN, L. S. (1972) *Social psychology in the seventies.* Monterey, Calif.: Brooks-Cole. **554**
WYATT, F. (1967) Clinical notes on the motives of reproduction. *Journal of Social Issues,* 23:29–56. **574**
YACORZYNSKI, G., see NEYMANN and YACORZYNSKI (1942).
YAKSH, T., see PLATT, YAKSH, and DARBY (1967).
YALOM, I. D. (1970) *The theory and practice of group psychotherapy.* N.Y.: Basic Books. **521**
YALOM, I. D., see LIEBERMAN, YALOM, and MILES (1973).
YERKES, R. M., and MORGULIS, S. (1909) The method of Pavlov in animal psychology. *Psychological Bulletin,* 6:257–73. **195**
YOUNISS, J., see ROBERTSON and YOUNISS (1969).
ZAJONC, R. B. (1966) *Social psychology: An experimental approach.* Monterey, Calif.: Brooks-Cole. **561**
ZAJONC, R. B. (1968) Attitudinal effects of mere exposure. *Journal of Personality and Social Psychology Monograph Supplement,* 9:1–27. **534**
ZAJONC, R. B., HEINGARTNER, A., and HERMAN, E. M. (1969) Social enhancement and impairment of performance in the cockroach. *Journal of Personality and Social Psychology,* 13:83–92. **545**
ZAJONC, R. B., see SAEGERT, SWAP, and ZAJONC (1973).
ZANNA, M. P., see KIESLER, NISBETT, and ZANNA (1969); see LEPPER, ZANNA, and ABELSON (1970).
ZAX, M., and COWEN, E. L. (1972) *Abnormal psychology: Changing conceptions.* N.Y.: Holt, Rinehart and Winston. **521**
ZEIGLER, H. P., and LEIBOWITZ, H. (1957) Apparent visual size as a function of distance for children and adults. *American Journal of Psychology,* 70:106–09. **133**
ZILBOORG, G., and HENRY, G. W. (1941) *A history of medical psychology.* N.Y.: Norton. **521**
ZIMBARDO, P., see MASLACH, MARSHALL, and ZIMBARDO (1972).
ZUBEK, J. P. (1969) *Sensory deprivation: Fifteen years of research.* N.Y.: Appleton-Century-Crofts. **329**

continued from page IV

15-1 Kroeber, T. C., The coping functions of the ego mechanisms. In R. W. White (ed.), *The study of lives.* Reprinted by permission of the publisher, Atherton Press, Inc. Copyright © 1968, Atherton Press, Inc., New York. All rights reserved.

16-1 Kleinmuntz, Benjamin, *Essentials of abnormal psychology.* New York: Harper & Row, 1974, p. 227, Table 9-1. **16-2** Carpenter, W. T., Strauss, J. S., and Bartko, J. J., Flexible system for the diagnosis of schizophrenia: Report from the WHO international pilot study of schizophrenia, *Science, 182* (December 21, 1973): 1275–78, Table 2. **16-4** Pitt, R. and Hage, J., Patterns of peer interaction during adolescence as prognostic indicators in schizophrenia. *The American Journal of Psychiatry, 120* (1964): 1089–96. Copyright 1964 the American Psychiatric Association and used by permission. **16-5** Gottesman, I. I., and Shields, J.; Genetic theorizing and schizophrenia. *British Journal of Psychiatry, 122* (1973): 15–30. **16-6** Heston, L. L., The genetics of schizophrenic and schizoid disease. *Science, 167* (January 16, 1970): 249–56, Table 4.

17-1 Lang, Peter J., Behavior therapy with a case of nervous anorexia. In Leonard Ullman and Leonard Krasner (eds.), *Case studies in behavior modification.* New York: Holt, Rinehart and Winston, Inc., 1965, p. 219. Reprinted by permission of Holt, Rinehart and Winston, Inc. **17-3** Colby, K. M. and Enea, H., Heuristic methods for computer understanding of natural language in context—restricted on-line dialogues. Originally appeared in *Mathematical Biosciences, 1:* No. 1. Published in 1967 by American Elsevier Publishing Company, Inc.

18-2 Ross, L., Lepper, M. R., and Hubbard, M. (1974) Perseverance in self-perception and social perception: Biased attributional processes in the debriefing paradigm (Unpublished manuscript). Stanford, Calif.: Sanford University. **18-3** Miller, N., and Campbell, D. T., Recency and primacy in persuasion as a function of the timing of speeches as measurements. *Journal of Abnormal and Social Psychology, 59:* 1–9. Copyright 1959 by the American Psychological Association and used by permission. **18-4** McGuire, E. J., and Papageoris, Relative efficacy of various types of prior belief-defense in producing immunity against persuasion. *Journal of Abnormal and Social Psychology, 62:* 327–37. Copyright 1961 by the American Psychological Association and used by permission.

19-1 Free, L. A., and Cantril, H., *The political beliefs of America.* New Brunswick, N.J.: Rutgers University Press, 1967.

Figures

1-5 Cates, J., Psychology's manpower: Report on the 1968 national register of scientific and technical personnel. *American Psychologist, 25:* 254–63. Copyright 1970 by the American Psychological Association and used by permission. **1-10** Hilgard, E. R., Hypnosis and experimental psychodynamics. In H. Brosen (ed.), *Lectures on experimental psychiatry.* Pittsburgh, Pa.: University of Pittsburgh Press, 1961.

2-5 From Eccles, J. C., *The physiology of imagination, 199:* 135–46. Copyright September 1958 by Scientific American, Inc. All rights reserved. **2-10** Penfield, W., and Rasmussen, T., *The cerebral cortex of man.* New York: Macmillan, 1950. **2-12** Sperry, R. W., Perception in the absence of neocortical commissures. In *Perception and its disorders,* Res. Publ. A.R.N.M.D., Vol. 48, The Association for Researchers in Nervous and Mental Diseases. Nebes, R. D. and Sperry, R. W. *Neuropsychologia, 9* (1971): 247. **2-13** Same as above (Figure 2-12). **2-14** Gazzaniga, Michael S., *The bisected brain.* New York: Plenum Publishing Company, 1970, p. 99. **2-18** Thompson, W. R., The inheritance and development of intelligence. *Proceedings of the Association for Research on Nervous and Mental Disease, 33* (1954): 209–31.

3-2 Frankenburg, W. K., and Dodds, J. B., The Denver Developmental Screening Test. *Journal of Pediatrics, 71* (1967): 181–91. **3-8** Maccoby, Eleanor E., and Feldman, Shirley S., Mother-attachment and stranger-reactions in the third year of life. *Monograph, of the Society for Research in Child Development, 37* (1972): 24, Ser. No. 146, Fig. 2. Copyright The Society for Research in Child Development. **3-10** DeLucia, Lenore A. The toy preference test: a measure of sex-role identification. *Child Development, 34* (1963): 107–17. Copyright 1964 by The Society for Research in Child Development, Inc. **3-11** Nisbett, R. E., Birth order and participation in dangerous sports. *Journal of Personality and Social Psychology, 8:* 351–53. Copyright 1968 by the American Psychological Association and used by permission. **3-12** Costanzo, Philip R., and Shae, Marvin E., Conformity as a function of age level. *Child Development, 37* (1966): 967–75. Fig. 1, p. 971. Copyright 1966 by The Society for Research in Child Development, Inc. **3-13** Tanner, Whitehouse, and Takaishi, M., Standards from birth to maturity for height, weight, height velocity, and weight velocity, *Archives of Disease in Childhood, 41* (1966): 467.

4-4 Hess, E. H., and Polt. J. M., Pupil size as related to the interest value of visual stimuli. *Science, 132* August 5, 1960): 349–50, Fig. 4-4. Copyright 1960 by the American Association for the Advancement of Science. **4-17** Cornsweet, T. N. *Stanford Research Institute Journal* (January 5, 1969).

5-2 Zeigler, H. D., and Leibowitz, H., Apparent visual size as a function of distance. *American Journal of Psychology, 70:* 106–09. Copyright 1957 by the University of Illinois Press. **5-3** Rock, I., and Harris, C. S., *Vision and Touch, 216:* 96–104. Copyright May 1967 by Scientific American, Inc. All rights reserved. **5-12** Brown, J. F., and Voth, A. C., The path of seen movement as a function of the vector field. *American Journal of Psychology, 49* (1937): 543–63. Copyright 1937 by the University of Illinois Press.

6-1 Williams, H. L., Lubin, A., and Goodnow, J. J., Impaired performance with acute sleep loss. *Psychological Monographs, 73*: No. 14. Copyright 1959 by the American Psychological Association and used by permission. **6-2** Slightly modified. Ludwig, A. M., Brandsma, J. M., Wilbur, C. B., Bendfeldt, F., and Jameson, D. H., The objective study of a multiple personality. *Archives of General Psychiatry, 26:* 298–310. Copyright 1972 by the American Medical Association. **6-3** Not modified. Same as Figure 6-2. **6-4** Kleitman, N., *Sleep and wakefulness,* Second Edition. Copyright 1939, © 1963 by The University of Chicago Press. **6-5** Klein, K. E., Wegmann, H. M., and Hunt, B. M., Desynchronization of body temperature and performance circadian rhythm as a result of outgoing and home-going transmeridian flights. *Aerospace Medicine, 43* (1972): 119–32. **6-6** Webb, W. B. and Agnew, H. W., Jr. In L. E. Abt and B. F. Riess (eds.), *Progress in clinical psychology,* Vol. 8, p. 15. New York: Grune and Stratton, 1968. **6-7** Adapted from Jim M'Guinness for The Portable Stanford volume *Some must watch while some must sleep* by William C. Dement. Stanford, Calif.: Stanford Alumni Association, 1972, Fig. 3, p. 111. **6-8** Williams, H. L., The problem of defining depth of sleep. In S. S. Kety, E. V. Evarts, and H. L. Williams, (eds.), *Sleep and altered states of consciousness* New York: Association for Research in Nervous and Mental Disease, 1967, pp. 277–87. **6-9** Hilgard, E. R., Weitzenhoffer, A. M., Landes, J., and Moore, R. K., The distribution of susceptibility to hypnosis in a student population: A study using the Stanford Hypnotic Susceptibility Scale. *Psychological Monographs, 75:* No. 512. Copyright 1961 by the American Psychological Association. **6-11** Wallace, Robert Keith, and Benson, Herbert, The physiology of meditation. Copyright February 1972, page 86, by Scientific American, Inc. All rights reserved. **6-13** Dupont, R. L. and Greene, M. H., The dynamics of a heroin addiction epidemic. *Science, 181* (August 24, 1973): 716–22, Fig. 6.

7-4 Pavlov, I. P., *Conditioned reflexes.* Oxford, England: The Clarendon Press, 1927. **7-6** Hovland, C. I., The generalization of conditioned responses: I. The sensory generalization of conditioned responses with varying frequencies of tone. *Journal of General Psychology, 17* (1937): 125–48. **7-7** Fuhrer, M. J., and Baer, P. E., Differential classical conditioning: Verbalization of stimulus contingencies. *Science, 150* (December 10, 1965): 1479–81. **7-10** Skinner, B. F., *The behavior of organisms.* New York: Appleton-Century-Crofts, 1938. Reproduced by permission of Prentice-Hall, Inc. **7-13** Miller N. E., and Banuazizi, A., Instrumental learning by curarized rats of a specific visceral response, intestinal or cardiac. *Journal of Comparative and Physiological Psychology, 65:* 1–7. Copyright 1968 by the American Psychological Association. **7-15A** Clayton, K. N., T-maze choice-learning as a joint function of the reward magnitudes of the alternatives. *Journal of Comparative and Physiological Psychology, 58:* 333–38. Copyright 1964 by the American Psychological Association. **7-16** From "Drives, Rewards, and the Brain" by James and Marianne Olds, in *New directions in psychology 2* by Frank Barron, William C. Dement, Ward Edwards, Harold Lindman, Lawrence D. Phillips, and James and Marianne Olds. Copyright © 1965 by Holt, Rinehart and Winston, Inc. Adapted and reprinted by permission of Holt, Rinehart and Winston, Inc. **7-18** Lorge, I., Influence of regularly interpolated time intervals on subsequent learning. Teachers College Contributions to Education, No. 438. New York: Teachers College Press, copyright 1930. Reprinted with permission of the publisher.

7-19 Bourne, L. E., Jr., and Archer, E. J. Time continuously on target as a function of distribution of practice. *Journal of Experimental Psychology, 51:* 25–33. Copyright 1956 by the American Psychological Association and used by permission. **7-25** Tolman, E. G., and Honzik, C. H., Introduction and removal of reward, and maze performance in rats. University of California Press Publications in Psychology, Vol. 4 (1930): 17. Originally published by the University of California Press; reprinted by permission of The Regents of the University of California.

8-1 Ebbinhaus, H. *Memory.* Translated by H. A. Ruger and C. E. Bussenius. New York: Teachers College Press, copyright 1913. **8-3** Collins, Allan M., and Quillian, M. Ross, Retrieval time from semantic memory. *Journal of Verbal Learning and Verbal Behavior, 8* (1969): 240–47. Reproduced by permission of Academic Press, Inc. **8-4** Same as Figure 8-3. **8-5** Jenkins, J. G., and Dallenbach, K. M., Oblivescence during sleep and waking. *American Journal of Psychology, 35* (1924): 605–12. Reproduced with the permission of the University of Illinois Press. **8-6** Underwood, B. J., Interference and forgetting. *Psychological Review, 64:* 49–60. Copyright 1957 by the American Psychological Association and used by permission. **8-7** Peterson, L. R., and Peterson, M. J., Short-term retention of individual verbal items. *Journal of Experimental Psychology, 58:* 193–98. Copyright 1959 by the American Psychological Association. **8-10** Craik, F., Immediate versus delayed recall. 1970. **8-12** Bower, G. H., Organizational factors in memory. *Journal of Cognitive Psychology, 1* (1970): Reproduced by permission of Academic Press, Inc. **8-13** Gates, A. I., Effects on retention of spending various proportions of study time in self-recitation rather than in silent study. *Archives of Psychology* (1917) No. 40. Reproduced by permission of the American Psychological Association. **8-14** Krueger, W. C. F., The effect of over-learning on retention. *Journal of Experimental Psychology, 12:* 71–78. Copyright 1929 by the American Psychological Association and used by permission.

9-3 Skinner, B. F., Teaching machines. *Science, 128* (October 24, 1958): 969–77, Table 2. **9-5** Davenport, J. W., Chamove, A. S., and Harlow, H. F., The semi-automatic Wisconsin general test apparatus. *Behavioral Research Methods and Instrumentation, 2* (1970): 135–38. **9-6** Harlow, H. F., The formation of learning sets. *Psychological Review, 56:* 51–65. Copyright 1949 by the American Psychological Association, and used by permission. **9-8** From Thorndyke, P., and Bower, G., Storage and retrieval processes in sentence memory. *Cognitive psychology*, in press. **9-10** Sarason, S. B., Mandler, G., and Craighill, P. G., The effect of differential instructions on anxiety and learning. *Journal of Abnormal and Social Psychology, 47:* 561–65. Copyright 1952 by the American Psychological Association, and used by permission. **9-11** Spielberger, D. C., The effects of manifest anxiety on the academic achievement of college students. *Mental Hygiene 46* (1962): 420–26.

10-2 Maclay, H., and Ware, E. E., Cross-cultural use of the semantic differential. Reprinted from *Behavioral Science, 6* (1961): No. 3, by permission of the managing editor. **10-4** Heidbreder, E., The attainment of concepts: III. The problem. *Journal of Psychology, 24* (1947): 93–138, adaptation of Table 1 and Figure 1. **10-8** Brown, R., Word order and meaning. From *A first language.* Cambridge, Mass.: Harvard University Press, 1973, p. 159, Figure 8. **10-9** Same as above, p. 55, Figure 1. **10-10** Gardner, Beatrice T., and Gardner, R. Allen, Comparing the early utterances of child and chimpanzee. In Pick (ed.), *1973 Minnesota symposium on child psychology.* **10-11** Kuenne, M. R., Experimental investigation of the relation of language to transposition behavior in young children. *Journal of Experimental Psychology, 36:* 471–90. Copyright 1946 by the American Psychological Association and used by permission.

11-3 Hoebel, B. G. and Teitelbaum, P., Effects of force feeding and starvation on food intake and body weight of a rat with ventromedial hypothalamic lesions. *Journal of Comparative and Physiological Psychology, 61:* 189–93. Copyright 1966 by the American Psychological Association and used by permission. **11-4** Powley, T. L., and Keesey, R. E., Body weight and the lateral hypothalamic feeding syndrome. *Journal of Comparative and Physiological Psychology, 70:* 25–36. Copyright 1970 by the American Psychological Association and used by permission. **11-5** Epstein, A. N., and Teitelbaum, J., Of food regulation without the benefits of taste and olfactory cues. *Journal of Comparative and Physiological Psychology, 55:* 753–59. Copyright 1962 by the American Psychological Association and used by permission. **11-6** Schachter, S., and Gross, L., Manipulated time and eating behavior. From D. C. Glass (ed.), *Neurophysiology and emotion.* New York: Rockefeller University Press and the Russell Sage Foundation, 1967, p. 138. **11-7** Nisbett, R. C., Taste, deprivation and weight determinants of eating behavior. From D. C. Glass (ed.), *Neurophysiology and emotion.* New York: Rockefeller University Press and the Russell Sage Foundation, 1967, p. 217. **11-10** Hess, Eckhard H., Imprinting in animals. Copyright March 1958 by Scientific American, Inc. All rights reserved.

12-1 Maslow, A., *Motivation and personality.* New York: Harper & Row, 1954. **12-4** Bandura, A., *Aggression: A social learning analysis.* Englewood Cliffs, N.J.: Prentice-Hall, 1973, p. 54, Figure 1.1. **12-5** Bandura, A., *Aggression: A social learning analysis.* Englewood Cliffs, N.J.: Prentice-Hall, 1973, p. 75, Figure 2.2. Plotted from data from Bandura, Ross and Ross, Imitation of film-mediated aggressive models, 1963. **12-7** Eron, L., Huesmann, L., Lefkowitz, M., and Walder, L., Does television violence cause aggression? *American Psychologist, 27:* 253–63. Copyright 1972 by the American Psychological Association and used by permission. **12-11** After Schachter, S., 1971 and Hohmann, 1962. Schachter, S., The interaction of cognitive and physiological determinants of emotional state. In P. Herbert Leiderman and Daniel Shapiro (eds.), *Psychobiological approaches to social behavior.* Stanford, Calif.: Stanford University Press, 1964, p. 166. **12-13** Speisman, J. C., Lazarus, R. S., Davison, L., and Mordkoff, A. M., Experimental reduction of stress based on ego-defense theory. *Journal of Abnormal and Social Psychology, 68:* 367–80. Copyright 1964 by the American Psychological Association and used by permission. **12-15** Hebb, Donald, L., Emotional arousal and performance. From *Textbook of psychology,* Third Edition. Philadelphia, Pa.: W. B. Saunders Co., 1972, p. 199.

13-2 Neymann, Clarence A., and Yacorzynski, G. K., Studies of introversion-extroversion and conflict of motives in the psychoses. *Journal of General Psychology, 27:* 241–55. Copyright 1942 by The Journal Press. **13-3** Eysenck, H. J., and Eysenck, S. B. G., *The Eysenck Personality Inventory.* San Diego. Calif.: Educational and Industrial Testing Service; London: University of London Press, 1963. **13-4** Cattell, R. B., *Personality Profiles, 1973.* Champaign, Ill.: The Institute for Personality and Ability Testing. **13-5** Hathaway, S. R., and Monachesi, E. D., *Adolescent personality and behavior.* Minneapolis, Minn.: University of Minnesota Press. © copyright 1963 University of Minnesota. **13-7** Reproduced with permission from Kleinmuntz, B, *Personality measurement: An introduction* Homewood, Ill.: The Dorsey Press, 1967. **13-9** Allen, K. E., Hart, B., Buell, J. S., Harris, F. R., and Wolf, M. M., Effects of social reinforcement on isolate behavior of a nursery school child. *Child Development, 35:* 310, No. 2. Copyright 1964 by the Society for Research in Child Development, Inc.

14-2 Thurstone, L. L., and Thurstone, T. G., Factorial studies of intelligence. *Psychometric Monographs,* No. 2. Copyright 1941 by the University of Chicago. All rights reserved. **14-3** Terman, L. M., and Merrill, M. A., *Measuring intelligence.* Boston: Houghton Mifflin, 1937. Adaptation of Figure 1, p. 37. **14-6** Guilford, J. R., *The nature of human intelligence.* Copyright © 1967 by McGraw-Hill, Inc. **14-7** Same as Figure 14-6. **14-8** Same as Figure 14-6. **14-9** Baldwin, B. T., and Stecher, L. I., Mental growth curves of normal and superior children. *University of Iowa Studies in Child Welfare, 2* (1922): No. 1. **14-10** Thurstone, L. L., *The differential growth of mental abilities.* Chapel Hill, N.C.: University of North Carolina Psychometric Laboratory, 1955. **14-11** Bayley, Nancy, Development of mental abilities. In Paul Mussen (ed.), *Carmichael's manual of child psychology,* Vol. 1. New York: John Wiley and Sons, 1970, p. 1176. **14-12** Schaie, K. W., and Strother, C. R., A cross-sequential study of age changes in cognitive behavior. *Psychological Bulletin, 70:* 677. Copyright 1968 by the American Psychological Association and used by permission. **14-13** Erlenmeyer-Kimling, L., and Jarvik, L. F., Genetics and intelligence: A review. *Science, 142* (December 13, 1963): 1477–79, Fig. 1.

15-3 Brown, J. S., Gradients of approach and avoidance responses and their relation to motivation. *Journal of Comparative and Physiological Psychology, 41* (1948): 450–65. Copyright 1948 by the American Psychological Association and used by permission. **15-4** Epstein, S., and Fenz, W. D., Steepness of approach and avoidance gradients in humans as a function of experience. *Journal of Experimental Psychology, 70:* 1-12. Copyright 1965 by the American Psychological Association and used by permission. **15-8** Masserman, J. H., *Principles of dynamic psychiatry,* Second Edition. Philadelphia, Pa.: W. B. Saunders Co., 1961, p. 38.

16-2 From *Abnormal psychology and modern life,* Fourth Edition by James C. Coleman. Copyright © 1972 by Scott, Foresman and Company, Reprinted by permission of the publisher. **16-3** Laughlin, Henry P., *The neuroses.* Washington: Butterworth, Inc., 1967, pp. 324–25. **16-6** Kleinmuntz, Benjamin, *Essentials of abnormal psychology.* New York: Harper & Row, 1974. Abridged and adapted from Case Report 7-4, Phobic Neurosis. **16-6** Laughlin, Henry, P., *The neuroses.* Washington: Butterworth, Inc., 1967, pp. 673–74. **16-7** Kleinmuntz, Benjamin, *Essentials of abnormal psychology.* New York: Harper & Row, 1974. Abridged and adapted from Case Report 9-1, Manic-depressive psychosis. **16-8** In A. I. Rabin, A. Burton, and R. E. Harris, (eds.), *Case histories in clinical and abnormal psychology.* New York: Harper & Row, 1947, pp. 22–30. **16-10** Weiss, Jay M., Psychological factors in stress and disease, *Scientific American, 226:* 106. Copyright June 1972 by Scientific American, Inc., All rights reserved. **16-12** Maher, Brendan A., *Principles of psychopathology.* New York: McGraw-Hill, 1966, pp. 214–15.

17-2 Seeman, J., A study of the process of nondirective therapy. *Journal of Consulting Psychology, 13:* 157–68. Copyright 1949 by the American Psychological Association and used by permission. **17-5** Bandura, A., Blanchard, E. B., and Ritter, B., The relative efficacy of desensitization and modeling approaches for inducing behavioral, affective, and attitudinal changes. *Journal of Personality and Social Psychology, 13:* 173–99. Copyright 1969 by the American Psychological Association and used by permission.

18-1 Helmreich, R., Aronson, E., and Lefan, J., To err is humanizing—sometimes: Effects of self-esteem, competence, and a pratfall on interpersonal attraction. *Journal of Personality and Social Psychology, 16:* 259–64. Copyright 1970 by the American Psychological Association. **18-2** Festinger, L., and Carlsmith, J. M., Cognitive consequences of forced compliance. *Journal of Abnormal and Social Psychology, 58:* 203–10. Copyright 1959 by the American Psychological Association and used by permission. **18-4** Darley, J. M., and Latane, B., Bystander intervention in emergencies: Diffusion of responsibility. *Journal of Personality and Social Psychology, 8:* 377–83. Copyright 1968 by the American Psychological Association. **18-6** Milgram, S., Behavioral study of obedience. *Journal of Abnormal and Social Psychology, 67:* 371–78. Copyright 1963 by the American Psychological Association and used by permission.

19-2 Bem, S. L., and Bem, D. J., Does sex-biased job advertising "Aid and abet" sex discrimination? *Journal of Applied Social Psychology, 3* (1973): 6–18.

Picture

Page 5 Professor José M. R. Delgado. **6** (top) Historical Pictures Service. **6** (left) Mt. Zion Neurological Institute. **6** (right) Newsweek photo by Lester Sloan, Copyright 1971. **7** Rick Stafford. **9** Edmund Engelman. **10** Ian Berry, Magnum Photos, Inc. **15** Harbrace. **18** Eric Hamburg. **19** (top) Harbrace. **22** Illustration by Marilyn Grastorf. **34** United Press International. **37** The Granger Collection. **38 & 39** Martin Iger. **42** (top) Martha Swope. **42** (middle) Marlis Muller. **42** (bottom) Harbrace. **43** Richard Estes, Photo Researchers. **47** Illustration by Don MacKay, Copyright 1974 Newsweek. **49** Photograph by Peter Simon; Degas painting from Shostal Associates. **54** Drawing by Roy Doty. **59** Dr. Tijo. **60** Hank Morgan. **63** Sandiford, P. (1938) *Foundations of educational psychology.* New York: Longmans Green. **68** Mark N. Boulton from National Audubon Society. **69** Pro Pix from Monkmeyer Press Photo Service. **70** David Linton. **71** Hanna Schreiber, Rapho-Guillumette. **72** UNICEF Photo by Jean Speiser. **73** M. R. Rosenzweig. **75** The Menninger Foundation. **76** George Zimbel, Monkmeyer Press Photo Service. **77** Harbrace. **79** Norton Publishers. **82** Harry Harlow, Wisconsin Regional Primate Research Center. **85** Louis Goldman, Rapho-Guillumette. **87** Hella Hamid, Rapho-Guillumette. **88** (top) David Attie. **88** (bottom) DeWys, Monkmeyer Press Photo Service. **90** Paul Sequeira, Rapho-Guillumette. **93** Henry Moore, DPI. **118** T. N. Cornsweet. **120** Charles Gatewood. **121** Leannart Nilsson, Time-Life Picture Agency. **124** Leannart Nilsson, Time-Life Picture Agency. **125** Marc & Evelyn Bernheim, Woodfin Camp and Associates. **127** American Airlines. **130** Art Institute of Chicago. **135** (left) Arthur D. Little, Inc. **135** (top) M. C. Escher, "Circle limit IV," Escher Foundation—Haags Gemeentemuseum—The Hague. **135** (bottom) Salvador Dali, "The Slave Market with Disappearing Bust of Voltaire." Collection: Mr. and Mrs. A. Reynolds Morse. Photograph courtesy of Salvador Dali Museum, Cleveland, Ohio. **138** Harvey Stein. **139** Drawing by Miroslav Bartak, © 1972 DIKOBRAZ. **142** Satire on False Perspective, engraved by L. Sullivan after Hogarth. The Metropolitan Museum of Art, gift of Sarah Lazarus, 1891. **142** (bottom) M. C. Escher, "Waterfall, 1961," Escher Foundation—Haags Gemeente-museum—The Hague. **143** Fritz Goro, Time-Life Picture Agency. **147** Courtesy of the American Museum of Natural History. **148** William Vandivert. **149** William Vandivert. **162** Thomas Höpker, Woodfin Camp and Associates. **169** Bildarchiv Foto Marburg. **178** Bonnie Freer, Rapho-Guillumette. **180** Philip Daly, BBC. **182** Wide World Photos. **183** Wide World Photos. **185** North Carolina Department of Mental Health. **195** The Bettmann Archive. **198** Arlene H. Little, Brown University. **200** (top) Will Rapport. **200** (bottom) Drawing by Alan E. Cober. **201** Ralph Gerbrands Company. **202** Elliot Erwitt, Magnum Photos, Inc. **204** The New York Times. **205** (top) Yale Joel, Time-Life Picture Agency. **205** (bottom) Bill Huck, Marineland of Florida. **213** Harbrace. **215** Yerkes Regional Primate Center. **217** Lilo Hess, Three Lions. **219** Drawing by Sidney Harris. **225** The Bettmann Archive. **227** Drawing by Siggs. *The Best Cartoons from Punch.* Copyright 1952 Simon & Schuster. © Punch, London. **228** Culver Pictures, Inc. **229** Drawings by Bernarda Bryson to depict Descartes' Rule for the Direction of the Mind, described in "Information and Memory" by George A. Miller. Copyright August 1956 by Scientific American, Inc. All rights reserved. **235** From *De Humani Corporis Fabrica* of Andreas Vesalius. **242** McClure's Magazine, 1901. **248** Will Rapport. **249** (top) Illustration by Frank Modell. **249** (bottom) Harbrace. **250** Raimondo Borea. **252** Harbrace. **253** (top) IBM. **253** (middle) Harbrace. **253** (bottom) Illustration by Marilyn Grastorf. **254** Newsweek photo by Dan Bernstein. Copyright, 1974. **261** Center for the Study of Instruction, San Francisco. **262** (top) Sepp Seitz, Magnum Photos, Inc. **263** Reprinted from Higginson, George M., and Love, Reeve, The role of media in field testing or whatever happened to the simple life? *Audiovisual Instruction,* Volume XV, No. 5, May 1970, p. 35. **271** Clockwise beginning at top left: Dennis Stock, Magnum Photos, Inc. Wayne Miller, Magnum Photos, Inc. Abigail Heyman, Magnum Photos, Inc. Burt Glinn, Magnum Photos, Inc. Hiroji Kubota, Magnum Photos, Inc. Helen Faye. Center: Burk Uzzle, Magnum Photos, Inc. **273** Harry Harlow, Wisconsin Regional Primate Research Center. **275** Jeffrey Foxx, Woodfin Camp and Associates. **281** Thomas Höpker, Woodfin Camp and Associates. **287** (left) Burk Uzzle, Magnum Photos, Inc. **287** (middle) Burk Uzzle, Magnum Photos, Inc. **287** (right) Charles Harbutt, Magnum Photos, Inc. **289** B. T. Gardner. **290** R. C. Atkinson. **303** The Granger Collection. **306** Cornell Capa, Magnum Photos, Inc. **307** René Burri, Magnum Photos, Inc. **308** Dr. Neal E. Miller. **309** David Attie. **312** Hank Morgan. **323** Wisconsin Regional Primate Research Center. **324** Charles Gatewood, Magnum Photos, Inc. **325** (bottom) Mark Haven. **326** Thomas D. McAmroy, Time-Life Picture Agency. **328** Wisconsin Regional Primate Research Center. **329** A. T. & T., Bell Systems Science Services Film "Gateways of the Mind." **334** Brandeis University. **336** (top) Leonard Freed, Magnum Photos, Inc. **336** (bottom) David Hurn, Magnum Photos, Inc. **337** Bruce Davidson, Magnum Photos, Inc. **338** Professor José M. R. Delgado. **339** Professor José M. R. Delgado. **341** Professor Albert Bandura. **342** Richard C. Estes. **345** (top) Bob Adelman, Magnum Photos, Inc. **347** Safeguards Management Systems, Inc. **355** Hank Morgan. **365** Harbrace. **368** Edward Steichen, The Museum of Modern Art. **371** Starke R. Hathaway, Ph.D. and J. Charnley McKingley, M.D. **378** (left) Culver Pictures; (right) from *The Secret of the Golden Flower* translated by Richard Wilhelm and Cary Baynes. Harcourt Brace Jovanovich, Inc. and Routledge & Kegan Paul Ltd. **379** (top left) Culver Pictures. **379** (top right) Jill Krementz. **379** (bottom left) Karen Horney Clinic. **379** (bottom right) The New York Times. **380** Hans Huber Verlag, Switzerland. **381** George Roos. **382** Mark Haven. **384** Peter Simon. **389** Carl Rogers. **392** (top) Philippe Halsman. **392** (bottom) Mathew B. Brady, Meserve Collection. **393** Jodi Cobb. **395** Thomas Höpker, Woodfin Camp and Associates. **403** The Bettmann Archive. **406** Constantine Manos, Magnum Photos, Inc. **417** National Association for Retarded Citizens. **421** National Association for Retarded Citizens. **422** (top) Drawing by Frank Ansley, Center for the Study of Instruction. **422** (bottom) Stanford University. **431** John Rees, Black Star. **432** Dr. Neal E. Miller. **433** Jerry Irwin, Black Star. **437** M. Bourke-White. **439** Dr. N. R. F. Maier. **440** J. H. Masserman. *Principles of dynamic psychiatry.* Second edition. Philadelphia, Pa.: W. B. Saunders Co., 1961.

441 *Anxiety* by Edvard Munch. The Museum of Modern Art. **444** Jules Feiffer © 1960. **446** Poem and illustration from *When we were very young* by A. A. Milne, illustrated by E. H. Shepard. Copyright © 1924 by E. P. Dutton & Co., Inc. Renewal—1952 by A. A. Milne. **455** (top) Culver Pictures. **455** (bottom) The Bettmann Archive. **456** Joseph Farris. **462** Bersteins International Press Service. **470** Vincent Van Gogh, *Sorrow*. Photograph by Soichi Sunami, The Museum of Modern Art. **472** Museo del Prado. **473** Wide World Photos, Inc. **474** From an art therapy session conducted by NIMH by Harriet Wadeson, A.T.R. Appeared on cover of *Schizophrenic Bulletin*, No. 7, Winter 1973. **477** Bill Bridges, Globe Photos. **482** Medical Audio Visual Dept., Walter Reed Army Institute of Research. **494** (top) University Museum, Philadelphia. **494** (bottom) Culver Pictures. **495** (top left) The Bettmann Archive. **495** (bottom left) The Bettmann Archive. **495** (center) Culver Pictures. **495** (right) The Bettmann Archive. **496** (top) Jerry Cooke, Photo Researchers. **496** (bottom) Culver Pictures. **497** Burk Uzzle, Magnum Photos, Inc. **498** Edmund Engelman. **499** Courtesy University of Florida Clinical Psychology. Van Bucher, Photo Researchers. **506** Wide World Photos. **507** Photographs by Allan Grant. **508** J. Olin Campbell. **510** Harbrace. **511** Arthur Schatz, Time Magazine, 1970. **513** Allan Grant. **516** National Institute of Mental Health. **530** (top) George W. Gardner. **530** (top middle) Bob Adelman, Magnum Photos, Inc. **530** (bottom middle) Joan Sydlow, FPG. **530** (bottom) Michael Wayne, FPG. **531** United Press International. **535** Hugh Rogers. **537** Dr. Fritz Heider. **540** Harbrace. **544** Photo Researchers. **547** Shelley Rusten. **549** Charles Gatewood, Magnum Photos, Inc. **552** (top) Dr. Solomon Asch. **552** (bottom) William Vandivert. **553** Stanley Milgram. **555** Dr. Leon Festinger. **563** United Press International. **564** (top) Henri Cartier-Bresson, Magnum Photos, Inc. **564** (center) Olive Pierce, Photo Researchers. **564** (bottom) The Bettmann Archive. **565** N.O.W. Legal Defense and Education Fund. **567** United Press International. **571** Bob. Adelman, Magnum Photos, Inc. **576** C.A.R.E. Photo. **578** Photo by Louis W. Hine, George Eastman House.

Color Section

4-12 Fritz Goro for Life Magazine, © Time, Inc. **4-13** Harbrace Photo. **4-14** Courtesy American Optical Corp. Persian Miniature: Photo Brent Brolin-DPI.

index

Page numbers in *italics* refer to figures and tables.

A 4
B 5
C 6
D 7
E 8
F 9
G 0
H 1
I 2
J 3